The Thalamus

The thalamus is a key structure in the mammalian brain, providing a hub for communication within and across distributed forebrain networks. Research in this area has undergone a revolution in the last decade, with findings that suggest an expanded role for the thalamus in sensory processing, motor control, arousal regulation, and cognition. Moving beyond previous studies of anatomy and cell neurochemistry, scientists have expanded into investigations of cognitive function and harnessed new methods and theories of neural computation. This book provides a survey of topics at the cutting edge of this field, covering basic anatomy, evolution, development, physiology, and computation. It is also the first book to combine these disciplines in one place, highlighting the interdisciplinary nature of thalamus research, and will be an essential resource for students and experts in biology, medicine, and computer science.

Michael M. Halassa is an Associate Professor in the Department of Brain and Cognitive Sciences at the Massachusetts Institute of Technology. He received the Vilcek Prize for Creative Promise in the Biomedical Sciences, an award given to immigrants who have made "lasting contributions to American society through their extraordinary achievements in biomedical research."

The Thalamus

Edited by
Michael M. Halassa
Massachusetts Institute of Technology

Shaftesbury Road, Cambridge CB2 8EA, United Kingdom

One Liberty Plaza, 20th Floor, New York, NY 10006, USA

477 Williamstown Road, Port Melbourne, VIC 3207, Australia

314–321, 3rd Floor, Plot 3, Splendor Forum, Jasola District Centre, New Delhi – 110025, India

103 Penang Road, #05–06/07, Visioncrest Commercial, Singapore 238467

Cambridge University Press is part of Cambridge University Press & Assessment, a department of the University of Cambridge.

We share the University's mission to contribute to society through the pursuit of education, learning and research at the highest international levels of excellence.

www.cambridge.org
Information on this title: www.cambridge.org/9781108481564
DOI: 10.1017/9781108674287

© Cambridge University Press & Assessment 2023

This publication is in copyright. Subject to statutory exception and to the provisions of relevant collective licensing agreements, no reproduction of any part may take place without the written permission of Cambridge University Press & Assessment.

First published 2023 (version 2, March 2023)

Printed in the United Kingdom by TJ Books Limited, Padstow Cornwall, March 2023

A catalogue record for this publication is available from the British Library

Library of Congress Cataloging-in-Publication data
Names: Halassa, Michael, author.
Title: The Thalamus / edited by Michael M. Halassa, Massachusetts Institute of Technology.
Description: First edition. | Cambridge, United Kingdom ; New York, NY, USA : Cambridge University Press, 2023. | Includes bibliographical references and index.
Identifiers: LCCN 2022007328 (print) | LCCN 2022007329 (ebook) | ISBN 9781108481564 | ISBN 9781108722933 (paperback) | ISBN 9781108674287 (ebook)
Subjects: LCSH: Thalamus. | BISAC: PSYCHOLOGY / Cognitive Psychology & Cognition
Classification: LCC QP383.5 .H35 2023 (print) | LCC QP383.5 (ebook) | DDC 612.8/262–dc23/eng/20220329
LC record available at https://lccn.loc.gov/2022007328
LC ebook record available at https://lccn.loc.gov/2022007329

ISBN 978-1-108-48156-4 Hardback

Cambridge University Press & Assessment has no responsibility for the persistence or accuracy of URLs for external or third-party internet websites referred to in this publication and does not guarantee that any content on such websites is, or will remain, accurate or appropriate.

Contents

List of Contributors vii
Preface ix

Section 1: History

1. **A Brief History of Thalamus Research** 1
   Francisco Clascá

Section 2: Anatomy

2. **Organization of Thalamic Inputs** 27
   László Acsády

3. **Thalamic Output Pathways** 45
   Francisco Clascá

4. **Thalamocortical Circuitry Matters** 71
   S. Murray Sherman

Section 3: Evolution

5. **Morphological, Developmental, and Functional Evolution of the Thalamus** 91
   Ann B. Butler

6. **Lamprey Thalamus and Beyond** 125
   Shreyas M. Suryanarayana, Brita Robertson, Sten Grillner

Section 4: Development

7. **Development of the Thalamocortical Systems** 139
   Sara Bandiera, Zoltán Molnár

8. **Ontogeny of Thalamic GABAergic Neurons** 163
   Alessio Delogu

Section 5: Sensory Processing

9. **Thalamocortical Interactions in the Primary Visual Cortex** 187
   Jose-Manuel Alonso, Massimo Scanziani

10. **Corticothalamic Feedback in Vision** 206
    W. Martin Usrey

11. **The Vibrissa Sensorimotor System of Rodents: A View from the Sensory Thalamus** 214
    Martin Deschênes, David Kleinfeld

12. **Corticothalamic Pathways in the Somatosensory System** 221
    Alexander Groh, Rebecca Mease

13. **Thalamocortical Circuits for Auditory Processing, Plasticity, and Perception** 237
    Daniel B. Polley, Anne E. Takesian

Section 6: Motor Control

14. **Motor Thalamic Interactions with Brainstem and Basal Ganglia** 269
    Jesse H. Goldberg

15. **Cerebellar Regulation of the Thalamus** 284
    Freek E. Hoebeek, Henk-Jan Boele

Section 7: Cognition

16. **The Thalamus in Cognitive Control** 307
    Kai Hwang, Mark D'Esposito

17. **The Thalamus in Attention** 324
    Sabine Kastner, Michael J. Arcaro

18. **The Thalamus in Navigation** 340
    Adrien Peyrache

Section 8: Arousal

19. **The Thalamus and Sleep** 361
    Mattia Aime, Antoine R. Adamantidis

20 **Central Thalamic Contributions to Arousal Regulation** 382
Nicholas D. Schiff

Section 9: Computation

21 **A Dynamical Systems Perspective on Thalamic Circuit Function** 401
Qinglong L. Gu, John D. Murray

22 **Computational Contributions of the Thalamus to Learning and Memory** 416
Randall C. O'Reilly, Thomas E. Hazy

Index 432

Contributors

László Acsády, Head of the Laboratory of Thalamus Research Institute of Experimental Medicine at the Hungarian Academy of Sciences, Budapest

Antoine R. Adamantidis, Professor of System Neurophysiology (extraordinarius) and Director of the Center for Experimental Neurology (ZEN), University of Bern, Switzerland

Mattia Aime, Research Associate, University of Bern, Switzerland

Jose-Manuel Alonso, Distinguished Professor, College of Optometry, State University of New York

Michael J. Arcaro, Assistant Professor in the Department of Psychology, University of Pennsylvania

Sara Bandiera, graduate student, University of Oxford, United Kingdom

Henk-Jan Boele, Assistant Professor in the Department of Neuroscience at Erasmus University Medical Centre, Utrecht, Netherlands; visiting researcher at Princeton Neuroscience Institute, New Jersey; and Chief Executive Officer of BlinkLab

Ann B. Butler, Professor Emerita at Ivory Tower Neurobiology Institute, Bremen, Maine, and George Mason University, Fairfax, Virginia

Francisco Clascá, Professor of Human anatomy and Neuroscience at Autonoma de Madrid University Medical School, Madrid, Spain

Mark D'Esposito, Distinguished Professor of Neuroscience and Psychology, University of California, Berkeley.

Alessio Delogu, Associate Professor, King's College London, United Kingdom

Martin Deschênes, Professor at CERVO Brain Research Centre, University of Laval, Canada

Jesse H. Goldberg, Associate Professor and Robert R. Capranica Fellow, Director of Graduate Studies, Cornell University, New York

Sten Grillner, Professor of Neuroscience at the Karolinska Institute, Sweden

Alexander Groh, Professor at the Institute of Physiology and Pathophysiology, Universität Heidelberg, Germany

Qinglong L. Gu, Postdoctoral Associate in the Department of Psychiatry at Yale University, Connecticut

Thomas E. Hazy, Senior Research Associate at the Clinical and Cognitive Neuroscience Lab, Center for Neuroscience, University of California, Davis

Freek E. Hoebeek, Professor of Translational Research of Early Life Events, University Medical Center Utrecht, Brain Center and Wilhelmina Children's Hospital, Utrecht University, Netherlands.

Kai Hwang, Assistant Professor in Psychological and Brain Sciences, Iowa Neuroscience Institute, The University of Iowa

Sabine Kastner, Professor of Neuroscience and Psychology at the Princeton Neuroscience Institute and Department of Psychology, Scientific Director of Princeton's neuroimaging facility, and Head of the Neuroscience of Attention and Perception Laboratory, Princeton University, Princeton, New Jersey

David Kleinfeld, Professor of Physics and of Neurobiology, University of California, San Diego

Rebecca Mease, Research Associate at the Institute of Physiology and Pathophysiology, Universität Heidelberg, Germany

Zoltán Molnár, Professor of Developmental Neuroscience, Department of Physiology, Anatomy and Genetics, Oxford Martin School and St John's College, University of Oxford, United Kingdom; Einstein Visiting Fellow, Charité-Universitätsmedizin Berlin, Berlin Germany; Visiting Professor at Acibadem Mehmet Ali Aydinlar Üniversitesi, Istanbul, Turkey

John D. Murray, Associate Professor in the Department of Psychiatry at Yale University, Connecticut

Randall C. O'Reilly, Professor of Psychology and Computer Science at the Center for Neuroscience, University of California, Davis

Adrien Peyrache, Assistant Professor at McGill University, Canada

List of Contributors

Daniel B. Polley, Professor of Otolaryngology – head and neck surgery, Harvard Medical School, Massachusetts, and Director of the Lauer Tinnitus Research Center, Mass. Eye and Ear, Massachusetts

Brita Robertson, Research Engineer, Karolinska Institute, Sweden

Massimo Scanziani, Professor, Howard Hughes Medical Institute; investigator, University of California, San Francisco School of Medicine

Nicholas D. Schiff, Jerold B. Katz Professor of Neurology and Neuroscience in the Feil Family Brain and Mind Research Institute at Weill Cornell Medical College, New York; codirector of Consortium for the Advanced Study of Brain Injury (CASBI) at Weill Cornell Medical College

S. Murray Sherman, Chair of Neurobiology and Maurice Goldblatt Professor of Neurobiology at the University of Chicago, Illinois

Shreyas M. Suryanarayana, Postdoctoral Researcher, Karolinska Institute, Sweden and currently Postdoctoral Scholar at Duke Neurobiology, Duke University School of Medicine, Durham, NC, USA

Anne E. Takesian, Assistant Professor of Otolaryngology – head and neck surgery, Harvard Medical School, Massachusetts

W. Martin Usrey, Chair of the Department of Neurobiology, Physiology and Behavior; Professor and Barbara A. Horwitz and John M. Horowitz Endowed Chair in Physiology, College of Biological Sciences, University of California, Davis

Preface

The field of thalamus research has witnessed nothing short of a revolution over the last decade or so. Advances in interrogations of neural circuit structure and function have led to deeper insights into how the brain generally works, including the principles of thalamocortical organization. Around 2019, I was reflecting on this with my good friend, colleague, and mentor Murray Sherman while writing our review for *Neuron* (Halassa and Sherman, 2020). We were discussing how much the field has grown and how it has expanded its focus beyond sensory systems and arousal and into areas like cognition and its computational mechanisms. At one point, Murray paused, looked at me, and said, "Mike, I think our field needs an edited volume." This was the beginning of the effort to realize what is to come in this book.

I remain grateful to Murray for pointing this out, as well as for his constant guidance and encouragement over the years. I am also grateful to Ralf Wimmer for helping with putting this volume together into its current form. I am grateful to him, Brabeeba Wang, and Arghya Mukherjee for helping review and edit some of the chapters that I have received from the amazing group of scientists who have contributed to this book. It goes without saying that without the efforts of these authors, this work would not be possible. I thank them for their hard work, patience, and dedication. I am also very grateful that they have put their trust in me to curate this work. I look forward to serving our community by continuing to update this volume with new editions as our field continues expanding.

The book is divided into a total of nine sections that include twenty-two chapters. After a chapter that grounds the book in the *history of thalamus research*, three chapters outline the major principles behind the *structural organization* within the thalamus and thalamocortical loops. This is followed by two chapters on *thalamic evolution*. The *development* of the principal and reticular thalamus follows to round out an evo/devo perspective that is sorely needed to ground our understanding of thalamic structure and function. After these general chapters comes perhaps the best-studied topic in thalamus research (and neuroscience more generally): *sensory processing*. Five chapters straddle vision, somatosensation, and audition, highlighting both the feedforward and feedback features of the corresponding thalamocortical systems. *Motor control* follows, with two chapters that tackle thalamic motor function with respect to the basal ganglia and cerebellum. This leads to the section on *cognition*, with three chapters that teach us about the thalamus in relation to cognitive control, attention, and navigation. Next are two chapters about the role of the thalamus in *sleep and arousal*, an area that had traditionally received some attention but has recently expanded to some incredible clinical applications, such as deep-brain stimulation of the central thalamus, which has allowed patients in persistent vegetative states to regain some ability to interact with their environment. Last are two chapters on *computational roles* for the thalamus, providing a principled way to understand its contribution to forebrain function more generally.

The hope is that by putting this volume together, readers would be inspired by the following question: Why is there a thalamus in the middle of each of our brains in the first place? It is no secret that in addition to the revolution in neuroscience, there has been a revolution in artificial intelligence and the development of algorithms that rival human performance on certain tasks. The development of computational architectures, some of which were originally inspired by the brain, does not provide an answer to why our brains have a thalamus at this point. Would adding a thalamus-like structure to recurrent neural networks provide some computational advantage or perhaps some energy efficiency that would have real-world application and shed some light on why the brain is built the way it is? By putting together this volume, I hope that our current and future students, those at the intersection between biology and computation, will provide us with answers to these fascinating questions.

Section 1: **History**

Chapter 1

A Brief History of Thalamus Research

Francisco Clascá

Current knowledge about the thalamus is the outcome of a long process of data acquisition and conceptual refinement that is still ongoing. Strides along this process have been marked, to a large extent, by the introduction of new research tools. Here, I summarize this sequence of events along two main lines: (a) the identification of the thalamus and its constituent nuclei and (b) the development of conceptual frameworks about thalamus function.

1. Identification of the Thalamus and Its Constituent Nuclei

The word *thalamus* is a Latin transliteration of the ancient Greek θάλαμος, the name for a bridal bed and, by extension, for the recess or chamber in a mansion for such a bed. Although formal and dated, the word *tálamo* retains this meaning in modern Latin-derived languages, such as Spanish, Portuguese, and Italian. Its first recorded use for naming a brain structure is by the second-century CE Roman physician Claudius Galenus, who investigated brain anatomy by skillfully dissecting fresh animal brain specimens. When he mentioned a "thalamus of the ventricles," however, Galenus was not referring to what we today call the thalamus but to a recess of the lateral ventricles that, he surmised, contacted the end of the optic tract. Because Galenus believed that a "mind fluid" (*pneuma psychicon*) contained within the ventricles should somehow flow into the optic nerve toward the eye to make seeing possible, he regarded the identification of this point of contact as a major discovery (Rocca 2003).

Following Galenus's view, Mondino de Luzzi (thirteenth century), in his pioneering dissections of human brains, used a different term, "buttocks (*anche*) of the ventricles," to name the two round, adjoining masses he observed at the base of the lateral ventricles (Gailloud et al. 2003). Similar names were used by anatomists in the following three centuries (García-Cabezas et al. 2021). However, in their influential anatomical treatises, first Jean Riolan (1626) and then Thomas Willis (1664; Figure 1A) labeled the two round masses *thalami of the optic nerves*. Moreover, they attributed this denomination to Galenus himself, hence consolidating its usage in subsequent literature. The association with the optic nerves persisted in the anatomical literature, although already by 1775, Giovanni Domenico Santorini (1775) had shown that the optic tract actually terminates in the lateral geniculate body, a gray mass he described as adjacent to but separate from the rest of the human thalamus.

The introduction in the early nineteenth century of ethyl alcohol as tissue fixative and hardener allowed the first macroscopic descriptions of the inner structure of the thalamus. Applying this method to human brains and aided with a hand magnifying glass, Karl Friedrich Burdach (1822) identified the lamina medullaris interna within the gray mass of the thalamus and used this fiber tract as a reference to separate some of the main nuclear groups we recognize today, which he called *superior* (anterior), *internal* (medial), and *external* (ventral/lateral). He also named the pulvinar (Latin for "cushion") because of its shape as seen from behind, protruding in the quadrigeminal cistern. He confirmed Santorini's description of the medial and lateral geniculate bodies and noted that a *stratum corneum* (the external medullary lamina) wrapped them together with the rest of the thalamus.

The next advance was the combination by Gerlach (1858) of a fixative (chromic acid) with a dye (carmine-gelatin) to increase the contrast between tissue regions. The neurologist Julius Bernard Luys (1865) applied Gerlach's method to identify the cell groups or *cèntres* (centers) that, he supposed, should exist within the thalamus to act as separate conduits for the sensory pathways to the cerebral cortex. Luys's delineation of four "centers" and their associated sensory channels was not confirmed by subsequent studies, but his *cèntre median* label remains in use for a nucleus that is prominent in the thalamus of humans and other primates (numbered 10 and 10' in Figure 1B).

In the second half of the nineteenth century, the introduction of improved light microscopes, along with sliding microtomes, tissue embedding in paraffin, mounting media, and new synthetic chemicals able to selectively stain specific tissue components, allowed an increasingly refined microscopical analysis of the brain. Employing potassium dichromate and gold chloride to selectively stain myelin, Theodor Meynert (1872) was able to identify and name in human and monkey brains most of the major myelinated fiber tracts entering or surrounding the thalamus, such as the optic tract, ansa peduncularis, fornix, brachium of the inferior colliculus, and habenulo-interpeduncular tract. He also identified the habenula and subdivided the *external* mass of Burdach into a lateral and a ventral portion (the modern lateral posterior and ventral posterior nuclei) because of the high prevalence of myelinated fiber bundles in the latter. Meynert's student Auguste Forel (1877) published the first complete collection of drawings of myelin-stained thalamus sections and reviewed and modified Meynert's nomenclature. In doing so, Forel's name became attached to some reticular regions ("fields") of the ventral thalamus.

History

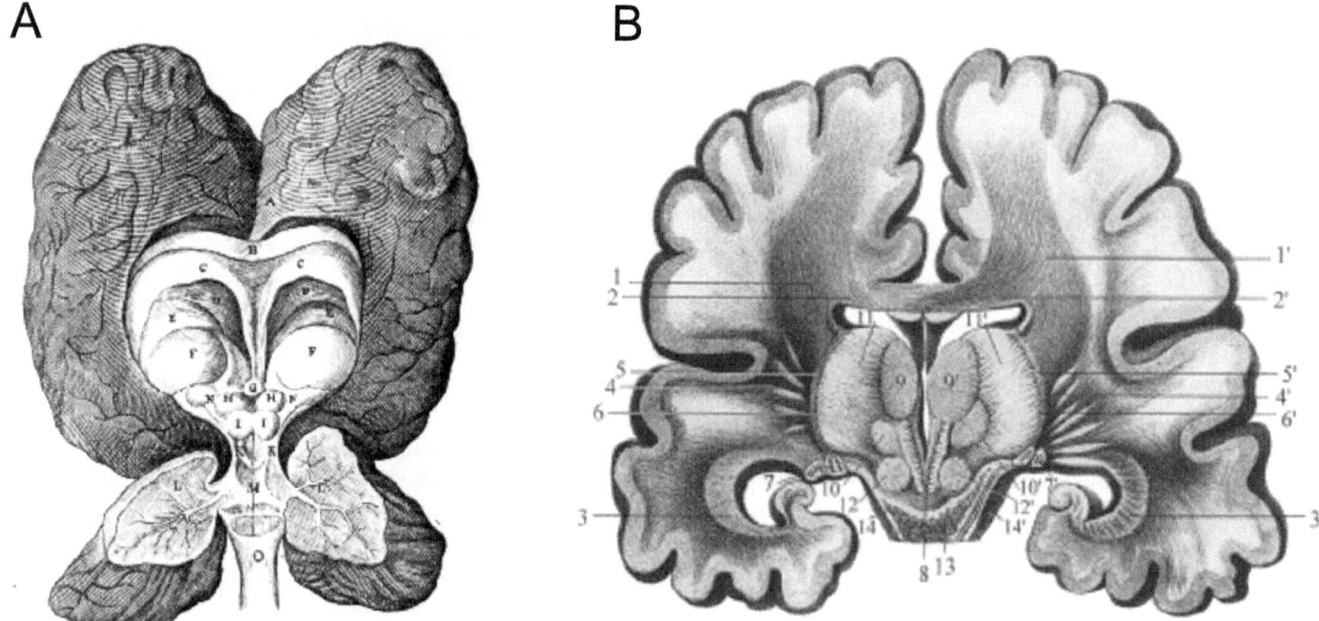

Figure 1 **Macroscopic identification of the thalamus.**
A. Posterior view of a dissected brain and cerebellum, with the cerebral hemispheres lifted dorsally and the posterior end of the lateral ventricles open along the choroid fissure. Letter "F" was labeled "Thalamus Nervorum Opticorum" (thalamus of the optic nerves). From Thomas Willis (1664); drawing by Christopher Wren.
B. Coronal diagram of a human brain section by Luys (1865) showing two of his four main thalamic centers: 9-9', *Cèntres Moyens*, and 10-10', *Cèntres Médians*. Drawing based on thick tissue sections stained with the Gerlach method.

In 1894, as he was still a medical student in Munich, Franz Nissl (1894) discovered that cresyl violet, an aniline dye derived from tar, could be applied on glass-mounted thin tissue sections to selectively stain acidic cell structures such as polyribosomes (known today as *Nissl's bodies*), nuclear chromatin, and nucleoli in the neuronal cell somata and the glial and endothelial cells. His method was rapidly adopted by others and remains in wide use. The method allowed a delineation of brain cell masses based on population-level differences in their packing density, soma size, and/or staining intensity, as seen under low or medium light-microscope magnification. Using this so-called cytoarchitectonic approach, Nissl later published a complete description of the nuclei of the rabbit thalamus (Nissl 1913).

In the following decades, thalamus research focused mainly on cytoarchitectonic and myelin architecture studies in different mammal species. As studies were conducted in different institutions by researchers writing in English, French, or German, they led to a proliferation of inconsistent delineations and terminologies. Finally, a comprehensive review on the structure and connections of the thalamus by Wilfrid Le Gros Clark (1932) opened a gradual process of consolidation that led to the adoption of a common nomenclature for about thirty nuclei in the thalamus of laboratory species such as rats, rabbits, cats, and dogs. Consensus took longer to emerge for the thalamus of nonhuman primates (Vogt 1909; Friedemann 1912; Walker 1938; Jones 2007), mainly because of the complexities involved in subdividing the massive ventral and lateral posterior-pulvinar nuclei of primates.

Meanwhile, the nomenclature and delineation of the human thalamus followed an independent path for most of the twentieth century, as it remained mainly defined by neuropathological studies or stereotaxic atlases devised to guide selective "thalamotomies" intended as surgical treatments for depression, psychosis, pain, and movement disorders (Dèjerine 1901; Vogt & Vogt 1941; Schaltenbrand & Wahren 1977). After the decline of such methods in the 1970s and the introduction of modern brain-imaging techniques, a nomenclature consistent with that used in nonhuman primates was finally extended to the human thalamus (Hirai & Jones 1989; Morel et al. 2007, Mai & Majtanik 2019). Based on multiarchitectonic data and on an extrapolation from connectivity data in nonhuman primates, this new nomenclature is now accepted as the international standard in the *Terminologia Neuroanatomica* (FIPAT 2017).

In the twentieth century, the application of increasingly sensitive connection labeling methods confirmed the heuristic value of the classic "cytoarchitectonic" nuclei delineations as a key principle of the functional organization of the thalamus. For example, studies of *input* pathways from the brainstem or retina revealed that the terminal distribution of these pathways largely matches nuclear boundaries. In addition, these studies redefined some boundaries and identified new subdivisions, such as the lateral geniculate domains receiving either retinal or tectal inputs (Kaas et al. 1972, 1978) and the pulvinar subnuclei receiving tectal inputs (Kaas & Lyon 2007). Additional histochemical and immunolabeling methods developed in this period provided new references for nuclei delineation (Graybiel & Berson 1980; Rausell & Jones 1991; Kuramoto et al. 2009). From these studies, a consensus on nuclei layout and terminology based on cyto- and chemoarchitectonics as well as on connectivity criteria is now widely shared for the main animal model species (mouse: Paxinos & Franklin 2019; Allen Mouse Common Coordinate Framework and Reference Atlas v.3 2017; rat: Paxinos & Watson 2007; marmoset: Paxinos et al. 2012; ferret: Radtke-Schuller 2018). Even in these best-studied species, however, some nuclei boundaries and/or subdivision denominations remain unsettled.

Studies of the thalamic output pathways showed that the cells in each thalamic nucleus selectively send their axons to one area or group of cortical areas and often also to other forebrain structures such as the striatum. Studies with single-cell-resolution methods have in recent years revealed that a relatively small number of high-level cell classes are found repeatedly throughout the thalamus. These cell classes are each characterized by a distinct axon wiring and transcriptomic profile (Phillips et al. 2019; see Chapter 3 in this volume). The same cell class is often found in nuclei that are separate and receive different inputs. Interestingly, recent developmental cell lineage studies (Shi et al. 2017; Nakagawa 2019) suggest that these common cell classes may reflect a deep level of thalamic cell diversity that is related to the clonal origins and migration of young neurons in the developing thalamus, well before the arrival of input connections or the emergence of cytoarchitectonically distinct nuclei.

2. Thalamic Circuits and Functional Frameworks

As for other brain systems, the delineation of connections and electrophysiological properties is key for mechanistically defining the functioning of the thalamus and its contributions to behavior. A comprehensive framework for thalamic functions has been slow to emerge and is still being actively discussed. Historically, advances followed from three main research approaches: (a) observation of the effects of spontaneous or experimental lesions; (b) connection tracing; and (c) electrical recording, often in combination with the other two methods.

2.1 Lesion Studies

In the early nineteenth century, postmortem pathological reports became an increasingly common part of clinical practice. Some such reports linked, for the first time, lesions in the thalamus with premortem focal sensory and motor deficits (Bright 1837; Jackson 1864). However, because of the nonselective nature of the lesions, usually vascular in origin, and the proximity to the thalamus of the internal capsule, the symptoms reported were quite variable. Likewise, experimental lesion studies conducted in frogs, birds, and mammals produced inconsistent behavioral effects (Flourens 1824; Nothnagel 1873). As a result, the idea of the thalamus as a sensory-related structure gained acceptance only slowly (Luys 1865; Jackson 1866, Ferrier 1886) against the alternative view that the thalamus was one more of the basal ganglia and primarily motor in function (Magendie 1841; Vulpian 1866; Meynert 1885).

As noted earlier, Luys (1865) was an early proponent of the thalamus as a gateway for sensory information to the cortex. As was common at the time, Luys assumed that brain cells formed continuous syncytia. Emboldened by the then-recent finding by Paul Broca (1861) of a brain "center" for speech, Luys envisioned the thalamus as consisting of separate "centers" whose cells would "condense," "store," and "elevate" the sensory impressions they received from the "purely reflex" brainstem levels. Via the thalamic radiations, the centers would then convey this "energy" to particular regions of the cortex to excite or awaken ("erect") them (Figure 2). Multisensory convergence could then occur in the upper layers of the cortex via tangential connections (Parent & Parent 2011). Although prescient, Luys's views were largely bold intuitions based on the case-report medical literature, as well as his knowledge of macroscopic brain anatomy and cellular theory, without much experimental support.

A few years later, Nothnagel (1873) reported a persistent loss of visual responses in rabbits following thalamus lesions, along with somatic sensory-motor deficits. After the demonstration by Fritsch and Hitzig (1870) of the electrical excitability of the motor cortex, several researchers performed electric stimulation experiments in the thalamus, without conclusive motor effects. As part of one of these studies, David Ferrier (1886) performed a selective surgical ablation of the posterior thalamus in a monkey and observed a clear lack of response to cutaneous stimuli in the contralateral hemibody. This led him

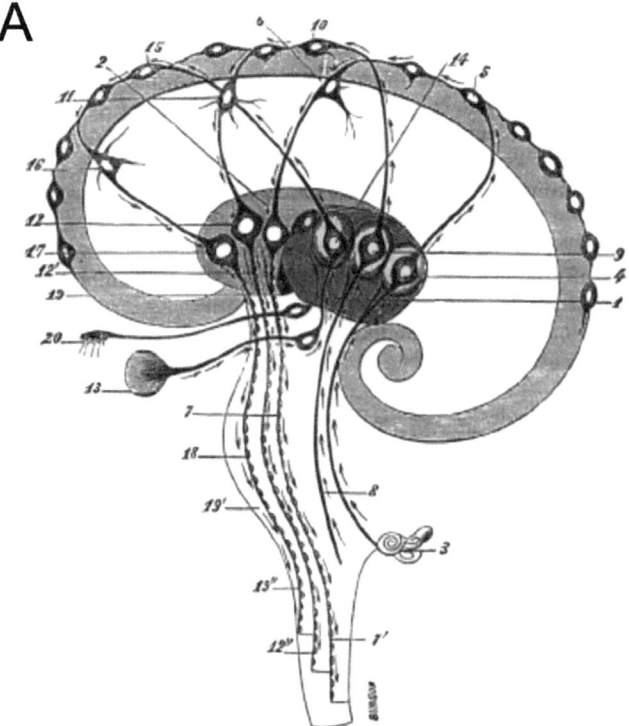

Figure 2 An early functional interpretation of thalamic function.
Diagram by Luys (1865) depicting his hypothesized main cellular centers (labeled *19*, *14*, *9*, and *4*), each conducting sensations, from the olfactory bulb (*20*), the retina (*13*), the spinal cord (*8*), or the inner ear (*3*). Neurons were envisioned as forming syncytial chains. Arrows indicate the presumed direction of impulse flow. For clarity, the contour of the thalamus is shaded in magenta.

to conclude that the thalamus should be involved in somatic sensation, although his overall interpretation remained that it would receive the sensory information in a top-down manner from the sensory areas of the cortex. In Ferrier's view, the thalamus was primarily involved in the guidance of voluntary movement through interactions with the striatum. A parallel line of early evidence for the implication of the thalamus in sensation came from clinical descriptions of numbness followed by persistent central pain (hyperalgesia and allodynia) associated with isolated infarctions of the posterolateral thalamus (Déjerine & Roussy 1906). This *thalamic pain syndrome* (*Déjerine-Roussy syndrome*) is today recognized as an infrequent but well-defined neurological condition. Pain is believed to arise from multilevel plastic changes in the somatic sensory pathways, set in motion by the thalamic lesion (Hong et al. 2010).

2.2 Connection-Tracing Studies

Correct delineation of neural circuits is a prerequisite for mechanistically understanding their function. Not surprisingly, therefore, insights on thalamic functions have, to a large extent, followed from the application of new methods able to resolve the highly diverse neural connections of the thalamus with increasing precision.

2.2.1 Early Lesion Degeneration and Golgi Studies

As soon as Franz Nissl discovered cresyl violet staining, his mentor, Bernhard von Gudden, realized its potential for neural connection tracing. Hence, following a selective lesion in a part of the brain, Gudden (1870) was able to detect changes in cellular morphology and subsequent neuronal loss and gliosis in distant brain regions. Such changes were most evident when the lesions were performed in very young animals later examined as adults. Cell loss could be interpreted as evidence that the region had been selectively connected at a distance with the lesioned area (Figure 3A). Using this experimental approach by lesioning different cortical areas of cats, dogs, and rabbits and identifying which thalamus nuclei showed retrograde neuronal degeneration, Constantin Von Monakow (1895) soon was able to delineate a first general topography of the thalamocortical connections.

Later, Wilfried Le Gros Clark (1932; Le Gros Clark & Boggon 1935; Le Gros Clark & Northfield 1937; Le Gros Clark & Powell 1953) and A. Earl Walker (1938) refined the method further and charted the projections of the thalamic nuclei to the cerebral cortex of monkeys. Other researchers extended the method to additional animal species, and by the 1960s, a general plan of the thalamocortical projection became established in the literature. However, the low sensitivity and indirect nature of the retrograde degeneration data fostered the image of a point-to-point, low-complexity wiring of the thalamocortical system (Walker 1938, Figure 3B). Moreover, the degeneration results suggested that the thalamic axons reached some cortical areas of the cerebral hemisphere, but not others (Walker 1938; Akert 1964; Locke 1967; Figure 3C). Likewise, the notion that some thalamic nuclei mainly innervate the striatum remained controversial for a long time (Rose & Woolsey 1943). Besides, the observation that some thalamic nuclei degenerated massively following a lesion to a single cortical area, whereas others degenerated to a lesser extent or only when several areas were simultaneously lesioned, led to an influential distinction between thalamocortical projections that were "essential" to a given area (those that degenerated following a lesion limited to the area) versus those that were just "sustaining" to the area (which required the lesioning of several areas to produce detectable degeneration; Rose & Woolsey 1949a, 1958). This distinction hinted at the possibility that some thalamocortical pathways might be more widely spread than others across the cortical mantle.

Improving on an impregnation method originally devised by Camillo Golgi (1873), Santiago Ramón-y-Cajal visualized, for the first time, the basic neuronal circuitry of the thalamus (1900, 1903; Figure 4A). The Golgi impregnation process stains at random, but entirely, a limited number of cells with a black silver precipitate, hence revealing dendrites, somata, and unmyelinated axons in exquisite detail. However, the myelinated part of long-range axons is mostly not impregnated; thus, Cajal's discoveries centered on the thalamic gray matter (Figure 4A and B). These included the selective and orderly arborization within the thalamus of the ascending sensory and corticothalamic input fiber systems. He also noted the presence of projection neurons and local interneurons (Figure 4A) and even commented on the scarcity of the latter in rodents compared with carnivores. In addition, Cajal emphasized that the prethalamic reticular nucleus cell axons project back into the dorsal thalamus, but not toward the cortex (Figure 4C). Cajal also noted that axon-to-dendrite contacts (later called *synapses*) were never observed between the projection neurons.

Working with the Golgi method on embryonic and neonatal brains, whose white-matter tracts are still incompletely myelinated, Cajal and his collaborators were even able to visualize, in part, the thalamocortical and corticothalamic axons (Figure 4A). In a late review of his earlier Golgi work as a young student at Cajal's laboratory, Rafael Lorente de No (1938) presumed that two types of axons innervating the cortex might come from the thalamus. The first type, which he called "specific" ("a" and "b" in Figure 4D), directly entered the cortex and arborized profusely in a single spot of the cortex middle layers. The second type, which he called "nonspecific" ("c" and "d" in Figure 4C), gave off a collateral branch that entered the cortex while the main trunk extended farther afield, toward other cortical regions. This collateral branch formed a simpler arborization that reached up to the pial surface. Because Lorente's observations were limited to Golgi-stained material, the origins of these axons could not be established with certainty.

Vittorio Marchi and Giovanni Algieri (1885) introduced an empirical method using osmium salts in the presence of an oxidizing agent to selectively stain myelin sheaths in their process of post-lesion breakup but not in the normal tissue. This method could thus be applied on serial brain tissue sections to track myelinated fiber bundles degenerating after experimental brain lesions, from the lesion site to the vicinity

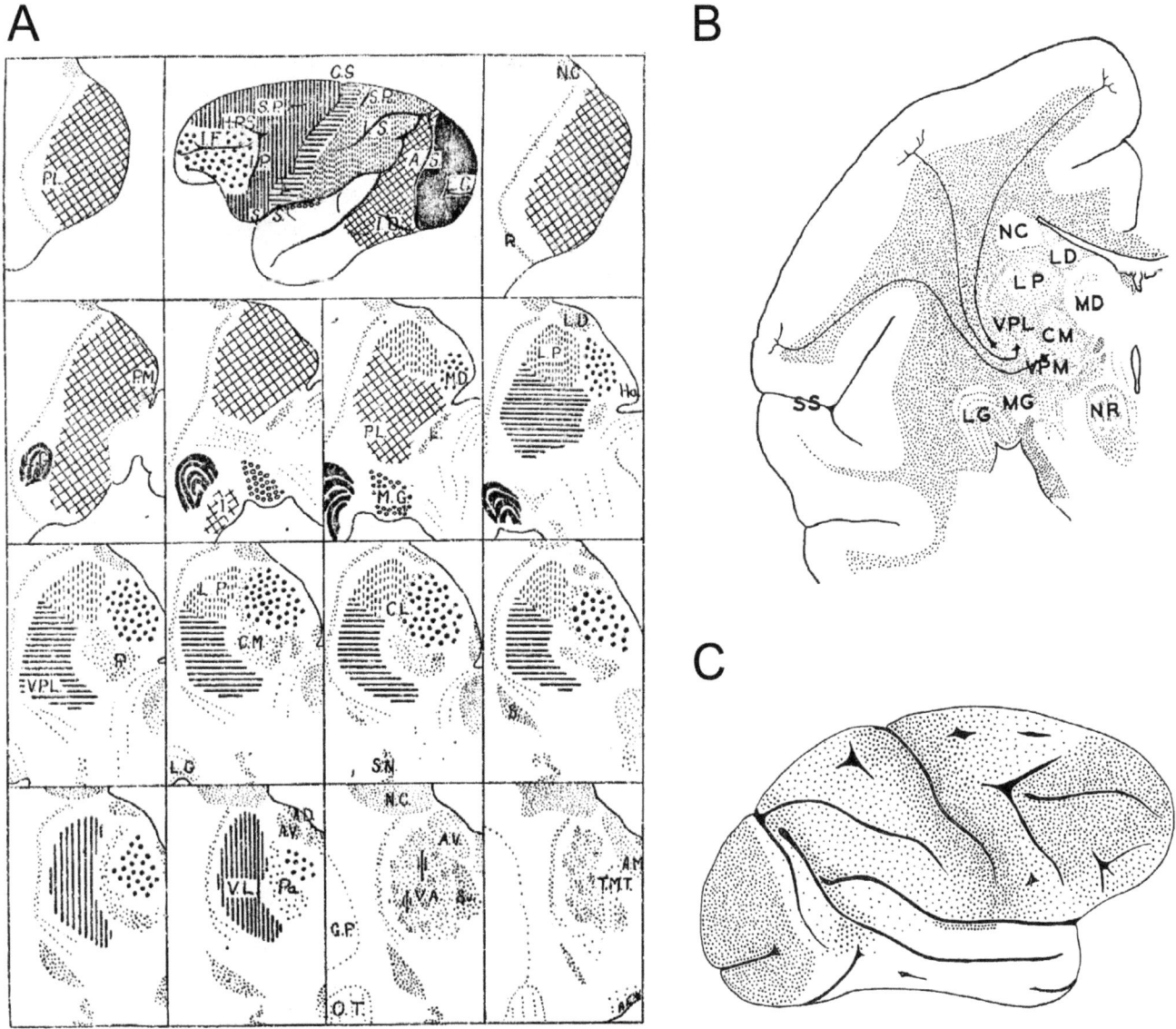

Figure 3 Global map of the thalamocortical projection derived from lesion-degeneration studies in macaque brains (Walker 1938, 1966).

A. Summary diagram of the correspondence observed between lesioned territories of the macaque cerebral cortex and the thalamic nuclei showing degeneration in the thalamus.

B. Topographic correspondence between the various parts of the postcentral (somatic) sensory cortex and the ventral posterior subnuclei.

C. Interpretation of supposed differences in the "intensity of the thalamic projection" (stippling) to different regions of the macaque cerebral cortex. The cortical zones with sparse or no stippling were believed to receive only a few or no thalamic connections because their lesioning did not produce a clear retrograde degeneration in the thalamus.

of their target territory. However, because the terminal axon arborizations lack myelin ensheathing, axons could not be tracked to their end with this method. Nevertheless, "Marchi's method" was instrumental to resolve disputes regarding the general sites of termination in the thalamus of the main subcortical input systems (Vogt 1909; Economo 1911; Walker 1938). Specifically, the method showed that the subcortical afferent systems always terminated in some nucleus of the thalamus without extending to the cerebral cortex (Mott 1892; Monakow 1895). Along with Cajal's Golgi observations, these studies definitively established the notion of the thalamus as a relay structure for sensory and motor subcortical inputs en route to the cortex.

In the 1950s, new methods based on metal impregnation were developed that allowed direct visualization of the degenerating axons themselves, including their terminal branches (Nauta & Gygax 1954; Fink & Heimer 1967). This allowed a more accurate mapping of the distribution of afferent and efferent thalamic connections (Guillery 1967; Montero & Guillery 1968). In the same years, the introduction of electron microscopy for the study of brain tissue ultrastructure made possible the first descriptions of thalamic and cortical synapses (Szentagotai 1963; Colonnier & Guillery 1964). Electron microscopy was soon shown to be useful for detecting synapses undergoing degenerative changes produced by a lesion in a distant brain region

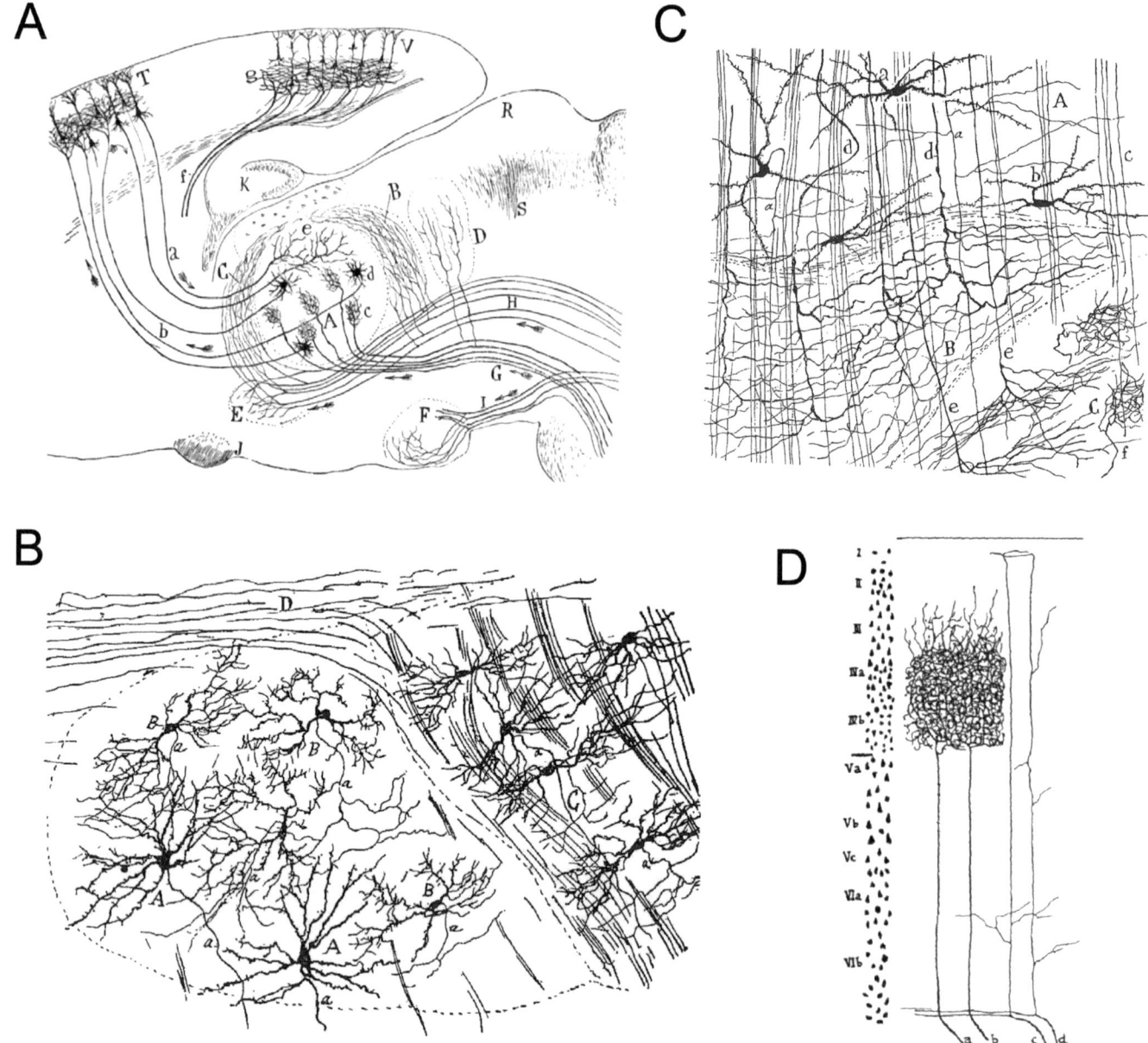

Figure 4 Golgi-stained studies of the thalamic neurons and their axons.

A. Circuit diagram by Cajal (1900) based on Golgi studies. A parasagittal section outline of the rodent brain is shown in the background. Rostral is to the left. Ascending brainstem axons (G) terminate within a somatic sensory nucleus (A) as dense focal arborizations (c). Multipolar thalamocortical neurons receiving these impulses then send their axons (b) to a specific cortical somatomotor "focus" (T) and terminate in a dense arborization confined to the middle cortical layers. In turn, corticothalamic projections originating in deep-layer pyramidal cells reciprocally innervate the same thalamic nucleus that originated the projection, forming arborizations that are relatively widespread but confined to the nucleus. A second set of axons (f) coming or going between an occipital visual area (V) and its corresponding thalamic nucleus (not shown) are also depicted.

B. Cajal's (1900) drawing of the cell types visible in a frontal section from a thalamic nucleus of an eight-day-old cat. Projection cells with their long axons extending out of the nucleus (A) and intrinsic interneurons with axons arborizing within the nucleus (B) are depicted. In all cells, the axon is labeled a.

C. Cajal's (1903) drawing of a detail from a horizontal section of a twenty-day-old mouse thalamus. The cerebral cortex is situated beyond the top of the image, and the thalamus is at the bottom. The upper part of the image (A) represents a part of the prethalamic reticular nucleus; a thin dashed line separates it from the external medullary lamina (B; fiber plexus in the center of the image). The lower-left corner (C) of the image represents a portion of the ventroposterior lateral nucleus. The vertical bundles are axons extending between the thalamus and the cortex. Prethalamic reticular nucleus neurons are represented with their long dendrites extended orthogonal to the plane of these fiber bundles. Cajal remarked that their axons (a) never extend toward the cortex and innervate other thalamic nuclei instead.

D. Rafael Lorente de No's (1938) depiction of two different types of putative thalamocortical axons entering the mouse cortex. a, b: "specific thalamic afferents"; c, d: "unspecific or pluriareal" afferents. On the left, a thin column of Nissl-stained cell somata is diagrammatically depicted. For clarity, this illustration is cropped from a larger page-wide original, which included many other cortical cell types.

(Gray & Hamlyn 1962). This approach provided the first descriptions of synapses established by specific cortical and subcortical axon systems onto thalamic cells (Colonnier & Guillery 1964; Jones & Powell 1970), as well as the identification of the cells and dendritic domains postsynaptic to thalamic axons in the cortex (Jones & Powell 1970; Strick & Sterling 1974; White 1978) or striatum (Kemp & Powell 1971b; Chung et al. 1977).

2.2.2 The Axonal-Transport-Tracing Revolution

In the early 1970s, entirely new kinds of connection-tracing methods that exploited the neuronal mechanisms for transmembrane uptake and axonal transport were developed. Each of these methods allowed the visualization of a particular exogenous molecule that, when deposited into the living nervous tissue, could be internalized by the local neuronal bodies and dendrites and actively transported to their distant axonal arborizations (anterograde transport) or be taken by the axons in the deposit region and transported to their parent cell bodies (retrograde transport), or both. Some of these methods remain in wide use. Detection of the transported substance was usually performed on thin tissue sections (Figure 5A–F). Depending on the substance injected, autoradiography (Cowan et al. 1972), histochemistry (LaVail & LaVail 1972; Gonatas et al. 1979), epifluorescence (Bentivoglio et al. 1980; Kuypers et al. 1980; Katz et al. 1984; Ju et al. 1989; Nance & Burns 1990), or immunolabeling with specific antibodies (Gerfen & Sawchenko 1984; Veenman et al. 1992; Angelucci et al. 1996) was required for detection (reviewed in Lanciego & Wouterlood 2020). Besides, key insights on the embryonic development of thalamus connections were gained through the application of highly lipophilic fluorescent substances that, when deposited into fixed embryonic brain specimens, spread selectively and over relatively long distances along axons by simple passive diffusion (Figure 5G; Godement et al. 1987; Molnár & Blakemore 1995; Clascá et al. 1995).

Because of their sensitivity and versatility, the axonal transport methods helped to resolve long-standing questions about the circuitry of the thalamus. First, they established that thalamic projection cells target the ipsilateral cerebral hemisphere and that, in contrast, the prethalamic reticular nucleus cells project instead to the nuclei of the dorsal thalamus (Jones 1975). Likewise, these methods showed that all areas of the neocortex, as well as some hippocampal and olfactory areas, receive thalamic connections (Figure 5I) and that some thalamic nuclei innervate subcortical structures such as the striatum, accumbens, and amygdala (Jones & Leavitt 1974).

Second, axonal transport tracing studies clarified the extent and complexity of the corticothalamic projection. Corticothalamic connections were found to arise from two different cortical layers. One projection system arises from cortical layer 6 pyramidal neurons. All thalamic nuclei were found to receive massive numbers of these layer 6 connections, which may arise from the same cortical areas innervated by the cells of a given nucleus ("reciprocity principle"; Diamond et al. 1969) but also from other functionally related cortical areas ("parity principle"; Deschênes et al. 1998), including even some in the contralateral cerebral hemisphere. Moreover, both the thalamocortical axons exiting a given thalamic nucleus and the layer 6 corticothalamic axons innervating that nucleus pierce the same region of the prethalamic reticular nucleus and leave branches in it; as a result, that reticular nucleus sector is functionally associated with that particular set of cortical and thalamic regions (Figures 5I and 10A; Jones 1975; Sherman & Guillery 1996).

A second corticothalamic projection system was found to originate in layer 5b pyramidal cells. These cells target the association nuclei but not the sensory relay nuclei of the thalamus (Gilbert & Kelly 1975; Catsman-Berrevoets & Kuypers 1978). Subsequent studies revealed that the differences between the two corticothalamic systems are profound. For example, layer 5 cells innervate the thalamus through branches of axons that also target the brainstem, whereas layer 6 cell axons target only the thalamus (Ojima 1994). In addition, each system establishes synapses onto different regions of the thalamic projection neuron dendrites (Guillery 1995). Moreover, the axon growth cones of each projection system invade the thalamus at markedly different ages during development (Clascá et al. 1995).

Third, the axonal transport methods detected a marked variability in the convergence–divergence of the pathways originating in different nuclei. Cells from some nuclei could be retrogradely labeled from many cortical regions, indicating that their axons reach wide swaths of the cortical mantle, whereas cells in other nuclei were only labeled from a particular area or subarea, thus indicating that their axons make a more focal and non-overlapping targeting (Herkenham 1986; Macchi et al. 1986; Figure 5H). Moreover, every cortical area was found to receive, as a rule, convergent inputs from more than one nucleus, in characteristic proportions (Clascá et al. 1997). Double-labeling strategies based on detecting the accumulation within the same cell body of two distinguishable retrograde tracers injected in distant points of the nervous tissue (Rosina et al. 1980) were used to investigate the possibility that some cells branched their axons to target separate cortical areas. In most such experiments, double-labeled cells were observed in small numbers, and only in some thalamic nuclei, suggesting that the divergently branched thalamocortical axons were unusual (Asanuma et al. 1985; Minciacchi et al. 1986; Spreafico et al. 1987; Kishan et al. 2008; Cappe et al. 2009; Figure 5H).

Fourth, bulk-injected anterograde tracers in the thalamus revealed that the axons from different nuclei terminate in the cortex in specific laminar patterns (Herkenham 1980, 1986; Killackey & Ebner 1972, 1973; Burton & Jones 1976), indicating that they may each target specific cell populations and/or dendritic domains within the cortical circuits. Based on a large collection of tracing experiments in the rat, Herkenham (1986) proposed a tripartite grouping of thalamic nuclei attending to these laminar patterns (Figure 6A and B).

Other studies examined this same issue by comparing the cells retrogradely labeled in the thalamus by tracer deposits limited to cortical layer 1 versus those involving the deeper layers. These confirmed that only some nuclei contain neurons that innervate layer 1 and often found differences in the soma size (Carey et al., 1979a, 1979b; Rausell & Avendaño 1985) and/or calcium-binding protein content (Hashikawa et al. 1991; Rausell et al. 1992; Hendry & Yoshioka 1994) of the neurons innervating layer 1 versus those targeting only deeper cortical layers.

Drawing from the reports mentioned previously and from his own observations in macaque brains, Edward Jones (Rausell & Jones 1991; Jones 1998, 2007) proposed, as a fundamental principle of thalamus organization, the existence of two major systems: (a) a broad class of neurons spread as a "matrix" across the thalamus and characterized by their widely spread axons

History

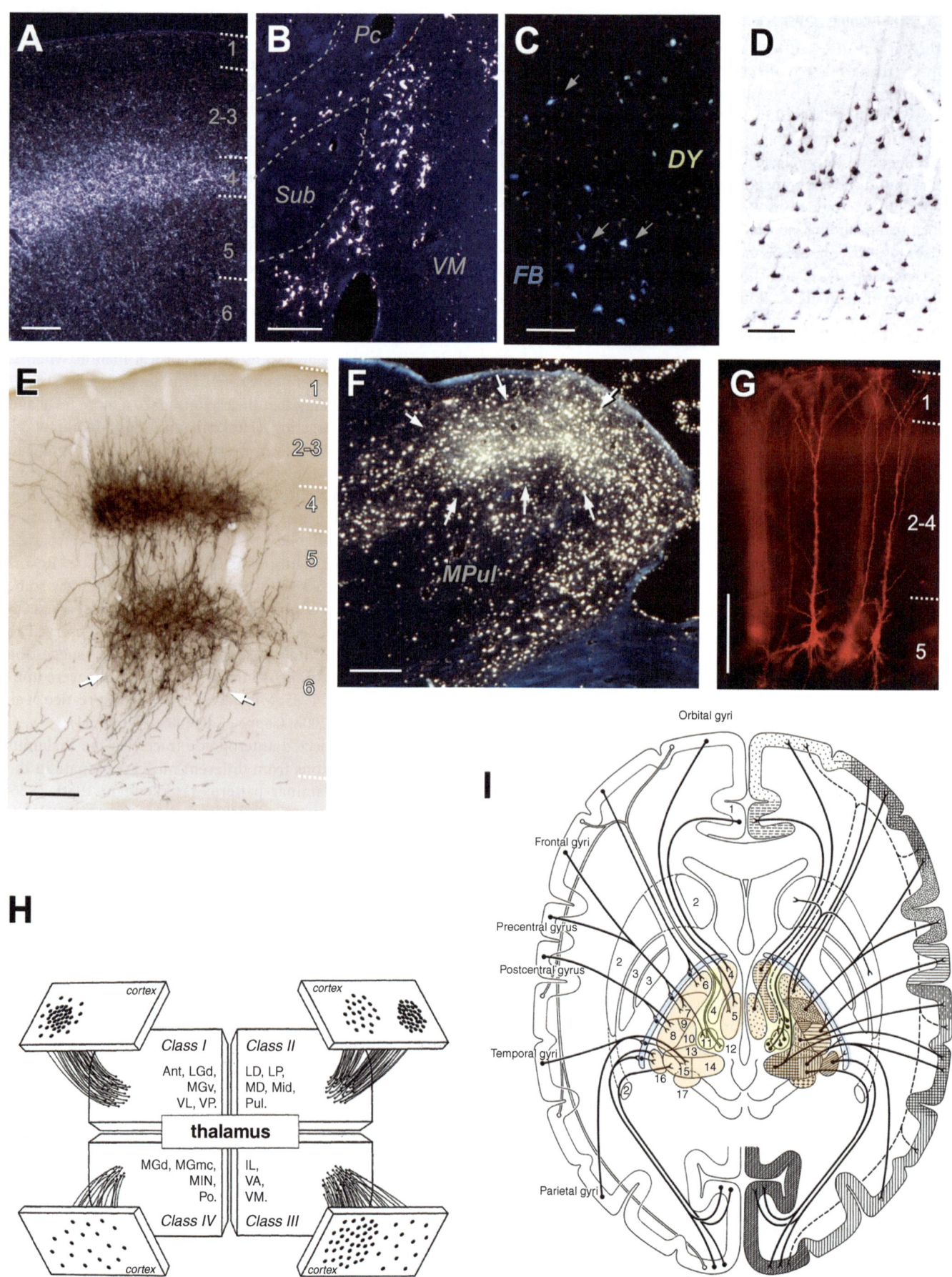

Figure 5 Bulk-injected chemical axonal tracers redefined the understanding of thalamic connectivity.

A. Autoradiographic labeling in cortical area 5a produced by a tritiated proline injection in the lateral intermediate nucleus of a cat. Darkfield optics. Note the silver nitrate grains in the photographic emulsion glowing brightly in layers 4–3. Bar = 250μm directed to the superficial layers of the cortex, and (b) another class of "core" cells present only in some thalamic nuclei characterized by focal axons centered in the cortex middle layers (Figure 7C). Jones emphasized that, at least in macaques, such two-cell populations each express specific calcium-binding proteins. Although later studies have shown the matrix-core hypothesis to be overly simplified, it provided an important conceptual framework for modeling the interactions between the thalamus and cortex, beyond those of simple relay (Kuramoto et al. 2009; Bonjean et al. 2012; Cruikshank et al. 2012; Krishnan et al. 2018; Müller et al. 2020; see Section 2.3.2).

At the turn of this century, the technical possibilities for selective pathway tracing were multiplied by the introduction of a variety of recombinant viral vectors able to drive the expression of high levels of fluorescent proteins in neurons and their long-distance axons, either constitutively (Chamberlin et al. 1998; Furuta et al. 2001), or in a Cre-recombinase–dependent fashion (Atasoy et al. 2008). Other vectors were engineered to label pathways as they spread selectively across synapses (see reviews in Xu et al. 2020; Saleeba et al. 2019). And yet other vectors were created to drive the expression of both a fluorescent tag and a light-sensitive optogenetic probe in the transfected axons, hence making possible the simultaneous interrogation of thalamic axon wiring and synaptic effects with unprecedented resolution and flexibility (see, e.g., Cruikshank et al. 2012; Zhou et al. 2018; Collins et al. 2018).

2.2.3 Neurochemical Characterization of Thalamic Circuits

In parallel with the advent of axonal transport connection-tracing methods, a variety new histochemical, immunolabeling, and in situ messenger RNA (mRNA) hybridization methods became available in the 1980s and 1990s. These revealed the existence of diverse molecular mechanisms for signal transmission and allowed their mapping at the cellular and subcellular levels. As a result, we now know that the projection neurons in all dorsal thalamic nuclei use mostly glutamate as a neurotransmitter. Corticothalamic and most subcortical thalamus input pathways are glutamatergic as well. Interestingly, the glutamate transporters in the synaptic vesicles of the thalamocortical and subcortical afferent axon terminals are different from those employed in the corticothalamic terminals (Fujiyama et al. 2001). In contrast, the intrinsic interneurons and prethalamic reticular nucleus cells utilize the inhibitory gamma-amino butyric acid (GABA). Some subcortical pathways also signal to thalamic neurons through inhibitory synapses, using GABA or glycine (reviewed in Halassa & Acsàdy 2016). Other studies detected the selective expression of proteins with specific calcium-binding dynamic profiles (calbindin28K, parvalbumin, calretinin) in different thalamic cell subpopulations (Rausell & Jones 1991; Jones & Hendry 1989).

Immunolabeling studies also revealed a variety of "diffuse" brainstem input pathways to the thalamus, each identified by their use of a specific neurotransmitter, as well as by their origin in a different brainstem cell population. Specific antibodies against the neurotransmitter itself, its pathway enzymes, or its membrane transporters became key tools to map these systems in different species. The diffuse input pathways included the cholinergic axons from the peribrachial region and laterodorsal nucleus of the pons (Saper & Loewy 1980; Ahlsén 1984; Hallanger et al. 1987), the noradrenergic axons from the locus coeruleus (Pickel et al. 1974; Leger et al. 1975; Swanson & Hartman 1975), and the serotonergic axons from the dorsal and median nucleus of the raphe (Conrad 1974; Morrison & Foote 1986; Rico & Cavada 1998). In addition, a substantial dopaminergic system and several peptidergic systems were described in the primate thalamus (Lechner et al. 1993; García-Cabezas et al. 2009). All components of the thalamus, including the dorsal thalamus and the prethalamic reticular nucleus, were found to be innervated by these pathways in

---

Caption for Figure 5 (cont.)

B. Thalamocortical cell somata retrogradely labeled in the ventromedial nucleus of a cat after an injection of horseradish peroxidase in the insular cortex. Tetramethyl benzidine histochemistry. Darkfield optics + polarized light. Bar = 150 μm.

C. Thalamocortical cell somata in the medial dorsal nucleus of a macaque labeled by retrograde transport of the fluorochromes fast blue (FB) and diamidino yellow (DY) following separate injections of the tracers in the orbitofrontal cortex. Arrows point to double-labeled cells. Bar = 100 μm.

D. Layer 6 corticothalamic cells labeled in the temporal cortex of a marmoset monkey following an injection of cholera toxin subunit B in the pulvinar nucleus. Immunostaining with avidin-biotin peroxidase and diaminobenzidine-nickel. Bar = 100 μm.

E. Terminal axon arborizations in the primary somatosensory cortex of a mouse labeled by an injection of biotinylated dextran amine 10,000 MW in the ventral posterior nucleus. Avidin-biotin peroxidase and diaminobenzidine-nickel stain. The arrows point to some retrogradely labeled layer 6 corticothalamic cells that reveal the reciprocal nature of these connections. Bar = 100 μm.

F. Overlapped labeling of thalamocortical somata (large dots) and anterogradely labeled corticothalamic terminals (fine dust-like stain, arrows) in the medial pulvinar nucleus of a macaque following an injection in the orbitofrontal cortex. Wheat germ agglutinin-conjugated horseradish peroxidase visualized with tetramethylbenzidine histochemistry and darkfield + polarized light optics. Again, the pattern reveals a reciprocal connection between the thalamus and cortex. Bar = 300 μm.

G. Corticothalamic layer 5 pyramidal cells labeled in the suprasylvian cortex of eight-day postnatal ferret labeled by the passive diffusion of a carbocyanine dye (DiI) deposited in the thalamus. Bar = 50 μm.

H. Diagram by Macchi et al. (1986) that summarizes their view on thalamocortical-pathway-layout-derived experiments with dual-retrograde tracer injections in the cat cortex (see panel B). These authors proposed the existence of four main "classes" of thalamic nuclei, according to their targeting of one or more areas and the density of each projection.

I. Highly schematic diagram of corticothalamic (right hemisphere) and thalamocortical (left hemisphere) pathways in the human brain (data extrapolated from animal axonal transport tracing studies; Nieuwenhuys et al. 2008). For clarity, the main thalamic gray masses are highlighted in orange, the internal medullary lamina in yellow, and the prethalamic reticular nucleus in blue. Note that each nucleus is reciprocally connected with a region of the cortex. Note also that all pathways coming and going from the cortex to the thalamus cross the prethalamic reticular nucleus and leave a collateral connection in it. Prethalamic Reticular nucleus neurons in turn project to the corresponding thalamic nucleus. Widely-spread "nonspecific" thalamocortical connections (dashed lines) are depicted as arising from the intralaminar nuclei.

Panel A: Courtesy of Dr. C. Avendaño; panels C and D: courtesy of Dr. C. Cavada.

History

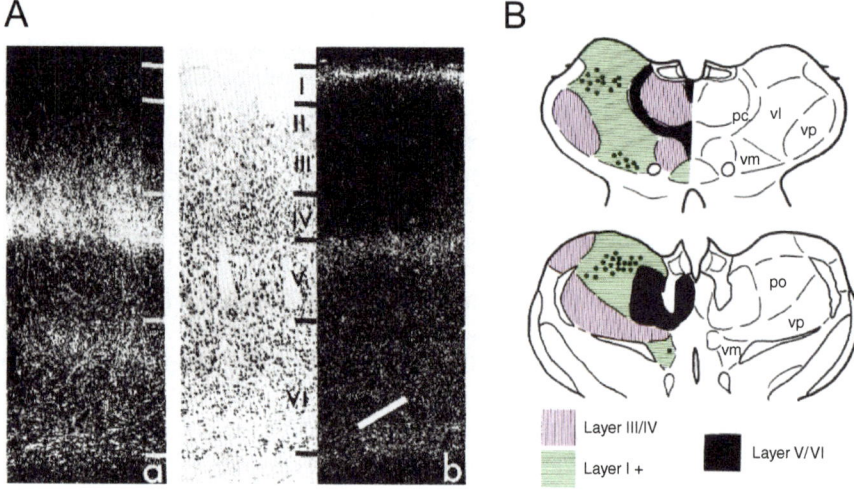

Figure 6 Herkenham's tripartite classification of thalamic nuclei according to the laminar distribution of their axons in the cortex.

A. Columnar samples of the rat somatosensory cortex showing the autoradiographic labeling of thalamocortical arborizations produced by the transport of tritiated amino acids that were previously injected in two different thalamic nuclei. Under darkfield optics, the autoradiography silver grains appear as white dots. In each column, the pial surface is at the top. Panel A shows the labeling produced by an amino acid injection in the ventral posteromedial nucleus. For reference, a bright-field image of the same sample, counterstained with Nissl stain and with the cortical laminae 1–6 (I–VI) indicated, is also included. Panel B shows the labeling produced by an injection in the posterior thalamic nucleus. Note the strikingly different laminar distribution of the autoradiography grains. Bar = 500 µm. From Herkenham (1980).

B. Two coronal section diagrams of the rat thalamus illustrating the three main classes of thalamic nuclei. Vertical grating and magenta shade: nuclei innervating mainly cortical layers ("4–3" class). Horizontal grating and green shade: nuclei innervating cortical layer 1 and, to a variable extent, other layers ("1+" class). Black shade: nuclei targeting mainly cortical layers 5 and 6 ("5–6" class). Modified from Herkenham (1986).

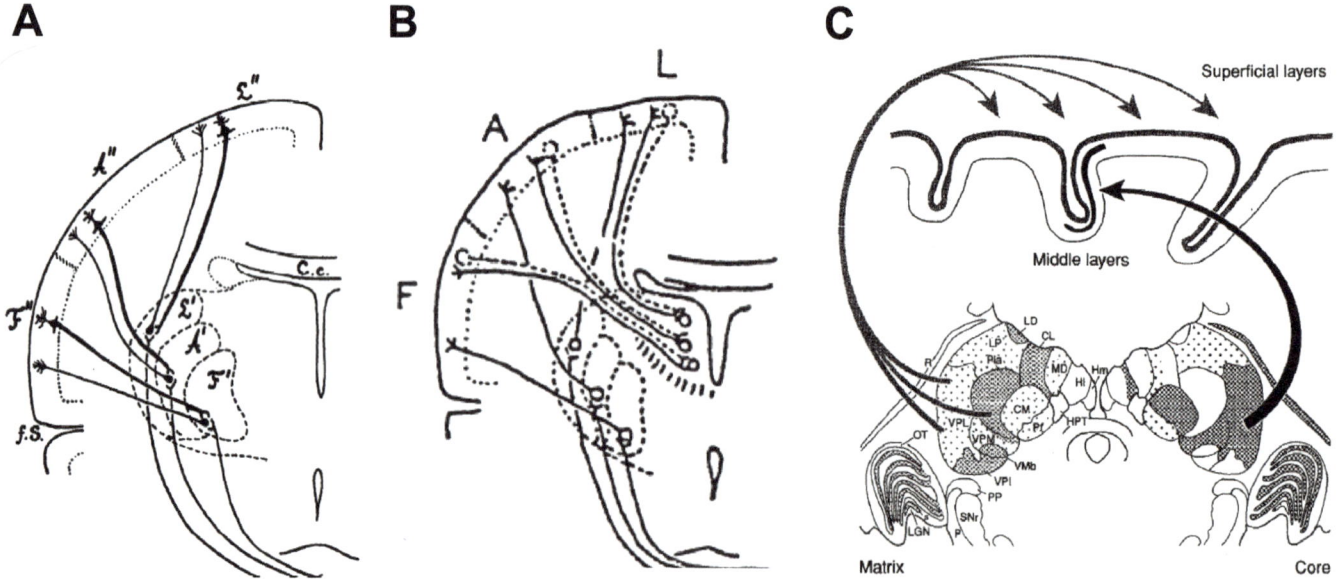

Figure 7 Models of thalamocortical wiring: topographic versus diffuse thalamocortical projection systems.

A. A strictly reciprocal thalamocortical wiring model proposed by Dusser de Barenne and McCulloch (1938) based on their strychnine stimulation studies of the sensory cortex and degeneration mapping studies by others.

B. Dempsey and Morison (1942) model postulating the existence of both point-to-point specific axons arising in the ventral nuclei as well as a diffuse, "nonspecific" type of axons arising from the medial and intralaminar nuclei. This model was proposed to account for the observed effects on the electroencephalogram activity of direct electrical stimulation in different thalamic nuclei. F, A, and L indicate regions carrying somatic information from the face, arm, and leg, respectively.

C. Diagram by Jones (2007) of his dual matrix-core model (*right*) represented on a frontal section through a macaque monkey thalamus. The distribution and relative concentration of calbindin-expressing matrix-type thalamic neurons (left thalamus) or parvalbumin-expressing core-type thalamic neurons (right thalamus) are indicated by different shading and stippling. A projection of the matrix-type cells to superficial layers of cortex over a relatively wide extent and unconstrained by borders between areas is also shown (*top*). Core-type cells restricted to individual nuclei project in a topographically ordered manner to the middle layers of single functional cortical fields.

a highly uneven fashion, as the axons branch profusely and cross nuclear boundaries. Studies combining immunolabeling and electron microscopy revealed that the distribution of these brainstem axons onto the thalamic cells and their presynaptic structure is specific (Raczkowski & Fitzpatrick 1989; Nothias et al. 1988).

The expression of receptors for each of the various neurotransmitters is highly heterogeneous across thalamic territories as well (Pérez-Santos et al. 2021). Overall, these discoveries have revealed a rich combinatorial matrix of modulatory inputs superimposed onto that of the main, signal-carrying afferent pathways.

2.2.4 Single-Cell Labeling Studies

Although dendritic and local axon morphologies had been amenable to study since the introduction of the Golgi method, techniques able to reveal the entire axonal tree of individual long-range projection neurons did not become available until the late 1990s (Deschênes et al. 1994; Pinault 1996). The first technique published required electroporation, under extracellular recording conditions, of a histochemically detectable marker molecule such as biocytin. This "juxtacellular labeling" strategy allowed the first visualizations of the complete morphology of individual thalamocortical, corticothalamic, and reticulo-thalamic neurons (Deschênes et al. 1998, Figure 8A–C). In the 2010s, new viral vectors (Kuramoto et al. 2009) or combinations of vectors (Economo et al. 2016) able to drive the expression of high levels of different fluorescent proteins in isolated cells expanded the array of tools available for visualizing complete thalamic projection neuron morphologies. To date, the method of single-cell tracing and reconstruction has been applied to a number of nuclei and cortical areas of the thalamus, mainly in rats and mice.

The most relevant insights gleaned to date from the single-cell studies regard the prevalence and specificity of branched axons. For example, many thalamic axons were found to innervate the cortex and striatum and/or amygdala simultaneously, dispelling the notion of strictly separate thalamocortical, thalamostriatal, and thalamoamygdaloid circuits. Within the cortex, branched axons were found to target separate areas, to arborize in different layers in each area, and to establish structurally diverse synapses that engage specific cell populations and receptor mechanisms (Kuramoto et al. 2009; Rodriguez-Moreno et al. 2020). These findings upended the dual matrix-core model. Overall, the single-cell labeling data made it clear that the thalamic projection neurons are a diverse cell population that encompasses several major cell classes, each characterized by their axonal architecture as well as other differences in somato-dendritic morphology and calcium-binding protein expression. The same basic cell types are found across different functional systems (see Chapter 3, in this book).

Likewise, branching in corticothalamic pathways was found to be highly specific. For example, the layer 5 projection to the thalamus is established exclusively via collateral branches from axons directed to brainstem motor centers; remarkably, these axons leave few or no branches in the prethalamic reticular nucleus. In contrast, corticothalamic layer 6 projections are established by axons that arborize only in the thalamus and reticular nucleus. The arborization patterns and presynaptic specializations of layer 5 and layer 6 inputs in the thalamus are strikingly different (Bourassa et al. 1995; Deschênes et al. 1998, Kakei et al. 2001, Guillery & Sherman 2002a; see Section 2.3.3).

2.3 Electrical Recording Studies and Theories of Thalamic Function

The technological effort around the Second World War led to the development of new systems capable of electrical recording, feedback, and amplification at the scales required for investigating the activity of neuronal populations or individual cells in the thalamus. Starting in the 1940s, these studies developed around two main themes: (a) the properties of thalamic neurons related to their role as relay stations for ascending information to the cerebral cortex and (b) the involvement of the thalamus in the synchronous activities of large numbers of forebrain neurons associated with different states of consciousness and sleep.

2.3.1 Functional Studies of the Thalamic Sensory Relay

Relay function studies recorded changes evoked by sensory stimulation in the membrane potential of thalamic and cortical cells. The emphasis of this approach was mainly on the mapping of topographical representations of the skin surface, visual field, and auditory periphery in the principal relay nuclei and on the receptive fields and response properties of neurons in these nuclei. Prominent researchers in this field were Vernon Mountcastle and colleagues in the somatosensory system (Rose & Mountcastle 1952; Poggio & Mountcastle 1963), David Hubel and Torsten Wiesel (1961) in the visual system, and Jerzy Rose and Clinton Woolsey (1958) in the auditory system.

Thalamic sensory nuclei were found to be ideal experimental models because of the ease of controlling input parameters during recording to gain insight into the specific functions performed in these circuits. An additional advantage is that neurons in sensory relay nuclei usually remain responsive under light anesthesia. Progress in electrophysiology created a positive-feedback loop for increasingly sophisticated structural and/or neurochemical investigations of the sensory nuclei and their connections. Eventually, the study of thalamic sensory pathways and their relay nuclei came to dominate thalamus research almost completely for several decades, even though these nuclei represent just one part of the thalamus and a relatively small one in humans (Guillery 1995).

The development of intracellular glass microelectrodes in the 1960s expanded the sensitivity and resolution of electrophysiological thalamic relay function studies. Such electrodes, applied in vivo or on brain slices, allowed the characterization of the functional properties of thalamic circuits at the single-cell level. In subsequent years, the microelectrodes were filled with marker substances that diffused, while recording, into the cells or terminal axons. This allowed detailed visualization of the recorded cells or axons under light and electron microscopy. This approach revealed, for example, the specific terminal morphologies of different retinofugal axon types in the dorsal lateral geniculate nucleus (Bowling & Michael 1980, 1984), the synaptic relationships of interneurons in this nucleus (Hamos et al. 1985, 1987), or the existence of three cells subclasses in the dorsal lateral geniculate nucleus, each carrying different signals from the retina and arborizing in specific layers of the primary visual cortex (Friedlander et al. 1981; Stanford et al. 1981, 1983; Sur & Sherman 1982).

Likewise, microelectrode studies established the existence of an extensive and functionally diverse set of corticothalamic connections. These were later shown to be excitatory but to elicit mainly inhibitory effects in the thalamic cells through a parallel activation of inhibitory neurons in the prethalamic reticular nucleus as well as of intrinsic interneurons in the relay nuclei (Swadlow 1994; Steriade 2001a, 2001b; Sirota et al. 2005; Briggs 2020).

History

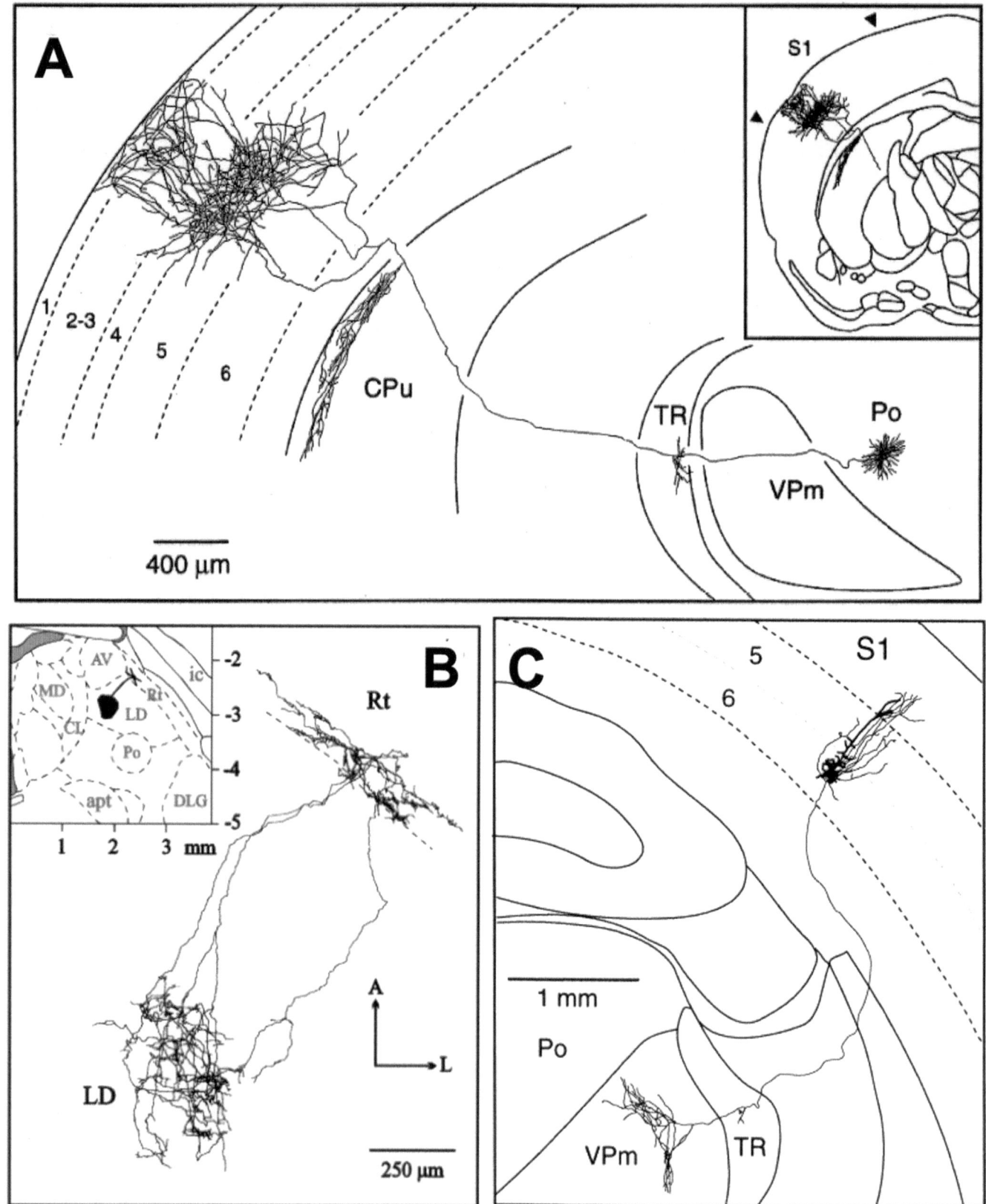

Figure 8 Complete morphology visualization of rat neurons labeled using juxtacellular microinjections of biocytin.

A. Thalamic posterior nucleus projection cell whose axons branch to arborize in the prethalamic reticular nucleus (TR), the striatum (CPu), and the primary somatosensory S1 cortex. The cell is represented on a coronal section contour.

B. Prethalamic nucleus cell innervating the laterodorsal thalamic nucleus. A horizontal section diagram of the thalamus (*inset*) is provided for orientation.

C. Corticothalamic layer 6 neuron from the primary somatosensory cortex (S1) innervating the ventral posteromedial nucleus (VPm). Note also the small collateral branch in the reticular prethalamic nucleus (TR).

Panels A and C taken from Deschênes et al. (1998); panel B taken from Pinault and Deschênes (1998).

Intracellular recordings in thalamus slices by Rodolfo Llinás and coworkers (Jahnsen & Llinás 1984a, 1984b) made the crucial discovery that all the thalamic relay cells have in their membranes an unusual type of calcium channel (transient T-type Ca^{2+} channels). These channels mediate, in a voltage-dependent manner, an inward current (I_T) that produces a transient depolarization of the cell (Figure 9A). Although T channels are common to neurons everywhere, what sets the thalamic projection neurons cell apart is that they exhibit a sufficiently dense distribution of T channels in their somata and dendrites that initiation of I_T generally leads to an all-or-none Ca^{2+} spike propagated throughout the soma and dendritic arbor. This is seen only rarely in other neuronal types in the central nervous system (Sherman 2001a).

It was subsequently shown that as a result of having these channels, a thalamic projection neuron cell can respond to incoming excitatory stimuli in one of two very different modes, depending on its recent voltage history (Sherman 2001b; Figure 9B). In the "tonic" mode, when the cell is near the resting membrane potential (approximately –60 mV), T channels go along with the rest of membrane conductances, allowing the projection neuron to fire action potentials at frequencies linearly proportional to the amplitude of the stimuli it receives. Thus, while in tonic mode, thalamic projection neurons faithfully relay ascending sensory or motor information.

In contrast, the same cells enter "burst" mode at more hyperpolarized (–70 mV) membrane potentials. In this situation, the T channels open again, allowing a calcium spike that is sufficiently large (typically 25–40 mV) to trigger a transient, high-frequency burst of two to ten action potentials. Bursting is an all-or-none activity, and its temporal profile follows mainly from the T-channel dynamics. As a result, during bursting, signals are nonlinearly relayed, and information may be lost. In addition, burst firing provides a much higher signal-to-noise ratio in the incoming flow of signals to the cortex than tonic firing, implying that an evoked burst is more likely to be detected by the cortex and may be used as a "wake-up call" for novel, potentially relevant stimuli (Sherman 2001b; Swadlow & Gusev 2001).

2.3.2 Studies of Thalamus-Driven Large-Scale Oscillations

In parallel with the studies of the thalamus as a relay, other electrophysiological studies examined a possible role of the thalamus in the generation of coordinated activity across widespread brain cell populations. This activity, detectable through

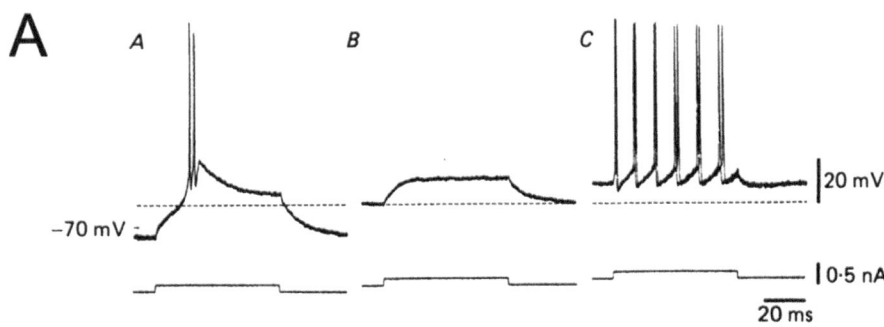

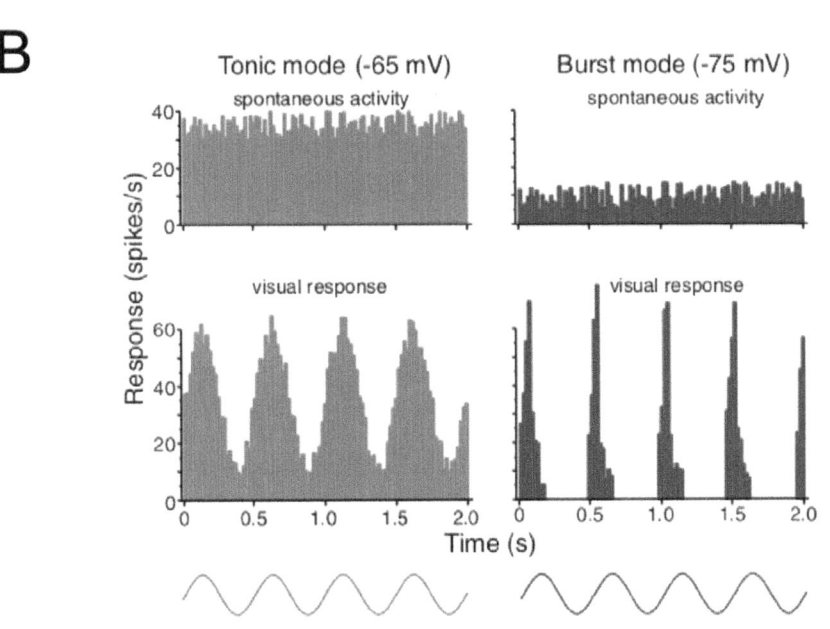

Figure 9 Intrinsic properties of burst and tonic firing in thalamic relay cells.

A. Responses of a cell recorded in vitro in a slice, showing the different response of the cell to the same depolarizing current injection (*bottom trace*) while a holding current was applied to change the standing membrane potential to hyperpolarization (*A*), resting potential (*B*), and subthreshold depolarization (*C*). From Jahnsen and Llinás (1984a).

B. Response differences for dorsal lateral geniculate relay neurons in the cat between tonic and burst modes recorded in vivo. Current injected through the intracellular recording electrode was used to bias membrane potential to more depolarized (65 mV), producing tonic firing, or more hyperpolarized (75 mV), producing burst firing. The responses are shown as average response histograms. Top histograms show spontaneous activity; bottom ones show responses to a sinusoidal grating drifted through the receptive field. The sine waves under each set of histograms show the contrast changes as the grating drifts through the receptive field. From Sherman (2001b).

macroelectrodes applied on the scalp or in the brain, had been shown to consist of large-scale voltage waves comprising different types of low-frequency and high-frequency oscillations that changed according to the state of consciousness (Berger 1929).

Interest in the thalamus as a potential source for some of these widespread oscillations arose from reports in the early 1940s that linked the thalamus with a type of slow (7- to 14-Hz) high-voltage waxing and waning wave burst that repeated spontaneously over wide zones of the cortex and thalamus during the entry or recovery from slow-wave sleep or under barbiturate anesthesia. These bursts, later known as *spindles* because of their appearance in the electroencephalogram (EEG), were first recorded in mesencephalon-transected cats (Bremer 1937) or in barbiturate-anesthetized animals after sensory stimulation (Adrian 1941). Intriguingly, spindles were observed to disappear from the cortex after transections of the underlying white matter (Bremer 1937; Morison et al. 1943; Burns 1950), yet they persisted in the thalamus even after complete decortication and extensive thalamic deafferentation (Morison et al. 1943; Morison & Basett 1945). These observations were interpreted as evidence that the thalamus could, in some circumstances, act as a pacemaker for cortical activity. Interest in this hypothesis was in part spurred by the assumption, later dismissed, that spindle activity could bear relation to the generation of the EEG alpha rhythm that characterizes relaxed wakefulness.

Another type of rhythmic activity associated with the thalamus was first reported in studies in barbiturate-anesthetized cats that recorded two different types of electrical activity "responses" on the cortical surface following the application of repeated low-frequency trains of electrical pulses in the thalamus (Dempsey & Morison 1942). The first or "primary" response, appearing at a short latency (around 3 ms) in primary sensory or motor areas after stimulation of their corresponding relay nuclei, consisted of a biphasic positive–negative that "augmented" in amplitude and cortical spread with pulse repetition. It is now known that this wave pattern reflects the distribution of some thalamocortical terminals in the middle layers of the cortex and their short-term synaptic plasticity mechanisms. The second ("recruiting") type of response appeared at longer latencies (around 20–35 ms) over much wider territories as high-voltage surface-negative waves that waxed and waned recurrently. Remarkably, this recruiting response was reported to be best elicited by stimulation in the medial and intralaminar nuclei, often following a single stimulus, and appeared mainly in the same frontoparietal areas where the spontaneous spindle activity was usually observed (Verzeano et al. 1953).

The significance of spindles and recruiting responses remains unclear, and they may actually be epiphenomenal effects of thalamic cell membrane properties and synaptic wiring (see later discussion); however, they were profoundly influential in generating experiments that uncovered important aspects of the functional connectivity of the thalamus.

The pursuit of the mechanism of this recruiting response attracted much attention in the 1940s and 1950s. The surface-negative wave profile of the response was interpreted as evidence of its origin near the cortical surface (Jasper 1949). Despite the long latencies, Dempsey and Morison (1942) favored the interpretation that it should involve a direct projection from a diffuse, thin-axon thalamocortical system preferentially targeting layer 1 (Figure 7B). Multidisciplinary approaches were unusual at the time, and these electrophysiology researchers apparently took at face value the opinion by Lorente de No that some of the "nonspecific" thalamocortical fibers he had observed in Golgi samples while at Cajal's lab might originate in the intralaminar nuclei (Lorente de No 1938, Figure 4B).

Hence, the notion was born that the intralaminar nuclei would innervate layer 1 in a diffuse manner and be the substrate for the recruiting responses. Remarkably, functional studies of this hypothetical system eventually came to absorb a substantial effort of thalamus research well until the early 1960s. Other authors posited that the intralaminar nuclei of the thalamus would represent, together with the prethalamic reticular nucleus, a rostral extension of a multisynaptic "ascending reticular activating system" (a concept in vogue at the time; Moruzzi & Magoun 1949) that would spread excitatory brainstem activity to the cortex for the regulation of consciousness and sleep.

Recruiting-response studies produced the first functional investigations of nonsensory thalamic nuclei in the medial and intralaminar regions of the thalamus, emphasizing their possible role in cortical arousal and EEG desynchronization (Jasper 1949, 1960). Additionally, because these nuclei could not be selectively driven by peripheral sensory stimulation, this line of research required the development of new fine bipolar electrodes for deep-brain stimulation and lesioning. It also fostered the publication of the first stereotaxic brain atlases to guide the positioning of deep electrodes in experimental animals (Jasper & Ajmone-Marsan 1954; Reinoso-Suárez 1961). As years passed, however, spindle activity was found to be evoked by microstimulation also in lateral nuclei such as the medial geniculate (Galambos et al. 1952) or the ventrobasal complex (Andersen & Sears 1964) and even in nonthalamic regions. Eventually, interest in the nonspecific / intralaminar system waned. In the following decades, axonal transport studies would reveal that the intralaminar nuclei do not target the superficial layers of the cortex and mostly innervate relatively restricted cortical territories (Herkenham 1986; Groenewegen & Berendse 1994; Deschênes et al. 1996).

In the 1990s and 2000s, the notion of a widely spread, upper-layer–directed thalamocortical system was revived within the "core-matrix" model of thalamocortical pathways of Edward Jones (Llinás et al. 1998; Jones 2001, 2007, 2009 Figure 7C). However, Jones remarked that the projection neurons originating this system were not located in the intralaminar nuclei but spread instead across many other thalamic nuclei. Jones speculated that the "matrix" projection neurons would propagate synchronous oscillations across wide assemblies of cortical and thalamic cells. Taking into the model some then recently published single-cell tracing data on corticothalamic pathways (Bourassa et al. 1995; Veinante et al. 2000; Figure 8B), he postulated that the double reciprocal pathways linking the thalamus and cortex, along with the widely projecting matrix thalamocortical cells, could be the substrate for the spread of coherent activity throughout the thalamocortical network (Jones 2001, 2009). However, rather than relating this effect to slow cortical oscillations as in the 1940s, Jones posited that the matrix thalamocortical system might facilitate the propagation of oscillations at faster frequencies (~40 Hz) across the network. These fast oscillations, known to originate in the cortex, had been associated a few years earlier with conscious sensory experiences in humans (Desmedt & Tomberg 1994; Tononi & Edelman 1998; Llinás et al. 1998). A link between the matrix cell pathway with reports of behavioral improvement in minimally conscious patients with brain injuries after thalamic stimulation was also proposed (Schiff et al. 2007).

In addition, Jones noted that the complementary laminar termination upon cortical pyramidal cells of "matrix" and "core" axons laid the wiring for a coincidence detector (Figure 10B). Based on this model, it was also speculated that pathological alterations disrupting the low- and high-frequency oscillatory rhythms of the thalamocortical network could ultimately underlie some of the clinical manifestations of conditions as diverse as neurogenic pain, tinnitus, Parkinson's disease, and depression (Llinás et al. 1999; Jones 2009).

2.3.3 Studies of the Thalamic Pacemaker Mechanisms

The notion that the thalamus was a pacemaker for some rhythmic EEG activities also triggered a search for the mechanisms that could generate such rhythmicity. First, Dempsey and Morison (1942) posited the existence in the medial and intralaminar nuclei of some cells with spontaneous rhythmic discharges that would be able to influence cells in other nuclei by means of hypothetical internuclear connections and/or corticothalamic feedback. Subsequent studies specifically aimed at testing these ideas combined microstimulation of the medial-intralaminar nuclei while intracellularly recording in the more lateral thalamic nuclei in awake, paralyzed animals (Purpura & Cohen 1962; Purpura & Shofer 1963).

During these experiments, large inhibitory postsynaptic potentials (IPSPs) were observed in the thalamic projection neurons following the thalamic stimulus. These potentials were long (80–200 ms) and effectively suppressed the spontaneous discharge of the neurons. Shorter excitatory postsynaptic potentials (EPSPs) alternated with them in a stereotyped fashion. Moreover, the stereotyped sequence also occurred spontaneously during spindles. At the time, it was proposed that these sequences and the ensuing synchronization in the EEG were generated in reciprocally interconnected excitatory neurons in medial and lateral thalamic nuclei (Purpura 1972).

Evidence for connections between dorsal thalamic nuclei was not substantiated by subsequent anatomical investigations with axonal transport labeling methods, and the notion was abandoned. However, these studies brought the role of inhibition in the generation of rhythmic thalamocortical cell oscillations to the forefront of research. In this vein, Andersen and colleagues (Andersen & Sears 1964; Andersen & Andersson 1968) observed the same type of alternating excitation and inhibition sequences following peripheral nerve stimulation in the ventroposterior nucleus of barbiturate-anesthetized cats. Their interpretation was that the thalamic spindle sequence would start with the firing of a projection neuron produced spontaneously or by extrinsic inputs. The activity would then be propagated within the nucleus through the supposed collaterals of the projection cell axon inside the nucleus to inhibitory local circuit interneurons. These would fire repetitively and induce the long IPSPs in a population of surrounding projection cells. After the IPSPs, the projection cells would rebound, firing axon potentials that would again reach, via their supposed axon collaterals, a wider group of interneurons, which would in turn recruit a larger number of thalamic cells, and so on, in cyclic fashion. The sequence would wane after a number of cycles because differences in IPSP duration would decouple the oscillations in the cell population. According to this view, any nucleus could become a pacemaker and propagate its activity to the cerebral cortex.

In the following decades, however, the same observations were reinterpreted in the light of new functional, anatomical, and neurochemical discoveries. These showed that projection neuron axons do not leave collateral branches inside the thalamus. Instead, the long IPSPs actually depend on the collaterals of the projection axons exciting prethalamic reticular nucleus cells (Figure 10A). The reticular cells were shown to be GABAergic (Houser et al. 1980) and to project back, in topographical fashion, to the thalamic nucleus that innervates them (Jones 1975; Steriade et al. 1987). Moreover, prethalamic reticular nucleus cells were shown to fire prolonged bursts of high-frequency action potentials during the spindles. Such bursts are enhanced by GABAergic connections between prethalamic reticular nucleus cells and the excitatory corticothalamic input to the nucleus.

In contrast, thalamic interneuron axons were found to remain confined to individual nuclei near their parent cell soma or to be missing altogether, as most interneuron synapses are dendro-dendritic (Jones 2007; Cox 2014). Because the thalamic projection cells do not connect directly to each other, local-scale connections within the thalamus are dominated by these resident inhibitory neurons (Sherman 2004; Hirsch et al. 2015). Remarkably, interneuron numbers and distribution vary widely across mammalian phyla, being virtually absent from some or most nuclei of the thalamus in some species, such as small rodents, marsupials, and bats. This observation suggests that the local interneurons are an optional part of the thalamic networks, and they may be flexibly modified to develop specific evolutionary adaptations (Arcelli et al. 1997; Letinic & Rakic 2001; Rikhye et al. 2018; Jager et al. 2021).

Studies in the 1980s and 1990s firmly established that the prethalamic reticular nucleus is the pacemaker for the thalamic-generated spindles and revealed the circuit and intrinsic cell properties of the reticular nucleus and thalamic cells from which it arises. The rebound discharges of thalamic cells were shown to depend on the expression, in thalamic cells of the T channels, the voltage-dependent conductances described in Section 2.3.2 (Jahnsen & Llinás 1984a, 1984b; Roy et al. 1984). During the spindling activity, low-threshold spikes and bursts occur in the projection cell as they recover from the strong

History

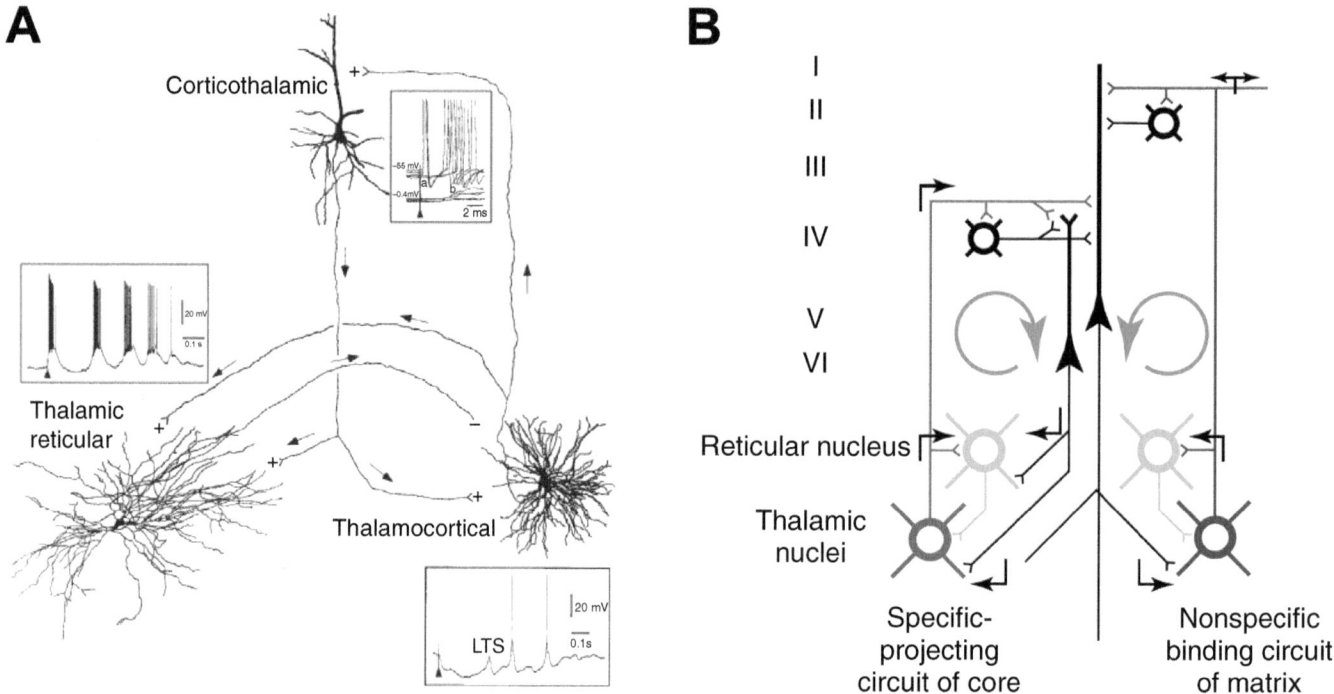

Figure 10 Neuronal loops in corticothalamic networks implicated in coherent oscillations.

A. Diagram by Steriade (1999). The three neuronal morphologies shown were actual cells recorded and stained intracellularly in anesthetized cats. The direction of action potential propagation their axons is indicated by arrows. The insets represent their responses to thalamic and cortical stimulation (arrowheads point to stimulus artifacts).

B. Model diagram by Jones (2001). Inputs from core (*left*) and matrix (*right*) cells oscillating at high frequencies were hypothesized to be integrated over the dendritic tree of cortical pyramidal cells (middle top) and promote oscillatory activity in the cortical cells, activity that would be further promoted by feedback to the initiating thalamic nucleus by layer 6 corticothalamic cells.

inhibition imposed by the prethalamic reticular nucleus cells. Thalamic projection cells burst and then excite prethalamic reticular nucleus cells, and the cycle starts again (Bal & McCormick 1993). Importantly, the thalamic cells do not oscillate at spindle frequencies when deprived of inhibitory input from the prethalamic reticular nucleus (Steriade et al. 1987). The population-level spindle waxes as more reticular nucleus and projection cells are recruited and wanes as the two populations become out of step. Beyond the spindle phenomenon, however, the most relevant effect of the prethalamic reticular nucleus-imposed inhibition on projection cells during normal information transmission probably occurs on those cells that are firing out of synchrony with the most activated projection cell population. In this way, activity in particular regions of the reticular nucleus can powerfully "focus" the flow of information through the thalamus (Crick 1984; Steriade 1999).

Overall, these investigations revealed that the dorsal thalamus and the prethalamic reticular nucleus form a tightly integrated functional network and that inhibition plays a major role in shaping thalamic cells' responses. Changes in prethalamic reticular nucleus inhibitory activity under modulation from the thalamus, cortex, and brainstem cholinergic and monoaminergic systems thus may even be causal to changes in arousal states (Dingledine & Kelly 1977; Beierlein 2014; Lewis et al. 2015).

2.3.4 The Guillery and Sherman Synthesis

In the late 1990s, a comprehensive new synthesis of thalamus structure and function was proposed by Ray Guillery and Murray Sherman and subsequently elaborated over the course of a long collaboration (Guillery 1995; Sherman & Guillery 1996, 1998, 2005, 2012; Guillery & Sherman 2002). This multi-pronged model was based on both electron microscopic and microelectrode recording data from their own laboratories, mainly on sensory relay nuclei, as well as on insightful analysis of the literature.

On the anatomical side, a fundamental distinction was made between the "first-order relay" (FO) thalamic nuclei that relay to the cortex ascending signals from the subcortical sensory or motor systems versus the "higher-order relay" (HO) nuclei that relay back to the cortex signals received from the cortex itself, via collaterals of layer 5 axons primarily directed to the brainstem (Guillery 1995). It was also pointed out that because the layer 5 pathway originating in a given primary sensory cortical area is not directed to the FO nucleus that innervates it but to a nearby HO nucleus, a potential route for transthalamic communication between cortical areas is created (Guillery 1995). Direct evidence in support of this hypothesis was subsequently obtained on mouse brain slice preparations with preserved connections between the cortex and thalamus (Theyel et al. 2010).

A second tenet of the proposal was that the layer 5 input would represent the "primary source" of information for HO nuclei cells in a manner equivalent to what subcortical sensory inputs are for FO nuclei cells (Guillery 1995). This conclusion was based on the fact that both layer 5 axon branches and ascending sensory axons reaching the thalamus form clustered large terminal boutons on proximal projection cell dendrites

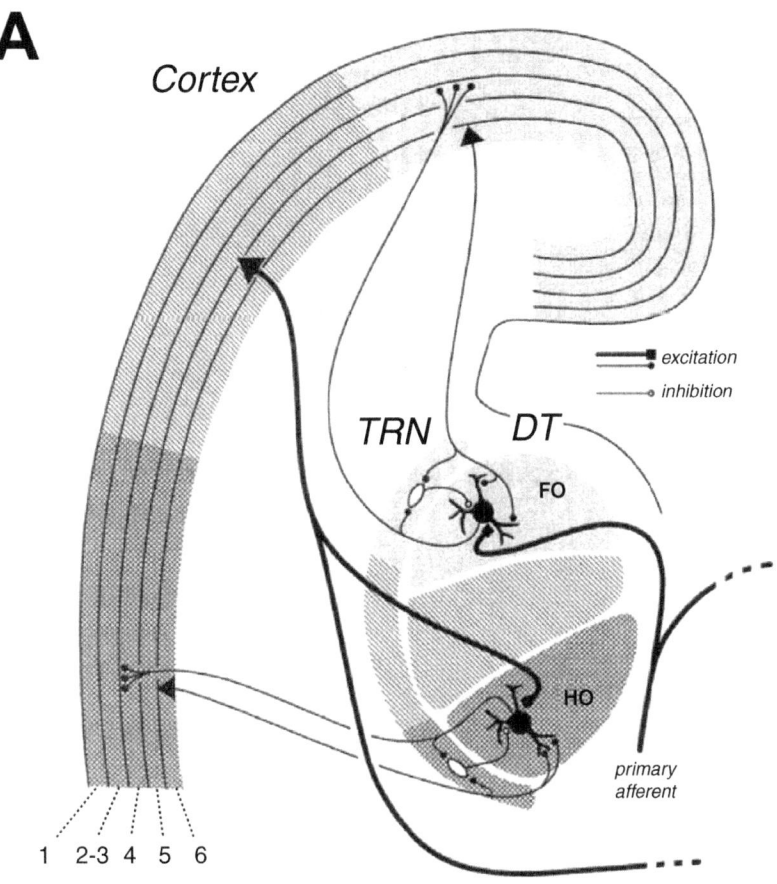

Figure 11 Sherman and Guillery's functional diagrams of the thalamo-cortico-thalamic network.

A. Diagram summarizing the major neuronal pathways involved in thalamocortical interactions. Three relay nuclei of the dorsal thalamus (DT), three regions of the prethalamic reticular nucleus (TRN), and three areas of cerebral cortex (cortex) are shown. Associated regions of the DT, TRN, and cortex share the same shading pattern, and some of the key interconnections are shown. From Sherman and Guillery (1996).

B. Diagram of the network created by direct and transthalamic corticocortical pathways. Information relayed to the cortex through the thalamus is brought to thalamus via class 1 axons, most or all of which branch, with the extrathalamic branch innervating brainstem or spinal cord motor centers. This applies to inputs to both first-order (FO) and higher-order (HO) thalamic relays. From Sherman and Guillery (2011).

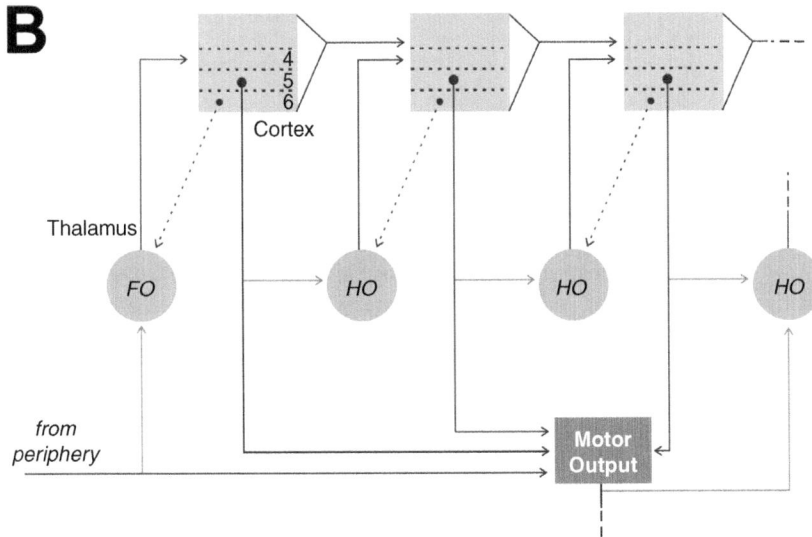

(Hoogland et al. 1987) that show virtually identical synaptic ultrastructures (Colonnier & Guillery 1964; Mathers 1972a, 1972b). Perceptively, Sherman & Guillery (1996) also remarked that, according to information in the literature, both the layer 5 corticothalamic and the peripheral sensory input systems to the thalamus are, as a rule, collateral branches of axons that simultaneously innervate lower (motor) centers. The functional implication is that the main content of information flowing through the thalamus must be about ongoing cortical or subcortical motor instructions (Figure 11B; Guillery & Sherman 2002b).

In striking contrast, the layer 6 cell corticothalamic axons were identified as a functionally different pathway that provides a highly convergent reciprocal feedback loop. Layer 6 axons terminate exclusively in the thalamus and the prethalamic reticular nucleus (Figures 8B and 11A), and they

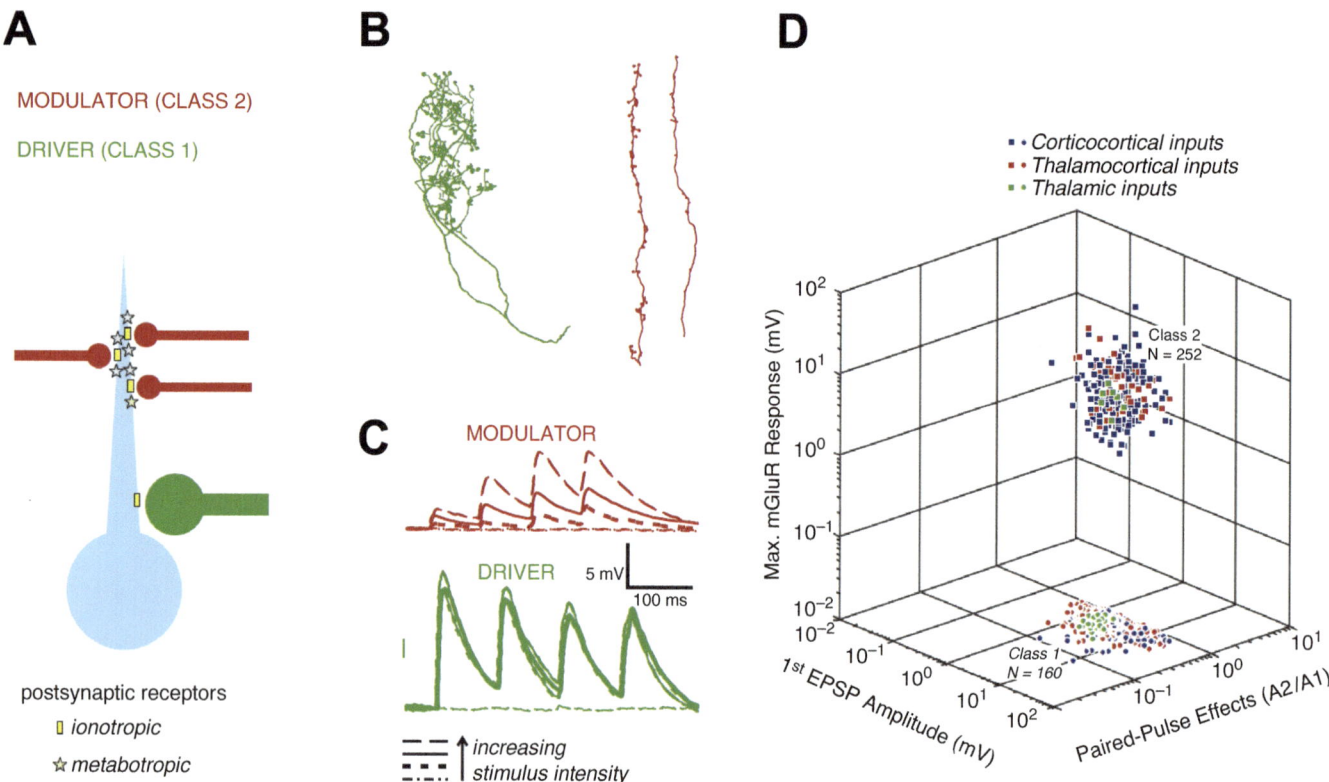

Figure 12 Distinguishing driver (class 1, *green*) from modulator (class 2, *red*) inputs.

A. Highly simplified diagram showing the position along a single dendrite of a relay cell (*blue contour*) of the various synapse and receptors. Modulator synapses are shown contacting more peripheral dendrites than do drivers. Also, drivers activate only ionotropic glutamate receptors, whereas modulators also activate metabotropic glutamate receptors.

B. Light microscopic tracings of a retinogeniculate axon from the cat and a corticogeniculate axon from layer 6 of the cat.

C. Effects of repetitive stimulation on EPSP amplitude: for modulators, it produces paired-pulse facilitation (increasing EPSP amplitudes during the stimulus train), whereas for drivers, it produces paired-pulse depression (decreasing EPSP amplitudes during the stimulus train). Also, increasing stimulus intensity for modulators (shown as different line styles) produces increasing EPSP amplitudes overall, whereas for drivers, it does not; this indicates more convergence of modulator inputs compared with driver inputs. From Sherman and Guillery (2011).

D. Three-dimensional scatter plot showing clustering of selected properties for different class 1 and 2 inputs. From Sherman and Guillery (2011).

form disperse small terminal varicosities that establish synapses only on distal dendritic domains of the thalamic projection neurons (Robson 1983; Guillery 1969).

The third element in the synthesis pertained to the dynamics of signal transmission of the various inputs reaching the thalamic projection neurons. Again, the activities evoked by the ascending subcortical inputs in FO nuclei neurons or layer 5 corticothalamic inputs in HO nuclei neurons were found to be identical. In contrast, the activities evoked by layer 6 corticothalamic inputs were markedly different. For example, in vitro studies showed that HO and layer 5 synapses produced fast-rising, large EPSPs that depressed with paired-pulse repetition, whereas the layer 6 corticothalamic synapses produced smaller, slower-rising currents that increased in amplitude with repetition and lasted longer (Figure 12C and D). Moreover, the application of selective channel blockers revealed that the ascending subcortical inputs to FO neurons and layer 5 corticothalamic inputs to HO neurons were both mediated only by ionotropic glutamate receptors, whereas the layer 6 corticothalamic inputs were mediated by ionotropic as well as metabotropic receptors.

An important generalization to other glutamatergic systems of the forebrain followed from these observations in the thalamus: that the glutamatergic synapses can be consistently separated into two large classes based on their functional impact on postsynaptic cells, subcellular structure, and electrophysiological parameters (Figure 12A–D). Sherman and Guillery (1998, 2011) coined the term *driver* for the glutamatergic synapses capable of reliably transmitting their information content (e.g., receptive field properties) to the postsynaptic cells, and they used the term *modulator* for all other synapses capable of altering the probability of certain aspects of that transmission. In the thalamus, the ascending glutamatergic inputs to FO nuclei and the layer 5 corticothalamic inputs to HO nuclei were both identified as "driver" synapses, whereas the layer 6 corticothalamic were identified as "modulator" synapses. As a result of the different functional impact of each, although the HO thalamic relay is massively dominated in terms of numbers by layer 6 corticothalamic synapses, it is the driver subcortical or cortical layer 5 synapses that determine the main content of the information relayed to the cortex. In subsequent studies, the driver/modulator analysis was extended to thalamocortical synapses (Viaene et al. 2011a, 2011b; Rodriguez-Moreno et al. 2020) and even to some of the afferent subcortical inputs to the thalamus (Lee & Sherman 2010).

Over the past two decades, the conceptual framework proposed by Guillery and Sherman has been profoundly influential. Specifically, it has brought into focus the importance of advancing knowledge on the HO nuclei. As a result, inroads are being made in the understanding of the structural and functional diversity of HO thalamocortical circuits (Rovó et al. 2012; Groh et al. 2014; Rodriguez-Moreno et al. 2020). In parallel, new in vivo experimental approaches are being specifically devised to investigate the roles that HO thalamic cell subnetworks may play in complex functions, such as the control of information transfer between cortical areas, spatial navigation, attention, and cognitive flexibility (Purusothaman et al. 2012; Saalman et al. 2012; Saalman & Kastner 2015; Schmitt et al. 2017). In the coming years, the combination of such approaches may provide important new clues about the functional diversity of thalamic circuits and their role within large-scale multiregional brain networks. Thalamus research history remains in the making.

———————

This work was supported by funding from the European Union's Horizon 2020 Research and Innovation Programme (Grant Agreement No. 945539 HBP SGA3). Additional support was provided by Spain's Ministerio de Ciencia, Innovación y Universidades (PID2020-115780GB-I00) to the author.

References

Adrian ED. (1941) Afferent discharges to the cerebral cortex from peripheral sense organs. J Physiol. **100**:159–191. doi: 10.1113/jphysiol.1941.sp003932.

Ahlsén G. (1984) Brain stem neurones with differential projection to functional subregions of the dorsal lateral geniculate complex in the cat. Neuroscience. **12**:817–838. doi: 10.1016/0306-4522(84)90173-8.

Akert K. (1964) Comparative anatomy of the frontal cortex and thalamocortical connections. In JM Warren and K Akert (eds.), The frontal granular cortex and behavior. New York: McGraw-Hill, pp. 372–396.

Allen Mouse Common Coordinate Framework and Reference Atlas. (October 2017) Technical White paper. v.3. alleninstitute.org.

Andersen P, Andersson SA. (1968) Physiological basis of the alpha rhythm. New York: Appleton-Century-Crofts.

Andersen P, Sears TA. (1964) The role of inhibition in the phasing of spontaneous thalamo-cortical discharge. J Physiol. **173**:459–480. doi:10.1113/jphysiol.1964.sp007468.

Angelucci A, Clascá F, Sur M. (1996) Anterograde axonal tracing with the subunit B of cholera toxin: a highly sensitive immunohistochemical protocol for revealing fine axonal morphology in adult and neonatal brains. J Neurosci Methods. **65**:101–112. doi: 10.1016/0165-0270(95)00155-7.

Arcelli P, Frassoni C, Regondi MC, Biasi SD, Spreafico R. (1997) GABAergic neurons in mammalian thalamus: a marker of thalamic complexity? Brain Res Bull. **42**:27–37. DOI: 10.1016/S0361-9230(96)00107-4

Asanuma C, Andersen RA, Cowan WM. (1985) The thalamic relations of the caudal inferior parietal lobule and the lateral prefrontal cortex in monkeys: divergent cortical projections from cell clusters in the medial pulvinar nucleus. J Comp Neurol. **241**(3):357–381. doi: 10.1002/cne.902410309.

Atasoy D, Aponte Y, Su HH, Sternson SM. (2008) A FLEX switch targets Channelrhodopsin-2 to multiple cell types for imaging and long-range circuit mapping. J. Neurosci. **28**, 7025–7030. doi:10.1523/JNEUROSCI.1954-08.2008.

Bal T, McCormick DA. (1993) Mechanisms of oscillatory activity in guinea-pig nucleus reticularis thalami in vitro: a mammalian pacemaker. J Physiol. **468**:669–91. doi: 10.1113/jphysiol.1993.sp019794.

Beierlein M. (2014) Synaptic mechanisms underlying cholinergic control of thalamic reticular nucleus neurons. J Physiol. Oct 1;**592**(19):4137–4145. doi: 10.1113/jphysiol.2014.277376.

Bentivoglio M, Kuypers HG, Catsman-Berrevoets CE, Loewe H, Dann O. (1980) Two new fluorescent retrograde neuronal tracers which are transported over long distances. Neurosci Lett. **18**:25–30. doi: 10.1016/0304-3940(80)90208-6.

Berger H. (1929) Uber das Elektrenkephalogramm des Menschen. Archiv Psychiat Nervenkr. **87**:527–570.

Bonjean M, Baker T, Bazhenov M, Cash S, Halgren E, Sejnowski T. (2012) Interactions between core and matrix thalamocortical projections in human sleep spindle synchronization. J Neurosci. **32**:5250–5263. doi: 10.1523/JNEUROSCI.6141-11.2012.

Bourassa J, Pinault D, Deschênes M. (1995) Corticothalamic projections from the cortical barrel field to the somatosensory thalamus in rats: a single-fibre study using biocytin as an anterograde tracer. Eur J Neurosci. **7**:19–30. doi: 10.1111/j.1460-9568.1995.tb01016.x.

Bowling DB, Michael CR. (1980) Projection patterns of single physiologically characterized optic tract fibres in cat. Nature. **286**:899–902. doi: 10.1038/286899a0.

Bowling DB, Michael CR. (1984) Terminal patterns of single, physiologically characterized optic tract fibers in the cat's lateral geniculate nucleus. J Neurosci. **4**:198–216. doi: 10.1523/JNEUROSCI.04-01-00198.1984.

Bremer F. (1937) L'activité cèrèbrale au cours du sommeil et de la narcose. Contribution à l'êtude du mêcanisme du sommeil. Bull Acad Roy Med Belg. **4**: 68–86.

Briggs F. (2020) Role of feedback connections in central visual processing. Annu Rev Vis Sci. **6**:313–334. doi: 10.1146/annurev-vision-121219-081716.

Bright R. (1837) Cases and observations illustrative of diagnosis where tumors are situated at the base of the brain; or where other parts of the brain and spinal cord suffer lesion from disease. Guy's Hosp Rep. **2**:279–310 (cited by Jones 2007).

Broca P. (1861). Perte de la parole, ramollissement chronique et destruction partielle du lobe antérieur gauche. Bulletin de la Société d'Anthropologie **2**: 235–238.

Burdach KF. (1822) Vom Baue und Leben des Gehirns. Vol 2. Leipzig: Dyk'schen Buchhandlung.

Burns BD. (1950) Some properties of the cat's isolated cerebral cortex. J Physiol. **111**:50–68. doi: 10.1113/jphysiol.1950.sp004463.

Burton H, Jones EG. (1976) The posterior thalamic region and its cortical projection in New World and Old World monkeys. J Comp Neurol. **168**:249–301. doi: 10.1002/cne.901680204.

Cajal S. Ramón y. (1900) Contribución al estudio de la via sensitiva centgraly estructura del tálamo óptico. Rev Trim Micrograf **5**:185–198.

Cajal S. Ramón y. (1903) Estudios talámicos. Trab lab Invest Biol Univ Madrid **2**:31–69.

Cappe C, Morel A, Barone P, Rouiller EM. (2009) The thalamocortical projection systems in primate: an anatomical support for multisensory and sensorimotor interplay. Cereb Cortex. **19**:2025–2037. doi: 10.1093/cercor/bhn228.

Carey RG, Fitzpatrick D, Diamond IT. (1979a) Layer I of striate cortex of Tupaia glis and Galago senegalensis: projections from thalamus and claustrum revealed by retrograde transport of horseradish peroxidase. J Comp Neurol. **186**:393–437. doi: 10.1002/cne.901860306.

Carey RG, Fitzpatrick D, Diamond IT. (1979b) Thalamic projections to layer I of striate cortex shown by retrograde transport of horseradish peroxidase. Science. **203**:556–559. doi: 10.1126/science.760205.

Catsman-Berrevoets CE, Kuypers HG. (1978). Differential laminar distribution of corticothalamic neurons projecting to the VL and the center median. An HRP study in the cynomolgus monkey. Brain Res. **154**:359–365. doi: 10.1016/0006-8993(78)90706-0.

Chamberlin NL, Du B, de Lacalle S, Saper CB. (1998) Recombinant adeno-associated virus vector: use for transgene expression and anterograde tract tracing in the CNS. Brain Res. **793**(1–2), 169–175. doi:10.1016/s0006-8993(98)00169-3.

Chung JW, Hassler R, Wagner A. (1977) Degeneration of two of nine types of synapses in the putamen after center median coagulation in the cat. Exp Brain Res. **28**:345–361. doi: 10.1007/BF00235716.

Clascá F, Angelucci A, Sur M. (1995) Layer-specific programs of development in neocortical projection neurons. Proc Natl Acad Sci USA. **92**:11145–11149. doi: 10.1073/pnas.92.24.11145.

Clascá F, Llamas A, Reinoso-Suárez F. (1997) Insular cortex and neighboring fields in the cat: a redefinition based on cortical microarchitecture and connections with the thalamus. J Comp Neurol. **384**:456–482. doi: 10.1002/(sici)1096-9861(19970804)384:3<456::aid-cne10>3.0.co;2-h.

Collins DP, Anastasiades PG, Marlin JJ, Carter AG. (2018) Reciprocal circuits linking the prefrontal cortex with dorsal and ventral thalamic nuclei. Neuron. **98**:366–379. doi: 10.1016/j.neuron.2018.03.024.

Colonnier M, Guillery RW. (1964) Synaptic organization in the lateral geniculate nucleus of the monkey. Z Zellforsch Mikrosk Anat. **62**:333–355. doi: 10.1007/BF00339284.

Conrad LC, Leonard CM, Pfaff DW. (1974) Connections of the median and dorsal raphe nuclei in the rat: an autoradiographic and degeneration study. J Comp Neurol. **156**:179–205. doi: 10.1002/cne.901560205.

Cowan WM, Gottlieb DI, Hendrickson AE, Price JL, Woolsey TA. (1972) The autoradiographic demonstration of axonal connections in the central nervous system. Brain Res. **37**(1):21–51. doi:10.1016/0006-8993(72)90344-7.

Cox CL. (2014) Complex regulation of dendritic transmitter release from thalamic interneurons. Curr Opin Neurobiol. **29**:126–132. doi: 10.1016/j.conb.2014.07.004.

Crick F. (1984) Function of the thalamic reticular complex: the searchlight hypothesis. Proc Natl Acad Sci USA. **81**:4586–4590. doi: 10.1073/pnas.81.14.4586.

Cruikshank SJ, Ahmed OJ, Stevens TR, Patrick SL, Gonzalez AN, Elmaleh M, Connors BW. (2012). Thalamic control of layer 1 circuits in prefrontal cortex. J Neurosci. **32**:17813–17823. doi: 10.1523/JNEUROSCI.3231-12.2012.

de Barenne JG Dusser, McCulloch WS. (1938) The direct functional interrelation of sensory cortex and optic thalamus. J Neurophysiol. **1**:176–186. doi:10.1152/jn.1938.1.2.176.

Déjerine J, Roussy G. (1906) Le syndrome thalamique. Revue de Neurologie (Paris). **14**: 1–32.

Déjerine JJ. (1901) Anatomie des centres nerveux (with AM Dejerine-Klumpke). París: J. Rueff.

Dempsey, EW, Morison RS. (1942) The production of rhythmically recurrent cortical potentials after localized thalamic stimulation. Amer J Physiol. **135**:293–300.

Deschênes M, Bourassa J, Doan VD, Parent A. (1996) A single-cell study of the axonal projections arising from the posterior intralaminar thalamic nuclei in the rat. Eur J Neurosci. **8**:329–343. doi: 10.1111/j.1460-9568.1996.tb01217.x.

Deschênes M, Bourassa J, Pinault D. (1994) Corticothalamic projections from layer V cells in rat are collaterals of long-range corticofugal axons. Brain Res. **664**:215–219. doi: 10.1016/0006-8993(94)91974-7.

Deschênes M, Veinante P, Zhang ZW. (1998) The organization of corticothalamic projections: reciprocity versus parity. Brain Res Brain Res Rev. **28**:286–308. doi: 10.1016/s0165-0173(98)00017-4.

Desmedt JE, Tomberg C. (1994) Transient phase-locking of 40 Hz electrical oscillations in prefrontal and parietal human cortex reflects the process of conscious somatic perception. Neurosci Lett. Feb 28;**168**(1–2):126–129. doi: 10.1016/0304-3940(94)90432-4.

Diamond IT, Jones EG, Powell TPS. (1969) The projection of the auditory cortex upon the diencephalon and brainstem in the cat. Brain Res. **15**:305–340.

Dingledine R, Kelly JS. (1977) Brain stem stimulation and the acetylcholine-evoked inhibition of neurones in the feline nucleus reticularis thalami. J Physiol. Sep;**271**(1):135–154. doi: 10.1113/jphysiol.1977.sp011994.

Economo, C. von. (1911) Über dissoziierte Empfindungslähmung bei Ponstumoren und über die zentralen Bahnen des sensiblen Trigeminus. Jahrb Psychiatr Neurol **32**: 107–138.

Economo MN, Clack NG, Lavis LD, Gerfen CR, Svoboda K, Myers EW, Chandrashekar J. (2016) A platform for brain-wide imaging and reconstruction of individual neurons. eLife. Jan 20;**5**:e10566. doi: 10.7554/eLife.10566.

Ferrier D. (1886) The functions of the brain, 2nd ed. London: Smith Elder.

Fink RP, Heimer L. (1967) Two methods for selective silver impregnation of degenerating axons and their synaptic endings in the central nervous system. Brain Res. **4**:369–374. doi: 10.1016/0006-8993(67)90166-7.

FIPAT. (February 2017) Terminologia Neuroanatomica. FIPAT.library.dal.ca. Federative International Programme for Anatomical Terminology, Ch. 1, pp. 55–57.

Flourens P. (1824) Recherches Experimentales Sur Les Proprietes Et Les Fonctions Du Systeme Nervoux, Dans Les Animaux Vertebres. Kessinger Publishing LLC (facsímil) 2010.

Forel, A. (1877) Untersuchungen über die Haubenregion und ihre oberen Verknüpfungen im Gehirne des Menschen und einiger Säugethiere, mit Beiträgen zu den Methoden der Gehirnuntersuchung. Archiv für Psychiatrie und Nervenkrankheiten **7**:393–495. doi: 10.1007/BF02041873.

Friedemann M. (1912) Die Cytoarchitektonik des Zwischenhirns der Cercopitheken, mit besonderer Berücksichtigung des Thalamus opticus. J für Psychologie Neurologie (Leipzig) **18**:309–378.

Friedlander MJ, Lin CS, Stanford LR, Sherman SM. (1981) Morphology of functionally identified neurons in lateral geniculate nucleus of the cat. J Neurophysiol. **46**:80–129. doi: 10.1152/jn.1981.46.1.80.

Fritsch G, Hitzig E. (1870) Ueber die elektrische Erregbarkeit des Grosshirns. Arch Anat Physiol Wiss Med. **37**:300–332.

Fujiyama F, Furuta T, Kaneko T. (2001) Immunocytochemical localization of candidates for vesicular glutamate transporters in the rat cerebral cortex. J Comp Neurol. **435**:379–387.

Furuta T, Tomioka R, Taki K, Nakamura K, Tamamaki N, Kaneko T. (2001). In vivo transduction of central neurons using recombinant Sindbis virus: Golgi-like labeling of dendrites and axons with membrane-targeted fluorescent proteins. J Histochem Cytochem. **49**:1497–1508.

Gailloud P, Carota A, Bogousslavsky J, Fasel J. (2003) Histoire de l'anatomie du thalamus de l'antiquité à la fin du XIXe siècle. Schw Arch Nerorl Psychiatr. **154**:49–58.

Galambos R, Rose JE, Bromiley RB, Hughes JR. (1952) Microelectrode studies on medial geniculate body of cat. II. Response to clicks. J Neurophysiol. **15**:359–380. doi: 10.1152/jn.1952.15.5.359.

García-Cabezas MA, Martínez-Sánchez P, Sánchez-González MA, Garzón M, Cavada C. (2009) Dopamine innervation in the thalamus: monkey versus rat. Cereb Cortex. **19**:424–434. doi: 10.1093/cercor/bhn093.

García-Cabezas MA, Pérez-Santos I, Cavada C. (2021) The epic of the thalamus in anatomical language. Front Neuroanat. **15**:744095. doi: 10.3389/fnana.2021.744095.

Gerfen CR, Sawchenko PE. (1984) An anterograde neuroanatomical tracing method that shows the detailed morphology of neurons, their axons and terminals: immunohistochemical localization of an axonally transported plant lectin, Phaseolus vulgaris leucoagglutinin (PHA-L). Brain Res. **290**:219–238. doi: 10.1016/0006-8993(84)90940-5.

Gerlach J. (1858) Mikroskopische Studien aus dem Gebiet der Menschlichen Morphologie. Erlange: Enke.

Gilbert CD, Kelly JP. (1975) The projections of cells in different layers of the cat's visual cortex. J Comp Neurol. **163**:81–105. doi: 10.1002/cne.901630106.

Godement P, Vanselow J, Thanos S, Bonhoeffer F. (1987) A study in developing visual systems with a new method of staining neurones and their processes in fixed tissue. Development. **101**:697–713.

Golgi, C. (1873). Sulla Struttura della Sostanza Grigia del Cervello. Gazzetta Medica Italiana-Lombardia.**33**:244–246.

Gonatas NK, Harper C, Mizutani T, Gonatas JO. (1979) Superior sensitivity of conjugates of horseradish peroxidase with wheat germ agglutinin for studies of retrograde axonal transport. J Histochem Cytochem. **27**(3):728–734. doi:10.1177/27.3.90065.

Gray EG, Hamlyn LH. (1962) Electron microscopy of experimental degeneration in the avian optic tectum. J Anat. **96**:309–316.5.

Graybiel AM, Berson DM. (1980) Histochemical identification and afferent connections of subdivisions in the lateralis posterior-pulvinar complex and related thalamic nuclei in the cat. Neuroscience. **5**:1175–238. doi: 10.1016/0306-4522(80)90196-7.

Groenewegen HJ, Berendse HW. (1994) The specificity of the "nonspecific" midline and intralaminar thalamic nuclei. Trends Neurosci. **17**:52–57. doi: 10.1016/0166-2236(94)90074-4.

Groh A, Bokor H, Mease RA, Plattner VM, Hangya B, Stroh A, Deschenes M, Acsády L. (2014) Convergence of cortical and sensory driver inputs on single thalamocortical cells. Cereb Cortex. **24**:3167–3179. doi: 10.1093/cercor/bht173.

Gudden, B. (1870) Experimental Untersuchungen über das peripherische und central Nervensystem, Arch Psychiat Nervenkr **2**:693–723.

Guillery RW. (1967) Patterns of fiber degeneration in the dorsal lateral geniculate nucleus of the cat following lesions in the visual cortex. J Comp Neurol. **130**:197–221. doi: 10.1002/cne.901300303.

Guillery RW. (1969) The organization of synaptic interconnections in the laminae of the dorsal lateral geniculate nucleus of the cat. Z Zellforsch Mikrosk Anat. **96**:1–38. doi: 10.1007/BF00321474.

Guillery RW. (1995) Anatomical evidence concerning the role of the thalamus in corticocortical communication: a brief review. J Anat. **187**:583–592.

Guillery RW, Sherman SM. (2002a) Thalamic relay functions and their role in corticocortical communication: generalizations from the visual system. Neuron. **33**:163–175. doi: 10.1016/s0896-6273(01)00582-7.

Guillery RW, Sherman SM. (2002b) The thalamus as a monitor of motor outputs. Philos Trans R Soc Lond B Biol Sci. **357**:1809–1821. doi: 10.1098/rstb.2002.1171.

Halassa MM, Acsády L. (2016) Thalamic inhibition: diverse sources, diverse scales. Trends Neurosci. **39**:680–693. doi: 10.1016/j.tins.2016.08.001.

Hallanger AE, Levey AI, Lee HJ, Rye DB, Wainer BH. (1987) The origins of cholinergic and other subcortical afferents to the thalamus in the rat. J Comp Neurol. **262**:105–24. doi: 10.1002/cne.902620109.

Hamos JE, Van Horn SC, Raczkowski D, Sherman SM. (1987) Synaptic circuits involving an individual retinogeniculate axon in the cat. J Comp Neurol. **259**:165–92. doi: 10.1002/cne.902590202

Hamos JE, Van Horn SC, Raczkowski D, Uhlrich DJ, Sherman SM. (1985) Synaptic connectivity of a local circuit neurone in lateral geniculate nucleus of the cat. Nature **317**:618–621. doi: 10.1038/317618a0.

Hashikawa T, Rausell E, Molinari M, Jones EG. (1991) Parvalbumin- and calbindin-containing neurons in the monkey medial geniculate complex: differential distribution and cortical layer specific projections. Brain Res. **544**:335–341. doi: 10.1016/0006-8993(91)90076-8.

Hendry SH, Yoshioka TA. (1994) neurochemically distinct third channel in the macaque dorsal lateral geniculate nucleus. Science **264**:575–577. doi: 10.1126/science.8160015.

Herkenham M. (1980) Laminar organization of thalamic projections to the rat neocortex. Science. **207**:532–535.

Herkenham M. (1986) New perspectives on the organization and evolution of nonspecific thalamocortical projections. In EG Jones and A Peters (eds.), Cerebral cortex, vol. **5**. New York: Plenum, pp. 403–445.

Hirai T, Jones EG. (1989) A new parcellation of the human thalamus on the basis of histochemical staining. Brain Res Brain Res Rev. **14**:1–34. doi: 10.1016/0165-0173(89)90007-6.

Hirsch JA, Wang X, Sommer FT, Martinez LM. (2015) How inhibitory circuits in the thalamus serve vision. Ann Rev Neurosci. **38**:309–329. DOI: 10.1146/annurev-neuro-071013-014229.

Hong JH, Bai DS, Jeong JY, Choi BY, Chang CH, Kim SH, Ahn SH, Jang SH. (2010) Injury of the spino-thalamo-cortical pathway is necessary for central post-stroke pain. Eur Neurol. **64**:163–168. doi: 10.1159/000319040.

Hoogland PV, Welker E, Van der Loos H. (1987) Organization of the projections from barrel cortex to thalamus in mice studied with phaseolus vulgaris-leucoagglutinin and

HRP. Exp Brain Res. **68**:73–87. doi: 10.1007/BF00255235.

Houser CR, Vaughn JE, Barber RP, Roberts E. (1980) GABA neurons are the major cell type of the nucleus reticularis thalami. Brain Res. **200**:341–354. doi: 10.1016/0006-8993(80)90925-7.

Hubel DH, Wiesel TN. (1961) Integrative action in the cat's lateral geniculate body J. Physiol. **155**:385–398.

Jackson JH. (1864) Illustrations on the diseases of the nervous system. London Hosp Clin Lect Rep. **3**:337–387 (cited by Jones 2007).

Jackson JH. (1866) Note on the functions of the optic thalamus. London Hosp Clin Lect. **3**:373–377.

Jager P, Moore G, Calpin P, Durmishi X, Salgarella I, Menage L, Kita Y, Wang Y, Kim DW, Blackshaw S, Schultz SR, Brickley S, Shimogori T, Delogu A. (2021) Dual midbrain and forebrain origins of thalamic inhibitory interneurons. eLife. **10**: e59272. doi: 10.7554/eLife.59272.

Jahnsen H, Llinás R. (1984a) Electrophysiological properties of guinea-pig thalamic neurones: an in vitro study. J Physiol. **349**:205–226. doi: 10.1113/jphysiol.1984.sp015153.

Jahnsen H, Llinás R (1984b) Ionic basis for the electro-responsiveness and oscillatory properties of guinea-pig thalamic neurones in vitro. J Physiol. **349**:227–247. doi: 10.1113/jphysiol.1984.sp015154.

Jasper H. (1949) Diffuse projection systems: the integrative action of the thalamic reticular system. Electroencephalogr Clin Neurophysiol. **1**:405–419; discussion 419–420.

Jasper H, Ajmone-Marsan C. (1954) A stereotaxic atlas of the diencephalon of the cat. Ottawa: Nat. Res. Council Canada.

Jasper HH. (1960) Unspecific thalamocortical relations. In J Field, HW Magoun, and VE Hall (eds.), Handbook of physiology. Section 1: Neurophysiology, Vol. II. Washington, DC: American Physiological Society, pp. 1307–1321.

Jones EG. (1975) Some aspects of the organization of the thalamic reticular complex. J Comp Neurol. **162**:285–308. doi: 10.1002/cne.901620302.

Jones EG. (1998) Viewpoint: the core and matrix of thalamic organization. Neuroscience. **85**:331–345. doi: 10.1016/s0306-4522(97)00581-2.

Jones EG. (2001) The thalamic matrix and thalamocortical synchrony. Trends Neurosci. **24**:595–601. doi: 10.1016/s0166-2236(00)01922-6.

Jones EG. (2007). The thalamus. 2nd ed. Cambridge: Cambridge University Press.

Jones EG. (2009) Synchrony in the interconnected circuitry of the thalamus and cerebral cortex. Ann N Y Acad Sci. **1157**:10–23. doi: 10.1111/j.1749-6632.2009.04534.x.

Jones EG, Hendry SH. (1989) Differential calcium binding protein immunoreactivity distinguishes classes of relay neurons in monkey thalamic nuclei. Eur J Neurosci. **1**:222–246. doi: 10.1111/j.1460-9568.1989.tb00791.x.

Jones EG, Leavitt RY. (1974) Retrograde axonal transport and the demonstration of non-specific projections to the cerebral cortex and striatum from thalamic intralaminar nuclei in the rat, cat and monkey. J Comp Neurol. **154**:349–377. doi: 10.1002/cne.901540402.

Jones EG, Powell TPS. (1970) Connexions of the somatic sensory cortex of the rhesus monkey. III. Thalamic connexions. Brain. **93**:37–56. doi: 10.1093/brain/93.1.37.

Ju G, Han ZS, Fan LZ. (1989). Fluorogold as a retrograde tracer used in combination with immunohistochemistry. J Neurosci Meth. **1**:69–72.

Kaas JH, Guillery RW, Allman JM. (1972) Some principles of organization in the dorsal lateral geniculate nucleus. Brain Behav Evol. **6**:253–299. doi: 10.1159/000123713.

Kaas JH, Huerta MF, Weber JT, Harting JK. (1978) Patterns of retinal terminations and laminar organization of the lateral geniculate nucleus of primates. J Comp Neurol. **182**:517–553. doi: 10.1002/cne.901820308.

Kaas JH, Lyon DC. (2007) Pulvinar contributions to the dorsal and ventral streams of visual processing in primates. Brain Res Rev. **55**:285–296. doi: 10.1016/j.brainresrev.2007.02.008. Epub 2007 Mar 12.

Kakei S, Na J, Shinoda Y. (2001) Thalamic terminal morphology and distribution of single corticothalamic axons originating from layers 5 and 6 of the cat motor cortex. J Comp Neurol. **437**:170–185. doi: 10.1002/cne.1277.

Katz LC, Burkhalter A, Dreyer WJ. (1984) Fluorescent latex microspheres as a retrograde neuronal marker for in vivo and in vitro studies of visual cortex. Nature **310**:498–500.

Kemp JM, Powell TPS. (1971a) The site of termination of afferent fibres in the caudate nucleus. Philos Trans R Soc Lond B Biol Sci. **262**:413–427. doi: 10.1098/rstb.1971.0104.

Kemp JM, Powell TPS. (1971b) The termination of fibres from the cerebral cortex and thalamus upon dendritic spines in the caudate nucleus: a study with the Golgi method. Philos Trans R Soc Lond B Biol Sci. **262**:429–439. doi: 10.1098/rstb.1971.0105.

Killackey HP, Ebner FF (1972) Two different types of thalamocortical projections to a single cortical area in mammals. Brain Behav Evol. **6**:141–169. doi: 10.1159/000123703.

Killackey H, Ebner F. (1973) Convergent projection of three separate thalamic nuclei on to a single cortical area. Science **179**:283–285. doi: 10.1126/science.179.4070.283.

Kishan AU, Lee CC, Winer JA. (2008) Branched projections in the auditory thalamocortical and corticocortical systems. Neuroscience. **154**:283–293. doi: 10.1016/j.neuroscience.2008.01.010.

Krishnan GP, Rosen BQ, Chen JY, Muller L, Sejnowski TJ, Cash SS, Halgren E, Bazhenov M. (2018) Thalamocortical and intracortical laminar connectivity determines sleep spindle properties. PLoS Comput Biol. **14**(6):e1006171. doi: 10.1371/journal.pcbi.1006171.

Kuramoto E, Furuta T, Nakamura KC, Unzai T, Hioki H, Kaneko T. (2009) Two types of thalamocortical projections from the motor thalamic nuclei of the rat: a single neuron-tracing study using viral vectors. Cereb Cortex. **19**:2065–2077. doi: 10.1093/cercor/bhn231.

Kuypers HG, Bentivoglio M, Catsman-Berrevoets CE, Bharos AT. (1980). Double retrograde neuronal labeling through divergent axon collaterals, using two fluorescent tracers with the same excitation wavelength which label different features of the cell. Exp Brain Res. **40**:383–392. doi: 10.1007/BF00236147.

Lanciego JL, Wouterlood FG. (2020) Neuroanatomical tract-tracing techniques that did go viral. Brain Struct Funct. **225**:1193–1224. doi: 10.1007/s00429-020-02041-6.

LaVail JH, LaVail MM. (1972) Retrograde axonal transport in the central nervous system. Science. **176**:1416–1417. https://doi.org/10.1126/science.176.4042.1416.

Le Gros Clark WE. (1932) The structure and connections of the thalamus. Brain. **55** (3):406–470. doi.org/10.1093/brain/55.3.406.

Le Gros Clark WE, Boggon RH. (1935) The thalamic connections of the parietal and frontal lobes of the brain in the monkey. Phil Trans. R Soc Lond. **141**:467–487. doi:10.1098/rstb.1935.0002.

Le Gros Clark WE, Northfield DWC. (1937) The cortical projection of the pulvinar in the macaque monkey Brain. **60**:126–142. doi: 10.1093/brain/60.1.126.

Le Gros Clark WE, Powell TPS. (1953) On the thalamo-cortical connexions of the general sensory cortex of Macaca. Proc R Soc Lond B Biol Sci. **141**:467–487. doi: 10.1098/rspb.1953.0054.

Lechner J, Leah JD, Zimmermann M. (1993) Brainstem peptidergic neurons projecting to the medial and lateral thalamus and zona incerta in the rat. Brain Res. **603**:47–56. doi: 10.1016/0006-8993(93)91298-7.

Lee CC, Sherman SM. (2010) Drivers and modulators in the central auditory pathways. Front Neurosci. Apr 15;4:79. doi: 10.3389/neuro.01.014.2010.

Leger L, Sakai K, Salvert D, Touret M, Jouvet M. (1975) Delineation of dorsal lateral geniculate afferents from the cat brain stem as visualized by the horseradish peroxidase technique. Brain Res. **93**:490–496. doi: 10.1016/0006-8993(75)90187-0.

Letinic K, Rakic P. (2001) Telencephalic origin of human thalamic GABAergic neurons. Nature Neuroscience. **4**:931–936. DOI: 10.1038/nn0901-931.

Lewis LD, Voigts J, Flores FJ, Schmitt LI, Wilson MA, Halassa MM, Brown EN. (2015) Thalamic reticular nucleus induces fast and local modulation of arousal state. eLife. Oct 13;4:e08760. doi: 10.7554/eLife.08760.

Llinás R, Ribary U, Contreras D, Pedroarena C. (1998) The neuronal basis for consciousness. Philos Trans R Soc Lond B Biol Sci. **353**:1841–1849. doi: 10.1098/rstb.1998.0336.

Llinás RR, Ribary U, Jeanmonod D, Kronberg E, Mitra PP. (1999) Thalamocortical dysrhythmia: A neurological and neuropsychiatric syndrome characterized by magnetoencephalography. Proc Natl Acad Sci USA. **96**:15222–15227. doi: 10.1073/pnas.96.26.15222.

Locke S. (1967) Thalamic connections to insular and opercular cortex of monkey. J Comp Neurol. **129**:219–240. doi: 10.1002/cne.901290302.

Lorente de No R. (1938) Cerebral cortex: architecture, intracortical connections, motor projections. In J Fulton (ed.), Physiology of the nervous system. London: Oxford University Press, pp. 291–340.

Luys JB. (1865) Recherches sur la système nerveux cerébrospinal: sa structure, ses functions, et ses maladies. Paris: Germer-Baillière.

Marchi V, Algeri G (1885) Sulle degenerazioni descendenti consecutive a lesioni sperimentale in diverse zone della corteccia cerebrale. Riv Freniat **11**:492–494.

Macchi G, Bentivoglio M, Minciacchi D, Molinari M. (1986) Organisation des connexions thalamiques. Rev Neurol (Paris). **142**:267–282.

Magendie F. (1841) Leçons sur les Fonctions et les Maladies du Système Nerveux. Paris: Lecaplain. https://gallica.bnf.fr/ark:/12148/bpt6k61492609/f17.item.texteImage.

Mai JK, Majtanik M. (2019) Toward a common terminology for the thalamus. Front Neuroanat. Jan 11;**12**:114. doi: 10.3389/fnana.2018.00114.

Mathers LH. (1972a) Ultrastructure of the pulvinar of the squirrel monkey. J Comp Neurol. **146**:15–42. doi: 10.1002/cne.901460103.

Mathers LH. (1972b) The synaptic organization of the cortical projection to the pulvinar of the squirrel monkey. J Comp Neurol. **146**:43–60. doi: 10.1002/cne.901460104.

Meynert T. (1872) Vom Gehirne des Säugetiere. In S. Stricker (ed.), Handbuch der Lehre von den Geweben des Menschen und der Thiere. Leipzig: Engelman, pp. 694–808.

Meynert T. (1885) Psychiatry. A clinical treatise on diseases of the forebrain. London: Putnam's Sons.

Minciacchi D, Bentivoglio M, Molinari M, Kultas-Ilinsky K, Ilinsky IA, Macchi G. (1986) Multiple cortical targets of one thalamic nucleus: the projections of the ventral medial nucleus in the cat studied with retrograde tracers. J Comp Neurol. **252**:106–129. doi: 10.1002/cne.902520107.

Molnár Z, Blakemore C. (1995) How do thalamic axons find their way to the cortex? Trends Neurosci. **18**:389–397. doi: 10.1016/0166-2236(95)93935-q.

Monakow C Von. (1895). Experimentelle und pathologisch-anatomische Untersuchungen über die Haubenregion, den Sehhügel und die Regio subthalamica, nebst Beiträgen zur Kenntniss früh erworbener Gross- und Kleinhirn-defecte. Archiv f. Psychiatrie. **27**:1–128 doi: 10.1007/BF02076254.

Montero VM, Guillery RW. (1968) Degeneration in the dorsal lateral geniculate nucleus of the rat following interruption of the retinal or cortical connections. J Comp Neurol. **134**:211–242. doi: 10.1002/cne.901340208.

Morel A, Magnin M, Jeanmonod D. (2007) Multiarchitectonic and stereotactic atlas of the human thalamus. J Comp Neurol. **387**:588–630. doi: 10.1002/(sici)1096-9861(19971103)387:4<588::aid-cne8>3.0.co;2-z.

Morison RS, Bassett, DL. (1945) Electrical activity of the thalamus and basal ganglia in decorticate cats. J Neurophysiol. **8**:309–314.

Morison RS, Finley, KH, Lothrop, GN. (1943). Spontaneous electrical activity of the thalamus and other forebrain structures. J Neurophysiol. **6**:243–254.

Morrison JH, Foote SL. (1986) Noradrenergic and serotoninergic innervation of cortical, thalamic, and tectal visual structures in Old and New World monkeys. J Comp Neurol. **243**:117–138. doi: 10.1002/cne.902430110.

Moruzzi G, Magoun HW. (1949) Brain stem reticular formation and activation of the EEG. Electroencephalogr Clin Neurophysiol. **1**:455–473.

Mott FW. (1892) Ascending degenerations resulting from lesions of the spinal cord in monkeys. Brain **15**:215–229. https://doi.org/10.1093/brain/15.2.215.

Müller EJ, Munn B, Hearne LJ, Smith JB, Fulcher B, Arnatkevičiūtė A, Lurie DJ, Cocchi L, Shine JM. (2020) Core and matrix thalamic sub-populations relate to spatio-temporal cortical connectivity gradients. Neuroimage. **222**:117224. doi: 10.1016/j.neuroimage.2020.117224.

Nakagawa Y. (2019) Development of the thalamus: From early patterning to regulation of cortical functions. Wiley Interdiscip Rev Dev Biol. Sep;**8**(5):e345. doi: 10.1002/wdev.345.

Nance DM, Burns J. (1990) Fluorescent dextrans as sensitive anterograde neuroanatomical tracers: applications and pitfalls. Brain Res Bull. **25**:139–145. doi: 10.1016/0361-9230(90)90264-z.

Nauta WJ, Gygax PA. (1954) Silver impregnation of degenerating axons in the central nervous system: a modified technic. Stain Technol. **29**:91–93. https://doi.org/10.3109/10520295409115448.

Nieuwenhuys R, Voogd J, Van Huijzen C. (2008) The human central nervous system: a synopsis and atlas, 4th ed. Berlin: Springer.

Nissl F. (1894) Uber eine neue Untersuchungmethode des Centralorgans speciell zur Feststellung der Localisation der Nervenzellen. Neurol Centralblatt. **13**:507–508.

Nissl F. (1913) Die Grosshirnanteile des Kaninchens. Archiv f. Psychiatrie **52**:867–953. https://doi.org/10.1007/BF02160485.

Nothias F, Onteniente B, Roudier F, Peschanksi M. (1988) Immunocytochemical study of serotoninergic and noradrenergic innervation of the ventrobasal complex of the rat thalamus. Neurosci Lett. **95**:59–63. doi: 10.1016/0304-3940(88)90632-5.

Nothnagel CWH. (1873) Experimentelle Untersuchunge über dei Funktion des Gehirs. Virchows Ach path Anat. **57**:184–214.

Ojima H. (1994) Terminal morphology and distribution of corticothalamic fibers originating from layers 5 and 6 of cat primary auditory cortex. Cereb Cortex. **4**:646–663. doi: 10.1093/cercor/4.6.646.

Parent M, Parent A. (2011) Jules Bernard Luys in Charcot's penumbra. Front Neurol Neurosci. **29**:125–136. doi: 10.1159/000321782.

Paxinos G, Franklin K. (2019) Paxinos and Franklin's the mouse brain in stereotaxic coordinates, 5th ed. London: Academic Press–Elsevier.

Paxinos G, Watson C. (2007). The rat brain in stereotaxic coordinates. San Diego: Academic Press.

Paxinos G, Watson C, Petrides M, Rosa M, Tokuno H. (2012) The marmoset brains in stereotaxic coordinates. London: Academic Press.

Pérez-Santos I, Palomero-Gallagher N, Zilles K, Cavada C. (2021) Distribution of the noradrenaline innervation and adrenoceptors in the macaque monkey thalamus. Cerebral Cortex. **31**(9):4115–4139.

Phillips JW, Schulmann A, Hara E, Winnubst J, Liu C, Valakh V, Wang L, Shields BC, Korff W, Chandrashekar J, Lemire AL, Mensh B, Dudman JT, Nelson SB, Hantman AW. (2019) A repeated molecular architecture across thalamic pathways. Nat Neurosci. **22**:1925–1935. doi: 10.1038/s41593-019-0483-3.

Pickel VM, Segal M, Bloom FE. (1974) A radioautographic study of the efferent pathways of the nucleus locus coeruleus. J Comp Neurol. **155**:15–42. doi: 10.1002/cne.901550103.

Pinault D. (1996) A novel single-cell staining procedure performed in vivo under electrophysiological control: morpho-functional features of juxtacellularly labeled thalamic cells and other central neurons with biocytin or Neurobiotin. J Neurosci Methods. **65**:113–136. doi: 10.1016/0165-0270(95)00144-1.

Pinault D, Deschênes M. (1998) Projection and innervation patterns of individual thalamic reticular axons in the thalamus of the adult rat: a three-dimensional, graphic, and morphometric analysis. J Comp Neurol. **391**:180–203. doi: 10.1002/(sici)1096-9861(19980209)391:2<180::aid-cne3>3.0.co;2-z.

Poggio GF, Mountcastle VB. (1963) The functional properties of ventrobasal thalamic neurons studied in unanesthetized monkeys. J Neurophysiol. **26**:775–806. doi: 10.1152/jn.1963.26.5.775.

Purpura DP. (1972) Intracellular studies of synaptic organization in the mammalian brain. In GD Pappas and DP Purpura (eds.), Structure and function of synapses. New York: Raven, pp. 257–302.

Purpura DP, Cohen B. (1962) Intracellular recording from thalamic neurons during recruiting responses. J Neurophysiol. **25**:621–635. doi: 10.1152/jn.1962.25.5.621.

Purpura DP, Shofer RJ. (1963) Intracellular recording from thalamic neurons during reticulocortical activation. J Neurophysiol. **26**:494–505. doi: 10.1152/jn..26.3.494.

Purushothaman G, Marion R, Li K, Casagrande VA. (2012) Gating and control of primary visual cortex by pulvinar. Nat Neurosci. **15**:905–912. doi: 10.1038/nn.3106.

Raczkowski D, Fitzpatrick D. (1989) Organization of cholinergic synapses in the cat's dorsal lateral geniculate and perigeniculate nuclei. J Comp Neurol. **288**:676–690. doi: 10.1002/cne.902880412.

Radtke-Schuller S. (2018) Cyto- and myeloarchitectural brain atlas of the ferret (*Mustela putorius*) in MRI aided stereotaxic coordinates. New York: Springer.

Rausell E, Avendaño C. (1985) Thalamocortical neurons projecting to superficial and to deep layers in parietal, frontal and prefrontal regions in the cat. Brain Res. **347**:159–165. doi: 10.1016/0006-8993(85)90905-9.

Rausell E, Bae CS, Viñuela A, Huntley GW, Jones EG. (1992) Calbindin and parvalbumin cells in monkey VPL thalamic nucleus: distribution, laminar cortical projections, and relations to spinothalamic terminations. J Neurosci. **12**:4088–4111. doi: 10.1523/JNEUROSCI.12-10-04088.

Rausell E, Jones EG. (1991) Chemically distinct compartments of the thalamic VPM nucleus in monkeys relay principal and spinal trigeminal pathways to different layers of the somatosensory cortex. J Neurosci. **11**:226–237. doi: 10.1523/JNEUROSCI.11-01-00226.1991.

Reinoso-Suárez F. (1961) Topographischer Hirnatlas der Katze. Darmstadt: E. Merck.

Rico B, Cavada C. (1998) Adrenergic innervation of the monkey thalamus: an immunohistochemical study. Neuroscience. **84**:839–847. doi: 10.1016/s0306-4522(97)00549-6.

Rikhye RV, Wimmer RD, Halassa MM. (2018) Toward an integrative theory of thalamic function. Ann Rev Neurosci. **41**:163–183. doi: 10.1146/annurev-neuro-080317-062144.

Riolan J. (1626) Antropograhia et ostheologia. Paris: Moreau.

Robson JA. (1983) The morphology of corticofugal axons to the dorsal lateral geniculate nucleus in the cat. J Comp Neurol. **216**:89–103. doi: 10.1002/cne.902160108.

Rocca J. (2003) Galen on the brain: anatomical knowledge and physiological speculation in the second century AD, Studies in Ancient Medicine, vol. **26**. Leiden: Brill.

Rodriguez-Moreno J, Porrero C, Rollenhagen A, Rubio-Teves M, Casas-Torremocha D, Alonso-Nanclares L, Yakoubi R, Santuy A, Merchan-Pérez A, DeFelipe J, Lübke JHR, Clascá F. (2020) Area-specific synapse structure in branched posterior nucleus axons reveals a new level of complexity in thalamocortical networks. J Neurosci. **40**:2663–2679. doi: 10.1523/JNEUROSCI.2886-19.2020.

Rose JE, Mountcastle VB. (1952) The thalamic tactile region in rabbit and cat. J Comp Neurol. **97**:441–489. doi: 10.1002/cne.900970303.

Rose JE, Woolsey CN. (1943) A study of thalamo-cortical relations in the rabbit. Bull Johns Hopkins Hosp. **73**:65–128.

Rose JE, Woolsey CN. (1949a) Organization of the mammalian thalamus and its relationships to the cerebral cortex. Electroencephalogr Clin Neurophysiol. **1**:391–403.

Rose JE, Woolsey CN. (1949b) The relations of thalamic connections, cellular structure and evocable electrical activity in the auditory region of the cat. J Comp Neurol. **91**:441–466. doi: 10.1002/cne.900910306.

Rose, JE, Woolsey, CN. (1958) Cortical connections and functional organization of thalamic auditory system in the cat. In HF Harlow and CN Woolsey (eds.), Biological and biochemical bases of behavior. Madison: University of Wisconsin Press, pp. 127–150.

Rosina A, Provini L, Bentivoglio M, Kuypers HG. (1980) Ponto-neocerebellar axonal branching as revealed by double fluorescent retrograde labeling technique. Brain Res. **195**:461–466. doi: 10.1016/0006-8993(80)90080-3.

Rovó Z, Ulbert I, Acsády L. (2012) Drivers of the primate thalamus. J Neurosci. **32**:17894–17908. doi: 10.1523/JNEUROSCI.2815-12.2012.

Roy JP, Clercq M, Steriade M, Deschênes M. (1984) Electrophysiology of neurons of lateral thalamic nuclei in cat: mechanisms of long-lasting hyperpolarizations.

J Neurophysiol. **51**:1220–1235. doi: 10.1152/jn.1984.51.6.1220.

Saalmann YB, Kastner S. (2015) The cognitive thalamus. Front Syst Neurosci. Mar 17;**9**:39. doi: 10.3389/fnsys.2015.00039.

Saalmann YB, Pinsk MA, Wang L, Li X, Kastner S. (2012) The pulvinar regulates information transmission between cortical areas based on attention demands. Science. **337**:753–756. doi: 10.1126/science.1223082.

Saleeba C, Dempsey B, Le S, Goodchild A, McMullan S. (2019). A student's guide to neural circuit tracing. Front Neurosci. **13**. https://doi.org/10.3389/fnins.2019.00897 art 897.

Santorini GD. (1775) Tabulae anatomicae. Parma: Regia Typographia.

Saper CB, Loewy AD. (1980) Efferent connections of the parabrachial nucleus in the rat. Brain Res. **197**:291–317. doi: 10.1016/0006-8993(80)91117-8.

Schaltenbrand G, Wahren W. (1977) Atlas for stereotaxy of the human brain. Stuttgart: Thieme.

Schiff ND, Giacino JT, Kalmar K, Victor JD, Baker K, Gerber M, Fritz B, Eisenberg B, Biondi T, O'Connor J, Kobylarz EJ, Farris S, Machado A, McCagg C, Plum F, Fins JJ, Rezai AR. (2007) Behavioural improvements with thalamic stimulation after severe traumatic brain injury. Nature. **448**:600–603. doi: 10.1038/nature06041.

Schmitt LI, Wimmer RD, Nakajima M, Happ M, Mofakham S, Halassa MM. (2017) Thalamic amplification of cortical connectivity sustains attentional control. Nature. **545**:219–223. doi: 10.1038/nature22073.

Sherman SM. (2001a) Tonic and burst firing: dual modes of thalamocortical relay. Trends Neurosci. **24**:122–126. doi: 10.1016/s0166-2236(00)01714-8.

Sherman SM. (2001b) A wake-up call from the thalamus. Nat Neurosci. **4**:344–346. doi: 10.1038/85973.

Sherman SM. (2004) Interneurons and triadic circuitry of the thalamus. Trends Neurosci. **27**:670–675. DOI: https://doi.org/10.1016/j.tins.2004.08.003.

Sherman SM, Guillery RW. (1996) Functional organization of thalamocortical relays. J Neurophysiol. **76**:1367–1395. doi: 10.1152/jn.1996.76.3.1367.

Sherman SM, Guillery RW. (1998) On the actions that one nerve cell can have on another: distinguishing "drivers" from "modulators." Proc Natl Acad Sci USA. **95**:7121–7126. doi: 10.1073/pnas.95.12.7121.

Sherman SM, Guillery RW. (2005) Exploring the thalamus and its role in cortical function. Boston: MIT Press.

Sherman SM, Guillery RW. (2011) Distinct functions for direct and transthalamic corticocortical connections. J Neurophysiol. **106**:1068–1077. doi: 10.1152/jn.00429.2011.

Sherman SM Guillery RW. (2012) Functional connections of cortical areas. A new view from the thalamus. Boston: MIT Press.

Shi W, Xianyu A, Han Z, Tang X, Li Z, Zhong H, Mao T, Huang K, Shi SH. (2017) Ontogenetic establishment of order-specific nuclear organization in the mammalian thalamus. Nat Neurosci. **20**:516–528. doi: 10.1038/nn.4519.

Sirota MG, Swadlow HA, Beloozerova IN. (2005) Three channels of corticothalamic communication during locomotion. J Neurosci. **25**:5915–5925. doi: 10.1523/JNEUROSCI.0489-05.2005.

Spreafico R, Barbaresi P, Weinberg RJ, Rustioni A. (1987) SII-projecting neurons in the rat thalamus: a single- and double-retrograde-tracing study. Somatosens Res. **4**:359–475. doi: 10.3109/07367228709144614.

Stanford LR, Friedlander MJ, Sherman SM. (1981) Morphology of physiologically identified W-cells in the C laminae of the cat's lateral geniculate nucleus. J Neurosci. **1**:578–584. doi: 10.1523/JNEUROSCI.01-06-00578.1981.

Stanford LR, Friedlander MJ, Sherman SM. (1983) Morphological and physiological properties of geniculate W-cells of the cat: a comparison with X- and Y-cells. J Neurophysiol. **50**:582–608. doi: 10.1152/jn.1983.50.3.582.

Steriade M. (1999) Coherent oscillations and short-term plasticity in corticothalamic networks. Trends Neurosci. **22**:337–345. doi: 10.1016/s0166-2236(99)01407-1.

Steriade M. (2001a) The GABAergic reticular nucleus: a preferential target of corticothalamic projections. Proc Natl Acad Sci USA. **98**:3625–3627. doi: 10.1073/pnas.071051998.

Steriade M. (2001b) Impact of network activities on neuronal properties in corticothalamic systems. J Neurophysiol. **86**:1–39. doi: 10.1152/jn.2001.86.1.1.

Steriade M, Parent A, Paré D, Smith Y. (1987) Cholinergic and non-cholinergic neurons of cat basal forebrain project to reticular and mediodorsal thalamic nuclei. Brain Res. **408**:372–376. doi: 10.1016/0006-8993(87)90408-2.

Strick PL, Sterling P. (1974) Synaptic termination of afferents from the ventrolateral nucleus of the thalamus in the cat motor cortex. A light and electron microscopy study. J Comp Neurol. **153**:77–106. doi: 10.1002/cne.901530107.

Sur M, Sherman SM. (1982) Retinogeniculate terminations in cats: morphological differences between X and Y cell axons. Science. **218**:389. doi: 10.1126/science.7123239.

Swadlow HA. (1994) Efferent neurons and suspected interneurons in motor cortex of the awake rabbit: axonal properties, sensory receptive fields, and subthreshold synaptic inputs. J Neurophysiol. **71**:437–453. doi: 10.1152/jn.1994.71.2.437.

Swadlow HA, Gusev AG. (2001) The impact of "bursting" thalamic impulses at a neocortical synapse. Nat Neurosci. **4**:402–408. doi: 10.1038/86054.

Swanson LW, Hartman BK. (1975) The central adrenergic system. An immunofluorescence study of the location of cell bodies and their efferent connections in the rat utilizing dopamine-beta-hydroxylase as a marker. J Comp Neurol. **163**:467–505. doi: 10.1002/cne.901630406.

Szentagothai J. (1963) The structure of the synapse in the lateral geniculate body. Acta Anat (Basel). **55**:166–185.

Theyel BB, Llano DA, Sherman SM. (2010) The corticothalamocortical circuit drives higher-order cortex in the mouse. Nat Neurosci. **13**:84–8. doi: 10.1038/nn.2449.

Tononi G, Edelman GM. (1998) Consciousness and complexity. Science. **282**:1846–1851. doi: 10.1126/science.282.5395.1846.

Veenman CL, Reiner, A, Honig, MG. (1992) Biotinylated dextran amine as an anterograde tracer for single- and double-labeling studies. J Neurosci Methods. **41**:239–254. https://doi.org/10.1016/0165-0270(92)90089-v.

Veinante P, Lavallée P, Deschênes M. (2000) Corticothalamic projections from layer 5 of the vibrissal barrel cortex in the rat. J Comp Neurol. **424**:197–204. doi: 10.1002/1096-9861(20000821)424:2<197::aid-cne1>3.0.co;2-6.

Verzeano M, Lindsey DB, Magoun HW. (1953) Nature of recruiting response. J Neurophysiol. **16**:183–195. doi: 10.1152/jn.1953.16.2.183.

Viaene AN, Petrof I, Sherman SM. (2011a) Properties of the thalamic projection from the posterior medial nucleus to primary and secondary somatosensory cortices in the mouse. Proc Natl Acad Sci USA. **108**:18156–18161. doi: 10.1073/pnas.1114828108.

Viaene AN, Petrof I, Sherman SM. (2011b) Synaptic properties of thalamic input to layers 2/3 and 4 of primary somatosensory and auditory cortices. J Neurophysiol. **105**:279–292. doi: 10.1152/jn.00747.2010.

Vogt C. (1909) La myéloarchitecture du thalamus du cercophitèque. J Psychol Neurol. (Berl.). **12**:285–324.

Vogt C, Vogt O. (1941) Thalamusstudien I-III (Mit 140 Abbildungen). J Psychol Neurol. **50**:31–154.

Vulpian A. (1866) Leçons sur la physiologie générale et comparée du système nerveux. Paris: Germer Baillière.

Walker AE. (1938). The primate thalamus. Chicago: Univ. Chicago Press.

Walker AE. (1966). Internal structure and afferent-efferent relations of the thalamus. In DP Purpura and MD Yahr (eds.), The thalamus. New York: Columbia University Press, pp. 1–11.

White EL. (1978) Identified neurons in mouse SmI cortex which are postsynaptic to thalamocortical axon terminals: a combined Golgi-electron microscopic and degeneration study. J Comp Neurol. **181**:627–661. doi: 10.1002/cne.901810310.

Willis T. (1664)/(1965). Anatomy of the brain and nerves: Volumes 1 and 2. Montreal: McGill University Press.

Xu X, Holmes TC, Luo MH, Beier KT, Horwitz GD, Zhao F, Zeng W, Hui M, Semler BL, Sandri-Goldin RM. (2020) Viral vectors for neural circuit mapping and recent advances in trans-synaptic anterograde tracers. Neuron. **107**:1029–1047. doi: 10.1016/j.neuron.2020.07.010.

Zhou N, Masterson SP, Damron JK, Guido W, Bickford ME. (2018) The mouse pulvinar nucleus links the lateral extrastriate cortex, striatum, and amygdala. J Neurosci. **38**:347–362. doi: 10.1523/JNEUROSCI.1279-17.2017.

Section 2: Anatomy

Chapter 2

Organization of Thalamic Inputs

László Acsády

1. Introduction

The organization of thalamic afferents solves a computational constraint introduced by a peculiar feature of the vertebrate forebrain systems. In all vertebrate species studied so far (including basal branches like *Cyclostomata*, the lampreys; Suryanarayana et al., 2017, 2020), the top-level information processor (i.e., the cortex, or pallium) has very little direct access to fast, accurate excitatory (i.e., glutamatergic) inputs from subcortical (subpallial) structures besides the thalamus. In other words, the cortex has minimal precisely timed information about the rest of the brain without a thalamic transfer. Because the thalamus has virtually no local axon collaterals, its inputs and the integration of these inputs will define the message the cortex will work on.

Thalamic inputs can be of cortical or subcortical origin (Sherman & Guillery, 2005). Subcortical inputs to the thalamus carry information about the outside world as well as the inner state of the animal (including motor, motivational, anxiety states, etc.); as a consequence, this information is extremely diverse by nature (Jones 2007a, 2007c). This results in versatile representations and *complex integration* of subthalamic inputs at the level of the thalamus. Many of these subcortical inputs are involved in cortico-subcortico-cortical loops (e.g., basal ganglia, the cerebellar loop, or the Papez circuit) closed via the thalamus through pathways utilizing various transmitters and terminal types (Guillery & Sherman, 2011).

Thalamic activity requires a constant and immediate update from the target region of the thalamus, the cortex. Similar to subcortical pathways, corticothalamic pathways display great diversity (Rouiller & Welker, 2000) and are combined with ascending information in many distinct ways (Groh et al., 2014; Blot et al., 2020). Certain thalamic regions are dedicated to transferring cortical information only (Rovó et al., 2012). Indeed, state-dependent thalamic information transfer and cortico-cortical communication critically depend on the top-down cortical inputs (Halassa & Kastner, 2017; Schmitt et al., 2017; Rikhye et al., 2018).

The past hundred years of thalamic research focused on the *relay* of sensory information to the cortex (Steriade et al., 1997b). This led to thalamic neurons being termed as *relay cells* and thalamic regions as *relay nuclei*. Whereas the thalamic relay was admittedly modulated by many factors, *integration of qualitatively different information* originating in *different regions of the brain* has not been considered as a major thalamic function. This is about to change now. The first description of the convergence of two driving inputs originating in different brain regions on single thalamocortical cells was published in 2014 (Groh et al., 2014). Since then, we have begun to realize that in the majority of the thalamus, *the integration, not the relay, of information* is the general mode of function (Otis et al., 2019; Barsy et al., 2020; Blot et al., 2020). Indeed, primary sensory nuclei consist of no more than 20% of the thalamic volume (Rovó et al., 2012). Acknowledging this new line of research, this chapter will refrain from using the term *relay neurons* and will refer to thalamic cells as *thalamocortical neurons*.

The study of the integrative role of the thalamus is in its infancy. The entire field is largely data deficient because relatively few experiments were performed outside the three main sensory nuclei (lateral, medial geniculate, and ventrobasal complex). Still, the available data indicate that thalamic afferents, which arise in a hugely diverse input space and display great diversity in the *structure* of the terminals, can be combined in multiple ways. This makes the *thalamus a hotspot of afferent diversity in the brain*.

1.1 Sort, Weigh, and Integrate

As indicated previously, the computational problem of vertebrate forebrains is that the cortex has very few direct glutamatergic inputs to update itself and accurately match its own activity with the environment and the behavioral needs of the animal. For proper cortical activity, the thalamus is the structure that provides almost all of this fast, versatile information. Needless to say, the cortex receives extrathalamic inputs, mainly from the brainstem and basal forebrain nuclei, that innervate large cortical areas (Steriade et al., 1997a). These well-studied inputs, however, differ hugely from thalamic inputs in their temporal and spatial domains of action. These afferents (i.e., serotonergic, noradrenergic, cholinergic, dopaminergic, and histaminergic neurons), although able to exert rapid actions on cortical interneurons (Varga et al., 2009; Lovett-Barron et al., 2014), for cortical principal cells, they mainly utilize slow neurotransmission, which mostly acts in a nonsynaptic manner via metabotropic receptors (Vizi & Lábos, 1991; Steriade et al., 1997a). These subcortical neurons form diffuse axon arbors that can span several cortical areas. As a consequence, whereas they are extremely important in general control of the cortex (Constantinople & Bruno, 2011), they are unable to perform point-to-point information transfer with millisecond time precision. This leaves the thalamus to collect subthalamic information, combine these inputs with cortical signals (and with each other if necessary), and transfer

Anatomy

this multiplexed information to the cortex in a spatiotemporally well-coordinated manner. In order to solve this problem, the thalamus needs to properly *sort, weigh, and integrate* all of its afferents. This task, however, poses particular challenges for the organization of thalamic afferents. I describe here three sets of requirements:

1. To properly inform the cortex about the activity in the rest of the brain, the thalamus needs to receive inputs from a vast number of brain regions. The thalamus is probably the structure innervated by the highest number of other brain regions in the brain (Figure 1). Thus, the first task is to organize inputs arising from many centers in space.
2. Inputs to the thalamus should be weighed. Not all inputs have an equal influence on thalamic activity. Thus, the second task is that both excitatory and inhibitory inputs should be scaled according to how strongly the input spike pattern should be represented in the output train.
3. Different inputs need the appropriate level of segregation and/or integration. Certain types of inputs require accurate, spatially restricted representation, whereas others need to be combined with information arising in different brain centers. Thus, the third task is to organize inputs relative to each other in order to allow for the combination of their influences.

The thalamus meets these challenges with its huge variability in the organization of afferents via the evolution of three major morphological characteristics that differentiate the thalamus not only from the cortex but also from most other brain regions: (1) heterogeneity of input space, (2) heterogeneity of terminal types, and (3) heterogeneity of input integration.

Heterogeneity of Input Space

Distinct thalamic regions evolved to process information arising from different parts of the brain (Jones 2007a). With the exception of direct monosynaptic inputs from the olfactory bulb, the thalamus is in connection with all major brain systems; thus, the input space of the thalamus involves almost the entire neuraxis (Sherman & Guillery, 2005) (Figure 1). As indicated previously, by comparison, the neocortex receives afferents only from a very limited set of brainstem and forebrain structures. Thus, the critical problem to solve, first, is how to organize afferents arising from multiple regions of the brain. The thalamus solves this problem via the well-known areal segregation of inputs in the thalamus (Jones 2007a).

Heterogeneity of Terminal Types

The thalamus is the brain region that probably has the highest variability in the size and complexity of both excitatory and inhibitory terminal types (Sherman & Guillery, 1998; Halassa & Acsády, 2016) (Figure 2). The vast majority of axon terminals in the brain establish one or two synapses on their postsynaptic targets, with a few notable exceptions (e.g., mossy terminals of the dentate granule cells, climbing fibers of the cerebellum, or the calyx of Held; Rollenhagen & Lübke, 2006). Variability of excitatory terminal types is the rule rather than the exception in the thalamus. In addition, unlike in any other brain region, the thalamus has huge variability in the complexity of inhibitory terminals. With very few notable exceptions,

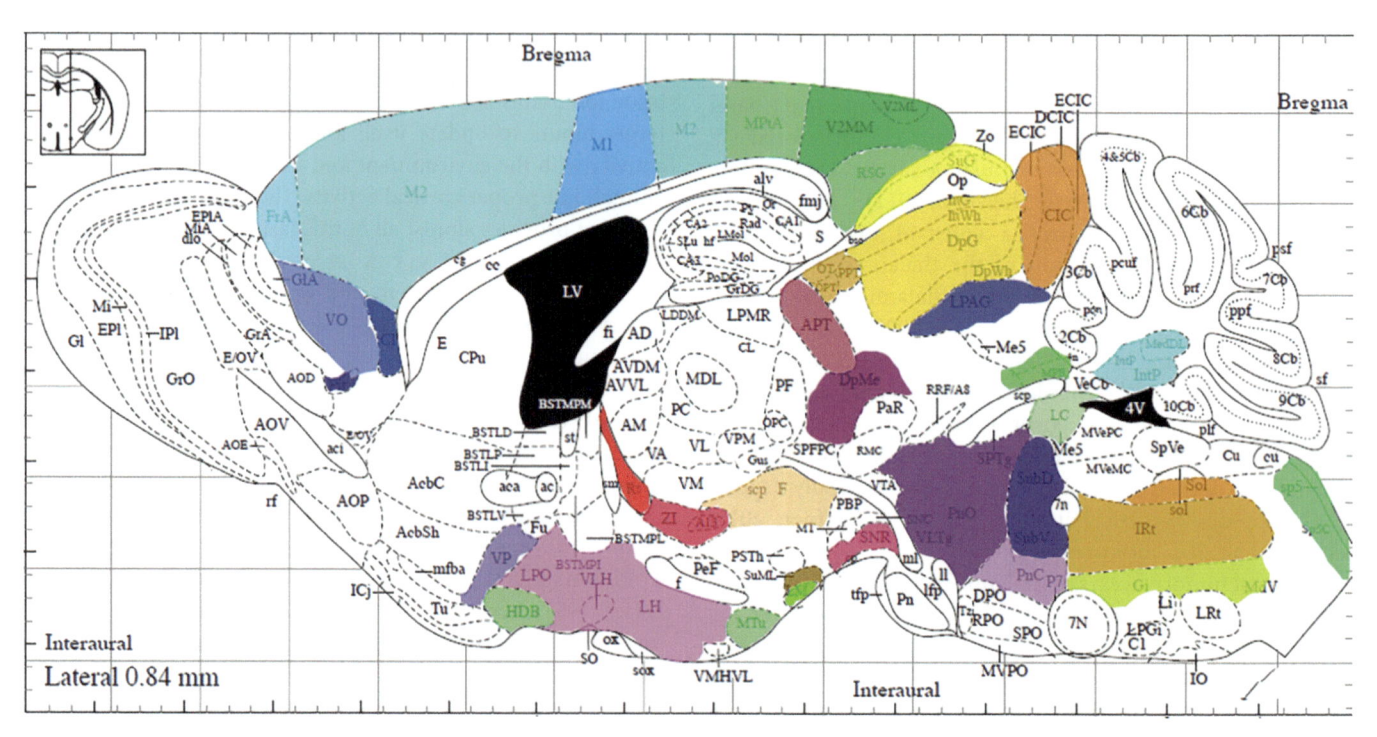

Figure 1 Input regions of the thalamus.

Parasagittal, stereotactic map of the mouse brain close to the midline. Anterior is to the left. Colored cortical and subcortical regions provide direct monosynaptic inputs to the thalamus. Most hypothalamic and brainstem inputs innervate the midline and/or the intralaminar nuclei. Not all input regions are present at this level. Note that the actual input space is much larger because, for example, in the case of the basal ganglia and the cerebellum, only the output nuclei of these systems (SNR and IntP, MedDL) are colored and encompass the entire neuraxis.

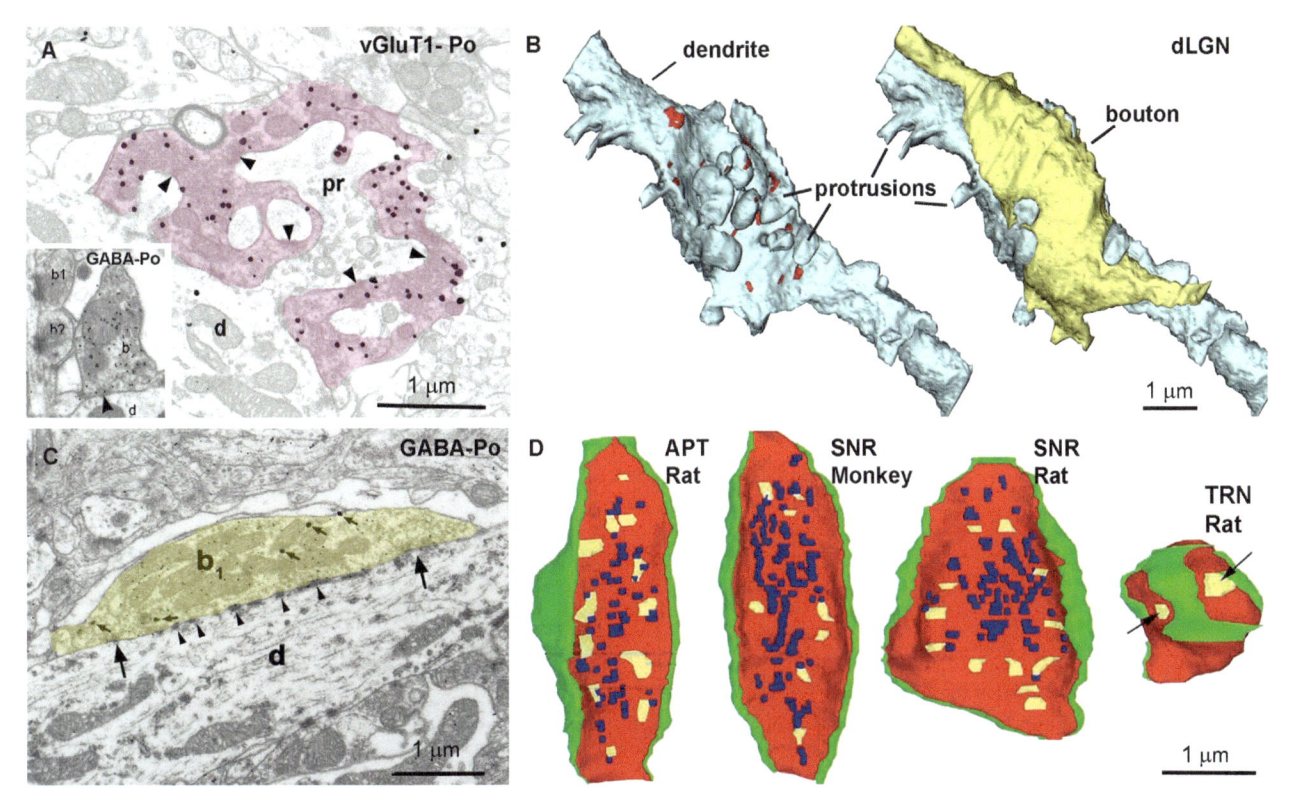

Figure 2 Variability of GABAergic and glutamatergic terminals types in the thalamus.

A. Large cortical multisynaptic glutamatergic terminal (*pink shading*) in rat Po labeled by preembedding silver-intensified immunogold method (*black dots*) for vGluT1. Note that the thick proximal dendrite (*d*) emits a complex protrusion (*pr*), which greatly enlarges the surface available for synapses (*arrowheads*). Inset: A small GABAergic bouton (*b*), labeled by postembedding immunogold for gamma-amino butyric acid (GABA) (*small dots*) and two small GABA-negative axon terminals (*b1* and *b2*) from the same nucleus using the same magnification for comparison.

B. Three-dimensional (3D) electron microscope (EM) reconstruction of a giant retinal axon terminal in the dorsal lateral geniculate nucleus (dLGN). Note the multiple dendritic protrusions. Some of the synapses (*red dots*) are established on the dendritic shaft, not on the protrusions.

C. Giant multisynaptic GABAergic axon terminal in the rat Po arising from the anterior pretectal nucleus. Note the multiple puncta adherentia (*arrowheads*) between the synapses (*large arrows*). Small arrows indicate silver-intensified immunogold labeling of the anterograde tracer.

D. 3D EM reconstructions of large multisynaptic GABAergic terminals arising from extrathalamic sources and a small GABAergic terminal from the thalamic reticular nucleus (TRN) for comparison. Red, membrane of the terminals; yellow, synapses; green, glial cover; blue, puncta adherentia. Note consistent structure of the multisynaptic terminals between systems and taxa. When TRN terminals establish more than one synapse (*arrows*), they innervate two different dendrites, whereas all contacts of a single multisynaptic terminal always converge on one target. SNR, substantia nigra pars reticulata; APT, anterior pretectal nucleus.

all thalamic regions have both giant and small excitatory and/or inhibitory terminals and, in several regions, large variability in intermediate terminal sizes (Rouiller & Welker, 2000; Rovó et al., 2012; Bickford et al., 2015). The thalamus utilizes this feature to weigh its inputs relative to each other and fine-tune the dynamics of thalamic information transfer.

Heterogeneity of Input Integration

The most complex and least-understood task of the thalamus is the integration of various inputs. The paucity of this knowledge has a historical reason. For a neuroscientist, studying simple, replicable, and reliable neuronal activity has always been alluring. This led to a highly intensive investigation of three types of sensory information transfer in the thalamus: vision, audition, and touch. Clarification of the principles of sensory relay not only *led* but also *misled* thalamic research in the past one hundred or so years. As it turns out, sensory relay is an important but minor and highly specialized form of cortical update performed by the thalamus. The highly specialized properties of sensory thalamic relays are a consequence of the fact that in the case of these three modalities, information coded by peripheral receptors is distributed along a two-dimensional (2D) receptor surface. The exact position of the receptors in these 2D surfaces (i.e., retina, organ of Corti, and skin) is critical to decoding the signal. Studying this type of information transfer *led* to critical insights into the structural and functional basis of receptive field formation in the thalamus and some understanding of the integration of top-down cortical signals with the ascending sensory information. Studying sensory transmission, however, also *misled* thalamic research because we predicted that the rest of the thalamus works along the same principles. Recent data indicate that this is not the case. In most other thalamic regions, inputs are not organized according to a simple 2D logic, and as indicated in the Introduction, integrating different information rather than relaying a single piece of information is likely the rule. Thus, the most challenging aspect of thalamic organization, what is at the forefront of current research now, is how the thalamus integrates information from different sources. The emerging theme is that thalamic integration can take place in a perplexingly complex manner that displays great heterogeneity within the structure. There appears to be no "canonical" method of input integration within the thalamus with repeated

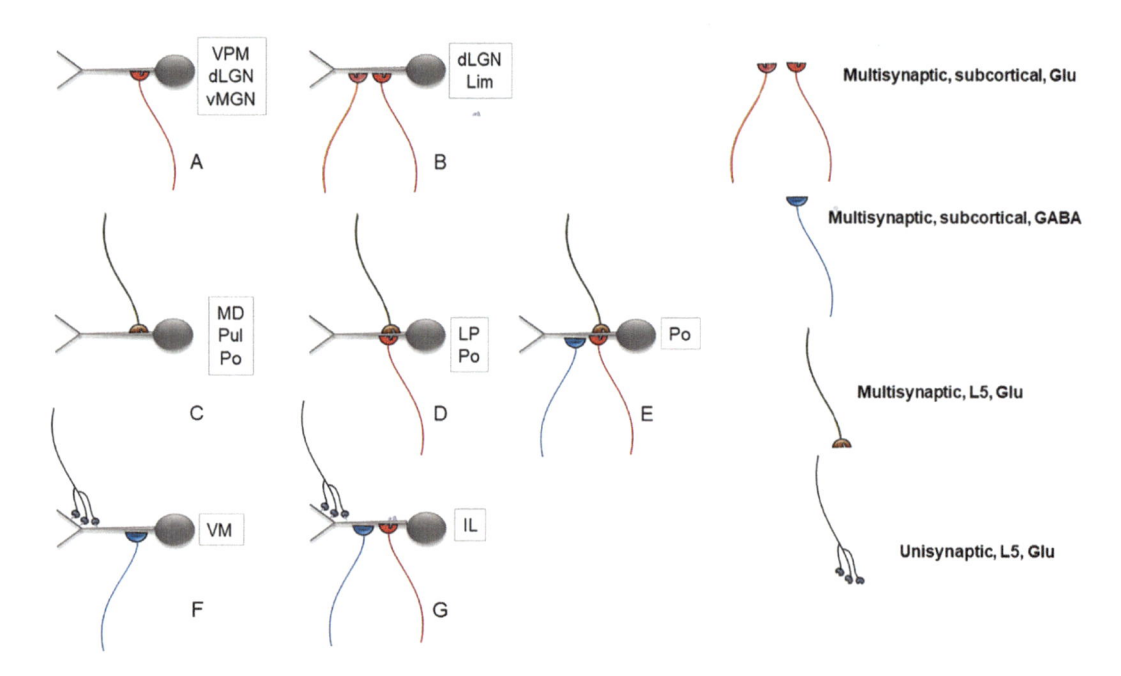

Figure 3 Variability of input integration in the thalamus.

A–G. Thalamocortical cells receiving inputs from variable combinations of terminal types that arise from different sources (subcortical vs. L5 cortical) display different complexity (uni- or multisynaptic) and use different transmitters (glutamate or GABA). Note that the final output of the thalamocortical cell depends on the varied integration of these inputs. For details, see the text.

modular units (for details, see later discussion). On the contrary, there seem to be large *intranuclear* and *internuclear* differences among thalamocortical cells in how they combine converging inputs (Figure 3). Although it may sound trivial that inputs arising from numerous brain centers, having different transmitters and terminal types and integrated in multiple ways, will result in highly diverse thalamic computation, the units deciphering the rules of integration remain to be determined.

2. Heterogeneity of Input Space

2.1 Subcortical Inputs

If the thalamus needs to handle inputs arising from almost the entire brain, it has to appropriately sort them. Indeed, large thalamic regions can be characterized by the locus of their afferents. Nuclear definition is always a hot topic in thalamic research, but one way to categorize thalamic regions is by their major afferents (Jones 2007b). Accordingly, several thalamic regions (nuclei) can be defined by their subthalamic, excitatory, or inhibitory inputs (e.g., Percheron et al., 1996). The best-characterized subcortical afferents carry somatosensory information from the spinal cord and trigeminal nuclei; visual and auditory information from the retina and inferior colliculus, respectively; and gustatory afferents from the nucleus tractus solitarii (Sherman & Guillery, 2005). A critical feature of these pathways is that distinct submodalities (e.g., touch and pain in the case of somatosensation, X and Y pathways in the case of vision) are carried by parallel ascending pathways that do not mix at the thalamic level (Friedlander et al., 1981; Hamos et al., 1987; Usrey et al., 1999). In one of the best-studied sensory modalities, the whisker system of rodents, up to four distinct pathways have been described that integrate vibrissal sensory signals in a different manner and are kept separate in the thalamus (Yu et al., 2006; Urbain & Deschênes, 2007a; Bokor et al., 2008) (see also Chapter 11). In this case, these afferents parcellate the somatosensory nucleus into four subregions. However, recent morphological data in the mouse dorsolateral geniculate nucleus challenge the segregated view of sensory inputs and indicate the convergence of retinal ganglion cells with distinct tuning properties on single thalamocortical cells (Morgan et al., 2016; Rompani et al., 2017). The abundance, the functional consequence of this integration, and its relevance to other taxa remain to be determined.

Other major sources of glutamatergic inputs that reach large, congruent thalamic territories include the mammillary body (anterior nuclear group) (Vicq d'Azyr, 1786; Guillery, 1956) and the cerebellum (ventral lateral nucleus) (Percheron et al., 1996). Cerebellar and mammillary afferents, rather than carrying simple sensory inputs, are parts of the multiple embedded loops that carry information about the action of the cortex on subcortical centers and are involved in complex functions such as movement organization and memory formation, respectively (Bubb et al., 2017; De Zeeuw et al., 2021). Although these afferents are still organized in a topographic manner, their point-to-point precision is far less precise than that of the sensory afferents (Asanuma et al., 1983), and even their primary action on thalamocortical cells may differ (Pare et al., 1991). As a consequence, their thalamic targets likely integrate these inputs differently. Unlike in the case of sensory inputs, where afferents with similar tuning properties converge on one thalamic neuron, in cerebellar and mammillary systems, thalamocortical cells probably combine differentially tuned subcortical inputs. The paucity of data on these systems, however, does not presently allow us to draw more firm conclusions.

Besides the inputs listed previously, several other subthalamic centers specifically target mainly two dedicated nuclear groups, the intralaminar nuclei and the midline nuclear group, making these regions a hotspot for integration (Van der Werf et al., 2002; Kirouac, 2015). Unlike in earlier accounts that lumped these nuclei, it is clear now that intralaminar and midline nuclei form distinct systems. The main sources of these inputs include the hypothalamus, the superior colliculus, the reticular formation, the periaqueductal gray matter, and the parabrachial nucleus (Van der Werf et al., 2002; Kirouac, 2015). The spatial organization of these systems is very little understood. The superior colliculus also provides important inputs to various visual thalamic nuclei, which, together with cortical inputs, are used to parcellate these regions (Bennett et al., 2019).

Like glutamatergic inputs, GABAergic afferents also reach the thalamus from several extrathalamic sources. The most important of these arise from the output nuclei of the basal ganglia (substantia nigra pars reticulata and internal globus pallidus) (Ilinsky et al., 1985, 1997; Percheron et al., 1996; Bodor et al., 2008), but many others originate from the ventral pallidum, the hypothalamus, the ventral and caudal diencephalon (zona incerta, anterior pretectum, ventral lateral geniculate body) (Moore et al., 2000; Barthó et al., 2002; Bokor et al., 2005), the deep layers of the superior colliculus, and the rostral reticular formation (Giber et al., 2015). The real function and the mode of action of these afferents are poorly studied, but the available data and models suggest that they are involved in complex behaviors and integrative functions (Lavallée et al., 2005).

A second set of very important GABAergic inputs to the thalamus arises from the thalamic reticular nucleus (TRN) (Pinault, 2004; Halassa & Acsády, 2016). Although the TRN has the same embryological origin as the other two extrathalamic GABAergic inputs (the zona incerta and the ventral lateral geniculate nucleus), it is traditionally regarded as an intrathalamic input because, unlike the other two nuclei, it not only projects to the thalamus but also receives dense excitatory thalamic feedback. The axon arbors of most TRN cells are restricted to a single thalamic nucleus (Pinault & Deschênes, 1998).

Modulatory inputs to the thalamus arise from the dorsal raphe (serotonergic), pedunculopontine tegmental nucleus and laterodorsal tegmental nucleus (cholinergic), locus coeruleus (noradrenergic), tuberomammillary nucleus (histaminergic), and in the case of the primate thalamus, the ventral tegmental area (dopaminergic) (Steriade et al., 1997a). Almost all thalamic nuclei receive these inputs, but the density of terminals displays great variability among the nuclei. As indicated previously, rather than carrying precisely timed information to a specific thalamic nucleus, these afferents are involved in setting the membrane potential of thalamocortical cells via metabotropic receptors, which allows the emergence of state-dependent firing patterns (burst vs. tonic firing) (Steriade et al., 1997a).

2.2 Cortical Inputs

In the simplified textbook view, the thalamus relays sensory information carried by large (see later discussion) glutamatergic terminals to the cortex. Now, if we map these glutamatergic terminals in a primate thalamus, they cover no more than 40% of the entire structure (Rovó et al., 2012). Half of these regions are dedicated to sensory information; the rest of them convey cerebellar and mammillary messages (Rovó et al., 2012). In other words, in primates, only the smaller portion of the thalamus is in position to transfer precise subcortical glutamatergic information to the cortex; the larger part of the thalamus cannot fulfill this classical role because it lacks large subcortical glutamatergic input. The reason for this discrepancy between textbooks and reality (besides the paucity of research) is the huge expansion of thalamic territories where cortical, not subcortical, glutamatergic afferents provide the major source of excitation.

All cortical regions receive thalamic inputs (with the notable exception of the dentate gyrus of the hippocampus), all cortical regions project back to the thalamus, and no thalamic region is free of cortical inputs (Deschênes et al., 1998; Sherman & Guillery, 2005; Jones, 2007b). The only cortical region that does not reciprocate thalamic inputs is the basolateral amygdala (BLA). Although earlier reports describe an amygdalo-thalamic pathway (Krettek & Price, 1977), a recent reinvestigation demonstrated that in the mouse, this originates from a small subcortical center, the ventral endopyriform nucleus, a region adjacent to the BLA, not from the BLA itself (Mátyás et al., 2014).

Cortical afferents in the thalamus are among the densest in the brain. Cortical terminals far outnumber any other terminals in the thalamus by an order of magnitude (Liu et al., 1995; Erişir et al., 1997; Deschênes et al., 1998). Cortical influence on various thalamic functions varies greatly from no detectable influence on the sensory-evoked response (Diamond, Armstrong-James, & Ebner, 1992) to one-to-one mapping of cortical-to-thalamic activity (Guo et al., 2017) or the emergence of a distinct thalamic code upon cortical influence (Schmitt et al., 2017), depending on the system and paradigm used. Thalamocortical and corticothalamic pathways together form the most widespread and least understood loop in the brain, the thalamocortical circuit. The real function of the intimate, mutually interdependent relationship between the cortex and thalamus is still a mystery.

Corticothalamic inputs arise from at least three distinct cortical cell types: layer 6a, layer 6b, and layer 5b (Bourassa et al., 1995; Rouiller & Welker, 2000; Kakei et al., 2001; Hoerder-Suabedissen et al., 2018). The cells of origin, distribution, structure, and organization of the terminals are all characteristically different in these three sets of corticothalamic routes. Large thalamic territories receive inputs from all three types of terminals, which indicates significant interactions among them. The interaction among various types of cortical afferents on thalamic neurons is presently completely unexplored.

The most traditional cortical inputs arise from the corticothalamic cells of layer 6a (Jacobson & Trojanowski, 1975;

Lund et al., 1975). The axons of these neurons densely and topographically innervate the entire thalamus (Jones, 2007b). Axon arbors of single cells are usually large; for example, in the case of the somatosensory system, they encompass the representation of several whiskers (i.e., barreloids) (Bourassa et al., 1995). The terminals are small, rarely contain mitochondria, and innervate mostly the distal dendrites of thalamocortical cells (Sherman & Guillery, 2005). An important feature of layer 6a fibers is that they do not innervate subcortical structures other than the thalamus, and layer 6a corticothalamic axons emit a collateral in the TRN "en route" to the thalamus (Bourassa et al., 1995; Kakei et al., 2001).

Layer 6b cells are the remnants of the cortical subplate, and their thalamic projections have only been recently described in detail (Bourassa et al., 1995; Hoerder-Suabedissen et al., 2018). They are similar to layer 6a cells in that they innervate only the thalamus and no other subcortical structure, but their axon arbors were reported to be restricted only to a subpopulation of nuclei (also innervated by layer 5b; see later discussion), and their collaterals were reported to spare the TRN (Hoerder-Suabedissen et al., 2018). Their axon arbor is even wider than those of layer 6a, indicating that any single thalamic region is receiving inputs from layer 6b of large cortical territories. No functional data are available on the action of layer 6b cells on the thalamus.

The third type of cortical input to the thalamus arises from the large pyramidal cells of layer 5b (also called *pyramidal tract* [PT] neurons) (Ojima, 1994; Bourassa et al., 1995; Harris et al., 2019). Thalamic projecting PT cells form only a subpopulation of layer 5b (Harris et al., 2019). Unlike layer 6 cells, besides thalamic collaterals, they have huge subcortical axon arbors (Guillery & Sherman, 2011). Indeed, each layer 5b neuron having a thalamic collateral innervates various combinations of other subcortical structures (e.g., striatum, zona incerta, subthalamic nucleus, or superior colliculus) (Deschênes et al., 1994; Guillery & Sherman, 2011). Apparently, the classical PT neurons innervating the spinal cord arise from a distinct population of 5b cells, and these cells rarely, if ever, have thalamic collaterals (Economo et al., 2018). During a motor task involving working memory, thalamic projecting and spinal cord projecting neurons are activated in a sequential manner (Economo et al., 2018). Within the thalamus, a single layer 5b axon can innervate multiple functionally related nuclei (e.g., in the case of layer 5b of the frontal cortex) (Kakei et al., 2001) or can have precise topographically aligned termination within one nucleus (e.g., somatosensory cortex) (Sumser et al., 2017). Layer 5 inputs are used to define the so-called higher-order nuclei, indicating a major cortical influence on their activity as opposed to "first-order" nuclei, which are driven by subcortical inputs (Sherman & Guillery, 1996; Reichova & Sherman, 2004). Like layer 6b fibers, layer 5b axons also traverse the TRN without emitting collaterals, at least in the case of parietal cortices (Bourassa et al., 1995; Kakei et al., 2001). Recent data indicate, however, that the frontal cortical layer 5b does innervate the rostral sector of the TRN (Hádinger et al., 2022). The terminals of layer 5b in the thalamus are large and display structural and physiological features similar to those of the large subcortical glutamatergic terminals (Hoogland et al., 1991; Vidnyánszky et al., 1996; Negyessy et al., 1998). This organization has the interesting functional consequence that the impact of layer 5b cells on 5b recipient thalamic neurons is as decisive on their outputs as the retinal input on retino-recipient thalamic neurons (Reichova & Sherman, 2004). Thus, in layer 5b–driven thalamic regions, the "receptive field properties" of thalamocortical cells are entirely inherited from the top-down, highly processed output of layer 5b (Guillery & Sherman, 2002). The proportion of the thalamus dedicated entirely to dealing with layer 5b inputs and not with subcortical inputs is greatly enlarged in primates, as indicated earlier (Rovó et al., 2012). The real function of this short, effective cortico-thalamo-cortical loop is unexplored.

Finally, it has to be noted that not all cortical regions that project to the thalamus (e.g., subiculum, presubiculum, prelimbic, infralimbic cortices) have well-defined, distinct layers 5 and 6. Classical layer 5b–type terminals have already been described arising from paleocortical regions (Pelzer et al., 2017), but whether all these "nonneocortical" inputs can be compared to any of the three corticothalamic pathways described previously or represent novel types of inputs remains to be determined.

2.3 Dynamic Stability of Thalamic Afferents during Evolution

In contrast to earlier notions indicating that the thalamocortical (i.e., thalamo-pallial) system became significant later in vertebrate evolution, new data indicate that the principal elements of thalamocortical organization are present in jawless fish (*Cyclostomata* or lampreys), the most ancient vertebrates alive today (Suryanarayana et al., 2020) (see Chapter 6). Combined morphological and physiological data clearly indicate that lampreys have a proper, functioning, light-sensitive retino-thalamo-pallial pathway distinct from a parallel somatosensory trigemino-thalamo-pallial pathway (Suryanarayana et al., 2020). The system is complemented by pallio-thalamic feedback. In essence, these data show that thalamus and thalamic afferent systems were present at the emergence of vertebrates (~600 million years ago).

Thalamocortical cells and retinal afferents are clearly different in lampreys and primates, reflecting million steps of adaptations. Apparently, one of the key features that allowed the spectacular diversification of vertebrates was the fast coevolution of thalamic inputs, thalamic territories, and the cortex. This was able to rapidly match the challenges of the environment and allowed coping of the nervous system. Maintaining the key logic of thalamic organization and its afferents, the thalamocortical system was able to rapidly and dynamically diversify, elaborate, increase, or shrink in a region-specific manner according to the behavioral niche of the animal. Remarkable examples of adaptations have been described, for instance, in the somatosensory system of the platypus (Mikula et al., 2008) and the visual thalamus of the blind mole rat (Cooper et al., 1993). Obviously, evolutionary changes are not restricted to subcortical sensory inputs. As indicated previously, the cortical input space also changed dynamically during evolution.

Regions dedicated to subcortical, *inhibitory* inputs follow the same principle, too: maintain the main logic but accommodate to behavioral needs. In the case of the GABAergic inputs from the basal ganglia or the pontine reticular formation, the size, shape, and position of innervated thalamic regions have changed between rodents and primates, but the principles of organization remain the same (Percheron et al., 1996; Bodor et al., 2008; Giber et al., 2015).

Thus, the general conclusion so far is that the high number of noncanonical inputs to the thalamus arising from multiple brain centers generate *a thalamic mosaic* rather than a canonical structure. The properties of this mosaic-like organization significantly differ from those of much better-studied brain structures containing canonical inputs that are present throughout the entire structure.

3. Heterogeneity of Terminal Types

3.1 Axon Terminals with Single and Multiple Synapses

The vast majority of glutamatergic and GABAergic axon terminals in the brain establish a single synapse on their postsynaptic targets. As a result, vesicle docking, release, and synaptic transmission are largely defined by a single pre- and postsynaptic element. In a few notable cases, presynaptic terminals become giant, and a single terminal establishes dozens of synapses, mostly on a single postsynaptic target (Rollenhagen & Lübke, 2006). Famous multisynaptic excitatory terminals are the mossy terminals of the hippocampus, the climbing fibers of the cerebellum, and the calyx of Held (Rollenhagen & Lübke, 2006). In these cases, special requirements at this point of the network resulted in a hugely effective yet highly controllable synaptic transmission (Rollenhagen & Lübke, 2006). Large terminals are unique because release sites interact both within the terminals (Budisantoso et al., 2012) and on the postsynaptic surfaces (Telgkamp et al., 2004), influencing the probability and amplitude of release as well as its short-term plasticity. Indeed, the exact position of active zones has a strong impact on the properties of synaptic transmission (Cathala et al., 2005). Thus, the brain does use *variable terminal size and complexity* but apparently uses it sparingly. In the thalamus, however, this variable is overexploited. All thalamic nuclei studied so far contain both large and small excitatory terminals of some type (Colonnier & Guillery, 1964; Szentágothai et al., 1966; Ralston, 1969; Jones & Rockel, 1971; Rinvik & Grofová, 1974b, 1974a; Dekker & Kuypers, 1976; Harding & Powell, 1977; Hoogland et al., 1991; Rovó et al., 2012; Bickford, 2019). Moreover, the thalamus displays huge variability in the complexity of inhibitory terminals as well (Halassa & Acsády, 2016). Besides classical unisynaptic inhibitory terminals, the largest multisynaptic inhibitory terminals presently known in the brain have also been described in the thalamus (Barthó et al., 2002; Bokor et al., 2005; Bodor et al., 2008; Giber et al., 2015) (Figure 2C and D). These can form up to 16 synapses with their postsynaptic targets. The only other GABAergic axon terminals with several zones are the boutons of Purkinje cells in the deep cerebellar nuclei (Telgkamp et al., 2004).

The critical questions are: Why is it advantageous to have 10–30 synapses formed by a single large terminal? Can we consider transmission via uni- and multisynaptic terminals as distinct forms of computation? Does the heterogeneity of terminals add to the complexity of neurotransmission in the thalamus? The trivial answer is that the simultaneous release of many vesicles at different synapses increases both the probability of the release as well as the size of the postsynaptic current. Indeed, thalamic giant terminals, both excitatory and inhibitory, have a high initial probability of release and large-amplitude responses (Turner & Salt, 1998; Veinante & Deschênes, 2003; Bokor et al., 2005; Groh et al., 2008; Wanaverbecq et al., 2008; Budisantoso et al., 2012). This, coupled with the preferential location of these contacts on proximal dendrites (Liu et al., 1995; Barthó et al., 2002; Groh et al., 2014), results in a large impact on their targets. In the case of excitatory giant terminals in the thalamus, this synaptic arrangement is responsible for the effective spike coupling between pre- and postsynaptic activity, resulting in the well-studied faithful relay of ascending sensory information to the cortex (Friedlander et al., 1981; Maendly et al., 1981; Deschênes et al., 2003; Hirsch, 2003). In the case of inhibitory terminals, the activation of a single inhibitory input can result in a rebound burst of the postsynaptic target in vitro (Bokor et al., 2005). In vivo, the giant GABAergic basal ganglia inputs in the bird thalamus effectively pattern the action potential trains of their postsynaptic targets, which is necessary for proper song production (Goldberg et al., 2013), and in the case of the rodent incerto-thalamic pathway, large GABAergic terminals are able to completely block sensory transmission (Lavallée et al., 2005). In sum, both the large excitatory and inhibitory large terminals are critical elements of the thalamic network, and variability of terminal dimensions seems to be an essential feature of thalamic computation.

3.2 Uni- and Multisynaptic Inhibitory Terminals

Almost all extrathalamic GABAergic inputs studied so far (substantia nigra pars reticulata, internal globus pallidus, ventral pallidum, zona incerta, anterior pretectum, rostral reticular formation) establish multisynaptic terminals on the proximal dendrites of thalamocortical cells (for a review, see Halassa & Acsády, 2016) (Figure 2C and D). They are also called *F3* terminals because they contain flattened vesicles and are the third GABAergic terminal type described in the thalamus (Halassa & Acsády, 2016). All these inputs target thalamic regions with higher-order functions (Halassa & Acsády, 2016). In contrast, the vast majority of TRN terminals establish a single synapse on their postsynaptic target (Wanaverbecq et al., 2008) and innervate all thalamic nuclei (Pinault & Deschênes, 1998). These boutons are termed *F1* terminals. If large terminals evolved only to evoke large responses, then in theory, 10 unisynaptic terminals along the same axon and converging on the same target could match the effect of one large terminal with 10 synapses. Besides the number of synapses, however, the key determinant that defines the dynamics of transmission in the case of large terminals is the exact three-dimensional (3D) position of the synapses relative to each other. This will largely influence the postsynaptic responses to trains of presynaptic activity (Telgkamp et al., 2004; Wanaverbecq et al., 2008; Giber et al., 2015).

In a fortuitous case, the properties of unisynaptic and multisynaptic GABAergic terminals could be directly compared (Wanaverbecq et al., 2008). In Po cells, unisynaptic terminals from the TRN evoked similar-sized inhibitory postsynaptic responses as large multisynaptic terminals arising from the anterior pretectal nucleus (APT) (Wanaverbecq et al., 2008). Quantal analysis and serial 3D electron microscope (EM) reconstructions clarified why the unisynaptic input is able to evoke a comparable response to its multisynaptic counterpart. It was established that on average, eight small unisynaptic TRN terminals situated on one TRN axon contacted a single Po cell, whereas in the case of the APT, it was on average one large terminal with eight synapses (Wanaverbecq et al., 2008). This arrangement obviously negated the "large terminal evolved to evoke large effect" argument. The real difference between the two types of inputs emerged using trains of stimulations. Stimulation frequencies above 10 Hz in the case of the TRN resulted in a pronounced short-term depression and diminished inhibitory charge transfer, whereas APT terminals were able to maintain (or even surpass) the initial current even at 100 Hz, resulting in a constant, strong inhibitory barrage during the train (Wanaverbecq et al., 2008). Indeed, high-frequency firing is a main feature of the parent cells sending multisynaptic GABAergic boutons to the thalamus (Bokor et al., 2005; Giber et al., 2015). In the case of the zona incerta, this approaches the theoretical maximum firing of 1,000 Hz (Barthó et al., 2007). Thus, the strong, persistent inhibition at these terminals at high firing frequency is highly relevant biologically. Modeling studies clarified the role of multisynaptic GABAergic terminals with closely situated synapses in persistent inhibition at high presynaptic activity (Telgkamp et al., 2004). The data showed that gamma-amino butyric acid (GABA) released from one active zone is able to diffuse to several synapses *of the same terminal* within one millisecond. Thus, failure of release at one or two (or even at several) release sites will not result in a diminished postsynaptic current because even a single active release site will provide sufficient GABA for GABA receptors located in the nearby synapses (Telgkamp et al., 2004). This certainly will not happen with unisynaptic terminals because the release sites are much farther apart.

In conclusion, variability in GABAergic bouton complexity will result in distinct inhibitory functions. The strongly maintained inhibition of multisynaptic systems is involved in the timing of thalamocortical activity (Goldberg et al., 2013) focally, whereas the depressing, unisynaptic TRN may not affect precise spike timing but participates in gain control and more global actions, such as oscillations (Halassa & Acsády, 2016).

3.3 Uni- and Multisynaptic Excitatory Terminals

As described earlier, not only inhibitory but also excitatory afferents establish giant, multisynaptic terminals in the thalamus (termed *RL* terminals because they contain **r**ound vesicles and are **l**arge) (Figure 2A and B). These types of boutons transfer subcortical sensory inputs arising from all modalities, as well as the cerebellar and mamillary afferents (Colonnier & Guillery, 1964; Szentágothai et al., 1966; Ralston, 1969; Jones & Rockel, 1971; Rinvik & Grofová, 1974a, 1974b; Dekker & Kuypers, 1976; Harding & Powell, 1977). Large and small cortical terminals have been described in the posterior, the lateroposterior, the dorsal medial geniculate, and the mediodorsal nuclei arising from the somatosensory (Hoogland et al., 1991), visual (Vidnyánszky et al., 1996), auditory (Ojima, 1994), piriform (Pelzer et al., 2017), and frontal (Schwartz et al., 1991; Negyessy et al., 1998) cortices, respectively, in all mammalian species studied so far (for a review, see Rouiller & Welker, 2000). The cortex seems to be the only source of large excitatory terminals in the primate lateral pulvinar and mediodorsal nucleus (Rovó et al., 2012). The origin of large terminals is confined to layer 5 (Bourassa & Deschênes, 1995; Bourassa et al., 1995; Kakei et al., 2001). There appears to be no major structural or physiological difference between top-down cortical and bottom-up subcortical large glutamatergic terminals other than the type of vesicular glutamate transporter they express (vGluT1 and vGluT2, respectively) (Reichova & Sherman, 2004; Sherman & Guillery, 2005; Rovó et al., 2012). It is important to emphasize, though, that both the information content of the neuronal message carried by these afferents and the properties of convergence on thalamocortical cells differ between cortical and subcortical multisynaptic terminals; thus, their integration by thalamocortical cells cannot be regarded as identical.

Giant excitatory terminals are even larger (2–10 μm) than their inhibitory counterparts and may establish up to 30–50 synapses per target (Mason et al., 1996; Budisantoso et al., 2012). A peculiar feature of these inputs is that the postsynaptic proximal dendrite protrudes dendritic appendages into the giant terminal, and many synapses contact these structures. In species and nuclei that contain thalamic interneurons, the vesicles bearing filopodial dendrites of interneurons (called *F2* terminals) receive many inputs from the large terminals and, in turn, synapse on the thalamocortical neurons, forming the famous "triads" described in the pioneering EM studies of the 1960s (Colonnier & Guillery, 1964; Szentágothai et al., 1966; Ralston, 1969). Thus, triads may qualify for one of the longest-standing riddles in neuroscience, described over 50 years ago, and their function is still unexplained today. It is interesting to note that even within the same nucleus, afferents with distinct origins (e.g., X and Y retinal ganglion cells) may or may not form triads. Three-dimensional EM reconstruction revealed that in the case of cerebellar inputs, the three partners (i.e., afferent terminal, thalamocortical dendrite, and interneuron dendrite) may establish quite variable assemblies (Mason et al., 1996).

The vast majority of small unisynaptic excitatory terminals (called *RS*; **r**ound vesicle, **s**mall terminals) originate in layer 6

(L6) (Bourassa & Deschênes, 1995; Bourassa et al., 1995). By far, these are the most numerous inputs and blanket the entire thalamus (Sherman & Guillery, 2005). L6 terminals are less than 1 μm, rarely contain mitochondria, and establish a single contact, mostly on the distal dendritic shafts of their targets (Hoogland et al., 1991; Liu et al., 1995; Vidnyánszky et al., 1996). L6 boutons never form triads.

As expected, the large glutamatergic terminals in the thalamus evoke large-amplitude, fast-rising currents that may reach the action potential threshold (Deschênes et al., 2003; Groh et al., 2008; Pelzer et al., 2017). This is why they are called "detonator" or "driver" inputs and, in general, are thought to be responsible for faithful transmission. Driver inputs, however, are strongly depressing even in the case of only a slight increase in presynaptic activity (5–10 Hz) (Turner & Salt, 1998; Castro-Alamancos, 2002b; Reichova & Sherman, 2004). Two questions arise, then. What is the mechanism of depression, and why does a faithful pathway display strong depression? The answer to the first question lies in the structure of the terminals, as in the case of the large inhibitory terminals. Interestingly, however, because of the different properties of GABAergic and glutamatergic transmission, exactly the same type of structure (i.e., closely arranged release sites) results in the opposite effect (Telgkamp et al., 2004; Budisantoso et al., 2012). In the case of excitatory terminals, intraterminal spillover of glutamate among the many release sites causes the desensitization of AMPA receptors. A high initial release probability and multivesicular release strongly contribute to this depression (Budisantoso et al., 2012). Recently, the auxiliary subunit of the AMPA receptor (CKAMP44) has also been identified, which is responsible for a reduction in the rate of recovery from desensitization (Chen et al., 2018).

The second question, the function of the strong short-term depression and hence strong low-pass filtering of the incoming signal, is less clear. It is somewhat counterintuitive for a structure designed for faithful relay. One influential theory holds that faithful thalamic relays work only if the membrane potential of the thalamocortical cells is close to threshold (Castro-Alamancos, 2002a). In this way, the heavily depressed excitatory postsynaptic potentials (EPSPs) late in the trains will also reach threshold and evoke postsynaptic action potentials. When, however, the thalamic cell is more hyperpolarized, only the first spike that goes through the train will not be transmitted, and this will not result in a sensory percept (Castro-Alamancos, 2002a). In the case of sensory transmission, this would be a mechanism for selective attention, whereby only attended modalities pass the thalamic gate, and the others are filtered out. Adjusting the membrane potential could be achieved by nucleus selective modulation of TRN inputs or by any other modulator (e.g., acetylcholine). According to the second theory (developed largely for cortical terminals), in the case of depressed EPSPs, thalamocortical cells become coincidence detectors (Groh et al., 2008). Depressed EPSPs will reach threshold only if two different inputs are coactive. Thus, this theory emphasizes the importance of presynaptic timing. It is evident, though, that more work is needed to decipher the real function of these most peculiar giant but heavily depressing terminals.

In contrast to the giants, small excitatory terminals evoke small postsynaptic currents and have a facilitating role in the thalamus (Reichova & Sherman, 2004). This clearly shows that small and large terminals are not two ends of a spectrum but are different entities. The function of these weak distal synapses and their facilitation is less clear. We know very little about the activity of L6 cells, but in several situations, they are very silent (Sirota et al., 2005). In general, a paucity of data and theories surround the most numerous inputs to the thalamus.

The conclusion is that, like in the case of inhibitory terminals, the exact structure of the terminals has a strong functional consequence on their actions. Giant terminals may be optimized for state-dependent relay or coincidence detection, whereas small terminals are probably involved in a hitherto little-understood modulation of thalamic states.

3.4 Variability of Terminals

Studies of the size of excitatory terminals in the thalamus of primates led to interesting insights into the variability of terminal types. Measuring the diameter of cortical terminals at the EM level disclosed that large thalamic regions have multisynaptic terminals of intermediate sizes (Rovó et al., 2012). For example, the two important sectors of the pulvinar, lateral and medial, could be clearly differentiated based on the size of cortical terminals even at the light microscopic level (Rovó et al., 2012). Besides the small L6 terminals, the lateral pulvinar displayed the classical giant multisynaptic layer 5b terminals. In the medial pulvinar, the size of multisynaptic boutons was significantly smaller (by 50%) (Rovó et al., 2012). Small multisynaptic terminals have also been described in rodents. Glutamatergic terminals from the superior colliculus were significantly smaller in the dorsolateral geniculate nucleus than the retino-geniculate terminals (Bickford et al., 2015; Barsy et al., 2020). Small multisynaptic terminals were termed *RM* terminals (**r**ound vesicles, **m**edium size), as opposed to RL and RS terminals, because their size is significantly larger than RS terminals but smaller than RL terminals (Rovó et al., 2012).

Small and large *multisynaptic terminals* are apparently not simply transients along a size spectrum but distinct entities. Certain pathways evidently use only small but not large multisynaptic terminals (Bickford et al., 2015; Barsy et al., 2020). Fewer synapses will result in a lower release probability, leading to less saturation of neighboring synapses. Indeed, small multisynaptic terminals displayed significantly smaller short-term depression than large ones in the same system (Bickford et al., 2015). Small multisynaptic terminals are also clearly distinct from small unisynaptic terminals because the latter is facilitating, as described earlier. In sum, the data indicate that small multisynaptic terminals perform input–output transformation that is different from that of both large multisynaptic and small unisynaptic terminals.

Finally, in the entire basal ganglia recipient ventral anterior nucleus with known layer 5b inputs, no multisynaptic excitatory terminals of any type could be resolved, indicating that layer 5b boutons in this nucleus are actually small (Rovó et al., 2012). Unisynaptic layer 5b terminals have recently been confirmed in rodents using cell-type–specific tracing (Bokor et al.,

2016). Preliminary data indicate that small unisynaptic layer 5b terminals are not facilitating like the small unisynaptic layer 6 terminals. Excitatory terminals, which deviate from the accepted small–large distinction, as described previously, are not few in number, nor do they cover tiny, unimportant thalamic regions. Close to 40% of the primate thalamus is innervated by "nonconventional" excitatory terminals (Rovó et al., 2012).

As described earlier, the exact number and position of synapses relative to each other have important functional consequences. The data listed previously indicate that the terminal structure will mainly influence the state-dependent transmission of spike trains. Because this input–output transformation crucially affects the timing of thalamic messages to the cortex, the exact structure of the terminals in any thalamic input is an important variable in the thalamus. Smaller terminals are always more numerous than larger ones (although this has to be quantified in the future); thus, besides input–output transformation, terminal size will indirectly affect the other critical variable of thalamic transmission, *the degree of convergence*.

3.5 Stability of Terminal Complexity during Evolution

In mammals, both the giant excitatory and inhibitory terminals appear to be quite rigid during evolution. In all of the model species studied so far (rodents, cats, primates), subcortical excitatory inputs display complex synaptic arrangements. Dual (large layer 5 and small layer 6) corticothalamic inputs are also present in every case (Rouiller & Welker, 2000). The structure of the multisynaptic GABAergic inputs from the basal ganglia is remarkably similar between rodents and primates (Bodor et al., 2008) (Figure 2D). Finally, the GABA-glycinergic ascending afferents from the rostral reticular formation display similar organization in the mouse and humans (Giber et al., 2015).

Concerning reptiles, the synaptic organization of the turtle lateral geniculate nucleus (LGN), in essence, replicates the mammalian visual thalamus, down to the presence of vesicle-bearing interneurons and triads (Kenigfest et al., 1995). Because turtles are one of the most ancient reptilian lineages and parallel evolution of such a complex system is unlikely, these structural data indicate that complex synaptic structures and variability of terminal types in the thalamus predate the split of mammalian–reptilian branches in the Permian. Further back in time, as indicated previously, primary somatosensory and visual thalamic sectors have been identified in the most primitive vertebrate alive today, the lamprey (Suryanarayana et al., 2020). Although EM analysis of the afferents is not yet available, the light microscopic data show that the structure of the retino-geniculate contacts is different from that of mammals; they target more distal dendrites with smaller terminals (Suryanarayana et al., 2020). This indicates that the variability of terminal structures in the thalamus may have evolved after the bifurcation of jawless fish early in vertebrate evolution.

4. Heterogeneity of Input Integration

All neurons in the brain perform local computation by integrating several different inputs. Consider now the thalamus. Similar to other neurons in the brain, every thalamic cell receives inputs from several sources, so thalamic cells also perform input integration to generate an output. What differentiates the thalamus from the rest of the brain is *the variability of input integration among its neurons*. Most of the thalamic inputs target only some of its sectors. In addition, unlike in any other brain region, terminal types also display great variability. Thus, different thalamic cells will display qualitatively different types of integration because axons converging on different thalamocortical cells arise from different sets of sources and from different types of boutons (Figure 3).

In most other brain regions (e.g., hippocampus, cerebellum, striatum), inputs are present in the entire structure and innervate all principal cells with the same terminal type. As a consequence, these inputs are canonical, and the individual cells of a region (e.g., CA1 pyramidal cells) will perform canonical input integration. Thus, when we consider how hippocampal function is implemented, we should consider only the *variability in the strength of the inputs* on CA1 pyramidal cells, not the *variability of the input space* itself. This is why we call the CA1 region, and many other intensively studied networks, a *canonical* or *modular* network. In these networks, however complex the canonical unit is, the origin and types of afferents and, as a consequence, their integration do not display qualitative differences between the elements.

In the thalamus, presently, only L6 and TRN inputs can be considered as canonical (i.e., innervating the entire structure with similar terminals). Recent splitting of TRN cells with distinct termination patterns, however, may further reduce canonical elements in the thalamus (Clemente-Perez et al., 2017; Li et al., 2020; Martinez-Garcia et al., 2020). Thus, as opposed to many other brain regions, due to the variability of inputs, the thalamus cannot be considered as a modular network because it is not possible to identify a canonical unit with canonical inputs performing canonical integration for the entire structure.

How many types of input integration are present in the thalamus is an exciting question, but presently, it is not possible to determine this clearly because the entire field is largely data deficient. Functional investigation of the nonsensory thalamus started in earnest only in the second half of the past decade, but still, the origin, types, and number of inputs converging on any single thalamic neuron outside sensory nuclei are poorly known. As a first attempt, in the next section, I provide one approach to start to investigate the problem. As indicated previously, the entire problem of regional variability in input space and type within a structure is largely nonexistent in other brain regions; thus, approaches to this question may rapidly change in the future as more data will start filling the gaps in our knowledge.

4.1 Types of Integration

In order to assess the types of thalamic integration, inputs will be described by three features: origin, transmitter, and type of terminals (Figure 3). For now, I will consider only two types of origin (*cortical layer 5b and subcortical*), two types of neurotransmitters (*glutamate and GABA*), and two types of terminals (*large multisynaptic and small unisynaptic terminals*). These terminal types can be present alone or in combination with others in a thalamic region. Later in the chapter, I discuss some of the known types of thalamic input integration (computational units or modules) described so far and indicate if physiological data are available concerning the function of this integration. *My main argument here* is that because of the difference in source, transmitter, degree of convergence, and properties of synaptic transmission, *the exact computation performed by thalamic neurons while integrating these inputs in order to generate a spike output will differ*. The list that follows is certainly not complete; it merely aims to represent the heterogeneity of input integration in the thalamus.

4.2 Large Multisynaptic Subcortical Glutamatergic Inputs (Figure 3A)

The prototypical sensory nuclei receive only large multisynaptic subcortical terminals from a single source. In these cases, the activity of layer 5b or large GABAergic inputs is not integrated into the thalamic message. Integration of inputs occurs only among similar inputs. The general interpretation of this arrangement is that primary sensory cortices require a faithful representation of subthalamic sensory activity; thus, spike timing reaches the cortex unaltered by other strong excitatory or inhibitory influences. State-dependent transmission, as described previously, however, can strongly influence the relay of the trains. Dense 3D EM reconstruction data in the visual thalamus recently indicated that the size of retinal inputs can be highly variable, demonstrating that variability of input integration may take place even in these circuits thought to be "prototypical" so far (Morgan et al., 2016).

In general, cerebellar and mammillary territories are also considered to belong to this category, and indeed, layer 5b input seems to be negligible in cerebellar regions (Yamawaki & Shepherd, 2015), at least from M1. In the case of the mammillary recipient anterior nuclear group, however, the postsubicular influence on thalamic activity strongly shapes the angular tuning of the head-direction cells in the anterodorsal nucleus (Goodridge & Taube, 1997; Peyrache et al., 2015). This influence is more compatible with a strong layer 5 than a week L6 influence; as a consequence, in the future, mammillary territories may be considered as being of the convergent-integration type, as described later in the chapter. The detailed study of both the parent cells and the terminal types along cortical pathways to the anterior thalamus is still missing. Thalamic regions that receive only small multisynaptic or unisynaptic glutamatergic terminals from subcortical centers and no other input types have not been described so far.

4.3 Integration of Multisynaptic Subcortical Glutamatergic Terminals with Distinct Origin (Figure 3B)

Recent data indicate that two subcortical inputs arising from different subcortical centers and carrying distinct messages can be integrated at the level of the thalamus. These types of integration have never been considered to be performed by the thalamus before.

In the case of conditioned fear, the association of a conditioned stimulus (CS; e.g., a sound) and a painful unconditioned stimulus (US; e.g., foot shock) were traditionally thought to take place in the lateral amygdala. Recent data, however, indicate that integration *and* association of the CS and US take place first in the thalamus, not in the amygdala (Barsy et al., 2020). This study demonstrates that the associative amygdalar representation of conditioned fear critically depends on the upstream, integrated thalamic input. In order to solve this computation, calretinin-positive thalamic neurons in the suprageniculate–limitans complex are contacted by small multisynaptic terminals arising from the inferior colliculus (these carry the auditory signals) *and* similar boutons from the deep layers of the superior colliculus (carrying the pain information) (Barsy et al., 2020). During CS-US association, these neurons undergo plastic changes that are essential for this type of associative fear memory, and the final output of these thalamocortical cells represents integrated information. These data not only show the importance of integration of qualitatively different information in thalamic function but also bring down another important conceptual wall of thalamic activity—the claim that the thalamus is immune to plastic changes.

Integration of subcortical inputs with different sources has been observed in the visual system as well. Thalamic neurons in the outer layers of the rodent LGN have been shown to be contacted both by giant retinal terminals and small multisynaptic collicular inputs (Bickford et al., 2015). Although clear differences in the short-term dynamics of these two terminal types have been described, the functional significance of this integration requires further studies.

4.4 Large Multisynaptic Cortical Glutamatergic Inputs (Figure 3C)

In the primate thalamus, large territories receive glutamatergic multisynaptic terminals exclusively from layer 5b of the cortex (Rovó et al., 2012). These regions receive no glutamatergic inputs of any type from subcortical centers (Rovó et al., 2012). In essence, this means that these territories are entirely dedicated to cortico-thalamo-cortical communication. Large multisynaptic terminals prevail in the lateral pulvinar and the mediodorsal nucleus, whereas small multisynaptic terminals are abundant in the medial pulvinar (Rovó et al., 2012). Large and small multisynaptic terminals not only differ in size and short-term plasticity (Bickford et al., 2015) but also in the degree of convergence; however, hard data on this matter are still missing. In rodents, the caudal, ventral part of Po that is not innervated by trigeminal terminals (Groh et al., 2014) is also dedicated purely to cortico-thalamo-cortical communication, similar to the primate pulvinar. The large multisynaptic terminals arrive from the S1 cortex in this case. Large terminals in rodents are also abundant in the submedial and mediodorsal nucleus originating in the orbitofrontal and piriform cortex, but whether and to what extent they intermingle with other terminals require clarification.

Several hypotheses have been put forward to explain the role of the L5-thalamic, top-down organization, but because clear identification of purely cortically driven versus convergent zones (see following discussion) in physiological experiments is mostly missing, tests of these hypotheses await further data. In the visual sector of the lateral pulvinar, clear retinotopic organization has been described (Bender, 1981; Purushothaman et al., 2012). This activity cannot originate in the colliculus (or the retina) because no subcortical terminals are present in this region (Rovó et al., 2012), and the colliculus targets the inferior, not the lateral pulvinar. This suggests that retinotopic organization in the lateral pulvinar is conveyed by large top-down multisynaptic terminals of layer 5b origin. Indeed, recently, layer 5b input from V2 has been described for this region (Moore et al., 2019). The precise role of this activity is unclear, but proper pulvinar input back to V1 is essential to maintain V1 activity, indicating a reverberating, mutually interdependent V1–lateral pulvinar circuitry (Purushothaman et al., 2012). Reverberating pulvinar–V1 activity is clearly only the tip of the iceberg because the cortically driven pulvinar is apparently involved in more complex functions, such as selective attention (Komura et al., 2013; Zhou et al., 2016), as well.

4.5 Integration of Multisynaptic Cortical and Multisynaptic Subcortical Glutamatergic Inputs (Figure 3D)

The first unequivocal evidence of the convergence of two multisynaptic terminals from distinct (cortical *and* subcortical) origins was described in 2014 (Groh et al., 2014). In this case, large multisynaptic cortical terminals from the S1 cortex converged with large multisynaptic subcortical terminals from the spinal trigeminal nucleus on thalamocortical cells in Po (Groh et al., 2014). Timed subthreshold stimulation of the two inputs separately in vivo demonstrated that Po cells integrate the two inputs in a supralinear manner (Groh et al., 2014). Interestingly, integration time windows displayed great cell-to-cell variability. The study also demonstrated that whereas all Po cells display the physiological signature of large layer 5 cortical inputs, large subcortical inputs are confined to the lateral and dorsal parts of the nucleus. In essence, this means that the nucleus can be divided into a cortically driven sector and a convergent sector.

Two types of hypotheses were put forward to explain the function of the convergent inputs. Po cells may work as a conditional relay, allowing subcortical signals to reach the cortex only if they are coactive with top-down cortical inputs (e.g., during active touch by whiskers) (Mátyás et al., 2010). According to the other idea, Po cells may multiplex the two types of signals and transfer one *or* the other, depending on the circumstances. In this latter case, the downstream target of Po (S1 and M1 cortex) should be clearly informed of whether there is a Po transfer cortical or subcortical signal in a given moment.

A similar organization has been recently demonstrated in the case of the visual system. In this case, thalamocortical cells of the lateral posterior nucleus (LP) integrate cortical information arriving from layer 5b of V1 via large multisynaptic terminals with other signals, some of which originate in the subcortical structure of the superior colliculus (Blot et al., 2021). Collicular terminals are known to form small multisynaptic terminals in the thalamus (Bickford et al., 2015). In this case, the function of thalamic integration is also to link perception and action. The output of LP cells reaches the higher-order visual area (AL), and the LP provides information to the AL cortex about visual motion with high temporal frequencies (Blot et al., 2021). Furthermore, the LP is also able to integrate visual signals with the animal's running speed. LP input is very effective and greatly defines the receptive field properties of the AL. The critical thing is that the LP message is not simply a "relay" of top-down V1 information to AL; it contains a substantial subcortical, precisely timed update of this cortical message (Blot et al., 2021). Note that the primary sensory cortico-cortical signal (V1 to AL) does not contain the motion information because it has no direct access to the direct collicular output. V1 information needs to descend to the thalamus, where it can be integrated with a subcortical input.

Convergence of cortical and subcortical information, each of which is necessary for proper function, has recently been described in the motor thalamus (Guo et al., 2017; Gao et al., 2018) as well. In this very nice example of multiple embedded loops, both the cortico-thalamo-cortical loop and the cortico-subcortico-thalamic loop targeting the same thalamic population were shown to be essential to maintain cortical persistent activity during the delay period of a tactile discrimination task with a delayed directional response (licking). First, it was shown that the cortex and thalamus were mutually interdependent on each other's activity and that their reciprocal strong excitation was necessary for a proper behavioral response (Guo et al., 2017). Next, the same thalamic population was shown to be targeted by the fastigial nucleus of the cerebellum (Gao et al., 2018). The cerebellum was driven by the cortical persistent activity via the pontine nuclei and reciprocated this input back to the cortex via the motor thalamus (Gao et al., 2018). The thalamus thus integrated delay activity from both the cortex and the cerebellum. The individual contributions of these pathways to thalamic activity are presently unclear.

These three examples from three systems clearly show that the integration of strong and fast excitatory inputs from cortical *and* subcortical sources is an important mode of thalamic function during which a cortical descending signal can be updated with subcortical information before it reenters the cortex.

4.6 Integration of Multisynaptic GABAergic and Multisynaptic Glutamatergic Inputs (Figure 3E)

Two parallel ascending whisker pathways in rodents, the lemniscal and the paralemniscal, evoke characteristically different responses in the thalamus despite the fact that they both establish strong multisynaptic excitatory inputs on their targets (Diamond, Armstrong-James, & Ebner, 1992). The lemniscal arises from the principal trigeminal nucleus and evokes prototypical fast sensory responses with the well-known topographic receptive field properties (barreloids) in the ventral posteromedial nucleus (VPM). The paralemniscal, from the spinal trigeminal nucleus, however, has almost zero early response in Po (Diamond, Armstrong-James, Budway, et al., 1992). Po neurons only have a delayed multiwhisker response to whisker stimulation, which depends on their strong layer 5b inputs from the cortex (Kuroda & Price, 1991). In intracellular recording from Po cells after whisker stimulation, the first response is, curiously, an inhibitory postsynaptic potential (IPSP), which is followed by an EPSP; however, as a result of the early inhibition, it rarely reaches the firing threshold (Lavallée et al., 2005). The source of this IPSP is an extremely fast and effective feedforward inhibition, which, perhaps uniquely in the brain, overtakes feedforward excitation and prevents its action on the postsynaptic cell (Lavallée et al., 2005). The source of this input is the zona incerta, which establishes multisynaptic GABAergic terminals on Po cells (Barthó et al., 2002). Lesions of this input result in a fast, effective sensory response in Po (Lavallée et al., 2005). What might be the function of inhibiting sensory responses at the level of the thalamus? Some data indicate that the circuit may work with disinhibition and top-down cortical signals (Barthó et al., 2007) and may shut down the incerto-Po inhibitory pathway via intra-incertal communication during active whisking (Urbain & Deschênes, 2007b). The critical thing is that the final output of the thalamic cell is determined by the interaction of the multisynaptic excitatory and multisynaptic inhibitory signals. Because, apparently, all Po cells receive layer 5b input (Groh et al., 2014), most probably, integration of three major pathways—cortical and subcortical multisynaptic and inhibitory multisynaptic terminals—takes place in Po cells. Finally, to add a final touch, inhibitory multisynaptic terminals arise not only from the zona incerta but also from the anterior pretectal nucleus to Po (Bokor et al., 2005; Wanaverbecq et al., 2008), so how the final output is computed is still unresolved.

Similar interactions between large GABAergic and other large terminals may take place in several other regions (e.g., ventral pallidal and cortical terminals in the mediodorsal nucleus) (Kuroda & Price, 1991), but no other system has been studied in detail.

4.7 Integration of Multisynaptic Inhibitory and Unisynaptic Excitatory Inputs (Figure 3F)

Ultrastructural investigation of the basal ganglia recipient primate thalamus revealed that it contains only small unisynaptic excitatory terminals, along with the large multisynaptic GABAergic ones that arise from the basal ganglia (Rovó et al., 2012). Because in addition to layer 6, layer 5 also heavily innervates this region, the conclusion is that in these territories, unlike in the examples listed so far, layer 5 establishes unisynaptic terminals where interaction among the release sites cannot take place. This assumption has recently been demonstrated in rodents with cell-type–specific labeling. Small layer 5 terminals are apparently also very effective in driving thalamic neurons (Bokor et al., 2016) and thalamic activity indeed heavily depends on the cortical inputs in these regions (Guo et al., 2017). The real computational advantage of this computational unit is presently unknown. Considering the size and importance (Parkinson's disease) of this region, in the near future, we will certainly see a rapid increase in our knowledge.

Interactions of extrathalamic GABAergic signals and cortical inputs were also observed recently in the paraventricular nucleus, which forms the largest member of the dorsal midline region. In a reward association licking task, the response properties of dorsal midline thalamic neurons displayed dissociable components (Otis et al., 2019). After several days of learning, the activity of midline neurons could be used to predict both the timing of CS+ and the behavioral response (licking frequency). Ca-imaging of afferents arising from two distinct brain regions (prefrontal cortex and lateral hypothalamus) demonstrated that cue–reward association arises from glutamatergic prefrontal cortical neurons, whereas licking information originates in the GABAergic cells of the lateral hypothalamus. Optogenetic interference with prefrontal inputs selectively impaired the coding of cue–reward associations in dorsal midline thalamic neurons and reduced the ability to appropriately respond to CS+. Interestingly, after disruption of the cortical signal, the prediction of licking frequency remained intact in the thalamic cells (it actually got better because the cue–reward association no longer interfered with the licking signal), demonstrating proper hypothalamic signaling. These data clearly show that thalamic neurons do integrate information arising from different sources and are able to generate a multiplexed signal. This is an excellent example of how a highly derived top-down cortical signal (Pavlovian conditioning) is integrated and updated with a bottom-up state or motivational signal from the hypothalamus. It is important to keep in mind that the cortex has no direct access to these motivational signals because GABAergic hypothalamic cells do not have extensive cortical projections. Because cortically projecting dorsal midline neurons innervate many other forebrain targets with branching collaterals (Mátyás et al., 2018), the multiplexed signal generated in the thalamus is transferred to widespread brain regions.

4.8 Hubs of Integration—the Intralaminar Nuclei and the Midline Nuclear Group (Figure 3G)

The complexity of thalamic integration reaches its pinnacles in two little-understood nuclear groups: the intralaminar and the midline nuclei (Van der Werf et al., 2002). Unfortunately, earlier accounts brought these cell groups under the same umbrella, but it has to be emphasized that they are characteristically distinct, and besides some common inputs, they share very few features. One of these features is that both intralaminar and midline nuclei are contacted by terminals originating in many distinct brain centers. Up till now, we investigated cases when a thalamic neuron integrated noncanonical inputs originating from two or three brain regions. In midline and intralaminar nuclei, this number certainly has to be multiplied—by how many is still unknown because of the paucity of data.

The intralaminar nuclei are contacted by the cerebellum, the basal ganglia, the superior colliculus, the reticular formation, and the lateral pain pathway, among others (Van der Werf et al., 2002). Their output mainly targets frontal motor cortical regions, and they also heavily innervate the dorsal striatum (Steriade & Glenn, 1982). Their activity has been tightly linked to conscious states (Morgan et al., 2016). Just like their input space, terminal types in the intralaminar nuclei are also highly variable. They are contacted both by large and small multisynaptic subcortical glutamatergic terminals (Rovó et al., 2012) and by multisynaptic GABAergic terminals from the pontine reticular formation (Giber et al., 2015) and the basal ganglia (Percheron et al., 1996). Activation of the brainstem GABAergic inputs in the intralaminar nuclei induces complete behavioral arrest and a switch of awake cortical activity to a low-frequency oscillation for the duration of the stimulus (Giber et al., 2015), indicating a powerful effect of one of its many inputs. Intralaminar nuclei also receive small layer 5 inputs from premotor cortices.

The input/output space of midline nuclei is different, and its dorsal (paraventricular nucleus) and ventral (reuniens nucleus) members are apparently involved in different brain circuits (Van der Werf et al., 2002). The paraventricular nucleus is a hub for the representation of the inner state, arousal, saliency of the stimuli, and stress levels (Kirouac, 2015; Penzo & Gao, 2021). It receives inputs from periaqueductal gray matter, the parabrachial nucleus, several nuclei and cell types of the hypothalamus, and the bed nucleus of the stria terminalis (Kirouac, 2015). The output of midline nuclei is also highly unusual because in addition to providing widespread cortical outputs, it also targets almost all subcortical centers in the forebrain (Mátyás et al., 2018). This truly hub-like organization allows dorsal midline nuclei to control complex behavioral responses, which requires the orchestration of many different brain centers.

In contrast to its dorsal counterpart, the reuniens nucleus is mainly involved in prefrontal–hippocampal loops; it receives strong inputs from the frontal cortex, and in addition to widespread neocortical outputs, it sends a pronounced projection to the CA1 region of the hippocampus (Van der Werf et al., 2002). This prefrontal-thalamo-hippocampal pathway is apparently involved in prospective hippocampal coding in goal-directed tasks (Ito et al., 2015) and fear generalization (Xu & Südhof, 2013).

Subcortical inputs also differ between the dorsal and ventral midline nuclei. A pronounced excitatory input to the nucleus reuniens arises from the supramammillary nucleus of the hypothalamus, which also innervates the hippocampus (Maglóczky et al., 1994) and is a key pacemaker of the hippocampal theta oscillation. In a nice example of cortical–subcortical interaction in the thalamus, this supramammillary input to the nucleus reuniens was found to orchestrate the timing of spike trains in the transthalamic prefronto-hippocampal pathway in the theta frequency range (Ito et al., 2018). Concerning subcortical GABAergic inputs, I already described the role of the hypothalamic afferents in a reward-associated licking task (Otis et al., 2019).

In the case of both the intralaminar and the midline nuclei, the critical question is, How many input regions converge on single thalamocortical cells? Are there parallel pathways with thalamic neurons displaying a low degree of convergence, or rather, do these neurons function as real hubs by integrating the activity of many brain centers? Depending on the experimental approaches, these centers are apparently involved in widely different behavioral functions that do not have a common denominator. Deciphering the rules of convergence and integration may be one tool to disentangle this diverse array of functions.

5. Conclusions

According to the data noted previously, mosaic-like, noncanonical organization is the rule rather than the exception in the thalamus. The degree of input complexity varies among different thalamic nuclei, but no single connectional rule applies to all thalamocortical cells. The true functional relevance of this unique complexity is presently unclear, but the computational logic of this thalamic organization clearly differs from that of the cortex. The cortex is characterized by few input sources and few terminal types but great neuronal diversity and complex interactions among them. In the cortex, the basic canonical module is relatively unaltered in the entire structure. In contrast, the thalamus has a large number of input sources, variable terminal types, almost no neuronal diversity, and no recurrent intrathalamic communication. The basic computational unit, however, displays huge variability, resulting in a noncanonical, mosaic-like organization.

The nonmodular organization of the thalamus might be one answer to the fundamental question of why the modular cortex, with its neat areal segregation, is nearly isolated from direct subcortical glutamatergic inputs, and these are first processed in the thalamus. It is tempting to speculate that the highly diverse subcortical input patterns need to be preprocessed and appropriately integrated with cortical spike trains before entering the cortex. The thalamus is, thus, a preprocessing interface of the cortex. *The advantage of this forebrain organization for the cortex is that rather than having multitudes of inputs with different requirements for spatial and temporal representations, thalamic transfer will result in a relatively homogeneous neuronal code constantly updated with the inner state, cortical rhythms, sensory information, motor commands, and so forth. Thus, inputs arising from nearly every part of the brain are integrated and translated in the thalamus to a unified, fast glutamatergic code for the cortex.*

References

Asanuma, C., Thach, W.T., & Jones, E.G. (1983) Anatomical evidence for segregated focal groupings of efferent cells and their terminal ramifications in the cerebellothalamic pathway of the monkey. *Brain Res. Rev.*, **5**, 267–297.

Barsy, B., Kocsis, K., Magyar, A., Babiczky, Á., Szabó, M., Veres, J.M., Hillier, D., Ulbert, I., Yizhar, O., & Mátyás, F. (2020) Associative and plastic thalamic signaling to the lateral amygdala controls fear behavior. *Nat. Neurosci.*, **23**, 625–637.

Barthó, P., Freund, T.F., & Acsády, L. (2002) Selective GABAergic innervation of thalamic nuclei from zona incerta. *Eur. J. Neurosci.*, **16**, 999–1014.

Barthó, P., Slézia, A., Varga, V., Bokor, H., Pinault, D., Buzsáki, G., & Acsády, L. (2007) Cortical control of zona incerta. *J. Neurosci.*, **27**, 1670–1681.

Bender, D.B. (1981) Retinotopic organization of macaque pulvinar. *J. Neurophysiol.*, **46**, 672–693.

Bennett, C., Gale, S.D., Garrett, M.E., Newton, M.L., Callaway, E.M., Murphy, G.J., & Olsen, S.R. (2019) Higher-order thalamic circuits channel parallel streams of visual information in mice. *Neuron*, **102**, 477–492.e5.

Bickford, M.E. (2019) Synaptic organization of the dorsal lateral geniculate nucleus. *Eur. J. Neurosci.*, **49**, 938–947.

Bickford, M.E., Zhou, N., Krahe, T.E., Govindaiah, G., & Guido, W. (2015) Retinal and tectal "driver-like" inputs converge in the shell of the mouse dorsal lateral geniculate nucleus. *J. Neurosci.*, **35**, 10523–10534.

Blot, A., Roth, M., Gasler, I., Javadzadeh, M., Imhof, F., & Hofer, S. (2020) Visual intracortical and transthalamic pathways carry distinct information to cortical areas. *bioRxiv*, 2020.07.06.189902.

Blot, A., Roth, M.M., Gasler, I., Javadzadeh, M., Imhof, F., & Hofer, S.B. (2021) Visual intracortical and transthalamic pathways carry distinct information to cortical areas. *Neuron*, **109**, 1996–2008.

Bodor, Á.L., Giber, K., Rovó, Z., Ulbert, I., & Acsády, L. (2008) Structural correlates of efficient GABAergic transmission in the basal ganglia-thalamus pathway. *J. Neurosci.*, **28**, 3090–3102.

Bokor, H., Acsády, L., & Deschênes, M. (2008) Vibrissal responses of thalamic cells that project to the septal columns of the barrel cortex and to the second somatosensory area. *J. Neurosci.*, **28**, 5169–5177.

Bokor, H., Frère, S.G.A., Eyre, M.D., Slézia, A., Ulbert, I., Lüthi, A., & Acsády, L. (2005) Selective GABAergic control of higher-order thalamic relays. *Neuron*, **45**, 929–940.

Bokor, H., Hádinger, N., & Acsády, L. (2016) Efficient cortical control of basal ganglia recipient motor thalamus. *Soc. Neurosci. Abs.*, 720.18/SS16.

Bourassa, J., & Deschênes, M. (1995) Corticothalamic projections from the primary visual cortex in rats: a single fiber study using biocytin as an anterograde tracer. *Neuroscience*, **66**, 253–263.

Bourassa, J., Pinault, D., & Deschênes, M. (1995) Corticothalamic projections from the cortical barrel field to the somatosensory thalamus in rats: a single-fibre study using biocytin as an anterograde tracer. *Eur. J. Neurosci.*, **7**, 19–30.

Bubb, E.J., Kinnavane, L., & Aggleton, J.P. (2017) Hippocampal–diencephalic–cingulate networks for memory and emotion: an anatomical guide. *Brain Neurosci. Adv.*, **1**, 239821281772344.

Budisantoso, T., Matsui, K., Kamasawa, N., Fukazawa, Y., & Shigemoto, R. (2012) Mechanisms underlying signal filtering at a multisynapse contact. *J. Neurosci.*, **32**, 2357–2376.

Castro-Alamancos, M.A. (2002a) Different temporal processing of sensory inputs in the rat thalamus during quiescent and information processing states in vivo. *J. Physiol.*, **539**, 567–578.

Castro-Alamancos, M.A. (2002b) Properties of primary sensory (lemniscal) synapses in the ventrobasal thalamus and the relay of high-frequency sensory inputs. *J. Neurophysiol.*, **87**, 946–953.

Cathala, L., Holderith, N.B., Nusser, Z., DiGregorio, D.A., & Cull-Candy, S.G. (2005) Changes in synaptic structure underlie the developmental speeding of AMPA receptor-mediated EPSCs. *Nat. Neurosci.*, **8**, 1310–1318.

Chen, X., Aslam, M., Gollisch, T., Allen, K., & Von Engelhardt, J. (2018) CKAMP44 modulates integration of visual inputs in the lateral geniculate nucleus. *Nat. Commun.*, **9**, 261.

Clemente-Perez, A., Makinson, S.R., Higashikubo, B., Brovarney, S., Cho, F.S., Urry, A., Holden, S.S., Wimer, M., Dávid, C., Fenno, L.E., Acsády, L., Deisseroth, K., & Paz, J.T. (2017) Distinct thalamic reticular cell types differentially modulate normal and pathological cortical rhythms. *Cell Rep.*, **19**, 2130–2142.

Colonnier, M., & Guillery, R.W. (1964) Synaptic organization in the lateral geniculate nucleus of the monkey. *Zeitschrift für Zellforsch. und Mikroskopische Anat.*, **62**, 333–355.

Constantinople, C.M., & Bruno, R.M. (2011) Effects and mechanisms of wakefulness on local cortical networks. *Neuron*, **69**, 1061–1068.

Cooper, H.M., Herbin, M., & Nevo, E. (1993) Visual system of a naturally microphthalmic mammal: The blind mole rat, Spalax ehrenbergi. *J. Comp. Neurol.*, **328**, 313–350.

De Zeeuw, C.I., Lisberger, S.G., & Raymond, J.L. (2021) Diversity and dynamism in the cerebellum. *Nat. Neurosci.*, **24**, 160–167.

Dekker, J.J., & Kuypers, H.G.J.M. (1976) Morphology of rat's AV thalamic nucleus in light and electron microscopy. *Brain Res.*, **117**, 387–398.

Deschênes, M., Bourassa, J., & Pinault, D. (1994) Corticothalamic projections from layer V cells in rat are collaterals of long-range corticofugal axons. *Brain Res.*, **664**, 215–219.

Deschênes, M., Timofeeva, E., & Lavallée, P. (2003) The relay of high-frequency sensory signals in the whisker-to-barreloid pathway. *J. Neurosci.*, **23**, 6778–6787.

Deschênes, M., Veinante, P., & Zhang, Z.W. (1998) The organization of corticothalamic projections: reciprocity versus parity. *Brain Res. Brain Res. Rev.*, **28**, 286–308.

Diamond, M.E., Armstrong-James, M., Budway, M.J., & Ebner, F.F. (1992) Somatic sensory responses in the rostral sector of the posterior group (POm) and in the ventral posterior medial nucleus (VPM) of the rat thalamus: dependence on the barrel field cortex. *J. Comp. Neurol.*, **319**, 66–84.

Diamond, M.E., Armstrong-James, M., & Ebner, F.F. (1992) Somatic sensory responses in the rostral sector of the posterior group (POm) and in the ventral posterior medial nucleus (VPM) of the rat thalamus. *J. Comp. Neurol.*, **318**, 462–476.

Economo, M.N., Viswanathan, S., Tasic, B., Bas, E., Winnubst, J., Menon, V., Graybuck, L.T., Nguyen, T.N., Smith, K.A., Yao, Z., Wang, L., Gerfen, C.R., Chandrashekar, J., Zeng, H., Looger, L.L., & Svoboda, K. (2018) Distinct descending motor cortex pathways and their roles in movement. *Nature*, **563**, 79–84.

Erişir, A., Van Horn, S.C., & Sherman, S.M. (1997) Relative numbers of cortical and brainstem inputs to the lateral geniculate nucleus. *Proc. Natl. Acad. Sci. U. S. A.*, **94**, 1517–1520.

Friedlander, M.J., Lin, C.S., Stanford, L.R., & Sherman, S.M. (1981) Morphology of functionally identified neurons in lateral geniculate nucleus of the cat. *J. Neurophysiol.*, **46**, 80–129.

Gao, Z., Davis, C., Thomas, A.M., Economo, M.N., Abrego, A.M., Svoboda, K., De Zeeuw, C.I., & Li, N. (2018) A cortico-cerebellar loop for motor planning. *Nature*, **563**, 113–116.

Giber, K., Diana, M.A., M Plattner, V., Dugué, G.P., Bokor, H., Rousseau, C. V., Maglóczky, Z., Havas, L., Hangya, B., Wildner, H., Zeilhofer, H.U., Dieudonné, S., & Acsády, L. (2015) A subcortical inhibitory signal for behavioral arrest in the thalamus. *Nat. Neurosci.*, **18**, 562–568.

Goldberg, J.H., Farries, M.A., & Fee, M.S. (2013) Basal ganglia output to the thalamus: still a paradox. *Trends Neurosci.*, **36**, 695–705.

Goodridge, J.P. & Taube, J.S. (1997) Interaction between the postsubiculum and anterior thalamus in the generation of head direction cell activity. *J. Neurosci.*, **17**, 9315–9330.

Groh, A., Bokor, H., Mease, R.A., Plattner, V. M., Hangya, B., Stroh, A., Deschênes, M., & Acsády, L. (2014) Convergence of cortical and sensory driver inputs on single thalamocortical cells. *Cereb. Cortex*, **24**, 3167–3179.

Groh, A., de Kock, C.P.J., Wimmer, V.C., Sakmann, B., & Kuner, T. (2008) Driver or coincidence detector: modal switch of a corticothalamic giant synapse controlled by spontaneous activity and short-term depression. *J. Neurosci.*, **28**, 9652–9663.

Guillery, R.W. (1956) Degeneration in the post-commissural fornix and the mamillary peduncle of the ratNo Title. *J. Anat.*, **90**, 350–370.

Guillery, R.W. & Sherman, S.M. (2002) Thalamic relay functions and their role in corticocortical communication: generalizations from the visual system. *Neuron*, **33**, 163–175.

Guillery, R.W. & Sherman, S.M. (2011) Branched thalamic afferents: what are the messages that they relay to the cortex? *Brain Res. Rev.*, **66**, 205–219.

Guo, Z. V., Inagaki, H.K., Daie, K., Druckmann, S., Gerfen, C.R., & Svoboda, K. (2017) Maintenance of persistent activity in a frontal thalamocortical loop. *Nature*, **545**, 181–186.

Hádinger, N., Bősz, E., Tóth, B., Vantomme, G., Lüthi, A., & Acsády, L. (2022) Region selective cortical control of the thalamic reticular nucleus. BioRxiv, 2022.01.17.476335. https://doi.org/10.1101/2022.01.17.476335

Halassa, M.M., & Acsády, L. (2016) Thalamic inhibition: diverse sources, diverse scales. *Trends Neurosci.*, **39**, 680–693.

Halassa, M.M., & Kastner, S. (2017) Thalamic functions in distributed cognitive control. *Nat. Neurosci.*, **20**, 1669–1679.

Hamos, J.E., VanHorn, S.C., Raczkowski, D., & Sherman, S.M. (1987) Synaptic circuits involving an individual retinogeniculate axon in the cat. *J. Comp. Neurol.*, **259**, 165–192.

Harding, B.N., & Powell, T.P. (1977) An electron microscopic study of the centre-median and ventrolateral nuclei of the thalamus in the monkey. *Philos. Trans. R. Soc. Lond. B. Biol. Sci.*, **279**, 357–412.

Harris, J.A., Mihalas, S., Hirokawa, K.E., Whitesell, J.D., Choi, H., Bernard, A., Bohn, P., Caldejon, S., Casal, L., Cho, A., Feiner, A., Feng, D., Gaudreault, N., Gerfen, C.R., Graddis, N., Groblewski, P.A., Henry, A.M., Ho, A., Howard, R., Knox, J.E., Kuan, L., Kuang, X., Lecoq, J., Lesnar, P., Li, Y., Luviano, J., McConoughey, S., Mortrud, M.T., Naeemi, M., Ng, L., Oh, S. W., Ouellette, B., Shen, E., Sorensen, S.A., Wakeman, W., Wang, Q., Wang, Y., Williford, A., Phillips, J.W., Jones, A.R., Koch, C., & Zeng, H. (2019) Hierarchical organization of cortical and thalamic connectivity. *Nature*, **575**, 195–202.

Hirsch, J.A. (2003) Synaptic physiology and receptive field structure in the early visual pathway of the cat. In *Cerebral Cortex*. Oxford University Press, pp. 63–69.

Hoerder-Suabedissen, A., Hayashi, S., Upton, L., Nolan, Z., Casas-Torremocha, D., Grant, E., Viswanathan, S., Kanold, P.O., Clascá, F., Kim, Y., & Molnár, Z. (2018) Subset of cortical layer 6b neurons selectively innervates higher order thalamic nuclei in mice. *Cereb. Cortex*, **28**, 1882–1897.

Hoogland, P. V, Wouterlood, F.G., Welker, E., & Van der Loos, H. (1991) Ultrastructure of giant and small thalamic terminals of cortical origin: a study of the projections from the barrel cortex in mice using Phaseolus vulgaris leuco-agglutinin (PHA-L). *Exp. Brain Res.*, **87**, 159–172.

Ilinsky, I.A., Jouandet, M.L., & Goldman-Rakic, P.S. (1985) Organization of the nigrothalamocortical system in the rhesus monkey. *J. Comp. Neurol.*, **236**, 315–330.

Ilinsky, I.A., Yi, H., & Kultas-Ilinsky, K. (1997) Mode of termination of pallidal afferents to the thalamus: a light and electron microscopic study with anterograde tracers and immunocytochemistry in Macaca mulatta. *J. Comp. Neurol.*, **386**, 601–612.

Ito, H.T., Moser, E.I., & Moser, M.B. (2018) Supramammillary nucleus modulates spike-time coordination in the prefrontal-thalamo-hippocampal circuit during navigation. *Neuron*, **99**, 576–587.e5.

Ito, H.T., Zhang, S.J., Witter, M.P., Moser, E. I., & Moser, M.B. (2015) A prefrontal-thalamo-hippocampal circuit for goal-directed spatial navigation. *Nature*, **522**, 50–55.

Jacobson, S., & Trojanowski, J.Q. (1975) Corticothalamic neurons and thalamocortical terminal fields: An investigation in rat using horseradish peroxidase and autoradiography. *Brain Res.*, **85**, 385–401.

Jones, E.G. (2007a) Descriptions of thalamus in representative mammals. In *The Thalamus*, 2nd ed. Cambridge University Press, pp. 43–87.

Jones, E.G. (2007b) Principles of thalamic organization. In *The Thalamus*, 2nd ed. Cambridge University Press, pp. 87–171.

Jones, E.G. (2007c) Thalamic neurons, synaptic organization, and functional properties. In *The Thalamus*, 2nd ed. Cambridge University Press, pp. 171–318.

Jones, E.G., & Rockel, A.J. (1971) The synaptic organization in the medial geniculate body of afferent fibres ascending from the inferior colliculus. *Zeitschrift für Zellforsch. und Mikroskopische Anat.*, **113**, 44–66.

Kakei, S., Na, J., & Shinoda, Y. (2001) Thalamic terminal morphology and distribution of single corticothalamic axons originating from layers 5 and 6 of the cat motor cortex. *J. Comp. Neurol.*, **437**, 170–185.

Kenigfest, N.B., Repérant, J., Rio, J. -P, Belekhova, M.G., Tumanova, N.L., Ward, R., Vesselkin, N.P., Herbin, M., Chkeidze, D.D., & Ozirskaya, E. V. (1995) Fine structure of the dorsal lateral geniculate nucleus of the turtle, Emys orbicularis: A Golgi, combined hrp tracing and GABA immunocytochemical study. *J. Comp. Neurol.*, **356**, 595–614.

Kirouac, G.J. (2015) Placing the paraventricular nucleus of the thalamus within the brain circuits that control behavior. *Neurosci. Biobehav. Rev.*, **56**, 315–329.

Komura, Y., Nikkuni, A., Hirashima, N., Uetake, T., & Miyamoto, A. (2013) Responses of pulvinar neurons reflect a subject's confidence in visual categorization. *Nat. Neurosci.*, **16**, 749–755.

Krettek, J.E. & Price, J.L. (1977) Projections from the amygdaloid complex to the cerebral cortex and thalamus in the rat and cat. *J. Comp. Neurol.*, **172**, 687–722.

Kuroda, M., & Price, J.L. (1991) Synaptic organization of projections from basal forebrain structures to the mediodorsal thalamic nucleus of the rat. *J. Comp. Neurol.*, **303**, 513–533.

Lavallée, P., Urbain, N., Dufresne, C., Bokor, H., Acsády, L., & Deschênes, M. (2005) Feedforward inhibitory control of sensory information in higher-order thalamic nuclei. *J. Neurosci.*, **25**, 7489–7498.

Li, Y., Lopez-Huerta, V.G., Adiconis, X., Levandowski, K., Choi, S., Simmons, S.K., Arias-Garcia, M.A., Guo, B., Yao, A.Y., Blosser, T.R., Wimmer, R.D., Aida, T., Atamian, A., Naik, T., Sun, X., Bi, D., Malhotra, D., Hession, C.C., Shema, R., Gomes, M., Li, T., Hwang, E., Krol, A., Kowalczyk, M., Peça, J., Pan, G., Halassa, M. M., Levin, J.Z., Fu, Z., & Feng, G. (2020) Distinct subnetworks of the thalamic reticular nucleus. *Nature*, **583**, 819–824.

Liu, X.B., Honda, C.N., & Jones, E.G. (1995) Distribution of four types of synapse on physiologically identified relay neurons in the ventral posterior thalamic nucleus of the cat. *J. Comp. Neurol.*, **352**, 69–91.

Lovett-Barron, M., Kaifosh, P., Kheirbek, M. A., Danielson, N., Zaremba, J.D., Reardon, T. R., Turi, G.F., Hen, R., Zemelman, B. V., & Losonczy, A. (2014) Dendritic inhibition in the hippocampus supports fear learning. *Science*, **343**, 857–863.

Lund, J.S., Lund, R.D., Hendrickson, A.E., Bunt, A.H., & Fuchs, A.F. (1975) The origin of efferent pathways from the primary visual cortex, area 17, of the macaque monkey as shown by retrograde transport of horseradish peroxidase. *J. Comp. Neurol.*, **164**, 287–303.

Maendly, R., Ruegg, D.G., Wiesendanger, M., Lagowska, J., & Hess, B. (1981) Thalamic relay for group I muscle afferents of forelimb nerves in the monkey. *J. Neurophysiol.*, **46**, 901–917.

Maglóczky, Z., Acsády, L., & Freund, T.F. (1994) Principal cells are the postsynaptic targets of supramammillary afferents in the hippocampus of the rat. *Hippocampus*, **4**, 322–334.

Martinez-Garcia, R.I., Voelcker, B., Zaltsman, J.B., Patrick, S.L., Stevens, T.R., Connors, B.W., & Cruikshank, S.J. (2020) Two dynamically distinct circuits drive inhibition in the sensory thalamus. *Nature*, **583**, 813–818.

Mason, A., Ilinsky, I.A., Beck, S., & Kultas-Ilinsky, K. (1996) Reevaluation of synaptic relationships of cerebellar terminals in the ventral lateral nucleus of the rhesus monkey thalamus based on serial section analysis and three-dimensional reconstruction. *Exp. Brain Res.*, **109**, 219–239.

Mátyás, F., Komlósi, G., Babiczky, Á., Kocsis, K., Barthó, P., Barsy, B., Dávid, C., Kanti, V., Porrero, C., Magyar, A., Szűcs, I., Clascá, F., & Acsády, L. (2018) A highly collateralized thalamic cell type with arousal-predicting activity serves as a key hub for graded state transitions in the forebrain. *Nat. Neurosci.*, **21**, 1551–1562.

Mátyás, F., Lee, J., Shin, H.-S., & Acsády, L. (2014) The fear circuit of the mouse forebrain: connections between the mediodorsal thalamus, frontal cortices and basolateral amygdala. *Eur. J. Neurosci.*, **39**, 1810–1823.

Mátyás, F., Sreenivasan, V., Marbach, F., Wacongne, C., Barsy, B., Mateo, C., Aronoff, R., & Petersen, C.C.H. (2010) Motor control by sensory cortex. *Science*, **330**, 1240–1243.

Mikula, S., Manger, P.R., & Jones, E.G. (2008) The thalamus of the monotremes: Cyto- and myeloarchitecture and chemical neuroanatomy. *Philos. Trans. R. Soc. B Biol. Sci.*, **363**, 2415–2440.

Moore, B., Li, K., Kaas, J.H., Liao, C.C., Boal, A.M., Mavity-Hudson, J., & Casagrande, V. (2019) Cortical projections to the two retinotopic maps of primate pulvinar are distinct. *J. Comp. Neurol.*, **527**, 577–588.

Moore, R.Y., Weis, R., & Moga, M.M. (2000) Efferent projections of the intergeniculate leaflet and the ventral lateral geniculate nucleus in the rat. *J. Comp. Neurol.*, **420**, 398–418.

Morgan, J.L., Berger, D.R., Wetzel, A.W., & Lichtman, J.W. (2016) The Fuzzy logic of network connectivity in mouse visual thalamus. *Cell*, **165**, 192–206.

Negyessy, L., Hamori, J., & Bentivoglio, M. (1998) Contralateral cortical projection to the mediodorsal thalamic nucleus: origin and synaptic organization in the rat. *Neuroscience*, **84**, 741–753.

Ojima, H. (1994) Terminal morphology and distribution of corticothalamic fibers originating from layers 5 and 6 of cat primary auditory cortex. *Cereb. Cortex*, **4**, 646–663.

Otis, J.M., Zhu, M.H., Namboodiri, V.M.K., Cook, C.A., Kosyk, O., Matan, A.M., Ying, R., Hashikawa, Y., Hashikawa, K., Trujillo-Pisanty, I., Guo, J., Ung, R.L., Rodriguez-Romaguera, J., Anton, E.S., & Stuber, G.D. (2019) Paraventricular thalamus projection neurons integrate cortical and hypothalamic signals for cue-reward processing. *Neuron*, **103**, 423–431.e4.

Pare, D., Dossi, R.C., & Steriade, M. (1991) Three types of inhibitory postsynaptic potentials generated by interneurons in the anterior thalamic complex of cat. *J. Neurophysiol.*, **66**, 1190–1204.

Pelzer, P., Horstmann, H., & Kuner, T. (2017) Ultrastructural and functional properties of a giant synapse driving the piriform cortex to mediodorsal thalamus projection. *Front. Synaptic Neurosci.*, **9**, 3.

Penzo, M.A., & Gao, C. (2021) The paraventricular nucleus of the thalamus: an integrative node underlying homeostatic behavior. *Trends Neurosci.*, **44**, 538–549.

Percheron, G., Franqois, C., Talbi, B., Yelnik, J., & Ffnelon, G. (1996) The primate motor thalamus. *Brain*, **22**, 93–181.

Peyrache, A., Lacroix, M.M., Petersen, P.C., & Buzsáki, G. (2015) Internally organized mechanisms of the head direction sense. *Nat. Neurosci.*, **18**, 569–575.

Pinault, D. (2004) The thalamic reticular nucleus: structure, function and concept. *Brain Res. Brain Res. Rev.*, **46**, 1–31.

Pinault, D., & Deschênes, M. (1998) Projection and innervation patterns of individual thalamic reticular axons in the thalamus of the adult rat: a three-dimensional, graphic, and morphometric analysis. *J. Comp. Neurol.*, **391**, 180–203.

Purushothaman, G., Marion, R., Li, K., & Casagrande, V.A. (2012) Gating and control of primary visual cortex by pulvinar. *Nat. Neurosci.*, **15**, 905–912.

Ralston, H.J. (1969) The synaptic organization of lemniscal projections to the ventrobasal thalamus of the cat. *Brain Res.*, **14**, 99–115.

Reichova, I., & Sherman, S.M. (2004) Somatosensory corticothalamic projections: distinguishing drivers from modulators. *J. Neurophysiol.*, **92**, 2185–2197.

Rikhye, R. V., Wimmer, R.D., & Halassa, M. M. (2018) Toward an integrative theory of thalamic function. *Annu. Rev. Neurosci.*, **41**, 163–183.

Rinvik, E., & Grofová, I. (1974a) Cerebellar projections to the nuclei ventralis lateralis and ventralis anterior thalami – Experimental electron microscopical and light microscopical studies in the cat. *Anat. Embryol. (Berl).*, **146**, 95–111.

Rinvik, E., & Grofová, I. (1974b) Light and electron microscopical studies of the normal nuclei ventralis lateralis and ventralis anterior thalami in the cat. *Anat. Embryol. (Berl).*, **146**, 57–93.

Rollenhagen, A., & Lübke, J.H.R. (2006) The morphology of excitatory central synapses: From structure to function. *Cell Tissue Res.*, **326**, 221–237.

Rompani, S.B., Müllner, F.E., Wanner, A., Zhang, C., Roth, C.N., Yonehara, K., & Roska, B. (2017) Different modes of visual integration in the lateral geniculate nucleus revealed by single-cell-initiated transsynaptic tracing. *Neuron*, **93**, 767–776.e6.

Rouiller, E.M., & Welker, E. (2000) A comparative analysis of the morphology of corticothalamic projections in mammals. *Brain Res. Bull.*, **53**, 727–741.

Rovó, Z., Ulbert, I., & Acsády, L. (2012) Drivers of the primate thalamus. *J. Neurosci.*, **32**, 17894–17908.

Schmitt, L.I., Wimmer, R.D., Nakajima, M., Happ, M., Mofakham, S., & Halassa, M.M. (2017) Thalamic amplification of cortical connectivity sustains attentional control. *Nature*, **545**, 219–223.

Schwartz, M.L., Dekker, J.J., & Goldman-Rakic, P.S. (1991) Dual mode of corticothalamic synaptic termination in the mediodorsal nucleus of the rhesus monkey. *J. Comp. Neurol.*, **309**, 289–304.

Sherman, S.M., & Guillery, R.W. (1996) Functional organization of thalamocortical relays. *J. Neurophysiol.*, **76**, 1367–1395.

Sherman, S.M., & Guillery, R.W. (1998) On the actions that one nerve cell can have on another: distinguishing "drivers" from "modulators." *Proc. Natl. Acad. Sci. USA*, **95**, 7121–7126.

Sherman, S.M., & Guillery, R.W. (2005) The afferent axons to the thalamus: their structure and connections. In *Exploring the Thalamus and Its Role in Cortical Functions*. MIT Press, pp. 77–137.

Sirota, M.G., Swadlow, H.A., & Beloozerova, I.N. (2005) Three channels of corticothalamic communication during locomotion. *J. Neurosci.*, **25**, 5915–5925.

Steriade, M., & Glenn, L.L. (1982) Neocortical and caudate projections of intralaminar thalamic neurons and their synaptic excitation from midbrain reticular core. *J. Neurophysiol.*, **48**, 352–371.

Steriade, M., Jones, E.G., & McCormick, D. A. (1997a) Diffuse regulatory system of the thalamus. In *Thalamus*. Elsevier, pp. 269–339.

Steriade, M., Jones, E.G., & McCormick, D. A. (1997b) The relay function of the thalamus during brain activation. In *Thalamus*. Elsevier, pp. 393–533.

Sumser, A., Mease, R.A., Sakmann, B., & Groh, A. (2017) Organization and somatotopy of corticothalamic projections from L5B in mouse barrel cortex. *Proc. Natl. Acad. Sci. USA*, **114**, 8853–8858.

Suryanarayana, S.M., Pérez-Fernández, J., Robertson, B., & Grillner, S. (2020) The evolutionary origin of visual and somatosensory representation in the vertebrate pallium. *Nat. Ecol. Evol.*, **4**, 639–651.

Suryanarayana, S.M., Robertson, B., Wallén, P., & Grillner, S. (2017) The lamprey Pallium provides a blueprint of the mammalian layered cortex. *Curr. Biol.*, **27**, 3264–3277.e5.

Szentágothai, J., Hámori, J., & Tömböl, T. (1966) Degeneration and electron microscope analysis of the synaptic glomeruli in the lateral geniculate body. *Exp. Brain Res.*, **2**, 283–301.

Telgkamp, P., Padgett, D.E., Ledoux, V.A., Woolley, C.S., & Raman, I.M. (2004) Maintenance of high-frequency transmission at Purkinje to cerebellar nuclear synapses by spillover from boutons with multiple release sites. *Neuron*, **41**, 113–126.

Turner, J.P., & Salt, T.E. (1998) Characterization of sensory and corticothalamic excitatory inputs to rat thalamocortical neurones in vitro. *J. Physiol.*, **510**, 829–843.

Urbain, N., & Deschênes, M. (2007a) A new thalamic pathway of vibrissal information modulated by the motor cortex. *J. Neurosci.*, **27**, 12407–12412.

Urbain, N., & Deschênes, M. (2007b) Motor cortex gates vibrissal responses in a thalamocortical projection pathway. *Neuron*, **56**, 714–725.

Usrey, W.M., Reppas, J.B., & Reid, R.C. (1999) Specificity and strength of retinogeniculate connections. *J. Neurophysiol.*, **82**, 3527–3540.

Van der Werf, Y.D., Witter, M.P., & Groenewegen, H.J. (2002) The intralaminar and midline nuclei of the thalamus. Anatomical and functional evidence for participation in processes of arousal and awareness. *Brain Res. Brain Res. Rev.*, **39**, 107–140.

Varga, V., Losonczy, A., Zemelman, B. V, Borhegyi, Z., Nyiri, G., Domonkos, A., Hangya, B., Holderith, N., Magee, J.C., & Freund, T.F. (2009) Fast synaptic subcortical control of hippocampal circuits. *Science*, **326**, 449–453.

Veinante, P., & Deschênes, M. (2003) Single-cell study of motor cortex projections to the barrel field in rats. *J. Comp. Neurol.*, **464**, 98–103.

Vicq d'Azyr, F. (1786) *Traite d'Anatomie et de Physiologie*. Didot.

Vidnyánszky, Z., Gorcs, T., Negyessy, L., Borostyankoi, Z., Knopfel, T., & Hamori, J. (1996) Immunocytochemical visualization of the mGluR1a metabotropic glutamate receptor at synapses of corticothalamic terminals originating from area 17 of the rat. *Eur. J. Neurosci.*, **8**, 1061–1071.

Vizi, E.S., & Lábos, E. (1991) Non-synaptic interactions at presynaptic level. *Prog. Neurobiol.*, **37**, 145–163.

Wanaverbecq, N., Bodor, Á.L., Bokor, H., Slézia, A., Lüthi, A., & Acsády, L. (2008) Contrasting the functional properties of GABAergic axon terminals with single and multiple synapses in the thalamus. *J. Neurosci.*, **28**, 11848–11861.

Xu, W., & Südhof, T.C. (2013) A neural circuit for memory specificity and generalization. *Science*, **339**, 1290–1295.

Yamawaki, N., & Shepherd, G.M.G. (2015) Synaptic circuit organization of motor corticothalamic neurons. *J. Neurosci.*, **35**, 2293–2307.

Yu, C., Derdikman, D., Haidarliu, S., & Ahissar, E. (2006) Parallel thalamic pathways for whisking and touch signals in the rat. *PLoS Biol.*, **4**,e124.

Zhou, H., Schafer, R.J., & Desimone, R. (2016) Pulvinar-cortex interactions in vision and attention. *Neuron*, **89**, 209–220.

Chapter 3

Thalamic Output Pathways

Francisco Clascá

Introduction

The thalamus is the central hub of forebrain networks. It receives orderly inputs from a wide variety of sources, and in turn, it innervates multiple structures of the forebrain. These output pathways have traditionally been described and investigated as more or less independent systems (thalamocortical, thalamostriatal, thalamo-amygdaloid, etc.) at the large-cell-population scale. However, new anatomical and molecular methods now allow the analysis of brain connections at the single-cell level. These methods reveal an unsuspected diversity among thalamic projection neurons (TPNs), as well as the involvement of many of these cells, via branched axons, in more than one of the classic pathways.

The TPNs, also known as *principal* or *relay cells*, constitute the vast majority of thalamus neurons (70–100%, depending on the nucleus and species). TPN dendrites are directly contacted by all the input systems reaching the thalamus, and their axons are the only pathway for thalamus output. Because TPNs do not establish local reentrant excitatory circuits between them, the thalamus could be envisioned, on a first approximation, as a multichannel relay station. In addition to the TPNs, a smaller population of GABAergic interneurons is present in the thalamus; however, their axons remain confined to individual nuclei.

Developmental studies have shown that the TPNs in all the nuclei of the dorsal thalamus arise from a single neuroepithelial domain (Puelles & Rubenstein 2003; Nakagawa 2019). In contrast, interneurons migrate tangentially into the dorsal thalamus from nearby segments of the neural tube (Jager et al. 2021). Reflecting their common lineage, adult TPN across the thalamus share many basic features, such as glutamatergic neurotransmission, membrane conductances, and somatodendritic appearance.

Likewise, their axons display many common traits, such as (a) targeting the prethalamic reticular nucleus and one or more structures of the anterior forebrain, (b) arborizing in highly specific terminal patterns, and (c) never crossing the midline or entering in the hypothalamus. However, the application of single-cell labeling methods has in recent years revealed that despite the similarities, TPN axons are far more complex and diverse than previously understood. Differences include both the cell-level axon branching and arborization and the subcellular-level structure of their synapses (Casas-Torremocha et al. 2019; Rodriguez-Moreno et al. 2020).

Compared to axons, variation in TPN somatodendritic morphology is modest. The same basic dendrite arborization pattern is found across the thalamus, in cells that differ broadly in their axonal architectures or that carry out different signal-processing roles (e.g., single-input relay vs. multiple-input integration; Groh et al. 2014; Sampathkumar et al. 2021). Likewise, the electrotonic properties and membrane conductances in the somatodendritic domain are basically the same (Llinás & Jahnsen 1982; Jahnsen & Llinás 1984a; Sheroziya & Timofeev 2014), with variations that are mainly quantitative (Landisman & Connors 2007; Nakamura et al. 2014; Phillips et al. 2019; Desai & Varela 2021).

Genomic techniques now allow for the characterization of single-cell-level gene-expression data. In the case of TPNs, these studies have revealed genomic profile groups that align loosely with axonal/functional morphotypes (Phillips et al. 2019), and gene-expression differences that are mostly gradual and highly combinatorial.

In the following sections, I review the range of structural, functional, and gene-expression variations observed among TPNs. Based on these differences, I propose a tentative catalog consisting of six main cell profiles as a framework for the analysis of thalamic output pathways. The data reviewed mainly pertain to lab rodents; cat and nonhuman primate data are discussed when appropriate. The terminal synaptic specializations of TPN axons in their various target structures are not covered in detail here; reviews on this topic can be found in Castro-Alamancos & Connors (1997), Jones (2007a), and Smith et al. (2014).

1. TPN Somatodendritic Morphology

The TPN cell bodies are polygonal or fusiform and relatively large, although they show noticeable variations across thalamic nuclei and even within the same nucleus (Figure 1). In fact, differences in cell soma sizes were a key criterion for classic Nissl-based nuclear delineations (see Chapter 1). Subsequent retrograde tracer studies showed that the TPN soma size differences are often correlated with functionally relevant features. For example, in the motor, sensory, and associative thalamic nuclei of carnivores and primates, the neurons innervating layer 1 (L1) show, on average, smaller soma sizes than those in the same nucleus innervating only deeper cortical layers (LeVay & Gilbert 1976; Carey et al. 1979a, 1979b; Penny et al. 1982; Fitzpatrick et al. 1983; Rausell & Avendaño 1985; Mitani et al. 1987; Avendaño et al. 1990; Rausell et al. 1992; Hendry & Yoshioka 1994). Likewise, there are consistent differences in the sizes of cells carrying different types of retinal information in the lateral geniculate nuclei of carnivores and primates (Boyd & Matsubara 1996; Figure 2).

Until quite recently, dendrite arbor morphologies were studied almost exclusively in sensory or motor relay nuclei,

Anatomy

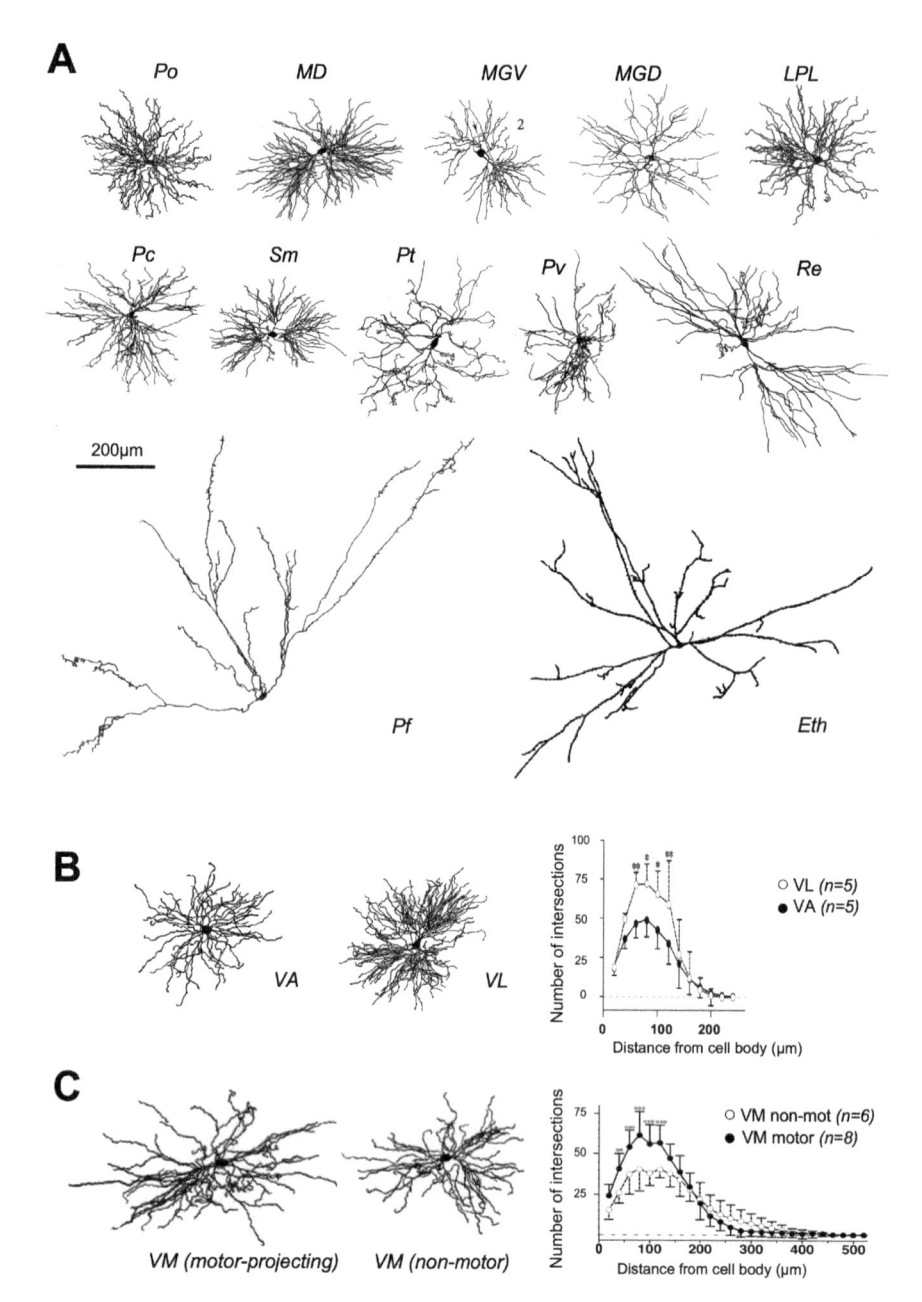

Figure 1 Somatodendritic morphology variation across rat thalamic nuclei.

A. Representative individual morphologies of PTNs from different nuclei. Cells were reconstructed after in vivo transfection-labeling with Sindbis viral vectors in all cases except for the ethmoid (Eth) nucleus cell, which was juxtacellularly injected with biocytin and the MGV and MGD cells, which were intracellularly filled with biocytin. All cells are represented at the same scale. See the list at the end of the chapter for other abbreviations.

B. Two representative neurons from the ventral anterior (VA) or ventral lateral (VL) nuclei. Comparison of the number of dendrite intersections at different distances from the cell body as measured in a Scholl test in five cells from VA and VL. This comparison revealed that VL secondary dendrites were significantly more numerous at distances of 40–120 μm away from the cell body.

C. Two representative PTNs from different portions of the ventromedial (VM) nucleus (one that projected to motor cortex and another that innervated medial non-motor areas of the frontal cortex). A comparison of dendritic structure between VM neurons with motor versus nonmotor cortical projection patterns reveals a small but statistically significant greater abundance of secondary dendrites in the motor-projecting VM neurons. Circles and bars in B and C indicate mean and standard deviation (SD), respectively, and asterisks point to the statistical significance (*$P < 0.05$, ** < 0.01, ***$P < 0.001$ by Bonferroni multiple comparison test).

Images taken from: Po: Ohno et al. (2012); MD: Kuramoto, Pan, et al. (2017); LPL: Nakamura et al. (2015); Sm: Kuramoto, Iwai, et al. (2017); Pc, Pt, Pv, Re, and Pf: modified from Unzai et al. (2017); MGv and MGD: modified from Bartlett and Smith (1999); Eth: modified from Deschênes, Bourassa, Doan, et al. (1996); VA, VL, and corresponding chart: modified from Kuramoto et al. (2009); VM and corresponding chart: taken from Kuramoto et al. (2015).

first with Golgi stains (Ramón y Cajal, 1904; Morest 1964; Scheibel and Scheibel 1966) or by intracellular filling with dyes such as horseradish peroxidase (HRP) during electrophysiological recording (Friedlander et al. 1981; Stanford et al. 1983). With the introduction of vector-mediated transfection labeling, small numbers of complete dendrite morphologies from many other nuclei of the thalamus have begun to be reported (Figure 1).

From these observations, it is now clear that TPN somatodendritic morphologies across the rodent dorsal thalamus are basically similar. Multiple (up to about 12) thick primary dendrites can sprout from the cell body in multipolar or slightly bi-tufted arrangements. After a short stretch, each primary dendrite divides again into several thinner secondary branches that diverge in a radial fashion for about 100–250 μm and that together give TPNs their typical "bushy" dendritic tree appearance. The secondary dendrites may have irregularly spaced appendages resembling slender spines or stubby protrusions, which in some TPNs may be clustered together (Guillery 1966; Jones 2007a).

Although the sample of morphologies is still small, some consistent variations between TPNs have been detected in the average number and length of their secondary branches. For example, they tend to be overall shorter and/or more numerous in the neurons that relay ascending signals from a single source with minimal convergence (be it sensory, such as neurons in the dorsal lateral geniculate [DLG], ventral posterior [VP], ventral medial geniculate [MGV], or motor, such as neurons in the ventrolateral nucleus [VL]) than in the neurons in nuclei receiving more diverse and convergent sets of cortical

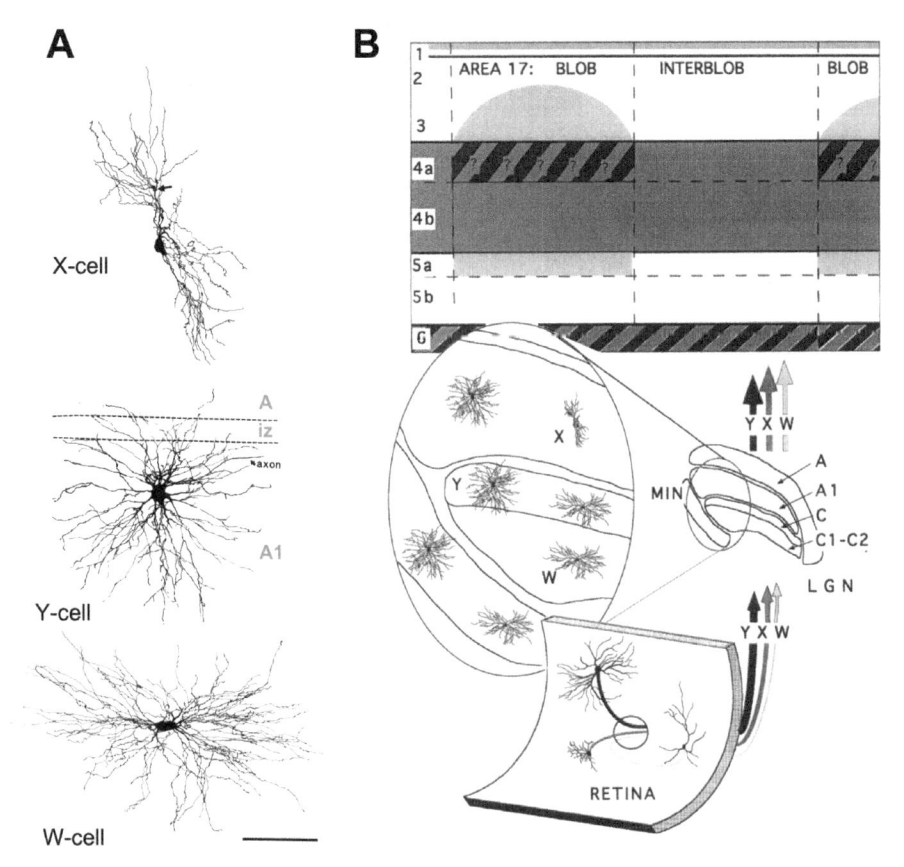

Figure 2 Small-scale somatodendritic morphology variation in the PTNs of the cat's visual DLG and its relation-specific retinofugal information channels.

A. Archetypal morphologies of the three PTN subclasses identified in the cat's DLG reconstructed after intracellular filling with HRP during in vivo intracellular recordings. Large and complex protrusions are frequently present near bifurcation points in the X-cell dendrites; one of them is indicated by an arrow. These protrusions are part of synaptic glomeruli. The dendrites of the Y-cell subclass often extend across the interlaminar zone (iz) separating the parvocellular A and A1 layers. Taken from Friedlander et al. (1981) and Stanford et al. (1983).

B. Diagram representation of the three main structurally and functionally separate pathways arising from the retina (X, Y, and Z classes) and relying on specific cell subclasses of the DLG (here abbreviated "LGN"), which in turn relay the information to partly segregated layers (1–6) or subdomains (blobs/interblobs) in a column of the primary visual cortex ("Area 17"). Taken from Boyd and Matsubara (1996).

and/or subcortical inputs (Figure 1; Bartlett and Smith 2002; Kuramoto et al. 2009; Kuramoto, Iwai, et al. 2017).

A consistent exception from the typical bushy morphology is observed in most TPNs of the posterior intralaminar (centromedian-parafascicular, ethmoid-limitans, and posterior intralaminar) thalamic nuclei, both in rodents and primates (Deschênes, Bourassa, & Parent 1996; Parent & Parent 2005; Smith et al. 2006). The primary dendrites of these TPNs are few, but they extend for long distances; give off few, if any, secondary branches; and have frequent spines and appendages (Figure 2A). This overall appearance has been called "reticular-like" (Deschênes, Bourassa, Doan, et al. 1996) or "diffuse" (Lacey et al. 2007; Beatty et al. 2009). Likewise, the axonal architecture and functional properties of these neurons are substantially different from other TPNs (see Section 3 in this chapter).

In the intensively studied first-order sensory relay nuclei, some variations in somatodendritic morphology have been linked to specific functional subspecializations. For example, in the DLG of cats, three main morphological cell subtypes, named X, Y, and Z, each with slightly different mean soma sizes, dendritic tree morphologies, and axon calibers, were described (Guillery 1966; Friedlander et al. 1981; Figure 2). Each subtype relays mainly a specific set of retinal ganglion cell signals and tends to distribute its dendrites in arrangements adapted to maximize the selective sampling of its specific inputs, keeping convergence to a minimum. These subtypes even show slightly different membrane conductances (Friedlander et al. 1981; Crunelli et al. 1987). However, numerous cells with features intermediate between these "types" are present in the same nucleus (Friedlander et al. 1981). Comparable, albeit less stereotyped, differences have been reported in rodent and primate DLGs (Jones 2007a; Kerschensteiner & Guido 2017). Variations in somatodendritic morphology related to the selective sampling of particular auditory frequency ranges were also described with Golgi methods in the MGB (Clerici et al. 1990).

2. TPN Axon Morphology

2.1 TPN Axon Architecture Diversity

Instead of a similar wiring pattern being repeated across the thalamus, axonal morphologies vary widely between nuclei and often even between TPN populations in the same nucleus. As a result, several very differently wired circuits link the thalamus to its various forebrain targets. Moreover, several different TPN circuits may converge on the same region in intricate and complementary terminal patterns, setting the stage for complex interactions with the cortical or striatal circuits (Jones 2001; Ellender et al. 2013).

Because they involve the simultaneous labeling of many cells together, bulk-injected chemical tracers used in the 1970s, 1980s and 1990s were unsuitable to fully elucidate the complex organization of these pathways. Nevertheless, evidence for the existence of diverse TPN axon wiring motifs accumulated over the years, first from studies that made selective lesions or anterograde tracer injections in individual thalamic nuclei and observed different patterns of tangential spread and/or laminar labeling in the cortex (Killackey & Ebner 1972, 1973; Jones & Burton 1976; Herkenham 1978, 1979, 1980, 1986; Donoghue & Ebner 1981), and then from studies that made retrograde tracer injections limited to some cortical layers and observed labeling in specific thalamic cell populations (Le Vay & Gilbert 1976; Ferster & Le Vay 1978; Leventhal 1979; Penny et al. 1982; Mitani et al. 1987; Rausell & Avendaño 1985; Avendaño et al. 1990; Rausell & Jones 1991; Hashikawa et al. 1991). In addition, some studies that made tracer injections in separate areas for double-retrograde labeling concluded that some TPN axons should branch to target separate regions, although their prevalence was deemed very low overall (Macchi et al. 1984; Miciacchi et al. 1986; Spreafico et al. 1987; Asanuma et al. 1985). Besides, terminal arborization morphologies were visualized by direct infusion with HRP during intraaxonal electrophysiological axonal recordings (Humphrey et al. 1985; Garraghty & Sur 1990) or by bulk-labeling axons with sensitive anterograde tracers such as PHA-L and dextrans (Vertes et al. 2006, 2012; Van Groen & Wyss 1995; Van Groen et al. 1999; Shibata 1993a, 1993b; Vertes & Hoover 2008; Van der Werf et al. 2002; Wouterlood et al. 1990; Huang & Winer 2000). Other studies confirmed the existence of thalamic projections to the striatum (Jones & Leavitt 1974; Herkenham 1978; Van der Werf et al. 2002) or to the amygdala (Yasui et al. 1987; Namura et al. 1997; Doron and Ledoux 1999), although it remained controversial whether such TPNs were always the same when projecting to the cortex or were different cell populations.

It was only with the introduction of single-cell labeling methods able to reveal the whole morphology of individual long-range projection cell axons (Pinault 1996; Furuta et al. 2001) that the complexity and diversity of TPN pathways came into full view (Figure 3). Data accumulating from these studies rendered obsolete previous conceptualizations of the global organization of thalamic output pathways (Herkenham 1986; Macchi et al. 1996; Avendaño et al. 1990; Jones 1998, 2007a; Guillery & Sherman 2002; see Chapter 1).

Adoption of the single-cell labeling methods, however, remained limited, probably because of the low yield of the labeling experiments and the amount of histological and microscope work required to manually reconstruct large axon arbors from a multitude of submicron-thin micron-thin fragments scattered over dozens of serial brain sections. As a result, data from less than 200 single-cell TPN axon morphologies, in total, have been reported in peer-reviewed journals over more than two decades. Some thalamic nuclei have been barely explored, or not explored at all, with these new methods. Almost all these studies were conducted in rats (Deschênes, Bourassa, and Parent 1996; Deschênes, Bourassa, Doan, et al. 1996; Deschênes et al. 1998; Kuramoto et al. 2009, 2015; Kuramoto, Pan, et al. 2017; Kuramoto, Iwai, et al. 2017; Noseda et al. 2010, 2011; Ohno et al. 2012; Nakamura et al. 2015; Unzai et al. 2017) or mice (Gheorghita et al. 2006; Phillips et al. 2019; Rodriguez-Moreno et al. 2020). Some studies included quantifications of branch length and estimations of the numbers of axonal varicosities (putative synaptic sites). A single study has investigated TPN axons in a primate with these methods (Figure 8B–D; Parent & Parent 2005).

In recent years, large-scale research initiatives explicitly aimed at producing large numbers of long-range projection neuron morphologies registered to a standard digital three-dimensional (3D) brain framework (Wang et al. 2020) have been launched (Harris et al. 2019; Winnubst et al. 2019). Instead of one or few cells per brain, these projects combine sparse viral vector–mediated fluorescent labeling (several dozen cells per brain) with high-end automated sectioning and imaging platforms and advanced 3D reconstruction software tools. At the time of this writing, several hundred TPN morphologies obtained from these pipelines are already available as online databases (Figure 4). A limitation is that the morphologies are not yet as thoroughly analyzed and curated for completeness or precision as those described in the published papers. For maximal consistency, morphologies are all derived only from young adult mice. Parallel efforts are underway to elucidate PTN transcriptomic profiles with single-cell resolution. The expectation is that quantitatively robust samples of morphological phenotypic traits and transcriptomic data may be combined to provide a comprehensive classification of mice TPN cell and circuit diversity (Winnubst et al. 2020).

2.2 General Layout of the TPN Axons

In the adult, all TPN axons leaving their parent cell bodies first run out of the thalamus in an anteroventral/lateral direction. They soon become myelinated and leave no significant branches in their own or in other nuclei of the dorsal thalamus.

Subsequently, all TPN axons pierce the prethalamic reticular nucleus (TRN) orthogonally to the nucleus curved surface. As they do so, axons issue one or several thin varicose branches that exit from the main axon trunk at right angles. These branches form flat and relatively simple arborizations near the point where the axon trunk crosses the TRN. These arborizations may sublaminate across the thickness of TRN in a nuclei-specific fashion (Li et al. 2020).

Some TPN neurons send varicose branches to basal forebrain structures such as the substantia innominata, central amygdala, lateral preoptic area, ventral pallidum, or

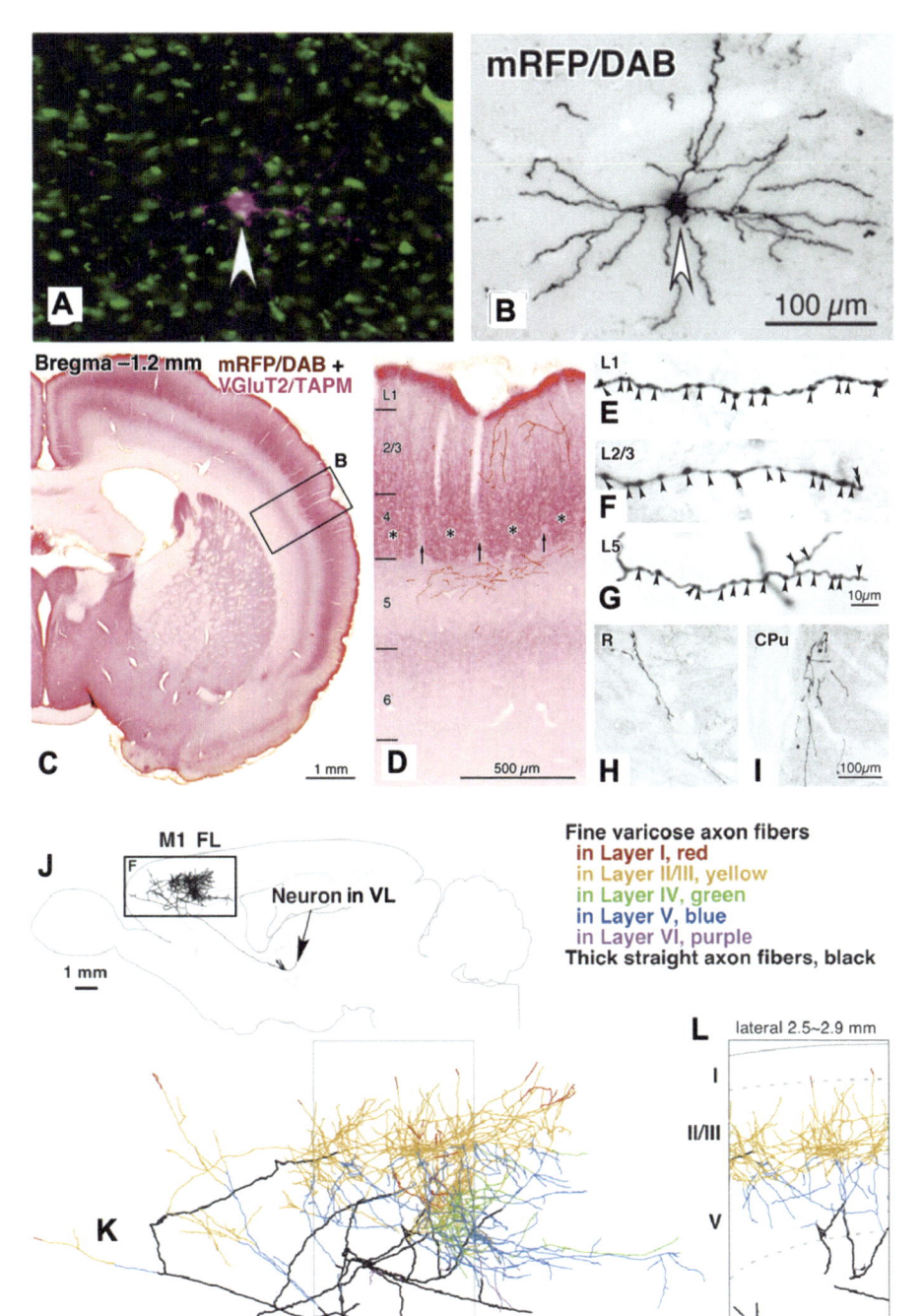

Figure 3 The full morphology of isolated PTN axons visualized by single-cell transfection with Sindbis-Pal-gfp viral vectors.

A–I. An individually transfected PTN in the rat posterior nucleus.

A. Red fluorescence (*magenta*) from the labeled cell amid a general green fluorescence Nissl counterstain.

B. DAB-HRP–enhanced visualization of the same labeling, in bright field.

C and D. Axon branch segments as seen in a coronal 50-μm section. Vesicular glutamate 2 transporter immunolabeling is used as a counterstain to delineate cortical compartments such as S1 barrels (*asterisks*).

E–G. High-magnification detail of three branches of the labeled cell axon. Individual varicosities (putative synaptic sites) are indicated by arrowheads.

H. A branch from the same axon in the TRN.

I. A branch from the same axon in the caudate-putamen (CPu). Modified from Ohno et al. (2012).

J. Reconstruction of the entire axonal arborization from a neuron individually transfected in the VL is represented within the contour or a sagittal rat brain section. An axon arborization in the forelimb region of the motor cortex (M1-FL) is represented, enlarged, in panels K–L. Modified from Kuramoto et al. (2009).

subthalamic nucleus (Unzai et al. 2017; Lanciego et al. 2004; see following discussion). The axons giving off these branches travel in the most anteroventral part of the internal capsule, near the medial forebrain bundle; from there, their branches cover relatively short distances to reach these basal forebrain structures. The same branch often innervates several structures in succession, for example, first the entopeduncular nucleus, then the subthalamic nucleus, and finally the substantia nigra (Deschênes, Bourassa, Doan, et al. 1996).

Axons from all thalamic nuclei extend along the internal capsule while following progressively divergent trajectories. In the medial part of the internal capsule, axons accumulate in a tight bundle and keep a strict topological order according to their origin in the thalamus. Axons from anterior and medial nuclei travel in rostral and ventral portions of the internal capsule. In rodents, these fibers rapidly split into small bundles as they enter the striatal gray matter. Axons originating from ventral or lateral thalamic nuclei occupy progressively more lateral portions of the internal capsule. This stereotyped arrangement reflects the constraints that thalamic axon growth cones must overcome to cross this basal forebrain region early in development (López-Bendito et al. 2006), as well as the

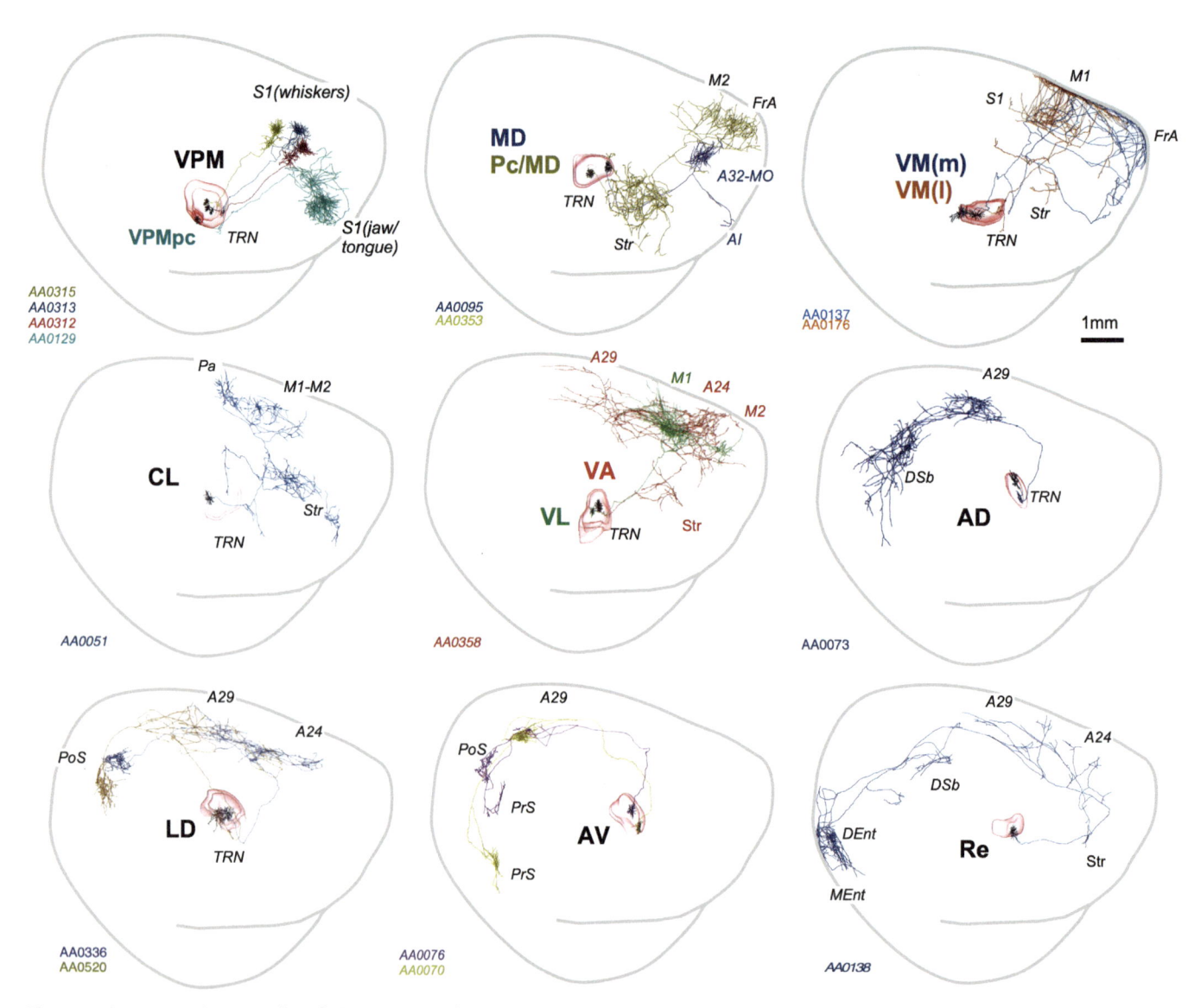

Figure 4 Representative examples of 3D reconstructed mouse single-cell PTN morphologies.

Two-dimensional (2D) lateral projection captures of computer visualizations of the cells displayed in a five-point (spherical) perspective are presented within simple outlines of the right cerebral hemisphere. One or several cells from the same or adjacent nuclei (in different colors) are shown within each hemisphere. Cell bodies and dendritic trees are shown in a semitransparent lateral projection of each nucleus (*pink contours*; right and left nuclei contours are visualized). The areas targeted by the axon terminal branches are indicated. Reconstruction images taken from the Janelia Research Campus Mouselight database (Winnubst et al. 2019; https://www.janelia.org/project-team/mouselight). The reference numbers for each cell in the database are indicated in matching colors. Because of the spherical perspective, the calibration provided by the bar is only approximate.

A24: cingulate cortex area 24; A29: cingulate cortex area 29; A32-MO: cingulate cortex area 32 (prelimbic cortex) and medial orbital cortex; AI: agranular insular cortex; Dent: dorsal entorhinal area. DSb: dorsal subiculum; FrA: frontal agranular area; M2: motor cortex area 2; MEnt: medial entorhinal area; MI1: motor cortex area 1; Pa: posterior parietal area; PoS: posubiculum; PrS: presubiculum; S1: primary somatosensory area; Str: striatum. See list at the end of the chapter for other abbreviations.

presence of gradient-based molecular sorting mechanisms (Adams et al. 1997; López-Bendito & Molnar 2003; Vanderhaeghen & Polleux 2004; Molnár et al. 2012).

Although some TPN axons cross the internal capsule without branching at all, other axons emit one or more collateral branches in this region. Such branches emerge perpendicularly from the main axon trunk and are relatively thin and varicose and extend to innervate different portions of the striatum (caudate-putamen, nucleus accumbens, and olfactory tubercle). As will be discussed later, for many TPN axons, these striatal arborizations are their largest and most profuse.

After crossing the striato-pallial angle and entering the pallial white matter, the TPN axon trunks fan out in divergent trajectories toward their target areas, extending tangentially in the superficial portion of the subcortical white matter and deep layer 6. The trajectories still maintain a general topographic arrangement; however, axon trajectories are not always the most direct possible. For example, axons directed to the dorsolateral and frontal areas of the hemisphere fan out in straight or gently arched trajectories to their targets, whereas the axons directed to parahippocampal and hippocampal areas in the medial and caudal areas of the hemisphere first extend out of the internal capsule in a rostral direction, then turn medially around the anterior horn of the lateral ventricle, and finally continue backward in the cingulum bundle to reach their target cortical areas (Figure 4). Moreover, axon trajectories often become circuitous in their final approximation to the target area; for example, adjacent axons may diverge widely to finally converge on the same area(s). Most axons issue several collateral branches to the cortex. Some branches extend into the upper layers of the cortex and arborize profusely and in layer-specific patterns, but others remain simple, displaying a "stunted" adult appearance that is reminiscent of immature postnatal axons (Catalano et al. 1996; Galazo et al. 2008; Figure 6).

Terminal axon arborizations in the cortical middle layers tend to be focal; the branches forming these arborizations tend to spread obliquely or orthogonally to the columnar arrangement of the cortex and for relatively short distances. In contrast, arborizations in L1 or in the molecular layer of the parahippocampal areas are more widespread and extend as flat canopies in the outer, subpial half the layer.

2.3 TPN Axon Wiring Motifs

Although individual TPN axon morphologies may at first seem quite disparate, a comparison of large numbers of them reveals that just a few basic motifs are repeated across neurons in different nuclei and functional systems (Figures 7 and 8). The diverse axon-wiring motifs are functionally relevant because they constrain the role that each TPN population can play within forebrain networks. For example, some motifs naturally create focal, point-to-point circuits with minimal convergence able to faithfully preserve topological information within an input matrix, whereas other motifs create branched point-to-multipoint circuits suitable for signal broadcasting, synchronization, or cross-correlation between separate target cell populations. In addition, differences in the cell types or dendritic domains targeted by different axons and/or separate branches of the same axons, as well as in the structure and receptor mechanisms of their synapses, may expand, in a pleiotropic fashion, the functional complexity of TPN axon circuits (Casas-Torremocha et al. 2019; Rodriguez-Moreno et al. 2020).

The thalamic nuclei containing cells with the same basic wiring motif are clustered in a nonrandom fashion (Figure 9). There is now evidence that cells in these nuclei clusters might be derived from common neuroepithelial precursors (Shi et al. 2017; Wong et al. 2018; Figure 5). Moreover, in the adult, they show similar global transcriptomic profiles (Nagalski et al. 2016; Phillips et al. 2019; Figure 13B) and often play comparable computational roles in their respective functional systems (e.g., low-convergence subcortical information relay vs. multi-area broadcasting and/or synchronization) (Groh et al. 2014; Sampathkumar et al. 2021). Because the axon wiring motifs

vary widely, are quantifiable and relatively stable, and functionally relevant, they provide a key axis of variation for the definition of TPN cell types.

At a basic level, the various axon architectures share the same general layout: axons extend from the thalamus to a point in the cerebral cortex, giving off some varicose collateral branches along the way. Differences between motifs are largely due to variation in these branches (Figures 7 and 8). The spectrum of variation can be split into at least six discrete major "high-level" axon wiring profiles. Nested levels of diversity (submotifs) are detectable within some of the main profiles; they may eventually be classified as separate motifs as larger morphology datasets become available.

In addition, considerable fine-grain variation is observed at the single-cell level, even between cells that are adjacent to each other within a nucleus and target the same structures, for example, in the precise number and trajectory of branches or in the profusion of a particular terminal arborization. Such differences are always present and are most evident in axons with widely spread branches. They probably represent slightly variable end results from the protracted and sequential interplay between cell-specific gene-expression patterns and non–cell-autonomous local signals that, during development, sculpt the axonal tree morphology (López-Bendito & Molnar 2003; Clascá et al. 2016). Likewise, there is evidence that specific activity patterns driven by postnatal and even adult experience may dynamically modify the terminal branching and local synapse number of TPN axons (Oberlaender et al. 2012; Martini et al. 2021), further contributing to their structural diversification.

Some TPNs innervate only the cerebral cortex, a few innervate only the striatum, and many others innervate both, albeit in widely variable proportions. A first general distinction can be thus made between thalamocortical axons, which have most of their varicose branches (synaptic regions) in the cerebral cortex (neocortex, parahippocampal cortex, or hippocampus), and the thalamostriatal axons, which have most of their branches in the striatum (dorsal striatum, nucleus accumbens, or olfactory tubercle). Under each of these two primary groupings, three motifs or morphotypes can be consistently distinguished. They are briefly described in the following discussion. See also Figures 7, 8 and Table 1.

2.3.1 Unifocal Thalamocortical Axons

Unifocal thalamocortical axons arborize heavily and focally in a single area of the cerebral cortex and do not target subcortical structures except for the TRN (In red ink in Figures 7 and 8). Axons of this type have historically been the focus of most of the structural, developmental, and functional studies of thalamic pathways and are variously referred to as *specific* (Lorente de No 1938), *core* (Jones 1998, 2001), or *C-type* (Clascá et al. 2012). They are typically found in *first-order relay* nuclei (Guillery 1995; Guillery & Sherman 2002).

As they cross cortical layer 6 (L6) and layer 5 (L5), unifocal thalamocortical axons may divide several times; some of these branches finally arborize profusely in layer 4 (L4) to layer 3 (L3), either within a single focus or in several discrete clusters within the same area. Additional simpler terminal arborizations may be

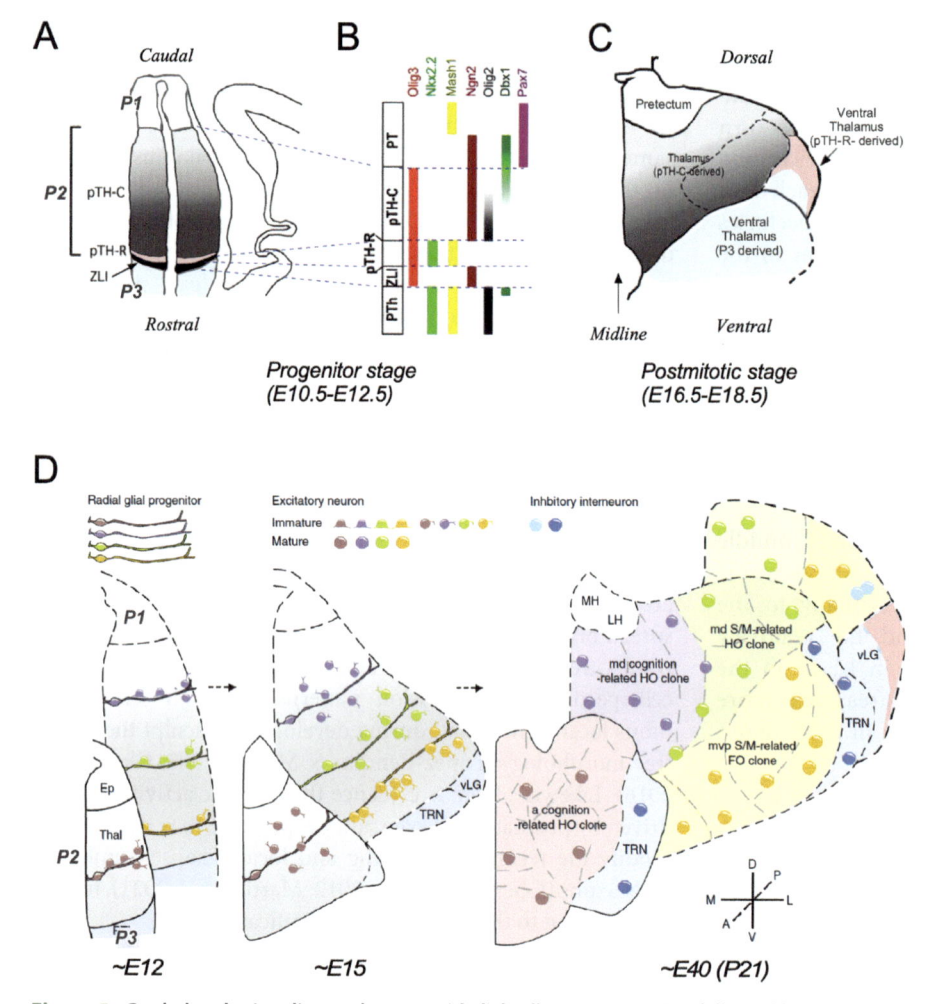

Figure 5 Graded early signaling and neuroepithelial cell gene expression followed by radial clonal dispersion of intermediate precursors and postmitotic cells may lay the basic blueprint for PTN class distribution across the adult thalamus.

A. Diagram showing an idealized frontal section of the embryonic diencephalon at postconceptional day (E)10.5–12.5. In this diagram, the top part (prosomere 1, P1) is more caudal in the neuraxis, than the bottom part (prosomere 3, P3). Neural progenitors in the thalamus are exposed to graded concentration levels of Sonic Hedgehog (Shh) signaling that diffuses from the zona limitans interthalamica (ZLI; black in A). The ZLI forms the border between P3 and prosomere 2 (P2). Shades of gray represent graded levels of Shh signaling. Caudal (pTH-C) and rostral (pTH-R) progenitor domains are established within P2 at this age.

B. Diagram showing the gradients of selective expression of early marker genes, including some transcription factors, along the rostrocaudal axis of the three diencephalic prosomeres at the same early stage.

C. A coronal section diagram of the diencephalon at a later embryonic age, when PTNs are already postmitotic. The pTH-C neuroepithelial precursors originate, directly or through intermediate precursors, all the PTNs of the adult dorsal thalamus.

D. A diagram illustration of the general layout of ontogenetic columns that generate PTNs (Thal) and their relation to the main adult cytoarchitectonic and functional nuclei groups. S/M: sensory and motor; HO: higher-order nuclei; FO: first-order nuclei. "P" indicates postnatal age in days. See end-of-chapter list for other abbreviations.

Panels A–C: Modified from Vue et al. (2009). Panel D: Modified from Shi et al. (2017).

present in L6. In their terminal branches, the axons form abundant *en passant* varicosities of relatively large size. These varicosities often correspond to simple or complex multisynaptic arrangements that target glutamatergic cortical cell spines as well as GABAergic cortical cell dendrites (Familtsev et al. 2016; Rodriguez-Moreno et al. 2018, 2020) mediated by ionotropic receptors (Guillery and Sherman 2002). Some unifocal axon branches may reach cortical L1 but do not arborize significantly in this layer.

Most neurons in the VP, DLG, the ventral division of the MGV, and the dorsal part of the nucleus submedius (SMd) display a unifocal thalamocortical motif. Observations of intraaxonally labeled distal axon fragments from equivalent nuclei in primates and carnivores reveal similar patterns (Humphrey et al. 1985; Garraghty & Sur 1990). In primates, the unifocal axons from different DLG projection neuron subtypes display a remarkable degree of terminal sublamination in cortical layers 4 and 3b (Fitzpatrick et al. 1983; Lund 1988).

2.3.2 Multifocal Thalamocortical Axons

Multifocal thalamocortical axons characteristically have several (usually two to five) primary branches arborizing in separate points of the isocortex and, in some cases, also of the

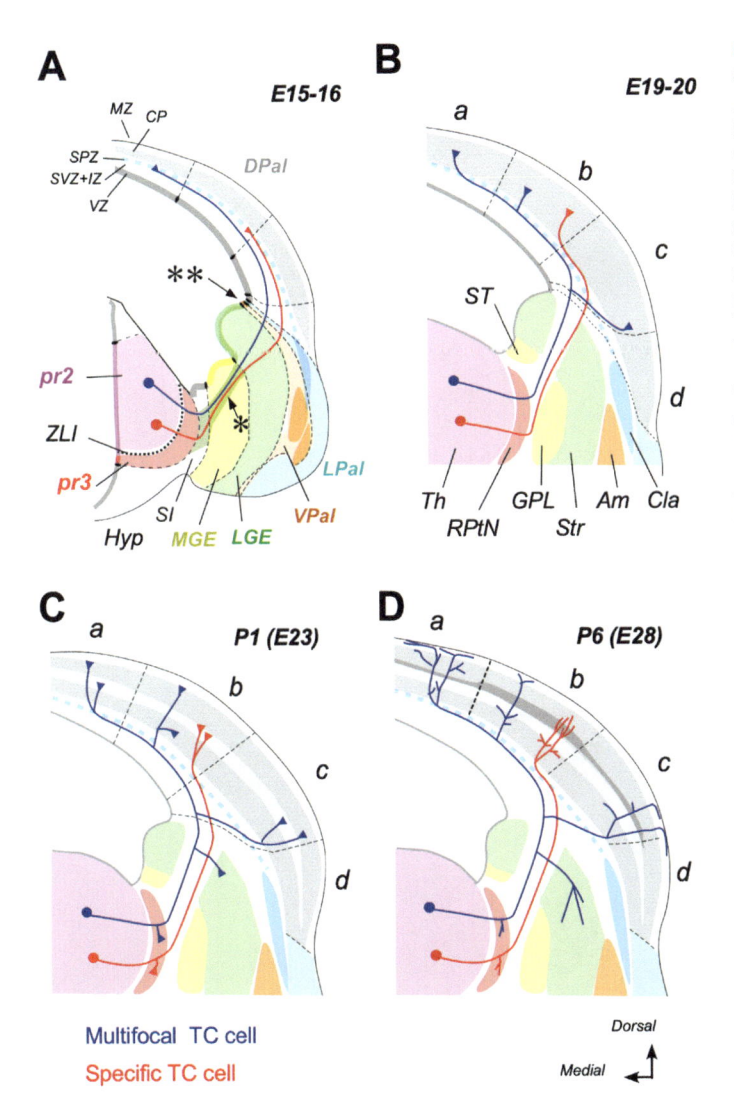

Figure 6 Temporal sequences of sprouting, growth, and arborization of axon branches from different PTNs.

A monofocal thalamocortical (TC) (red) and a multifocal thalamocortical (blue) PTN are represented in highly schematic form. Cartoon sections of the prenatal (A and B) and postnatal (C and D) rat forebrain are represented. The filled circles represent the neuronal cell body in the thalamus (Th). Triangles at the tip of the lines indicate patent axonal growth cones. The structures derived from the same histogenetic compartments are labeled with shades of the same color. *: Corridor compartment; **: pallio-subpallial boundary. In panels A–C, the general trajectory of the pial processes of radial precursors at the borders of prospective cortical areas is indicated by dashed lines. Numbers preceded by "E" indicate embryonic age in days (rat), and numbers preceded by "P" indicate the age in postnatal days. Note also delayed sprouting of collateral branches to lateral cortical areas (panel B) and the even more delayed sprouting of branches to the striatum (Str) and reticular prethalamic nucleus (RPtN; panel C). Other abbreviations: Am: amygdala; CP: cortical plate; DCla: dorsal claustrum; DPal: dorsal pallium; GPL: lateral globus pallidus; Hyp: hypothalamus; LGE: lateral ganglionic eminence; LPal: lateral pallium; MGE: medial ganglionic eminence; MZ: marginal zone; pr2: prosomere 2; Pr3: prosomere 3; SI: substantia innominata; SPZ: subplate zone; ST: stria terminalis; Str: striatum; SVZ+IZ: subventricular zone + intermediate zone fiber layer; VPAL: ventral pallium; VZ: ventricular zone; ZLI: zona limitans intrathalamica. Taken from Clascá et al. (2016).

perirhinal and parahippocampal cortex as well (In blue ink in Figures 7 and 8). In this way, multifocal thalamocortical axons can innervate at least two cortical areas that are contiguous or may diverge widely to innervate areas that are far from each other. The density of cortical branches and their laminar arborization patterns may vary markedly between areas. For example, they can be concentrated in L4–L3 in one area while targeting layer 5a (L5a) and L1 in another (Ohno et al. 2012; Nakamura et al. 2015; Rodriguez-Moreno et al. 2020). In the parahippocampal areas, terminal arborizations are focused mostly in L1 and layer 3 (L3). Importantly, the separate branches of these axons can establish markedly different presynaptic arrangements and contact different cell classes in each target area, and their effects can be mediated by different ionotropic or glutamatergic receptor mechanisms (Casas-Torremocha et al. 2019; Rodriguez-Moreno et al. 2020).

Many of these axons issue additional arborizations in the striatum. These are usually modest, but in some cells, they may be substantial. The striatal branches are markedly thinner than the parent axon, with numerous *en passant* varicosities; are distributed in loose patterns ("type I thalamostriatal" axons of Deschênes et al. 1995); and remain largely confined to the matrix compartment of the striatum.

In rodents, multifocal axon wiring is the predominant motif for TPNs in nuclei such as the posterior nucleus (Po), lateral posterior-pulvinar (LP), dorsal medial geniculate (MGD), VL, lateral dorsal (LD), and mediodorsal (MD). The limited single-cell evidence available indicates that the anteroventral (AV), anteromedial (AM), and anterodorsal (AD) nuclei also show this axon wiring motif (Figure 4, 7–9).

As defined here, the multifocal motif allows room for considerable variation. For example, some of the aforementioned nuclei target only isocortical areas (Po, LP, MGD, MDVL), whereas others target both isocortical and parahippocampal areas (LD, AV, AM, AD). In any case, because of their multifocal axonal wiring, the neurons in these nuclei all share a capacity for acting as cellular backbones in specific multiple-area functional subnetworks.

Anatomy

THALAMO-CORTICAL (TC): *(most varicosities in cortex)*

Monofocal TC — VP, DLG, MGV, VL

Multifocal TC — Po, LP-Pul, LD, MD, MGD, AD, AM, AV

Subpial TC — VM, VA, PoT, MGM, [Re]

THALAMO-STRIATAL (TS): *(most varicosities in striatum)*

Anterior TS — CL, PC, CeM, Rh

Midline TS — Pt, Pv, IMD, SPf

Posterior TS — Pf-CM, Eth, PIL

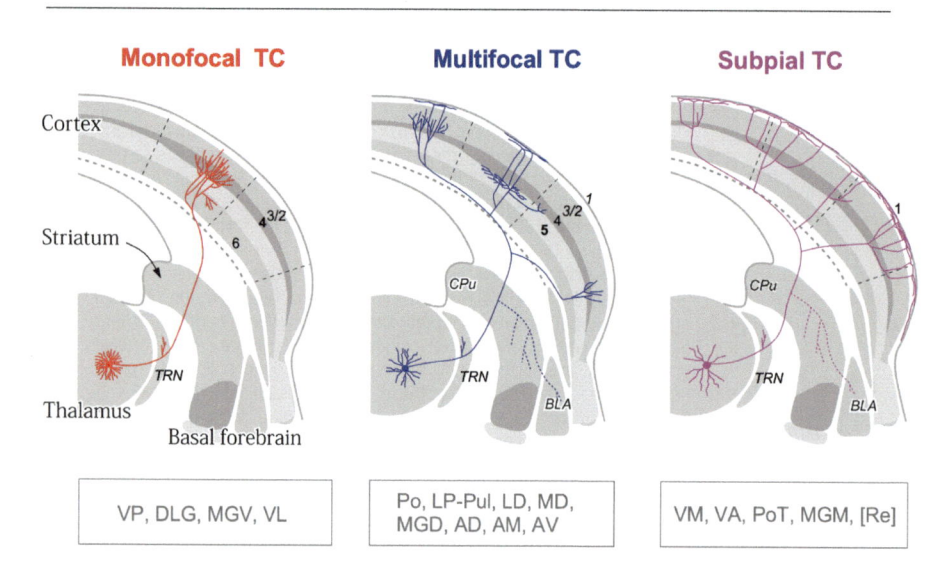

Figure 7 Cartoon summary of the features characterizing each of the main axon wiring motifs observed in rodent PTNs.

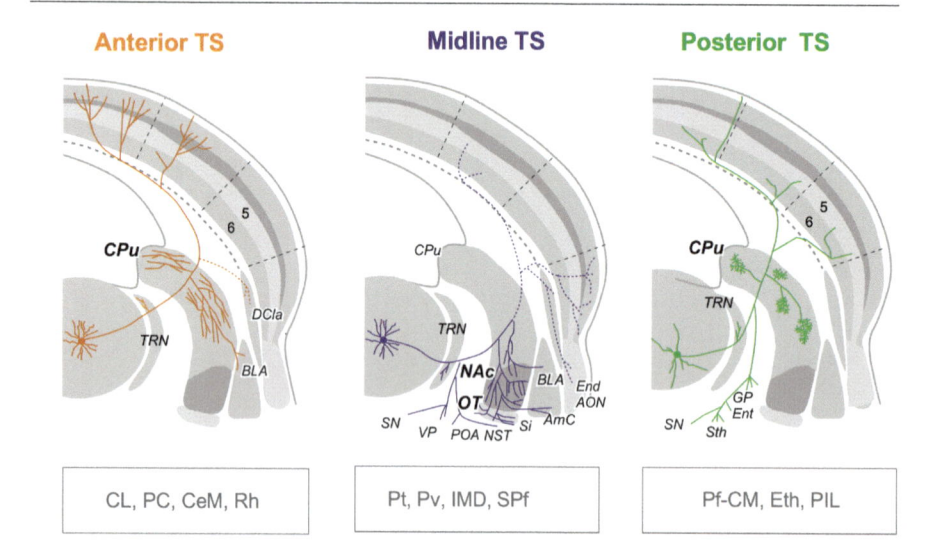

Idealized neurons representing each axonal morphotype are drawn on a diagram of the forebrain (see Figure 6). Dashed lines indicate branches that may often be absent in some cells within a morphotype. The structures receiving the heaviest innervation in each case are highlighted in boldface. Mouse thalamic nuclei that predominantly or exclusively contain cells showing the corresponding motif are listed under each figure.

2.3.3 Subpial Thalamocortical Axons

The subpial thalamocortical axons have a predominant arborization in cortical L1, where they form "flat" canopies of subpial branches (in magenta ink in Figures 7 and 8). Subpial thalamocortical axons have also been referred to as *matrix axons* (Jones 1998, 2001, 2007a) or *M-type axons* (Clascá et al. 2012). The subpial plexus from one of these axons may extend over a large region in the cerebral hemisphere (Rubio-Garrido et al. 2009; Kuramoto et al. 2015; Nakamura et al. 2015). In their course along the subcortical white matter/deep L6, the subpial thalamocortical axons typically give off numerous (often over a dozen) separate primary branches that climb up radially into the gray matter. As they cross layers 6–2, they can give off additional branches that also climb radially toward L1. Upon reaching L1, most branches make a 90-degree turn and extend tangentially, often running in relatively straight trajectories for hundreds or even thousands of microns as poorly branched varicose processes. The evidence available indicates that these axon terminals preferentially target spines in the apical dendritic tufts of pyramidal cells reaching L1 (Arbuthnott et al. 1990), as well as the interneurons present in the layer (Cruickshank et al. 2012).

In addition to the cortex, some cells with subpial thalamocortical axons form small type I (Deschênes et al. 1995) arborizations in the striatum.

Subpial thalamocortical wiring is the norm among TPNs in the ventromedial (VM) and ventral anterior (VA) medial division of the medial geniculate (MGM), the posterior triangular (PoT), and the reuniens (Re) nuclei. In addition, cells with wiring motifs that may be considered intermediate between subpial thalamocortical and multifocal thalamocortical are frequent in the caudal zone of Po and in the lateral posterior medial (LPM) nucleus (Figures 7–9).

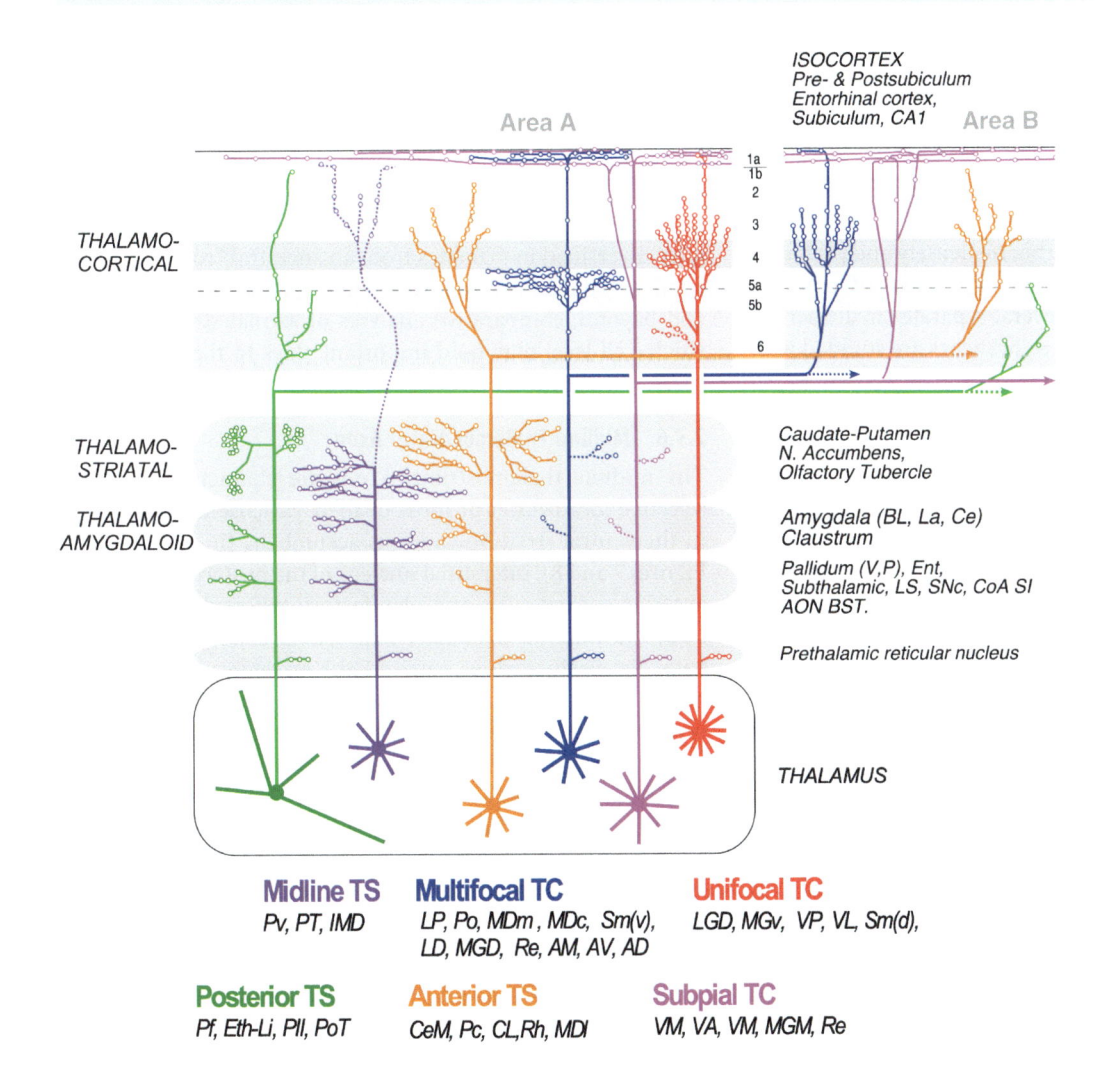

Figure 8 Summary diagram of the main cell types contributing to the various thalamic output pathways.

Schematic comparison of the axon architectures of the main PTN cell classes. Color coded as in Figures 7 and 9. Open circles indicate the distribution of axon varicosities (putative synaptic regions). The diagram reveals the fundamental similarity in the layout of all PTN axons, as well as their distinctive branching motifs. Note that all PTN axons leave small branches in the prethalamic reticular nucleus. Arrows indicate axons that extend farther to innervate more than two cortical areas. Dashed lines indicate branches often absent in the PTNs of a particular class. Cell bodies and dendritic arbors are represented in simplified form. Compare with Figure 1.

Midline TS
Pv, PT, IMD

Multifocal TC
LP, Po, MDm, MDc, Sm(v), LD, MGD, Re, AM, AV, AD

Unifocal TC
LGD, MGv, VP, VL, Sm(d)

Posterior TS
Pf, Eth-Li, PII, PoT

Anterior TS
CeM, Pc, CL, Rh, MDl

Subpial TC
VM, VA, VM, MGM, Re

In addition to innervating L1 in neocortical, entorhinal, and subicular areas, Re cell axons arborize heavily in the deep layers of the entorhinal cortex and often reach the stratum lacunosum-moleculare of the hippocampus field CA1 as well. Such unusual features, along with a peculiar transcriptomic profile (Phillips et al. 2019; see Section 4 and Figure 13C), suggest that the subpial-thalamocortical projection Re neurons may be considered a subclass of their own.

2.3.4 Anterior Thalamostriatal Axons

Anterior thalamostriatal axons are characterized by a robust arborization in the dorsal striatum (caudate-putamen) that consists of multiple widely spread and finely varicose branches ("type I" thalamostriatal axons; Deschênes et al. 1995), along with a substantial arborization in the cerebral cortex (In orange ink in Figures 7 and 8). Anterior thalamostriatal axons are widespread, yet they show rough topographic distributions in the dorsal striatum, according to their nucleus of origin (Van del Werf et al. 2002; Erro et al. 2002). Their axonal varicosities are primarily localized in the matrix compartment (Deschênes, Bourassa, & Parent 1996; Lacey et al. 2007; Unzai et al. 2017), selectively target the spine heads of striatal medium spiny neurons, and are mediated predominantly by N-methyl-D-aspartate (NMDA) receptor mechanisms (Lacey et al. 2007; Beatty et al. 2009; Smith et al. 2014).

The cortical arborizations of anterior thalamostriatal axons are most numerous in layers 5–3 and limited to just a few areas; occasional branches may reach L1 but do not arborize tangentially into it (Deschênes, Bourassa, Doan, et al. 1996; Deschênes, Bourassa, & Parent, 1996; Parent & Parent 2005). The arborizations may sometimes cluster focally, resembling those of some multifocal thalamocortical axons.

In rodents, the TPN neurons in the anterior intralaminar nuclei (namely, the central lateral [CL], paracentral [PC], and central medial [CeM]), as well as most neurons in the lateral portion of the mediodorsal nucleus (MDl), display this wiring motif (Figures 4 and 7–9). Many of the cells in CeM send, in addition, axon branches to the lateral and basolateral amygdaloid nuclei, whereas cells in the CL frequently send an axon branch to the dorsal claustrum (Unzai et al. 2017; see also Carey & Neal 1986; Kaufman & Rosenquist 1985; Real et al. 2006; Van der Werf et al. 2002).

2.3.5 Posterior Thalamostriatal Axons

Posterior thalamostriatal axons arborize densely and preferentially in the dorsal striatum, where they give off complex terminal branches clustered in several separate small foci (In green ink in Figures 7 and 8). These branches are studded with varicose swellings and short, club-ended processes ("type 2" thalamostriatal arborization; Deschênes, Bourassa, Doan, et al. 1996; Lacey et al. 2007; Beatty et al. 2009). In the striatum, these axons' synapses have been reported to be established on both the medium spiny neurons and cholinergic interneurons. The synapses are established mainly on the shafts of the spiny neurons and are mediated mainly by non-NMDA glutamate receptor systems (Smith et al. 2014). Despite a substantial dispersal of the terminal clusters formed by the individual axons (Deschênes, Bourassa, Doan, et al. 1996), a crude topographic mediolateral segregation across the striatum is evident (Erro et al. 2002; Mandelbaum et al. 2019). The posterior thalamostriatal axon terminals almost exclusively target the matrix compartment of the striatum (Deschênes, Bourassa, Doan, et al. 1996; Unzai et al. 2017).

In addition to the dorsal striatum, rodent posterior thalamocortical axons typically send a branch to the cerebral cortex. In contrast to the striatal branches, however, this cortical branch establishes a relatively simple and loosely spread arborization whose terminal branches are mainly located in layers 5 and 6.

In rodents, neurons exhibiting a posterior thalamostriatal wiring pattern are typically found along the caudomedial edge of the dorsal thalamus in the parafascicular (Pf) (Lacey et al. 2007; Beatty et al. 2009), ethmoid-limitans (Eth; Deschênes, Bourassa, Doan et al. 1996), and posterior intralaminar nuclei (Smith et al. 2006). In both rodents and primates, the parent cells of these axons possess few, very long, and poorly branched dendrites with occasional spines, a feature that sets them apart from all other neurons of the thalamus (Section 1). Remarkably, however, not all the cells in the rodent Pf nucleus display a posterior thalamostriatal wiring and reticular-like dendritic morphology: about a third of Pf TPNs show a projection pattern similar to those of the anterior intralaminar type and exhibit bushy somatodendritic morphologies (Deschênes, Bourassa, Doan, et al. 1996; Deschênes, Bourassa, & Parent 1996; Beatty et al. 2009; Unzai et al. 2017).

A single-cell labeling study in squirrel monkeys (*Saimiri sciureus*) has examined TPNs in the centromedian-parafascicular (CM-Pf) nucleus, which is regarded as an equivalent of the rodent Pf (Smith et al. 2014). This study found that 25/25 cells exhibited "reticular-like" somatodendritic morphologies similar to those observed in the rodent Pf. However, these cells showed a diverse spectrum of wiring architectures (Figure 10). For example, the axons of some cells terminated in a patchy fashion in the striatum and globus pallidus but did not continue toward the cortex. Other cell axons left patchy arborizations in the striatum and a loosely branched axon in the cerebral cortex. And yet another population of CM-Pf cells had axons that did not branch in the striatum but arborized extensively in cortical layers 5 and 6. Although limited, these observations hint at the possibility that new axon subtypes (and, hence, new multiregional forebrain subnetworks) may have diversified in primates from an ancestral "root" TPN type similar to the one present in modern rodents. In the thalamus and beyond, comparative analyses of axonal structure at the single-cell level may hold important clues to the evolution of brain function and behavior (Clascá et al. 2016).

2.3.6 Midline Thalamostriatal Axons

The midline thalamostriatal axons are characterized by the selective localization of most of their varicose axon branches in the ventral striatum (nucleus accumbens (in purple ink in Figures 7 and 8), interstitial nucleus of the posterior limb of the anterior commissure, and/or olfactory tuberculum). In addition, the midline thalamostriatal axons usually target other basal forebrain regions, such as the amygdala, endopyrifom nucleus, ventral pallidum, substantia innominata, lateral septum, and preoptic area; in some cases, they may even reach, through relatively simple branches, the periaqueductal gray of the mesencephalon (Unzai et al. 2017). Midline thalamostriatal innervation of the cortex is relatively limited targeting only the medial ventromedial frontal and perirhinal cortices, mostly in layers 1 and 3 (Van der Werf et al. 2002). The segment of the axon directed to the cortex may even be absent in some cells.

3. TPN Cell Membrane Properties

Studies that directly compared the membrane properties of TPNs in different thalamic nuclei have repeatedly confirmed they are essentially similar (Llinás & Jahnsen 1982; Jahnsen & Llinás, 1984a, 1984b; Sheroziya & Timofeev 2014; Desai & Varela 2021). These include a resting potential of around −60 mV (Turner et al. 1997; Aguilar et al. 2008; Li et al. 2003; Bartlett & Smith 1999; Smith et al. 2006), a firing threshold of about −40 mV (Turner et al. 1997), and a similar range of input resistances (Turner et al. 1997; Smith et al. 2006; Sheroziya & Timofeev 2014).

Conductances are also widely shared across TPNs. These prominently include a low-threshold, transient calcium current (IT) that operates via T-type Ca^{2+} channels (IT-type Ca^{2+} channels) located in the membranes of the soma and dendrites. These channels mediate, in a voltage-dependent manner, an inward current (I_T) that produces a transient depolarization of the cell. Although T-type channels are common to neurons everywhere, in TPNs, they have a sufficiently dense distribution that the initiation of I_T generally leads to an all-or-none Ca^{2+} spike (low-threshold calcium spike [LTS]) that propagates throughout the soma and dendritic arbor. This is seen only rarely in other neuronal types in the central nervous system. (Sherman 2001b). These channels are inactivated by depolarization, and they are de-inactivated by hyperpolarization; at hyperpolarized voltages (−70 or below), they can be activated by an excitatory postsynaptic potential (EPSP)

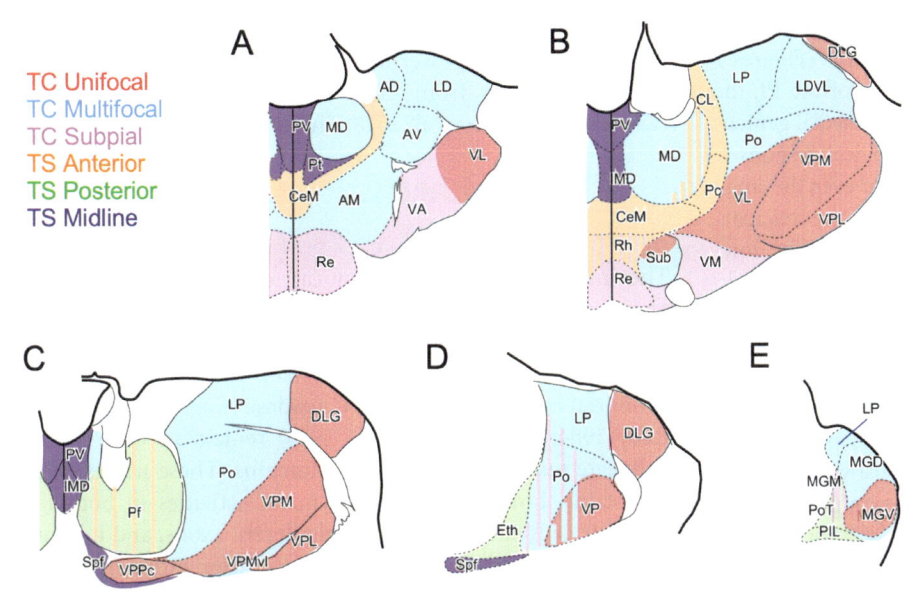

Figure 9 Simplified diagram representation of the general distribution across the mouse thalamus nuclei of the six high-level PTN profiles listed in Table 1. Banded patterns indicate regions with a high prevalence of intermingled PTN types or transitional profiles.

TC Unifocal
TC Multifocal
TC Subpial
TS Anterior
TS Posterior
TS Midline

depolarization. When I_T is thus activated, the interaction of the LTS it creates with other Na⁺ channels can elicit multiple sodium-dependent action potentials, often at a high frequency; these are collectively known as a *burst*.

As a result, TPNs fire in two fundamentally different modes. Regular, or tonic, firing is elicited when the neuron is depolarized from a resting membrane potential near −55 mV. At this depolarized potential, I_T is inactivated, and the discharge frequency is linearly related to the magnitude of membrane depolarization, thus facilitating accurate transmission of presynaptic information (Guido et al. 1992; Guido & Weyand 1995; Reinagel et al. 1999; Llinás & Steriade 2006; Wang et al. 2007; Whitmire et al. 2016; Crunelli et al. 2018). In contrast, if the membrane potential is below −70 mV, activation of the low-threshold, transient Ca²⁺ current, I_T, can occur, and the same depolarizing stimulus may now trigger a burst of action potentials (Jahnsen & Llinás 1984b; Huguenard 1996; Gutierrez et al. 2001; Perez-Reyes 2003). The transient bursts are stereotyped signals whose discharge rate is independent of presynaptic input intensity. During wakefulness, bursting has been shown to provide enhanced detectability of salient shifts in a stimulus or new sensory stimuli (Swadlow & Gusev 2001; Sherman 2001a). During some phases of sleep, reciprocal interactions between TPNs and the cells in the prethalamic reticular nucleus may also lead to rhythmic bursting; under this condition, bursting may strongly interfere with peripheral signal transmission to the cerebral cortex.

Other common conductances are a mixed cation conductance (I_H) that prevents membrane hyperpolarization and a transient K⁺ conductance that delays spike firing (I_A). Interactions between all these membrane conductances allow TPNs to display different intrinsic rhythms, such as the slow (0.5- to 4-Hz) (Nuñez et al. 1992), very slow (0.05- to 0.2-Hz) (Leresche et al. 1991), or spontaneous high-frequency (20- to 80-Hz) oscillations at membrane potentials of −45 mV (Pedroarena & Llinás 1997).

Beyond the fundamental similarity just described, small yet functionally relevant differences have been reported between TPNs in different nuclei (Figure 11). For example, as a rule, action potentials are slightly narrower, depolarization thresholds are lower, and frequencies of tonic firing are higher in the cells of nuclei that relay peripheral sensory and cerebellar inputs than in cells in higher-order sensory nuclei and midline-intralaminar nuclei (Landisman & Connors 2007; Nakamura et al. 2014; Phillips et al. 2019). Other differences have been observed less consistently or only for some nuclei. In the visual thalamus, there are reports of a T-current in the TPNs of the LP nucleus larger than that in the cells of the adjacent DLG, which can make LP cells more likely to fire a series of rebound bursts instead of a single one and thus be more prone to rhythmic bursting (Li et al. 2003; Wei et al. 2011). In contrast, TPNs in the centromedian thalamic nucleus have been reported to exhibit very little I_H and an elevated tonic firing threshold (Jhangiani-Jashanmal et al. 2016).

Recent in vivo and in vitro studies have directly compared the bursting responses in several thalamic nuclei, for example, between first-order/primary and higher-order/association nuclei of the same modality or across sensory modalities. These studies have reported consistent differences in the number of spikes fired on bursts. Likewise, differences have been observed in the latency with which bursts are produced after a hyperpolarization (Landisman & Connors 2007; Slézia et al. 2011; Sheroziya & Timofeev 2014; Desai & Varela 2021, Figure 9A and B). Compartmental modeling simulations indicate that the latter differences may simply result from variations in the abundance and/or spatial distribution of active T channels in the neuron's soma and dendrites (Desai & Varela 2021).

In consonance with their peculiar somatodendritic morphology (Figure 1; see Section 1) and axon-wiring motifs (Figures 7 and 8; see Section 2.3.5), the reticular-like TPNs of the Pf, the Eth, and the paralaminar regions adjacent to the medial geniculate complex (PoT, PIl) show unique physiological responses. Compared to the bushy neurons in other nuclei or even the small population of bushy neurons present within the Pf, the reticular-like cells show a reduction or complete absence of the low-threshold, voltage-sensitive calcium conductance. As a result, the voltage-dependent burst response in these cells is minimal or absent, even when given a depolarizing step from hyperpolarized membrane potentials (Smith et al. 2006; Lacey et al. 2007; Beatty et al. 2009). In those reticular-like Pf TPNs that do show some bursting, the number of action potentials per burst is significantly less than that observed in the bushy neurons of the Pf or from other nuclei. Moreover, the resting potentials of these TPNs are often more depolarized than those seen in bushy cells, and their action potentials are larger and can show biphasic or monophasic afterhyperpolarization. The input resistance of the reticular-like TPNs has been reported to be, as a rule, significantly lower than that of bushy TPNs (Smith et al. 2006; Lacey et al. 2007; Beatty et al. 2009; Sheroziya & Timofeev 2014).

Less striking, but still consistent differences have been observed between bushy cells in other thalamic nuclei. For example, in the visual and somatic relay nuclei, specific subsets of thalamocortical neurons respond to brief peripheral stimuli with rapidly adapting (transient) discharges, whereas other neurons respond with slowly adapting (sustained) discharges (Yen et al. 1985; Turner et al. 1994, 1997; Friedlander et al. 1981).

Although fragmentary, the evidence available thus suggests that upon a fundamental similarity, the combined effect of relatively small differences in the number and/or distribution of conductances and receptors may create significant diversity in the dynamic behaviors of different TPN populations. By influencing the specific bandpass filter and oscillatory properties of thalamic neurons, these differences may turn out to be relevant in the regulation of information flow through the thalamus within multiregional forebrain networks (Bonnefond et al. 2017; Fiebelkorn et al. 2019; Jaramillo et al. 2019).

An additional and important layer of complexity in the response properties of TPNs may follow from the uneven expression of receptors to different modulatory neurotransmitters. Although the data available on this topic are fragmentary, there is already evidence that the effects of these neuromodulators may differ widely between TPNs of different nuclei and even between cells in the same nucleus. For example, serotonin hyperpolarizes some higher-order nuclei instead of enhancing I_H as it does in first-order relays (Monckton & McCormick 2002; Varela & Sherman 2009). Further, in the rat auditory system, acetylcholine hyperpolarizes neurons in the higher-order thalamus but depolarizes them in the first-order thalamus (Mooney et al. 2004). The same difference has been observed between the bushy and the reticular-like TPNs, respectively, of the rat Pf nucleus (Beatty et al. 2009). TPNs in the midline and intralaminar nuclei, as a whole, display a wider diversity of neuromodulator receptors, often in a combinatorial fashion. Physiological responses in the TPNs in these nuclei are powerfully modified by neurotransmitter-specific pathways from the brainstem and basal forebrain (Kirouac 2015; Ren et al. 2018; Phillips et al. 2019).

4. TPN Neurochemical and Gene-Expression Diversity

The introduction of histochemical techniques in the 1970s revealed remarkable heterogeneities in the distribution of some enzymatic activities across the thalamus. Stainings for acetylcholinesterase (Graybiel & Berson 1980) or for the mitochondrial enzyme cytochrome C-oxidase (Kageyama & Wong-Riley 1984; Land & Simmons 1985) remain in wide use to delineate nuclei and nuclear subdomains. These neurochemical stains, however, reveal enzymatic activities in both the thalamic cells and in the terminal afferent axons, and they are strongly modified by fixatives. Thus, the information that these stainings provide about the actual molecular diversity of TPNs is limited (see Jones 2007b for a review).

In the 1980s and 1990s, immunohistochemical methods with a variety of antibodies against specific neuronal proteins, as well as in situ hybridization methods for the identification of specific gene transcripts, became available. These methods revealed a much more diverse and complex molecular landscape across the thalamus (reviewed in Jones 2007b). Studies using these methods were conducted in a variety of species, ages, and experimental conditions; they made crucial discoveries, such as the GABAergic phenotype of thalamic interneurons and the cells in the prethalamic reticular nucleus (Houser et al. 1980) and the selective expression of glutamate transporter 2 in most TPNs (Fujiyama et al. 2001; Barroso-Chinea et al. 2007). They were also very useful for consistent comparisons across species. Overall, however, the "neurochemical" mapping studies produced a large body of research, whose accumulating results became increasingly difficult to compare and systematize because of the fragmentary nature of the studies and the wide diversity of probes, protocols, and animal species employed (see Jones 2007b for a review).

Some antibodies introduced in the late 1980s against the calcium-binding proteins calbindin 28K and parvalbumin revealed diverse and often complementary patterns of distribution of these proteins across the thalamus in different species. Interest in these proteins was subsequently fostered by the discovery that, in the thalamus of macaque monkeys, calbindin 28K is expressed by the TPNs innervating cortical L1 but not those innervating cortical layers 3 and 4. In contrast, parvalbumin was found to be expressed in groups of TPNs complementary to those expressing calbindin 28K and innervating L2–L4 (Rausell et al. 1992; Hashikawa et al. 1991; Jones 2001, 2007a). At a time in which systematic large-scale gene expression analyses were not available, these proteins thus came to be regarded as key molecular "markers" for specific thalamic cell populations (Jones 1998, 2007a, 2007b). Likewise, other calcium-binding proteins, such as calretinin (Baimbridge et al. 1992), calcium-dependent calmodulin kinase 2a (Hendry & Yoshioka 1994), and the calmodulin-binding protein Purkinje cell protein 4

(PCP4; Murray et al. 2007), were found to have heterogeneous and often nucleus-specific expression patterns.

In recent years, systematic genome-wide in situ hybridization and transcriptomic analyses have finally become possible. These studies have greatly expanded the number of genes (to about 4,000) whose expression varies across the thalamus (Nagalski et al. 2016; Phillips 2019). Remarkably, the differences detected are mostly gradual and highly combinatorial in nature at the single-cell level (Figure 12). Thus, at least in the mouse thalamus, gene-expression patterns are best viewed as a variation across a continuum rather than specific genes sharply delineating cell classes. Interestingly, these studies have shown that the heterogeneous expression of calcium-binding proteins actually involves many different such proteins instead of just two or three. The correlation of calcium-binding proteins with particular thalamic cell classes or nuclei thus seems to be quite complex.

An unsupervised nearly full-genome analysis of these gene profiles across nuclei (Phillips et al. 2019) was able to detect three main groupings, which roughly aligned with some, but not all, axonal morphotypes. Cells in the same transcriptomic grouping were found across multiple nuclei and functional systems (Figure 13A and B). The main component of variation detected in this analysis included gene classes encoding proteins known to be involved in synaptic vesicle release, metabolic enzymes, kinases, and calcium-binding proteins. However, the most enriched were genes encoding neurotransmitter receptors, ion channels, and signaling molecules (Figure 13E), indicating that the differences are related to functions such as neuronal excitability and synaptic transmission.

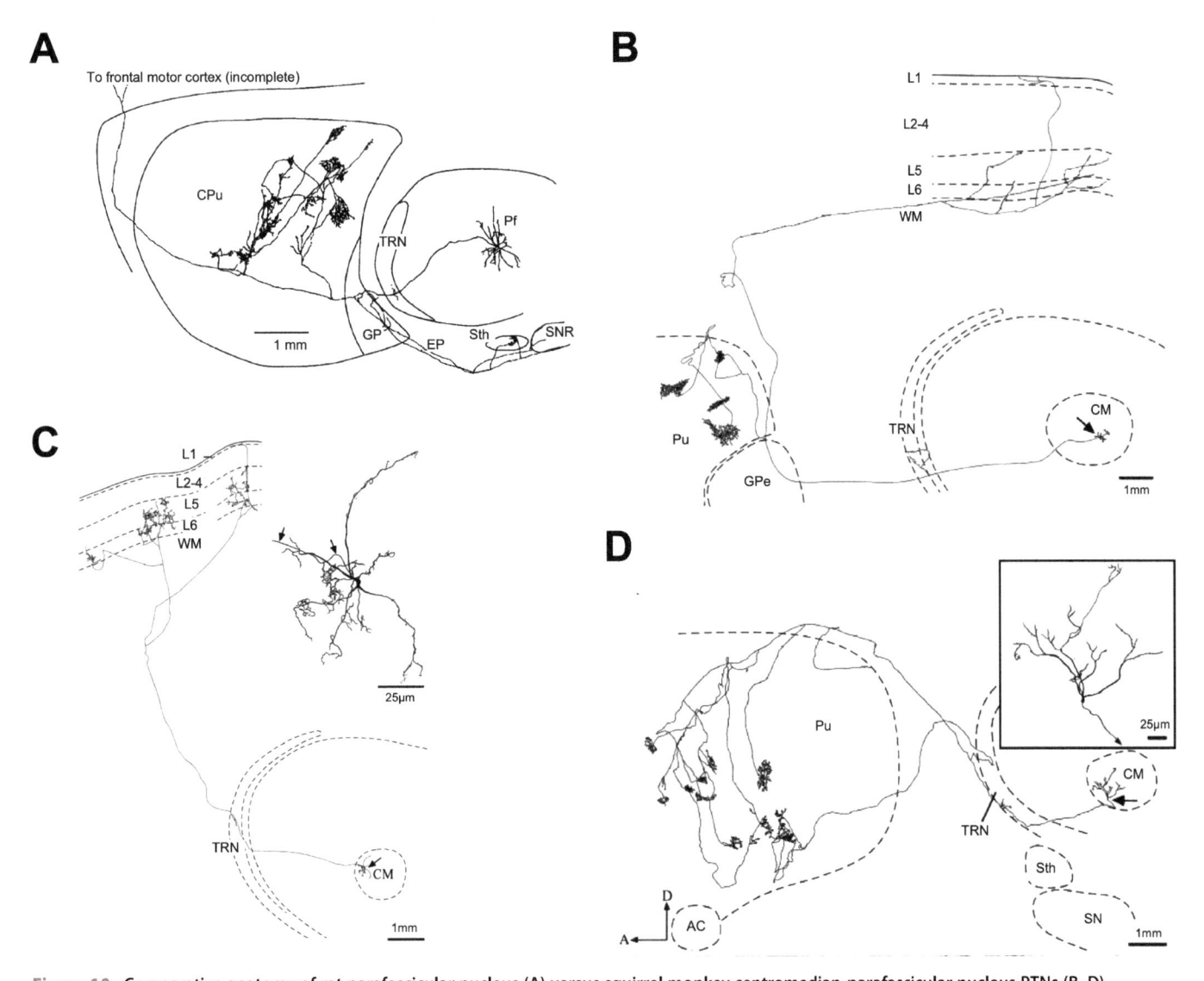

Figure 10 Comparative anatomy of rat parafascicular nucleus (A) versus squirrel monkey centromedian-parafascicular nucleus PTNs (B–D).
Camera lucida reconstructions of the whole-cell morphologies are shown on a sagittal diagram of the forebrain. Pu: putamen; CM: centromedian nucleus; AC: anterior commissure. For other abbreviations, see the list at the end of the chapter.
Panel A: Modified from Deschênes, Bourassa, Doan, et al. (1996). Panels C and D: Modified from Parent and Parent (2005).

Anatomy

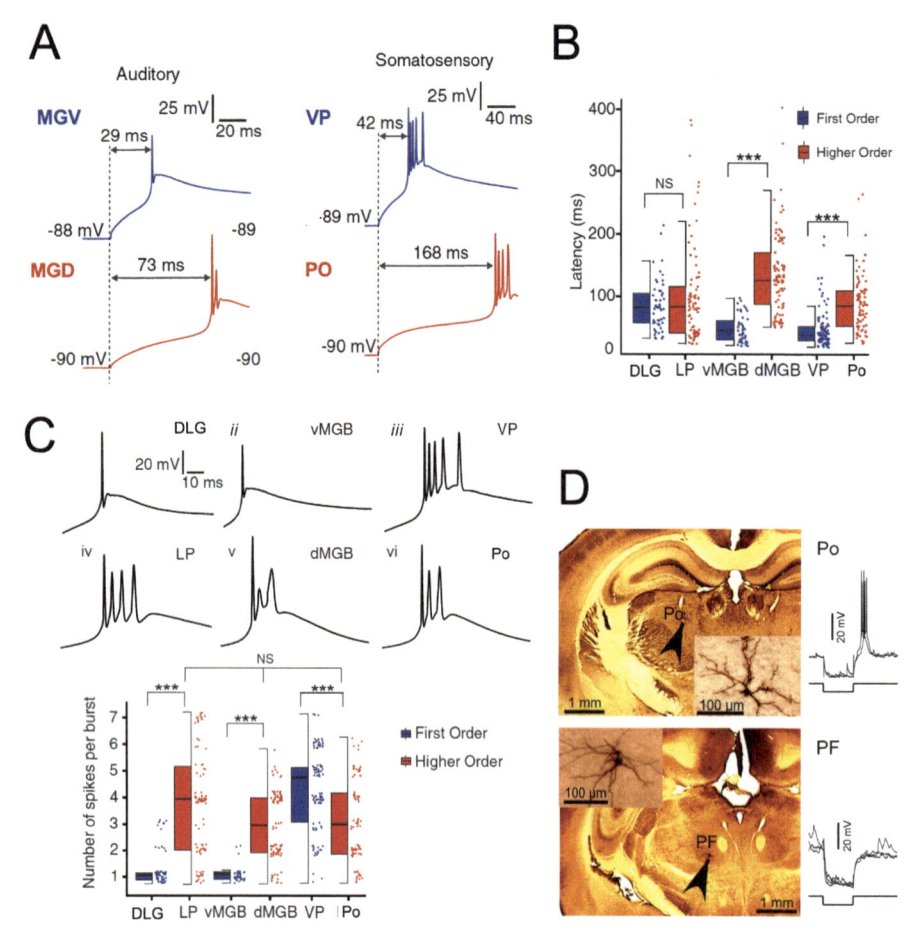

Figure 11 Differences in bursting behavior of PTNs in different thalamic nuclei.

A and B. Bursts evoked from similar hyperpolarization levels in typical cells of the rat auditory and somatosensory systems recorded in vitro. Cells in first-order nuclei (MGV, VP) display a shorter latency than in the corresponding high-order relay nucleus (MGB, Po).

B. Population distribution of the latency values for all evoked bursts in the study.

C. Number of spikes in bursts evoked by hyperpolarization of thalamocortical cells in different nuclei. Top: Examples of bursts from six representative thalamic cells from different nuclei show different numbers of spikes/bursts at similar hyperpolarization levels prior to the burst (average = 90.92 ± 0.90 mV SD). Distributions of numbers of spikes/bursts for all bursts across the population of thalamic cells in first-order relay (*blue*) and higher-order relay (*red*) nuclei. Boxes indicate the median and 25–75% quartiles. Modified from Desai and Varela (2021).

D. In vivo recordings of representative cells in the mouse Po nucleus (*top*) and parafascicular (Pf) nucleus (*bottom*). Left, light microscopic images of the intracellularly stained neurons (*inset*), shown on a coronal slice containing the cell. Cytochrome-oxidase counterstain. In contrast to Po neurons, the Pf neuron did not produce a low-threshold spike in response to hyperpolarizing (100-ms, 1-nA) current pulses. From Sheroziya and Timofeev (2014).

More detailed and complete transcriptomic analyses in rodents and other species, including single-cell transcriptomes, are expected to eventually provide a definitive and consistent foundation for the understanding of TPN cell diversity (Winnubst et al. 2020). Many of these differences in gene expression are probably at the root of the distinctive morphology, response properties, and connectivity that characterize the various TPN classes. However, it is far from clear that axonal morphology, a fundamental trait of long-range projection neurons, may be directly predicted by reading the adult cell gene-expression profile because the architecture of each axon branch reflects a complex developmental history (Clascá et al. 2016; Winnubst et al. 2020; Figure 6). Other factors, such as the activity of the neurons during development (reviewed in Martini et al. 2021) and the sequential and in part random interactions of the axon growth cones with multiple membrane-bound or diffusible guidance signals found along their path (reviewed in Garel & López-Bendito 2014), could be equally important. Moreover, the gene-expression patterns critical for selective axon branching and/or targeting during development may not persist into adulthood. In fact, there is recent evidence that projection neuronal cell groups from within a single transcriptomic cluster can be further separated based on their anatomical projections and connectivity patterns (Kim et al. 2020). These results indicate that connectivity is an important feature for cell-type identification in long-range projection neurons and that gene expression alone cannot be used to fully annotate cell types. To arrive at meaningful descriptions of TPN types, therefore, gene expression must be linked to structural and functional properties.

5. A Catalog of Top-Level TPN Cell Classes

Single-cell data regarding TPN morphologies and gene-expression profiles have increased rapidly in recent years but are still far from complete, even for rodent model species. For example, the number of morphologies is low overall and not yet available for some nuclei. Likewise, gene expression has been mostly analyzed on large-scale nucleus-level samples, and this has not been done for every thalamic nucleus. Thus, at present, TPN profiles can be defined with confidence only for high-level classes based on major, clear-cut differences.

Here I propose a tentative a catalog of such six top-level classes. It considers the architecture of the TPN axons as a primary axis of variation, as discussed in the previous sections (Table 1). Available data on somatodendritic morphology, synaptic properties, and molecular markers are also considered. There is a strong correlation between these high-level TPN profiles and cytoarchitectonic nuclei and/or functional systems, albeit not a simple or strict one. For example, a specific TPN profile predominates in each nucleus or nuclear subdivision; however, the same profile is often repeated in nuclei that receive very different inputs and are part of different functional systems. Besides, there is already conclusive evidence that, at least in some nuclei, such as in the Pf, cells of two different top level-classes are intermingled (Table 1, Figure 9).

This catalog is based on data from about 400 rat and mouse single-cell morphologies, both from peer-reviewed studies (Deschênes, Bourassa, Doan, et al. 1996; Deschênes, Bourassa, & Parent 1996; Deschênes et al. 1998; Kuramoto et al. 2009, 2015; Kuramoto, Pan, et al. 2017, Kuramoto, Iwai, et al. 2017; Ohno et al. 2012; Noseda et al. 2010; 2011; Nakamura et al. 2015; Unzai et al. 2017, Gheorghita et al. 2006; Phillips et al. 2019; Rodriguez-Moreno et al. 2020), available open-access online repositories (Mouselight Project at Janelia Research Campus, Winnubst et al. 2019; Allen Institute Mouse Connectivity Atlas; Oh et al. 2014), and unpublished material from our own. These data cover virtually all nuclei of the rodent thalamus, albeit with very variable saturation. For some nuclei for which single-cell morphologies are still scant or unavailable, information is derived from small-population tract-tracing studies with sensitive anterograde tracers (Van de Werf et al. 2002; Van Groen & Wyss 1995; Van Groen et al. 1999; Shibata 1993a, 1993b; Vertes et al. 2006; Vertes & Hoover 2008). It is thus reasonable to assume that the present classification may already capture the full gamut of TPN cell variation. Nevertheless, as higher numbers of single-cell morphologies and molecular profiles become available, new subclasses may be delineated within these top-level classes in the future.

The catalog provides a unified framework of cell classes in the lab rodent thalamus that are named and organized primarily around structural motifs but is also consistent with currently available data on development, gene expression, and synaptic and cell membrane properties, as reviewed in the previous sections of this chapter.

The various TPN classes combined in different patterns together constitute the "classic" large-scale thalamic output pathways, such as the thalamocortical, thalamostriatal, thalamoamygdaloid, and so forth. The signals conveyed through these pathways may thus be differently distributed, combined, and filtered according to the specific cell properties of the various TPN populations involved.

Table 1. A Catalog of Top-Level PTN Cell Classes Present in the Rodent (Rat/Mouse) Thalamus

Each cell class is identified by its axon wiring motif and linked to other traits such as somatodendritic morphology, membrane properties, and calcium-binding protein-expression patterns. For the latter, just the differential expression of five different proteins is indicated; they are chosen as an example because, historically, some of these (CB and PV) have been widely used as specific markers for thalamic cell types. Data given in brackets indicate features present only in cells of a particular nucleus within the class. CB: calbindin 28K; PV: parvalbumin; CR: calretinin; N-EFCaBP: N-terminal EF-hand calcium-binding protein (see also Figure 12); PH: parahippocampal areas. Names in *italics* indicate nuclei for which only population-level data are currently available on cell morphologies.

PROFILE	Main Varicose Axon Domain	Nuclei Where Prevalent	Shape	Membrane Properties	Ca2+ BP Expression	Subcortical Targets											Cortex Targets	
						TRN	SN	Sth	EP	GP	Sl-VP	Cd-Pu	Acd-TuO IPAC	CoA AoN BST LPO	Cla End	BLA End	No. of Areas/ Patterns	Main Layers
TC UNIFOCAL	Neocortex	VP, MGV, VL, DLG Sm(d)	Bushy	Fast firing Short-latency bursts	PV +++/0 Troponin++ +	+											1 Focal +++	4-3, 6
TC MULTIFOCAL	Neocortex [PH]	Po, MD, LP, *MGD*, *Sm(v)* [LD, AV, AD, AM]	Bushy	Reg. firing Long-latency bursts?	CB+ PV+ Troponin 1 + +	+						+/0 Spread				+	2–3 Variable +++	1, 3–5a [1,3 PH]
TC SUBPIAL	Neocortex [PH]	VA, VM, *MGM* [Re]	Bushy	Reg. firing Long-latency bursts?	CB +++ CR +++ [Re]	+						+/0 Spread					≥2 Spread +++	1 [1,3 PH]
TS ANTERIOR	Dorsal striatum	CL, Pc, CeM Rh; some Pf	Bushy	Reg. firing Long-latency bursts?	CB+ PV+ N-EFCaBP++	+						+++ Spread			+	+	≥2 Spread +++	3–5a
TS MIDLINE	Ventral striatum and TuO	PVA, pt, IMD Spf	Bushy	?	CR ++ CB+++ N-EFCaBP++	+	+	+	+		+	+ Spread	+++ Spread	++	+	++	+/0	6, 3, 1
TS POSTERIOR	Dorsal striatum and TuO	Pf, Eth, PoT, PiL	Reticular-like	Slow firing No/ weak bursts	CB++ CR +++	+	+	+	+	+	+	+++ Patchy			+	+	≥2 Spread +	6, 5b

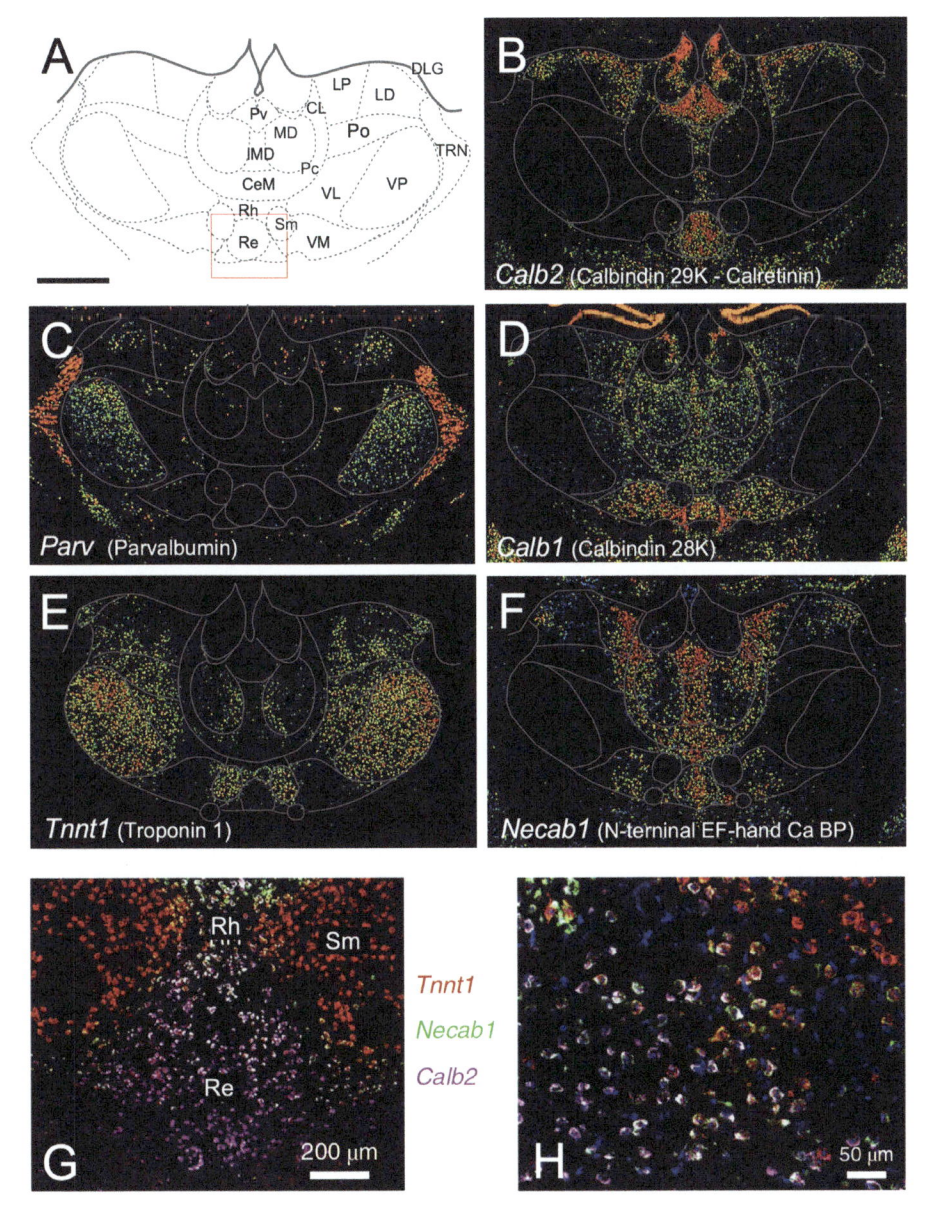

Figure 12 Combinatorial and heterogeneous expression of calcium-binding protein genes across the mouse thalamus.

A–F. Each panel shows, on a representative thalamus section of the same approximate coronal level, the normalized in situ hybridization signal for the gene coding for each calcium-binding protein. Each dot is a cell. Levels of messenger RNA (mRNA) hybridization are color-coded from high (*red*) to low (*blue*). Expression images taken from the Allen Institute Mouse Brain Mouse ISH Atlas (Experiments #71717640, #79556738, #79556672, #77280576, and #696671899).

G–H. Multiple fluorescence in situ hybridizations (FISH) against three of the aforementioned genes. A region of the ventral midline of the thalamus (inset in panel A) is illustrated in panel G, and a higher magnification detail is provided in panel H. Note that some cells simultaneously express more than one of the mRNAs tested (white signals), whereas others express only one. From Phillips et al. (2019).

Anatomy

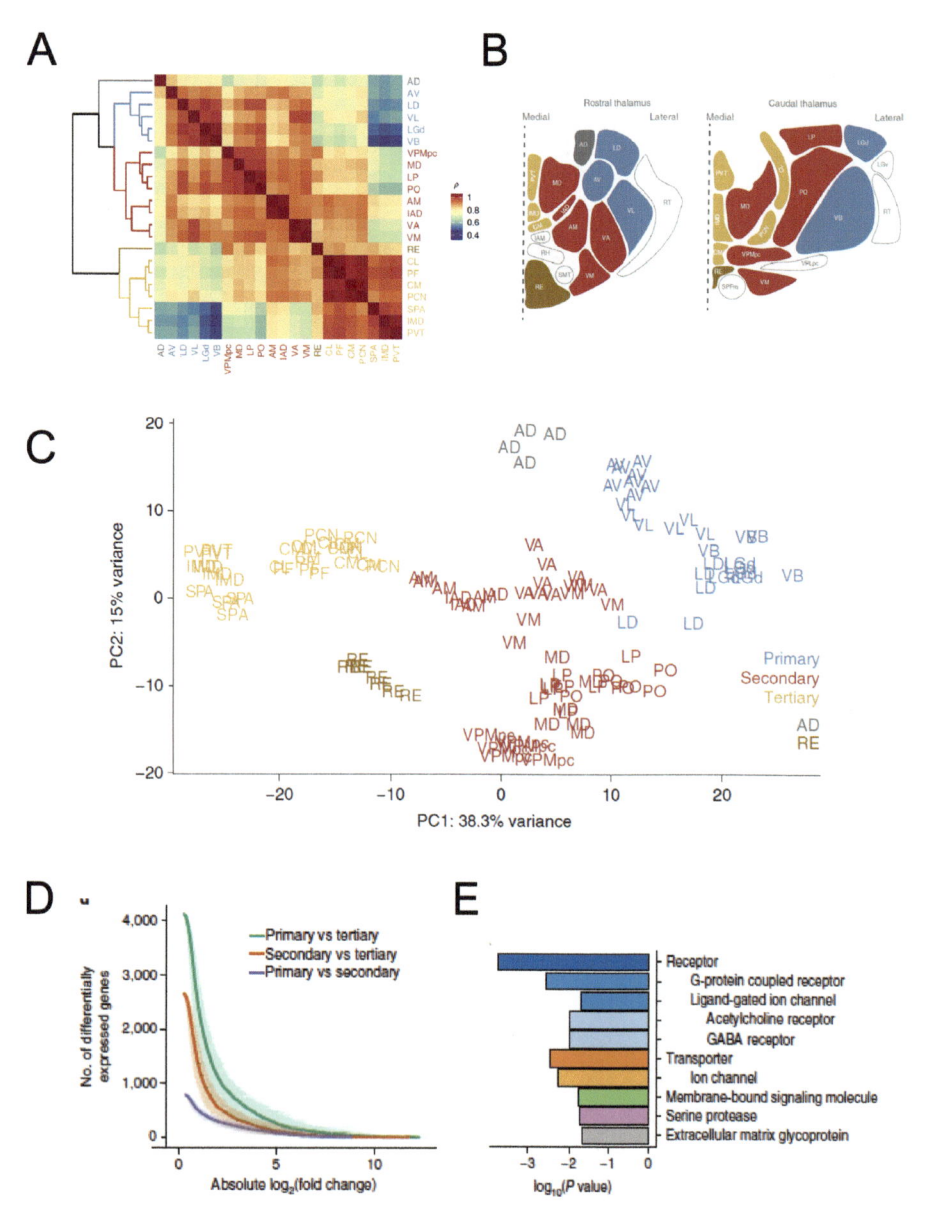

Figure 13 Unbiased clustering analysis reveals gene-expression differences conserved across different functional systems and nuclei.

A. Hierarchical clustering of thalamic nuclei using Spearman's correlation (ρ) of the top 500 most differentially expressed genes across all 22 nuclei (total n = 120 samples; using the mean of 3–8 replicates per nucleus). Major profiles were defined as the top five branches of the cluster dendrogram.

B. Topographical localization of gene-expression profiles in the thalamus.
Coronal thalamic section schematics with nuclei colored as in panel A. Unsampled nuclei are left uncolored.

C. Principal component (PC) analysis showing the separation of functional nuclear profiles in the first two PCs. The underlying gene set, sample set, and color scheme are the same as in panel B.

D. The differential gene-expression number is larger between primary and tertiary nuclei than between primary and secondary or secondary and tertiary nuclei. The plot shows the number of differentially expressed genes at each $\log^2$ (fold change) for the three comparison levels (shown as the mean ± SD of bootstrapped values).

E. Genes relevant to neurotransmission are overrepresented among genes with high PC1 loadings in the analyzed dataset. The 10 most highly overrepresented protein class terms are shown. P values are based on a two-sided Fisher's exact test for each term. Overrepresentation in the top 200 genes with the highest absolute PC1 loading was assessed. The background gene pool included all expressed genes (n = 16,538). Indentation indicates gene subfamily.

Acknowledgments

Supported by funding from the European Union's Horizon 2020 Research and Innovation Programme (Grant Agreement No. 945539 HBP SGA3), Spain's Ministerio de Ciencia, and Innovación y Universidades (PCI-111900-2 and 2019-PID2020-115780GB-I00).

List of Abbreviations

AD: Anterodorsal nucleus
AM: Anteromedial nucleus
AV: Anteroventral nucleus
CA1: Cornu ammonis sector 1 of the hippocampus
CeM: Central medial nucleus
CL: Central lateral nucleus

CM-Pf:	Centromedian-parafascicular nucleus	Re:	Reuniens nucleus
DLG:	Dorsal lateral geniculate nucleus	Rh:	Rhomboid nucleus
Eth:	Ethmoidal thalamic nucleus	Spf:	Subparafascicular nucleus
IMD:	Intermediodorsal nucleus	Sub:	Submedius nucleus
LD:	Laterodorsal nucleus	TC:	Thalamocortical
LP:	Lateral posterior (pulvinar) nucleus	TPN:	Thalamic projection neuron
MD:	Mediodorsal nucleus	TRN:	Prethalamic reticular nucleus
MD(l):	Lateral region of the mediodorsal nucleus	TS:	Thalamostriatal
MD(m):	Medial region of the mediodorsal nucleus	VA:	Ventral anterior nucleus
MGD:	Dorsal division of the medial geniculate complex	VL:	Ventral lateral nucleus
MGM:	Medial division of the medial geniculate complex	VM:	Ventromedial nucleus
MGV:	Ventral division of the medial geniculate complex	VM(m):	Medial region of the ventromedial nucleus
Pf:	Parafascicular nucleus	VM(l):	Lateral region of the ventromedial nucleus
PIL:	Posterior intralaminar nucleus	VP:	Ventroposterior nucleus
Po:	Posterior nucleus	VPL:	Ventroposterior lateral nucleus
PoT:	Triangular portion of the posterior nucleus	VPM:	Ventroposterior medial nucleus
PT:	Paratenial nucleus	VPMvl:	Ventrolateral region of the ventroposterior medial nucleus
PV:	Paraventricular nucleus	VPPc:	Parvocellular ventroposterior medial nucleus

References

Adams NC, Lozsádi, DA, Guillery RW. (1997) Complexities in the thalamocortical and corticothalamic pathways. Eur J Neurosci. 9:204–209.

Aguilar J, Morales-Botello ML, Foffani, G. (2008) Tactile responses of hindpaw, forepaw and whisker neurons in the thalamic ventrobasal complex of anesthetized rats. Eur J Neurosci. 27:378–387.

Arbuthnott GW, MacLeod NK, Maxwell DJ, Wright AK. (1990) Distribution and synaptic contacts of the cortical terminals arising from neurons in the rat ventromedial thalamic nucleus. Neuroscience. 38:47–60.

Asanuma C, Andersen RA, Cowan WM. (1985) The thalamic relations of the caudal inferior parietal lobule and the lateral prefrontal cortex in monkeys: divergent cortical projections from cell clusters in the medial pulvinar nucleus. J Comp Neurol. 241:357–381. doi: 10.1002/cne.902410309.

Avendaño C, Stepniewska I, Rausell E, Reinoso-Suárez F. (1990) Segregation and heterogeneity of thalamic cell populations projecting to superficial layers of posterior parietal cortex: a retrograde tracer study in cat and monkey. Neuroscience. 39:547–559.

Baimbridge KG, Celio MR, Rogers JH. (1992) Calcium-binding proteins in the nervous system. Trends Neurosci. 15:303–308. doi: 10.1016/0166-2236(92)90081-i.

Barroso-Chinea P, Castle M, Aymerich MS, Pérez-Manso M, Erro E, Tuñon T, Lanciego JL. (2007) Expression of the mRNAs encoding for the vesicular glutamate transporters 1 and 2 in the rat thalamus. J Comp Neurol. 501:703–715. doi: 10.1002/cne.21265.

Bartlett EL, Smith PH. (1999) Anatomic, intrinsic, and synaptic properties of dorsal and ventral division neurons in rat medial geniculate body. J Neurophysiol. 81:1999–2016. doi: 10.1152/jn.1999.81.5.1999.

Bartlett EL, Smith PH. (2002) Effects of paired-pulse and repetitive stimulation on neurons in the rat medial geniculate body. Neuroscience. 113:957–974. doi: 10.1016/s0306-4522(02)00240-3.

Beatty JA, Sylwestrak EL, Cox CL. (2009) Two distinct populations of projection neurons in the rat lateral parafascicular thalamic nucleus and their cholinergic responsiveness. Neuroscience. 162:155–173. doi: 10.1016/j.neuroscience.2009.04.043.

Bonnefond M, Kastner S, Jensen O. (2017) Communication between brain areas based on nested oscillations. eNeuro. Mar 27;4(2):ENEURO.0153-16.2017. doi: 10.1523/ENEURO.0153-16.2017.

Boyd JD, Matsubara JA. (1996) Laminar and columnar patterns of geniculocortical projections in the cat: relationship to cytochrome oxidase. J Comp Neurol. 365:659–682.

Carey RG, Fitzpatrick D, Diamond IT. (1979a) Thalamic projections to layer I of striate cortex shown by retrograde transport of horseradish peroxidase. Science. 203:556–559.

Carey RG, Fitzpatrick D, Diamond IT. (1979b) Layer I of striate cortex of *Tupaia glis* and *Galago senegalensis*: projections from thalamus and claustrum revealed by retrograde transport of horseradish peroxidase. J Comp Neurol. 186:393–437.

Carey RG, Neal TL. (1986) Reciprocal connections between the claustrum and visual thalamus in the tree shrew (*Tupaia glis*). Brain Res. 386:155–168.

Casas-Torremocha D, Porrero C, Rodriguez-Moreno J, García-Amado M, Lübke JHR, Núñez Á, Clascá F. (2019) Posterior thalamic nucleus axon terminals have different structure and functional impact in the motor and somatosensory vibrissal cortices. Brain Struct Funct. 224:1627–1645.

Castro-Alamancos MA, Connors BW. (1997) Thalamocortical synapses. Prog Neurobiol. 51(6):581–606. doi: 10.1016/s0301-0082(97)00002-6.

Catalano SM, Robertson RT, Killackey HP. (1996) Individual axon morphology and thalamocortical topography in developing rat somatosensory cortex. J Comp Neurol. 367:36–53. doi: 10.1002/(SICI)1096-9861(19960325)367:1<36::AID-CNE4>3.0.CO;2-K.

Clascá F, Porrero C, Galazo, M, Rubio-Garrido P, Evangelio M. (2016) Anatomy and development of multi-specific thalamocortical axons: implications for cortical dynamics and evolution. In KS Rockland (ed.), Axons and Brain Architecture. Amsterdam: Elsevier, pp. 69–92. doi: 10.1016/B978-0-12-801393-9.00004-9.

Clascá F, Rubio-Garrido P, Jabaudon D. (2012). Unveiling the diversity of thalamocortical neuron subtypes. Eur J Neurosci. 35:1524–1532.

Clerici WJ, McDonald AJ, Thompson R, Coleman JR. (1990) Anatomy of the rat medial geniculate body: II. Dendritic morphology. J Comp Neurol. 297:32–54.

Cruikshank SJ, Ahmed OJ, Stevens TR, Patrick SL, Gonzalez AN, Elmaleh M, Connors BW. (2012) Thalamic control of layer 1 circuits in prefrontal cortex. J Neurosci. 32:17813–17823. doi: 10.1523/JNEUROSCI.3231-12.2012.

Crunelli V, Leresche N, Parnavelas JG. (1987) Membrane properties of morphologically identified X and Y cells in the lateral geniculate nucleus of the cat in vitro. J Physiol. **390**:243–256. doi: 10.1113/jphysiol.1987.sp016697.

Crunelli V, Lorincz ML, Connelly WM, David F, Hughes SW, Lambert RC, Leresche N, Errington AC. (2018) Dual function of thalamic low-vigilance state oscillations: Rhythm-regulation and plasticity. Nat Rev Neurosci. **19**:107–118. doi: 10.1038/nrn.2017.151

Desai NV, Varela C. (2021) Distinct burst properties contribute to the functional diversity of thalamic nuclei. J Comp Neurol. **529**(17): 3726–3750.

Deschênes M, Bourassa J, Doan VD, Parent A. (1996) A single-cell study of the axonal projections arising from the posterior intralaminar thalamic nuclei in the rat. Eur J Neurosci. **8**:329–343.

Deschênes M, Bourassa J, Parent A. (1995) Two different types of thalamic fibers innervate the rat striatum. Brain Res. **701**:288–292.

Deschênes M, Bourassa J, Parent A. (1996) Striatal and cortical projections of single neurons from the central lateral thalamic nucleus in the rat. Neuroscience. **72**:679–687.

Deschênes M, Veinante P, Zhang ZW. (1998) The organization of corticothalamic projections: reciprocity versus parity. Brain Res Brain Res Rev. **28**:286–308. doi: 10.1016/s0165-0173(98)00017-4.

Donoghue JP, Ebner FF. (1981) The laminar distribution and ultrastructure of fibers projecting from three thalamic nuclei to the somatic sensory-motor cortex of the opossum. J Comp Neurol. **198**:389–420. doi: 10.1002/cne.901980303.

Doron NN, Ledoux JE. (2000) Cells in the posterior thalamus project to both amygdala and temporal cortex: a quantitative retrograde double-labeling study in the rat. J Comp Neurol. **425**:257–274.

Ellender TJ, Harwood J, Kosillo P, Capogna M, Bolam JP. (2013) Heterogeneous properties of central lateral and parafascicular thalamic synapses in the striatum. J Physiol. **591**:257–272. doi: 10.1113/jphysiol.2012.245233.

Erro M, Lanciego JL, Gimenez-Amaya JM. (2002) Re-examination of the thalamostriatal projections in the rat with retrograde tracers. Neurosci Res. **42**:45–55. doi: 10.1016/s0168-0102(01)00302-9.

Familtsev D, Quiggins R, Masterson SP, Dang W, Slusarczyk AS, Petry HM, Bickford ME. (2016) Ultrastructure of geniculocortical synaptic connections in the tree shrew striate cortex. J Comp Neurol. **524**:1292–1306. doi: 10.1002/cne.23907.

Ferster D, LeVay S. (1978) The axonal arborizations of lateral geniculate neurons in the striate cortex of the cat. J Comp Neurol. **182**:923–944. doi: 10.1002/cne.901820510.

Fiebelkorn IC, Pinsk MA, Kastner S. (2019) The mediodorsal pulvinar coordinates the macaque fronto-parietal network during rhythmic spatial attention. Nat Commun. **10**:215. doi: 10.1038/s41467-018-08151-4.

Fitzpatrick D, Itoh, K, Diamond IT. (1983) The laminar organization of the lateral geniculate body and the striate cortex in the squirrel monkey (*Saimiri sciureus*). J Neurosci. **3**:673–702.

Friedlander MJ, Lin CS, Stanford LR, Sherman SM. (1981) Morphology of functionally identified neurons in lateral geniculate nucleus of the cat. J Neurophysiol. **46**:80–129. doi: 10.1152/jn.1981.46.1.80.

Fujiyama F, Furuta T, Kaneko T. (2001) Immunocytochemical localization of candidates for vesicular glutamate transporters in the rat cerebral cortex. J Comp Neurol. **435**:379–387. doi: 10.1002/cne.1037.

Furuta T, Tomioka R, Taki K, Nakamura K, Tamamaki N, Kaneko T. (2001) In vivo transduction of central neurons using recombinant Sindbis virus: Golgi-like labeling of dendrites and axons with membrane-targeted fluorescent proteins. J Histochem Cytochem. **49**:1497–1508. doi: 10.1177/002215540104901203.

Galazo MJ, Martinez-Cerdeño V, Porrero C, Clascá F. (2008) Embryonic and postnatal development of the layer I-directed ("matrix") thalamocortical system in the rat. Cereb Cortex. **18**:344–363.

Garel S, López-Bendito G. (2014) Inputs from the thalamocortical system on axon pathfinding mechanisms. Curr Opin Neurobiol. **27**:143–150. doi: 10.1016/j.conb.2014.03.013.

Garraghty PE, Sur M. (1990) Morphology of single intracellularly stained axons terminating in area 3b of macaque monkeys. J Comp Neurol. **294**:583–593. doi: 10.1002/cne.902940406. PMID: 2341626.

Gheorghita F, Kraftsik R, Dubois R, Welker E. (2006) Structural basis for map formation in the thalamocortical pathway of the barrelless mouse. J Neurosci. **26**:10057–10067. doi: 10.1523/JNEUROSCI.1263-06.2006.

Graybiel AM, Berson DM. (1980) Histochemical identification and afferent connections of subdivisions in the lateralis posterior-pulvinar complex and related thalamic nuclei in the cat. Neuroscience. **5**:1175–1238. doi: 10.1016/0306-4522(80)90196-7.

Groh A, Bokor H, Mease RA, Plattner VM, Hangya B, Stroh A, Deschênes M, Acsády L. (2014) Convergence of cortical and sensory driver inputs on single thalamocortical cells. Cereb Cortex. **24**:3167–3179.

Guido W, Lu SM, Sherman SM. (1992) Relative contributions of burst and tonic responses to the receptive field properties of lateral geniculate neurons in the cat. J Neurophysiol. **68**, 2199–2211. doi:10.1152/jn.1992.68.6.2199.

Guido W, Weyand T. (1995) Burst responses in thalamic relay cells of the awake behaving cat. J Neurophysiol. **74**:1782–1786.

Guillery RW. (1966) A study of Golgi preparations from the dorsal lateral geniculate nucleus of the adult cat. J Comp Neurol. **128**:21–50. doi: 10.1002/cne.901280104.

Guillery RW. (1995) Anatomical evidence concerning the role of the thalamus in corticocortical communication: a brief review. J Anat. **187**:583–592.

Guillery RW, Sherman SM. (2002) Thalamic relay functions and their role in corticocortical communication: generalizations from the visual system. Neuron. **33**:163–175. doi: 10.1016/s0896-6273(01)00582-7.

Gutierrez C, Cox CL, Rinzel J, Sherman SM. (2001) Dynamics of low-threshold spike activation in relay neurons of the cat lateral geniculate nucleus. J Neurosci. **21**:1022–1032.

Harris JA, Mihalas S, Hirokawa KE, Whitesell JD, Choi H, Bernard A, Bohn P, Caldejon S, Casal L, Cho A, Feiner A, Feng D, Gaudreault N, Gerfen CR, Graddis N, Groblewski PA, Henry AM, Ho A, Howard R, Knox JE, Kuan L, Kuang X, Lecoq J, Lesnar P, Li Y, Luviano J, McConoughey S, Mortrud MT, Naeemi M, Ng L, Oh SW, Ouellette B, Shen E, Sorensen SA, Wakeman W, Wang Q, Wang Y, Williford A, Phillips JW, Jones AR, Koch C, Zeng H. (2019) Hierarchical organization of cortical and thalamic connectivity. Nature. **575**:195–202. doi: 10.1038/s41586-019-1716-z.

Hashikawa T, Rausell E, Molinari M, Jones EG. (1991) Parvalbumin- and calbindin-containing neurons in the monkey medial geniculate complex: differential distribution and cortical layer specific projections. Brain Res. **544**:335–341. doi: 10.1016/0006-8993(91)90076-8.

Hendry SH, Yoshioka T. (1994) A neurochemically distinct third channel in the macaque dorsal lateral geniculate nucleus. Science. 264:575–577.

Herkenham M. (1978) The connections of the nucleus reuniens thalami: evidence for a direct thalamo-hippocampal pathway in the rat. J Comp Neurol. 177:589–610.

Herkenham M. (1979) The afferent and efferent connections of the ventromedial thalamic nucleus in the rat. J Comp Neurol. 183:487–517.

Herkenham M. (1980) Laminar organization of thalamic projections to the rat neocortex. Science. 207:532–535.

Herkenham M. (1986) New perspectives on the organization and evolution of nonspecific thalamocortical projections. In EG Jones (ed.), Cerebral Cortex, Vol 5. New York: Plenum Press, 1985, pp. 403–445.

Houser CR, Vaughn JE, Barber RP, Roberts E. (1980) GABA neurons are the major cell type of the nucleus reticularis thalami. Brain Res. 200:341–354.

Huang CL, Winer JA. (2000) Auditory thalamocortical projections in the cat: laminar and areal patterns of input. J Comp Neurol. 427:302–331. doi: 10.1002/1096-9861(20001113)427:2<302::aid-cne10>3.0.co;2-j.

Huguenard JR. (1996) Low-threshold calcium currents in central nervous system neurons. Ann Rev Physiol. 58:329–348. doi:10.1146/annurev.ph.58.030196.001553

Humphrey AL, Sur M, Uhlrich DJ, Sherman SM. (1985) Termination patterns of individual X- and Y-cell axons in the visual cortex of the cat: projections to area 18, to the 17/18 border region, and to both areas 17 and 18. J Comp Neurol. 233:190–212. doi: 10.1002/cne.902330204.

Jager P, Moore G, Calpin P, Durmishi X, Salgarella I, Menage L, Kita Y, Wang Y, Kim DW, Blackshaw S, Schultz SR, Brickley S, Shimogori T, Delogu A. (2021) Dual midbrain and forebrain origins of thalamic inhibitory interneurons. eLife. Feb 1;10:e59272. doi: 10.7554/eLife.59272.

Jahnsen H, Llinás R. (1984a) Electrophysiological properties of guinea-pig thalamic neurones: an in vitro study. J Physiol. 349:205–226. doi: 10.1113/jphysiol.1984.sp015153.

Jahnsen H, Llinás R. (1984b) Voltage-dependent burst-to-tonic switching of thalamic cell activity: An in vitro study. Arch Ital Biol. 122:73–82.

Jaramillo J, Mejias, JF, Wang, X-J. (2019) Engagement of pulvinocortical feedforward and feedback pathways in cognitive computations. Neuron. 101:321–336. doi: 10.1016/j.neuron.2018.11.023.

Jhangiani-Jashanmal IT, Yamamoto R, Gungor NZ, Paré D. (2016) Electroresponsive properties of rat central medial thalamic neurons. J Neurophysiol. 115:1533–1541. doi: 10.1152/jn.00982.2015.

Jones EG. (1998) Viewpoint: the core and matrix of thalamic organization. Neuroscience. 85:331–345.

Jones EG. (2001) The thalamic matrix and thalamocortical synchrony. Trends Neurosci. 24, 595–601.

Jones EG. (2007a) Thalamic neurons, synaptic organization, and functional properties. In The Thalamus, 2nd ed., Vol. 1. Cambridge: Cambridge University Press, Ch. 4, pp. 171–317.

Jones EG. (2007b) The chemistry of the thalamus. In The Thalamus, 2nd ed., Vol. 1. Cambridge: Cambridge University Press, Ch. 5, pp. 318–478.

Jones EG, Burton H. (1976) Areal differences in the laminar distribution of thalamic afferents in cortical fields of the insular, parietal and temporal regions of primates. J Comp Neurol. 168: 197–247.

Jones EG, Leavitt RY. (1974) Retrograde axonal transport and the demonstration of non-specific projections to the cerebral cortex and striatum from thalamic intralaminar nuclei in the rat, cat and monkey. J Comp Neurol. 154:349–377. doi: 10.1002/cne.901540402.

Kageyama GH, Wong-Riley MT. (1984) The histochemical localization of cytochrome oxidase in the retina and lateral geniculate nucleus of the ferret, cat, and monkey, with particular reference to retinal mosaics and ON/OFF-center visual channels. J Neurosci. 4:2445–2459. doi: 10.1523/JNEUROSCI.04-10-02445.1984.

Kaufman EF, Rosenquist AC. (1985) Efferent projections of the thalamic intralaminar nuclei in the cat. Brain Res. 335, 257–279.

Kerschensteiner D, Guido W. (2017) Organization of the dorsal lateral geniculate nucleus in the mouse. Vis Neurosci. Jan;34: E008. doi: 10.1017/S0952523817000062.

Killackey H, Ebner F. (1972) Two different types of thalamocortical projections to a single cortical area in mammals. Brain Behav Evol. 6:141–69.

Killackey H, Ebner F. (1973) Convergent projection of three separate thalamic nuclei on to a single cortical area. Science. 179, 283–285.

Kim EJ, Zhang Z, Huang L, Ito-Cole T, Jacobs MW, Juavinett AL, Senturk G, Hu M, Ku M, Ecker JR, Callaway EM. (2020) Extraction of distinct neuronal cell types from within a genetically continuous population. Neuron. 107:274–282. doi: 10.1016/j.neuron.2020.04.018.

Kirouac GJ. (2015) Placing the paraventricular nucleus of the thalamus within the brain circuits that control behavior. Neurosci Biobehav Rev. 56:315–329. doi: 10.1016/j.neubiorev.2015.08.005.

Kuramoto E, Furuta T, Nakamura KC, Unzai T, Hioki H, Kaneko T. (2009) Two types of thalamocortical projections from the motor thalamic nuclei of the rat: a single neuron-tracing study using viral vectors. Cereb Cortex. 19:2065–2077.

Kuramoto E, Iwai H, Yamanaka A, Ohno S, Seki H, Tanaka YR, Furuta T, Hioki H, Goto T. (2017) Dorsal and ventral parts of thalamic nucleus submedius project to different areas of rat orbitofrontal cortex: A single neuron-tracing study using virus vectors. J Comp Neurol. 525:3821–3839. doi: 10.1002/cne.24306. Epub 2017.

Kuramoto E, Ohno S, Furuta T, Unzai T, Tanaka YR, Hioki H, Kaneko, T. (2015) Ventral medial nucleus neurons send thalamocortical afferents more widely and more preferentially to layer 1 than neurons of the ventral anterior–ventral lateral nuclear complex in the rat. Cereb Cortex. 25:221–235.

Kuramoto E, Pan S, Furuta T, Tanaka YR, Iwai H, Yamanaka A, Ohno S, Kaneko T, Goto T, Hioki H. (2017) Individual mediodorsal thalamic neurons project to multiple areas of the rat prefrontal cortex: a single neuron-tracing study using virus vectors. J Comp Neurol. 525:166–185. doi: 10.1002/cne.24054.

Lacey CJ, Bolam JP, Magill PJ. (2007) Novel and distinct operational principles of intralaminar thalamic neurons and their striatal projections. J Neurosci. 27:4374–4384. doi: 10.1523/JNEUROSCI.5519-06.2007.

Lanciego JL, Gonzalo N, Castle M, Sanchez-Escobar C, Aymerich MS, Obeso JA. (2004) Thalamic innervation of striatal and subthalamic neurons projecting to the rat entopeduncular nucleus. Eur J Neurosci. 19:1267–1277. doi: 10.1111/j.1460-9568.2004.03244.x.

Land PW, Simons DJ. (1985) Metabolic and structural correlates of the vibrissae representation in the thalamus of the adult rat. Neurosci Lett. 60:319–324. doi: 10.1016/0304-3940(85)90597-x.

Landisman CE, Connors BW. (2007) VPM and PoM nuclei of the rat somatosensory thalamus: Intrinsic neuronal properties and corticothalamic feedback. Cereb Cortex.

17:2853–2865. https://doi.org/10.1093/cercor/bhm025

Leresche N, Lightowler S, Soltesz I, Jassik-Gerschenfeld D, Crunelli V. (1991) Low-frequency oscillatory activities intrinsic to rat and cat thalamocortical cells. J Physiol. 441:155–174.

LeVay S, Gilbert CD. (1976) Laminar patterns of geniculocortical projection in the cat. Brain Res. 113:1–19.

Leventhal AG. (1979) Evidence that the different classes of relay cells of the cat's lateral geniculate nucleus terminate in different layers of the striate cortex. Exp Brain Res. 37:349–372. doi: 10.1007/BF00237719.

Li J, Bickford ME, Guido W. (2003) Distinct firing properties of higher order thalamic relay neurons. J Neurophysiol. 90:291–299. doi: 10.1152/jn.01163.2002

Li Y, Lopez-Huerta VG, Adiconis X, Levandowski K, Choi S, Simmons SK, Arias-Garcia MA, Guo B, Yao AY, Blosser TR, Wimmer RD, Aida T, Atamian A, Naik T, Sun X, Bi D, Malhotra D, Hession CC, Shema R, Gomes M, Li T, Hwang E, Krol A, Kowalczyk M, Peça J, Pan G, Halassa MM, Levin JZ, Fu Z, Feng G. (2020) Distinct subnetworks of the thalamic reticular nucleus. Nature. 583:819–824. doi: 10.1038/s41586-020-2504-5.

Llinás R, Jahnsen H. (1982) Electrophysiology of mammalian thalamic neurones in vitro. Nature. 297:406–408. doi: 10.1038/297406a0.

Llinás RR Steriade M. (2006) Bursting of thalamic neurons and states of vigilance. J Neurophysiol. 95:3297–3308. doi:10.1152/jn.00166.2006.

López-Bendito G, Cautinat A, Sánchez JA, Bielle F, Flames N, Garratt AN, Talmage DA, Role LW, Charnay P, Marín O, Garel S. (2006) Tangential neuronal migration controls axon guidance: a role for neuregulin-1 in thalamocortical axon navigation. Cell. 125:127–142. doi: 10.1016/j.cell.2006.01.042.

López-Bendito G, Molnar, Z. (2003) Thalamocortical development: how are we going to get there? Nat Rev Neurosci. 4:276–289. doi:10.1038/nrn1075.

Lorente de No R. (1938) Cerebral cortex: architecture, intracortical connections, motor projections. In J Fulton (ed.), Physiology of the nervous system. London: Oxford University Press. pp. 291–340.

Lund JS. (1988) Anatomical organization of macaque monkey striate visual cortex. Annu Rev Neurosci. 11:253–288. doi: 10.1146/annurev.ne.11.030188.001345.

Macchi G, Bentivoglio M, Minciacchi D, Molinari M. (1996) Trends in the anatomical organization and functional significance of the mammalian thalamus. Ital J Neurol Sci. 17:105–129. doi: 10.1007/BF02000842.

Macchi G, Bentivoglio M, Molinari M, Minciacchi D. (1984) The thalamo-caudate versus thalamo-cortical projections as studied in the cat with fluorescent retrograde double labeling. Exp Brain Res. 54:225–239. doi: 10.1007/BF00236222.

Mandelbaum G, Taranda J, Haynes TM, Hochbaum DR, Huang KW, Hyun M, Umadevi Venkataraju K, Straub C, Wang W, Robertson K, Osten P, Sabatini BL. (2019) Distinct cortical-thalamic-striatal circuits through the parafascicular nucleus. Neuron. 102:636–652. doi: 10.1016/j.neuron.2019.02.035.

Martini FJ, Guillamón-Vivancos T, Moreno-Juan V, Valdeolmillos M, López-Bendito G. (2021) Spontaneous activity in developing thalamic and cortical sensory networks. Neuron. 109:2519–2534. doi: 10.1016/j.neuron.2021.06.026.

Minciacchi D, Bentivoglio M, Molinari M, Kultas-Ilinsky K, Ilinsky IA, Macchi G. (1986) Multiple cortical targets of one thalamic nucleus: the projections of the ventral medial nucleus in the cat studied with retrograde tracers. J Comp Neurol. 252:106–129.

Mitani A, Itoh K, Mizuno N. (1987) Distribution and size of thalamic neurons projecting to layer I of the auditory cortical fields of the cat compared to those projecting to layer IV. J Comp Neurol. 257:105–121.

Molnár Z, Garel S, López-Bendito G, Maness P, Price DJ. (2012) Mechanisms controlling the guidance of thalamocortical axons through the embryonic forebrain. Eur J Neurosci. 35:1573–1585. doi: 10.1111/j.1460-9568.2012.08119.x

Monckton JE, McCormick DA. (2002) Neuromodulatory role of serotonin in the ferret thalamus. J Neurophysiol. 87:2124–2136. doi: 10.1152/jn.00650.2001.

Morest DK. (1964) The neuronal architecture of the medial geniculate body of the cat. J Anat. 98:611–630. PMID: 14229992.

Murray KD, Choudary, PV, Jones EG. (2007) Nucleus- and cell-specific gene expression in monkey thalamus. Proc Natl Acad Sci USA. 104:1989–1994.

Nagalski A, Puelles L, Dabrowski M, Wegierski T, Kuznicki J, Wisniewska MB. (2016) Molecular anatomy of the thalamic complex and the underlying transcription factors. Brain Struct Funct. 221:2493–2510. doi: 10.1007/s00429-015-1052-5.

Nakagawa Y. (2019) Development of the thalamus: From early patterning to regulation of cortical functions. Wiley Interdiscip Rev Dev Biol. Sep;8(5):e345. doi: 10.1002/wdev.345.

Nakamura H, Hioki H, Furuta T, Kaneko T. (2015) Different cortical projections from three subdivisions of the rat lateral posterior thalamic nucleus: a single-neuron tracing study with viral vectors. Eur J Neurosci. 41:1294–1310.

Nakamura KC, Sharott A, Magill PJ. (2014) Temporal coupling with cortex distinguishes spontaneous neuronal activities in identified basal ganglia-recipient and cerebellar-recipient zones of the motor thalamus. Cereb Cortex. 24:81–97. doi: 10.1093/cercor/bhs287.

Namura S, Takada M, Kikuchi H, Mizuno N. (1997) Collateral projections of single neurons in the posterior thalamic region to both the temporal cortex and the amygdala: a fluorescent retrograde double-labeling study in the rat. J Comp Neurol. 384:59–70.

Noseda R, Jakubowski M, Kainz V, Borsook D, Burstein R. (2011) Cortical projections of functionally identified thalamic trigeminovascular neurons: implications for migraine headache and its associated symptoms. J. Neurosci. 31:14204–14217.

Noseda R, Kainz V, Jakubowski M, Gooley JJ, Saper CB, Digre K, Burstein R. (2010) A neural mechanism for exacerbation of headache by light. Nat. Neurosci. 13:239–245. doi: 10.1038/nn.2475. Epub 2010 Jan 10.

Nuñez A, Amzica F, Steriade M. (1992) Intrinsic and synaptically generated delta (1–4 Hz) rhythms in dorsal lateral geniculate neurons and their modulation by light-induced fast (30–70 Hz) events. Neuroscience. 51:269–284.

Oberlaender M, Ramirez A, Bruno RM. (2012) Sensory experience restructures thalamocortical axons during adulthood. Neuron. 74, 648–655.

Oh SW, Harris JA, Ng L, Winslow B, Cain N, Mihalas S, Wang Q, Lau C, Kuan L, Henry AM, Mortrud MT, Ouellette B, Nguyen TN, Sorensen SA, Slaughterbeck CR, Wakeman W, Li Y, Feng D, Ho A, Nicholas E, Hirokawa KE, Bohn P, Joines KM, Peng H, Hawrylycz MJ, Phillips JW, Hohmann JG, Wohnoutka P, Gerfen CR, Koch C, Bernard A, Dang C, Jones AR, Zeng H. (2014) A mesoscale connectome of the mouse brain. Nature. 508:207–214. doi: 10.1038/nature13186.

Ohno S, Kuramoto, E, Furuta T, Hioki H, Tanaka YR, Fujiyama F, Sonomura T, Uemura M, Sugiyama K, Kaneko T. (2012) A morphological analysis of thalamocortical axon fibers of rat posterior thalamic nuclei: a single neuron tracing study with viral vectors. Cereb Cortex. **22**: 2840–2857.

Parent M, Parent A. (2005) Single-axon tracing and three-dimensional reconstruction of centre median-parafascicular thalamic neurons in primates. J Comp Neurol. **481**:127–144. doi: 10.1002/cne.20348.

Pedroarena, C. Llinás, R. (1997) Dendritic calcium conductances generate high-frequency oscillation in thalamocortical neurons. Proc Natl Acad Sci USA. **94**:724–728.

Penny GR, Itoh K, Diamond IT. (1982) Cells of different sizes in the ventral nuclei project to different layers of the somatic cortex in the cat. Brain Res. **242**:55–65. doi: 10.1016/0006-8993(82)90495-4.

Perez-Reyes E. (2003) Molecular physiology of low-voltage-activated t-type calcium channels. Physiol Rev. **83**:117–161. doi: 10.1152/physrev.00018.2002.

Phillips JW, Schulmann A, Hara E, Winnubst J, Liu C, Valakh V, Wang L, Shields BC, Korff W, Chandrashekar J, Lemire AL, Mensh B, Dudman JT, Nelson SB, Hantman AW. (2019) A repeated molecular architecture across thalamic pathways. Nat Neurosci. **22**:1925–1935. doi: 10.1038/s41593-019-0483-3.

Pinault, D. (1996) A novel single-cell staining procedure performed in vivo under electrophysiological control: morpho-functional features of juxtacellularly labeled thalamic cells and other central neurons with biocytin or Neurobiotin. J Neurosci Meth. **65**:113–136.

Puelles L, Rubenstein JL. (2003) Forebrain gene expression domains and the evolving prosomeric model. Trends Neurosci. **26**:469–476.

Ramón y Cajal S (1904) *Textura del Sistema Nervioso del Hombre y de los Vertebrados. II Parte.*, Vol. 2. Madrid: Imprenta Nicolás Moya.

Rausell E, Avendaño C. (1985) Thalamocortical neurons projecting to superficial and to deep layers in parietal, frontal and prefrontal regions in the cat. Brain Res. **347**:159–165.

Rausell E, Bae CS, Viñuela A, Huntley GW, Jones EG. (1992) Calbindin and parvalbumin cells in monkey VPL thalamic nucleus: distribution, laminar cortical projections, and relations to spinothalamic terminations. J Neurosci. **12**:4088–4111.

Rausell E, Jones EG. (1991) Histochemical and immunocytochemical compartments of the thalamic VPM nucleus in monkeys and their relationship to the representational map. J Neurosci. **11**:210–225. doi: 10.1523/JNEUROSCI.11-01-00210.1991.

Real MA, Dávila JC, Guirado S. (2006) Immunohistochemical localization of the vesicular glutamate transporter VGLUT2 in the developing and adult mouse claustrum. J Chem Neuroanat. **31**:169–177.

Reinagel P, Godwin D, Sherman SM, Koch C. (1999) Encoding of visual information by LGN bursts. J Neurophysiol. **81**:2558–2569. doi: 10.1152/jn.1999.81.5.2558

Ren S, Wang Y, Yue F, Cheng X, Dang R, Qiao Q, Sun X, Li X, Jiang Q, Yao J, Qin H, Wang G, Liao X, Gao D, Xia J, Zhang J, Hu B, Yan J, Wang Y, Xu M, Han Y, Tang X, Chen X, He C, Hu Z. (2018) The paraventricular thalamus is a critical thalamic area for wakefulness. Science. **362**:429–434. doi: 10.1126/science.aat2512.

Rodriguez-Moreno J, Porrero C, Rollenhagen A, Rubio-Teves M, Casas-Torremocha D, Alonso-Nanclares L, Yakoubi R, Santuy A, Merchan-Pérez A, DeFelipe J, Lübke JHR, Clascá F. (2020) Area-specific synapse structure in branched posterior nucleus axons reveals a new level of complexity in thalamocortical networks. J Neurosci. **40**:2663–2679. doi: 10.1523/JNEUROSCI.2886-19.2020.

Rodriguez-Moreno J, Rollenhagen A, Arlandis J, Santuy A, Merchan-Pérez A, DeFelipe J, Lübke JHR, Clascá F. (2018) Quantitative 3D ultrastructure of thalamocortical synapses from the "lemniscal" ventral posteromedial nucleus in mouse barrel cortex. Cereb Cortex. **28**:3159–3175. doi: 10.1093/cercor/bhx187.

Rubio-Garrido P, Pérez-de-Manzo F, Porrero C, Galazo MJ, Clascá F. (2009) Thalamic input to distal apical dendrites in neocortical layer 1 is massive and highly convergent. Cereb Cortex. **19**:2380–2395. doi: 10.1093/cercor/bhn259.

Sampathkumar V, Miller-Hansen A, Sherman SM, Kasthuri N. (2021) Integration of signals from different cortical areas in higher order thalamic neurons. Proc Natl Acad Sci USA. **118**(30):e2104137118. doi: 10.1073/pnas.2104137118.

Scheibel ME, Scheibel AB. (1966) The organization of the ventral anterior nucleus of the thalamus. A Golgi study. Brain Res. **1**:250–268. doi: 10.1016/0006-8993(66)90091-6.

Sherman SM. (2001a) A wake-up call from the thalamus. Nat Neurosci. **4**:344–346. doi: 10.1038/85973.

Sherman SM. (2001b) Tonic and burst firing: dual modes of thalamocortical relay. Trends Neurosci. **24**:122–126. doi: 10.1016/s0166-2236(00)01714-8.

Sheroziya M, Timofeev I. (2014) Global intracellular slow-wave dynamics of the thalamocortical system. J Neurosci. **34**:8875–8893. doi: 10.1523/JNEUROSCI.4460-13.2014.

Shi W, Xianyu A, Han Z, Tang X, Li Z, Zhong H, Mao T, Huang K, Shi SH. (2017) Ontogenetic establishment of order-specific nuclear organization in the mammalian thalamus. Nat Neurosci. **20**:516–528. doi: 10.1038/nn.4519.

Shibata H. (1993a) Direct projections from the anterior thalamic nuclei to the retrohippocampal region in the rat. J Comp Neurol. **337**:431–445. doi: 10.1002/cne.903370307.

Shibata H. (1993b) Efferent projections from the anterior thalamic nuclei to the cingulate cortex in the rat. J Comp Neurol. **330**:533–542. doi: 10.1002/cne.903300409.

Slézia A, Hangya B, Ulbert I, Acsády L. (2011) Phase advancement and nucleus-specific timing of thalamocortical activity during slow cortical oscillation. J Neurosci. **31**:607–617. doi: 10.1523/JNEUROSCI.3375-10.2011.

Smith PH, Bartlett EL, Kowalkowski A. (2006) Unique combination of anatomy and physiology in cells of the rat paralaminar thalamic nuclei adjacent to the medial geniculate body. J Comp Neurol. **496**:314–334. doi: 10.1002/cne.20913.

Smith Y, Galvan A, Ellender TJ, Doig N, Villalba RM, Huerta-Ocampo I, Wichmann T, Bolam JP. (2014) The thalamostriatal system in normal and diseased states. Front Syst Neurosci. Jan 30;**8**:5. doi: 10.3389/fnsys.2014.00005.

Stanford LR, Friedlander MJ, Sherman SM. (1983) Morphological and physiological properties of geniculate W-cells of the cat: a comparison with X- and Y-cells. J Neurophysiol. **50**:582–608. doi: 10.1152/jn.1983.50.3.582.

Swadlow HA, Gusev AG. (2001) The impact of "bursting" thalamic impulses at a neocortical synapse. Nat Neurosci. **4**:402–408. doi: 10.1038/86054.

Turner JP, Anderson CM, Williams SR, Crunelli V. (1997) Morphology and membrane properties of neurones in the cat ventrobasal thalamus in vitro. J Physiol. **505**:707–726.

Turner JP, Leresche N, Guyon A, Soltesz I, Crunelli V. (1994) Sensory input and burst firing output of rat and cat thalamocortical cells: the role of NMDA and non-NMDA receptors. J Physiol. 480:281–295.

Unzai T, Kuramoto E, Kaneko T, Fujiyama F. (2017) Quantitative analyses of the projection of individual neurons from the midline thalamic nuclei to the striosome and matrix compartments of the rat striatum. Cereb Cortex. 27:1164–1181. doi: 10.1093/cercor/bhv295.

Van der Werf YD, Witter MP, Groenewegen HJ. (2002) The intralaminar and midline nuclei of the thalamus. Anatomical and functional evidence for participation in processes of arousal and awareness. Brain Res Brain Res Rev. 39:107–140. doi: 10.1016/s0165-0173(02)00181-9.

Van Groen T, Kadish I, Wyss JM. (1999) Efferent connections of the anteromedial nucleus of the thalamus of the rat. Brain Res Brain Res Rev. 30:1–26. doi: 10.1016/s0165-0173(99)00006-5.

Van Groen T, Wyss JM. (1995) Projections from the anterodorsal and anteroventral nucleus of the thalamus to the limbic cortex in the rat. J Comp Neurol. 358:584–604. doi: 10.1002/cne.903580411.

Vanderhaeghen P, Polleux F. (2004) Developmental mechanisms patterning thalamocortical projections: intrinsic, extrinsic and in between. Trends Neurosci. 27:384–391.

Varela C, Sherman SM. (2009) Differences in response to serotonergic activation between first and higher order thalamic nuclei. Cereb Cortex. 19:1776–1786. doi: 10.1093/cercor/bhn208.

Vertes RP, Hoover WB. (2008) Projections of the paraventricular and paratenial nuclei of the dorsal midline thalamus in the rat. J Comp Neurol. 508:212–237. doi: 10.1002/cne.21679.

Vertes RP, Hoover WB, Do Valle AC, Sherman A, Rodriguez JJ. (2006) Efferent projections of reuniens and rhomboid nuclei of the thalamus in the rat. J Comp Neurol. 499:768–96. doi: 10.1002/cne.21135.

Vertes RP, Hoover WB, Rodriguez JJ. (2012) Projections of the central medial nucleus of the thalamus in the rat: node in cortical, striatal and limbic forebrain circuitry. Neuroscience. 219:120–136. doi: 10.1016/j.neuroscience.2012.04.067.

Vue TY, Aaker J, Taniguchi A, Kazemzadeh C, Skidmore JM, Martin DM, Martin JF, Treier M, Nakagawa Y. (2007) Characterization of progenitor domains in the developing mouse thalamus. J Comp Neurol. 505:73–91. doi: 10.1002/cne.21467.

Wang Q, Ding SL, Li Y, Royall J, Feng D, Lesnar P, Graddis N, Naeemi M, Facer B, Ho A, Dolbeare T, Blanchard B, Dee N, Wakeman W, Hirokawa KE, Szafer A, Sunkin SM, Oh SW, Bernard A, Phillips JW, Hawrylycz M, Koch C, Zeng H, Harris JA, Ng L. (2020) The Allen mouse brain common coordinate framework: A 3D reference atlas. Cell. 181:936–953.e20. doi: 10.1016/j.cell.2020.04.007.

Wang X, Wei Y, Vaingankar V, Wang Q, Koepsell K, Sommer FT, Hirsch JA. (2007) Feedforward excitation and inhibition evoke dual modes of firing in the cat's visual thalamus during naturalistic viewing. Neuron. 55:465–478. doi: 10.1016/j.neuron.2007.06.039.

Wei H, Bonjean M, Petry HM, Sejnowski, TJ, Bickford, ME. (2011) Thalamic burst firing propensity: A comparison of the dorsal lateral geniculate and pulvinar nuclei in the tree shrew. J Neurosci. 31:17287–17299. doi: 10.1523/JNEUROSCI.6431-10.2011

Whitmire CJ., Waiblinger C, Schwarz C, Stanley GB. (2016) Information coding through adaptive gating of synchronized thalamic bursting. Cell Rep. 14:795–807. doi: 10.1016/j.celrep.2015.12.068.

Winnubst J, Bas E, Ferreira TA, Wu Z, Economo MN, Edson P, Arthur BJ, Bruns C, Rokicki K, Schauder D, Olbris DJ, Murphy SD, Ackerman DG, Arshadi C, Baldwin P, Blake R, Elsayed A, Hasan M, Ramirez D, Dos Santos B, Weldon M, Zafar A, Dudman JT, Gerfen CR, Hantman AW, Korff W, Sternson SM, Spruston N, Svoboda K, Chandrashekar J. (2019) Reconstruction of 1,000 projection neurons reveals new cell types and organization of long-range connectivity in the mouse brain. Cell. 179:268–281. doi: 10.1016/j.cell.2019.07.042.

Winnubst J, Spruston N, Harris JA. (2020) Linking axon morphology to gene expression: a strategy for neuronal cell-type classification. Curr Opin Neurobiol. 65:70–76. doi: 10.1016/j.conb.2020.10.006.

Wong SZH, Scott EP, Mu W, Guo X, Borgenheimer E, Freeman M, Ming G, Wu QF, Song H, Nakagawa Y. (2018) In vivo clonal analysis reveals spatiotemporal regulation of thalamic nucleogenesis. PLoS Biol. 16(4):e2005211. doi: 10.1371/journal.pbio.2005211.

Wouterlood FG, Saldana E, Witter MP. (1990) Projection from the nucleus reuniens thalami to the hippocampal region: light and electron microscopic tracing study in the rat with the anterograde tracer phaseolus vulgaris-leucoagglutinin. J Comp Neurol. 296:179–203. doi: 10.1002/cne.

Yasui Y, Itoh K, Sugimoto T, Kaneko T, Mizuno N. (1987) Thalamocortical and thalamo-amygdaloid projections from the parvicellular division of the posteromedial ventral nucleus in the cat. J Comp Neurol. 257:253–268. doi: 10.1002/cne.902570210.

Yen CT, Conley M, Jones EG. (1985) Morphological and functional types of neurons in cat ventral posterior thalamic nucleus. J Neurosci. 5:1316–1338.

Chapter 4

Thalamocortical Circuitry Matters

S. Murray Sherman

Introduction

Until fairly recently, the thalamus was written off as merely a machine-like relay of peripheral information to the cortex. That is how textbooks still generally depict the thalamus, if they do so at all. However, work in the past few decades has made clear that the thalamus has complex intrinsic circuitry and connections with the cortex that belie any such simple function. Indeed, we now appreciate that the thalamus plays a major role in cortical functioning beyond the relay of peripheral information to the cortex. In this account, I start with an overview of thalamic circuitry. I then move on to details of thalamocortical and corticothalamic organization, starting with a cataloguing of synaptic types involved in this circuitry and finishing with speculations about what some of these details mean writ large. I will try to separate actual experimental data from speculation and hypothesis.

Overview of Thalamic Circuitry: The Cat's Lateral Geniculate Nucleus

The best-studied model of the functional circuitry of the thalamus remains the cat's lateral geniculate nucleus. Unfortunately, work on this nucleus has come to a virtual stop, with very few laboratories continuing to study the cat brain, and so we have not much advanced our knowledge of thalamic circuitry in the past decade or so. Relevant work today centers on the use of mice or monkeys, and it will be some time before the study of the thalamus in these species catches up to the knowledge base amassed for the cat.

The schema of Figure 1A shows the main inputs to geniculate relay cells, with some pathways omitted for simplicity. To a first approximation, the circuitry shown here is conserved for the thalamus across nuclei and mammalian species, with the exception that for different nuclei, the retinal input would be replaced by a different information source to be relayed. Thus, for the ventral posterior nucleus, which relays somatosensory information, retinal input would be replaced by input from the medial lemniscus; for the medial geniculate nucleus, the input would be from the inferior colliculus; and so forth. Some exceptions to this general plan of thalamic circuitry are considered later in the chapter, and further details of thalamic circuitry can be found in Sherman and Guillery (1996, 2013).

Inputs to Geniculate Relay Cells

Although textbook accounts often mention only retinal inputs to geniculate relay cells, there are a number of other inputs. These include local inputs from interneurons and thalamic reticular cells, layer 6 of the visual cortex, and the brainstem, mostly from a midbrain area known as the *brainstem reticular formation*.[1] The left key in Figure 1A shows the neurotransmitters involved: glutamate by retinal and cortical input, γ-aminobutyric acid (GABA) by the interneurons and reticular cells, and mostly acetylcholine (ACh) by brainstem input. Note that the local GABAergic inputs are also innervated by the same cortical and brainstem sources that innervate relay cells. Thus, these extrinsic inputs can affect relay cells directly or indirectly via local GABAergic circuitry.

Postsynaptic Receptors on Relay Cells

All of the synapses onto relay cells shown in Figure 1A are standard chemical synapses. This means that they affect relay cells by releasing neurotransmitters that operate through various postsynaptic receptors. These receptors are of two main types, ionotropic and metabotropic, and both types are involved in the postsynaptic responses of relay cells. Examples of the relevant ionotropic receptors are alpha-amino-3-hydroxy-5-methyl-4-isoxazole propionic acid (AMPA) and *N*-methyl-D-aspartate (NMDA) for glutamate, nicotinic for acetylcholine, and the $GABA_A$ receptor. Examples of metabotropic receptors are various metabotropic glutamate receptors, various muscarinic receptors for acetylcholine, and the $GABA_B$ receptor.

There are many differences between ionotropic and metabotropic receptors, and only some are considered here (for details, see Nicoll et al., 1990; Mott and Lewis, 1994; Pin and Duvoisin, 1995; Recasens and Vignes, 1995; Brown et al., 1997; Viaene et al., 2013). Ionotropic receptors are simpler in construction and function, and the receptor protein itself usually contains the ion channel it controls. Binding of the neurotransmitter to the ionotropic receptor causes an alteration of the receptor shape, which in turn exposes and opens the ion channel. This allows ions to flow down their electrochemical gradients, leading to an excitatory postsynaptic potential (EPSP) or inhibitory postsynaptic potential (IPSP). Metabotropic receptor functioning is

---

[1] Other terms often applied to this area include *pedunculopontine tegmental nucleus* and *parabrachial region*. I prefer *brainstem reticular formation* because, in many or most species, the cells that innervate the thalamus from this area do not have a clear nuclear boundary and instead are found scattered around the brachium conjunctivum.

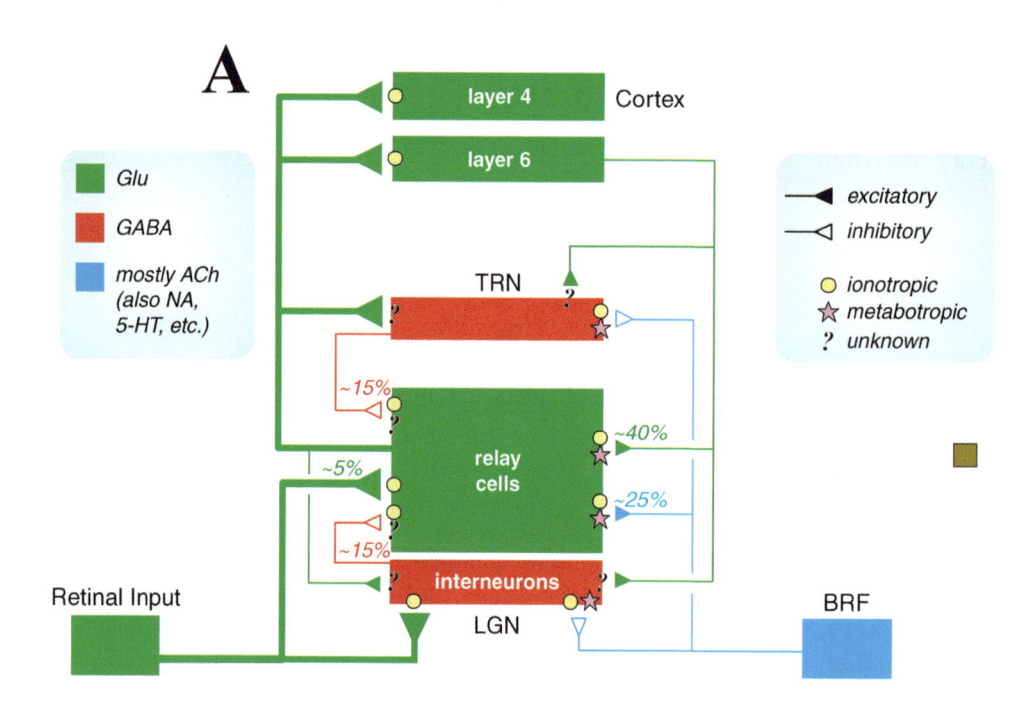

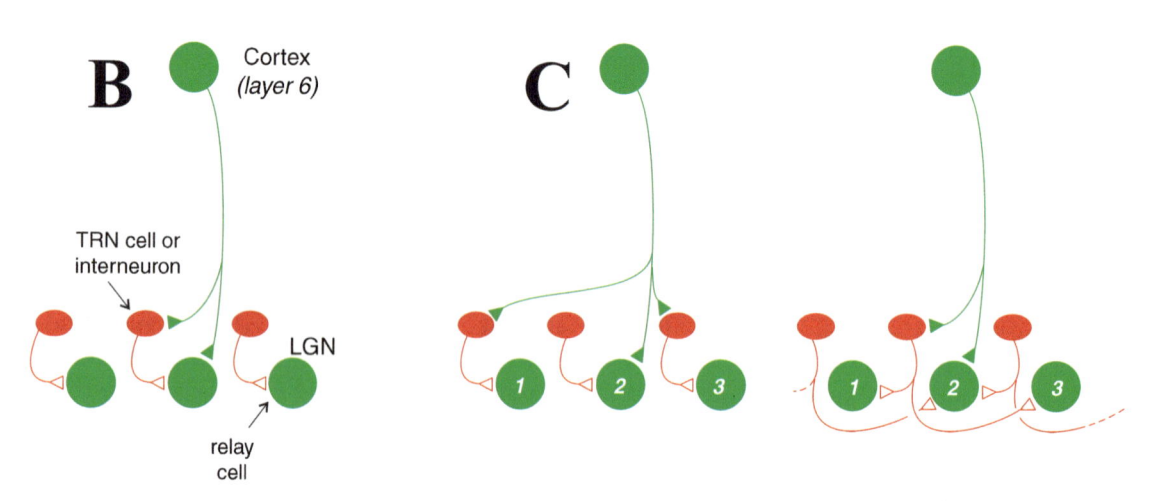

Figure 1 Circuitry of the lateral geniculate nucleus.

A. Major circuit features of the lateral geniculate nucleus with related postsynaptic receptors present on relay cells. Other thalamic nuclei seem to be organized along a similar pattern. The key to the left indicates the major transmitter systems involved, and that to the right indicates the postsynaptic receptors involved and whether the input is excitatory or inhibitory. The retinal input activates only ionotropic receptors (*yellow circles*), whereas all nonretinal inputs activate metabotropic receptors (*purple stars*) and often ionotropic receptors as well. The question marks related to interneurons indicate uncertainty of whether metabotropic receptors are involved. Percentages indicate, for each input to the relay cell, the relative number of synapses provided to that input. Abbreviations: *5-HT*, serotonin; *ACh*, acetylcholine; *BRF*, brainstem reticular formation; *GABA*, γ-aminobutyric acid; *Glu*, glutamate; *LGN*, lateral geniculate nucleus; *NA*, noradrenaline; *TRN*, thalamic reticular nucleus.

B and C. Two possible patterns among others for corticothalamic projection from layer 6.

B. Pattern of simple excitation and feedforward inhibition.

C. More complicated pattern in which activation of a cortical axon can excite some relay cells directly (*cell 2*) and inhibit others (*cells 1 and 3*) through activation of interneurons or thalamic reticular cells. This could be done via several circuitry variants, and two examples are shown here. Further details in the text. Abbreviations for panels B and C are as in panel A.

more complicated because the receptor is indirectly linked to ion channels via second-messenger systems, and in thalamic relay cells, this usually involves a G-protein and ultimately opens or closes K$^+$ channels. Opening of K$^+$ channels causes K$^+$ to flow out of the cell, producing an IPSP, whereas closing of these channels stops leakage of K$^+$, leading to an EPSP.

Two other differences between receptor types bear emphasis. First, ionotropic PSPs typically occur with brief latencies (<1 msec) and durations (mostly over in 10 or a few 10s of msec), whereas metabotropic PSPs have longer latencies (~10 msec or so) and durations (100s of msec to several sec). Second, whereas the low firing rates of an afferent input, even a single action potential, can activate ionotropic receptors, higher firing rates are generally needed to activate metabotropic receptors. Apparently, this results from metabotropic receptors being located perisynaptically and thus farther from neurotransmitter release sites than are ionotropic receptors (Lujan et al., 1996), and thus higher firing rates are needed to release sufficient neurotransmitter to reach metabotropic receptors. However, as few as two action potentials separated by 100 msec or less in the afferent can begin to activate metabotropic glutamate receptors, although higher rates or more action potentials increasingly activate more of these receptors (Viaene et al., 2013).

Note that the extrinsic nonretinal inputs innervate not only relay cells but also interneurons and reticular cells, and individual axons usually do so via branches. The right key of Figure 1A shows the overall general effects of these extrinsic inputs on relay cells. Brainstem input, in general excites relay cells directly and inhibits interneurons and reticular cells, and often the same brainstem axon branches, to achieve all of these effects. This means that activity in this pathway excites relay cells both directly and indirectly, the latter by inhibiting inhibitory inputs to relay cells. This neat trick is achieved by cholinergic input activating different muscarinic (metabotropic or M) receptors on the different cell types. On relay cells, M1 receptors are activated, leading to prolonged EPSPs, whereas on interneurons and reticular cells, M2 receptors are activated, leading to prolonged IPSPs. However, these cholinergic inputs also activate nicotinic (ionotropic) receptors on all these target cells, producing a brief EPSP in them. As noted previously, activation of metabotropic receptors requires higher rates of firing of the afferent input, and so it is when these brainstem cholinergic inputs fire at higher rates that the muscarinic responses will begin to dominate and persist.

Whereas brainstem input, when more active, clearly excites relay cells directly and indirectly, the action of the layer 6 glutamatergic input is harder to predict, because all the target cells are excited. Thus, both monosynaptic excitation and disynaptic inhibition of relay cells are possible. However, the actual effect of this input on relay cells depends critically on details of circuitry, as illustrated in Figure 1B and C. Figure 1B shows the often-assumed configuration in which layer 6 activation monosynaptically excites relay cells and disynaptically inhibits them. Figure 1C shows a very different configuration: here, a layer 6 axon directly excites some relay cells (i.e., cell 2) and disynaptically inhibits surrounding ones (i.e., cells 1 and 3). Other patterns not shown in Figure 1B and C can also be imagined. Clearly, uncovering the details of this circuitry is key to understanding the function of this layer 6 corticothalamic pathway. It should be noted that if the pattern of Figure 1C exists, and evidence for this is available (Lam and Sherman, 2010; Wang et al., 2006; Legendy et al., 1978; Tsumoto et al., 1978), large-scale topographic excitation or suppression of this pathway, such as by optogenetics, lesion, chemical manipulation, and so forth, would obscure the details of Figure 1C and effectively not distinguish between Figure 1B and many other patterns, such as that in Figure 1C.

Thalamic Cell Properties

Neurons express many voltage- and time-gated ionic membrane conductances, and this includes thalamic relay cells. The action potential, which is based on voltage- and time-gated Na^+ and K^+ conductances, is the best-known example. There is also a variety of other Na^+, K^+, and Ca^{2+} conductances, and more detailed accounts can be found elsewhere (Jack et al., 1975; Hille, 1992; Levitan and Kaczmarek, 2002; Sherman and Guillery, 2006, 1996). Because of these conductances, membrane voltage and its temporal pattern play important roles in relay cell functioning. Although most of these conductances are ubiquitous to neurons everywhere, one in particular, a voltage-gated Ca^{2+} conductance that operates via T-type Ca^{2+} channels, is particularly important to relay cell function and relatively specific to thalamic neurons (for details, see Sherman and Guillery, 2006; Sherman, 2001; Sherman and Guillery, 1996). Because the properties of this Ca^{2+} channel are qualitatively so similar to those underlying the conventional action potential, we shall start with a brief review of the action potential shown in Figure 2A.

The Action Potential

The Na^+ channel has two voltage- and time-regulated gates, an *activation gate* and an *inactivation gate*. Both gates must be open for Na^+ to flow into the cell and depolarize it. When the activation gate is open, the channel is said to be *activated*; when closed, it is *de-activated*. Likewise for the inactivation gate: when open, the channel is *de-inactivated*, and when closed, *inactivated*. The K^+ channel has only an activation gate and thus can be *activated* or *de-activated*.

At normal resting potentials, the inactivation gate is open, but the activation gate is closed, preventing entry of Na^+ (Figure 2A[i]). From this level, a sufficient depolarization will open the activation gate, leading to the up swing of the action potential (Figure 2A[ii]). After about 1msec, this depolarizing spike inactivates the channel (i.e., the inactivation gate closes), meaning that *both* sufficient depolarization *and* sufficient time are needed for inactivation. This inactivation of the Na^+ channel, along with activation of the somewhat slower K^+ channel, prevents further depolarization (Figure 2A[iii]) and repolarizes the cell to its original resting potential (Figure 2A[iv]). However, even with this repolarization to the original level, the Na^+ channel remains inactivated for another 1 msec or so (i.e., the inactivation gate remains closed), after which the channel becomes de-inactivated (i.e., the inactivation gate opens); this underlies the refractory period of 1 msec or so during which no further action potentials can be evoked. In principle, this limits the cell's firing rate to 1 kHz, but in practice, other factors limit the firing of most cells to a few hundred hertz. An important point worth emphasizing here is that the inactivation gate has both voltage and time requirements: inactivation requires sufficient depolarization for at least about 1 msec; de-inactivation requires sufficient hyperpolarization, again for at least about 1 msec.

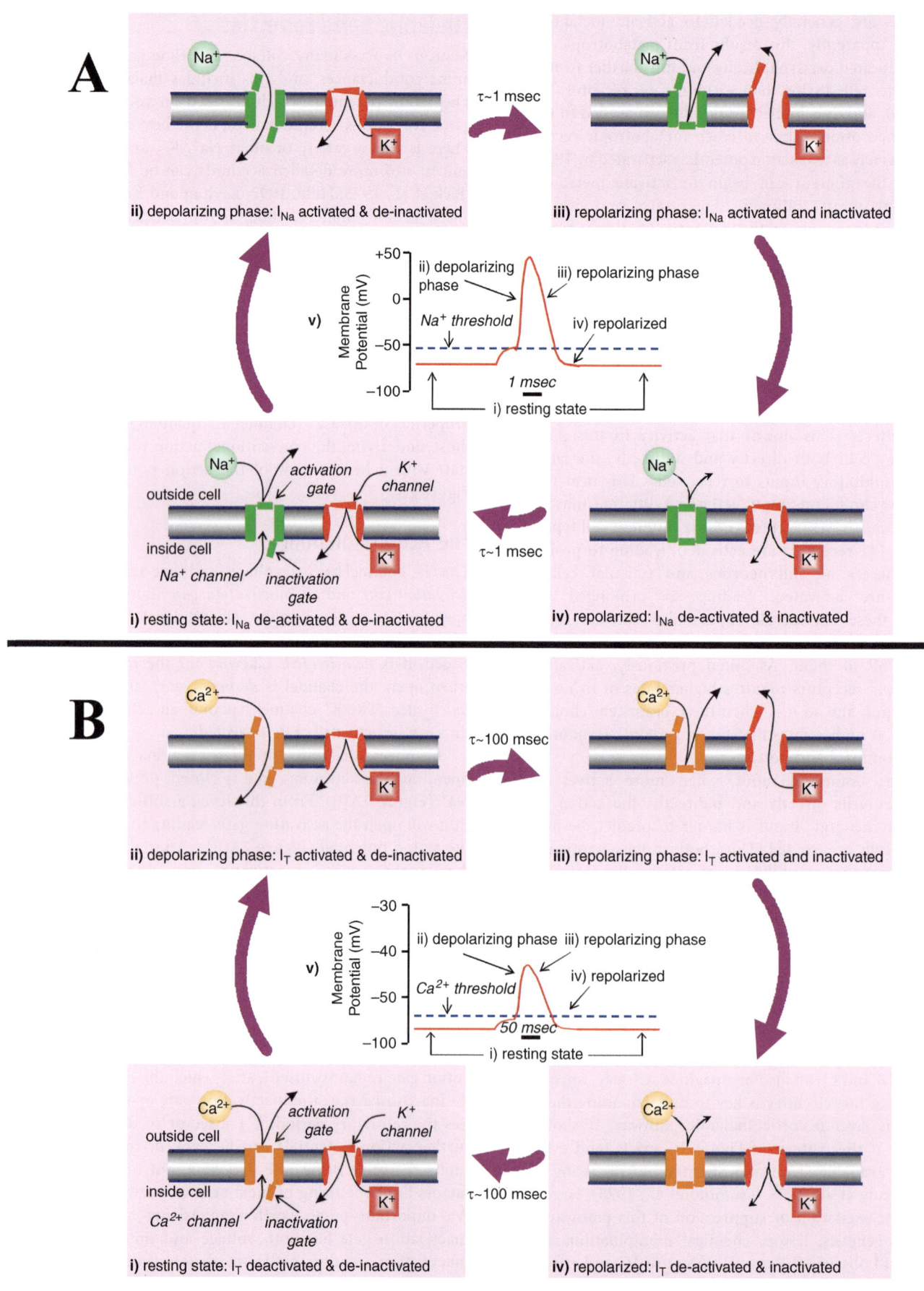

Figure 2 Schematic representation of qualitatively similar voltage- and time-gated ion channels underlying the conventional action potential and low-threshold Ca^{2+} spike.

The Low-Threshold Ca^{2+} Spike

The voltage and time dependencies of T-type[2] Ca^{2+} channels are qualitatively like those of the Na^+ channels, with similar activation and inactivation gates (Sherman & Guillery, 2013; Sherman, 2001; Jahnsen and Llinás, 1984a, 1984b; McCormick and Huguenard, 1992). Figure 2B illustrates these properties. At rest, which is slightly more hyperpolarized than the example for the Na^+ channel in Figure 2A, the inactivation gate is open but the activation gate is closed; the channel is thus both de-inactivated and de-activated (Figure 2B[i]). Following sufficient depolarization, the activation gate opens, and Ca^{2+} flows into the cell, leading to a depolarizing spike, and so the Ca^{2+} channel is activated and de-inactivated (Figure 2B[ii]). This Ca^{2+} spike is often termed the *low-threshold spike* because the activation threshold for the Ca^{2+} channel is hyperpolarized with respect to that for the Na^+ channel underlying the action potential. After roughly 100 msec of depolarization, the Ca^{2+} channel inactivates[3] (Figure 2B[iii]), and this, combined with activation of a slower series of K^+ conductances, repolarizes the neuron (Figure 2B[iv]). However, the T-type Ca^{2+} channel remains inactivated (Figure 2B[iv]) for another 100 msec or so, after which time the original state of Figure 2B(i) is restored. The two gates of the T-type Ca^{2+} channel have opposite voltage dependencies, but while the activation gate responds quickly to voltage change, the inactivation gate is slower, requiring roughly 100 msec of polarization change to open or close. Note that the roughly 100 msec of hyperpolarization needed to de-inactivate the T-type Ca^{2+} channel provides a refractory period limiting low-threshold Ca^{2+} spiking to roughly 10 Hz. Most voltage- and time-gated conductances have rather long time constants for inactivation kinetics; thus, the T-type Ca^{2+} channel is rather typical in this regard, and the Na^+ channel underlying the action potential is a rather fast outlier. This means that to control most of these active channels requires rather long-lasting changes in membrane voltage.

T-type Ca^{2+} channels are common to neurons throughout the central nervous system. However, in the cases of both the Na^+ and Ca^{2+} channels discussed here, their density must be relatively high to generate an all-or-none propagating spike. The high density of Na^+ channels in the axon and often in the cell body and dendrites allows the propagation of the action potential. Regarding the T-type Ca^{2+} channels, their density in the soma and dendrites (but not along the axon!) of thalamic relay cells is typically high enough to support such spiking (Huguenard, 1996; Huguenard and McCormick, 1994). Because these Ca^{2+} channels are not found along the axon, such Ca^{2+} spikes are not propagated to any postsynaptic targets; however, the Na^+ action potentials they evoke at the axon hillock are so propagated. In most neurons outside of the thalamus, the density of these channels is too low for spiking, and so for these other neurons, activation of these channels leads to modest depolarizations that spread electrotonically.

Burst and Tonic Firing

The properties of T-type Ca^{2+} channels underlie two different response modes, *burst* or *tonic*, that characterize the firing properties of thalamic relay cells. Which of these response modes prevails at any time is an important variable in the nature of information transmission to the cortex (Sherman and Guillery, 2013; Sherman, 2001; Bezdudnaya et al., 2006; Swadlow and Gusev, 2001; MacLean et al., 2005).

Caption for Figure 2 (cont.)

A. For the action potential, (i)–(iv) depict the channel events, and (v) shows the effects on membrane potential. The Na^+ channel has two voltage-dependent gates: an *activation gate* that opens at depolarized levels and closes at hyperpolarized levels and an *inactivation gate* with the opposite voltage dependency. For the inward, depolarizing Na^+ current (I_{Na}) to flow, both gates must be open at the same time. The K^+ channel (here, an imaginary combination of different K^+ channels) has a single activation gate with slower kinetics than for the Na^+ gates, and when it opens at depolarized levels, an outward, hyperpolarizing K^+ current is activated. (i) At the resting membrane potential, the activation gate of the Na^+ channel is closed, and so it is de-activated, but the inactivation gate is open, and so it is also de-inactivated. The single gate for the K^+ channel is closed, and so the K^+ channel is also de-activated. (ii) With sufficient depolarization to reach its threshold, the activation gate of the Na^+ channel opens, and Na^+ flows into the cell (i.e., I_{Na} flows). This depolarizes the cell, leading to the upswing of the action potential. (iii) The inactivation gate of the Na^+ channel closes after the depolarization is sustained for approximately 1 msec ("approximately" because inactivation is a complex function of time and voltage), and the slower K^+ channel also opens. These combined channel actions lead to the repolarization of the cell. While the inactivation gate of the Na^+ channel is closed, the channel is inactivated. (iv) Even though the initial resting potential is reached, the Na^+ channel remains inactivated because it takes approximately 1 msec of hyperpolarization for de-inactivation to occur. (v) Membrane voltage changes showing action potential corresponding to the events in (i)–(iv).

B. For the representation of actions of voltage-dependent T-type Ca^{2+} and K^+ channels underlying the low-threshold Ca^{2+} spike, the conventions are as in panel A, and so (i)–(iv) show the channel events, and (v) shows the effects on membrane potential. Note the strong qualitative similarity between the behavior of the T-type Ca^{2+} channel and the Na^+ channel shown in panel A, including the presence of both activation and inactivation gates with similar relative voltage dependencies. (i) At a membrane potential more hyperpolarized than the normal resting potential, the activation gate of the T-type Ca^{2+} channel is closed, but the inactivation gate is open, and so the channel is both de-activated and de-inactivated. The K^+ channel is also de-activated. (ii) With sufficient depolarization to reach its threshold, the activation gate of the T-type Ca^{2+} channel opens, allowing Ca^{2+} to flow into the cell. This depolarizes the cell, providing the upswing of the low-threshold Ca^{2+} spike. (iii) The inactivation gate of the T-type Ca^{2+} channel closes after approximately 100 msec ("approximately" because, as for the Na^+ channel in panel A, closing of the channel is a complex function of time and voltage), inactivating the T-type Ca^{2+} channel, and the K^+ channel also opens. (iv) These combined actions repolarize the cell, but after repolarization, it takes approximately 100 msec for de-inactivation to occur. Redrawn from Sherman and Guillery (2013).

---

[2] There are numerous types of Ca^{2+} channels found in neuronal membranes. The T-type channel is so named for its "transience." In addition are other, much higher-threshold Ca^{2+} channels that are located in dendrites and synaptic terminals (Johnston et al., 1996; Llinás, 1988; Hille, 1992). One involves the L-type Ca^{2+} channel (*L* for *long-lasting* because it slowly inactivates) and the other, the N-type channel (*N*, wryly, for *neither*, being neither T nor L type; it inactivates more rapidly than the L-type channel). Other types of high-threshold Ca^{2+} channels also exist (Wu et al., 1998; Hille, 1992; Snutch & Reiner, 1992).

[3] Control of the inactivation gate is a complex function of voltage and time (Jahnsen & Llinás, 1984b, 1984a; Zhan et al., 1999) so that the more depolarized (or hyperpolarized), the more quickly the gate closes (or opens), but the important point is that under normal conditions, roughly 100 msec is required for these actions.

Anatomy

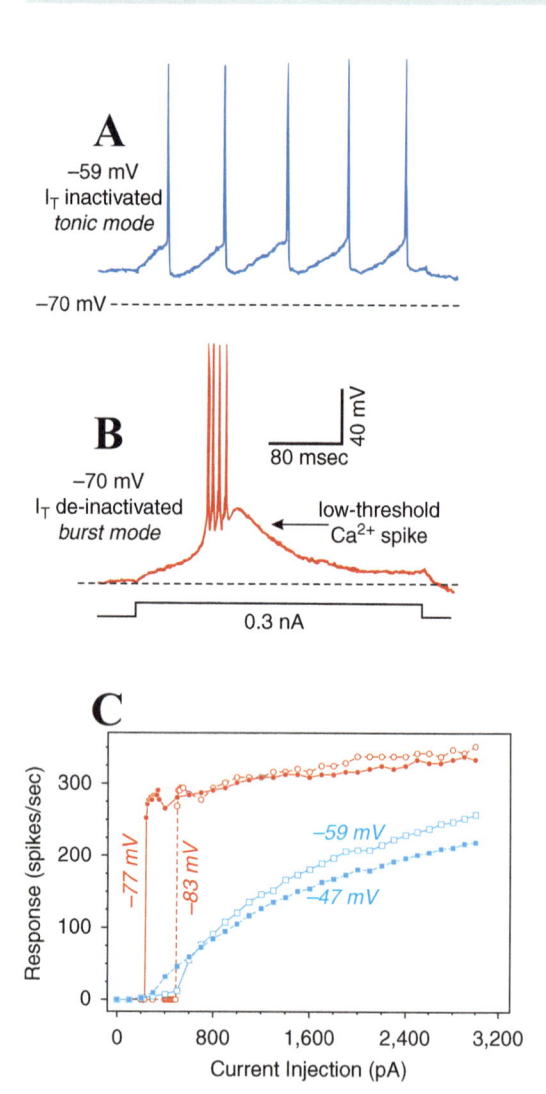

Figure 3 Properties related to T-type Ca^{2+} channels.

All examples are from relay cells of the cat's lateral geniculate nucleus recorded intracellularly in in vitro slice preparations.

A and B. Voltage dependency of the Ca^{2+} low-threshold spike. Responses are shown to the same depolarizing current injection delivered intracellularly from two different initial holding potentials. At a relatively depolarized level (A), most Ca^{2+} channels are inactivated, and the cell responds with a stream of unitary action potentials as long as the stimulus is suprathreshold for firing. This is the *tonic mode* of firing. At a relatively hyperpolarized level (B), most Ca^{2+} channels are de-inactivated, and the current pulse activates a low-threshold Ca^{2+} spike with four action potentials riding its crest. This is the *burst mode* of firing.

C. Input–output relationship for another cell. The input variable is the amplitude of the depolarizing current pulse (labeled "Current Injection"), and the output is the firing frequency of the cell (labeled "Response"). To compare burst and tonic firing, the firing frequency was determined by the first six action potentials of the response because this cell usually exhibited six action potentials per burst in this experiment. The initial holding potentials are shown, and −47 mV and −59 mV reflect tonic mode, whereas −77 mV and −83 mV reflect burst mode. Redrawn from Sherman and Guillery (2013).

Burst and tonic firing properties. Figure 3 shows many of the properties that distinguish burst from tonic firing. Panels A and B of Figure 3 show that the same input (e.g., a current injection in this case, but it could also be an excitatory postsynaptic current [EPSC] from the retina in a geniculate relay cell) evokes a very different postsynaptic response during the two firing modes. When the cell is relatively depolarized (Figure 3A), the Ca^{2+} channels are mostly inactivated and thus play little or no role. Under these conditions, the depolarization evokes firing as long as it remains above threshold; this is tonic firing. When the same cell is relatively hyperpolarized (Figure 3B), these channels are de-inactivated, and the exact same depolarizing current injection now activates them, producing a spike upon which rides a brief burst of action potentials; this is burst firing.

Significance of burst and tonic firing. Burst and tonic firing modes are important for thalamic relay functions for at least three reasons. Figure 3C shows the first: tonic mode provides a more linear relay of information (Zhan et al., 1999). During tonic firing, there is a relatively direct relationship between the input depolarization (e.g., an EPSP) and evoked action potentials, and so the firing rate rises monotonically and thus fairly linearly with the size of the EPSP. However, during burst firing, action potentials are not evoked directly from the EPSP but, rather, from the Ca^{2+} spike, and because this is an all-or-none spike, once the EPSP is large enough to reach threshold for this spike, larger EPSPs do not evoke larger Ca^{2+} spikes, and so the input–output relationship is more like a step function, which is highly nonlinear. Second, burst firing can only occur after a period of hyperpolarization needed to de-inactivate the Ca^{2+} channels, and there can be no neuronal firing during such hyperpolarization. Therefore, the burst of action potentials occurs against a background of low spontaneous firing compared to tonic mode. Spontaneous firing can be regarded as noise, and as such, the signal-to-noise ratio of burst firing is considerably greater than that of tonic firing, so the thalamic response, and thus the signal that is passed to the cortex, is more detectable (Sherman, 1996). The third reason is again related to the requisite period of hyperpolarization and lack of action potentials before a burst can be evoked. Geniculocortical synapses show the property of paired-pulse depression (reviewed in Sherman and Guillery, 2013), meaning that an action potential produces a smaller EPSP if it follows another within about 100 msec or so. During tonic mode, when geniculate firing rates usually exceed 10 action potentials/sec, the geniculocortical synapse will usually be depressed; however, a burst of action potentials would arrive at the thalamocortical synapse after the requisite silent period of 100 msec or longer, which means that the thalamocortical synapse has been relieved of depression, and thus the postsynaptic response evoked would be greater. This, in turn, predicts that the first action potentials in a burst should evoke a greater response in the cortex than a typical tonic action potential, and this indeed occurs (Swadlow et al., 2002; Swadlow and Gusev, 2001).

These differences between firing modes suggest that burst firing produces a larger signal that is more readily detected in the cortex compared to tonic firing. However, the more linear input–output function during tonic firing suggests that it represents a more faithful relay mode for information transfer. These differences have led to the hypothesis that burst firing can provide a "wake-up call" to the cortex to strongly signal that a novel stimulus has occurred after a quiescent period. Once this signal has been detected, the circuitry can then be brought to bear to depolarize the relay cell (e.g., depolarization from corticogeniculate feedback that activates metabotropic glutamate receptors, leading to a prolonged depolarization to inactivate the underlying Ca^{2+} channels; see next section) to switch to tonic mode so that further details of the novel stimulus can be faithfully relayed (Sherman, 1996). This idea remains a hypothesis to be tested, and other hypotheses do exist (e.g., Kim et al., 2015).

One final point needs to be emphasized. Although burst and tonic firing modes are often referred to as completely distinct, there is a sort of intermediate stage. If a relay cell is held at a sufficiently depolarized level to inactivate virtually all T-type Ca^{2+} channels, the neuron's response is strictly in tonic mode. Likewise, if the neuron is held sufficiently hyperpolarized to bring an adequate number or density of these Ca^{2+} channels into play to activate a low-threshold spike, burst firing ensues. However, there exist less hyperpolarized levels at which some of these Ca^{2+} channels will be de-inactivated, but their density is insufficient to activate an all-or-none low-threshold spike. In this case, activation of these Ca^{2+} channels will evoke a relatively small depolarization that propagates only electrotonically but that can nonetheless affect the neuron's responsiveness (Deleuze et al., 2012; Alitto et al., 2019).

Control of burst and tonic firing. A relay cell's firing mode is dictated by its recent voltage history: sufficiently long relative depolarization produces tonic firing, and hyperpolarization produces burst firing. Because of the temporal requirement, it would appear that activation of metabotropic receptors presents the most efficient route for controlling firing mode. Figure 1A shows the likely candidates. Layer 6 feedback activates metabotropic glutamate receptors on relay cells that depolarize them sufficiently in time and amount to promote tonic firing, and evidence for this exists (Godwin et al., 1996; Andolina et al., 2013). Likewise, $GABA_B$ receptors on relay cells activated from thalamic reticular neurons (Ulrich et al., 2007; Huguenard and Prince, 1994; Crunelli and Leresche, 1991; Soltész et al., 1989) and possibly interneurons would hyperpolarize them sufficiently in time and amount to promote burst firing. Figure 1C shows how a likely corticogeniculate circuit would depolarize some cells (e.g., *cell 2*) to promote tonic firing and hyperpolarize others (e.g., *cells 1* and *3*) to promote burst firing.

Glutamatergic Drivers and Modulators

Despite the many different inputs to relay cells, it is the retinal input alone that carries the main information relayed to the cortex. A consideration of receptive field properties underscores this fact because these properties of the relay cell identify the information it relays. This is shown in Figure 4. The receptive fields of geniculate relay cells are remarkably like those of their retinal afferents, having basically the same monocularly driven, center/surround configuration (Usrey et al., 1999; Hubel and Wiesel, 1961). In contrast, these relay cell receptive fields are unlike those of extraretinal afferents: the receptive fields of corticogeniculate afferents are characteristically binocularly driven and selective for orientation and often direction, properties typical of visual cortical neurons (Gilbert, 1977), and brainstem inputs are not plausible sources of such clear center/surround properties. If retinal input alone provides the information to be

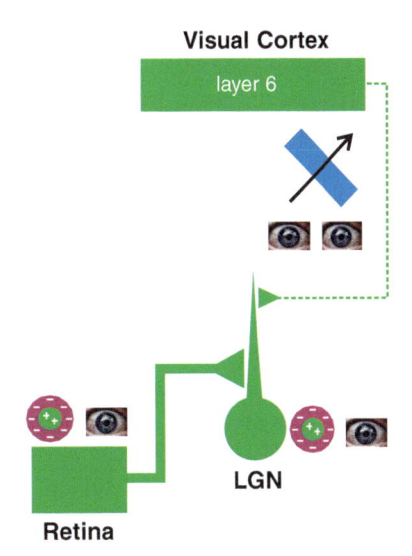

Figure 4 Different functions for glutamatergic retinal and cortical inputs to the lateral geniculate nucleus.

The receptive field of the retinal input (monocular, center/surround) is very similar to that of the geniculate relay cell, whereas the cortical cell's receptive field (binocular, specificity for orientation, direction, etc.) is not. This suggests that the retinal input carries the information to be relayed, whereas the cortical input has a very different function. See text for details.

relayed, then the nonretinal inputs must have another function. Clearly, then, retinogeniculate and layer 6 corticogeniculate inputs, which are both glutamatergic, have very different functions.

This, plus a number of morphological, pharmacological, and physiological differences that distinguish retinal and nonretinal afferents to relay cells, has led to the idea that these can be functionally divided: the retinal inputs are the information-bearing drivers (so called because one of their properties is the very strong postsynaptic drive of their target relay cells), whereas all the nonretinal inputs serve to modulate retinogeniculate transmission (reviewed in Sherman and Guillery, 1998, 2013). A modulatory function for GABAergic and classic modulatory afferents like cholinergic, noradrenergic, and so forth is clearly not a novel idea. However, it follows from this argument that the cortical layer 6 feedback input, which, like the retinal input, is glutamatergic, is also a modulator.

Drivers and Modulators in Thalamus

The concept of a division of glutamatergic inputs being classified as drivers or modulators originated with consideration, as just discussed, of the very different properties of retinal versus layer 6 cortical input to geniculate relay cells (Sherman and Guillery, 1998). This spawned experiments identifying different properties among glutamatergic afferents in the thalamus and cortex, which in turn led to their classification into drivers and modulators (reviewed in Sherman and Guillery, 2013). Many properties distinguish glutamatergic drivers from modulators in the thalamus, and the number will likely increase as we learn more about this issue. The following list, which is not meant to be exhaustive, summarizes seven distinguishing features in a roughly decreasing order of importance:

1. Drivers activate only ionotropic receptors; modulators activate metabotropic receptors as well.
2. Driver synapses show a high probability of neurotransmitter release and paired-pulse depression; modulator synapses show the opposite properties of low release probability and paired-pulse facilitation (Dobrunz and Stevens, 1997; Dittman et al., 2000; Branco and Staras, 2009).
3. Drivers evoke larger initial EPSPs than do modulators.
4. Driver inputs show less convergence onto their targets than do modulators.
5. Driver inputs produce a small minority (2–5%) of the synapses onto thalamic relays cells, whereas layer 6 cortical input produces 30–50% of such synapses (Wang et al., 2002; Van Horn et al., 2000; Van Horn and Sherman, 2007).
6. Drivers tend to form larger terminals on more proximal dendrites than do modulators.
7. Drivers tend to have thicker axons and denser terminal arbors than do modulators.

The main point is that not all anatomical pathways are functionally equivalent, acting in some sort of anatomical democracy so that the numerically largest glutamatergic input is the most important. This old notion is strongly challenged by a consideration of the lateral geniculate nucleus, where the number of layer 6 cortical synaptic inputs exceeds that of retinal inputs by roughly an order of magnitude, and the conclusion based on this notion of information magnitude being determined by the size of the input is that the layer 6 input provides relay cells with information to be fed back to the cortex, whereas the retinal input is too small to be of much importance. Clearly, this conclusion is wrong. Thus, if one is to understand the functional organization of the thalamus, and especially the identity of the input being relayed to the cortex, one must identify and characterize the driver input.

Drivers and Modulators in the Cortex

The classification of drivers and modulators among glutamatergic circuits has been extended to the cortex (reviewed in Sherman and Guillery, 2013). This includes thalamocortical (Mo and Sherman, 2019; Lee and Sherman, 2012; Covic and Sherman, 2011; Viaene et al., 2011a, 2011b, 2011c; Lee and Sherman, 2008), local intraareal corticocortical (Lam and Sherman, 2019; DePasquale and Sherman, 2012; Lee and Sherman, 2008, 2009), and interareal corticocortical pathways (Petrof et al., 2015; Covic and Sherman, 2011; DePasquale and Sherman, 2011, 2013).

The three-dimensional scatterplot of Figure 5 shows certain quantitative features of this classification for the thalamus and cortex. Each point represents a single thalamic or cortical neuron recorded in a mouse brain slice for which a glutamatergic input was identified as driver or modulator. The scatterplot suggests three conclusions. First, the driver-versus-modulator classification is clearly robust. Thus, whereas the functional significance of the duality of glutamatergic synapses may still be open to question, the presence of this duality seems quite clear. Second, so far only two main classes of glutamatergic synapse have been described in the

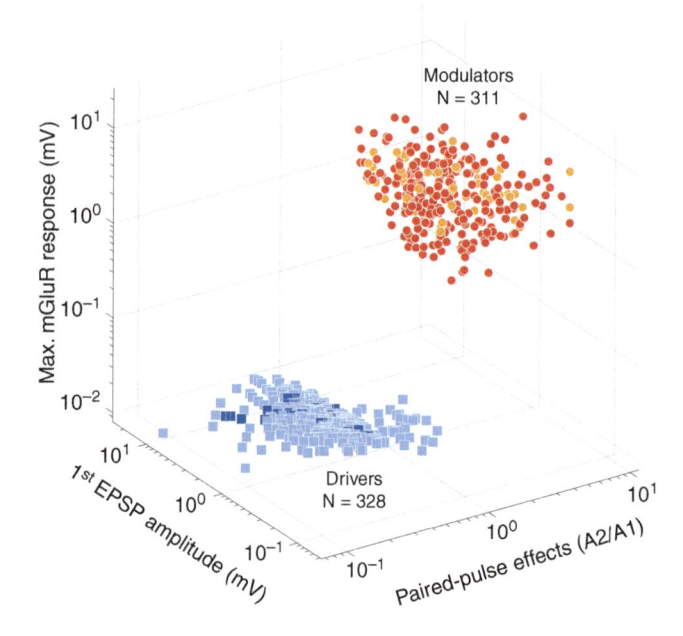

Figure 5 Three-dimensional scatterplot for inputs classified as driver or modulator to cells of thalamus and cortex; data from in vitro slice experiments in mice from the author's laboratory.

Each point is a single cell for which a glutamatergic input was identified as driver or modulator, and the key below the graph indicates whether the cell was thalamic or cortical. The parameters for the three axes are (1) the amplitude of the first EPSP elicited in a train at a stimulus level just above threshold; (2) a measure of paired-pulse effects (the amplitude of the second EPSP divided by the first [A2 divided by A1] for stimulus trains of 10–20 Hz; and (3) a measure of the response to synaptic activation of metabotropic glutamate receptors, taken as the maximum depolarization or hyperpolarization evoked during the 300-msec postsynaptic response period to tetanic stimulation in the presence of AMPA and NMDA blockers. Pathways tested here include various inputs to the thalamus from the cortex and subcortical sources, various thalamocortical pathways, and various intracortical pathways. From Sherman (2016).

thalamus and cortex, although there is evidence that driver synapses in the cortex may be further subdivided (Viaene et al., 2011c). Third, the basic properties of a glutamatergic driver or modulator synapse appear to be fundamentally the same in the thalamus and cortex.

Why Have Glutamatergic Modulators?

Given the presence of so many classic modulatory systems (e.g., cholinergic, noradrenergic, serotonergic), what is the point of adding glutamatergic modulators to the mix? I suggest an answer based both on topography and the control of the modulation. Classical modulatory systems have little or no topography in their projections patterns, affecting much of the neuraxis when active, although recent evidence does indicate some topography in the cholinergic input from the basal forebrain to the cortex (Zaborszky et al., 2018). Thus, for the most part, the function of classic modulatory systems seems more related to overall behavioral state: alertness, sleep, and so forth. Only glutamatergic modulatory pathways possess a high degree of topography, and such topographic modulation is needed for processes that require localized effects, such as focal or covert attention, adaptation, and learning and memory. Furthermore, classic modulatory systems originate subcortically and thus do not have the benefit of thalamocortical processing, which is the source of most of the glutamatergic inputs discussed here, and such processing would obviously be important for modulation related to higher cognitive functioning.

First and Higher Order Thalamic Relays

A major function of a thalamic relay is determined by its driver input. Thus, we can define the function of the lateral geniculate nucleus or the ventral posterior nucleus as relaying retinal or medial lemniscal information, respectively. However, until recently, the driver inputs of many thalamic relays were undefined, and thus their functions in this sense had been unclear. We now know that a major source of driver input to many thalamic nuclei originates in layer 5 of various cortical areas (Prasad et al., 2020; Kita and Kita, 2012; Bourassa and Deschênes, 1995; Bourassa et al., 1995; Deschênes et al., 1994; Economo et al., 2018; reviewed in Sherman and Guillery, 2013). This is illustrated in Figure 6A, using the visual system as an example. Figure 6B generalizes the patterns of Figure 6A to the thalamus more broadly.

Thalamic relays can be divided based on the source of their driver input: *first order* relays receive driver input from a subcortical source, whereas *higher order* relays receive driver input from layer 5 of the cortex (Sherman and Guillery, 2013; Guillery, 1995). These layer 5 inputs to relay cells have the same properties as do the subcortical drivers, such as retinal input to the lateral geniculate nucleus. A first order example is the lateral geniculate nucleus, which receives driving subcortical input from the retina, and a higher order example is the pulvinar, which receives driving input from layer 5 of the visual cortex (Figure 6A). This pattern is not limited to the visual

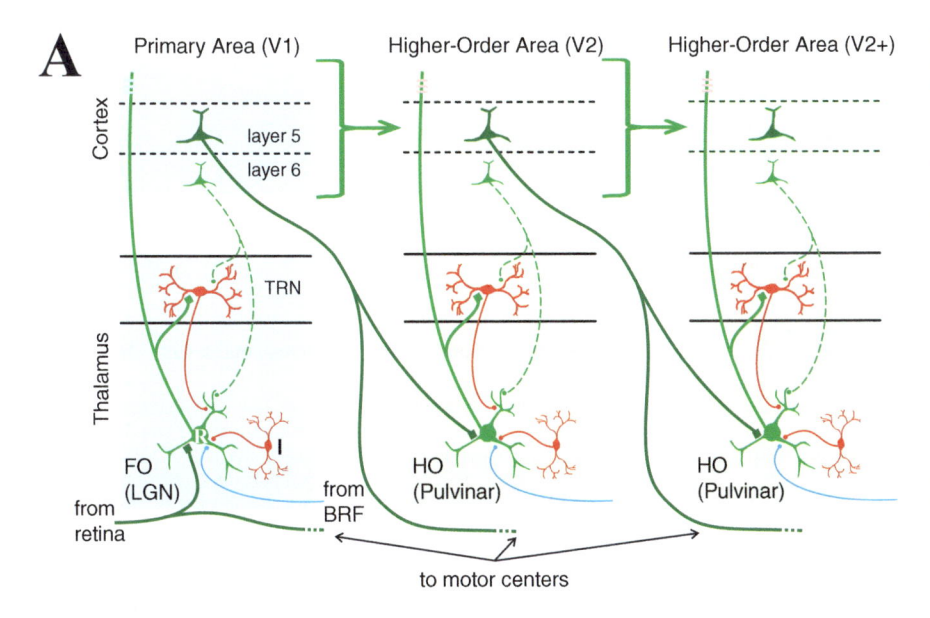

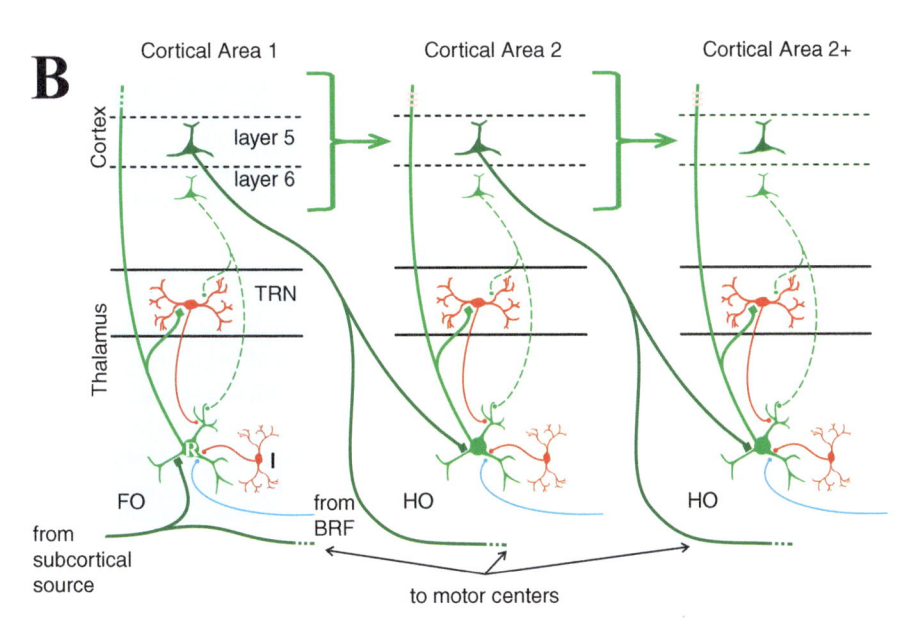

Figure 6 Schematic diagram showing organizational features of first and higher order thalamic relays.

A. Examples from the visual system. The first order nucleus (FO; lateral geniculate nucleus) relays subcortical (retinal) input to the primary visual cortex. A higher order nucleus (HO; pulvinar) relays information from layer 5 of one visual cortical area to another; this is a transthalamic corticocortical circuit. This relay can be between first and higher order visual areas or between two higher order visual areas. The important difference between first and higher order relays is the driver input, which is subcortical (retinal) for a first order thalamic nucleus and from layer 5 of the cortex for a higher order one. Note that both types of thalamic nuclei receive an input from layer 6 of the cortex, which is modulatory and mostly feedback, but higher order nuclei additionally receive a layer 5 input from the cortex, which, in these examples, is feedforward. Note also that the driver inputs, both subcortical and from layer 5, are typically from branching axons, the significance of which is elaborated in the text.

B. Generalization for thalamus from example in the visual system shown in panel A.

Abbreviations: *BRF*, brainstem reticular formation; *FO*, first order; *HO*, higher order; *I*, interneuron; *LGN*, lateral geniculate nucleus; *R*, relay cell; *TRN*, thalamic reticular nucleus. Redrawn from Sherman (2005).

system, as shown in Figure 6B: for the somatosensory system, the ventral posterior nucleus is first order, and the posterior medial nucleus is higher order; for the auditory system, the ventral division of the medial geniculate nucleus is first order, and the dorsal division is higher order (details reviewed in Sherman and Guillery, 2013). This classification has been extended to most of the thalamus, and in this regard, most of the thalamus, by volume, is higher order (Sherman and Guillery, 2013). It appears that all thalamic nuclei receive a corticothalamic projection from layer 6 that is a modulator, but higher order relays receive another cortical input, a driver input from layer 5 (Figure 6).

As indicated in Figure 6, the non-driver inputs to first and higher order thalamic relays are similar, with some quantitative differences, some of which are noted later in the discussion. One implication is that all thalamic relays receive a modulator layer 6 corticothalamic projection, but higher order relays receive another cortical input, from layer 5, that is a driver. Another implication is that higher order relays serve as a thalamic hub in transthalamic corticocortical communication. Figure 6 also shows that cortical areas connected via transthalamic pathways also have direct connections. This parallel organization has been seen for direct and transthalamic connections in the mouse between V1 and V2, S1 and S2, A1 and A2 (reviewed in Sherman and Guillery, 2013), and S1 and M1 (Mo and Sherman, 2019; Petrof et al., 2015).

It should be clear from Figure 6 that higher order relays are organized to provide a route for corticocortical communication. Given the preponderance of higher order relays in the thalamus (Sherman and Guillery, 2013; Prasad et al., 2020), such transthalamic circuits likely play an important and only recently recognized role in overall cortical functioning. The patterns seen in Figure 6 raise three critical questions for which we now have no clear answers:

- How often is this parallel pattern of direct and transthalamic connections seen between cortical areas, or how often are cortical areas connected by just one or the other?
- What is different in the nature of the messages sent via the direct versus transthalamic pathways?
- Why is one path of corticocortical communication routed through the thalamus?

Feedforward versus Feedback Transthalamic Pathways

The transthalamic pathways shown in Figure 6 represent feedforward examples that ascend a cortical hierarchy. Figure 7A shows feedforward transthalamic pathways that have been identified to date in the mouse cortex (Sherman and Guillery, 2013; Mo and Sherman, 2019), and these are color coded in the diagram. These include V1 to V2 via the pulvinar; S1 to S2 and S1 to M1, both via the posterior medial nucleus; and A1 to A2 via the dorsal division of the medial geniculate nucleus.

The possibility that transthalamic circuits may be involved in feedback corticocortical communication remains a possibility that, to date, has received little attention. Recent evidence for

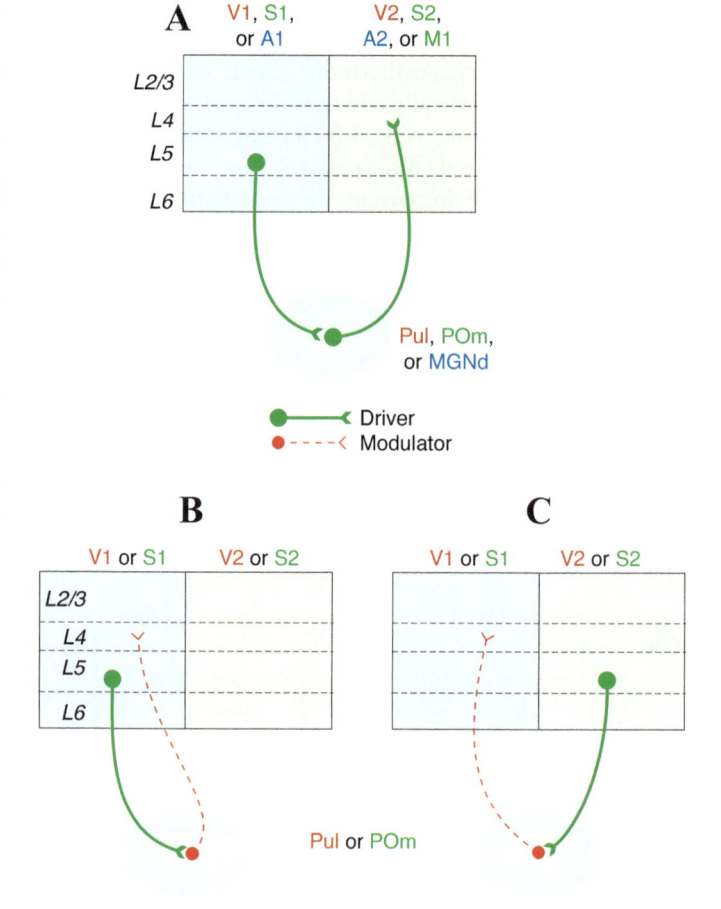

Figure 7 Feedforward and feedback transthalamic circuits identified to date in the mouse.

A. Examples of feedforward transthalamic circuits. These are from primary to secondary cortical areas (visual, V1 and V2; somatosensory, S1 and S2; auditory, A1 and A2) through higher order thalamic relays (pulvinar [Pul] for vision, posterior medial nucleus [POm] for somatosensation, dorsal division of the medial geniculate nucleus [MGNd] for audition); also, there is a transthalamic pathway from S1 to M1 via POm. All inputs shown are driver. The color coding shows the cortical and thalamic relationships.

B and C. Examples of feedback transthalamic circuits; color coding and abbreviations as in panel A. Note that the thalamocortical inputs here are modulatory.

B. Feedback from primary sensory area to itself.

C. Feedback from secondary sensory area to primary sensory area.
Abbreviations: *MGNd*, dorsal division of medial geniculate nucleus; *POm*, posterior medial nucleus; *Pul*, pulvinar.

a transthalamic feedback circuit has been presented for the visual cortex and the somatosensory cortex (Miller-Hansen and Sherman, 2022) and is summarized in Figure 7B and C. In both cases, the feedback targets the primary sensory cortex. Figure 7B shows a layer 5 driving input from V1 or S1 to the higher order thalamic relay, the pulvinar or the posterior medial nucleus, with the latter providing a modulatory input back to V1 or S1. Figure 7C shows a feedback arrangement starting with a driving input from layer 5 of V2 or S2 to the pulvinar or the posterior medial nucleus and, from there, a modulatory input to V1 or S1. What is particularly interesting in the transthalamic pathways shown in Figure 7 is that the feedforward ones provide driving input to the target cortical area, whereas the feedback ones provide modulatory input to the target cortical area. The examples so far are few, and so we need many more examples to test the generality of these patterns.

Some Differences between First and Higher Order Thalamic Nuclei

Figure 6 suggests that the only difference between first and higher order thalamic nuclei is the nature of their driver input: subcortical for first order and cortical layer 5 for higher order. However, several differences, mostly quantitative, between them have been documented. These are simply listed as follows:

- Higher order nuclei have relatively fewer driver synapses than do first order nuclei, at roughly 2% of all synapses versus 7% (Van Horn and Sherman, 2007; Van Horn et al., 2000; Wang et al., 2002). This suggests more modulation of higher order relay cells.
- Serotonergic and cholinergic inputs from the brainstem depolarize all first order relay cells, but a significant minority (1/4 to 1/3) of those in higher order nuclei are hyperpolarized by these inputs; this results from different postsynaptic receptors to these neurotransmitters (Varela and Sherman, 2008; Varela and Sherman, 2007).
- Higher order thalamic nuclei receive substantial GABAergic inputs from the zona incerta, substantia nigra, basal ganglia, and pretectal region that do not extensively innervate first order nuclei (Bokor et al., 2005; Gulcebi et al., 2011; Lavallée et al., 2005; Kuramoto et al., 2011; Sakai et al., 1996).
- Bursting based on activation of T-type Ca^{2+} channels is more frequent among higher order relay cells (Ramcharan et al., 2005; Sherman, 2001). This may be related to the previously noted points that higher order relays receive more hyperpolarizing inputs via GABAergic, serotonergic, and cholinergic innervation, which serves to de-inactivate T-type Ca^{2+} channels in more relay cells, thereby promoting more burst firing.
- First order nuclei appear to be strictly first order, meaning that they all receive subcortical driver inputs, but nuclei identified as higher order appear to include some first order circuits. Thus, the superior colliculus seems to provide driving input to some cells of the pulvinar and medial dorsal nucleus, as does the spinal trigeminal nucleus for some cells of the posterior medial nucleus (Groh et al., 2013; Kelly et al., 2003; Berman and Wurtz, 2010; Sommer and Wurtz, 2004; Mo et al., 2017).
- First order relays innervate the cortex in a feedforward manner because they are the first relay of a particular kind of information to the cortex and predominantly innervate primary cortical areas. However, as indicated by Figure 7, some relay cells of the pulvinar, posterior medial nucleus, and dorsal division of the medial geniculate nucleus innervate primary visual, somatosensory, and auditory cortices, as well as higher areas, indicating that some higher order inputs to the cortex are links in feedback circuitry.
- First order relay cells generally transfer information from one or a few driver inputs without further significant elaboration of the information carried (but see Bickford et al., 2015; Litvina and Chen, 2017), whereas evidence exists for such elaboration for some higher order relay cells, where single neurons in the posterior medial nucleus or pulvinar are innervated both by layer 5 and subcortical driver inputs (Groh et al., 2014). This is a critical issue and needs indisputable confirmation because current ideas of thalamic processing do not include the elaboration of information based on a significant convergence of driver inputs.

Do Driver Afferents to the Thalamus Carry Efference Copy Information?

Efference Copies

Every eye movement creates a sensory signal on the retina that the visual scene has moved in the opposite direction. We typically scan scenes with rapid eye movements known as *saccades* three to five times per second, and yet we do not normally perceive the world as spinning about when this occurs. This is because neural circuits are set up to anticipate these eye movements and eliminate the sensory consequences of them from our perception. All self-generated movements, not just eye movements, create such circuits. Such a process is required to disambiguate sensory stimulation due to self-generated movements from that caused by actual changes in the environment, an absolute requirement for any organism moving about in its environment. This requires a prediction, or "forward model," of what will occur because of the impending motion, but any sensory feedback that can indicate the position of the eyes or any joint would occur after the movement and be too late for this purpose (Sommer and Wurtz, 2008).

These anticipatory circuits depend on efference copies (also known as *corollary discharges*), which are messages sent from motor areas of the brain back into appropriate sensory processing streams to anticipate impending self-generated behaviors. Details of efference copies can be found elsewhere (Wolpert and Flanagan, 2010; Sommer and Wurtz, 2008; Crapse and Sommer, 2008a, 2008b); here, the focus is on the possible role of efference copies in thalamocortical processing.

Coordinated motor performance of any motile animal without efference copies is implausible. Indeed, the presence of efference copies was predicted in the nineteenth century (von Graefe, 1854). It took nearly another century for experimental evidence to be found for efference copies in fishes and flies (Sperry, 1950; von Holst and Mittelstaedt, 1950), and this indicates that it must occur widely in the animal kingdom and be a core part of our early evolutionary heritage. It thus logically follows that any message generated anywhere in the central nervous system that leads to a change in motor behavior must have associated with it an efference copy. In the next section, I suggest that branching axons associated with thalamocortical relationships might serve a role in the processing of some efference copies.

Axonal Branching

Axonal branching is a ubiquitous feature of the central nervous system. Because of the high safety factor in propagating action potentials in mammalian axons, it seems clear that the exact same temporal pattern of action potentials will be conducted along all branches of the axon to its terminations (Raastad and

Anatomy

Shepherd, 2003; Cox et al., 2000). This does not mean that the message has the same effect on all of its targets because different synaptic properties at different targets likely exist, and these lead to postsynaptic variation in responses. Nonetheless, a branching axon is the most efficient and effective way to share a single message with multiple targets.

Some Axonal Branching Could Subserve Efference Copies

Over a century ago, Cajal (1911) emphasized the omnipresence of branching axons in the central nervous system. Figure 8A is a reproduction of one of his drawings from Golgi impregnations in which he pointed out that every primary afferent entering the spinal cord branches, with one branch innervating the ventral horn, where motoneurons live, and the other ascending to the brain. Figure 8B is a version of this pattern shown more schematically. The branch carrying the message toward motoneurons can be considered a motor command, but the branch ascending to the brain carries the exact same message. This ascending message is conventionally thought of as a sensory message, conveying information about a change in skin depression, a joint angle, and so forth. However, this message is also an exact copy of a message targeting motor neurons, that is, a motor message, and a copy of a motor message is a definition of an efference copy. An important point about the ascending axon branch is that it carries a single message. This message can be interpreted by some postsynaptic targets as sensory information and by others as an efference copy.

Axonal Branching of Driver Afferents to Thalamus

Figure 6 shows that axons providing the driver inputs to both first and higher order relay cells branch, with extrathalamic branches innervating targets in the brainstem and spinal cord that are often motor in nature (Sherman and Guillery, 2013; Guillery, 2003, 2005). Figure 9 shows specific examples of this. Most or all retinogeniculate axons branch to innervate the pretectum and/or superior colliculus (Sur et al., 1987; Tamamaki et al., 1995), areas involved in the control of head and eye movements, pupillary size, focusing, and so forth (Figure 9A). Other examples in Figure 9 include cerebellar axons innervating the ventral anterior/ventral lateral complex of the motor thalamus and branching to innervate bulbospinal control centers (Figure 9B), and layer 5 pyramidal tract axons from the motor cortex that branch to innervate the thalamus plus many motor targets in the brainstem, as well as entering the spinal cord (Figure 9C).

So far, the evidence is that all layer 5 corticofugal axons branch to innervate numerous targets, and those that innervate the thalamus also innervate extrathalamic targets; these latter targets include supraspinal control centers and often the spinal cord itself. In any case, this branching pattern of driver inputs to the thalamus, with some extrathalamic branches targeting subcortical motor structures, seems to be a ubiquitous feature of thalamic circuitry. An interesting feature of these layer 5 corticothalamic axons is that regardless of the cortical area of origin, the layer 5 projections to the thalamus all have extrathalamic branches, and most or all of these innervate the superior colliculus (Prasad et al., 2020; Economo et al., 2018).

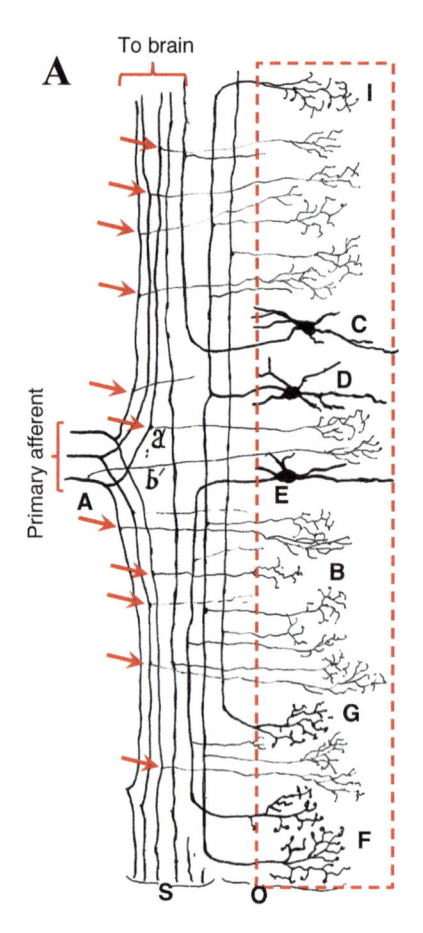

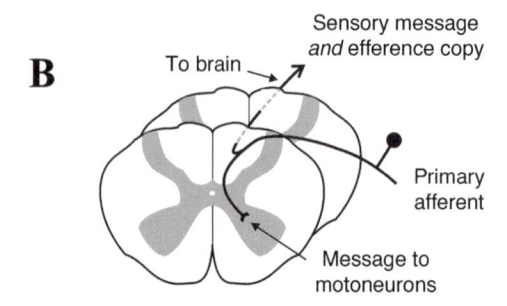

Figure 8 Examples of branching primary afferents to spinal cord.
A. Cajal illustration (Cajal, 1911) of primary axons entering the spinal cord and branching to innervate the spinal gray matter and brain areas. The red arrows indicate branch points.
B. Schematic interpretation of panel A. From Sherman (2016).

One interpretation of this pattern of branching driver afferents to the thalamus shown in Figure 6 is that the messages relayed by the thalamus can relate to motor commands and thus serve as efference copies. However, as explained by the example of Figure 8B, these messages can be interpreted by different targets groups in different ways, with only some postsynaptic circuitry treating them as efference copies.

Logic of Cortically Related Efference Copies

These ideas of efference copies related to thalamic afferents may at first seem unfettered and purely speculative, but there is a plausible line of reasoning that supports this hypothesis. The

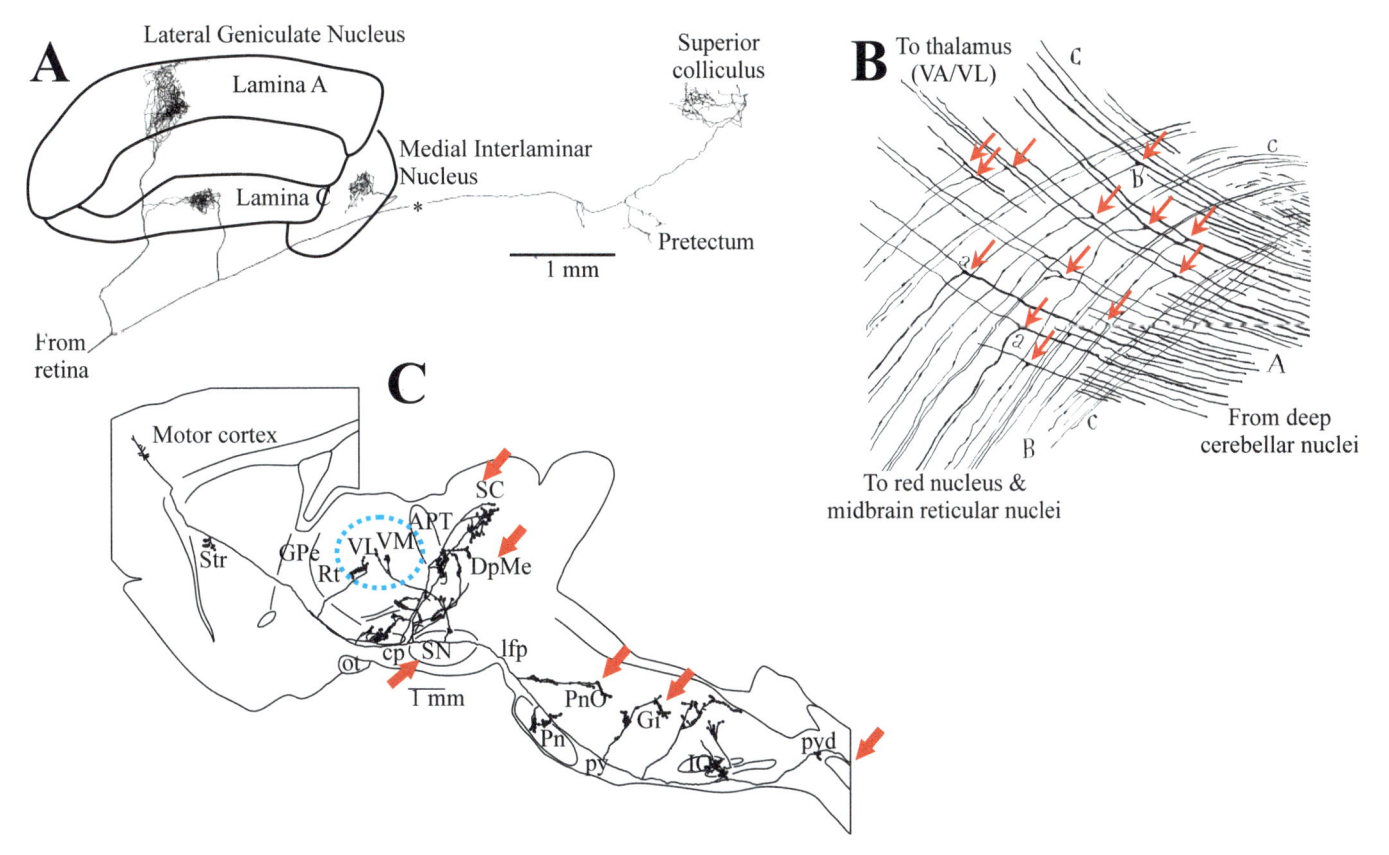

Figure 9 Examples of branching axons of driver inputs to the thalamus.

A. Example from retinogeniculate axon of cat; redrawn from Tamamaki et al. (1995).

B. Cajal illustration (Cajal, 1911) showing that innervation of the ventral anterior–ventral lateral (VA-VL) thalamic complex from the cerebellum involves axons that branch (*red arrows*) to innervate other brainstem structures as well.

C. Example from layer 5 pyramidal tract cell of rat motor cortex; redrawn from Kita and Kita (2012). Branches innervating the thalamus are indicated by the dashed blue circle, and brainstem motor regions are indicated by red arrows. Abbreviations: *DpMe*, deep mesencephalic nuclei; *Gi*, gigantocellular reticular nucleus; *GPe*, globus pallidus external segment; *ic*, internal capsule; *IO*, inferior olive; *MIN*, medial interlaminar nucleus (part of the lateral geniculate nucleus); *Pn*, pontine nucleus; *PnO*, pontine reticular nucleus, oral part; *py*, medullary pyramid; *pyd*, pyramidal decussation; *Rt*, reticular thalamic nucleus; *SC*, superior colliculus; *SN*, substantia nigra; *Str*, striatum; *VL*, ventrolateral thalamic nucleus; *VM*, ventromedial thalamic nucleus. From Sherman (2016).

cortex clearly evolved to affect behavior in more flexible and effective ways than had been possible with only subcortical circuitry. Nonetheless, much behavior is accomplished without significant cortical participation: think of chewing gum, breathing, or walking up a familiar flight of stairs. Yet the cortex is required for many high-level behaviors, such as when attention is focused on a new task. But the only effective pathway for the cortex to affect behavior is through its layer 5 projections to the brainstem and spinal motor centers. The cortex, with all of its beautiful circuitry and computational power, would be pretty useless without these layer 5 outputs.

Thus, the cortex influences behavior by using layer 5 projections, meaning that the messages carried by these axons in at least some cases are read as motor commands. If the cortex does act to create a new behavior, it follows that it must also create a related efference copy to be fed back into the cortical circuitry so that further cortical processing can disambiguate the environmental effects of any new movement from independent environmental changes. The branches from these layer 5 axons that innervate the thalamus seem like an ideal candidate for an efference copy route because, as noted, the branch to the thalamus carries an exact copy of the message also being transmitted to subcortical motor centers.

It should also be noted again that an efference copy, to be effective, must create a forward model of the expected behavior, and this must occur with minimal latency. Therefore, any efference copies generated downstream from these layer 5 outputs, for instance, from target brainstem or spinal centers, might be too late by the time they reach the cortex. Again, the idea is that layer 5 corticofugal branches that innervate the thalamus seem to fit the bill quite nicely.

Although evidence does indicate that virtually every layer 5 axon that innervates the thalamus branches to innervate other subcortical sites, the obverse is not the case: some of the layer 5 corticofugal axons avoid targeting the thalamus (Economo et al., 2018). This indicates an important proviso to these ideas about efference copies because if these neurons carry a motor message like other layer 5 corticofugal projections, their innervation patterns offer no clear route for an efference copy back to the cortex that can quickly produce the needed forward model. At least three possible explanations for this pattern can be proposed. First, these projections that avoid the thalamus may modulate rather than drive their subcortical targets and thus would not carry a message requiring an efference copy. Second, perhaps an efference copy originates from one of their targets, such as the superior colliculus (see later discussion), and the extra synaptic delay still permits a timely efference copy. Indeed, evidence exists for efference copies being sent from the superior colliculus to the thalamus (Sommer and Wurtz, 2004). Third, these ideas about efference copies may simply be wrong.

Other Aspects of Layer 5 Corticofugal Projections

The evolution of the cortex occurred without coevolution of motor circuitry to which the cortex has unique access. That is, except in rare examples in primates, there is no direct pathway from the cortex to motoneurons (Isa et al., 2013; Rathelot and Strick, 2009). This means that layer 5 outputs of the cortex must operate through older circuitry in the brainstem and spinal cord if they are to influence behavior.

Bursting in Layer 5 Corticofugal Cells

Both tonic and burst firing also exist in layer 5 corticofugal cells that in many ways resemble these different firing modes in thalamic relay cells, although different Ca^{2+} channels are involved (Larkum et al., 1999, 2007; Llano and Sherman, 2009; Suzuki and Larkum, 2020). One similarity is that these layer 5 cells must be suitably hyperpolarized for a period of time to de-inactivate the Ca^{2+} channels so that a burst can be evoked, and during such hyperpolarization, these cells would not fire action potentials. Because the layer 5 inputs to higher order thalamic relay cells have driver characteristics showing paired-pulse depression (Sherman, 2016; Sherman and Guillery, 2013), and because the requisite period of hyperpolarization and lack of firing would relieve such depression, it follows that a burst would maximally activate the corticothalamic synapses, just as bursting thalamic relay cells do so in the cortex (Swadlow et al., 2002; Swadlow and Gusev, 2001). Perhaps this acts as a "wake-up call" for the transthalamic pathway much as it does for thalamocortical processing, as suggested previously.

Several unresolved issues arise with this speculation. One is that bursting in these cells, as in thalamic relay cells, likely involves nonlinear distortion in the message being transmitted. Second, because these layer 5 projections involve branching to many extrathalamic motor sites as well as the thalamus, what is the implication of this strong activation of these sites by the bursts? Is this a way to "jump-start" the initial phase of a motor action? Clearly, there is a great deal we need to learn about the properties of these layer 5 corticofugal cells, especially because they are the sole means by which the cortex can influence behavior.

We have discussed earlier how the burst/tonic transition in thalamic relay cells might be controlled (e.g., via layer 6 feedback circuitry). There are several pieces of evidence for the control of bursting in these layer 5 cells, largely from the work of Matthew Larkum and his colleagues (Suzuki and Larkum, 2020; Larkum et al., 1999, 2004). Bursting in these cells occurs when there is conjoint synaptic activation of their apical dendritic tufts in layer 1 and input to more proximal dendrites. The summed resultant depolarization, which typically involves a backpropagating action potential, is sufficient to activate the Ca^{2+} spike in the apical dendrite, thereby producing a burst. This requires coupling between the apical dendritic tufts in layer 1 and the main shaft of the apical dendrite. This coupling can be broken by anesthetics but, more interestingly, also by blockers of metabotropic receptors for either acetylcholine (i.e., muscarinic receptors) or glutamate (i.e., metabotropic glutamate receptors) (Suzuki and Larkum, 2020). It thus follows that cholinergic input from the basal forebrain, which corresponds mostly to overall behavioral state, or that from glutamatergic modulators, which can provide more specific and topographic control of activity in these layer 5 corticofugal cells, can provide necessary conditions for bursting in these cells. Given the importance of these layer 5 cells for the execution of cortical control of behavior, it is of obvious importance to better understand the response properties of these cells and, in particular, the inputs that activate metabotropic glutamate receptors that control bursting.

Layer 5 Projections to the Midbrain

It seems reasonable to assume that in doing so, the cortex would preferentially operate through circuits more advanced in evolutionary terms rather than having to "reinvent the wheel" by accessing older circuitry in the spinal cord and brainstem. In this regard, the most advanced sensorimotor center in nonmammalian vertebrates is the optic tectum and associated midbrain regions, structures that remain in mammals as a major center for controlling head and body movements (Stein et al., 2009; Stein and Gaither, 1983; Gaither and Stein, 1979; Suzuki et al., 2019).

From this perspective, we suggest that the most efficient way for the cortex to influence many or most behaviors is by operating through these midbrain circuits. It is thus particularly interesting that most or all cortical areas for which layer 5 projections have been defined innervate the midbrain (Prasad et al., 2020; Kita and Kita, 2012; Bourassa and Deschênes, 1995; Bourassa et al., 1995; Deschênes et al., 1994; Economo et al., 2018). Also, these studies indicate that most or all layer 5 axons that innervate the midbrain branch to innervate the thalamus.

Layer 5 Projections and Attention

Mechanisms underlying attention have long been a main focus of neuroscience research. A detailed discussion of the neuronal bases of attention is beyond the scope of this account, and many excellent reviews on the subject are available (Nobre et al., 2014; Maunsell and Treue, 2006; Posner, 2012; Desimone and Duncan, 1995; Petersen and Posner, 2012; Reynolds and Chelazzi, 2004). Much research on underlying mechanisms of attention has been directed at putative bottom-up and/or top-down circuits that enable a brain region, typically cortical, to enhance processing of the attended object (Awh et al., 2012; Desimone and Duncan, 1995). Mechanisms for this that have been identified to date include, among others, enhanced responses to attended stimuli (Lee and Maunsell,

2010; Suzuki et al., 2019; Mineault et al., 2016; Maunsell and Treue, 2006); less noise correlation in firing among neurons in the attending circuit (Cohen and Maunsell, 2009); coherent, rhythmic neuronal firing across cortical areas (Fries, 2005; Suzuki et al., 2019; Chalk et al., 2010; Miller and Buschman, 2013;); and enhancement of thalamocortical synaptic efficacy (Suzuki et al., 2019; Briggs et al., 2013).

Why does attention reduce cognitive abilities to unattended objects? The explanation for attentional mechanisms is that it enables our brains to focus on environmental events of particular importance to our survival. For instance, a rabbit traveling through bushland might attend with its visual system on the lookout for hovering hawks. However, attention comes at a price because that rabbit, by emphasizing visual stimuli, may be less responsive to auditory cues that could signal a stalking fox. Even within vision, there may be a price to be paid: by concentrating on upper visual fields where hawks fly, the rabbit might miss observing the fox in its lower visual field. This raises the question: Given the extensive cortical circuitry subserving its enormous computational power, why cannot all areas of the cortex function all the time in an attentive-like mode so that the rabbit can be maximally sensitive to all sensory stimuli simultaneously? I believe that an evolutionary perspective offers a plausible answer to this question (Sherman and Usrey, 2021).

As noted earlier, the cortex evolved without the evolution of motor circuitry to which it has unique access. This means that cortical areas can only influence behavior by projections from layer 5 that activate older motor centers in the brainstem and spinal cord. These older motor centers may be seen as a bottleneck through which the cortex must operate. This presents a problem. If, as suggested previously, every cortical area operated at maximum capacity to turn its inputs into layer 5 motor commands, these would all compete for control through the same subcortical intermediaries, and chaos would ensue. There clearly needs to be some selective process that ensures that only the cortical areas engaged in analyzing those environmental objects that are the most important, or the most crucial to survival, are permitted to control subcortical motor centers. This is where "attention" comes in. Somehow, via top-down or bottom-up processes (Awh et al., 2012; Desimone and Duncan, 1995), the appropriate region or regions of cortex are engaged, and their layer 5 corticofugal projections are allowed to dominate subcortical motor regions; other areas of cortex (and their layer 5 outputs) dealing with less critical environmental events are suppressed.

Attention is not just cortical. Most of the literature on attention is concerned only with cortical contributions thereof. However, an evolutionary perspective suggests a more complex view. Just as attention seems necessary to ensure that the appropriate cortical regions take control of behavior, more primitive species had to deal with the same problem but without a cortex. For example, the highest level of behavioral control for nonmammalian vertebrates would be various brainstem motor areas, and I have argued earlier that the highest level of motor control for nonmammalian vertebrates is located in the midbrain. These centers, like the mammalian cortex, also had to operate through older bulbospinal and spinal centers, and the same problem as suggested earlier had to be overcome: that is, to avoid chaos, something like attentional mechanisms would be required to filter out inappropriate midbrain centers from controlling behavior (Sherman and Usrey, 2021).

One general rule of the evolution of the nervous system is that these older circuits are not discarded as newer ones evolve, and furthermore, these older circuits continue to function in current species, including humans. Indeed, for example, the mammalian superior colliculus has been shown to be involved in various attentional and other cognitive processes (Suzuki et al., 2019; Basso and May, 2017; Krauzlis et al., 2013; Wang et al., 2020; Herman et al., 2018; Wang and Krauzlis, 2018). It thus seems likely that the attentional mechanisms in our brains are not limited to cortical circuitry but involve older, subcortical circuits as well, and these all must operate in a coordinated fashion.

Concluding Remarks

Figure 10 contrasts the conventional view of thalamocortical processing (Figure 10A) with the alternative view offered here (Figure 10B). The conventional view is that information from the periphery is initially relayed by the thalamus to the sensory cortex and passes up a cortical hierarchy from sensory areas to sensorimotor areas and finally to some executive motor area from which an output is finally produced to activate motor centers and affect behavior (Figure 10A). Also, it is only at this final stage of sensorimotor processing that an efference copy is created, but the circuitry of Figure 10A offers no plausible route for this information to reach the cortex in a timely manner, a *sine qua non* for continued effective cortical involvement in ongoing behavior. Another problem with Figure 10A is that it provides no specific role for most of the thalamus (indicated by question marks), which we have defined as higher order. Perhaps even more important as a criticism, the circuitry of Figure 10A seems an implausible result of evolution. That is, anytime a new sensory receptor or circuit evolves, it will have no survival value if it lacks a fairly immediate motor output. Whereas an intelligent designer might design a circuit like Figure 10A, it seems unlikely that evolution would produce one that takes so long to yield a relevant behavioral response to a sensory stimulus.

The alternative view (Figure 10B) differs significantly and does so from the very beginning of the sensorimotor processing stream. The initial information to be relayed via a first order thalamic nucleus is a copy of the information sent to motor structures. From the primary cortex, information can be relayed to other cortical areas not only via direct projections but also via higher order thalamic nuclei, and this continues through the various hierarchical stages. Also, these transthalamic pathways involve layer 5 corticothalamic axons that branch to innervate extrathalamic motor structures. Thus, this circuitry provides a credible route for efference copies to be effectively incorporated into further cortical processing.

Figures 6 and 10B show that most or all driving inputs to the thalamus, even to first order relays, branch to innervate extrathalamic motor centers. The branches related to first order relays are perhaps quite crude commands that are

Anatomy

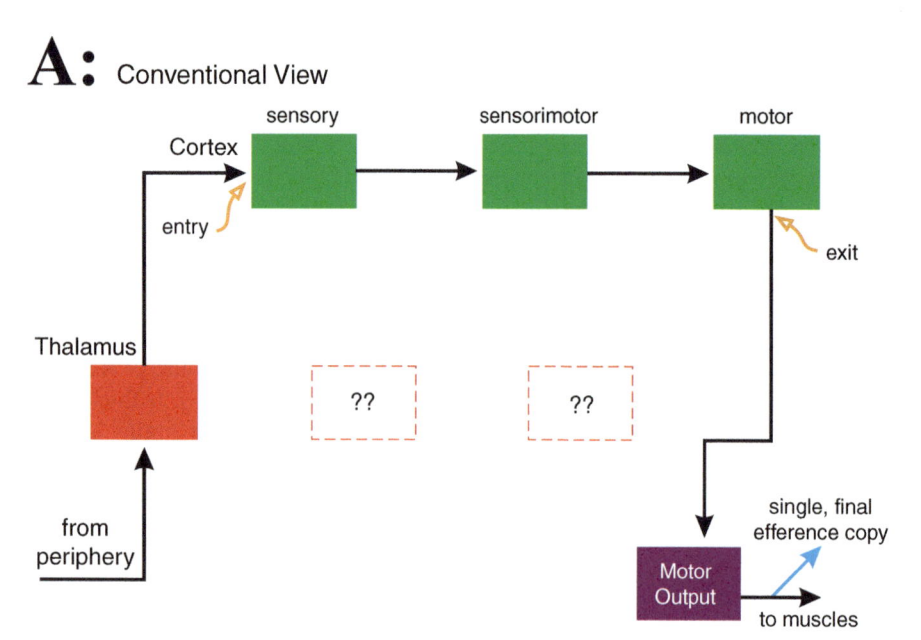

A: Conventional View

Figure 10 Comparison of conventional view (A) with the alternative view proposed here (B).
Abbreviations: *FO*, first order; *HO*, higher order. Further details in the text. Reproduced from Sherman (2005).

B: Alternative View

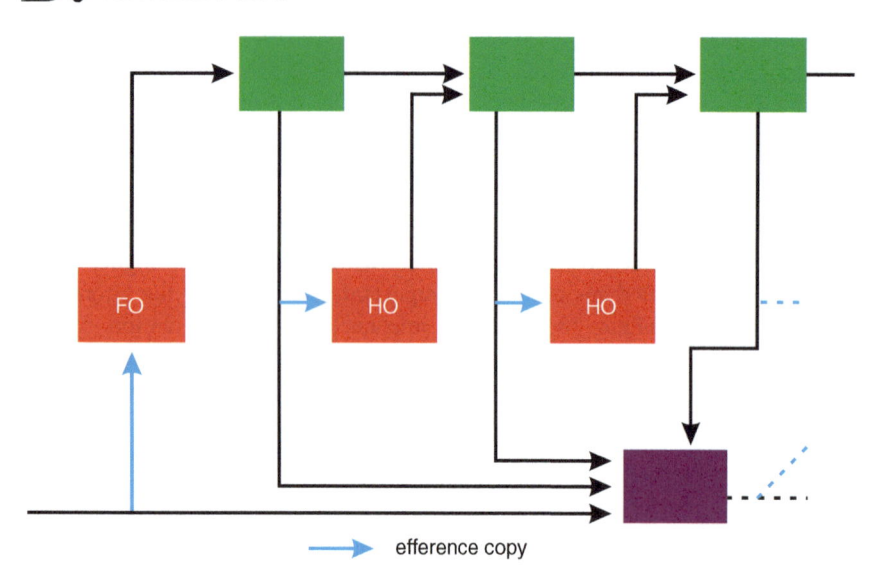

efference copy

constantly upgraded with further cortical processing and effected via higher order layer 5 cortical outputs. An observation consistent with but far from proving this scenario was made in monkeys trained to pursue a moving target that suddenly appeared in their visual fields (Osborne et al., 2007). After fixing the target, each monkey pursued it with smooth eye movements, but the accuracy of the smooth pursuit was initially poor and improved asymptotically over the next 50–100 msec of pursuit.

This interpretation clearly stands the conventional view of early visual processing on its head. That is, conventionally, the primary visual cortex (V1) is generally viewed as a purely sensory structure, and this view seems at odds with the idea that V1 is processing motor information. Furthermore, as already noted, V1 (and indeed, all cortical areas so far studied) has a layer 5 projection that branches to innervate pulvinar and extrathalamic motor targets (Prasad et al., 2020; Kita and Kita, 2012; Bourassa and Deschênes, 1995; Bourassa et al., 1995; Deschênes et al., 1994; Economo et al., 2018), so even the corticofugal outputs of V1 have a motor tag according to this perspective. The conventional wisdom that V1 or any other visual, auditory, or somatosensory area is purely "sensory" is thus challenged by this observation that all of these areas have motor outputs. Indeed, as suggested previously, the idea that evolution would produce cortical areas that have no fairly immediate motor effect seems unlikely. By this way of thinking, the current view that some cortical areas are "sensory" and others "motor" is misleading. Finally, Figure 10B offers a more plausible route for efference copies to be integrated into cortical processing.

The bottom line is that higher order thalamic nuclei play an important and still largely unappreciated role in corticocortical communication. Thus, the thalamus is not there just to get information to the cortex in the first place but, rather, continues to play a role in further cortical processing of that information. What is less clear is the different roles of the direct and transthalamic corticocortical pathways, their relationship to each other, and why one route involves a thalamic relay.

Outstanding Questions

I conclude this chapter with a list of questions, the answers to which are as yet unavailable but that I consider to be of special importance.

1. Why do we have a thalamus?
2. Among glutamatergic inputs in the thalamus, those of modulators greatly outnumber those of drivers, measured either by the number of afferent axons or the number of synaptic terminals, but what are the relative numbers for cortical circuitry?
3. How common is the pattern whereby two cortical areas are connected in parallel by both direct and transthalamic pathways, or are some connected only by one or the other? Does this pattern apply equally to feedforward and feedback transthalamic pathways?
4. What is different in the nature of the messages carried by direct versus transthalamic corticocortical pathways?
5. Why do the messages carried by transthalamic pathways pass through a thalamic relay?
6. Given that some layer 5 corticofugal axons that innervate subcortical motor centers have branches that innervate higher order relays and others lack these branches, what are the functional differences between these two types of layer 5 cells? Do they send different messages to the lower motor centers?
7. What is the significance of the pattern of branching axons that provide driver input to the thalamus and also innervate extrathalamic targets? (Remember that the suggestion that these relate to efference copies is merely a hypothesis.)
8. Why does attention reduce awareness of unattended features in the environment?
9. What is the significance of bursting in layer 5 corticofugal cells, and how is it controlled?

References

Alitto, H., Rathbun, D. L., Vandeleest, J. J., Alexander, P. C., & Usrey, W. M. (2019). The augmentation of retinogeniculate communication during thalamic burst mode. *Journal of Neuroscience*, **39**, 5710.

Andolina, I. M., Jones, H. E., & Sillito, A. M. (2013). Effects of cortical feedback on the spatial properties of relay cells in the lateral geniculate nucleus. *Journal of Neurophysiology*, **109**, 889–899.

Awh, E., Belopolsky, A. V., & Theeuwes, J. (2012). Top-down versus bottom-up attentional control: A failed theoretical dichotomy. *Trends in Cognitive Sciences*, **16**, 437–443.

Basso, M. A., & May, P. J. (2017). Circuits for action and cognition: A view from the superior colliculus. *Annual Review of Vision Science*, **3**, 197–226.

Berman, R. A., & Wurtz, R. H. (2010). Functional identification of a pulvinar path from superior colliculus to cortical area MT. *Journal of Neuroscience*, **30**, 6342–6354.

Bezdudnaya, T., Cano, M., Bereshpolova, Y., Stoelzel, C. R., Alonso, J. M., & Swadlow, H. A. (2006). Thalamic burst mode and inattention in the awake LGNd. *Neuron*, **49**, 421–432.

Bickford, M. E., Zhou, N., Krahe, T. E., Govindaiah, G., & Guido, W. (2015). Retinal and tectal "driver-like" inputs converge in the shell of the mouse dorsal lateral geniculate nucleus. *Journal of Neuroscience*, **35**, 10523–10534.

Bokor, H., Frere, S. G. A., Eyre, M. D., Slezia, A., Ulbert, I., Luthi, A., et al. (2005). Selective GABAergic control of higher-order thalamic relays. *Neuron*, **45**, 929–940.

Bourassa, J., & Deschênes, M. (1995). Corticothalamic projections from the primary visual cortex in rats: A single fiber study using biocytin as an anterograde tracer. *Neuroscience*, **66**, 253–263.

Bourassa, J., Pinault, D., & Deschênes, M. (1995). Corticothalamic projections from the cortical barrel field to the somatosensory thalamus in rats: A single-fibre study using biocytin as an anterograde tracer. *European Journal of Neuroscience*, **7**, 19–30.

Branco, T., & Staras, K. (2009). The probability of neurotransmitter release: variability and feedback control at single synapses. *Nature Reviews Neuroscience*, **10**, 373–383.

Briggs, F., Mangun, G. R., & Usrey, W. M. (2013). Attention enhances synaptic efficacy and the signal-to-noise ratio in neural circuits. *Nature*, **499**, 476–480.

Brown, D. A., Abogadie, F. C., Allen, T. G., Buckley, N. J., Caulfield, M. P., Delmas, P., Haley, J. E., Lamas, J. A., & Selyanko, A. A. (1997). Muscarinic mechanisms in nerve cells. *Life Sciences*, **60**, 1137–1144.

Cajal, S. R. y. (1911). *Histologie du Système Nerveaux de l'Homme et des Vertébrés*. Paris: Maloine.

Chalk, M., Herrero, J. L., Gieselmann, M. A., Delicato, L. S., Gotthardt, S., & Thiele, A. (2010). Attention reduces stimulus-driven gamma frequency oscillations and spike field coherence in V1. *Neuron*, **66**, 114–125.

Cohen, M. R., & Maunsell, J. H. (2009). Attention improves performance primarily by reducing interneuronal correlations. *Nature Neuroscience*, **12**, 1594–1600.

Covic, E. N., & Sherman, S. M. (2011). Synaptic properties of connections between the primary and secondary auditory cortices in mice. *Cerebral Cortex*, **21**, 2425–2441.

Cox, C. L., Denk, W., Tank, D. W., & Svoboda, K. (2000). Action potentials reliably invade axonal arbors of rat neocortical neurons. *Proceedings of the National Academy of Sciences of the United States of America*, **97**, 9724–9728.

Crapse, T. B., & Sommer, M. A. (2008a). Corollary discharge across the animal kingdom. *Nature Reviews Neuroscience*, **9**, 587–600.

Crapse, T. B., & Sommer, M. A. (2008b). Corollary discharge circuits in the primate brain. *Current Opinion in Neurobiology,* **18,** 552–557.

Crunelli, V., & Leresche, N. (1991). A role for GABA$_B$ receptors in excitation and inhibition of thalamocortical cells. *Trends in Neurosciences,* **14,** 16–21.

Deleuze, C., David, F., Behuret, S., Sadoc, G., Shin, H. S., Uebele, V. N., et al. (2012). T-type calcium channels consolidate tonic action potential output of thalamic neurons to neocortex. *Journal of Neuroscience,* **32,** 12228–12236.

DePasquale, R., & Sherman, S. M. (2011). Synaptic properties of corticocortical connections between the primary and secondary visual cortical areas in the mouse. *Journal of Neuroscience,* **31,** 16494–16506.

DePasquale, R., & Sherman, S. M. (2012). Modulatory effects of metabotropic glutamate receptors on local cortical circuits. *Journal of Neuroscience,* **32,** 7364–7372.

DePasquale, R., & Sherman, S. M. (2013). A modulatory effect of the feedback from higher visual areas to V1 in the mouse. *Journal of Neurophysiology,* **109,** 2618–2631.

Deschênes, M., Bourassa, J., & Pinault, D. (1994). Corticothalamic projections from layer V cells in rat are collaterals of long-range corticofugal axons. *Brain Research,* **664,** 215–219.

Desimone, R., & Duncan, J. (1995). Neural mechanisms of selective visual attention. *Annual Reviews in Neuroscience,* **18,** 193–222.

Dittman, J. S., Kreitzer, A. C., & Regehr, W. G. (2000). Interplay between facilitation, depression, and residual calcium at three presynaptic terminals. *Journal of Neuroscience,* **20,** 1374–1385.

Dobrunz, L. E., & Stevens, C. F. (1997). Heterogeneity of release probability, facilitation, and depletion at central synapses. *Neuron,* **18,** 995–1008.

Economo, M. N., Viswanathan, S., Tasic, B., Bas, E., Winnubst, J., Menon, V., et al. (2018). Distinct descending motor cortex pathways and their roles in movement. *Nature,* **563,** 79–84.

Fries, P. (2005). A mechanism for cognitive dynamics: neuronal communication through neuronal coherence. *Trends in Cognitive Sciences,* **9,** 474–480.

Gaither, N. S., & Stein, B. E. (1979). Reptiles and mammals use similar sensory organizations in the midbrain. *Science,* **205,** 595–597.

Gilbert, C. D. (1977). Laminar differences in receptive field properties of cells in cat primary visual cortex. *Journal of Physiology (London),* **268,** 391–421.

Godwin, D. W., Vaughan, J. W., & Sherman, S. M. (1996). Metabotropic glutamate receptors switch visual response mode of lateral geniculate nucleus cells from burst to tonic. *Journal of Neurophysiology,* **76,** 1800–1816.

Groh, A., Bokor, H., Mease, R. A., Plattner, V. M., Hangya, B., Stroh, A., et al. (2013). Convergence of cortical and sensory driver inputs on single thalamocortical cells. *Cerebral Cortex,* **24,** 3167–3179.

Groh, A., Bokor, H., Mease, R. A., Plattner, V. M., Hangya, B., Stroh, A., et al. (2014). Convergence of cortical and sensory driver inputs on single thalamocortical cells. *Cerebral Cortex,* **24,** 3167–3179.

Guillery, R. W. (1995). Anatomical evidence concerning the role of the thalamus in corticocortical communication: A brief review. *Journal of Anatomy,* **187,** 583–592.

Guillery, R. W. (2003). Branching thalamic afferents link action and perception. *Journal of Neurophysiology,* **90,** 539–548.

Guillery, R. W. (2005). Anatomical pathways that link action to perception. *Progress in Brain Research,* **149,** 235–256.

Gulcebi, M. I., Ketenci, S., Linke, R., Hacioglu, H., Yanali, H., Veliskova, J., et al. (2011). Topographical connections of the substantia nigra pars reticulata to higher-order thalamic nuclei in the rat. *Brain Research Bulletin,* **87,** 312–318.

Herman, J. P., Katz, L. N., & Krauzlis, R. J. (2018). Midbrain activity can explain perceptual decisions during an attention task. *Nature Neuroscience,* **21,** 1651–1655.

Hille, B. (1992). *Ionic channels of excitable membranes.* Sunderland, MA: Sinauer Associates.

Hubel, D. H., & Wiesel, T. N. (1961). Integrative action in the cat's lateral geniculate body. *Journal of Physiology (London),* **155,** 385–398.

Huguenard, J. R. (1996). Low-threshold calcium currents in central nervous system neurons. *Annual Review of Physiology,* **58,** 329–348.

Huguenard, J. R., & McCormick, D. A. (1994). *Electrophysiology of the neuron.* New York: Oxford: Oxford University Press.

Huguenard, J. R., & Prince, D. A. (1994). Clonazepam suppresses GABA$_B$-mediated inhibition in thalamic relay neurons through effects in nucleus reticularis. *Journal of Neurophysiology,* **71,** 2576–2581.

Isa, T., Kinoshita, M., & Nishimura, Y. (2013). Role of direct vs. indirect pathways from the motor cortex to spinal motoneurons in the control of hand dexterity. *Frontiers in Neurology,* **4,** 191.

Jack, J. J. B., Noble, D., & Tsien, R. W. (1975). *Electric current flow in excitable cells.* Oxfrod: Oxford University Press.

Jahnsen, H., & Llinás, R. (1984a). Electrophysiological properties of guinea-pig thalamic neurones: An in vitro study. *Journal of Physiology (London),* **349,** 205–226.

Jahnsen, H., & Llinás, R. (1984b). Ionic basis for the electroresponsiveness and oscillatory properties of guinea-pig thalamic neurones in vitro. *Journal of Physiology (London),* **349,** 227–247.

Johnston, D., Magee, J. C., Colbert, C. M., & Christie, B. R. (1996). Active properties of neuronal dendrites. *Annual Review of Neuroscience,* **19,** 165–186.

Kelly, L. R., Li, J., Carden, W. B., & Bickford, M. E. (2003). Ultrastructure and synaptic targets of tectothalamic terminals in the cat lateral posterior nucleus. *Journal of Comparative Neurology,* **464,** 472–486.

Kim, H. R., Hong, S. Z., & Fiorillo, C. D. (2015). T-type calcium channels cause bursts of spikes in motor but not sensory thalamic neurons during mimicry of natural patterns of synaptic input. *Frontiers in Cellular Neuroscience,* **9,** 428.

Kita, T., & Kita, H. (2012). The subthalamic nucleus is one of multiple innervation sites for long-range corticofugal axons: a single-axon tracing study in the rat. *Journal of Neuroscience,* **32,** 5990–5999.

Krauzlis, R. J., Lovejoy, L. P., & Zenon, A. (2013). Superior colliculus and visual spatial attention. *Annual Reviews in Neuroscience,* **36,** 165–182.

Kuramoto, E., Fujiyama, F., Nakamura, K. C., Tanaka, Y., Hioki, H., & Kaneko, T. (2011). Complementary distribution of glutamatergic cerebellar and GABAergic basal ganglia afferents to the rat motor thalamic nuclei. *European Journal of Neuroscience,* **33,** 95–109.

Lam, Y. W., & Sherman, S. M. (2010). Functional organization of the somatosensory cortical layer 6 feedback to the thalamus. *Cerebral Cortex,* **20,** 13–24.

Lam, Y. W., & Sherman, S. M. (2019). Convergent synaptic inputs to layer 1 cells of mouse cortex. *European Journal of Neuroscience,* **49,** 1399.

Larkum, M. E., Senn, W., & Luscher, H. R. (2004). Top-down dendritic input increases the gain of layer 5 pyramidal neurons. *Cerebral Cortex,* **14,** 1059–1070.

Larkum, M. E., Waters, J., Sakmann, B., & Helmchen, F. (2007). Dendritic spikes in apical dendrites of neocortical layer 2/3 pyramidal neurons. *Journal of Neuroscience,* **27,** 8999–9008.

Larkum, M. E., Zhu, J. J., & Sakmann, B. (1999). A new cellular mechanism for coupling inputs arriving at different cortical layers. *Nature*, **398**, 338–341.

Lavallée, P., Urbain, N., Dufresne, C., Bokor, H., Acsády, L., & Deschênes, M. (2005). Feedforward inhibitory control of sensory information in higher-order thalamic nuclei. *Journal of Neuroscience*, **25**, 7489–7498.

Lee, C. C., & Sherman, S. M. (2008). Synaptic properties of thalamic and intracortical inputs to layer 4 of the first- and higher-order cortical areas in the auditory and somatosensory systems. *Journal of Neurophysiology*, **100**, 317–326.

Lee, C. C., & Sherman, S. M. (2009). Modulator property of the intrinsic cortical projection from layer 6 to layer 4. *Frontiers in Systems Neuroscience*, **3**, 1–5.

Lee, C. C., & Sherman, S. M. (2012). Intrinsic modulators of auditory thalamocortical transmission. *Hearing Research*, **287**, 43–50.

Lee, J., & Maunsell, J. H. R. (2010). Attentional modulation of MT neurons with single or multiple stimuli in their receptive fields. *Journal of Neuroscience*, **30**, 3058–3066.

Levitan, I. B., & Kaczmarek, L. K. (2002). *The neuron: Cell and molecular biology*. New York: Oxford University Press.

Litvina, E. Y., & Chen, C. (2017). Functional convergence at the retinogeniculate synapse. *Neuron*, **96**, 330–338.

Llano, D. A., & Sherman, S. M. (2009). Differences in intrinsic properties and local network connectivity of identified layer 5 and layer 6 adult mouse auditory corticothalamic neurons support a dual corticothalamic projection hypothesis. *Cerebral Cortex*, **19**, 2810–2826.

Llinás, R. (1988). The intrinsic electrophysiological properties of mammalian neurons: insights into central nervous system. *Science*, **242**, 1654–1664.

Lujan, R., Nusser, Z., Roberts, J. D., Shigemoto, R., Somogyi P. (1996). Perisynaptic location of metabotropic glutamate receptors mGluR1 and mGluR5 on dendrites and dendritic spines in the rat hippocampus. *European Journal of Neuroscience*, **8**, 1488–1500.

MacLean, J. N., Watson, B. O., Aaron, G. B., & Yuste, R. (2005). Internal dynamics determine the cortical response to thalamic stimulation. *Neuron*, **48**, 811–823.

Maunsell, J. H., & Treue, S. (2006). Feature-based attention in visual cortex. *Trends in Neuroscience*, **29**, 317–322.

McCormick, D. A., & Huguenard, J. R. (1992). A model of the electrophysiological properties of thalamocortical relay neurons. *Journal of Neurophysiology*, **68**, 1384–1400.

Miller-Hansen, A.J., and Sherman, S.M. (2022) Conserved patterns of functional organization between cortex and thalamus in mice. Proc. Natl. Acad. Sci. (USA), in press.

Miller, E. K., & Buschman, T. J. (2013). Cortical circuits for the control of attention. *Current Opinion in Neurobiology*, **23**, 216–222.

Mineault, P. J., Tring, E., Trachtenberg, J. T., & Ringach, D. L. (2016). Enhanced spatial resolution during locomotion and heightened attention in mouse primary visual cortex. *Journal of Neuroscience*, **36**, 6382–6392.

Mo, C., & Sherman, S. M. (2019). A sensorimotor pathway via higher-order thalamus. *Journal of Neuroscience*, **39**, 692–704.

Mott, D. D., & Lewis, D. V. (1994). The pharmacology and function of central $GABA_B$ receptors. *International Review of Neurobiology*, **36**, 97–223.

Nicoll, R. A., Malenka, R. C., & Kauer, J. A. (1990). Functional comparison of neurotransmitter receptor subtypes in mammalian central nervous system. *Physiology Review*, **70**, 513–565.

Nobre, K., Nobre, A., & Kastner, S. (2014). *The Oxford handbook of attention*. Oxford: Oxford University Press.

Osborne, L. C., Hohl, S. S., Bialek, W., & Lisberger, S. G. (2007). Time course of precision in smooth-pursuit eye movements of monkeys. *Journal of Neuroscience*, **27**, 2987–2998.

Petersen, S. E., & Posner, M. I. (2012). The attention system of the human brain: 20 years after. *Annual Reviews in Neuroscience*, **35**, 73–89.

Petrof, I., Viaene, A. N., & Sherman, S. M. (2012). Synaptic properties of the lemniscal and paralemniscal somatosensory inputs to the mouse thalamus. *Proceedings of the National Academy of Sciences of the United States of America*, **114**, E6212–E6221.

Petrof, I., Viaene, A. N., & Sherman, S. M. (2015). Properties of the primary somatosensory cortex projection to the primary motor cortex in the mouse. *Journal of Neurophysiology*, **113**, 2652.

Pin, J. P., & Duvoisin, R. (1995). The metabotropic glutamate receptors: structure and functions. *Neuropharmacology*, **34**, 1–26.

Posner, M. I. (2012). *Cognitive neuroscience of attention*. New York: Guilford Press.

Prasad, J. A., Carroll, B. J., & Sherman, S. M. (2020). Layer 5 corticofugal projections from diverse cortical areas: variations on a pattern of thalamic and extra-thalamic targets. *Journal of Neuroscience*, **40**, 5785–5796.

Raastad, M., & Shepherd, G. M. (2003). Single-axon action potentials in the rat hippocampal cortex. *Journal of Physiology*, **548**, 745–752.

Ramcharan, E. J., Gnadt, J. W., & Sherman, S. M. (2005). Higher-order thalamic relays burst more than first-order relays. *Proceedings of the National Academy of Sciences of the United States of America*, **102**, 12236–12241.

Rathelot, J. A., & Strick, P. L. (2009). Subdivisions of primary motor cortex based on cortico-motoneuronal cells. *Proceedings of the National Academy of Sciences of the United States of America*, **106**, 918–923.

Recasens, M., & Vignes, M. (1995). Excitatory amino acid metabotropic receptor subtypes and calcium regulation. *Annals of the New York Academy of Sciences*, **757**, 418–429.

Reynolds, J. H., & Chelazzi, L. (2004). Attentional modulation of visual processing. *Annual Review of Neuroscience*, **27**, 611–647.

Sakai, S. T., Inase, M., & Tanji, J. (1996). Comparison of cerebellothalamic and pallidothalamic projections in the monkey (*Macaca fuscata*): A double anterograde labeling study. *Journal of Comparative Neurology*, **368**, 215–228.

Sherman, S. M. (1996). Dual response modes in lateral geniculate neurons: mechanisms and functions. *Visual Neuroscience*, **13**, 205–213.

Sherman, S. M. (2001). Tonic and burst firing: Dual modes of thalamocortical relay. *Trends in Neurosciences*, **24**, 122–126.

Sherman, S. M. (2005). Thalamic relays and cortical functioning. *Progress in Brain Research*, **149**, 107–126.

Sherman, S. M. (2016). Thalamus plays a central role in ongoing cortical functioning. *Nature Neuroscience*, **19**, 533–541.

Sherman, S. M., & Guillery, R. W. (1996). The functional organization of thalamocortical relays. *Journal of Neurophysiology*, **76**, 1367–1395.

Sherman, S. M., & Guillery, R. W. (1998). On the actions that one nerve cell can have on another: Distinguishing "drivers" from "modulators." *Proceedings of the National Academy of Sciences of the United States of America*, **95**, 7121–7126.

Sherman, S. M., & Guillery, R. W. (2006). *Exploring the thalamus and its role in cortical function* (2nd ed.). Cambridge, MA: MIT Press.

Sherman, S. M., & Guillery, R. W. (2013). *Functional connections of cortical areas: a new view from the thalamus.* Cambridge, MA: MIT Press.

Sherman SM, Usrey WM (2021) Cortical control of behavior and attention from an evolutionary perspective. Neuron 109: 3048–3064.

Snutch, T. P., & Reiner, P. B. (1992). Ca^{2+} channels: Diversity of form and function. *Current Opinion in Neurobiology*, **2**, 247–253.

Soltész, I., Lightowler, S., Leresche, N., & Crunelli, V. (1989). On the properties and origin of the $GABA_B$ inhibitory postsynaptic potential recorded in morphologically identified projection cells of the cat dorsal lateral geniculate nucleus. *Neuroscience*, **33**, 23–33.

Sommer, M. A., & Wurtz, R. H. (2004). What the brain stem tells the frontal cortex. II. Role of the SC-MD-FEF pathway in corollary discharge. *Journal of Neurophysiology*, **91**, 1403–1423.

Sommer, M. A., & Wurtz, R. H. (2008). Brain circuits for the internal monitoring of movements. *Annual Review of Neuroscience*, **31**, 317–338.

Sperry, R. W. (1950). Neural basis of the spontaneous optokinetic response produced by visual inversion. *Journal of Comparative Neurology*, **43**, 482–489.

Stein, B. E., & Gaither, N. S. (1983). Receptive-field properties in reptilian optic tectum: some comparisons with mammals. *Journal of Neurophysiology*, **50**, 102–124.

Stein, B. E., Stanford, T. R., & Rowland, B. A. (2009). The neural basis of multisensory integration in the midbrain: Its organization and maturation. *Hearing Research*, **258**, 4–15.

Sur, M., Esguerra, M., Garraghty, P. E., Kritzer, M. F., & Sherman, S. M. (1987). Morphology of physiologically identified retinogeniculate X- and Y-axons in the cat. *Journal of Neurophysiology*, **58**, 1–32.

Suzuki, D. G., Perez-Fernandez, J., Wibble, T., Kardamakis, A. A., & Grillner, S. (2019). The role of the optic tectum for visually evoked orienting and evasive movements. *Proceedings of the National Academy of Sciences of the United States of America*, **116**, 15272–15281.

Suzuki, M., & Larkum, M. E. (2020). General anesthesia decouples cortical pyramidal neurons. *Cell*, **180**, 666–676.

Swadlow, H. A., & Gusev, A. G. (2001). The impact of "bursting" thalamic impulses at a neocortical synapse. *Nature Neuroscience*, **4**, 402–408.

Swadlow, H. A., Gusev, A. G., & Bezdudnaya, T. (2002). Activation of a cortical column by a thalamocortical impulse. *Journal of Neuroscience*, **22**, 7766–7773.

Tamamaki, N., Uhlrich, D. J., & Sherman, S. M. (1995). Morphology of physiologically identified retinal X and Y axons in the cat's thalamus and midbrain as revealed by intra-axonal injection of biocytin. *Journal of Comparative Neurology*, **354**, 583–607.

Ulrich, D., Besseyrias, V., & Bettler, B. (2007). Functional mapping of GABA(B)-receptor subtypes in the thalamus. *Journal of Neurophysiology*, **98**, 3791–3795.

Usrey, W. M., Reppas, J. B., & Reid, R. C. (1999). Specificity and strength of retinogeniculate connections. *Journal of Neurophysiology*, **82**, 3527–3540.

Van Horn, S. C., Erisir, A., & Sherman, S. M. (2000). The relative distribution of synapses in the A-laminae of the lateral geniculate nucleus of the cat. *Journal of Comparative Neurology*, **416**, 509–520.

Van Horn, S. C., & Sherman, S. M. (2007). Fewer driver synapses in higher order than in first order thalamic relays. *Neuroscience*, **475**, 406–415.

Varela, C., & Sherman, S. M. (2007). Differences in response to muscarinic agonists between first and higher order thalamic relays. *Journal of Neurophysiology*, **98**, 3538–3547.

Varela, C., & Sherman, S. M. (2008). Differences in response to serotonergic activation between first and higher order thalamic nuclei. *Cerebral Cortex*, **19**, 1776–1786.

Viaene, A. N., Petrof, I., & Sherman, S. M. (2011a). Properties of the thalamic projection from the posterior medial nucleus to primary and secondary somatosensory cortices in the mouse. *Proceedings of the National Academy of Sciences of the United States of America*, **108**, 18156–18161.

Viaene, A. N., Petrof, I., & Sherman, S. M. (2011b). Synaptic properties of thalamic input to layers 2/3 in primary somatosensory and auditory cortices. *Journal of Neurophysiology*, **105**, 279–292.

Viaene, A. N., Petrof, I., & Sherman, S. M. (2011c). Synaptic properties of thalamic input to the subgranular layers of primary somatosensory and auditory cortices in the mouse. *Journal of Neuroscience*, **31**, 12738–12747.

Viaene, A. N., Petrof, I., & Sherman, S. M. (2013). Activation requirements for metabotropic glutamate receptors. *Neuroscience Letters*, **541**, 67–72.

von Graefe, A. (1854). Beiträge zur Physiologie und Pathologie der schiefen Augenmuskeln. *Archiv für Opthlalmologie*, **1**, 1–81.

von Holst, E., & Mittelstaedt, H. (1950). The reafference principle. Interaction between the central nervous system and the periphery. In *Selected papers of Erich von Holst: The behavioural physiology of animals and man* (R. Martin, Trans.; Vol. **1**, pp. 139–173). Coral Gables, FL: University of Miami Press.

Wang, L., & Krauzlis, R. J. (2018). Visual selective attention in mice. *Current Biology*, **28**, 676–685.

Wang, L., McAlonan, K., Goldstein, S., Gerfen, C. R., & Krauzlis, R. J. (2020). A causal role for mouse superior colliculus in visual perceptual decision-making. *Journal of Neuroscience*, **40**, 3768–3782.

Wang, S., Eisenback, M. A., & Bickford, M. E. (2002). Relative distribution of synapses in the pulvinar nucleus of the cat: Implications regarding the "driver/modulator" theory of thalamic function. *Journal of Comparative Neurology*, **454**, 482–494.

Wang, W., Jones, H. E., Andolina, I. M., Salt, T. E., & Sillito, A. M. (2006). Functional alignment of feedback effects from visual cortex to thalamus. *Nature Neuroscience*, **9**, 1330–1336.

Wolpert, D. M., & Flanagan, J. R. (2010). Motor learning. *Current Biology*, **20**, R467–R472.

Wu, L. G., Borst, J. G., & Sakmann, B. (1998). R-type Ca^{2+} currents evoke transmitter release at a rat central synapse. *Proceedings of the National Academy of Sciences of the United States of America*, **95**, 4720–4725.

Zaborszky, L., Gombkoto, P., Varsanyi, P., Gielow, M. R., Poe, G., Role, L. W., et al. (2018). Specific basal forebrain-cortical cholinergic circuits coordinate cognitive operations. *Journal of Neuroscience*, **38**, 9446–9458.

Zhan, X. J., Cox, C. L., Rinzel, J., & Sherman, S. M. (1999). Current clamp and modeling studies of low threshold calcium spikes in cells of the cat's lateral geniculate nucleus. *Journal of Neurophysiology*, **81**, 2360–2373.

Section 3: Evolution

Chapter 5
Morphological, Developmental, and Functional Evolution of the Thalamus

Ann B. Butler

1. Introduction
1.1 Overview

The thalamus comprises two divisions, the dorsal thalamus, or thalamus, which develops embryologically along with the epithalamus from prosomere 2, and the ventral thalamus, or prethalamus, which lies rostral to the thalamus and develops from prosomere 3. The ventral thalamus predominantly contains GABAergic neurons and exerts regulatory control of dorsal thalamic activity. The dorsal thalamus of vertebrates contains nuclei with predominantly glutamatergic neurons that project to the telencephalon. It needs to be understood from several different perspectives that all yield heuristically informative models but only partially or marginally overlap each other. Traditional anatomical divisions are now joined by developmental divisions, functional divisions, and evolutionary divisions. The evolution of the dorsal thalamus is inextricably tied to the evolution of both the pallium (the dorsal portion of the telencephalic hemispheres) and the striatum (a subpallial component in the ventral portion of the telencephalon). The pallium is now recognized to have a tetrapartite organization with medial, dorsal, lateral, and ventral sectors, which are differentially elaborated in the sauropsids (reptiles and birds) and mammals. The dorsal pallial sector is most expanded and elaborated in the latter, forming the neocortex, whereas the lateral and ventral pallial sectors dominate the sauropsid telencephalon, forming a large nuclear region, the dorsal ventricular ridge (DVR). The hypothesis of pallial evolution in amniotes that was originally proposed by Harvey Karten (1969) and his colleagues was based on hodology (the patterns of the ascending, intrinsic, and descending connections) and posited that the DVR is homologous to the regions of the neocortex that are in receipt of ascending sensory information relayed from the midbrain roof to the thalamus and thence to the cortex. This hypothesis was first challenged by Laura Bruce and Tim Neary on cytoarchitectural grounds and other known data and subsequently by Luis Puelles and his colleagues with developmental molecular studies that indicated homology of parts of the DVR to the claustrum and parts of the pallial amygdala of mammals rather than to the neocortex. The latter hypothesis has most commonly been referred to as the *claustroamygdalar hypothesis*. The possible homologous relationships of dorsal thalamic nuclei were caught in a circular argument about the pallial homologies because the identities of dorsal thalamic nuclei are linked to their respective pallial targets. The possible homology of the DVR to mammalian pallial components is crucial as to whether the midbrain-relaying dorsal thalamic nuclei in sauropsids are homologous to first-order mammalian nuclei such as the lateral posterior (LP)/pulvinar and the medial geniculate nucleus pars ventralis or to the nuclei that comprise the posterior nuclear group and project to the basolateral part of the pallial amygdala. Although recent work definitively shows the lateral/ventral pallial origin of the DVR (from which the claustrum and, possibly, the basolateral amygdala, respectively, develop in mammals) early in the developmental sequence, epigenetic regulatory factors that are expressed later during development endow the DVR with neocortical-like neuronal types and synaptology, resolving the two hypotheses by appreciating that a combination of early genetic and subsequent epigenetic developmental events are involved. These findings support my hypothesis of two evolutionary divisions of the dorsal thalamus with one modification that clarifies it.

The two evolutionary divisions, the lemnothalamus and collothalamus, are present across vertebrate clades, and they were separately elaborated with different time courses in the sauropsid and mammalian lineages. In mammals, the lemnothalamus—involved in hippocampal, geniculostriate, and somatosensory circuitry—enlarged first and empowered the early mammals with allocentric spatial mapping abilities for foraging and expanding their territorial range. Collothalamic elaboration followed, reaching its apex in primates with the greatly expanded pulvinar. In sauropsids, the collothalamus first elaborated and was involved in egocentric spatial mapping, later enhanced with lemnothalamic elaboration, particularly in birds. As a result of the new developmental information on both the pallium and the thalamus, the original collothalamic part of the hypothesis is slightly revised to reconcile the competing Karten and claustroamygdalar hypotheses.

Current views of functional divisions and how thalamocortical circuit motifs function to produce complex cognitive abilities and consciousness in *mammals* may be informed and bolstered by identifying commonalities with the thalamopallial circuitry in nonmammalian vertebrates. In comparing the circuitry, some features are clearly in common, whereas a number of others are different or altogether lacking. Some of the surprisingly high-level cognitive abilities evinced by some birds and even by some fishes may suggest that there may be more than one neuronal circuit design capable of supporting these functions.

1.2 Background

In his first edition of *The Thalamus*, Ted Jones (1985) included a chapter on the comparative structure of the thalamus across vertebrates and summarized the currently available information on its components and connections across fishes, amphibians, and tetrapods. He noted that, in general, the patterns of sensory afferents to individual dorsal thalamic nuclei and their projections to circumscribed parts of the telencephalon are similar across all vertebrates and exhibit much greater similarity than earlier researchers had been aware of. These patterns are of the greatest similarity between sauropsids (reptiles, including birds) and mammals, but nevertheless, Jones correctly questioned whether this similarity could be the result of a common origin (i.e., homology) or more simply the result of parallelism. Although Jones noted that the thalamic nuclei and their connections are similar enough between birds and other reptiles as to appear homologous, he also stated that "even the least differentiated mammalian thalamus bears so little resemblance to that of any living nonmammal that it is virtually impossible to detect among the nonmammals features that would suggest the evolutionary history of the mammalian thalamus" (1985, pp. 769–770).

Although the basic pattern of ascending sensory pathways through the dorsal thalamus to the telencephalon in amniotes had been documented by the time of Jones's first edition (1985), some afferent projections to the dorsal thalamus of relevance to its evolutionary history were still unknown. Also, an extensive and critical examination of this question of homology, considering not only connectional but also embryological data, had not been undertaken. Because of its reduced size and complexity in amphibians and, in contrast, its apparently widely divergent evolution across fishes and, separately, across amniotes, the evolution of the dorsal thalamus remained a challenging puzzle until a good comparative understanding of its numerous connections and also of its embryological development was achieved.

As will be discussed later in the chapter, the evolutionary history of the mammalian thalamus has been masked by the traditional anatomical divisions of primary, or first-order, and association, or higher-order, nuclei that cut across the two evolutionary divisions now recognized and combine some nuclei from both divisions as primary and others from each division as association. Likewise, early developmental events, such as the site of generation of particular sets of neurons, do not correlate with the evolutionary divisions, which are specified at a later time in development by epigenetic mechanisms, particularly by regulatory influences that determine whether particular genes are expressed or not. This sequence applies to both the dorsal thalamic nuclei and to the parts of the telencephalon to which they project. Thus, both the development and homologous relationships of the telencephalic targets across amniotes and of the dorsal thalamic nuclei that project to them are crucial to illuminating dorsal thalamic evolution.

For discussing thalamic evolution across vertebrates, the terms *pallium* and *subpallium* for the dorsal and ventral parts of the telencephalic hemispheres need to be used. The pallium is the dorsal part of the telencephalon, and part of it in tetrapods (and in some instances in anamniotes) consists of cortex, that is, a cytoarchitecture of layers of neuronal cell bodies between (or superficial to) a layer or layers of axonal fibers and dendritic processes. An example of the simplest architecture of the pallium occurs in amphibians for their ventral, lateral, and dorsal cortices, which consist of only two layers—a periventricular neuronal cell layer deep to a layer of fibers (Figure 1A). The most elaborate is the six-layered neocortex of mammals. Other parts of the pallium can assume a nuclear configuration, such as the dorsal ventricular ridge in sauropsids (Figure 1B)—although recent findings using three-dimensional (3D) imaging, which will be discussed later in the chapter, indicate the cryptic presence of cortical organization in this pallial component as well.

In mammals, the dorsal thalamus is most extensively interconnected with the neocortex, but various thalamic nuclei also project to other telencephalic components as well (Jones, 2007). The neocortex is the largest part of the pallium, which also includes the pallial amygdala (including its olfactory and basolateral components), endopiriform nuclei, and claustrum laterally, as well as the hippocampal formation medially. In addition to the neocortex, some of these other pallial components receive dorsal thalamic projections. Of particular importance to discerning the evolution of thalamic nuclei is that the basolateral amygdala receives projections from the posterior nuclear group—including the limitans/suprageniculate nucleus and the medial division of the medial geniculate nucleus (Jones, 2007; Bruce and Neary, 1995). In contrast, the thalamic nuclei that relay unimodal sensory information from the midbrain roof predominantly to the neocortex include LP/pulvinar and the ventral division of the medial geniculate nucleus (Jones, 2007). Comparing these two sets of mammalian thalamic nuclei to the thalamic nuclei in sauropsids and anamniotes has been a major focus of contention that has, as Jones (2007) noted, made the evolutionary history of the mammalian thalamus so refractive to illumination.

Neocortex is unique to mammals, however, and the question of which sector or sectors of the pallium in nonmammalian vertebrates is/are homologous to it has long been debated—and these homologous relationships are crucially related to the homologies and thus the evolution of the dorsal thalamic nuclei. As will be discussed further later in the chapter, four pallial sectors are now recognized across all gnathostomes (jawed vertebrates) (Smith-Fernandez et al., 1998; Puelles et al., 2000): in mammals, the medial sector gives rise to the hippocampal formation; the dorsal sector to most of the neocortex; the lateral sector to the claustrum, dorsal endopiriform nucleus, and insula; and the ventral sector to several structures, including the ventral endopiriform nucleus and olfactory cortex (Puelles et al., 2016, 2017). It is possible that the ventral pallium also gives rise to the pallial basolateral amygdala, but because the latter is *Emx1*-positive, whereas other ventral pallial derivatives are not, further study is needed to resolve this question (Puelles et al., 2017).

In discussing the evolution of both the dorsal and ventral parts of the thalamus, the issue of homology itself and the criteria for recognizing it need to be considered. This methodology allows for distinguishing which characters, or features, are shared among phylogenetic groups and thus likely ancestral and homologous and which are unique specializations.

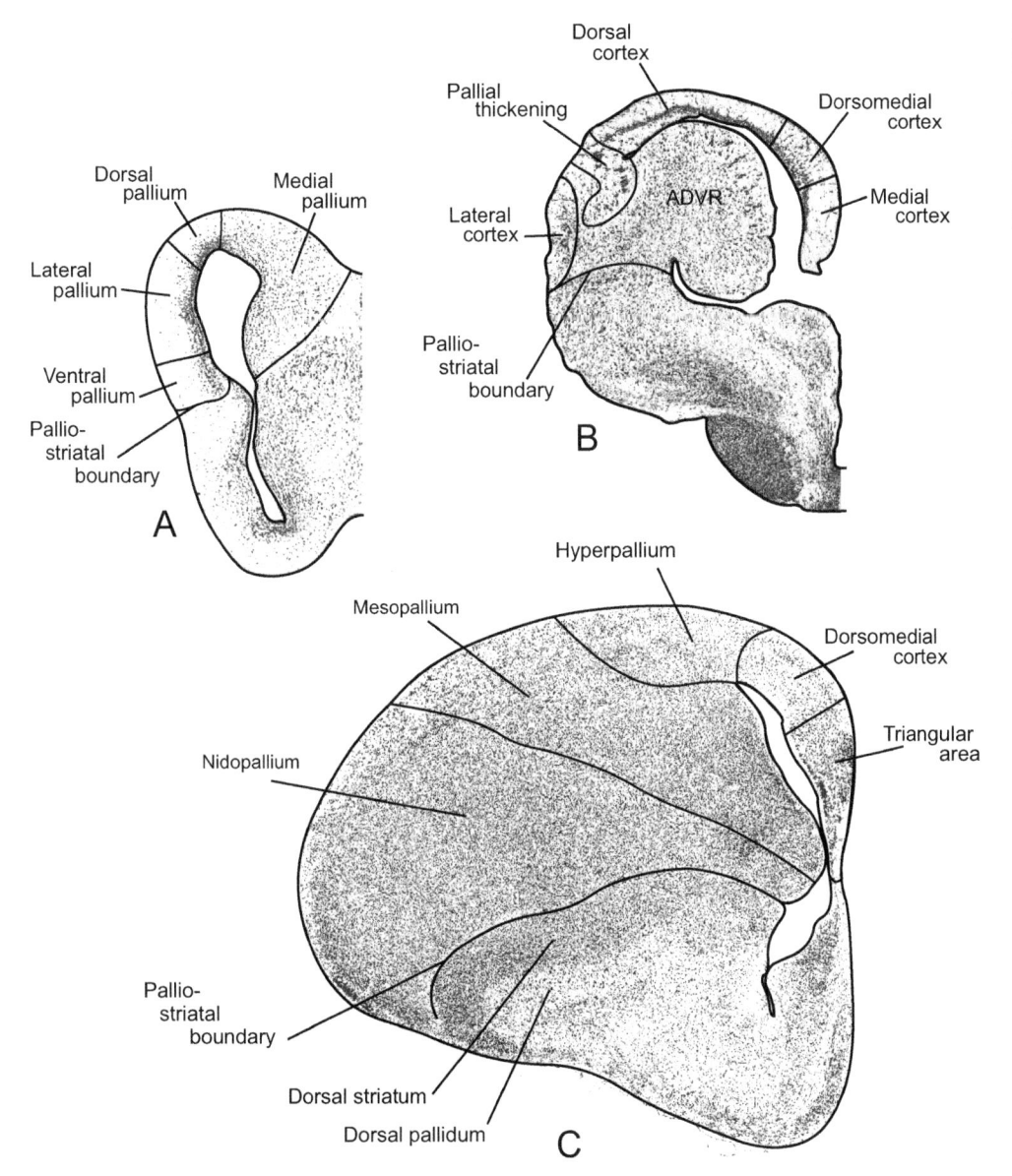

Figure 1 Nissl-stained transverse hemisections (left side) through mid-telencephalic levels in (A) an amphibian (the bullfrog, *Rana catesbeiana*), (B) a reptile (the turtle, *Pseudemys scripta*), and (C) a bird (the pigeon, *Columba livia*). Figure modified from Butler, A.B. (2008b) Evolution of the thalamus: a morphological and functional review. Thalamus & Related Systems, 24 pp, DOI 10.1017/S1472928808000356, used with permission of Cambridge University Press, Cambridge, UK

Questions about perceptual and cognitive functions and consciousness itself can then be informed by integrated models of structure and function. The dorsal thalamus, which is deeply involved, in concert with the pallium, in these functions, will therefore be the main focus of this chapter, and those nuclei that are involved in the major ascending pathways and thalamo-telencephalic circuits will be discussed here rather than an exhaustive survey of all the nuclei. The evolution of the ventral thalamus, which plays crucial regulatory roles for the dorsal thalamic nuclei, particularly in mammals, will be considered in Section 9. The regulatory functions of the ventral thalamus via its GABAergic, inhibitory projections to the dorsal thalamus are common to most if not all vertebrates (Butler and Hodos, 2005) and serve to moderate the activity of otherwise-positive feedback loops between the glutamatergic, excitatory activity of the dorsal thalamic and cortical neurons, just as intrinsic GABAergic neurons regulate glutamatergic pallial projection neurons (Steriade et al., 1997).

2. Methodology: Cladistic Analysis and Homology

The technique for the reconstruction of the evolutionary history of any character is cladistic analysis—the identification of homologous characters across a taxon, that is, a phylogenetic group of animals such as a phylum, class, order, or genus (see Butler and Hodos, 2005). For structures that fossilize, such as bones, one can survey not only extant taxa but also the sometimes-rich collection of samples from extinct species. Because the internal anatomy of brains cannot be gleaned from fossils, one is limited to studying only the extant taxa. Characters that occur in most or all members of a group are most likely ancestral for that group. By comparing the features of the thalamic nuclei that groups have in common, one can reconstruct a hypothesized model of the common ancestor and, from that model, then identify the particular specializations that are unique to each group. Similarly, and of significance for understanding thalamic evolution, one can compare features among the different groups of reptiles and, likewise, among the orders of mammals to note the subsequent evolutionary specializations within each, of which there are many.

2.1 Criteria for Homology

In 1843, the British comparative anatomist Richard Owen defined homology as "the same organ in different animals under every variety of form and function" (Panchen, 1999, p. 40). Several criteria are commonly applied for recognizing homologous characters, including how minute the resemblance is and how many features of similarity are found (Simpson, 1961). For neural structures, location within the neuraxis, embryological origin, the sets of afferent and efferent connections, neurochemistry, cytoarchitecture, and neuronal subtypes can all be considered (Hodos and Campbell, 1969; Campbell and Hodos, 1970; Northcutt, 1984, 1985). For the thalamus, especially the dorsal thalamus, this has been particularly challenging because the identification of homologous nuclei in the adult brains of extant vertebrates has been anything but obvious. For several decades, hodology (the pattern of connections) was the principal criterion applied, but more recently, immunohistochemical features and embryological origin have come to be regarded as equally or more important (Puelles et al., 2017; García-Moreno and Molnár, 2020). Further, the differential elaboration of different parts of the dorsal thalamus and pallial sectors over different time courses, both between reptiles (including birds) and mammals and also among different groups of mammals, had to be recognized and sorted.

2.2 Field Homology

The concept of field homology was introduced by Hobart Smith (1967), who defined it as "derivation of structures, however similar or dissimilar, from . . . the same ontogenetic source" (p. 102). The usefulness of the field homology concept has been questioned on the basis that it can be too broadly applied by using very early developmental precursor regions and that it does not account for instances where nonhomologous precursor regions give rise to clearly homologous adult features, such as the vertebrate gut but, rather, requires a strict linkage of developmental and adult homology (Striedter, 1999; Striedter and Northcutt, 2020). The latter cases are rare and not well accounted for by field, iterative, or discrete homology but are perhaps best addressed by the biological homology concept of Wagner (1999, 2014), which focuses on epigenetic stabilization of a character in the phylogeny and will be discussed further in Section 4.5. In most instances of homology, however, the requirement of homologous developmental regions for homologous adult structures has become more firmly entrenched with the recent plethora of studies on gene-expression patterns (for discussion, see García-Moreno and Molnár, 2020). Field homology is indeed not useful if taken too far back in the embryological developmental sequence, but the concept of a developmental, morphogenetic field is a fundamental tenet of biology (see Gilbert, 1994). By specifying the field, just as Campbell and Hodos (1970) have posited for specifying any homology, overgeneralizations can be avoided. For example, the lateral pallial sector is homologous across jawed vertebrates as a discrete developmental field, whereas the individual adult derivatives of it that vary across vertebrates are not homologous as discrete structures but only as different groups of structures independently derived from the field.

As we will see later in the chapter, the field homology approach (Puelles and Medina, 2002; Butler and Hodos, 2005; Butler, 2009) is inescapable for the sets of adult derivatives of both the pallial sectors and the evolutionary divisions of the dorsal thalamus across vertebrates and, both across and within orders of mammals, even for the microstructure of individual nuclei, such as the layers of the dorsal lateral geniculate nucleus (DLGN). It is also fully compatible with and complementary to the hypothesis of parcellation of Ebbesson (1980, 1984, 2020), whereby sets of inputs initially targeting one population of neurons become segregated according to modality or other afferent input patterns as the one field differentiates into multiple nuclei in a different or descendant taxon. Further, rather than obscuring major innovations, as Striedter and Northcutt (2020) have concerns about, I would argue that it identifies them. The set of six main layers of the dorsal lateral geniculate nucleus in primates cannot be compared as discretely homologous, layer by layer, to the five (two A and three C) main DLGN layers in carnivores or to the much less differentiated DLGN in rodents. The multiple components of the DLGN in these different orders are innovations in themselves, as independently derived sets from the DLGN pronucleus (Rose, 1942).

3. The Thalamus in Tetrapods—Introduction

Vertebrates arguably comprise four major groups (Figure 2)—the jawless fishes, or cyclostomes (lampreys and hagfishes);

Box 1. Epigenetics

Epigenetics is the study of developmental events that are caused by activating or suppressing gene expression rather than heritable alterations of the genes themselves (i.e., genetics). Homeobox and related gene families identified by particular DNA sequences are involved in patterning the organism (Lichtneckert and Reichert, 2005), such as genes that promote the development of various parts of the organism, such as the limb buds, and include genes that specify various parts of the brain, including the sectors of the pallium. Subsequently in the developmental sequence, epigenetic factors affect the specific developmental path of the various regions. Transcription factors, which control the production of RNA from DNA, and other proteins affect the size, particular neuronal phenotypes, and other characters of the developing sector or area. The recent review of García-Moreno and Molnár (2020) gives an excellent overview of the genetic and epigenetic events that influence the development of the telencephalon in amniotes.

muscles were bowed out over the outside of the skull surface. It is important to realize that the ancestral mammalian stock of synapsids did not arise from diapsids, but rather, the two groups independently arose from an ancestral tetrapod stock. In fact, the earliest synapsid fossils marginally predate those of diapsids (Reisz, 1997; Evans, 2000). Thus, using the term *mammal-like reptile* to refer to any mammalian ancestor is inaccurate and misleading and should be avoided. The two groups—and their sets of dorsal thalamic nuclei and pallial sectors—separately diverged from their common ancestral condition, retaining some shared features but independently elaborating many others.

3.1 Different Perspectives on Dorsal Thalamic Components

To understand the dorsal thalamus, one must consider its organization from several different perspectives, only some of which partially overlap. All yield heuristically informative divisional schemes. Several views of the functional divisions of the dorsal thalamus have been proposed. Other divisions can be recognized from studies of development, only some of which are congruent with the two major evolutionary divisions.

3.2 Focus on Dorsal Thalamus in Tetrapods

We will focus on the dorsal thalamus in tetrapods. The thalamic nuclei of mammals are discussed elsewhere in this volume, so those in sauropsids will be reviewed here, and then both of these amniote groups will be contrasted with the condition in extant amphibians. We will then consider the thalamus in the outgroups among fishes in Section 8 (see also Chapter 6 of this book). These outgroups offer only limited insight into the complexities of the thalamus and thalamopallial connections in amniotes but, importantly, do reveal that the dorsal thalamus consistently comprises two evolutionarily distinct divisions, a rostral and a caudal one, across at least all jawed vertebrates and likely also in lampreys among the cyclostomes (Suryanaraya et al., 2020). Further, the dorsal thalamic–pallial pathways support sophisticated cognitive abilities not only in mammals but also in birds and even in some of the ray-finned fishes. These findings both inform and challenge current attempts in mammals to identify and understand the structural/functional bases for them.

Before comparing thalamic nuclei and their evolution across amniotes, however, we need to first consider the evolution of ideas and insights into pallial organization and the homologies of the thalamic nuclei that project to them, particularly among amniotes. The pallium in mammals is substantially divergent from that in reptiles, and the homologous relationships of some of its components have been in dispute for several decades. Recent gene-expression data have now allowed a new perspective that recognizes some of the components as being homologous as derivatives of particular pallial segments but not as discrete structures. The issue of homology is not yet fully resolved, however, as discussed in Section 4.5.

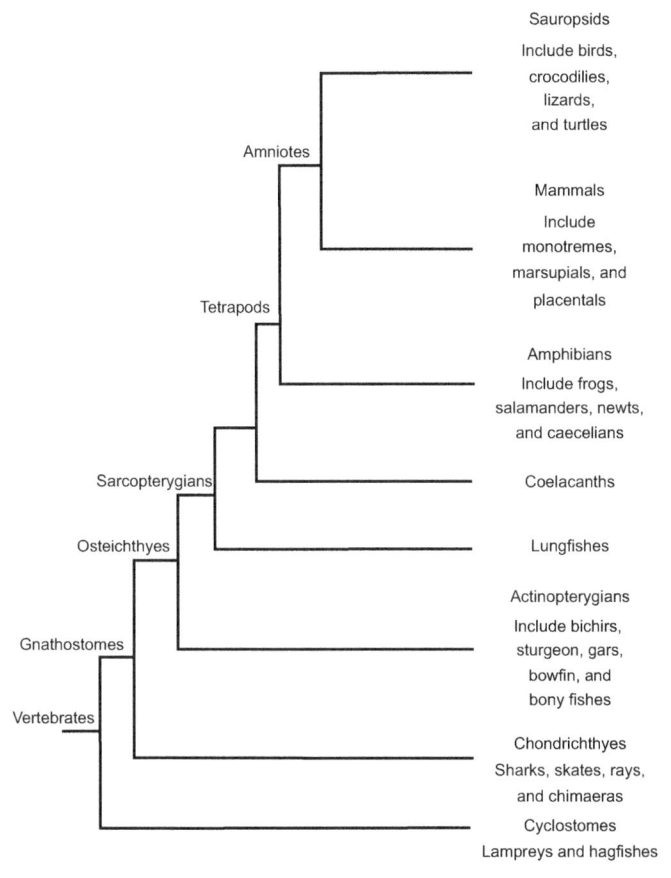

Figure 2 Dendrogram of the phylogenetic relationships of the major groups of vertebrates.

Vertebrates comprise jawless vertebrates—lampreys and hagfishes—and the jawed vertebrates, or gnathostomes. The latter comprises cartilaginous fishes and all the rest of gnathostomes, classified as *Osteichthyes*, meaning "bony fish." Osteichthyes comprise two groups, the ray-finned fishes, or *Actinopterygii*, and the lobe-finned fishes, which comprise lungfishes, the coelacanth *Latimeria*, and the tetrapods.

chondrichthyans, or cartilaginous fishes (sharks, skates, and rays); ray-finned fishes, or actinopterygians (a large group that includes over 20,000 species of bony fishes); and the lobe-finned fishes, or sarcopterygians—lungfishes, the coelacanth *Latimeria*, and the tetrapod descendants (Liem et al., 2001). Within amniotes, the radiation of reptiles originated with a basal stock characterized by the presence of two openings, or fenestrae, enclosed by bony arches in the temporal part of the skull, and hence called *diapsids*, meaning "two arches." Some of the extant reptiles lack both these arches, having lost one or both secondarily, but based on their phylogenetic history and genetic analyses, they are all classified as part of that group. Extant diapsids include lizards, snakes, the tuatara *Sphenodon punctatus*, turtles, crocodiles, and birds. In this chapter, although the clade referred to as reptiles is now understood to include birds, the word *reptile* will be used from here on to denote non-avian reptiles only.

The diapsid condition contrasts with mammals, which are derived from *synapsid* stock, referring to the presence of just one arch, the zygomatic arch, and fenestra in the temporal region. It allows some of the powerful muscles of mastication to pass through it for better mechanical advantage than if the

4. Relationship of Dorsal Thalamic Evolution to Pallial Evolution

In amphibians, the medial pallium, which comprises the dorsomedial and medial cortices, is the only elaborated pallial component, with modest, periventricularly bound pallial areas lateral to it (Figure 1A). In reptiles (Figure 1B), the pallium includes medial, dorsal, and lateral cortical regions, characterized by three layers rather than six—a cellular layer of variable compactness sandwiched between two layers of fibers and neuropil. A large pallial area that bulges medially from the lateral aspect of the hemisphere is also present and called the dorsal ventricular ridge (DVR), which has anterior (ADVR) (Figure 1B) and posterior (PDVR) divisions. Dorsal to the ADVR is an additional cortical area called the *pallial thickening*. In reptiles, the dorsomedial and medial cortices are homologous, respectively, to Ammon's horn and the dentate gyrus (Tosches et al., 2018). Likewise, in birds (Figure 1C), the dorsomedial cortex is homologous to Ammon's horn, and the medial cortex, which lies in a triangular area with a V-shaped cell layer, is homologous to the dentate gyrus (Atoji et al., 2016). The dorsal cortex (DC) of reptiles is enlarged in birds and referred to as the *Wulst* (meaning "bulge") or the *hyperpallium*. The ADVR is called the *nidopallium*, the PDVR is called the *arcopallium* (caudal to the level shown in Figure 1C), and the area that is homologous to the pallial thickening (Pth) is called the *mesopallium* (Reiner et al., 2004) (Figure 1C). In contrast, the pallium in mammals is dominated by the neocortex. It also includes the hippocampal formation and transitional cortices (entorhinal and subicular cortices) medially and, lateral to the neocortex, the pallial amygdala, claustrum, endopiriform nuclei, bed nucleus of the external capsule, and piriform cortex. The pallial part of the amygdala consists of the olfactory amygdala superficially and the deeper-lying basolateral complex of nuclei (Swanson and Petrovich, 1998; Martínez-García et al., 2002, 2007; Medina et al., 2017).

4.1 The Original Karten Hypothesis of Pallial Evolution in Sauropsids

The Karten hypothesis (Karten, 1969; Karten et al., 1973, 1978; Zeier and Karten, 1971) comprised five main points. The first three points concerned ascending sensory pathways to the pallium (Figure 3): (1) The mesopallium (Pth), nidopallium (ADVR), and arcopallium (PDVR) of birds (previously called terms with the misleading suffix "striatum" [Reiner et al., 2004]) were pallial regions rather than striatal, based on the paucity of acetylcholinesterase (AChE) expression. (2) Based on hodology, the sensory-recipient parts of the nidopallium (ADVR) were homologous to various neocortical areas—a region called the *entopallium* receiving visual projections (Karten and Hodos, 1970) to extrastriate cortices, an auditory-recipient region called *Field L* (Karten, 1968) to the primary auditory cortex, and a somatosensory-recipient region (Wild, 1987) to the secondary somatosensory cortex. (3) The caudal part of the overlying Wulst, or hyperpallium, was homologous to the primary visual cortex (Karten et al., 1973), with a rostral, primary somatosensory homologue (Karten et al., 1978), later studied in detail (e.g., Delius and Bennetto, 1972; Wild, 1987, 1997). Homologous ascending pathways are also present in reptiles.

The auditory-, visual-, and somatosensory-recipient regions of the ADVR in a turtle are shown for comparison in Figure 4, which also shows the dorsal striatum and pallidum immediately ventral to the pallial-subpallial boundary (Ulinski, 1983; Powers and Reiner, 1980). The striatum also receives inputs from collothalamic and intralaminar nuclei, and this region will be discussed later in the chapter in relation to the different routes that the ascending sensory axons take during development in sauropsids and mammals to reach their telencephalic targets.

The Karten hypothesis also postulated that (4) the arcopallium (PDVR) was homologous to the pallial amygdala (Zeier and Karten, 1971), and the findings in sauropsids of efferent projections from it and a laterally neighboring region to the striatal amygdala and medial hypothalamus (Martínez-Garcia et al., 2002; Novejarque et al., 2004) supported this contention. (5) The fifth—and currently most cogent—postulate was that individual populations of pallial neurons—afferent-recipient, intrapallial, and efferent—were homologous across amniotes, forming canonical processing pathways. In other words, intrapallial circuitry similar to that within mammalian neocortex is present in the pallium of sauropsids and may, at least for some of its components, have been inherited in both taxa from the common ancestral stock.

These postulates involve the nuclei of the sauropsid dorsal thalamus, some of which are diagrammed in Figure 3 and shown in Figure 5. Several of these include nuclei that receive most of their input from the midbrain roof, such as nuclei rotundus and ovoidalis in birds (Figure 5). Other nuclei receive little or no input from the midbrain roof, such as the dorsal lateral geniculate nucleus (DLGN), ventrointermediate area (VIA), and nuclei dorsalis intermedius ventralis anterior (DIVA), dorsomedialis anterior, and dorsolateralis anterior. Terminology varies for some of these nuclei in reptiles (Figure 5), where the nucleus ovoidalis is called the *nucleus medialis* or *reuniens pars compacta*, and another nucleus that receives somatosensory input from the midbrain roof, the cDLP (the caudal part of nucleus dorsolateralis posterior) in birds (which lies caudal to the levels shown in Figure 5), is called the *nucleus medialis posterior* in reptiles. The Karten hypothesis inferred that the sauropsid dorsal thalamic nuclei relaying sensory information to the pallium (Figure 3) were homologous to mammalian nuclei as follows (here using avian terminology):

- The DLGN, which relays visual information to the caudal part of the hyperpallium, to the DLGN of mammals
- The DIVA, which relays somatosensory information to the rostral hyperpallium, to the ventral posterior lateral nucleus (VPL)
- The nucleus rotundus, which projects to the visual entopallium, to the LP/pulvinar complex

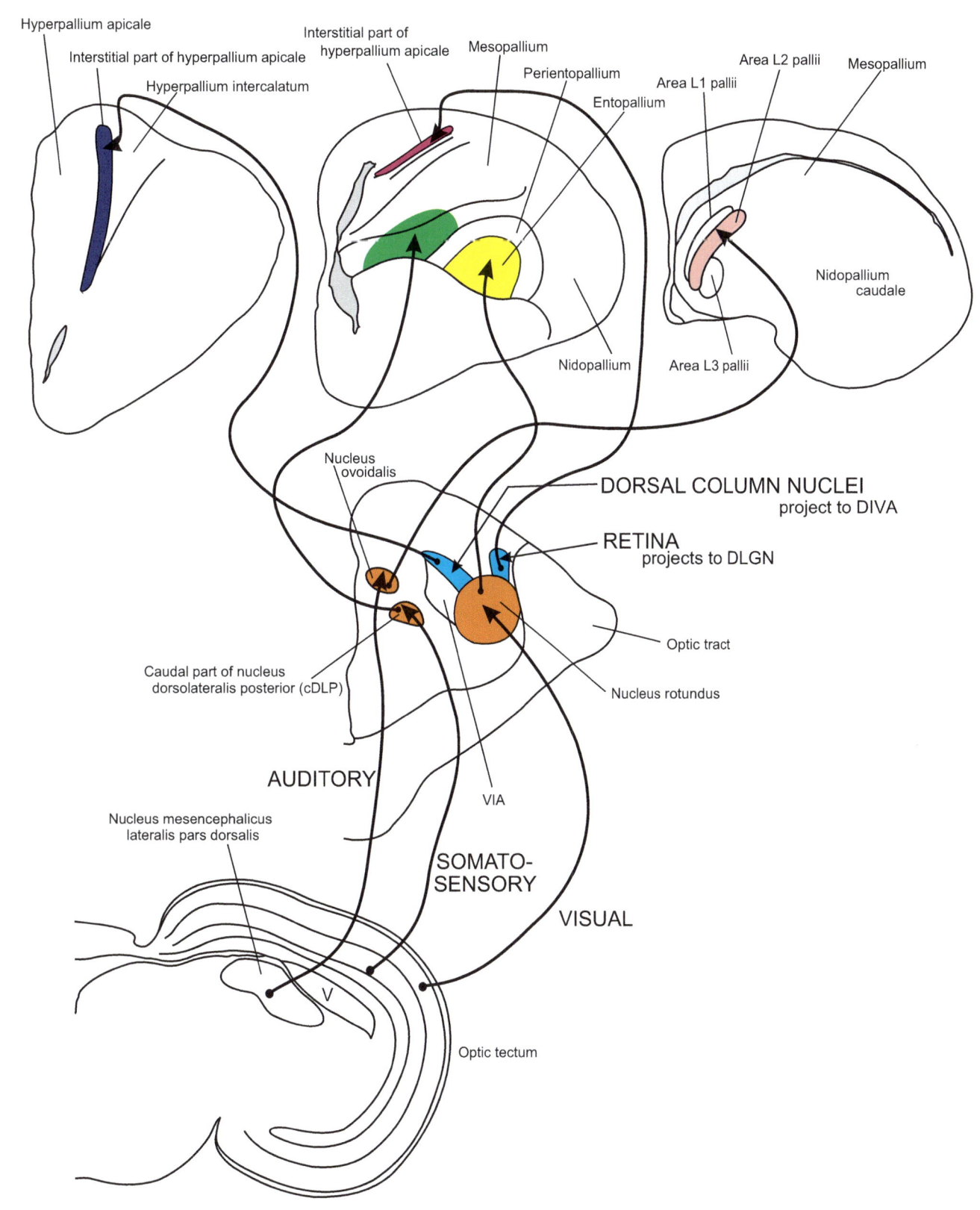

Figure 3 Schematic representation of ascending sensory pathways in a bird, the pigeon *Columba livia*.

Top row: Drawings of transverse hemisections of the right telencephalon from rostral (left) to caudal (right). Middle row: Drawing of transverse hemisection of the right diencephalon showing the thalamic relay nuclei involved in some of the pathways to the pallium. Bottom: Drawing of transverse hemisection through the right midbrain. The ascending collothalamic pathways shown here are (1) visual from the superficial optic tectum to nucleus rotundus (*orange*) to the entopallium (*yellow*) in the center telencephalic hemisection, (2) auditory from the homologue of the inferior colliculus (nucleus mesencephalicus lateralis pars dorsalis) to nucleus ovoidalis (*orange*) to Field L (*pink*) in the right hemisection, and (3) somatosensory from the deep optic tectum to the cDLP (*orange*) to the somatosensory-recipient part of the nidopallium (*green*) in the center hemisection. The ascending lemnothalamic pathways shown here are (1) visual from the DLGN (*blue*) to a subdivision of the caudal Wulst (*magenta*) and (2) somatosensory from DIVA (*blue*) to the same subdivision of the Wulst but at a more rostral level in the left hemisection (*dark blue*). Figure based on references discussed in the text.

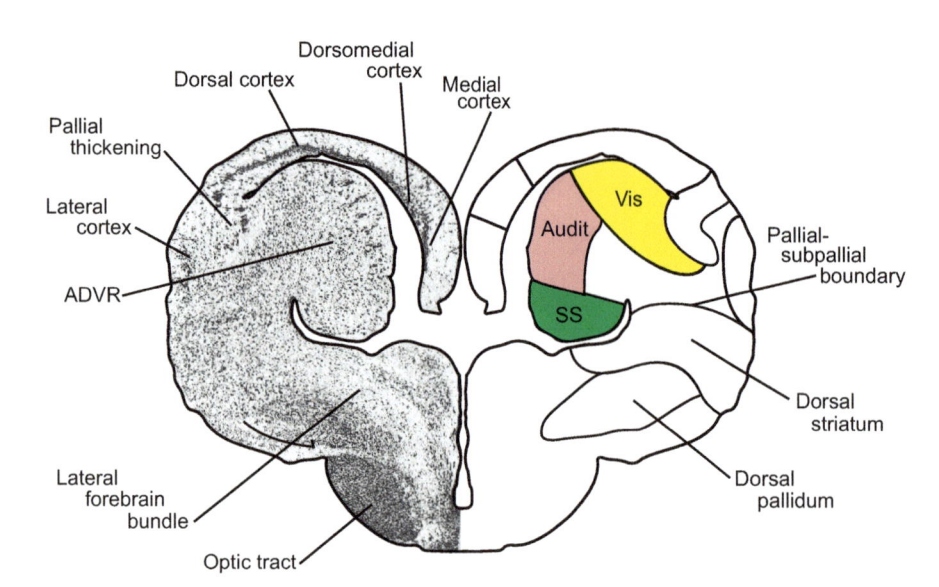

Figure 4 Transverse, Nissl-stained hemisection of the turtle (*Pseudemys scripta*) telencephalon on the left with a drawing on the right showing the areas in the ADVR that receive visual (Vis), auditory (Audit), and somatosensory (SS) inputs relayed from the midbrain roof through collothalamic nuclei.

- The nuclei ovoidalis, which projects to the auditory Field L, to the medial geniculate nucleus pars ventralis (MGv)
- The caudal part of nucleus dorsolateralis posterior (cDLP), which relays somatosensory information to the limitans/suprageniculate nuclei in the posterior nuclear group

As will be properly introduced and discussed later in the chapter, Butler (1994a, 1994b) identified the thalamic pathways to the DVR and their nuclei of origin as collothalamic, based on the observation that these thalamic nuclei (such as the nuclei rotundus, ovoidalis, and cDLP) receive substantial input from the midbrain roof, among other shared features, and their pallial targets as collopallial. In contrast, the thalamic nuclei that do not receive their major inputs from the midbrain roof but directly via lemniscal pathways (such as the medial lemniscus to the DIVA and the retinogeniculate pathway) were termed *lemnothalamic* and their pallial targets as *lemnopallial*. These terms are mentioned here for use in discussing these hypotheses of pallial relationships because it is the collothalamic nuclei that project to the nidopallium (ADVR) and, in mammals, to the lateral nucleus of the amygdala (LA) and/or auditory cortex and to the extrastriate visual, secondary somatosensory, and temporal and parietal association cortices (Jones, 2007).

4.2 Developmental Studies of Pallial Segments

Beginning with the insightful contention of Bruce and Neary (1995), based on adult cytoarchitecture and hodology, that all of the DVR was, in fact, a homologue of the mammalian pallial amygdala, the parts of the Karten hypothesis on DVR homology were challenged. This position was supported by the division of the developing pallial mantle into four segments (Figure 6) rather than the previously recognized three—medial (MPall), dorsal (DPall), and lateral (LPall). Smith-Fernandez et al. (1998) and Puelles et al. (2000) discovered a ventral pallial sector (VPall) in chicken and mouse embryos that is distinguished from the rest of the pallium by the lack of expression of the transcription factor *Emx1*. Other molecular markers have subsequently supported recognition of the VPall (Szele et al., 2002; Chen et al., 2013; Jarvis et al., 2013; Puelles et al., 2015; Desfilis et al., 2017; Medina et al., 2017; Puelles et al., 2017). Combinatorial patterns of regulatory gene expression have resulted in a now well-established and accepted view of homologies across amniotes for the adult derivatives of most but not all pallial segments.

The MPall derivatives, particularly Ammon's horn and the dentate gyrus, have now been identified across reptiles, birds, and mammals and are homologous as discrete characters (Bingman et al., 2017; Tosches et al., 2018). The visual- and somatosensory-recipient parts of the dorsal cortex of reptiles (which lie rostral to a transitional area homologous to the subiculum [Hoogland and Vermeulen-Van der Zee, 1989; Tosches et al., 2018]) are discretely homologous to the visual and somatosensory parts of the Wulst (hyperpallium) of birds and to the primary visual and somatosensory parts of neocortex, respectively. The pallial thickening of reptiles and mesopallium of birds are homologous to each other discretely and, as field derivatives of the LPall, to the claustrum (Cl), insula (I), and dorsal entopeduncular nucleus (EPd) of mammals (Puelles et al., 2016, 2017). The homology of the collothalamic-recipient ADVR in reptiles and nidopallium in birds has not been fully clarified, but the entire ADVR appears to be a VPall derivative. In mammals, the VPall field develops into the bed nucleus of the external capsule (BEC), the ventral endopiriform nucleus (EPv), and at least a substantial part of the pallial amygdala, although the basolateral amygdala, which receives dorsal thalamic projections, is *Emx1*-positive, which is a not a ventral pallial character. The latter may receive a contribution from a fifth ventrocaudal pallial developmental region (Desfilis et al., 2017; Medina et al., 2017; Puelles et al., 2017).

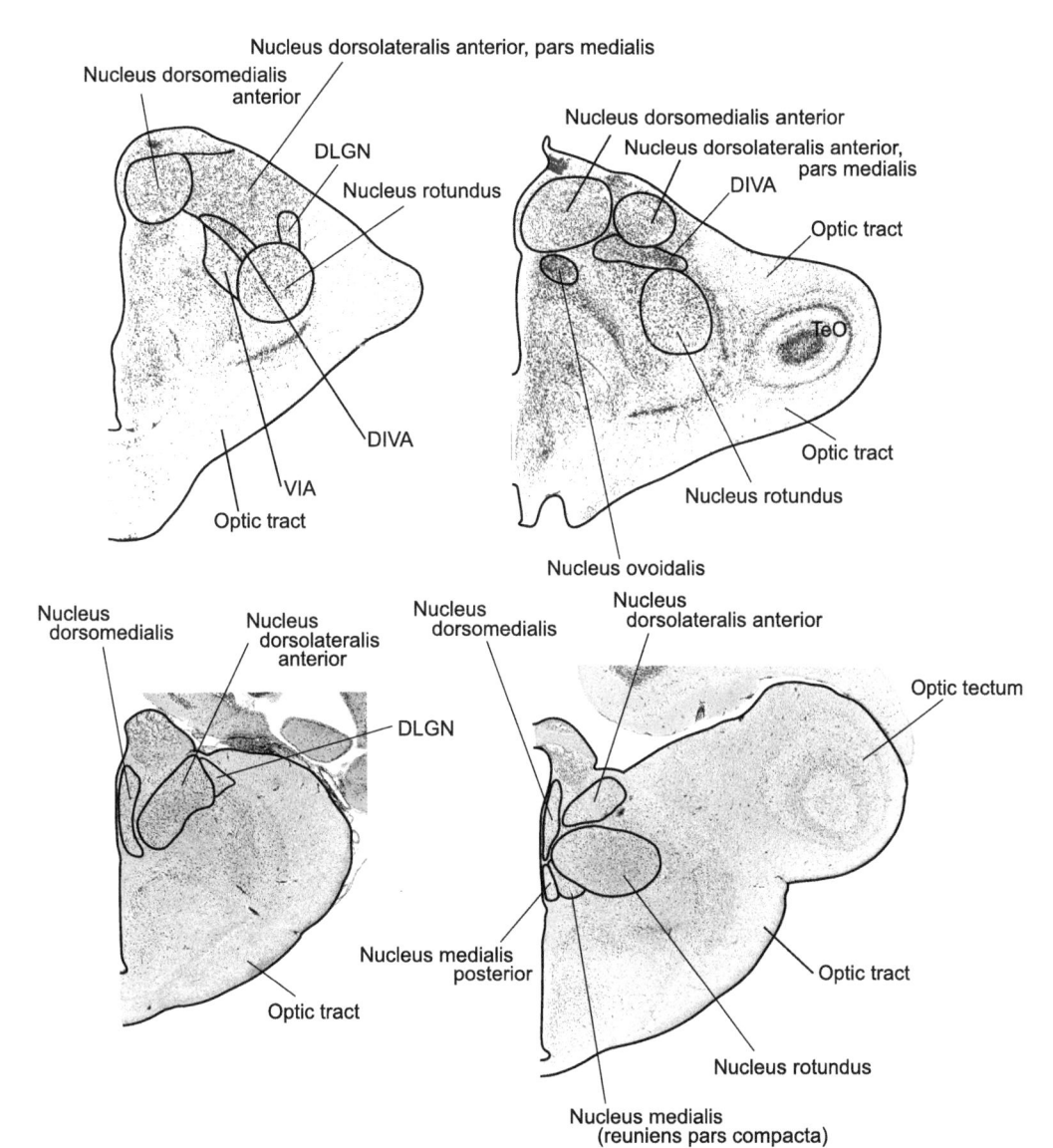

Figure 5 Two transverse, Nissl-stained hemisections through the right thalamus of a pigeon (*Columba livia*) (*top*) and two transverse, Bodian-stained hemisections through the right thalamus of a lizard (*Iguana iguana*) at comparable levels (*bottom*) with some of the dorsal thalamic nuclei labeled.

The Karten hypothesis (Karten, 1969; Butler et al., 2011) had indicated that in sauropsids, the nuclei rotundus, ovoidalis, and cDLP (avian terminology) were homologous to the LP/pulvinar, the ventral division of the medial geniculate nucleus, and the limitans/suprageniculate nucleus, respectively. Based on the hypothesis that the sauropsid DVR was homologous to the amygdala, Bruce and Neary (1995) postulated changes to these hypotheses of homology with mammalian nuclei such that the sauropsid nuclei rotundus, ovoidalis, and cDLP, which project to the DVR, were instead all homologous as a group to the posterior nuclear group of mammals. This issue has persisted for decades as the fundamental obstacle to understanding dorsal thalamic evolution.

4.3 Elaboration of Pallial Segment Derivatives in Sauropsids

In addition to evolutionary changes in the thalamus, the pallium has obviously become enlarged and elaborated within both the synapsid and diapsid lines. The evolution of the neocortex in mammals has been extensively studied (see Kaas, 2017a, 2017b; Krubitzer and Seelke, 2012; Raghanti et al., 2017 and references therein). Of particular note here is the extensive elaboration of the visual and auditory areas of the DVR in birds. Although the hypothesis that the DVR is an amygdalar homologue (Bruce and Neary, 1995) is supported by its putative VPall developmental origin, the sensory-recipient areas within it are strikingly similar to neocortical areas. The DVR sensory areas are unimodal, whereas the sensory-recipient areas of the pallial amygdala are multimodal (Morrow et al., 2019). The thalamic nuclear projections to the areas in the DVR are dedicated ones (Figures 3 and 5) (i.e., each to only one unimodal pallial locus), unlike the multimodal posterior group nuclei that project to the amygdala as well as to multiple cortical areas (Jones, 2007). The circuitry of the auditory and visual areas in the avian nidopallium is highly elaborate, with extensive similarities to the auditory and visual neocortical areas (e.g., Karten et al., 1968; Karten and Hodos,

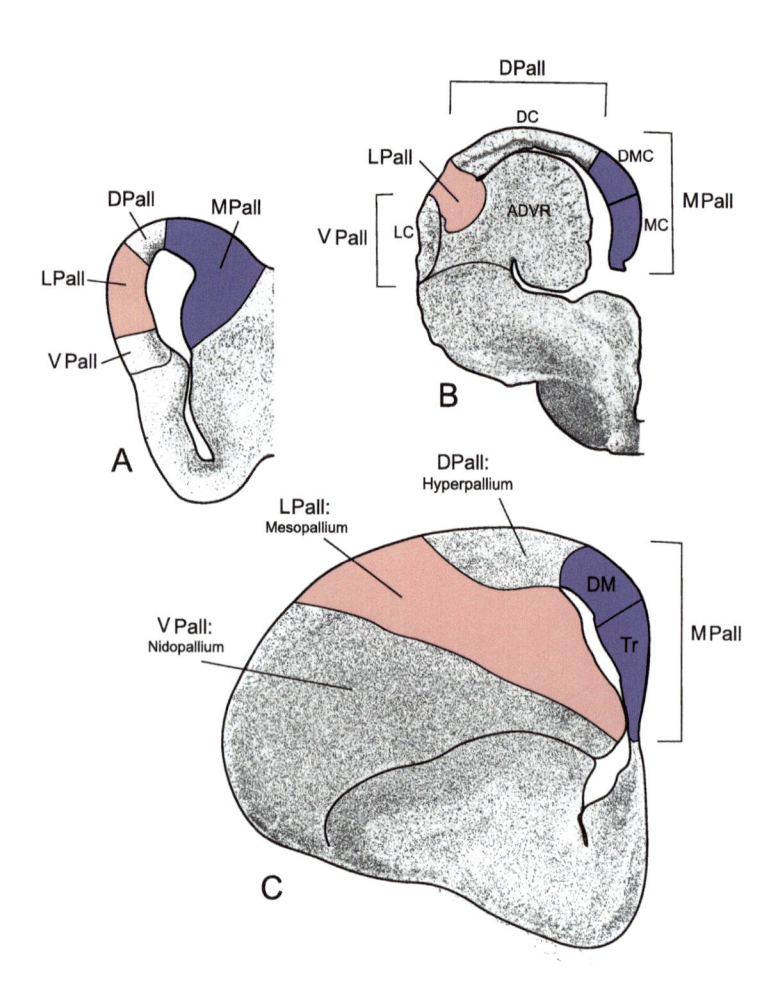

Figure 6 Nissl-stained transverse hemisections (*left side*) through mid-telencephalic levels in (A) amphibian (the bullfrog, *Rana catesbeiana*), (B) a reptile (the turtle, *Pseudemys scripta*), and (C) a bird (the pigeon, *Columba livia*).

The medial (*MPall*) (*blue*), dorsal (*DPall*), lateral (*LPall*) (*pink*), and ventral (*VPall*) sector derivatives are indicated. In the reptile (B), the ventral pallial derivatives include the lateral (piriform) cortex and the DVR. In the bird (C), the ventral pallial derivatives include the nidopallium as shown and also the lateral (piriform) cortex that lies at a more caudal level. Figure modified from Butler, A.B. (2008b) Evolution of the thalamus: a morphological and functional review. Thalamus & Related Systems, 24 pp, DOI 10.1017/S1472928808000356, used with permission of Cambridge University Press, Cambridge, UK.

1970; Zeier and Karten, 1971; Wild et al., 1993; Karten et al., 1997; Husband and Shimizu, 1999; Reiner et al., 2005; Yamamoto and Reiner, 2007; Butler et al., 2011; Fernández et al., 2019). Additionally, a recent study using 3D polarized light imaging (Stacho et al., 2020) has revealed the presence in birds of canonical neocortical-like circuitry that, despite developmental differences, has both laminar-like tangential organization and columnar-like orthogonal organization. These findings apply to both the Wulst, or hyperpallium, and the DVR and imply that birds actually do have a "cerebral cortex" and can sustain the correlates of consciousness, as Herculano-Houzel (2020) has made a strong case for. This functional architecture is augmented by the findings of Olkowicz et al. (2016) that birds have both higher neuronal packing densities and higher proportions of their neurons located in the pallium than mammals, including primates, so that those species among avians with relatively large brains—parrots and corvids—have neuron counts that are equal to or even greater than those of primates.

Furthermore, some sauropsid pallial cell components similar to neocortical components are also either homologous as discrete neuronal types or independently gained in the sauropsid line. In a large-scale study of adult pallial transcriptomes, Belgard et al. (2013) found that although a module of mouse striatal genes overlapped with two chicken striatal modules, as did mouse and chicken hippocampal gene modules, modules from non-hippocampal pallial regions did not show significant overlap. The hippocampal and striatal overlaps were associated, however, with shared functional, neurophysiological roles, indicating possible conservation of function rather than homology per se. In a different study using single-cell transcriptomes, Tosches et al. (2018) found similarities in gene-expression patterns and clusters between the sauropsid MPall derivatives and the hippocampus, the posterior part of the dorsal cortex and subiculum (supporting the previous hypothesis of Hoogland and Vermeulen-Van der Zee, 1989), the pallial thickening and claustrum, the PDVR and pallial amygdalar nuclei except the lateral amygdala (LA), the ADVR and LA, and the anterior dorsal cortex and neocortex. Further, neurons in the anterior DC express a variety of markers identical to those of neurons in neocortical layers (L)—L2/3, L4, and L5a intratelencephalic neurons and L5b and L6 corticofugal projection neurons.

These populations of neurons might have been present in the common amniote ancestor or evolved in parallel in the diapsid and synapsid lines. Suzuki et al. (2012) also had identified upper-layer neocortical-like neurons in the mesopallium of chicks and found that they were generated in the same sequence as in mammals after lower layer-like neurons in a more medial region. Similarly, and building on previous work by Dugas-Ford et al. (2012) and Dugas-Ford and Ragsdale (2015), Briscoe et al. (2018) found that the mesopallium in both chicks and crocodiles (Pth) shares a transcription factor network with the canonical neocortical circuitry between the supragranular and infragranular layers, indicating parallel expansions of homologous cell populations in both birds and mammals—particularly primates—that support their higher cognitive abilities. These laminar-similarity findings support the fifth—and sometimes ignored—part of Karten's (1969) original hypothesis: that of conserved circuitry of thalamic-recipient cells, intrapallial processing cells, and output cells (Reiner, 2012; Briscoe et al., 2018). Dugas-Ford and Ragsdale (2015) refer to this as the *Strong Karten Hypothesis*—that of homology of cell types.

In discussing pallial evolution in amniotes, Reiner (2012) postulated that the common ancestor had relatively small and simple pallial segments and lacked elaboration of any of them into a Wulst (hyperpallium), DVR, or neocortex. Focusing on just the ADVR and in agreement with Reiner (2012) and Striedter and Northcutt (2020), it seems highly likely that the common amniote ancestor had neither a sauropsidian-like nor a mammalian-like elaboration of the ventral pallium. Attempts to identify parts or all of the DVR as discretely homologous to specific parts of the neocortex or of the amygdala are therefore arguments about a false dichotomy.

4.4 Value of Specifying the Homology

The resolution may be in simply specifying the homology (Campbell and Hodos, 1970). The classic example is that of the wing of a bird and the upper limb (arm, forearm, and hand) of a human. Neither of these structures is homologous as either wings or upper limbs. They are homologous as derivatives of the embryonic, rostral limb bud. In the case of pallial evolution among amniotes, the question of homology can likewise be clarified, as also discussed by García-Moreno and Molnár (2020). The DVR of sauropsids and the VPall structures of mammals both develop from the same VPall zone, and earlier- versus later-generated populations can be distinguished (Puelles et al., 2017). However, assigning mammalian names to individual sauropsid pallial components (Puelles et al., 2017) implies discrete homology rather than field homology. These structures evolved independently from the condition in the common ancestor, just as wings and upper limbs evolved from the rostral forelimbs of the common amniote ancestor. Although they share an embryological origin, they differ in many respects, as noted previously. As Simpson (1961) recognized, multiplicity of similarity and minuteness of resemblance are crucial to discrete homology and include specific neuronal components, hodology, and other features in addition to shared developmental origin. Further, as Northcutt discussed (2003), adult structures that arise from the same developmental anlage (embryological primordium for developing structures, such as the rostral limb bud) in different taxa are not necessarily homologous. They also must undergo homologous stages in their development. This second criterion is in agreement with Wagner's concept of biological homology (Wagner, 1999, 2014) discussed later in the chapter. For these reasons, the current hypothesis (Puelles, 2017) might profit by being renamed, simply, the *developmental pallial evolution hypothesis*. The same cautions and comparisons apply to the sets of dorsal thalamic nuclei.

4.5 Not a Slam Dunk: An Alternative Possibility

Ascending dorsal thalamic pathways and pallial circuitry that support cognitive processing have arisen multiple times with varying degrees of independence across phyla. Features in common across those phyla are good candidates for being essential components supporting this complex function, and there also may be more than one circuit configuration that is sufficient for it, albeit to varying degrees and abilities. Identifying the crucial features of circuit motifs requires a clear understanding of the full evolutionary and developmental sequences for both the dorsal thalamic nuclei and their telencephalic projection targets. The neuronal phenotypes that are necessary and sufficient for complex cognitive abilities that are produced either by genetic or epigenetic mechanisms, whether the result of historical homology or parallelism, can then be discerned.

Although the developmental pallial evolution hypothesis is in the ascendant, it does not rule out an alternative possibility. Just as homologous anlagen can give rise to nonhomologous adult structures (Northcutt, 2003), it also is well established that nonhomologous anlagen sometimes give rise to homologous structures in adult organisms, as noted in Section 2.2. While Raff (1996) noted that commonality of development strongly supports a hypothesis of homology, he also recognized that clearly homologous structures can arise in different ways during development. The biological homology concept of Wagner (1999, 2014) allows for different developmental anlagen to give rise to homologous characters. Examples include axial segmental contributions to forelimbs (de Beer, 1971), lens development in amphibians (Hall, 1992), and teleost pectoral fin regeneration (Wagner and Misof, 1992). Biological homologues only have to share those developmental mechanisms that produce their particular shared adult features (Wagner, 1999, 2014).

This possibility is not being considered in most of the current discussion on the neocortical-like ventral and lateral pallial derivatives of sauropsids hypothesized to be homologous to derivatives of the same pallial segments in mammals. Thus, an alternative hypothesis, supported by this body of observation, is that the sauropsid ventral and lateral pallial derivatives and the collothalamic-recipient neocortical areas might constitute an example of biological homology (Wagner, 1999, 2014). The striking and extensive similarity of neuronal components, unimodal thalamic inputs, and neocortical-like circuitry in sensory areas of the DVR in birds all clearly involve epigenetic contributions to the differentiating pallial tissue, just as are addressed by the biological homology concept.

Raff (1996, p. 34) noted that although outcomes are determined by both gene expression and epigenetic events, the process is not a straightforward one, and no simple answer can explicate the complex choreography involved in the developmental process. However, Nomura and Hirata (2017) have recently offered a solution to reconcile the various criteria. They proposed that the mechanism of birth-order neurogenesis (Okano and Temple, 2009), which is conserved and shared across amniotes but context-dependent for expression (Suzuki et al., 2012), would allow the development of neocortical-like circuitry in sauropsids as well as in mammals (Suzuki and Hirata, 2012, 2013), irrespective of the pallial segmental origin and thus bridging the divide between homology based solely on developmental criteria and homology based on hodology. This is in accord with the discussion of "levels" of homology by Dugas-Ford and Ragsdale (2015) for the homology of cell types (Karten, 1969), interpreted here as derived from nonhomologous anlagen but developing into the "same" cell types through epigenetic mechanisms.

A straightforward way to express the relationships may lie in the generative homology, or syngeny, concept (Butler and Saidel, 2000) that directly addresses both genetic and epigenetic levels. For example, the eyes of fruit flies and mammals are syngenous (arising from the same genes) as eyes engendered by the expression of *Pax6*, but they are allogenous (arising from different genes) as ommatidial versus retinal eyes. Likewise, the collothalamic-recipient areas in the sauropsid DVR and collothalamic-recipient areas of the neocortex in mammals are allogenous as pallial sector derivatives but syngenous in regard to the generation of a number of their specific neuronal components and synaptology.

5. Evolutionary and Embryological Divisions of the Dorsal Thalamus in Amniotes

In 1942, Jerzy Rose published a study of the embryological development of the dorsal thalamus in the rabbit. He identified a set of what he termed *pronuclei* (Figure 7A,B), which, as development proceeded, differentiated into one or more daughter nuclei. His dorsal lateral geniculate and medial geniculate pronuclei give rise to the respective individual adult nuclei; the medial pronucleus to nuclei including the parataenial, medioventral, parafascicular, and mediodorsal; the central pronucleus to the anterior, anterior intralaminar, and ventral groups; and the dorsal pronucleus to the lateral and posterior nuclear groups. Thus, the dorsal and medial geniculate pronuclei of Rose gives rise to nuclei in the adult that predominantly receive ascending input from the midbrain roof, whereas the remaining pronuclei give rise to nuclei that receive either minor or no tectal inputs but, rather, are characterized by direct lemniscal inputs that bypass the midbrain roof and terminate directly within them, including the medial lemniscus, the retinogeniculate pathway, and olfactory and basal ganglia circuit inputs.

5.1 Dual Elaboration Hypothesis of Dorsal Thalamic Evolution

In an attempt to reconstruct the evolution of the dorsal thalamus across vertebrates (Butler, 1994b, 1995, 2007, 2008b), I recognized that there were two divisions that had undergone different patterns of elaboration in the line to sauropsids versus that to mammals and thus formulated the dual elaboration hypothesis. I noted the dominance of midbrain roof input to the derivatives of the dorsal and medial geniculate pronuclei of Rose (1942), among other common factors, and so called that group of nuclei the *collothalamus*. Likewise, the other three pronuclei give rise to the lemnothalamus, that is, nuclei that receive most of their inputs directly via lemniscal (meaning "ribbon-like") pathways from the retina, the dorsal column nuclei, the basal ganglia, and other sources and have little to no midbrain roof input (see Kenigfest et al., 2007). They also have multiple other features in common that distinguish them from collothalamic nuclei (Butler, 1994b). With the exception of the rostral intralaminar nuclei, lemnothalamic nuclei do not project to the striatum, in contrast to striatal projections arising from all collothalamic nuclei. These two divisions were independently deduced by Martínez-de-la-Torre (1985), Caballero-Bleda (1988), Guillén (1991), working in the laboratory of Luis Puelles, and are present in all gnathostomes and in lampreys (Nieuwenhuys et al., 1998; Suryanarayana et al., 2020).

Regarding the terms chosen, it should be noted that the lateral lemniscus carries auditory inputs directly (and thus ribbon-like) to the inferior colliculus but does not supply lemniscal input to any part of the dorsal thalamus. Thus, the auditory relay to the medial geniculate body (MGB) is a collothalamic pathway, and the MGB is a part of the collothalamus. Of the many choices considered, using *lemnothalamus* for the more rostral division was not ideal but, rather, the least problematic.

Although other evolutionary divisions of the dorsal thalamic nuclei have been proposed, most have relied heavily on the pattern of thalamotelencephalic and telencephalothalamic connections, as discussed by Pritz (2015). Such schemes are not in conflict with the lemnothalamic and collothalamic divisions, however. The six subdivisions proposed by Pritz (2015) in crocodiles, for example, based predominantly on telencephalic connections, comprise four subdivisions (his 1–4) of the lemnothalamus and two subdivisions (his 5 and 6) of the collothalamus. The lemnothalamic and collothalamic divisions were discerned by taking into account the fundamental importance of the relative magnitude of midbrain roof inputs to the different dorsal thalamic nuclei, which exhibit less variation across taxa, in addition to the somewhat more variable telencephalic circuitry and additional anatomical and developmental features.

The crucial issue for comparing dorsal thalamic evolution across amniotes was to realize that the two divisions had undergone different paths of elaboration over different time courses within the diapsid line leading to modern reptiles and the synapsid line leading to mammals (Figure 8). In the synapsid line leading to mammals, the lemnothalamus was elaborated first and was related to the visual, somatosensory and motor, and limbic systems for the allocentric spatial orientation functions favorable to occupying a crepuscular, foraging niche with greater mobility and agility (Liem et al., 2001; Kemp, 2005; Rowe, 2017; Striedter and Northcutt, 2020). Secondarily in the synapsid line, after the split of stem mammals into modern orders, the collothalamus was elaborated, initially relating to

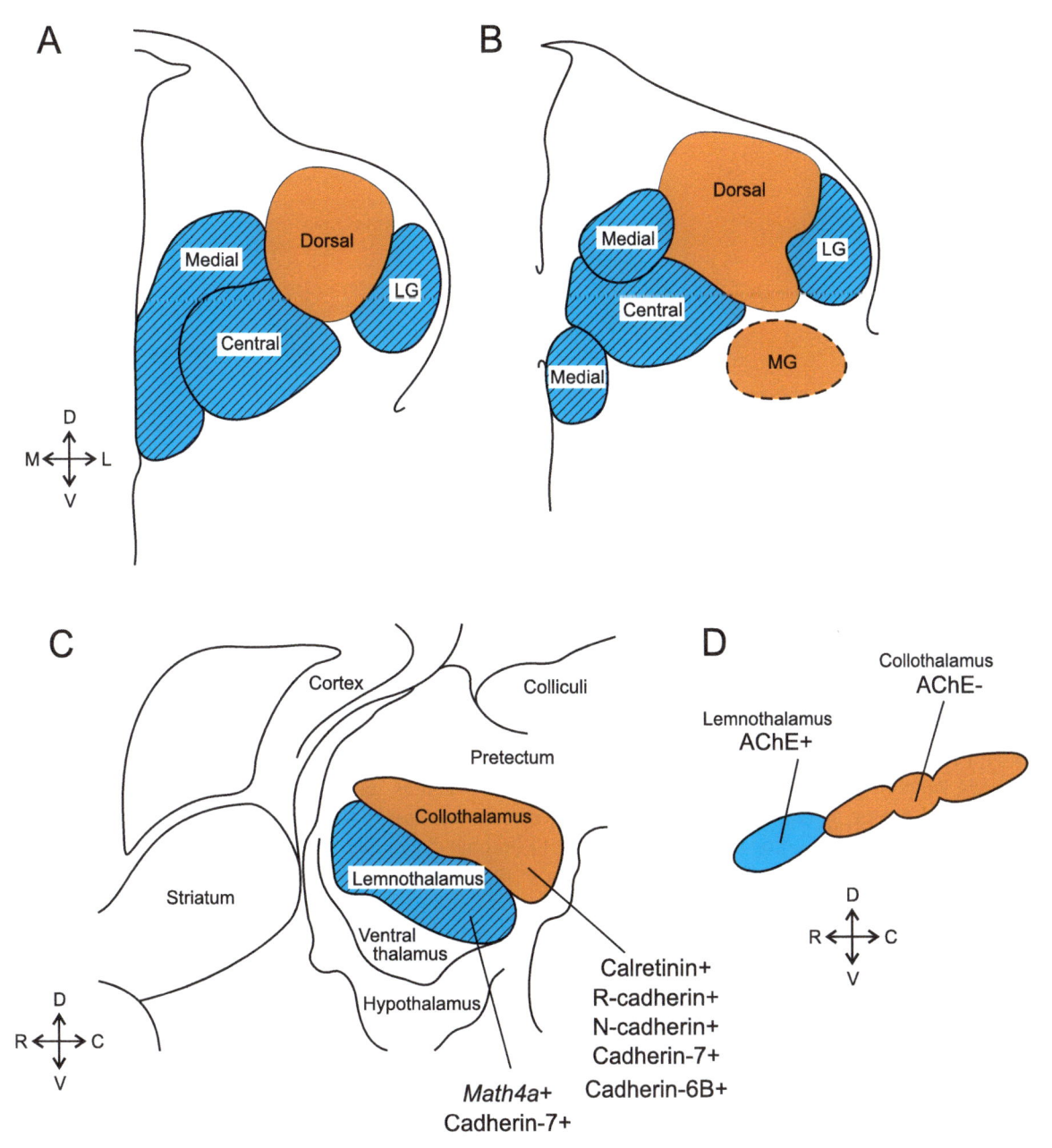

Figure 7 (A) and B) Semi-schematic drawings of transverse hemisections on the right side of the developing brain showing the locations of the pronuclei in the dorsal thalamus of a rabbit embryo, based on findings of Rose (1942). (B) is slightly caudal to (A). Collothalamic pronuclei are indicated by orange shading and lemnothalamic pronuclei in blue. Abbreviations: *LG*, dorsal lateral geniculate pronucleus; *MG*, medial geniculate pronucleus. (C) Semi-schematic drawing of a parasagittal section through the diencephalon of a mouse embryo showing the collothalamic territory (*orange*) positive for calretinin and four cadherins and the lemnothalamic territory (*blue*) positive for Math4a and cadherin-7 based on findings of González et al. (2002) and Redies et al. (2000). (D) Sagittal schematic representation of the dorsal thalamus in an adult amphibian with the lemnothalamus shaded blue and strong AChE positivity in its neuropil regions and the collothalamus shaded orange, with only faint AChE reactivity, based on the findings of Puelles et al. (1996). Figure modified from Butler, A.B. (2008b) Evolution of the thalamus: a morphological and functional review. Thalamus & Related Systems, 24 pp, DOI 10.1017/S1472928808000356, used with permission of Cambridge University Press, Cambridge, UK.

egocentric functions, along with further elaboration of the lemnothalamus. Noting the allocentric functions of the limbic, somatomotor, and geniculostriate systems versus the egocentric functions of the ascending collicular systems (Stein and Meredith, 1993) is obviously a generalization, and both sets of systems are present in extant reptiles and mammals, as they were in the common ancestral stock before the split into the diapsid and synapsid lineages. Nonetheless, it was the different and independent courses of elaboration of the lemnothalamic and collothalamic moieties in each lineage that had made comparisons and recognition of homologous nuclei challenging.

5.2 Lemnothalamic and Collothalamic Elaboration in Mammals

At the systems level in mammals, the effects of climate, ecological niche, and many somatic evolutionary changes, as discussed in detail by Striedter and Northcutt (2020),

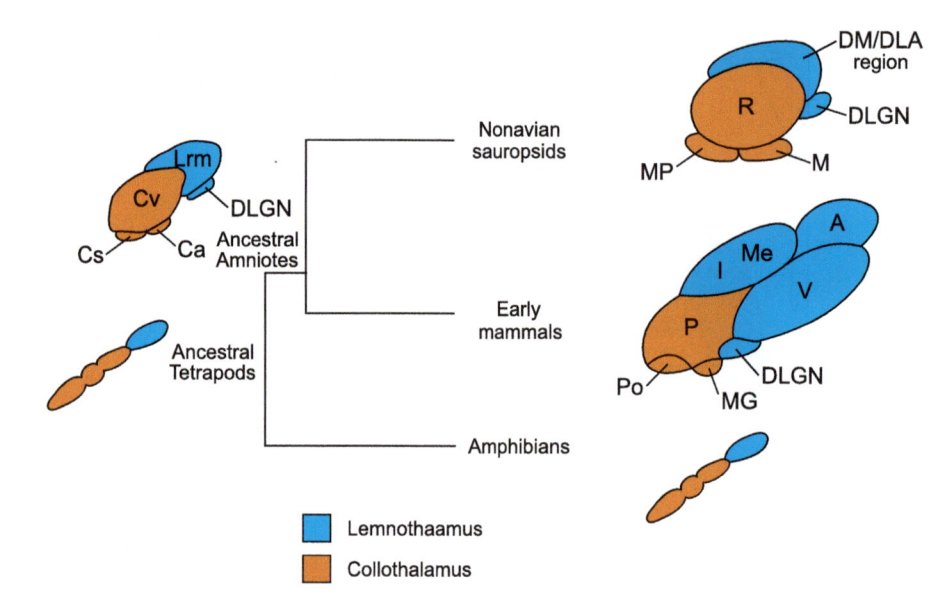

Figure 8 Schematic representations of the differential elaboration of the lemnothalamus (*blue*) and collothalamus (*orange*) from the ancestral tetrapod unelaborated condition (*lower left*) to the retention of this condition in extant amphibians (*lower right*) (although with modification of sensory inputs to the ventral thalamus rather than directly to the dorsal thalamus) and to the condition in ancestral amniotes with a modest elaboration of both divisions (*upper left*). The latter gave rise to an initially more elaborated collothalamus in the diapsid line to sauropsids (*upper right*) and independently to the initially more elaborated lemnothalamus in the synapsid line to mammals (*middle right*). For all schematic representations, dorsal is toward the top and rostral is toward the right.

accompanied lemnothalamic and lemnopallial elaborations. The loss of scales and the gain of hair and whiskers allowed for much more discriminative somatosensation and elaboration of the lemniscal somatosensory pathways, and elaboration of the motor pathways involving an expanded cerebellum and basal ganglia control also occurred. The hippocampal formation and its ascending afferent innervation supported the allocentric functions for foraging that the enhanced somatosensory and motor systems allowed, and enhancement of the olfactory system, including elaboration of the mediodorsal (MD) thalamic nucleus, further contributed to these functions. The enlargement and subdivision of the MD neuronal components are likewise related to the elaboration of the lemnopallial prefrontal cortex. The subsequent elaboration of the collothalamus, on the other hand, culminated in the extensive elaboration of the pulvinar complex and a plethora of extrastriate visual and temporoparietal association cortical areas in primates. Clearly, much of the collothalamic elaboration occurred after the evolutionary divergence of the orders of mammals, as a differential elaboration of many of the collothalamic-recipient cortical areas occurred independently in rodents, carnivores, primates, and other orders as well, as also for the gain of association cortical areas in the temporal and parietal lobes of primates that have reciprocal connections with divisions of the elaborated pulvinar (Harting et al., 1972; Jones, 2007; Baldwin et al., 2017).

At the intranuclear level in mammals, independent elaborations also occurred within orders. The magnocellular and parvocellular components of the lemnothalamic MD and the divisions of the collothalamic pulvinar are two examples. Perhaps most dramatic example is the elaboration of the individual layers of the lemnothalamic DLGN, as noted previously in the section on field homology. The DLGN has a relatively simple anatomical configuration in some mammals, such as rodents, but is enlarged and differentiated into multiple layers in carnivores and primates. However, the individual layers in these orders are not discretely homologous but, rather, homologous only as a set of derivatives of the DLGN pronucleus (Rose, 1942; Jones, 2007).

5.3 Collothalamic and Lemnothalamic Elaboration in Sauropsids

In the diapsid line leading to modern reptiles, both divisions of the dorsal thalamus also were elaborated, but in reverse sequence. In sauropsids, the collothalamus (Table 1) was the first to become elaborated, with the optic tectum (the homologue of the mammalian superior colliculus) enlarging and, as in mammals, in receipt of visual information in its superficial layers and ascending somatosensory inputs to its deeper layers. The elaboration of the torus semicircularis (the homologue of the mammalian inferior colliculus) was arguably less dramatic but nonetheless contributed to spatial mapping and localization functions. The dorsal thalamus in extant sauropsids is dominated by the large, centrally located nucleus rotundus, named for its shape in transverse section and constituting the relay for ascending visual input from the tectum to the ADVR/entopallium (within the nidopallium). The auditory pathway to the ADVR/Field L (within the nidopallium) is via the nucleus reuniens pars compacta in reptiles and the nucleus ovoidalis in birds. A somatosensory pathway from the deep tectal layers is likewise present to a third part of the nidopallium via the nucleus medialis posterior (alternately called the *nucleus caudalis* or the *medialis complex*) in reptiles and the cDLP (the caudal part of nucleus dorsolateralis posterior) in birds (see Butler [1994b], Butler and Hodos [2005], and references therein). Further, Veenman et al. (1997) identified midbrain roof-recipient, laterally lying nuclei in birds as comparable to the posterior intralaminar nuclei of mammals, a distinction not made in the original hypothesis (Butler, 1994b).

Subsequently over evolution and to a different degree in the different groups of reptiles, the lemnothalamus also elaborated. Shared features of lemnothalamic nuclei in mammals include bilaterality in some of their projections to the pallium

Table 1. Connections of the Main Collothalamic Nuclei in Reptiles and Birds

Main Afferent Source	Dorsal Thalamic Relay in Reptiles	Pallial Target in Reptiles	Dorsal Thalamic Relay in Birds	Pallial Target in Birds
Optic tectum—superficial layers	Nucleus rotundus	Pallial visual area in the ADVR and striatum	Nucleus rotundus	Entopallium (within nidopallium) and striatum
Optic tectum—deep layers	Nucleus medialis posterior	Somatosensory area in the ADVR and striatum	cDLP (the caudal part of nucleus dorsolateralis posterior)	Somatosensory area in nidopallium and striatum
Torus semicircularis (nucleus mesencephalicus lateralis pars dorsalis in birds)	Nucleus reuniens pars compacta	Auditory area in the ADVR and striatum	Nuclei ovoidalis	Field L in nidopallium and striatum

Table 2. Hypothesis of Homologues for Major Lemnothalamic Nuclei in Birds and Mammals (Butler, 1994b; Veenman et al., 1997; and references in text)

Main Afferent Sources	Pronucleus of Rose (1942)	Main Thalamic Targets in Birds	Main Telencephalic Targets in Birds	Main Thalamic Targets in Mammals	Main Telencephalic Targets in Mammals
Retina Raphe	Lateral geniculate pronucleus	DLGN	Wulst	DLGN	Primary visual cortex
Cortex Globus pallidus Ventral striatum Septum Hypothalamus Raphe Spinal cord	Medial and central pronuclei	Dorsal thalamic zone (DTZ; including dorsomedialis and dorsolateralis anterior)	Wulst and nidopallium and dorsal and ventral striatum	Rostral nuclein including anterior intralaminar and mediodorsal nuclei	Prefrontal and sensorimotor cortices and dorsal and ventral striatum
Dorsal column nuclei	Central pronucleus	DIVA	Rostral Wulst	VPL	Primary somatosensory cortex
Principal trigeminal nucleus		—	Nucleus basorostralis pallii	VPM	Primary somatosensory cortex
Globus pallidus		VIA	Rostral Wulst	VA/VL	Primary motor cortex

(Herkenham, 1978; Preuss and Goldman-Rakic, 1987; Dermon and Barbas, 1994; Dinopoulos, 1994; Caretta et al., 1996), as is also the case in sauropsids (Karten et al., 1973; Lohman and van Woerden-Verkley, 1978), in contrast to solely ipsilateral collothalamic projections (Harting et al., 2001). Also shared among lemnothalamic nuclei in amniotes and in contrast to the collothalamus are serotoninergic innervation from the raphe and, except for the rostral intralaminar nuclei, the lack of any projections to the striatum (see Butler [1994b] and references therein).

Lemnothalamic elaboration among sauropsids is most strikingly observed in birds (Table 2), in which the homologue of the mammalian dorsal lateral geniculate nucleus (DLGN), now called by the same name (Reiner et al., 2004), relays visual input to a different part of the pallium, the visual part of the Wulst (Karten et al., 1973). Additionally, lemniscal somatosensory inputs from the dorsal column nuclei to the thalamus, to a nucleus called the *DIVA* (nucleus dorsalis intermedius ventralis anterior) in birds, is relayed to the more rostrally lying, somatosensory part of the Wulst (Wild, 1997), which then gives rise to a pyramidal-like tract (Wild and Williams, 2000).

Although the DIVA is clearly the homologue of the mammalian VPL, no homologue of the mammalian trigeminorecipient thalamic nucleus, the ventral posterior medial

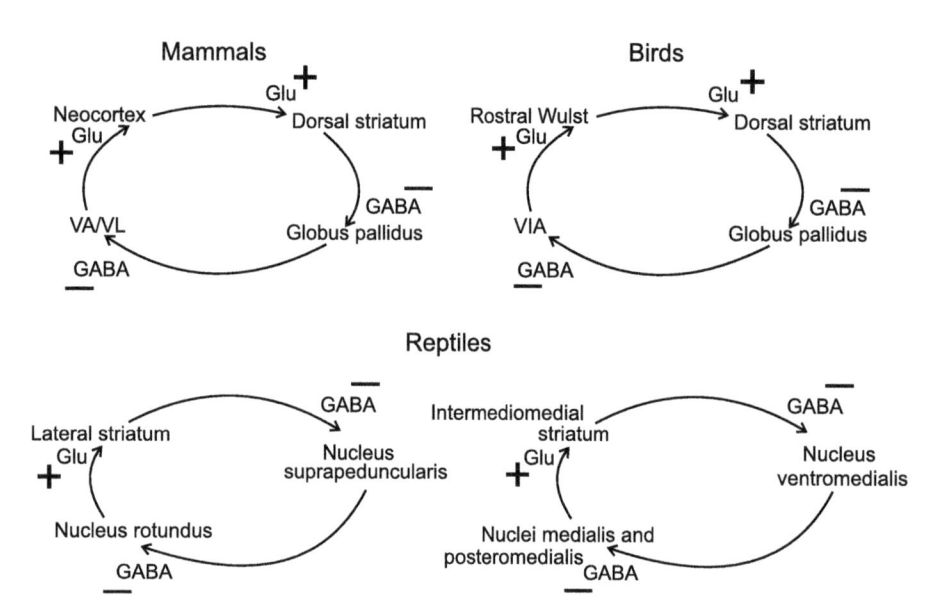

Figure 9 Diagrams of the direct loop circuits in amniotes.

The neurotransmitters glutamate (Glu) or gamma-aminobutyric acid (GABA) are indicated along with plus and minus signs, respectively, to indicate their excitatory or inhibitory function. The direct loop for birds is identical in synaptology and function for the promotion of movement to that in mammals. In reptiles, the two three-component circuits have been identified that also serve to promote movement. All four circuits involve inhibition of inhibition for a net excitatory influence.

nucleus (VPM), exists in birds. Instead of synapsing anywhere in the diencephalon, the ascending trigeminal tract in birds continues straight on through and terminates in a telencephalic nucleus, the nucleus basorostralis pallii (formerly, *nucleus basalis*) (Wild et al., 1985). Because the tract connects the trigeminal nucleus directly with this nucleus in the telencephalon, it is called the *quintofrontal tract*. This synaptology may be unique to birds and thus an evolutionary novelty because trigeminal projections have been found in a lizard to part of nucleus dorsolateralis anterior (Desfilis et al., 1998), which would thus be a homologue of the mammalian VPM.

In birds as in mammals, a direct loop, the striatopallidothalamic circuit, is relayed through a neighboring nucleus, the VIA (Medina et al., 1997; Reiner et al., 1998; Reiner, 2002), which is comparable to the mammalian ventral anterior/ventral lateral nuclei (VA/VL). The pathway comprises projections from the striatum to the globus pallidus to the VIA to the somatosensory Wulst and back to the striatum and functions to promote movement (Figure 9). The VIA has yet to be definitively identified in reptiles but may, along with the DIVA, be located in the region of two perirotundal nuclei, the nucleus intermedius dorsalis thalami and nucleus ventralis (with somewhat variable terminology across species) (see Medina et al. [1997] and references therein).

However, Suárez et al. (2002) identified two striatothalamic pathways that may serve the direct loop function in a lizard (Figure 9). The lateral striatum projects to the ventral thalamic suprapeduncular nucleus (nSP), which reciprocally influences the lateral striatum via a relay through the nucleus rotundus. The intermediomedial striatum projects to the ventral thalamic nucleus ventromedialis, which directly projects back to the intermediomedial striatum via a relay through ventral tier-like dorsal thalamic nuclei. Because these pathways both involve inhibition of inhibition, as does the direct loop in mammals, they would serve to promote movement. Substance P-positive neurons are abundant in the globus pallidus in both birds and reptiles, as they are in mammals for the direct loop circuit (Reiner et al., 1998). Additionally, the nSP also projects to the medial cortex (Zhu et al., 2005) and sends descending projections to the red nucleus (Herrick and Keifer, 1997; Keifer and Lustig, 2000), further contributing to motor system regulation.

Nuclei that resemble the anterior interlaminar, midline, and mediodorsal nuclei of mammals are present in an area dorsal to the nucleus rotundus in birds (Veenman et al., 1997; Montagnese et al., 2003; Csillag and Montagnese, 2005). These nuclei lie in a dorsal thalamic zone; have connections with the striatum, pallidum, and various brainstem regions; and project topographically to the pallium (Veenman et al., 1997), resembling the so-called diffuse, nonspecific intralaminar projections in mammals that are now also known to be topographically organized (Sherman and Guillery, 2013). Bilateral, intralaminar-like projections to the pallium have been found in lizards (Lohman and Van Woerden-Verkley, 1978; Desfilis et al., 2002), so some of the components are clearly there and thus likely to have been established in the deep common amniote ancestor.

In contrast to mammals, reptiles exhibit fewer reciprocal, glutamatergic pallial projections to the dorsal thalamus (Pritz, 1995; Nieuwenhuys et al., 1998; Butler and Hodos, 2005). In turtles, the dorsal cortex projects reciprocally to the DLGN and to the nuclei dorsolateralis anterior and ventralis (Hall et al., 1977), all three nuclei a part of the lemnothalamus. Likewise, the cortex projects to the nucleus dorsolateralis anterior in lizards (Hoogland and Vermeulen-Van der Zee, 198). Suárez et al. (2002) identified two striatothalamic pathways that may serve the direct loop function in a lizard (Figure 9); Bruce and Butler, 1984). As Pritz (1995) notes, however, it has not been established that these projections are truly reciprocal. In birds, the visual and somatosensory parts of the Wulst do project reciprocally to the DLGN and DIVA, respectively, but even so, reciprocal palliothalamic projections are substantially less extensive than in mammals (Karten et al., 1973; Watanabe, 1987; Wild and Williams, 2000). Thus, even though some diffuse (i.e., widespread) thalamopallial projections are present in sauropsids, the reciprocal projections to the thalamus that mammals utilize for the modulator functions (Sherman and Guillery, 2013) are not as prominent.

The dual elaboration hypothesis was formulated entirely in the context of the Karten (1969) hypothesis and so led to the recognition of the lemnothalamic-recipient neocortical areas as the lemnocortex (lemnopallium) and the collothalamic-recipient neocortical areas as the collocortex (collopallium) in amniotes (Butler, 1994a). These pallial divisions were independently identified by Reiner (1993) using a different analytical approach. The revision of DVR homologies discussed earlier in the chapter now requires a revision of the collopallial part of the dual elaboration hypothesis but otherwise leaves the thalamic divisions and the recognition of the lemnopallium across amniotes intact. Within the pallium of mammals, the collothalamic nuclei project not only to ventral and lateral pallial derivatives but also to an apparently novel and large region derived from the dorsal pallium, that is, the collothalamic-recipient neocortex.

5.4 The Dual Elaboration Hypothesis and Developmental Studies

5.4.1 Studies That Are Congruent with the Dual Elaboration Hypothesis

The two evolutionary compartments are marked by the differential expression of two molecular markers in the dorsal thalamus of the 14.5-day embryonic mouse brain (González et al., 2002; Moreno et al., 2017) (Figure 7C). The proneural gene *Math4a*, a transcription factor that is requisite for the determination of neural fate (Brown et al., 2001), is confined to the rostral lemnothalamic compartment, and the expression of calretinin, also called *calbindin 2* or *calbindin-D29k*, which is a calcium-binding protein, is confined to the caudal collothalamic compartment. The *Math4a*-positive component is a field that gives rise to the nuclei that include the dorsal lateral geniculate nucleus, anterior nuclear group, and ventrobasal complex, whereas the calretinin-positive component, which consists of the caudoventral and ventral regions (distinguished from each other by the density of calretinin staining in cells and/or neuropil), differentiates into the components of the collothalamus, including the LP/pulvinar, the posterior nuclear group, and the medial geniculate body.

These findings of González et al. (2002) and Moreno et al. (2017) confirmed and extended the results of Dávila et al. (2000) and Redies et al. (2000), who, using antibodies to calretinin and several cadherins, both found differential expression patterns within the developing dorsal thalamus in a lizard and chicken embryos, respectively, and recognized three tiers—dorsal, intermediate, and ventral—with the dorsal tier appearing to correspond to the *Math4a*-positive lemnothalamus and the intermediate and ventral tiers to the calretinin-positive collothalamus. For example, the dorsal tier predominantly expresses only cadherin-7, whereas various parts of the intermediate and ventral tiers express cadherin-6B, R-cadherin, and N-cadherin in addition to cadherin-7 (Redies et al., 2000) (Figure 7C).

In a study using bromodeoxyuridine, Lynn et al. (2015) found that the time course of neuronal generation and gradients in the developing avian (chicken) dorsal thalamus is very similar to those seen in the developing rodent thalamus (Bayer and Altman, 1995). They identified lateral-to-medial, dorsal-to-ventral, and posterior-to-anterior gradients. Although their data did not differentiate between radial units, they were applicable to the three-tier scheme of Redies et al. (2000) and Dávila et al. (2000), with the dorsal tier containing nuclei that project to the hyperpallium, including the Wulst, and the intermediate and ventral tier nuclei projecting to the dorsal ventricular ridge.

These two evolutionary divisions are likewise present in frogs. Puelles et al. (1996) analyzed the prosomeric organization of the diencephalon in the bullfrog *Rana perezi* using acetylcholinesterase histochemistry (Figure 7D). They found the anterior nucleus, which comprises the lemnothalamus in amphibians, to be strongly positive for AChE in its neuropil. In contrast, the caudal, collothalamic region expressed very low levels of AChE. Thus, the proneural gene *Math4a*, calretinin, several cadherins, and AChE are all expressed differentially in the lemnothalamus versus the collothalamus in various tetrapods.

5.4.2 Other Developmental Studies

Not all studies examining regulatory gene-expression patterns or other immunohistochemically active molecules align with the evolutionary divisions of the dorsal thalamus. For example, Nakagawa and O'Leary (2001) documented the expression patterns of five LIM-homeodomain and three other genes (*Gbx2*, *Ngn2*, and *Pax6*)—all of which encode transcription factors that influence the translation of DNA to messenger RNA and are involved in patterning and cell fate specification, including connectivity (e.g., Bachy et al., 2001; Bulchand et al., 2001; Moreno et al., 2004). In mouse embryos, the expression regions of these genes overlap, each being expressed in some of the lemnothalamic and some of the collothalamic nuclei. Thus, these genes appear to be involved in regulating the development of internal nuclear or other features that are shared across the two divisions.

In a recent clonal lineage study, Shi et al. (2017) identified three clonal subclusters in the developing mouse dorsal thalamus, but two include elements of both evolutionary divisions. Their anterior cluster appears to include only lemnothalamic nuclei, whereas their mediodorsal subcluster mainly comprises collothalamic nuclei but includes the lemnothalamic mediodorsal nucleus. Likewise, the medial ventral posterior subclusters comprise elements of both evolutionary divisions, including the DLGN and MGv.

These gene-expression and clonal analyses clearly focus on early developmental events that do not differentiate the evolutionary divisions. In contrast, the differential expression of *Math4a*, calretinin, calbindins, and AChE in the mouse dorsal thalamic divisions and the physical groupings of neurons into the pronuclei that Rose (1942) identified in a rabbit are the result of later epigenetic regulation of cell differentiation and telencephalic target selections that distinguish the two evolutionary divisions. This situation is like that in the developing pallium whereby epigenetic regulation of cell differentiation and connectivity results in neocortical-like neuronal components and connections in the ventral and lateral pallial derivatives in sauropsids. Just as for these pallial areas, the sets of collothalamic and lemnothalamic nuclei each have some components that are allogenous (produced by different generative zones) but syngenous in regard to epigenetic regulatory events that specify a number of their features, particularly in regard to their evolutionary histories and synaptology. Likewise, the traditional anatomical divisions of the dorsal thalamus, such as the "primary" sensory pathways that group the medial geniculate nucleus with the lateral geniculate nucleus and somatosensory relay nuclei, and the functional divisions of the dorsal thalamus, such as the core and matrix concept (Jones, 2007), apply across both the lemnothalamic and collothalamic nuclei and mask their evolutionary history.

5.5 Anatomical and Functional Divisions of the Dorsal Thalamus

The traditional anatomical classifications of thalamic nuclei do not correlate with the lemnothalamic and collothalamic evolutionary divisions. The anatomical grouping of "primary" sensory pathways in mammals—visual via the DLGN, somatosensory via the VPL, and auditory via the MGv—clearly involves components of both and simply reflects the relay of information to areas that are considered "primary" cortices rather than whether the sensory input to the thalamus is via the midbrain roof or not. In fact, ironically, this anatomical perspective on dorsal thalamic organization actually obscured the evolutionary history of differential innervation patterns and different time courses for lemnothalamic versus collothalamic elaboration in the sauropsid and mammalian lineages. Studying the outgroups to amniotes, especially amphibians, allowed the evolutionary divisions and their differential histories to be discerned.

Functional systems, such as those of Jones (2007), Macchi et al. (1996), and Sherman and Guillery (2013), also do not correlate with, or at best only partially overlap, the evolutionary divisions. These perspectives are based mainly on features that have become elaborated within the mammalian lineage. Because some of these features are shared by some components of both the lemnothalamus and collothalamus, they do not distinguish them. For example, three of the four classes of thalamocortical projection patterns noted by Macchi et al. (1996) include some diffuse (i.e., widespread) projections, as does the matrix portion of the core and the matrix concept of Jones (2007). Such projections are present in sauropsids from lemnothalamic nuclei but not from collothalamic nuclei and only to a moderate degree. In birds, Csillag and Montagnese (2005) found projections from the DLGN to three laminae within the hyperpallium and a projection from what may be the best candidate for an anterior intralaminar homologue within the dorsal thalamic zone (DTZ) (Veenman et al., 1997) to one of the same laminae and also to the outermost hyperpallial lamina. Such projections are moderately diffuse (i.e., to a broader area of the pallium than the unimodal sensory system projections) but nonetheless topographic like the mammalian intralaminar projections. Nevertheless, the clear presence of the four classes of Macchi et al. would be difficult to defend in sauropsids.

The drivers-versus-modulators distinction for first- and higher-order nuclei of Sherman and Guillery (2013) similarly involves both evolutionary divisions and also may be predominantly a mammalian specialization. The modulator system reaches its apex with the extensive elaboration of the pulvinar components in primates that are involved solely in thalamo-corticothalamic loops (Jones, 2007). Further, Bickford (2016) notes that there are a number of variations in thalamic circuits that do not easily fit the driver/modulator model, such as tectothalamic projections that exhibit differences in their synaptic terminal morphology and presynaptic proteins, as well as converging terminations on individual neurons. The tectothalamic terminals are medium-sized, with round vesicles, unlike the larger-sized retinogeniculate driver terminals, for example. In contrast, in a lizard, tectothalamic projections to the nucleus rotundus are via very thin, unmyelinated fibers whose small boutons with round synaptic vesicles terminate on the dendrites of rotundal neurons, on which unlabeled terminal boutons (i.e., from a non-tectal source) converge (Dávila et al., 2002). More studies at the electron microscopic level need to be done in sauropsids to determine the degrees of differences and similarities.

Physiological studies of sensory relay neurons in the thalamus of birds have shown that they have tonic firing that converts to burst discharges with depolarizing input, similar to the burst-spiking behavior of mammalian thalamic neurons (Steriade et al., 1997; Steriade and Paré, 2007; Rikhye et al., 2018). Neurons in the auditory relay nucleus, the nucleus ovoidalis, for example, behave in this way and may thus modulate the relay of auditory information to the pallium (Ströhmann et al., 1994). In the tectal visual relay nucleus, the nucleus rotundus, Hu and Wang (2001) found at least one type of neuron that, with depolarizing input, changed its firing pattern from a single spike to late spiking to fast spiking as the current intensity was increased. In contrast, a second type of cell, not distinguishable on morphological grounds, gave a "hump-like" discharge followed by one or two spikes followed by inactivation.

Some similarities to the physiological mechanisms for mammalian sleep (Steriade et al., 1997; Steriade and Paré, 2007) also are present in birds. Ovoidalis neurons exhibit hyperpolarization-activated inward rectification (Ströhmann et al., 1994), resembling the thalamic hyperpolarization-activated current responsible for sleep regulation. Further, van der Meij et al. (2019) found some similarities and some differences in wave propagation during non–rapid eye movement sleep (NREM) and also in the transition from NREM to REM. During NREM and similar to neocortex behavior, slow-wave activity propagated through the hyperpallium and was primarily confined to the thalamic input layers as in mammals, but spindles were not detected in either the hyperpallium or the thalamus. Thus, at least some functional similarities are shared by birds and mammals in sleep mechanisms driven by the thalamus.

Functional models are, of course, the key to illuminating how complex cognitive abilities and consciousness are generated by the thalamocortical system in mammals and, perhaps involving some different features, those functions in nonmammals. In considering functional models, the relative paucity of diffuse, matrix-like projections and loop systems in sauropsids—and in fishes, for that matter—needs to be weighed against the surprisingly high level of cognitive capabilities in some members of both of these taxa, as discussed later in the chapter. A number of features of the integrated models of thalamocortical function in mammals, including the hierarchical convolutional neural networks (HCNNs) proposed by Rikyhe et al. (2018), particularly involving the extensive thalamocorticothalamic recurrent circuitry of the mediodorsal nucleus and various divisions of the pulvinar and/or of thalamic computational models (Halassa and Sherman, 2019), may be lacking in nonmammals. Nonetheless, the surprisingly high-level cognitive abilities displayed by diverse nonmammalian taxa, discussed in Section 10, are somehow supported by their ascending thalamopallial systems.

6. Dual Elaboration Hypothesis in Light of Tetrapartite Pallial Evolution

How did the elaborated pallial areas and their multiple thalamic afferent nuclei arise in amniotes? Insights into the evolutionary origin of collothalamic-recipient neocortices and the lateral amygdala in mammals, the DVR in sauropsids, and the collothalamic nuclei that project to them, as well as the multiple lemnothalamic nuclei and lemnopallial areas, can be gleaned from available data. Differential expression of dorsalizing and ventralizing molecular cues account for the differences in pallial sector elaboration (e.g., Medina and Abellán, 2009; García-Moreno and Molnár, 2020). Minor differences in molecular axonal guidance cues (Bielle et al., 2011; Tosa et al., 2015) account for the difference in the thalamic axonal pathway through the ventral telencephalon via an external route in sauropsids (Cordery and Molnár, 1999) and the internal capsule in mammals (López-Bendito and Molnár, 2003, López-Bendito et al., 2007; Molnár et al., 2012; see also Chapter 7 of this book) and thus to different thalamo-recipient pallial areas in mammals and sauropsids. The parcellation hypothesis posited by Sven Ebbesson (1980, 1984, 2020) can be invoked to account for the gain of multiple thalamic nuclei in both divisions in both sauropsids and mammals.

An early amniote ancestor would likely have had four (Smith-Fernandez et al., 1998; Puelles et al., 2000, 2017) only modestly developed pallial sectors and relatively simple thalamic organization (Reiner, 1993, 2012; Butler, 1994a, 1994b; Striedter and Northcutt, 2020). It is important to recall that neither the diapsid nor synapsid line was, at any point, ancestral to the other, so the differences in pallial and thalamic elaboration were independently evolved. The growth cones of the thalamic corticopetal axons would have been repelled from the hypothalamus by the midline repellent Slit2 toward a lateral position in the diencephalon, as this mechanism is common to both sauropsids and mammals (Bielle et al., 2011; Tosa et al., 2015), but then reached the pallium via the lateral forebrain bundle (LFB), as is the case in the outgroup, the amphibians (Laberge et al., 2008), and lemnothalamic projections to the medial pallium would have invaded the modestly increased dorsal pallial area as well. A few projections to the striatum might also have been present from the emerging lemnothalamic, rostral intralaminar nuclei. Most if not all collothalamic projections, at this point, would have been restricted to the striatum, also via the LFB.

Within the synapsid line, the dorsal pallial sector gave rise to a greatly expanded region as a result of molecular dorsalizing influences (Aboitiz et al., 2003; Sur and Rubenstein, 2005; Medina and Abellán, 2009; Montiel and Aboitiz, 2015; García-Moreno and Molnár, 2020). Upon entering the ventral telencephalon, the thalamic projections to this sector would have entered a permissive corridor that had newly become displaced medially by the short-range repellent effect of Slit2 on the migration of the corridor cells. This expression and action of Slit2 in the ventral telencephalon is absent in sauropsids (Lopez-Bendito et al., 2007; Bielle et al., 2011; Tosa et al., 2015). Because of the position of the corridor, the collothalamic axons thus access the cortex, the lateral amygdala, and striatum via the internal capsule (see Chapter 7 of this book).

With elaboration of the lemnothalamus initially greater than that of the collothalamus, these projections would carry information predominantly to the hippocampus and the primary visual and somatosensory cortices, as well as relaying olfactory information to the more rostral cortex via the lemnothalamic, mediodorsal nucleus. As Aboitiz et al. (2003) and Montiel and Aboitiz (2015) have discussed, these inputs would allow for allocentric spatial mapping (Rodríguez et al., 2002; Bingman et al., 2017) and episodic memory, with the olfactory and primary visual information enhancing those functions. The former authors postulated a confluence of the lemnothalamic and collothalamic pathways in this scenario, which would likely have been sequential. Further expansion of the dorsal pallial sector would have created additional "real estate" for existing but minor collopallial pathways to expand into. The propensity of collothalamic-recipient cortical areas to multiply within different orders is clearly high, reaching its apex in primates with the many extrastriate cortices and other association cortical areas that reciprocally connect with the non-sensory pulvinar divisions (Kaas, 2017a; Sherman and Guillery, 2013).

Within the diapsid line, the dorsal pallial sector initially remained modest, whereas the lateral and ventral pallial sectors expanded as a result of molecular ventralizing influences (Aboitiz et al., 2003; Montiel and Aboitiz, 2015; García-Moreno and Molnár, 2020). Upon entering the ventral telencephalon, the thalamic projections to all four sectors would have remained within the LFB because of a lack of Slit2 expression to repel migrating corridor cells medially (Bielle et al., 2011; Tosa et al., 2015). The initially greater elaboration of the collothalamus into separate visual-, auditory-, and somatosensory-relaying nuclei would have

Table 3. Revised Hypothesis of Homologies for Collothalamic Nuclei in Amniotes

Major Afferent Source	Pronucleus of Rose (1942)	Thalamic Nucleus(i) in Reptiles (and Birds)	Pallial Targets in Reptiles (and Birds)	Thalamic Nucleus(i) in Mammals	Pallial Targets in Mammals
Tectum/superior colliculus	Dorsal pronucleus	Nuclei rotundus and nucleus medialis posterior (cDLP)	Visual and somatosensory areas of ADVR (entopallium and caudomedial nidopallium) and striatum	LP/pulvinar complex and posterior nuclear group	Extrastriate cortices, secondary somatosensory cortex (SII), amygdala, and striatum
Torus semicircularis (nucleus mesencephalicus lateralis pars dorsalis)	Medial geniculate pronucleus	Nucleus medialis (nucleus ovoidalis)	Auditory area of ADVR (Field L) and striatum	Medial geniculate body (MGm, MGd, and MGv)	Auditory cortex, amygdala, and striatum

resulted in the respective unimodal projections to the ADVR, whereas relatively modest lemnothalamic projections would have reached the medial and dorsal pallia. Later, as archosaurs arose and gave rise to extant crocodiles and birds, elaboration of the lemnothalamus occurred, including the visual and somatosensory projections to the Wulst.

This scenario (Table 3) implies that the tectal-recipient collothalamic nuclei—the nucleus rotundus and nucleus medialis posterior (cDLP in birds)—are homologous as derivatives of a field (the dorsal pronucleus of Rose [1942]) to both the LP/pulvinar complex and the posterior group nuclei, including the limitans/suprageniculate nucleus, of mammals. The many features that the tectorotundal pathway shares with *both* the tectoposterior group pathway (Dávila et al., 2002) and the tecto-LP/pulvinar pathway (Karten et al., 1997; Luksch et al., 1998), in addition to the deeper-layer tecto-somatosensory pathway, support this hypothesis. Likewise, the toral-recipient (auditory) collothalamic relay nucleus of sauropsids—the nucleus reuniens pars compacta (nucleus medialis) of reptiles and the nucleus ovoidalis of birds—is homologous as a derivative of a field (the medial geniculate pronucleus of Rose [1942]) to the multiple divisions of the medial geniculate body. Alternatively for the latter, as Striedter and Northcutt (2020) have discussed, the auditory relay nuclei in the sauropsid and mammalian lines may have evolved independently.

But how did the separate but different sets of nuclei in both the lemnothalamus and collothalamus in both the synapsid and diapsid lines arise? Where two pallial targets (e.g., the collothalamic-recipient neocortex and the lateral amygdala) rather than one were gained, the added target could have initially attracted collaterals from a single thalamic nucleus. Subsequently, the elaboration of the nucleus could have occurred by the process of parcellation (Ebbesson, 1980, 1984, 2020) such that neurons projecting solely to each of the two targets, rather than giving rise to collateral branches, would be gained and then separate into two separate nuclei within the thalamus. This type of scenario was anticipated by Dávila et al. (2000) in their calcium-binding protein study. They proposed that deep in the stem synapsid line leading to mammals, late-born tecto-LP–projecting neurons may have been acquired in addition to older tectoposterior-/tectorotundic-projecting neurons. This is only slightly different from the idea here of a dorsal pronucleus giving rise in this manner to both the posterior group and LP/pulvinar in mammals and, independently, to the nuclei rotundus and medialis posterior in sauropsids.

This two-step transition phase would then result in separate, novel cortical areas and the lateral amygdala in mammals and separate DVR areas in sauropsids, each in receipt of ascending projections from novel, dedicated thalamic nuclei. That collateralization is possible is supported by the fact that some collothalamic nuclei in mammals give rise to collaterals to both the lateral amygdala and auditory cortex (Kudo et al., 1986; Doron and LeDoux, 2000)—perhaps a trace remnant of evolutionary history.

7. Amphibians

The thalamus across the two major divisions of tetrapods—amphibians and amniotes—is different in several major respects. Whether the thalamus of the basal tetrapod stock resembled either of these conditions or had some features of one combined with some of the other is unknowable. The thalamus in amphibians is arguably much simpler than that in amniotes, with substantially fewer nuclei—a lemnothalamic anterior nucleus and two collothalamic nuclei, the anterior lateral and central nuclei. However, it is different enough to question whether what we see in extant amphibians is like that of ancestral tetrapods or at least partly the result of secondary simplification combined with some unique specializations. Of particular note in that regard is that although the anterior nucleus does not receive substantial midbrain tectal input

Table 4 Ascending Projections through the Dorsal Thalamus of Amphibians

Afferent Source(s)	Dorsal Thalamic Nucleus(i)	Telencephalic Target(s)
Retina Thalamus Hypothalamus Pretectum Optic tectum Obex Raphe Medial pallium	Nucleus anterior via GABAergic relay in ventral thalamus	Medial and/or dorsal pallium
Optic tectum	Anterior lateral nucleus via GABAergic relay in ventral thalamus	Striatum
Torus semicircularis	Central nucleus via GABAergic relay in ventral thalamus	Striatum

and thus qualifies as lemnothalamic, it also does not transmit any unimodal information to the pallium, as Laberge et al. (2008) point out, which is in marked contrast to other lemnothalamic systems in other vertebrates.

From the revision of collothalamic nuclei homologues shown in Table 3, it is not a far leap to postulate that the dorsal and medial geniculate pronuclei of Rose (1942) and their various derivatives in amniotes would be homologous, again as derivatives of the pronuclear fields, to the tectal-recipient anterior lateral and toral-recipient central nuclei of amphibians, respectively.

Amphibians have both dorsal and ventral divisions of the thalamus. The evolution of the ventral thalamus is discussed in Section 9 but, uniquely, is a crucial and integral part of the dorsal thalamic circuitry in amphibians because of the synaptology of sensory afferents. The several ventral thalamic nuclei contain GABAergic neurons and, uniquely in amphibians, are the only thalamic components that are in direct receipt of somatosensory inputs from spinal and trigeminal nerves, vestibular inputs, and visual inputs (Roth et al., 2003; Westhoff et al., 2004), as studied in the fire-bellied toad, *Bombina orientalis*. These ventral thalamic inputs are relayed to discrete, largely non-overlapping territories within the dorsal thalamus (Table 4). Direct glutamatergic sensory inputs to the dorsal thalamus are sparse to absent, in marked contrast to amniotes. This means that the sensory-thalamic-pallial circuitry in amphibians is a marked exception to that in all other vertebrate phyla.

The anterior nucleus projects to multiple sites in the telencephalon, predominantly the medial pallium (Laberge et al., 2008), relaying the multisensory information to it. The medial pallium in mammals comprises the hippocampal formation, and the medial pallium in other vertebrates, including amphibians, is its homologue on topological and embryological grounds. In contrast, in amphibians, the dorsal and lateral pallia are much smaller and not in receipt of significant direct thalamic sensory inputs.

This ascending pathway for multiple sensory systems is thus quite unlike the thalamopallial pathways in amniotes, which receive direct sensory inputs from glutamatergic neurons. A further marked difference between amphibians and amniotes is the lack of both reciprocal, pallial projections to dorsal thalamic nuclei and a GABAergic thalamic reticular nucleus in the ventral thalamus. Thus, amphibians lack the several hallmark features of thalamic and pallial circuitry present in amniotes.

8. Dorsal Thalamic Evolution in Fishes

In fishes, there are also marked differences in the dorsal thalamic components and, in ray-finned fishes, other related but independently evolved nuclei (see Nieuwenhuys et al. [1998], Butler and Hodos [2005], Striedter and Northcutt [2020], and references therein).

The lobe-finned fishes comprise extant lungfishes, the coelacanth *Latimeria chalumnae*, and the descendant tetrapods covered earlier. Lungfishes are divided into two orders, one of which contains the Australian lungfish of the genus *Neoceratodus* and the other the South American lungfish, genus *Lepidosiren*, and the African lungfish, genus *Protopterus*. The dorsal thalamic organization in lungfishes is similar to that in amphibians in being divisible into prosomeres on the basis of calbindin and calretinin immunoreactivity, including dorsal thalamic (or thalamic) and ventral thalamic (prethalamic) divisions, but the lack of migration of neurons from the periventricular surface does not allow recognition of specific nuclei except in *Protopterus*, where immunohistochemical studies allow recognition of three regions (López et al., 2017; Moreno et al., 2018). Retinal projections were traced into the dorsal thalamus by Northcutt (1977, 1980), and cytoarchitectural and immunohistochemical studies of the telencephalon suggest that it is organized in a manner similar to that in tetrapods, with pallial, striatopallidal, and amygdalar components (Northcutt, 2009), but little additional information is available relative to thalamic and pallial relationships.

Ray-finned fishes, or actinopterygians, have some marked differences from the other vertebrate clades in how they relay sensory information to the telencephalon. Ray-finned fishes are an extremely diverse and extremely large group, and there is substantial variation in their forebrains within the group as well as outside it. The dorsal portions of the telencephalic hemispheres appear to be everted in the adult phenotype, rather than evaginated as is the case in other vertebrate clades, such that the topographic relationships are preserved in the basal telencephalon but have long been believed to be reversed (lateral to medial) for the pallial regions, nevertheless with preservation of the topologic relationships. The topographically medial region, Dm, has been posited to be homologous to the pallial amygdala and the lateral region, Dl, to the hippocampus (Braford, 1995). Recent studies, however, indicate that the developmental process is not one of simple eversion after all and that the topographic and topologic relationships are preserved in the pallium (Dirian et al., 2014; Vernier, 2017). These findings are relevant here because the amygdalar-like functions of the Dm (Portavella et al., 2004) and the hippocampal-like functions of the Dl (Rodriguez et al., 2002; Broglio et al., 2010; Bingman et al., 2017) are consistent with the eversion hypothesis. It is possible that epigenetic effects during neurogenesis account for these functional analogies (Vernier, 2017) because the neurogeneic gradient develops in the opposite direction in teleosts and mammals, and signaling molecules from the roof plate in teleosts and the cortical hem in mammals may specify the neuronal populations of Dm and Dl (Folgueira et al., 2012). This would thus be the same developmental process involving epigenetic determination of pallial region identity as occurs in sauropsids and mammals in the development of the collothalamic-recipient pallia.

In the diencephalon of ray-finned fishes, dorsal thalamic nuclei are present and can be divided into the two evolutionary divisions. The rostral lemnothalamic division, the nucleus anterior, receives robust retinal inputs and serotoninergic inputs from the raphe, but its projections to the pallium are few, if any. The caudal collothalamic division consists of the dorsal posterior nucleus, which receives tectal input, and a central posterior nucleus, which receives and relays auditory information to the pallium and the striatum. The dorsal thalamus as a whole is smaller than a more caudal structure, the preglomerular nuclear complex (PGC), which lies between the dorsal thalamus and the pretectum. The PGC has multiple components that separately relay some of the ascending sensory information to the telencephalon, including gustatory, lateral line, and acoustic. The lateral part of the PGC projects to the pallium and the striatum, mimicking the collothalamus. This nuclear complex is thus similar to but not homologous to the collothalamus and was clearly independently evolved in the ancestral gnathostome lineage because cartilaginous fishes also may have nuclei in this location that are either homologous to the PGC of ray-finned fishes or gained independently (see Butler [1994b] and references therein; Striedter and Northcutt, 2020).

The forebrain organization in cartilaginous fishes, or chondrichthyans, is similar to that in the other non-actinopterygian vertebrate clades (Rodríguez-Moldes et al., 2017). The pallial regions are relatively elaborated in the Group II cartilaginous fishes—those with larger, more complex brains than those in Group I (Northcutt, 1989), so it is still challenging to identify homologies to amniote pallial areas with confidence. Ascending visual pathways to the telencephalon are relayed from the retina through the rostral part of the dorsal thalamus—via a putative homologue of the DLGN and via the retinotectothalamic system, as well as ascending somatosensory information. The main targets of the two visual pathways are different but overlapping parts of a large pallial formation called the *central nucleus*. The study of these pathways formed the starting point for Ebbesson's parcellation hypothesis (Ebbesson, 2020). Electrosensory information is relayed to an area identified as the medial pallium via a more posteriorly lying dorsal thalamic nucleus (Hofmann and Northcutt, 2012). Thus, although more studies of these systems in this clade would be helpful, the presence of the lemno- and collothalamic divisions is indicated.

The jawless fishes, or cyclostomes, comprise lampreys and hagfishes. In comparison to lampreys, hagfishes have a greatly expanded and elaborated forebrain, but relatively little is known about its organization, connections, or development (Sugahara et al., 2013, 2016, 2017; Pombal and Megías, 2017; Striedter and Northcutt, 2020). The forebrain in lampreys appears to be more like the forebrains of gnathostomes (Sugahara et al., 2017) and so is more relevant to illuminating thalamic and pallial evolution. The molecular evidence indicates that lampreys lack a developmentally homologous dorsal pallial sector and may also lack a medial pallial sector, but they have lateral (dorsolateral) and ventral (ventrolateral) pallia (Pombal et al., 2009; Martínez-de-la-Torre et al., 2011; Puelles, 2011; Pombal and Megías, 2017; Striedter and Northcutt, 2020). As in gnathostomes, lemnothalamic (or lemnothalamic-like) visual and somatosensory dorsal thalamic nuclei project to the pallium in a highly ordered, topographic manner (Suryanarayana et al., 2017, 2020; see also Chapter 6 of this book). They terminate in the dorsolateral pallium, which is laminated and has the canonical pallial circuit of thalamo-recipient, intrapallial, and efferent motor system neurons (Suryanarayana et al., 2017, 2020; see also Chapter 6 of this book). The latter references and other papers (Polenova and Vesselkin, 1993; Northcutt and Wicht, 1997; González et al., 1999) indicate that the dorsal thalamus in lampreys comprises both lemnothalamic and collothalamic divisions. Thus, the thalamopallial canonical circuitry for processing sensory information from the two evolutionary divisions of the dorsal thalamus apparently has evolved multiple times independently and to different pallial sectors as the opportunity presents itself in each clade.

9. Evolution of the Ventral Thalamus across Vertebrates

Most anamniotes have multiple nuclei in the ventral thalamus (the prethalamus of segmental terminology, prosomere 3 [Moreno et al., 2017]), several of which are in receipt of retinal projections, including an apparent homologue of the ventral lateral geniculate nucleus of amniotes. A number of the connections of these nuclei remain to be identified (Moreno et al., 2017). As noted earlier, amphibians have several ventral thalamic nuclei that contain GABAergic neurons; are in receipt of somatosensory inputs from spinal and trigeminal nerves, vestibular inputs, and visual inputs; and project to the anterior dorsal thalamus for relay to the medial pallium (Roth et al., 2003; Westhoff et al., 2004). However, a thalamic reticular nucleus (TRN) has not been found in amphibians studied to date or in other anamniotes.

Within amniotes, the ventral thalamus is most elaborated in mammals. Striatopallidal-thalamic circuits that involve only dorsal thalamic nuclei in birds and mammals instead involve ventral thalamic nuclei in reptiles (Suárez et al., 2002), as discussed previously. Some direct loop or direct loop–like circuitry in the stem amniote ancestor would have allowed for greater control and promotion of movements as they invaded the land (Reiner et al., 1998; Reiner, 2002; Striedter and Northcutt, 2020), perhaps including substance P–positive pallidal neurons participating in it. It would nonetheless have required several changes in circuitry from the three-component loop in lizards with two inhibitory elements (striatum inhibitory to VM, VM inhibitory to ventral tier, and the latter excitatory back to striatum) to change to the canonical, four-component direct loop circuit that includes the dorsal pallidum and excludes the ventral thalamus.

In contrast to the direct loop, an indirect loop utilizing enkephalin (ENK)-positive pallidal neurons and glutamatergic subthalamic neurons has been identified in both reptiles and birds, as well as in mammals, and thus was likely present in the stem amniote ancestor. The homologue of the mammalian subthalamic nucleus in birds is the anterior nucleus of the ansa lenticularis (ALa). It contains glutamatergic neurons, receives dorsal pallidal ENK+ projections, and projects back to it (Jiao et al., 2000). In reptiles, the anterior entopeduncular nucleus (ENa) is in the same location as Ala (prosomere 4, topographically in the hypothalamus but traditionally included in the ventral thalamus [Puelles et al., 1987; Reiner et al., 1998]), has glutamatergic neurons, is projected to by the ENK+ pallidal neurons, and projects back to the pallidum (Reiner et al., 1998; Jiao et al., 2000).

A nomenclatural issue needs to be noted here. Another, different nucleus but of the same name—the anterior entopeduncular nucleus—has been identified in reptiles. This nucleus is located rostrolaterally, contains GABAergic neurons, and receives projections from the lateral part of the dorsal striatum (Hoogland, 1977; Nieuwenhuys et al., 1998; Suárez et al., 2002), in addition to the suprapeduncular and ventromedial nuclei discussed in Section 5.3. This ENa is most likely homologous to the medial part of the mammalian globus pallidus (Suárez et al., 2002) and should not be confused with the ALa-like ENa that participates in the indirect loop.

Sauropsids lack GABAergic interneurons within most dorsal thalamic nuclei (Pritz and Stritzel, 1988, 1994; Belekhova et al., 1991; Rio et al., 1992; Pritz 2015). They do, however, have a TRN, which, as is the case in mammals, surrounds the dorsal thalamus, contains GABAergic neurons, and projects to it in sectors (Pritz, 1995, 2015). Díaz et al. (1994) identified three nuclei as components of the TRN in a lizard. They have reciprocal connections with dorsal thalamic nuclei such that the so-called *dorsolateral hypothalamic nucleus* interconnects with the dorsal tier, the ventromedial nucleus with the middle tier, and the suprapeduncular nucleus (nSP) with the ventral tier. The view that the nSP is part of the TRN might be revised, however, in view of its dorsal loop-like involvement (Suárez et al., 2002) and projections to both the medial cortex and the red nucleus, as discussed previously.

A TRN is also present in birds, where it is also called the *superior reticular nucleus* (Mpodozis et al., 1996), and in crocodiles (Pritz and Stritzel, 1990; Pritz, 1995) and turtles (Kenigfest et al., 2005). Thus, it would appear that a TRN was present in the stem amniote stock and contributed to dorsal thalamic functions and interactions with the pallium as these animals emerged from an aquatic habitat and expanded into the terrestrial environment.

Figure 10 schematically shows the circuitry of the midbrain and forebrain discussed here across gnathostomes. The details of these pathways are discussed in the caption, but arguably most relevant for understanding thalamocortical circuit motifs (Halassa and Sherman, 2019) is to note the absence of a TRN in anamniotes and the relative paucity of reciprocal palliothalamic projections in sauropsids and anamniotes. (Even lampreys have GABAergic neurons in the region of their ventral thalamus, but whether these neurons participate in TRN-like circuitry is not known [Meléndez-Ferro et al., 2002].) Also of note is the different circuitry involving diencephalic-pallial projections in ray-finned fishes, most of which are via the preglomerular nuclear complex rather than the dorsal thalamus, in view of the admittedly limited but nonetheless rather surprising cognitive abilities in this clade. The complex cognitive abilities and consciousness in both birds and mammals and, to some degree, in reptiles and ray-finned and cartilaginous fishes may be produced by different mechanisms, understanding all of which will illuminate how these abilities arise from neuronal activity.

10. How Understanding Thalamic Evolution, Organization, and Circuitry with the Pallium Informs (or Does Not Yet Inform) Our Understanding of Perception, Cognition, and Consciousness

As shown in Figure 10 and discussed previously and in the figure caption, the thalamopallial and palliothalamic connections vary considerably across vertebrates. Features common to most include ascending, unimodal sensory pathways—as well as some multimodal pathways—and some features of intrapallial circuitry. How some cognitive abilities are supported by these various connectivities, even to some degree in some taxa of fishes, needs to be considered in the quest to explain the neuronal bases for those abilities and for

Evolution

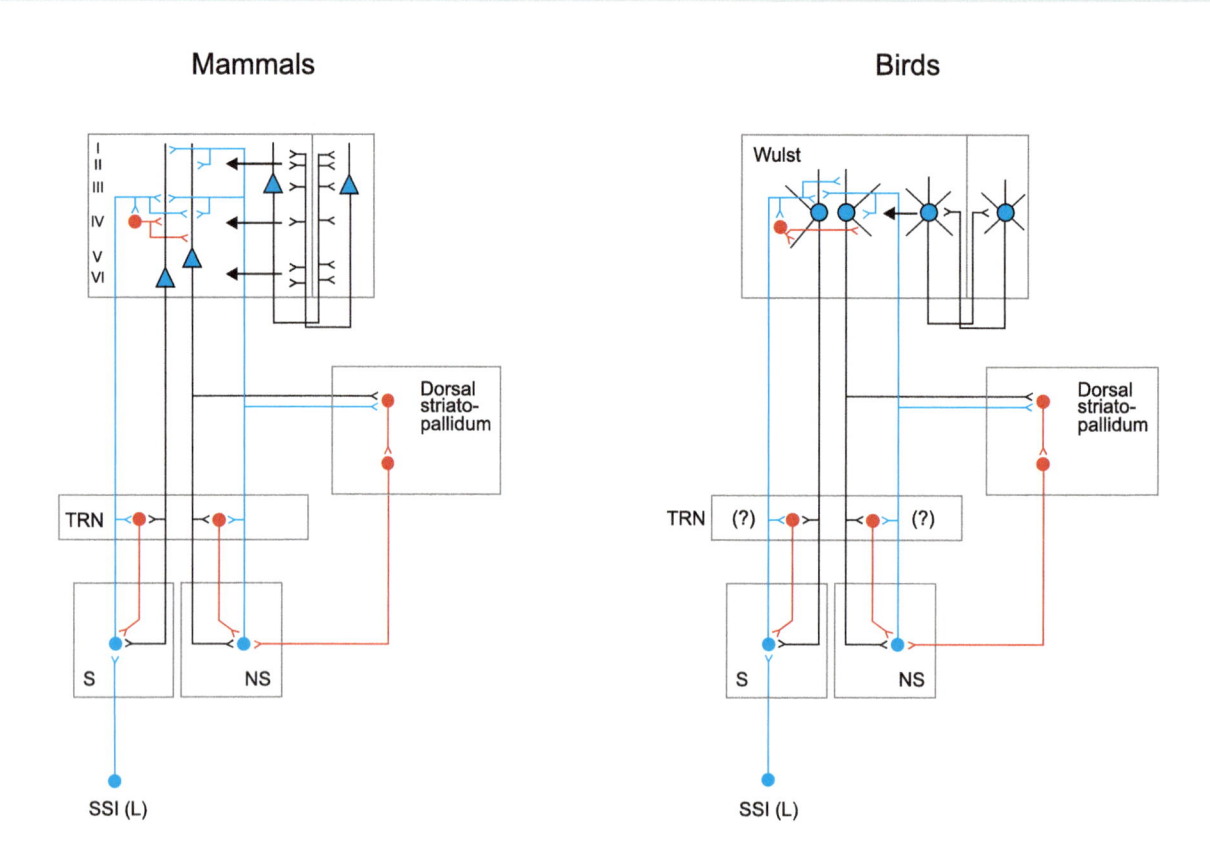

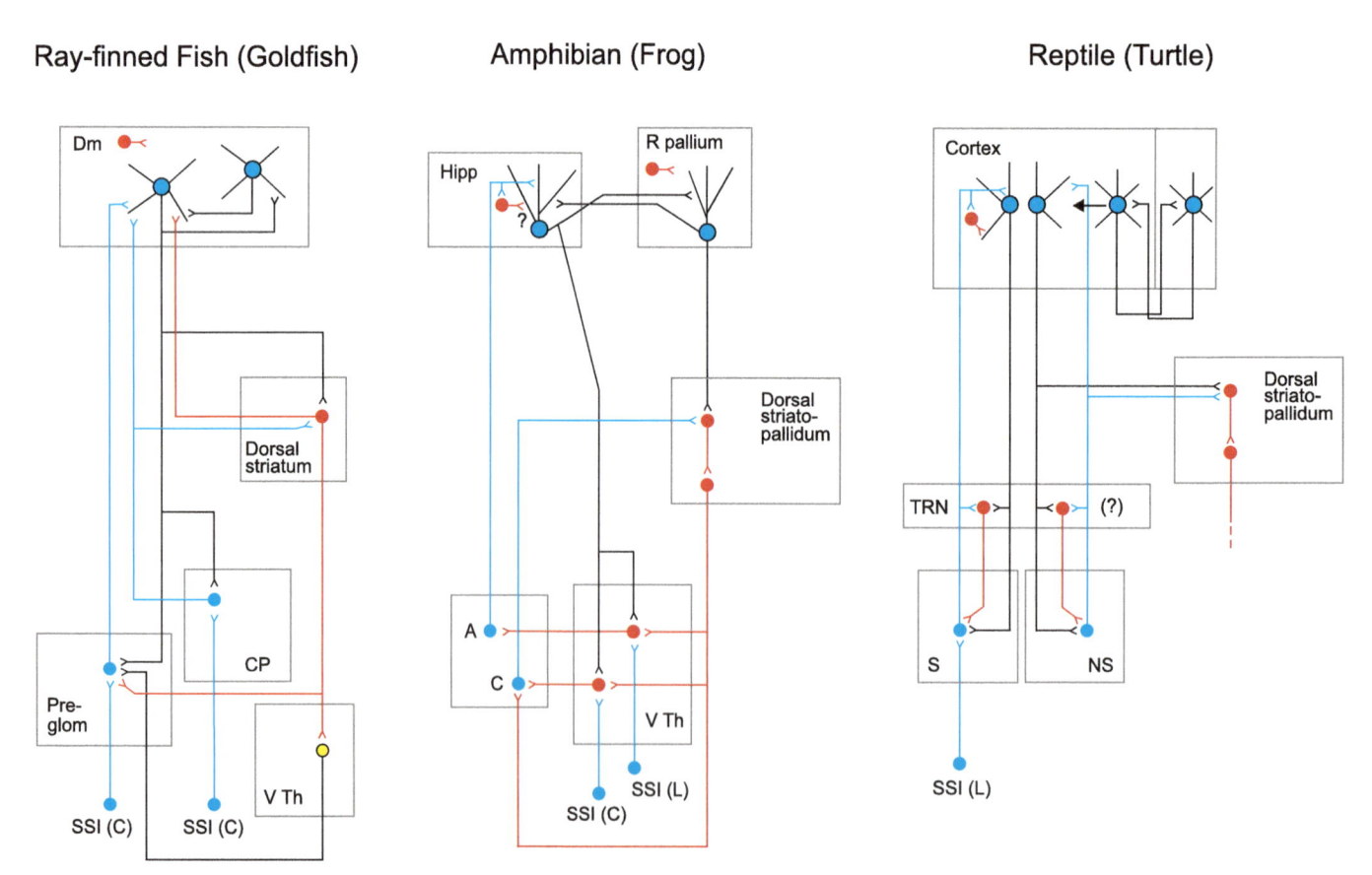

Figure 10 Summary diagrams of the thalamocortical (TC) circuitry in mammals and non-mammals, including birds (drawn mainly from studies of pigeons), reptiles (turtle), ray-finned fish (mainly drawn from studies on goldfish) and amphibians (frog).

Most circuitry is based on lemnothalamic sensory input to its part of the thalamus, and in birds and turtles, it is based on the retinogeniculopallial pathway. The reciprocal palliothalamic projections shown for this pathway are not present for all sensory systems in birds and are present exclusively for this pathway in turtles. The contralateral component of lemnothalamic-pallial projections (present to a substantial degree in amphibians, birds, and reptiles and to a minor degree, in mammals) consciousness (Butler, 2008a). More than one pattern of connectivity may be able to support these functions.

The abilities of birds and some fishes will be focused on here, but cognitive abilities, to a greater or lesser degree, have been found across diverse taxa of vertebrates and invertebrates alike (Iwaniuk, 2017; Gómez-Laplaza and Gerlai, 2020). Although some birds far outshine reptiles in their cognitive abilities, it should be mentioned that reptiles do have some level of cognitive processing (Northcutt, 2013; Roth et al., 2019). Their abilities include problem solving, such as monitor lizards being able to retrieve prey placed in a closed, transparent plastic tube (Manrod et al., 2008). Other abilities include reversal learning, sensory discrimination, and spatial learning (see Iwaniuk, 2017). Likewise, amphibians can make quantity discriminations (Krusche et al., 2010; Stancher et al., 2015), although their pallia are not elaborated but likely secondarily reduced, and their thalamopallial circuitry is markedly different than in other tetrapods, as noted earlier in the chapter.

10.1 Complex Cognitive Abilities of Birds

Numerous studies have now revealed and documented a host of very high-level cognitive abilities in birds, particularly in corvids (crows, jays, jackdaws, magpies), Psittaciformes (parrots), and other taxa, including hummingbirds and pigeons (see Pepperberg, 1999, 2006, 2013, 2020; Heinrich, 1999; Kirsch et al., 2008; Emery and Clayton, 2016; Pepperberg and Nakayama, 2016; Güntürkün, 2020). These abilities include working memory, which Baars (2003) has argued requires conscious processes. Pigeons, for example, are able to do delayed match-to-sample tasks (Diekamp et al., 2002a), and neurons in an area designated the *nidopallium caudolaterale* (NCL) that seems to be analogous (but not homologous) to the prefrontal cortex (PFC) sustain their firing during the delay period (Diekamp et al., 2002b), as do neurons in the PFC during this task. Even more PFC-like, the activity of these delay-active neurons accurately predicts a choice to be made in the delay period between two locations (Rinnert et al., 2019).

Other compelling examples of working memory have been demonstrated involving representations of numerosity. Single-neuron recordings of responses in the NCL during delayed match-to-sample tasks were predictive of the crow's number discrimination ability across a broad range of numerosities regardless of the physical appearance of the items, indicating sensory encoding and memorization processes that are highly similar to those in mammals and other vertebrates as well (Ditz

Caption for Figure 10 (cont.)

is omitted. Glutamate-containing neurons are indicated by blue cell bodies, with blue axons for thalamic neurons and black dendrites and axons for pallial neurons; GABA-containing neurons are indicated by red cell bodies and axons. Dendrites are omitted for all except glutamate-containing pallial neurons. References for many of the connections shown are listed in the text (and see Butler, 2008b), and additional references are provided here, particularly for pallial and striatopallidal features. In mammals (Llinás and Paré, 1991; Llinás et al., 1998, 2005; Llinás and Steriade, 2006; Jones, 2007), specific lemnothalamic sensory input (SSI [L]) is shown to the specific nuclei (S) of the dorsal thalamus, and ascending thalamocortical projections are shown for both the specific and nonspecific (NS; i.e., intralaminar) nuclei to pyramidal neurons in layers V and VI of the neocortex (the main input to layer IV and lower III is omitted), along with inhibitory input to the pyramidal neurons from local circuit GABA-containing neurons in layer IV. Reciprocal corticocortical association connections are indicated to the right in the box representing neocortex; the black arrows indicate that these connections involve the thalamo-recipient neurons. The feedback circuit from the cortex through the dorsal striatopallidum to the intralaminar nuclei is included, as is the reciprocal pathway through the TRN and its other connections with the thalamic nuclei. Intrinsic GABAergic neurons within the dorsal thalamus, which are present in most if not all taxa, are omitted.

Many similar elements of the mammalian TC circuit are present in birds. The layering of the neocortex is absent in the pallium, however, as indicated by multipolar neurons in a single region. As for the mammalian diagram, the pallial circuitry is somewhat simplified. GABAergic neurons are present and included in the circuitry here (Suárez et al., 2005, 2006), but question marks in parentheses in the TRN indicate that the specific connectivities have not yet been fully elucidated. Palliopallial reciprocal connections are indicated as for mammals. The presence of the nonspecific thalamopallial circuitry is based on Veenman et al. (1997). Elements of basal ganglia circuitry in bird and other vertebrates are based on Reiner et al. (1998) and other references as given later in the caption.

In the turtle, as for the bird, the lemnothalamic visual pathway is used as the basis for the circuitry shown. Nonspecific-like (but nonetheless topographic and bilateral [Veenman et al., 1997]) projections to the pallium are included for both turtle and bird, but they terminate in a different part of the pallium than the visual pathway, so they are shown to a neighboring but different pallial neuron. Palliopallial interconnections are indicated, as for birds and mammals. GABAergic pallial neurons are present and implicated in feedforward inhibition to glutamatergic pallial neurons, which exhibit regular spiking in their firing patterns (Mancilla and Ulinski, 2001; Colombe et al., 2004). The TRN circuitry shown is based mainly on Kenigfest et al. (2005); the question mark in parentheses indicates uncertainty about the circuitry of possible nonspecific reciprocal projections. In contrast to other tetrapods, reptiles lack pallidothalamic projections (Reiner et al., 1998), so pallidal projections to other targets are indicated by the dashed end of the axon.

In amphibians, as exemplified here by frogs, the circuitry is markedly different. As discussed in the text, the ascending sensory inputs are restricted to GABAergic ventral thalamic neurons (V Th), which project to the dorsal thalamus. For this taxon, both the lemnothalamic pathway through the rostral thalamus (A; nucleus anterior) to the medial hippocampal pallium (hipp) and the collothalamic pathway with its sensory input (SSI [C]) relayed through the central (auditory relay) nucleus (C) to the striatum are shown. GABAergic neurons are present in the pallial areas (Hollis and Boyd, 2005), although the question mark indicates that their precise circuitry remains to be defined. The medial (hippocampal) pallium is reciprocally connected with the rostral pallium (R pallium) (Roth et al., 2007), which in turn projects to the dorsal striatum (Endepols et al., 2004; Roth et al., 2007). The latter projects to a population identified as pallidal neurons, which in turn project to both the ventral thalamus (ventromedial nucleus) and the central nucleus of the dorsal thalamus (Endepols et al., 2004).

In ray-finned fishes (with most data from goldfish), the afferent thalamic circuitry is more amniote-like, with direct sensory inputs to dorsal thalamic nuclei, for which the collothalamic (auditory) input to the central posterior nucleus (CP) is shown. However, in contrast to amniotes, the projection from the CP to the medial part of the pallium (Dm) is very sparse (Northcutt, 2006). The central posterior nucleus also projects to the striatum (Striedter, 1991). The major ascending relay to the Dm, which most likely corresponds to the pallial (lateral) amygdala of amniotes, is via the preglomerular nuclear complex (Preglom) (Northcutt, 2006), which also receives midbrain-roof input ("collogomerular"). GABAergic neurons are present in the pallium (Crespo et al., 1999), but the details of their circuitry remain to be worked out, as indicated in the figure by their offset position. Reciprocal palliopallial connections are present for most areas, including the Dm (Northcutt, 2006), as are reciprocal connections with the dorsal striatum (Northcutt, 2006). Also, the Dm gives rise to sparse reciprocal projections back to the CP and more robust reciprocal projections to the preglomerular nuclei (Northcutt, 2006). In contrast to other vertebrates, ray-finned fishes lack any population of pallidal neurons; instead, the striatum directly gives rise to descending projections to the ventral thalamus and the preglomerular nuclear complex (Rink and Wullimann, 2004). Also, the ventral thalamus lacks GABAergic neurons in some fish, such as the tench, *Tinca tinca* (Crespo et al., 1999), which is closely related to goldfish, even though they are present in others, such as eels (Médina et al., 1994), so the neurotransmitter involved is uncertain, as indicated by the yellow cell body.

Figure from Butler, A.B. (2008b) Evolution of the thalamus: a morphological and functional review. Thalamus & Related Systems, 24 pp, DOI 10.1017/S1472928808000356, used with permission of Cambridge University Press, Cambridge, UK.

and Nieder, 2016). In a more recent study, Nieder et al. (2020) have demonstrated a direct correlate of consciousness in crows. They trained crows to report whether visual stimuli near their perception threshold were present or absent in a delayed detection task, and a choice of which motor action was to be used by the crow to report presence or absence was not given until after the delay, thus preventing the neuronal activity from involving preparation of the motor response. During the stimulus presentation and delay period, the initial single-neuron activity component was correlated with the stimulus intensity, but a second component was predictive of the perceptual report, indicating that the latter activity—in accordance with criteria established by studies in primates—is a direct correlate of consciousness.

Episodic memory, another manifestation of working memory, has been demonstrated in scrub jays, which are corvids that naturally cache their food. Using multiple paradigms, scrub jays have been shown to be capable of "mental time travel" with respect to the relative time of caching and the various items cached (Clayton and Dickinson, 1998, 1999; Griffiths et al., 1999; Clayton et al., 2001, 2003a, 2003b). Episodic memory has also been demonstrated in hummingbirds, which can adjust the pattern and timing of their visits to artificial flowers with sucrose solution by learning and remembering the different time intervals for each flower when a dose of the solution will become available (Henderson et al., 2006). Transitive inference (TI), which requires the subject to infer relationships using previously obtained information retrieved from working memory, has been demonstrated in pigeons (von Fersen et al., 1990), pinyon jays (Paz-y-Miño et al., 2004), and great tits, which are passerines (Peake et al., 2001, 2002). Pigeons are also able to form categories, another high-level cognitive ability. Pigeons trained to discriminate pairs of abstract paintings by Picasso versus Monet were able to transfer the learned discrimination and apply it to paintings by either Braque or Matisse versus Renoir (Watanabe et al., 1995). New Caledonian crows not only make tools but can create novel compound tools to use to retrieve food targets, an ability otherwise known only to humans and a few examples in captive apes (von Bayern et al., 2018; Gruber et al., 2019). Alex and other parrots in the laboratory of Irene Pepperberg have demonstrated a host of complex cognitive abilities, including spoken words, phoneme understanding, numerical abilities, Piagetian object permanence, shape and color discriminations, and an understanding of the concept of zero (Pepperberg, 1999).

The studies compel one to recognize that birds are indeed capable of thinking, understanding concepts, reasoning, planning, remembering relative durations of time, and theory of mind. Those features of mammalian thalamocortical circuitry (Rikhye et al., 2018; Halassa and Sherman, 2019) that birds also possess may be of particular importance for these functions.

10.2 Surprising Cognitive Abilities of Some Fishes

Ray-finned fishes are a very large and diverse taxon, and a range of cognitive abilities has been found among them (Patton and Braithwaite, 2015; Yamamoto and Bloch, 2017). Goldfish exhibit allocentric spatial memory abilities (Rodríguez et al., 2002; Broglio et al., 2010; Durán et al., 2010) and conditioned fear responses (Portavella et al., 2004). Numerical abilities of judging more versus less or the group size of sholes have been documented in a variety of taxa among ray-finned fishes (see Agrillo and Bisazza, 2017), including guppies (Dadda et al., 2015), angelfish (Gómez-Laplaza and Gerlai, 2020), and other species (Dadda et al., 2009).

Numerical discrimination has even been found in Port Jackson sharks (Vila Pouca et al., 2019). Although the brains of cartilaginous fishes differ substantially from those of ray-finned fishes (Butler and Hodos, 2005; Striedter and Northcutt, 2020), they vary in the degree of elaboration. Interestingly, the Port Jackson sharks are heterodontids and among those with lesser development of the pallium (Northcutt, 1989; Striedter and Northcutt, 2020). Thus, one would predict even greater cognitive abilities in those taxa with larger and more elaborate forebrains.

A much more sophisticated ability, that of transitive inference, has been demonstrated in labrid (*Labridae*) fishes—a cichlid (Grosenick et al., 2007) and a cleaner wrasse (Hotta et al., 2020). A different species of wrasse, the sixbar wrasse, exhibits tool-use–like behavior (Pasko, 2010). In its aquarium, the wrasse used a rock as an anvil to successfully break up too-large food pellets and repeatedly selected the same rock for the job. Recently, cleaner wrasses have been reported to have self-recognition in a mirror, a cognitive ability considered to be of a very high order. The wrasses show reactions to mirrors, including social reactions, repeated idiosyncratic reactions, and frequent observation. When a colored mark is applied and the fish are subsequently in the presence of the mirror, the fish repeatedly scrape the body—apparently attempting to remove the mark—a behavior that does not occur in the absence of the mirror (Kohda et al., 2019). Although this finding needs to be replicated, it is certainly intriguing. In correlation with these elevated cognitive abilities, at least for transitive inference, labrid fishes have a greatly enlarged pallium in comparison to many other euteleosts (Yamamoto and Bloch, 2017).

Perhaps equally compelling are findings that some fish perceive illusory contours and exhibit other perceptual abilities (Agrillo et al., 2013). Illusory contour perception has been demonstrated in goldfish (Wyzisk and Neumeyer, 2007) and in redtail splitfins (Sovrano and Bisazza, 2009), which are both euteleosts but phylogenetically distant (Nelson, 1994), as also are groupers and parrotfish, who attack their own mirror image even when it is fragmented but do not attack control stimuli (Darmaillacq et al., 2011), thus exhibiting amodal completion—the ability to perceive a whole when parts of it are concealed—which also has been found in redtail splitfins (Sovrano and Bisazza, 2008).

10.3 Summary: Circuit Motifs across Vertebrates That May Support Cognition and Consciousness

These findings suggest conscious perceptual processes. The thalamopallial and palliopallial circuitry available to support them in these fishes is, however, markedly different from that in both birds and mammals (Figure 10). The questions are as follows: What features of circuitry, neurotransmitter patterns, and combinatorial interactions occur that result in these abilities across vertebrates, and how do each of these sets of features compare with the features of mammalian thalamocortical circuit motifs? As noted previously, the major features of the thalamopallial circuitry across vertebrates are shown in Figure 10, with references in this text and in its caption. In all jawed vertebrates, lampreys, and likely in hagfishes, dorsal thalamic nuclei relay sensory information to glutamatergic neurons in the telencephalic pallium. In fishes, some additional sensory information is relayed through a more caudal part of the diencephalon, the PGC, but this is dorsal thalamic–like and not a significant departure in terms of circuitry. GABAergic pallial neurons are present, but the details of their circuitry have not been worked out. Reciprocal palliothalamic glutamatergic projections are present to one of the collothalamic nuclei and to the PGC. The dorsal striatum—but not the pallium—projects to the ventral thalamus, which in turn projects to the PGC, but the ventral thalamic nuclei are known to lack GABA in at least some fish, so a TRN-like circuit appears to be absent.

Thalamopallial circuitry is much more similar across amniotes than across all vertebrates and even more similar between birds and mammals. Very similar ascending sensory projections are present across amniotes for the visual, auditory, and somatosensory systems, in addition to intralaminar projections, with mammals having relatively more of the latter. Direct loop pathways for the promotion of movement involving four components are shared by mammals and birds, while two three-loop pathways are present in reptiles. A TRN has been identified in a reptile but not definitively in birds. Mammals have far more palliothalamic glutamatergic projections than either birds or reptiles, which have some but comparatively few. The association, or higher-order, nuclei are substantially better developed in mammals, reaching their apogee in primates, with their capacity to extensively interconnect cortical areas and regulate cortical focus. GABAergic neurons are present in the pallium and regulate pallial glutamatergic neuronal activity across amniotes.

Thus, the key shared features across amniotes are the ascending systems, at least some intralaminar distributed projections, intrinsic pallial GABAergic neurons, at least some palliothalamic reciprocity, and likely, a TRN. Extensive intrapallial circuitry is a key feature in both birds and mammals, and it is highly likely that the functions of complex cognition and consciousness emerge from this complex interconnectivity. Finally, the sheer number of neurons in the pallium may well be an important contributing factor, as present in corvids, parrots, and primates, allowing for an exponential increase in the number of combinatorial interactions among them.

Acknowledgments

The author notes with sadness the recent death, in the summer of 2021, of Laura Bruce, who was a postdoctoral fellow in her laboratory at Georgetown University in the late 1970s and who, during the course of her long career, made major and insightful contributions to the spirited, sometimes heated, and always lively debates about forebrain evolution among amniotes. She will be greatly missed by all her colleagues, family, and friends.

The author wishes to thank Zoltán Molnár, Fernando García-Moreno, Sten Grillner, and Mac Shine for helpful discussions and exchanges of ideas in the preparation of this chapter. She thanks Michael Halassa and Arghya Mukherjee for their helpful editing and suggestions that substantially enhanced it. She also thanks the librarian at George Mason University, Carl Leak, for assistance with literature access. This work was supported by the author.

References

Aboitiz, F., Morales, D., & Montiel, J. (2003) The evolutionary origin of the mammalian neocortex: towards an integrated developmental and functional approach. Behav Brain Sci 26:535–586.

Agrillo, C., & Bisazza, A. (2017) Understanding the origin of number sense: a review of fish studies. Phil Trans Roy Soc B 373:20160511. doi:10.1098/rstb.2016.0511.

Agrillo, A., Petrazzini, M.E., & Dadda, M. (2013) Illusory patterns are fishy for fish, too. Front Neur Circ 7. doi:10.3389/fncir.2013.00137.

Atoji, Y., Sarkar, S., & Wild, J.M. (2016) Proposed homologue of the dorsomedial subdivision and V-shaped layer of the avian hippocampus to Ammon's horn and dentate gyrus, respectively. Hipp 26:1608–1617.

Baars, B.J. (2003) Working memory requires conscious processes, not vice versa. In: Osaka, N. (Ed.), Neural Basis of Consciousness. John Benjamins Publishing Co., Amsterdam, pp. 11–26.

Bachy, I., Vernier, P., & Rétaux, S. (2001) The LIM-homeodomain gene family in the developing Xenopus brain: conservation and divergences with the mouse related to the evolution of the forebrain. J Neurosci 21:7620–7629.

Baldwin, M.K.L., Balaram, P., and Kaas, J.H. (2017) The evolution and functions of nuclei of the visual pulvinar in primates. J Comp Neurol 525:3207–3226.

Belekhova, M.G., Kratskin, I.L., Repérant, J., Pierre, J., Vesselkin, N.P., Kenigfest, N.B., Tumanova, N.L., & Chkheidze, D.D. (1991) Localization of GABA-immunoreactive elements in the thalamus of the tortoise Emys orbicularis. Zh Evol Biokhim Fiziol 27:676–685.

Belgard, T.G., Montiel, J.F., Wang, W.Z., García-Moreno, F., Margulies, E.H., Ponting, C.P., & Molnár, Z. (2013) Adult pallial transcriptomes surprise in not reflecting predicted homologies across diverse chicken and mouse pallial sectors. Proc Nat Acad Sci 110:13150–13155.

Bickford, M.E. (2016) Thalamic circuit diversity: modulation of the driver/modulator framework. Front Neural Circ 9, Art. 86, doi:10.3389/fncir.2015.00086.

Bielle, F., Marcos-Mondejar, P., Keita, M., Mailhes, C., Verney, C., Nguyen Ba-Chavet, K., Tessier-Lavigne, M., Lopez-Bendito, G., & Garel, S. (2011) Slit2 activity in the migration of guidepost neurons shapes thalamic projections during development and evolution. Neuron 69:1085–1098.

Bingman, V.P., Rodríguez, F., & Salas, C. (2017) The hippocampus of nonmammalian vertebrates. In: Kaas, J.H., & Striedter, G. (Eds.), Evolution of Nervous Systems. Vol. 1: The Evolution of the Nervous Systems in

Nonmammalian Vertebrates, 2nd ed. Elsevier, Amsterdam, pp. 479–489.

Braford, M.R., Jr. (1995) Comparative aspects of forebrain organization in the ray-finned fishes: touchstone or not? Brain Behav Evol 46:259–274.

Briscoe, S.D., Albertin, C.B., Rowell, J.J., & Ragsdale, C.W. (2018) Neocortical association cell types in the forebrain of birds and alligators. Curr Biol 28:686–696.

Broglio, C., Rodriguez, F., Gomez, A., Arias, J.L., & Salas, C. (2010) Selective involvement of goldfish lateral pallium in spatial memory. Behav Brain Res 210:191–201.

Brown, M., Keynes, R., & Lumsden, A. (2001) The Developing Brain. Oxford University Press, Oxford, UK.

Bruce, L.L., & Butler, A.B. (1984) Telencephalic connections in lizards. I. Projections to cortex. J Comp Neurol 229:585–601.

Bruce, L.L., & Neary, T. (1995) The limbic system of tetrapods: a comparative analysis of cortical and amygdalar populations. Brain Behav Evol 46:224–234.

Bulchand, S., Grove, E.A., Porter, F.D., & Tole, S. (2001) LIM-homeodomain gene Lhx2 regulates the formation of the cortical hem. Mech Dev 100:165–175.

Butler, A.B. (1994a) The evolution of the dorsal pallium in the telencephalon of amniotes: cladistic analysis and a new hypothesis. Brain Res Rev 19:66–101.

Butler, A.B. (1994b) The evolution of the dorsal thalamus of jawed vertebrates, including mammals: cladistic analysis and a new hypothesis. Brain Res Rev 19:29–65.

Butler, A.B. (1995) The dorsal thalamus of jawed vertebrates: a comparative viewpoint. Brain Behav Evol 46:209–223.

Butler, A.B. (2007) The dual elaboration hypothesis of the evolution of the dorsal thalamus. In Krubitzer, L.A., & Kaas, J.H. (Eds.), Evolution of Nervous System in Mammals. Elsevier, Amsterdam, pp. 517–523.

Butler, A.B. (2008a) Evolution of brains, cognition, and consciousness. Brain Res Bull 75:442–449.

Butler, A.B. (2008b) Evolution of the dorsal thalamus: a morphological-functional review. Thalamus Relate Sys 4:35–58.

Butler, A. B. (2009) Evolution and the concept of homology. In: Binder, M.D., Hirokawa, N., & Windhorst, U. (Eds.), Encyclopedic Reference of Neuroscience. Springer, New York, pp. 1208–1212.

Butler, A.B., & Hodos, W. (2005) Comparative Vertebrate Neuroanatomy, 2nd ed. John Wiley & Sons, Hoboken, NJ.

Butler, A.B., Reiner, A., & Karten, H.J. (2011) Evolution of the amniote pallium and the origins of mammalian neocortex. Ann NY Acad Sci 1225:14–27.

Butler, A.B., & Saidel, W.M. (2000) Defining sameness: historical, biological, and generative homology. BioEssays 22:846–853.

Caballero-Bleda, M. (1988) Región alar del diencéfalo y mesencéfalo en el conejo : quimioarquitectonía de AChE y NADH-diaforasa como contribución a su neuroanatomíca comparada. PhD thesis, Universidad de Murcia.

Campbell, C.B.G., & Hodos, W. (1970) The concept of homology and the evolution of the nervous system. Brain Behav Evol 3:353–367.

Caretta, D., Sbriccoli, A., Santarelli, M., Pinto, F., Granato, A., & Minciacchi, D. (1996) Crossed thalamo-cortical and cortico-thalamic projections in adult mice. Neurosci Lett 204:69–72.

Chen, C.C., Winkler, C.M., Pfenning, A.R., & Jarvis, E.D. (2013) Molecular profiling of the developing avian telencephalon: regional timing and brain subdivision continuities. J Comp Neurol 521:3666–3701.

Clayton, N.S., Bussey, T.J., & Dickinson, A. (2003a) Can animals recall the past and plan for the future? Nat Rev Neurosci 4:685–691.

Clayton, N.S., Bussey, T.J., & Dickinson, A. (2003b) Prometheus to Proust: the case for behavioural criteria for "mental time travel." Trends Cogn Sci 7:436–437.

Clayton, N.S., & Dickinson, A. (1998) Episodic-like memory during cache recovery by scrub jays. Nature 395:272–274.

Clayton, N.S., & Dickinson, A. (1999) Scrub jays (*Aphelocoma coerulescens*) remember the relative time of caching as well as the location and content of their caches. J Comp Psychol 113:403–416.

Clayton, N.S., Griffiths, D.P., Emery, N.J., & Dickinson, A. (2001) Elements of episodic-like memory in animals. Phil Trans Roy Soc Lond B 356:1483–1491.

Colombe, J.B., Sylvester, J., Block, J., & Ulinski, P.S. (2004) Subpial and stellate cells: two populations of interneurons in turtle visual cortex. J Comp Neurol 471:333–351.

Cordery, P., & Molnár, Z. (1999) Embryonic development of connections in turtle pallium. J Comp Neurol 413:26–54.

Crespo, C., Porteros, A., Arévalo, R., Briñón, J.G., Aijón, J., & Alonso, J. R. (1999) Distribution of parvalbumin immunoreactivity in the brain of the tench (*Tinca tinca* L., 1758). J Comp Neurol 413:549–571.

Csillag, A., & Montagnese, C.M. (2005) Thalamotelencephalic organization in birds. Brain Res Bull 66:303–310.

Dadda, M., Agrillo, C., Bisazza, A., & Brown, C. (2015) Laterality enhances numerical skills in the guppy, *Poecilia reticulata*. Front Behav Neurosci 9:285. doi:10.3389/fnbeh.2015.00285.

Dadda, M., Piffer, L., Agrillo, C., & Bisazza, A. (2009). Spontaneous number representation in mosquitofish. Cogn 122:343–348.

Darmaillacq, A.S., Dickel, L., Rahmani, N., & Shashar, N. (2011) Do reef fish, *Variola louit* and *Scarus niger*, perform amodal competition? Evidence from a field study. J Comp Psychol 125:273–277.

Dávila, J.C., Andreu, M.J., Real, A., Puelles, L., & Guirado, S. (2002) Mesencephalic and diencephalic afferent connections to the thalamic nucleus rotundus in the lizard, *Psammodromus algirus*. Europ J Neurosci 16:267–282.

Dávila, J.C., Guirado, S., & Puelles, L. (2000) Expression of calcium-binding proteins in the diencephalon of the lizard *Psammodromus algirus*. J Comp Neurol 427:67–92.

de Beer, G. (1971) Homology, an unsolved problem. In: Head, J.J., & Lowenstein, O.E. (Eds.), Oxford Biology Readers, No. 11. Oxford University Press, London.

Delius, J.D., & Bennetto, K. (1972) Cutaneous sensory projections to the avian forebrain. Brain Res 37:205–222.

Derman, C.R., & Barbas, H. (1994) Contralateral thalamic projections predominantly reach transitional cortices in rhesus monkey. J Comp Neurol 344:508–531.

Desfilis, E., Abellán, A., Sentandreu, V., & Medina, L. (2017) Expression of regulatory genes in the embryonic brain of a lizard and implications for understanding pallial organization and evolution. J Comp Neurol 526:166–202.

Desfilis, E., Font, E., Belekhova, M., & Kenigfest, N. (2002) Afferent and efferent projections of the dorsal anterior thalamic nuclei in the lizard *Podarcis hispanica* (*Sauria, Lacertidae*). Brain Res Bull 57: 477–450.

Desfilis, E., Font, E., & Garcia-Verdugo, J.M. (1998) Trigeminal projections to the dorsal thalamus in a lacertid lizard, *Podarcis hispanica*. Brain Behav Evol 52:99–110.

Díaz, C., Yanes, C., Trujillo, C.M., & Puelles, L. (1994) The lacertidian reticular thalamic nucleus projects topographically upon the dorsal thalamus: experimental study in *Gallotia galloti*. J Comp Neurol **343**:193–208.

Diekamp, B., Gagliardo, A., & Güntürkün, O. (2002a) Nonspatial and subdivision-specific working memory deficits after selective lesions of the avian prefrontal cortex. J Neurosci **22**:9573–9580.

Diekamp, B., Kalt, T., & Güntürkün, O. (2002b) Working memory neurons in pigeons. J Neurosci **22**:1–5.

Dinopoulos, A. (1994) Reciprocal connections of the motor neocortical area with the contralateral thalamus in the hedgehog (*Erinaceus europaeus*) brain. Europ J Neurosci **6**:374–380.

Dirian, L., Galant, S., Coolen, M., Chen, W., Bedu, S., Houart, C., Bally-Cuif, L., & Foucher, I. (2014) Spatial regionalization and heterochrony in the formation of adult pallial neural stem cells. Dev Cell **30**:123–136.

Ditz, H.M., & Nieder, A. (2016) Sensory and working memory representations of small and large numerosities in the crow forebrain. J Neurosci **36**:12044–12052.

Doron, N.N., & LeDoux, J.E. (2000) Cells in the posterior thalamus project to both amygdala and temporal cortex: a quantitative retrograde double-labeling study in the rat. J Comp Neurol **425**:257–274.

Dugas-Ford, J., & Ragsdale, C.W. (2015) Levels of homology and the problem of neocortex. Annu Rev Neurosci **38**:351–368.

Dugas-Ford, J., Rowell, J.J., & Ragsdale, C.W. (2012) Cell-type homologies and the origins of neocortex. Proc Nat'l Acad Sci **109**:16974–16979.

Durán, E., Ocaña, F.M., Broglio, C., Rodríguez, F., & Salas, C. (2010) Lateral but not medial telencephalic pallium ablation impairs the use of goldfish spatial allocentric strategies in a "hole-board" task. Behav Brain Res **214**:480–487.

Ebbesson, S.O.E. (1980) The parcellation theory and its relation to interspecific variability in brain organization, evolutionary and ontogenetic development and neuronal plasticity. Cell Tiss Res **213**:179–212, doi:10.1007/BF00234781.

Ebbesson, S.O.E. (1984) An update of the parcellation theory. Behav Brain Sci **7**:350–366, doi:10.1017/S0140525X00018628.

Ebbesson, S.O.E. (2020) How the parcellation theory of comparative forebrain specialization emerged from the Division of Neuropsychiatry at the Walter Reed Army Institute of Research. J Hist Neurosci **30**:24–55, doi:10.1080/0964704X.2020.1763759.

Emery, N.J., & Clayton, N.S. (2016) An avian perspective on stimulating other minds Learn Behav **44**:203–204.

Endepols, H., Roden, K., Luksch, H., Dicke, U., & Walkowiak, W. (2004) Dorsal striatopallidal system in anurans. J Comp Neurol **468**:299–310.

Evans, S.E. (2000) Amniote evolution. In: Bock, G.R., & Cardew, G. (Eds.), Evolutionary Developmental Biology of the Cerebral Cortex (Novartis Foundation Symposium 228). John Wiley & Sons, Ltd., Chichester, pp. 109–113.

Fernández, M., Ahumada-Galleguillos, P., Marían, G., & Mpodozis, J. (2019) Intratelencephalic projections of the avian visual dorsal ventricular ridge: laminarly segregated, reciprocally and topographically organized. J Comp Neurol **413**:26–54.

Folgueira, M., Bayley, P., Navratilova, P., Becker, T.S., Wilson, S.W., & Clarke, J.D.W. (2012) Morphogenesis underlying the development of the everted teleost telencephalon. Neural Dev **7**:32.

García-Moreno, F., & Molnár, Z. (2020) Variations of telencephalic development that paved the way for neocortical evolution. Progr Neurobiol **194**:101865, doi:10.1016/j.pneurobio.2020.101865.

Gilbert, S.R. (1994) Developmental Biology, 4th ed. Sinauer Associates, Inc., Sunderland MA.

Gómez-Laplaza, L.M., & Gerlai, R. (2020) Food density and preferred quantity: discrimination of small and large numbers in angelfish (*Pterophyllum scalare*). Sci Rep **9**:15305. doi:10.1007/s10071-0C20-01355-6.

González, G., Puelles, L., & Medina, L. (2002). Organization of the mouse dorsal thalamus based on topology, calretinin immunostaining, and gene expression. Brain Res Bull **57**:439–442.

González, M.J., Yáñez, J., and Anadón, R. (1999) Afferent and efferent connections of the torus semicircularis in the sea lamprey: an experimental study. Brain Res **826**:83–94.

Griffiths, D., Dickinson, A., & Clayton, N. (1999) Episodic memory: what can animals remember about their past? Trends Cogn Sci **3**:74–80.

Grosenick, L., Clement, T.S., & Fernald, R.D. (2007) Fish can infer social rank by observation alone. Nature **445**:429–432.

Gruber, R., Schiesti, M., Boeckle, M., Frohnwieser, A., Miller, R., Gray, R.D., Clayton, N.S., & Taylor, A.H. (2019) New Caledonian crows use mental representations to solve metatool problems. Curr Biol **29**:686–692.

Guillén, M. (1991) Estructura del epitálamo y complejo superior del talámo dorsal en aves: studio embryológico. Posibles homologies con mamíferos. PhD thesis, Universidad de Murcia.

Güntürkün, O. (2020) The surprising power of the avian mind. Sci Am **322**:48–55.

Halassa, M.M., & Sherman, S.M. (2019) Thalamocortical circuit motifs: a general framework. Neuron **103**:762–770.

Hall, B.K. (1992) Evolutionary Developmental Biology. Chapman & Hall, London.

Hall, J.A., Foster, R.E., Ebner, F.F., & Hall, W.C. (1977) Visual cortex in a reptile, the turtle (*Pseudemys scripta* and *Chrysemys picta*). Brain Res **130**:197–216.

Harting, J.K., Hall, W.C., & Diamond, I.T. (1972) Evolution of the pulvinar. Brain Behav Evol **6**:424–452.

Harting, J.K., Updyke, B.V., & van Lieshout, D.P. (2001) Striatal projections from the cat visual thalamus. Europ J Neurosci **14**:893–896.

Heinrich, B. (1999) The Mind of a Raven. Harper Collins Publishers, New York.

Henderson, J., Hurly, T.A., Bateson, M., & Healy, S.D. (2006) Timing in free-living rufous hummingbirds, *Selasphorus rufus*. Curr Biol **16**:512–515.

Herculano-Houzel, S. (2020) Birds do have a brain cortex—and think. Sci **369**:1567–1568.

Herkenham, M. (1978) The connections of the nucleus reuniens thalami: evidence for a direct thalamo-hippocampal pathway in the rat. J Comp Neurol **177**:589–610.

Herrick, J.L., & Keifer, J. (1997) A hypothalamic projection to the turtle red nucleus: An anterograde and retrograde tracing study. Exp Brain Res **116**:556–560.

Hodos, W., & Campbell, C.B.G. (1969) Scala naturae: why there is no theory in comparative psychology. Psychol Rev **76**:337–350.

Hofmann, M.H., & Northcutt, R.G. (2012) Forebrain organization in elasmobranchs. Brain Behav Evol **80**:142–151.

Hollis, D.M., & Boyd, S.K. (2005) Distribution of GABA-like immunoreactive cell bodies in the brains of two amphibians, *Rana catesbeiana* and *Xenopus laevis*. Brain Behav Evol **65**:127–142.

Hoogland, P.V. (1977) Efferent connections of the striatum in *Tupinambis nigropunctatus*. J Morphol **152**:229–246.

Hoogland, P.V., & Vermeulen-Van der Zee (1989) Efferent connections of the dorsal cortex of the lizard *Gekko gecko* studied with *Phaseolus vulgaris*-leucoagglutinin. J Comp Neurol **285**:289–303.

Hotta, T., Ueno, K., Hataji, Y., Kuroshima, H., Fujita, K., & Kohda, M. (2020) Transitive inference in cleaner wrasses (*Labroides dimidiatus*). PLoSONE **15**(8): e0237817. doi:10.1371/journal.pone.0237817.

Hu, J., & Wang, S.-R. (2001) Firing patterns and morphological features of neurons in the pigeon nucleus rotundus. Brain Behav Evol **57**:343–348.

Husband, S., & Shimizu, T. (1999) Efferent projections of the ectostriatum in the pigeon (*Columba livia*). J Comp Neurol **406**:329–345.

Iwaniuk, A.N. (2017) The evolution of cognitive brains in non-mammals. In: Watanabe, S., Hofman, M.A., & Shimizu, T. (Eds.), Evolution of the Brain, Cognition, and Emotion in Vertebrates. Springer Japan KK, Tokyo, pp. 101–124.

Jarvis, E.D., Yu, J., Rivas, M.V., Horita, H., Feenders, G., Whitney, O., Jarvis, S.C., Jarvis, E.R., Kubikova, L., Puck, A.E.P., Siang-Bakshi, C., Martin, S., McElroy, M., Hara, E., Howard, J., Pfenning, A., Mouritsen, H., Chen, C.-C., & Wada, K. (2013) Global view of the functional molecular organization of the avian cerebrum: mirror images and functional columns. J Comp Neurol **521**:3614–3665.

Jiao, Y., Medina, L., Veenman, L.C., Toledo, C., Puelles, L., & Reiner, A. (2000) Identification of the anterior nucleus of the ansa lenticularis in birds as the homologue of the mammalian subthalamic nucleus. J Neurosci **20**:6998–7010.

Jones, E.G. (1985) The Thalamus. Plenum Press, New York.

Jones, E.G. (2007) The Thalamus, 2nd ed. Cambridge University Press, Cambridge, UK.

Kaas, J.H. (2017a) Evolution of the visual cortex in primates. In: Kaas, J.H., & Krubitzer, L. (Eds.), *Evolution of Nervous Systems*. Vol. *3: The Nervous Systems of Non-human Primates*, 2nd ed. Elsevier, Amsterdam, pp. 187–201.

Kaas, J.H. (2017b) The organization of neocortex in early mammals. In: Kaas, J.H., & Herculano-Houzel, S. (Eds.), Evolution of Nervous Systems. Vol. 2: The Nervous Systems of Early Mammals and Their Evolution, 2nd ed. Elsevier, Amsterdam, pp. 87–101.

Karten, H.J. (1968) The ascending auditory pathways in the pigeon (*Columba livia*): II. Telencephalic projections of the nucleus ovoidalis thalami. Brain Res **11**:134–153.

Karten, H.J. (1969) The organization of the avian telencephalon and some speculations on the phylogeny of the amniote telencephalon. Ann NY Acad Sci **167**:164–179.

Karten, H.J., Cox, K., & Mpodozis, J. (1997) Two distinct populations of tectal neurons have unique connections within the retinotectorotundal pathway of the pigeon (*Columba livia*). J Comp Neurol **387**: 449–465.

Karten, H.J., & Hodos, W. (1970) Telencephalic projections of the nucleus rotundus in the pigeon (*Columba livia*). J Comp Neurol **140**:35–52.

Karten, H.J., Hodos, W., Nauta, W.H.J., & Revzin, A. (1973) Neural connections of the "visual Wulst" of the avian telencephalon: experimental studies in the pigeon (*Columba livia*) and owl (*Speotyto cunicularia*). J Comp Neurol **150**:253–278.

Karten, H.J., Konishi, M., & Pettigrew, J.D. (1978) Somatosensory representation in the anterior Wulst of the owl *Speotyto cunicularis*. Soc Neurosci Abstr 4:554.

Keifer, J., & Lustig, D.G. (2000) Comparison of cortically and subcortically controlled motor systems. II. Distribution of anterogradely labeled terminal boutons on intracellularly filled rubrospinal neurons. J Comp Neurol **416**:101–111.

Kemp, T.S. (2005) The *Origin* and *Evolution* of *Mammals*. Oxford University Press, Oxford, UK.

Kenigfest, N., Belekhova, M., Repérant, J., Rio, J.-P., Ward, R., & Vesselkin, N. (2005) The turtle thalamic anterior entopeduncular nucleus shares connectional and neurochemical characteristics with the mammalian thalamic reticular nucleus. J Chem Neuroanat **30**:129–143.

Kenigfest, N., Repérant, J., Belekhova, M., Rio, J.-P., & Ward, R. (2007) Evolution of the visual tectogeniculate and pretectogeniculate pathways in the brain of amniote vertebrates. In: Kaas, J.H., & Bullock, T.H. (Eds.), Evolution of Nervous Systems: A Comprehensive Reference. Vol. 2, Nonmammalian Vertebrates. Elsevier, Amsterdam, pp. 459–467.

Kirsch, J.A., Güntürkün, O., & Rose, J. (2008) Insight without cortex: lessons from the avian brain. Consc Cogn **17**:475–483.

Kohda, M., Hotta, T., Takeyama, T., Awata, S., Tanaka, H., Asai, J., & Jordan, A.L. (2019) If a fish can pass the mark test, what are the implications for consciousness and self-awareness testing in animals? PLoS Biol **17**: e3000021. doi:10.1371/journal.pbio.3000021.

Krubitzer, L., & Seelke, A.M.H. (2012) Cortical evolution in mammals: the bane and beauty of phenotypic variability. Proc Nat Acad Sci USA **109**, Suppl. 1:10647–10654.

Krusche, P., Uller, C., & Dicke, U. (2010) Quantity discrimination in salamanders. J Exp Biol **213**:1822–1828.

Kudo, M., Glendenning, K.K., Frost, S.B., & Masterton, R.B. (1986) Origin of mammalian thalamocortical projections. I. Telencephalic projections of the medial geniculate body in the opossum (*Didelphis virginiana*). J Comp Neurol **245**:176–197.

Laberge, F., Mühlenbrock-Lenter, S., Dicke, U., & Roth, G. (2008) Thalamo-telencephalic pathways in the fire-bellied toad *Bombina orientalis*. J Comp Neurol **508**:806–823.

Lichtneckert, R., & Reichert, H. (2005) Insights into the urbilaterian brain: conserved genetic patterning mechanisms in insect and vertebrate brain development. Heredity **94**:465–477.

Liem, K.F., Bemis, W.E., Walker, W.F., Jr., & Grande L. (2001) Functional Anatomy of the Vertebrates: An Evolutionary Perspective. Harcourt College Publishers, Fort Worth.

Llinás, R., & Paré, D. (1991) Coherent oscillations in specific and nonspecific thalamocortical networks and their role in cognition. In Steriade, M., Jones, E.G., & McCormick, D.A. (Eds.), Thalamus. Vol. II: Experimental and Clinical Aspects. Elsevier, Amsterdam, pp. 501–516.

Llinás, R., Ribary, U., Contreras, D., & Pedroarena, C. (1998) The neuronal basis for consciousness. Phil Trans Roy Soc Lond **353**:1841–1849.

Llinás, R.R., & Steriade, M. (2006) Bursting of thalamic neurons and states of vigilance. J Neurophysiol **95**:3297–3308.

Llinás, R.R., Urbano, F.J., Leznik, E., Ramírez, R.R., & van Marle, H.J.F. (2005) Rhythmic and dysrhythmic thalamocortical dynamics: GABA systems and the edge effect. Trends Neurosci **28**:325–333.

Lohman, A.H.M., & Van Woerden-Verkley (1978) Ascending connections to the forebrain in the tegu lizard. J Comp Neurol **182**:555–594.

López, J.M., Morona, R., Moreno, N., & González, A. (2017) The organization of the central nervous system of lungfishes: an immunohistochemical approach. In: Kaas, J.H., & Striedter, G. (Eds.), Evolution of Nervous Systems. Vol. 1: The Evolution of the Nervous Systems in Nonmammalian

Vertebrates, 2nd ed. Elsevier, Amsterdam, pp. 121–139.

López-Bendito, G., Flames, N., Ma, L., Fouquet, C., Di Medlio A., Tessier-Lavigne, M., & Marín, O. (2007) Robo1 and Robo2 cooperate to control the guidance of major axonal tracts in the mammalian forebrain. J Neurosci **27**:3395–3407.

López-Bendito, G., & Molnár, Z. (2003) Thalamocortical development: how are we going to get there? Nat Rev Neurosci **4**:276–289.

Luksch, H., Cox, K., & Karten, H.J. (1998) Bottlebrush dendritic endings and large dendritic fields: motion-detecting neurons in the tectofugal pathway. J Comp Neurol **396**:399–414.

Lynn, A.M., Schneider, D.A., & Bruce, L. L. (2015) Development of the avian dorsal thalamus: patterns and gradients of neurogenesis. Brain Behav Evol **86**:94–109.

Macchi, G., Bentivoglio, M., Minciacchi, D., & Molinari, M. (1996) Trends in the anatomical organization and functional significance of the mammalian thalamus. Ital J Neurol Sci **17**:105–129.

Mancilla, J.G., & Ulinski, P.S. (2001) Role of GABA(A)-mediated inhibition in controlling the responses of regular spiking cells in turtle visual cortex. Vis Neurosci **18**:9–24.

Manrod, J.D., Hartdegen, R., & Burghardt, G.M. (2008) Rapid solving of a problem apparatus by juvenile black-throated monitor lizards (*Varanus albigularis albigularis*). Anim Cogn **11**:267–273.

Martínez-de-la-Torre, M. (1985) Estructura del mesencéfalo y diencéfalo en aves y reptiles: aportaciones a una síntesis en la búsqueda de homologías. PhD thesis, Universidad de Murcia.

Martínez-de-la-Torre, M., Pombol, M.A., & Puelles, L., (2011) Distal-less-like protein distribution in the larval lamprey forebrain. Neurosci **178**:270–284.

Martínez-García, F., Martínez-Marcos, A., & Lanuza, E. (2002) The pallial amygdala of amniote vertebrates: evolution of the concept, evolution of the structure. Brain Res Bull **57**:463–4

Martínez-García, F., Novejarque, A., & Lanuza, E. (2007) Evolution of the amygdala in vertebrates. In: Kaas, J.H., & Bullock, T.H. (Eds.), Evolution of Nervous Systems: A Comprehensive Reference. Vol. 2, Nonmammalian Vertebrates. Elsevier, Amsterdam, pp. 255–334.

Medina, L., & Abellán, A. (2009) Development and evolution of the pallium. Sem Cell Devel Biol **20**:698–711.

Medina, L., Abellán, A., Vicario, A., Castro-Robles, B., & Desfilis, E. (2017) The amygdala. In: Kaas, J.H., & Striedter, G. (Eds.), Evolution of Nervous Systems. Vol. 1: The Evolution of the Nervous Systems in Nonmammalian Vertebrates, 2nd ed. Elsevier, Amsterdam, pp. 427–478.

Medina, L., Veenman, C.L., & Reiner, A. (1997). Evidence for a possible avian dorsal thalamic region comparable to the mammalian ventral anterior, ventral lateral, and oral ventroposterolateral nuclei. J Comp Neurol **384**:86–108.

Médina, M., Repérant, J., Dufour, S., Ward, R., Le Belle, N., & Miceli, D. (1994) The distribution of GABA-immunoreactive neurons in the brain of the silver eel (*Anguilla anguilla* L.). Anat Embryol **189**:25–39.

Meléndez-Ferro, M., Pérez-Costas, E., Villar-Cheda, Abalo, X.M., Rodriguez-Muñoz, R., Rodicio, M.C., & Anadón, R. (2002) Ontogeny of γ-aminobutyric acid-immunoreactive neuronal populations in the forebrain and midbrain of the sea lamprey. J Comp Neurol **446**:360–376.

Molnár, Z., Garel, S., López-Bendito, G., Maness, P., & Price, D.J. (2012) Mechanisms controlling the guidance of thalamocortical axons through the embryonic forebrain. Europ J Neurosci **35**:1573–1585.

Montagnese, C.M., Mezey, S.E., & Csillag, A. (2003) Efferent connections of the dorsomedial thalamic nuclei of the domestic chick (*Gallus domesticus*). J Comp Neurol **459**:301–326.

Montiel, J.F., & Aboitiz, F. (2015) Pallial patterning and the origin of the isocortex. Front Neurosci **9**. doi: 10.3389/fnins.2015.00377.

Moreno, N., Bachy, I., Rétaux, S., & González, A. (2004) LIM-homeodomain genes as developmental and adult genetic markers of *Xenopus* forebrain functional subdivisions. J Comp Neurol **472**:52–72.

Moreno, N., Morona, R., López, J.M., and González, A. (2017) The diencephalon and hypothalamus of nonmammalian vertebrates: evolutionary and developmental traits. In: Kaas, J.H., & Striedter, G. (Eds.), Evolution of Nervous Systems. Vol. 1: The Evolution of the Nervous Systems in Nonmammalian Vertebrates, 2nd ed. Elsevier, Amsterdam, pp. 409–426.

Morrow, J., Mosher, C., & Gothard, K. (2019) Multisensory neurons in the primate amygdala. J Neurosci **39**:3663–3675.

Mpodozis, J., Cox, K., Shimizu, T., Bischoff, H.J., Woodson, W., & Karten, H.J. (1996) GABAergic inputs to the nucleus rotundus (pulvinar inferior) of the pigeon (*Columba livia*). J Comp Neurol **374**:204–222.

Nakagawa, Y., & O'Leary, D.D.M. (2001) Combinatorial expression patterns of LIM-homeodomain and other regulatory genes parcellate developing thalamus. J Neurosci **21**.2711–2725.

Nelson, J.S. (1994) Fishes of the World, 3rd ed., John Wiley & Sons, New York.

Nieder, A., Wagener, L., & Rinnert, P. (2020) A neural correlate of sensory consciousness in a corvid bird. Sci **369**:1626–1629.

*Nieuwenhuys, R., ten Donkelaar, H.J., & Nicholson, C. (1998) The Central Nervous System of Vertebrates, Vol. **1**. Springer-Verlag, Berlin.

*Nieuwenhuys, R., ten Donkelaar, H.J., & Nicholson, C. (1998) The Central Nervous System of Vertebrates. Springer-Verlag, Berlin.

Nomura, T., & Hirata, T. (2017) The neocortical homologues in nonmammalian amniotes: bridging the hierarchical concepts of homology through comparative neurogenesis. In: Kaas, J.H., & Herculano-Houzel, S. (Eds.), Evolution of Nervous Systems. Vol. 2: The Nervous Systems of Early Mammals and Their Evolution, 2nd ed. Elsevier, Amsterdam, pp. 195–204.

Northcutt, R.G. (1977) Retinofugal projections in the lepidosirenid lungfishes. J Comp Neurol **174**:553–574.

Northcutt, R.G. (1980) Retinal projections in the Australian lungfish. Brain Res **185**:85–90.

Northcutt, R.G. (1984) Evolution of the vertebrate central nervous system: patterns and processes. Amer Zool **24**:701–716.

Northcutt, R.G. (1985) Central nervous system phylogeny: evaluation of hypotheses. Fortsch Zool **30**:497–505.

Northcutt, R.G. (1989) Brain variation and phylogenetic trends in elasmobranch fishes. J Exp Zool Suppl **2**:83–100.

Northcutt, R.G. (2003) The use and abuse of developmental data. Behav Brain Sci **26**:565–566.

Northcutt, R.G. (2006) Connections of the lateral and medial divisions of the goldfish telencephalic pallium. J Comp Neurol **494**:903–943.

Northcutt, R.G. (2009) Telencephalic organization in the spotted African lungfish, *Protopterus dolloi*: a new cytological model. Brain Behav Evol **73**:59–80.

Northcutt, R.G. (2013) Variations in reptilian brains and cognition. Brain Behav Evol **82**:45–54.

Northcutt, R.G., & Wicht, H. (1997) Afferent and efferent connections of the lateral and medial pallia of the silver lamprey. Brain Behav Evol **49**:1–19.

Novejarque, A., Lanuza, E., & Martínez-Garcia, F. (2004) Amygdalostriatal projections in reptiles: a tract-tracing study in the lizard *Podarcis hispanica*. J Comp Neurol **479**:287–308.

Okano, H., & Temple, S. (2009) Cell types to order: temporal specification of CNS stem cells. Curr Opin Neurobiol **19**:112–119.

Olkowicz, S., Kocourek, M., Lučan, R.K., Porteš, M., Fitch, W.T., Herculano-Houzel, S., & Němec, P. (2016) Birds have primate-like numbers of neurons in the forebrain. Proc Nat Acad Sci USA **113**:7255–7260.

Panchen, A.L. (1999) Homology—history of a concept. In: Bock G.R., & Cardew, G. (Eds.), Homology: Novartis Foundation Symposium 222. John Wiley & Sons, Chichester.

Pasko, L., (2010) Tool-like behavior in the sixbar wrasse, *Thalassoma hardwicke* (Bennett, 1830). Zool Biol **29**:767–773.

Patton, B.W., & Braithwaite, V.A. (2015) Changing tides: ecological and historical perspectives on fish cognition. WIREs Cogn Sci **6**:159–176. doi:10.1002/wcs.1337.

Paz-y-Miño, G., Bond, A.B., Kamil, A.C., & Balda, R.P. (2004) Pinyon jays use transitive inference to predict social dominance. Nature **430**:778–781.

Peake, T.M., Terry, A.M.R., McGregor, P.K., & Dabelsteen, T. (2001) Male great tits eavesdrop on simulated male-to-male vocal interactions. Proc Roy Soc Lond B **268**:1183–1187.

Peake, T.M., Terry, A.M.R., McGregor, P.K., & Dabelsteen, T. (2002) Do great tits assess rivals by combining direct experience with information gathered by eavesdropping? Proc Roy Acad Lond B **269**:1925–1929.

Pepperberg, I.M. (1999) The Alex Studies: Cognitive and Communicative Abilities of Grey Parrots. Harvard University Press, Cambridge, MA.

Pepperberg, I.M. (2006) Grey parrot (*Psittacus erithacus*) numerical abilities: addition and further experiments on a zero-like concept. J Comp Psychol **120**:1–11.

Pepperberg, I.M. (2013) Abstract concepts: data from a grey parrot. Behav Proc **93**:82–90.

Pepperberg, I.M. (2020) The comparative psychology of intelligence: some thirty years later. Front Psychol **11**. doi:10.3389/fpsyg.2020.00973.

Pepperberg, I.M., & Nakayama, K. (2016) Robust representation of shape in a grey parrot (*Psittacus erithacus*). Cogn **153**:146–160.

Polenova, O.A., & Vesselkin, N.P. (1993) Olfactory and nonolfactory projections in the river lamprey (*Lampetra fluviatilis*) telencephalon. J Hirnforsch **34**:261–279.

Pombal, M.A., & Megías, M. (2017) The nervous system of jawless vertebrates. In: Kaas, J.H., & Striedter, G. (Eds.), Evolution of Nervous Systems. Vol. 1: *The Evolution of the Nervous Systems in Nonmammalian Vertebrates*, 2nd ed. Elsevier, Amsterdam, pp. 37–57.

Pombal, M.A., Megías, M., Bardet, S.M., & Puelles, L. (2009) New and old thoughts on the segmental organization of the forebrain in lampreys. Brain Behav Evol **74**:7–19.

Portavella, M., Torres, B., & Salas, C. (2004) Avoidance response in goldfish: emotional and temporal involvement of medial and lateral telencephalic pallium. J Neurosci **24**:2335–2342.

Powers, A.S., & Reiner, A. (1980) A stereotaxic atlas of the forebrain and midbrain of the Eastern painted turtle (*Chrysemys picta picta*). J Hirnforsch **21**:125–159.

Preuss, T.M., & Goldman-Rakic, P.S. (1987) Crossed corticothalamic and thalamocortical connections of macaque prefrontal cortex. J Comp Neurol **257**:269–281.

Pritz, M.B. (1995) The thalamus of reptiles and mammals: similarities and differences. Brain Behav Evol **46**:197–208.

Pritz, M.B. (2015) Crocodilian forebrain: evolution and development. *Integrative Comp Biol* **55**:949–961.

Pritz, M.B., & Stritzel, M.E. (1988) Thalamic nuclei that project to reptilian telencephalon lack GABA and GAD immunoreactive neurons and puncta. Brain Res **457**:154–159.

Pritz, M.B., & Stritzel, M.E. (1990) A different type of vertebrate thalamic organization. Brain Res **525**:330–334.

Pritz, M.B., & Stritzel, M.E. (1994) Glutamic acid decarboxylase immunoreactivity in some dorsal thalamic nuclei in *Crocodilia*. Neurosci Lett **165**:109–112.

Puelles, L., (2011) Pallio-pallial tangential migrations and growth signaling: new scenario for cortical evolution? Brain Behav Evol **78**:108–127.

Puelles, L., Amat, J.A., & Martínez-de-la-Torre, M. (1987) Segment-related, mosaic neurogenetic pattern in the forebrain and mesencephalon of early chick embryos: I. Topography of AChE-positive neuroblasts up to stage HH18. J Comp Neurol **266**:247–268.

Puelles, L., Ayad, A., Alonso, A., Sandoval, J.E., Martínez-de-la-Torre, M., Medina, L., & Ferran, J.L. (2016) Selective early expression of the orphan nuclear receptor *Nr4a2* identifies the claustrum homolog in the avian mesopallium: impact on sauropsidian/mammalian pallium comparisons. J Comp Neurol **524**:665–703.

Puelles, L., Kuwana, E., Puelles, E., Bulfone, A., Shimamura, K., Keleher, J., Smiga, S., & Rubenstein, J.L. (2000) Pallial and subpallial derivatives of the embryonic chick and mouse telencephalon, traced by the expression of genes *Dlx-2*, *Emx-1*, *Nkx-2.1*, *Pax-6*, and *TBR-1*. J Comp Neurol **424**:409–438.

Puelles, L., & Medina, L. (2002) Field homology as a way to reconcile genetic and developmental variability with adult homology. Brain Res Bull **57**:243–255.

Puelles, L., Medina, L., Borello, U., Legaz, I., Teissier, A., Pierani, A., & Rubenstein, J.L.R. (2015) Radial derivatives of the mouse ventral pallium traced with *Dbx1-LacZ* reporters. J Chem Neuroanat **75**:2–19.

Puelles, L., Milán, F.J., & Martínez-de-la-Torre, M. (1996) A segmental map of architectonic subdivisions in the diencephalon of the frog *Rana perezi*: acetylcholinesterase-histochemical observations. Brain Behav Evol **47**:279–310.

Puelles, L., Sandoval, J.E., Ayad, A., del Corral, R., Alonso, A., Ferran, J.L., & Martínez-de-la-Torre (2017) The pallium in reptiles and birds in the light of the updated tetrapartite pallium model. In: Kaas, J.H., & Striedter, G. (Eds.), Evolution of Nervous Systems. Vol. 1: The Evolution of the Nervous Systems in Nonmammalian Vertebrates, 2nd ed.Elsevier, Amsterdam, pp. 519–555.

Raff, R.A. (1996) The Shape of Life: Genes, Development, and the Evolution of Animal Form. University of Chicago Press, Chicago.

Raghanti, M.A., Munger, E.L., Wicinski, B., Butti, C., & Hof, P.R. (2017) Comparative structure of the cerebral cortex in large mammals. In: Kaas, J.H., & Herculano-Houzel, S. (Eds.), Evolution of Nervous Systems. Vol. 2: The Nervous Systems of Early Mammals and Their Evolution, 2nd ed. Elsevier, Amsterdam, pp. 267–289.

Redies, C., Ast, M., Nakagawa, S., Takeichi, M., Martínez-de-la-Torre, M., & Puelles, L. (2000) Morphogenetic fate of diencephalic prosomeres and their subdivisions revealed by mapping cadherin expression. J Comp Neurol **421**:481–514.

Reiner, A. (1993) Neurotransmitter organization and connections of turtle cortex: implications for the evolution of mammalian isocortex. Comp Biochem Physiol A **104**:735–748.

Reiner, A. (2002) Functional circuitry of the avian basal ganglia: implications for basal ganglia organization in stem amniotes. Brain Res Bull **57**:513–528.

Reiner, A. (2012) You are who you talk with a commentary on Dugas-Ford et al. PNAS, 2012. Brain Behav Evol **81**:146–149 doi:10.1159/000348281.

Reiner, A., Medina, L., & Veenman, L.C. (1998) Structural and functional evolution of the basal ganglia in vertebrates. Brain Res Rev **28**:235–285.

Reiner, A., Perkel, D.J., Bruce, L.L., Butler, A. B., Csillag, A., Kuenzel, W., Medina, L., Paxinos, G., Shimizu, T., Striedter, G., Wild, M., Ball, G.F., Durand, S., Güntürkün, O., Lee, D.W., Mello, C.V., Powers, A., White, S.A., Hough, G., Kubikova, L., Smulders, T.V., Wada, K., Dugas-Ford, J., Husband, S., Yamamoto, K., Yu, J., Siang, C., & Jarvis, E.D. (2004) Avian Brain Nomenclature Forum. Revised nomenclature for avian telencephalon and some related brainstem nuclei. J Comp Neurol **473**:377–414.

Reiner, A., Yamamoto, K., & Karten, H.J. (2005) Organization and evolution of the avian forebrain. Anat Rec **287A**:1080–1102.

Reisz, R.R. (1997) The origin and early evolutionary history of amniotes. Trends Ecol Evol **12**:218–222.

Rikhye, R.V., Wimmer, R.D., & Halassa, M. M. (2018) Toward an integrative theory of thalamic function. Annu Rev Neurosci **41**:163–183. doi:10.1146/annurev-neuro-080317-062144.

Rink, E., & Wullimann, M.F. (2004) Connections of the ventral telencephalon (subpallium) in the zebrafish (*Danio rerio*). Brain Res **1011**:206–220.

Rinnert, P., Kirschhock, M.E., & Nieder, A. (2019) Neuronal correlates of spatial working memory in the endbrain of crows. Curr Biol **29**:2616–2624.

Rio, J.-P., Repérant, J., Ward, R., Miceli, D., & Medina, M. (1992) Evidence of GABA-immunopositive neurons in the dorsal part of the lateral geniculate nucleus of reptiles: morphological correlates with interneurons. Neurosci **47**:395–407.

Rodríguez, F., López, J.C., Vargas, J.P., Broglio, C., Gómez, Y., & Salas, C. (2002) Spatial memory and hippocampal pallium through vertebrate evolution: insights from reptiles and teleost fish. Brain Res Bull **57**:499–503.

Rodríguez-Moldes, I., Santos-Durán, G.N., Pose-Méndez, S., Quintana-Urzainqui, I., & Candal, E. (2017) The brains of cartilaginous fishes. In: Kaas, J.H., & Striedter, G. (Eds.), Evolution of Nervous Systems. Vol. 1: *The Evolution of the Nervous Systems in Nonmammalian Vertebrates*, 2nd ed. Elsevier, Amsterdam, pp. 77–97.

Rose, J.E. (1942) The ontogenetic development of the rabbit's diencephalon. J Comp Neurol **77**:61–129.

Roth, G., Grunwald, W., & Dicke, U. (2003) Morphology, axonal projection pattern, and responses to optic nerve stimulation of thalamic neurons in the fire-bellied toad *Bombina orientalis*. J Comp Neurol **461**:91–110.

Roth, G., Laberge, F., Mühlenbrock-Lenter, S., & Grunwald, W. (2007) Organization of the pallium in the fire-bellied toad *Bombina orientalis*. I: morphology and axonal projection pattern of neurons revealed by intracellular biocytin labeling. J Comp Neurol **501**:443–464.

Roth, T.C. II, Krochmal, A.R., & LaDage, L. D. (2019) Reptilian cognition: a more complex picture via integration of neurological mechanisms, behavioral constraints, and evolutionary context. BioEssays **41**. doi:10.1002/bies.201900033.

Rowe, T.B. (2017) The emergence of mammals. In: Kaas, J.H., & Herculano-Houzel, S. (Eds.), Evolution of Nervous Systems. Vol. 2: The Nervous Systems of Early Mammals and Their Evolution, 2nd ed. Elsevier, Amsterdam, pp. 1–52.

Sherman, S.M., & Guillery, R.W. (2013) Functional Connections of Cortical Areas: A New View *from* the Thalamus. MIT Press, Cambridge, MA.

Shi, W., Xianyu, A., Han, Z., Tang, X., Li, Z., Zhong, H., Mao, T., Huang, K., & Shi, S.-H. (2017) Ontogenetic establishment of order-specific nuclear organization in the mammalian thalamus. Nat Neurosci **20**:516–528.

Simpson, G.G. (1961) Principles of Animal Taxonomy. Columbia University Press, New York.

Smith, H. (1967) Biological similarities and homologies. Syst Biol **16**:101–102.

Smith-Fernandez, A., Pieau, C., Repérant, J., Boncinelli, E., & Wassef, M. (1998) Expression of the *Emx-1* and *Dlx-1* homeobox genes define three molecularly distinct domains in the telencephalon of mouse, chick, turtle and frog embryos: implications for the evolution of telencephalic subdivisions in amniotes. Devel **2111**:2099–2111.

Sovrano, V.A., & Bisazza, A. (2008) Recognition of partly occluded objects by fish. Anim Cogn **11**:161–166.

Sovrano, V.A., & Bisazza, A. (2009) Perception of subjective contours in fish. Percep **38**:579–590.

Stacho, M., Herold, C., Rook, N., Wagner, H., Axer, M., Amunts, K., & Gunturkun, O. (2020) A cortex-like canonical circuit in the avian forebrain. Sci **369**:eabc5534.

Stancher, G., Rugani, R., Regolin, L., & Vallortigara, G. (2015) Numerical discrimination by frogs (*Bombina orientalis*). Anim Cogn **18**:219–229.

Stein, B.E., & Meredith, M.A. (1993) The Merging of the Senses. MIT Press, Cambridge, MA.

Steriade, M., Jones, E.G., & McCormick, D. A. (1997) Thalamus. Vol. 1: Organization and Function. Elsevier, Amsterdam.

Steriade, M., & Paré, D. (2007) Gating in Cerebral Networks. Cambridge University Press, Cambridge, UK.

Striedter, G. (1991) Auditory, electrosensory, and mechanosensory lateral line pathways through the forebrain in channel catfishes. J Comp Neurol **312**:311–331.

Striedter, G.F. (1999) Homology in the nervous system: of characters, embryology and levels of analysis. In: Bock, G.R., & Cardew, G. (Eds.), Homology (Novartis Foundation Symposium 222). John Wiley & Sons, Chichester, UK, pp. 158–172.

Striedter, G.F., & Northcutt, R.G. (2020) Brains *through* Time: A Natural History of Vertebrates. Oxford University Press, Oxford, UK.

Ströhmann, B., Schwarz, D.W.F., & Puil, E. (1994) Mode of firing and rectifying properties of nucleus ovoidalis neurons in the avian auditory thalamus. J Neurophysiol **71**:1351–1360.

Suárez, J., Andreu, M.J., Heredia, R., Dávila, J.C., & Guirado, S. (2002) A putative striato-dorsal thalamic pathway in lizards. Brain Res Bull **57**:533–535.

Suárez, J., Dávila, J.C., Real, M.Á., & Guirado, S. (2005) Distribution of GABA, calbindin and nitric oxide synthase in the developing chick entopallium. Brain Res Bull **66**:441–444.

Suárez, J., Dávila, J.C., Real, M.Á., Guirado, S., & Medina, L. (2006) Calcium-binding proteins, neuronal nitric oxide synthase, and GABA help to distinguish different pallial areas in the developing and adult chicken. I. Hippocampal formation and hyperpallium. J Comp Neurol **497**:751–771.

Sugahara, F., Murakami, Y., Adachi, N., & Kuratani, S. (2013) Evolution of the regionalization and patterning of the vertebrate telencephalon: what can we learn from cyclostomes? Curr Opin Genet Devel **23**:475–483.

Sugahara, F., Murakami, Y., Pascual-Anaya, J., & Kuratani, S. (2017) Reconstructing the ancestral vertebrate brain. Develop Growth Differ **59**:163–174.

Sugahara, F., Pascual-Anaya, J., Oisi, Y., Kuraku, S., Aota, S., Adachi, N., Takagi, W., Hirai, T., Sato, H., Murakami, Y., & Kuratani, S. (2016) Evidence from cyclostomes for complex regionalization of the ancestral vertebrate brain. Nature **531**: 97–100.

Sur, M., & Rubenstein, J.L.R. (2005) Patterning and plasticity of the cerebral cortex. Sci **310**:805–810.

Suryanarayana, S.M., Pérez-Fernández, J., Robertson, B., & Grillner, S. (2020) The evolutionary origin of visual and somatosensory representation in the vertebrate pallium. Nat Ecol Evol **4**:639–651.

Suryanarayana, S.M., Robertson, B., Wallén, P., & Grillner, S. (2017) The lamprey pallium provides a blueprint of the mammalian layered cortex. Curr Biol **27**:3264–3277.

Suzuki, I.K., & Hirata, T. (2012) Evolutionary conservation of neocortical neurogenetic program in the mammals and birds. Bioarchitec **2**: 124–129.

Suzuki, I.K., & Hirata, T. (2013) Neocortical neurogenesis is not really "neo": a new evolutionary model derived from a comparative study of chick pallial development. Dev Growth Differ **55**:173–187.

Suzuki, I.K., Kawasaki, T., Gojobori, T., & Hirata, T. (2012) The temporal sequence of the mammalian neocortical neurogenic program drives mediolateral pattern in the chick pallium. Dev Cell **22**:863–870.

Swanson, L.W., & Petrovich, G.D. (1998) What is the amygdala? Trends Neurosci **21**:323–331.

Szele, F.G., Chin, H.K., Rowlson, M.A., & Cepko, C.L. (2002) Sox-9 and cDachsund-2 expression in the developing chick telencephalon. Mech Dev **112**:179–182.

Tosa, Y., Hirao, A., Matsubara, I., Kawaguchi, M., Fukui, M., Kuratani, S., & Murakami, Y. (2015) Development of the thalamo-dorsal ventricular ridge tract in the Chinese soft-shelled turtle, *Pelodiscus sinensis*. Develop Growth Differ **57**:40–57.

Tosches, M.A., Yamawaki, T.M., Naumann, R.K., Jacobi, A.A., Tushev, G., & Laurent, G. (2018) Evolution of pallium, hippocampus, and cortical cell types revealed by single-cell transcriptomes in reptiles. Sci **360**:881–888.

Ulinski, P.S. (1983) *Dorsal Ventricular Ridge: A Treatise on Forebrain Organization in Reptiles and Birds*. John Wiley, New York.

van der Meij, J., Martinez-Gonzalez, D., Beckers, G.J.L., & Rattenborg, N.C. (2019) Intra-"cortical" activity during avian non-REM and REM sleep: variant and invariant traits between birds and mammals. Sleep J **42**:1–13.

Veenman, C.L., Medina, L., & Reiner, A. (1997) Avian homologues of mammalian intralaminar, mediodorsal and midline thalamic nuclei: immunohistochemical and hodological evidence. Brain Behav Evol **49**:78–98.

Vernier, P. (2017) The brains of teleost fishes. In: Kaas, J.H., & Striedter, G. (Eds.), Evolution of Nervous Systems. Vol. 1: *The Evolution of the Nervous Systems in Nonmammalian Vertebrates*, 2nd ed. Elsevier, Amsterdam, pp. 59–75.

Vila Pouca, C., Gervais, C., Reed, J., Michard, J., & Brown, C. (2019) Quantity discrimination in Port Jackson sharks incubated under elevated temperatures. Behav Ecol Sociobiol **73**:93. doi:10.1007/s00265-019-2706-8.

von Bayern, A.M.P., Danel, S., Auersperg, A.M.I., Mioduszewska, B., & Kacelnik, A. (2018) Compound tool construction by New Caledonian crows. Sci Reports **8**:15676. doi:10.1038/s41598-018-33458-z.

von Fersen, L., Wynne, C.D.L., & Delius, J.D. (1990) Deductive reasoning in pigeons. Naturwissench **77**:548–549.

Wagner, G.P. (1999) A research programme for testing the biological homology concept. In Bock, G.R., & Cardew, G. (Eds.), Homology (Novartis Foundation Symposium 222). John Wiley & Sons, Chichester, pp. 125–140.

Wagner, G.P. (2014) *Homology, Genes, and Evolutionary Innovation*. Princeton University Press, Princeton, NJ.

Wagner, G.P., & Misof, B.Y. (1992) Evolutionary modification of regenerative capability in vertebrates: a comparative study on teleost pectoral fin regeneration. J Exp Zool **261**:62–78.

Watanabe, M. (1987) Synaptic organization of the nucleus dorsolateralis anterior thalami in the Japanese quail (*Coturnix coturnis japonica*). Brain Res **401**:92–112.

Watanabe, S., Sakamoto, J., & Wakita, M. (1995) Pigeons' discrimination of paintings by Monet and Picasso. J Exp Anal Behav **63**:165–174.

Westhoff, G., Roth, G., & Straka, H. (2004) Topographic representation of vestibular and somatosensory signals in the anuran thalamus. Neurosci **124**:669–683.

Wild, J.M. (1987) The avian somatosensory system: connections of regions of body representation in the forebrain of the pigeon. Brain Res **412**:205–223.

Wild, J.M. (1997) The avian somatosensory system: the pathway from wing to Wulst in a passerine (*Chloris chloris*). Brain Res **759**:122–134.

Wild, J.M., Arends, J.J., & Zeigler, H.P. (1985) Telencephalic connections of the trigeminal system in the pigeon (*Columba livia*): a trigeminal sensorimotor circuit. J Comp Neurol **234**:441–464.

Wild, J.M., Karten, H.J., & Frost, B.J. (1993) Connections of the auditory forebrain in the pigeon (*Columba livia*). J Comp Neurol **337**:32–62.

Wild, J.M., & Williams, M.N. (2000) Rostral Wulst in passerine birds. I. Origin, course, and termination of an avian pyramidal tract. J Comp Neurol **416**:429–450.

Wyzisk, K., & Neumeyer, C. (2007) Perception of illusory surfaces and contours in goldfish. Vis Neurosci **24**:291–298.

Yamamoto, K., & Bloch, S. (2017) Overview of brain evolution: lobe-finned fish vs. ray-finned fish. In: Watanabe, S., Hofman, M.A., & Shimizu, T. (Eds.), Evolution of the Brain, Cognition, and Emotion in Vertebrates. Springer Japan KK, Tokyo, pp. 3–33.

Yamamoto, K., & Reiner, A. (2007) Is the avian dorsal ventricular ridge (DVR) homologous to the mammalian cerebral cortex or to the amygdala? Evaluating hypotheses by assessing homologous projection pathways to the telencephalon. In Watanabe, S., & Hofman, M.A. (Eds.), Integration of Comparative Neuroanatomy and Cognition. Keio University Press, Tokyo, pp. 75–96.

Zeier, H., & Karten, H.J. (1971) The archistriatum of the pigeon: organization of afferent and efferent connections. Brain Res **31**:313–326.

Zhu, D., Lustig, K.H., Bifulco, K., & Keifer, J. (2005) Thalamocortical connections in the pond turtle Pseudemys scripta elegans. Brain Behav Evol **65**:278–292.

Chapter 6

Lamprey Thalamus and Beyond

Shreyas M. Suryanarayana, Brita Robertson, and Sten Grillner

Introduction

Cyclostomes (jawless fishes) are the earliest group of vertebrates with two extant species—hagfish and lamprey. Phylogenetically, cyclostomes have an important position, with molecular and fossil evidence indicating a monophyly (Heimberg et al., 2010; Miyashita et al., 2019; Sugahara et al., 2017, 2016). It is therefore interesting to examine the organisation of the thalamus and compare it with that of other classes of vertebrates. However, any comparative inquiry into the organisation of the thalamus inevitably brings in other parts of the forebrain, in particular, the question of the pallium, which, along with the striatum, is the major target of the thalamus. We will begin with an overview of telencephalic organisation in cyclostomes.

The lamprey forebrain has recently been shown to be organised with many similarities to that of mammals. The pallium consists of a three-layered cortex with a microcircuit, including pyramidal tract (PT), intratelencephalic (IT), and thalamorecipient-equivalent neuronal subtypes, and GABAergic interneurons (Suryanarayana et al., 2017). There is also a sensory-motor topography in the dorsolateral pallium with a retinotopic visual area, a somatosensory area with distinct representations of the head and the body, and a motor area that can elicit well-delineated movements of the eyes, mouth, and body and locomotion. Moreover, the PT neurons project to motor centres in the midbrain, brainstem, and spinal cord, as in mammals (Ocana et al., 2015; Suryanarayana et al., 2020). The ventral part of the pallium processes olfactory input, with a short latency similar to the mammalian piriform cortex, and relays it via secondary projections to the dorsolateral pallium (Suryanarayana et al., 2021). Furthermore, the basal ganglia are also conserved in considerable detail (Grillner and Robertson, 2016). The organisation of the thalamus is, therefore, a pertinent question.

As in other vertebrates, the lamprey thalamus is located in the diencephalon in prosomere p2 (Pombal and Puelles, 1999) and divided into a periventricular zone of densely packed neurons and, lateral to this, an area of loosely arranged cells (Nieuwenhuys et al., 1998; Northcutt and Wicht, 1997; Pombal and Puelles, 1999; Suryanarayana et al., 2020; Villar-Cervino et al., 2011) (Figure 1a–d). The thalamopallial neurons are glutamatergic and excitatory (Suryanarayana et al., 2017) and located in both the periventricular and lateral parts of the thalamus and are interspersed with GABAergic neurons (Figure 1e–h). The thalamus does not appear to form distinct nuclei. It is now apparent that the thalamus has a relay function for both visual and somatosensory information forwarded to the pallium/cortex and also receives projections from the optic tectum/superior colliculus, and there is also a thalamostriatal projection from the periventricular area (Capantini et al., 2017; Heier, 1948; Nieuwenhuys and Nicholson, 1998; Ocana et al., 2015; Stephenson-Jones et al., 2011; Suryanarayana et al., 2020, 2017). Another characteristic feature of vertebrate thalamic neurons that target the pallium/cortex is that they express calretinin, which also applies to the thalamopallial neurons in the lamprey (Figure 1i–j). This is essentially the same building blocks as in other vertebrates (Butler, 1995; see also Chapter 5 in this volume), but thalamus is much smaller than in mammals.

In the evolutionary lineage before vertebrates, the tunicates and the amphioxus have few traces of a forebrain and no trace of a thalamus (Benito-Gutiérrez et al., 2018). The evolutionary stages between tunicates and lamprey (cyclostomes) are largely unknown, although there are fossil records of early cyclostomes (Feinberg and Mallatt, 2017; Miyashita et al., 2019). Cyclostomes diverged from the evolutionary line 560 million years ago (Kumar and Hedges, 1998), and this suggests that what is common between the lamprey and mammals, in terms of the detailed organisation of the forebrain, had evolved very early in vertebrate evolution. In the next section, we will review the organisation of the lamprey thalamus and initially make a comparison with mammals and other classes of vertebrates (see also Chapter 5 in this volume).

Somatosensory Transmission from the Spinal Cord and Trigeminal Area to the Thalamus and Cortex/Pallium

A major aspect of the thalamic pathways is that somatosensory information from the dorsal column nuclei to the thalamus is relayed to the cortex. The lamprey dorsal column conveys sensory information from touch and pressure receptors in the skin, and their axons terminate in the dorsal column nucleus (DCN) located at the transition between the spinal cord and the lower brainstem (Dubuc et al., 1993a, 1993b), wherein they synapse onto the dendrites of DCN neurons projecting to the thalamus (Suryanarayana et al., 2020). The axons of the DCN, in turn, cross at the lower-brainstem level and continue as a medial lemniscal bundle to terminate in the thalamus (Suryanarayana et al., 2020)(Figure 2a–e). These DCN axons synapse onto the dendrites of thalamopallial neurons in the lateral regions of the thalamus (Figure 2f).

Evolution

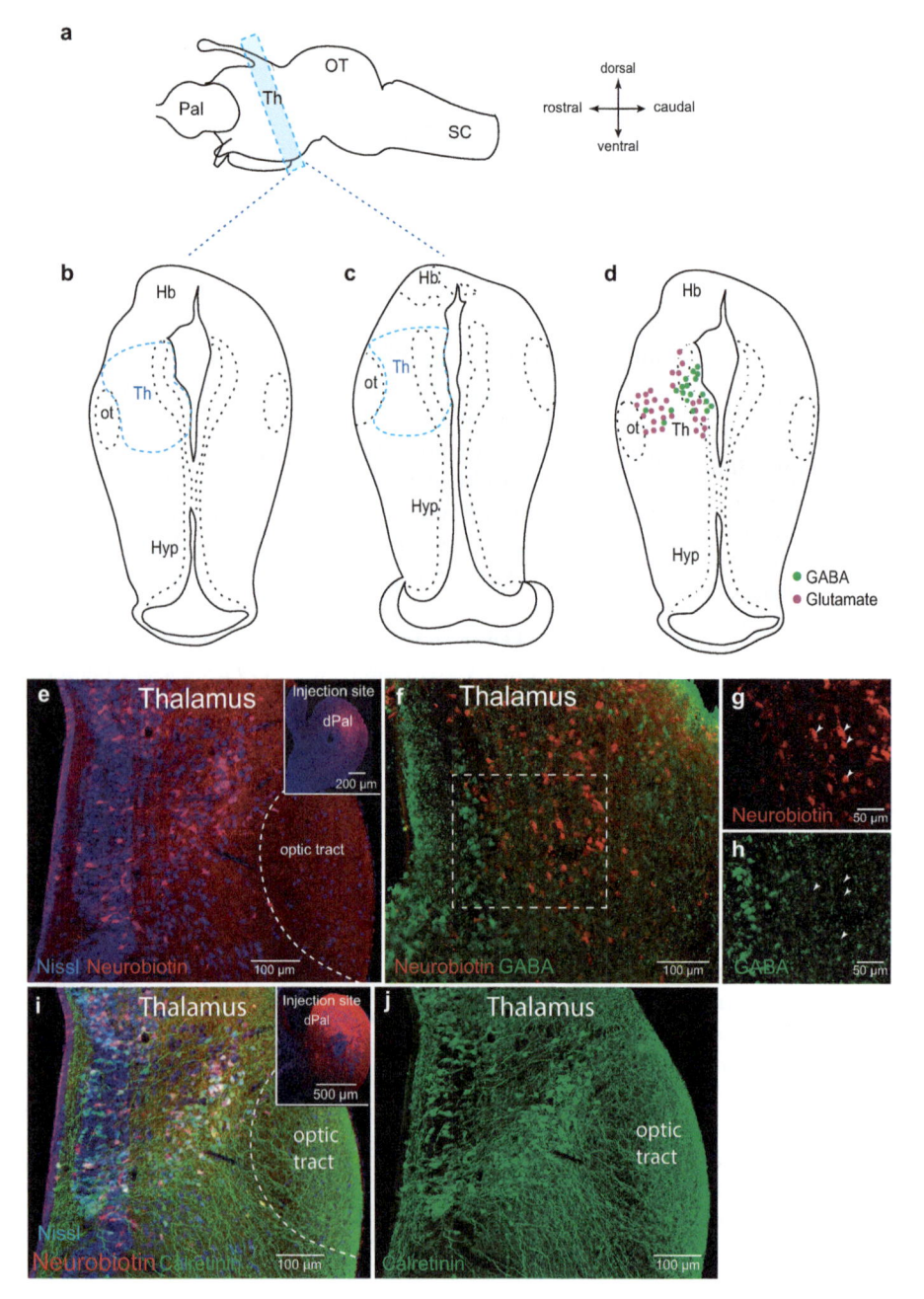

Figure 1 The lamprey thalamus.

(a) Schematic drawing of a sagittal view of the lamprey brain with the blue rectangle indicating the location of the thalamus. **(b and c)** Transverse sections showing the location of the thalamus. **(d)** Schematic of a transverse section of the thalamus indicating the location of GABAergic and glutamatergic cells. **(e)** Retrogradely labelled cells (*magenta*) in the thalamus after injection of Neurobiotin (*inset*) in the dorsal pallium (dPal). Nissl stain in blue. **(f–h)** Thalamic cells that target dPal do not express GABA (*arrowheads*). **(i)** Thalamic cells that target dPal express calretinin. **(j)** Calretinin-immunopositive cells in the thalamus. *Hb*, habenula; *Hyp*, hypothalamus; *OT*, optic tectum; *ot*, optic tract; *Pal*, pallium; *SC*, spinal cord; *STN*, subthalamic nucleus; *Th*, thalamus.

The medial lemniscal pathway relaying somatosensory information from the DCN and spinal cord to the thalamus and further to the cortex is thus present in the lamprey (Figure 2g). The DCN projections are largely to the contralateral thalamus, although a sparse projection exists to the ipsilateral side. The thalamic projections, however, are in their entirety to the ipsilateral pallium (Suryanarayana et al., 2020).

The other known somatosensory pathway is the input from the head region mediated via the trigeminal nerve and the trigeminal sensory nucleus (TSN) to the thalamus (Figure 3a). The trigeminal afferents terminate on neurons in the TSN that target the contralateral thalamus (Figure 3a–c). There is thus a corresponding pathway for trigeminal afferents to the TSN and contralateral thalamus (Figure 3d), as for the dorsal column afferents.

As indicated by the anatomical connectivity, electrical stimulations of the dorsal column and the trigeminal sensory nerve elicit robust field potential responses in the pallium (Figure 3e and f). The somatosensory information is represented in a discrete area in the dorsolateral pallium with distinct representations of the dorsal column (body) and trigeminal inputs (head), constituting a basic somatotopy, within the somatosensory area (Figure 3g)(Suryanarayana et al., 2020). This somatosensory area is located in the dorsolateral part of the lamprey dorsal pallium (Suryanarayana et al., 2020).

In mammals, the somatosensory thalamus consists of the ventroposterior inferior, ventroposterior, and ventroposterior superior nuclei. The ventroposterior nucleus represents a major relay of somatosensory information to

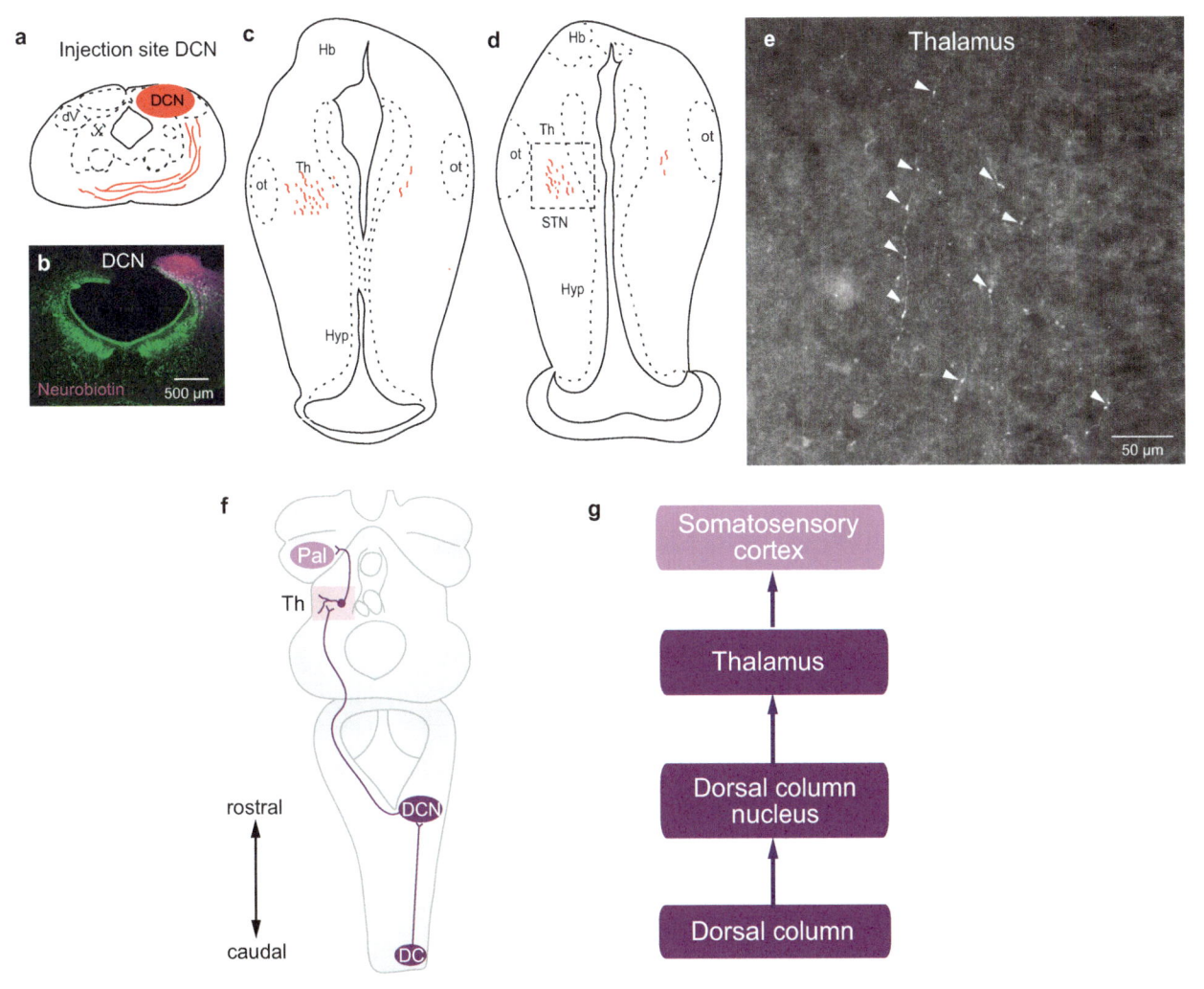

Figure 2 The medial lemniscal pathway in the lamprey.

(**a and b**) Schematic drawing and a transverse section showing the injection site of the tracer Neurobiotin in the contralateral DCN. (**c and d**) Schematic drawings of transverse sections of the thalamus indicating in red the termination area of afferent fibres from the DCN. (**e**) Photomicrograph of the thalamus showing afferent fibres (*arrows*) from the DCN. (**f**) Schematics of the lamprey brain showing the somatosensory pathway from the dorsal column to the DCN that then transmits information via the medial lemniscal pathway to thalamus and further to the somatosensory area in the dorsal pallium. (**g**) Schematic diagram showing the somatosensory pathway from the dorsal column to the pallium.

the primary somatosensory cortex and has been identified in all examined mammals (Kaas, 2004). This has been divided broadly into two subnuclei, and the cutaneous input from the contralateral body is relayed via the dorsal column systems to the ventroposterior lateral subnucleus. The larger ventroposterior medial nucleus represents cutaneous information from the different branches of the trigeminal nerve, which is relayed via the trigeminal brainstem complex. The topography of cutaneous input from different parts of the body is maintained through the thalamus to be represented as such in the primary somatosensory cortex (Kaas, 2004; Kaas et al., 1979). Other than the primary somatosensory cortex, the secondary somatosensory areas and some parietal areas also receive inputs from the somatosensory thalamic nuclei. The ventroposterior nucleus also projects to the thalamic reticular nucleus, which projects back and supplies GABAergic input. In primates, the ventroposterior inferior nucleus receives direct spinothalamic projections, but this has not been identified in all mammals (Krubitzer and Kaas, 1992). In non-mammalian amniotes (reptiles and birds), there are also equivalent somatosensory lemniscal pathways. In birds, lemniscal input reaches a thalamic nucleus called the nucleus dorsalis intermedius ventralis anterior (DIVA) that in turn relays it to a distinct area in the Wulst, which is a dorsal pallial derivative (Karten, 2015; Medina and Reiner, 2000; Puelles, 2017; Wild, 1997). Although much less is known about somatosensory representation in the dorsal cortex of reptiles, there is some evidence of a similar pathway wherein somatosensory information is relayed via the ventral areas of the thalamus to a specific region in the rostral parts of the dorsal cortex (Dugas-Ford and Ragsdale, 2015; Reiner, 1993).

In conclusion, as in other vertebrates, the lamprey somatosensory inputs are mediated via the trigeminal sensory nucleus and the dorsal column nucleus, respectively, to separate neuronal populations within the dorsal thalamus. They in turn project to separate adjacent parts of the dorsal pallium to provide a somatotopic representation.

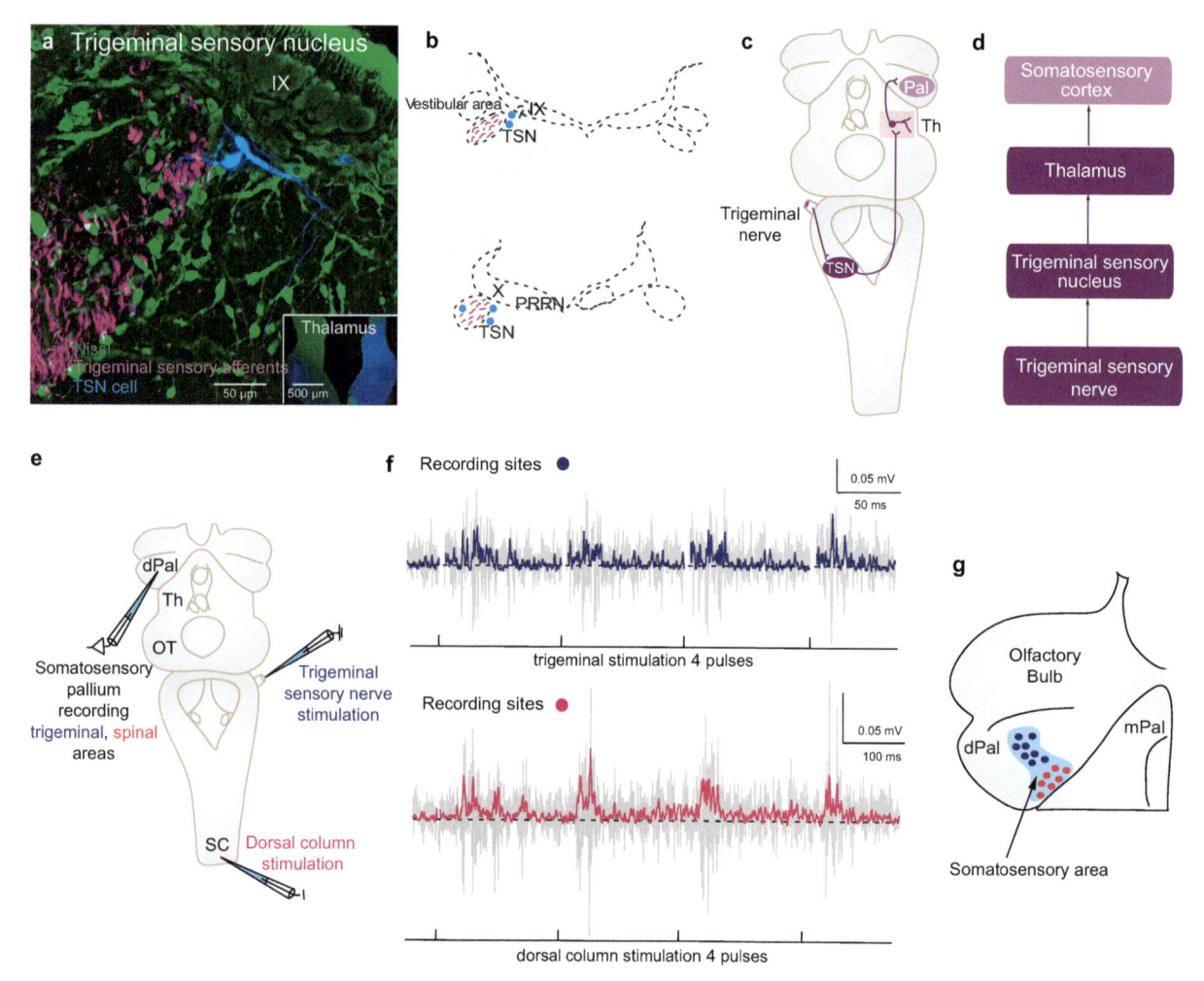

Figure 3 Sensory trigeminal input to the thalamus.
(a) Photomicrograph showing retrogradely labelled neurons in the trigeminal sensory nucleus (*blue*) following injection of tracer into the thalamus (*inset*). Trigeminal sensory afferents are labelled by dextran application to the sensory nerve (*magenta*). (b) Transverse schematics showing the location of retrogradely labelled neurons projecting to the contralateral thalamus (*blue dots*) in the trigeminal sensory nucleus, as well as the descending root of the trigeminal nerve (*magenta*). (c) Schematics of the lamprey brain showing the trigeminal sensory pathway from the trigeminal sensory nerve to the trigeminal sensory area in the dorsal pallium. (d) Box diagram showing the trigeminal sensory pathway from the trigeminal sensory nerve to the somatosensory cortex. (e) Schematic showing the in vitro preparation and the recording and stimulation points used. (f) Responses recorded in the dorsal pallium following extracellular repetitive stimulation (four pulses) of the trigeminal sensory nerve (*blue trace*) and the dorsal column (*pink trace*). (g) Dorsal pallial areas responding to trigeminal and dorsal column stimulation are located adjacent to each other (*blue and pink dots, respectively*), forming the somatosensory area (*pale blue*). IX, glossopharyngeal motor nucleus; X, vagus motor nucleus; Pal, pallium; PRRN, posterior rhombencephalon reticular nucleus; Th, thalamus; TSN, trigeminal sensory nucleus.

Retinotopic Representation in the Thalamus and Pallium/Cortex

The fact that afferents from the lamprey retina enter the thalamus through the optic tract and send projections to the lateral thalamus was suggested early on by Heier (1948)(Figure 4a). In addition, thalamocortical cells receive retinal input onto their dendrites, which extend into the optic tract, where they form synapses with retinal afferents (Figure 4b and c). There is also a retinotopic organisation in the optic tract (Figure 4d), with retinal afferents targeting the rostral and caudal optic tectum represented in distinct parts of the optic tract (Jones et al., 2009). A thalamic neuron is thus only activated by stimulation in one location in the optic tract (*green trace*), with almost no effect in the adjacent location (*red trace*), when the neuron is held near its resting potential (Figure 4e and f). However, when the neuron is more depolarised and (Figure 4g) spontaneously actively spiking, the stimulation instead leads to inhibition from both locations. This implies that the stimulation leads to both excitation and inhibition in the green location, whereas the red trace from the inefficient location in the optic tract (*red*) leads to inhibition. This suggests the presence of lateral inhibition within the thalamus from the local GABAergic neurons. The effective retinal afferent stimulation leads to monosynaptic excitation and then a short latency by inhibition (Figure 4h and i).

The visuo-thalamopallial neurons have a pronounced afterhyperpolarisation following an action potential, and they fire with little adaptation during continuous activation through direct current injection and display postinhibitory rebound (Figure 4j–m). These neurons are glutamatergic and located both in the periventricular and lateral areas. The short-latency inhibition observed after optic tract stimulation is due to the local GABAergic neurons also present within the thalamus (see Figure 1d–h). A removal of thalamic

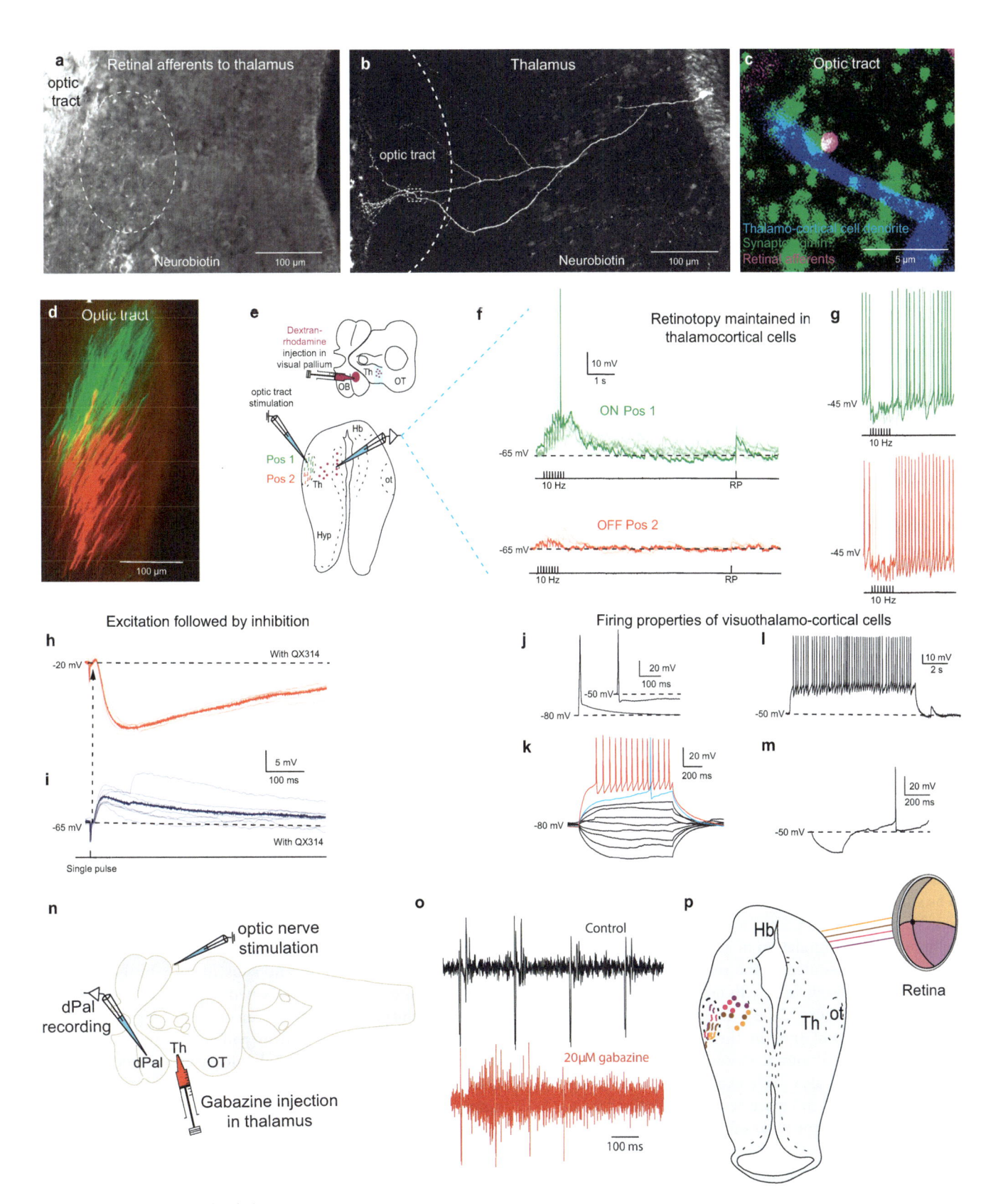

Figure 4 Visual input to the thalamus.

(a) Retinal afferents in the lamprey thalamus after injection of Neurobiotin in the retina. (b) Morphology of the thalamopallial cell intracellularly filled with Neurobiotin. Note that the dendrites extend into the optic tract. (c) High-magnification image of the dashed square in panel b, showing optic tract axon (*magenta*) synapses onto a dendrite (*blue*), as indicated by synaptotagmin (*green*). (d) Retinotopic organisation in the optic tract following injections of dextran-rhodamine and dextran-fluorescein isothiocyanate (FITC) into the caudal and rostral optic tectum, respectively. (e) Schematics showing injection of dextran-rhodamine to retrogradely prelabel cells in the thalamus for recordings (*upper panel*) and site of stimulation and recording in the thalamus (*lower panel*). (f) Repetitive stimulation in one position of the optic tract elicits excitatory postsynaptic potentials (EPSPs)/spiking (ON pos 1) in a thalamopallial neuron while another position provides very small EPSPs (OFF pos 2). (g) Holding the cell at a more depolarised membrane potential elicits spiking, which is silenced by stimulation of both optic tract positions. (h and i) The onsets of single-pulse EPSPs and inhibitory postsynaptic potentials (IPSPs) (*arrow*) show that excitation precedes inhibition. (j) Firing properties of thalamopallial neurons. Spikes were elicited in response to a brief (5-ms) suprathreshold current pulse, showing the afterhyperpolarisation. (k) Membrane potential responses to 1-s hyperpolarising and depolarising current pulses (step: 10 pA) showing threshold (*blue trace*) and suprathreshold response (*red trace*). (l) A long suprathreshold (10-s) pulse elicits non-adapting regular spiking behaviour. (m) A hyperpolarising pulse elicits postinhibitory rebound spiking. (n) Schematic of the lamprey brain showing the recording, stimulation, and gabazine-injection sites. (o) Local gabazine injection in the thalamus resulted in large responses (*red trace*) compared to control after optic nerve stimulation. (p) Schematic of the thalamus showing distinct thalamocortical cells receiving inputs from distinct retinal quadrants.

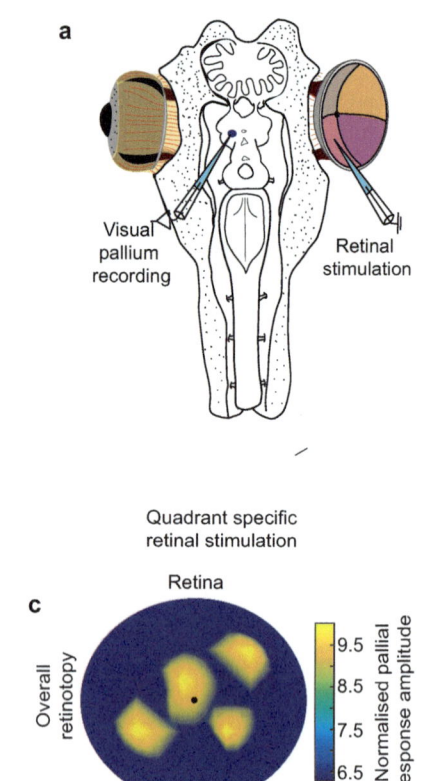

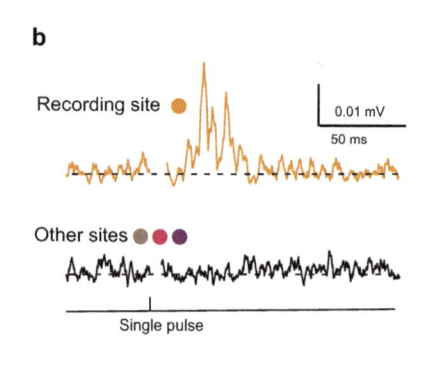

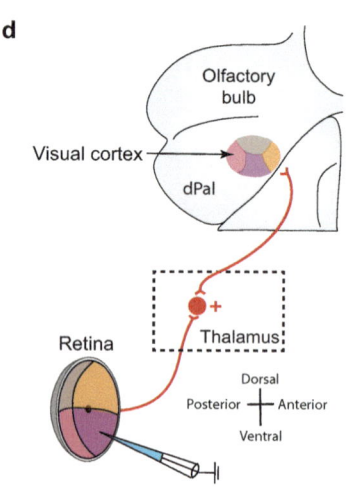

Figure 5 A visual region in the dorsal pallium responds to retinal stimulation with retinotopy.

(a) Schematic showing the in vitro eye–brain preparation used to stimulate the retina while recording in the dorsal pallium. (b) For each recording site, only stimulation of a specific location in the retina evoked responses (*colour coded*), whereas stimulation of other retinal areas did not (*black trace*). (c) Heatmap of the retina showing normalised amplitudes of activity evoked in the visual pallium in response to stimulation in multiple retinal locations for each of the recorded areas in visual pallium (*colour coded*). (d) Dorsal view of the pallium showing the visual area and the recording sites (*colour coded*).

GABA$_A$-mediated synaptic transmission with gabazine results in a very prominent activation of the pallium in comparison with the short-latency bursts occurring during control conditions (Figure 4n and o).

The retinotopic specificity seen in the thalamus (Figure 4p) is relayed to and maintained in the visual pallium. By using an eye–brain preparation (Figure 5a), different parts of the retina could be stimulated, which resulted in an activation of neurons in a specific area located medial to the somatosensory area in the pallium/cortex. Stimulation of each of the different quadrants of the retina resulted in the selective activation of one specific part of the visual field, with no effects produced in the other quadrants (Figure 5a–d). In other words, there is a retinotopic representation in the pallium/cortex, due in turn to a hardwired retinotopic representation of the thalamic relay neurons. This is also made explicit by the heatmap and summarising drawings in Figure 5c and d. With regard to the retinal input, six different types of retinal ganglion cells with selective projection patterns to the tectum and pretectum have been described, presumably forwarding different types of specific information (Jones et al., 2009). It is, however, not known how they are represented in the thalamus.

Interactions between the Tectum and Thalamus

In addition to the retinothalamic pathways, there are also projections to the thalamus from the roof of the midbrain, particularly the optic tectum (superior colliculus) and pretectum. These projections relay processed information from the tectum to the cortex (Butler, 1994, 2008; Butler and Hodos, 2005). The tectal output neurons projecting to reticulospinal neurons in the lamprey are involved in the control of the eye and in orienting or evasive movements, and they also send collaterals to the thalamus (Capantini et al., 2017)(Figure 6a–d). In the same way, neurons in the pretectum, which send axonal branches to reticulospinal neurons, also send collaterals to the thalamus (Capantini et al., 2017). The type of information forwarded to the thalamus and subsequently to the cortex is most likely motor commands issued from the tectum that are fed back to the pallium/cortex as an efference copy, also called a *corollary discharge*, to inform pallial structures about the commands issued. The tectothalamic pathway is mediated via thalamic nuclei distinct from the retinothalamic pathway in amniotes (see Chapter 5 in this volume). Whether there are separate thalamopallial relay neurons for the tectothalamic and retinothalamic pathways in the lamprey is not yet known, although separate projections have been identified in other vertebrate groups (see later discussion).

Conversely, there are also thalamotectal projections. Some of the thalamopallial neurons send collaterals to the optic tectum, with two distinct subpopulations targeting the rostral and caudal tectum, respectively (Figure 6e–j). It is noteworthy that thalamocortical neurons in the rodent lateral geniculate complex also send axonal branches to the superior colliculus (Comoli et al., 2012).

Visual Pathway in Other Vertebrates

In mammals, there are also two visual systems (Schneider, 1969). The first is the visual pathway that relays retinal information via the dorsal lateral geniculate nucleus of the thalamus to the primary visual cortex. Neurons in the visual cortex form a general retinotopic map with clustering of neurons to a preferred orientation observed in carnivores and primates (Drager, 1975). The dorsal lateral geniculate nucleus in carnivores and primates is also expanded and laminated, and there is an almost a one-to-one topographic specificity from the retinal ganglion cells onto cells in the dorsal lateral geniculate (Cleland et al., 1971; Sincich et al., 2009).

The other visual pathway relays processed information from the superior colliculus (tectum) to the lateral posterior nucleus of the thalamus, which in turn relays it to the extrastriate visual cortex (Schneider, 1969). Both these visual systems also exist in birds and non-avian reptiles, wherein the visual pathway relays retinal information via the lateral geniculate nucleus to the posterior parts of the Wulst and to the dorsal cortex, respectively. With regard to retinotopic topography in turtles, the visual dorsal cortex has been reported not to be retinotopically organised because the receptive fields of neurons in this area cover the entire contralateral visual field (Fournier et al., 2018). The tectothalamic pathway in birds and non-avian reptiles is relayed via the nucleus rotundus in the thalamus to terminate in pallial visual areas in the dorsoventricular ridge (DVR).

Thalamus and the Basal Ganglia

The basal ganglia in the lamprey are organised in a similar way to that of mammals, with an input from the pallium/cortex and with the same two types of projection neurons in the striatum (D1 and D2 spiny projection neurons) and a dopamine innervation from the substantia nigra pars compacta (SNc) (Grillner and Robertson, 2016; Perez-Fernandez et al., 2017, 2014; Stephenson-Jones et al., 2012, 2011). As in other vertebrates, there is also a thalamostriatal projection, which originates from the periventricular areas of the thalamus (Figure 7a and b). The input to the thalamostriatal neurons has not been defined in the lamprey, and whether the input to the thalamus from the optic tectum and pretectum targets the thalamostriatal neurons in the lamprey as in other vertebrates is not known. In rodents, the thalamostriatal parafascicular and central lateral nuclei receive input from the superior colliculus, the pedunculopontine, and the basal ganglia output nuclei (Grillner et al. 2020). In birds and non-avian

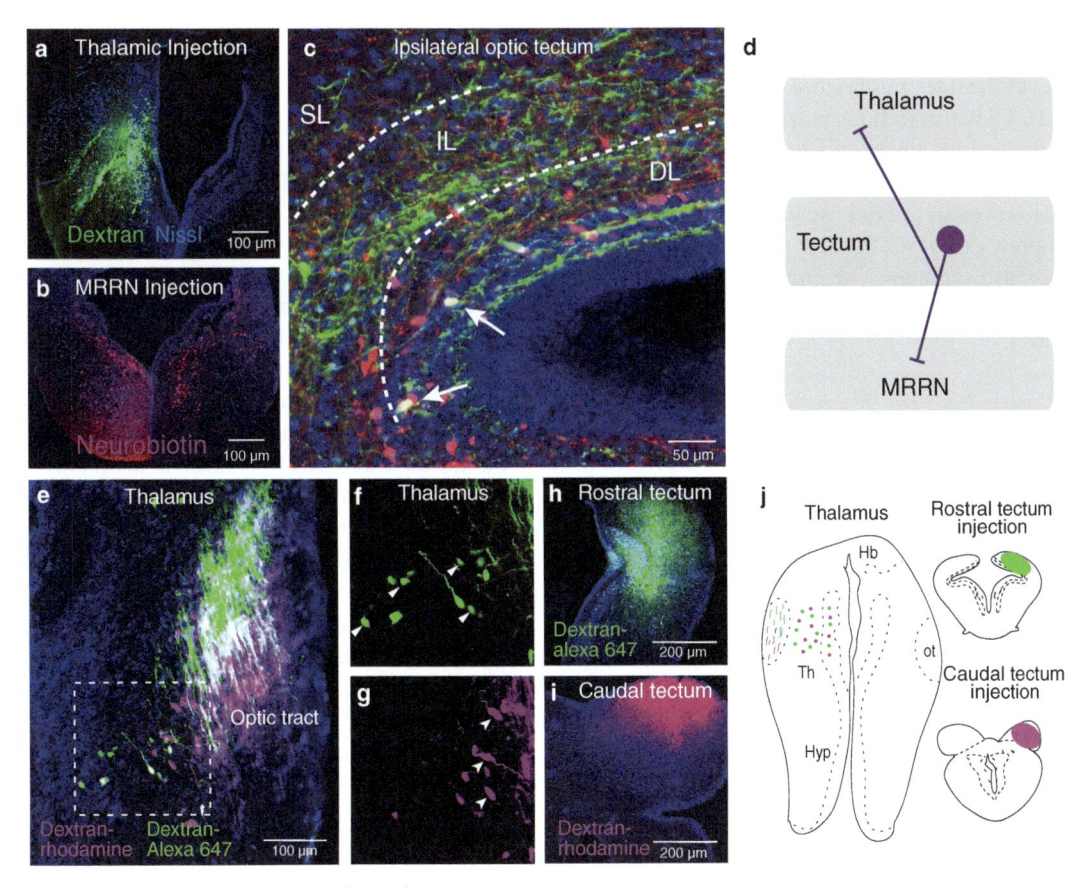

Figure 6 Tectal interactions with the thalamus.

(a) Dextran injection in the thalamus. (b) Neurobiotin injection in the middle rhombencephalic reticular nucleus (MRRN). (c) Retrogradely labelled cells in the deep motor layer (DL) of the optic tectum. Arrows point to cells that target the thalamus and send a collateral to the MRRN. (d) Box diagram showing the tectal deep motor layer projecting to both the thalamus and MRRN (e) Retrogradely labelled cells in the thalamus that target the tectum. Note that cells that project to the rostral tectum (f) are a separate subpopulation from those that target the caudal tectum (g). (h) Injection site in the rostral tectum following injection of dextran-Alexa 647. (i) Injection site in the caudal tectum following injection of dextran-rhodamine. (j) Schematic showing the location of thalamic cells that target the rostral (*green*) and caudal (*magenta*) optic tectum. *IL*, intermediate layer; *pv*, periventricular layer; *SL*, superficial layer.

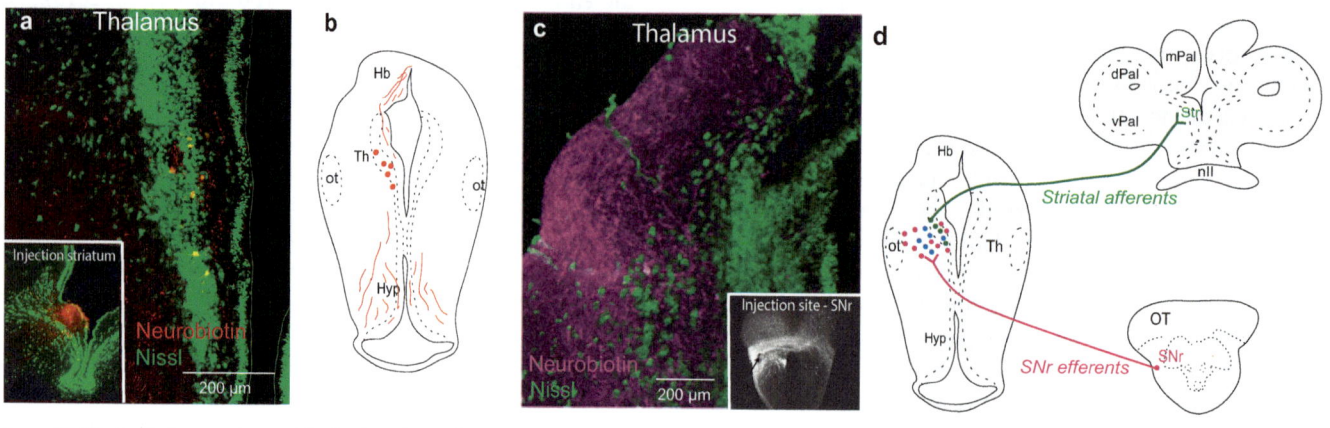

Figure 7 Thalamic interactions with the basal ganglia.
(a) Retrogradely labelled cells (*red*) in the periventricular thalamic area following injection in the striatum. Nissl stain in green. Injection site in striatum (*inset, red*). (b) Schematic drawing of a transverse section of the thalamus showing the location of thalamic cells that target the striatum. (c) Fibres and presumed terminals (*magenta*) in the thalamus after injection in the SNr. The SNr injection site (*inset*). (d) Schematic illustrating the thalamic interactions with the lamprey basal ganglia. GP, globus pallidus; OT, optic tectum; PPN, pedunculopontine nucleus; PT, pretectum; SNc, substantia nigra pars compacta; STN, subthalamic nucleus.

reptiles, the thalamostriatal pathways arise from the nucleus rotundus, the medial complex, and the posterior dorsolateral nucleus. These nuclei also send projections to the pallial dorso-ventricular ridge.

The output nuclei of the basal ganglia, notably the substantia nigra pars reticulata (SNr), which projects to different midbrain and brainstem motor centres in the lamprey, as well as mammals, also sends axonal branches to the thalamus (Figure 7c and d)(Stephenson-Jones et al., 2011). These projections may correspond to the prominent SNr projections in mammals to the ventrolateral nuclei that forwards information back to the frontal lobe (Grillner et al., 2020). However, at present, we have no detailed information in the lamprey, except for the SNr projections to the thalamus. This may also represent efference copy information concerning the basal ganglia commands issued to midbrain/brainstem motor centres.

Pallial/Cortical Projections to the Lamprey Thalamus

The lamprey dorsolateral pallium has projection neurons (PT-type) that target all downstream motor centres, including the thalamus and the brainstem (Figure 8a–c)(Ocana et al., 2015). In mammals, there is an extensive thalamo-specific projection from layer 6 in the neocortex that affects not least the reticular thalamus (Crabtree, 2018; Erisir et al., 1997) and may serve to control the "thalamic gate"—that is how much of the sensory information that reaches the thalamus is transmitted further to the cortex (Guillery, 2017). In addition, a large number of the layer 5B pyramidal neurons on their way to the brainstem centres give off collaterals directly to thalamic nuclei, in particular, the higher-order nuclei (Bourassa and Deschênes, 1995; Deschênes et al., 1994; Guillery, 2017) that project back to association areas in the neocortex. In the lamprey, the pallial efferents that innervate the thalamus may correspond to mammalian layer 5B neurons (Suryanarayana et al., 2017). Whether there are specific pallial projection neurons targeting the thalamus exclusively is not known. In birds, projection neurons in the Wulst and DVR target the thalamus, the brainstem, and the rostral spinal cord (Reiner et al., 2005). The dorsal cortex in reptiles is also known to project to the thalamus and brainstem (Hall et al., 1977; Ulinski, 1986).

Thalamus in Other Anamniotes (cyclostomes to amphibians)

Cartilaginous Fish

The first group of jawed vertebrates, the elasmobranchs (sharks, skates, and rays) and the extant holocephalians, including the rat and elephant fishes, evolved around 420 million years ago. The available data are largely from studies on sharks. In general, the thalamus of cartilaginous fish has a periventricular part and a lateral part with larger cells. In some species, dorsal and ventral subdivisions have been identified (Smeets, 1982, 1992). The caudal part of the dorsal periventricular thalamus receives tectal input, and the periventricular part is also known to project back to the tectum (Smeets, 1982). The periventricular thalamus is known to project to both the dorsal and medial pallium (Luiten, 1981a, 1981b) but also in some species to the subpallium (Butler, 1994). The lateral thalamus receives contralateral retinal input (Smeets, 1982, 1992), and a visual area has been identified in the shark dorsal telencephalon; however, whether there is a topography of this visual input is not known (Cohen et al., 1973). With regard to somatosensory inputs, spinothalamic projections have been reported (Ebbesson and Hodde, 1981). There is clearly a need for more data, but it seems that the thalamus serves as an important relay of sensory information to the telencephalon (Ebbesson and Schroeder, 1971).

The Gar—a Basic Ray-Finned Fish

The gar belongs to the family of Holosteans, which diverged before the teleost gene duplication. Recent genome studies in the gar have revealed that they have a slow rate of genome evolution and serve as a vital bridge to understanding the orthology of genes between teleosts, amphibians, and

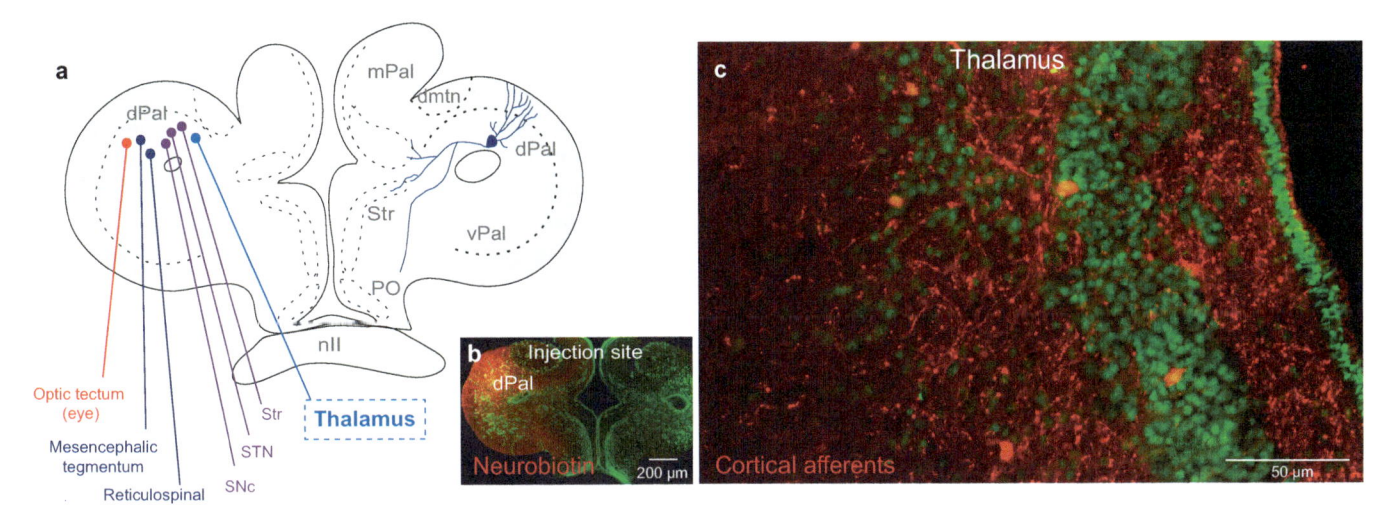

Figure 8 Dorsal pallial projections to the thalamus and beyond.
(a) Schematic that illustrates areas that receive projections from the dorsal pallium (dPal). (b) Neurobiotin injection site in the dorsal pallium. (c) Retrogradely labelled cells (red) in the periventricular and lateral area of the thalamus. Nissl stain in green.

mammals (Braasch et al., 2016; Parichy, 2016). This is in contrast to the majority of current teleosts that have undergone additional gene duplications. In the longnose gar, the thalamus is known to receive retinal afferents (Northcutt and Butler, 1976), as well as input from the optic tectum. The longnose gar, like the teleosts, has a preglomerular complex, which receives tectal input. It is not known whether it receives direct visual input via dendrites extending into the optic tract (Northcutt and Butler, 1980).

Modern Teleosts—Bony Fish

The bony fishes are a diverse group of vertebrates consisting of the lobe- and ray-finned fishes. We will focus here on modern teleosts (goldfish and zebrafish) (Nieuwenhuys et al., 1998), which are by themselves a very diverse group and constitute half of all extant vertebrates (Ravi and Venkatesh, 2018). The teleosts have undergone an additional gene duplication (Braasch et al., 2016; Ravi and Venkatesh, 2018). The thalamus is involved in relaying sensory input to the telencephalon, but along with the thalamus, there is a ventrolaterally located preglomerular complex caudal to the thalamus, which is also a major source of ascending projections to the telencephalon (Bloch et al., 2020; Butler, 1994; Mueller, 2012; Wullimann and Mueller, 2004; Wullimann and Northcutt, 1990; Yamamoto and Ito, 2008).

The thalamus consists of the anterior, central, and dorsal posterior nuclei (Braford and Northcutt, 1983; Nieuwenhuys et al., 1998; Striedter, 1990a, 1990b) and is located just ventral to the habenula. The anterior nucleus consists of cells with laterally projecting dendrites that might receive direct retinal inputs, given their terminal fields in the nucleus opticus dorsolateralis (Butler and Saidel, 1993; Medina et al., 1993), which is known to receive retinal input and is also topographically organised (Butler and Saidel, 1993; Medina et al., 1993; Nieuwenhuys et al., 1998). It projects to pallial areas (medial and dorsal pallium) (Echteler and Saidel, 1981).

A recent study in larval zebrafish using restricted transneuronal anterograde labelling (Mundell et al., 2015) also found axonal terminations of retinorecipient cells in the pallium (Ma et al., 2019). Input from the tectum, on the other hand, targets the dorsal posterior nucleus (Butler, 1994; Luiten, 1981a, 1981b). The dorsal posterior thalamic nucleus projects, in turn, to the dorsomedial pallium (Echteler and Saidel, 1981). Conversely, the thalamic nuclei are known to project to the tectum and have been shown to transmit luminance information (Heap et al., 2018; Helmbrecht et al., 2018; Kunst et al., 2019).

The Preglomerular Relay Nuclei—a Teleost Feature

In addition to the thalamus, a prominent relay of sensory information to the telencephalon is through the preglomerular nuclei. They are reciprocally connected with the dorsomedial and dorsolateral pallium (Mueller, 2012; Wullimann and Northcutt, 1990; Yamamoto and Ito, 2008) and consist of several subdivisions. The anterior nucleus receives auditory inputs while the lateral nucleus receives visual, lateral line, and auditory ascending inputs (Mueller, 2012; Yamamoto and Ito, 2008). The homology of the preglomerular complex remains a matter of debate, and some propose it as homologous to the thalamus proper (Ishikawa et al., 2007; Mueller, 2012), whereas others have suggested a midbrain origin of the majority of the cells of the preglomerular complex rather than from the diencephalon (Bloch et al., 2020).

It is important to note that both amphibians and more basal vertebrate groups such as cartilaginous fishes and cyclostomes and also basal ray-finned fishes generally do not have a preglomerular complex. It thus appears that the preglomerular complex is a unique feature of modern teleosts and an additional source of sensory relay to the telencephalon.

Amphibians

Modern amphibians form a diverse order of terrestrial vertebrates with three broad groups. Urodeles consist of salamanders and newts, anurans consist of frogs and toads, and the last group consists of caecilians or serpentine amphibians. They diverged from the main vertebrate line over 340 million years ago. They have been of interest to comparative neuroanatomists, given that they are critical for understanding the anamniote-to-amniote transition, as well as the transition from water to land-dwelling vertebrates. The brain of the tiger salamander, *Ambystoma tigrinum*, was examined by Herrick, who suggested that it is a simplified version of the common brain architecture found across vertebrates (Herrick, 1948). Although all major regions of amniote brains are recognised in the amphibian brain, they have been thought to have a much simpler brain than what their phylogenetic position would entail, also described as a *secondary simplification* (Nieuwenhuys et al., 1998; Northcutt and Kicliter, 1980; Roth et al., 1995, 1993; ten Donkelaar, 1998).

The thalamus in amphibians, as in other vertebrates, is located in the prosomere p2, which forms the middle segment of the diencephalon. The dorsal thalamus, with regard to patterns of cell migrations, has been divided into a medial and a lateral nucleus corresponding to the periventricular and superficial nuclei (González et al., 2020; Nieuwenhuys et al., 1998). The anterior nuclei have strong calretinin immunoreactivity in some parts and calbindin immunoreactivity in others (Morona and Gonzalez, 2008; Morona et al., 2011), and they are bilaterally connected with the medial and dorsal pallium both in urodeles and anurans (González et al., 2020; Westhoff and Roth, 2002). The central thalamic nuclei show intense calretinin immunoreactivity and receive inputs from the dorsal column nuclei, the superior olivary nucleus, and the lateral line system (González et al., 2020; Matesz and Szekely, 1978; Munoz et al., 1995; Westhoff et al., 2004; Wicht and Himstedt, 1988). They project to the striatum and central amygdala and have been compared to the thalamic areas in reptiles that project to the dorsoventricular ridge, whereas the equivalent pathways in mammals have been thought of as the lateral thalamic nuclei, including the sensory and associative nuclei.

The lateral or superficial thalamic nuclei consist of neurons that extend their dendrites into the optic tract but also have a strong reciprocal connection with the nucleus of Bellonci (González et al., 2020). Other than the thalamus, direct retinal input and secondary visual input from the optic tectum reach the thalamus in its lateral part. The tectal inputs also reach the medial portions. The ventromedial and ventrolateral nuclei receive somatosensory inputs from the spinal cord and the dorsal column nuclei (Munoz et al., 1995; Westhoff et al., 2004; Wicht and Himstedt, 1988). The thalamus, furthermore, innervates the striatum and the nucleus accumbens (Marin et al., 1997a, 1997b).

Conclusion

From the recent data obtained in the lamprey showing the topographic visual and somatosensory projections from the thalamus to the pallium, as well as the presence of thalamic projections to the striatum, and the presence of a similar organisation in elasmobranchs, teleosts, and amphibians, one can conclude that the thalamus, as a relay of ascending sensory information to the pallium and subpallium, constitutes a fundamental feature of the general anamniote forebrain organisation.

Comparing Thalamic Pathways

The thalamic relay nuclei include both the periventricular and lateral cell groups, which have been classified as distinct nuclei in some anamniotes with variations, as well as in amniotes. However, in several species there is relatively less migration of cells to the lateral parts of the thalamus, and therefore comparing these as distinct "nuclei" is not straightforward. This applies more so when comparing with the mammalian condition where there is extensive migration of cell groups and the presence of several nuclei, some of which are also mammalian-specific evolutionary innovations.

Although distinct thalamic nuclei are difficult to discern and compare between different vertebrate classes, the sensory pathways are more readily comparable. In lamprey, visual and somatosensory information is relayed by both periventricular and lateral cells in the thalamus to distinct parts of the dorsal pallium, and furthermore, thalamic neurons projecting to different parts of pallium are distinct but are partially overlapping in their location in the thalamus (Suryanarayana et al., 2020). The lamprey data agree with the retinothalamic and somatosensory lemniscal pathways as being consistent across vertebrates from the lamprey and elasmobranchs to basic teleosts (e.g., gar), amphibians, and amniotes. Modern teleosts have, in addition, evolved a novel sensory relay, the preglomerular nuclei, which may be of midbrain developmental origin (Bloch et al., 2020). This, as concluded earlier, could be a unique and largely teleost-specific evolutionary innovation. The tectothalamic pathway, consisting of relayed sensory information from the roof of the midbrain (Butler, 1994, 1995), targets the recipient neurons in the thalamus, which are also generally periventricular nuclei but, in some cases, also consist of the lateral parts. This segregation is apparent in mammals with distinct targets in the different sensory and higher-order cortices as well as in non-mammalian amniotes, wherein these two pathways are also segregated by their differential targeting in the dorsal cortex/Wulst and the dorsal ventricular ridge (birds and reptiles). In anamniotes, although tectal projections to the thalamus are present, the organisation in the thalamus needs to be clarified in greater detail (Briscoe and Ragsdale, 2019; Puelles, 2017). In the lamprey, there is evidence that tectal deep-layer motor cells projecting to reticulospinal nuclei send collaterals to the thalamus (Capantini et al., 2017).

The other pathway that is prominent in most anamniote species is the thalamic projections to the tectum, which is topographically arranged in the lamprey (Suryanarayana et al., 2020). A subset of these neurons has been shown to transmit luminance information in the zebrafish (Heap et al., 2018). Thalamic projections to the tectum also exist in amniotes (Comoli et al., 2012; Ito and Atoji, 2016; Kenigfest and Belekhova, 2009; Patel et al., 2017).

Concluding Remarks

The previous discussion has shown that in all classes of vertebrates, the thalamus is an essential part of the forebrain and vital as a sensory relay to the pallium/cortex and the striatum, both with regard to the sensory pathways from the retina and other senses and also information from the superior colliculus/tectum (see also Chapter 5 in this volume; Kaas, 2004). Figure 9 summarises the findings in the different vertebrate groups. The most complete information is available for mammals and the lamprey, in which there is a topographic representation for both vision and somatosensory information in the pallium/cortex, whereas in other groups, a topographic representation has not been demonstrated, although a visual thalamopallial relay is present in most cases. A tectothalamic and a thalamostriatal projection has been reported in all amniotes and in the lamprey. The latter pathway is also present in amphibians, possibly in sharks, and lastly, in modern teleosts via the preglomerular nucleus. A palliothalamic projection has been demonstrated in all amniotes and the lamprey, and a thalamotectal pathway is present in practically all vertebrate groups. With everything taken together, the evidence is striking for a conservation of the general organisation of the thalamus with its input and output within amniotes and the lamprey. Certain pieces of information are, however, lacking in certain groups, such as fish and amphibians, and thus a detailed analysis with modern techniques should be performed in these vertebrates. Although the basic design is conserved, many species have developed impressive behavioural specialisations, such as echolocation in bats and many other examples from the animal kingdom, humans included. This, of course, required new features to be added to the basic neural organisation.

A new image is emerging, suggesting that not only the thalamus, with its input–output relations, but also the bauplan of the entire forebrain was developed very early in vertebrate evolution, at the stage when lamprey diverged from the evolutionary line leading to mammals (see also Lamanna et al., 2022). This includes the sensory and motor areas of the pallium/cortex, the basal ganglia, the dopamine system, and the habenula, areas that play a fundamental role in the control of action and decision-making in the vertebrate nervous system.

Acknowledgements

The support of the Swedish Medical Research Council (VR-M-K2013-62X-03026, VR-M-2015–02816, VR-M-2018–02453); EU/FP7 Moving Beyond grant ITN-No-316639; European Union Seventh Framework Programme (FP7/2007–2013) under grant agreement no. 604102 (HBP); EU/Horizon 2020 no. 720270 (HBP SGA1), no. 785907 (HBP SGA2), and no. 945539 (HBP SGA3); and the Karolinska Institutet is gratefully acknowledged.

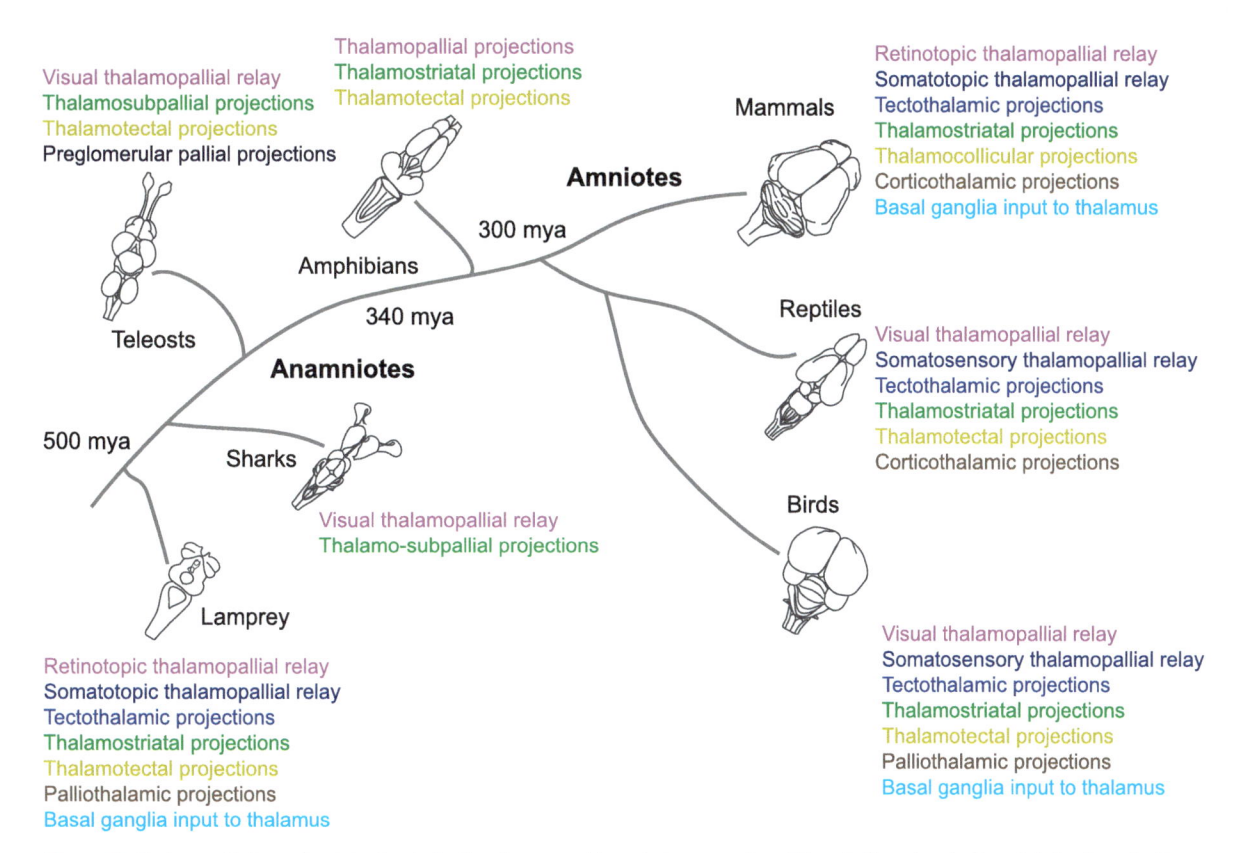

Figure 9 Phylogenetic tree of vertebrates, indicating the current knowledge regarding different afferent and efferent thalamic projections.

References

Benito-Gutiérrez, È., Stemmer, M., Rohr, S.D., Schuhmacher, L.N., Tang, J., Marconi, A., Jékely, G., and Arendt, D. (2018). Patterning of a telencephalon-like region in the adult brain of amphioxus. bioRxiv, 307629.

Bloch, S., Hagio, H., Thomas, M., Heuze, A., Hermel, J.M., Lasserre, E., Colin, I., Saka, K., Affaticati, P., Jenett, A., et al. (2020). Non-thalamic origin of zebrafish sensory nuclei implies convergent evolution of visual pathways in amniotes and teleosts. eLife 9, e54945.

Bourassa, J., and Deschênes, M. (1995). Corticothalamic projections from the primary visual cortex in rats: a single fiber study using biocytin as an anterograde tracer. Neuroscience 66, 253–263.

Braasch, I., Gehrke, A.R., Smith, J.J., Kawasaki, K., Manousaki, T., Pasquier, J., Amores, A., Desvignes, T., Batzel, P., Catchen, J., et al. (2016). The spotted gar genome illuminates vertebrate evolution and facilitates human-teleost comparisons. Nat Genet 48, 427–437.

Braford, M.R.J., and Northcutt, R.G. (1983). Organization of the diencephalon and pretectum of the ray-finned fishes. In Neurobiology, Vol 2: Higher Brain Areas and Functions, R.E. Davis, and R.G. Northcutt, eds. (Ann Arbor: University of Michigan Press), pp. 117–164.

Briscoe, S.D., and Ragsdale, C.W. (2019). Evolution of the chordate telencephalon. Curr Biol 29, R647–R662.

Butler, A.B. (1994). The evolution of the dorsal thalamus of jawed vertebrates, including mammals: cladistic analysis and a new hypothesis. Brain Res Brain Res Rev 19, 29–65.

Butler, A.B. (1995). The dorsal thalamus of jawed vertebrates: a comparative viewpoint. Brain Behav Evol 46, 209–223.

Butler, A.B. (2008). Evolution of brains, cognition, and consciousness. Brain Res Bull 75, 442–449.

Butler, A.B., and Hodos, W. (2005). Comparative Vertebrate Neuroanatomy: Evolution and Adaptation, 2nd edn (New Jersey: Wiley).

Butler, A.B., and Saidel, W.M. (1993). Retinal projections in teleost fishes: Patterns, variations, and questions. Comp Biochem Physiol Part A 104, 431–442.

Capantini, L., von Twickel, A., Robertson, B., and Grillner, S. (2017). The pretectal connectome in lamprey. J Comp Neurol 525, 753–772.

Cleland, B.G., Dubin, M.W., and Levick, W.R. (1971). Simultaneous recording of input and output of lateral geniculate neurones. Nat New Biol 231, 191–192.

Cohen, D.H., Duff, T.A., and Ebbesson, S.O. (1973). Electrophysiological identification of a visual area in shark telencephalon. Science 182, 492–494.

Comoli, E., Das Neves Favaro, P., Vautrelle, N., Leriche, M., Overton, P.G., and Redgrave, P. (2012). Segregated anatomical input to sub-regions of the rodent superior colliculus associated with approach and defense. Front Neuroanat 6, 9.

Crabtree, J.W. (2018). Functional diversity of thalamic reticular subnetworks. Front Syst Neurosci 12, 41.

Deschênes, M., Bourassa, J., and Pinault, D. (1994). Corticothalamic projections from layer V cells in rat are collaterals of long-range corticofugal axons. Brain Res 664, 215–219.

Drager, U.C. (1975). Receptive fields of single cells and topography in mouse visual cortex. J Comp Neurol 160, 269–290.

Dubuc, R., Bongianni, F., Ohta, Y., and Grillner, S. (1993a). Anatomical and physiological study of brainstem nuclei relaying dorsal column inputs in lampreys. J Comp Neurol 327, 260–270.

Dubuc, R., Bongianni, F., Ohta, Y., and Grillner, S. (1993b). Dorsal root and dorsal column mediated synaptic inputs to reticulospinal neurons in lampreys: involvement of glutamatergic, glycinergic, and GABAergic transmission. J Comp Neurol 327, 251–259.

Dugas-Ford, J., and Ragsdale, C.W. (2015). Levels of homology and the problem of neocortex. Annu Rev Neurosci 38, 351–368.

Ebbesson, S.O., and Hodde, K.C. (1981). Ascending spinal systems in the nurse shark, *Ginglymostoma cirratum*. Cell Tissue Res 216, 313–331.

Ebbesson, S.O., and Schroeder, D.M. (1971). Connections of the nurse shark's telencephalon. Science 173, 254–256.

Echteler, S.M., and Saidel, W.M. (1981). Forebrain connections in the goldfish support telencephalic homologies with land vertebrates. Science 212, 683–685.

Erisir, A., Van Horn, S.C., and Sherman, S.M. (1997). Relative numbers of cortical and brainstem inputs to the lateral geniculate nucleus. Proc Natl Acad Sci USA 94, 1517–1520.

Feinberg, T.E., and Mallatt, J. (2017). Corrigendum to "The Nature of Primary Consciousness. A New Synthesis" [Conscious Cogn. 43 (2016) 113–127]. Conscious Cogn 48, 293.

Fournier, J., Muller, C.M., Schneider, I., and Laurent, G. (2018). Spatial information in a non-retinotopic visual cortex. Neuron 97, 164–180 e167.

González, A., Lopez, J.M., Morona, R., and Moreno, N. (2020). The organization of the central nervous system of amphibians. In Evolutionary Neuroscience, J.H. Kaas, ed. (Oxford: Academic Press), pp. 125–157.

Grillner, S., and Robertson, B. (2016). The basal ganglia over 500 million years. Curr Biol 26, R1088–R1100.

Grillner, S., Robertson, B., and Kotaleski Hellgren, J. (2020). Basal ganglia—a motion perspective. Compr Physiol 10, 1241–1275.

Guillery, R. (2017). The Brain as a Tool. A Neuroscientist's Account (Oxford: Oxford University Press).

Hall, J.A., Foster, R.E., Ebner, F.F., and Hall, W.C. (1977). Visual cortex in a reptile, the turtle (*Pseudemys scripta* and *Chrysemys picta*). Brain Res 130, 197–216.

Heap, L.A.L., Vanwalleghem, G., Thompson, A.W., Favre-Bulle, I.A., and Scott, E.K. (2018). Luminance changes drive directional startle through a thalamic pathway. Neuron 99, 293–301 e294.

Heier, P. (1948). Fundamental properties in the structure of the brain. A study of the brain of *Petromyzon marinus*. Acta Anat 8, 3–213.

Heimberg, A.M., Cowper-Sal-lari, R., Semon, M., Donoghue, P.C., and Peterson, K.J. (2010). microRNAs reveal the interrelationships of hagfish, lampreys, and gnathostomes and the nature of the ancestral vertebrate. Proc Natl Acad Sci USA 107, 19379–19383.

Helmbrecht, T.O., Dal Maschio, M., Donovan, J.C., Koutsouli, S., and Baier, H. (2018). Topography of a visuomotor transformation. Neuron 100, 1429–1445 e1424.

Herrick, C.J. (1948). The Brain of the Tiger Salamander, *Ambystoma tigrinum* (Chicago: University of Chicago Press).

Ishikawa, Y., Yamamoto, N., Yoshimoto, M., Yasuda, T., Maruyama, K., Kage, T., Takeda, H., and Ito, H. (2007). Developmental origin of diencephalic sensory relay nuclei in teleosts. Brain Behav Evol 69, 87–95.

Ito, T., and Atoji, Y. (2016). Tectothalamic inhibitory projection neurons in the avian torus semicircularis. J Comp Neurol 524, 2604–2622.

Jones, M.R., Grillner, S., and Robertson, B. (2009). Selective projection patterns from subtypes of retinal ganglion cells to tectum and pretectum: distribution and relation to behavior. J Comp Neurol **517**, 257–275.

Kaas, J.H. (2004). Somatosensory *system*. In The *Human Nervous System*, G. Paxinos, and J.K. Mai, eds. (New York: Elsevier), pp. 1059–1092.

Kaas, J.H., Nelson, R.J., Sur, M., Lin, C.S., and Merzenich, M.M. (1979). Multiple representations of the body within the primary somatosensory cortex of primates. Science **204**, 521–523.

Karten, H.J. (2015). Vertebrate brains and evolutionary connectomics: on the origins of the mammalian "neocortex." Philos Trans R Soc Lond B Biol Sci **370**.

Kenigfest, N.B., and Belekhova, M.G. (2009). [Evolutionary significance of reciprocal connections in the turtle tectofugal visual system]. Zh Evol Biokhim Fiziol **45**, 334–342.

Krubitzer, L.A., and Kaas, J.H. (1992). The somatosensory thalamus of monkeys: cortical connections and a redefinition of nuclei in marmosets. J Comp Neurol **319**, 123–140.

Kumar, S., and Hedges, S.B. (1998). A molecular timescale for vertebrate evolution. Nature **392**, 917–920.

Kunst, M., Laurell, E., Mokayes, N., Kramer, A., Kubo, F., Fernandes, A.M., Forster, D., Dal Maschio, M., and Baier, H. (2019). A Cellular-resolution atlas of the larval zebrafish brain. Neuron **103**, 21–38 e25.

Lamanna F, Hervas-Sotomayor F, A.P. O, Jandzik D, Sobrido-Cameán D, Martik ML, Green SA, Brüning T, Mößinger K, Schmidt J, et al.: Reconstructing the ancestral vertebrate brain using a lamprey neural cell type atlas. *BioRxiv* 2022.

Luiten, P.G. (1981a). Two visual pathways to the telencephalon in the nurse shark (*Ginglymostoma cirratum*). I. Retinal projections. J Comp Neurol **196**, 531–538.

Luiten, P.G. (1981b). Two visual pathways to the telencephalon in the nurse shark (*Ginglymostoma cirratum*). II. Ascending thalamo-telencephalic connections. J Comp Neurol **196**, 539–548.

Ma, M., Kler, S., and Pan, Y.A. (2019). Structural neural connectivity analysis in zebrafish with restricted anterograde transneuronal viral labeling and quantitative brain mapping. Front Neural Circuits **13**, 85.

Marin, O., Gonzalez, A., and Smeets, W.J. (1997a). Basal ganglia organization in amphibians: afferent connections to the striatum and the nucleus accumbens. J Comp Neurol **378**, 16–49.

Marin, O., Gonzalez, A., and Smeets, W.J. (1997b). Basal ganglia organization in amphibians: efferent connections of the striatum and the nucleus accumbens. J Comp Neurol **380**, 23–50.

Matesz, C., and Szekely, G. (1978). The motor column and sensory projections of the branchial cranial nerves in the frog. J Comp Neurol **178**, 157–176.

Medina, L., and Reiner, A. (2000). Do birds possess homologues of mammalian primary visual, somatosensory and motor cortices? Trends Neurosci **23**, 1–12.

Medina, M., Reperant, J., Ward, R., Rio, J.P., and Lemire, M. (1993). The primary visual system of flatfish: an evolutionary perspective. Anat Embryol (Berl) **187**, 167–191.

Miyashita, T., Coates, M.I., Farrar, R., Larson, P., Manning, P.L., Wogelius, R.A., Edwards, N.P., Anne, J., Bergmann, U., Palmer, A.R., *et al.* (2019). Hagfish from the Cretaceous Tethys Sea and a reconciliation of the morphological-molecular conflict in early vertebrate phylogeny. Proc Natl Acad Sci USA **116**, 2146–2151.

Morona, R., and Gonzalez, A. (2008). Calbindin-D28k and calretinin expression in the forebrain of anuran and urodele amphibians: further support for newly identified subdivisions. J Comp Neurol **511**, 187–220.

Morona, R., Lopez, J.M., and Gonzalez, A. (2011). Localization of calbindin-d28k and calretinin in the brain of *Dermophis mexicanus* (amphibia: gymnophiona) and its bearing on the interpretation of newly recognized neuroanatomical regions. Brain Behav Evol **77**, 231–269.

Mueller, T. (2012). What is the thalamus in zebrafish? Front Neurosci **6**, 64.

Mundell, N.A., Beier, K.T., Pan, Y.A., Lapan, S.W., Goz Ayturk, D., Berezovskii, V.K., Wark, A.R., Drokhlyansky, E., Bielecki, J., Born, R.T., *et al.* (2015). Vesicular stomatitis virus enables gene transfer and transsynaptic tracing in a wide range of organisms. J Comp Neurol **523**, 1639–1663.

Munoz, A., Munoz, M., Gonzalez, A., and Ten Donkelaar, H.J. (1995). Anuran dorsal column nucleus: organization, immunohistochemical characterization, and fiber connections in *Rana perezi* and *Xenopus laevis*. J Comp Neurol **363**, 197–220.

Nieuwenhuys, R., and Nicholson, C. (1998). Lampreys (*Petromyzontoidea*). In The Central Nervous System of Vertebrates, R. Nieuwenhuys, H.J.T. Donkelaar, and C. Nicholson, eds. (Berlin, Heidelberg: Springer), pp. 397–495.

Nieuwenhuys, R., ten Donkelaar, H.J., and Nicholson, C. (1998). The Central Nervous System of Vertebrates (Berlin, Heidelberg: Springer).

Northcutt, R.G., and Butler, A.B. (1976). Retinofugal pathways in the lingnose gar *Lepisosteus osseus* (linnaeus). J Comp Neurol **166**, 1–15.

Northcutt, R.G., and Butler, A.B. (1980). Projections of the optic tectum in the longnose gar, *Lepisosteus osseus*. Brain Res **190**, 333–346.

Northcutt, R.G., and Kicliter, E. (1980). Organization of the amphibian telencephalon. In Comparative Neurology of the Telencephalon, S.O.E. Ebbesson, ed. (Boston, MA: Springer).

Northcutt, R.G., and Wicht, H. (1997). Afferent and efferent connections of the lateral and medial pallia of the silver lamprey. Brain Behav Evol **49**, 1–19.

Ocana, F.M., Suryanarayana, S.M., Saitoh, K., Kardamakis, A.A., Capantini, L., Robertson, B., and Grillner, S. (2015). The lamprey pallium provides a blueprint of the mammalian motor projections from cortex. Curr Biol **25**, 413–423.

Parichy, D.M. (2016). The gar is a fish... is a bird... is a mammal? Nat Genet **48**, 344–345.

Patel, M.B., Sons, S., Yudintsev, G., Lesicko, A.M., Yang, L., Taha, G.A., Pierce, S.M., and Llano, D.A. (2017). Anatomical characterization of subcortical descending projections to the inferior colliculus in mouse. J Comp Neurol **525**, 885–900.

Perez-Fernandez, J., Kardamakis, A.A., Suzuki, D.G., Robertson, B., and Grillner, S. (2017). Direct dopaminergic projections from the SNc modulate visuomotor transformation in the lamprey tectum. Neuron **96**, 910–924 e915.

Perez-Fernandez, J., Stephenson-Jones, M., Suryanarayana, S.M., Robertson, B., and Grillner, S. (2014). Evolutionarily conserved organization of the dopaminergic system in lamprey: SNc/VTA afferent and efferent connectivity and D2 receptor expression. J Comp Neurol **522**, 3775–3794.

Pombal, M.A., and Puelles, L. (1999). Prosomeric map of the lamprey forebrain based on calretinin immunocytochemistry, Nissl stain, and ancillary markers. J Comp Neurol **414**, 391–422.

Puelles, L. (2017). Comments on the updated tetrapartite pallium model in the mouse and chick, featuring a homologous claustro-insular complex. Brain Behav Evol **90**, 171–189.

Ravi, V., and Venkatesh, B. (2018). The divergent genomes of teleosts. Annu Rev Anim Biosci 6, 47–68.

Reiner, A. (1993). Neurotransmitter organization and connections of turtle cortex: implications for the evolution of mammalian isocortex. Comp Biochem Physiol Comp Physiol 104, 735–748.

Reiner, A., Yamamoto, K., and Karten, H.J. (2005). Organization and evolution of the avian forebrain. Anat Rec A Discov Mol Cell Evol Biol 287, 1080–1102.

Roth, G., Blanke, J., and Ohle, M. (1995). Brain size and morphology in miniaturized plethodontid salamanders. Brain Behav Evol 45, 84–95.

Roth, G., Nishikawa, K.C., Naujoks-Manteuffel, C., Schmidt, A., and Wake, D.B. (1993). Paedomorphosis and simplification in the nervous system of salamanders. Brain Behav Evol 42, 137–170.

Schneider, G.E. (1969). Two visual systems. Science 163, 895–902.

Sincich, L.C., Zhang, Y., Tiruveedhula, P., Horton, J.C., and Roorda, A. (2009). Resolving single cone inputs to visual receptive fields. Nat Neurosci 12, 967–969.

Smeets, W.J. (1982). The afferent connections of the tectum mesencephali in two chondrichthyans, the shark *Scyliorhinus canicula* and the ray *Raja clavata*. J Comp Neurol 205, 139–152.

Smeets, W.J. (1992). Comparative aspects of basal forebrain organization in vertebrates. Eur J Morphol 30, 23–36.

Stephenson-Jones, M., Ericsson, J., Robertson, B., and Grillner, S. (2012). Evolution of the basal ganglia: dual-output pathways conserved throughout vertebrate phylogeny. J Comp Neurol 520, 2957–2973.

Stephenson-Jones, M., Samuelsson, E., Ericsson, J., Robertson, B., and Grillner, S. (2011). Evolutionary conservation of the basal ganglia as a common vertebrate mechanism for action selection. Curr Biol 21, 1081–1091.

Striedter, G.F. (1990a). The diencephalon of the channel catfish, *Ictalurus punctatus*. I. Nuclear organization. Brain Behav Evol 36, 329–354.

Striedter, G.F. (1990b). The diencephalon of the channel catfish, *Ictalurus punctatus*. II. Retinal, tectal, cerebellar and telencephalic connections. Brain Behav Evol 36, 355–377.

Sugahara, F., Murakami, Y., Pascual-Anaya, J., and Kuratani, S. (2017). Reconstructing the ancestral vertebrate brain. Dev Growth Differ 59, 163–174.

Sugahara, F., Pascual-Anaya, J., Oisi, Y., Kuraku, S., Aota, S., Adachi, N., Takagi, W., Hirai, T., Sato, N., Murakami, Y., *et al.* (2016). Evidence from cyclostomes for complex regionalization of the ancestral vertebrate brain. Nature 531, 97–100.

Suryanarayana, S.M., Perez-Fernandez, J., Robertson, B., and Grillner, S. (2020). The evolutionary origin of visual and somatosensory representation in the vertebrate pallium. Nat Ecol Evol 4, 639–651.

Suryanarayana, S.M., Pérez-Fernández, J., Robertson, B., and Grillner, S. (2021). Olfaction in lamprey pallium revisited—dual projections of mitral and tufted cells. Cell Reports 34.

Suryanarayana, S.M., Robertson, B., Wallen, P., and Grillner, S. (2017). The lamprey pallium provides a blueprint of the mammalian layered cortex. Curr Biol 27, 3264–3277 e3265.

ten Donkelaar, H.J. (1998). Urodeles. In The Central Nervous System of Vertebrates, R. Nieuwenhuys, H.J. ten Donkelaar, and C. Nicolson, eds. (Berlin, Heidelberg: Springer), pp. 1045–1150.

Ulinski, P.S. (1986). Organization of corticogeniculate projections in the turtle, *Pseudemys scripta*. J Comp Neurol 254, 529–542.

Villar-Cervino, V., Barreiro-Iglesias, A., Mazan, S., Rodicio, M.C., and Anadon, R. (2011). Glutamatergic neuronal populations in the forebrain of the sea lamprey, Petromyzon marinus: an in situ hybridization and immunocytochemical study. J Comp Neurol 519, 1712–1735.

Westhoff, G., and Roth, G. (2002). Morphology and projection pattern of medial and dorsal pallial neurons in the frog *Discoglossus pictus* and the salamander *Plethodon jordani*. J Comp Neurol 445, 97–121.

Westhoff, G., Roth, G., and Straka, H. (2004). Topographic representation of vestibular and somatosensory signals in the anuran thalamus. Neuroscience 124, 669–683.

Wicht, H., and Himstedt, W. (1988). Topologic and connectional analysis of the dorsal thalamus of *Triturus alpestris* (amphibia, urodela, salamandridae). J Comp Neurol 267, 545–561.

Wild, J.M. (1997). The avian somatosensory system: the pathway from wing to Wulst in a passerine (*Chloris chloris*). Brain Res 759, 122–134.

Wullimann, M.F., and Mueller, T. (2004). Teleostean and mammalian forebrains contrasted: Evidence from genes to behavior. J Comp Neurol 475, 143–162.

Wullimann, M.F., and Northcutt, R.G. (1990). Visual and electrosensory circuits of the diencephalon in mormyrids: an evolutionary perspective. J Comp Neurol 297, 537–552.

Yamamoto, N., and Ito, H. (2008). Visual, lateral line, and auditory ascending pathways to the dorsal telencephalic area through the rostrolateral region of the lateral preglomerular nucleus in cyprinids. J Comp Neurol 508, 615–647.

Section 4: Development

Chapter 7

Development of the Thalamocortical Systems

Sara Bandiera and Zoltán Molnár

1. Introduction

The thalamus and the cortex form a network of connections that functions as a close unit (Sherman and Guillery 1996). The reciprocal thalamocortical connectivity is important for trans-thalamic cortical communications and cortical integration, brain state control, and plasticity. Previous chapters of this book described that the thalamus is not merely a relay station passing on information to the cortex; rather, the thalamus and cortex represent an integrated processing unit that dynamically regulates the thalamic transmission of peripherally derived data for cortical processing (Sherman and Guillery 1998).

Corticothalamic connectivity largely outnumbers the sensory input to the thalamus, providing essential feedforward and feedback mechanisms (Mitrofanis and Guillery 1993). The thalamus integrates cortico-cortical interactions through the direct innervation of higher-order (HO) thalamic nuclei by layer 5 neurons in primary cortical areas; the HO nuclei then project into other cortical areas. This provides trans-thalamic cortico-cortical communication and integration of disparate cortical areas into a global network (Guillery and Sherman 2002). This network provides a substrate for the widespread synchronization of cortical and thalamic cell populations. As such, cortical innervation of the thalamus is highly important, yet its development has received little attention.

The development and evolution of the cortex cannot be understood without considering its connections to the thalamus (Grant et al. 2012; Molnár et al. 2012; Deck et al. 2013; Hunnicutt et al. 2014; Horvath et al., 2022). The development of connections between the developing thalamus and cortex starts at an early stage, and the two structures influence each other. The earliest thalamic input reaches the cortex before the peak of cortical neurogenesis, neuronal migration, and cytoarchitectonic differentiation. Therefore, early thalamic inputs might have a major effect in orchestrating the formation and arealization of cortical circuitry (O'Leary 1989; Dehay and Kennedy 2007). Although some of these events are determined by intrinsic programs, the input from each thalamic nucleus can act as a local "extrinsic signal," influencing the outcomes of the intrinsic cortical neurogenic program (Goldman-Rakic 1987; O'Leary 1989; Grove and Fukuchi-Shimogori 2003; Dehay and Kennedy 2007; Sansom and Livesy 2009; Cadwell et al. 2019).

Finally, the developmental mechanisms that govern the interconnection between the thalamus and the cortex have great evolutionary relevance because the increased complexity of cortical representations has been accompanied by impressive changes in the structure of the thalamus (Butler and William 2005; Kaas and Lyon 2007; see Chapter 5 in this volume). The thalamus and cortex co-evolved to form more sophisticated circuits. This allowed primates to expand the trans-thalamic cortico-cortical circuits, with a large increase in the proportions of the HO versus first-order thalamic nuclei. Primates have exceptionally expanded cortices relative to the amount of direct sensory inputs they receive through the first-order thalamic nuclei (Halley and Krubitzer 2019).

1.1 Complexities of the Adult Thalamocortical Relations

The thalamus is divided into more than 40 nuclei distinguished according to their position in the diencephalon, their cytoarchitecture, gene-expression patterns, anatomical connectivity, and function (Jones 2007; see Chapters 2 and 4 in this volume). First-order thalamic nuclei contain thalamic relay cells that receive direct sensory input, mostly originating from layer 6 cortical projecting neurons (Figure 1). HO thalamic nuclei contain matrix cells with diffuse projections (i.e., widespread but nonetheless topographic) that relay cortico-cortical information between different cortical areas (Guillery and Sherman 2002; Jones 2002). All cortical areas receive thalamic input and send projections to the thalamus (Caviness and Frost 1980). The sensory input to the thalamus is outnumbered by the corticothalamic projections by a factor of 10 (Sherman 2005). The formation of the reciprocal connectivity between the thalamus and the cortex and its subsequent experience-dependent refinement results in the orchestrated development of sensory circuits (Katz and Shatz 1996; Molnár 1998; Sur and Rubenstein 2005; Molnár et al. 2020).

1.2 Transformation of the Adult Representations and Developmental Explanations

The relationships between the thalamus and cortex follow basic principles (Caviness and Frost 1980; Behrens et al. 2003), but the fine detail of topography is complex because of transformations of representations and differences in scaling and innervation densities. The routes taken by thalamocortical fibers in the adult brain can be tortuous, with sharp bends and rotations of the array around one axis. Moreover, a single thalamic nucleus can project to more than one cortical area in addition to subcortical targets, such as the striatum, and each cortical field can have several thalamic inputs. The topographic order of projections from a single nucleus can change

Development

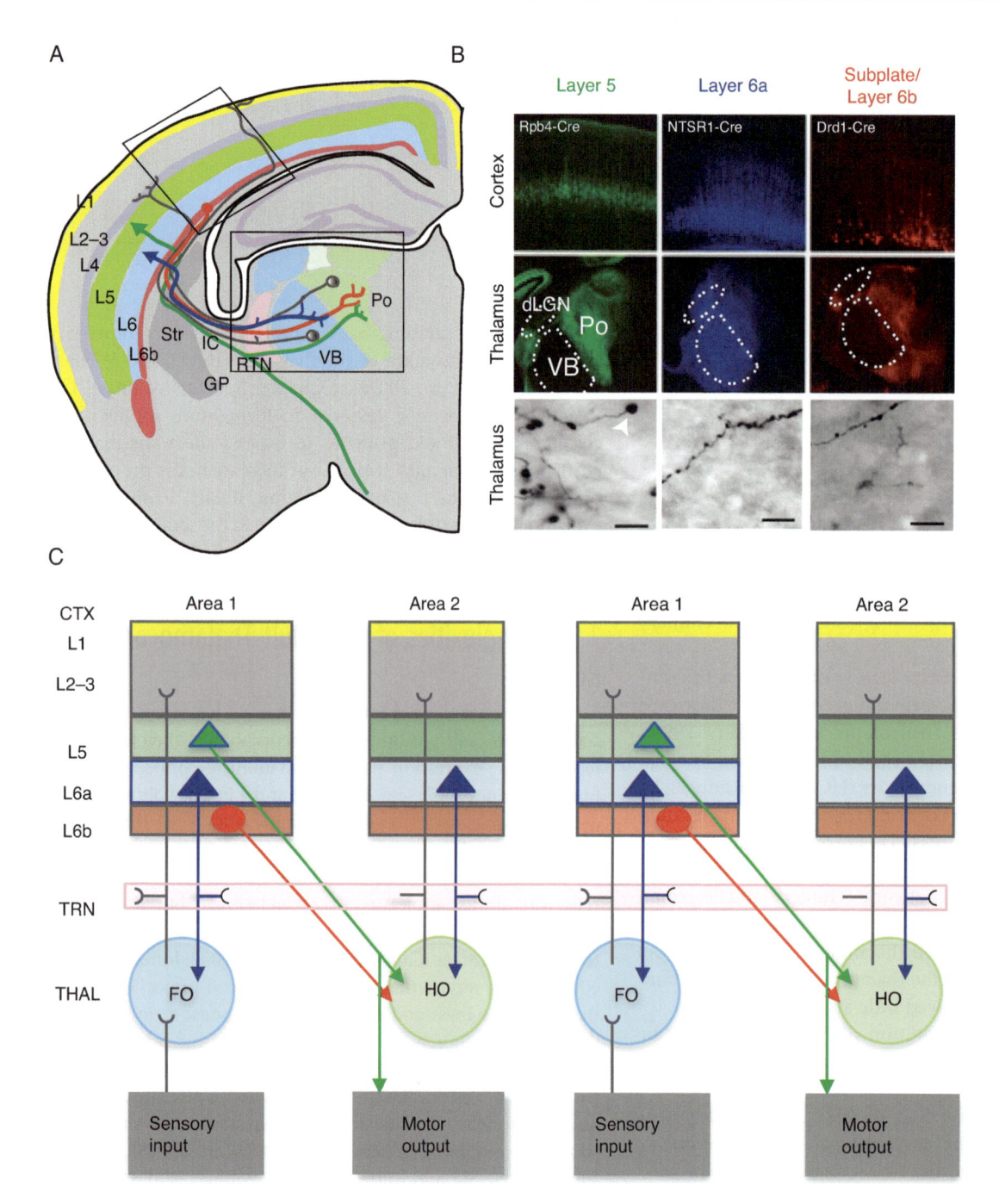

Figure 1 The specificity of the connections between the cortex and thalamus using the mouse somatosensory system as an example.

A. Schematic summary of the complexities of the thalamocortical connectivity in the adult mouse on an idealized section of mouse brain containing somatosensory cortical connections. The first-order ventral posterior thalamic nucleus (VP) receives somatosensory peripheral input (*not indicated*). The VP then projects axons (*black*) to layer 4 of the primary somatosensory cortex S1. Layer 6 (L6) "modulator" neurons (*dark blue*) in S1 project back to the VP. Layer 5 (L5) neurons (*light green*) in S1 project to subcerebral structures and send a collateral branch to an HO thalamic nucleus, for example, the posterior thalamic nucleus (Po). L6 projections innervate both nuclei, whereas some subgroups of layer 6b selectively innervate HO thalamic nuclei (Grant et al. 2016; Hoerder-Suabedissen et al. 2018).

B. Transgenic mouse lines enabled the study of selective innervation of first- and higher-order thalamic nuclei. White circles illustrate the dorsolateral geniculate nucleus (dLGN) and VP. L5 (Rbp4-Cre) and L6b (Drd1a-Cre) projections selectively innervate HO thalamic nuclei, whereas L6a (Ntsr1-Cre) lack such preference. The L5 terminals from S1 to Po are larger than the L6a or L6b terminals from S1 to VP (Grant et al. 2012, 2016; Hoerder-Suabedissen et al. 2018; Hayashi et al. 2020).

C. Schematic illustration of the possible functional circuits generated by this open-loop connectivity and how subplate (SP) neurons can regulate the trans-thalamic cortico-cortical communication through their projections (*bright pink*) to HO thalamic nuclei. Sensory information is relayed through a first-order thalamic nucleus to the cortex (*red*). This cortical area then projects from L6 reciprocally back to the first-order nucleus (*light green*). Each area is also non-reciprocally connected to an HO thalamic nucleus. The L5 input to the thalamus (*dark green*) is an "efference copy" of the L5 output to the motor system in the brainstem and spinal cord. This copy is forwarded to a higher cortical area (*blue*). Some persistent SP cells in layer 6b selectively project to HO thalamic nuclei and are in a position to regulate the trans-thalamic cortico-cortical communication. Direct cortico-cortical connections are also depicted between cortical layers and cortical areas (*pale-gray lines*). These circuits enable cortical areas to act with other cortical areas and motor apparatus in a coordinated manner. *CP*, cerebral peduncle; *FO*, first-order thalamic nuclei; *GP*, globus pallidus; *HO*, higher-order thalamic nuclei; *ic*, internal capsule; *RTN*, reticular thalamic nuclei; *SP*, subplate; *Str*, striatum; *S1*, primary somatosensory cortex; *S2*, secondary association somatosensory cortex; *Po*, posterior thalamic nucleus; *VP*, ventral lateral thalamic nucleus. Figure is modified from Grant et al. (2012), which was inspired by Guillery and Sherman (2002) and modified based on the results of Hoerder-Suabedissen et al. (2018). Panel modified from Molnár (2019).

abruptly at the borders of adjacent cortical areas (e.g., there is a reversal of the retinotopic map between the primary and secondary visual areas) (Molnár et al. 2012; Molnár 1998; see Chapter 3 in this volume).

What developmental mechanisms govern these complex thalamocortical trajectory arrangements? In considering this question, it is important not to infer complexity during development from the appearance in the mature animal. Many perplexing features of thalamocortical organization (convoluted paths taken by individual axons, rotations of axon arrays, and irregular topology between the thalamus and cortex) might be produced after the initial establishment of connections. Coarse reciprocal connections are established during early development when distances are minimal (Molnár and Blakemore 1995; Grant et al. 2016). Fine-tuning of representations occurs subsequently, closer to the target regions. Thalamocortical projections accumulate in the subplate (SP) before they invade the cortex and synapse on their final cortical target cells. These transient circuits assist the formation and maturation of the earliest cortical circuits (Kostovic and Rakic 1990; Allendoerfer and Shatz 1994; Kanold and Luhmann 2010; Molnár et al. 2020). The transient circuits that the corticothalamic projections form in close proximity to the thalamus are less understood (Grant et al. 2012, 2016). Mitrofanis and Guillery (1993) suggested that during development, the perireticular and the thalamic reticular nuclei (PRN and TRN, respectively) serve as compartments where such rearrangements of corticothalamic projections occur (Mitrofanis and Guillery 1993; Chou et al. 2013) (Figure 2). These compartments share compelling similarities: they are both more extensive during development than adulthood, they share some gene-expression patterns, and they both contain transient cellular populations that contribute to the formation of the earliest circuits between the thalamus and the cortex (Montiel et al. 2011; Wang et al. 2011; Grant et al. 2012).

Thalamocortical interactions have been studied in numerous species and have species-specific differences. The mouse model provides unparalleled genetic tools to selectively monitor and manipulate specific cell populations during development. Here we will focus on the developmental principles revealed in the mouse while also pointing out some species-specific differences, especially similarities and differences with humans. We shall concentrate on the neurogenesis, molecular and cellular patterning of thalamic nuclei, thalamocortical and corticothalamic development, and plasticity. The migration of GABAergic neurons and the specific development of the thalamic reticular nucleus (TRN) are discussed in Chapter 8 of this volume.

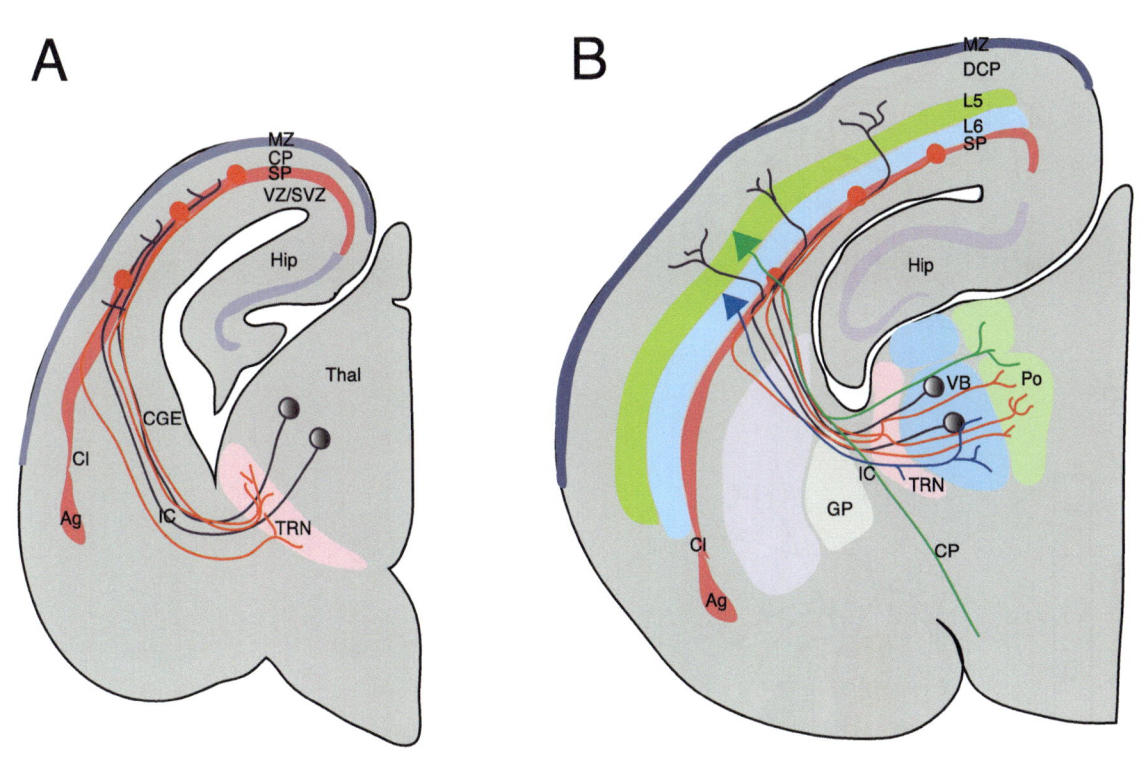

Figure 2 Interactions of the developing thalamocortical projections with the cortical SP zone and interactions of corticothalamic projections with the thalamic reticular nucleus during mouse development at E15 (A) and P4 (B).

A. Corticofugal (*red*) and thalamocortical (*black*) axons extend toward each other at early stages during embryonic development and arrive close to their targets by E15. However, they both stop short of their ultimate targets: corticofugal projections from the SP and layer 6 accumulate in the thalamic reticular nucleus (TRN; *pink*), whereas thalamocortical projections stall in the SP (*red*). Both compartments contain largely transient cells that get integrated into circuits during these early stages.

B. During the first postnatal week, corticofugal and corticopetal axons enter the thalamus (Thal) and dense cortical plate (DCP), respectively, where they arborize and establish their contacts with their ultimate targets. There are signs of fiber decussating in the TRN and in the SP, indicating some rearrangements during development. Red areas (amygdala [Ag], subplate claustrum [Cl], and TRN) represent brain regions sharing gene-expression patterns. *Ag*, amygdala; *Cl*, claustrum; *Hip*, hippocampus; *CGE*, caudal ganglionic eminence; *MZ*, marginal zone (*dark gray/blue area*); *GP*, globus pallidus; *IC*, internal capsule, next to green fibers; the cerebral peduncle is indicated *CP*. Modified from Montiel et al. (2011).

2. Development of the Thalamus

2.1 Molecular Patterning of the Early Thalamus

During early development, diffusible signaling molecules (bone morphogenetic proteins [BMPs], wingless-INT proteins [Wnts], and fibroblast growth factor proteins [FGFs]) released from signaling centers provide positional information for the subdivision of the anterior neural plate and neural tube into regions that express different combinations of high-level transcription factors, often referred to as *master regulators* (Lim and Golden 2007; Scholpp and Lumdsen 2010; Chatterjee and Li 2012; Martinez-Ferre and Martinez 2012; Puelles et al. 2013). According to the "prosomeric model" (Puelles and Rubenstein 2003), the diencephalon develops into three transverse segments, the pretectum (p1), thalamus (p2), and prethalamus (p3), with distinct morphological boundaries and regulatory genes, such as *Pax6*, *Dlx2*, and *Wnt3* (Figure 3A). By embryonic day (E)12.5 in mice, the thalamic formation is completed, with thalamic nuclei arising from the alar plate of the thalamic anlage (P2) (Puelles and Rubenstein 2003). The thalamus is topographically determined by specific transcription factors, including *Otx2*, *Irx1*, *Gbx2*, and *Pax6*, as well as by the *zona limitans intrathalamica* (ZLI), a forebrain organizing center that acts as a boundary between thalamic P2 and prethalamic P3 anlagen by promoting Sonic hedgehog *Shh* expression (Nakagawa and O'Leary 2001; Price et al. 2002).

The thalamus develops from neural progenitor cells located within the p2 domain of the alar plate of the caudal diencephalon (Angevine 1970; Puelles and Rubenstein 1993, 2003).

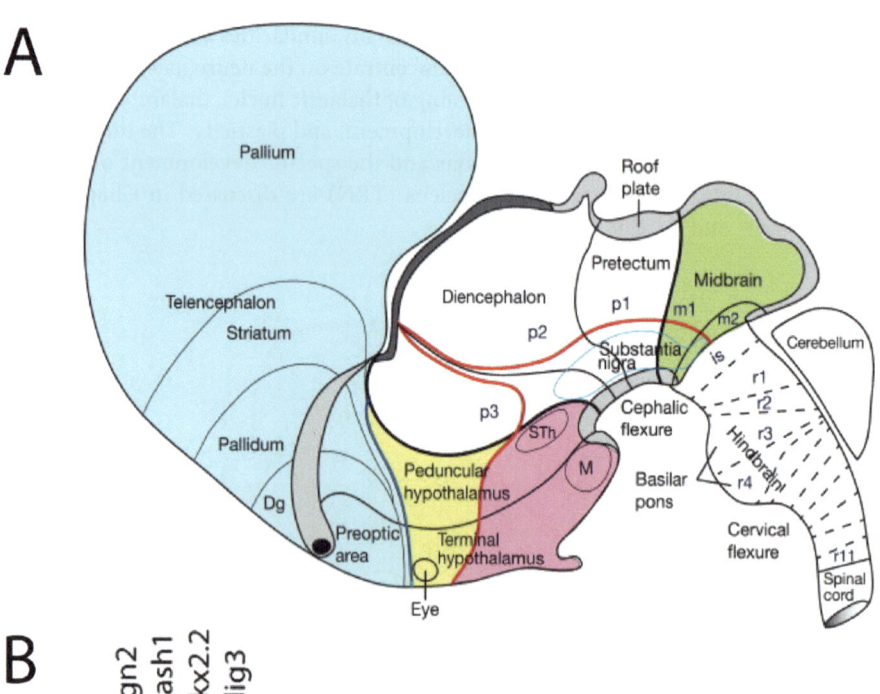

Figure 3 **(A)** Schematic representation of the sagittal view of the developing mouse brain showing the subdivisions of the brainstem and forebrain organization, following the prosomeric model of Puelles and Rubenstein (2003). The diagram shows the boundaries of the diencephalic prosomeres (p3, p2, and p1). Adapted from Puelles et al. (2012).

(B) Schematic representation of diencephalic progenitor domains with examples of expression patterns of transcription factors. The thalamus is divided into the large caudal-posterior progenitor domain (pTH-C; *orange*) and a small rostral-anterior progenitor domain (pTH-R; *blue*). *PT*, pretectum; *PTh*, prethalamus; *ZLI*, zona limitans intrathalamica. Panel B is from Price et al. (2012), and it was originally inspired by Vue et al. (2007).

In the mouse, thalamic neurogenesis takes place in the ventricular zone from E10.5 to E16.5 (Angevine 1970). The thalamus develops from two progenitor domains distinguished by their expression of different combinations of transcription factors: the caudal progenitor thalamic domain (pTh-C) lies caudal to the ZLI and expresses *Neurogenin 1* and *2*, *Gbx2*, *Olig3*, and *Sox2*, whereas the smaller rostral progenitor thalamic domain (pTh-R) lies rostral to the ZLI and expresses *Ascl1*, *Mash1*, and *Nkx2.2* (Figure 3B) (Vue et al. 2007; Price et al. 2012).

Although some molecules that influence the patterning of the diencephalon have been identified, less is known about how the distinct postmitotic thalamic nuclei emerge from discrete developmental units (Scholpp and Lumsden 2010). As in the neocortex and other brain regions, molecules secreted by signaling centers organize the patterning and growth of specific compartments. The ZLI organizes thalamic development by secretion of Sonic hedgehog (Shh), as well as Wnts and FGFs. Although Wnt signaling is important for setting up the initial rostrocaudal regionalization (Salinas and Nusse 1992; Murray et al. 2007; Quinlan et al. 2009), it remains unknown whether this is directly required for thalamic specification. FGF signaling has also been implicated in organizing diencephalic development. FGF15 and FGF19 function downstream of Shh and are implicated in some aspects of thalamic development (Miyake et al. 2005; Gimeno and Martinez 2007). Based on in utero manipulations, FGF8 has also been shown to control the patterning of thalamic nuclei (Kataoka and Shimogori 2008).

Shh is the principal determinant of cell-fate specification during thalamic development, with at least three Shh-dependent steps in patterning of the thalamic anlage. Through induction of specific transcription factors (TFs), Shh determines cell specification (Scholpp and Lumsden 2010). Ectopic activation of thalamic markers such as Gbx2, oligodendrocyte transcription factor-2 (Otx2), and neurogenin-2 (Neurog2) and oligodendrocyte transcription factor-3 in the mouse pretectum demonstrate that Shh plays a crucial role in patterning thalamic progenitor domains (Vue et al. 2009).

2.2 Thalamic Neurogenesis and Nuclei Specification

Temporal, spatial, and lineage-dependent variables interact in the generation of discrete thalamic nuclei. [3H]-thymidine birth-dating in rats showed that TRN neurons have temporally and spatially diverse origins (Altman and Bayer 1988a, 1988b, 1988c). Other studies showed that glutamatergic neurons populating first-order (FO) thalamic nuclei arise from the pTh-C earlier (E10.5–15.5) than those contributing to HO nuclei (Vue et al. 2007; Nakagawa and Shimogori 2012; Gezelius and Lopez-Bendito 2017).

Lineage-tracing studies suggested that separation of the sensory- and motor-related nuclei is highly lineage related (Shi et al. 2017). Individual progenitors arising from the thalamic ventricular zone (VZ) produce neurons that are preferentially located in specific sets of nuclei with distinct ontogeny and functional characteristics (Figure 4). Labeled thalamic clones segregated into anterior and medial-dorsal clones that occupied sensory-, motor- and cognition-related HO nuclei. The medial-ventral-posterior clones principally clustered to sensory- and motor-related FO nuclei. Rostrally located clones occupied FO sensory nuclei, whereas caudally located clones contributed to HO caudo-dorsal nuclei, indicating that the location of progenitor cells predicts the set of nuclei they preferentially generate (Wong et al. 2018).

The lineage-related functional organization revealed by Shi et al. (2017) suggests that the clonal relationship is not only coupled to anatomical and nuclear allocation but also linked to functional organization, with the differential origin of the functionality of thalamic neurons and clonal segregation between the FO and HO sensory- and motor-related nuclei across different modalities. FO nuclei are transcriptionally more similar to each other across modalities than they are to HO nuclei of the same modality (Frangeul et al. 2016). Shi et al. (2017) emphasize that although there is a strong predisposition for distinct nuclei, this clonal and nuclear allocation is not absolute, and clones within individual clonal clusters show some variability. Shi et al. (2017) also demonstrated that the GABAergic interneurons for the TRN and LGN arise from separate lineages. This is discussed further in Chapter 8 of this volume.

3. Development of Connections between Thalamus and Cortex

3.1 Early Outgrowth from the Thalamus toward the Cortex Encounters Various Sectors of the Diencephalon and Telencephalon

Shortly after thalamic neurogenesis, the first thalamic projections descend to and cross the diencephalic–telencephalic boundary (DTB), enter the internal capsule, and advance laterally through the pallial subpallial boundary (PSPB) (Molnár et al. 2012). Along their path to their final targets, they use various guidance cues. To understand these mechanisms, the cellular and molecular characterization of these domains are required. Some of them underwent great transformations during mammalian evolution (Molnár et al. 2002; Garcia-Moreno and Molnár 2020). Both early thalamocortical and corticofugal projections are guided by other preexisting projections (in the prethalamus and internal capsule) and by migratory paths defined by specific guidepost cells known as *corridor cells* (Mitrofanis et al. 1995; Molnár and Blakemore 1995; Metin and Godement 1996; Lopez-Bendito et al. 2006; Molnár et al. 2012) (Figure 5). Border zones contribute to thalamocortical and corticothalamic guidance in three ways: (1) generating physical boundaries that can be appropriately permissive or restrictive depending on developmental stage; (2) acting as decision points for major trajectory changes; (3) setting up important patterns of guidance molecules. There are numerous mouse mutants where, as a result of the altered gene-expression patterns, the timing, arrangements, and synchronization of guidance mechanisms are perturbed, which

Development

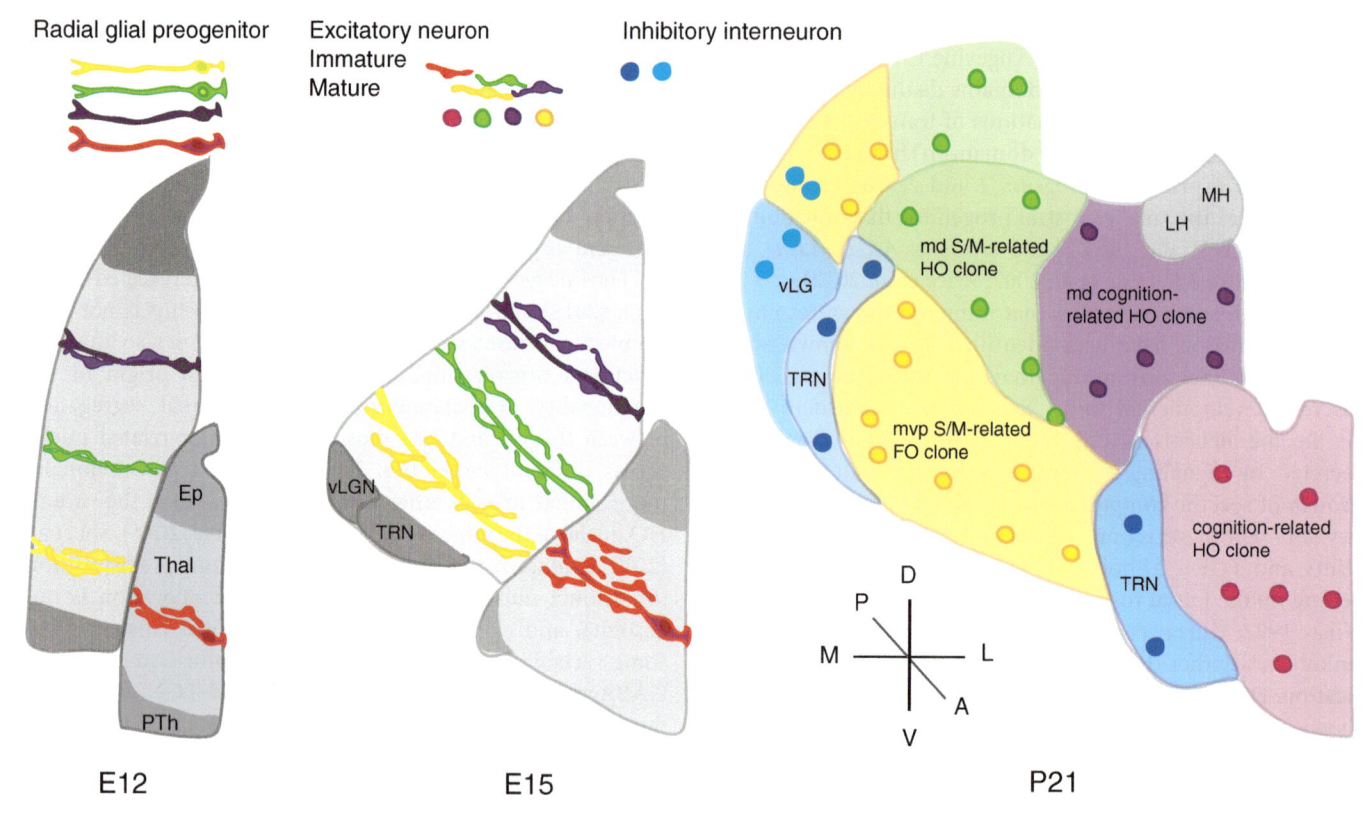

Figure 4 Lineage relationships influence the functional organization of the thalamus.

The inhibitory neurons and neurons contributing to TRN (*blue*) have a separate origin. Schematic representations of thalamic hemispheres containing a mosaic analysis with double markers (MADM)–labeled clones in mice at E12, E15, and P21. Radial progenitors in the thalamic ventricular zone divide to produce a cohort of neuronal progeny (E12–E15). The panels demonstrate the correlation between the ontogenetic origin and emerging organization of thalamic nuclei according to function at P21. *Ep*, epithalamus; *Thal*, thalamus; *PTh*, prethalamus; *TRN*, thalamic reticular nucleus; *vLG*, ventral geniculate nucleus; *MH*, medial habenula; *LH*, lateral habenula; *md*, mediodorsal); *S/M-related*, somatosensory–motor related. Modified from Shi et al. (2017).

leads to abrupt termination or disruption of the developing pathways (Lopez-Bendito et al. 2006). Growing axons get derailed or stall, most commonly at the DTB or PSPB. To what extent those boundaries contribute to the guidance of thalamocortical axonal connections is still under investigation in more refined mouse genetic models where early neuronal populations in these regions are monitored and modulated (Molnár 1998; Molnár et al. 2012; Garcia-Moreno and Molnár 2020; Molnár et al. 2020).

3.2 Guidance Mechanisms for Crossing the Diencephalon–Telencephalon Boundary

The DTB lies anterolaterally to the thalamus and prethalamus (Figure 5). Its genetic-identity boundary is not fully established, and it is identified by nearby anatomical landmarks, including the prethalamus (Lopez-Bendito and Molnár 2003; Garel and Rubenstein 2004; Hanashima et al. 2006). After crossing the DTB, thalamocortical projections turn laterally to enter the internal capsule (E12 in Figure 5). At the same turning points at later stages, the corticothalamic axons (CTAs) reroute dorsally to invade the thalamus, whereas other corticofugal axons (originating from cortical layer 5) initiate their descent through the cerebral peduncle to the brainstem and spinal cord (E18 in the mouse; Mitrofanis and Baker 1993; Mitrofanis and Guillery 1993; Agmon et al. 1995; Lozsadi et al. 1996; Molnár, Adams, and Blakemore 1998; Molnár Adams, Goffinet, et al. 1998; Molnár, Knott, et al. 1998). This region appears important for sorting subpopulations of cortical projections according to their target destination. Disruption of pioneer axons or disruption of co-fasciculation of early corticothalamic projections with thalamic axons prevents CTAs from entering the diencephalon or invading the thalamus correctly (McConnell et al. 1994; Hevner et al. 2002).

Métin and Godement (1996) proposed that the thalamic projections extend along the preexisting pioneer reciprocal projections between the prethalamus and ventral telencephalon in hamsters. Similar arrangements were subsequently found in rat and mouse embryos (Molnár, Adams, and Blakemore 1998; Molnár Adams, Goffinet, et al. 1998; Molnár, Knott, et al. 1998; Braisted et al. 1999; Molnár and Cordery 1999), in a region described by Mitrofanis (1992) as the *perireticular nucleus*. These studies suggested that the ventral telencephalic neurons may belong to the globus pallidus rather than being perireticular cells because perireticular cells were retrogradely labeled from the thalamus in postnatal but not embryonic rats (Mitrofanis and Baker, 1993) and ferrets (Mitrofanis 1994a, 1994b). The spatial and temporal features of the axonal projection of the prethalamus to the dorsal

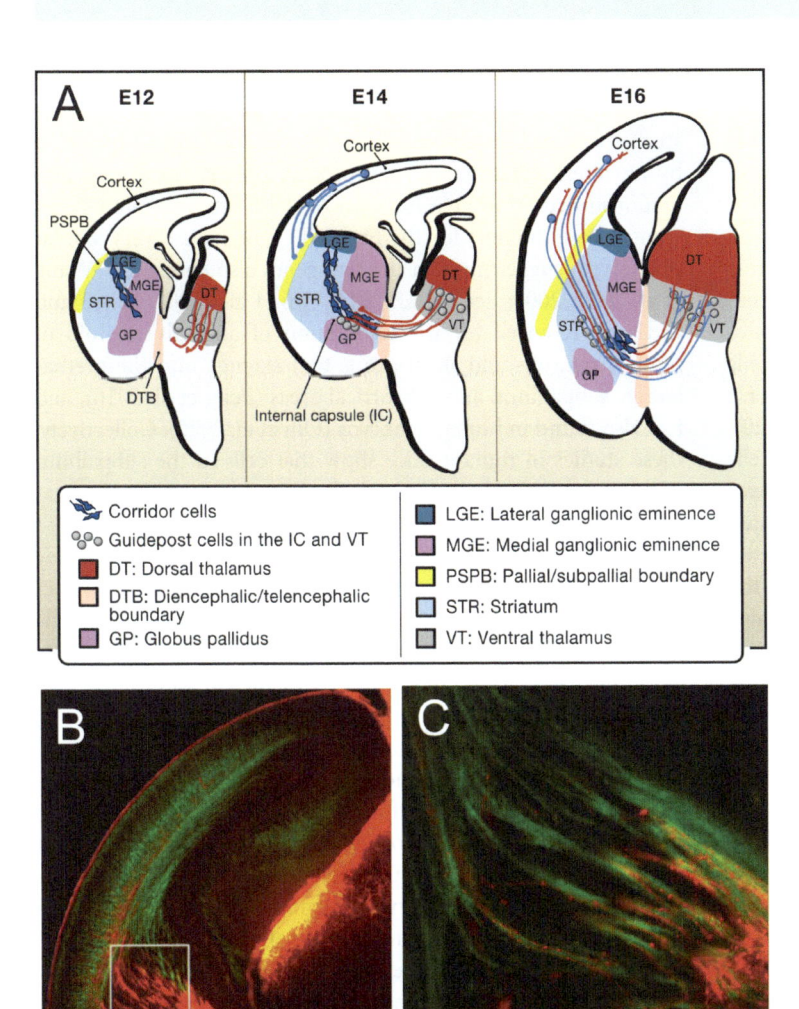

Figure 5 Multiple factors involved in the development of early thalamocortical connectivity.

A. Three stages of the early establishment of reciprocal connections between the dorsal thalamus and cortex in the mouse. At E12–E14, the ventral thalamus (current preferred name is *prethalamus*) and internal capsule contain guidepost cells (*gray*) that already developed projections to the dorsal thalamus (Braisted et al. 2000) and guide the thalamic projections toward the internal capsule through the DTB. Corridor cells (*dark blue*) originate from the lateral ganglionic eminence (LGE) at embryonic day 12 (E12) and migrate tangentially toward the diencephalon, where they form a permissive "corridor" for the thalamic projections (*red*) to navigate through the internal capsule. Perireticular cells have been proposed to regulate the entrance of thalamocortical axons (TCAs) into the subpallium (Metin and Godement 1996; Molnár, Adams, and Blakemore 1998; Molnár Adams, Goffinet, et al. 1998; Molnár, Knott, et al. 1998; Molnár and Cordery 1999; Tuttle et al. 1999), whereas corridor cells orient the internal pathfinding of TCAs inside the medial ganglionic eminence (MGE) (Lopez-Bendito et al. 2006). Subsequently, the early corticothalamic projections guide the thalamic projections through the PSPB as originally proposed in the handshake hypothesis (Molnár and Blakemore 1995).

B and C. Between E14 and E16, the thalamocortical projections reach the PSPB and cross this frontier by associating to the early corticothalamic projections mostly originating from the subplate. Thalamic projections were labeled with DiI (*red*) in an E15 Golli-tau eGFP mouse, where the lower layers 6b and some 6a express GFP (Pinon et al. 2009). The diagrams show the co-fasciculation of the thalamic and early corticofugal projections. The boxed area in panel A is enlarged in panel B. Scale 80 μm and 15μm, respectively. Panel A is from Hanashima et al. (2006); panels B and C are unpublished from the study of Pinon et al. (2009).

thalamus (Braisted et al. 1999, 2009, 2000) are consistent with the idea that this axonal projection, and possibly the cell bodies themselves, may act as a scaffold to guide thalamocortical axons (TCAs) through the developing prethalamus and toward the DTB, as well as other axons in the opposite direction, including the later developing corticothalamic fibers (Mitrofanis 1994a, 1994b). Consistent with this hypothesis, in Ascl1−/− and Pax6−/− embryos where the population of VTel-Th cells appears to be missing, TCAs fail to extend into the ventral telencephalon (VTel) (Tuttle et al. 1999; Bishop et al. 2000; Lopez-Bendito et al. 2002; Pratt et al. 2002; Lakhina et al. 2007). Recent work by Quintana-Urzainqui et al. (2020) demonstrated the importance of the thalamic gene-expression gradients and their responsiveness to guidance queues during early TCA pathfinding. Their study reported thalamocortical projection errors upon disruption of diencephalic development by Pax6 deletion. This mapping error was not due to the disruption of pioneer projections from the prethalamus to the thalamus but, rather, to altered molecular cues in the thalamus itself. The authors suggest that each subset of thalamic axons maintains the expression of the same combination of axon-guidance receptors along the route and therefore shows the same differential chemotactic response when confronting gradients of signaling cues, such as netrin 1 and semaphorin 3a. The responsiveness of the TCAs to guidance molecules seems to be important from these earliest stages of their growth.

3.3 Role of "Corridor" Cells in Delineating the Path of Thalamocortical Axons in the Subpallium

A distinct population of tangentially migrating guidepost cells ("corridor" cells) controls the pathfinding of TCAs within the subpallium (Lopez-Bendito et al. 2006). These cells are GABAergic neurons that originate from the lateral ganglionic eminence (LGE) and migrate into the medial ganglionic eminence (MGE) (from E11.5 to E14), where they form a permissive "corridor" between the proliferative zones of the MGE and the globus pallidus (GP), enabling the growth of TCAs through MGE-derived, nonpermissive cell areas (Figure 5). The nonpermissive nature of this environment is indicated by the fact that thalamic projections fasciculate into large bundles all the way to the PSPB, where they break up into individual fibers (Molnár, Adams, and Blakemore 1998; Molnár Adams, Goffinet, et al. 1998; Molnár, Knott, et al. 1998;). Corridor cells express a membrane-bound isoform of neuregulin-1 (NRG1), whereas TCAs express its receptor ErbB4, thereby creating a permissive environment where they can extend. Interestingly, corridor cells have been conserved during evolution and observed in diverse species (Bielle et al. 2011), including humans (Qin et al. 2020). The relationship between corridor cells and other guidepost cells in the perireticular/internal capsule is still not clear. Perireticular/internal capsule and corridor cells are not located in exactly the same regions; some perireticular cells are in the prethalamus or in its vicinity, whereas corridor cells are in the MGE. Some back-labeled neurons from the thalamus are also found in the corridor and lateral ganglionic eminence, raising the possibility that perireticular and corridor cells may be related (Figure 5). The fate of the corridor cells is also not known. Further analyses are needed to define the molecular nature of back-labeled cells in the internal capsule and thereby reveal whether some corridor cells may settle in that region and act by axon-mediated contact.

The perireticular/internal capsule and corridor cells provide a permissive path for the thalamocortical and corticofugal axons amongst the nonpermissive territory of the subpallium. Moreover, the perireticular and internal capsule cells constitute an intermediate target for these projections (Metin and Godement 1996; Braisted et al. 1999; Garel and Rubenstein 2004). Analyses of mutant mice in which the regionalization and development of the subpallium are affected (Marin 2002) have assessed the relative importance of the LGE and MGE in corticofugal and thalamocortical axon pathfinding. In particular, mutations affecting the development of the LGE, such as in Ebf1 or Gsh1−/−;Gsh2−/− double mutants, severely impair TCA navigation, in contrast to mutations that perturb MGE development, such as in Nkx2.1 mutants (Garel et al. 1999; Sussel et al. 1999; Marin 2002; Yun et al. 2003). Specifically, the GP and the MGE proliferative zones exert repulsive activities that are likely to channel TCAs along an internal route (Lopez-Bendito et al. 2006). Analyses of mice carrying mutations for guidance-cue molecules or their receptors have implicated netrin-1, Slit1, and Slit2 and their receptors Robo1 and Robo2, as well as semaphorin 6A, in the general pathfinding of TCAs in the subpallium (Braisted et al. 2000; Leighton et al. 2001; Bagri et al. 2002; Bonnin et al. 2007; Lopez-Bendito et al. 2007; Powell et al. 2008; Braisted et al. 2009; Little et al. 2009). Members of the protocadherin family play essential roles in TCA guidance and internal capsule formation (Tissir et al. 2005; Uemura et al. 2007; Zhou et al. 2008, 2009). Celsr3, a seven-pass cadherin orthologue of *Drosophila* flamingo, is widely expressed in the mantle of the telencephalon and forebrain. Its inactivation in the subpallium and prethalamus severely impairs the formation of the thalamocortical connections: TCAs stall in the ventral subpallium just after crossing the DTB, whereas corticofugal axons stall in the proximal part of the LGE after crossing the PSPB (Zhou et al. 2008, 2009). These studies revealed an absolute requirement for Celsr3 expression by an intermediate target that acts at a short range and also demonstrated an in vivo function of these intermediate targets. Constitutive mutants for the Frizzled3 gene have a very similar phenotype, suggesting that the two genes also cooperate (Wang et al. 2002, 2006; Feng et al. 2016; Qin et al. 2020). Celsr3 and Fzd3 are required for the elaboration of an early scaffold of pioneer neurons and short axons that extends into the prethalamus, subpallium, and subcortical areas (Feng et al. 2016), and it is also found in human embryos (Qin et al. 2020). Collectively, these studies in mutant mice show that cells in the subpallium express a series of secreted and transmembrane molecules that contribute to TCA pathfinding.

As TCAs travel internally through the subpallium, they spread rostrocaudally in a fan-like manner, allowing distinct TCAs (which are already segregated inside the tract) to navigate toward different cortical areas. Analyses of mouse mutants with anomalies in the development of the subpallium or thalamus showed that the initial thalamocortical topography is largely controlled by information contained within the subpallium, and it is chiefly independent of cortical regionalization (Garel et al. 2002; Dufour et al. 2003; Garel et al. 2003; Seibt et al. 2003; Shimogori et al. 2004). The topographic sorting of presegregated TCAs inside the internal capsule is mediated by complementary gradients of ligand–receptor systems expressed by TCAs and cells in the VTel. Key determinants of initial TCA divergence include ephrinAs/EphAs, netrin-1/DCC/Unc5a–c, class III semaphorins (Sema3s)/neuropilins (Npns), and the L1 family of cell adhesion molecules (L1-CAMs), which specify sorting of distinct TCA contingents (Vanderhaeghen and Polleux 2004; reviewed in Molnár et al. 2012).

3.4 "Handshake" of the Thalamocortical and Corticothalamic Projections Guide Projections through the Pallial–Subpallial Boundary

The PSPB is another key anatomical border zone that CTAs and TCAs encounter along their path (Molnár and Butler 2002). Comparisons of avian, reptilian, and mammalian telencephalic development demonstrated that this region undergoes great changes during evolution (Garcia-Moreno and Molnár 2020). There is a great difference in the relative position of the thalamocortical projections in relation to the subpallium in reptiles and birds (Cordery and Molnár 1999). This transformation at the PSPB may have allowed the increase in thalamocortical reciprocal connectivities in mammals (Molnár and Butler 2002). The PSPB plays a critical role during CTA and TCA development, as shown by studies of numerous mutants with axon-guidance defects at the boundary (Molnár 1998; Lopez-Bendito and Molnár 2003). The PSPB (see Figure 5) represents a graduated overlapping gene-expression domain separating the developing cortex from the striatum (hence its alternative name, the *cortico-striatal boundary*). It is primarily generated and maintained by opposing gradients of

Pax6 and Gsh2 expression: Pax6 is highly expressed in the dorsal pallium, and conversely, Gsh2 is highly expressed in the subpallium (Carney et al. 2009).

Early patterning of the pallium and subpallium by organizer genes, such as Pax6 and Gsh2, determines expression guidance molecules. Pax6 is especially important for the generation of the PSPB. In Pax6 knock-out (KO) mice, the expression of corticofugal guidance cues Netrin-1, Sema3C, and Sema5A is disrupted (Jones 2002). Furthermore, the PSPB may be a temporary physical barrier. Some subpallium-derived cells migrate ventrolaterally along the palisade of radial glia at the PSPB, forming the lateral cortical stream (LCS). This heterogeneous migrating cell population includes Pax6+ pallium-derived and Dlx2+ subpallium-derived cells (Carney et al. 2006, 2009). This lateral migratory stream may generate a physical boundary preventing axons from crossing into the subpallium until appropriate cues or a physical bridge becomes available. Evidence for this hypothesis is provided by studies of the Pax6−/− mouse, where CTAs fail to cross the PSPB and are derailed ventrally and follow the LCS. The fibers that succeed in crossing do so in abnormally large fascicles (Hevner et al. 2002; Jones 2002). Pax6−/− mice have a higher cellular density at the PSPB, suggesting the mutation may enhance a normal anatomical barrier and prevent crossing (Jones 2002; Pinon et al. 2008). This physical barrier may be overcome by time-dependent mechanisms such as axon–axon fasciculation, thus enabling precise temporal control of corticofugal guidance. Indeed, this is supported by work showing thalamic axons require cortical axons in order to cross the PSPB (Chen et al. 2012; Molnár et al. 2012). The PSPB is an important decision point where early corticofugal projections turn sharply from their original ventrolateral trajectory to a medial one to enter the subpallium (Agmon et al. 1995; Molnár and Cordery 1999).

TCAs encounter the PSPB just before reaching the cerebral cortex. When thalamic axons approach the pallium (E13 in mouse; GW 10–11 in human), the PSPB has developed a striking cell-dense radial glial palisade perpendicular to the trajectory of TCAs (Chapouton et al. 2001; Carney et al. 2006, 2009; Krsnik et al. 2017). It has been suggested that these features make this region hostile to the passage of thalamic axons. Pioneer descending corticofugal axons arrive at the PSPB before the thalamic axons (E12 in mouse; GW 11.5–13 in human) and may be needed and assist TCAs to cross the otherwise-hostile PSPB (Molnár, Adams, and Blakemore 1998; Molnár Adams, Goffinet, et al. 1998; Molnár, Knott, et al. 1998; Molnár and Butler 2002).

In the reeler mouse, the SP scaffold originates from the superplate, from the surface of the cerebral cortex, and thalamocortical projections travel through the cortical plate in close association with this scaffold (Molnár, Adams, and Blakemore 1998; Molnár Adams, Goffinet, et al. 1998; Molnár, Knott, et al. 1998;). The thalamocortical projections follow the developmental algorithm but in relation to the displaced SP cells. The TCA defects observed in some mutant mice might be explained by the breakdown of that interaction (Molnár, Adams, and Blakemore 1998; Molnár Adams, Goffinet, et al. 1998; Molnár, Knott, et al. 1998; Hevner et al. 2002; Jones 2002; Lopez-Bendito et al. 2002; Lopez-Bendito and Molnár 2003; Dwyer et al. 2011). The "handshake hypothesis" of Molnár and Blakemore (1995) has been tested with conditional mutagenesis both in vivo and in co-culture organotypic slices. A block of corticofugal axonal development, without disruption of the thalamus, subpallium, or PSPB, is observed in Emx1Cre;APCloxP/loxP mutants (Chen et al. 2012). In those animals, thalamic axons still progress within the subpallium in topographic order, yet they fail to cross the PSPB. By providing evidence against alternative explanations and by showing that replacement of mutant cortex with control cortex restored corticofugal efferents and allowed thalamic axons from conditional mutants to cross the PSPB, this work provided the most compelling evidence to date that cortical efferents are required to guide TCAs across the PSPB, even though the molecular mechanisms involved require further investigation. These studies are aided by our better understanding of cortical and thalamic gene-expression patterns (Osheroff and Hatten 2009; Oeschger et al. 2012).

3.5 The First Interactions of Thalamocortical Axons with Cortical Subplate

Thalamocortical projections arrive at the telencephalon in a ventro-dorsal and antero-posterior temporal progression, in a topographically organized fashion. At this stage, the preplate is already split into the SP and marginal zone by the migrating cortical plate neurons (Molnár, Adams, Goffinet, et al. 1998). Thalamic axons accumulate below the cortex prior to the birth of the majority of cortical neurons and before their migration is complete (Rakic 1976; Shatz and Luskin 1986). At the peak of cortical neurogenesis and neuronal migration, the germinative and intermediate zones undergo highly dynamic changes. The compartment of still-migrating cortical cells, the cortical plate, is increasing in thickness, and new cells are added to it in an inside-first and outside-last fashion. The SP below the cortical plate is generated earliest and provides a relatively stable platform in the developing cortex during this period (Marin-Padilla 1971; Lund et al. 1977; De Carlos and O'Leary 1992; Kostovic 2020). The SP contains the earliest postmigratory, mature neurons that develop functional synapses (Molliver and Van der Loos 1970; Kostovic and Rakic 1990; Friauf and Shatz 1991; Higashi et al. 2001; Kostovic 2020; Molnár et al. 2020). Once they reach the telencephalon, the ingrowing thalamocortical projections accumulate in the SP before reaching their final target in the cortical plate. The time spent by TCAs within the SP (so-called waiting period) varies considerably among species and underwent a great protraction during evolution within the primate lineage (from one day in the mouse to a few weeks in primates) (Rakic 1976; Shatz and Luskin 1986; Catalano et al. 1991; Molnár, Adams, Goffinet, et al. 1998).

From the time of arrival, thalamic projections form synapses with SP neurons. This was recorded by current source density (CSD) and optical recording in rat thalamocortical slices (Friauf et al. 1990; Higashi et al. 2002; Molnár et al. 2003). As shown in Figure 6, sustained depolarization indicating postsynaptic responses appears in SP cells before the thalamic projections enter the cortical plate. These responses are blocked upon application of both α-amino-3-hydroxy-5-methyl-4-isoxazolepropionic acid (AMPA)/kainite receptor antagonist 6,7-dinitroquinoxaline-2,3-dione (DNQX) and N-methyl-D-aspartate (NMDA) receptor antagonist (APV) (Higashi et al. 2002). The pattern of these responses changes rapidly: they extend to the entire thickness of the cortical plate before birth, and the elicited depolarization strengthens after birth, with a columnar organization apparent from P2 and more confined to layers 4 and 6 by P10 (Higashi et al. 2002). There is sustained depolarization within the anlage of the globus pallidus and putamen, but it is currently not known whether the perireticular and internal capsule neurons are involved in these responses (Higashi et al. 2002).

3.6 Earliest Thalamocortical Connectivity Is Established in an Autonomous Fashion

The initial matching between the cells in the three-dimensional volume of the thalamus to the two-dimensional sheet of the cerebral cortex is established before the thalamic projections enter the cortical plate (Molnár, Adams, and Blakemore 1998; Molnár Adams, Goffinet, et al. 1998; Molnár, Knott, et al. 1998;). Labeling experiments with multiple carbocyanine dyes in the cortex showed that an anteroposterior direction along the convexity of the cortex resulted in a mediolateral direction of distribution of back-labeled thalamic neurons, and a ventrodorsal direction along the cortex corresponded to an anteroposterior direction of distribution of back-labeled

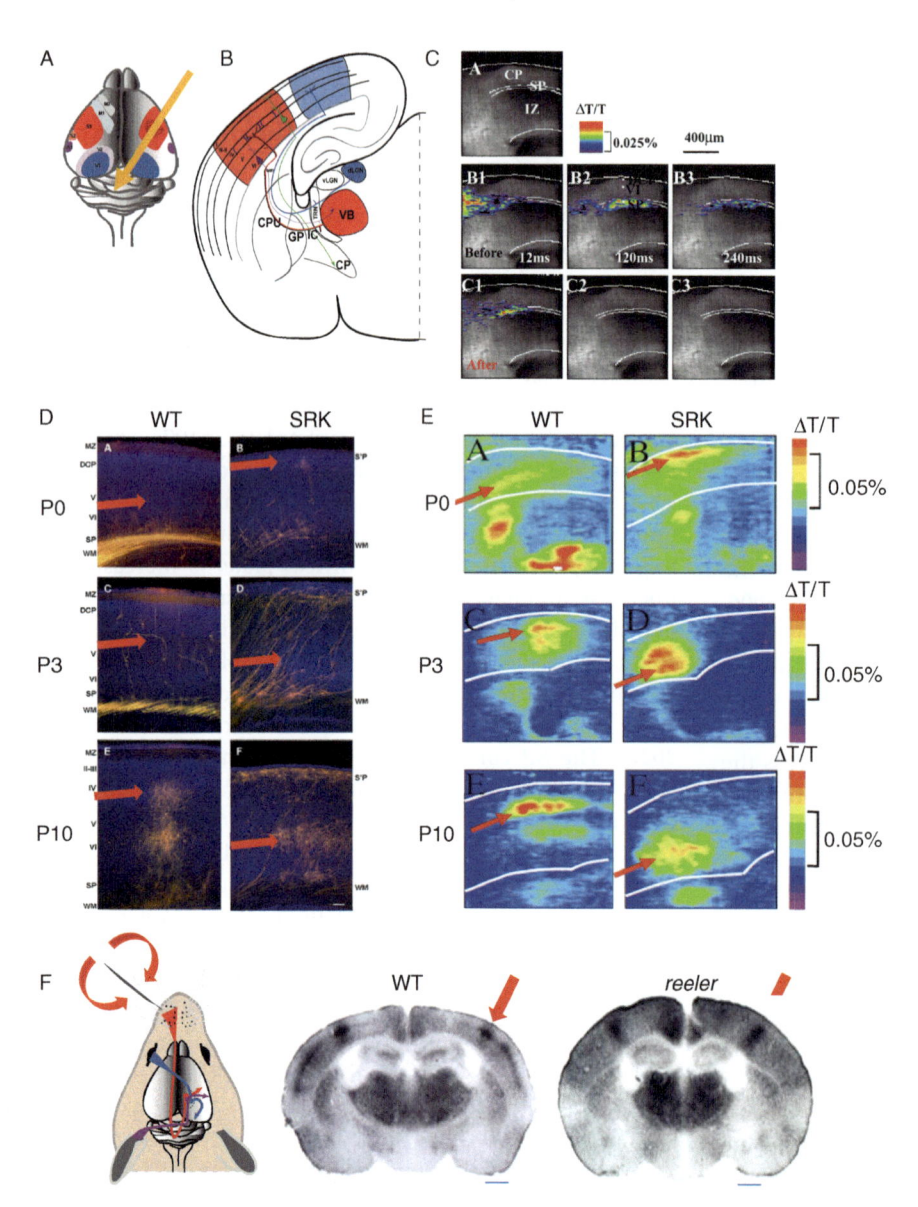

Figure 6 Inversion of the neurogenic gradient alters the thalamocortical targeting and sequence of development but still produces normal areal activation in the adult.

A and B. Schematic representation of the preparation of the thalamocortical slices based on Agmon and Connors (1991).

C. The earliest sustained activation patterns revealed with optical recording with voltage-sensitive dyes in the subplate of embryonic WT rat primary somatosensory cortex after thalamic stimulation in thalamocortical slice preparations. A frame of the recording was selected at the peak of the response (time in milliseconds) viewed with ×4 objectives on the Fuji Deltaron 1700 image-acquisition system. The lower row indicates the image obtained under similar conditions, after the bath application of DNQX and APV. Short depolarizations, probably representing spikes, reach the cortex by E17. The sustained, long-lasting depolarization (up to 240 ms) was blocked with a cocktail of glutamate receptor antagonists. Adapted from Higashi et al. (2002).

D. In the "reeler"-type rat mutant, Shaking Rat Kawasaki (SRK), the thalamocortical projections first target the superplate and then develop branches in the region that is equivalent to layer 4 following the same pattern of algorithms as in WT, but in relation to the displaced cells. From Molnár et al. (2006).

E. The activation pattern follows the same pattern as the thalamic fibers in WT and SRK. First, the sustained depolarization, corresponding to postsynaptic responses, appears in the SP. There is also sustained depolarization within the anlage of the globus pallidus and putamen. All of these are blocked after the application of DNQX and APV (not shown). At postnatal ages, the response is stronger than at prenatal stages, and periphery-related columnar patterning was apparent from P2, which is refined to layers 4 and 6 by P10. Figure based on Higashi et al. (2002) from Molnár et al. (2006).

F. Single- or double-row stimulation combined with [14C]-2-deoxyglucose–uptake methodology (Zhang et al. 2003) revealed normal areal activation in the primary somatosensory cortex on coronal sections of the WT and reeler mouse mutant (Bronchti, Welker and Molnár, 1999, unpublished).

neurons (Molnár, Adams, and Blakemore 1998; Molnár Adams, Goffinet, et al. 1998; Molnár, Knott, et al. 1998; Molnár et al. 2012). At early stages, most thalamocortical projections are still in the intermediate zone and SP, below the cortical plate. These early connections are rearranged and redefined before the final innervation pattern of the cortical plate is achieved. TCAs initially overshoot their targets and develop transient side branches in the intermediate zone and SP on the more proximal segments of their path through delayed branching (Naegele et al. 1988). These side branches extend over considerable distances and have been considered to be the anatomical substrate for the rearrangements of cortical maps during normal development (Molnár, Adams, and Blakemore 1998; Molnár Adams, Goffinet, et al. 1998; Molnár, Knott, et al. 1998; Molnár 2000). Early manipulations of gene expression or cortical lesions can substantially rearrange the thalamocortical topography at these early stages, and these extended side branches could be involved (Huffman et al. 1999; Shimogori et al. 2005). However, the mechanisms that guide the thalamic projections and initiate their accumulation below the cortical plate are considered to be largely autonomous (Price et al. 2006; Molnár et al. 2020). Studies in mice that lack the ability to release synaptic vesicles in an organized fashion (Snap25 or Munc13 knocked out) suggest that the early ingrowth of the thalamic axons does not depend on neuronal communication through regulated or spontaneous vesicular release (Molnár et al. 2002; Blakey et al. 2012; Hoerder-Suabedissen et al. 2018) but that later, an activity-dependent mechanism may start to dominate (Catalano and Shatz 1998; Molnár et al. 2002; Uesaka et al. 2006, 2007; Yamada et al. 2010) (Figure 7).

3.7 Thalamic Axon Innervation of the Subplate and Cortical Plate and Emergence of Areal Differences in Thalamocortical Topographic Organization

The organization of thalamocortical afferents changes during normal development and can be altered through (i) manipulations of the early guidance mechanisms in the subpallium (Bonnin et al. 2007), (ii) manipulations of the early cortical regionalization, or (iii) changing the flow of sensory input from the sense organs (Garel et al. 2003; Rash and Grove 2006; O'Leary and Sahara 2008; Molnár et al. 2020). Although the subpallium controls the early guidance of TCAs, cortical regionalization, which is controlled by the morphogen FGF8 and gradients of TFs (Pax6, COUP-TFI, Emx2, and Sp8), is sufficient to reorient the thalamocortical map within the neocortex. Areal differences in the density, topographic precision, and maturity of thalamocortical projections (Molnár, Adams, and Blakemore 1998; Molnár Adams, Goffinet, et al. 1998; Molnár, Knott, et al. 1998;) are particularly visible as the TCAs move from the SP to innervate the cortical plate. Similar carbocyanine dye injected into the primary somatosensory cortex labels 2–5 times more thalamic projection neurons that are tightly segregated into two back-labeled groups of thalamic neurons in the VB than similar pairs of crystal placements into the primary visual cortex, which reveal a smaller number of, but more scattered and intermingled, thalamic neuronal populations (Agmon et al. 1993; Molnár, Adams, and Blakemore 1998). The deployment and initial entry of thalamocortical projections to the SP zone is considerably modified as the TCAs enter the cortical plate in cortical areas, such as V1 of rodents (Naegele et al. 1988; Krug et al. 1998; Ravary et al. 2003), whereas the topography of TCAs is essentially established immediately after entry into the primary somatosensory cortex in the mouse (Agmon et al. 1993, 1995). The period during which rearrangements can be obtained via sensory manipulation varies considerably in visual and somatosensory cortical areas, which we shall discuss in the plasticity section. Rearrangement in the organization of these early thalamocortical connections can be obtained by manipulating the expression gradients of patterning genes such as FGF8. Altering early cortical FGF8 expression patterns imposes shifts or even two opposing cortical gradients, with corresponding shifts and duplications of thalamocortical projections (Shimogori and Grove 2005), whereas changes in Pax6 gradients in the cortex fail to elicit substantial changes in thalamocortical topography (Pinon et al. 2008). FGF8 gradient alterations can lead to duplication of the thalamic input from the same VP nucleus into multiple areas.

As they first accumulate in the SP, TCAs develop additional branches within this region and interact functionally with SP neurons. This synaptic interaction eventually orchestrates the TCAs' invasion of the cortical plate in the appropriate manner (Allendoerfer and Shatz 1994; Kanold and Luhmann 2010; Kostovic 2020). The transient circuits between SP neurons, thalamic afferents, and layer 4 neurons are now widely recognized as constituting a key mechanism for early circuit formation (Allendoerfer and Shatz 1994; Kanold and Luhmann 2010; Hoerder-Suabedissen and Molnár 2015; Kostovic 2020; Molnár et al. 2020). SP neurons integrate into the cortical circuits in an age-specific and area-specific dynamic fashion (Little et al. 2009; Hoerder-Suabedissen and Molnár 2012; Tolner et al. 2012; Viswanathan et al. 2012; Molnár et al. 2020) (Figure 8). Changing or ablating the sensory input to the barrel field of the primary somatosensory cortex around birth can change the stage-specific rearrangement of the SP projections within the somatosensory cortex (Little et al. 2009). Initially (P0–P4), these projections target the marginal zone, then layer 4 within the barrel, but by P8–10, they retract to the layer 4–5 boundary within the barrel and remain in layer 4 in the septa. Altering the whisker pattern can alter this rearrangement of SP projections, indicating that there is a dynamic interplay between thalamic afferents, the SP, and layer 4 neurons. The recognition of the ultimate target neurons within layer 4 relies on multiple cellular and molecular mechanisms. Thalamocortical projections recognize layer 4 neurons in organotypic co-cultures even if they lose their ability to

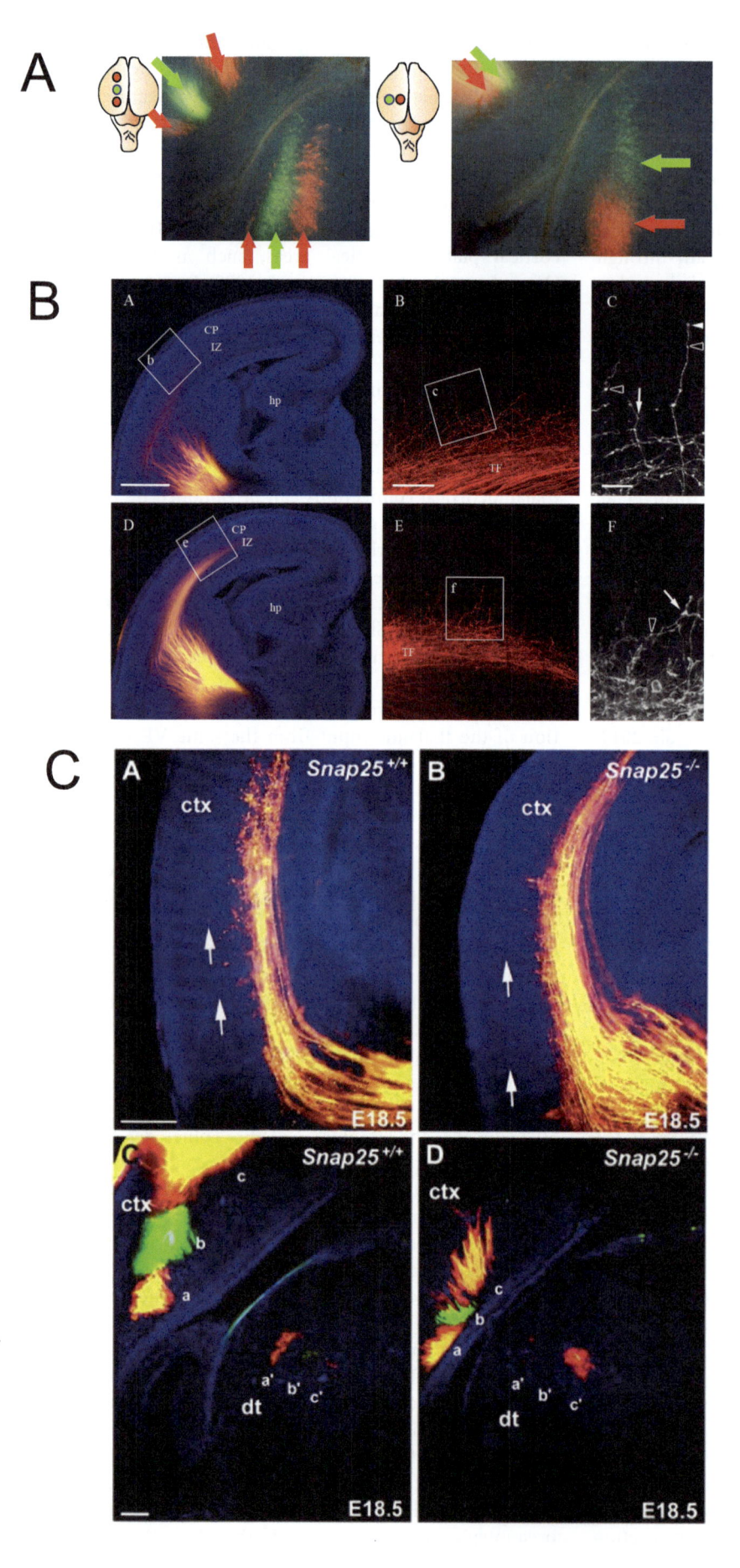

Figure 7. The early basic topography of thalamocortical projections is established at the time of fiber arrival to the cortex (A), and it does not depend on synaptic vesicular release demonstrated in the Munc13-1,2,3 triple KO (B) and in the Snap25 KO (C) using anterograde and retrograde carbocyanine dye tracing.

A. Placement of carbocyanine dyes into the embryonic cortex in an anteroposterior or ventrodorsal fashion and back-labeled thalamic projection neurons in mediolateral and anteroposterior fashion, respectively (Molnár, Adams, and Blakemore 1998).

B. Fiber outgrowth and accumulation in the SP of the early innervation of the cortex does not require regulated synaptic vesicular release, as demonstrated in Munc13-1,2,3 triple KO at E18.5 (Blakey 2007). Thalamic projections were revealed with carbocyanine dye injected into the dorsal thalamus. Coronal sections reveal the layering using bisbenzimide counterstain (*blue*) and the DiI labeling (*orange/red*). Thalamic axons traverse the internal capsule as an organized array of fiber bundles, then defasciculate and turn dorsally to extend through the intermediate zone and SP below the cortical plate. Boxed areas are enlarged to the right. There is no noticeable difference between Munc13-1,2,3$^{+/+}$ (*upper row in panel B*) and Munc13-1,2,3$^{-/-}$ (*lower row*) brains in the state of advancement (*arrows*) and branch formation of thalamocortical fibers.

C. Similar results were obtained in the E18.5 Snap25+/+ (*left*) and Snap25–/– (*right*) brains for thalamocortical fiber invasion (*upper row*) and cortical targeting (*lower row*). Thalamic axons were revealed from multiple anteroposterior carbocyanine dye placements into the cortex at E18.5. Posterior cortical crystal placement (a) revealed a group of cells in the lateral thalamus (a′), whereas progressively more anterior crystal placements (b, c) labeled more medial thalamic regions (b′, c′). The pattern was identical in wild-type and mutants. Scale bar: 200 m. Figure is based on Molnár et al. (2002).

Development of the Thalamocortical Systems

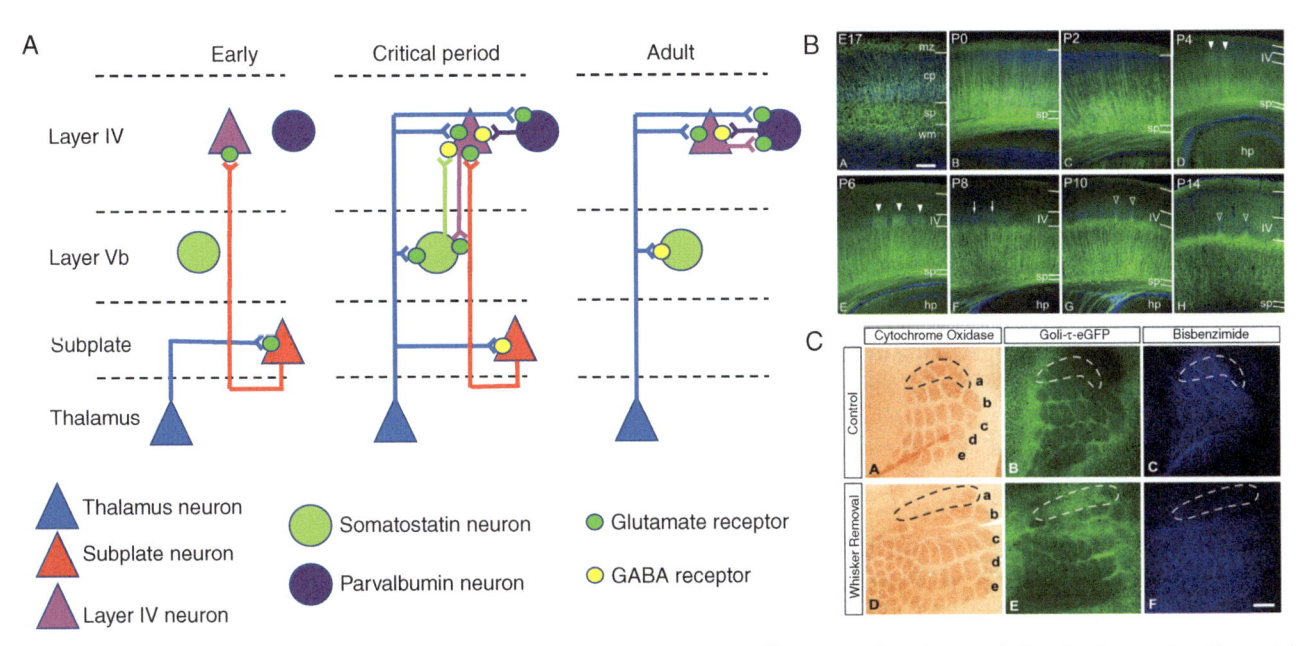

Figure 8 SP neurons integrate into the developing cerebral cortex in a stage-specific manner that changes during development and is modulated by sensory input.

A. Diagram illustrating the changing pattern of thalamocortical ingrowth, SP neurons, and GABAergic neurons during development and in the adult. In the earliest phase of thalamocortical circuit establishment, SP neurons (*white triangle*) receive inputs from the thalamus and project axons to layer 4. At the onset of the critical period, both SP neurons and the thalamus project to layer 4. In the adult, SP neurons have been eliminated by programmed cell death, and layer 4 neurons receive inputs directly from the thalamus (adapted from Kanold 2009). This classical view has been augmented by the inclusion of GABA-ergic layer 5b interneurons, which have been demonstrated to contribute to thalamocortical circuitry development in somatosensory mouse cortex (Marques-Smith et al. 2016; Tuncdemir et al. 2016). Figure adapted from (Millar et al. 2017).

B. Sections through the developing barrel cortex of the Golli-tau-eGFP (GTE) mouse at ages E17–P14 (A–H). GFP neurites are shown in green and the bisbenzimide nuclear counterstain in blue. GFP-labeled neurites extend radially toward the pial surface from cell bodies situated in the SP and, to a lesser extent, in the cortical plate (layer 6). By P4 and P6, GFP-positive fibers cluster in layer 4, but subsequently, this pattern is changed by the retraction of the GFP-labeled neurites from the hollows of layer 4. Filled arrowheads in D and E indicate intra-barrel GFP densities; arrows in F indicate barrel septa; open arrowheads in G and H indicate inter-barrel GFP concentration. From (Pinon et al. 2009).

C. Age-specific rearrangement of the GFP-positive neurites and the effect of whisker removal at birth. The initially homogeneous distribution of SP neurites changes to hollow, then to septa by P10. However, the effect of neonatal removal of a row of whiskers alters the neurite patterning in the P10 barrel cortex. Bright-field and fluorescence micrographs comparing the two barrel cortices in the tangential sections of a Golli-tau-eGFP mouse at P10. Upper panels are from the control side (ipsilateral to the whisker removal), and lower panels are from the same mouse contralateral to the whisker ablation from row "a" at P0. Dashed rings encircle the row "a" region of the barrel cortex. Scale bar 300 m. From Pinon et al. (2009).

release synaptic vesicles in a regulated fashion (Molnár and Blakemore 1991; Blakey et al. 2012; Yamamoto et al. 2012). In addition to SP neurons, layer 5b somatostatin+ GABAergic neurons also form transient projections that are important for the consolidation of layer-specific thalamic input (Marques-Smith et al. 2016; Tuncdemir et al. 2016) (Figure 8).

4. Development of Connections from Cortex to Thalamus

4.1 Complexities of the Adult Corticothalamic Inputs Arise during Development

In adult mammals, the corticothalamic inputs outnumber the inputs from the sensory periphery by 10 to 1 (Sherman and Guillery 1996). The anatomical and physiological properties of CTAs and their synapses have distinctive characteristics (Usrey and Sherman 2019). Corticothalamic projections arise from three cortical layers (5, 6a, and 6b), and they all have different targeting, anatomical, and physiological properties. Layer 5 projection neurons provide feedforward "driver inputs" to the HO thalamic nuclei, which do not receive direct input from the sensory periphery (Reichova et al. 2004; Sherman and Guillery 2013; Sherman 2016). Driver input is provided to FO thalamic nuclei by sensory afferents (Sherman and Guillery 1996) (Figure 1). Layer 6 provides "modulator inputs" to all thalamic nuclei, with their synapses occupying roughly 40–50% of the total contacts formed onto relay cells (Sherman and Guillery 1996; Reichova et al. 2004; Usrey and Sherman 2019). Subtypes of layer 6b projections provide selective input to HO thalamic nuclei. These form small boutons in the thalamus, but they do not provide collaterals to the thalamic reticular nucleus, and they have specificity according to their cortical origin (Hoerder-Suabedissen et al. 2018). How does this complex corticothalamic innervation pattern develop? Exploring these questions revealed that corticothalamic projections accumulate in compartments that are close to the thalamus, possibly in the perireticular and reticular nucleus of the thalamus. This is similar to the thalamocortical projections that accumulate close to the cortex in the SP. As we discussed in Figure 1, these regions are ideally situated to allow rearrangements and transformations during the waiting period.

4.2 Early Outgrowth of Corticothalamic Projections

The earliest corticothalamic projections toward the thalamus emerge from the first postmitotic neurons that form the preplate, around embryonic day E10. They form before the newly born cortical neurons have left the intermediate zone (between the germinal zone and cortical plate) (Noctor et al. 2004; Lickiss et al. 2012). Preplate neurite extension proceeds laterally, medially, rostrally, or caudally, depending on TF expression. Ctip2 is highly expressed in laterally projecting corticofugals, with complementary high Satb2 expression in callosal projections (Molyneaux et al. 2007; Fishell and Hanashima 2008). These corticofugal projections extend through the intermediate zone, deep to the cortex, until they reach the lateral internal capsule between E13 and E15.5 (Auladell et al. 2000; Jacobs et al. 2007). The lateral fibers arrive first and briefly pause until dorsally derived fibers have grown the extra distance (De Carlos and O'Leary 1992; Molnár and Cordery 1999). From E13, these projections resume extension, cross the (PSPB), and enter the internal capsule. They reach the DTB around E15 before entering the prethalamus, where they encounter the cells of the PRN and TRN at E16. Here, there is a second pause in their progression until E17.5 (Molnár and Cordery 1999; Jacobs et al. 2007). During this pause, the heterogeneous corticofugal projections are "sorted" and separated, with some then continuing to the cerebral peduncle (layer 5) and others entering the thalamus (layer 6 and layer 5 collaterals). The site of this sorting lies within the PRN and TRN (Mitrofanis and Guillery, 1993).

4.3 Early Transient Circuits before Corticothalamic Innervation

The development and behavior of corticofugal projections have been studied using labeling methods, time-lapse videomicroscopy, and transgenic mouse lines that express reporter genes in subtypes of cortical neurons (Grant et al. 2012, 2016). Shatz and Rakic (1981) demonstrated with orthogradely transported tritiated proline injected into the occipital cortex of fetal rhesus monkeys that the development of corticofugal projections is synchronous with the development of thalamocortical pathways and that the corticofugal projections from V1 accumulate outside the LGN for a protracted period (Shatz and Rakic 1981). They proposed that the "waiting period" for the corticothalamic projections outside the thalamus is similar, analogous to the waiting period of thalamocortical projections as they arrive below the cortex (Rakic 1976; Allendoerfer and Shatz 1994). The exact timing and pattern of the early SP, layer 6, and layer 5 fibers projecting subcortically and entering the thalamus have been explored with various reporter gene–expressing mouse lines (Grant et al. 2016; Hoerder-Suabedissen et al. 2018, 2019), but the earliest stages are still not fully established. Clascá and colleagues observed that in spite of the early outgrowth from the SP toward the thalamus, in ferrets, the earliest projections that invade the thalamus originate from layer 5 (Clascá et al. 1995). They suggested that fibers slow down or wait in the intermediate zone or lateral internal capsule. Using carbocyanine dye tracing from various points of the telencephalon and diencephalon, the thalamic reticular nucleus was also proposed as a possible waiting compartment (Molnár and Cordery 1999; Grant et al. 2012). Cortical stimulation can elicit sustained depolarization in the thalamic reticular nucleus at early postnatal stages (Grant et al. 2012). Analysis of the distribution of these mixed corticofugal projections demonstrated two waiting periods, the first as the fiber front reaches the lateral internal capsule and the second as it arrives at the DTB. These tau-eGFP fibers that originate from layers 6 and 6b enter the thalamus in a clear temporal sequence, depending on the thalamic nucleus to be innervated (Grant et al. 2012). However, it has been debated whether subplate projections ever enter the dorsal thalamus at all (Allendoerfer and Shatz 1994). Work on the subpopulation of layer 6b (Drd1a-cre) neurons that represent the remnants of subplate neurons demonstrated selective innervation of the HO thalamic nuclei in the adult, but the development has not been studied yet (Hoerder-Suabedissen et al. 2018).

4.4 The Role of Spontaneous and Sensory-Driven Activity in the Development of Early Thalamocortical Connectivity

Spontaneous activity is a general feature of developing nervous systems in all animals studied so far, including the zebrafish (Zhang et al. 2010), the mouse (Ackman et al. 2012), the rat (Colonnese and Khazipov 2010), and humans (Colonnese et al. 2010; Kirkby and Feller 2013). Spontaneous activity patterns were initially demonstrated in the visual system. Maffei and Galli-Resta (1990) observed that intrinsic activity in the form of spontaneous waves is present in the retina, prior to eye opening, before any visual experience. Subsequently, it was demonstrated that retinal axons make mature synapses that can transmit spontaneous waves from the retina to the dLGN at birth (Mooney et al. 1996; Ackman et al. 2012), and at the same time, thalamic projections are able to elicit long-lasting sustained depolarization in the developing cortex (Higashi et al. 2002). There are different forms of spontaneous waves: embryonic calcium waves mediated by gap junctions, waves mediated by cholinergic transmission from birth, and waves mediated by glutamatergic transmission from P10 (Feller et al. 1996; Syed et al. 2004; Firth et al. 2005; Ackman et al. 2012). Spontaneous calcium waves have been associated with the refinement of sensory pathways (Ackman et al. 2012). The activity-dependent regulation of TCA sprouting is mediated by receptors such as DCC and Robo1 (Mire et al. 2012; Castillo-Paterna et al. 2015).

Several lines of evidence indicated that spontaneous retinal activity is essential for eye-specific segregation and the formation of ocular dominance columns. Blocking spontaneous waves by tetrodotoxin (TTX) intraocular injections in cats (Shatz and Stryker 1988) as well as epibatidine administration in ferrets (Penn et al. 1998) disturbed eye-specific and ocular dominance column segregation and caused an increase of receptive field size in the visual cortex (Huberman et al. 2006). Majdan and Shatz (2006) explored gene-expression changes in the visual cortex of mice after monocular enucleation at various developmental stages. The downregulated genes included brain-derived neurotropic factor (BDNF), the early growth factors (Egr) 1 and 2, and the transcription factor Fos, many of which are regulated by the MAPK signaling pathway (Majdan and Shatz 2006). Binocular enucleation experiments in mice showed downregulation in the expression of ephrinA5 in the enucleated dLGN (Dye et al. 2012). Genetic ablation of retinal ganglion cells (RGCs) also induced differential expression of Adamts metalloproteinases in the deprived dLGN, indicating a role of retinal activity in the gene expression of dLGN (Brooks et al. 2013).

5. Plasticity of Thalamocortical Connectivity

5.1 Sensory Induced Plasticity of Thalamocortical Connectivity

Sensory experience is essential in shaping the structural and functional connectivity in the cortex. The sensory afferents reach the thalamus after some of the circuits have already been established. For instance, retinal projections reach the dLGN at E14–E16, when the early thalamocortical connections have already formed (see Figure 7A). Therefore, sensory afferents join thalamocortical circuits that are partially established independently of external stimuli in an autonomous fashion (Molnár and Blakemore 1995; Molnár et al. 2020). Later in development, these early connections and representations change depending on peripheral stimuli, thus exhibiting their intrinsic "plasticity." The plastic nature of the thalamocortical and corticothalamic projections has been demonstrated in various models where, upon peripheral deprivation, such as deafness or blindness, processing of inputs corresponding to the remaining modalities increased to compensate for the loss of the other sense (Huberman et al. 2008; Thompson et al. 2016). This phenomenon is known as *cross-modal plasticity* (Figure 9B).

In addition to cross-modal plasticity, sensory deprivation induces changes in the corticothalamic projections. Layer 5 projections that normally innervate the HO thalamic nuclei now innervate the FO thalamic nuclei that no longer receive peripheral sensory input. This form of plasticity was termed *cross-hierarchical corticothalamic plasticity* (Grant et al. 2016; Giasafaki et al., 2022; Horvath et al., 2022). Both forms of plasticity were detected in the visual cortex following visual deprivation and were suggested to arise through enhancement of cortical intermodal connections, unmasking of already-existent cortical connections, and sprouting of novel cortical connections (Bavelier and Neville 2002; Pascual-Leone et al. 2005). Plasticity may also arise through sprouting of corticofugal projections from layer 5 driver inputs to additional thalamic nuclei (Grant et al. 2012, 2016)(Figure 9C).

5.2 Cross-Modal Plasticity of Thalamocortical Connectivity

Cross-modal plasticity is defined by the ability of a particular sensory system to be influenced by the activation/modulation of another sensory modality. For example, cross-modality plasticity has been demonstrated in visually deprived animals after enucleation at birth or congenital blindness, with the visual cortex becoming activated by auditory or somatosensory stimuli (Toldi et al. 1994; Rauschecker 1995; Toldi et al. 1996; Yaka et al. 1999; Negyessy et al. 2000; Bronchti et al. 2002; Izraeli et al. 2002; Chabot et al. 2007; Piche et al. 2007). Charbonneau et al. (2012) provided evidence of direct projections from auditory and somatosensory cortices to V1 in visually deprived mice, both congenitally anophthalmic and perinatally enucleated (Charbonneau et al. 2012). Strikingly, auditory stimuli were found to activate the occipital cortex and dorsal lateral geniculate nucleus in the blind mole rat (Bronchti et al. 1989). Laramee et al. (2014) also revealed a disorganization of projections from V1 to the corpus callosum and extrastriate areas in the blind mole rat. Cross-modal plasticity has also been investigated at the level of the thalamus. Sur and colleagues used "rerouting surgery" in juvenile ferrets by removing the cochlea and inferior colliculus and inducing retinal fibers to project to the MGN in addition to the dLGN (Sur et al. 1988; Roe et al. 1992; Angelucci et al. 1997, 1998). Gene-expression analysis showed that the rewired MGN had a transcriptional profile similar to the control dLGN, indicating that peripheral input can influence the modality-specific gene expression of an FO thalamic nucleus (Horng et al. 2009). Furthermore, in adult congenitally blind mice, ascending somatosensory projections innervate and arborize into the dLGN (Asanuma and Stanfield 1990).

The influence of spontaneous activity on the formation of the thalamocortical circuits starts early. In mice, neonatal binocular enucleation alters the expression of genes involved in the establishment of cortical maps at P10, a stage when sensory experience has not started (Dye et al. 2012). Neonatal enucleations in rats resulted in increased barrel size in the whisker representation of the primary somatosensory cortex, indicating cross-modal plasticity between the visual and somatosensory systems before active sensory whisking occurs (Fetter-Pruneda et al. 2013). These experience-independent mechanisms of cross-modal plasticity might be induced by spontaneous activity through changes in the propagation of retinal waves, which are involved in the regulation of cortical arealization before the onset of sensory experience (Huberman et al. 2006; Espinosa and Stryker 2012). Moreno-Juan et al. (2017) demonstrated changes in gene expression and TCA sprouting in the highly reorganized somatosensory cortex as early as P4. The same results were also shown following the silencing of thalamic spontaneous retinal waves, which induced alterations in the size of primary cortical areas prior to sensory experience (Moreno-Juan et al. 2017).

Development

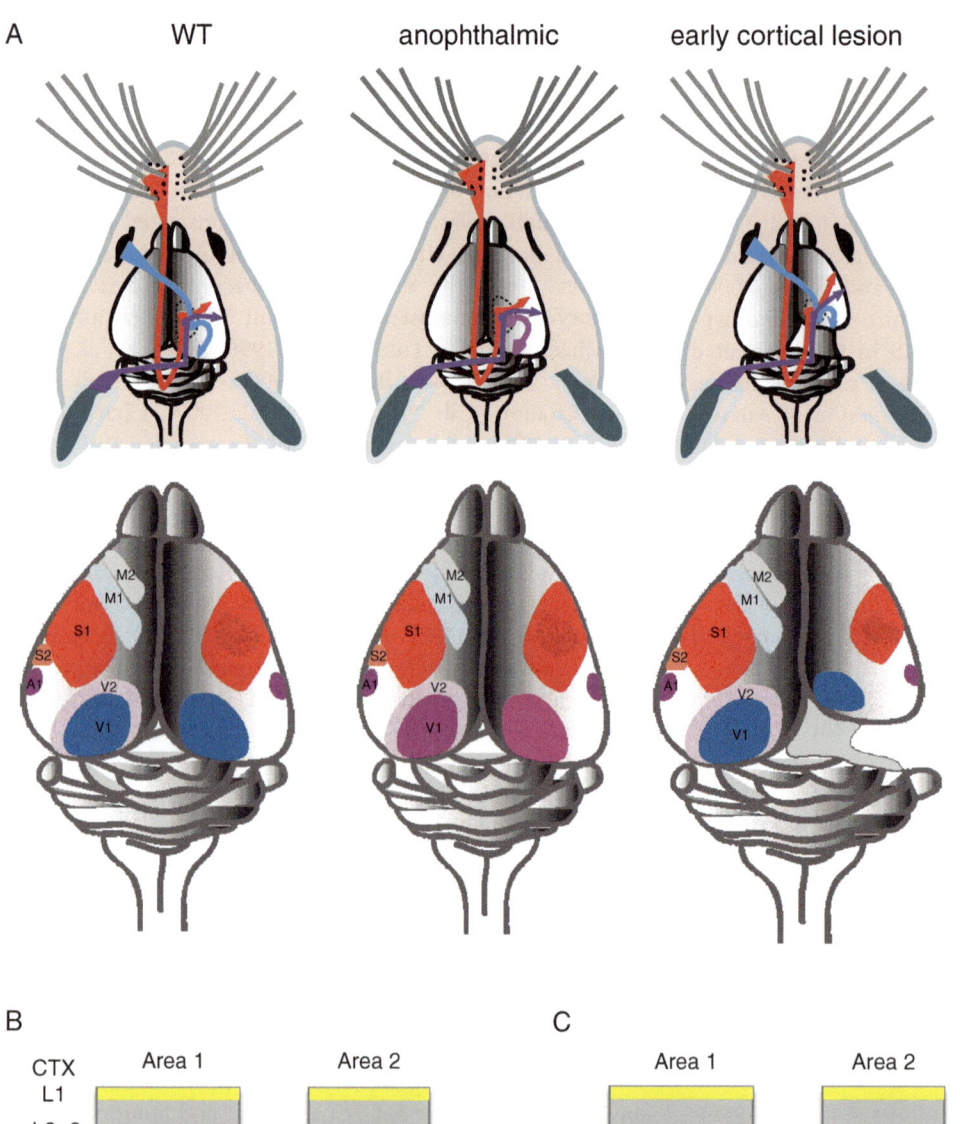

Figure 9 Changes in thalamocortical relationships after sensory manipulations or thalamic or cortical lesions include both cross-modal and cross-hierarchical plasticity.

A. The plastic nature of the thalamocortical and corticothalamic projections has been demonstrated in various systems in which, upon peripheral deprivation such as blindness, processing of inputs was increased to the remaining modalities as a compensatory mechanism to the loss of the other sense. Very early cortical lesions can change the thalamocortical relationships (Huffman et al. 1999). Figure adopted from Molnár et al. (2006) from the book by Erzurumlu et al. (2006).

B. After a lesion in the sensory periphery, the particular FO thalamic nucleus can now receive sensory input from a different sensory organ. For example, after enucleation, auditory and/or somatosensory input can target the dLGN, and the thalamocortical circuits of V1 can now process different modalities. This form of cross-modal plasticity can have subcortical, thalamic, and cortical components.

C. Only the HO thalamic nuclei receive layer 5 corticothalamic input. However, after losing sensory input (e.g., after neonatal enucleation), the FO thalamic nucleus (dLGN) now receives layer 5 driver input (Grant et al., 2016). Because there is a switch between the layer 5 targeting of HO to an FO thalamic nucleus, this form of plasticity is called *cross-hierarchical plasticity* (Grant et al. 2016; Molnár et al. 2020; Giasafaki et al., 2022).

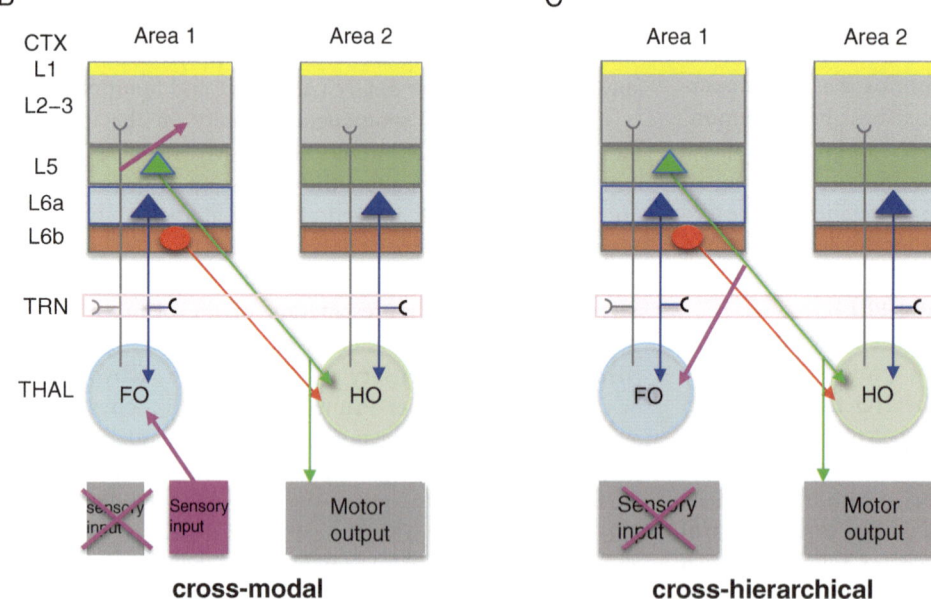

5.3 Cross-Hierarchical Plasticity of Corticothalamic Projections

The FO and HO thalamic nuclei develop from different sets of progenitors, and it is believed that their identity is determined from the early stages (Figure 4). The corticofugal projections from layer 5 selectively target the FO thalamic nuclei, whereas projections from layer 6 innervate both sets of nuclei. However, after sensory deprivation, both FO and HO thalamic nuclei change their connectivity and gene-expression pattern, and it has been described that corticofugal projections change their thalamic targeting (Mooney and Rhoades 1983). Detailed analysis after neonatal enucleation demonstrated that the FO dLGN receives layer 5 projections, and its gene-expression patterns become more similar to the ones associated with the LP, an HO nucleus (Pouchelon et al. 2014). Moreover, in the absence of FO thalamic input, the primary sensory cortices acquire the transcriptional characteristics of associative secondary cortical areas, indicating the importance of thalamic input in the development and determination of primary cortical identity (Chou et al. 2013; Vue et al. 2013; Pouchelon et al. 2014). Pouchelon and collaborators have demonstrated rewiring of TCAs from the Po to layer 4 of S1 after genetic ablation of the VPM, with deprived S1 circuits acquiring S2-like properties (Pouchelon et al. 2014). Moreover, monocular enucleation at birth, causing loss of retinal input, results in premature layer 5 and 6 projection ingrowth to the dLGN (Grant et al. 2016). Additionally, layer 5 CTAs rearrange and arborize aberrantly inside the FO dLGN after visual deprivation, with branches forming synapses at P8. These effects were also observed after blocking spontaneous retinal waves with epibatidine in layer 6–labeled transgenic mice (Golli-tau-eGFP), indicating that intrinsic activity might be involved in the establishment of FO or HO thalamic identity (Grant et al. 2016). These data indicate cross-hierarchical rewiring of thalamocortical and corticothalamic projections following sensory deprivation.

Early layer 6 axonal projection to the dLGN was described by Seabrook et al. (2013) upon retinal input suppression, either surgically with binocular enucleation at birth or genetically, in math5-/- mutant mice. Using the same models of retinogeniculate axon depletion, Brooks et al. (2013) described a temporal regulation of the innervation of layer 6 CTAs to the dLGN controlled by aggrecan, indicating the role of guidance cues in the regulation of corticothalamic ingrowth (Brooks et al. 2013).

Studies in the somatosensory and visual systems showed that peripheral input contributes to the transcriptional identity of the thalamic projection nuclei. Frangeul et al. (2016) ablated sensory input to the VPM at birth by infraorbital nerve section, as well as retinal input to the dLGN by bilateral enucleation, and demonstrated that the FO thalamic nuclei lacking peripheral input have a gene-expression profile similar to that of HO nuclei, suggesting that HO gene expression is a default state from which FO identity emerges in an input-dependent manner (Bishop et al. 1959; Butler 2008; Frangeul et al. 2016). The bilateral optic nerve section at P0 affects the migration of dLGN interneurons at P20, indicating the importance of peripheral input in the incorporation of interneurons into the dLGN (Golding et al. 2014). By blocking spontaneous waves with TTX, the same study also showed that spontaneous activity affects dLGN interneuron migration (Golding et al. 2014).

Studies of the plasticity that follows input changes focused mainly on the peripheral afferents to the subcortical structures, mostly the thalamus. How inputs affect the areal targeting of TCAs within the sensory-specific cortices and which mechanisms mediate corticothalamic plasticity are standing questions that need further investigation.

Summary

Although the adult organization of the thalamocortical projections is intriguingly complex, we are beginning to understand how the initial layout of this system is constructed with a cascade of relatively simple developmental events. Multiple developmental mechanisms are involved, and some may be dominant at a particular stage. They follow a well-choreographed and integrated algorithm that reflects the evolutionary changes of the forebrain. Both thalamocortical and corticothalamic projections are laid down very early, when the distances are minimal. Their development relies on precocious transient axonal bundles that form scaffolds and on streams of guidepost cells. These transient structures assist the crossing of diencephalic and telencephalic boundaries. The initial deployment and topographic organization of early axons are guided by diencephalic and telencephalic molecular gradients, and the connectivity is established in an autonomous fashion before the afferents from the sensory periphery reach the dorsal thalamus. However, local and peripheral neuronal activity patterns presumably modify this topography soon after initial thalamocortical targeting, during thalamocortical and corticothalamic fiber ingrowth and arborization. In particular, thalamocortical projections rearrange in the subplate before their final ingrowth into the cortical plate, whereas some corticofugal projections also stall and wait near the thalamus before they enter dorsal thalamic nuclei. Mouse transgenic models enable us to dissect mechanisms such as various forms of early neural activities, and it will be a major challenge to understand how external influence is translated into cellular and molecular cues that organize circuits. Both thalamocortical and corticothalamic projections are plastic and can remodel after alterations in sensory input or various lesions. Understanding these mechanisms is critical to fostering and recruiting the plasticity of cortical representations in the context of therapy of disease or lesions.

Acknowledgments

Some of the ideas and concepts reviewed in this chapter relied heavily on our previous publications: Molnár and Blakemore 1995; Molnár 1998; Molnár, Adams, and Blakemore 1998; Molnár Adams, Goffinet, et al. 1998; Molnár, Knott, et al. 1998; López-Bendito and Molnár, 2003; Molnár et al. 2012; Hoerder-Suabedissen and Molnár 2015; Grant et al. 2016; Molnár et al. 2020. We are grateful to all previous and current laboratory members for comments and discussions. We are indebted to Ann Butler and André Goffinet for critical comments on an earlier version of this manuscript.

The work in the laboratory of Zoltán Molnár has been funded by the Medical Research Council (MRC), Biotechnology and Biological Sciences Research Council (BBSRC), Royal Society, Wellcome Trust, Oxford Martin School, Anatomical Society, and St. John's College. Zoltán Molnár is associated to Charité-Universitätsmedizin Berlin (Host Prof Britta Eickholt) as Einstein Visiting Fellow (2020–2024).

Abbreviations

DTB: diencephalic–telencephalic boundary
Ep: epithalamus
FO: first-order thalamic nucleus
HO: higher-order thalamic nucleus
Ic: internal capsule
LGE: lateral ganglionic eminence
LH: lateral habenula
MADM: mosaic analysis with double markers
md: mediodorsal
MGE: medial ganglionic eminence
MGN: medial geniculate nucleus
MH: medial habenula
PRN: perireticular nucleus
PSPB: pallial–subpallial boundary
PTh: prethalamus
RGPs: radial progenitors
RTN: reticular thalamic nucleus
S/M-related: somatosensory–motor related
St: striatum
SuP: subpallium
TCAs: thalamocortical axons
Thal: thalamus
TRN: thalamic reticular nucleus
VB: ventrobasal nucleus
VL: ventrolateral nucleus
vLG: ventral geniculate nucleus
VZ: ventricular zone

References

Ackman, J. B., T. J. Burbridge and M. C. Crair (2012). "Retinal waves coordinate patterned activity throughout the developing visual system." Nature 490 (7419): 219–225.

Agmon, A. and B. W. Connors (1991). "Thalamocortical responses of mouse somatosensory (barrel) cortex in vitro." Neuroscience 41(2–3): 365–379.

Agmon, A., L. T. Yang, E. G. Jones and D. K. O'Dowd (1995). "Topological precision in the thalamic projection to neonatal mouse barrel cortex." J Neurosci 15 (1 Pt 2): 549–561.

Agmon, A., L. T. Yang, D. K. O'Dowd and E. G. Jones (1993). "Organized growth of thalamocortical axons from the deep tier of terminations into layer IV of developing mouse barrel cortex." J Neurosci 13(12): 5365–5382.

Allendoerfer, K. L. and C. J. Shatz (1994). "The subplate, a transient neocortical structure: its role in the development of connections between thalamus and cortex." Annu Rev Neurosci 17: 185–218.

Altman, J. and S. A. Bayer (1988a). "Development of the rat thalamus: I. Mosaic organization of the thalamic neuroepithelium." J Comp Neurol 275(3): 346–377.

Altman, J. and S. A. Bayer (1988b). "Development of the rat thalamus: II. Time and site of origin and settling pattern of neurons derived from the anterior lobule of the thalamic neuroepithelium." J Comp Neurol 275(3): 378–405.

Altman, J. and S. A. Bayer (1988c). "Development of the rat thalamus: III. Time and site of origin and settling pattern of neurons of the reticular nucleus." J Comp Neurol 275(3): 406–428.

Angelucci, A., F. Clascá, E. Bricolo, K. S. Cramer and M. Sur (1997). "Experimentally induced retinal projections to the ferret auditory thalamus: development of clustered eye-specific patterns in a novel target." J Neurosci 17(6): 2040–2055.

Angelucci, A., F. Clascá and M. Sur (1998). "Brainstem inputs to the ferret medial geniculate nucleus and the effect of early deafferentation on novel retinal projections to the auditory thalamus." J Comp Neurol 400(3): 417–439.

Angevine, J. B., Jr. (1970). "Time of neuron origin in the diencephalon of the mouse. An autoradiographic study." J Comp Neurol 139 (2): 129–187.

Asanuma, C. and B. B. Stanfield (1990). "Induction of somatic sensory inputs to the lateral geniculate nucleus in congenitally blind mice and in phenotypically normal mice." Neuroscience 39(3): 533–545.

Auladell, C., P. Perez-Sust, H. Super and E. Soriano (2000). "The early development of thalamocortical and corticothalamic projections in the mouse." Anat Embryol (Berl) 201(3): 169–179.

Bagri, A., O. Marin, A. S. Plump, J. Mak, S. J. Pleasure, J. L. Rubenstein and M. Tessier-Lavigne (2002). "Slit proteins prevent midline crossing and determine the dorsoventral position of major axonal pathways in the mammalian forebrain." Neuron 33(2): 233–248.

Bavelier, D. and H. J. Neville (2002). "Cross-modal plasticity: where and how?" Nat Rev Neurosci 3(6): 443–452.

Behrens, T. E., H. Johansen-Berg, M. W. Woolrich, S. M. Smith, C. A. Wheeler-Kingshott, P. A. Boulby, G. J. Barker, E. L. Sillery, K. Sheehan, O. Ciccarelli, A. J. Thompson, J. M. Brady and P. M. Matthews (2003). "Non-invasive mapping of connections between human thalamus and cortex using diffusion imaging." Nat Neurosci 6(7): 750–757.

Bielle, F., P. Marcos-Mondejar, M. Keita, C. Mailhes, C. Verney, K. Nguyen Ba-Charvet, M. Tessier-Lavigne, G. Lopez-Bendito and S. Garel (2011). "Slit2 activity in the migration of guidepost neurons shapes thalamic projections during development and evolution." Neuron 69(6): 1085–1098.

Bishop, K. M., G. Goudreau and D. D. O'Leary (2000). "Regulation of area identity in the mammalian neocortex by Emx2 and Pax6." Science 288(5464): 344–349.

Bishop, P. O., W. Burke and R. Davis (1959). "Activation of single lateral geniculate cells by stimulation of either optic nerve." Science 130(3374): 506–507.

Blakey, D. (2007). The Role of Neural Activity in the Development of Thalamocortical Connections. D.Phil, University of Oxford.

Blakey, D., M. C. Wilson and Z. Molnár (2012). "Termination and initial branch formation of SNAP-25-deficient thalamocortical fibres in heterochronic organotypic co-cultures." Eur J Neurosci 35 (10): 1586–1594.

Bonnin, A., M. Torii, L. Wang, P. Rakic and P. Levitt (2007). "Serotonin modulates the response of embryonic thalamocortical axons to netrin-1." Nat Neurosci 10(5): 588–597.

Braisted, J. E., S. M. Catalano, R. Stimac, T. E. Kennedy, M. Tessier-Lavigne,

C. J. Shatz and D. D. O'Leary (2000). "Netrin-1 promotes thalamic axon growth and is required for proper development of the thalamocortical projection." J Neurosci 20(15): 5792–5801.

Braisted, J. E., T. Ringstedt and D. D. O'Leary (2009). "Slits are chemorepellents endogenous to hypothalamus and steer thalamocortical axons into ventral telencephalon." Cereb Cortex 19 Suppl 1: i144–151.

Braisted, J. E., R. Tuttle and D. O'Leary D (1999). "Thalamocortical axons are influenced by chemorepellent and chemoattractant activities localized to decision points along their path." Dev Biol 208(2): 430–440.

Bronchti, G., P. Heil, R. Sadka, A. Hess, H. Scheich and Z. Wollberg (2002). "Auditory activation of 'visual' cortical areas in the blind mole rat (*Spalax ehrenbergi*)." Eur J Neurosci 16(2): 311–329.

Bronchti, G., P. Heil, H. Scheich and Z. Wollberg (1989). "Auditory pathway and auditory activation of primary visual targets in the blind mole rat (*Spalax ehrenbergi*): I. 2-deoxyglucose study of subcortical centers." J Comp Neurol 284 (2): 253–274.

Brooks, J. M., J. Su, C. Levy, J. S. Wang, T. A. Seabrook, W. Guido and M. A. Fox (2013). "A molecular mechanism regulating the timing of corticogeniculate innervation." Cell Rep 5(3): 573–581.

Butler, A. B. (2008). "Evolution of the thalamus: a morphological and functional review." Thalamus & Related Systems 4(1): 35–58.

Butler, A. B. and H. William (2005). Comparative Vertebrate Neuroanatomy: Evolution and Adaptation. Hoboken, NJ: Wiley-Liss.

Cadwell, C. R., A. Bhaduri, M. A. Mostajo-Radji, M. G. Keefe and T. J. Nowakowski (2019). "Development and arealization of the cerebral cortex." Neuron 103(6): 980–1004.

Carney, R. S., T. B. Alfonso, D. Cohen, H. Dai, S. Nery, B. Stoica, J. Slotkin, B. S. Bregman, G. Fishell and J. G. Corbin (2006). "Cell migration along the lateral cortical stream to the developing basal telencephalic limbic system." J Neurosci 26 (45): 11562–11574.

Carney, R. S., L. A. Cocas, T. Hirata, K. Mansfield and J. G. Corbin (2009). "Differential regulation of telencephalic pallial-subpallial boundary patterning by Pax6 and Gsh2." Cereb Cortex 19(4): 745–759.

Castillo-Paterna, M., V. Moreno-Juan, A. Filipchuk, L. Rodriguez-Malmierca,

R. Susin and G. Lopez-Bendito (2015). "DCC functions as an accelerator of thalamocortical axonal growth downstream of spontaneous thalamic activity." EMBO Rep 16(7): 851–862.

Catalano, S. M., R. T. Robertson and H. P. Killackey (1991). "Early ingrowth of thalamocortical afferents to the neocortex of the prenatal rat." Proc Natl Acad Sci USA 88 (8): 2999–3003.

Catalano, S. M. and C. J. Shatz (1998). "Activity-dependent cortical target selection by thalamic axons." Science 281(5376): 559–562.

Caviness, V. S., Jr. and D. O. Frost (1980). "Tangential organization of thalamic projections to the neocortex in the mouse." J Comp Neurol 194(2): 335–367.

Chabot, N., S. Robert, R. Tremblay, D. Miceli, D. Boire and G. Bronchti (2007). "Audition differently activates the visual system in neonatally enucleated mice compared with anophthalmic mutants." Eur J Neurosci 26(8): 2334–2348.

Chapouton, P., C. Schuurmans, F. Guillemot and M. Gotz (2001). "The transcription factor neurogenin 2 restricts cell migration from the cortex to the striatum." Development 128(24): 5149–5159.

Charbonneau, V., M. E. Laramee, V. Boucher, G. Bronchti and D. Boire (2012). "Cortical and subcortical projections to primary visual cortex in anophthalmic, enucleated and sighted mice." Eur J Neurosci 36(7): 2949–2963.

Chatterjee, M. and J. Y. Li (2012). "Patterning and compartment formation in the diencephalon." Front Neurosci 6: 66.

Chen, Y., D. Magnani, T. Theil, T. Pratt and D. J. Price (2012). "Evidence that descending cortical axons are essential for thalamocortical axons to cross the pallial-subpallial boundary in the embryonic forebrain." PLoS One 7(3): e33105.

Chou, S. J., Z. Babot, A. Leingartner, M. Studer, Y. Nakagawa and D. D. O'Leary (2013). "Geniculocortical input drives genetic distinctions between primary and higher-order visual areas." Science 340 (6137): 1239–1242.

Clascá, F., A. Angelucci and M. Sur (1995). "Layer-specific programs of development in neocortical projection neurons." Proc Natl Acad Sci USA 92(24): 11145–11149.

Colonnese, M. T., A. Kaminska, M. Minlebaev, M. Milh, B. Bloem, S. Lescure, G. Moriette, C. Chiron, Y. Ben-Ari and R. Khazipov (2010). "A conserved switch in sensory processing prepares developing neocortex for vision." Neuron 67(3): 480–498.

Colonnese, M. T. and R. Khazipov (2010). "'Slow activity transients' in infant rat visual cortex: a spreading synchronous oscillation patterned by retinal waves." J Neurosci 30 (12): 4325–4337.

Cordery, P. and Z. Molnár (1999). "Embryonic development of connections in turtle pallium." J Comp Neurol 413(1): 26–54.

De Carlos, J. A. and D. D. O'Leary (1992). "Growth and targeting of subplate axons and establishment of major cortical pathways." J Neurosci 12(4): 1194–1211.

Deck, M., L. Lokmane, S. Chauvet, C. Mailhes, M. Keita, M. Niquille, M. Yoshida, Y. Yoshida, C. Lebrand, F. Mann, E. A. Grove and S. Garel (2013). "Pathfinding of corticothalamic axons relies on a rendezvous with thalamic projections." Neuron 77(3): 472–484.

Dehay, C. and H. Kennedy (2007). "Cell-cycle control and cortical development." Nat Rev Neurosci 8(6): 438–450.

Dufour, A., J. Seibt, L. Passante, V. Depaepe, T. Ciossek, J. Frisen, K. Kullander, J. G. Flanagan, F. Polleux and P. Vanderhaeghen (2003). "Area specificity and topography of thalamocortical projections are controlled by ephrin/Eph genes." Neuron 39(3): 453–465.

Dwyer, N. D., D. K. Manning, J. L. Moran, R. Mudbhary, M. S. Fleming, C. B. Favero, V. M. Vock, D. D. O'Leary, C. A. Walsh and D. R. Beier (2011). "A forward genetic screen with a thalamocortical axon reporter mouse yields novel neurodevelopment mutants and a distinct emx2 mutant phenotype." Neural Dev 6: 3.

Dye, C. A., C. W. Abbott and K. J. Huffman (2012). "Bilateral enucleation alters gene expression and intraneocortical connections in the mouse." Neural Dev 7: 5.

Erzurumlu, R., W. Guido and Z. Molnár (2006). Development and Plasticity in Sensory Thalamus and Cortex. Boston, MA, Springer US.

Espinosa, J. S. and M. P. Stryker (2012). "Development and plasticity of the primary visual cortex." Neuron 75(2): 230–249.

Feller, M. B., K. R. Delaney and D. W. Tank (1996). "Presynaptic calcium dynamics at the frog retinotectal synapse." J Neurophysiol 76 (1): 381–400.

Feng, J., Q. Xian, T. Guan, J. Hu, M. Wang, Y. Huang, K. F. So, S. M. Evans, G. Chai, A. M. Goffinet, Y. Qu and L. Zhou (2016). "Celsr3 and Fzd3 organize a pioneer neuron scaffold to steer growing thalamocortical axons." Cereb Cortex 26(7): 3323–3334.

Fetter-Pruneda, I., H. Geovannini-Acuna, C. Santiago, A. S. Ibarraran-Viniegra,

Development

E. Martinez-Martinez, M. Sandoval-Velasco, L. Uribe-Figueroa, P. Padilla-Cortes, G. Mercado-Celis and G. Gutierrez-Ospina (2013). "Shifts in developmental timing, and not increased levels of experience-dependent neuronal activity, promote barrel expansion in the primary somatosensory cortex of rats enucleated at birth." PLoS One 8(1): e54940.

Firth, S. I., C. T. Wang and M. B. Feller (2005). "Retinal waves: mechanisms and function in visual system development." Cell Calcium 37(5): 425–432.

Fishell, G. and C. Hanashima (2008). "Pyramidal neurons grow up and change their mind." Neuron 57(3): 333–338.

Frangeul, L., G. Pouchelon, L. Telley, S. Lefort, C. Luscher and D. Jabaudon (2016). "A cross-modal genetic framework for the development and plasticity of sensory pathways." Nature 538(7623): 96–98.

Friauf, E., S. K. McConnell and C. J. Shatz (1990). "Functional synaptic circuits in the subplate during fetal and early postnatal development of cat visual cortex." J Neurosci 10(8): 2601–2613.

Friauf, E. and C. J. Shatz (1991). "Changing patterns of synaptic input to subplate and cortical plate during development of visual cortex." J Neurophysiol 66(6): 2059–2071.

Garcia-Moreno, F. and Z. Molnár (2020). "Variations of telencephalic development that paved the way for neocortical evolution." Prog Neurobiol: 101865.

Garel, S., K. J. Huffman and J. L. Rubenstein (2003). "Molecular regionalization of the neocortex is disrupted in Fgf8 hypomorphic mutants." Development 130(9): 1903–1914.

Garel, S., F. Marin, R. Grosschedl and P. Charnay (1999). "Ebf1 controls early cell differentiation in the embryonic striatum." Development 126(23): 5285–5294.

Garel, S. and J. L. Rubenstein (2004). "Intermediate targets in formation of topographic projections: inputs from the thalamocortical system." Trends Neurosci 27(9): 533–539.

Garel, S., K. Yun, R. Grosschedl and J. L. Rubenstein (2002). "The early topography of thalamocortical projections is shifted in Ebf1 and Dlx1/2 mutant mice." Development 129(24): 5621–5634.

Gezelius, H. and G. Lopez-Bendito (2017). "Thalamic neuronal specification and early circuit formation." Dev Neurobiol 77(7): 830–843.

Giasafaki, C., Grant, E., Hoerder-Suabedissen, A., Hayashi, S., Lee, S., Molnár, Z., (2022) Cross-hierarchical plasticity of corticofugal projections to dLGN after neonatal monocular enucleation. J Comp Neurol THAL-JCN-21-0096 Specialissue on Thalamus for the Journal of Comparative Neurology Editors: William Guido and AndrewHuberman https://onlinelibrary.wiley.com/doi/epdf/10.1002/cne.25304

Gimeno, L. and S. Martinez (2007). "Expression of chick Fgf19 and mouse Fgf15 orthologs is regulated in the developing brain by Fgf8 and Shh." Dev Dyn 236(8): 2285–2297.

Golding, B., G. Pouchelon, C. Bellone, S. Murthy, A. A. Di Nardo, S. Govindan, M. Ogawa, T. Shimogori, C. Luscher, A. Dayer and D. Jabaudon (2014). "Retinal input directs the recruitment of inhibitory interneurons into thalamic visual circuits." Neuron 81(6): 1443.

Goldman-Rakic, P. S. (1987). "Development of cortical circuitry and cognitive function." Child Dev 58(3): 601–622.

Grant, E., A. Hoerder-Suabedissen and Z. Molnár (2012). "Development of the corticothalamic projections." Front Neurosci 6: 53.

Grant, E., A. Hoerder-Suabedissen and Z. Molnár (2016). "The regulation of corticofugal fiber targeting by retinal inputs." Cereb Cortex 26(3): 1336–1348.

Grove, E. A. and T. Fukuchi-Shimogori (2003). "Generating the cerebral cortical area map." Annu Rev Neurosci 26: 355–380.

Guillery, R. W. and S. M. Sherman (2002). "Thalamic relay functions and their role in corticocortical communication: generalizations from the visual system." Neuron 33(2): 163–175.

Halley, A. C. and L. Krubitzer (2019). "Not all cortical expansions are the same: the coevolution of the neocortex and the dorsal thalamus in mammals." Curr Opin Neurobiol 56: 78–86.

Hanashima, C., Z. Molnár and G. Fishell (2006). "Building bridges to the cortex." Cell 125(1): 24–27.

Hayashi, S., A. Hoerder-Suabedissen, E. Kiyokage, C. Maclachlan, K. Toida, G. Knott and Z. Molnár (2020). "Maturation of complex synaptic connections of layer 5 cortical axons in the posterior thalamic nucleus requires SNAP25." Cerebral Cortex. 31(5):2625–2638.

Hevner, R. F., E. Miyashita-Lin and J. L. Rubenstein (2002). "Cortical and thalamic axon pathfinding defects in Tbr1, Gbx2, and Pax6 mutant mice: evidence that cortical and thalamic axons interact and guide each other." J Comp Neurol 447(1): 8–17.

Higashi, K., A. Fujita, A. Inanobe, M. Tanemoto, K. Doi, T. Kubo and Y. Kurachi (2001). "An inwardly rectifying K(+) channel, Kir4.1, expressed in astrocytes surrounds synapses and blood vessels in brain." Am J Physiol Cell Physiol 281(3): C922–931.

Higashi, S., Z. Molnár, T. Kurotani and K. Toyama (2002). "Prenatal development of neural excitation in rat thalamocortical projections studied by optical recording." Neuroscience 115(4): 1231–1246.

Hoerder-Suabedissen, A., S. Hayashi, L. Upton, Z. Nolan, D. Casas-Torremocha, E. Grant, S. Viswanathan, P. O. Kanold, F. Clascá, Y. Kim and Z. Molnár (2018). "Subset of cortical layer 6b neurons selectively innervates higher order thalamic nuclei in mice." Cereb Cortex 28(5): 1882–1897.

Hoerder-Suabedissen, A., K. V. Korrell, S. Hayashi, A. Jeans, D. M. O. Ramirez, E. Grant, H. C. Christian, E. T. Kavalali, M. C. Wilson and Z. Molnár (2019). "Cell-specific loss of SNAP25 from Cortical projection neurons allows normal development but causes subsequent neurodegeneration." Cereb Cortex 29(5): 2148–2159.

Hoerder-Suabedissen, A. and Z. Molnár (2012). "Morphology of mouse subplate cells with identified projection targets changes with age." J Comp Neurol 520(1): 174–185.

Hoerder-Suabedissen, A. and Z. Molnár (2015). "Development, evolution and pathology of neocortical subplate neurons." Nat Rev Neurosci 16(3): 133–146.

Horng, S., G. Kreiman, C. Ellsworth, D. Page, M. Blank, K. Millen and M. Sur (2009). "Differential gene expression in the developing lateral geniculate nucleus and medial geniculate nucleus reveals novel roles for Zic4 and Foxp2 in visual and auditory pathway development." J Neurosci 29(43): 13672–13683.

Horváth, T.L., J. Hirsch, Z. Molnár (2022) Body, Brain, Behavior, Three Views and a Conversation Academic Press, An imprint of Elsevier; ISBN: 9780128180938 pp:444

Huberman, A. D., M. B. Feller and B. Chapman (2008). "Mechanisms underlying development of visual maps and receptive fields." Annu Rev Neurosci 31: 479–509.

Huberman, A. D., C. M. Speer and B. Chapman (2006). "Spontaneous retinal activity mediates development of ocular dominance columns and binocular receptive fields in v1." Neuron 52(2): 247–254.

Huffman, K. J., Z. Molnár, A. Van Dellen, D. M. Kahn, C. Blakemore and L. Krubitzer (1999). "Formation of cortical fields on a reduced cortical sheet." J Neurosci 19(22): 9939–9952.

Hunnicutt, B. J., B. R. Long, D. Kusefoglu, K. J. Gertz, H. Zhong and T. Mao (2014). "A comprehensive thalamocortical projection map at the mesoscopic level." Nat Neurosci 17(9): 1276–1285.

Izraeli, R., G. Koay, M. Lamish, A. J. Heicklen-Klein, H. E. Heffner, R. S. Heffner and Z. Wollberg (2002). "Cross-modal neuroplasticity in neonatally enucleated hamsters: structure, electrophysiology and behaviour." Eur J Neurosci 15(4): 693–712.

Jacobs, E. C., C. Campagnoni, K. Kampf, S. D. Reyes, V. Kalra, V. Handley, Y. Y. Xie, Y. Hong-Hu, V. Spreur, R. S. Fisher and A. T. Campagnoni (2007). "Visualization of corticofugal projections during early cortical development in a tau-GFP-transgenic mouse." Eur J Neurosci 25(1): 17–30.

Jones, E. G. (2002). "Thalamic circuitry and thalamocortical synchrony." Philos Trans R Soc Lond B Biol Sci 357(1428): 1659–1673.

Jones, E. G. (2007). The Thalamus. Cambridge, Cambridge University Press.

Kaas, J. H. and D. C. Lyon (2007). "Pulvinar contributions to the dorsal and ventral streams of visual processing in primates." Brain Res Rev 55(2): 285–296.

Kanold, P. O. (2009). "Subplate neurons: crucial regulators of cortical development and plasticity." Front Neuroanat 3: 16.

Kanold, P. O. and H. J. Luhmann (2010). "The subplate and early cortical circuits." Annu Rev Neurosci 33: 23–48.

Kataoka, A. and T. Shimogori (2008). "Fgf8 controls regional identity in the developing thalamus." Development 135(17): 2873–2881.

Katz, L. C. and C. J. Shatz (1996). "Synaptic activity and the construction of cortical circuits." Science 274(5290): 1133–1138.

Kirkby, L. A. and M. B. Feller (2013). "Intrinsically photosensitive ganglion cells contribute to plasticity in retinal wave circuits." Proc Natl Acad Sci USA 110(29): 12090–12095.

Kostovic, I. (2020). "The enigmatic fetal subplate compartment forms an early tangential cortical nexus and provides the framework for construction of cortical connectivity." Prog Neurobiol: 101883.

Kostovic, I. and P. Rakic (1990). "Developmental history of the transient subplate zone in the visual and somatosensory cortex of the macaque monkey and human brain." J Comp Neurol 297(3): 441–470.

Krsnik, Z., V. Majic, L. Vasung, H. Huang and I. Kostovic (2017). "Growth of thalamocortical fibers to the somatosensory cortex in the human fetal brain." Front Neurosci 11: 233.

Krug, K., A. L. Smith and I. D. Thompson (1998). "The development of topography in the hamster geniculo-cortical projection." J Neurosci 18(15): 5766–5776.

Lakhina, V., A. Falnikar, L. Bhatnagar and S. Tole (2007). "Early thalamocortical tract guidance and topographic sorting of thalamic projections requires LIM-homeodomain gene Lhx2." Dev Biol 306(2): 703–713.

Laramee, M. E., G. Bronchti and D. Boire (2014). "Primary visual cortex projections to extrastriate cortices in enucleated and anophthalmic mice." Brain Struct Funct 219(6): 2051–2070.

Leighton, P. A., K. J. Mitchell, L. V. Goodrich, X. Lu, K. Pinson, P. Scherz, W. C. Skarnes and M. Tessier-Lavigne (2001). "Defining brain wiring patterns and mechanisms through gene trapping in mice." Nature 410(6825): 174–179.

Lickiss, T., A. F. Cheung, C. E. Hutchinson, J. S. Taylor and Z. Molnár (2012). "Examining the relationship between early axon growth and transcription factor expression in the developing cerebral cortex." J Anat 220(3): 201–211.

Lim, Y. and J. A. Golden (2007). "Patterning the developing diencephalon." Brain Res Rev 53(1): 17–26.

Little, G. E., G. Lopez-Bendito, A. E. Runker, N. Garcia, M. C. Pinon, A. Chedotal, Z. Molnár and K. J. Mitchell (2009). "Specificity and plasticity of thalamocortical connections in Sema6A mutant mice." PLoS Biol 7(4): e98.

Lopez-Bendito, G., A. Cautinat, J. A. Sanchez, F. Bielle, N. Flames, A. N. Garratt, D. A. Talmage, L. W. Role, P. Charnay, O. Marin and S. Garel (2006). "Tangential neuronal migration controls axon guidance: a role for neuregulin-1 in thalamocortical axon navigation." Cell 125(1): 127–142.

Lopez-Bendito, G., C. H. Chan, A. Mallamaci, J. Parnavelas and Z. Molnár (2002). "Role of Emx2 in the development of the reciprocal connectivity between cortex and thalamus." J Comp Neurol 451(2): 153–169.

Lopez-Bendito, G., N. Flames, L. Ma, C. Fouquet, T. Di Meglio, A. Chedotal, M. Tessier-Lavigne and O. Marin (2007). "Robo1 and Robo2 cooperate to control the guidance of major axonal tracts in the mammalian forebrain." J Neurosci 27(13): 3395–3407.

Lopez-Bendito, G. and Z. Molnár (2003). "Thalamocortical development: how are we going to get there?" Nat Rev Neurosci 4(4): 276–289.

Lozsadi, D. A., J. Gonzalez-Soriano and R. W. Guillery (1996). "The course and termination of corticothalamic fibres arising in the visual cortex of the rat." Eur J Neurosci 8(11): 2416–2427.

Lund, R. D. and M. J. Mustari (1977). "Development of the geniculocortical pathway in rats." J Comp Neurol 173(2): 289–306.

Maffei, L. and L. Galli-Resta (1990). "Correlation in the discharges of neighboring rat retinal ganglion cells during prenatal life." Proc Natl Acad Sci U S A 87(7): 2861–2864.

Majdan, M. and C. J. Shatz (2006). "Effects of visual experience on activity-dependent gene regulation in cortex." Nat Neurosci 9(5): 650–659.

Marin, O. (2002). "[Origin of cortical interneurons: basic concepts and clinical implications]." Rev Neurol 35(8): 743–751.

Marin-Padilla, M. (1971). "Early prenatal ontogenesis of the cerebral cortex (neocortex) of the cat (*Felis domestica*). A Golgi study. I. The primordial neocortical organization." Z Anat Entwicklungsgesch 134(2): 117–145.

Marques-Smith, A., D. Lyngholm, A. K. Kaufmann, J. A. Stacey, A. Hoerder-Suabedissen, E. B. Becker, M. C. Wilson, Z. Molnár and S. J. Butt (2016). "A transient translaminar GABAergic interneuron circuit connects thalamocortical recipient layers in neonatal somatosensory cortex." Neuron 89(3): 536–549.

Martinez-Ferre, A. and S. Martinez (2012). "Molecular regionalization of the diencephalon." Front Neurosci 6: 73.

McConnell, S. K., A. Ghosh and C. J. Shatz (1994). "Subplate pioneers and the formation of descending connections from cerebral cortex." J Neurosci 14(4): 1892–1907.

Metin, C. and P. Godement (1996). "The ganglionic eminence may be an intermediate target for corticofugal and thalamocortical axons." J Neurosci 16(10): 3219–3235.

Millar, L. J., L. Shi, A. Hoerder-Suabedissen and Z. Molnár (2017). "Neonatal hypoxia ischaemia: mechanisms, models, and therapeutic challenges." Front Cell Neurosci 11: 78.

Mire, E., C. Mezzera, E. Leyva-Diaz, A. V. Paternain, P. Squarzoni, L. Bluy, M. Castillo-Paterna, M. J. Lopez, S. Peregrin, M. Tessier-Lavigne, S. Garel, J. Galceran, J. Lerma and G. Lopez-Bendito (2012). "Spontaneous activity regulates Robo1 transcription to mediate a switch in thalamocortical axon growth." Nat Neurosci 15(8): 1134–1143.

Mitrofanis, J. (1992). "Patterns of antigenic expression in the thalamic reticular nucleus of developing rats." J Comp Neurol 320(2): 161–181.

Mitrofanis, J. (1994a). "Development of the pathway from the reticular and perireticular nuclei to the thalamus in ferrets: a DiI study." Eur J Neurosci 6(12): 1864–1882.

Mitrofanis, J. (1994b). "Development of the thalamic reticular nucleus in ferrets with special reference to the perigeniculate and perireticular cell groups." Eur J Neurosci 6(2): 253–263.

Mitrofanis, J. and G. E. Baker (1993). "Development of the thalamic reticular and perireticular nuclei in rats and their relationship to the course of growing corticofugal and corticopetal axons." J Comp Neurol 338(4): 575–587.

Mitrofanis, J. and R. W. Guillery (1993). "New views of the thalamic reticular nucleus in the adult and the developing brain." Trends Neurosci 16(6): 240–245.

Mitrofanis, J., D. A. Lozsadi and K. A. Coleman (1995). "Evidence for a projection from the perireticular thalamic nucleus to the dorsal thalamus in the adult rat and ferret." J Neurocytol 24(12): 891–902.

Miyake, A., Y. Nakayama, M. Konishi and N. Itoh (2005). "Fgf19 regulated by Hh signaling is required for zebrafish forebrain development." Dev Biol 288(1): 259–275.

Molliver, M. E. and H. Van der Loos (1970). "The ontogenesis of cortical circuitry: the spatial distribution of synapses in somesthetic cortex of newborn dog." Ergeb Anat Entwicklungsgesch 42(4): 5–53.

Molnár, Z. (1998). Development of Thalamocortical Connections. Oxford, Springer.

Molnár, Z. (2000). "Development and evolution of thalamocortical interactions." Eur J Morphol 38(5): 313–320.

Molnár, Z. (2019). "Cortical layer with no known function." Eur J Neurosci 49(7): 957–963.

Molnár, Z., R. Adams and C. Blakemore (1998). "Mechanisms underlying the early establishment of thalamocortical connections in the rat." J Neurosci 18(15): 5723–5745.

Molnár, Z., R. Adams, A. M. Goffinet and C. Blakemore (1998). "The role of the first postmitotic cortical cells in the development of thalamocortical innervation in the reeler mouse." J Neurosci 18(15): 5746–5765.

Molnár, Z. and C. Blakemore (1991). "Lack of regional specificity for connections formed between thalamus and cortex in coculture." Nature 351(6326): 475–477.

Molnár, Z. and C. Blakemore (1995). "How do thalamic axons find their way to the cortex?" Trends Neurosci 18(9): 389–397.

Molnár, Z. and A. B. Butler (2002). "The corticostriatal junction: a crucial region for forebrain development and evolution." Bioessays 24(6): 530–541.

Molnár, Z. and P. Cordery (1999). "Connections between cells of the internal capsule, thalamus, and cerebral cortex in embryonic rat." J Comp Neurol 413(1): 1–25.

Molnár, Z., S. Garel, G. Lopez-Bendito, P. Maness and D. J. Price (2012). "Mechanisms controlling the guidance of thalamocortical axons through the embryonic forebrain." Eur J Neurosci 35(10): 1573–1585.

Molnár, Z., G. W. Knott, C. Blakemore and N. R. Saunders (1998). "Development of thalamocortical projections in the South American gray short-tailed opossum (Monodelphis domestica)." J Comp Neurol 398(4): 491–514.

Molnár, Z., T. Kurotani, S. Higashi and K. Toyama (2003). "Development of functional thalamocortical synapses studied with current source density analysis in whole forebrain slices." Brain Res Bull 60(4): 355–372.

Molnár Z, López-Bendito G, Blakey D, Thompson A, and Higashi S (2006) The Earliest Thalamocortical Interactions. In Development and Plasticity in Sensory Thalamus and Cortex (Editors: R. Erzurumlu, W. Guido, Z. Molnár). New York: Springer, 54–78.

Molnár, Z., G. Lopez-Bendito, J. Small, L. D. Partridge, C. Blakemore and M. C. Wilson (2002). "Normal development of embryonic thalamocortical connectivity in the absence of evoked synaptic activity." J Neurosci 22(23): 10313–10323.

Molnár, Z., H. J. Luhmann and P. O. Kanold (2020). "Transient cortical circuits match spontaneous and sensory-driven activity during development." Science 370(6514).

Molyneaux, B. J., P. Arlotta, J. R. Menezes and J. D. Macklis (2007). "Neuronal subtype specification in the cerebral cortex." Nat Rev Neurosci 8(6): 427–437.

Montiel, J. F., W. Z. Wang, F. M. Oeschger, A. Hoerder-Suabedissen, W. L. Tung, F. Garcia-Moreno, I. E. Holm, A. Villalon and Z. Molnár (2011). "Hypothesis on the dual origin of the Mammalian subplate." Front Neuroanat 5: 25.

Mooney, R., A. A. Penn, R. Gallego and C. J. Shatz (1996). "Thalamic relay of spontaneous retinal activity prior to vision." Neuron 17(5): 863–874.

Mooney, R. D. and R. W. Rhoades (1983). "Neonatal enucleation alters functional organization in hamster's lateral posterior nucleus." Brain Res 285(3): 399–404.

Moreno-Juan, V., A. Filipchuk, N. Anton-Bolanos, C. Mezzera, H. Gezelius, B. Andres, L. Rodriguez-Malmierca, R. Susin, O. Schaad, T. Iwasato, R. Schule, M. Rutlin, S. Nelson, S. Ducret, M. Valdeolmillos, F. M. Rijli and G. Lopez-Bendito (2017). "Prenatal thalamic waves regulate cortical area size prior to sensory processing." Nat Commun 8: 14172.

Murray, K. D., P. V. Choudary and E. G. Jones (2007). "Nucleus- and cell-specific gene expression in monkey thalamus." Proc Natl Acad Sci USA 104(6): 1989–1994.

Naegele, J. R., S. Jhaveri and G. E. Schneider (1988). "Sharpening of topographical projections and maturation of geniculocortical axon arbors in the hamster." J Comp Neurol 277(4): 593–607.

Nakagawa, Y. and D. D. O'Leary (2001). "Combinatorial expression patterns of LIM-homeodomain and other regulatory genes parcellate developing thalamus." J Neurosci 21(8): 2711–2725.

Nakagawa, Y. and T. Shimogori (2012). "Diversity of thalamic progenitor cells and postmitotic neurons." Eur J Neurosci 35(10): 1554–1562.

Negyessy, L., V. Gal, T. Farkas and J. Toldi (2000). "Cross-modal plasticity of the corticothalamic circuits in rats enucleated on the first postnatal day." Eur J Neurosci 12(5): 1654–1668.

Noctor, S. C., V. Martinez-Cerdeno, L. Ivic and A. R. Kriegstein (2004). "Cortical neurons arise in symmetric and asymmetric division zones and migrate through specific phases." Nat Neurosci 7(2): 136–144.

O'Leary, D. D. (1989). "Do cortical areas emerge from a protocortex?" Trends Neurosci 12(10): 400–406.

O'Leary, D. D. and S. Sahara (2008). "Genetic regulation of arealization of the neocortex." Curr Opin Neurobiol 18(1): 90–100.

Oeschger, F. M., W. Z. Wang, S. Lee, F. Garcia-Moreno, A. M. Goffinet, M. L. Arbones, S. Rakic and Z. Molnár (2012). "Gene expression analysis of the embryonic subplate." Cereb Cortex 22(6): 1343–1359.

Osheroff, H. and M. E. Hatten (2009). "Gene expression profiling of preplate neurons destined for the subplate: genes involved in transcription, axon extension, neurotransmitter regulation, steroid hormone signaling, and neuronal survival." Cereb Cortex 19 Suppl 1: i126–134.

Pascual-Leone, A., A. Amedi, F. Fregni and L. B. Merabet (2005). "The plastic human brain cortex." Annu Rev Neurosci 28: 377–401.

Penn, A. A., P. A. Riquelme, M. B. Feller and C. J. Shatz (1998). "Competition in retinogeniculate patterning driven by spontaneous activity." Science 279(5359): 2108–2112.

Piche, M., N. Chabot, G. Bronchti, D. Miceli, F. Lepore and J. P. Guillemot (2007). "Auditory responses in the visual cortex of neonatally enucleated rats." Neuroscience 145(3): 1144–1156.

Pinon, M. C., A. Jethwa, E. Jacobs, A. Campagnoni and Z. Molnár (2009). "Dynamic integration of subplate neurons into the cortical barrel field circuitry during postnatal development in the Golli-tau-eGFP (GTE) mouse." J Physiol 587(Pt 9): 1903–1915.

Pinon, M. C., T. C. Tuoc, R. Ashery-Padan, Z. Molnár and A. Stoykova (2008). "Altered molecular regionalization and normal thalamocortical connections in cortex-specific Pax6 knock-out mice." J Neurosci 28(35): 8724–8734.

Pouchelon, G., F. Gambino, C. Bellone, L. Telley, I. Vitali, C. Luscher, A. Holtmaat and D. Jabaudon (2014). "Modality-specific thalamocortical inputs instruct the identity of postsynaptic L4 neurons." Nature 511 (7510): 471–474.

Powell, A. W., T. Sassa, Y. Wu, M. Tessier-Lavigne and F. Polleux (2008). "Topography of thalamic projections requires attractive and repulsive functions of Netrin-1 in the ventral telencephalon." PLoS Biol 6(5): e116.

Pratt, T., J. C. Quinn, T. I. Simpson, J. D. West, J. O. Mason and D. J. Price (2002). "Disruption of early events in thalamocortical tract formation in mice lacking the transcription factors Pax6 or Foxg1." J Neurosci 22(19): 8523–8531.

Price, D. D. and G. N. Verne (2002). "Does the spinothalamic tract to ventroposterior lateral thalamus and somatosensory cortex have roles in both pain sensation and pain-related emotions?" J Pain 3(2): 105–108; discussion 113–104.

Price, D. J., J. Clegg, X. O. Duocastella, D. Willshaw and T. Pratt (2012). "The importance of combinatorial gene expression in early Mammalian thalamic patterning and thalamocortical axonal guidance." Front Neurosci 6: 37.

Price, D. J., H. Kennedy, C. Dehay, L. Zhou, M. Mercier, Y. Jossin, A. M. Goffinet, F. Tissir, D. Blakey and Z. Molnár (2006). "The development of cortical connections." Eur J Neurosci 23(4): 910–920.

Puelles, L., M. Harrison, G. Paxinos and C. Watson (2013). "A developmental ontology for the mammalian brain based on the prosomeric model." Trends Neurosci 36 (10): 570–578.

Puelles, L. and J. L. Rubenstein (1993). "Expression patterns of homeobox and other putative regulatory genes in the embryonic mouse forebrain suggest a neuromeric organization." Trends Neurosci 16(11): 472–479.

Puelles, L. and J. L. Rubenstein (2003). "Forebrain gene expression domains and the evolving prosomeric model." Trends Neurosci 26(9): 469–476.

Puelles, L. M. Martinez-de-la-Torres, J.-L. Ferran and C. Watson (2012). Diencephalon. In The Mouse Nervous System (Editors: Charles Watson, George Paxinos, Luis Puelles). New York: Academic Press, 313–336.

Qin, J., M. Wang, T. Zhao, X. Xiao, X. Li, J. Yang, L. Yi, A. M. Goffinet, Y. Qu and L. Zhou (2020). "Early forebrain neurons and scaffold fibers in human embryos." Cereb Cortex 30(3): 913–928.

Qin, Y., N. Zhang, Y. Chen, X. Zuo, S. Jiang, X. Zhao, L. Dong, J. Li, T. Zhang, D. Yao and C. Luo (2020). "Rhythmic network modulation to thalamocortical couplings in epilepsy." Int J Neural Syst 30(11): 2050014.

Quinlan, R., M. Graf, I. Mason, A. Lumsden and C. Kiecker (2009). "Complex and dynamic patterns of Wnt pathway gene expression in the developing chick forebrain." Neural Dev 4: 35.

Quintana-Urzainqui, I., P. Hernandez-Malmierca, J. M. Clegg, Z. Li, Z. Kozic and D. J. Price (2020). "The role of the diencephalon in the guidance of thalamocortical axons in mice." Development 147(12).

Rakic, P. (1976). "Prenatal genesis of connections subserving ocular dominance in the rhesus monkey." Nature 261(5560): 467–471.

Rash, B. G. and E. A. Grove (2006). "Area and layer patterning in the developing cerebral cortex." Curr Opin Neurobiol 16(1): 25–34.

Rauschecker, J. P. (1995). "Compensatory plasticity and sensory substitution in the cerebral cortex." Trends Neurosci 18(1): 36–43.

Ravary, A., A. Muzerelle, D. Herve, V. Pascoli, K. N. Ba-Charvet, J. A. Girault, E. Welker and P. Gaspar (2003). "Adenylate cyclase 1 as a key actor in the refinement of retinal projection maps." J Neurosci 23(6): 2228–2238.

Reichova, I. and S. M. Sherman (2004). "Somatosensory corticothalamic projections: distinguishing drivers from modulators." J Neurophysiol 92(4): 2185–2197.

Roe, A. W., S. L. Pallas, Y. H. Kwon and M. Sur (1992). "Visual projections routed to the auditory pathway in ferrets: receptive fields of visual neurons in primary auditory cortex." J Neurosci 12(9): 3651–3664.

Salinas, P. C. and R. Nusse (1992). "Regional expression of the Wnt-3 gene in the developing mouse forebrain in relationship to diencephalic neuromeres." Mech Dev 39 (3): 151–160.

Sansom, S. N. and F. J. Livesey (2009). "Gradients in the brain: the control of the development of form and function in the cerebral cortex." Cold Spring Harb Perspect Biol 1(2): a002519.

Scholpp, S. and A. Lumsden (2010). "Building a bridal chamber: development of the thalamus." Trends Neurosci 33(8): 373–380.

Seabrook, T. A., T. E. Krahe, G. Govindaiah and W. Guido (2013). "Interneurons in the mouse visual thalamus maintain a high degree of retinal convergence throughout postnatal development." Neural Dev 8: 24.

Seibt, J., C. Schuurmans, G. Gradwhol, C. Dehay, P. Vanderhaeghen, F. Guillemot and F. Polleux (2003). "Neurogenin2 specifies the connectivity of thalamic neurons by controlling axon responsiveness to intermediate target cues." Neuron 39(3): 439–452.

Shatz, C. J. and M. B. Luskin (1986). "The relationship between the geniculocortical afferents and their cortical target cells during development of the cat's primary visual cortex." J Neurosci 6(12): 3655–3668.

Shatz, C. J. and P. Rakic (1981). "The genesis of efferent connections from the visual cortex of the fetal rhesus monkey." J Comp Neurol 196(2): 287–307.

Shatz, C. J. and M. P. Stryker (1988). "Prenatal tetrodotoxin infusion blocks segregation of retinogeniculate afferents." Science 242(4875): 87–89.

Sherman, S. M. (2005). "Thalamic relays and cortical functioning." Prog Brain Res 149: 107–126.

Sherman, S. M. (2016). "Thalamus plays a central role in ongoing cortical functioning." Nat Neurosci 19(4): 533–541.

Sherman, S. M. and R. W. Guillery (1996). "Functional organization of thalamocortical relays." J Neurophysiol 76(3): 1367–1395.

Sherman, S. M. and R. W. Guillery (1998). "On the actions that one nerve cell can have on another: distinguishing 'drivers' from 'modulators.'" Proc Natl Acad Sci USA 95 (12): 7121–7126.

Sherman, S. M. and R. W. Guillery (2013). Functional Connections of Cortical Areas: A New View from the Thalamus. London: MIT Press.

Shi, W., A. Xianyu, Z. Han, X. Tang, Z. Li, H. Zhong, T. Mao, K. Huang and S. H. Shi (2017). "Ontogenetic establishment of order-specific nuclear organization in the mammalian thalamus." Nat Neurosci **20**(4): 516–528.

Shimogori, T., V. Banuchi, H. Y. Ng, J. B. Strauss and E. A. Grove (2004). "Embryonic signaling centers expressing BMP, WNT and FGF proteins interact to pattern the cerebral cortex." Development **131**(22): 5639–5647.

Shimogori, T. and E. A. Grove (2005). "Fibroblast growth factor 8 regulates neocortical guidance of area-specific thalamic innervation." J Neurosci **25**(28): 6550–6560.

Sur, M., P. E. Garraghty and A. W. Roe (1988). "Experimentally induced visual projections into auditory thalamus and cortex." Science **242**(4884): 1437–1441.

Sur, M. and J. L. Rubenstein (2005). "Patterning and plasticity of the cerebral cortex." Science **310**(5749): 805–810.

Sussel, L., O. Marin, S. Kimura and J. L. Rubenstein (1999). "Loss of Nkx2.1 homeobox gene function results in a ventral to dorsal molecular respecification within the basal telencephalon: evidence for a transformation of the pallidum into the striatum." Development **126**(15): 3359–3370.

Syed, M. M., S. Lee, S. He and Z. J. Zhou (2004). "Spontaneous waves in the ventricular zone of developing mammalian retina." J Neurophysiol **91**(5): 1999–2009.

Thompson, A. D., N. Picard, L. Min, M. Fagiolini and C. Chen (2016). "Cortical feedback regulates feedforward retinogeniculate refinement." Neuron **91**(5): 1021–1033.

Tissir, F., I. Bar, Y. Jossin, O. De Backer and A. M. Goffinet (2005). "Protocadherin Celsr3 is crucial in axonal tract development." Nat Neurosci **8**(4): 451–457.

Toldi, J., T. Farkas and B. Volgyi (1994). "Neonatal enucleation induces cross-modal changes in the barrel cortex of rat. A behavioural and electrophysiological study." Neurosci Lett **167**(1–2): 1–4.

Toldi, J., O. Feher and J. R. Wolff (1996). "Neuronal plasticity induced by neonatal monocular (and binocular) enucleation." Prog Neurobiol **48**(3): 191–218.

Tolner, E. A., A. Sheikh, A. Y. Yukin, K. Kaila and P. O. Kanold (2012). "Subplate neurons promote spindle bursts and thalamocortical patterning in the neonatal rat somatosensory cortex." J Neurosci **32**(2): 692–702.

Tuncdemir, S. N., B. Wamsley, F. J. Stam, F. Osakada, M. Goulding, E. M. Callaway, B. Rudy and G. Fishell (2016). "Early somatostatin interneuron connectivity mediates the maturation of deep layer cortical circuits." Neuron **89**(3): 521–535.

Tuttle, R., Y. Nakagawa, J. E. Johnson and D. D. O'Leary (1999). "Defects in thalamocortical axon pathfinding correlate with altered cell domains in Mash-1-deficient mice." Development **126**(9): 1903–1916.

Uemura, M., S. Nakao, S. T. Suzuki, M. Takeichi and S. Hirano (2007). "OL-Protocadherin is essential for growth of striatal axons and thalamocortical projections." Nat Neurosci **10**(9): 1151–1159.

Uesaka, N., Y. Hayano, A. Yamada and N. Yamamoto (2007). "Interplay between laminar specificity and activity-dependent mechanisms of thalamocortical axon branching." J Neurosci **27**(19): 5215–5223.

Uesaka, N., E. S. Ruthazer and N. Yamamoto (2006). "The role of neural activity in cortical axon branching." Neuroscientist **12**(2): 102–106.

Usrey, W. M. and S. M. Sherman (2019). "Corticofugal circuits: communication lines from the cortex to the rest of the brain." J Comp Neurol **527**(3): 640–650.

Vanderhaeghen, P. and F. Polleux (2004). "Developmental mechanisms patterning thalamocortical projections: intrinsic, extrinsic and in between." Trends Neurosci **27**(7): 384–391.

Viswanathan, S., S. Bandyopadhyay, J. P. Kao and P. O. Kanold (2012). "Changing microcircuits in the subplate of the developing cortex." J Neurosci **32**(5): 1589–1601.

Vue, T. Y., J. Aaker, A. Taniguchi, C. Kazemzadeh, J. M. Skidmore, D. M. Martin, J. F. Martin, M. Treier and Y. Nakagawa (2007). "Characterization of progenitor domains in the developing mouse thalamus." J Comp Neurol **505**(1): 73–91.

Vue, T. Y., K. Bluske, A. Alishahi, L. L. Yang, N. Koyano-Nakagawa, B. Novitch and Y. Nakagawa (2009). "Sonic hedgehog signaling controls thalamic progenitor identity and nuclei specification in mice." J Neurosci **29**(14): 4484–4497.

Vue, T. Y., M. Lee, Y. E. Tan, Z. Werkhoven, L. Wang and Y. Nakagawa (2013). "Thalamic control of neocortical area formation in mice." J Neurosci **33**(19): 8442–8453.

Wang, W. Z., F. M. Oeschger, J. F. Montiel, F. Garcia-Moreno, A. Hoerder-Suabedissen, L. Krubitzer, C. J. Ek, N. R. Saunders, K. Reim, A. Villalon and Z. Molnár (2011). "Comparative aspects of subplate zone studied with gene expression in sauropsids and mammals." Cereb Cortex **21**(10): 2187–2203.

Wang, Y., N. Thekdi, P. M. Smallwood, J. P. Macke and J. Nathans (2002). "Frizzled-3 is required for the development of major fiber tracts in the rostral CNS." J Neurosci **22**(19): 8563–8573.

Wang, Y., J. Zhang, S. Mori and J. Nathans (2006). "Axonal growth and guidance defects in Frizzled3 knock-out mice: a comparison of diffusion tensor magnetic resonance imaging, neurofilament staining, and genetically directed cell labeling." J Neurosci **26**(2): 355–364.

Wong, S. Z. H., E. P. Scott, W. Mu, X. Guo, E. Borgenheimer, M. Freeman, G. L. Ming, Q. F. Wu, H. Song and Y. Nakagawa (2018). "In vivo clonal analysis reveals spatiotemporal regulation of thalamic nucleogenesis." PLoS Biol **16**(4): e2005211.

Yaka, R., U. Yinon and Z. Wollberg (1999). "Auditory activation of cortical visual areas in cats after early visual deprivation." Eur J Neurosci **11**(4): 1301–1312.

Yamada, A., N. Uesaka, Y. Hayano, T. Tabata, M. Kano and N. Yamamoto (2010). "Role of pre- and postsynaptic activity in thalamocortical axon branching." Proc Natl Acad Sci USA **107**(16): 7562–7567.

Yamamoto, N. and G. Lopez-Bendito (2012). "Shaping brain connections through spontaneous neural activity." Eur J Neurosci **35**(10): 1595–1604.

Yun, M. E., R. R. Johnson, A. Antic and M. J. Donoghue (2003). "EphA family gene expression in the developing mouse neocortex: regional patterns reveal intrinsic programs and extrinsic influence." J Comp Neurol **456**(3): 203–216.

Zhang, J. S., J. A. Kaltenbach, J. Wang and G. Bronchti (2003). "Changes in [14 C]-2-deoxyglucose uptake in the auditory pathway of hamsters previously exposed to intense sound." Hear Res **185**(1–2): 13–21.

Zhang, R. W., H. P. Wei, Y. M. Xia and J. L. Du (2010). "Development of light response and GABAergic excitation-to-inhibition switch in zebrafish retinal ganglion cells." J Physiol **588**(Pt 14): 2557–2569.

Zhou, L., A. M. Goffinet and F. Tissir (2008). "[Role of the cadherin Celsr3 in the connectivity of the cerebral cortex]." Med Sci (Paris) **24**(12): 1025–1027.

Zhou, L., Y. Qu, F. Tissir and A. M. Goffinet (2009). "Role of the atypical cadherin Celsr3 during development of the internal capsule." Cereb Cortex **19 Suppl 1**: i114–119.

Chapter 8

Ontogeny of Thalamic GABAergic Neurons

Alessio Delogu

1. Introduction

This chapter describes the ontogeny of the neurons that express the neurotransmitter gamma-aminobutyric acid (GABA) and that are present within the boundaries of the adult mammalian thalamus. The definition of the developing thalamus and its topological relationship with other diencephalic structures is based on the prosomeric model (Puelles et al., 2013; Puelles and Rubenstein, 1993, 2003; Rubenstein et al., 1994), which stems from knowledge accumulated over the past 40 years on the molecular organisation of the embryonic brain and is therefore best suited to describing the ontogenetic events and underlying mechanisms that result in the mature anatomy of the thalamus (Puelles, 2019).

The prosomeric model takes its name from the realisation of the segmental organisation of the developing neural tube into functional developmental units called *neuromeres* (Lumsden and Krumlauf, 1996) or, specifically in the diencephalon, *prosomeres*. Each prosomere consists of longitudinal bands from dorsal to ventral: roof, alar, basal, and floor plate. The rostral most prosomere 3 (p3) consists of the prethalamic neuroepithelium that generates from its alar plate GABAergic structures, including the thalamic reticular nucleus (RT), the zona incerta (ZI), and the ventral lateral geniculate (LGv). The alar plate of the second prosomere (p2) generates all the thalamocortical glutamatergic neurons (thalamocortical relay cells [TRCs]) and a cohort of projection GABAergic neurons mostly, but not exclusively, found in the intergeniculate leaflet (IGL). The caudal-most first prosomere (p1) coincides with the pretectum, and its alar plate generates glutamatergic neurons in its rostral portion and GABAergic neurons in the caudal portion (Martinez-Ferre and Martinez, 2012). Embryonic folding of the neural tube and asymmetric growth push the prethalamus ventrally underneath the thalamus so that prethalamus and thalamus correspond broadly to the ventral thalamus and dorsal thalamus definitions of the columnar model of diencephalic organisation.

Hence, in this chapter, the thalamus is intended as the portion of the diencephalon delimited rostrally by the zona limitans intrathalamica (ZLI) that marks the boundary between p3 and p2, caudally by the fasciculus retroflexus that extends between p2 and p1, dorsally by the epithalamic habenular complex, and ventrally by the combined basal and floor plate derivatives of the tegmentum [see also (Figure 3A)].

Within p2 derivatives, Thalamic GABAergic neurons can be divided into two main classes: local circuit neurons, or interneurons, and projection neurons that extend axons across thalamocortical nuclear boundaries and to extra-thalamic structures. This subdivision of thalamic GABAergic neurons is not only convenient to organise this chapter, but it also reflects the author's interpretation of the current and yet incomplete evidence available on the ontogeny of thalamic GABAergic neurons, whereby the fate of GABAergic progenitors in p2 is restricted to GABAergic projection neurons, whereas GABAergic interneurons are specified at multiple locations outside p2 and invade the thalamus via tangential migration.

1.1 Interneurons

The first description of cells with distinctive short-axon morphology in the thalamus was made more than a century ago on Golgi preparations by Ramon y Cajal (Cajal, 1911). In the last decades of 1900s, an increasing number of observations, based mostly on the cat's first-order visual thalamus, the dorsal lateral geniculate (LGd), helped define some of the distinctive morphological properties of interneurons, including a small, ovoidal soma and a short, branched axon contained within the radius of the dendritic arbor (Cajal, 1911; Szentagothai, 1967; Tombol, 1967); dendritic enlargements containing loosely packed synaptic vesicles known as *F2 terminals* (Famiglietti, 1970; Famiglietti and Peters, 1972; Guillery, 1966, 1969; Majorossy and Kiss, 1976; Morest, 1971; Peters and Palay, 1966; Scheibel et al., 1972); the expression of the GABA biosynthetic enzyme glutamic acid decarboxylase (Gad) or GABA-containing vesicles in their neurites (Fitzpatrick et al., 1984; Montero, 1986; Sterling and Davis, 1980); and the lack of retrograde labelling following tracer injection in the cortex (Geisert, 1980; Weber and Kalil, 1983).

A distinctive feature of thalamic interneurons in sensory pathways is the observation of intermingled synaptic input and output on segments of their dendrites. Different synaptic arrangements are present in LGd interneurons, most commonly of a triadic type, where an interneuron's F2 type dendritic terminal is postsynaptic to an incoming retinal ganglion cell (RGC) axon and presynaptic to a TRC dendrite. These multi-synaptic complexes are ensheathed by glia to form glomeruli (Blitz and Regehr, 2005; Cox and Sherman, 2000; Govindaiah and Cox, 2004).

Extensive investigation of the synaptic organisation of interneurons in the LGd allows for the formulation of a standard connectivity module that enables retina-driven feedforward inhibition onto TRCs for contrast gain control, shaping of receptive fields, and fine temporal regulation (Hirsch et al., 2015; Sherman, 2004; Steriade, 2004). The fundamental elements of this organisational scheme are of broader validity for interneurons located in other principal sensory nuclei across small- and large-brained mammalian species (Guillery and Sherman, 2002; Montero and Singer, 1985; Ohara et al., 1989). However, interneuron subtypes may exist that do not follow this synaptic organisation, for instance, neurons that are allocated to associative thalamo-cortical networks.

Interneurons in the LGd receive driver input from RGCs along thick axons that form restricted clusters of larger boutons (Guillery, 1966; Sherman and Guillery, 1998) and target virtually all dendrites of an interneuron (Morgan and Lichtman, 2020). Retinal input accounts for the majority of synapses onto interneurons (Montero, 1991; Morgan and Lichtman, 2020; Van Horn et al., 2000), arising from different classes of RGCs with a high degree of convergence onto an individual interneuron (Acuna-Goycolea et al., 2008; Seabrook et al., 2013b). The majority of RGC contacts are at glia-encapsulated F2-type terminals (Hamos et al., 1985; Montero, 1991; Morgan and Lichtman, 2020).

Input from other interneurons, often reciprocal, is common in the LGd and involves mostly dendritic GABA release at F2-type terminals, although conventional axonal F1-type terminals are also observed (Morgan and Lichtman, 2020). Such interneuron-to-interneuron communication is not only restricted to cells in close proximity to each other but also can engage distant interneurons too, therefore potentially linking inhibitory activity in different functional subdivisions of the LGd (Morgan and Lichtman, 2020).

Cortical input involves thin axons that extend short lateral branches ending in small boutons (Guillery, 1966) with a modulatory function (Sherman and Guillery, 1998). Cortical input is less frequent on interneurons than it is on TRCs (Van Horn et al., 2000) and preferentially found on an interneuron's dendritic shaft, rather than at F2 terminals (Montero, 1991; Weber et al., 1989).

Ascending neuromodulatory input arises mostly from the cholinergic parabrachial region (Erisir et al., 1997; McCormick and Pape, 1988) and possibly also from serotonergic and noradrenergic subcortical sources (Feig and Harting, 1994; Fitzpatrick et al., 1989) to target mostly F2 terminals.

GABAergic neurons of the nucleus of the optic tract (NOT) in the pretectum synapse onto F2-type terminals (Born and Schmidt, 2007; Cucchiaro et al., 1993; Wang et al., 2002) and dendritic shafts (Wang et al., 2002). This pretectal input is distinct from that generated by neurons in the anterior pretectal area that exclusively targets TRCs in higher-order nuclei (Bokor et al., 2005).

Although a potential additional GABAergic input from the reticular thalamic nucleus (RT) has been proposed on theoretical grounds (Steriade et al., 1986), empirical validation is limited: no such inhibitory input was detected on rodent LGd interneurons (Campbell et al., 2020) but has been reported for interneurons of the motor thalamus and of associative nuclei in non-human primates (Ilinsky et al., 1999; Kultas-Ilinsky et al., 1995; Tai et al., 1995). Hence, interneurons are under inhibitory control from at least two sources (i.e., other interneurons and pretectal nuclei), whereas inhibitory input from the RT may be restricted to selected sub-circuitries and animal species.

In summary, within first-order sensory nuclei, interneuron dendrites support a broad range of synaptic motifs and—at least in rodents—the dendrites of an individual interneuron may provide access to the full thalamocortical nucleus (Grimes et al., 2010; Morgan and Lichtman, 2020; Seabrook et al., 2013b; Williams et al., 1996), enabling a single interneuron to potentially participate simultaneously in parallel circuitries. Hence, neurites of interneurons may be considered functional units with local specificity and control on the backdrop of a highly promiscuous connectivity pattern at the whole-cell level. However, evidence suggests that species-specific differences also exist, even for the well-described neurons of the LGd (Montero, 1989; Montero and Zempel, 1985, 1986; Wilson, 1986)

Far less is known about the synaptic organisation of interneurons in the associative nuclei of the thalamus and further comparative studies are needed to understand how evolutionary adaptation of a basic interneuron connectivity module enabled species-specific sensory abilities.

1.2 Projection Neurons

In addition to interneurons engaged in local connectivity, within the thalamus are also GABAergic neurons that extend a long axon to target other thalamic and extra-thalamic structures. Rather than being scattered within thalamocortical nuclei, these cells form dense cell clusters at the rostroventral of the thalamus bordering the prethalamus, to form the IGL and at the dorsocaudal edge of the thalamus to contribute to the recently described perihabenula nucleus (pHB) (An et al., 2020; Fernandez et al., 2018). The IGL lies between the prethalamic LGv and the LGd. The pHB—so far described only in the mouse thalamus—occupies a superficial position next to the lateral subdivision of the habenular complex, dorsal to the central lateral nucleus (CL) and extending further in the caudal direction, medial to the LP.

Both the IGL and pHB are part of a subcortical visual network that receives non–image-forming retinal input from intrinsically photosensitive RGCs (ipRGCs) (Beier et al., 2020; Fernandez et al., 2018; Guler et al., 2008; Hattar et al., 2006). IpRGCs are a functionally heterogeneous class of retinal ganglion cells defined genetically by expression of the opsin gene *Opn4* and accounting for about 3% of all RGCs (Guler et al., 2008). The IGL and pHB participate in limbic functions, including mood regulation (An et al., 2020; Fernandez et al., 2018; Huang et al., 2019), circadian physiology (Fernandez et al., 2020; Harrington and Rusak, 1986; Janik and

Mrosovsky, 1994; Johnson et al., 1989; Lewandowski and Usarek, 2002), and sleep (Shi et al., 2020).

Besides retinal input, IGL neurons are defined by orexinergic, serotonergic, and cortical input (Blasiak and Lewandowski, 2003; Marchant et al., 1997; Meyer-Bernstein and Morin, 1996; Smith et al., 2015; Vrang et al., 2003). Output is broad and includes the master circadian pacemaker in the hypothalamus, the contralateral IGL, the pretectum, and superficial layers of the superior colliculus (Moore et al., 2000; Morin and Blanchard, 2005). Recently, neurons in the IGL/LGv region were shown to exert direct control of the nucleus reuniens, a thalamocortical relay with strong connections to the hippocampal formation (Huang et al., 2021), therefore introducing a new paradigm for the modulation of thalamocortical plasticity by light. As expected from the diversity of connections and functions, neurons in the IGL are heterogenous, including neuropeptide Y and enkephalin-secreting types (Morin and Blanchard, 1995; Sabbagh et al., 2020).

In contrast to the IGL, which is described across mammals (Babb, 1980; Lima et al., 2012; Moore, 1989) and has homologs in other amniotes (Garcia-Lopez et al., 2004; Yoon et al., 2000), the existence and features of the pHB in larger-brained mammals and non-mammalian species are currently unknown. Within the mouse pHB, GABAergic interneurons occupy the dorsal-most portion and project to the nucleus accumbens (An et al., 2020); other neurons in the ventral subdivision of the pHB connect to the medial prefrontal cortex (Fernandez et al., 2018).

2. Distribution and Diversity of Thalamic Interneurons

Within the broader thalamocortical system, there are two striking attributes of thalamic interneurons that distinguish them from their cortical counterpart: an apparent lack of broad cell type diversity and a high degree of variability in density between mammalian orders.

2.1 Distribution of Thalamic Interneurons

Interneurons are abundant and ubiquitous in the thalamus of carnivores and primates but scarce and inhomogeneously distributed in rodents, so a division is often made between species with larger brains having proportionally far more thalamic interneurons than species with smaller brains, where they are grouped mostly in the visual nuclei. However, the recent application of sensitive and accurate detection methods to the mouse thalamus suggests that, albeit in low numbers, interneurons are present also within associative thalamocortical nuclei previously thought not to contain any (Jager et al., 2021). A shift in thinking may be required to reflect the fact that interneurons are present in the mammalian thalamus irrespective of sensory modality or hierarchical order. Although interneurons in rodents are mostly very rare, their sparsity may be to some degree compensated their broad dendritic coverage and dendritic neurotransmitter release sites—as described in Section 1.1—so that even a few interneurons may suffice to provide inhibition to several TRCs and to parallel sub-circuitries within a thalamocortical nucleus.

Several studies in the 1980s and 1990s have investigated the proportion of interneurons in some of the larger thalamocortical nuclei and are summarised in the following paragraphs. These studies document the striking difference in interneuron densities and distribution in the thalamus of primates, carnivores, and other mammals. However, the quantitative data they report are, in some cases, likely conditioned by the technologies available at the time and should be taken with the awareness that actual numbers may differ.

A distinguishing feature of human and non-human primates is the ubiquitous and abundant presence of interneurons across sensory and associative areas of the thalamus (Braak and Weinel, 1985), perhaps to enable the behavioural flexibility characteristic of these animals. Although estimates vary, in the primate thalamus, interneurons are thought to account for between 25% and 50% of all neurons. The anterior thalamus in particular appears to contain the highest proportion of interneurons in both humans and macaques (Dixon and Harper, 2001; Hunt et al., 1991). Variations in interneuron density are reported between different thalamocortical nuclei (Braak and Weinel, 1985; Clark et al., 1989; Hunt et al., 1991) and within subnuclear structures, such as the laminae and interlaminae of the LGd (Benson et al., 1991; Braak and Bachmann, 1985; Braak and Braak, 1984; Hunt et al., 1991; Montero and Zempel, 1986; Smith et al., 1987).

In the carnivore thalamus, early studies in cats identified interneurons in all the first-order sensory relay nuclei, where they account for 20–30% of all neurons (Fitzpatrick et al., 1984; Majorossy and Kiss, 1976; Pasik et al., 1973; Penny et al., 1983; Spreafico et al., 1983) and in smaller numbers in the anterior and intralaminar thalamus (Bentivoglio et al., 1991; Penny et al., 1983; Rinvik et al., 1987). Overall, in carnivores, interneuron densities within and between thalamocortical nuclei appear to exhibit greater variation than in the primate thalamus (Herron et al., 1997; Rinvik et al., 1987).

Lagomorphs, such as the rabbit, present a further reduction in distribution and higher variability in the abundance of interneurons across thalamocortical nuclei. The highest density of interneurons is found in the LGd, a feature shared with smaller-brained mammals, including rodents. Interneurons are also detected in other principal sensory relays: the ventroposterior (VP) and, in smaller numbers, the medial geniculate (MG). Interneurons are not restricted to first-order relays; they are also found in the higher-order LP and posterior (PO) nuclei. However, in these early studies, interneurons were not detected in some sectors of the thalamus, including the anterior, midline, and intralaminar thalamus (Penny et al., 1984), possibly reflecting lower density rather than a complete absence. Comparable densities and distributions of interneurons are described in the thalamus of the rodent guinea pig, with the highest density in the LGd (20%) followed by the VP (15%). Very sparse interneurons (less than 1%) are reported in the ventrobasal complex (VB) and the laterodorsal nucleus (LD) (Spreafico et al., 1994).

Similar to the guinea pig, the rat thalamus displays the highest density of interneurons in the LGd (Benson et al.,

1992; Harris and Hendrickson, 1987; Ohara et al., 1983; Ottersen and Storm-Mathisen, 1984; Spreafico et al., 1992) and very sparse interneurons in the motor nuclei (Gonzalo-Ruiz et al., 1996; Sawyer et al., 1991).

The organisation of the interneurons in the mouse and rat thalamus may resemble that in primitive mammalian species, as suggested by comparison with the thalamus of the opossum, a living marsupial related to fossil didelphids and retaining characteristics of these early mammals. In the opossum, interneurons are reported in the LGd and LP and in greater sparsity in the VB and the LD (Penny et al., 1984).

More recently, the increased availability of transgenic reporter mice and the development of new whole-brain imaging techniques have enabled a reassessment of interneuron numbers and distribution in the mouse thalamus. Block face optical laser microscopy of the entire thalamus of juvenile *Sox14Gfp* transgenic reporter mice, where approximately 80% of all thalamic interneurons are fluorescently labelled, resulted in a total count of about 7000 cells across both thalamic hemispheres (Figure 1A) (Jager et al., 2021). In the LGd, there are approximately 1200 *Sox14* interneurons per hemisphere, matching an independent stereological quantification in the LGd of C57Bl/6 mice (Evangelio et al., 2018) and therefore confirming that all LGd interneurons belong to the *Sox14* class (Figure 1A and B). In decreasing numbers, *Sox14* interneurons are found in the LP (about 400 per hemisphere), the somatosensory VPM and VPL (approximately 250 and 100 respectively), the higher-order PO (about 100), the auditory ventral medial geniculate (MGv; about 50) and higher-order dorsal medial geniculate (MGd; about 20), the LD and parafascicular (PF; about 20 each), the caudal end of the mediodorsal (MD; about 10); and lastly, the ventral anterior lateral (VAL) and ventral medial (VM; about 5 cells each) (Jager et al., 2021). The residual 20% of all thalamic interneurons (*Sox14*-negative), not included in this systematic count, is found in associative nuclei, including the MD, LD, LP, and PO, but not in the first-order sensory nuclei (Figure 1C and D) (Jager et al., 2021). An indirect rough estimate would put the total number of all thalamic interneurons across both hemispheres of the mouse thalamus just short of 9000 cells.

A unifying theme of all mammals, which extends to other amniotes, is the presence of interneurons in the visual thalamus, albeit in variable numbers: about 6% in mouse LGd (Evangelio et al., 2018) but 25–35% in the LGd of carnivores and primates (Montero and Zempel, 1986). The prevalence of interneurons in this first-order sensory relay and the presence of interneurons in somatosensory and auditory nuclei more generally, even in the rodent thalamus, suggests that a level of local control is required in sensory relays and in fact may be essential for a refined interaction with the environment. It remains unclear whether a local source of inhibition is dispensable in other thalamocortical networks or whether very few interneurons are sufficient to regulate activity in a large number of TRCs.

Further studies are needed to understand what unique properties emerge in animal species with a higher representation of local interneurons in thalamocortical networks.

2.2 Molecular Diversity of Thalamic Interneurons

Compared to other GABAergic systems, there are currently few molecular markers available to classify thalamic interneurons. The calcium-binding proteins calbindin (Calb1) and parvalbumin (Pvalb), which are expressed by different GABAergic cell types in the cortex (Celio, 1986; Celio and Heizmann, 1981; Demeulemeester et al., 1989; Hendry et al., 1989), have a less clear correlation with neurotransmitter expression in the thalamus, and their cell-type–specific expression is not conserved across mammals. In primates, expression of Calb1 or Pvalb correlates with patterns of cortical projections of glutamatergic TRCs, supporting the matrix-core model of thalamic organisation (Hashikawa et al., 1991; Jones and Hendry, 1989; Munkle et al., 2000; Rausell et al., 1992). Early studies in primates did not detect Calb1 expression in thalamic interneurons and only rarely Pvalb expression, specifically in the principal laminae of the LGd and in the magnocellular MG (Jones and Hendry, 1989). This paucity of Pvalb interneurons detected in primates contrasts with an abundance of Pvalb interneurons in all laminae of the cat's LGd (Stichel et al., 1988) and the pulvinar (Batini et al., 1991). The LGd interneurons in cats can be further subdivided according to the concomitant expression of Calb1 (Demeulemeester et al., 1991; Demeulemeester et al., 1989). In the interlaminae of the LGd, interneurons are sparser and thought to only express Pvalb (Montero, 1989; Sanchez-Vives et al., 1996). Double-positive Pvalb/Calb1 interneurons were also described in the intralaminar thalamus (Molinari et al., 1994) but not in the pulvinar (Palestini et al., 1993).

Nitric oxide synthase (Nos) expression defines interneuron subsets in carnivores. Nos1-positive but Calb1-negative interneuron subsets are present in the VB (Meng et al., 1996), the pulvinar/LP, and in the laminar structures of the LGd (Bickford et al., 1999). Specific functional properties may be associated with these molecularly defined subclasses (Carden and Bickford, 2002; McCauley et al., 2003). Nitric oxide biosynthetic markers have been reported in subsets of LGd interneurons of the rodent thalamus (Gabbott and Bacon, 1994; Leist et al., 2016), where they are proposed to correlate with specific electrical properties of the cell membrane (Leist et al., 2016).

There is, however, no clear evidence for multiple interneuron classes in the mouse LGd, as all its interneurons express the transcription factor genes *Sox14*, *Gata3*, and *Otx2* and the nicotinic cholinergic receptor subunit *Chrna6* (Bakken et al., 2020; Golding et al., 2014; Jager et al., 2021, 2016). When the location of *Chrna6*- expressing neurons is mapped across the entire mouse thalamus, a clear spatial segregation of *Chrna6*-positive and *Chrna6*-negative interneurons emerges, wherein the lateral and caudal thalamus is enriched for *Chrna6*-positive neurons, whereas the anterior and medial thalamus is enriched for the *Chrna6*-negative type (Figure 1E and F) (Jager et al., 2021). Although such clear anatomical segregation observed in the mouse thalamus is suggestive of functional compartmentalisation (Figure 1C), recent comparative analysis in the New World monkey marmoset (Jager et al., 2021), the Old World

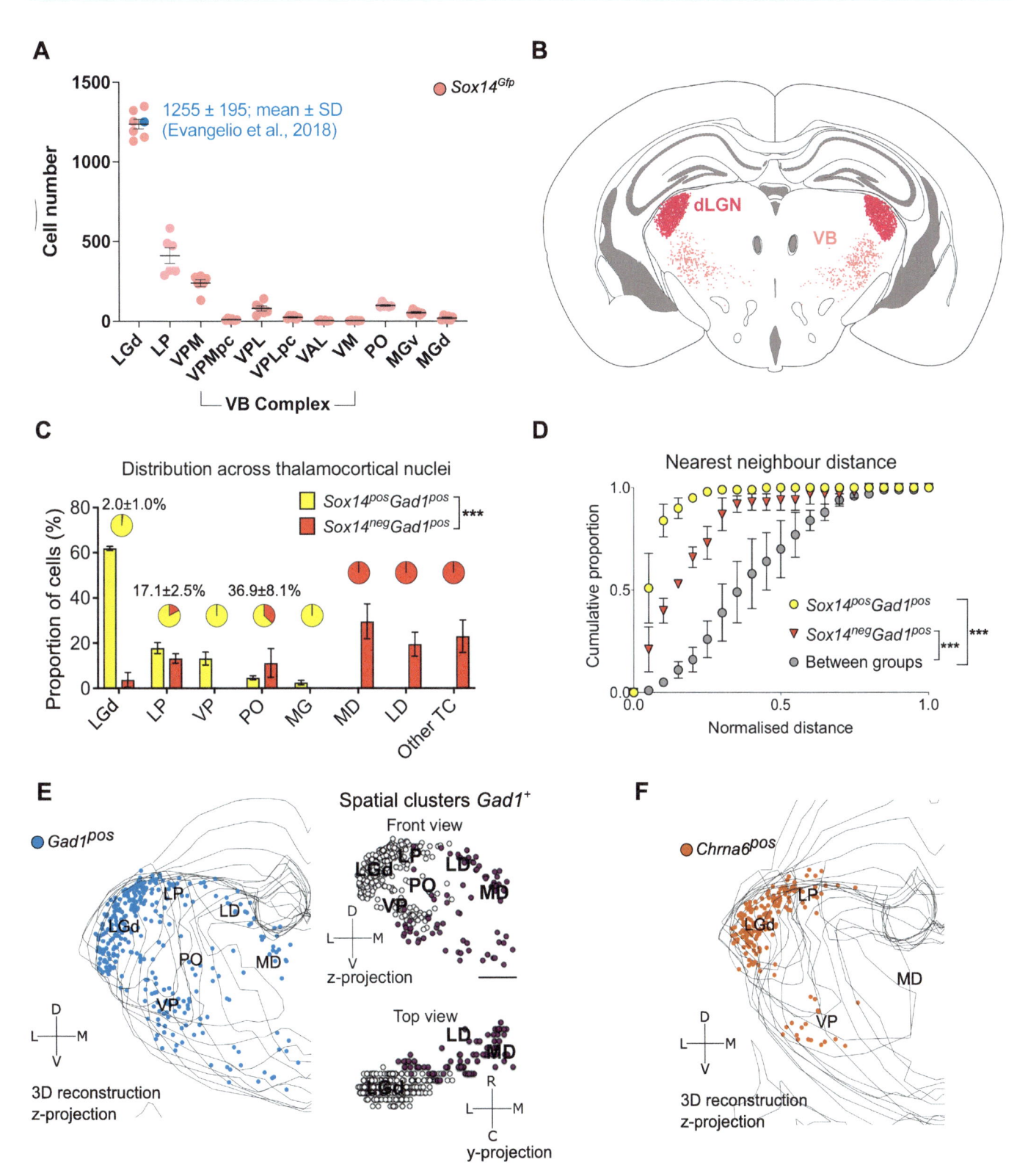

Figure 1 Spatial organisation of interneurons in the mouse thalamus.

In **A**, quantification of GFP+ cells in thalamocortical nuclei (per hemisphere) based on automated detection from serial two-photon imaging of the thalamus of Sox14$^{Gfp/+}$ reporter mice at three weeks of age. Automated count of GFP+ cells in the LGd at 1234 ± 82 (mean ± standard deviation [SD]) is consistent with a previous stereological quantification by Evangelio et al. (2018) of 1255 ± 195 (mean ± SD) interneurons (*blue*) in this nucleus. Images were registered to the Allen Institute for Brain Science CCF3 atlas for identification of all anatomical structures according to the Institute's hierarchical taxonomy. In **B**, all GFP+ cells detected in the LGd and VB complex are projected on a representative coronal section of the mouse brain. In **C**, although Sox14 marks the largest fraction of thalamic interneurons, about 20% of interneurons do not express Sox14. The histogram shows the distribution of Sox14+Gad1+ and Sox14−Gad1+ cells across thalamocortical nuclei in the Sox14$^{GFP/+}$ brains at P14, plotted as a proportion of all the cells for each interneuron class (mean ± standard error of the mean [SEM]; $n = 3$ brains). Sox14+Gad1+ and Sox14−Gad1+ populations have distinct distributions ($p < 10^{-3}$ chi-squared test) that appear to correlate with anatomical/functional divisions of the thalamus. Pie charts show the proportion (mean ± SEM) of the two interneuron classes within each nucleus. The category "other TC" refers to regions where nuclear boundaries cannot be defined precisely at two weeks of age and that are likely to contain VAL, VM, CL, IMD, PF, RE, RH, SPF, SPA, CM, and AM. In **D**, normalised nearest-neighbour distance within each interneuron class and between monkey macaque, and the human (Bakken et al., 2020) points to a more homogenous distribution of the two interneuron classes in primates, across thalamocortical modalities and hierarchies.

Expression of the *Sox14*, *Otx2*, and *Gata3* markers by the *Chrna6*-positive interneuron class appears to be conserved across the mouse, macaque, and human thalamus (Bakken et al., 2020). In the mouse, the *Chrna6*-negative class expresses a high level of *Pvalb* (Jager et al., 2021), but cell-type–specific expression of *Pvalb* is not conserved across mammals. Large-scale single-cell gene-expression libraries (Bakken et al., 2020; Kalish et al., 2018; Saunders et al., 2018; Zeisel et al., 2018) may reveal new molecularly defined interneuron subtypes, allowing for comparative studies in key reference species with evolutionary significance.

3. Multiple Sources of Thalamic GABA Neurons

The current understanding of the developmental complexity of thalamic GABA neurons is incomplete and based on a limited number of studies. It follows that any attempt at extrapolating a conserved developmental logic of general mammalian validity must be intended as speculative. This chapter follows a working model whereby interneurons are specified outside of the thalamus and migrate tangentially to reach their target thalamocortical nuclei, whereas GABA projection neurons are specified within the thalamus and distribute radially and tangentially to their definitive locations.

3.1 Extra-Thalamic Origin of Interneurons

Interneurons appear in the thalamus late in development, when the thalamocortical nuclei are already delineated and morphogenetic processes have reshaped the histological organisation of p2. Interneurons are first observed at the end of the second gestational quarter in the rhesus monkey (Jones, 2002), at birth in ferrets (Jones, 2002), and shortly before birth in mice (Golding et al., 2014; Jager et al., 2021, 2016; Su et al., 2020). Despite their late appearance, birth dating of interneurons by S-phase incorporation of modified deoxynucleotides in dividing cells indicates that they are generated early, at E24–E30 in the cat (Weber et al., 1986) and E10.5–E12.5 in the mouse (Jager et al., 2016), within the general time window of neurogenesis of both the glutamatergic TRCs (Altman and Bayer, 1988a, 1988b, 1989a, 1989b, 1989c; Angevine, 1970) and the GABAergic neurons of the prethalamus (Altman and Bayer, 1988c; Inamura et al., 2011). The delay between the time of their specification and their appearance in the thalamus corroborates an emerging picture whereby interneurons are not the result of intrinsic thalamic neurogenetic programs but, rather, of extra-thalamic GABAergic neurogenesis that takes place in other embryonic subdivisions.

An extra-thalamic origin of interneurons may seem counterintuitive because the neuroepithelium of p2 contains in its rostral-most region a narrow GABAergic progenitor domain (pTH-R; Figure 2A) (Vue et al., 2007); however, lineage tracing and time-lapse imaging in mice suggests that rather than generating GABA interneurons, the pTH-R gives rise to projection GABA neurons that migrate radially to the IGL and tangentially to the lateral sector of the LGv and to other structures at the dorsal and caudal edges of p2, including the pHB (Figure 2B) (Bluske et al., 2009; Delogu et al., 2012; Vue et al., 2007). Although there is no evidence from mouse studies indicating that the pTH-R also generates local circuit interneurons, there remains the theoretical possibility that this may occur in other species such as humans.

Adjoining the pTH-R domain of p2 is the rostrally positioned prethalamic p3 domain, known to generate diverse GABAergic cell types that populate the RT, the LGv, and the ZI (Inamura et al., 2011; Puelles et al., 2020). Long thought to be the main source of thalamic interneurons, the prethalamus contributes only a small fraction of these cells (Figure 2C). Evidence from lineage-tracing experiments in transgenic reporter mice with the rostral forebrain (ventral telencephalon, p3, and hypothalamus) *Dlx5/6Cre*-driver line and with a p3 and hypothalamic-restricted *Foxd1Cre* line label the Pvalb-expressing-but *Chrna6*-negative-subtype of thalamic interneurons, which accounts for just 20% of all thalamic interneurons, as discussed in Section 2.2 (Jager et al., 2021). In mice, this interneuron class is not found in the LGd or in other primary sensory nuclei but is restricted to higher-order and associative thalamocortical nuclei (Figure 1C and D) (Jager et al., 2021). In the mouse, fate-mapping experiments with *Nkx2.1Cre* and *Lhx6Cre* driver lines exclude a contribution from telencephalic or hypothalamic progenitor domains, pointing instead to the *Dlx5/6;Foxd1*-positive prethalamus as the likely source of this class of thalamic interneurons (Jager et al., 2021). In humans, however, additional developmental complexity has been observed: fate mapping by deposition of fluorescent lipophilic dye crystals demonstrates that the human ganglionic eminences of the telencephalon—likely the medial component—contribute a subtype of thalamic interneurons to associative nuclei, including the pulvinar and MD (Figure 2C) (Letinic and Rakic, 2001; Mojsilovic and Zecevic, 1991; Rakić and Sidman, 1969).

Caption for Figure 1 (cont.)

the two classes, expressed as a cumulative proportion of cells from P14 Sox14$^{GFP/+}$ mice. Larger distances are more common between groups than within each group ($p < 1.4 \times 10^{-30}$, two-sample Kolmogorov–Smirnov test, $n = 3$ brains). In **E**, spatial segregation into two clusters is also observed in adult C57BL/6J mice (P56) when Gad1$^+$ cells are mapped in thalamocortical space (unsupervised k-means algorithm; $k = 2$, silhouette score 0.512). The largest cluster occupies the lateral and caudal sectors of the thalamus, whereas the smaller cluster occupies mostly the rostral and medial sectors of the thalamus. In **F**, interneurons that express Chrna6 are mostly in the lateral and caudal sector of the adult C57BL/6J mouse thalamus (P56). In situ data for **E** and **F** were downloaded from the Allen Mouse Brain Atlas (Allen Institute for Brain Science). One dot represents one neuron from every eight 25-μm-thick coronal section. Figure from data in Jager et al. (2021).

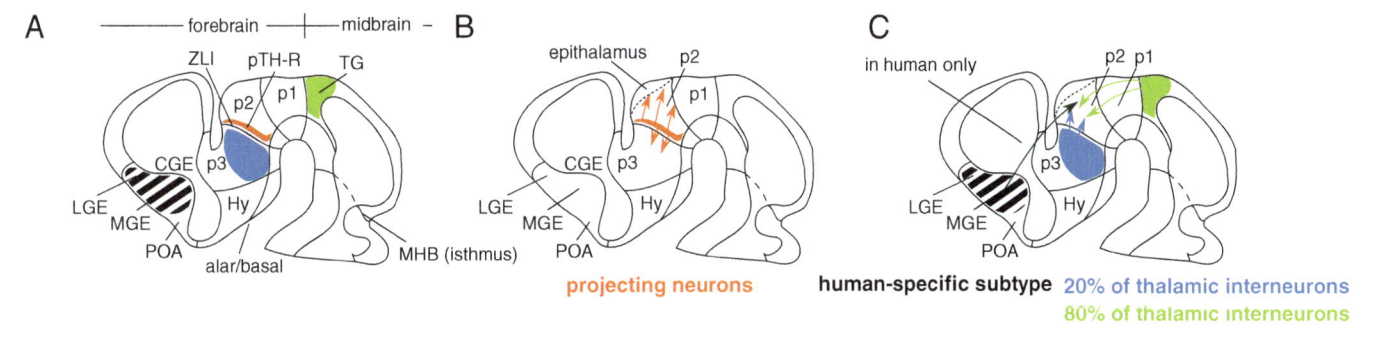

Figure 2 Thalamic and Extra-thalamic origins of GABA neurons.

In **A**, a schematic drawing representing a parasagittal section through the embryonic mouse brain at the peak of neurogenesis, with the boundaries of the prospective thalamic territory in the alar portion of p2, preceded rostrally by the prethalamic p3 and followed caudally by the pretectal p1. The locations of other relevant GABAergic neurogenic territories are also labelled: the subpallium of the telencephalon with the lateral, medial, and caudal divisions of the ganglionic eminences (LGE, MGE, and CGE, respectively) and the POA; the dorsal grey in the dorsal midbrain; the basal and narrow alar domain of the hypothalamus (Hy). Local organisers ZLI and midbrain–hindbrain boundary (MHB) are marked as transversal bold lines separating p3 and p2 and the midbrain and hindbrain, respectively. In the mouse, the prethalamus (*blue*) contributes about 20% of all thalamic interneurons, whereas the rostral and dorsal midbrain (*green*) contributes the remaining 80%. Marked in black and white stripes is the region of the ganglionic eminences that generates a subset of thalamic interneurons in humans only; the overall proportion of these cells is not known. The GABAergic pTH-R domain of p2 that generates the GABA projection neurons of the thalamus, including those in the IGL and the pHB, is depicted in orange. In **B** and **C**, coloured arrows indicate the direction of tangential migration from the three different GABAergic domains and, for humans only, from the telencephalic MGE.

In the mouse, the majority of thalamic interneurons (approximately 80%), and including those of the LGd, do not originate from any of the forebrain subdivisions but are specified in the *En1*-positive region of the developing neural tube (mesencephalon and rhombomere 1) (Figure 2A and C) (Jager et al., 2021, 2016). Fate mapping with an *En1Cre* driver line labels interneurons that populate the LGd and other first-order relays as well as higher-order nuclei, including the LP and PO (Jager et al., 2021, 2016), essentially overlapping with the *Sox14*; *Chrna6*-positive class described in Section 2.2. The precise location of the GABAergic progenitors for this larger class of thalamic interneurons is not known. However, focal labeling of the embryonic rostral and dorsal midbrain prior to the onset of tangential migration recapitulates the fate mapping observed with *En1Cre*, therefore providing strong evidence that this portion of the neuroepithelium generates the bulk of thalamic interneurons. In consideration of its rostral position in the midbrain, the territory could be part of the presumptive tectal grey of the dorsal midbrain (Figure 2C). The midbrain-derived class of thalamic interneurons appears homogenous at early postnatal stages because all cells express key developmental transcriptional regulators *Otx2*, *Gata3*, and *Sox14* (Jager et al., 2021, 2016), consistent with the limited molecular and functional diversity of thalamic interneurons so far observed in adult tissue.

Gene expression analysis in the New World monkey marmoset identified *SOX14* transcripts in about 90% of all thalamic interneurons, broadly distributed across virtually all sensory and associative thalamocortical nuclei, regardless of hierarchy or modality (Jager et al., 2021). Recent single-cell transcriptomics analysis of the lateral thalamus in the mouse, macaque, and human identified GABAergic neuron types with transcriptional profiles consistent with either a rostral forebrain or midbrain origin (Bakken et al., 2020). Therefore, the dual forebrain and midbrain origin of thalamic interneurons described by fate mapping in the mouse (Jager et al., 2021) may represent the common developmental plan for all mammalian species.

The dramatic increase in thalamic interneuron numbers that characterises carnivores and primates is interpreted as a key event that enabled more complex behaviours (Arcelli et al., 1997; Butler, 2008; Letinic and Rakic, 2001; Rikhye et al., 2018). The available lineage-tracing and genoarchitectonic evidence implicates that the mechanism for the massive increase in thalamic interneuron numbers observed in carnivores and primates is to be found in the species-specific regulation of midbrain GABAergic neurogenesis, rather than of the forebrain one. An increase in cell-type diversity, however, may also depend—as demonstrated for humans (Figure 2C)—on the contribution of a novel neuronal progenitor domain. Future comparative work within mammals and with other amniotes may further corroborate and extend the validity of this interpretation.

Irrespective of the specific developmental origin of interneurons, colonisation of the thalamus from extra-thalamic regions depends on long-distance tangential migration (Jager et al., 2021, 2016; Jones, 2002; Letinic and Rakic, 2001; Rakić and Sidman, 1969). By contrast, the differentiation of glutamatergic TRCs proceeds along radial trajectories within p2, with limited tangential dispersion (Golden et al., 1997; Shi et al., 2017; Wong et al., 2018). Admittedly, a full understanding of the migratory routes taken by thalamic interneuron precursors to reach the thalamus is still missing, and the current knowledge is certainly not comparable to the detailed picture already available for cortical interneuron migration.

In the days preceding birth, migrating interneuron precursors cross the pretectal territory from the midbrain along the pial surface of the NOT, directed to the laterally positioned LP and LGd. By the time interneurons are first detected in the LGd and LP, they are also present in more medially positioned VPL, VPM, and PO, consistent with the existence of multiple migratory avenues from the midbrain to the thalamus (Jager et al., 2021). These midbrain-derived precursors express *Sox14* and *Otx2*, two transcription factor genes loosely implicated in the regulation of tangential migration (Delogu et al., 2012; Golding et al., 2014; Inverardi et al., 2007). *Sox14*-expressing cells accumulate at the dorsal and lateral edge of the LGd and only enter the LGd after birth (Jager et al., 2016), but the molecular switch that signals entry into the LGd remains elusive. It is likely that activity-dependent mechanisms participate in the finer control of interneuron dispersion and synaptic maturation, as discussed in Section 5 of this chapter.

Less is known about other systems, but the progressive appearance of interneurons from the caudal to rostral regions of the thalamus observed in non-human primates and carnivores (Jones, 2002) is consistent with conserved migration from the midbrain across mammals.

Tracing of the precise migratory pathway of prethalamus-derived interneurons in the mouse is complicated by the small size of this population and the lack of specific markers to distinguish it from the bulk of the GABAergic precursors in the adjoining prethalamus. *Gad1*-expressing cells begin dispersing in the MD from birth (Jager et al., 2021), consistent with the notion that thalamic interneurons colonise the thalamus during early postnatal life. Although not formally demonstrated, the possibility of scattered GABAergic neurons entering the thalamus from functionally distinct sectors of the presumptive RT has been proposed by some authors (Jones, 2007; Puelles et al., 2020; Sanchez-Vives et al., 1996).

In humans, the diverse types of forebrain-derived interneurons must take substantially different routes to reach their final destinations, reflecting their different developmental origins in the telencephalic GE and, presumably, the prethalamus. Tangential migration into the human thalamus was first proposed to explain the protracted growth of the pulvinar, well past the neurogenic period of the thalamic primordium. Indeed, GABAergic neuronal precursors undergo collective migration along a transient structure named the *gangliothalamic body* that joins the proliferative zone of the ganglionic eminences—likely the MGE—to the thalamus (Letinic and Kostovic, 1997; Rakić and Sidman, 1969). Forming at the 18th gestational week, the gangliothalamic body extends along GFAP astroglia bundles under the pial surface of the thalamus to reach the pulvinar and medial thalamic territory. This transient structure is four to six cells thick at its onset, increasing in size over the course of the following three months, to recede before birth. Cells within the gangliothalamic body express neuronal markers Map2, TuJ, and PSA-NCAM positive (Letinic and Kostovic, 1997; Letinic and Rakic, 2001) and the forebrain GABAergic markers DLX1/2 and GABA (Letinic and Rakic, 2001), and undergo morphological maturation from an immature neuroblast morphology in its lateral sector to more mature dendritic branching in its medial sector (Rakić and Sidman, 1969). Because the gangliothalamic body is present at all rostrocaudal levels of the developing human thalamus, it is possible that GE-derived interneurons contribute to other thalamocortical nuclei in addition to the pulvinar and MD (Letinic and Kostovic, 1997).

A structure equivalent to the gangliothalamic body has not been found in non-human species (Letinic and Rakic, 2001), supporting the view that the migration of telencephalic interneurons into the associative human thalamus is an evolutionary innovation. In vitro experiments revealed a key difference in the chemotactic properties of the human and mouse GE-derived neuronal precursors, demonstrating that mouse GE neurons, but not human ones, are repelled by the subthalamic and choroid tissue separating the proliferative zones of the GE from the thalamus (Letinic and Rakic, 2001).

Investigation of the migratory routes and the identification of the repulsive and attractant molecular cues required to correctly home interneurons to first- and higher-order thalamocortical nuclei must take into consideration the major histogenic processes that alter the initial simpler organisation of the neural tube. For instance, the glutamatergic progenitors that differentiate in the TCRs of the LGd and MG are located in the rostral portion of the alar p2, nearest to its anterior border, from where they radially migrate to occupy a lateral position close to the pial surface (Shi et al., 2017; Wong et al., 2018); however, these sensory nuclei are pushed farther caudally by the subsequent expansion of the thalamic and telencephalic mass that takes place in larger-brained species (Puelles, 2019). In humans, the selective expansion of the pulvinar complex forces the LGd and MD farther into a ventral position (Rakić and Sidman, 1969). The subthalamic nucleus, which is proposed to act as a barrier preventing the migration of GE-derived interneurons to the thalamus in mice (Letinic and Rakic, 2001), is specified in the caudal hypothalamus (Puelles, 2019) but shifted dorsally toward the prethalamus by the time interneurons migrate from the ganglionic eminences into the thalamus. Similar topological considerations apply to prethalamic and pretectal territories that surround the thalamus and must be crossed by incoming thalamic interneurons; here, too, the completion of major histological rearrangements may provide migratory avenues or barriers to the late-coming interneurons. It cannot be excluded that the notable variation in the distribution of thalamic interneurons across species is partly due to the distinctive histological organisation of their diencephalons.

3.2 Thalamic Origin of GABA Projection Neurons

Detailed characterisation in mice indicates that the pTH-R domain is the only GABAergic territory of the thalamic p2, where it occupies its rostral most portion, separated from the prethalamus by the diencephalic organiser ZLI (Figure 2A) (Kataoka and Shimogori, 2008; Vue et al., 2007). During the neurogenic period, p2 is marked by high expression of *Olig3* (Vue et al., 2007). Neurogenesis across p2 proceeds in a rostroventral to dorsocaudal direction, with onset in the rostrally positioned pTH-R detected already by E10.5 (Vue et al., 2007). Restricted expression of transcriptional regulators and availability of transgenic reporter lines have been instrumental in mapping the fate of the pTH-R territory. Combinatorial fate mapping using the *Olig3* and *Ascl1* promoters (Vue et al., 2007) or *Tal1*-driven Cre recombinase expression (Jeong et al., 2011) and time-lapse imaging with a *Sox14Gfp* reporter (Delogu et al., 2012) traced pTH-R derived precursors migrating radially to form—by E14.5—a compact mass of GABAergic neurons in the lateral portion of the mantle zone and an elongated band of more medially positioned GABAergic cells in the ventral-most extent of p2. This rostrally positioned mass of pTH-R–derived neurons will eventually differentiate to acquire, postnatally, the stereotypical flattened appearance of the IGL and, in addition, of a thin strip of sparse GABAergic neurons lining the boundary between p3 and p2, dorsal to the prethalamic ZI. Over the period E11.5 to E16.5, however, from the laterally positioned mass of pTH-R–derived neurons, at least two subsets of precursors migrate tangentially along two distinct sequential streams, indicative of cell lineage complexity in the apparently homogenous pTH-R. Between E11.5 and E13.5, a first wave of migration is directed toward the caudal and dorsal edges of the developing thalamus, spanning the entire longitudinal extension of the thalamus (Figure 2B) (Delogu et al., 2012; Vue et al., 2007). Rather than resulting in scattering of isolated GABAergic precursors across the intervening thalamic territory, these tangentially migrating cells accumulate to form a continuous structure of densely packed neurons lining the caudal edge of the embryonic thalamus just anterior to the pretectum and extending dorsally, to line the *Olig3*-negative epithalamic territory that will subsequently differentiate into the habenular complex (Delogu et al., 2012; Vue et al., 2007). This pTH-R–derived dorsal group of GABAergic neurons contributes to the pHB, a retinorecipient thalamic nucleus with limbic functions (An et al., 2020; Fernandez et al., 2018). The fate of the pTH-R–derived neurons that condense at the border with p1 is less clear. A corresponding GABAergic mass is not detected after E16.6, and it is likely that further lateromedial dispersion into the thalamus or pretectum occurs, possibly contributing to the nucleus posterior limitans (Delogu et al., 2012).

The second wave of tangential migration involves a subset of pTH-R precursors in the presumptive IGL that, starting from E14.5 and for the following two days, seeds the prethalamic region that will later differentiate into the LGv (Figure 2B). These p2-derived GABAergic neurons are therefore found within prethalamic territory, where they occupy the lateral division of the LGv in the mature brain (Delogu et al., 2012; Jeong et al., 2011; Virolainen et al., 2012; Vue et al., 2007).

Despite radically different topology of thalamic nuclei in non-mammalian species, the pTH-R appears to be a conserved progenitor domain of all vertebrates and has been described in teleost fish (Scholpp et al., 2009, 2006) and birds (Kiecker and Lumsden, 2004; Robertshaw et al., 2013; Vieira and Martinez, 2006). Furthermore, the caudally oriented tangential migration of pTH-R–derived precursors is particularly obvious in birds (Robertshaw et al., 2013; Sellers et al., 2014), in accordance with the view that this domain does not generate thalamic local interneurons but participates instead in the formation of thalamic projections that are distinct from and complementary to thalamocortical networks.

4. Transcriptional Control of GABAergic Neurogenesis

The current understanding of the molecular control of GABAergic neurogenesis in mammals is mostly based on the mouse system and, historically, on shared principles with the avian system. Intrinsic control of GABAergic neurogenesis depends on the spatial and temporal expression of key transcription factors. This combinatorial expression partitions the rostral neural tube into three broad anteroposterior GABAergic domains delineated by the two secondary organisers: the ZLI at the p3–p2 boundary and the isthmus at the midbrain–hindbrain boundary (MHB) (Figure 3A). The ZLI separates a rostral GABAergic region that spans the telencephalic ganglionic eminences and p3 from a mesodiencephalic GABAergic region comprising p2, p1, and the midbrain (Figure 3B). The MHB marks the transition from the mesodiencephalic GABAergic domain to a caudal GABAergic domain in the hindbrain. Each domain depends on different lineage selector genes: *Dlx1/2* in the rostral domain, *Gata2* in the intermediate domain, and *Ptf1a* and *Tal1* in the caudal domain (Figure 3B and C). This neurogenic organisation reflects an underlying patterning scheme common to all vertebrates, whereby the midbrain and caudal diencephalon appear to be part of a coherent developmental unit (Albuixech-Crespo et al., 2017). In the context of the ontogeny of thalamic GABA neurons, the implications are twofold: firstly, the molecular control of thalamic interneurons specified anterior to the ZLI is drastically different than the one of thalamic interneurons specified in the midbrain, and secondly, that differentiation of thalamic GABA projection neurons in the pTH-R of p2 impinges on a pool of transcriptional regulators largely shared with the midbrain-derived thalamic interneurons.

4.1 Transcriptional Regulation of GABAergic Neurogenesis in the Rostral Forebrain

In the mouse, most forebrain-derived thalamic interneurons are specified in a *Dlx5/6;Foxd1*-positive and *Nkx2.1;Lhx6*-negative region of the rostral diencephalon, essentially overlapping with the prethalamus (Jager et al., 2021). Additionally, in humans only, some forebrain-derived interneurons are specified in the *DLX1/2*-positive GE of the telencephalon, likely the MGE (Letinic and Rakic, 2001; Letinic et al., 2002). GABAergic lineages derived from *Dlx*-expressing precursors can be grossly allocated to two neuroepithelial domains, one defined by expression of the homeodomain transcription factor gene *Nkx2.1* and the other, much broader and heterogenous, by expression of the homeodomain transcription factor genes Gs*x1/2* (Corbin et al., 2003). The transcriptional regulation of *Nkx2.1* lineages is relevant for the human-specific type of GE-derived thalamic interneurons but not for the forebrain-derived thalamic interneurons described in the mouse, because these were not labelled by fate mapping with *Nkx2.1Cre* (Jager et al., 2021). Unfortunately, there is currently limited information available on human-specific transcriptional regulation of *NKX2.1* progenitors; hence, mouse data will be described instead.

In mice, expression of *Nkx2.1* is first detected at E10.5 in the ventral hypothalamus and one day later in the subpallium (Lazzaro et al., 1991), where it marks progenitors in the MGE and preoptic area (POA) (Figure 3B and C) (Shimamura et al.,

1995; Sussel et al., 1999). MGE progenitors differentiate into several cortical interneuron types, including the fast-spiking Pvalb interneurons and the somatostatin (SST) interneurons (Fogarty et al., 2007; Pleasure et al., 2000; Xu et al., 2004, 2008). The POA progenitors add developmental complexity, contributing to about 10% of all cortical interneurons (Gelman et al., 2011, 2009). From E12.5, *Nkx2.1* progenitors support gliogenesis (Kessaris et al., 2006; Minocha et al., 2017, 2015) with direct Nkx2.1 binding on the *Gfap* promoter (Minocha et al., 2017). Glia precursors tangentially migrate to enter the pallium and septal region, and *Nkx2.1*-derived glia is also present in the mouse thalamus (Jager et al., 2021). Within the GABAergic domains of the developing forebrain, *Nkx2.1* loss of function results in changes in regional identity: in the subpallium, in the conversion of the MGE into lateral ganglionic eminence (LGE) identity (Sussel et al., 1999) and in the rostral diencephalon, in conversion of the hypothalamus into prethalamus (Kim et al., 2020). Although not directly involved in regulating the expression of genes in the GABA biosynthesis pathway, *Nkx2.1* controls the migratory behaviour of postmitotic GABAergic precursors (Nobrega-Pereira et al., 2008). The *Nkx2.1* loss-of-function mutation results in the depletion of several interneuron classes (Butt et al., 2008; Pleasure et al., 2000; Sussel et al., 1999) and of ventral hypothalamic identity (Kimura et al., 1996). It is possible, but not yet tested, that the conversion of hypothalamic territory into a prethalamic one in the *Nkx2.1* loss-of-function mutant mouse (Kim et al., 2020) leads to an increase in the number of prethalamus-derived thalamic interneurons.

In view of the extensive evidence for the essential role of *Nkx2.1* in forebrain interneuron development in mice, it could be postulated that mutations in human *NKX2.1* should also affect differentiation of thalamic interneurons directed to the human pulvinar and MD.

Expression of *Gsx2* (*Gsh2*) is detected by E9.5 in the ventricular zone (VZ) and extending further than *Nkx2.1* to include the GABAergic neurogenic domains in the LGE and the prethalamus (Hsieh-Li et al., 1995) and is therefore a candidate developmental regulator also for the prethalamus-derived thalamic interneurons; *Gsx1* (*Gsh1*) expression is even broader, including the caudal diencephalon and midbrain (Figure 3B and C) (Valerius et al., 1995). Gsx1 and Gsx2 have different roles in the maturation of GABAergic progenitors, where Gsx1 promotes differentiation and Gsx2 maintenance of the undifferentiated state (Pei et al., 2011). Graded *Gsx2* expression is required to establish dorsoventral regional identity in the LGE and in the caudal ganglionic eminence (CGE) and for the generation of cortical interneurons, olfactory bulb interneurons, and striatal projection neurons (Waclaw et al., 2009; Yun et al., 2003), a role also mediated by downstream activation of the transcription factors Sp8 and Sp9 in intermediate progenitors (Figure 3C) (Li et al., 2018; Wei et al., 2019; Zhang et al., 2016). The impact of the *Gsx2* loss-of-function mutation on GABAergic neurogenesis is also explained by the ventral shift of the pallium–subpallium boundary (Carney et al., 2009; Szucsik et al., 1997), likely via dis-inhibition of the pallial marker *Pax6* (Toresson et al., 2000; Waclaw et al., 2009; Yun et al., 2001). The *Gsx1* loss-of-function mutation displays less severe phenotypes (Yun et al., 2003). Ectopic Gsx2 expression activates key regulators of GABAergic differentiation, including the proneural basic helix loop helix (bHLH) transcription factor gene *Ascl1* and the lineage-selector genes of the *Dlx* family (Figure 3C) (Waclaw et al., 2009). Ascl1 controls cell cycle progression and cell cycle exit via direct and sequential transcriptional regulation of cell cycle genes (Castro et al., 2011) and contributes to maintaining neighbouring neural stem cells in an undifferentiated state; this is achieved via repression of the SoxB1 transcription factors required to maintain the undifferentiated state (Bylund et al., 2003; Graham et al., 2003) and upregulation of Notch ligands for lateral inhibition (Casarosa et al., 1999; Henke et al., 2009; Yun et al., 2002).

Upregulation of the proneural *Ascl1* gene (Wang et al., 2009) is a hallmark of GABAergic differentiation across all brain vesicles (Figure 3C), albeit with regional differences, dictated by putative cofactors (Parras et al., 2002). However, and in contrast with GABAergic neurogenesis in the mesodiencephalic domain, here, Ascl1 directly activates the *Dlx1/2* genes, binding at intergenic enhancers that also contain autoregulatory Dlx-binding sites and putative Nkx2.1-binding sites (Poitras et al., 2007). By E12.5, *Dlx2* expression is well established in the VZ and subventricular zone (SVZ) and is followed by activation of *Dlx1* in the same proliferative zones; both transcription factors participate in the activation of the paralogous genes *Dlx5* in the SVZ and *Dlx6* in the mantle zone (MZ) (Figure 3C) (Liu et al., 1997). The *Dlx1/2/5/6* genes are expressed in all GABAergic domains of the telencephalon, hypothalamus, and prethalamus (Bulfone et al., 1993; Simeone et al., 1994) and encode for homeodomain transcription factors that control multiple aspects of GABAergic differentiation (Lindtner et al., 2019).

The compounded *Dlx1/2* loss-of-function mutant mouse also lacks *Dlx5/6* expression and displays severely impaired GABAergic differentiation of the striatum and of the cortical and olfactory interneurons (Anderson et al., 1997b; Long et al., 2007; Wang et al., 2010). It is possible that *Dlx1/2* mutations will also affect the forebrain-derived thalamic interneurons; however, this has not been tested yet. GABAergic differentiation by Dlx factors is in part achieved in conjunction with Ascl1 function (Long, Cobos, et al., 2009, Long, Swan, et al., 2009b; Yun et al., 2002). Dlx1/2 activate genes required for GABA biosynthesis (Anderson et al., 1997a; Le et al., 2017) and for cell migration (Pleasure et al., 2000), as exemplified by the activation of the transcription factor gene *Arx* (Figure 3C) (Cobos et al., 2005) and of chemokine signalling receptor genes (Wang et al., 2010, 2011). The Dlx1/2 factors suppress alternative lineage fates (Petryniak et al., 2007), and in the context of thalamic inhibitory subtypes, they suppress a latent pTH-R potential in the prethalamus (Delogu et al., 2012).

A more refined description of the transcriptional regulators for the *Dlx5/6;Foxd1*-derived thalamic interneurons is currently not possible. The recent implementation of single-cell transcriptomics on the developing hypothalamus and prethalamus (Kim

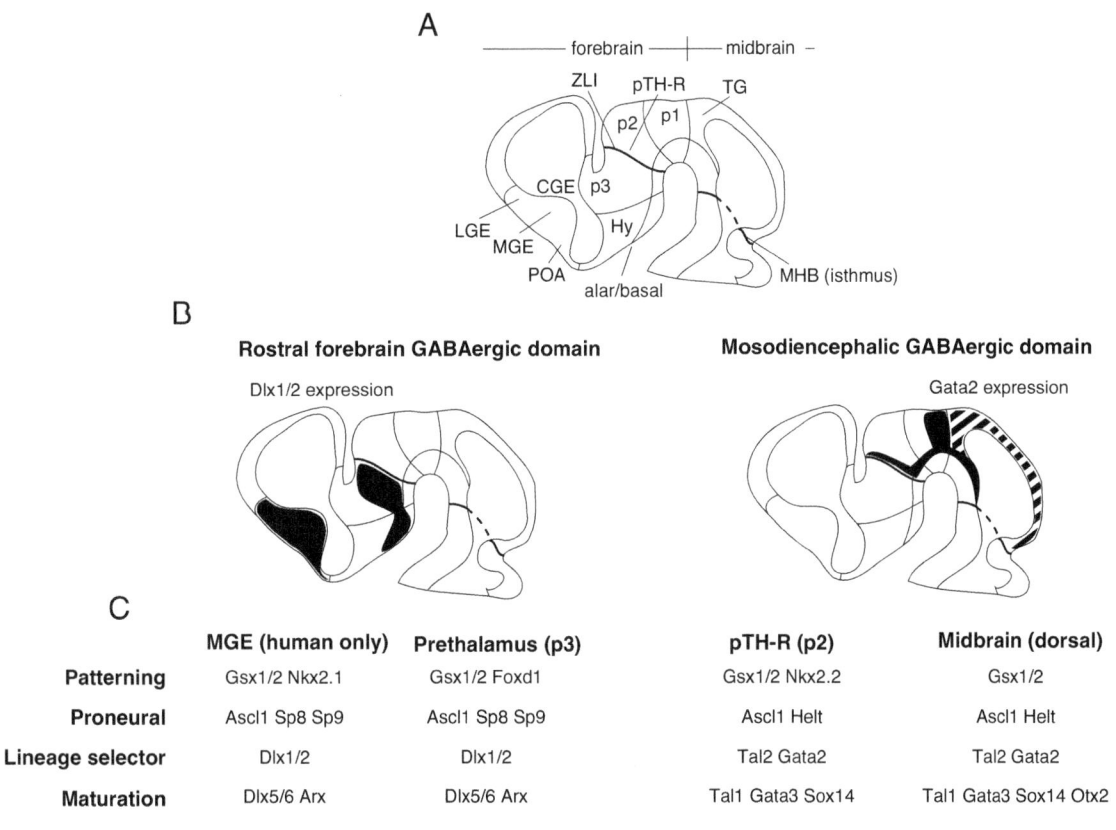

Figure 3 Rostral forebrain and mesodiencephalic GABAergic neurogenesis.

In **A**, the embryonic mouse brain at about E12.5, with its major subdivisions. In **B**, marked in black, the areas of GABAergic neurogenesis in the rostral forebrain (*left*), which extend caudally to the ZLI and are defined by *Dlx1/2* expression, and the areas of GABAergic neurogenesis in the mesodiencephalic compartment (*right*), between the ZLI and the MHB and defined by *Gata2* expression. Black and white stripes indicate the intermingled GABAergic and glutamatergic neurogenesis that takes place in the dorsal midbrain. In **C**, a selection of well-characterised transcription factors that guide GABAergic differentiation in the territories that contribute GABA neurons to the mature thalamus. Within the rostral forebrain domain, *Nkx2.1* and *Foxd1* define two distinct sources of thalamic interneurons, although the *Nkx2.1* source is thought to only exist in the human brain. *Dlx1/2* confer neurotransmitter identity and are therefore considered lineage selectors. In the mesodiencephalic domain, *Nkx2.2* distinguishes the region giving rise to the GABA projection neurons of the IGL, LGv, and pHB, whereas postmitotic expression of *Otx2* is restricted to thalamic interneurons. *Gata2* and, to a lesser extent *Tal2*, are the lineage selectors for neurotransmitter fate in these regions.

et al., 2020) may already contain information on the molecular determinants that set progenitors of the thalamic interneurons on a different differentiation path from the other prethalamic lineages; however, mining single-cell transcriptomics data for such a minor population presents technical challenges.

4.2 Transcriptional Regulation of GABAergic Neurogenesis in the Midbrain

The embryonic midbrain neuroepithelium is patterned by longitudinal and transversal spatiotemporal gradients of morphogens that provide the spatial coordinates for the expression of transcription factors, often of the homeodomain family. The anteroposterior axis of the midbrain is predominantly patterned by fibroblast growth factors (FGFs) released by the notochord and subsequently by the isthmic organiser at the MHB (Crossley et al., 1996; Shamim et al., 1999). The dorsoventral axis is patterned by opposing SHH and BMP gradients secreted from the floor plate and underlying chord and the roof plate, respectively (Perez-Balaguer et al., 2009). It ensues the emergence of progenitor domains along the dorsoventral axis of the mesencephalon (Sanders et al., 2002), with neurogenesis proceeding from a proliferative VZ to the MZ, through an intervening intermediate zone (IZ) (Arimura et al., 2019). The combinatorial pattern of transcription factor gene expression in the ventricular and mantle zones defines seven progenitor domains. Numbered from dorsal to ventral, domains m1 and m2 fall within the alar (dorsal) plate, the m3–m5 within the basal (ventral) plate, and m6 and m7 are contained within the floor plate. GABAergic neurogenesis takes place in all these domains except for the ventral-most m6 and m7. Midbrain-derived thalamic interneurons are likely specified within the m1 and m2 progenitor domains of the dorsal midbrain (Jager et al., 2016), which also generate GABAergic neurons of the superior colliculus, the inferior colliculus, and part of the dorsal periaqueductal grey. Birth dating of thalamic interneurons (Jager et al., 2016) broadly correlates with neurogenesis of the superior colliculus (Edwards et al., 1986). A peculiarity of the m1 and m2 domains is that glutamatergic and GABAergic fates are interspersed rather than segregated in neurotransmitter-specific spatial subdomains (Figure 3B), possibly reflecting the presence of neuronal progenitors with excitatory and inhibitory potential.

Similar to other GABAergic neurogenic domains across the embryonic brain, progenitors in the VZ of m1 and m2 express the transcription factor Ascl1 (Figure 3C) (Miyoshi et al., 2004). GABAergic neurogenesis in the m1 and m2 domains is strictly dependent on Ascl1 (Miyoshi et al., 2004), whereas it is only partially so in the ventral m3–m5 domains (Peltopuro et al., 2010), suggesting the presence of redundant mechanisms in m3–m5 that are instead absent in the dorsal midbrain.

The GABAergic progenitors in the dorsal and ventral midbrain and caudal diencephalon share expression of the bHLH/ORANGE transcriptional repressor *Helt* (Heslike, Megane; Figure 3B and C) (Guimera et al., 2006a; Miyoshi et al., 2004). *Helt* expression follows *Ascl1*, first in the ventral midbrain at E9.5 and two days later in the dorsal midbrain (Miyoshi et al., 2004). *Helt* plays a direct role in promoting GABAergic neurogenesis by repressing the glutamatergic proneural genes *Neurog1* and *Neurog2* (Guimera et al., 2006b; Nakatani et al., 2007), and ectopic expression of *Helt* is sufficient to force GABAergic differentiation at the expenses of glutamatergic differentiation (Nakatani et al., 2007; Sellers et al., 2014) or to enhance it within GABAergic domains (Miyoshi et al., 2004).

Similar to the *Ascl1* loss-of-function phenotype (Peltopuro et al., 2010), *Helt* loss-of-function mutations lead to a complete failure of GABAergic neurogenesis in m1 and m2 and in all the ventral domains, except for m5 (Guimera et al., 2006b; Nakatani et al., 2007). Residual GABAergic neurogenesis in some domains of the ventral midbrain in the *Ascl1* or *Helt* knockout, but complete loss in the compounded knockout (Wende et al., 2015) indicates a degree of redundancy between the two factors in the ventral but not in the dorsal midbrain (Song et al., 2015; Wende et al., 2015). These data suggest that midbrain-derived thalamic interneurons are dependent on *Helt* and *Ascl1* function, although formal validation is currently lacking.

Upon cell cycle exit and transition into the IZ, *Ascl1* and *Helt* are downregulated concomitantly with upregulation of two key lineage selector genes: the bHLH transcription factor *Tal2* (Mori et al., 1999) and the zinc finger transcription factor *Gata2* (Figure 3C) (Kornhauser et al., 1994; Nardelli et al., 1999); both control important steps in the acquisition of GABAergic lineage identity, including expression of the GABA biosynthetic enzymes (Achim et al., 2013; Kala et al., 2009; Virolainen et al., 2012). *Tal2* expression is detected already by E10.5 in the VZ, with its expression spreading from ventral to dorsal (Bucher et al., 2000) and preceding the onset of *Gata2* expression (Achim et al., 2013). *Tal2* loss of function impacts the formation of the superior and inferior colliculi (Bucher et al., 2000) and severely affects GABAergic differentiation in all but the m5 domain. Although expression of the progenitor genes *Ascl1* and *Helt* and cell cycle progression are unaffected in *Tal2* mutants, the glutamatergic marker *Scl17a6* (*Vglut2*) and glutamatergic lineage transcription factors are ectopically induced (Achim et al., 2013).

In keeping with the ventral-to-dorsal direction of the neurogenic wave, strong expression of *Gata2* in the IZ of the m1 and m2 domains is first detected only by E12.5 (Herberth et al., 2005; Kala et al., 2009). The *Gata2* loss-of-function mutation is more severe than the *Tal2* one, causing a complete failure of GABAergic neurogenesis in all domains of the midbrain while preserving progenitor gene expression intact (Kala et al., 2009; Willett and Greene, 2011). Consequently, midbrain-derived thalamic interneurons are dramatically reduced in the midbrain-specific *Gata2* loss-of-function mutant (Jager et al., 2016). Although both *Tal2* and *Gata2* genes emerge as critical regulators of the GABAergic fate in the midbrain, their activation is independent of each other (Achim et al., 2013). The role of *Tal2* and *Gata2* as lineage selector genes is confirmed by ectopic expression experiments, which interfere with the glutamatergic differentiation programme and force expression of GABAergic genes (Achim et al., 2013; Kala et al., 2009). It is currently unknown if such gain-of-function experiments are sufficient to increase thalamic interneuron numbers.

Although *Tal2* and *Gata2* expression in the MZ is not sustained, *Tal2* and *Gata2* control the expression of the other gene family members *Tal1* and *Gata3* and of *Sox14* that define more mature precursors and display sustained temporal expression (Figure 3C) (Achim et al., 2013; Jager et al., 2016; Kala et al., 2009; Ogilvy et al., 2007; van Doorninck et al., 1999; van Eekelen et al., 2003; Zhao et al., 2008). Because of their protracted expression window, they can be used to monitor the migration of midbrain-derived interneurons into the thalamic territory (Jager et al., 2016). *Tal1* loss of function preserves GABAergic differentiation (Achim et al., 2013) but may be required for survival of the GABAergic neurons in the superior colliculus during late embryogenesis and early postnatal life (Bradley et al., 2006). Constitutive inactivation of *Gata3* leads to multiple broad defects in the developing brain (Pandolfi et al., 1995), but its conditional inactivation in the midbrain does not impede GABAergic differentiation (Achim et al., 2012).

Expression of *Sox14* marks all midbrain-derived thalamic interneurons (Chrna6-positive class, see also Figure 1) throughout embryonic development and the juvenile stages (Jager et al., 2021, 2016). *Sox14* encodes for an HMG box transcription factor and together with *Sox21*, they form the SOXB2 family of *Sox* genes (Uchikawa et al., 1999). The two paralogue genes have partially overlapping expression and non-redundant functions: expression of *Sox21* is broader than that of *Sox14*, extending throughout the VZ, IZ, and MZ (Makrides et al., 2018); *Sox14* expression is restricted to postmitotic precursors in the MZ (Jager et al., 2016; Makrides et al., 2018) and requires *Tal2* (Achim et al., 2013) and *Gata2* (Jager et al., 2016). Loss-of-function mutation of *Sox14* severely impairs terminal differentiation of GABAergic neurons in the dorsal midbrain (Makrides et al., 2018), which correlates with a 90% reduction in midbrain-derived thalamic interneurons in the postnatal mouse brain (Jager et al., 2016). In the dorsal midbrain, *Sox14* controls the GABAergic gene *Gad2* and is required for robust induction of *Gata3* expression; however, contrary to lineage-selector genes such as *Tal2* and *Gata2*, its function does not appear to include suppression of a late glutamatergic potential (Makrides et al., 2018).

Gata2 induces the expression of additional transcription factor genes, including *Lhx1* and *Pitx2* (Kala et al., 2009). *Lhx1* and *Pitx2* identify different GABAergic subtypes in the dorsal midbrain, but *Pitx2* is also expressed in some glutamatergic neuron types in the ventral midbrain (Waite et al., 2011).

Otx2 is expressed together with *Sox14* in thalamic interneuron precursors that migrate into the diencephalon perinatally (Figure 3C) (Jager et al., 2016). Otx2 is a homeobox transcription factor with multiple developmental roles, including the positioning of the MHB organiser prior to the onset of neurogenesis. From E10.5 onward, *Otx2* is required for neurogenesis and cell-lineage identity in the midbrain (Vernay et al., 2005), including the regulation of GABAergic differentiation in the dorsal midbrain (Di Giovannantonio et al., 2014). Conditional inactivation of Otx2 at birth leads to a dramatic reduction in thalamic interneurons (Golding et al., 2014). The transcriptional activity of Otx2 is regulated by interaction with Meis2, a TALE subtype homeobox transcription factor required for dorsal midbrain specification (Agoston and Schulte, 2009) whose expression is retained postnatally in midbrain-derived thalamic interneurons (Golding et al., 2014). Although Gata2, Sox14, and Otx2 are important molecular players in the differentiation of the midbrain-derived thalamic interneurons, the specific determinants that set this particular lineage on its own developmental trajectory, distinct from other midbrain-resident GABAergic cells, remain to be identified.

4.3 Transcriptional Regulation of Neurogenesis in the Thalamic Primordium

GABA projection neurons in the IGL and those migrating from the embryonic IGL into the LGv and pHB are specified in the pTH-R domain of p2. Despite proximity with the GABAergic neuroepithelium of p3, from which it is separated by the thin layer of the ZLI (Figure 2A, 3A), the transcriptional profile of the precursors in pTH-R more closely resembles the one observed in the GABAergic progenitor domains of the dorsal midbrain than the one in p3 (Figure 3B and C). Rostrocaudal patterning of the prospective p3 and p2 prior to the establishment of the local organiser ZLI and the onset of diencephalic neurogenesis (Hirata et al., 2006; Kobayashi et al., 2002; Martinez-Ferre et al., 2013; Mattes et al., 2012; Shimamura et al., 1995) contributes to the subsequent differential interpretation of morphogenic molecules secreted by the ZLI that result in the acquisition of different GABAergic subtype identity in p3 and pTH-R; these secreted molecules include sonic hedgehog (SHH) (Jeong et al., 2011; Kiecker and Lumsden, 2004; Scholpp et al., 2006; Vieira and Martinez, 2006; Vue et al., 2009), FGF8 (Kataoka and Shimogori, 2008; Martinez-Ferre and Martinez, 2009), and members of the Wnt family (Bluske et al., 2009, 2012; Martinez-Ferre et al., 2013; Quinlan et al., 2009).

The GABAergic progenitors in p3 and pTH-R share expression of *Ascl1*, and *Nkx2.2* is expressed in the pTH-R as well as in the proximal region of p3, but high expression of *Helt* is only observed in pTH-R (Delogu et al., 2012; Kitamura et al., 1997; Miyoshi et al., 2004; Vue et al., 2007). However, divergence in transcriptional programs becomes evident as progenitors exit the cell cycle and begin post-mitotic differentiation and radial migration into the MZ (Figure 3C). Precursors in pTH-R, but not in p3, activate *Gata2* and *Tal2* and, subsequently, *Gata3*, *Tal1*, and *Sox14* (Delogu et al., 2012; Guo and Li, 2019; Kataoka and Shimogori, 2008; Virolainen et al., 2012; Vue et al., 2007), recapitulating the transcriptional cascade observed during GABAergic neurogenesis in p1 and the dorsal midbrain. In contrast, p3 neurogenesis proceeds with activation of the *Dlx1/2/5/6* regulated programs, as discussed earlier.

Within the large GABAergic territory that spans p3 and pTH-R, *Dlx1/2* and *Gata2* regulate alternative GABAergic subtype fate. This is demonstrated by the ectopic activation of pTH-R markers, including *Gata2*, *Tal1*, and *Sox14*, in the p3 of the *Dlx1/2* loss-of-function mutant (Delogu et al., 2012; Sellers et al., 2014) and, conversely, by the ectopic activation of p3 markers, including *Dlx1/2* and *Arx*, in the pTH-R domain of *Gata2* mutant animals (Virolainen et al., 2012).

Despite the apparent homogeneity of pTH-R precursors, additional mechanisms must exist that lead to the acquisition of the diverse migratory properties, axonal projections, and synaptic specificity observed in the pTH-R–derived neurons of the IGL, LGv, and pHB. These additional lineage regulators remain currently unknown, and further investigation is needed to reveal the extent to which immature patterns of neuronal activity contribute to the recruitment of GABA projection neurons into larger networks during development.

5. Activity-Dependent Control of Interneuron Development

The visual pathway is a well-established system to model the maturation of sensory circuitry in the thalamus (Figure 4) (Shatz, 1996) and the availability of genetic tools makes the mouse a particularly powerful system for dissecting the underlying molecular mechanisms (Huberman et al., 2008; Seabrook et al., 2017). In the LGd, interneurons undergo a lengthy process of maturation that extends to the first few weeks of postnatal life (Charalambakis et al., 2019; Golding et al., 2014; Jager et al., 2016). This developmental window coincides with broader circuit maturation events that are often driven by spontaneous or elicited neuronal activity and glia–neuron interactions (Clarke and Barres, 2013; Hong and Chen, 2011; Pan and Monje, 2020; Shatz, 1996).

The late arrival of interneurons and delayed establishment of local inhibition in the thalamus reflect a general scheme that appears geared to privilege excitation during the early stages of thalamocortical circuit maturation (Anton-Bolanos et al., 2019; Moreno-Juan et al., 2017), followed by remodelling of inhibitory circuits to coincide with the switch from immature to adult-like patterns of activity (Colonnese and Phillips, 2018).

Retinal afferentiation precedes the formation of other non-retinal inputs (Figure 4), which are established when visually evoked activity is already present and the retinogeniculate tract is undergoing pruning (Bickford et al., 2010; El-Danaf et al., 2015). The use of *Math5* mutant animals has been instrumental in studying the role of retinal afferents in the maturation of the LGd circuitry. *Math5* is a proneural bHLH transcription factor required in the retina for differentiation of RGCs, so that *Math5* mutant animals display an 80% reduction in RGC numbers and the failure to extend axons toward the brain (Brown

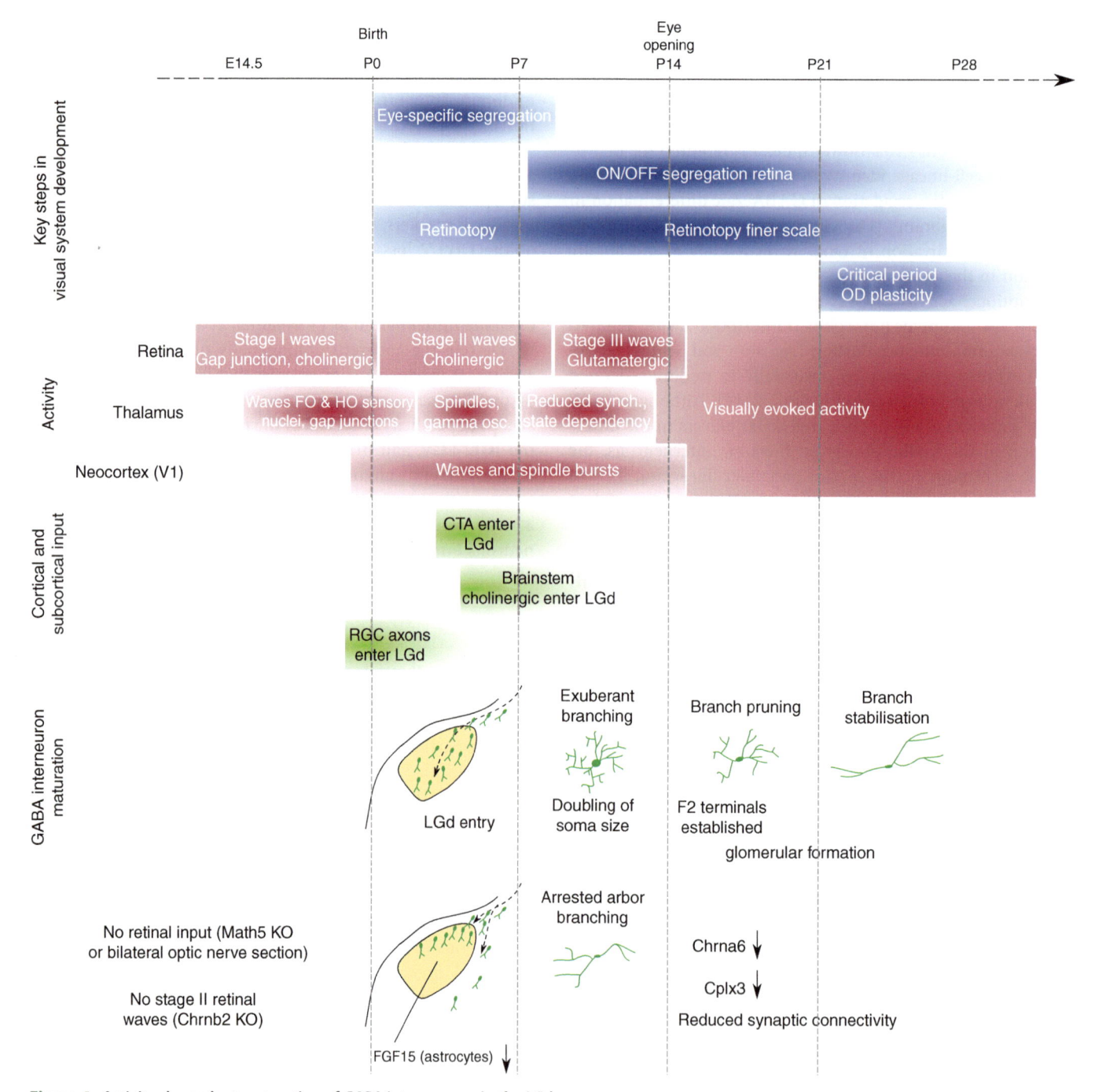

Figure 4 Activity-dependent maturation of GABA interneurons in the LGd.

Timing of the main events in the mouse visual circuit development are presented in blue. Spontaneous and coordinated patterns of neuronal activity in the retina, thalamus (including the LGd), and primary visual cortex (V1) begin before birth and are replaced by visually evoked activity around the time of eye opening (red). The timeline of driver and modulatory incoming axonal projections into the LGd is presented in green. Note the early appearance of retinal afferents that precedes cortical layer 6 input and ascending modulatory input from the cholinergic brainstem. The normal progression of interneuron maturation and functional integration in the LGd microcircuitry begins at the time of birth and continues for the first two to three weeks postnatally. The presence of an intact retinal input is essential for interneuron migration, dendritic growth and pruning, the establishment of F2 contacts, and gene expression of key synaptic components. Sources: Anton-Bolanos et al. (2018, 2019), Charalambakis et al. (2019), Huberman et al. (2008), Moreno-Juan et al. (2017), Su et al. (2020).

et al., 2001; Wang et al., 2001). Studies based on the *Math5* loss-of-function mutant indicate that the early appearance of retinal synapses is required for subsequent maturation of LGd connectivity: accordingly, ascending cholinergic neuromodulatory input (Sokhadze et al., 2018) and the timing of descending cortical layer 6 input (Brooks et al., 2013; Grant et al., 2016; Seabrook et al., 2013a) depend on an intact and functional retinal innervation. Retinal input induces chromatin reorganisation (He et al., 2019) and regulates transcription of key genes involved in the maturation of the LGd circuitry (Brooks et al., 2013; Cheadle et al., 2018).

Recent experimental evidence suggests that retinal signals also contribute to defining the finer positioning of thalamic interneurons and their functional integration into the thalamocortical visual circuitry (Figure 4). Interneurons enter the LGd from the first postnatal day, from a dorsolateral location (Jager et al., 2016), and over the first postnatal week spread progressively in a ventromedial direction to disperse homogeneously throughout the LGd (Charalambakis et al., 2019; Golding et al., 2014; Jager et al., 2016). Dendritic arbour maturation proceeds first with a period of exuberant branching in the second postnatal week, before interneurons acquire their stereotypic mature bipolar morphology during the third postnatal week (Figure 4) (Charalambakis et al., 2019). Although connectivity with incoming retinal axons is established early (Seabrook et al., 2013b), the integration of interneurons within local thalamic circuitry, formation of F2-type synapses, and ensuing inhibitory responses in TCRs are reliably detected only by the time of eye opening (Figure 4) (Bickford et al., 2010; Charalambakis et al., 2019; Golding et al., 2014).

Intact retinal input is required for correct positioning of interneurons, which fail to distribute evenly along the lateromedial axis of the LGd in mice enucleated at birth or when cholinergic type II retinal waves are inhibited while preserving the retinogeniculate tract intact (Figure 4) (Golding et al., 2014). Recruitment of interneurons to the LGd requires expression of the secreted factor Fgf15 in the LGd and along the migratory trajectory to the nucleus (Figure 4) (Su et al., 2020). In *Math5* and *Fgf15* mutants, homing of interneurons appears aberrant, with cells diverted into the contiguous VB complex. Intriguingly, retinal input appears to regulate *Fgf15* transcription in astrocytes rather than in neuronal cells (Su et al., 2020), an indication of the complex and yet poorly understood interactions underlying the maturation of the LGd circuitry. In addition to cell migration, the synaptic maturation process, too, requires retinal input. In *Math5* mutant mice, interneurons fail to undergo the transient increase in dendritic branching normally observed during the second postnatal week, display abnormal intrinsic membrane properties, and fail to establish F2-type synapses (Figure 4) (Charalambakis et al., 2019). Similar effects are observed upon bilateral optic nerve section (ONS). Interneurons do not complete their migration to spread evenly throughout the LGd when ONS is performed at birth, whereas migration is normal but the establishment of inhibitory control on TCRs is impaired when ONS is performed at P8; interestingly, by P12, none of these effects is observed, suggesting closure of a developmental window for plasticity (Golding et al., 2014). In keeping with the activity-dependent establishment of F2 contacts in the LGd, ONS at P1 or P8 eliminates the enhanced inhibitory responses normally observed in TCRs upon treatment with the metabotropic glutamate receptor type I agonist DHPG (Golding et al., 2014). Indicative of underlying activity-dependent transcriptional regulation, suppression of type II retinal waves or ONS at birth prevented activation of the *Cplx3* and *Chrna6* genes, encoding for presynaptic and postsynaptic components of interneurons, respectively (Figure 4) (Golding et al., 2014).

Sensory afferentiation is required at perinatal age to impose hierarchical identity to TRCs so that within a modality-specific thalamocortical loop, the absence of sensory drive converts a first-order identity into a higher-order one (Frangeul et al., 2016), this is also reflected in the acquisition of stereotypical higher-order connectivity with the neocortex (Frangeul et al., 2016; Grant et al., 2016). Whether local interneurons respond similarly by displaying ectopic patterns of connectivity that reflect a change in hierarchy is still unknown.

Further work is required to assess the role of activity-dependent mechanisms in the maturation and recruitment of interneurons in associative higher-order nuclei.

6. Concluding Remarks

The embryonic origin of thalamic GABAergic interneurons has long been the subject of speculation that focused primarily on the GABAergic progenitor domains of the forebrain. Recently obtained experimental evidence in mice, however, identified the midbrain as the main source of thalamic interneurons. Forebrain progenitors migrating into the thalamus from the prethalamus make a minor contribution to the diversity of thalamic interneurons. The observation that proximal GABAergic progenitors can contribute to thalamic interneurons but do so only to a minor extent, whereas more distant sources generate the largest fraction of thalamic interneurons, is intriguing and invites further investigation.

The presence of a GABAergic domain within the embryonic thalamus, the pTH-R, which is conserved among amniotes but does not generate thalamic interneurons, may reflect a primordial form of thalamic organisation that lacked local inhibitory control. The evolution of increasingly more elaborated and reciprocal connectivity between the thalamus and an expanding cortex in the mammalian lineage may have generated the conditions for the invasion and integration of interneurons, primarily from the midbrain.

The high variability in interneuron content and distribution across thalamocortical nuclei in different mammalian species may also be interpreted in the context of the evolution of an elaborated thalamocortical system. The functional implications of varying densities of thalamic interneurons in sensory perception and cognition are not fully understood. Recent data illustrating the existence of different developmental programs for thalamic interneurons that impinge on distinct transcriptional regulators pave the way for future investigation into the specific connectional and functional properties of interneuron subtypes within thalamocortical networks.

References

Achim, K., Peltopuro, P., Lahti, L., Li, J., Salminen, M., and Partanen, J. (2012). Distinct developmental origins and regulatory mechanisms for GABAergic neurons associated with dopaminergic nuclei in the ventral mesodiencephalic region. Development **139**, 2360–2370.

Achim, K., Peltopuro, P., Lahti, L., Tsai, H. H., Zachariah, A., Astrand, M., Salminen, M., Rowitch, D., and Partanen, J. (2013). The role of Tal2 and Tal1 in the differentiation of midbrain GABAergic neuron precursors. Biol Open **2**, 990–997.

Acuna-Goycolea, C., Brenowitz, S.D., and Regehr, W.G. (2008). Active dendritic conductances dynamically regulate GABA release from thalamic interneurons. Neuron **57**, 420–431.

Agoston, Z., and Schulte, D. (2009). Meis2 competes with the Groucho co-repressor Tle4 for binding to Otx2 and specifies tectal fate without induction of a secondary midbrain-hindbrain boundary organizer. Development **136**, 3311–3322.

Albuixech-Crespo, B., Lopez-Blanch, L., Burguera, D., Maeso, I., Sanchez-Arrones, L., Moreno-Bravo, J.A., Somorjai, I., Pascual-Anaya, J., Puelles, E., Bovolenta, P., et al. (2017). Molecular regionalization of the developing amphioxus neural tube challenges major partitions of the vertebrate brain. PLoS Biol **15**, e2001573.

Altman, J., and Bayer, S.A. (1988a). Development of the rat thalamus: I. Mosaic organization of the thalamic neuroepithelium. J Comp Neurol **275**, 346–377.

Altman, J., and Bayer, S.A. (1988b). Development of the rat thalamus: II. Time and site of origin and settling pattern of neurons derived from the anterior lobule of the thalamic neuroepithelium. J Comp Neurol **275**, 378–405.

Altman, J., and Bayer, S.A. (1988c). Development of the rat thalamus: III. Time and site of origin and settling pattern of neurons of the reticular nucleus. J Comp Neurol **275**, 406–428.

Altman, J., and Bayer, S.A. (1989a). Development of the rat thalamus: IV. The intermediate lobule of the thalamic neuroepithelium, and the time and site of origin and settling pattern of neurons of the ventral nuclear complex. J Comp Neurol **284**, 534–566.

Altman, J., and Bayer, S.A. (1989b). Development of the rat thalamus: V. The posterior lobule of the thalamic neuroepithelium and the time and site of origin and settling pattern of neurons of the medial geniculate body. J Comp Neurol **284**, 567–580.

Altman, J., and Bayer, S.A. (1989c). Development of the rat thalamus: VI. The posterior lobule of the thalamic neuroepithelium and the time and site of origin and settling pattern of neurons of the lateral geniculate and lateral posterior nuclei. J Comp Neurol **284**, 581–601.

An, K., Zhao, H., Miao, Y., Xu, Q., Li, Y.F., Ma, Y.Q., Shi, Y.M., Shen, J.W., Meng, J.J., Yao, Y.G., et al. (2020). A circadian rhythm-gated subcortical pathway for nighttime-light-induced depressive-like behaviors in mice. Nat Neurosci **23**, 869–880.

Anderson, S.A., Eisenstat, D.D., Shi, L., and Rubenstein, J.L. (1997a). Interneuron migration from basal forebrain to neocortex: dependence on Dlx genes. Science **278**, 474–476.

Anderson, S.A., Qiu, M., Bulfone, A., Eisenstat, D.D., Meneses, J., Pedersen, R., and Rubenstein, J.L. (1997b). Mutations of the homeobox genes Dlx-1 and Dlx-2 disrupt the striatal subventricular zone and differentiation of late born striatal neurons. Neuron **19**, 27–37.

Angevine, J.B., Jr. (1970). Time of neuron origin in the diencephalon of the mouse. An autoradiographic study. J Comp Neurol **139**, 129–187.

Anton-Bolanos, N., Espinosa, A., and Lopez-Bendito, G. (2018). Developmental interactions between thalamus and cortex: a true love reciprocal story. Curr Opin Neurobiol **52**, 33–41.

Anton-Bolanos, N., Sempere-Ferrandez, A., Guillamon-Vivancos, T., Martini, F.J., Perez-Saiz, L., Gezelius, H., Filipchuk, A., Valdeolmillos, M., and Lopez-Bendito, G. (2019). Prenatal activity from thalamic neurons governs the emergence of functional cortical maps in mice. Science **364**, 987–990.

Arcelli, P., Frassoni, C., Regondi, M.C., De Biasi, S., and Spreafico, R. (1997). GABAergic neurons in mammalian thalamus: a marker of thalamic complexity? Brain Research Bulletin **42**, 27–37.

Arimura, N., Dewa, K.I., Okada, M., Yanagawa, Y., Taya, S.I., and Hoshino, M. (2019). Comprehensive and cell-type-based characterization of the dorsal midbrain during development. Genes Cells **24**, 41–59.

Babb, R.S. (1980). The pregeniculate nucleus of the monkey (*Macaca mulatta*). I. A study at the light microscopy level. J Comp Neurol **190**, 651–672.

Bakken, T.E., van Velthoven, C.T.J., Menon, V., Hodge, R.D., Yao, Z., Nguyen, T.N., Graybuck, L.T., Horwitz, G.D., Bertagnolli, D., Goldy, J., et al. (2020). Single-cell RNA-seq uncovers shared and distinct axes of variation in dorsal LGN neurons in mice, non-human primates and humans. bioRxiv.

Batini, C., Guegan, M., Palestini, M., and Thomasset, M. (1991). The immunocytochemical distribution of calbindin-D28k and parvalbumin in identified neurons of the pulvinar-lateralis posterior complex of the cat. Neurosci Lett **130**, 203–207.

Beier, C., Zhang, Z., Yurgel, M., and Hattar, S. (2020). The projections of ipRGCs and conventional RGCs to retinorecipient brain nuclei. bioRxiv.

Benson, D.L., Isackson, P.J., Gall, C.M., and Jones, E.G. (1992). Contrasting patterns in the localization of glutamic acid decarboxylase and Ca^{2+}/calmodulin protein kinase gene expression in the rat central nervous system. Neuroscience **46**, 825–849.

Benson, D.L., Isackson, P.J., Hendry, S.H., and Jones, E.G. (1991). Differential gene expression for glutamic acid decarboxylase and type II calcium-calmodulin-dependent protein kinase in basal ganglia, thalamus, and hypothalamus of the monkey. J Neurosci **11**, 1540–1564.

Bentivoglio, M., Spreafico, R., Minciacchi, D., and Macchi, G. (1991). GABAergic interneurons and neuropil of the intralaminar thalamus: an immunohistochemical study in the rat and the cat, with notes in the monkey. Exp Brain Res **87**, 85–95.

Bickford, M.E., Carden, W.B., and Patel, N.C. (1999). Two types of interneurons in the cat visual thalamus are distinguished by morphology, synaptic connections, and nitric oxide synthase content. J Comp Neurol **413**, 83–100.

Bickford, M.E., Slusarczyk, A., Dilger, E.K., Krahe, T.E., Kucuk, C., and Guido, W. (2010). Synaptic development of the mouse dorsal lateral geniculate nucleus. J Comp Neurol **518**, 622–635.

Blasiak, T., and Lewandowski, M.H. (2003). Dorsal raphe nucleus modulates neuronal activity in rat intergeniculate leaflet. Behav Brain Res **138**, 179–185.

Blitz, D.M., and Regehr, W.G. (2005). Timing and specificity of feed-forward inhibition within the LGN. Neuron **45**, 917–928.

Bluske, K.K., Kawakami, Y., Koyano-Nakagawa, N., and Nakagawa, Y. (2009). Differential activity of Wnt/beta-catenin signaling in the embryonic mouse thalamus. Dev Dyn **238**, 3297–3309.

Bluske, K.K., Vue, T.Y., Kawakami, Y., Taketo, M.M., Yoshikawa, K., Johnson, J.E., and Nakagawa, Y. (2012). beta-Catenin signaling specifies progenitor cell identity in parallel with Shh signaling in the developing mammalian thalamus. Development **139**, 2692–2702.

Bokor, H., Frere, S.G., Eyre, M.D., Slezia, A., Ulbert, I., Luthi, A., and Acsady, L. (2005). Selective GABAergic control of higher-order thalamic relays. Neuron **45**, 929–940.

Born, G., and Schmidt, M. (2007). GABAergic pathways in the rat subcortical visual system: a comparative study in vivo and in vitro. Eur J Neurosci 26, 1183–1192.

Braak, H., and Bachmann, A. (1985). The percentage of projection neurons and interneurons in the human lateral geniculate nucleus. Hum Neurobiol 4, 91–95.

Braak, H., and Braak, E. (1984). Neuronal types in the lateral geniculate nucleus of man. A Golgi-pigment study. Cell Tissue Res 237, 509–520.

Braak, H., and Weinel, U. (1985). The percentage of projection neurons and local circuit neurons in different nuclei of the human thalamus. J Hirnforsch 26, 525–530.

Bradley, C.K., Takano, E.A., Hall, M.A., Gothert, J.R., Harvey, A.R., Begley, C.G., and van Eekelen, J.A. (2006). The essential haematopoietic transcription factor Scl is also critical for neuronal development. Eur J Neurosci 23, 1677–1689.

Brooks, J.M., Su, J., Levy, C., Wang, J.S., Seabrook, T.A., Guido, W., and Fox, M.A. (2013). A molecular mechanism regulating the timing of corticogeniculate innervation. Cell Rep 5, 573–581.

Brown, N.L., Patel, S., Brzezinski, J., and Glaser, T. (2001). Math5 is required for retinal ganglion cell and optic nerve formation. Development 128, 2497–2508.

Bucher, K., Sofroniew, M.V., Pannell, R., Impey, H., Smith, A.J., Torres, E.M., Dunnett, S.B., Jin, Y., Baer, R., and Rabbitts, T.H. (2000). The T cell oncogene Tal2 is necessary for normal development of the mouse brain. Dev Biol 227, 533–544.

Bulfone, A., Puelles, L., Porteus, M.H., Frohman, M.A., Martin, G.R., and Rubenstein, J.L. (1993). Spatially restricted expression of Dlx-1, Dlx-2 (Tes-1), Gbx-2, and Wnt-3 in the embryonic day 12.5 mouse forebrain defines potential transverse and longitudinal segmental boundaries. J Neurosci 13, 3155–3172.

Butler, A.B. (2008). Evolution of the thalamus: a morphological and functional review. In Thalamus & Related Systems (Cambridge University Press), pp. 35–58.

Butt, S.J., Sousa, V.H., Fuccillo, M.V., Hjerling-Leffler, J., Miyoshi, G., Kimura, S., and Fishell, G. (2008). The requirement of Nkx2-1 in the temporal specification of cortical interneuron subtypes. Neuron 59, 722–732.

Bylund, M., Andersson, E., Novitch, B.G., and Muhr, J. (2003). Vertebrate neurogenesis is counteracted by Sox1-3 activity. Nat Neurosci 6, 1162–1168.

Cajal, S.R.y. (1911). Histologie du Systeme Nerveux de l' Homme et des Vertebres, Vol 2 (Maloine).

Campbell, P.W., Govindaiah, G., Masterson, S.P., Bickford, M.E., and Guido, W. (2020). Synaptic properties of the feedback connections from the thalamic reticular nucleus to the dorsal lateral geniculate nucleus. J Neurophysiol 124, 404–417.

Carden, W.B., and Bickford, M.E. (2002). Synaptic inputs of class III and class V interneurons in the cat pulvinar nucleus: differential integration of RS and RL inputs. Vis Neurosci 19, 51–59.

Carney, R.S., Cocas, L.A., Hirata, T., Mansfield, K., and Corbin, J.G. (2009). Differential regulation of telencephalic pallial-subpallial boundary patterning by Pax6 and Gsh2. Cereb Cortex 19, 745–759.

Casarosa, S., Fode, C., and Guillemot, F. (1999). Mash1 regulates neurogenesis in the ventral telencephalon. Development 126, 525–534.

Castro, D.S., Martynoga, B., Parras, C., Ramesh, V., Pacary, E., Johnston, C., Drechsel, D., Lebel-Potter, M., Garcia, L.G., Hunt, C., et al. (2011). A novel function of the proneural factor Ascl1 in progenitor proliferation identified by genome-wide characterization of its targets. Genes Dev 25, 930–945.

Celio, M.R. (1986). Parvalbumin in most gamma-aminobutyric acid-containing neurons of the rat cerebral cortex. Science 231, 995–997.

Celio, M.R., and Heizmann, C.W. (1981). Calcium-binding protein parvalbumin as a neuronal marker. Nature 293, 300–302.

Charalambakis, N.E., Govindaiah, G., Campbell, P.W., and Guido, W. (2019). Developmental remodeling of thalamic interneurons requires retinal signaling. J Neurosci 39, 3856–3866.

Cheadle, L., Tzeng, C.P., Kalish, B.T., Harmin, D.A., Rivera, S., Ling, E., Nagy, M.A., Hrvatin, S., Hu, L., Stroud, H., et al. (2018). Visual experience-dependent expression of Fn14 is required for retinogeniculate refinement. Neuron 99, 525–539, e510.

Clark, A.S., Schwartz, M.L., and Goldman-Rakic, P.S. (1989). GABA-immunoreactive neurons in the mediodorsal nucleus of the monkey thalamus. J Chem Neuroanat 2, 259–267.

Clarke, L.E., and Barres, B.A. (2013). Emerging roles of astrocytes in neural circuit development. Nat Rev Neurosci 14, 311–321.

Cobos, I., Broccoli, V., and Rubenstein, J.L. (2005). The vertebrate ortholog of Aristaless is regulated by Dlx genes in the developing forebrain. J Comp Neurol 483, 292–303.

Colonnese, M.T., and Phillips, M.A. (2018). Thalamocortical function in developing sensory circuits. Curr Opin Neurobiol 52, 72–79.

Corbin, J.G., Rutlin, M., Gaiano, N., and Fishell, G. (2003). Combinatorial function of the homeodomain proteins Nkx2.1 and Gsh2 in ventral telencephalic patterning. Development 130, 4895–4906.

Cox, C.L., and Sherman, S.M. (2000). Control of dendritic outputs of inhibitory interneurons in the lateral geniculate nucleus. Neuron 27, 597–610.

Crossley, P.H., Martinez, S., and Martin, G.R. (1996). Midbrain development induced by FGF8 in the chick embryo. Nature 380, 66–68.

Cucchiaro, J.B., Uhlrich, D.J., and Sherman, S.M. (1993). Ultrastructure of synapses from the pretectum in the A-laminae of the cat's lateral geniculate nucleus. J Comp Neurol 334, 618–630.

Delogu, A., Sellers, K., Zagoraiou, L., Bocianowska-Zbrog, A., Mandal, S., Guimera, J., Rubenstein, J.L., Sugden, D., Jessell, T., and Lumsden, A. (2012). Subcortical visual shell nuclei targeted by ipRGCs develop from a Sox14$^+$ GABAergic progenitor and require Sox14 to regulate daily activity rhythms. Neuron 75, 648–662.

Demeulemeester, H., Arckens, L., Vandesande, F., Orban, G.A., Heizmann, C.W., and Pochet, R. (1991). Calcium binding proteins as molecular markers for cat geniculate neurons. Exp Brain Res 83, 513–520.

Demeulemeester, H., Vandesande, F., Orban, G.A., Heizmann, C.W., and Pochet, R. (1989). Calbindin D-28K and parvalbumin immunoreactivity is confined to two separate neuronal subpopulations in the cat visual cortex, whereas partial coexistence is shown in the dorsal lateral geniculate nucleus. Neurosci Lett 99, 6–11.

Di Giovannantonio, L.G., Di Salvio, M., Omodei, D., Prakash, N., Wurst, W., Pierani, A., Acampora, D., and Simeone, A. (2014). Otx2 cell-autonomously determines dorsal mesencephalon versus cerebellum fate independently of isthmic organizing activity. Development 141, 377–388.

Dixon, G., and Harper, C.G. (2001). Quantitative analysis of glutamic acid decarboxylase-immunoreactive neurons in the anterior thalamus of the human brain. Brain Res 923, 39–44.

Edwards, M.A., Caviness, V.S., Jr., and Schneider, G.E. (1986). Development of cell and fiber lamination in the mouse superior colliculus. J Comp Neurol 248, 395–409.

El-Danaf, R.N., Krahe, T.E., Dilger, E.K., Bickford, M.E., Fox, M.A., and Guido, W.

(2015). Developmental remodeling of relay cells in the dorsal lateral geniculate nucleus in the absence of retinal input. Neural Dev **10**, 19.

Erisir, A., Van Horn, S.C., Bickford, M.E., and Sherman, S.M. (1997). Immunocytochemistry and distribution of parabrachial terminals in the lateral geniculate nucleus of the cat: a comparison with corticogeniculate terminals. J Comp Neurol **377**, 535–549.

Evangelio, M., García-Amado, M., and Clascá, F. (2018). Thalamocortical projection neuron and interneuron numbers in the visual thalamic nuclei of the adult C57BL/6 mouse. Frontiers in Neuroanatomy **12**, 27.

Famiglietti, E.V., Jr. (1970). Dendro-dendritic synapses in the lateral geniculate nucleus of the cat. Brain Res **20**, 181–191.

Famiglietti, E.V., Jr., and Peters, A. (1972). The synaptic glomerulus and the intrinsic neuron in the dorsal lateral geniculate nucleus of the cat. J Comp Neurol **144**, 285–334.

Feig, S., and Harting, J.K. (1994). Ultrastructural studies of the primate lateral geniculate nucleus: morphology and spatial relationships of axon terminals arising from the retina, visual cortex (area 17), superior colliculus, parabigeminal nucleus, and pretectum of *Galago crassicaudatus*. J Comp Neurol **343**, 17–34.

Fernandez, D.C., Fogerson, P.M., Lazzerini Ospri, L., Thomsen, M.B., Layne, R.M., Severin, D., Zhan, J., Singer, J.H., Kirkwood, A., Zhao, H., et al. (2018). Light affects mood and learning through distinct retina-brain pathways. Cell **175**, 71–84 e18.

Fernandez, D.C., Komal, R., Langel, J., Ma, J., Duy, P.Q., Penzo, M.A., Zhao, H., and Hattar, S. (2020). Retinal innervation tunes circuits that drive nonphotic entrainment to food. Nature **581**, 194–198.

Fitzpatrick, D., Diamond, I.T., and Raczkowski, D. (1989). Cholinergic and monoaminergic innervation of the cat's thalamus: comparison of the lateral geniculate nucleus with other principal sensory nuclei. J Comp Neurol **288**, 647–675.

Fitzpatrick, D., Penny, G.R., and Schmechel, D.E. (1984). Glutamic acid decarboxylase-immunoreactive neurons and terminals in the lateral geniculate nucleus of the cat. J Neurosci **4**, 1809–1829.

Fogarty, M., Grist, M., Gelman, D., Marin, O., Pachnis, V., and Kessaris, N. (2007). Spatial genetic patterning of the embryonic neuroepithelium generates GABAergic interneuron diversity in the adult cortex. J Neurosci **27**, 10935–10946.

Frangeul, L., Pouchelon, G., Telley, L., Lefort, S., Luscher, C., and Jabaudon, D. (2016). A cross-modal genetic framework for the development and plasticity of sensory pathways. Nature **538**, 96–98.

Gabbott, P.L., and Bacon, S.J. (1994). Two types of interneuron in the dorsal lateral geniculate nucleus of the rat: a combined NADPH diaphorase histochemical and GABA immunocytochemical study. J Comp Neurol **350**, 281–301.

Garcia-Lopez, R., Vieira, C., Echevarria, D., and Martinez, S. (2004). Fate map of the diencephalon and the zona limitans at the 10-somites stage in chick embryos. Dev Biol **268**, 514–530.

Geisert, E.E., Jr. (1980). Cortical projections of the lateral geniculate nucleus in the cat. J Comp Neurol **190**, 793–812.

Gelman, D., Griveau, A., Dehorter, N., Teissier, A., Varela, C., Pla, R., Pierani, A., and Marin, O. (2011). A wide diversity of cortical GABAergic interneurons derives from the embryonic preoptic area. J Neurosci **31**, 16570–16580.

Gelman, D.M., Martini, F.J., Nobrega-Pereira, S., Pierani, A., Kessaris, N., and Marin, O. (2009). The embryonic preoptic area is a novel source of cortical GABAergic interneurons. J Neurosci **29**, 9380–9389.

Golden, J.A., Zitz, J.C., McFadden, K., and Cepko, C.L. (1997). Cell migration in the developing chick diencephalon. Development **124**, 3525–3533.

Golding, B., Pouchelon, G., Bellone, C., Murthy, S., Di Nardo, A.A., Govindan, S., Ogawa, M., Shimogori, T., Lüscher, C., Dayer, A., et al. (2014). Retinal input directs the recruitment of inhibitory interneurons into thalamic visual circuits. Neuron **81**, 1057–1069.

Gonzalo-Ruiz, A., Sanz, J.M., and Lieberman, A.R. (1996). Immunohistochemical studies of localization and co-localization of glutamate, aspartate and GABA in the anterior thalamic nuclei, retrosplenial granular cortex, thalamic reticular nucleus and mammillary nuclei of the rat. J Chem Neuroanat **12**, 77–84.

Govindaiah, and Cox, C.L. (2004). Synaptic activation of metabotropic glutamate receptors regulates dendritic outputs of thalamic interneurons. Neuron **41**, 611–623.

Graham, V., Khudyakov, J., Ellis, P., and Pevny, L. (2003). SOX2 functions to maintain neural progenitor identity. Neuron **39**, 749–765.

Grant, E., Hoerder-Suabedissen, A., and Molnar, Z. (2016). The regulation of corticofugal fiber targeting by retinal inputs. Cereb Cortex **26**, 1336–1348.

Grimes, W.N., Zhang, J., Graydon, C.W., Kachar, B., and Diamond, J.S. (2010). Retinal parallel processors: more than 100 independent microcircuits operate within a single interneuron. Neuron **65**, 873–885.

Guillery, R.W. (1966). A study of Golgi preparations from the dorsal lateral geniculate nucleus of the adult cat. J Comp Neurol **128**, 21–50.

Guillery, R.W. (1969). The organization of synaptic interconnections in the laminae of the dorsal lateral geniculate nucleus of the cat. Z Zellforsch Mikrosk Anat **96**, 1–38.

Guillery, R.W., and Sherman, S.M. (2002). Thalamic relay functions and their role in corticocortical communication: generalizations from the visual system. Neuron **33**, 163–175.

Guimera, J., Vogt Weisenhorn, D., Echevarria, D., Martinez, S., and Wurst, W. (2006a). Molecular characterization, structure and developmental expression of Megane bHLH factor. Gene **377**, 65–76.

Guimera, J., Weisenhorn, D.V., and Wurst, W. (2006b). Megane/Heslike is required for normal GABAergic differentiation in the mouse superior colliculus. Development **133**, 3847–3857.

Guler, A.D., Ecker, J.L., Lall, G.S., Haq, S., Altimus, C.M., Liao, H.W., Barnard, A.R., Cahill, H., Badea, T.C., Zhao, H., et al. (2008). Melanopsin cells are the principal conduits for rod-cone input to non-image-forming vision. Nature **453**, 102–105.

Guo, Q., and Li, J.Y.H. (2019). Defining developmental diversification of diencephalon neurons through single cell gene expression profiling. Development **146**.

Hamos, J.E., Van Horn, S.C., Raczkowski, D., Uhlrich, D.J., and Sherman, S.M. (1985). Synaptic connectivity of a local circuit neurone in lateral geniculate nucleus of the cat. Nature **317**, 618–621.

Harrington, M.E., and Rusak, B. (1986). Lesions of the thalamic intergeniculate leaflet alter hamster circadian rhythms. J Biol Rhythms **1**, 309–325.

Harris, R.M., and Hendrickson, A.E. (1987). Local circuit neurons in the rat ventrobasal thalamus–a GABA immunocytochemical study. Neuroscience **21**, 229–236.

Hashikawa, T., Rausell, E., Molinari, M., and Jones, E.G. (1991). Parvalbumin- and calbindin-containing neurons in the monkey medial geniculate complex: differential distribution and cortical layer specific projections. Brain Res **544**, 335–341.

Hattar, S., Kumar, M., Park, A., Tong, P., Tung, J., Yau, K.W., and Berson, D.M. (2006). Central projections of melanopsin-expressing retinal ganglion cells in the mouse. J Comp Neurol **497**, 326–349.

He, J., Xu, X., Monavarfeshani, A., Banerjee, S., Fox, M.A., and Xie, H. (2019). Retinal-input-induced epigenetic dynamics in the developing mouse dorsal lateral geniculate nucleus. Epigenetics Chromatin **12**, 13.

Hendry, S.H., Jones, E.G., Emson, P.C., Lawson, D.E., Heizmann, C.W., and Streit, P. (1989). Two classes of cortical GABA neurons defined by differential calcium binding protein immunoreactivities. Exp Brain Res **76**, 467–472.

Henke, R.M., Meredith, D.M., Borromeo, M.D., Savage, T.K., and Johnson, J.E. (2009). Ascl1 and Neurog2 form novel complexes and regulate Delta-like3 (Dll3) expression in the neural tube. Dev Biol **328**, 529–540.

Herberth, B., Minko, K., Csillag, A., Jaffredo, T., and Madarasz, E. (2005). SCL, GATA-2 and Lmo2 expression in neurogenesis. Int J Dev Neurosci **23**, 449–463.

Herron, P., Baskerville, K.A., Chang, H.T., and Doetsch, G.S. (1997). Distribution of neurons immunoreactive for parvalbumin and calbindin in the somatosensory thalamus of the raccoon. J Comp Neurol **388**, 120–129.

Hirata, T., Nakazawa, M., Muraoka, O., Nakayama, R., Suda, Y., and Hibi, M. (2006). Zinc-finger genes Fez and Fez-like function in the establishment of diencephalon subdivisions. Development **133**, 3993–4004.

Hirsch, J.A., Wang, X., Sommer, F.T., and Martinez, L.M. (2015). How inhibitory circuits in the thalamus serve vision. Annu Rev Neurosci **38**, 309–329.

Hong, Y.K., and Chen, C. (2011). Wiring and rewiring of the retinogeniculate synapse. Curr Opin Neurobiol **21**, 228–237.

Hsieh-Li, H.M., Witte, D.P., Szucsik, J.C., Weinstein, M., Li, H., and Potter, S.S. (1995). Gsh-2, a murine homeobox gene expressed in the developing brain. Mech Dev **50**, 177–186.

Huang, L., Xi, Y., Peng, Y., Yang, Y., Huang, X., Fu, Y., Tao, Q., Xiao, J., Yuan, T., An, K., et al. (2019). A visual circuit related to habenula underlies the antidepressive effects of light therapy. Neuron **102**, 128–142 e128.

Huang, X., Huang, P., Huang, L., Hu, Z., Liu, X., Shen, J., Xi, Y., Yang, Y., Fu, Y., Tao, Q., et al. (2021). A visual circuit related to the nucleus reuniens for the spatial-memory-promoting effects of light treatment. Neuron **109**, 347–362 e347.

Huberman, A.D., Feller, M.B., and Chapman, B. (2008). Mechanisms underlying development of visual maps and receptive fields. Annu Rev Neurosci **31**, 479–509.

Hunt, C.A., Pang, D.Z., and Jones, E.G. (1991). Distribution and density of GABA cells in intralaminar and adjacent nuclei of monkey thalamus. Neuroscience **43**, 185–196.

Ilinsky, I.A., Ambardekar, A.V., and Kultas-Ilinsky, K. (1999). Organization of projections from the anterior pole of the nucleus reticularis thalami (NRT) to subdivisions of the motor thalamus: light and electron microscopic studies in the rhesus monkey. J Comp Neurol **409**, 369–384.

Inamura, N., Ono, K., Takebayashi, H., Zalc, B., and Ikenaka, K. (2011). Olig2 lineage cells generate GABAergic neurons in the prethalamic nuclei, including the zona incerta, ventral lateral geniculate nucleus and reticular thalamic nucleus. Dev Neurosci **33**, 118–129.

Inverardi, F., Beolchi, M.S., Ortino, B., Moroni, R.F., Regondi, M.C., Amadeo, A., and Frassoni, C. (2007). GABA immunoreactivity in the developing rat thalamus and Otx2 homeoprotein expression in migrating neurons. Brain Res Bull **73**, 64–74.

Jager, P., Moore, G., Calpin, P., Durmishi, X., Salgarella, I., Menage, L., Kita, Y., Wang, Y., Kim, D.W., Blackshaw, S., et al. (2021). Dual midbrain and forebrain origins of thalamic inhibitory interneurons. *eLife* **10**.

Jager, P., Ye, Z., Yu, X., Zagoraiou, L., Prekop, H.T., Partanen, J., Jessell, T.M., Wisden, W., Brickley, S.G., and Delogu, A. (2016). Tectal-derived interneurons contribute to phasic and tonic inhibition in the visual thalamus. Nat Commun **7**, 13579.

Janik, D., and Mrosovsky, N. (1994). Intergeniculate leaflet lesions and behaviorally-induced shifts of circadian rhythms. Brain Res **651**, 174–182.

Jeong, Y., Dolson, D.K., Waclaw, R.R., Matise, M.P., Sussel, L., Campbell, K., Kaestner, K.H., and Epstein, D.J. (2011). Spatial and temporal requirements for sonic hedgehog in the regulation of thalamic interneuron identity. Development **138**, 531–541.

Johnson, R.F., Moore, R.Y., and Morin, L.P. (1989). Lateral geniculate lesions alter circadian activity rhythms in the hamster. Brain Res Bull **22**, 411–422.

Jones, E. (2002). Dichronous appearance and unusual origins of GABA neurons during development of the mammalian thalamus. Thalamus & Related Systems **1**, 283–288.

Jones, E.G. (2007). The *Thalamus* (Cambridge University Press).

Jones, E.G., and Hendry, S.H. (1989). Differential calcium binding protein immunoreactivity distinguishes classes of relay neurons in monkey thalamic nuclei. Eur J Neurosci **1**, 222–246.

Kala, K., Haugas, M., Lillevali, K., Guimera, J., Wurst, W., Salminen, M., and Partanen, J. (2009). Gata2 is a tissue-specific post-mitotic selector gene for midbrain GABAergic neurons. Development **136**, 253–262.

Kalish, B.T., Cheadle, L., Hrvatin, S., Nagy, M.A., Rivera, S., Crow, M., Gillis, J., Kirchner, R., and Greenberg, M.E. (2018). Single-cell transcriptomics of the developing lateral geniculate nucleus reveals insights into circuit assembly and refinement. Proc Natl Acad Sci *USA* **115**, E1051–E1060.

Kataoka, A., and Shimogori, T. (2008). Fgf8 controls regional identity in the developing thalamus. Development **135**, 2873–2881.

Kessaris, N., Fogarty, M., Iannarelli, P., Grist, M., Wegner, M., and Richardson, W.D. (2006). Competing waves of oligodendrocytes in the forebrain and postnatal elimination of an embryonic lineage. Nat Neurosci **9**, 173–179.

Kiecker, C., and Lumsden, A. (2004). Hedgehog signaling from the ZLI regulates diencephalic regional identity. Nat Neurosci **7**, 1242–1249.

Kim, D.W., Washington, P.W., Wang, Z.Q., Lin, S.H., Sun, C., Ismail, B.T., Wang, H., Jiang, L., and Blackshaw, S. (2020). The cellular and molecular landscape of hypothalamic patterning and differentiation from embryonic to late postnatal development. Nat Commun **11**, 4360.

Kimura, S., Hara, Y., Pineau, T., Fernandez-Salguero, P., Fox, C.H., Ward, J.M., and Gonzalez, F.J. (1996). The T/ebp null mouse: thyroid-specific enhancer-binding protein is essential for the organogenesis of the thyroid, lung, ventral forebrain, and pituitary. Genes Dev **10**, 60–69.

Kitamura, K., Miura, H., Yanazawa, M., Miyashita, T., and Kato, K. (1997). Expression patterns of Brx1 (Rieg gene), Sonic hedgehog, Nkx2.2, Dlx1 and Arx during zona limitans intrathalamica and embryonic ventral lateral geniculate nuclear formation. Mech Dev **67**, 83–96.

Kobayashi, D., Kobayashi, M., Matsumoto, K., Ogura, T., Nakafuku, M., and Shimamura, K. (2002). Early subdivisions in the neural plate define distinct competence for inductive signals. Development **129**, 83–93.

Kornhauser, J.M., Leonard, M.W., Yamamoto, M., LaVail, J.H., Mayo, K.E., and Engel, J.D. (1994). Temporal and spatial changes in GATA transcription factor expression are coincident with development of the chicken optic tectum. Brain Res Mol Brain Res **23**, 100–110.

Kultas-Ilinsky, K., Yi, H., and Ilinsky, I.A. (1995). Nucleus reticularis thalami input to the anterior thalamic nuclei in the monkey: a light and electron microscopic study. Neurosci Lett **186**, 25–28.

Lazzaro, D., Price, M., de Felice, M., and Di Lauro, R. (1991). The transcription factor TTF-1 is expressed at the onset of thyroid and lung morphogenesis and in restricted regions of the foetal brain. Development **113**, 1093–1104.

Le, T.N., Zhou, Q.P., Cobos, I., Zhang, S., Zagozewski, J., Japoni, S., Vriend, J., Parkinson, T., Du, G., Rubenstein, J.L., et al. (2017). GABAergic interneuron differentiation in the basal forebrain is mediated through direct regulation of glutamic acid decarboxylase isoforms by Dlx homeobox transcription factors. J Neurosci **37**, 8816–8829.

Leist, M., Datunashvilli, M., Kanyshkova, T., Zobeiri, M., Aissaoui, A., Cerina, M., Romanelli, M.N., Pape, H.C., and Budde, T. (2016). Two types of interneurons in the mouse lateral geniculate nucleus are characterized by different h-current density. Sci Rep **6**, 24904.

Letinic, K., and Kostovic, I. (1997). Transient fetal structure, the gangliothalamic body, connects telencephalic germinal zone with all thalamic regions in the developing human brain. J Comp Neurol **384**, 373–395.

Letinic, K., and Rakic, P. (2001). Telencephalic origin of human thalamic GABAergic neurons. Nat Neurosci **4**, 931–936.

Letinic, K., Zoncu, R., and Rakic, P. (2002). Origin of GABAergic neurons in the human neocortex. Nature **417**, 645–649.

Lewandowski, M.H., and Usarek, A. (2002). Effects of intergeniculate leaflet lesions on circadian rhythms in the mouse. Behav Brain Res **128**, 13–17.

Li, J., Wang, C., Zhang, Z., Wen, Y., An, L., Liang, Q., Xu, Z., Wei, S., Li, W., Guo, T., et al. (2018). Transcription Factors Sp8 and Sp9 coordinately regulate olfactory bulb interneuron development. Cereb Cortex **28**, 3278–3294.

Lima, R.R., Pinato, L., Nascimento, R.B., Engelberth, R.C., Nascimento, E.S., Cavalcante, J.C., Britto, L.R., Costa, M.S., and Cavalcante, J.S. (2012). Retinal projections and neurochemical characterization of the pregeniculate nucleus of the common marmoset (*Callithrix jacchus*). J Chem Neuroanat **44**, 34–44.

Lindtner, S., Catta-Preta, R., Tian, H., Su-Feher, L., Price, J.D., Dickel, D.E., Greiner, V., Silberberg, S.N., McKinsey, G.L., McManus, M.T., et al. (2019). Genomic resolution of DLX-orchestrated transcriptional circuits driving development of forebrain GABAergic neurons. Cell Rep **28**, 2048–2063 e2048.

Liu, J.K., Ghattas, I., Liu, S., Chen, S., and Rubenstein, J.L. (1997). Dlx genes encode DNA-binding proteins that are expressed in an overlapping and sequential pattern during basal ganglia differentiation. Dev Dyn **210**, 498–512.

Long, J.E., Cobos, I., Potter, G.B., and Rubenstein, J.L. (2009). Dlx1&2 and Mash1 transcription factors control MGE and CGE patterning and differentiation through parallel and overlapping pathways. Cereb Cortex **19** *Suppl 1*, i96–106.

Long, J.E., Garel, S., Alvarez-Dolado, M., Yoshikawa, K., Osumi, N., Alvarez-Buylla, A., and Rubenstein, J.L. (2007). Dlx-dependent and -independent regulation of olfactory bulb interneuron differentiation. J Neurosci **27**, 3230–3243.

Long, J.E., Swan, C., Liang, W.S., Cobos, I., Potter, G.B., and Rubenstein, J.L. (2009). Dlx1&2 and Mash1 transcription factors control striatal patterning and differentiation through parallel and overlapping pathways. J Comp Neurol **512**, 556–572.

Lumsden, A., and Krumlauf, R. (1996). Patterning the vertebrate neuraxis. Science **274**, 1109–1115.

Majorossy, K., and Kiss, A. (1976). Types of interneurons and their participation in the neuronal network of the medial geniculate body. Exp Brain Res **26**, 19–37.

Makrides, N., Panayiotou, E., Fanis, P., Karaiskos, C., Lapathitis, G., and Malas, S. (2018). Sequential role of SOXB2 factors in GABAergic neuron specification of the dorsal midbrain. Front Mol Neurosci **11**, 152.

Marchant, E.G., Watson, N.V., and Mistlberger, R.E. (1997). Both neuropeptide Y and serotonin are necessary for entrainment of circadian rhythms in mice by daily treadmill running schedules. J Neurosci **17**, 7974–7987.

Martinez-Ferre, A., and Martinez, S. (2009). The development of the thalamic motor learning area is regulated by Fgf8 expression. J Neurosci **29**, 13389–13400.

Martinez-Ferre, A., and Martinez, S. (2012). Molecular regionalization of the diencephalon. Front Neurosci **6**, 73.

Martinez-Ferre, A., Navarro-Garberi, M., Bueno, C., and Martinez, S. (2013). Wnt signal specifies the intrathalamic limit and its organizer properties by regulating Shh induction in the alar plate. J Neurosci **33**, 3967–3980.

Mattes, B., Weber, S., Peres, J., Chen, Q., Davidson, G., Houart, C., and Scholpp, S. (2012). Wnt3 and Wnt3a are required for induction of the mid-diencephalic organizer in the caudal forebrain. Neural Dev **7**, 12.

McCauley, A.K., Carden, W.B., and Godwin, D.W. (2003). Brain nitric oxide synthase expression in the developing ferret lateral geniculate nucleus: analysis of time course, localization, and synaptic contacts. J Comp Neurol **462**, 342–354.

McCormick, D.A., and Pape, H.C. (1988). Acetylcholine inhibits identified interneurons in the cat lateral geniculate nucleus. Nature **334**, 246–248.

Meng, X.W., Ohara, P.T., and Ralston, H.J., 3rd (1996). Nitric oxide synthase immunoreactivity distinguishes a sub-population of GABA-immunoreactive neurons in the ventrobasal complex of the cat. Brain Res **728**, 111–115.

Meyer-Bernstein, E.L., and Morin, L.P. (1996). Differential serotonergic innervation of the suprachiasmatic nucleus and the intergeniculate leaflet and its role in circadian rhythm modulation. J Neurosci **16**, 2097–2111.

Minocha, S., Valloton, D., Arsenijevic, Y., Cardinaux, J.R., Guidi, R., Hornung, J.P., and Lebrand, C. (2017). Nkx2.1 regulates the generation of telencephalic astrocytes during embryonic development. Sci Rep **7**, 43093.

Minocha, S., Valloton, D., Ypsilanti, A.R., Fiumelli, H., Allen, E.A., Yanagawa, Y., Marin, O., Chedotal, A., Hornung, J.P., and Lebrand, C. (2015). Nkx2.1-derived astrocytes and neurons together with Slit2 are indispensable for anterior commissure formation. Nat Commun **6**, 6887.

Miyoshi, G., Bessho, Y., Yamada, S., and Kageyama, R. (2004). Identification of a novel basic helix-loop-helix gene, Heslike, and its role in GABAergic neurogenesis. J Neurosci **24**, 3672–3682.

Mojsilovic, J., and Zecevic, N. (1991). Early development of the human thalamus: Golgi and Nissl study. Early Hum Dev **27**, 119–144.

Molinari, M., Leggio, M.G., Dell'Anna, M.E., Giannetti, S., and Macchi, G. (1994). Chemical compartmentation and relationships between calcium-binding protein immunoreactivity and layer-specific cortical caudate-projecting cells in the anterior intralaminar nuclei of the cat. Eur J Neurosci **6**, 299–312.

Montero, V.M. (1986). Localization of gamma-aminobutyric acid (GABA) in type 3 cells and demonstration of their source to F2 terminals in the cat lateral geniculate nucleus: a Golgi-electron-microscopic GABA-immunocytochemical study. J Comp Neurol **254**, 228–245.

Montero, V.M. (1989). The GABA-immunoreactive neurons in the interlaminar regions of the cat lateral geniculate nucleus: light and electron microscopic observations. Exp Brain Res **75**, 497–512.

Montero, V.M. (1991). A quantitative study of synaptic contacts on interneurons and relay cells of the cat lateral geniculate nucleus. Exp Brain Res **86**, 257–270.

Montero, V.M., and Singer, W. (1985). Ultrastructural identification of somata and neural processes immunoreactive to antibodies against glutamic acid decarboxylase (GAD) in the dorsal lateral geniculate nucleus of the cat. Exp Brain Res **59**, 151–165.

Montero, V.M., and Zempel, J. (1985). Evidence for two types of GABA-containing interneurons in the A-laminae of the cat lateral geniculate nucleus: a double-label HRP and GABA-immunocytochemical study. Exp Brain Res **60**, 603–609.

Montero, V.M., and Zempel, J. (1986). The proportion and size of GABA-immunoreactive neurons in the magnocellular and parvocellular layers of the lateral geniculate nucleus of the rhesus monkey. Exp Brain Res **62**, 215–223.

Moore, R.Y. (1989). The geniculohypothalamic tract in monkey and man. Brain Res **486**, 190–194.

Moore, R.Y., Weis, R., and Moga, M.M. (2000). Efferent projections of the intergeniculate leaflet and the ventral lateral geniculate nucleus in the rat. J Comp Neurol **420**, 398–418.

Moreno-Juan, V., Filipchuk, A., Anton-Bolanos, N., Mezzera, C., Gezelius, H., Andres, B., Rodriguez-Malmierca, L., Susin, R., Schaad, O., Iwasato, T., et al. (2017). Prenatal thalamic waves regulate cortical area size prior to sensory processing. Nat Commun **8**, 14172.

Morest, D.K. (1971). Dendrodendritic synapses of cells that have axons: the fine structure of the Golgi type II cell in the medial geniculate body of the cat. Z Anat Entwicklungsgesch **133**, 216–246.

Morgan, J.L., and Lichtman, J.W. (2020). An individual interneuron participates in many kinds of inhibition and innervates much of the mouse visual thalamus. Neuron **106**, 468–481 e462.

Mori, S., Sugawara, S., Kikuchi, T., Tanji, M., Narumi, O., Stoykova, A., Nishikawa, S.I., and Yokota, Y. (1999). The leukemic oncogene tal-2 is expressed in the developing mouse brain. Brain Res Mol Brain Res **64**, 199–210.

Morin, L.P., and Blanchard, J. (1995). Organization of the hamster intergeniculate leaflet: NPY and ENK projections to the suprachiasmatic nucleus, intergeniculate leaflet and posterior limitans nucleus. Vis Neurosci **12**, 57–67.

Morin, L.P., and Blanchard, J.H. (2005). Descending projections of the hamster intergeniculate leaflet: relationship to the sleep/arousal and visuomotor systems. J Comp Neurol **487**, 204–216.

Munkle, M.C., Waldvogel, H.J., and Faull, R.L. (2000). The distribution of calbindin, calretinin and parvalbumin immunoreactivity in the human thalamus. J Chem Neuroanat **19**, 155–173.

Nakatani, T., Minaki, Y., Kumai, M., and Ono, Y. (2007). Helt determines GABAergic over glutamatergic neuronal fate by repressing Ngn genes in the developing mesencephalon. Development **134**, 2783–2793.

Nardelli, J., Thiesson, D., Fujiwara, Y., Tsai, F.Y., and Orkin, S.H. (1999). Expression and genetic interaction of transcription factors GATA-2 and GATA-3 during development of the mouse central nervous system. Dev Biol **210**, 305–321.

Nobrega-Pereira, S., Kessaris, N., Du, T., Kimura, S., Anderson, S.A., and Marin, O. (2008). Postmitotic Nkx2-1 controls the migration of telencephalic interneurons by direct repression of guidance receptors. Neuron **59**, 733–745.

Ogilvy, S., Ferreira, R., Piltz, S.G., Bowen, J.M., Gottgens, B., and Green, A.R. (2007). The SCL +40 enhancer targets the midbrain together with primitive and definitive hematopoiesis and is regulated by SCL and GATA proteins. Mol Cell Biol **27**, 7206–7219.

Ohara, P.T., Chazal, G., and Ralston, H.J., 3rd (1989). Ultrastructural analysis of GABA-immunoreactive elements in the monkey thalamic ventrobasal complex. J Comp Neurol **283**, 541–558.

Ohara, P.T., Lieberman, A.R., Hunt, S.P., and Wu, J.Y. (1983). Neural elements containing glutamic acid decarboxylase (GAD) in the dorsal lateral geniculate nucleus of the rat; immunohistochemical studies by light and electron microscopy. Neuroscience **8**, 189–211.

Ottersen, O.P., and Storm-Mathisen, J. (1984). GABA-containing neurons in the thalamus and pretectum of the rodent. An immunocytochemical study. Anat Embryol (Berl) **170**, 197–207.

Palestini, M., Guegan, M., Saavedra, H., Thomasset, M., and Batini, C. (1993). Glutamate, GABA, calbindin-D28k and parvalbumin immunoreactivity in the pulvinar-lateralis posterior complex of the cat: relation to the projection to the Clare-Bishop area. Neurosci Lett **160**, 89–92.

Pan, Y., and Monje, M. (2020). Activity shapes neural circuit form and function: a historical perspective. J Neurosci **40**, 944–954.

Pandolfi, P.P., Roth, M.E., Karis, A., Leonard, M.W., Dzierzak, E., Grosveld, F.G., Engel, J.D., and Lindenbaum, M.H. (1995). Targeted disruption of the GATA3 gene causes severe abnormalities in the nervous system and in fetal liver haematopoiesis. Nat Genet **11**, 40–44.

Parras, C.M., Schuurmans, C., Scardigli, R., Kim, J., Anderson, D.J., and Guillemot, F. (2002). Divergent functions of the proneural genes Mash1 and Ngn2 in the specification of neuronal subtype identity. Genes Dev **16**, 324–338.

Pasik, P., Pasik, T., Hamori, J., and Szentagothai, J. (1973). Golgi type II interneurons in the neuronal circuit of the monkey lateral geniculate nucleus. Exp Brain Res **17**, 18–34.

Pei, Z., Wang, B., Chen, G., Nagao, M., Nakafuku, M., and Campbell, K. (2011). Homeobox genes Gsx1 and Gsx2 differentially regulate telencephalic progenitor maturation. Proc Natl Acad Sci USA **108**, 1675–1680.

Peltopuro, P., Kala, K., and Partanen, J. (2010). Distinct requirements for Ascl1 in subpopulations of midbrain GABAergic neurons. Dev Biol **343**, 63–70.

Penny, G.R., Conley, M., Schmechel, D.E., and Diamond, I.T. (1984). The distribution of glutamic acid decarboxylase immunoreactivity in the diencephalon of the opossum and rabbit. J Comp Neurol **228**, 38–56.

Penny, G.R., Fitzpatrick, D., Schmechel, D.E., and Diamond, I.T. (1983). Glutamic acid decarboxylase-immunoreactive neurons and horseradish peroxidase-labeled projection neurons in the ventral posterior nucleus of the cat and Galago senegalensis. J Neurosci **3**, 1868–1887.

Perez-Balaguer, A., Puelles, E., Wurst, W., and Martinez, S. (2009). Shh dependent and independent maintenance of basal midbrain. Mech Dev **126**, 301–313.

Peters, A., and Palay, S.L. (1966). The morphology of laminae A and A1 of the dorsal nucleus of the lateral geniculate body of the cat. J Anat **100**, 451–486.

Petryniak, M.A., Potter, G.B., Rowitch, D.H., and Rubenstein, J.L. (2007). Dlx1 and Dlx2 control neuronal versus oligodendroglial cell fate acquisition in the developing forebrain. Neuron **55**, 417–433.

Pleasure, S.J., Anderson, S., Hevner, R., Bagri, A., Marin, O., Lowenstein, D.H., and Rubenstein, J.L. (2000). Cell migration from the ganglionic eminences is required for the development of hippocampal GABAergic interneurons. Neuron **28**, 727–740.

Poitras, L., Ghanem, N., Hatch, G., and Ekker, M. (2007). The proneural determinant MASH1 regulates forebrain Dlx1/2 expression through the I12b intergenic enhancer. Development **134**, 1755–1765.

Puelles, L. (2019). Survey of midbrain, diencephalon, and hypothalamus neuroanatomic terms whose prosomeric definition conflicts with columnar tradition. Front Neuroanat **13**, 20.

Puelles, L., Diaz, C., Stuhmer, T., Ferran, J.L., Martinez-de la Torre, M., and Rubenstein, J.L.R. (2020). LacZ-reporter mapping of Dlx5/6 expression and genoarchitectural analysis of the postnatal mouse prethalamus. J Comp Neurol **529**, 367–420.

Puelles, L., Harrison, M., Paxinos, G., and Watson, C. (2013). A developmental ontology for the mammalian brain based on the prosomeric model. Trends Neurosci **36**, 570–578.

Puelles, L., and Rubenstein, J.L. (1993). Expression patterns of homeobox and other putative regulatory genes in the embryonic mouse forebrain suggest a neuromeric organization. Trends Neurosci **16**, 472–479.

Puelles, L., and Rubenstein, J.L. (2003). Forebrain gene expression domains and the evolving prosomeric model. Trends Neurosci **26**, 469–476.

Quinlan, R., Graf, M., Mason, I., Lumsden, A., and Kiecker, C. (2009). Complex and dynamic patterns of Wnt pathway gene expression in the developing chick forebrain. Neural Dev **4**, 35.

Rakić, P., and Sidman, R.L. (1969). Telencephalic origin of pulvinar neurons in the fetal human brain. Z Anat Entwicklungsgesch **129**, 53–82.

Rausell, E., Bae, C.S., Vinuela, A., Huntley, G.W., and Jones, E.G. (1992). Calbindin and parvalbumin cells in monkey VPL thalamic nucleus: distribution, laminar cortical projections, and relations to spinothalamic terminations. J Neurosci **12**, 4088–4111.

Rikhye, R.V., Wimmer, R.D., and Halassa, M.M. (2018). Toward an integrative theory of thalamic function. Annu Rev Neurosci **41**, 163–183.

Rinvik, E., Ottersen, O.P., and Storm-Mathisen, J. (1987). Gamma-aminobutyrate-like immunoreactivity in the thalamus of the cat. Neuroscience **21**, 781–805.

Robertshaw, E., Matsumoto, K., Lumsden, A., and Kiecker, C. (2013). Irx3 and Pax6 establish differential competence for Shh-mediated induction of GABAergic and glutamatergic neurons of the thalamus. Proc Natl Acad Sci USA **110**, E3919–3926.

Rubenstein, J.L., Martinez, S., Shimamura, K., and Puelles, L. (1994). The embryonic vertebrate forebrain: the prosomeric model. Science **266**, 578–580.

Sabbagh, U., Govindaiah, G., Somaiya, R.D., Ha, R.V., Wei, J.C., Guido, W., and Fox, M.A. (2020). Diverse GABAergic neurons organize into subtype-specific sublaminae in the ventral lateral geniculate nucleus. J Neurochem **159**, 479–497.

Sanchez-Vives, M.V., Bal, T., Kim, U., von Krosigk, M., and McCormick, D.A. (1996). Are the interlaminar zones of the ferret dorsal lateral geniculate nucleus actually part of the perigeniculate nucleus? J Neurosci **16**, 5923–5941.

Sanders, T.A., Lumsden, A., and Ragsdale, C.W. (2002). Arcuate plan of chick midbrain development. J Neurosci **22**, 10742–10750.

Saunders, A., Macosko, E.Z., Wysoker, A., Goldman, M., Krienen, F.M., de Rivera, H., Bien, E., Baum, M., Bortolin, L., Wang, S., et al. (2018). Molecular diversity and specializations among the cells of the adult mouse brain. Cell **174**, 1015–1030, e1016.

Sawyer, S.F., Martone, M.E., and Groves, P.M. (1991). A GABA immunocytochemical study of rat motor thalamus: light and electron microscopic observations. Neuroscience **42**, 103–124.

Scheibel, M.E., Davies, T.L., and Scheibel, A.B. (1972). On dendrodendritic relations in the dorsal thalamus of the adult cat. Exp Neurol **36**, 519–529.

Scholpp, S., Delogu, A., Gilthorpe, J., Peukert, D., Schindler, S., and Lumsden, A. (2009). Her6 regulates the neurogenetic gradient and neuronal identity in the thalamus. Proc Natl Acad Sci USA **106**, 19895–19900.

Scholpp, S., Wolf, O., Brand, M., and Lumsden, A. (2006). Hedgehog signalling from the zona limitans intrathalamica orchestrates patterning of the zebrafish diencephalon. Development **133**, 855–864.

Seabrook, T.A., Burbridge, T.J., Crair, M.C., and Huberman, A.D. (2017). Architecture, function, and assembly of the mouse visual system. Annu Rev Neurosci **40**, 499–538.

Seabrook, T.A., El-Danaf, R.N., Krahe, T.E., Fox, M.A., and Guido, W. (2013a). Retinal input regulates the timing of corticogeniculate innervation. J Neurosci **33**, 10085–10097.

Seabrook, T.A., Krahe, T.E., Govindaiah, G., and Guido, W. (2013b). Interneurons in the mouse visual thalamus maintain a high degree of retinal convergence throughout postnatal development. Neural Dev **8**, 24.

Sellers, K., Zyka, V., Lumsden, A.G., and Delogu, A. (2014). Transcriptional control of GABAergic neuronal subtype identity in the thalamus. Neural Dev **9**, 14.

Shamim, H., Mahmood, R., Logan, C., Doherty, P., Lumsden, A., and Mason, I. (1999). Sequential roles for Fgf4, En1 and Fgf8 in specification and regionalisation of the midbrain. Development **126**, 945–959.

Shatz, C.J. (1996). Emergence of order in visual system development. Proc Natl Acad Sci USA **93**, 602–608.

Sherman, S.M. (2004). Interneurons and triadic circuitry of the thalamus. Trends Neurosci **27**, 670–675.

Sherman, S.M., and Guillery, R.W. (1998). On the actions that one nerve cell can have on another: distinguishing "drivers" from "modulators." Proc Natl Acad Sci USA **95**, 7121–7126.

Shi, H.Y., Xu, W., Guo, H., Dong, H., Qu, W.M., and Huang, Z.L. (2020). Lesion of intergeniculate leaflet GABAergic neurons attenuates sleep in mice exposed to light. Sleep **43**.

Shi, W., Xianyu, A., Han, Z., Tang, X., Li, Z., Zhong, H., Mao, T., Huang, K., and Shi, S.H. (2017). Ontogenetic establishment of order-specific nuclear organization in the mammalian thalamus. Nat Neurosci **20**, 516–528.

Shimamura, K., Hartigan, D.J., Martinez, S., Puelles, L., and Rubenstein, J.L. (1995). Longitudinal organization of the anterior neural plate and neural tube. Development **121**, 3923–3933.

Simeone, A., Acampora, D., Pannese, M., D'Esposito, M., Stornaiuolo, A., Gulisano, M., Mallamaci, A., Kastury, K., Druck, T., Huebner, K., et al. (1994). Cloning and characterization of two members of the vertebrate Dlx gene family. Proc Natl Acad Sci USA **91**, 2250–2254.

Smith, V.M., Jeffers, R.T., and Antle, M.C. (2015). Serotonergic enhancement of circadian responses to light: role of the raphe and intergeniculate leaflet. Eur J Neurosci 42, 2805–2817.

Smith, Y., Seguela, P., and Parent, A. (1987). Distribution of GABA-immunoreactive neurons in the thalamus of the squirrel monkey (*Saimiri sciureus*). Neuroscience 22, 579–591.

Sokhadze, G., Seabrook, T.A., and Guido, W. (2018). The absence of retinal input disrupts the development of cholinergic brainstem projections in the mouse dorsal lateral geniculate nucleus. Neural Dev 13, 27.

Song, H., Lee, B., Pyun, D., Guimera, J., Son, Y., Yoon, J., Baek, K., Wurst, W., and Jeong, Y. (2015). Ascl1 and Helt act combinatorially to specify thalamic neuronal identity by repressing Dlxs activation. Dev Biol 398, 280–291.

Spreafico, R., De Biasi, S., Battaglia, G., and Rustioni, A. (1992). GABA- and glutamate-containing neurons in the thalamus of rats and cats: an immunocytochemical study. Epilepsy Res Suppl 8, 107–115.

Spreafico, R., Frassoni, C., Arcelli, P., and De Biasi, S. (1994). GABAergic interneurons in the somatosensory thalamus of the guinea-pig: a light and ultrastructural immunocytochemical investigation. Neuroscience 59, 961–973.

Spreafico, R., Schmechel, D.E., Ellis, L.C., Jr., and Rustioni, A. (1983). Cortical relay neurons and interneurons in the N. ventralis posterolateralis of cats: a horseradish peroxidase, electron-microscopic, Golgi and immunocytochemical study. Neuroscience 9, 491–509.

Steriade, M. (2004). Local gating of information processing through the thalamus. Neuron 41, 493–494.

Steriade, M., Domich, L., and Oakson, G. (1986). Reticularis thalami neurons revisited: activity changes during shifts in states of vigilance. J Neurosci 6, 68–81.

Sterling, P., and Davis, T.L. (1980). Neurons in cat lateral geniculate nucleus that concentrate exogenous [3H]-gamma-aminobutyric acid (GABA). J Comp Neurol 192, 737–749.

Stichel, C.C., Singer, W., and Heizmann, C.W. (1988). Light and electron microscopic immunocytochemical localization of parvalbumin in the dorsal lateral geniculate nucleus of the cat: evidence for coexistence with GABA. J Comp Neurol 268, 29–37.

Su, J., Charalambakis, N.E., Sabbagh, U., Somaiya, R.D., Monavarfeshani, A., Guido, W., and Fox, M.A. (2020). Retinal inputs signal astrocytes to recruit interneurons into visual thalamus. Proc Natl Acad Sci USA 117, 2671–2682.

Sussel, L., Marin, O., Kimura, S., and Rubenstein, J.L. (1999). Loss of Nkx2.1 homeobox gene function results in a ventral to dorsal molecular respecification within the basal telencephalon: evidence for a transformation of the pallidum into the striatum. Development 126, 3359–3370.

Szentagothai, J. (1967). Models of specific neuron arrays in thalamic relay nuclei. Acta Morphol Acad Sci Hung 15, 113–124.

Szucsik, J.C., Witte, D.P., Li, H., Pixley, S.K., Small, K.M., and Potter, S.S. (1997). Altered forebrain and hindbrain development in mice mutant for the Gsh-2 homeobox gene. Dev Biol 191, 230–242.

Tai, Y., Yi, H., Ilinsky, I.A., and Kultas-Ilinsky, K. (1995). Nucleus reticularis thalami connections with the mediodorsal thalamic nucleus: a light and electron microscopic study in the monkey. Brain Res Bull 38, 475–488.

Tombol, T. (1967). Short neurons and their synaptic relations in the specific thalamic nuclei. Brain Res 3, 307–326.

Toresson, H., Potter, S.S., and Campbell, K. (2000). Genetic control of dorsal-ventral identity in the telencephalon: opposing roles for Pax6 and Gsh2. Development 127, 4361–4371.

Uchikawa, M., Kamachi, Y., and Kondoh, H. (1999). Two distinct subgroups of Group B Sox genes for transcriptional activators and repressors: their expression during embryonic organogenesis of the chicken. Mech Dev 84, 103–120.

Valerius, M.T., Li, H., Stock, J.L., Weinstein, M., Kaur, S., Singh, G., and Potter, S.S. (1995). Gsh-1: a novel murine homeobox gene expressed in the central nervous system. Dev Dyn 203, 337–351.

van Doorninck, J.H., van Der Wees, J., Karis, A., Goedknegt, E., Engel, J.D., Coesmans, M., Rutteman, M., Grosveld, F., and De Zeeuw, C.I. (1999). GATA-3 is involved in the development of serotonergic neurons in the caudal raphe nuclei. J Neurosci 19, RC12.

van Eekelen, J.A., Bradley, C.K., Gothert, J.R., Robb, L., Elefanty, A.G., Begley, C.G., and Harvey, A.R. (2003). Expression pattern of the stem cell leukaemia gene in the CNS of the embryonic and adult mouse. Neuroscience 122, 421–436.

Van Horn, S.C., Erisir, A., and Sherman, S.M. (2000). Relative distribution of synapses in the A-laminae of the lateral geniculate nucleus of the cat. J Comp Neurol 416, 509–520.

Vernay, B., Koch, M., Vaccarino, F., Briscoe, J., Simeone, A., Kageyama, R., and Ang, S.L. (2005). Otx2 regulates subtype specification and neurogenesis in the midbrain. J Neurosci 25, 4856–4867.

Vieira, C., and Martinez, S. (2006). Sonic hedgehog from the basal plate and the zona limitans intrathalamica exhibits differential activity on diencephalic molecular regionalization and nuclear structure. Neuroscience 143, 129–140.

Virolainen, S.M., Achim, K., Peltopuro, P., Salminen, M., and Partanen, J. (2012). Transcriptional regulatory mechanisms underlying the GABAergic neuron fate in different diencephalic prosomeres. Development 139, 3795–3805.

Vrang, N., Mrosovsky, N., and Mikkelsen, J.D. (2003). Afferent projections to the hamster intergeniculate leaflet demonstrated by retrograde and anterograde tracing. Brain Res Bull 59, 267–288.

Vue, T.Y., Aaker, J., Taniguchi, A., Kazemzadeh, C., Skidmore, J.M., Martin, D.M., Martin, J.F., Treier, M., and Nakagawa, Y. (2007). Characterization of progenitor domains in the developing mouse thalamus. J Comp Neurol 505, 73–91.

Vue, T.Y., Bluske, K., Alishahi, A., Yang, L.L., Koyano-Nakagawa, N., Novitch, B., and Nakagawa, Y. (2009). Sonic hedgehog signaling controls thalamic progenitor identity and nuclei specification in mice. J Neurosci 29, 4484–4497.

Waclaw, R.R., Wang, B., Pei, Z., Ehrman, L.A., and Campbell, K. (2009). Distinct temporal requirements for the homeobox gene Gsx2 in specifying striatal and olfactory bulb neuronal fates. Neuron 63, 451–465.

Waite, M.R., Skidmore, J.M., Billi, A.C., Martin, J.F., and Martin, D.M. (2011). GABAergic and glutamatergic identities of developing midbrain Pitx2 neurons. Dev Dyn 240, 333–346.

Wang, B., Waclaw, R.R., Allen, Z.J., 2nd, Guillemot, F., and Campbell, K. (2009). Ascl1 is a required downstream effector of Gsx gene function in the embryonic mouse telencephalon. Neural Dev 4, 5.

Wang, S., Eisenback, M., Datskovskaia, A., Boyce, M., and Bickford, M.E. (2002). GABAergic pretectal terminals contact GABAergic interneurons in the cat dorsal lateral geniculate nucleus. Neurosci Lett 323, 141–145.

Wang, S.W., Kim, B.S., Ding, K., Wang, H., Sun, D., Johnson, R.L., Klein, W.H., and Gan, L. (2001). Requirement for math5 in the development of retinal ganglion cells. Genes Dev 15, 24–29.

Wang, Y., Dye, C.A., Sohal, V., Long, J.E., Estrada, R.C., Roztocil, T., Lufkin, T., Deisseroth, K., Baraban, S.C., and Rubenstein, J.L. (2010). Dlx5 and Dlx6 regulate the development of parvalbumin-expressing cortical interneurons. J Neurosci 30, 5334–5345.

Wang, Y., Li, G., Stanco, A., Long, J.E., Crawford, D., Potter, G.B., Pleasure, S.J., Behrens, T., and Rubenstein, J.L. (2011). CXCR4 and CXCR7 have distinct functions in regulating interneuron migration. Neuron 69, 61–76.

Weber, A.J., and Kalil, R.E. (1983). The percentage of interneurons in the dorsal lateral geniculate nucleus of the cat and observations on several variables that affect the sensitivity of horseradish peroxidase as a retrograde marker. J Comp Neurol 220, 336–346.

Weber, A.J., Kalil, R.E., and Behan, M. (1989). Synaptic connections between corticogeniculate axons and interneurons in the dorsal lateral geniculate nucleus of the cat. J Comp Neurol 289, 156–164.

Weber, A.J., Kalil, R.E., and Hickey, T.L. (1986). Genesis of interneurons in the dorsal lateral geniculate nucleus of the cat. J Comp Neurol 252, 385–391.

Wei, S., Du, H., Li, Z., Tao, G., Xu, Z., Song, X., Shang, Z., Su, Z., Chen, H., Wen, Y., et al. (2019). Transcription factors Sp8 and Sp9 regulate the development of caudal ganglionic eminence-derived cortical interneurons. J Comp Neurol 527, 2860–2874.

Wende, C.Z., Zoubaa, S., Blak, A., Echevarria, D., Martinez, S., Guillemot, F., Wurst, W., and Guimera, J. (2015). Hairy/enhancer-of-split MEGANE and proneural MASH1 factors cooperate synergistically in midbrain GABAergic neurogenesis. PLoS One 10, e0127681.

Willett, R.T., and Greene, L.A. (2011). Gata2 is required for migration and differentiation of retinorecipient neurons in the superior colliculus. J Neurosci 31, 4444–4455.

Williams, S.R., Turner, J.P., Anderson, C.M., and Crunelli, V. (1996). Electrophysiological and morphological properties of interneurones in the rat dorsal lateral geniculate nucleus in vitro. J Physiol 490 (Pt 1), 129–147.

Wilson, J.R. (1986). Synaptic connections of relay and local circuit neurons in the monkey's dorsal lateral geniculate nucleus. Neurosci Lett 66, 79–84.

Wong, S.Z.H., Scott, E.P., Mu, W., Guo, X., Borgenheimer, E., Freeman, M., Ming, G.L., Wu, Q.F., Song, H., and Nakagawa, Y. (2018). In vivo clonal analysis reveals spatiotemporal regulation of thalamic nucleogenesis. PLoS Biol 16, e2005211.

Xu, Q., Cobos, I., De La Cruz, E., Rubenstein, J.L., and Anderson, S.A. (2004). Origins of cortical interneuron subtypes. J Neurosci 24, 2612–2622.

Xu, Q., Tam, M., and Anderson, S.A. (2008). Fate mapping Nkx2.1-lineage cells in the mouse telencephalon. J Comp Neurol 506, 16–29.

Yoon, M.S., Puelles, L., and Redies, C. (2000). Formation of cadherin-expressing brain nuclei in diencephalic alar plate divisions. J Comp Neurol 427, 461–480.

Yun, K., Fischman, S., Johnson, J., Hrabe de Angelis, M., Weinmaster, G., and Rubenstein, J.L. (2002). Modulation of the notch signaling by Mash1 and Dlx1/2 regulates sequential specification and differentiation of progenitor cell types in the subcortical telencephalon. Development 129, 5029–5040.

Yun, K., Garel, S., Fischman, S., and Rubenstein, J.L. (2003). Patterning of the lateral ganglionic eminence by the Gsh1 and Gsh2 homeobox genes regulates striatal and olfactory bulb histogenesis and the growth of axons through the basal ganglia. J Comp Neurol 461, 151–165.

Yun, K., Potter, S., and Rubenstein, J.L. (2001). Gsh2 and Pax6 play complementary roles in dorsoventral patterning of the mammalian telencephalon. Development 128, 193–205.

Zeisel, A., Hochgerner, H., Lonnerberg, P., Johnsson, A., Memic, F., van der Zwan, J., Haring, M., Braun, E., Borm, L.E., La Manno, G., et al. (2018). Molecular Architecture of the Mouse Nervous System. Cell 174, 999–1014 e1022.

Zhang, Q., Zhang, Y., Wang, C., Xu, Z., Liang, Q., An, L., Li, J., Liu, Z., You, Y., He, M., et al. (2016). The zinc finger transcription factor Sp9 is required for the development of striatopallidal projection neurons. Cell Rep 16, 1431–1444.

Zhao, G.Y., Li, Z.Y., Zou, H.L., Hu, Z.L., Song, N.N., Zheng, M.H., Su, C.J., and Ding, Y.Q. (2008). Expression of the transcription factor GATA3 in the postnatal mouse central nervous system. Neurosci Res 61, 420–428.

Section 5: Sensory Processing

Chapter 9: Thalamocortical Interactions in the Primary Visual Cortex

Jose-Manuel Alonso and Massimo Scanziani

Introduction

All information about the visual world reaches the cortex via the thalamus. Thalamic neurons receive direct input from axons originating in the retina of the eye and, in turn, send their axons to the cortex. Thus, the thalamic input is the obligatory entry point into the cortex for any signal about the visual world. A mechanistic understanding of how the cortex contributes to vision thus necessitates a thorough knowledge of what visual information the thalamus sends to the cortex and how this visual information enters the cortex. Because of the massive evolutionary expansion of the cortex in mammals and the vast amount of cortical real estate dedicated to vision in some mammals, including humans (Mazade and Alonso, 2017; Van Essen et al., 2018), the logic of this entry point of visual information has stimulated curiosity and triggered the imagination of scores of scientists for many decades. Through this effort, the structure and function of thalamocortical communication in the visual system are probably the best understood among all sensory modalities.

Several thalamic nuclei receive visual information ascending from the periphery, yet the transmission of this information to the visual cortex relies mainly on two nuclei, the dorsolateral geniculate nucleus (dLGN) and the pulvinar nucleus. The dLGN is the recipient of the vast majority of retinal axons targeting the thalamus and, accordingly, is considered the primary visual nucleus of the thalamus. The dLGN, in turn, projects to the primary visual cortex (V1), also known as the *striate cortex* because of a band or "stria" in the middle cortical layers (layer 4B) that is visible to the naked eye and was first observed by the anatomist Francesco Gennari at the University of Parma (Gennari, 1782). The dLGN projects to V1, giving rise to the "geniculo-striate" pathway and, to a lesser extent, several other visual cortical areas (Bienkowski et al., 2019; Kawano, 1998; Sincich et al., 2004). In contrast to the dLGN, the pulvinar nucleus receives its main ascending visual input from the superior colliculus (Zhou et al., 2017) and, in small part, also directly from the retina (Cowey et al., 1994; Morin and Studholme, 2014; Warner et al., 2015). It then distributes its output to several visual cortical areas (Adams et al., 2000; Berman and Wurtz, 2008; Zhou et al., 2017), giving rise to the extra-geniculate pathway. The logic of the dLGN input to V1 in mammals is far better understood than any other visual input to the cortex and is the focus of this review.

We will describe the main principles in the organization of the dLGN-to-V1 pathways and highlight how structure relates to function. We will compare specific aspects of this organization between model organisms to underline or qualify their generality. Finally, we will point toward critical unanswered questions to inspire future research. We believe that several aspects of the dLGN-to-V1 communication discussed in this review likely apply to other sensory modalities and may thus represent general principles for how the sensory world enters the mammalian cortex.

Parallel Pathways

Signals originating from distinct sensory modalities, for example, vision and sound, travel into and through the brain via separate, anatomically defined "pathways," that is, routes along chains of synaptically connected neurons. These pathways can remain separate through many sensory processing steps, consistent with the fact that vision and audition are clearly distinct perceptual experiences. The coherence of our sensory world, however, also relies on the eventual merger of these separate pathways. The merger of pathways allows us to extract meaning. For example, the identification of a bird in a tree may depend on both its appearance and its vocalizations. The combination of signals from distinct sensory modalities also occurs when those signals are strongly correlated. For example, the perception of speech can rely on the visual input of the movements of the mouth, as exemplified by the McGurk effect (McGurk and MacDonald, 1976). Even a specific sensory modality, like vision, encompasses distinct "parallel" (i.e., separate) pathways (Callaway, 2005; Livingstone and Hubel, 1988; Merigan and Maunsell, 1993). Within the visual system, parallel pathways often segregate anatomically into different layers or zones within the dLGN and V1 based on properties such as the spatial location, eye of origin, and response to stimulus polarity (light or dark). Within each pathway, an individual axon signals a specific combination of stimulus properties, such as the position of a dark stimulus in the left eye. The organization of visual pathways as relatively independent signaling channels underlies much of the logic of communication between the dLGN and V1. In this section, we will discuss the main parallel pathways of geniculo-striate communication, with particular attention to those that are conserved among most mammalian species studied so far (Figure 1). In the next section, we will provide examples of how the merger of these pathways in V1 enables the visual cortex to extract specific features of the visual environment.

Sensory Processing

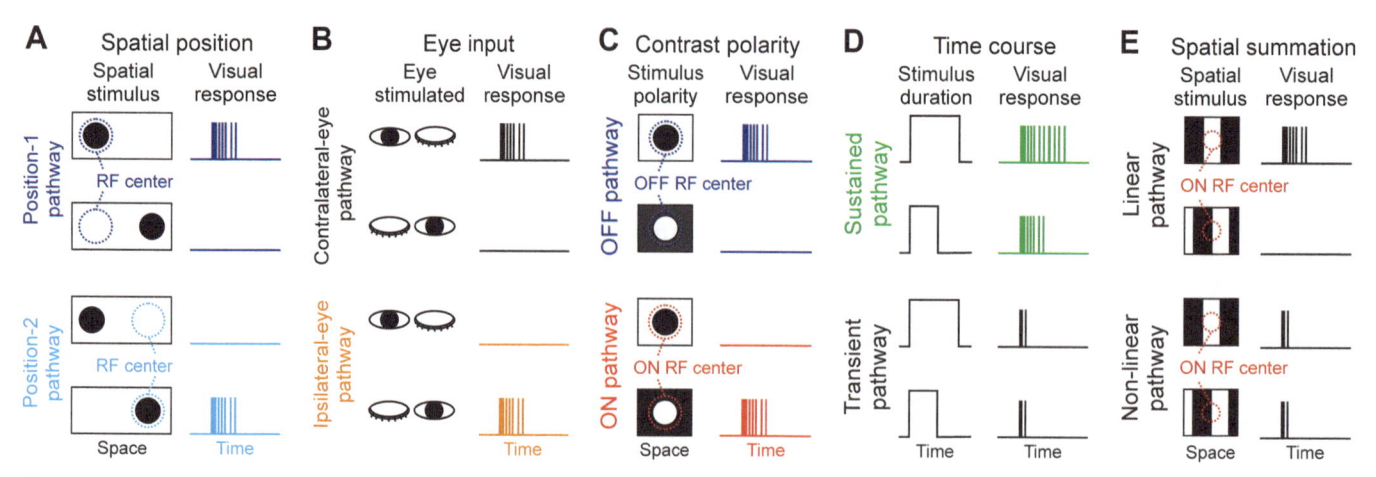

Figure 1 Parallel pathways most conserved among mammalian species.

A. The stimulus position is processed in parallel by neurons with receptive fields (RFs) on different locations of visual space (position 1 at the top and 2 at the bottom).

B. Eye input is independently processed by neurons responding to stimulation of the eye contralateral (*top*) or ipsilateral (*bottom*) to their brain hemisphere.

C. Stimulus polarity is processed in parallel by neurons responding to dark (*top*) or light (*bottom*) stimuli.

D. The stimulus time course is processed by pathways signaling stimulus duration with sustained responses (*top*) or stimulus onset with transient responses (*bottom*). Some of these neurons also signal the time when the stimulus is turned off (*not shown*).

E. Certain mammals (e.g., carnivores) have separate pathways for linear and non-linear spatial summation. Linear neurons respond as if they were linearly summing the light (+1) and dark (−1) pixels of the stimulus (*top*) and do not respond when the stimulus has an equal number of light and dark pixels (1 − 1 = 0 response). Conversely, non-linear neurons respond to a large variety of stimuli that have equal numbers of light and dark pixels (1 − 1 > 0 response). See text for more detail.

Parallel Pathways in Visual Space

The parcellation of visual space along parallel signaling pathways (Figure 1A) is one of the best-preserved properties in thalamocortical communication. In the dLGN, each neuron "looks" at a portion of visual space determined by the inputs it gets from the retina. These retinal inputs generate the receptive field of the dLGN neuron, namely, the region of visual space where a stimulus can drive action potentials (Hartline, 1938). Because neighboring dLGN neurons "look" at neighboring portions of visual space and project their axons to neighboring regions in the primary visual cortex, the thalamus projects a map of visual space onto the cortex (Malpeli and Baker, 1975; Van Essen et al., 1984). Visual space is not homogeneously covered by dLGN neurons. In fact, retinal variations in image sampling are closely associated with variations in the number of thalamocortical axons signaling each portion of visual space. For example, the human fovea (i.e., the retinal region sampling the center of visual space) has narrow and tightly packed photoreceptors (Curcio et al., 1990) that communicate with area V1 through separate and independent pathways (Kolb and Dekorver, 1991; Masri et al., 2020) that operate as private lines (Figure 2). Through this parallel thalamocortical parcellation of visual space, humans enjoy exquisite visual acuity at the center of vision. These private lines allow humans to discriminate very small differences between images, such as the letters *e* and *c* on this page. Similarly, in macaques, the vast majority of thalamocortical axons signal spatial locations at the center of vision and, consequently, the cortical space dedicated to this small sector of the image is much larger than the space dedicated to more peripheral sectors of the visual field. For example, a central patch of just 10 degrees (e.g., a face at a distance of 0.5 meters) occupies less than 1/50th

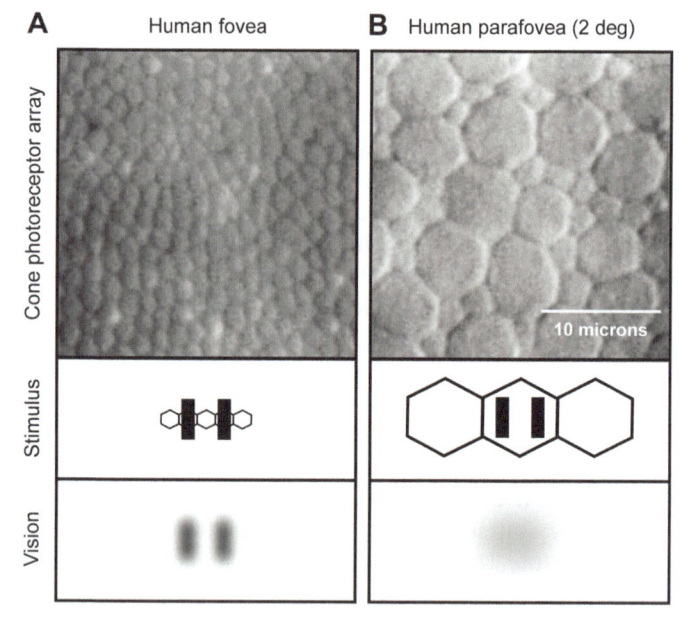

Figure 2 Parallel pathways in visual space.

A. Each small cone in the human fovea (*top*) transmits signals through a private line to area V1. These private lines make it possible to discriminate (*bottom*) narrow gaps between closely spaced lines (*middle*).

B. Outside the fovea, cones are larger (*top*) and no longer have private lines, limiting the discrimination (*bottom*) of narrow gaps between closely spaced lines (*middle*). Cone arrays from Curcio et al. (1990) with permission from John Wiley and Sons, copyright 1990.

of the visual image but nearly 1/2 of dLGN and V1 volume (Figure 3). Maintaining this exquisite spatial resolution throughout the entire retina would require having one dedicated pathway for each of the 125 million photoreceptors of the human retina, that is, two orders of magnitude more fibers

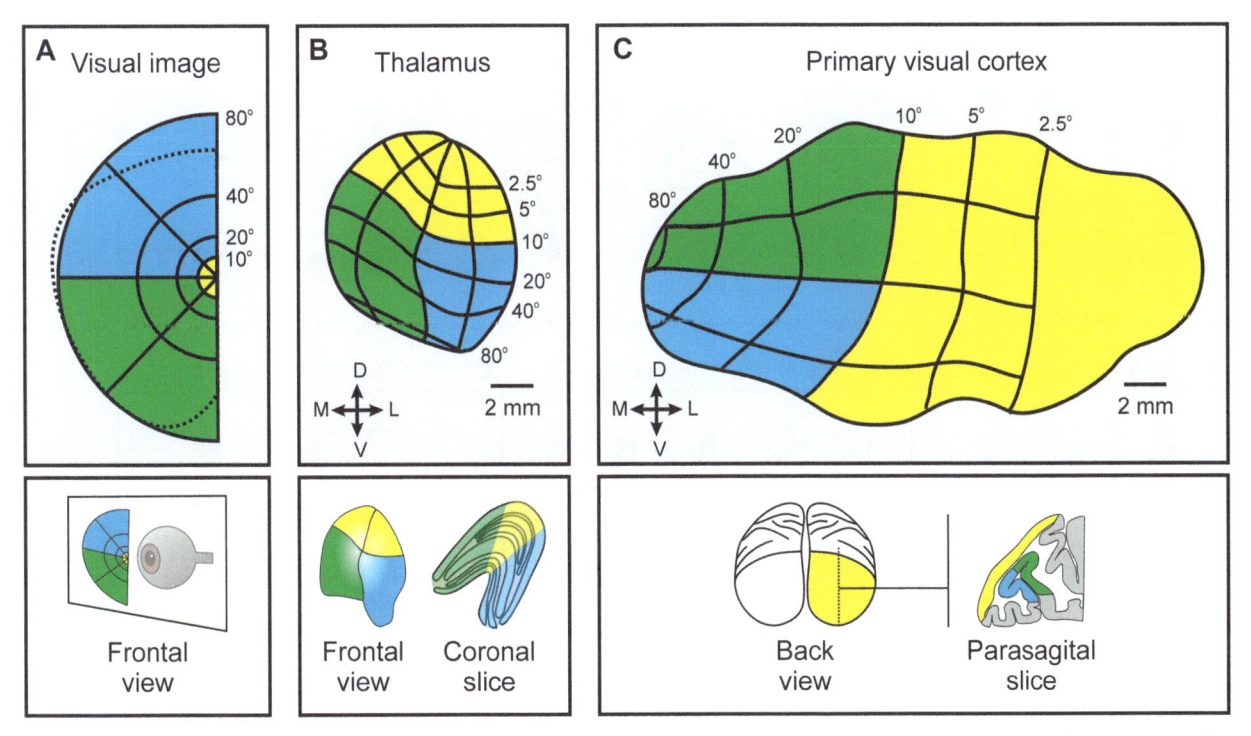

Figure 3 Parallel pathways in visual space are organized in brain maps that dedicate a disproportionate amount of space to central vision.
A. Half of the human visual field (*top, dotted line*) seen with an eye fixating at the center (*bottom*). The upper visual field is shown in blue, the lower visual field in green, and the central 10 degrees in yellow.
B. Map of visual space in macaque dLGN in a flattened frontal view (*top*), a three-dimensional frontal view (*bottom left*), and a coronal slice (*bottom right*).
C. Map of visual space in macaque V1 in a flattened view (*top*), back view (*bottom left*), and parasagittal slice (*bottom right*). D: dorsal, L: lateral, V: ventral, M: medial.

than those actually present in the human optic nerve (Curcio and Allen, 1990; Kolb, 1995; Mazade and Alonso, 2017; Osterberg, 1935). Therefore, in the visual periphery, each pathway receives convergent input from multiple, wider photoreceptors, resulting in a decrease in spatial resolution. In fact, spatial resolution already starts falling within a fraction of a millimeter away from the fovea (Curcio et al., 1990), as the reader can verify by fixating the eyes on one letter of this page. Without moving the eyes, the letters in the words adjacent to the point of fixation are almost impossible to resolve.

Parallel Ocular Pathways

The anatomical segregation of the two pathways originating from each eye (Figure 1B) is another striking property of the organization of thalamocortical communication. In animals with lateral eyes, like mice and tree shrews, each of the two eyes samples a largely non-overlapping hemifield of visual space, resulting in independent pathways that represent different portions of the image both in the dLGN and V1 (Conway and Schiller, 1983; Ji et al., 2015; Kaas et al., 1972; Kerschensteiner and Guido, 2017). Through the midline crossing of the optic nerve, the left and right brain hemispheres receive signals from the right and left hemifield of visual space, respectively. However, the midline crossing of the optic nerve is not complete (Jeffery and Erskine, 2005; Murcia-Belmonte and Erskine, 2019). Some retinal axons do not cross the midline, and the number of those axons increases with the size of the binocular field (i.e., the portion of the visual field seen with both eyes). As a consequence, the dLGN of a hemisphere receives axons from both retinas, which segregate in different dLGN layers or zones (Figure 4) (Rakic, 1977; Shatz, 1983; Sretavan and Shatz, 1986). In animals with frontal eyes, and hence with a much larger binocular field, the ocular separation of pathways is largely preserved also in V1 (Figure 5). For example, in humans, macaques, and cats, the afferents carrying signals from the two eyes are segregated in both separate dLGN layers and "ocular dominance" V1 columns (Adams et al., 2007; Anderson et al., 1988). The ocular dominance column describes a fundamental aspect of the functional organization of V1, namely, that neurons located along the radial dimension or depth of V1 (the "column") all preferentially respond to the stimulation of the same eye. The ocular preference of these columns alternates along the tangential plane of V1, forming three-dimensional shapes that resemble the curve-shaped pillars from the architect Santiago Calatrava more than a classic cylindrical column. The shape of the ocular dominance columns can vary greatly across animals. When seen from the brain surface, the columns appear as long stripes in humans and macaques (Adams et al., 2007), shorter blobs in cats (Anderson et al., 1988) or nearly circular domains in some types of rats (Laing et al., 2015). Importantly, the separation according to ocular origin is not absolute in V1. Neurons located at the transition between ocular dominance columns respond with similar strength to stimulation of the two eyes (Kara and Boyd, 2009), a fact that endows these neurons with remarkable functional properties (see Combining Pathways).

Sensory Processing

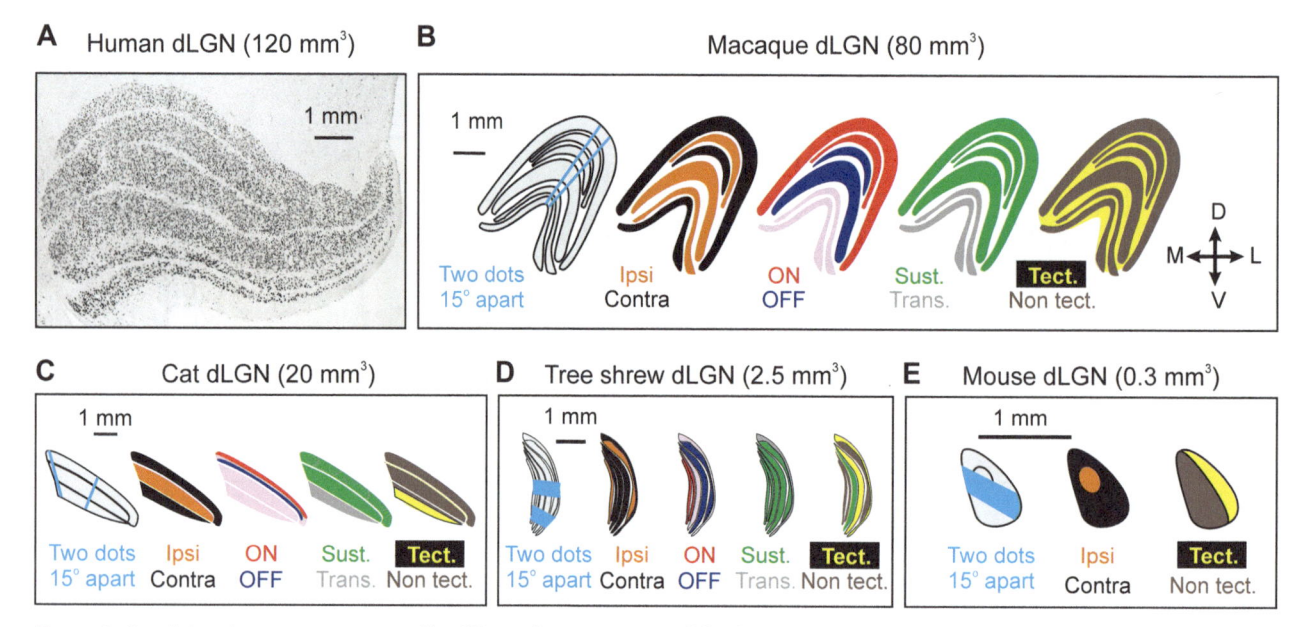

Figure 4 Parallel pathways are segregated in different layers or zones of the dLGN.

A. Coronal section of human dLGN from Andrews et al. (1997) and total volume in mm³. All volume values from Mazade and Alonso (2017).

B. Cartoon of macaque dLGN illustrating the segregation of parallel pathways by visual space (activation of dLGN by two dots separated 15 degrees apart), eye input (contra: contralateral eye in black; ipsi: ipsilateral eye in orange), light–dark polarity (predominance of ON neurons in red, predominance of OFF neurons in blue, similar number of ON and OFF neurons in pink), response time course (Sust: sustained response in green, Trans: transient response in gray), and tectal input (tect: layers receiving tectal input; non-tect: layers not receiving tectal input).

C. Same as panel B for the cat. In sustained/transient, the layers illustrated in green are dominated by sustained neurons but also include a minority of transient neurons.

D and E. Same as panel B for tree shrew and mouse.

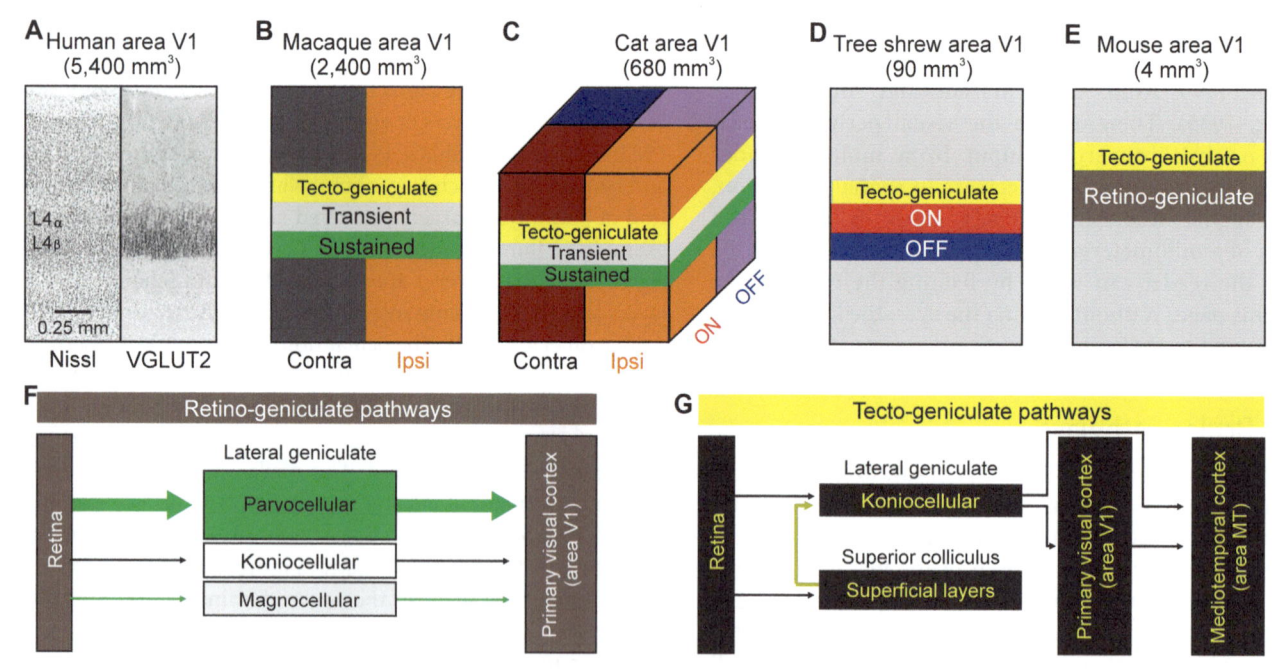

Figure 5 Parallel pathways are segregated in different layers or zones of the primary visual cortex (area V1).

A. Coronal section of human area V1 from Bryant et al. (2012) with permission from Karger Publishers, copyright 2012, and total volume in mm³. All V1 volumes from Mazade and Alonso (2017).

B. Cartoon of coronal slice from macaque area V1 showing segregation by eye input (contra: contralateral in black; ipsi: ipsilateral in orange), response time course (sustained in green, transient in gray), and tecto-geniculate pathways (yellow).

C. Same as panel B for cat area V1 but showing a cube instead of a coronal slice to illustrate the segregation by light–dark polarity (ON: responses to light stimuli in red/orange, OFF: responses to dark stimuli in blue/purple).

D. Same as panel B for tree shrew.

E. Same as panel B for mouse (yellow: tecto-geniculate pathway, brown: retino-geniculate pathway).

F and G. Cartoons illustrating the anatomy of retino-geniculate (F) and tecto-geniculate (G) pathways.

An important consequence of having segregated ocular pathways is that each eye can see the visual world relatively independently, even in animals with frontal eyes. This eye independence could have an evolutionary advantage because it helps to continuously track a target when moving among obstacles that may momentarily occlude the view of one eye or the other. For example, when the view from one eye is occluded in a competitive environment (e.g., by a hand in a fight between two monkeys competing for food), the non-occluded eye can operate independently until recovering binocular vision. If the fight takes a turn for the worse and one eye is lost, the visual input to the brain is reduced by half, but vision through the spared eye can still operate independently to coordinate an escape to safety. Monocular vision is a serious disability in humans but is not invalidating. Johnny Depp, the famous actor of *Pirates of the Caribbean* (2003), is legally blind in his left eye since birth. However, few of his fans know that he is only seeing with one eye, the one that could not be covered by a pirate patch.

Parallel ON and OFF Pathways

A conserved function of visual thalamocortical pathways is to signal the polarity of the stimulus (i.e., light or dark), defined as the stimulus luminance at the receptive field center relative to its surround. The parallel signaling of light and dark (Figure 1C) is very well preserved throughout the animal kingdom and is carried by two pathways that Hartline called ON and OFF because they each respond to light turned on or off within the receptive field (Hartline, 1938). The receptive fields of dLGN thalamic neurons have the same center-surround structure discovered by Kuffler in retinal neurons (Kuffler, 1953). In both the retina and the dLGN, the receptive fields are organized as two concentric circular regions, with the center region being about three times smaller in diameter than the surround (Kuffler, 1953). The receptive field surround responds to the opposite contrast polarity than the center and suppresses the neuronal response when stimulated with its non-preferred polarity. For example, OFF neurons respond strongest when a dark stimulus, presented in the center of their receptive field, is surrounded by a bright background (e.g., a fly against a bright sky), and the response decreases when the dark stimulus also covers the surround (e.g., when closing the eyes). Conversely, ON neurons respond strongest when a bright stimulus, presented in the center of their receptive field, is surrounded by a dark background (e.g., a star in a dark night sky), and the response decreases when the bright stimulus also covers the surround (e.g., a patch of a bright sky). Thus, ON and OFF neurons signal local differences in luminance between the receptive field center and surround (i.e., luminance contrast), and their responses become stronger as the luminance difference increases. The increase in response strength makes stimuli with high contrast (e.g., a dark letter on a bright screen) easier to see than stimuli with low contrast (e.g., a dark letter on a dim screen).

ON and OFF pathways are present in all animals that can form retinal images, from invertebrates to humans (Dacey and Petersen, 1992; Joesch et al., 2010; Kremkow and Alonso, 2018), and their separation starts at the very first synapse of the visual pathway, between photoreceptors and bipolar cells in the retina (Kolb et al., 1995–; Rodieck, 1998). ON and OFF pathways remain fully segregated in the dLGN at the level of single neurons in all mammals (Figure 4). The segregation also remains largely, yet not entirely, preserved in area V1 of many mammals, including cats, ferrets, minks, tree shrews, and primates (Figure 5) (Chatterjee and Callaway, 2003; Jin et al., 2008; Kremkow et al., 2016; McConnell and LeVay, 1984; Norton et al., 1985; Zahs and Stryker, 1988). In fact, as we will see later in the chapter, the merger of ON and OFF pathways in V1 endows neurons with very interesting properties. As with visual space and eye input, ON and OFF pathways operate in parallel and relatively independently. Humans can have productive lives without an ON pathway (Cammack et al., 2016; Dryja et al., 2005), and their visual function is only seriously compromised at night (night blindness) or in low-light environments (e.g., finding a seat in a movie theater when the lights are off). Similarly, the loss of the ON visual pathway in monkeys is associated with pronounced visual deficits when seeing light stimuli in dark backgrounds but not dark stimuli in light backgrounds (Schiller et al., 1986). Indeed, experimental inactivation of the ON visual pathway does not greatly affect most of the receptive field properties of cortical neurons, such as orientation and direction selectivity in macaques, cats, and mice (Sarnaik et al., 2014; Schiller, 1982; Sherk and Horton, 1984).

ON and OFF pathways are not simple mirror versions of each other. The ON thalamocortical pathway has higher contrast sensitivity (i.e., responds to smaller luminance differences between the center and the surround), has a lower spatial resolution (i.e., larger receptive fields), and prefers slower changes in luminance than the OFF pathway (Komban et al., 2014; Kremkow et al., 2014; Mazade et al., 2019). Most of these differences originate in the retina and appear well preserved across species. For example, dendritic fields are larger in ON than OFF retinal ganglion cells in humans, non-human primates, cats, and rats (Dacey and Petersen, 1992; Peichl, 1989; Wassle et al., 1981). Consequently, the receptive fields are also larger in ON than OFF cells in the retina, dLGN, and area V1 of different species (Chichilnisky and Kalmar, 2002; Kremkow et al., 2014). Consistent with the differences in contrast sensitivity and spatial resolution, a loss of ON pathway function in humans is associated with a loss of contrast sensitivity that leaves visual acuity relatively well preserved (Cammack et al., 2016; Dryja et al., 2005). In all mammals, the ON pathway is also slower (i.e., responds with a longer delay to a stimulus) than the OFF pathway at its very first synapse between the photoreceptor and the bipolar cell. The transmitter released by the depolarization of a photoreceptor to a dark stimulus depolarizes OFF bipolar cells via fast ionotropic receptors while hyperpolarizing ON cells via slow metabotropic receptors (Kolb et al., 1995–; Rodieck, 1998). These differences in response timing are maintained along the thalamocortical pathway. As a consequence, in cats, OFF thalamocortical pathways respond faster to stimuli and follow higher temporal fluctuations in luminance contrast than ON pathways (Jin, Wang, Lashgari, et al., 2011; Komban et al., 2014; Rekauzke et al., 2016). Similarly, OFF neurons in the lobula plate of flies respond to faster stimuli than ON neurons (Leonhardt et al., 2016). Humans are also more accurate at discriminating slowly moving stimuli when they are light and fast-moving stimuli when they are dark (Komban et al., 2011; Luo-Li et al., 2018). Moreover, the human visual cortex responds to dark stimuli with a shorter latency than to light stimuli (Norcia et al., 2020).

Parallel Transient and Sustained Pathways

Most visual stimuli with ethological relevance are not static but are continuously changing position in the visual environment. When a fly is hovering in front of a frog, it is important for the frog brain to signal its spatial location with a sustained response that can guide a tongue launch before the fly leaves that location. Conversely, when a rapid change in the environment precedes a threat, it is important to signal its transient location with a transient response (Figure 1D). In mammals, a prolonged visual stimulus generates a transient response in some dLGN neurons (i.e., drives action potentials at the stimulus onset) and a sustained response in other dLGN neurons (i.e., drives action potentials for as long as the stimulus is present), a property that, like ON and OFF responses, is inherited from the retina. In macaques, cats, tree shrews, and many other mammals, transient and sustained neurons are segregated in different layers of the dLGN and V1 (Figures 4 and 5) (Cleland et al., 1971; Conway and Schiller, 1983; Schiller and Malpeli, 1978; Stoelzel et al., 2008; Van Hooser et al., 2003). Parallel transient and sustained pathways are also well preserved across the entire animal kingdom and have been described in birds, fish, reptiles, amphibians, and invertebrates (Cleland et al., 1971; Emran et al., 2007; Granda and Fulbrook, 1989; Honegger, 1978; Maturana et al., 1960; Miles, 1972; Schiller and Malpeli, 1978; Stoelzel et al., 2008; Van Hooser et al., 2003).

As mentioned earlier, each dLGN neuron signals a specific combination of response properties that represent the intersection among several independent pathways (e.g., a light stimulus seen by the contralateral eye for a sustained period of time). However, not all possible pathway combinations exist. In macaques, for example, neurons in one of the three main layers of the primate's dLGN, the parvocellular layers, respond in a sustained manner and can signal both luminance and color contrast (i.e., color difference between receptive field center and surround). However, neurons in one of the other main dLGN layers, the magnocellular layer, respond in a transient manner and only signal luminance contrast (Schiller and Malpeli, 1978; Wiesel and Hubel, 1966). Parvocellular dLGN neurons have higher spatial resolution, lower contrast sensitivity, and lower temporal resolution than magnocellular dLGN neurons (Livingstone and Hubel, 1988) and send their axons to a different sublamina of layer 4C in area V1 (the main recipient of thalamic input in macaques). The parvocellular dLGN neurons project at the bottom of layer 4C (4Cβ) and the magnocellular at the top (4Cα)(Blasdel and Lund, 1983).

Another example of pathway variations across species are the pathways showing "linear" (X) and "non-linear" (Y) spatial summation that were first described in the cat (Enroth-Cugell and Robson, 1966). In cats, most sustained ON and OFF dLGN neurons respond to dark–light spatial patterns in a so-called linear manner; they respond as if they were linearly summing the negative and positive portions of the stimulus (negative contrast: darks; positive contrast: lights). For example, an ideal ON-center dLGN neuron increases its firing rate when a light spot is presented at its receptive field center, it decreases the firing rate when the spot is dark, and it does not change its firing rate when half the spot is light and the other is dark (Figure 1E). Conversely, most transient ON and OFF dLGN neurons respond to dark–light spatial patterns in a non-linear manner; they respond as if they were weighting the light and dark portions of the stimulus differently. As a consequence of the differences in summation, an OFF linear neuron responds strongly to a dark stimulus that fully covers the receptive field center but does not respond at all to a stimulus pattern that is half-light and half-dark. Conversely, an OFF non-linear neuron responds strongly to a dark stimulus fully covering the receptive field center but also responds to many different light–dark stimulus patterns. Thus, non-linear dLGN neurons can reliably signal the appearance and disappearance of any stimulus pattern falling within the receptive field centers, even if the average pattern luminance across space and time is zero. Unlike transient and sustained pathways, pathways showing linear and non-linear spatial summation are not segregated in the dLGN layers of many species and can be very variable in number. Non-linear dLGN neurons are rare in macaques (Shapley et al., 1981) and squirrels (Van Hooser et al., 2003) but very abundant in cats (Friedlander et al., 1979; So and Shapley, 1979) and rabbits (Cano et al., 2006). Because these neurons signal the onset of multiple light–dark stimulus patterns, they may help to detect rapid stimulus changes when hunting or escaping from predators, which could explain their abundance in carnivores and lagomorphs.

Parallel Tecto-Geniculate Pathways

Ascending visual inputs reach the thalamus directly through the retina or indirectly through the superior colliculus (also called *tectum*). Whereas the superior colliculus projects mostly to the pulvinar nucleus of the thalamus, it also sends afferents to the dLGN, forming a tecto-geniculate pathway. These two thalamic nuclei, the dLGN and the pulvinar, thus represent the gateway for visual signals ascending from the superior colliculus to enter the cortex and together are the two thalamic nodes of the tecto-thalamocortical pathways. The tecto-geniculate-cortical pathway is well preserved across mammals (Harting et al., 1991) and can be seen as a small branch of the tecto-thalamocortical pathway present in many vertebrates. Tecto-thalamic circuits dominate vision in birds (Bischof and Watanabe, 1997), a species that navigates the environment at high speeds, and are very rudimentary in snakes (Ulinski, 1977), a species that navigates at very slow speed. Therefore, an interesting possibility is that the tecto-thalamocortical pathways of mammals play a role in processing vision while navigating at high speeds in the environment.

In mammals, dLGN neurons that receive input from the superior colliculus are part of a pathway that segregates in specific layers of the dLGN called *koniocellular* in primates, *C layers* in carnivores, and *dLGN shell* in mice (Figure 4). These layers also receive abundant afferents directly from the retina. Therefore, some of these neurons may integrate two input types, retinal and tectal. In fact, in the mouse, it has been shown that individual neurons in the shell of the dLGN can receive both strong retinal and tectal input (Bickford et al., 2015). The population of neurons in the koniocellular layers of primates is very heterogeneous. Many of them generate weak, variable responses with long latency to visual stimuli (Hendry and Reid, 2000). However, at least in marmosets, some koniocellular cells have response properties similar to those of tectal neurons. They respond strongly and transiently to both light and dark stimuli, have high contrast sensitivity, and show nonlinear spatial summation as Y dLGN cells in cats (Eiber et al., 2018). Unlike the koniocellular pathway of primates, most cells in the shell of the mouse dLGN are direction selective, a property that they directly inherit from the retina. The dLGN layers that receive tectal input project to the superficial layers of area V1 in macaques, cats, tree shrews, and mice (Figure 5) (Bickford et al., 2015; Boyd and Matsubara, 1996; Diamond et al., 1991; Hendry and Yoshioka, 1994; Usrey et al., 1992). They also project to other cortical areas, such as area 19 in cats and area MT in macaques (Kawano, 1998; Sincich et al., 2004). Because the superior colliculus plays an important role in orienting the eyes and body while navigating in the environment, tecto-geniculo-cortical pathways may be important to the processing of vision during self-motion. The fact that the tecto-geniculo-cortical pathway also sends visual information to cortical areas other than V1 makes it a potential anatomical substrate for the ability of cortically blind humans and nonhuman primates to respond to visual stimuli that they do not consciously perceive, a phenomenon referred to as *blindsight* (Stoerig and Cowey, 1997). Indeed, primate models of blindsight, in which V1 or part thereof has been ablated, indicate that the residual ability to respond to visual stimuli depends on the superior colliculus (Mohler and Wurtz, 1977) and the dLGN (Schmid et al., 2010), the two subcortical nodes of the tecto-geniculate pathway. Thus, visually guided behavior in subjects with V1 lesions may rely, at least in part, on the visual pathway linking the superior colliculus to the dLGN and the dLGN to extrastriate areas (Cowey, 2010).

Combining Pathways

"*It would be astonishing if such a structure [the cerebral cortex] did not profoundly modify the response patterns of fibers coming into it.*" With this sentence, Hubel and Wiesel (Hubel and Wiesel, 1962, p. 106) introduced the idea that neurons in the visual cortex transform the activity pattern they receive from the thalamus in response to a visual input rather than simply reproducing it. They proposed that visual cortical neurons integrate thalamic afferent inputs, thereby selectively responding to their combined activity. By responding to a diverse combination of thalamic inputs, some neurons in V1 extract specific features of the visual scene that are not encoded by their individual thalamic afferents (Priebe and Ferster, 2005, 2008; Stanley et al., 2012). Other V1 neurons, however, maintain roughly the same response properties of dLGN afferents, thus preserving the independence of parallel pathways, the "raw" data, even in the cortex. For example, while V1 neurons at the transition zone between ocular dominance columns merge signals from the two eyes, neurons at the center of the column preferentially respond to one or the other eye, thereby maintaining the separation of ocular pathways. Similarly, the signals from individual photoreceptors in the fovea can be transmitted through private lines, all the way to cortical neurons with very small receptive fields. In this section, we describe how neurons in V1 combine thalamic inputs across space, eyes, light–dark polarity, and time to extract very specific features of the visual scene.

Combining Pathways in Visual Space

A striking feature of neurons in V1 is their ability to preferentially respond to dark–light borders of a specific orientation (i.e., vertical, horizontal or anything in between), a property that is referred to as *orientation tuning*. Given that most dLGN neurons have approximately circular receptive fields and respond to any orientation of a dark–light edge, orientation tuning in cortical neurons is unlikely to be inherited from the dLGN. So, how do cortical neurons obtain orientation tuning? Hubel and Wiesel (1962) proposed a model in which neighboring dLGN neurons of a given polarity (either ON or OFF) with receptive fields aligned in visual space converge onto a cortical neuron, a model supported by functional studies in ferrets and cats (Alonso et al., 2001; Chapman et al., 1991; Reid and Alonso, 1995; Sedigh-Sarvestani et al., 2017). By responding to the combination of these dLGN inputs, the cortical neuron becomes tuned to the orientation of an edge, the preferred orientation being the main axis of the aligned dLGN receptive fields (Figure 6).

A consequence of the convergence from aligned dLGN neurons onto a cortical neuron is a transformation in the receptive field structure. In the cat, for example, the receptive fields of layer 4 neurons have ON and OFF subregions that are elongated and parallel instead of circular and concentric as in the dLGN. This type of cortical receptive field was named *simple* by Hubel and Wiesel (Hubel and Wiesel, 1962) because it can be explained as a simple linear sum of dLGN circular receptive fields (Figure 6). The optimal stimulus to drive a simple cell (i.e., a cell with a simple receptive field) is not a light spot on a dark background or a dark spot on a light background, as is the case for thalamic neurons. Instead, simple cells respond best to light–dark borders or bars with an orientation and width that properly overlap with the ON and OFF subregions of their receptive field. Thus, V1 neurons with simple receptive fields respond to bars of a specific orientation and width that properly match the alternation of the receptive field ON and OFF subregions.

Combining thalamic afferents in visual space also causes an enlargement of the cortical receptive field relative to previous

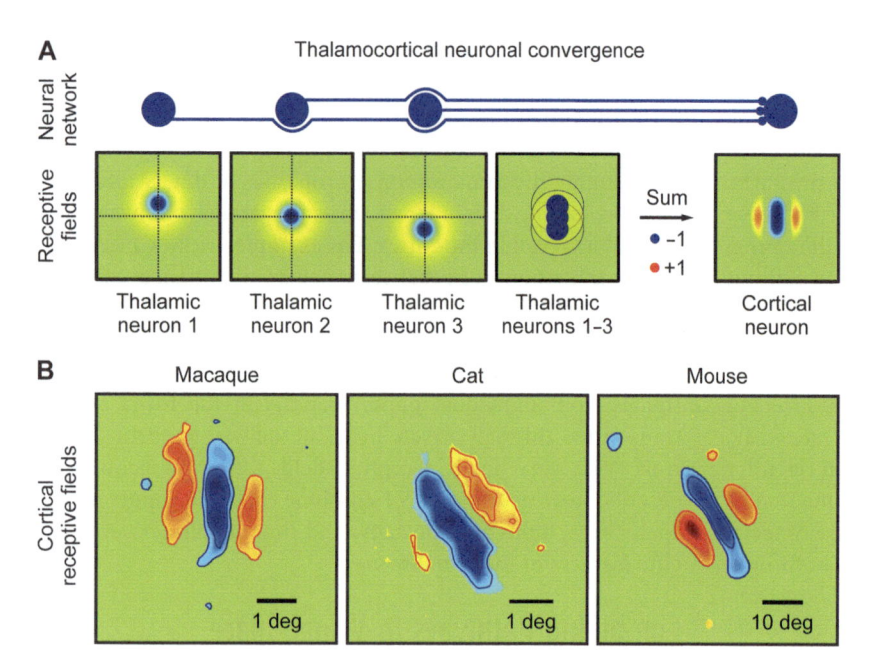

Figure 6 Thalamocortical convergence in visual space.

A. Connections (*top*) and receptive fields (*bottom*) from three OFF dLGN neurons (1, 2, and 3 on the left) targeting the same cortical neuron (*right*). The receptive fields are modeled as the difference of Gaussians (OFF center in blue, ON surround in red) normalized to a maximum value of 1 and minimum value of −1. The surround is weaker than the center. The dLGN receptive fields are shown in separate panels (*left*) and superimposed on the same panel (*right*). The cortical receptive field is calculated from a simple sum of the three dLGN receptive fields that pass a threshold. The sum of three OFF dLGN neurons (OFF-center, ON-surround) with receptive fields displaced along the vertical dimension of visual space generates an OFF-center cortical neuron (OFF center, ON flanks) that will be activated optimally with dark vertical stimuli (e.g., a black vertical line on a white background).

B. Examples of OFF-center cortical neurons from a macaque (*left*), a cat (*middle*), and a mouse (*right*). Iso-response lines mark 1/3 and 2/3 of maximum response. Data for mouse adapted from Niell and Stryker (2008) with permission from Cris Niell. Data for cat from Jin et al. (2008) and for macaque from Jansen et al. (2019).

stages of the visual pathway. In V1, this enlargement is, however, limited by the fact that most thalamic inputs converging at any given point in the cortex have receptive fields separated by a distance of not more than two receptive field centers (Jin, Wang, Swadlow, et al., 2011). Interestingly, when properly scaled by differences in retinal sampling, the size of V1 receptive fields is similar in macaques, cats, and mice (Figure 6). Therefore, limiting the size of cortical receptive fields helps preserve the spatial resolution of the cortical map and may also help to maximize visual acuity.

Combining Pathways from the Two Eyes

Whereas lagomorphs and rodents have vision covering nearly a 360-degree panoramic view, animals with frontal eyes (e.g., primates and carnivores) cannot see behind their heads. What advantage do frontal eyes provide that makes up for the loss of half of the visual field? Frontal eyes increase the fraction of the visual field that is binocular, suggesting that seeing the same scene with both eyes provides some benefit. Indeed, human V1 devotes more than 90% of its area to the binocular field (Figure 3), despite the fact that just half of the visual field is seen by both eyes.

How does the merger of pathways originating from the two eyes contribute to vision? An important consequence of this merger is visual depth perception. Stimuli at different visual depths from the point of fixation (e.g., farther or closer) are projected at slightly different retinal positions in each eye, a phenomenon known as *retinal disparity* (Figure 7). Thalamic inputs from the two eyes signaling slightly different receptive field positions converge on a V1 neuron, endowing the neuron with the ability to preferentially respond to stimuli at specific visual depths. Therefore, binocular neurons tuned to different retinal disparities provide a neuronal mechanism for stereopsis, the perception of visual depth through the merger of images taken from two slightly different positions (e.g., two horizontally separated eyes or cameras). Stereo images have been used by artists since first discovered by Charles Wheatstone in 1838 (Wheatstone, 1838) and are a common type of entertainment in movie theaters with IMAX 3D technology. Lack of stereovision in humans is not uncommon and is a symptom of 2–5% of humans with amblyopia (Holmes and Clarke, 2006). However, this visual deficit is not necessarily incapacitating because humans can use many other monocular cues to estimate visual depth. In fact, many humans discover that they cannot use stereovision late in life when sitting in front of a microscope or going to an IMAX theater.

The combination of ocular pathways provides other important advantages in addition to stereopsis. Binocular summation, for example, improves visual acuity and the signal-to-noise ratio in the perceived image. Humans looking at the world with both eyes have higher visual acuity than when looking with one eye only, and this difference increases as the contrast and signal-to-noise ratio of the stimulus are reduced (Banton and Levi, 1991). This binocular improvement in visual acuity has an interesting correlation with the architecture of V1. Binocular cortical neurons at the border of ocular dominance columns not only are tuned to retinal disparities (Kara and Boyd, 2009) but also have higher spatial resolution than monocular neurons at the center of the columns (Nauhaus et al., 2016).

Binocular neurons are also present in animals with lateral eyes. The lateral location of the eyes, however, reduces the size of the binocular visual field and compromises the spatial sampling of the image. This is because in animals with lateral eyes, the binocular field is projected onto the peripheral retina, which has a lower density of retinal ganglion cells than the central retina, even in the mouse (Drager and Olsen, 1981). The lateral location of the eyes also creates additional challenges in binocular processing (Figure 8). In animals with frontal eyes, stimuli moving away from the point fixation drift toward more peripheral retinal regions in both eyes.

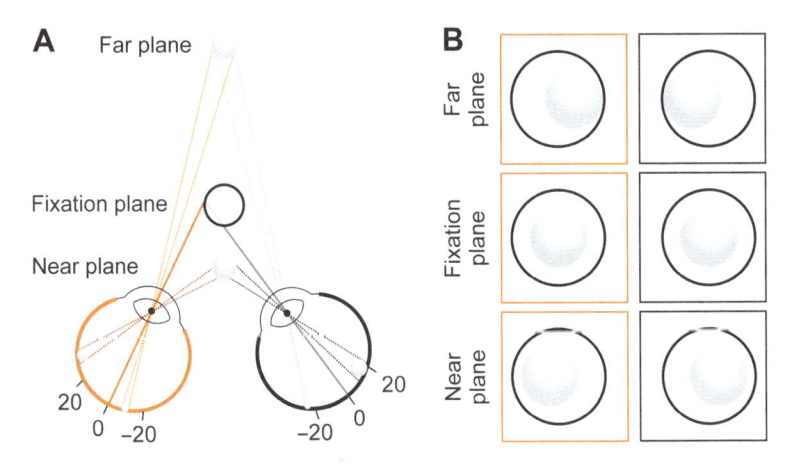

Figure 7 Combining ocular pathways: stereopsis.

A. The projection of a ball located at a closer (near plane) or farther (far plane) distance than the point of fixation (fixation plane) falls on different retinal locations (retinal disparities) in the left (*orange*) and right (*black*) eyes. In the near plane, the retinal location is at >20 degrees in the left eye and <20 degrees in the right eye. In the far plane, it is between 0 and −20 degrees in the left eye but at <−20 degrees in the right eye.

B. Images illustrating the retinal disparities. The images can be free-fused to perceive depth (i.e., crossing the eyes to fuse the left and right image). For simplicity, all the balls have the same size.

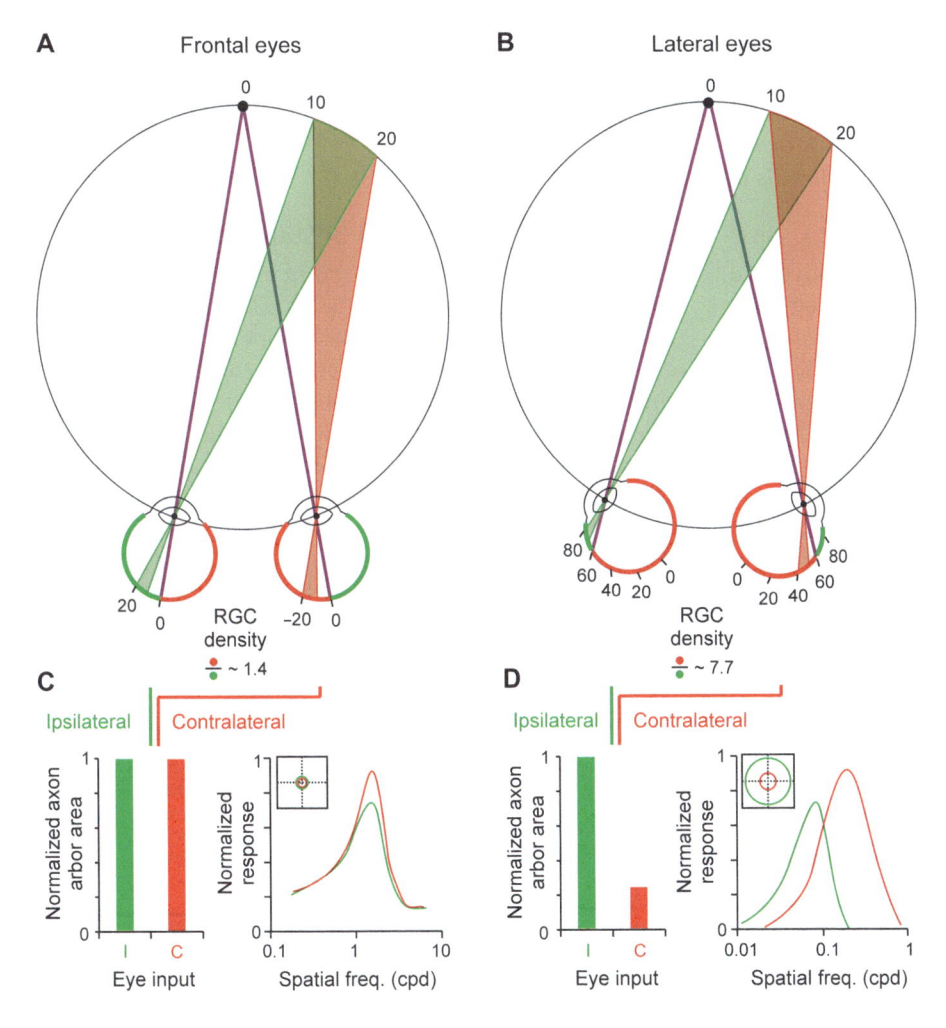

Figure 8 Thalamocortical convergence in binocular vision.

A. In animals with frontal eyes, the central point that divides the visual field into two equal halves falls at the center of the retina in both eyes. Stimuli moving away from this point fall at increasingly more peripheral regions in both retinas (retina projecting to ipsilateral cortex in green and to contralateral cortex in red). Because the cell density can be slightly higher in nasal than temporal retinas, the binocular ratio of cell density can also be slightly larger than 1.

B. In animals with lateral eyes, the central point falls in the peripheral retinas. Stimuli moving away from this point fall on more central retinal regions in one eye but more peripheral regions in the other. Because cell density is higher in the central retina, the stimuli fall in retinal areas with different cell density (~7.7 ratio assuming an animal with lateral eyes and human retinas).

C. In animals with frontal eyes, spatial resolution is binocularly matched. Therefore, the size of the dLGN axonal arbors and spatial frequency resolution of binocular cortical neurons are roughly matched across eyes.

D. In animals with lateral eyes, there is a mismatch in both dLGN axon arbor size and the spatial frequency resolution of binocular neurons across eyes.

Hence, the spatial resolution falls off similarly and remains roughly binocularly matched. The situation is different in animals with lateral eyes. As the stimulus moves away from the point of fixation, it drifts toward the retinal center of one eye but the retinal periphery of the other eye. Because the retinal periphery has lower cell density than the central retina, this creates a mismatch in the spatial resolution of the thalamocortical signals from the two eyes to the binocular cortex.

The binocular differences in retinal sampling should make the thalamic axonal arbors become larger (i.e., to cover a larger region of the retinotopic map) and the cortical spatial resolution lower for the ipsilateral than the contralateral eye. Consistent with this prediction, the thalamic axonal arbors from the ipsilateral eye are much larger than those from the contralateral eye in tree shrews (Raczkowski and Fitzpatrick, 1990). Moreover, the spatial resolution of binocular cortical neurons is lower for the ipsilateral than the contralateral eye in mice (Salinas et al., 2017). The differences in spatial resolution between contralateral and ipsilateral thalamic inputs compromise the stereo visual acuity of animals with lateral eyes. However, these animals may still be able to use ocular dominance convergence to signal coarse stereopsis (Samonds et al., 2019) and maximize the signal-to-noise ratio of the visual input.

Combining ON and OFF Pathways

The alternating and parallel ON and OFF receptive field structure of simple cells can be explained, as described earlier, by the combination of dLGN inputs of a given polarity with spatially aligned receptive fields. A complementary mechanism to obtain a similar receptive field structure is to combine spatially offset ON and OFF dLGN inputs. These two mechanisms are not mutually exclusive. It is likely that the receptive field structure of simple cells results from the combination of both the aligned receptive field of a given polarity along one spatial axis and the spatially offset ON and OFF receptive field along the orthogonal axis. This merger of ON and OFF dLGN receptive fields could help improve the sensitivity of simple cells to edges of luminance (Figure 9).

Evidence for the combination of ON and OFF dLGN afferents in V1 is supported by the mapping of dLGN receptive field afferents converging onto a column of cortical neurons that prefer a specific orientation. Indeed, the spatial organization and the polarity of the receptive field of these thalamic afferents predict the orientation preference of neurons in that cortical column (Jin, Wang, Swadlow, et al., 2011). But do individual neurons in a column combine thalamic inputs with distinct polarities to obtain their orientation tuning properties? Given that layer 4 simple cells receive the majority of synaptic inputs from other cortical neurons rather than from thalamic afferents, their receptive field structure could actually be entirely set by cortical rather than thalamic inputs. Several lines of evidence indicate that, at least in cats and rodents, this is not the case. First, even if one experimentally silences all activity in the visual cortex, such that layer 4 neurons are excited only by their thalamic afferents, the receptive field structure of the combined excitation that they receive from their thalamic afferents is still made of adjacent ON and OFF regions (Lien and Scanziani, 2013). Furthermore, the combined excitation of their thalamic afferents shows a clear preference for visual stimuli of a given orientation (Ferster et al., 1996; Lien and Scanziani, 2013). Finally, simultaneous recordings from thalamic neurons and their postsynaptic cortical targets demonstrate that the receptive field structure of cortical simple cells is made by the convergence of thalamic neurons with different polarities and spatially offset receptive fields (Alonso et al., 1996, 2001; Reid and Alonso, 1995; Sedigh-Sarvestani et al., 2017). Thus, by combining thalamic inputs in space with receptive fields that have the same polarity along one axis and different polarity along the orthogonal axis, cortical neurons can selectively respond to features of the visual world, like the orientation of a luminance edge, that are not explicitly encoded in any of their thalamic inputs (Priebe and Ferster, 2005, 2008; Stanley et al., 2012).

Combining Transient and Sustained Pathways

Things that move in the visual world make for salient visual stimuli. Early investigations in the visual cortex revealed that some cortical neurons preferentially respond to visual stimuli moving in a specific direction, a phenomenon called *direction selectivity* (Hubel and Wiesel, 1959, 1962). The mechanism underlying the direction selectivity of cortical neurons has triggered the curiosity of many investigators, and at least part of it relies on the combination of thalamic afferent inputs with distinct temporal response properties (Saul and Humphrey, 1992). The receptive field of a simple cell in the cortex is defined not only by its spatial structure, namely, the exact position of ON and OFF subregions, but also by its temporal structure (Albrecht and Geisler, 1991; DeAngelis et al., 1993;

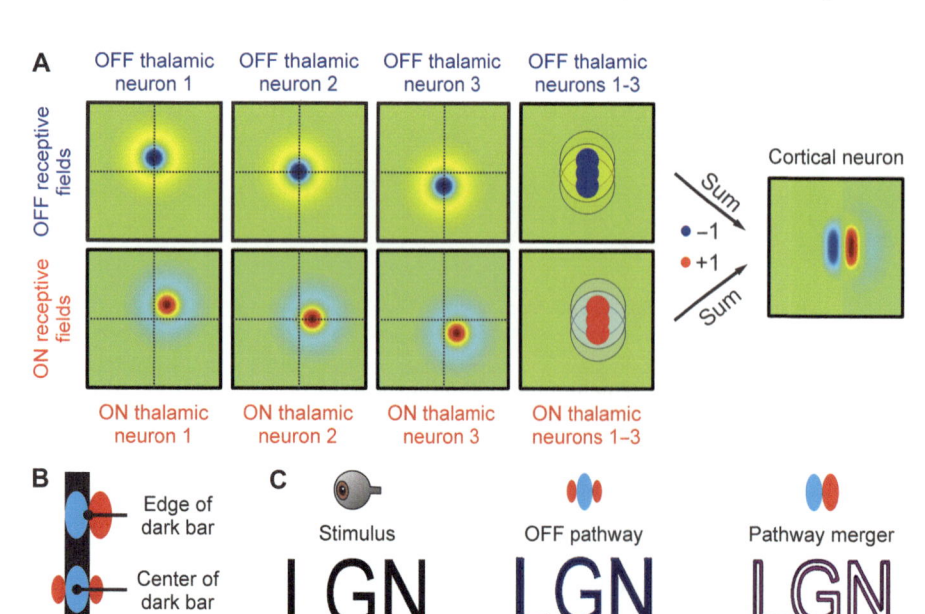

Figure 9 Combining ON and OFF pathways.

A. Left: Center-surround receptive fields from six dLGN neurons, three OFF-center (top, OFF in blue) and three ON-center (bottom, ON in red). Right: The sum of the six dLGN receptive fields generates a cortical receptive field with two parallel subregions of similar strength.

B. Cortical receptive fields made with a single row of OFF dLGN receptive fields are most strongly activated by the center of a dark bar. Those made with two rows (as in panel A) are most strongly activated by the edge of the bar.

C. Example of the acronym LGN (*left*) filtered with cortical receptive fields made of one (*middle*) or two dLGN rows (*right*). The one-row receptive field better signals the central sections of each letter, whereas the two-row field better signals the edges.

Jagadeesh et al., 1993, 1997; Livingstone, 1998; McLean and Palmer, 1989; Movshon et al., 1978; Reid et al., 1987, 1991; Saul and Humphrey, 1992). In other words, a stimulus presented at various positions within the receptive field of a simple cell does not only evoke responses of different magnitudes depending on whether the dark and light parts of the stimulus are properly matched with the ON and OFF subregions of the neuron's receptive field but also evokes responses with different time courses. In directionally selective simple cells, some stimulus positions trigger brisk transient responses, whereas other positions trigger slower, lasting responses. The magnitude and the time course of the response of a neuron relative to the position of a stimulus are referred to as the *spatio-temporal structure* of its receptive field (Jones and Palmer, 1987). At least in simple cells, the spatio-temporal structure of the receptive field represents the basis for their direction preference (Reid et al., 1987). Intuitively, a stimulus that moves across the receptive field of a neuron such as to first trigger a slow, sustained and then a fast, transient response will elicit a larger peak response than if it was moving in the opposite direction. This is because in the preferred direction of the neuron, the fast response will summate with the tail of the previously elicited sustained response. In the opposite, non-preferred direction, the transient response will have mostly subsided by the time the slow one is elicited, leading to a smaller peak response of the neuron. What determines the specific spatio-temporal receptive field structure of simple cells? As described in the previous section, thalamic neurons can differ in the temporal properties of their response to visual stimuli, with some responding in a transient manner while others respond in a sustained manner. The convergence of transient and sustained thalamic neurons whose spatial receptive fields are offset may thus endow cortical neurons with direction selectivity (Figure 10). Indeed, it has been shown that both transient and sustained thalamic neurons can converge on individual cells in layer 4 of cortex and that their spatial relationship predicts the direction preference of the cell they impinge on (Lien and Scanziani, 2018). At least in certain species, like the mouse, some components of direction selectivity can also be directly inherited from direction-selective ganglion cells in the retina, via the dLGN (Cruz-Martin et al., 2014; Hillier et al., 2017). Indeed, perturbations that abolish direction selectivity in the retina leave direction selectivity in layer 2/3 of V1 largely intact, but for responses to stimuli moving in the anterior–posterior direction, that is, the direction of lateral visual flow experienced by the animal as it moves forward (Hillier et al., 2017). Direction-selective neurons in the shell of the mouse dLGN are likely responsible for the transmission of this directional information to layer 2/3 neurons, through the pathway discussed previously (see parallel tecto-geniculate pathways).

Reading Pathway Convergence: The Cortical Targets

dLGN neurons that send their axons to V1 release the transmitter glutamate; that is, they exert an excitatory action on their postsynaptic targets. The axons of these dLGN neurons reach V1 through the optic radiation and enter V1 via the white matter. Once in V1, dLGN axons arborize throughout all layers, yet the highest axonal density occurs in layer 4 (Antonini et al., 1999; Blasdel and Lund, 1983; Humphrey et al., 1985; Raczkowski and Fitzpatrick, 1990), the so-called *main thalamic input layer*. Accordingly, although dLGN axons form synaptic contacts with neurons whose cells bodies reside across all cortical layers, the principal targets of dLGN axons in V1 are neurons located in layer 4. Thus, layer 4 is considered the site in which the first processing steps of visual information by the visual cortex take place. Importantly, dLGN afferents contact both excitatory (glutamatergic) and inhibitory (GABAergic) layer 4 neurons (Bereshpolova et al., 2019; Freund, Martin, Somogyi, et al., 1985; Freund, Martin, and Whitteridge, 1985; Ji et al., 2016; Martin et al., 1983; Sedigh-Sarvestani et al., 2017). That is, already at its onset, visual signaling in the cortex involves both excitation and inhibition. Excitatory neurons receive dLGN input via large presynaptic boutons contacting dendritic spines that are close to the soma (Freund, Martin, Somogyi, et al., 1985). dLGN inputs onto inhibitory neurons occur mainly on dendritic shafts and

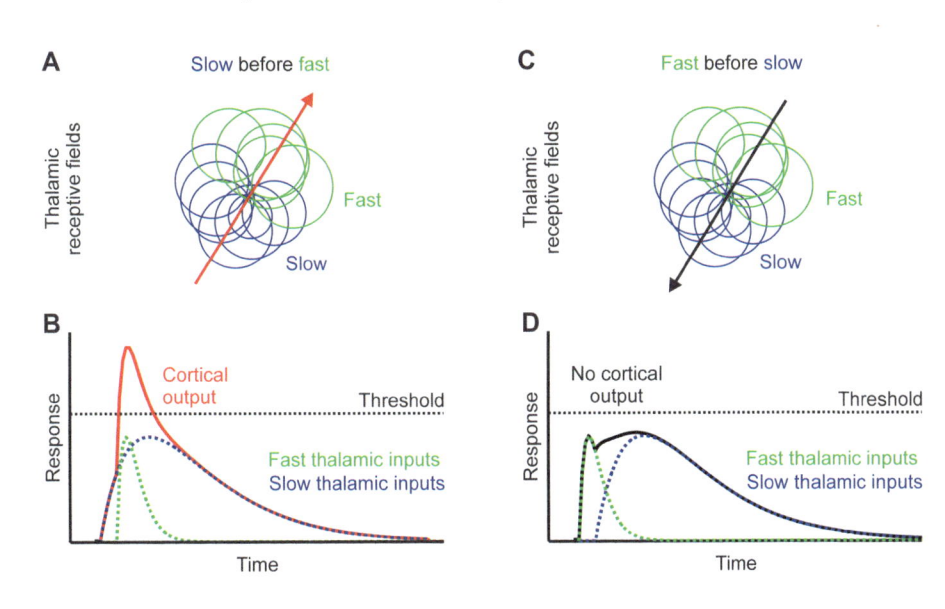

Figure 10 Thalamocortical convergence in response time course.

A. Receptive field centers of thalamic neurons converging on a cortical neuron that is direction selective (i.e., it responds more strongly to a stimulus moving upward than downward). The response time course is slower and more sustained for the thalamic receptive fields in the lower half (*blue*) than those in the upper half of the visual field (*green*).

B. When a stimulus moves upward, the slow thalamic inputs are activated before the fast ones, and their sum (*red*) reaches threshold and drives a cortical output.

C and D. When the stimulus moves downward (panel C), the fast thalamic inputs are activated before the slow ones, and the sum (*black*) does not cross threshold and does not generate a cortical output (panel D). Modified from Alonso (2018) with permission from Macmillan Publishers Ltd., copyright 2018.

somata (Freund, Martin, Somogyi, et al., 1985). In the mouse, it has been established that among the various types of cortical inhibitory neurons, only the neurons expressing parvalbumin (PV) are targeted by dLGN axons (Ji et al., 2016). Similarly, dLGN axons contact so-called "fast-spiking" cells in the cat and rabbit V1 (Bereshpolova et al., 2019; Sedigh-Sarvestani et al., 2017; Zhuang et al., 2013), fast spikes being the electrophysiological signature of PV-expressing inhibitory neurons (McCormick et al., 1985). Thus, dLGN axons target V1 with exquisite laminar and cellular specificity.

The arborization of a single dLGN afferent within V1 covers an area in the order of tens of thousands of square micrometers (Antonini et al., 1999; Blasdel and Lund, 1983; Humphrey et al., 1985; Raczkowski and Fitzpatrick, 1990). Although the order of magnitude of this coverage remains approximately the same from mice to monkeys (Figure 11), the fraction of visual cortical space covered by an individual dLGN arbor varies greatly across those species because V1 is three orders of magnitudes larger in monkeys than in mice. Thus, a dLGN arbor covers a much larger portion of visual space in mice than in monkeys, consistent with the higher visual acuity of the latter (Figure 11). However, irrespective of the species, there are many more dLGN neurons projecting to V1 than what would be strictly necessary for the arbors to tile the area. Thus, at any single point in V1, several dLGN arbors overlap, implying that any V1 neurons receive the convergent input of several dLGN afferents (Peters and Payne, 1993). Although dLGN axons represent the main sensory drive to V1 neurons, even among layer 4 excitatory neurons, their principal target in the cortex, they make up for only about 5–20% of all excitatory synapses (the rest of layer 4 excitatory synapses originating from neurons within layer 4 itself and of neurons from other layers) (Ahmed et al., 1994; Binzegger et al., 2004; Garcia-Marin et al., 2019). The exact number of thalamic afferents that converge onto an individual layer 4 excitatory neurons is, however, still a matter of great speculation, with estimates ranging from 7 to 120, depending on the approach and the species studied (Alonso et al., 2001; Garcia-Marin et al., 2019; Lien and Scanziani, 2018; Peters and Payne, 1993; Peters et al., 1994; Ringach 2021; Tanaka, 1983). Electrophysiological recordings between putative connected pairs of dLGN and V1 neurons in cats suggest that the convergence may be as low as 30 (Alonso et al., 2001); in the monkey, it has been even suggested that as little as 7–8 dLGN afferents converge onto individual cortical neurons (Garcia-Marin et al., 2019). In contrast, in mice, data indicate that during a visual stimulus, approximately 80 active dLGN axons converge onto an individual layer 4 excitatory neuron (Lien and Scanziani, 2018).

How many V1 neurons are contacted by a single dLGN afferent? This number is also still highly debated. In the cat, each dLGN afferent makes about 1,000–4,800 presynaptic boutons in V1 (Humphrey et al., 1985), and each bouton may form more than one synaptic contact (~1.5 on average) (Freund, Martin, and Whitteridge, 1985). Without an accurate estimate of the number of synaptic contacts existing between a dLGN axon and an excitatory neuron in layer 4, it is thus difficult to provide even a rough approximation of the number of neurons targeted by a given dLGN afferent in the cortex, at least through anatomical data. Functional data, on the other hand, may give us a hint at the fraction of targeted neurons rather than the absolute number. Recordings from dLGN–V1 pairs provide an estimate of the probability of a dLGN neuron contacting a layer 4 neuron. The probability depends on the alignment of the receptive fields of the dLGN and V1 neurons

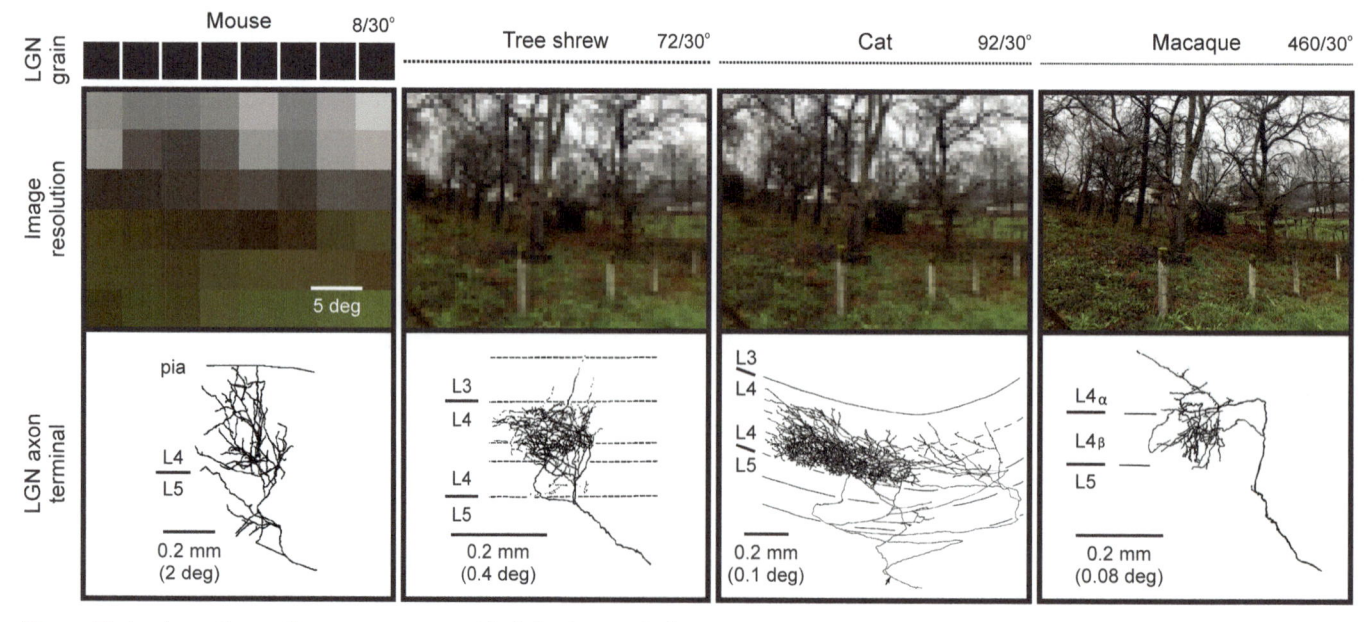

Figure 11 Implementing pathway convergence with thalamic axonal arbors.

Top: Number of dLGN axons (*squares*) needed to tile 30 degrees of visual space in four different species (e.g., 8/30 degrees in mouse).

Middle: An image sampled with a number of pixels equaling the number of dLGN axons estimated at the top for each species.

Bottom: A reconstruction from a single dLGN axonal arbor in each species. Axonal arbors for mouse and macaque reproduced from Antonini et al. (1999) and Blasdel and Lund (1983). Axonal arbors for tree shrew and cat reproduced from Raczkowski and Fitzpatrick (1990) and Humphrey et al. (1985) with permission from John Wiley and Sons, copyright 1990 and 1985.

(Alonso et al., 2001; Sedigh-Sarvestani et al., 2017). If the receptive fields are well matched in spatial position and contrast polarity, the probability of any dLGN afferent connecting with a given layer 4 neuron in the cat V1 can be as high as 40% (Alonso et al., 2001; Sedigh-Sarvestani et al., 2017). This probability, however, falls down quickly as the receptive fields become spatially offset, consistent with the fact that the receptive field location of V1 neurons is largely inherited from their dLGN afferents. At least in some species, the convergence from dLGN afferents is larger onto inhibitory as compared to excitatory neurons (Bereshpolova et al., 2020). The stronger and larger thalamocortical convergence onto inhibitory than excitatory neurons may be a general principle in thalamocortical organization because it appears to be well preserved across species and sensory systems (Alonso and Swadlow, 2005; Bagnall et al., 2011; Bruno and Simons, 2002; Cruikshank et al., 2007; Hull et al., 2009; Schiff and Reyes, 2012; Schmitt et al., 2017; Swadlow and Gusev, 2002). It is interesting that the main sensory input to the cortex ensures the transmission to inhibitory neurons better than to excitatory neurons. This may be the reason why in the cortex, excitation and inhibition are inseparable events.

It takes about 2 or 3 ms (mouse and cat, respectively) for an action potential in a dLGN neuron to propagate along its axon all the way to V1 and release glutamate (Lien and Scanziani, 2018; Sedigh-Sarvestani et al., 2017). There, upon activation of ionotropic glutamate receptors, each dLGN afferent triggers a relatively small "unitary" excitatory postsynaptic potential (uEPSP) on its target neuron. The amplitude of these uEPSPs recorded *in vivo* averages 0.4 mV in cats and 0.8 mV in mice, and individual values may vary from a tenth of a millivolt to a few millivolts (Lien and Scanziani, 2018; Sedigh-Sarvestani et al., 2017). Regardless of the exact amplitude, these small uEPSPs imply that a single dLGN afferent is very unlikely to depolarize the membrane of a V1 neuron sufficiently to reach spike threshold (Figure 12). In other words, V1 neurons rely on the combined activity of several dLGN afferents in order to reach threshold for action-potential generation in response to dLGN input. Furthermore, the combined activity of the dLGN afferents needs to occur within a time window of only a few milliseconds for the uEPSPs to efficiently summate. This time window is likely further narrowed by the occurrence of feedforward inhibition triggered by the dLGN input itself (Gabernet et al., 2005; Zhuang et al., 2013). This simple fact has very important functional consequences: it implies that if the dLGN neurons targeting a given V1 neuron each respond to distinct features of the visual world, a V1 neuron will only respond to a combination of at least some of those features.

Concluding Remarks and Open Questions

All geniculocortical pathways originate in the retina and merge in layer 4 of area V1. As they merge, they form new cortical pathways to signal multiple stimulus combinations that have ethological relevance. Pathways at the earliest stages of cortical processing have small receptive fields that signal basic stimulus attributes, such as spatial location, contrast polarity, orientation, motion, color, and depth. Pathways at later cortical stages have larger receptive fields that allow the signaling of more complex stimulus combinations and the extraction of features like faces or optic flow. As pathways merge, the cortex also retains the ability to signal the raw information from each geniculocortical pathway. For example, in primates, most neurons at later stages of cortical processing beyond V1 respond to the combined stimulation of the two eyes, but they can also respond equally strongly to the stimulation of one eye only, a flexibility of response signaling that probably requires the participation of some form of intracortical normalization (Heeger, 1992; Koch et al., 2016).

There is still much to learn about the anatomy and function of geniculocortical pathways and how they combine in the visual cortex. Over the past decades, we have made tremendous progress, but much more work is needed. Therefore, we finish

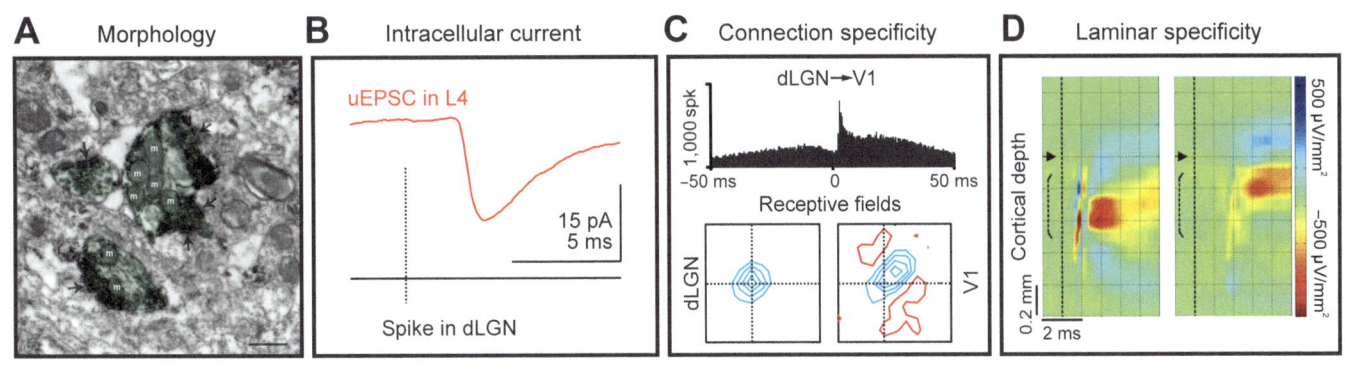

Figure 12 Reading pathway convergence at the cortical targets.

A. dLGN synaptic boutons in macaque area V1 (VGluT2 activity shown in green). Notice the large number of mitochondria (m) and the three different synapses made by the largest synaptic bouton at the center of the image (*black arrows*). Data from Garcia-Marin et al. (2019), reproduced with permission from Dr. Virginia Garcia-Marin.

B. Excitatory postsynaptic current (uEPSC in red) from a V1 neuron triggered by a single dLGN afferent (dotted line marks time of dLGN spike) in the mouse. Data from Lien and Scanziani (2018).

C. Cross-correlogram between the spikes from a V1 neuron and a single dLGN neuron in the cat (*top*) and receptive fields (dLGN OFF-center receptive field in blue; V1 OFF-center receptive field in blue with two ON flanks in red). Data from Alonso et al. (2001).

D. Current source density triggered by two dLGN afferents projecting at the top (afferent on the left) and bottom (afferent on the right) of layer 4 in rabbit V1. Dotted lines marks dLGN spike. Reproduced from Stoelzel et al. (2008).

this review by raising questions, one of the most powerful tools to stimulate and inspire future research. Although there is a long list of questions without answers that could be raised, we focus on a few that we think are fundamental to understanding the function of the geniculocortical pathways.

1. As was stated on Richard Feynman's blackboard at the time of his death, "What I cannot create, I do not understand." There are still many structural and functional properties of the dLGN-to-V1 pathway that we need to understand before our models will be able to accurately re-create thalamocortical communication. How many geniculate afferents converge on to a cortical neuron? How many cortical neurons receive input from the same geniculate afferent? How strong are geniculocortical connections? How many geniculate afferents are needed to drive a cortical neuron? Some of these questions have been addressed repeatedly in the past (which emphasizes their importance). However, we still do not have a reliable quantification that can be used to build realistic models of thalamocortical function.

2. What is the functional contribution of each geniculocortical pathway to visual perception and behavior? Classical studies in the past decades addressed these important questions by measuring the effect of restricted lesions in the dLGN or cortex on behavior (Baker et al., 1991; Merigan et al., 1991; Merigan and Maunsell, 1990; Newsome and Pare, 1988; Pasternak and Maunsell, 1992; Pasternak et al., 1995). We think that it is important to continue asking these questions. The development of modern genetic tools should provide new opportunities to address them with more precision than in the past (Liu et al., 2016; Tang and Higley, 2020). Finding molecular markers that identify specific pathways will also help to understand their roles and function.

3. Among geniculocortical pathways, the tecto-geniculate pathway is probably the least understood. What is the functional role of this mysterious pathway in vision? Does it play a role in blindsight? Why is it so well preserved? Why does it preferentially target the koniocellular dLGN layers of primates?

4. We always think about dLGN pathways reaching layer 4 of V1. However, it is well known that the dLGN also projects to layers above and below layer 4 as well as to higher cortical visual areas. What is the function of these projections?

5. We have discussed thalamocortical interactions as if they were mediated by a "one-way" street, from the dLGN to V1. However, V1 projects back to the dLGN via axons originating in layer 6. This is not a minor pathway. In fact, in terms of axon numbers, it is an order of magnitude larger than the retino-geniculate pathway. What is the role of this feedback? This pathway is discussed in detail in Chapter 10 of this volume.

6. Are there pathways that merge before entering V1? We have treated the dLGN as a simple relay node from the retina to the cortex, within which distinct pathways remain well separated. However, pathway integration occurs already in the dLGN. The possibility and the extent to which the dLGN contributes to the merger of independent pathways originating in the retina needs to be further explored.

7. The study of thalamocortical connectivity has greatly benefited from the use of diverse animal models. As an example, tecto-geniculate connections were thought to be an oddity of some species in earlier studies, but we now know that they are extremely well preserved across mammals. This conclusion arises in great part from a single paper that demonstrated these connections in 19 different species (Harting et al., 1991). Similar examples could be made with the discovery of the W/koniocellular pathways, their projection to the superficial layers of V1 and extra-striate cortex, and the clustering of ON and OFF dLGN afferents in the cortex. We think that it is extremely important to continue studying thalamocortical connections in multiple different species and value the power of diversity when revealing general principles of thalamocortical organization or evolutionary specializations.

References

Adams, D. L., Sincich, L. C., and Horton, J. C. (2007). Complete pattern of ocular dominance columns in human primary visual cortex. J Neurosci **27**, 10391–10403.

Adams, M. M., Hof, P. R., Gattass, R., Webster, M. J., and Ungerleider, L. G. (2000). Visual cortical projections and chemoarchitecture of macaque monkey pulvinar. J Comp Neurol **419**, 377–393.

Ahmed, B., Anderson, J. C., Douglas, R. J., Martin, K. A., and Nelson, J. C. (1994). Polyneuronal innervation of spiny stellate neurons in cat visual cortex. J Comp Neurol **341**, 39–49.

Albrecht, D. G., and Geisler, W. S. (1991). Motion selectivity and the contrast-response function of simple cells in the visual cortex. Vis Neurosci **7**, 531–546.

Alonso, J. M. (2018). Motion processing picks up speed in the brain. Nature **558**, 38–39.

Alonso, J. M., and Swadlow, H. A. (2005). Thalamocortical specificity and the synthesis of sensory cortical receptive fields. J Neurophysiol **94**, 26–32.

Alonso, J. M., Usrey, W. M., and Reid, R. C. (1996). Precisely correlated firing in cells of the lateral geniculate nucleus. Nature **383**, 815–819.

Alonso, J. M., Usrey, W. M., and Reid, R. C. (2001). Rules of connectivity between geniculate cells and simple cells in cat primary visual cortex. J Neurosci **21**, 4002–4015.

Anderson, P. A., Olavarria, J., and Van Sluyters, R. C. (1988). The overall pattern of ocular dominance bands in cat visual cortex. J Neurosci **8**, 2183–2200.

Andrews, T. J., Halpern, S. D., and Purves, D. (1997). Correlated size variations in human visual cortex, lateral geniculate nucleus, and optic tract. J Neurosci **17**, 2859–2868.

Antonini, A., Fagiolini, M., and Stryker, M. P. (1999). Anatomical correlates of functional plasticity in mouse visual cortex. J Neurosci **19**, 4388–4406.

Bagnall, M. W., Hull, C., Bushong, E. A., Ellisman, M. H., and Scanziani, M. (2011). Multiple clusters of release sites formed by individual thalamic afferents onto cortical interneurons ensure reliable transmission. Neuron **71**, 180–194.

Baker, C. L., Jr., Hess, R. F., and Zihl, J. (1991). Residual motion perception in a "motion-blind" patient, assessed with limited-lifetime random dot stimuli. J Neurosci **11**, 454–461.

Banton, T., and Levi, D. M. (1991). Binocular summation in vernier acuity. J Opt Soc Am A **8**, 673–680.

Bereshpolova, Y., Hei, X., Alonso, J. M. & Swadlow, H. A. Three rules govern thalamocortical connectivity of fast-spike inhibitory interneurons in the visual cortex. eLife **9**, doi:10.7554/eLife.60102 (2020), PMC7723404

Bereshpolova, Y., Stoelzel, C. R., Su, C., Alonso, J. M., and Swadlow, H. A. (2019). Activation of a visual cortical column by a directionally selective thalamocortical neuron. Cell Rep **27**, 3733–3740 e3733.

Berman, R. A., and Wurtz, R. H. (2008). Exploring the pulvinar path to visual cortex. Prog Brain Res **171**, 467–473.

Bickford, M. E., Zhou, N., Krahe, T. E., Govindaiah, G., and Guido, W. (2015). Retinal and tectal "driver-like" inputs converge in the shell of the mouse dorsal lateral geniculate nucleus. J Neurosci **35**, 10523–10534.

Bienkowski, M. S., Benavidez, N. L., Wu, K., Gou, L., Becerra, M., and Dong, H. W. (2019). Extrastriate connectivity of the mouse dorsal lateral geniculate thalamic nucleus. J Comp Neurol **527**, 1419–1442.

Binzegger, T., Douglas, R. J., and Martin, K. A. (2004). A quantitative map of the circuit of cat primary visual cortex. J Neurosci **24**, 8441–8453.

Bischof, H. J., and Watanabe, S. (1997). On the structure and function of the tectofugal visual pathway in laterally eyed birds. Eur J Morphol **35**, 246–254.

Blasdel, G. G., and Lund, J. S. (1983). Termination of afferent axons in macaque striate cortex. J Neurosci **3**, 1389–1413.

Boyd, J. D., and Matsubara, J. A. (1996). Laminar and columnar patterns of geniculocortical projections in the cat: relationship to cytochrome oxidase. J Comp Neurol **365**, 659–682.

Bruno, R. M., and Simons, D. J. (2002). Feedforward mechanisms of excitatory and inhibitory cortical receptive fields. J Neurosci **22**, 10966–10975.

Bryant, K. L., Suwyn, C., Reding, K. M., Smiley, J. F., Hackett, T. A., and Preuss, T. M. (2012). Evidence for ape and human specializations in geniculostriate projections from VGLUT2 immunohistochemistry. Brain Behav Evol **80**, 210–221.

Callaway, E. M. (2005). Structure and function of parallel pathways in the primate early visual system. J Physiol **566**, 13–19.

Cammack, J., Whight, J., Cross, V., Rider, A. T., Webster, A. R., and Stockman, A. (2016). Psychophysical measures of visual function and everyday perceptual experience in a case of congenital stationary night blindness. Clin Ophthalmol **10**, 1593–1606.

Cano, M., Bezdudnaya, T., Swadlow, H. A., and Alonso, J. M. (2006). Brain state and contrast sensitivity in the awake visual thalamus. Nat Neurosci **9**, 1240–1242.

Chapman, B., Zahs, K. R., and Stryker, M. P. (1991). Relation of cortical cell orientation selectivity to alignment of receptive fields of the geniculocortical afferents that arborize within a single orientation column in ferret visual cortex. J Neurosci **11**, 1347–1358.

Chatterjee, S., and Callaway, E. M. (2003). Parallel colour-opponent pathways to primary visual cortex. Nature **426**, 668–671.

Chichilnisky, E. J., and Kalmar, R. S. (2002). Functional asymmetries in ON and OFF ganglion cells of primate retina. J Neurosci **22**, 2737–2747.

Cleland, B. G., Dubin, M. W., and Levick, W. R. (1971). Sustained and transient neurones in the cat's retina and lateral geniculate nucleus. J Physiol **217**, 473–496.

Conway, J. L., and Schiller, P. H. (1983). Laminar organization of tree shrew dorsal lateral geniculate nucleus. J Neurophysiol **50**, 1330–1342.

Cowey, A. (2010). Visual system: how does blindsight arise? Curr Biol **20**, R702–704.

Cowey, A., Stoerig, P., and Bannister, M. (1994). Retinal ganglion cells labelled from the pulvinar nucleus in macaque monkeys. Neuroscience **61**, 691–705.

Cruikshank, S. J., Lewis, T. J., and Connors, B. W. (2007). Synaptic basis for intense thalamocortical activation of feedforward inhibitory cells in neocortex. Nat Neurosci **10**, 462–468.

Cruz-Martin, A., El-Danaf, R. N., Osakada, F., Sriram, B., Dhande, O. S., Nguyen, P. L., Callaway, E. M., Ghosh, A., and Huberman, A. D. (2014). A dedicated circuit links direction-selective retinal ganglion cells to the primary visual cortex. Nature **507**, 358–361.

Curcio, C. A., and Allen, K. A. (1990). Topography of ganglion cells in human retina. J Comp Neurol **300**, 5–25.

Curcio, C. A., Sloan, K. R., Kalina, R. E., and Hendrickson, A. E. (1990). Human photoreceptor topography. J Comp Neurol **292**, 497–523.

Dacey, D. M., and Petersen, M. R. (1992). Dendritic field size and morphology of midget and parasol ganglion cells of the human retina. Proc Natl Acad Sci USA **89**, 9666–9670.

DeAngelis, G. C., Ohzawa, I., and Freeman, R. D. (1993). Spatiotemporal organization of simple-cell receptive fields in the cat's striate cortex. II. Linearity of temporal and spatial summation. J Neurophysiol **69**, 1118–1135.

Diamond, I. T., Conley, M., Fitzpatrick, D., and Raczkowski, D. (1991). Evidence for separate pathways within the tecto-geniculate projection in the tree shrew. Proc Natl Acad Sci USA **88**, 1315–1319.

Drager, U. C., and Olsen, J. F. (1981). Ganglion cell distribution in the retina of the mouse. Invest Ophthalmol Vis Sci **20**, 285–293.

Dryja, T. P., McGee, T. L., Berson, E. L., Fishman, G. A., Sandberg, M. A., Alexander, K. R., Derlacki, D. J., and Rajagopalan, A. S. (2005). Night blindness and abnormal cone electroretinogram ON responses in patients with mutations in the GRM6 gene encoding mGluR6. Proc Natl Acad Sci USA **102**, 4884–4889.

Eiber, C. D., Rahman, A. S., Pietersen, A. N. J., Zeater, N., Dreher, B., Solomon, S. G., and Martin, P. R. (2018). Receptive field properties of koniocellular on/off neurons in the lateral geniculate nucleus of marmoset monkeys. J Neurosci **38**, 10384–10398.

Emran, F., Rihel, J., Adolph, A. R., Wong, K. Y., Kraves, S., and Dowling, J. E. (2007). OFF ganglion cells cannot drive the optokinetic reflex in zebrafish. Proc Natl Acad Sci USA **104**, 19126–19131.

Enroth-Cugell, C., and Robson, J. G. (1966). The contrast sensitivity of retinal ganglion cells of the cat. J Physiol **187**, 517–552.

Ferster, D., Chung, S., and Wheat, H. (1996). Orientation selectivity of thalamic input to simple cells of cat visual cortex. Nature **380**, 249–252.

Freund, T. F., Martin, K. A., Somogyi, P., and Whitteridge, D. (1985). Innervation of cat visual areas 17 and 18 by physiologically identified X- and Y- type thalamic afferents.

II. Identification of postsynaptic targets by GABA immunocytochemistry and Golgi impregnation. J Comp Neurol 242, 275–291.

Freund, T. F., Martin, K. A., and Whitteridge, D. (1985). Innervation of cat visual areas 17 and 18 by physiologically identified X- and Y- type thalamic afferents. I. Arborization patterns and quantitative distribution of postsynaptic elements. J Comp Neurol 242, 263–274.

Friedlander, M. J., Lin, C. S., and Sherman, S. M. (1979). Structure of physiologically identified X and Y cells in the cat's lateral geniculate nucleus. Science 204, 1114–1117.

Gabernet, L., Jadhav, S. P., Feldman, D. E., Carandini, M., and Scanziani, M. (2005). Somatosensory integration controlled by dynamic thalamocortical feed-forward inhibition. Neuron 48, 315–327.

Garcia-Marin, V., Kelly, J. G., and Hawken, M. J. (2019). Major feedforward thalamic input into layer 4C of primary visual cortex in primate. Cereb Cortex 29, 134–149.

Gennari, F. (1782). De peculiari structura cerebri nonnulisque ejus morbis. (Parma, Regio Typographeo).

Granda, A. M., and Fulbrook, J. E. (1989). Classification of turtle retinal ganglion cells. J Neurophysiol 62, 723–737.

Harting, J. K., Huerta, M. F., Hashikawa, T., and van Lieshout, D. P. (1991). Projection of the mammalian superior colliculus upon the dorsal lateral geniculate nucleus: organization of tectogeniculate pathways in nineteen species. J Comp Neurol 304, 275–306.

Hartline, H. K. (1938). The response of single optic nerve fibers of the vertebrate eye to illumination of the retina. Am J Physiol 121, 400–415.

Heeger, D. J. (1992). Normalization of cell responses in cat striate cortex. Vis Neurosci 9, 181–197.

Hendry, S. H., and Reid, R. C. (2000). The koniocellular pathway in primate vision. Annu Rev Neurosci 23, 127–153.

Hendry, S. H., and Yoshioka, T. (1994). A neurochemically distinct third channel in the macaque dorsal lateral geniculate nucleus. Science 264, 575–577.

Hillier, D., Fiscella, M., Drinnenberg, A., Trenholm, S., Rompani, S. B., Raics, Z., Katona, G., Juettner, J., Hierlemann, A., Rozsa, B., and Roska, B. (2017). Causal evidence for retina-dependent and -independent visual motion computations in mouse cortex. Nat Neurosci 20, 960–968.

Holmes, J. M., and Clarke, M. P. (2006). Amblyopia. Lancet 367, 1343–1351.

Honegger, H. W. (1978). Sustained and transient responding units in the medulla of the cricket Gryllus campestris. J Comp Physiol 125, 259–266.

Hubel, D. H., and Wiesel, T. N. (1959). Receptive fields of single neurones in the cat's striate cortex. J Physiol 148, 574–591.

Hubel, D. H., and Wiesel, T. N. (1962). Receptive fields, binocular interaction and functional architecture in the cat's visual cortex. J Physiol 160, 106–154.

Hull, C., Isaacson, J. S., and Scanziani, M. (2009). Postsynaptic mechanisms govern the differential excitation of cortical neurons by thalamic inputs. J Neurosci 29, 9127–9136.

Humphrey, A. L., Sur, M., Uhlrich, D. J., and Sherman, S. M. (1985). Projection patterns of individual X- and Y-cell axons from the lateral geniculate nucleus to cortical area 17 in the cat. J Comp Neurol 233, 159–189.

Jagadeesh, B., Wheat, H. S., and Ferster, D. (1993). Linearity of summation of synaptic potentials underlying direction selectivity in simple cells of the cat visual cortex. Science 262, 1901–1904.

Jagadeesh, B., Wheat, H. S., Kontsevich, L. L., Tyler, C. W., and Ferster, D. (1997). Direction selectivity of synaptic potentials in simple cells of the cat visual cortex. J Neurophysiol 78, 2772–2789.

Jansen, M., Jin, J., Li, X., Lashgari, R., Kremkow, J., Bereshpolova, Y., Swadlow, H. A., Zaidi, Q., and Alonso, J. M. (2019). Cortical balance between ON and OFF visual responses is modulated by the spatial properties of the visual stimulus. Cereb Cortex 29, 336–355.

Jeffery, G., and Erskine, L. (2005). Variations in the architecture and development of the vertebrate optic chiasm. Prog Retin Eye Res 24, 721–753.

Ji, W., Gamanut, R., Bista, P., D'Souza, R. D., Wang, Q., and Burkhalter, A. (2015). Modularity in the organization of mouse primary visual cortex. Neuron 87, 632–643.

Ji, X. Y., Zingg, B., Mesik, L., Xiao, Z., Zhang, L. I., and Tao, H. W. (2016). Thalamocortical innervation pattern in mouse auditory and visual cortex: laminar and cell-type specificity. Cereb Cortex 26, 2612–2625.

Jin, J., Wang, Y., Lashgari, R., Swadlow, H. A., and Alonso, J. M. (2011). Faster thalamocortical processing for dark than light visual targets. J Neurosci 31, 17471–17479.

Jin, J., Wang, Y., Swadlow, H. A., and Alonso, J. M. (2011). Population receptive fields of ON and OFF thalamic inputs to an orientation column in visual cortex. Nat Neurosci 14, 232–238.

Jin, J. Z., Weng, C., Yeh, C. I., Gordon, J. A., Ruthazer, E. S., Stryker, M. P., Swadlow, H. A., and Alonso, J. M. (2008). On and off domains of geniculate afferents in cat primary visual cortex. Nat Neurosci 11, 88–94.

Joesch, M., Schnell, B., Raghu, S. V., Reiff, D. F., and Borst, A. (2010). ON and OFF pathways in Drosophila motion vision. Nature 468, 300–304.

Jones, J. P., and Palmer, L. A. (1987). The two-dimensional spatial structure of simple receptive fields in cat striate cortex. J Neurophysiol 58, 1187–1211.

Kaas, J. H., Hall, W. C., Killackey, H., and Diamond, I. T. (1972). Visual cortex of the tree shrew (Tupaia glis): architectonic subdivisions and representations of the visual field. Brain Res 42, 491–496.

Kara, P., and Boyd, J. D. (2009). A micro-architecture for binocular disparity and ocular dominance in visual cortex. Nature 458, 627–631.

Kawano, J. (1998). Cortical projections of the parvocellular laminae C of the dorsal lateral geniculate nucleus in the cat: an anterograde wheat germ agglutinin conjugated to horseradish peroxidase study. J Comp Neurol 392, 439–457.

Kerschensteiner, D., and Guido, W. (2017). Organization of the dorsal lateral geniculate nucleus in the mouse. Vis Neurosci 34, E008.

Koch, E., Jin, J., Alonso, J. M., and Zaidi, Q. (2016). Functional implications of orientation maps in primary visual cortex. Nat Commun 7, 13529.

Kolb, H. (1995–). Facts and figures concerning the human retina. In Webvision: the organization of the retina and visual system, H. Kolb, E. Fernandez, and R. Nelson, eds. (Salt Lake City, University of Utah Health Sciences Center). Web. http://webvision.med.utah.edu/book/part-i-foundations/gross-anatomy-of-the-ey/.

Kolb, H., and Dekorver, L. (1991). Midget ganglion cells of the parafovea of the human retina: a study by electron microscopy and serial section reconstructions. J Comp Neurol 303, 617–636.

Kolb, H., Nelson, R., Fernandez, E., and Jones, B., eds. (1995–). Webvision: The organization of the retina and visual system. (Salt Lake City, University of Utah Health Sciences Center). Web. http://webvision.med.utah.edu/.

Komban, S. J., Alonso, J. M., and Zaidi, Q. (2011). Darks are processed faster than lights. J Neurosci **31**, 8654–8658.

Komban, S. J., Kremkow, J., Jin, J., Wang, Y., Lashgari, R., Li, X., Zaidi, Q., and Alonso, J. M. (2014). Neuronal and perceptual differences in the temporal processing of darks and lights. Neuron **82**, 224–234.

Kremkow, J., and Alonso, J. M. (2018). Thalamocortical circuits and functional architecture. Annu Rev Vis Sci **4**, 263–285.

Kremkow, J., Jin, J., Komban, S. J., Wang, Y., Lashgari, R., Li, X., Jansen, M., Zaidi, Q., and Alonso, J. M. (2014). Neuronal nonlinearity explains greater visual spatial resolution for darks than lights. Proc Natl Acad Sci USA **111**, 3170–3175.

Kremkow, J., Jin, J., Wang, Y., and Alonso, J. M. (2016). Principles underlying sensory map topography in primary visual cortex. Nature **533**, 52–57.

Kuffler, S. W. (1953). Discharge patterns and functional organization of mammalian retina. J Neurophysiol **16**, 37–68.

Laing, R. J., Turecek, J., Takahata, T., and Olavarria, J. F. (2015). Identification of eye-specific domains and their relation to callosal connections in primary visual cortex of long evans rats. Cereb Cortex **25**, 3314–3329.

Leonhardt, A., Ammer, G., Meier, M., Serbe, E., Bahl, A., and Borst, A. (2016). Asymmetry of *Drosophila* ON and OFF motion detectors enhances real-world velocity estimation. Nat Neurosci **19**, 706–715.

Lien, A. D., and Scanziani, M. (2013). Tuned thalamic excitation is amplified by visual cortical circuits. Nat Neurosci **16**, 1315–1323.

Lien, A. D., and Scanziani, M. (2018). Cortical direction selectivity emerges at convergence of thalamic synapses. Nature **558**, 80–86.

Liu, B. H., Huberman, A. D., and Scanziani, M. (2016). Cortico-fugal output from visual cortex promotes plasticity of innate motor behaviour. Nature **538**, 383–387.

Livingstone, M., and Hubel, D. (1988). Segregation of form, color, movement, and depth: anatomy, physiology, and perception. Science **240**, 740–749.

Livingstone, M. S. (1998). Mechanisms of direction selectivity in macaque V1. Neuron **20**, 509–526.

Luo-Li, G., Mazade, R., Zaidi, Q., Alonso, J. M., and Freeman, A. W. (2018). Motion changes response balance between ON and OFF visual pathways. Commun Biol **1**, 60.

Malpeli, J. G., and Baker, F. H. (1975). The representation of the visual field in the lateral geniculate nucleus of Macaca mulatta. J Comp Neurol **161**, 569–594.

Martin, K. A., Somogyi, P., and Whitteridge, D. (1983). Physiological and morphological properties of identified basket cells in the cat's visual cortex. Exp Brain Res **50**, 193–200.

Masri, R. A., Grunert, U., and Martin, P. R. (2020). Analysis of parvocellular and magnocellular visual pathways in human retina. J Neurosci **40**, 8132–8148.

Maturana, H. R., Lettvin, J. Y., McCulloch, W. S., and Pitts, W. H. (1960). Anatomy and physiology of vision in the frog (*Rana pipiens*). J Gen Physiol **43**(*6*)*Suppl*, 129–175.

Mazade, R., and Alonso, J. M. (2017). Thalamocortical processing in vision. Vis Neurosci **34**, E007.

Mazade, R., Jin, J., Pons, C., and Alonso, J. M. (2019). Functional specialization of ON and OFF cortical pathways for global-slow and local-fast vision. Cell Rep **27**, 2881–2894 e2885.

McConnell, S. K., and LeVay, S. (1984). Segregation of on- and off-center afferents in mink visual cortex. Proc Natl Acad Sci USA **81**, 1590–1593.

McCormick, D. A., Connors, B. W., Lighthall, J. W., and Prince, D. A. (1985). Comparative electrophysiology of pyramidal and sparsely spiny stellate neurons of the neocortex. J Neurophysiol **54**, 782–806.

McGurk, H., and MacDonald, J. (1976). Hearing lips and seeing voices. Nature **264**, 746–748.

McLean, J., and Palmer, L. A. (1989). Contribution of linear spatiotemporal receptive field structure to velocity selectivity of simple cells in area 17 of cat. Vision Res **29**, 675–679.

Merigan, W. H., Katz, L. M., and Maunsell, J. H. (1991). The effects of parvocellular lateral geniculate lesions on the acuity and contrast sensitivity of macaque monkeys. J Neurosci **11**, 994–1001.

Merigan, W. H., and Maunsell, J. H. (1990). Macaque vision after magnocellular lateral geniculate lesions. Vis Neurosci **5**, 347–352.

Merigan, W. H., and Maunsell, J. H. (1993). How parallel are the primate visual pathways? Annu Rev Neurosci **16**, 369–402.

Miles, F. A. (1972). Centrifugal control of the avian retina. I. Receptive field properties of retinal ganglion cells. Brain Res **48**, 65–92.

Mohler, C. W., and Wurtz, R. H. (1977). Role of striate cortex and superior colliculus in visual guidance of saccadic eye movements in monkeys. J Neurophysiol **40**, 74–94.

Morin, L. P., and Studholme, K. M. (2014). Retinofugal projections in the mouse. J Comp Neurol **522**, 3733–3753.

Movshon, J. A., Thompson, I. D., and Tolhurst, D. J. (1978). Spatial summation in the receptive fields of simple cells in the cat's striate cortex. J Physiol **283**, 53–77.

Murcia-Belmonte, V., and Erskine, L. (2019). Wiring the binocular visual pathways. Int J Mol Sci **20**, 3282.

Nauhaus, I., Nielsen, K. J., and Callaway, E. M. (2016). Efficient receptive field tiling in primate V1. Neuron **91**, 893–904.

Newsome, W. T., and Pare, E. B. (1988). A selective impairment of motion perception following lesions of the middle temporal visual area (MT). J Neurosci **8**, 2201–2211.

Niell, C. M., and Stryker, M. P. (2008). Highly selective receptive fields in mouse visual cortex. J Neurosci **28**, 7520–7536.

Norcia, A. M., Yakovleva, A., Hung, B., and Goldberg, J. L. (2020). Dynamics of contrast decrement and increment responses in human visual cortex. Transl Vis Sci Technol **9**, 6.

Norton, T. T., Rager, G., and Kretz, R. (1985). ON and OFF regions in layer IV of striate cortex. Brain Res **327**, 319–323.

Osterberg, G. (1935). Topography of the layer of rods and cones in the human retina. Acta Ophthalmologica Supplement **6**, 1–103.

Pasternak, T., and Maunsell, J. H. (1992). Spatiotemporal sensitivity following lesions of area 18 in the cat. J Neurosci **12**, 4521–4529.

Pasternak, T., Tompkins, J., and Olson, C. R. (1995). The role of striate cortex in visual function of the cat. J Neurosci **15**, 1940–1950.

Peichl, L. (1989). Alpha and delta ganglion cells in the rat retina. J Comp Neurol **286**, 120–139.

Peters, A., and Payne, B. R. (1993). Numerical relationships between geniculocortical afferents and pyramidal cell modules in cat primary visual cortex. Cereb Cortex **3**, 69–78.

Peters, A., Payne, B. R., and Budd, J. (1994). A numerical analysis of the geniculocortical input to striate cortex in the monkey. Cereb Cortex **4**, 215–229.

Priebe, N. J., and Ferster, D. (2005). Direction selectivity of excitation and inhibition in simple cells of the cat primary visual cortex. Neuron **45**, 133–145.

Priebe, N. J., and Ferster, D. (2008). Inhibition, spike threshold, and stimulus selectivity in primary visual cortex. Neuron **57**, 482–497.

Raczkowski, D., and Fitzpatrick, D. (1990). Terminal arbors of individual, physiologically identified geniculocortical axons in the tree shrew's striate cortex. J Comp Neurol **302**, 500–514.

Rakic, P. (1977). Prenatal development of the visual system in rhesus monkey. Philos Trans R Soc Lond B Biol Sci **278**, 245–260.

Reid, R. C., and Alonso, J. M. (1995). Specificity of monosynaptic connections from thalamus to visual cortex. Nature **378**, 281–284.

Reid, R. C., Soodak, R. E., and Shapley, R. M. (1987). Linear mechanisms of directional selectivity in simple cells of cat striate cortex. Proc Natl Acad Sci USA **84**, 8740–8744.

Reid, R. C., Soodak, R. E., and Shapley, R. M. (1991). Directional selectivity and spatiotemporal structure of receptive fields of simple cells in cat striate cortex. J Neurophysiol **66**, 505–529.

Rekauzke, S., Nortmann, N., Staadt, R., Hock, H. S., Schoner, G., and Jancke, D. (2016). Temporal asymmetry in dark-bright processing initiates propagating activity across primary visual cortex. J Neurosci **36**, 1902–1913.

Rodieck, R. W. (1998). The first steps in seeing (Sunderland, MA, Oxford University Press).

Salinas, K. J., Figueroa Velez, D. X., Zeitoun, J. H., Kim, H., and Gandhi, S. P. (2017). Contralateral bias of high spatial frequency tuning and cardinal direction selectivity in mouse visual cortex. J Neurosci **37**, 10125–10138.

Samonds, J. M., Choi, V., and Priebe, N. J. (2019). Mice discriminate stereoscopic surfaces without fixating in depth. J Neurosci **39**, 8024–8037.

Sarnaik, R., Chen, H., Liu, X., and Cang, J. (2014). Genetic disruption of the On visual pathway affects cortical orientation selectivity and contrast sensitivity in mice. J Neurophysiol **111**, 2276–2286.

Saul, A. B., and Humphrey, A. L. (1992). Evidence of input from lagged cells in the lateral geniculate nucleus to simple cells in cortical area 17 of the cat. J Neurophysiol **68**, 1190–1208.

Schiff, M. L., and Reyes, A. D. (2012). Characterization of thalamocortical responses of regular-spiking and fast-spiking neurons of the mouse auditory cortex in vitro and in silico. J Neurophysiol **107**, 1476–1488.

Schiller, P. H. (1982). Central connections of the retinal ON and OFF pathways. Nature **297**, 580–583.

Schiller, P. H., and Malpeli, J. G. (1978). Functional specificity of lateral geniculate nucleus laminae of the rhesus monkey. J Neurophysiol **41**, 788–797.

Schiller, P. H., Sandell, J. H., and Maunsell, J. H. (1986). Functions of the ON and OFF channels of the visual system. Nature **322**, 824–825.

Schmid, M. C., Mrowka, S. W., Turchi, J., Saunders, R. C., Wilke, M., Peters, A. J., Ye, F. Q., and Leopold, D. A. (2010). Blindsight depends on the lateral geniculate nucleus. Nature **466**, 373–377.

Schmitt, L. I., Wimmer, R. D., Nakajima, M., Happ, M., Mofakham, S., and Halassa, M. M. (2017). Thalamic amplification of cortical connectivity sustains attentional control. Nature **545**, 219–223.

Sedigh-Sarvestani, M., Vigeland, L., Fernandez-Lamo, I., Taylor, M. M., Palmer, L. A., and Contreras, D. (2017). Intracellular, in vivo, dynamics of thalamocortical synapses in visual cortex. J Neurosci **37**, 5250–5262.

Shapley, R., Kaplan, E., and Soodak, R. (1981). Spatial summation and contrast sensitivity of X and Y cells in the lateral geniculate nucleus of the macaque. Nature **292**, 543–545.

Shatz, C. J. (1983). The prenatal development of the cat's retinogeniculate pathway. J Neurosci **3**, 482–499.

Sherk, H., and Horton, J. C. (1984). Receptive field properties in the cat's area 17 in the absence of on-center geniculate input. J Neurosci **4**, 381–393.

Sincich, L. C., Park, K. F., Wohlgemuth, M. J., and Horton, J. C. (2004). Bypassing V1: a direct geniculate input to area MT. Nat Neurosci **7**, 1123–1128.

So, Y. T., and Shapley, R. (1979). Spatial properties of X and Y cells in the lateral geniculate nucleus of the cat and conduction velocities of their inputs. Exp Brain Res **36**, 533–550.

Sretavan, D. W., and Shatz, C. J. (1986). Prenatal development of retinal ganglion cell axons: segregation into eye-specific layers within the cat's lateral geniculate nucleus. J Neurosci **6**, 234–251.

Stanley, G. B., Jin, J., Wang, Y., Desbordes, G., Wang, Q., Black, M. J., and Alonso, J. M. (2012). Visual orientation and directional selectivity through thalamic synchrony. J Neurosci **32**, 9073–9088.

Stoelzel, C. R., Bereshpolova, Y., Gusev, A. G., and Swadlow, H. A. (2008). The impact of an LGNd impulse on the awake visual cortex: synaptic dynamics and the sustained/transient distinction. J Neurosci **28**, 5018–5028.

Stoerig, P., and Cowey, A. (1997). Blindsight in man and monkey. Brain **120** *(Pt 3)*, 535–559.

Swadlow, H. A., and Gusev, A. G. (2002). Receptive-field construction in cortical inhibitory interneurons. Nat Neurosci **5**, 403–404.

Tanaka, K. (1983). Cross-correlation analysis of geniculostriate neuronal relationships in cats. J Neurophysiol **49**, 1303–1318.

Tang, L., and Higley, M. J. (2020). Layer 5 circuits in V1 differentially control visuomotor behavior. Neuron **105**, 346–354 e345.

Ulinski, P. S. (1977). Tectal efferents in the branded water snake, *Natrix sipedon*. J Comp Neurol **173**, 251–274.

Usrey, W. M., Muly, E. C., and Fitzpatrick, D. (1992). Lateral geniculate projections to the superficial layers of visual cortex in the tree shrew. J Comp Neurol **319**, 159–171.

Van Essen, D. C., Donahue, C. J., and Glasser, M. F. (2018). Development and evolution of cerebral and cerebellar cortex. Brain Behav Evol **91**, 158–169.

Van Essen, D. C., Newsome, W. T., and Maunsell, J. H. (1984). The visual field representation in striate cortex of the macaque monkey: asymmetries, anisotropies, and individual variability. Vision Res **24**, 429–448.

Van Hooser, S. D., Heimel, J. A., and Nelson, S. B. (2003). Receptive field properties and laminar organization of lateral geniculate nucleus in the gray squirrel (*Sciurus carolinensis*). J Neurophysiol **90**, 3398–3418.

Warner, C. E., Kwan, W. C., Wright, D., Johnston, L. A., Egan, G. F., and Bourne, J. A. (2015). Preservation of vision by the pulvinar following early-life primary visual cortex lesions. Curr Biol **25**, 424–434.

Wassle, H., Boycott, B. B., and Illing, R. B. (1981). Morphology and mosaic of on- and off-beta cells in the cat retina and some functional considerations. Proc R Soc Lond B Biol Sci **212**, 177–195.

Wheatstone, C. (1838). Contributions to the physiology of vision. Part the first. On some remarkable, and hitherto unobserved, phenomena of binocular vision. Philos Trans R Soc **128**, 371–394.

Wiesel, T. N., and Hubel, D. H. (1966). Spatial and chromatic interactions in the lateral geniculate body of the rhesus monkey. J Neurophysiol **29**, 1115–1156.

Zahs, K. R., and Stryker, M. P. (1988). Segregation of ON and OFF afferents to ferret visual cortex. J Neurophysiol **59**, 1410–1429.

Zhou, N. A., Maire, P. S., Masterson, S. P., and Bickford, M. E. (2017). The mouse pulvinar nucleus: organization of the tectorecipient zones. Vis Neurosci **34**, E011.

Zhuang, J., Stoelzel, C. R., Bereshpolova, Y., Huff, J. M., Hei, X., Alonso, J. M., and Swadlow, H. A. (2013). Layer 4 in primary visual cortex of the awake rabbit: contrasting properties of simple cells and putative feedforward inhibitory interneurons. J Neurosci **33**, 11372–11389.

Chapter 10

Corticothalamic Feedback in Vision

W. Martin Usrey

Introduction

The dorsal thalamus and cerebral cortex are richly interconnected via a reciprocal organization of feedforward and feedback projections. Thalamic relay cells provide the cortex with feedforward information essential for cortical processing, and the cortex, in turn, provides extensive feedback to the thalamus to modulate feedforward processing. A subset of pyramidal neurons in layer 6 of the cortex is the source of corticothalamic feedback projections[1] (Gilbert & Kelly, 1975; Lund et al., 1975; Hendrickson et al., 1978). These layer 6 neurons project not only to the thalamus but also to the overlying cortical layers that receive thalamic input (Lund & Boothe, 1975; Fitzpatrick et al., 1985; Katz, 1987; Usrey & Fitzpatrick, 1996; Briggs et al., 2016). Based on their local and long-distance connections, corticothalamic feedback neurons are in a strategic position to influence the processing and transmission of signals en route from the thalamus to the cortex. Importantly, layer 6 corticothalamic feedback neurons in different cortical areas align with specific thalamic nuclei (reviewed in Jones, 2007; Usrey & Sherman, 2019). For instance, layer 6 neurons in the primary visual cortex send feedback axons to the lateral geniculate nucleus (LGN), a nucleus that receives feedforward input from the retina, whereas layer 6 neurons in the somatosensory cortex send axons to the ventral posterior nucleus, a nucleus that receives feedforward input from the head and body via the medial lemniscus. In a similar fashion, layer 6 neurons in the auditory cortex send feedback axons to the ventral division of the medial geniculate nucleus, a nucleus that receives feedforward auditory signals from the inferior colliculus. With these generalities and specifics noted, this chapter is focused on the structure and function of the corticothalamic feedback pathway from the primary visual cortex to the LGN, a pathway more specifically referred to as the *corticogeniculate* pathway. An emphasis is placed on results from studies examining corticogeniculate projections in cats and monkeys, two prominent model organisms for vision research, with additional results included from other model organisms.

Parallel Pathways from Retina to Cortex

The corticogeniculate feedback pathway is anchored in the parallel pathways of information flow from the retina to the LGN to the visual cortex, otherwise known as the *retinogeniculocortical pathway*. It is therefore important to first review these parallel pathways before considering the organization of corticogeniculate feedback projections.

Individual relay cells in the LGN receive visual input from just one of the distinct classes of retinal ganglion cells and relay these signals to specific laminar targets in the primary visual cortex. In cats and monkeys, these "parallel" pathways are the X, Y, and W pathways and the parvocellular, magnocellular, and koniocellular pathways, respectively (Usrey & Alitto, 2015). Estimates suggest that cats and monkeys shared a common ancestor approximately 80 million years ago. Since that time, their evolutionary paths have led to many species-specific differences. With this history in mind, the similarities between cat geniculate X and Y cells and monkey parvocellular and magnocellular neurons are noteworthy (reviewed in Stone, 1983; Sherman, 1985; Cleland, 1986; Schiller & Logothetis, 1990; Shapley, 1992; Merigan & Maunsell, 1993; Usrey & Alitto, 2015). For instance, cat X cells and monkey parvocellular neurons have smaller cell bodies, smaller receptive fields, slower conducting axons, slower visual responses, and more sustained visual responses than their Y-cell and magnocellular counterparts (Schiller & Malpeli, 1978; So & Shapley, 1979; Friedlander et al., 1981; Headon et al., 1985; Troy & Lennie, 1987; Saul & Humphrey, 1990; Croner & Kaplan, 1995; Maunsell et al., 1999; Usrey et al., 1999, 2000; Levitt et al., 2001; Alitto et al., 2011). The axons of cat geniculate X cells and monkey parvocellular neurons also share similarities in their patterns of synaptic input within cortical layer 4 (layer 4C for monkeys) that are distinct from their parallel counterparts, with the X-cell/parvocellular axons and making synapses beneath the Y-cell/magnocellular axons (Figure 1; Hendrickson et al., 1978; Blasdel & Lund, 1983; Diamond et al., 1985; Freund et al., 1985; Humphrey et al., 1985a, 1985b). In addition to these anatomical and physiological distinctions, molecular markers that are selective for X cells versus Y cells in the cat are also selective for parvocellular versus magnocellular neurons in the monkey (Hendry et al., 1984; Hockfield & Sur, 1990; Iwai et al., 2013). Taken together, the anatomy, physiology, and molecular markers provide compelling evidence for homology between cat geniculate X cells and monkey parvocellular neurons and between cat Y cells and monkey magnocellular neurons.

The members of the third group of geniculate cells, cat W cells and monkey koniocellular neurons, also share distinct properties in common with each other. Most notably, the axons of these cells pass through layer 4 of the cortex without making synapses and,

---

[1] The projections of layer 6 neurons to the thalamus are distinct from the projections of layer 5 neurons. Whereas layer 6 axons provide modulatory feedback input to first-order and higher-order thalamic neurons, layer 5 axons provide driving feedforward input only to higher-order thalamic nuclei. Additional details can be found in Usrey and Sherman (2019).

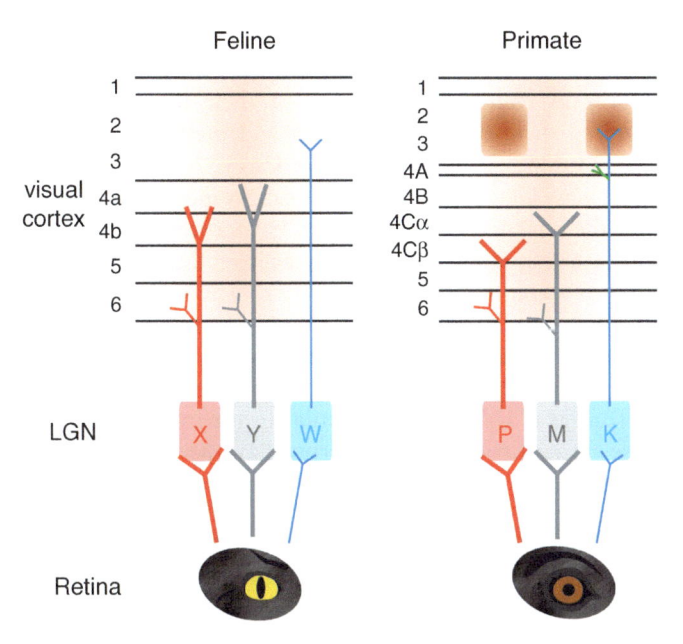

Figure 1 Schematic organization of the retino-geniculo-cortical pathway in the feline and primate.

In all mammals, including these examples, the majority of geniculo-cortical axons terminate in cortical layer 4, a minority of axons terminate in cortical layers 1–3 and 6. In feline, there are three major parallel pathways to the cortex – the X-cell pathway terminates in layer 4b, the Y-cell pathway terminates in layer 4a, and the W-cell pathway terminates in layers 1–3. There are also three parallel pathways in the primate – the parvocellular pathway (P) pathway terminates in layer 4 Cβ, the magnocellular pathway (M) pathway terminates in layer 4 Cα, and the koniocellular pathway (K) terminates in the layer 1–3 blobs. Adapted from Rathbun and Usrey (2009).

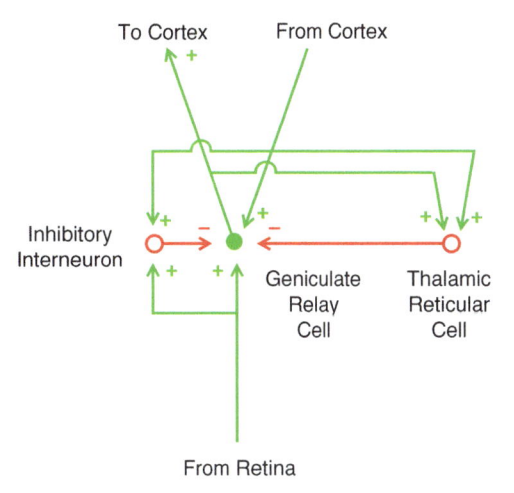

Figure 2 Schematic diagram of the connections involving geniculate relay cells.

Relay cells receive feedforward excitatory input from the retina and feedback excitation from the cortex. Relay cells also receive disynaptic inhibition from the retina and cortex.

instead, make synapses in the more superficial cortical layers (Figure 1; Levanthal, 1979; Fitzpatrick et al., 1983; Lachica & Casagrande, 1992; Usrey et al., 1992; Casagrande et al., 2007). W cells and koniocellular neurons also receive retinal input from distinct classes of ganglion cells (Calkins et al., 2005; Szmajda et al., 2008; Percival et al., 2014), in addition to input from neurons in the superior colliculus (Graham, 1977; Fitzpatrick et al., 1980; Lachica & Casagrande, 1993; Bickford et al., 2015), a source of input that is not shared with X/Y or parvocellular/magnocellular relay cells. Less is known about the physiology of W cells and koniocellular neurons (but see Xu et al., 2001) due, in part, to their limited distribution within the cat and monkey LGN and the likelihood that the category of W cells and koniocellular neurons is an umbrella category, being composed of many cell types. Here, it is hoped that studies from rodents, which can capitalize on molecular methods for cellular identification, will provide important information. Moreover, relay cells in the rodent with projections to the superficial layers of the cortex comprise a larger percentage of geniculate neurons than in the cat or monkey, which should further benefit studies examining these cell types that are less common in other species (reviewed in Huberman & Niell, 2011).

General Properties of Corticogeniculate Feedback

The single greatest source of synaptic input to LGN relay cells comes from corticogeniculate feedback axons (Guillery, 1969; Erisir, Van Horn, Bickford, et al., 1997; Erisir, Van Horn, & Sherman, 1997). In contrast to retinal inputs that can directly evoke action potentials in geniculate neurons (Hubel & Wiesel, 1961; Cleland et al., 1971a, 1971b; Kaplan & Shapley, 1984; Mastronarde, 1987; Usrey et al., 1998, 1999; Sincich et al., 2007; Weyand, 2007; Rathbun, Warland, et al., 2010; Rathbun, Alitto, et al., 2016), corticogeniculate feedback provides modulatory input, affecting how geniculate neurons respond to their retinal input (Sherman & Guillery, 1998). Geniculate relay cells, as well as local inhibitory interneurons, receive monosynaptic excitation from retinal ganglion cells and corticogeniculate axons (Figure 2). Corticogeniculate axons also target inhibitory neurons in the thalamic reticular nucleus, which also receive input from geniculate relay cells and, in turn, provide inhibition to LGN relay neurons (Figure 2). Corticogeniculate feedback therefore has a direct excitatory and disynaptic inhibitory influence on LGN relay neurons, presumably to increase or decrease their responsiveness (i.e., gain) to incoming retinal signals. Importantly, only a subset of the action potentials from a retinal ganglion cell will evoke geniculate action potentials (Wiesel & Hubel, 1961; Cleland et al., 1971a, 1971b; Kaplan & Shapley, 1984; Mastronarde, 1987; Usrey et al., 1998, 1999; Sincich et al., 2007; Weyand, 2007; Rathbun, Warland, et al., 2010; Rathbun, Alitto, et al., 2016). Consequently, corticogeniculate feedback can increase or decrease the successful communication of these action potentials, as well as play a role in determining whether geniculate neurons respond to retinal input with bursts or tonic responses (described later in the chapter).

Compared to retinal axons, corticogeniculate axons have a much larger terminal arborization, approximately two to three times the spread of retinal axons (Murphy & Sillito, 1996). Because of this, individual corticogeniculate axons not only influence the activity of a larger pool of LGN neurons than do individual retinal axons, but they also carry signals that arise from broader regions of visual space. Even though corticogeniculate synapses outnumber retinogeniculate synapses, the EPSPs from corticogeniculate axons are significantly smaller in amplitude than those from retinal axons (reviewed in Sherman & Guillery, 2009). In addition, corticogeniculate synapses are located more distally on relay-cell dendrites than are retinogeniculate synapses. For these reasons, and because the receptive fields of LGN neurons resemble those of retinal ganglion cells with center/surround receptive fields and not cortical cells with elongated and orientation selective receptive fields (Usrey et al., 1999), the corticogeniculate pathway is considered a modulatory pathway rather than a driving pathway (Sherman & Guillery, 1998, 2009).

Parallel Pathways for Corticogeniculate Feedback

In primates, corticogeniculate feedback respects the segregation of feedforward parallel pathways traversing the LGN. In particular, parvocellular LGN neurons receive cortical feedback from V1 pyramidal neurons whose cell bodies are located in the upper half of layer 6, whereas magnocellular neurons receive input from the pyramidal neurons in the lower half of layer 6 (Figure 3; Conley & Raczkowski, 1990, Fitzpatrick et al., 1994; Ichida et al., 2014). These divisions of layer 6 are also distinct based on their input from geniculate axons en route to layer 4, with parvocellular and magnocellular axons giving rise to branches that arborize in the top and bottom of layer 6, respectively (Hendrickson et al., 1978; Blasdel & Lund, 1983), and with respect to their intrinsic projections to the overlying cortical layers (Briggs et al., 2016). Corticogeniculate projections are not only anatomically separated but also physiologically distinct; feedback neurons supplying the parvocellular and magnocellular layers of the LGN have visual responses that share many features in common with those of their target neurons, including their contrast sensitivity and their temporal frequency tuning (Figure 4; Briggs & Usrey, 2009). Moreover, corticogeniculate neurons with visual responses that align with the magnocellular pathway have complex receptive fields (overlapping on and off receptive field subregions) and fast axon-conduction velocities, whereas those with visual responses that align with the parvocellular pathway have simple receptive fields (segregated on and off receptive field subregions) and slower axon-conduction velocities (Briggs & Usrey, 2009). Similar to the monkey, distinct classes of corticogeniculate neurons have been identified in the cat, with one having complex receptive fields and fast-conducting axons and the other having simple receptive fields and slower-conducting axons (Tsumoto & Suda, 1980). Lastly, a third group of corticogeniculate neurons has been identified in the monkey that has properties that align well with the koniocellular neurons in the LGN (Figure 3; Briggs & Usrey, 2009; Ichida et al., 2014). Most notably, these neurons have the slowest-conducting axons and receptive fields that include input from the short-wavelength (blue) cones in the retina (Briggs & Usrey, 2009). Although less is known about corticogeniculate neurons in other species, existing evidence from tree shrews, ferrets, and rabbits suggests that parallel pathways of corticogeniculate feedback may be typical for mammals (Usrey & Fitzpatrick, 1996; Briggs & Usrey, 2005; Stoelzel et al., 2017; Hasse et al., 2019). Importantly, taken together, these results indicate that corticogeniculate feedback exerts parallel, cell-class-specific influences on the feedforward transmission of visual signals to the cortex.

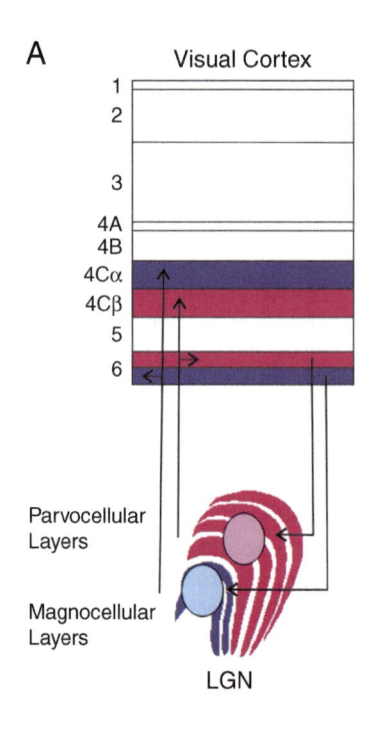

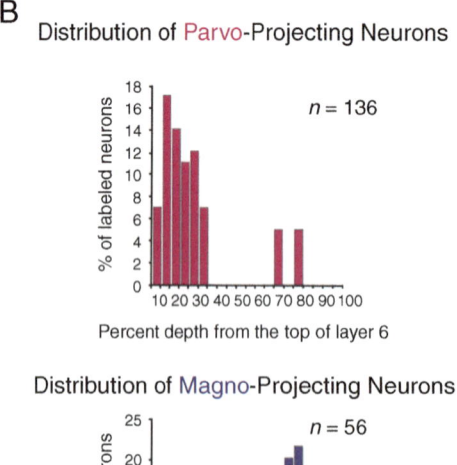

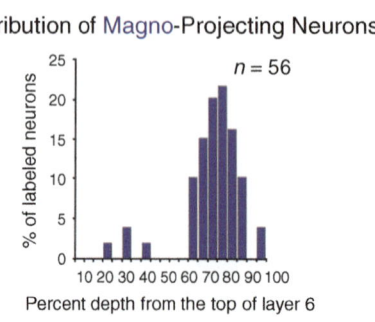

Figure 3 Sublaminar organization of corticogeniculate neurons projecting to the parvocellular and magnocellular layers of the LGN.

A. Circuit diagram illustrating the organization of feedforward geniculocortical projections. Axons from magnocellular neurons innervate neurons in cortical layer 4 Cα and lower layer 6; axons from parvocellular neurons innervate neurons in cortical layer 4 Cβ and upper layer 6. The koniocellular pathway is not shown in this figure; however, corticogeniculate input to the koniocellular layers is thought to arise from neurons in the bottom of layer 6. The colored ovals overlapping and restricted to the parvocellular (*pink*) and magnocellular (*lavender*) layers represent injection sites of retrograde tracers that labeled corticogeniculate neurons (panel B) in the upper and lower divisions of layer 6, respectively. Based on data from Fitzpatrick et al. (1994).

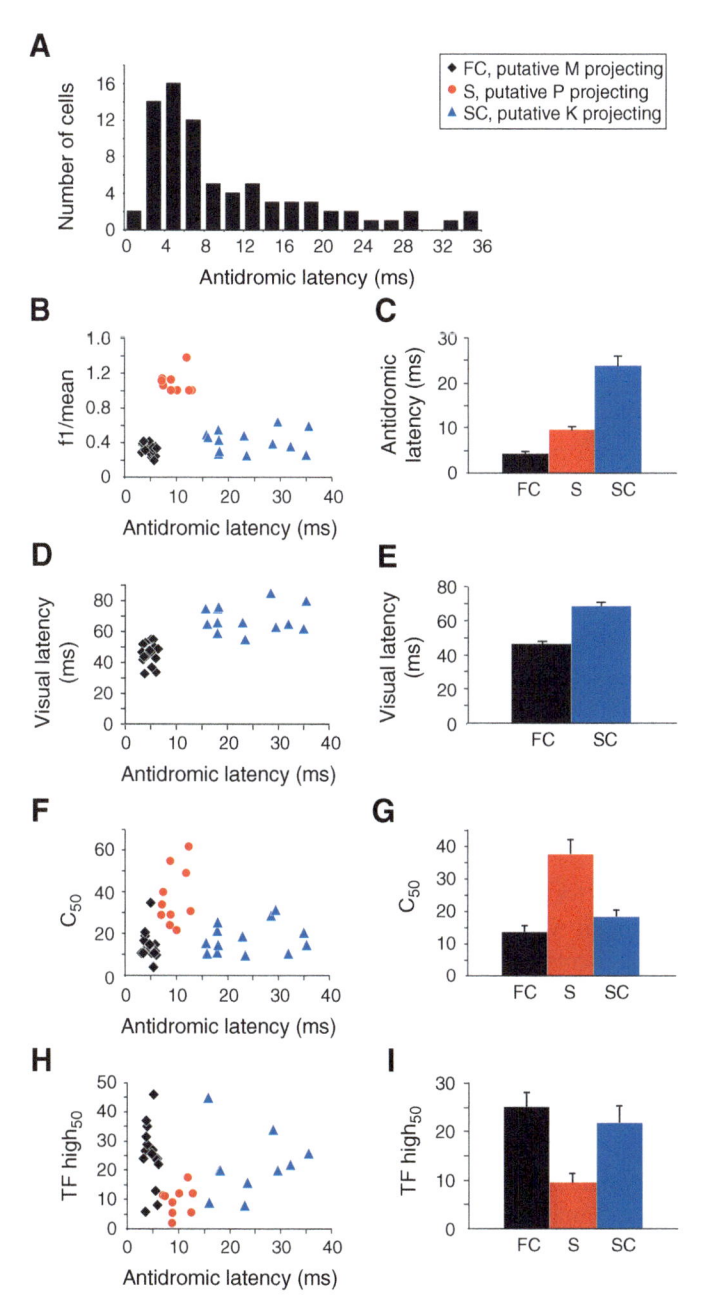

Figure 4 Physiological properties of identified corticogeniculate neurons in the alert monkey.

A. Distribution of antidromic response latencies for 78 corticogeniculate neurons.

B. f1 to f0 ratio of visual responses to drifting sinusoidal gratings versus antidromic latency for 40 corticogeniculate neurons. Neurons with ratios <1.0 are simple cells; neurons with ratios >1.0 are complex cells. Three distinct clusters of neurons are evident: fast complex cells (FC; black diamonds) with putative magnocellular projecting axons, simple cells (S; red circles) with putative parvocellular projecting axons, and slow complex cells (SC; blue triangles) with putative koniocellular projecting axons.

C. Average antidromic latencies of the fast complex, simple, and slow complex cells. All three classes of corticogeniculate neurons are significantly different from each other in terms of antidromic latency.

D. The two types of complex cells (FC, black diamonds and SC, blue triangles) are further distinguished from each other by their visual response latencies.

E. Average visual response latencies of fast complex and slow complex cells.

F. Comparison of the contrast to evoke a half-maximum response (C_{50}) versus antidromic latency for fast complex, simple, and slow complex cells. The fast complex cells (putative magnocellular projecting) are more sensitive to low-contrast stimuli than are the simple cells (putative parvocellular projecting).

G. Average C_{50} responses for fast complex, simple, and slow complex cells.

H. Comparison of the highest temporal frequencies to evoke a half-maximum response (TF high$_{50}$) versus antidromic latency for fast complex, simple, and slow complex cells. The fast complex cells (putative magnocellular projecting) follow stimuli at higher temporal frequencies than the simple cells (putative parvocellular projecting).

I. Average TF high$_{50}$ levels for fast complex, simple, and slow complex cells. For all histograms, error bars represent the standard error of the mean (SEM). Adapted from Briggs and Usrey (2009).

Corticogeniculate Effects on Visual Processing

Despite the anatomical strength of the corticogeniculate feedback pathway (e.g., individual LGN neurons receive two to five times more synapses from the cortex than from the retina), there is general agreement that feedback exerts a modulatory, rather than driving, influence on geniculate activity (Guillery, 1969; Erisir, Van Horn, Bickford, et al., 1997; Erisir, Van Horn, & Sherman, 1997; Sherman & Guillery, 1998). Proposed roles for corticogeniculate feedback can be sorted into two broad categories: (1) corticogeniculate feedback sharpens the receptive field boundaries of LGN neurons, and (2) corticogeniculate feedback adjusts temporal features (i.e., spike timing) of geniculate responses to influence the transmission of visual information from the LGN to the visual cortex.

Results from several studies support the idea that corticogeniculate feedback sharpens the receptive fields of LGN neurons by strengthening extraclassical surround suppression (Murphy & Sillito, 1987; Sillito & Jones, 2002; Born et al., 2020). Extraclassical surround suppression is the phenomenon in which responses to stimuli within a neuron's classical receptive field are suppressed by stimuli that extend into the extraclassical surround (Jones et al., 2000). Recent work further suggests that corticogeniculate feedback has a center/surround influence on geniculate activity, whereby feedback from cortical neurons with retinotopically overlapping receptive fields is net excitatory and feedback from neighboring neurons is net suppressive, presumably via disynaptic inhibition, either from local interneurons or neurons in the thalamic reticular nucleus (Born et al., 2020). Consequently, feedback augments geniculate responses to stimuli restricted to the classical receptive field as well as suppresses responses to stimuli that extend into the extraclassical surround. Both of these effects would serve to sharpen the spatial boundaries of LGN receptive fields. The idea that corticothalamic feedback sharpens receptive fields is also supported by work in the somatosensory system, where feedback has been shown to enhance the responses of thalamic neurons with matching receptive field properties and suppress the responses of neurons with mismatched properties (Temereanca & Simons, 2004; Li & Ebner, 2007).

Corticogeniculate feedback has been proposed to influence the transmission of visual information in several ways in the temporal domain. First, corticogeniculate feedback has been found to shift LGN neurons between burst and tonic activity modes (Andolina et al., 2013; Ortuño et al., 2014; Born et al., 2020). As with other thalamic neurons, geniculate neurons produce burst or tonic spikes depending on the inactivation state of the T-type Ca^{++} channels in their membranes (Jahnsen & Llinás, 1984a, 1984b). When geniculate neurons are hyperpolarized beyond typical resting levels (e.g., -75 mV versus -65 mV) for ~ 100 ms or longer, T-type channels become de-inactivated, and subsequent membrane depolarization leads to a low-threshold Ca^{++} spike, which then triggers a burst of Na^+-based spikes. In contrast, when geniculate neurons are less hyperpolarized, the T-type channels are in the inactivated state and unable to open in response to depolarizing input. Consequently, LGN neurons produce tonic spikes rather than burst spikes. Thus, based on the inactivation state of the T-type channels, LGN neurons operate either in burst mode or tonic mode (Sherman, 2001), the ramifications of which are important because bursts are particularly effective in evoking cortical responses to sensory stimulation and may serve to alert the cortex about new stimuli (Sherman 2001; Swadlow & Gusev, 2001; Alitto et al., 2019).

Corticogeniculate feedback has also been proposed to influence the transmission of visual information by enhancing geniculate response precision (Andolina et al., 2007; Hasse & Briggs, 2017; Murphy et al., 2020) and by synchronizing the firing of LGN neurons (Sillito et al., 1994). Although the source of this synchrony has been the subject of debate (Brody, 1998), studies demonstrate that near synchronous spikes from two thalamic neurons that provide convergent input to cortical target cells are more likely to evoke cortical responses than spikes displaced by little more than 10 msec (Usrey et al., 2000; Roy & Alloway, 2001). Thus, there is a mechanism to preferentially detect synchronous thalamic inputs to the cortex.

Corticogeniculate feedback is also thought to influence large-scale correlated activity among ensembles of thalamic neurons. In a model proposed by Destexhe and colleagues (1999), corticothalamic projections increased thalamic synchrony and, consequently, coherent oscillations in the cortico-thalamo-cortical loop. Soon thereafter, experimental evidence demonstrated that corticothalamic stimulation can trigger different patterns of correlated activity within the thalamus that is dependent on stimulation mode and inhibitory interactions involving the thalamic reticular nucleus (Blumenfeld & McCormick, 2000; see also Bastos et al., 2014). Moreover, certain patterns of thalamic activity were found to result in greater synchronization across neurons via a redistribution of spike times (Bal et al., 2000).

Finally, corticogeniculate feedback is thought to gate the flow of information from the retina to the cortex. As an extreme example, corticogeniculate projections contribute to the neuronal circuits that underlie sleep, a state where geniculocortical transmission is greatly diminished and disrupted (Livingstone & Hubel, 1981; Steriade, 2005). In contrast and during wakefulness, spatial attention is known to increase the activity of LGN neurons (O'Connor et al., 2002; McAlonan et al., 2006, 2008), an effect likely mediated by projections from corticogeniculate neurons (Béhuret et al., 2015). Lastly, corticogeniculate feedback may also increase the gain of LGN responses to otherwise weak stimuli, such as low-contrast visual stimuli (Przybyszewski et al., 2000; see also Olsen et al., 2012; Wang et al., 2018).

Summary and Concluding Remarks

Although we have a reasonably good understanding of the components and organization of the corticogeniculate feedback pathway, our understanding of the function of corticogeniculate feedback during visual processing is still rather limited. Evidence indicates that corticogeniculate feedback sharpens the spatial boundaries of geniculate receptive fields and adjusts the flow of information from the LGN to the cortex. Future advances in our understanding of how corticogeniculate feedback performs these and other, yet to be determined, functions will benefit greatly from methods that can spatially and temporally restrict manipulations on feedback neurons, which are needed to reveal the fine structure of feedback effects, such as details in the center/surround organization of feedback influence, rate-dependent interactions, and selective effects mediated by pathway-specific projections. Moreover, we have a very limited understanding of how corticogeniculate feedback contributes to processes involving attention and the analysis of visual scenes. However, we approach studying corticogeniculate feedback, it is clear that we need to view feedback as an integrated member of a much larger and time-varying dynamic network that includes retinal input, local thalamic interactions, brainstem modulation, cortical state, and behavior.

References

Alitto, H. J., Moore, B. D., Rathbun, D. L., & Usrey, W. M. (2011). A comparison of visual responses in the lateral geniculate nucleus of alert and anaesthetized macaque monkeys. *Journal of Physiology*, **589**(Pt 1), 87–99.

Alitto, H. J., Rathbun, D. L., Vandeleest, J. J., Alexander, P. C., & Usrey W. M. (2019). The augmentation of retinogeniculate communication during thalamic burst mode. *Journal of Neuroscience*, **39**, 5697–5710.

Andolina, I. M., Jones, H. E., Wang, W., & Sillito, A. M. (2007). Corticothalamic feedback enhances stimulus response precision in the visual system. *Proceedings of the National Academy of Sciences of the United States of America*, **104**, 1685–1690.

Andolina, I. M., Jones, H. E., & Sillito, A.M. (2013). Effects of cortical feedback on the spatial properties of relay cells in the lateral geniculate nucleus. *Journal of Neurophysiology*, **109**(3):889–99.

Bal, T., Debay, D., & Destexhe, A. (2000). Cortical feedback controls the frequency and synchrony of oscillations in the visual thalamus. *Journal of Neuroscience*, **20**, 7478–7488.

Bastos, A. M., Briggs, F., Alitto, H. J., Mangun, G. R., & Usrey, W. M. (2014). Simultaneous recordings from the primary visual cortex and lateral geniculate nucleus reveal rhythmic interactions and a cortical source for gamma-band oscillations. *Journal of Neuroscience*, **34**(22), 7639–7644.

Béhuret, S., Deleuze, C., & Bal, T. (2015). Corticothalamic synaptic noise as a mechanism for selective attention in thalamic neurons. *Frontiers in Neural Circuits*, **9**, 80.

Bickford, M. E., Zhou, N., Krahe, T. E., Govindaiah, G., & Guido, W. (2015). Retinal and tectal "driver-like" inputs converge in the shell of the mouse dorsal lateral geniculate nucleus. *Journal of Neuroscience*, **35**(29), 10523–10534.

Blasdel, G. G., & Lund, J. S. (1983). Termination of afferent axons in macaque striate cortex. *Journal of Neuroscience*, **3**, 1389–1413.

Blumenfeld, H., & McCormick, D.A. (2000). Corticothalamic inputs control the pattern of activity generated in thalamocortical networks. *Journal of Neuroscience*, **20**, 5153–5162.

Born, G., Erisken, S., Schneider, F. A., Klein, A., Mobarhan, M. H., Lao, C. L., Spacek, M. A. Einevoll, G. T., & Busse, L. (2020). Corticothalamic feedback sculpts visual spatial integration in mouse thalamus. bioRxiv. doi:10.1101/2020.05.19.104000.

Briggs, F., Kiley, C. W., Callaway, E. M., & Usrey, W. M. (2016). Morphological substrates for parallel streams of corticogeniculate feedback originating in both V1 and V2 of the macaque monkey. *Neuron*, **90**(2), 388–399.

Briggs, F., & Usrey, W. M. (2005). Temporal properties of feedforward and feedback pathways between the thalamus and visual cortex in the ferret. *Thalamus and Related Systems*, **3**(2), 133–139.

Briggs, F., & Usrey, W. M. (2009) Parallel processing in the corticogeniculate pathway of the macaque monkey. *Neuron* **62**, 135–146.

Brody, C. D. (1998). Slow covariations in neuronal resting potentials can lead to artefactually fast cross-correlations in their spike trains. *Journal of Neurophysiology*, **80**, 3345–3351.

Calkins, D. J., Sappington, R. M., & Hendry, S. H. (2005). Morphological identification of ganglion cells expressing the alpha subunit of type II calmodulin-dependent protein kinase in the macaque retina. *Journal of Comparative Neurology*, **481**(2), 94–209.

Casagrande, V. A., Yazar, F., Jones, K. D., & Ding, Y. (2007). The morphology of the koniocellular axon pathway in the macaque monkey. *Cerebral Cortex*, **17**(10), 2334–2345.

Cleland, B. G. (1986). The dorsal lateral geniculate nucleus of the cat. In J. D. Pettigrew, K. J. Sanderson, & W. R. Levick (Eds.), Visual Neuroscience (pp. 111–120). London: Cambridge University Press.

Cleland, B. G., Dubin, M. W., & Levick, W.R. (1971a). Simultaneous recording of input and output of lateral geniculate neurones. *Nature New Biology* **231**, 191–192.

Cleland, B. G., Dubin, M. W., & Levick, W.R. (1971b). Sustained and transient neurones in the cat's retina and lateral geniculate nucleus. *Journal of Physiology*, **217**, 473–496.

Conley, M., & Raczkowski, D. (1990). Sublaminar organization within layer VI of the striate cortex in *Galago*. *Journal of Comparative Neurology*, **302**(2), 425–436.

Croner, L. J. & Kaplan, E. (1995). Receptive fields of P and M ganglion cells across the primate retina. *Vision Research*, **35**, 7–24.

Destexhe, A., Contreras, D., & Steriade, M. (1999). Cortically-induced coherence of a thalamic-generated oscillation. *Neuroscience*, **92**, 427–443.

Diamond, I. T., Conley, M., Itoh, K., & Fitzpatrick, D. (1985). Laminar organization of geniculocortical projections in *Galago senegalensis* and *Aotus trivirgatus*. *Journal of Comparative Neurology*, **242**, 584–610.

Erisir, A., Van Horn, S. C., Bickford, M. E., & Sherman, S. M. (1997). Immunocytochemistry and distribution of parabrachial terminals in the lateral geniculate nucleus of the cat: a comparison with corticogeniculate terminals. *Journal of Comparative Neurology*, **377**, 535–549

Erisir, A., Van Horn, S. C., & Sherman, S. M. (1997). Relative numbers of cortical and brainstem inputs to the lateral geniculate nucleus. *Proceedings of the National Academy of Science*, **94**, 1517–1520.

Fitzpatrick, D., Carey, R. G., and Diamond, I. T. (1980). The projection of the superior colliculus upon the lateral geniculate body in *Tupaia glis* and *Galago senegalensis*. *Brain Research*, **194**, 494–499.

Fitzpatrick, D., Itoh, K., & Diamond, I. T. (1983). The laminar organization of the lateral geniculate body and the striate cortex in the squirrel monkey (*Saimiri sciureus*). *Journal of Neuroscience*, **3**(4), 673–702.

Fitzpatrick, D., Lund, J. S., & Blasdel, G. G. (1985). Intrinsic connections of macaque striate cortex. Afferent and efferent connections of lamina 4C. *Journal of Neuroscience*, **5**, 3329–3349.

Fitzpatrick, D., Usrey, W. M., Schofield, B. R., & Einstein, G. (1994). The sublaminar organization of corticogeniculate neurons in layer 6 of macaque striate cortex. *Visual Neuroscience*, **11**, 307–315.

Freund, T. F., Martin, K. A. C., & Whitteridge, D. (1985). Innervation of cat visual areas 17 and 18 by physiologically identified X- and Y-type thalamic afferents. I. Arborization patterns and quantitative distribution of postsynaptic elements. *Journal of Comparative Neurology*, **242**, 263–274.

Friedlander, M. J., Lin, C.-S., Stanford, L. R., & Sherman, S. M. (1981). Morphology of functionally identified neurons in lateral geniculate nucleus of the cat. *Journal of Neurophysiology*, **46**, 80–129.

Gilbert, C. D., & Kelly, J. P. (1975). The projections of cells in different layers of the cat's visual cortex. *Journal of Comparative Neurology*, **163**, 81–106.

Graham, J. (1977). An autoradiographic study of the efferent connections of the superior colliculus of the cat. *Journal of Comparative Neurology*, **173**, 629–654.

Guillery, R. W. (1969). A quantitative study of synaptic interconnections in the dorsal lateral geniculate nucleus of the cat. *Zeitschrift für Zellforschung und Mikroskopische Anatomie*. **96**, 39–48

Hasse, J. M., Bragg, E. M., Murphy, A. J., & Briggs, F. (2019). Morphological heterogeneity among corticogeniculate neurons in ferrets: quantification and comparison with a previous report in macaque monkeys. *Journal of Comparative Neurology*, **527**(3), 546–557.

Hasse, J. M., & Briggs, F. (2017). Corticogeniculate feedback sharpens the temporal precision and spatial resolution of visual signals in the ferret. *Proceedings of the National Academy of Science USA*, **114**(30), E6222–E6230.

Headon, M. P., Sloper, J. J., Hiorns, R. W., & Powell, T. P. S. (1985). Sizes of neurons in the primate lateral geniculate nucleus during normal development. *Developmental Brain Research*, **18**, 51–56.

Hendrickson, A. E., Wilson, J. R., & Ogren, M. P. (1978). The neuroanatomical organization of pathways between the dorsal lateral geniculate nucleus and visual cortex in Old World and New World primates. *Journal of Comparative Neurology*, **182**, 123–136.

Hendry, S. H. C., Hockfield, S., Jones, E. G., & McKay, R. (1984). Monoclonal antibody that identifies subsets of neurones in the central visual system of monkey and cat. *Nature*, **307**, 267–269.

Hockfield, S., & Sur, M. (1990). Monoclonal antibody cat-301 identifies Y-cells in the dorsal lateral geniculate nucleus of the cat. *Journal of Comparative Neurology*, **300**, 320–330.

Hubel, D. H., & Wiesel, T. N. (1961). Integrative action in the cat's lateral geniculate body. *Journal of Physiology*, **155**(2), 385–98.

Huberman, A. D., & Niell, C. M. (2011). What can mice tell us about how vision works? *Trends in Neuroscience*, **34**(9), 464–473.

Humphrey, A. L., Sur, M., Uhlrich, D. J., & Sherman, S. M. (1985a). Projection patterns of individual X- and Y-cell axons from the lateral geniculate nucleus to cortical area 17 in the cat. *Journal of Comparative Neurology*, **233**, 159–189.

Humphrey, A. L., Sur, M., Uhlrich, D. J., & Sherman, S. M. (1985b). Termination patterns of individual X- and Y-cell axons in the visual cortex of the cat: projections to area 18, to the 17-18 border region, and to both areas 17 and 18. *Journal of Comparative Neurology*, **233**, 190–212.

Ichida, J. M., Mavity-Hudson, J. A., & Casagrande, V. A. (2014). Distinct patterns of corticogeniculate feedback to different layers of the lateral geniculate nucleus. *Eye and Brain*, **2014**(6 Suppl 1), 57–73.

Iwai, L., Ohashi, Y., van der List, D., Usrey, W. M., Miyashita, Y., & Kawasaki, H. (2013). FoxP2 is a parvocellular-specific transcription factor in the visual thalamus of monkeys and ferrets. *Cerebral Cortex*, **23**(9), 2204–2212.

Jahnsen, H., & Llinás, R. (1984a). Electrophysiological properties of guinea-pig thalamic neurones: An in vitro study. *Journal of Physiology*, **349**, 205–226.

Jahnsen, H., & Llinás, R. (1984b). Ionic basis for the electroresponseiveness and oscillatory properties of guinea-pig thalamic neurones in vitro. *Journal of Physiology*, **349**, 227–247.

Jones, E. G. (2007). The Thalamus: Second Edition. Cambridge, UK: Cambridge University Press.

Jones, H. E., Andolina, I. M., Oakely, N. M., Murphy, P. C., & Sillito, A. M. (2000). Spatial summation in lateral geniculate nucleus and visual cortex. *Experimental Brain Research*, **135**, 279–284.

Kaplan, E., & Shapley, R. (1984). The origin of the S (slow) potential in the mammalian lateral geniculate nucleus. *Experimental Brain Research*, **55**, 111–116.

Katz, L. C. (1987). Local circuitry of identified projection neurons in cat visual cortex brain slices. *Journal of Neuroscience*, **4**, 1223–49.

Lachica, E. A., & Casagrande, V. A. (1992). Direct W-like geniculate projections to the cytochrome oxidase (CO) blobs in primate visual cortex: axon morphology. *Journal of Comparative Neurology*, **319**(1), 141–158.

Lachica, E. A., & Casagrande, V. A. (1993). The morphology of collicular and retinal axons ending on small relay (W-like) cells of the primate lateral geniculate nucleus. *Visual Neuroscience*, **10**(3), 403–418.

Leventhal, A. G. (1979). Evidence that the different classes of relay cells of the cat's lateral geniculate nucleus terminate in different layers of the striate cortex. *Experimental Brain Research*, **37**(2), 349–372.

Levitt, J. B., Schumer, R. A., Sherman, S. M., Spear, P. D., & Movshon, J. A. (2001). Visual response properties of neurons in the LGN of normally reared and visually deprived macaque monkeys. *Journal of Neurophysiology*, **85**, 2111–2129.

Li, L., & Ebner, F. F. (2007). Cortical modulation of spatial and angular tuning maps in the rat thalamus. *Journal of Neuroscience*, **27**, 167–179.

Livingstone, M. S., & Hubel, D. H. (1981). Effects of sleep and arousal on the processing of visual information in the cat. *Nature*, **291**(5816), 554–561.

Lund, J. S., & Boothe, R. (1975). Interlaminar connections and pyramidal neuron organization in the visual cortex, area 17, of the macaque monkey. *Journal of Comparative Neurology*, **159**, 305–334.

Lund, J. S., Lund, R. D., Hendrickson, A. E., Bunt, A. H., & Fuchs, A. F. (1975). The origin of efferent pathways from the primary visual cortex, area 17, of the macaque monkey. *Journal of Comparative Neurology*, **164**, 287–304.

Mastronarde, D. N. (1987). Two classes of single-input X-cells in cat lateral geniculate nucleus. II. Retinal inputs and the generation of receptive-field properties. *Journal of Neurophysiology*, **57**, 381–413

Maunsell, J. H. R., Ghose, G. M., Assad, J. A., McAdams, C. J., Boudreau, C. E., & Noerager, B. D. (1999). Visual response latencies of magnocellular and parvocellular LGN neurons in macaque monkeys. *Visual Neuroscience*, **16**, 1–14.

McAlonan, K., Cavanaugh, J., & Wurtz, R. H. (2006). Attentional modulation of thalamic reticular neurons. *Journal of Neuroscience*, **26**, 4444–4450.

McAlonan, K., Cavanaugh, J., & Wurtz, R. H. (2008). Guarding the gateway to cortex with attention in visual thalamus. *Nature*, **456**, 391–394.

Merigan, W. H., & Maunsell, J. H. R. (1993). How parallel are the primate visual pathways? *Annual Reviews in Neuroscience*, **16**, 369–402.

Murphy, A. J., Shaw, L., Hasse, J. M., Goris, R. L. T., & Briggs, F. (2020). Optogenetic activation of corticogeniculate feedback stabilizes response gain and increases information coding in LGN neurons. *Computational Neuroscience*. Online ahead of print. doi:10.1007/s10827-020-00754-5.

Murphy, P. C., & Sillito, A. M. (1996). Functional morphology of the feedback pathway from area 17 of the cat visual cortex to the lateral geniculate nucleus. *Journal of Neuroscience*, **16**, 1180–1192.

Murphy, P. C., & Sillito, A.M. (1987). Corticofugal feedback influences the generation of length tuning in the visual pathway. *Nature*, **329**, 727–729.

O'Connor, D. H., Fukui, M. M., Pinsk, M. A., & Kastner, S. (2002). Attention modulates responses in the human lateral geniculate nucleus. *Nature Neuroscience*, **5**, 1203–1209.

Olsen, S. R., Bortone, D., Adesnik, H., & Scanziani, M. (2012). Gain control by layer six in cortical circuits of vision. *Nature*, **483**(7387), 47–52.

Ortuño, T. Grieve, K. L., Cao, R., Cudeiro, J., & Rivadulla, C. (2014). Bursting thalamic responses in awake monkey contribute to visual detection and are modulated by corticofugal feedback. *Frontiers in Behavioral Neuroscience*, **8**, 198.

Percival, K. A., Koizumi, A., Masri, R. A., Buzás, P., Martin, P. R., & Grünert, U. (2014). Identification of a pathway from the retina to koniocellular layer K1 in the lateral geniculate nucleus of marmoset. *Journal of Neuroscience*, **34**(11), 3821–3825.

Przybyszewski, A. W., Gaska, J. P., Foote, W., & Pollen, D.A. (2000). Striate cortex increases contrast gain of macaque LGN neurons. *Visual Neuroscience*, 17(4), 485–494.

Rathbun, D. L., Alitto, H. J., Warland, D. K., & Usrey, W. M. (2016) Stimulus contrast and retinogeniculate signal processing. *Frontiers in Neural Circuits*, 10, 8. doi:10.3389/fncir.2016.00008.

Rathbun, D. L., Warland, D. K., & Usrey, W. M. (2010). Spike timing and information transmission at retinogeniculate synapses. *Journal of Neuroscience*, 30, 13558–13566.

Roy, S. A., & Alloway, K. D. (2001). Coincidence detection or temporal integration? What the neurons in somatosensory cortex are doing. *Journal of Neuroscience*, 21, 2462–2473.

Saul, A. B., & Humphrey, A. L. (1990). Spatial and temporal response properties of lagged and nonlagged cells in cat lateral geniculate nucleus. *Journal of Neurophysiology*, 64, 206–224.

Schiller, P. H., & Logothetis, N. K. (1990). The color-opponent and broad-band channels of the primate visual system. *Trends in Neurosciences*, 13, 392–398.

Schiller, P. H., & Malpeli, J. G. (1978). Functional specificity of lateral geniculate nucleus laminae of the rhesus monkey. *Journal of Neurophysiology*, 41, 788–797.

Shapley, R. M. (1992). Parallel retinocortical channels: X and Y and P and M. In J. Brannan (Ed.), Applications of Parallel Processing in Vision (pp. 3–36). New York: Elsevier.

Sherman, S. M. (1985). Functional organization of the W-, X-, and Y-cell pathways in the cat: a review and hypothesis. In J. M. Sprague & A. N. Epstein (Eds.), Progress in Psychobiology and Physiological Psychology, Vol. 11 (pp. 233–314). Orlando: Academic Press.

Sherman, S. M. (2001). Tonic and burst firing: dual modes of thalamocortical relay. *Trends in Neuroscience*, 24(2), 122–126.

Sherman, S. M., & Guillery, R. W. (1998). On the actions that one nerve cell can have on another: distinguishing "drivers" from "modulators." *Proceedings of the National Academy of Science USA*, 95(12), 7121–7126.

Sherman, S. M., & Guillery, R. W. (2009). Exploring the Thalamus and Its Role in Cortical Function. 2nd ed. Cambridge, MA: MIT Press.

Sillito, A. M., & Jones, H. E. (2002). Corticothalamic interactions in the transfer of visual information. *Philosophical Transactions of the Royal Society of London B: Biological Sciences*, 357, 1739–1752.

Sillito, A. M., Jones, H. E., Gerstein, G. L., & West, D. C. (1994). Feature-linked synchronization of thalamic relay cell firing induced by feedback from the visual cortex. *Nature*, 369, 479–482.

Sincich, L. C., Adams, D. L., Economides, J. R., & Horton, J. C. (2007). Transmission of spike trains at the retinogeniculate synapse. *Journal of Neuroscience*, 27, 2683–2692.

So, Y. T., & Shapley, R. (1979). Spatial properties of X and Y cells in the lateral geniculate nucleus of the cat and conduction velocities of their inputs. *Experimental Brain Research*, 36, 533–550.

Steriade, M. (2005). Sleep, epilepsy and thalamic reticular inhibitory neurons. *Trends in Neuroscience*, 28, 317–324.

Stoelzel, C. R., Bereshpolova, Y., Alonso, J.-M., & Swadlow, H. A. (2017). Axonal conduction delays, brain state, and corticogeniculate communication. *Journal of Neuroscience*, 37(26), 6342–6358.

Stone, J. (1983). Parallel Processing in the Visual System. New York: Plenum Press.

Swadlow, H. A., & Gusev, A.G. (2001). The impact of "bursting" thalamic impulses at a neocortical synapse. *Nature Neuroscience*, 4, 402–408.

Szmajda, B. A., Grünert, U., & Martin, P. R. (2008). Retinal ganglion cell inputs to the koniocellular pathway. *Journal of Comparative Neurology*, 510(3), 251–268.

Temereanca, S., & Simons, D.J. (2004). Functional topography of corticothalamic feedback enhances thalamic spatial response tuning in the somatosensory whisker/barrel system. *Neuron*, 41, 639–651.

Troy, J. B., & Lennie, P. (1987). Detection latencies of X and Y type cells of the cat's dorsal lateral geniculate nucleus. *Experimental Brain Research*, 65, 703–706.

Tsumoto, T., & Suda, K. (1980). Three groups of cortico-geniculate neurons and their distribution in binocular and monocular segments of cat striate cortex. *Journal of Comparative Neurology*, 193, 223–236.

Usrey, W. M., & Alitto, H. J. (2015). Visual functions of the thalamus. *Annual Review of Vision Science*, 1, 351–371.

Usrey, W. M., Alonso, J. M., & Reid, R.C. (2000). Synaptic interactions between thalamic inputs to simple cells in cat visual cortex. *Journal of Neuroscience*, 20, 5461–5467.

Usrey, W. M., & Fitzpatrick, D. (1996). Specificity in the axonal connections of layer VI neurons in tree shrew striate cortex: evidence for distinct granular and supragranular systems. *Journal of Neuroscience*, 16(3), 1203–1218.

Usrey, W. M., Muly, E., & Fitzpatrick, D. (1992). Lateral geniculate projections to the superficial layers of visual cortex in the tree shrew. *Journal of Comparative Neurology* 319, 159–171.

Usrey, W. M., Reppas, J. B., & Reid, R. C. (1998). Paired-spike interactions and synaptic efficacy of retinal inputs to the thalamus. *Nature*, 395, 384–387.

Usrey, W. M., Reppas, J. B., & Reid, R. C. (1999). Specificity and strength of retinogeniculate connections. *Journal of Neurophysiology*, 82, 3527–3540.

Usrey, W. M., & Sherman, S. M. (2019) Corticofugal circuits: Communication lines from the cortex to the rest of the brain. *Journal of Comparative Neurology*, 527, 640–650.

Wang, W., Andolina, I. M., Lu, Y., Jones, H. E., & Sillito, A. M. (2018). Focal gain control of thalamic visual receptive fields by layer 6 corticothalamic feedback. *Cerebral Cortex*, 28(1), 267–280.

Weyand, T. G. (2007). Retinogeniculate transmission in wakefulness. *Journal of Neurophysiology*, 98, 769–785.

Xu, X., Ichida, J. M., Allison, J. D., Boyd, J. D., Bonds, A. B., & Casagrande, V. A. (2001). A comparison of koniocellular, magnocellular and parvocellular receptive field properties in the lateral geniculate nucleus of the owl monkey (*Aotus trivirgatus*). *Journal of Physiology*, 531(Pt 1), 203–218.

Chapter 11
The Vibrissa Sensorimotor System of Rodents: A View from the Sensory Thalamus

Martin Deschênes and David Kleinfeld

The rat vibrissa system, with its tactile hairs and their associated neuronal architecture, is a prototypical sensorimotor system for the study of active sensation. Although nearly all mammalian species have vibrissae, many rodent species have specifically evolved the ability to sweep their vibrissae for a dynamic exploration of the environment (Knutsen et al., 2006; Metha and Kleinfeld, 2004; Metha et al., 2007). Thus, two aspects of signaling are involved in the vibrissa sensory pathway: one that signals touch and the other that signals self-motion (Kleinfeld and Deschênes, 2011; Prescott et al., 2011). In this chapter, we focus on the parallel streams of vibrissa information processing that are involved in vibrissa signaling (Figure 1), with an emphasis on the different signaling pathways to the thalamus and their roles in the behavior of rodents.

Background

On each side of the rodent's snout, in a region called the *mystacial pad*, there are five rows of vibrissae that form an ordered array of low-threshold mechanoreceptors (Figure 1A). The trigeminal ganglion cells that innervate these mechanoreceptors respond to the motion of only one vibrissa. The spatial arrangement of the vibrissae within the pad is mapped into homotopic aggregates of neurons from the trigeminal nuclei (Ma and Woolsey, 1984) (Figure 1B), up through the ventral posterior medial (VPM) nucleus of the thalamus (Van der Loos, 1976) (Figure 1C), and onto layer 4 of vibrissa primary somatosensory (vS1) cortex (Woolsey and Van der Loos, 1970) (Figure 1D). In mice, aggregates of neurons in the vS1 cortex consist of clusters of stellate cells surrounding a "hollow" core that is filled with dendrites, axons, and glial cells. Hence the term *barrel* was used to describe their structure (Woolsey and Van der Loos, 1970) (left image in Figure 1D). By extension, the cellular aggregates in the VPM thalamus and in the trigeminal brainstem subnuclei are denoted *barreloids* and *barrelettes*, respectively (Figure 1B and C). Thus, each vibrissa forms the start of a labeled line that includes a trigeminal barrelette, a thalamic barreloid, and a cortical barrel. This morphology makes the vibrissa system of rodents one of the most valuable models for research in sensory physiology, development, and experience-dependent synaptic plasticity. The advent of transgenic mice and the development of new imaging techniques have further contributed to promoting the popularity of this somatosensory system (Luo et al., 2008, 2018).

Ascending Streams of Vibrissa Information

Tract-tracing studies and studies that combined electrophysiological recording with single-cell labeling have led to the discovery of separate pathways of vibrissa information processing – designated as the *lemniscal*, *extralemniscal*, and *paralemniscal* pathways (Figure 1C). The lemniscal and extralemniscal pathways relay vibrissa information through different sectors of the VPM thalamus, whereas the paralemniscal pathway transits through the posterior group (Po) of the thalamus (for reviews, see Pouchelon et al., 2012; Deschênes and Urbain, 2016).

The lemniscal pathway. The lemniscal pathway arises from two populations of trigeminothalamic neurons. The first population consists of small-sized neurons that are clustered in modules (i.e., the barrelettes) within nucleus principalis (red arrow in Figure 1B and C). These cells have receptive fields that are dominated by a single vibrissa, and they account for about 75 percent of the projection cells in nucleus PrV (Minnery and Simons, 2003). They project only to the contralateral VPM thalamic nucleus, where they emanate small bushy terminal fields, which are approximately 80 μm in diameter, in the homologous barreloid. Sensory transmission along the lemniscal pathway retains a fine-grained map of vibrissa representation. Cells within a given PrV barrelette innervate the whole of a barreloid (left image in Figure 1C), and their projections show little convergence. On average, a VPM relay cell receives input from only one to two PrV neurons (Castro-Alamancos, 2002; Deschênes et al., 2003; Arsenault and Zhang, 2006). Synaptic transmission is mediated by physically large perisomatic synapses that ensure a fast and reliable relay of information (Spácek and Lieberman, 1974; Williams et al., 1994). These barreloid cells project to layers 4 and 6a in the granular zones of the vS1 cortex (Figure 1D).

The second population of trigeminothalamic neurons consists of physically large neurons in trigeminal nucleus PrV, whose somata are located in the septa between the barrelettes (Henderson and Jacquin, 1995; Lo et al., 1999) (blue arrow in Figure 1B and C). These neurons have multivibrissa receptive fields and project to the dorsal aspect of the barreloids near the border with the Po thalamus, which is referred to as the "head" of the barreloids, and more sparsely to the Po thalamus itself (Veinante and Deschênes, 1999). Thus, in contrast with the vast majority of barreloid cells whose receptive field is dominated by a single vibrissa, those situated in the head of barreloids respond equally well to multiple vibrissae (Ito, 1988; Sugitani et al., 1990; Urbain and Deschênes, 2007). These multivibrissa-responsive cells project preferentially to layers 4 and 6a in the dysgranular zone of the vS1 cortex (Furuta et al., 2009) (Figure 1D).

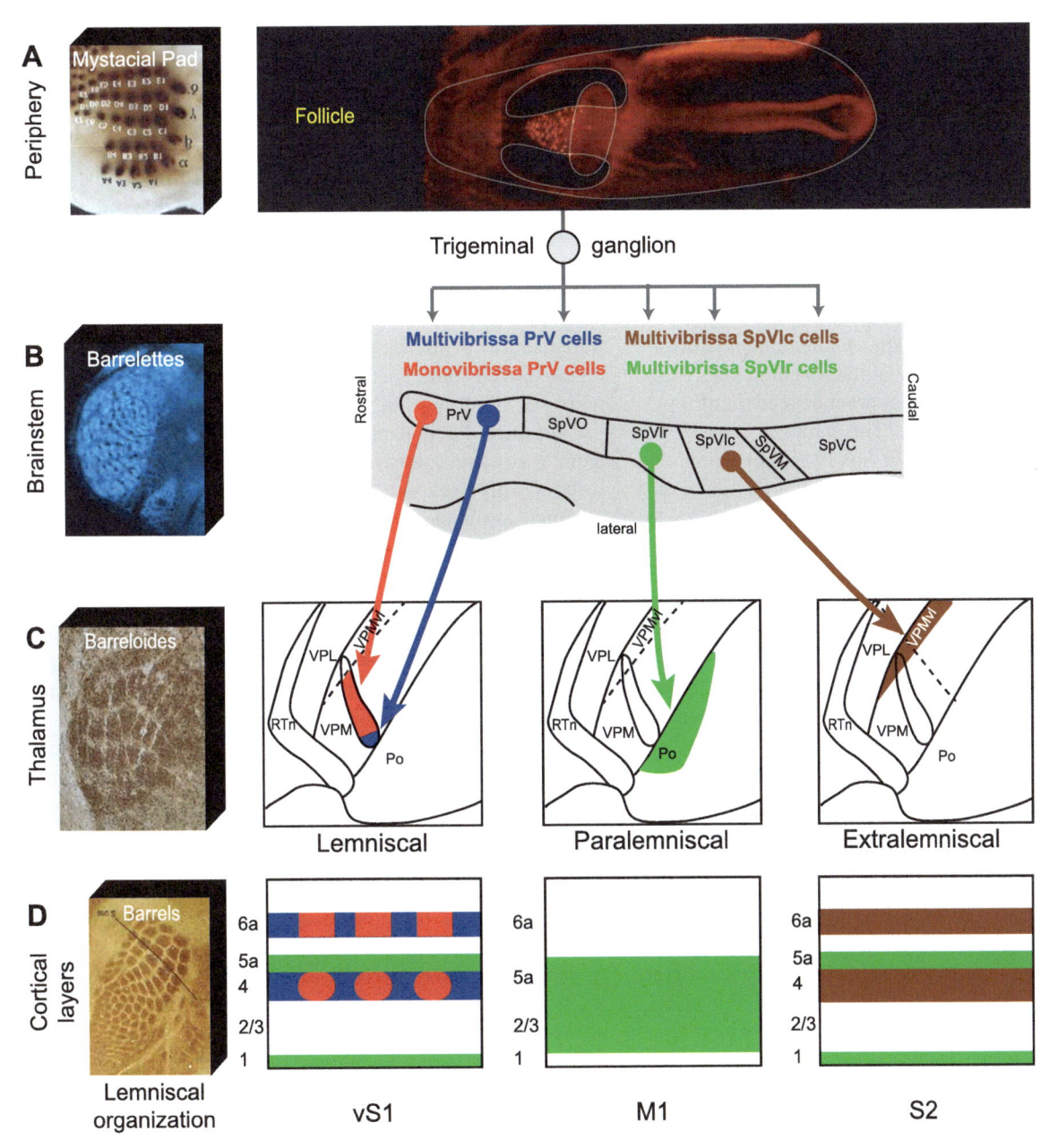

Figure 1 Schematic of the ascending pathways of vibrissa information processing.

Abbreviations: PrV, principal trigeminal nucleus; SpVO, spinal nucleus oralis; SpVIr and SpVIc, rostral and caudal divisions of spinal nucleus interpolaris, respectively; SpVM, spinal nucleus muralis, SpVC, spinal nucleus caudalis; VPM, ventral posterior medial nucleus of dorsal thalamus; VPMvl, ventrolateral aspect of the ventral posterior medial nucleus of dorsal thalamus; Po, medial division of the posterior group nucleus; RTn, nucleus reticularis; VPL, ventral posterior lateral nucleus of dorsal thalamus.

A. The periphery consists of vibrissae that are rhythmically swept by muscles in the mystacial pad and detection of touch by pressure sensors in the follicle. The image of the mystacial pad is adapted from Haidarliu et al. (2010), and that of the follicle is adapted from Whiteley et al. (2015).

B. The trigeminal subnuclei in the medulla receive input from the follicles in the mystacial pad that is transmitted by neurons in the trigeminal ganglion. The photomicrograph of barrelettes is unpublished work from Martin Deschênes; the photomicrograph of the trigeminus is adapted from Furuta et al. (2018).

C. The three main thalamic pathways. The photomicrograph of the barreloids in the core region of VPM thalamus is adapted from Haidarliu and Ahissar (2001).

D. The cortical target regions of the main thalamic pathways. The photomicrographs of vS1 cortex are unpublished work from Martin Deschênes.

The discovery of a multivibrissa pathway that transits through the head of the VPM barreloids (Urbain and Deschênes, 2007) raised the possibility that septal cells derive their receptive field input from this subpopulation of VPM neurons (blue in Figure 1C and D). Indeed, septal cells maintain their multivibrissa receptive field and response properties after a brainstem lesion that prevents vibrissa input from activating the paralemniscal pathway. Conversely, a lesion of the lemniscal pathway nearly completely abolishes vibrissa responses throughout the vS1 cortex. Finally, the labeling of single VPM cells revealed that multivibrissa cells in the head of the barreloids project principally to the dysgranular regions of the vS1 cortex (Furuta et al., 2009). In summary, barreloid cells project to layers 4 and 6a throughout the vS1 cortex via two separate streams that innervate the granular and dysgranular zones, respectively.

Prior studies in alert head-restrained rodents reported that VPM cells encode both self-generated vibrissa motion and touch (Moore et al., 2015; Urbain et al., 2015). Yet no clear spatial relationship was found between the location of a neuron within the VPM and the modulation of its firing rate. The coding and mixing of these touch and self-motion signals are an area of active research, with thalamic signals now imaged through the release of glutamate throughout all layers of the cortex (Liu et al., 2019).

The extralemniscal pathway. The extralemniscal pathway differs from the lemniscal pathway in that thalamic cells exhibit multivibrissa receptive fields that are independent of input from the PrV (Bokor et al., 2008). This pathway arises from cells located in the caudal sector of SpVI (SpVIc) (Veinante et al., 2000) that project to the VPMvl region of the thalamus, a crescent-shaped region that approximately corresponds to the lower tier of the VPM thalamus (brown arrow in Figure 1C). In contrast with the small size of the terminal field of nucleus PrV axons in a barreloid (i.e., a diameter of ~80 μm) (Veinante and Deschênes, 1999), individual SpVIc axons form larger, rostrocaudally oriented terminal fields in the VPMvl thalamus (i.e., size ~100 μm by 250 μm) (Veinante et al., 2000). This suggests a higher degree of input convergence on VPMvl neurons.

Relay cells in the VPMvl thalamus project principally to the second somatosensory (S2) cortical area and more sparsely to the dysgranular zone of the S1 cortex by means of axon collaterals (Pierret et al., 2000) (Figure 1D). The projection foci are dense in layers 4 and 6 of the S2 cortex and moderate in layers 3, 4, and 6 of the S1 cortex. A single study has addressed the role of this latter pathway (Yu et al., 2006). It was proposed that the extralemniscal pathway conveys vibrissa-contact signals for object localization in the whisking field (Yu et al., 2006). This result was obtained in anesthetized rats by means of artificial whisking (i.e., rhythmic electrical stimulation of the facial nerve) (Szwed et al., 2003). Additional experiments in alert rats are required to validate this suggestion, although object localization is lost by transient inactivation of the vS1 cortex (O'Connor, Clack, et al., 2010).

The paralemniscal pathway. The paralemniscal pathway arises from physically large, multivibrissa cells located in the rostral sector of subnucleus SpVI (SpVIr). In the Po thalamus, SpVIr axons terminate principally in a shell-like region over the dorsomedial aspect of the VPM thalamus, where they make large synaptic contacts with the proximal dendrites of relay neurons (Lavallée et al., 2005). The labeling of single axons that emanate from different parts of Po thalamus revealed heterogeneous neuronal populations that, collectively, project to the striatum and across the somatomotor regions of the neocortex, including S1, S2, and motor cortices (Deschênes et al., 1998; Ohno et al., 2012). The laminar distribution of terminal fields varies across areas, but layers 1 and 5a are the most densely innervated.

It was shown that Po thalamus contains a map of all body parts (Diamond et al., 1992). The vibrissae are represented in the most lateral sector near the VPM border (green region in Figure 1C), where cells receive vibrissa input from the trigeminal subnucleus SpVI, while the hindlimbs are represented in the most medial sector near the intralaminar nuclei. It is currently unclear whether Po neurons that are responsive to different body parts have similar projection patterns. It must be emphasized that the Po thalamus, as delineated in most stereotaxic atlases of rodents, is a large region with disparate prethalamic inputs and distinct clusters of relay cells, each characterized by a specific pattern of axonal projections to the cortex, striatum, and amygdala (Alloway et al., 2013; Ohno et al., 2012). Like the pulvinar in primates, this thalamic region remains ill-characterized both in terms of chemo-architecture and neuronal input–output relationships.

Although Po thalamic cells receive monosynaptic input from vibrissa-responsive trigeminal SpVIr neurons, they respond only weakly to vibrissa deflection. The responses are of much lower magnitude than those observed in the VPM thalamus and occur at long latencies (i.e., 16–20 ms) (Diamond et al., 1992; Sosnik et al., 2001). The reason for this weak response is that Po neurons receive a mixture of excitatory and feedforward inhibitory inputs. Most of the trigeminal axons that innervate the Po thalamus also project to the ventral division of the zona incerta (ZIv) (Barthó et al., 2002), and GABAergic ZIv cells project to Po neurons (Veinante et al., 2000). Silencing ZIv reinstates short-latency sensory transmission through the Po thalamus (Trageser and Keller, 2004; Lavallée et al., 2005). Thus, the relay of vibrissa inputs through the Po thalamus relies on disinhibition (i.e., inhibition of the inhibitory incerto-thalamic pathway). The behavioral conditions under which disinhibition operates and the types of vibrissa messages that are relayed through the Po thalamus are open questions.

Many dispelled conjectures complicate the understanding of the paralemniscal pathway. It was proposed that the paralemniscal pathway conveys information about whisking kinematics (Yu et al., 2006). However, subsequent studies found that encoding of whisking along the paralemniscal pathway is relatively poor (Moore et al., 2015; Urbain et al., 2015). It was also proposed that the paralemniscal pathway is specifically activated upon noxious stimulation (Masri et al., 2009; Frangeul et al., 2014). Yet, it has never been shown that trigeminal interpolaris cells that respond to vibrissa deflection are also activated by noxious stimuli. Lastly, a recurring notion is that vibrissa input to the dysgranular regions of the vS1 cortex process paralemniscal inputs. Although this proposal is inconsistent with the observation that the response of Po neurons to vibrissa deflection lags that of septal cells (Armstrong-James and Fox, 1987; Diamond et al., 1992; Brumberg et al., 1999), it has lingered in the literature for want of a better explanation.

A novel perspective on the function of the paralemniscal pathway was recently obtained on the basis of a virus-based tract-tracing study (Elbaz et al., 2022). We observed that SpVIr cells that project to the Po thalamus also innervate a number of regions involved in the control of autonomic functions and in the facial expression of emotional reactions. This suggests that the paralemniscal pathway is not involved in sensory processing per se but in signaling the valence of orofacial inputs and the triggering of adaptive behavioral reactions (Elbaz et al., 2022).

Are there other trigeminothalamic pathways? A thalamic projection from the oralis subnucleus of the trigeminal complex (SpVO) arises from large cells with multivibrissa receptive fields (Jacquin and Rhoades, 1990; Veinante et al., 2000). It is the least abundant trigeminothalamic projection and also the least studied. It terminates in the most posterior part of the thalamus, right in front of the pretectum, and also in a caudal thalamic region, intercalated between the pretectum and the medial geniculate nucleus. These thalamic regions are known to receive multisensory inputs (i.e., somatic, visceral, nociceptive, auditory) and to project to the perirhinal cortex, striatum, and amygdala (Groenewegen and Witter, 2004). Neurons in subnucleus oralis also provide a substantial projection to the superior colliculus. Although electrophysiological data are not yet available, we deem it likely that the subnucleus oralis projection constitutes a pathway to associate multiple sensory inputs and forward this information to the amygdala and limbic cortical areas involved in emotional reactions.

The caudalis subnucleus of the spinal trigeminal complex (SpVC) contains both mono- and multivibrissa-responsive cells (Renehan et al., 1986). Yet there is no evidence to date that these cells project to the thalamus.

Inhibitory Control of Thalamic Relay Cells

The VPM and Po thalamus in rodents do not contain local-circuit GABAergic cells. Inhibitory inputs arise from three sources: the reticular thalamic nucleus (RTn), the ZIv, and the anterior pretectal nucleus (Barthó et al., 2002; Bokor et al., 2005). Individual RTn cells receive input from thalamic relay cells and from layer 6 corticothalamic cells. Individual nRT cells project to specific sectors of the VPM and Po thalamus that relay vibrissa information from the lemniscal, extralemniscal, and paralemniscal pathways (Pinault et al., 1995). Although RTn terminals distribute over the distal half of the dendritic trees in both the VPM and the Po, incertal and pretectal axons make large synaptic contacts on the soma and proximal dendrites of Po cells.

Organization of Corticothalamic Pathways

Corticothalamic inputs arise from cortical layers 5 and 6. In the vibrissa system of rodents, the projection emanating from layer 5 cells is a collateral projection from long-range axons that project to the brainstem. These axons do not supply branches to the thalamic reticular nucleus or to neurons in the VPM thalamus. Rather, they arise from layer 5b in the vS1 cortex and project exclusively to the Po thalamus, where they make large synaptic contacts with the proximal dendrites of relay neurons. In contrast, layer 6 corticothalamic cells project to both the VPM and the Po thalamus (Bourassa et al., 1995; Killackey and Sherman, 2003). Those projecting to the VPM thalamus are located in the upper part of layer 6 (i.e., layer 6a), across the granular and dysgranular zones of the vS1 cortex. Those projecting to the Po thalamus reside in the lower part of layer 6 (i.e., layer 6b), across the granular and dysgranular zones of the S1 cortex, and in layer 6a of the dysgranular zone of the S1 cortex. In addition, the Po thalamus and the head of the barreloids receive corticothalamic input from layer 6 of the vibrissa motor cortex (Urbain and Deschênes, 2007). All layer 6 corticothalamic axons give off collaterals in the thalamic reticular nucleus and profusely innervate the distal dendrites of thalamic relay cells.

It is often said that the corticothalamic projections are organized in a manner that reciprocates the spatial distribution of thalamocortical pathways. Yet, over the years, some inconsistencies have been reported between the principle of reciprocity and the actual organization of corticothalamic projections. For instance, layer 6 cells of the vibrissa motor cortex innervate both the Po thalamus and the dorsal aspect of the thalamic barreloids (Urbain and Deschênes, 2007). Yet, there is no evidence that barreloid cells project to the motor cortex. Also, the vibrissa motor and premotor cortices project bilaterally in the thalamus, although these projections have not been shown to be matched by bilateral thalamocortical projections (Deschênes et al., 1998; Alloway et al., 2008). In view of these exceptions, it was proposed that the organization of corticothalamic connections complies with a more fundamental rule, called the *rule of parity* (Deschênes et al., 1998). This rule states that the distribution of layer 6 corticothalamic projections reciprocates the branching patterns of prethalamic afferents.

Corticothalamic axons make loops with the thalamocortical fibers. Yet, which elements in a loop act as the feedback as opposed to the feedforward path is largely a matter of viewpoint. It is reasonable to consider corticothalamic pathways as the feedback pathways in situations where sensory stimuli are delivered to a head-restrained or an anesthetized animal (Kleinfeld et al., 2002). Yet when animals search for specific stimuli, such as when foraging, the inverse viewpoint likely prevails as cortical activity models the desired stimulus and the corticothalamic pathway projects this pattern to the thalamus. The rule of parity considers the thalamus in terms of comparing the desired and stimulus-generated input, a viewpoint that is in line with psychophysical and behavioral evidence that perception is an active process intimately linked to the motor activities of the animal. A comprehensive exposé of this rule and its functional implications is found in the review by Deschênes et al. (1998).

Microvibrissae

The rat's microvibrissa somatosensory system is characterized by a vibrissa density that is about 40 times greater than that of the mystacial macrovibrissae (Brecht et al., 1997). The large expanse of the cortex devoted to representation of the microvibrissae points to the ethological importance of this fine-grained tactile system, which remains largely unexplored. We know of no systematic study that examined the encoding of signals from the microvibrissae in the brainstem and thalamus.

Video analysis shows that when a rat contacts an unexpected object with its macrovibrissae, it orients its nose to the nearest contact and dabs against the object with its microvibrissae at a rate of about 8 Hz (Grant et al., 2012; Parmiani et al., 2018). This rhythmic tactile sampling is phase-locked to sniffing and movement of the nose (Kurnikova et al., 2017). It was suggested that the microvibrissae are critically involved in object recognition and texture discrimination but are not essential for spatial tasks (Brecht et al., 1997). The robust and reliable encoding of differences in object textures by microvibrissa-responsive neurons in the barrel cortex supports this proposal (Kuruppath et al., 2014).

Functional Representation in Barrelettes, Barreloids, and Barrels

Neuronal receptive fields for touch within PrV barrelettes, VPM barreloids, and cortical barrels are dominated by a single principal vibrissa. What kinematic features are mapped by analogy with space-time patterns along pathways in the visual system? It was reported that cells with similar angular preference cluster together within a barrel or a barreloid in anesthetized rodents (Bruno et al., 2003; Timofeeva et al., 2003; Andermann and Moore, 2006), but no systematic map of angular tuning has yet emerged. The use of passive vibrissa deflection in anesthetized animals represents a major limitation in these studies, particularly because angular tuning may be secondary to encoding the phase of self-motion in the whisk cycle (Curtis and Kleinfeld, 2009). Because neurons along the lemniscal pathway robustly encode both touch and rhythmic whisking (Moore et al., 2015; Urbain et al., 2015), the whisking phase and vibrissa set point may be key parameters to consider. Inroads on the encoding of touch (de Kock et al., 2021; Brown et al., 2021; Harrell et al., 2021; Isett et al., 2009; Jadhav et al., 2009; O'Connor, Clack, et al., 2010; O'Connor, Perob, et al., 2010; Wolfe et al., 2008) and touch relative to self-motion (Cheung et al., 2020; Curtis and Kleinfeld, 2009; Isett and Feldman, 2020; Ranganathan et al., 2018; Severson et al., 2017; Xu, 2012), albeit not set point, have been made in the cortex. The mapping of touch kinematics and the logic of the interaction of the self-motion signal and set point represent work in progress at the level of the VPM thalamus (Liu, Yao, et al., 2019). Results obtained by means of advanced two-photon microscopy to image thalamocortical axons within a barrel (Liu et al., 2019) suggest that the phase in the whisk cycle is nominally mapped within a barrel, consistent with past studies on orientation preference (Furuta et al., 2011).

Open Questions and Missing Data

In the present review, we pointed out several anatomical and physiological issues that remain unanswered concerning the transmission of signals to and through thalamic nuclei in the vibrissa system (Figure 1). Until recently, most research has focused on the thalamus and cortex, with little attention paid to the brainstem trigeminal subnuclei that give rise to the ascending pathways. These subnuclei are richly interconnected and contain inhibitory circuits that operate both pre- and postsynaptically (Furuta et al., 2008; Bae and Yoshida, 2011). Although experimental studies of sensory processes in brainstem trigeminal nuclei are technically challenging, they are critical to understanding the role of the vibrissa system in rodents' behavior.

It is worth reminding that vibrissae are very sensitive organs. Without sensory filtering at the very first relay stations, the ascending pathways of vibrissa information would be overdriven. This could have disastrous consequences not only on sensory discriminative performance but also on the overall level of emotional stress of the animal. In this regard, we recall that sensory trigeminal nuclei receive inhibitory input from the Kölliker–Fuse nucleus (Geerling et al., 2017), an upper brainstem region involved in the control of autonomic reactions. The inhibitory connections from the Kölliker–Fuse nucleus may well gate sensory responses (Elbaz et al., 2022).

Acknowledgments

We thank the Canadian Institutes of Health Research (grant MI-5877) and the National Institutes of Health (grants U19 NS107466 and R35 NS097265) for their support.

References

Alloway KD, Olson ML, Smith JB (2008) Contralateral corticothalamic projections from M1 whisker cortex: potential route for modulating hemispheric interactions. J. Comp. Neurol. **510**: 100–116.

Alloway KD, Smith JB, Watson GDR (2013) Thalamostriatal projections from the medial posterior and parafascicular nuclei have distinct topographic and physiologic properties. J. Neurophysiol. **111**: 36–50.

Andermann ML, Moore CI (2006) A somatotopic map of vibrissa motion direction within a barrel column. Nat. Neurosci. **9**: 543–551.

Armstrong-James M, Fox K (1987) Spatiotemporal convergence and divergence in the rat S1 "barrel" cortex. J. Comp. Neurol. **263**: 265–281.

Arsenault D, Zhang, ZW (2006) Developmental remodeling of the lemniscal synapse in the ventral basal thalamus of the mouse. J. Physiol. **573**: 121–132.

Bae YC, Yoshida S (2011) Ultrastructure basis for craniofacial sensory processing in the brainstem. Int. Rev. Neurobiol. **97**: 99–141.

Barthó P, Freund TF, Acsády L (2002) Selective GABAergic innervation of thalamic nuclei from zona incerta. Eur. J. Neurosci. **16**: 999–1014.

Bokor H, Acsády L, Deschênes M (2008) Vibrissal responses of thalamic cells that project to the septal columns of the barrel cortex and to the second somatosensory area. J. Neurosci. **28**: 5169–5177.

Bokor H, Frère SGA, Eyre MD, Slézia A, Ulbert I, Luthi A, Acsady L (2005) Selective GABAergic control of higher thalamic relays. Neuron **45**: 929–940.

Bourassa J, Pinault D, Deschênes M (1995) Corticothalamic projections from the cortical barrel field to the somatosensory thalamus in rats: a single-fibre study using biocytin as an anterograde tracer. Eur. J. Neurosci. **7**: 19–30.

Brecht M, Preilowski B, Merzenich MM (1997) Functional architecture of the mystacial vibrissae. Behav. Brain Res. **84**: 81–97.

Brown J, Oldenburg IA, Telia GI, Griffin S, Voges M, Jain V, Adesnik H (2021) Spatial integration during active tactile sensation drives orientation perception. Neuron. **107**: 1707–1720.

Brumberg JC, Pinto, DJ, Simons, DJ (1999) Cortical columnar processing in the rat whisker-to-barrel system. J. Neurophysiol. **82**: 1808–1817.

Bruno RM, Khatri V, Land PW, Simons DJ (2003) Thalamocortical angular tuning domains within individual barrels of rat somatosensory cortex. J. Neurosci. **23**: 9565–9574.

Castro-Alamancos MA (2002). Properties of primary sensory (lemniscal) synapses in the ventrobasal thalamus and the relay of high-frequency sensory inputs. J. Neurophysiol. **87**: 946–953.

Cheung JA, Maire P, Kim J, Lee K, Flynn G, Hires SA (2020) Independent representations of self-motion and object location in barrel cortex output. PLoS Biol. **8**: e3000882.

Curtis JC, Kleinfeld D (2009) Phase to rate transformations encode touch in cortical neurons of a scanning sensorimotor system. Nat. Neurosci. **12**: 492–501.

de Kock CPJ, Pie J, Pieneman AW, Mease RA, Bast A, Guest JM, Oberlaender M Huibert D, Mansvelder HD, Sakmann B (2021) High-frequency burst spiking in layer 5 thick-tufted pyramids of rat primary somatosensory cortex encodes exploratory touch. Commun. Biol. **4**: 709.

Deschênes M, Timofeeva E, Lavallée, P (2003) The relay of high-frequency signals in the whisker-to-barrel pathway. J. Neurosci. **23**: 6778–6787.

Deschênes M, Urbain N (2016) Vibrissal afferents from trigeminus to cortices. In TJ Prescott et al. (eds), Scholarpedia of touch, Atlantis Press, pp. 657–672.

Deschênes M, Veinante P, Zhang ZW (1998) The organization of corticothalamic projections: reciprocity versus parity. Brain Res. Rev. **28**: 286–308.

Diamond ME, Armstrong-James M, Budway MJ, Ebner, FF (1992) Somatic sensory responses in the rostral sector of the posterior group (POm) and in the ventral posterior medial nucleus (VPM) of the rat thalamus: Dependence on the barrel field cortex. J. Comp. Neurol. **319**: 66–84.

Elbaz M, Callado-Pérez A, Demers M, Foo C, Kleinfeld D, Deschênes M (2022) A vibrissa pathway that activates the limbic system. eLife. **11**: e72096.

Frangeul L, Porrero C, Garcia-Amado M, Maimone B, Maniglier M, Clascá F,

Jabaudon D (2014) Specific activation of the paralemniscal pathway during nociception. Eur. J. Neurosci. **39**: 1455–1464.

Furuta T, Deschênes M, Kaneko T (2011) Anisotropic distribution of thalamocortical boutons in barrels. J. Neurosci. **31**: 6432–6439.

Furuta T, Kaneko T, Deschênes M (2009) Septal neurons in barrel cortex derive their receptive field input from the lemniscal pathway. J. Neurosci. **29**: 4089–4095.

Furuta T, Timofeeva E, Nakamura K, Okamoto-Furuta K, Togo M, Kaneko T, Deschênes M (2008) Inhibitory gating of vibrissal inputs in the brainstem. J. Neurosci. **28**: 1789–1797.

Geerling JC, Yokota S, Rikhadze I, Roe D, Chamberlin NL (2017) Kölliker-Fuse GABAergic and glutamatergic neurons project to distinct targets. J. Comp. Neurol. **525**: 1844–1860.

Grant RA, Sperber AL, Prescott TJ (2012) The role of orienting in vibrissal touch sensing. Front. Behav. Neurosci. **6**: 39. doi.org/10.3389/fnbeh.2012.00039.

Groenewegen HJ, Witter MP (2004) Thalamus. In G Paxinos (ed), The rat nervous system, 3rd edition, Academic Press, pp. 407–453.

Haidarliu S, Ahissar, E (2001) Size gradients of barreloids in the rat thalamus. J. Comp. Neurol. **429**: 372–387.

Haidarliu S, Simony E, Golomb D, Ahissar E (2010) Muscle architecture in the mystacial pad of the rat. Anat. Rec. **293**: 1192–1206.

Harrell ER, Renard A, Bathellier B (2021) Fast cortical dynamics encode tactile grating orientation during active touch. Sci. Adv. **7**. doi.org/10.1126/sciadv.abf7096.

Henderson, TA, Jacquin, MF (1995) What makes subcortical barrels? In EG Jones and IT Diamond (eds), Cerebral Cortex, the Barrel Cortex of Rodents, Vol. **11**, Plenum, pp. 123–187.

Isett, BR, Feasel, SH, Lane, MA, Feldman, DE (2018) Slip-based coding of local shape and texture in mouse S1. Neuron. **97**: 418–433.

Isett BR, Feldman DE (2020) Cortical coding of whisking phase during surface whisking. Curr. Biol. **30**: 3065–3074.

Ito M (1988) Response properties and topography of vibrissa-sensitive VPM neurons in the rat. J. Neurophysiol. **60**: 1181–1197.

Jacquin MF, Rhoades RW (1990) Cell structure and response properties in the trigeminal subnucleus oralis. Somatosens. Mot. Res. **7**: 265–288.

Jadhav SP, Wolfe J, Feldman DE (2009) Sparse temporal coding of elementary tactile features during active whisker sensation. Nat. Neurosci. **12**: 792–800.

Killackey HP, Sherman SM (2003) Corticothalamic projections from the rat primary somatosensory cortex. J. Neurosci. **23**: 7381–7384.

Kleinfeld D, Deschênes M (2011) Neuronal basis for object location in the vibrissa scanning sensorimotor system. Neuron **72**: 455–468.

Kleinfeld D, Sachdev RNS, Merchant LM, Jarvis MR, Ebner FF (2002) Adaptive filtering of vibrissa input in motor cortex of rat. Neuron **34**:1021–1034.

Knutsen PM, Pietr M, Ahissar E (2006) Haptic object localization in the vibrissal system: behavior and performance. J. Neurosci. **26**: 8451–8464.

Kurnikova A, Moore JD, Liao S-M, Deschênes M, Kleinfeld D (2017) Coordination of orofacial motor actions into exploratory behavior by rat. Curr. Biol. **27**: 688–696.

Kuruppath P, Gugig E, Azouz R (2014) Microvibrissae-based texture discrimination. J. Neurosci. **34**: 5115–5120.

Lavallée P, Urbain N, Dufresne C, Bokor H, Acsády L, Deschênes M (2005) Feedforward inhibitory control of sensory information in higher-order thalamic nuclei. J. Neurosci. **25**: 7489–7498.

Liu R, Li Z, Marvin JS, Kleinfeld D (2019) Direct wavefront sensing enables functional imaging of infragranular axons and spines. Nat. Meth. **16**: 615–618.

Liu R, Yao P, Deschênes M, Kleinfeld D (2019) Deep layer cortical circuits underlying active sensing revealed by two-photon adaptive optical imaging. Society for Neuroscience Annual Meeting (Chicago) poster 057.06.

Lo F-S, Guigo W, Erzurumlu RS (1999) Electrophysiological properties and synaptic responses of cells in the trigeminal principal sensory nucleus of postnatal rats. J. Neurophysiol. **82**: 2765–2775.

Luo L, Callaway EM, Svoboda K (2008) Genetic dissection of neural circuits. Neuron **57**: 634–660.

Luo L, Callaway EM, Svoboda K (2018) Genetic dissection of neural circuits: a decade of progress. Neuron **98**: 256–281.

Ma PM, Woolsey TA (1984) Cytoarchitectonic correlates of the vibrissae in the medullary trigeminal complex of the mouse. Brain Res. **306**: 374–379.

Masri R, Quiton RL, Lucas JM, Murray PD, Thompson SM, Keller A (2009) Zona incerta: a role in central pain. J. Neurophysiol. 102: 181–191.

Metha SB, Kleinfeld D (2004) Frisking the whiskers: patterned sensory input in the rat vibrissa system. Neuron 41:181–184.

Metha SB, Whitmer D, Figueroa R, Williams BA, Kleinfeld D (2007) Active spatial perception in the vibrissa scanning sensorimotor system. PLoS Biol. 5: 309–322.

Minnery BS, Simons DJ (2003) Response properties of whisker-associated trigeminothalamic neurons in rat nucleus principalis. J. Neurophysiol. 89: 40–56.

Moore JD, Mercer Lindsay N, Deschênes M, Kleinfeld D (2015) Vibrissa self-motion and touch are reliably encoded along the same somatosensory pathway from brainstem through thalamus. PLoS Biol. 13: e1002253.

O'Connor DH, Clack NG, Huber D, Komiyama T, Myers EW, Svoboda K (2010) Vibrissa-based object localization in head-fixed mice. J. Neurosci. 30: 1947–1967.

O'Connor DH, Peron SP, Huber D, Svoboda K (2010) Neural activity in barrel cortex underlying vibrissa-based object localization in mice. Neuron 67: 1048–1061.

Ohno S, Kuramoto E, Furuta T, Hioki H, Tanaka Y-R, Fujiyama F, Sonomura T, Uemura M, Sugiyama K, Kaneko T (2012) A morphological analysis of thalamocortical axon fibers of rat posterior thalamic nuclei: a single neuron tracing study with viral vectors. Cereb. Cortex 22: 2840–2857.

Parmiani P, Lucchette C, Franchi G (2018) Whisker and nose tactile sense guide rat behavior in a skilled reaching task. Front. Behav. Neurosci. 12: 24. doi.org/10.3389/fnbeh.2018.00024.

Pierret T, Lavallée P, Deschênes M (2000) Parallel streams for the relay of vibrissal information through thalamic barreloids. J. Neurosci. 20: 7455–7462.

Pinault D, Bourassa J, Deschênes M (1995) The axonal arborization of single thalamic reticular neurons in the somatosensory thalamus of the rat. Eur. J. Neurosci. 7: 31–40.

Pouchelon G, Frangeul L, Rijli F-M, Jabaudon D (2012) Patterning of pre-thalamic somatosensory pathways. Eur. J. Neurosci. 35: 1533–1539.

Prescott TJ, Diamond ME, Wing AM (2011) Active touch sensing. Phil. Trans. Roy. Soc. Lond. Biol. 366: 2989–2995.

Ranganathan GN, Apostolides PF, Harnett MT, Xu N-L, Druckmann S, Magee JC (2018) Active dendritic integration and mixed neocortical network representations during an adaptive sensing behavior. Nat. Neuro. 21: 1583–1590.

Renehan WE, Jacquin MF, Mooney RD, Rhoades RW (1986) Structure-function relationships in rat medullary and cervical dorsal horns. II. Medullary dorsal horn cells. J. Neurophysiol. 55: 1187–1201.

Severson KS, Xu D, Van de Loo M, Bai L, Ginty DD, O'Connor DH (2017) Active touch and self-motion encoding by Merkel cell-associated afferents. Neuron. 94: e669.

Severson KS, Xu D, Van de Loo M, Bai L, Ginty DD, O'Connor DH (2017) Active touch and self-motion encoding by Merkel cell-associated afferents. Neuron 94: 666–676.

Sosnik R, Haidarliu S, Ahissar E (2001) Temporal frequency of whisker movement. I. Representations in brain stem and thalamus. J. Neurophysiol. 86: 339–353.

Spácek J, Lieberman AR (1974). Ultrastructure and three-dimensional organization of synaptic glomeruli in rat somatosensory thalamus. J. Anat. 117: 487–516.

Sugitani M, Yano J, Sugai T, Ooyama H (1990) Somatotopic organization and columnar structure of vibrissae representation in the rat ventrobasal complex. Exp. Brain Res. 81: 346–352.

Szwed M, Bagdasarian K, Ahissar E (2003) Coding of vibrissal active touch. Neuron 40: 621–630.

Timofeeva E, Mérette C, Emond C, Lavallée P, Deschênes M (2003) A map of angular tuning preference in thalamic barreloids. J. Neurosci. 23:10717–10723.

Trageser JC, Keller A (2004) Reducing the uncertainty: gating of peripheral inputs by zona incerta. J. Neurosci. 24: 8911–8915.

Urbain N, Deschênes M (2007) A new thalamic pathway of vibrissal information modulated by the motor cortex. J. Neurosci. 27, 12407–12412.

Urbain N, Salin PA, Libourel P-A, Comte J-C, Gentet LJ, Petersen CCH (2015) Whisking-related changes in neuronal firing and membrane potential dynamics in the somatosensory thalamus of awake mice. Cell Rep. 13: 647–656.

Van der Loos H (1976) Barreloids in the mouse somatosensory. Neurosci. Let. 2: 1–6.

Veinante P, Deschênes M (1999) Single- and multi-whisker channels in the ascending projections from the principal trigeminal nucleus in the rat. J. Neurosci. 19: 5085–5095.

Veinante P, Jacquin M, Deschênes M (2000) Thalamic projections from the whisker sensitive regions of the spinal trigeminal complex in the rat. J. Comp. Neurol. 420: 233–240.

Whiteley SJ, Knutsen PM, Matthews DM, Kleinfeld D (2015) Deflection of a vibrissa leads to a gradient of strain across mechanoreceptors in the mystacial follicle. J. Neurophysiol. 114: 138–145.

Williams MN, Zahm DS, Jacquin MF (1994) Differential foci and synaptic organization of the principal and spinal trigeminal projections to the thalamus in the rat. Eur. J. Neurosci. 6: 429–453.

Wolfe J, Hill, DN, Pahlavan S, Drew PJ, Kleinfeld D, Feldman DE (2008) Texture coding in the rat whisker system: Slip-stick versus differential resonance. PLoS Bio. doi.org/10.1371/journal.pbio.0060215.

Woolsey TA, Van der Loos H (1970) The structural organization of layer IV in the somatosensory region (SI) of mouse cerebral cortex. The description of a cortical field composed of discrete cytoarchitectonic units. Brain Res. 17: 205–242.

Xu N-L, Harnett MT, Williams SR, Huber D, O'Connor DH, Svoboda K, Magee, JC (2012) Nonlinear dendritic integration of sensory and motor input during an active sensing task. Nature 492: 247–251.

Yu C, Derdikman D, Haidarliu S, Ahissar E (2006) Parallel thalamic pathways for whisking and touch signals in the rat. PLoS Biol. 4: 819–825.

Chapter 12: Corticothalamic Pathways in the Somatosensory System

Alexander Groh and Rebecca Mease

1. Introduction

The sense of touch arises from the dynamic physical interaction between external stimuli and sensors that transduce tactile stimuli into neural signals. Palpating fingers bounce across and catch on textures and deform soft materials in expected or surprising ways, and these stimulus–sensor interactions provide important information about the external world. Exquisite sensorimotor control of this system allows the same hands to craft a sculpture and recognize the curve of a loved one's cheek. These wide-ranging abilities arise from interactions between the details of the external world and internal representations of expectation arising from bodily movements and attention to relevant details. The brain's internal model guides actions and exploration, but to maintain behavioral flexibility, this model must be updated by the integration of novel, relevant external data. Solving this problem requires the ongoing integration of top-down cortical representations with "bottom-up" sensory stimuli in the thalamus.

In this chapter, we summarize how "top-down" streams of information from the cortex converge in and influence the thalamus in the somatosensory system. In addition to cortical inputs, somatosensory nuclei receive peripheral sensory information via parallel brainstem and spinothalamic tract pathways (see Chapter 2 in this volume). As a consequence of this convergence, the thalamus serves as an integrative hub for external and internal signals, which is a central feature for emerging theories of "closed-loop" perception (Ahissar & Assa, 2016), in which the cumulative acquisition of sensory signals is under active control and continually guided by the internal state. This framework suggests that perception is a process of iterative convergence, in which perceptual acuity gradually reaches an asymptotic maximum during the cyclical interplay between the nervous system and a sensory organ's dynamic report of the external world.

The mammalian sensory cortex connects to its associated thalamic structures via corticothalamic pathways, originating exclusively from the deepest cortical layers 5 and 6. These numerous cortical "feedback" inputs to the thalamus have been known since the time of Cajal (1906) and outnumber feedforward "sensory" inputs, such as those from the brainstem, by at least a factor of three (Sherman, 2001a). Although this anatomical scheme is common to many animals and sensory systems (Rouiller & Welker, 2000), the functions of these "feedback" pathways are only recently becoming understood in the context of sensory processing and cognitive tasks. Figure 1 presents an overview of the circuits discussed in this chapter, using the rodent primary somatosensory cortex (S1) as a model.

Studies combining cell-type-specific perturbations and high-resolution measurement of cortical and thalamic activity have elucidated the functional impact of descending cortical projections on thalamic activity and associated sensorimotor function, revealing diverse roles in receptive field sharpening and sensory gating, propagation of "efference" copies, and long-range communication between cortical regions. These findings thoroughly reject the historical view of the thalamus as a simple relay of ascending information from the sensory periphery to the cortex, demonstrating that thalamic spiking is strongly modulated and even driven by cortical signals and thus subject to strong, state-dependent control. Indeed, it is our view that the "feedforward" versus "feedback" dichotomy quickly becomes problematic beyond small local circuits or primary thalamic nuclei, and in the context of understanding thalamocortical signal processing, a strict hierarchical view of information flow from the periphery to the thalamus to cortex has more limitations than advantages.

In the following sections, we give a preview of useful terminology, concepts, and themes presented throughout the remaining sections of the chapter (Sections 2–4).

1.1 Cell-Type–Specific Cortical Innervation Patterns Define Higher- and First-Order Thalamic Nuclei

The somatosensory thalamus receives two discrete channels of corticothalamic input from distinct populations in the two deepest layers of the cortex (Figure 1), layer 6 (L6) and layer 5 (L5), each with distinct synaptic and connectivity properties (Figure 2). Here, we follow the terminology of Shepherd (2013), referring to input from L6 as "corticothalamic" (CT), to highlight that L6 cortical outputs are mostly restricted to the thalamus. In contrast, the L5 pyramidal tract (PT) targets the thalamus but also sends cortical information to other diverse subcortical structures, such as the striatum, pons, spinal cord, brainstem, and superior colliculus. Thus, whereas L6 circuits are local to the thalamocortical system, the L5–thalamus pathway is one branch of a larger L5–subcortical system. A particular point of contrast is synaptic strength: L6's weak but numerous "modulatory" synapses target all thalamic nuclei, whereas L5 inputs to the thalamus are restricted to higher-order regions and display "driver" functional properties typically seen in sensory

Sensory Processing

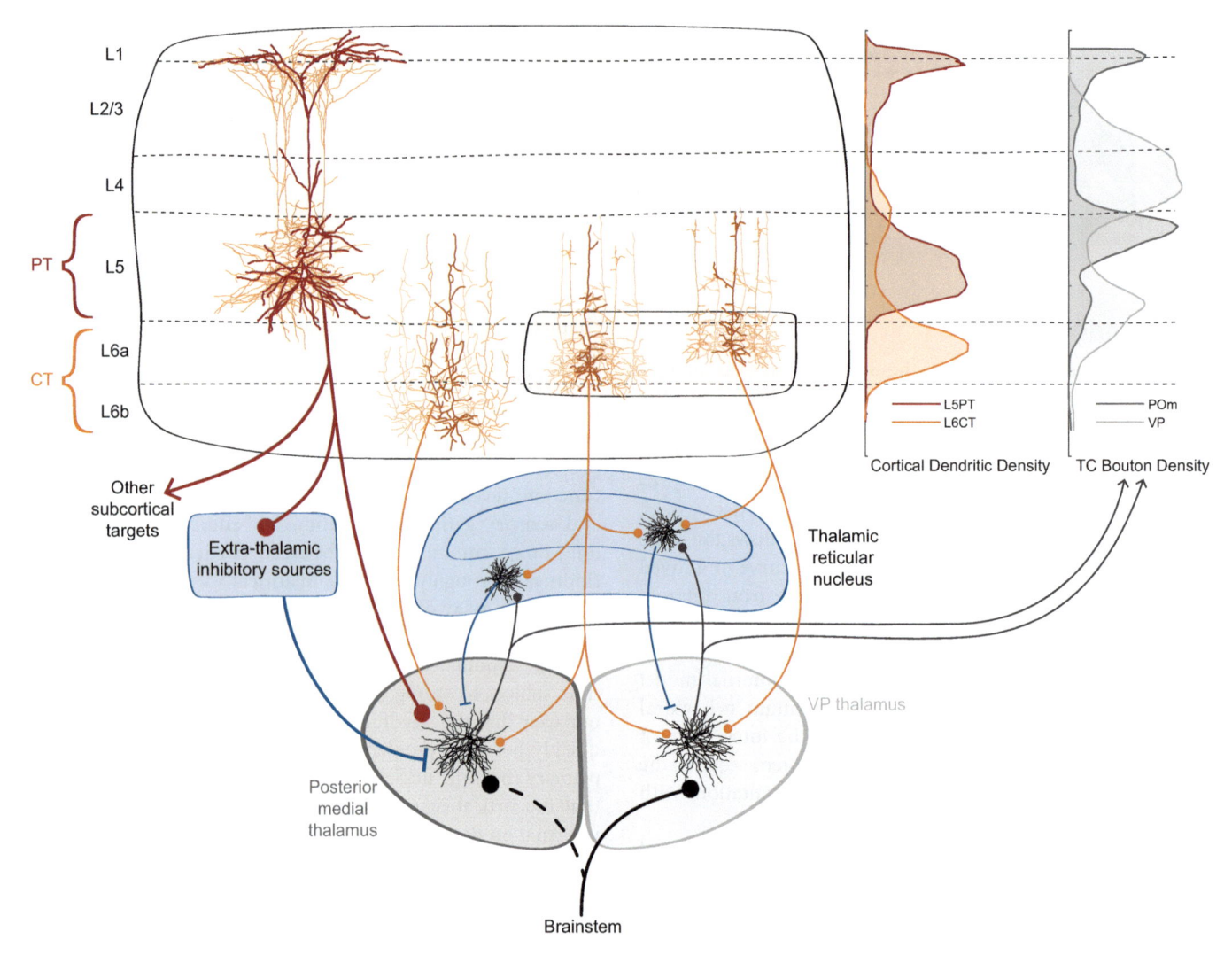

Figure 1 Schematic of the major corticothalamic pathways connecting the S1 barrel cortex to the somatosensory (ventral posterior [VP] and posterior medial [POm]) thalamus in rodents.

Excitatory connections shown as filled circles; inhibitory synapses as bars. Pyramidal tract projections (*red*): PT L5 neurons in L5B (*red*) target the POm, extrathalamic inhibitory (ETI) nuclei, and other subcortical regions. ETI nuclei (*blue*) provide strong inhibition to the POm. Corticothalamic projections (*orange*): Three populations in L6 project to the thalamus, with thalamic projection targets changing as a function of depth: upper L6A targets the VP and thalamic reticular nucleus (TRN), lower L6A targets the VP/POm and TRN. L6A CT neurons are arranging in "infrabarrels" (*rectangle*). L6B targets only the POm and does not make collaterals in the TRN. The inhibitory TRN is also engaged in specific intrathalamic loops with relay nuclei, with shell and core TRN neurons connected with the POm and VP, respectively. Upper right panels show PT and CT cortical dendritic density (*left*) and POm and VP thalamocortical bouton densities (*right*) as a function of cortical layer.

afferents (Sherman & Guillery, 1998, 2006; see Chapter 4 in this volume). These L5 driver synapses can robustly relay cortical signals via few but strong giant synapses. Thus, although the CT and PT pathways have some superficially analogous features – particularly engagement of feedforward inhibition (Figure 1) – they in fact differ in almost all properties characterized to date and have divergent structure, function, and evolutionary history.

Indeed, the different properties of the CT and PT pathways are the main criteria in the influential first-order/higher-order categorization scheme for thalamic nuclei proposed by Sherman and colleagues, defining thalamic nuclei according to their sources of "driving" (i.e., spike-evoking) input (Figure 1): higher-order (HO) thalamic nuclei receive both L6 CT and L5 PT inputs and are driven by PT inputs, whereas first-order (FO) nuclei are driven by ascending sensory input of subcortical origin and receive cortical input solely from L6 CT (Sherman, 2007). The HO-versus-FO distinction is convenient for this particular chapter; however, we emphasize that other useful and overlapping ontologies exist for understanding thalamocortical systems based on different criteria, such as thalamocortical projection patterns (Hanbery & Jasper, 1953) or molecular architecture (Phillips et al., 2019). For example, the cortical input-based FO and HO categories broadly align with the core/matrix and specific/nonspecific schemes (Jones, 1998). In general terms, FO nuclei propagate peripheral signals via anatomically confined thalamocortical projections, whereas HO nuclei are largely controlled by driving PT inputs and broadly distribute these signals to different cortical regions (see Chapter 3 in this volume).

As a well-characterized model of somatosensation, the rodent somatosensory system has proven a useful framework for

VP Relay Neuron   **POm Relay Neuron**

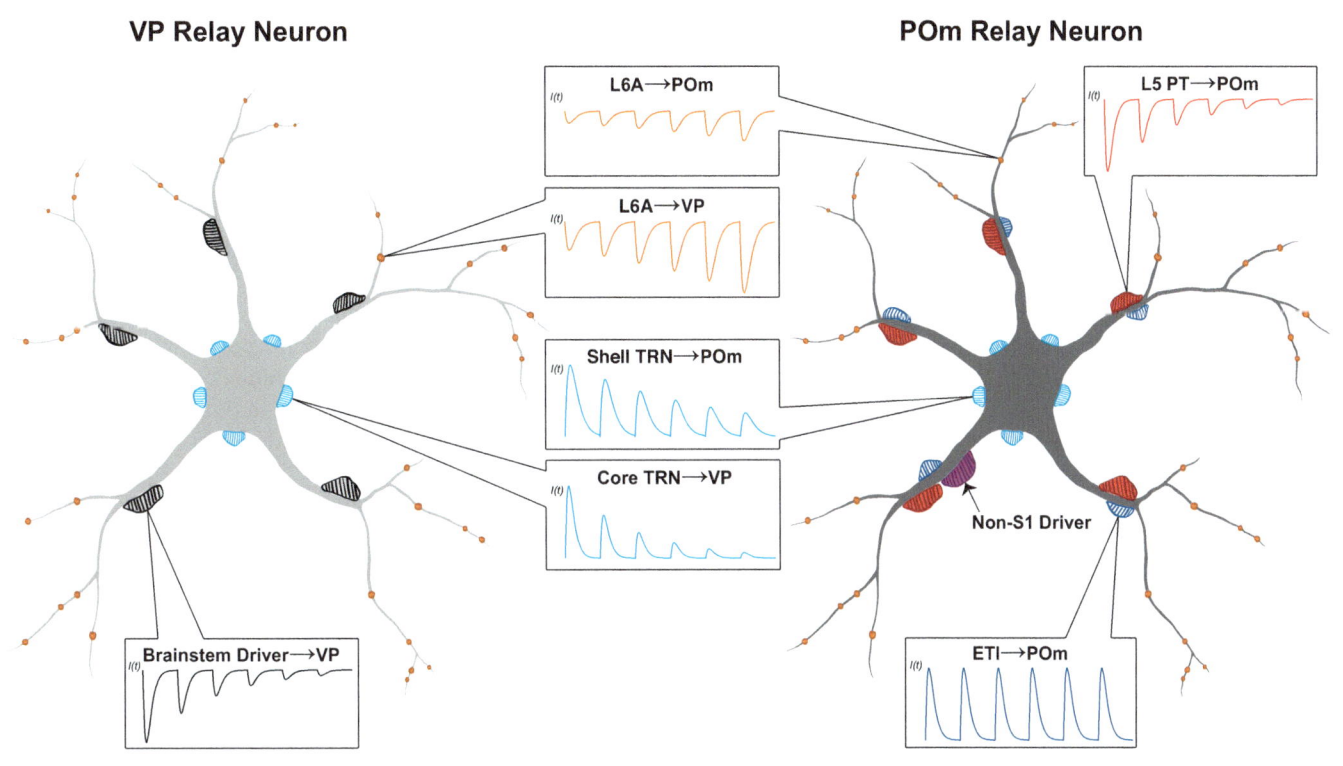

Figure 2 Locations and properties of synaptic inputs to relay neurons of the rodent somatosensory thalamus.

Call-outs show cartoons of short-erm synaptic dynamics (synaptic current vs. time) for repetitive stimulation. Both first-order VP (*left*) and higher-order POm (*right*) neurons receive CT input from S1 L6A via numerous small, excitatory synapses (*orange*), which target distal dendrites and show synaptic facilitation. Likewise, neurons of both regions receive TRN (*light blue*) input predominantly targeting the soma; synaptic dynamics are target specific. Following the first-order/higher-order framework, the VP and POm receive sparse excitatory driver inputs from, respectively, the brainstem (*black*) or S1 L5 PT (*red*); these powerful driver synapses show strong synaptic depression and target proximal dendrites. Some convergence regions of the POm integrate S1 L5 PT driver inputs with additional driver inputs (*magenta*) from, for example, M1, S2, the brainstem, and the cerebellum. The POm (but not the VP) also receives strong, non-depressing inhibitory input (*dark blue*) from extrathalamic inhibitory regions (e.g., zona incerta [ZI] or anterior pretectum [APT]), typically collocated with excitatory drivers on branch points of proximal dendrites.

understanding CT pathways and is the basis for most of this chapter's contents. In the somatosensory system, the two FO nuclei are ventroposteriolateral (VPL; body-related) and ventroposteriormedial (VPm; whisker-related) thalamus, together comprising the ventral posterior nucleus (VP) (Figure 1). The HO nucleus is the posterior medial (POm) thalamus, with both whisker- and non-whisker somatosensory regions (Diamond et al., 1992). Here, we largely focus on CT and PT projections from the primary somatosensory cortex (S1), which includes the barrel cortex (BC) (Figure 1). The understanding of the analogous circuits in non-rodent species is less complete, but we note that general corticothalamic organization seems to be conserved across species and modalities, with large and small terminals originating from L5 and L6, respectively (Rouiller & Welker, 2000).

1.2 Corticothalamocortical Loops: Closed or Open?

Neurons in the thalamus project back to the cortex, thereby forming corticothalamocortical (CTC) circuits with distinct HO and FO thalamocortical innervation patterns (Figure 1). Whereas the cortical projections of the VP are confined to S1, the POm's projections range widely, including S1, the secondary somatosensory cortex (S2), the motor cortex (M1), and other frontal areas (Clascá et al., 2016; Deschênes et al., 1998; Ohno et al., 2012). There are also clear differences in layer specificity: in the primary whisker system, POm TC afferents target L1 and L5 in the BC, interdigitating with VPm TC afferents, which mainly target L4 (Bruno et al., 2010; K. D. Harris & Shepherd, 2015). Consequent to these different connectivity patterns, there is emerging consensus that HO and FO nuclei and associated CTC circuits have very different information processing functions. However, the combination of cortical drive and widespread projections has made the HO thalamus less accessible to straightforward sensory physiology techniques involving experimental control of incoming sensory input.

To what degree CTC loops are "closed" or "open" is a useful framework within which to consider CTC information processing, as well as a topic of current research (Shepherd & Yamawaki, 2021). This distinction is typically based on connectivity between regions rather than between single neurons, but advances in high-spatial-resolution circuit mapping will likely sharpen our understanding of CTC circuit motifs in the future. In "closed" loops, CTC connections are reciprocal or recurrent, in that a thalamic region, targeted by a given cortical region, re-innervates the same cortical region, for example, S1–POm–S1. This architecture is found in both L5 and L6 CTC circuits and supports reverberating activity in the form of oscillations and short-term memory. Such recurrent information exchange between the cortex and sensory thalamic nuclei allows the integration of external signals with internal representation and can thereby provide a possible neuronal basis for context-dependent sensory processing. However, we are still learning to what extent sensory representations are affected by prior learning through recurrent loops.

In contrast, "open-loop" connectivity, which is often found in L5 CTC circuits, supports information transfer from one cortical region to another via thalamic connections, in parallel to ongoing cortico-cortico communication. Such "transthalamic" communication is based on the anatomical and functional input–output properties of open HO loops and suggests that HO nuclei can serve as communication routes between different cortical areas (Guillery, 1995). On the systems and behavioral levels, such open-loop CTC functions implicated in long-range communication between different brain areas are promising targets to better understand the network mechanisms underlying sensorimotor transformations, sensory perception, and cognition (Wolff et al., 2020).

1.3 Inhibitory Control via Somatosensory Corticothalamic Pathways

A final important theme is how the excitatory L6 CT and L5 PT pathways engage parallel inhibitory control of thalamic targets. This question is of particular importance in the somatosensory system because, in contrast to other sensory modalities, somatosensory relay nuclei in rodents contain very few (0–4%) local inhibitory interneurons (Arcelli et al., 1997; R. M. Harris & Hendrickson, 1987). Instead, inhibition of the somatosensory thalamus originates almost exclusively from distinct GABAergic nuclei, which are differently engaged by L5 PT and L6 CT (Halassa & Acsády, 2016). L6 targets the thalamic reticular nucleus (TRN), which in turn inhibits HO and FO nuclei (Pinault, 2004). L5 PT targets extrathalamic inhibitory (ETI) nuclei, which provide powerful inhibition exclusively to the POm. ETI sources comprise several inhibitory nuclei, of which the zona incerta (ZI) and the anterior pretectum (APT) are of particular interest for this chapter because they also receive cortical output from L5 PT (Bartho et al., 2007; Cadusseau & Roger, 1991; Foster et al., 1989; Sumser et al., 2017). Thus, S1 controls thalamic inhibition via two distinct corticothalamic circuits: L5–ETI–HO and L6–TRN–FO/HO. Both TRN and ETIs are engaged by subcortical cholinergic/modulatory circuits, further suggesting integration of cortical signals and lower-level arousal signals (see Chapter 2 in this volume).

For the remainder of the chapter, we discuss the connectivity and functional (synaptic, single-cell) properties of the L6 CT (Section 2) and L5 PT (Section 3) pathways. We close with a discussion of network-level information processing (Section 4).

2. Corticothalamic Pathways from Layer 6 of S1: Weak, Convergent, and Local

2.1 Layer 6: A Cortical Layer with Increasingly Known Function

Referred to as the "cortical layer with no known function" by Ray Guillery (Colello et al., 2018), intense research interest in this deepest layer of the cortex has revealed an increasingly sophisticated role for L6 in both cortical and thalamic information processing. In the rat whisker cortex, a full 25% of neurons in a column are in L6; indeed, out of all layers, L6 contains the largest number of neurons, followed closely by L4 (Meyer et al., 2010). This large cortical population is quite diverse, comprising heterogeneous neurons that participate in distinct local cortical and long-range cortical and thalamocortical circuits. Three major classes of excitatory L6 neurons have been distinguished to date: cortico-cortico, claustrum-projecting (Rouiller & Welker, 2000), and corticothalamic (CT) (Thomson, 2010). Furthermore, there is a functional and molecular division between the upper and lower L6A and L6B (deepest).

In the somatosensory thalamus, the VP, POm, and TRN receive CT input from L6A, with CT target specificity changing as a function of laminar depth (Figure 1). The upper L6A contains VPm-projecting CT neurons with developed apical tufts and axon collaterals terminating in L4. In contrast, CT neurons in the lower L6A project to both the VP and POm and have less developed apical tufts, with axon collaterals in L5A (Z. W. Zhang & Deschênes, 1997). In the whisker system, L6 CT projections are topographic, with a high degree of somatotopy in the FO thalamus, in that each barrel in BC projects largely to the corresponding barreloid in the VPm. A somatotopic organization of L6 CT projections to the POm is also evident, even though barreloid-analogous structures have not been described for the POm (Alloway et al., 2003; Bourassa et al., 1995; Hoogland et al., 1987).

L6A has a distinct columnar cytoarchitecture in the form of infrabarrels (Figure 1), precisely aligned with barrels in L4; each infrabarrel consists of a core of CT neurons surrounded by cortico-cortical (CC) neurons located in the septae. CT neurons receive weak input only from the VPm, whereas CC neurons receive strong input from the VPm and weak input from the POm (Crandall et al., 2017). L6A can be further subdivided into upper and lower lamina, with distinct subcircuits with different CT thalamic connectivity and engagement of distinct cortical inhibitory networks. L6A has CT and CC neurons in the upper and lower L6A (Frandolig et al., 2019) and shows varied dendritic morphologies, including a majority of short-tufted pyramidal neurons, along with inverted and spiny bipolar morphologies (Z. W. Zhang & Deschênes, 1997). VPm-/POm-projecting CT neurons in the lower L6A activate local inhibitory neurons, whereas VPm-projecting CT neurons in the upper L6A activate intralaminar (layers 1–6) inhibitory neurons. Thus, CT output specific to the VPm is paired with general inhibition of the cortical column, whereas CT output to the POm does not seem to be paired with cortical modulation (Ansorge et al., 2020; Frandolig et al., 2019).

The most recently described CT projection neurons are those in L6B (Figure 1); this layer is driven by long-range intracortical neurons and is responsive to wake-promoting orexin/hypocretin and thus may be involved in the coordination of brain states (Zolnik et al., 2020). In contrast to L6A CT projections targeting both the FO and HO thalamus

(Z. W. Zhang & Deschênes, 1997), CT neurons in L6B project exclusively to the POm (Hoerder-Suabedissen et al., 2018; Killackey & Sherman, 2003), with prominent apical dendrites terminating in L4 and no axon branching within the cortex. In contrast to CT innervation by L6A, these neurons do not send collaterals to the TRN. Thus, functionally, L6B seems to have no direct effect on cortical dynamics and a purely excitatory function in the POm (Ansorge et al., 2020). Although topography has not been explicitly demonstrated for L6B, it is likely to be similar to that of L6A because L6B was previously not differentiated from L6A in earlier experiments, and deviations have not been reported.

2.2 Synaptic Properties of L6 CT Pathways

The direct L6A–CT pathway forms numerous rod-like synapses with the distal dendrites of TC cells (Figure 2), with small (~0.6-μm diameter) varicosities providing weak excitatory input. These stereotypically modulatory L6–TC synapses are glutamatergic, activating both ionotropic and metabotropic glutamate receptors (iGluR and mGluR-I) in both the VPm and POm (Reichova, 2004). In fact, a main classification criterion for modulatory synapses is the presence of mGluR. Nevertheless, the majority of the current is carried by iGluR (α-amino-3-hydroxy-5-methyl-4-isoxazolepropionic acid receptor [AMPAR] and N-methyl-D-aspartate receptor [NMDAR]), and mGluR currents require sustained L6 activity. Functionally, activation of mGluRs prolongs excitatory postsynaptic potentials (EPSPs) and promotes the "tonic" spiking mode via depolarization-induced inactivation of intrinsic bursting mechanisms (Sherman & Guillery, 2006).

L6A CT inputs to the POm have many of the same morphological and physiological features as in the FO thalamus (J. Li et al., 2003; Reichova, 2004) and thus are hypothesized to exert similarly "modulatory" influence over both classes of thalamic nuclei (Sherman, 2016; Sherman & Guillery, 1998). However, voltage-clamp studies show that S1 L6 inputs to the VPL thalamus are approximately five times stronger than those to the PO thalamus (K. Guo et al., 2020).

Those L6B neurons specifically targeting the HO thalamus make excitatory *en passant* synapses onto the dendrites of relay neurons. Notably, in contrast to L6A, the L6B CT neurons do not send collaterals to the TRN and thereby do not engage feedforward inhibition. As with L6A, anatomical data suggest that these synapses are small boutons (<1 μm) (Hoerder-Suabedissen et al., 2018). At present, detailed synaptic physiology is lacking, but this is likely to rapidly change given targeted cell-type-specific tools to manipulate this pathway.

2.3 Engagement of Inhibitory Networks via L6 CT Pathways

Individual L6A CT axons form excitatory synapses on TC neurons and, via collaterals, on TRN neurons, which in turn form inhibitory synapses with TC neurons. Thereby, L6A CT-spiking activity results in a combination of monosynaptic feedforward excitation (CT–TC) and disynaptic feedforward inhibition (CT–TRN–TC) of TC neurons (Figure 1). Whether the balance between excitation and inhibition acting on a TC neuron depends on the topological alignment between the L6A and TC neuron is not entirely clear. Recordings of single TC neurons show that excitation and inhibition triggered by a particular region within L6 are mostly but not entirely aligned, suggesting that most TC neurons receive direct excitation and feedforward inhibition via the TRN from the same somatotopically aligned L6 population (Lam & Sherman, 2010).

L6 corticoreticular synapses produce excitatory postsynaptic currents (EPSCs) more than twice the amplitude of those produced by L6 synapses onto TC neurons (Golshani et al., 2001), suggesting that robust feedforward inhibition of TC neurons is an integral function of CT signaling. A more detailed look reveals fine-tuning of CT feedforward inhibition. For example, inputs to TRN neurons activate both mGluR-I and II, causing depolarization and hyperpolarization, respectively (Cox & Sherman, 1999). The TRN has heterogeneous cell composition and nucleus-specific subcircuits; the outer shell of the TRN has somatostatin-expressing cells and is reciprocally connected with the POm, whereas the calbindin-expressing central core of the TRN is reciprocally connected with the VP (Y. Li et al., 2020; Martinez-Garcia et al., 2020). It is currently a matter of conjecture whether or not CT collaterals to the TRN also follow this organization; based on the general somatotopy, it seems likely.

The interplay of simultaneous excitation and inhibition determines the overall functional impact of L6 CT input in regulating thalamic excitability and thus tailors afferent TC information transfer according to descending cortical signals. As a consequence of TC neurons' rich intrinsic excitability on slow and fast timescales, various combinations of CT excitatory and TRN inhibitory inputs can have diverse effects: hyperpolarization will prime bursting and response to low-frequencies via deinactivation and activation of voltage-dependent slow currents I_T and I_H, respectively; in contrast, depolarization will promote tonic firing via inactivation of I_T as well as decreased input resistance due to potassium channel activation; finally, balanced inhibition/excitation will still produce a shunting effect and decrease input resistance while leaving voltage-dependent excitability unchanged.

2.4 Short-Term Plasticity of L6 CT Pathways

The transfer of cortical signals to the thalamus via CT pathways is controlled by pronounced synaptic short-term dynamics (Figure 2). Recent studies combining cell-type specific and/or optogenetics with patch-clamp electrophysiology have begun to delineate the properties of different synapses within the circuit. Here we focus on L6A; the more recently described L6B has yet to be characterized at the level of synaptic properties.

With the combination of direct excitation and indirect inhibition, the overall effect of L6 CT on TC activity is neither simple suppression nor simple enhancement but rather depends on the balance of these inputs, which in turn is sculpted by frequency-dependent short-term synaptic dynamics (Figure 2). Both CT–TC and CT–TRN synapses show paired-pulse facilitation, although the latter has a larger initial effect but less facilitation (Jurgens et al., 2012); in contrast, the feedback TRN–TC synapses show strong paired-pulse depression. Functionally, the impact of these two inputs on single cells was dissected using dynamic clamp in combination with optogenetics (Crandall et al., 2015), demonstrating that distinct frequency-dependent plasticity creates a scenario in which the overall balance of excitation and inhibition is tuned by stimulation frequency: low-frequency (<~5 Hz) inputs from L6 provide net inhibitory input to TC neurons, whereas high-frequency L6 CT inputs provide net excitatory input. These complex synaptic dynamics likely explain the variability seen in in vivo manipulations of this pathway when pooling findings from the somatosensory and visual systems (Kirchgessner et al., 2020; Mease et al., 2014; Spacek et al., 2021).

These short-term dynamics of the feedforward pathways are also paralleled by differences in the short-term dynamics of intrathalamic feedback inhibition initiated by FO and HO TC–TRN–TC loops. TRN exhibits a transcriptomic gradient across core (targeted by FO VP) and shell (targeted by HO POm) neuronal populations, giving rise to different synaptic and intrinsic properties that subserve discrete inhibitory circuits. Whereas VP→TRN$_{core}$ synapses have rapid kinetics and stronger depression, POm→TRN$_{shell}$ synapses have slower kinetics and depress less; these distinct synaptic properties match the intrinsic excitability of recipient TRN neurons, supporting either phasic and precise or longer-lasting feedback inhibition for FO and HO TC neurons, respectively. It is currently unknown if the dynamics of TRN–TC (depression) and CT–TRN (facilitation) synapses show a similar distinction between FO and HO regions.

2.5 Long-Term Plasticity of L6 CT Pathways

Past work has brought to light a number of critical functions of CT pathways in sensory processing, such as modulating receptive field properties, temporal precision of sensory transmission, and sensory adaptation. These functions encompass dynamic control of sensory signaling in the thalamus on relatively short timescales. In contrast, long-term plastic changes in CT circuits are rather underexplored, especially the consequences of CT long-term plasticity on thalamocortical interactions, sensory-guided behavior, and memory. Both long-term strengthening (LTP) and weakening (LTD) of L6 CT pathways have been demonstrated in different parts of the L6 CT circuitry.

Glutamatergic synapses between L6 and VPm in mice undergo LTP upon stimulation of L6 axons at 10 Hz, whereas 1-Hz stimulation reverses this effect. This form of CT LTP is caused by presynaptic mechanisms that lead to enhanced transmitter release and reduced paired-pulse facilitation (Castro-Alamancos & Calcagnotto, 1999). In addition, L6 CT synapses either express LTP through a postsynaptic, NMDA-dependent mechanism triggered by 1-Hz presynaptic stimulation and postsynaptic depolarization or express LTD by simple repetitive depolarization of VPm neurons (Hsu et al., 2010). As discussed in the following, this bidirectional plasticity of the direct L6–VPm pathway is paralleled by additional plasticity mechanisms in the indirect inhibitory L6–CT pathway.

The L6–TRN (corticoreticular) pathway undergoes NMDA-dependent LTP upon theta-like stimulation of L6 neurons, and it was suggested that the resulting strengthening of the corticoreticular synapse leads to stronger cortical feedforward suppression of the VPm (Fernandez et al., 2017). In contrast, the TRN–VPm inhibitory synapse was shown to be weakened by burst-like presynaptic stimulation (Pigeat et al., 2015). Thus, several forms of homosynaptic plasticity with opposite signs are expressed along the L6–TRN–TC pathway, but the relationship between L6 activity and the net effect of interacting plasticity mechanisms in the circuitry on the VPm/VPL is currently not known. More importantly, the consequences of these long-term plastic changes on sensory transmission as well as possible heterosynaptic plastic changes have yet to be addressed.

3. Corticothalamic Inputs from Pyramidal Tract L5 of S1: Strong, Sparse, and Fast

Layer 5 pyramidal neurons are the powerful, wide-ranging control conduit of the cortex. Aside from L6's restricted projections, only L5 neurons are known to make synapses outside of the neocortex, and based on the number of subcortical targeted areas, L5 is the major cortical output pathway in mammals. Thus, L5 can be regarded as the exit point of cortical processing by which information is routed to subcortical circuits, many of which are related to motor control, such as the superior colliculus, pons, brainstem, and spinal cord. In the somatosensory system, this output class contains upper intratelencephalic neurons (L5A), which project to the striatum and contralateral cortex, as well as PT neurons in the deeper L5B (Groh et al., 2010). PT neurons have "thick-tufted" dendrites spanning all six cortical layers and nearly the width of a column (Figure 1), making L5B the primary neuronal substrate by which cortical information is integrated and then distributed outside of the cortex. In comparison to L6A neurons, L5 PT neurons show minimal axonal branching within the cortex, suggesting a smaller direct contribution to local cortical circuit dynamics (Narayanan et al., 2015). Within the somatosensory thalamus, L5 projections target the HO nucleus POm, whereas the FO nuclei VPm and VPL receive no or little L5 inputs and are driven exclusively by the brainstem. L5 projections also target diverse extrathalamic inhibitory (ETI) regions (Figure 1), which in turn provide the HO thalamus with inhibitory inputs in addition to intrathalamic inhibition from the TRN.

3.1 Layer 5 Subcortical Target Specificity

A currently unresolved question is whether distinct L5 populations project to single targets or, rather, send collaterals to different targets, thereby providing multiple structures with the same information. Axonal reconstructions can address this issue more clearly, but because of the technical demands of this low-throughput method, data are sparse. Notably, axon reconstructions of the L5 PT tend to reveal a high degree of branching (C. Guo et al., 2017; Kita & Kita, 2012; Veinante et al., 2000). On the other hand, retrograde tracer studies seem to systematically find little branching (Akintunde & Buxton, 1992; Groh et al., 2010; Rojas-Piloni et al., 2017) and thus support projection-specific subclasses of the L5B, which also differ in their dendritic morphology and firing patterns (Rojas-Piloni et al., 2017). An unresolved technical limitation of multicolor retrograde tracing is that double labeling to identify branching relies on targeting the correctly aligned subcortical areas, which may lead to systematic underestimation of branching. The degree of L5 multiregional innervation appears to vary across species, with greater branching observed in rodents and cats (Endo et al., 1973) compared to little branching in primates (Smith et al., 2014).

Although the degree of L5 target specificity remains to be fully resolved, the emerging scenario seems to be that PT neurons generally innervate several (C. Guo et al., 2017) – but not all – subcortical areas and that PT subclasses can be defined by certain subcortical target combinations. This picture will likely evolve rapidly, given the advent of high-throughput axon reconstruction efforts – such as the Mouse Light database (http://ml-neuronbrowser.janelia.org/) – leveraging transsynaptic viral tracing and automated reconstruction tools.

3.2 Relationship between PT Pathways and POm Sectors

Multiple lines of evidence support the view of the POm as a heterogeneous nucleus, composed of different sectors defined by distinct input–output connectivity, which may provide a basis for the diverse functional roles suggested for this nucleus (e.g., Ahissar et al., 2008; Masri et al., 2009). Criteria for the division include driver sources as well as thalamocortical innervation patterns, which co-vary with POm dendritic morphology, molecular markers, and somatotopy. A study of the somatotopy of L5 PT projections from the mouse BC to POm revealed the subdivision of the posterior group of the thalamus into four subnuclei (anterior, lateral, medial, and posterior), each containing a complete whisker map, imposed by driver inputs from the cortex (Sumser et al., 2017). Focusing on the outputs of the POm, Ohno et al. (2012) proposed a gradient along the anterior–posterior POm axis, with the anterior POm preferentially targeting L5 only and posterior POm targeting L1 and L5. Both anterior and posterior POm neurons projected to various cortical areas in addition to S1, in a similar anterior–posterior-specific way, with the anterior POm targeting deeper layers only (L4/L5) and the posterior POm targeting deeper layers and L1. The subdivision of the POm was also reflected by an increase in calbindin immunoreactivity and a decrease in dendritic complexity along the anterior–posterior axis (Ohno et al., 2012).

A split into the anterior and posterior POm was also seen by El-Boustani et al. (2020), who found anatomical and functional evidence for the existence of "FO" and "HO" subregions in the POm. According to this scheme, the anterior POm acts as an FO nucleus by routing brainstem signals from brainstem nucleus Sp5i to L4 in S2, whereas the posterior POm is targeted by S1–L5 and projects back to S1 L1 and L5A. In this scheme, only the posterior part of the POm is HO, that is, receives L5B-driver input from S1 but no brainstem input. Evidence for the anterior POm as more of a brainstem recipient was also described in an earlier study (Groh et al., 2014); however, in contrast to the proposal of a pure FO sector in the POm (El-Boustani et al., 2020), the anterior sector also receives PT input from the BC and thereby acts as an anatomical and functional convergence zone, comprising roughly one-third of the POm that integrates ascending whisker and descending cortical driver signals.

Considerable diversity in convergence and reciprocity has also been observed in descending PT signals from S1 and M1. Mo and Sherman (2019) found that S1 PT neurons in the BC innervate POm neurons that project to M1, thereby forming a transthalamic sensorimotor pathway from S1 to M1 via the POm. However, this transthalamic pathway contrasts findings from the hindlimb TC system in which M1 and S1 target largely segregated, non-overlapping subregions in the POm, which are reciprocally connected to their cortical partner (K. Guo et al., 2020). It is conceivable that specific transthalamic subzones exist within the POm, in which S1 inputs target M1-projecting POm neurons. Reminiscent of the converging brainstem and S1 inputs in the POm discussed earlier, Sampathkumar et al. (2021) report that roughly half of POm neurons receive convergent driver input from both S1 and M1, although M1 input was never observed without S1 input. Although further work remains, these studies underscore the POm's importance in transmitting signals from sensory and motor regions and as a possible integrator for sensorimotor signals (Krieger & Groh, 2015).

Overall, a subregional organization of the POm can be assumed, especially along the anterior–posterior axis. Less clear is how these subdivisions of the POm are related, some of which are possibly superimposed (i.e., CT whisker maps and POm thalamocortical innervation patterns), and yet others are more difficult to reconcile with the existing data (i.e., HO vs. FO, recurrent vs. transthalamic).

3.3 Synaptic Properties of the L5–POm Pathway

How is the connectivity between L5B and the POm organized? The number of L5B neurons converging onto a single POm neuron (convergence) and the number of POm neurons innervated by one L5B neuron (divergence) can be estimated for the mouse whisker system from functional and anatomical work (Mease, Sumser, et al., 2016b; Sumser et al., 2017). Around two or three L5B neurons converge onto one POm neuron, with each L5B neuron providing around three *en passant* giant boutons, summing up to around eight giant synapses per POm neuron. Each L5B neuron innervates only up to eight POm neurons. These estimates suggest very low divergence and convergence, indicating that the L5B-to-POm pathway is sparse and highly parallelized. Strikingly, low convergence and divergence for the corticothalamic L5 pathway are also proposed for the primate (Rockland, 2019). This connectivity scheme suggests that L5 PT neurons, at least in the BC, are the origin of a subcortical signal pathway organized by "labeled lines" with mostly parallel and topographic organization, which projects the cortical whisker map to the subcortical target nuclei (Sumser et al., 2017).

As driver synapses, the L5B inputs to the POm have very different properties than the L6 CT inputs discussed in Section 3.2. Here, we summarize the synaptic properties that give the L5–POm system distinct information-processing characteristics, focusing mostly on the S1 L5–POm pathway because it is, to date, the best characterized. L5B inputs to the POm form large, sparse boutons onto proximal dendrites near branch points (Hoogland et al., 1991; Reichova, 2004; Sumser et al., 2017) (Figure 2). L5B–POm bouton sizes vary widely (2 to in excess of 10+ μm), with larger "giant" boutons containing multiple contact sites (Hoerder-Suabedissen et al., 2018) forming large glomerular structures. Anatomical evidence shows that S1 L5 inputs to the POm are among the largest inputs from this cortical region to subcortical targets (Prasad et al., 2020).

L5B synapses in the POm are powerfully excitatory, with AMPA and NMDA components but, in contrast to L6 inputs, no mGluR, and are categorized as "driver" synapses (Groh et al., 2008; Hoogland et al., 1991; Reichova, 2004). The direct L5B–POm pathway activates high-conductance glutamate receptors electronically close to the soma (Figure 2). For the synaptic parameters of a single L5B–POm giant synapse in the rat, we estimate roughly 21 release sites, with a release probability of ~0.8 and a quantal size of ~64 pA. A single L5 fiber forms on average three *en passant* boutons onto one POm neuron, and single-fiber stimulation triggers EPSCs of ~3 nA (~200 up to ~800 pA in mouse). The AMPA receptors contain the subunit with the fastest kinetics (GluA4) mediating calcium permeability to produce fast (<1-ms rise time, decay <2 [rat] or <4 [mouse] ms), large EPSCs (Seol & Kuner, 2015). L5B-evoked POm–EPSPs are further enhanced by activation of Cav3.1 channels; functionally, this means that a single L5 spike can evoke bursts of spikes in a postsynaptic POm neuron (Mease, Sumser, et al., 2016b; Seol & Kuner, 2015).

3.4 Engagement of ETI Inhibitory Networks via L5 PT Pathways

L5 PT neurons' impact on the POm via powerful direct excitation is critically dependent on simultaneous monosynaptic excitation of unique, evolutionarily conserved ETI nuclei. Wide-ranging PT collaterals target diverse subcortical structures, and how cortical signals engage these targets is not completely understood; here, we restrict our discussion to two interconnected ETI nuclei that target the POm: the ZI and APT (Bartho et al., 2007; Cadusseau & Roger, 1991; Foster et al., 1989; Sumser et al., 2017). These GABAergic nuclei, in turn, project to the POm and have been suggested to be the sensory equivalent of basal ganglia inhibitory control in the motor system (Bokor et al., 2005). These non-reticular inhibitory inputs are another important distinguishing difference between POm and FO somatosensory nuclei. Whereas the PT–ETI–POm feedforward inhibition motif is similar to that of the CT–TRN–POm, the TRN receives reciprocal input from thalamic relay neurons, whereas ETIs do not.

PT innervation of the ETI. The extensive but only sparsely branched dendritic trees of ZI neurons integrate cortical signals from multiple areas, including S1 and M1, as well as ascending inputs from the brainstem. Cortico-incertal fibers make asymmetrical glutamatergic synapses with long active zones on the thick dendrites or spines of ZI neurons. These structural properties suggest that each cortical input will evoke a large postsynaptic current, and indeed, ZI neurons are driven by and highly synchronized with cortical activity (Bartho et al., 2007). The large areas spanned by ZI dendrites funnel and transform cortical input into powerful feedforward inhibition of POm via incerto-thalamic synapses.

PT collaterals also project to the APT, a heterogeneous nucleus comprising excitatory and inhibitory cell groups with different morphologies and firing patterns (Bokor et al., 2005). Fast-bursting inhibitory neurons project mainly to the POm, whereas tonic inhibitory and slow rhythmic excitatory neurons project to both the ZI and POm; ZI- and POm-projecting populations are intermingled within the APT, but single APT neurons project to either the POm or ZI (Giber et al., 2008). APT projections target the ventral ZI, the inhibitory incertal region that projects to the POm and also receives PT input. Furthermore, there is connectivity between ETI nuclei, with the APT providing inhibitory input to the ZI; thus, the APT, driven by PT inputs, could disinhibit the POm by inhibiting ZI spiking.

Both APT and ZI projections make large, multisynaptic GABAergic terminals on the proximal dendrites of POm neurons. These inhibitory inputs preferentially collocate with L5 PT glutamatergic inputs electrotonically close to the soma, suggesting an inhibitory complement to the giant excitatory terminals (Giber et al., 2008; Halassa & Acsády, 2016). However, in contrast to the fast depression of L5 PT–POm synapses, with several active zones and little synaptic depression, ETI–POm terminals support stable inhibition even at high frequencies (50+ Hz). For example, ZI single-fiber activation can elicit rebound bursting or complete silencing of POm spike generation with temporal precision at the level of single spikes (Bokor et al., 2005).

3.5 Short-Term Plasticity of the L5B–POm Pathway

In addition to exceptionally large, fast EPSCs, the L5B–POm pathway is characterized by rapid and pronounced frequency-dependent depression due to presynaptic mechanisms, namely, fast depletion of releasable vesicles (Groh et al., 2008) (Figure 2). At input frequencies greater than ~2 Hz, the L5B synapse depresses such that subsequent L5B inputs evoke smaller synaptic responses in the POm. For example, EPSC magnitudes decrease by 50% in response to a 20-Hz paired-pulse train. T-type calcium channels inactivate with depolarization, so the combination of synaptic depression and inactivation of T-type calcium channels makes the L5–POm pathway extremely sensitive to the statistics of L5B activity.

With the distinct profile of strong but depressing inputs, the functional impact of L5PT inputs on POm neurons is markedly different from that of modulatory L6. In vitro, stimulation of a single L5B fiber drives unitary large (>10-mV) EPSPs in the POm, robustly triggering action potentials, demonstrating the "driver" aspect of these synapses (Groh et al., 2008). Under circumstances of lower network activity in anesthetized animals corresponding to low levels of synaptic depression, single or a few L5B spikes can drive spikes in recipient POm neurons (Mease, Sumser, et al., 2016b). However, the combination of strong depression and voltage-dependent bursting makes the pathway highly adaptive, such that low levels of activity switch the pathway from high-fidelity driver to coincidence detection, in which two or more inputs are necessary to trigger POm action potentials (APs). Given the complex firing behavior of L5B neurons in vivo (de Kock et al., 2007; de Kock & Sakmann, 2009) and the impingement of many other synaptic inputs onto the POm in vivo, the balance of these two operational modes is likely highly dynamic.

3.6 Long-Term Plasticity of the L5–POm Pathway

It is currently unknown whether L5 CT synapses undergo similar long-term changes as L6 CT synapses. The particular driver properties of large L5 terminals support reliable transmission of cortical signals to subcortical targets, and extensive synaptic plasticity dynamics may be incompatible with a faithful transfer function, at least in the adult brain. Clues to possible mechanisms for plasticity come from recent developmental studies. L5 CT synapses in the mouse POm develop during the second and third postnatal weeks, and the maturation of giant synapses is use-dependent and under the control of the presynaptic SNAP25 (Hayashi et al., 2021). Intriguingly, ablation of somatosensory input in neonatal animals triggers genetic programs that convert the VPm's normal transcriptional profile into one more consistent with the HO thalamus, with putative cortical drive, although this result remains to be functionally characterized (Frangeul et al., 2016).

4. Functions of Corticothalamic Circuits in the Somatosensory System

Our knowledge about the anatomical and synaptic properties between CT pathways and their direct postsynaptic thalamic targets has grown to a point from which certain biological principles, such as the CT driver/modulator dichotomy, have been derived (Sherman & Guillery, 1998). Nevertheless, both L5 and L6 CT pathways are embedded in multi-regional circuits whose complex, long-range interactions are far from understood but are thought to give rise to sensory and behavioral functions. A difficulty for our understanding of L5 CT functions is the involvement of the enigmatic HO thalamic nuclei, which are far less understood than FO nuclei. Furthermore, L6 pathways in the somatosensory system may be embedded in simpler circuits than L5 and follow a more closed-loop arrangement compared to L5 circuits, which involve both closed loops and open loops extending beyond the thalamocortical system. Hence, to date, the involvement of L6 CT pathways in sensory functions is more defined than that of L5 CT pathways. Based on their closed-loop architecture, both CT pathways are involved in circuit synchronizations and oscillations (Crandall et al., 2015; Stroh et al., 2013). Distinct circuit functions seem to arise from the open-loop architectures of L5. In particular, the open-loop architecture of L5 pathways is the basis for a unique transthalamic signaling function, in which one cortical area connects to another cortical area via L5 CT pathways to HO nuclei (Guillery, 1995). Transthalamic signaling in the rodent somatosensory system has been demonstrated between S1and S2 (Theyel et al., 2010) as well as between S1 and M1 (Mo & Sherman, 2019).

The role of L5 in connecting to both sensory- and motor-related nuclei appears to be another contrasting feature of L5 in comparison to L6 and is thought to place L5 into a central position to mediate sensory–motor interactions, such as informing sensory circuits about motor commands via efference copies carried by L5 pathways. In contrast, L6 CT pathways in sensory circuits seem to be more confined within the thalamocortical system of their sensory modality and generally form closed-loops between somatotopically aligned cortical and thalamic neurons, making sensory L6 pathways less suitable for mediating transthalamic sensory–motor interactions. As a general theme, L6 CT feedback appears to be predominantly involved in modulating sensory signals en route to the cortex, such as modulating thalamic receptive fields, temporal precision, gain, and sensory adaptation.

4.1 Layer 6 Modulates Thalamic Firing, Gates Inputs, and Tunes Feature Selectivity

4.1.1 Modulation of Thalamic Receptive Fields by L6

L6 neurons evoke direct monosynaptic excitation and indirect disynaptic inhibition via the TRN in aligned VPm neurons. Furthermore, non-aligned VPm barreloids may be suppressed by lateral inhibition as a result of a less precisely organized topography between L6 and the TRN (Lam & Sherman, 2010). This slight offset in the topographical organization of L6 CT feedback pathways from S1 to the TRN compared to S1 to the VPm raised the hypothesis that cortical columns can individually control thalamocortical signal flow into their own and – through lateral inhibition – into neighboring columns. Indeed, it was shown that L6 CT feedback enhances whisker responses in aligned barreloids and suppresses responses in non-aligned barreloids (Temereanca & Simons, 2004). In addition to this spatial sharpening of individual whisker inputs, CT feedback via L6 also sharpens the temporal precision of whisker responses in the VPm (unpublished research) in a similar manner as was shown in the visual thalamus of ferrets (Hasse & Briggs, 2017). In contrast to the visual system, L6 activation does not seem to affect direction selectivity in the VPm (Pauzin et al., 2019).

4.1.2 Control of Thalamic Firing Mode by L6

A role for L6 in shifting thalamic firing from burst to tonic mode has been demonstrated in several studies from different labs for the VPm (Hirai et al., 2018; Mease et al., 2014) and LGN (Kirchgessner et al., 2020; Spacek et al., 2021). The underlying mechanism is the direct excitatory connection between L6 and the VPm, which moderately depolarizes the membrane potential of VPm neurons by a few millivolts, enough to inactivate burst-promoting T-type calcium channels. Importantly, as T-type calcium channels gradually inactivate with depolarization, they are not only available but also functionally relevant even at depolarized membrane potentials (Deleuze et al., 2012; Tscherter et al., 2011). Rather than abolishing I_T-mediated calcium spikes, CT feedback from L6 significantly decreases their amplitude, with the result that fewer burst spikes are fired. Hence, L6 shifts rather than switches VPm neurons toward tonic mode. Studies addressing CT feedback generally rely on mass activation or inactivation methods, such as optogenetic stimulation, which evokes a level of synchronized activity that is rarely, if at all, found in the awake cortex. The principal actions of L6 on thalamic input–output properties likely apply in awake conditions in a more refined and spatio-temporally precise manner, leading to more subtle burst-to-tonic shifts. Consistent with the graded availability of I_T, firing modes across the population of VPm neurons follow a continuum rather than a discrete thalamic burst state. The transitions between firing modes can be dynamic and extremely fast in the anesthetized and awake thalamus (Bezdudnaya et al., 2006; Guido et al., 1992). Therefore, it has been suggested that the L6 CT pathway underlies fast and topographically precise control over thalamic firing modes, whereas the spatially diffuse acetylcholine input from the brainstem represents the overall level of vigilance and modulates the thalamus more globally on slow timescales (Castro-Alamancos, 2002a; Lu et al., 1993; Mease et al., 2014).

In the framework of the wake-up-call hypothesis (Sherman, 2001b), thalamic bursts represent strong cortical activation as the thalamocortical firing rate transiently peaks and alerts the cortex that something new has occurred in the sensory scenery; indeed, functional in vivo measurements demonstrate that bursts powerfully activate cortical neurons in S1 (Swadlow & Gusev, 2001), although this effect has yet to be shown for particular cortical cell types and different TC synapses. Due to the highly nonlinear input–output properties of thalamic neurons in burst mode, it was suggested that bursty thalamic neurons lack encoding bandwidth to convey other information besides the occurrence of a new stimulus. Tonic mode, conversely, was suggested to enable increased coding bandwidth for the relay of stimulus details (e.g., size, shape, color, frequency) at the expense of smaller signal-to-noise ratios compared to burst mode. However, the strongly limited encoding power of thalamic bursts, and the related extreme view of the non-coding state of a bursty thalamus (Coenen & Vendrik, 1972; Livingstone & Hubel, 1981), has been called into question by the findings that thalamic bursts can convey very fine subthreshold temporal information and stimulus details (Butts et al., 2007, 2010; Lesica et al., 2006; Mease et al., 2017).

4.1.3 Control of Thalamic Sensory Adaptation by L6

Sensory adaptation, a general feature of sensory systems in which neural responses change for successive stimuli (Wark et al., 2007), is prominently observed in VPm responses to repetitive whisker stimulation (Ahissar et al., 2000; Castro-Alamancos, 2002b). Functionally, VPm adaptation has been shown to filter out whisker frequency information in the following way. Whereas the subthreshold activity of VPm neurons precisely reflects the frequency of trigemino-thalamic input from the brainstem, successive EPSPs become smaller as a result of presynaptic depression of trigemino-thalamic boutons (Castro-Alamancos, 2002a; Mease et al., 2014). In vivo stimulation of L6 in S1 served to overcome sensory adaptation by depolarizing VPm neurons, such that synaptically depressed EPSPs become more likely to trigger spikes as the membrane potential approaches spike threshold. As a result, the relay of frequency information from the whiskers can be dynamically gated by L6 CT feedback to the VPm (Mease et al., 2014). This CT gating function would be beneficial in light of limited attentional capacity in a multisensory world. L6 neurons in S1 would be able to function as a top-down attentional signal that turns on "fine-detail examination mode" for whisker signals to further explore behaviorally relevant signals, such as the texture of an object.

4.1.4 Control of Thalamic Gain by L6

L6 CT activity causes mixed excitation and inhibition in VPm neurons, which in turn affect VPm excitability and the relay of whisker information en route to S1 (Crandall et al., 2015; Lam & Sherman, 2010; Mease et al., 2014). This CT gain control is dependent on the firing rates of L6 CT neurons, with low firing rates decreasing thalamic gain and high firing rates increasing thalamic gain. The underlying mechanism is that the indirect inhibitory pathway shows short-term depression and thus quickly weakens during periods of enhanced L6 firing rates, giving way to the facilitating direct excitatory pathway that depolarizes the RMP (Crandall et al., 2015; Mease et al., 2014). However, the relationship between depolarization and VPm excitability is not as straightforward in the context of sensory transmission in vivo. Because T-type Ca channels inactivate upon depolarization, L6 CT input can effectively remove a depolarizing conductance from VPm neurons. In combination with a decrease in input resistance due to increased synaptic activities of both the direct and the indirect pathway via the TRN, L6 CT activity – even at high rates – leads to reduced VPm excitability. This scenario was demonstrated in intracellular recordings, in which L6 CT stimulation at high rates reduced the response probability of whisker stimulation and the overall thalamocortical spike rate (Mease et al., 2014).

Hence, moderate activation of the L6 CT circuitry may therefore generally reduce VPm gain as a result of reduced excitability and the shift toward tonic firing mode (Mease et al., 2014). Consistent with this suppressive role of L6, VPm gain was increased in awake rats after removing cortical feedback (Hirai et al., 2018). However, the role of L6 in controlling thalamic gain is still not resolved and may be modality-specific.

In the visual system, activation of L6 reduced thalamic gain, similar to the whisker system (Kirchgessner et al., 2020); however, V1 suppression also reduced LGN gain, arguing for a facilitatory role of L6 CT feedback.

4.2 Proposed Functions of the Layer 5 PT–POm Pathway

With their strong excitatory driver characteristics and the lack of TRN collaterals, L5 CT projections robustly transfer S1 cortical output to the POm (Mease, Sumser, et al., 2016a, 2016b). The POm, in turn, projects back to S1 (Figure 1) but also to other cortical and subcortical areas, thereby forming closed and open CTC loops, respectively. The POm targets mainly L1 and L5a, and innervates pyramidal neurons but also GABAergic circuits, which have been demonstrated to be involved in disinhibition of pyramidal neurons (Audette et al., 2018; Williams & Holtmaat, 2019). Hence, the closed loop (S1–POm–S1) has a primarily excitatory effect on cortical dynamics (Gambino et al., 2014; Mease, Metz, et al., 2016).

4.2.1 L5–POm CTC loop in learning and memory

Multiple lines of recent evidence unveiled a characteristic of POm input to S1 (Figure 1), which may turn out to be a breakthrough in our understanding of the POm and possibly the sensory HO in general. First, aspects of long-lasting excitation, such as plateau potentials, persistent activity, and oscillations, have been reported in independent studies of POm input to S1 (Gambino et al., 2014; Mease, Metz, et al., 2016; W. Zhang & Bruno, 2019) and point toward a role of POm inputs in the remodeling of cortical networks during learning. Moreover, it is conceivable that somatosensory closed-loop reverberating activity supports short-term memory in a similar manner as HO thalamocortical interactions in frontal TC loops (Bolkan et al., 2017; Z. V. Guo et al., 2017; Schmitt et al., 2017). A role for the POm–S1 circuitry in somatosensory learning via several synaptic and circuit mechanisms is increasingly evident (Mease & Gonzalez, 2021). POm inputs to S1 are involved in the long-term potentiation of pyramidal neurons and directly undergo LTP (Audette et al., 2019; Gambino et al., 2014). In an associative learning task in which a puff to the whiskers signaled a reward, POm – but not VPm – input to the BC strengthened, leading to increased cortical activity coinciding with learning the task (Audette et al., 2019).

4.2.2 L5–POm in Context-Dependent Sensory Processing

What signals are carried by the L5–POm pathway? Recently, it has been shown that L5 neurons specifically report changes in whisker touch conditions (Ayaz et al., 2019). The fact that whisking-related signals reach the whisker-sensitive part of the POm predominantly via the BC, demonstrated by the drastic effect of BC inactivation on POm-versus-VPm activity (Diamond et al., 1992; Mease, Sumser, et al., 2016a, 2016b) and the projection of the cortical whisker map to the POm via L5 (Sumser et al., 2017), highlight the role of the POm in relaying cortically computed signals rather than ascending sensory signals. Further corroborating a role for the POm in context-dependent sensory processing is the stark difference between POm and VPm sensitivity to physical stimulus parameters, as VPm activity more accurately captures whisking parameters, such as phase information, compared to the POm (Moore et al., 2015; Urbain et al., 2015). Thus, the POm is likely involved in context-dependent processes, such as goal-directed behavior (La Terra et al., 2022), rather than in simple peripheral information transfer. Taken together, the evidence suggests that the L5–POm pathway may specifically respond to salient tactile stimuli, such as unpredicted and/or behaviorally relevant signals.

Context-dependent processing of sensory stimuli by the POm likely involves state-specific activation patterns of PT inputs and ETI (ZI and APT) nuclei. There is evidence that direct brainstem signals reach ETI nuclei before the POm (Lavallée et al., 2005), creating a situation in which fast ETI-mediated feedforward inhibition of the POm may closely precede brainstem inputs, placing the POm under strong, default inhibitory control. Indeed, lesioning of the ZI enhances whisker responses in the POm (Trageser, 2004). The transmission of whisker signals would depend on delayed top-down PT signals because whisker-evoked PT input could both provide extra direct excitation to and trigger a "window of opportunity" by engaging disinhibitory mechanisms via either interconnected ETI nuclei (e.g., inhibition of the ZI by the APT) (Giber et al., 2008) or motor cortical drive of ETI local interneurons, resulting in POm disinhibition (Urbain & Deschênes, 2007). The interactions of these ascending and descending signals have yet to be disentangled in behaving animals.

The brain likely captures both salient and non-salient signals and subsequently prioritizes those signals that are salient and can eventually guide behavioral actions. Neural substrates for salience may be important in effective action selection, as behaving rodents follow an exploration strategy of maximizing novelty or accumulated information (Gordon et al., 2014). Distinct circuits in the TC system may differentially represent salient and non-salient stimuli in a context-dependent manner. In this framework, ascending TC pathways via the VPm robustly transfer sensory signals, whereas descending L5 CT pathways send cortically "interpreted" signals via the POm, including salience information. Receiving strong excitatory drive from L5 neurons in S1 and innervating association and motor cortices (Mo & Sherman 2019), the POm may serve as a link to inform executive circuits about salient events. In this speculative framework, salient tactile signals are specifically signaled via the L5–POm pathway to trigger appropriate actions and reshape cortical tactile representations in learning-dependent processes. The open-loop transthalamic signaling route instructs executive circuits (decision, valuation, motor) in order to respond optimally to a salient signal. In parallel, the closed-loop signaling route (S1–POm–S1) supports the formation of sensory memories of salient signals, which is advantageous in order to form or reshape associations to optimize future reactions to the same or similar signals (Wolff et al., 2020). Perceptual salience in the somatosensory system also arises from painful stimuli, which may explain why the POm and associated ETIs have been implicated in pain signaling (Masri et al., 2009).

4.2.3 L5–POm in Theories of Cortical Function

The recently discovered roles for POm TC inputs in sustained excitation (Mease, Metz, et al., 2016; W. Zhang & Bruno, 2019), learning (Audette et al., 2019; Williams & Holtmaat, 2019), and arousal (Suzuki & Larkum, 2020) underscore the importance of understanding the information transfer from L5 back to the cortex via the POm. Understanding the function of the L5 PT–POm pathway largely hinges on understanding which signals are carried in the output of L5 PT neurons (Mease & Gonzalez, 2021). This question is central to theories of cortical function; in brief, both precise temporal spiking patterns in single PT neurons and coherent activation of groups of PT neurons carry information. A long-standing and well-supported hypothesis is that high-frequency bursts in PT neurons encode coincident activation of apical and basal tufts that carry separate streams of information (Larkum et al., 1999). Indeed, apical activation in PT neurons underlies perception in tactile tasks (Takahashi et al., 2016), and PT bursts have recently been associated with active touch (de Kock et al., 2021), suggesting that bursts may be important signals for subcortical targets. Recent computational work examining bursting in the context of cortical ensembles also supports a role for bursts in encoding optimally segregated streams of information (Naud & Sprekeler, 2018).

Regardless of the exact nature of signals transmitted by PT spike output, the L5 PT–POm pathway will further transform these signals by strong synaptic depression and the nonlinear input/output properties of single POm neurons, under further control by TRN and ETI input. Recent information theoretic analysis suggests that POm neurons can transmit "multiplexed" information at different frequencies using a burst-based code (Mease et al., 2017): low-frequency (~5 Hz) stimuli are encoded by burst rate and spike count per burst, whereas high-frequency (~100–200 Hz) stimuli are encoded by precise spike times. These results suggest that POm spike trains have the capacity to encode diverse statistical features of presynaptic L5B spike trains (e.g., bursts and cortical synchrony), although this possibility has yet to be tested under naturalistic conditions (reviewed in Mease & Gonzalez, 2021).

Understanding the computation the POm performs in integrating cortical and subcortical inputs is another important open question because heterogeneous POm zones may integrate different combinations of cortical (S1, S2, M1) and subcortical (brainstem, cerebellar, collicular) inputs even on single neurons (Bickford, 2016; Groh et al., 2014; Sampathkumar et al., 2021) (Figure 2). One hypothesis for the POm's function in closed-loop computation centers on that subset of POm neurons that is targeted by both brainstem and PT inputs, with POm spiking reporting the relative timing between descending PT inputs and ascending sensory signals within a <50-ms window (Groh et al., 2014). It remains to be demonstrated how analogous computations are done with other driver combinations.

5. Conclusions

In conclusion, a deeper understanding of the role of CT and PT pathways in thalamocortical computations will benefit from emerging approaches to combine large-scale functional and anatomical data (Shepherd & Yamawaki, 2021). Recent large-scale studies measuring inferred cell-type-specific innervation (J. A. Harris et al., 2019), as well as transcription profiles and axonal morphologies (Phillips et al., 2019), have revealed a spectrum of connectivity and gene-expression patterns, thus allowing a finer-grained registration of various thalamic nuclei across modalities and functional systems. Categorization of thalamocortical systems by basic computational motifs has been recently suggested (Halassa & Sherman, 2019), and although the correlations between computational, molecular, and connectivity properties have yet to be fully established, it is clear that corticothalamic signal processing is deeply intertwined with these dimensions of variation.

Acknowledgments

The authors thank Heather Lou Mease for preparing the figures and Katharina Ziegler for assisting in preparing the manuscript. Rebecca Mease is supported by a Brigitte Schlieben Lange Fellowship from the Ministry of Science, Research, and Art of Baden-Württemberg.

References

Ahissar, E., & Assa, E. (2016). Perception as a closed-loop convergence process. *eLife*, **5**. https://doi.org/10.7554/eLife.12830

Ahissar, E., Golomb, D., Haidarliu, S., Sosnik, R., & Yu, C. (2008). Latency coding in POm: importance of parametric regimes [Review of *Latency coding in POm: importance of parametric regimes*]. *Journal of Neurophysiology*, **100**(2), 1152–1154; author reply 1155–1157.

Ahissar, E., Sosnik, R., & Haidarliu, S. (2000). Transformation from temporal to rate coding in a somatosensory thalamocortical pathway. *Nature*, **406**(6793), 302–306. https://doi.org/10.1038/35018568

Akintunde, A., & Buxton, D. F. (1992). Origins and collateralization of corticospinal, corticopontine, corticorubral and corticostriatal tracts: a multiple retrograde fluorescent tracing study. *Brain Research*, **586**(2), 208–218.

Alloway, K. D., Hoffer, Z. S., & Hoover, J. E. (2003). Quantitative comparisons of corticothalamic topography within the ventrobasal complex and the posterior nucleus of the rodent thalamus. *Brain Research*, **968**(1), 54–68.

Ansorge, J., Humanes-Valera, D., Pauzin, F. P., Schwarz, M. K., & Krieger, P. (2020). Cortical layer 6 control of sensory responses in higher-order thalamus. *The Journal of Physiology*, **598**(18), 3973–4001.

Arcelli, P., Frassoni, C., Regondi, M. C., de Biasi, S., & Spreafico, R. (1997). GABAergic neurons in mammalian thalamus: a marker of thalamic complexity? *Brain Research Bulletin*, **42**(1), 27–37. https://doi.org/10.1016/s0361-9230(96)00107-4

Audette, N. J., Bernhard, S. M., Ray, A., Stewart, L. T., & Barth, A. L. (2019). Rapid plasticity of higher-order thalamocortical inputs during sensory learning. *Neuron*, **103**

(2). 277–291.e4. https://doi.org/10.1016/j.neuron.2019.04.037

Audette, N. J., Urban-Ciecko, J., Matsushita, M., & Barth, A. L. (2018). POm thalamocortical input drives layer-specific microcircuits in somatosensory cortex. *Cerebral Cortex*, **28**(4), 1312–1328.

Ayaz, A., Stäuble, A., Hamada, M., Wulf, M.-A., Saleem, A. B., & Helmchen, F. (2019). Layer-specific integration of locomotion and sensory information in mouse barrel cortex. *Nature Communications*, **10**(1), 2585. https://doi.org/10.1038/s41467-019-10564-8

Bartho, P., Slezia, A., Varga, V., Bokor, H., Pinault, D., Buzsaki, G., & Acsady, L. (2007). Cortical control of zona incerta. *Journal of Neuroscience*, **27**(7), 1670–1681. https://doi.org/10.1523/jneurosci.3768-06.2007

Bezdudnaya, T., Cano, M., Bereshpolova, Y., Stoelzel, C. R., Alonso, J.-M., & Swadlow, H. A. (2006). Thalamic burst mode and inattention in the awake LGNd. *Neuron*, **49**(3), 421–432.

Bickford, M. E. (2016). Thalamic circuit diversity: Modulation of the driver/modulator framework. *Frontiers in Neural Circuits*, **9**. https://doi.org/10.3389/fncir.2015.00086

Bokor, H., Frère, S. G. A., Eyre, M. D., Slézia, A., Ulbert, I., Lüthi, A., & Acsády, L. (2005). Selective GABAergic control of higher-order thalamic relays. *Neuron*, **45**(6), 929–940.

Bolkan, S. S., Stujenske, J. M., Parnaudeau, S., Spellman, T. J., Rauffenbart, C., Abbas, A. I., Harris, A. Z., Gordon, J. A., & Kellendonk, C. (2017). Thalamic projections sustain prefrontal activity during working memory maintenance. *Nature Neuroscience*, **20**(7), 987–996. https://doi.org/10.1038/nn.4568

Bourassa, J., Pinault, D., & Deschênes, M. (1995). Corticothalamic projections from the cortical barrel field to the somatosensory thalamus in rats: A single-fibre study using biocytin as an anterograde tracer. *European Journal of Neuroscience*, **7**(1), 19–30.

Bruno, R. M., De Kock, C. P. J., Kuner, T., & Sakmann, B. (2010). Dimensions of a projection column and architecture of VPM and POm axons in rat vibrissal cortex. *Cerebral Cortex*, **20**(10), 2265–2276.

Butts, D. A., Desbordes, G., Weng, C., Jin, J., Alonso, J. M., & Stanley, G. B. (2010). The episodic nature of spike trains in the early visual pathway. *Journal of Neurophysiology*, **104**(6), 3371–3387.

Butts, D. A., Weng, C., Jin, J., Yeh, C. I., Lesica, N. A., Alonso, J. M., & Stanley, G. B. (2007). Temporal precision in the neural code and the timescales of natural vision. *Nature*, **449**(7158), 92–95.

Cadusseau, J., & Roger, M. (1991). Cortical and subcortical connections of the pars compacta of the anterior pretectal nucleus in the rat. *Neuroscience Research*, **12**(1), 83–100.

Cajal, S. R. y. (1906). *Santiago Ramón y Cajal—Nobel Lecture*. https://www.nobelprize.org/uploads/2018/06/cajal-lecture.pdf

Castro-Alamancos, M. A. (2002a). Different temporal processing of sensory inputs in the rat thalamus during quiescent and information processing states in vivo. *The Journal of Physiology*, **539**(Pt 2), 567–578.

Castro-Alamancos, M. A. (2002b). Properties of primary sensory (lemniscal) synapses in the ventrobasal thalamus and the relay of high-frequency sensory inputs. *Journal of Neurophysiology*, **87**(2), 946–953. https://doi.org/10.1152/jn.00426.2001

Castro-Alamancos, M. A., & Calcagnotto, M. E. (1999). Presynaptic long-term potentiation in corticothalamic synapses. *Journal of Neuroscience*, **19**(20), 9090–9097.

Clascá, F., Porrero, C., Galazo, M. J., Rubio-Garrido, P., & Evangelio, M. (2016). Anatomy and development of multispecific thalamocortical axons: Implications for cortical dynamics and evolution. In K. S. Rockland (Ed.), *Axons and Brain Architecture* (pp. 69–92). Academic Press.

Coenen, A. M., & Vendrik, A. J. (1972). Determination of the transfer ratio of cat's geniculate neurons through quasi-intracellular recordings and the relation with the level of alertness. *Experimental Brain Research*, **14**(3), 227–242.

Colello, R., Baker, G., Reese, B., Mitrofanis, J., Chan, H., & Joachim, L. (2018). Cortical layer with no known function. *European Journal of Neuroscience*, **49**(7), 957–963. https://doi.org/10.1111/ejn.13978

Cox, C. L., & Sherman, S. M. (1999). Glutamate inhibits thalamic reticular neurons. *Journal of Neuroscience*, **19**(15), 6694–6699.

Crandall, S. R., Cruikshank, S. J., & Connors, B. W. (2015). A corticothalamic switch: controlling the thalamus with dynamic synapses. *Neuron*, **86**(3), 768–782.

Crandall, S. R., Patrick, S. L., Cruikshank, S. J., & Connors, B. W. (2017). Infrabarrels are layer 6 circuit modules in the barrel cortex that link long-range inputs and outputs. *Cell Reports*, **21**(11), 3065–3078.

de Kock, C. P. J., Bruno, R. M., Spors, H., & Sakmann, B. (2007). Layer- and cell-type-specific suprathreshold stimulus representation in rat primary somatosensory cortex. *Journal of Physiology*, **581**(Pt 1), 139–154.

de Kock, C. P. J., Pie, J., Pieneman, A. W., Mease, R. A., Bast, A., Guest, J. M., Oberlaender, M., Mansvelder, H. D., & Sakmann, B. (2021). High-frequency burst spiking in layer 5 thick-tufted pyramids of rat primary somatosensory cortex encodes exploratory touch. *Communications Biology*, **4**(1), 1–14.

de Kock, C. P. J., & Sakmann, B. (2009). Spiking in primary somatosensory cortex during natural whisking in awake head-restrained rats is cell-type specific. *Proceedings of the National Academy of Sciences of the United States of America*, **106**(38), 16446–16450.

Deleuze, C., David, F., Béhuret, S., Sadoc, G., Shin, H.-S., Uebele, V. N., Renger, J. J., Lambert, R. C., Leresche, N., & Bal, T. (2012). T-type calcium channels consolidate tonic action potential output of thalamic neurons to neocortex. *Journal of Neuroscience*, **32**(35), 12228–12236.

Deschênes, M., Veinante, P., & Zhang, Z.-W. (1998). The organization of corticothalamic projections: Reciprocity versus parity. *Brain Research Reviews*, **28**(3), 286–308. https://doi.org/10.1016/s0165-0173(98)00017-4

Diamond, M. E., Armstrong-James, M., Budway, M. J., & Ebner, F. F. (1992). Somatic sensory responses in the rostral sector of the posterior group (POm) and in the ventral posterior medial nucleus (VPM) of the rat thalamus: Dependence on the barrel field cortex. *Journal of Comparative Neurology*, **319**(1), 66–84. https://doi.org/10.1002/cne.903190108

El-Boustani, S., Sermet, B. S., Foustoukos, G., Oram, T. B., Yizhar, O., & Petersen, C. C. H. (2020). Anatomically and functionally distinct thalamocortical inputs to primary and secondary mouse whisker somatosensory cortices. *Nature Communications*, **11**(1), 3342.

Endo, K., Araki, T., & Yagi, N. (1973). The distribution and pattern of axon branching of pyramidal tract cells. *Brain Research*, **57**(2), 484–491.

Fernandez, L. M. J., Pellegrini, C., Vantomme, G., Béard, E., Lüthi, A., & Astori, S. (2017). Cortical afferents onto the nucleus Reticularis thalami promote plasticity of low-threshold excitability through GluN2C-NMDARs. *Scientific Reports*, **7**(1), 12271.

Foster, G. A., Sizer, A. R., Rees, H., & Roberts, M. H. (1989). Afferent projections to the rostral anterior pretectal nucleus of the rat: a possible role in the processing of noxious stimuli. *Neuroscience*, **29**(3), 685–694.

Frandolig, J. E., Matney, C. J., Lee, K., Kim, J., Chevée, M., Kim, S.-J., Bickert, A. A., & Brown, S. P. (2019). The synaptic organization of layer 6 circuits reveals inhibition as a major output of a neocortical sublamina. *Cell Reports*, **28**(12), 3131–3143.e5.

Frangeul, L., Pouchelon, G., Telley, L., Lefort, S., Luscher, C., & Jabaudon, D. (2016). A cross-modal genetic framework for the development and plasticity of sensory pathways. *Nature*, **538**(7623), 96–98.

Gambino, F., Pagès, S., Kehayas, V., Baptista, D., Tatti, R., Carleton, A., & Holtmaat, A. (2014). Sensory-evoked LTP driven by dendritic plateau potentials in vivo. *Nature*, **515**(7525), 116–119. https://doi.org/10.1038/nature13664

Giber, K., Slézia, A., Bokor, H., Bodor, A. L., Ludányi, A., Katona, I., & Acsády, L. (2008). Heterogeneous output pathways link the anterior pretectal nucleus with the zona incerta and the thalamus in rat. *Journal of Comparative Neurology*, **506**(1), 122–140.

Golshani, P., Liu, X. B., & Jones, E. G. (2001). Differences in quantal amplitude reflect GluR4- subunit number at corticothalamic synapses on two populations of thalamic neurons. *Proceedings of the National Academy of Sciences of the United States of America*, **98**(7), 4172–4177.

Gordon, G., Fonio, E., & Ahissar, E. (2014). Learning and control of exploration primitives. *Journal of Computational Neuroscience*, **37**(2), 259–280. https://doi.org/10.1007/s10827-014-0500-1

Groh, A., Bokor, H., Mease, R. A., Plattner, V. M., Hangya, B., Stroh, A., Deschênes, M., & Acsády, L. (2014). Convergence of cortical and sensory driver inputs on single thalamocortical cells. *Cerebral Cortex*, **24**(12), 3167–3179.

Groh, A., de Kock, C. P. J., Wimmer, V. C., Sakmann, B., & Kuner, T. (2008). Driver or coincidence detector: Modal switch of a corticothalamic giant synapse controlled by spontaneous activity and short-term depression. *The Journal of Neuroscience: The Official Journal of the Society for Neuroscience*, **28**(39), 9652–9663.

Groh, A., Meyer, H. S., Schmidt, E. F., Heintz, N., Sakmann, B., & Krieger, P. (2010). Cell-type specific properties of pyramidal neurons in neocortex underlying a layout that is modifiable depending on the cortical area. *Cerebral Cortex*, **20**(4), 826–836.

Guido, W., Lu, S. M., & Sherman, S. M. (1992). Relative contributions of burst and tonic responses to the receptive field properties of lateral geniculate neurons in the cat. *Journal of Neurophysiology*, **68**(6), 2199–2211.

Guillery, R. W. (1995). Anatomical evidence concerning the role of the thalamus in corticocortical communication: a brief review. *Journal of Anatomy*, **187** (Pt 3), 583–592.

Guo, C., Peng, J., Zhang, Y., Li, A., Li, Y., Yuan, J., Xu, X., Ren, M., Gong, H., & Chen, S. (2017). Single-axon level morphological analysis of corticofugal projection neurons in mouse barrel field. *Scientific Reports*, **7**(1), 2846.

Guo, K., Yamawaki, N., Barrett, J. M., Tapies, M., & Shepherd, G. M. G. (2020). Cortico-thalamo-cortical circuits of mouse forelimb s1 are organized primarily as recurrent loops. *Journal of Neuroscience*, **40**(14), 2849–2858.

Guo, Z. V., Inagaki, H. K., Daie, K., Druckmann, S., Gerfen, C. R., & Svoboda, K. (2017). Maintenance of persistent activity in a frontal thalamocortical loop. *Nature*, **545**(7653), 181–186. https://doi.org/10.1038/nature22324

Halassa, M. M., & Acsády, L. (2016). Thalamic inhibition: Diverse sources, diverse scales. *Trends in Neurosciences*, **39**(10), 680–693.

Halassa, M. M., & Sherman, S. M. (2019). Thalamocortical circuit motifs: A general framework. *Neuron*, **103**(5), 762–770.

Hanbery, J., & Jasper, H. (1953). Independence of diffuse thalamo-cortical projection system shown by specific nuclear destructions. *Journal of Neurophysiology*, **16**(3), 252–271.

Harris, J. A., Mihalas, S., Hirokawa, K. E., Whitesell, J. D., Choi, H., Bernard, A., Bohn, P., Caldejon, S., Casal, L., Cho, A., Feiner, A., Feng, D., Gaudreault, N., Gerfen, C. R., Graddis, N., Groblewski, P. A., Henry, A. M., Ho, A., Howard, R., . . . Zeng, H. (2019). Hierarchical organization of cortical and thalamic connectivity. *Nature*, **575**(7781), 195–202.

Harris, K. D., & Shepherd, G. M. G. (2015). The neocortical circuit: Themes and variations. *Nature Neuroscience*, **18**(2), 170–181.

Harris, R. M., & Hendrickson, A. E. (1987). Local circuit neurons in the rat ventrobasal thalamus—a GABA immunocytochemical study. *Neuroscience*, **21**(1), 229–236.

Hasse, J. M., & Briggs, F. (2017). Corticogeniculate feedback sharpens the temporal precision and spatial resolution of visual signals in the ferret. *Proceedings of the National Academy of Sciences of the United States of America*, **114**(30), E6222–E6230.

Hayashi, S., Hoerder-Suabedissen, A., Kiyokage, E., Maclachlan, C., Toida, K., Knott, G., & Molnár, Z. (2021). Maturation of complex synaptic connections of layer 5 cortical axons in the posterior thalamic nucleus requires SNAP25. *Cerebral Cortex*, **31**(5), 2625–2638.

Hirai, D., Nakamura, K. C., Shibata, K.-I., Tanaka, T., Hioki, H., Kaneko, T., & Furuta, T. (2018). Shaping somatosensory responses in awake rats: Cortical modulation of thalamic neurons. *Brain Structure & Function*, **223**(2), 851–872.

Hoerder-Suabedissen, A., Hayashi, S., Upton, L., Nolan, Z., Casas-Torremocha, D., Grant, E., Viswanathan, S., Kanold, P. O., Clascá, F., Kim, Y., & Molnár, Z. (2018). Subset of cortical layer 6b neurons selectively innervates higher order thalamic nuclei in mice. *Cerebral Cortex*, **28**(5), 1882–1897.

Hoogland, P. V., Welker, E., & Van der Loos, H. (1987). Organization of the projections from barrel cortex to thalamus in mice studied with *Phaseolus vulgaris*-leucoagglutinin and HRP. *Experimental Brain Research*, **68**(1), 73–87.

Hoogland, P. V., Wouterlood, F. G., Welker, E., & Van der Loos, H. (1991). Ultrastructure of giant and small thalamic terminals of cortical origin: a study of the projections from the barrel cortex in mice using *Phaseolus vulgaris* leuco-agglutinin (PHA-L). *Experimental Brain Research*, **87**(1), 159–172.

Hsu, C.-L., Yang, H.-W., Yen, C.-T., & Min, M.-Y. (2010). Comparison of synaptic transmission and plasticity between sensory and cortical synapses on relay neurons in the ventrobasal nucleus of the rat thalamus. *Journal of Physiology*, **588**(Pt 22), 4347–4363.

Jones, E. G. (1998). Viewpoint: The core and matrix of thalamic organization. *Neuroscience*, **85**(2), 331–345.

Jurgens, C. W. D., Bell, K. A., McQuiston, A. R., & Guido, W. (2012). Optogenetic stimulation of the corticothalamic pathway affects relay cells and GABAergic neurons differently in the mouse visual thalamus. *PloS One*, **7**(9), e45717.

Killackey, H. P., & Sherman, S. M. (2003). Corticothalamic projections from the rat primary somatosensory cortex. *Journal of Neuroscience*, **23**(19), 7381–7384.

Kirchgessner, M. A., Franklin, A. D., & Callaway, E. M. (2020). Context-dependent and dynamic functional influence of corticothalamic pathways to first- and higher-order visual thalamus. *Proceedings of the National Academy of Sciences of the United States of America*, **117**(23), 13066–13077.

Kita, T., & Kita, H. (2012). The subthalamic nucleus is one of multiple innervation sites for long-range corticofugal axons: a single-axon tracing study in the rat. *Journal of Neuroscience*, **32**(17), 5990–5999.

Krieger, P., & Groh, A. (2015). *Sensorimotor Integration in the Whisker System*. Springer.

Lam, Y.-W., & Sherman, S. M. (2010). Functional organization of the somatosensory cortical layer 6 feedback to the thalamus. *Cerebral Cortex*, **20**(1), 13–24.

Larkum, M. E., Julius Zhu, J., & Sakmann, B. (1999). A new cellular mechanism for coupling inputs arriving at different cortical layers. *Nature*, **398**(6725), 338–341. https://doi.org/10.1038/18686

La Terra, D., Bjerre, A.-S., Rosier, M., Masuda, R., Ryan, T. J., and Palmer, L. M. (2022). The role of higher-order thalamus during learning and correct performance in goal-directed behavior. *Elife* 11, e77177.

Lavallée, P., Urbain, N., Dufresne, C., Bokor, H., Acsády, L., & Deschênes, M. (2005). Feedforward inhibitory control of sensory information in higher-order thalamic nuclei. *Journal of Neuroscience*, **25**(33), 7489–7498.

Lesica, N. A., Weng, C., Jin, J., Yeh, C. I., Alonso, J. M., & Stanley, G. B. (2006). Dynamic encoding of natural luminance sequences by LGN bursts. *PLoS Biology*, **4**(7), e209.

Li, J., Wang, S., & Bickford, M. E. (2003). Comparison of the ultrastructure of cortical and retinal terminals in the rat dorsal lateral geniculate and lateral posterior nuclei. *Journal of Comparative Neurology*, **460**(3), 394–409.

Li, Y., Lopez-Huerta, V. G., Adiconis, X., Levandowski, K., Choi, S., Simmons, S. K., Arias-Garcia, M. A., Guo, B., Yao, A. Y., Blosser, T. R., Wimmer, R. D., Aida, T., Atamian, A., Naik, T., Sun, X., Bi, D., Malhotra, D., Hession, C. C., Shema, R., ... Feng, G. (2020). Distinct subnetworks of the thalamic reticular nucleus. *Nature*, **583**(7818), 819–824.

Livingstone, M. S., & Hubel, D. H. (1981). Effects of sleep and arousal on the processing of visual information in the cat. *Nature*, **291**(5816), 554–561.

Lu, S.-M., Guido, W., & Sherman, S. M. (1993). The brain-stem parabrachial region controls mode of response to visual stimulation of neurons in the cat's lateral geniculate nucleus. *Visual Neuroscience*, **10**(4), 631–642. https://doi.org/10.1017/s0952523800005332

Martinez-Garcia, R. I., Voelcker, B., Zaltsman, J. B., Patrick, S. L., Stevens, T. R., Connors, B. W., & Cruikshank, S. J. (2020). Two dynamically distinct circuits drive inhibition in the sensory thalamus. *Nature*, **583**(7818), 813–818.

Masri, R., Quiton, R. L., Lucas, J. M., Murray, P. D., Thompson, S. M., & Keller, A. (2009). Zona incerta: A role in central pain. *Journal of Neurophysiology*, **102**(1), 181–191.

Mease, R. A., & Gonzalez, A. J. (2021). Corticothalamic pathways from layer 5: Emerging roles in computation and pathology. *Frontiers in Neural Circuits*, **15**, 88.

Mease, R. A., Krieger, P., & Groh, A. (2014). Cortical control of adaptation and sensory relay mode in the thalamus. *Proceedings of the National Academy of Sciences of the United States of America*, **111**(18), 6798–6803.

Mease, R. A., Kuner, T., Fairhall, A. L., & Groh, A. (2017). Multiplexed spike coding and adaptation in the thalamus. *Cell Reports*, **19**(6), 1130–1140.

Mease, R. A., Metz, M., & Groh, A. (2016). Cortical sensory responses are enhanced by the higher-order thalamus. *Cell Reports*, **14**(2), 208–215. https://doi.org/10.1016/j.celrep.2015.12.026

Mease, R. A., Sumser, A., Sakmann, B., & Groh, A. (2016a). Cortical dependence of whisker responses in posterior medial thalamus in vivo. *Cerebral Cortex*, **26**(8), 3534–3543. https://doi.org/10.1093/cercor/bhw144

Mease, R. A., Sumser, A., Sakmann, B., & Groh, A. (2016b). Corticothalamic spike transfer via the L5B-POm pathway in vivo. *Cerebral Cortex*, **26**(8), 3461–3475.

Meyer, H. S., Wimmer, V. C., Oberlaender, M., de Kock, C. P. J., Sakmann, B., & Helmstaedter, M. (2010). Number and laminar distribution of neurons in a thalamocortical projection column of rat vibrissal cortex. *Cerebral Cortex*, **20**(10), 2277–2286.

Mo, C., & Sherman, S. M. (2019). A sensorimotor pathway via higher-order thalamus. *Journal of Neuroscience*, **39**(4), 692–704.

Moore, J. D., Lindsay, N. M., Deschênes, M., & Kleinfeld, D. (2015). Vibrissa self-motion and touch are reliably encoded along the same somatosensory pathway from brainstem through thalamus. *PLOS Biology*, **13**(9), e1002253. https://doi.org/10.1371/journal.pbio.1002253

Narayanan, R. T., Egger, R., Johnson, A. S., Mansvelder, H. D., Sakmann, B., de Kock, C. P. J., & Oberlaender, M. (2015). Beyond columnar organization: cell type- and target layer-specific principles of horizontal axon projection patterns in rat vibrissal cortex. *Cerebral Cortex*, **25**(11), 4450–4468.

Naud, R., & Sprekeler, H. (2018). Sparse bursts optimize information transmission in a multiplexed neural code. *Proceedings of the National Academy of Sciences of the United States of America*, **115**(27), E6329–E6338. https://doi.org/10.1073/pnas.1720995115

Ohno, S., Kuramoto, E., Furuta, T., Hioki, H., Tanaka, Y. R., Fujiyama, F., Sonomura, T., Uemura, M., Sugiyama, K., & Kaneko, T. (2012). A morphological analysis of thalamocortical axon fibers of rat posterior thalamic nuclei: A single neuron tracing study with viral vectors. *Cerebral Cortex*, **22**(12), 2840–2857.

Pauzin, F. P., Schwarz, N., & Krieger, P. (2019). Activation of corticothalamic layer 6 cells decreases angular tuning in mouse barrel cortex. *Frontiers in Neural Circuits*, **13**, 67.

Phillips, J. W., Schulmann, A., Hara, E., Winnubst, J., Liu, C., Valakh, V., Wang, L., Shields, B. C., Korff, W., Chandrashekar, J., Lemire, A. L., Mensh, B., Dudman, J. T., Nelson, S. B., & Hantman, A. W. (2019). A repeated molecular architecture across thalamic pathways. *Nature Neuroscience*, **22**(11), 1925–1935. https://doi.org/10.1038/s41593-019-0483-3

Pigeat, R., Chausson, P., & Dreyfus, F. M. (2015). Sleep slow wave-related homo and heterosynaptic LTD of intrathalamic GABAAergic synapses: Involvement of T-type Ca^{2+} channels and metabotropic glutamate. *Journal of Neuroscience*, **35**(1), 64–73. https://www.jneurosci.org/content/35/1/64.short

Pinault, D. (2004). The thalamic reticular nucleus: structure, function and concept. *Brain Research. Brain Research Reviews*, **46**(1), 1–31.

Prasad, J. A., Carroll, B. J., & Sherman, S. M. (2020). Layer 5 corticofugal projections from diverse cortical areas: Variations on a pattern of thalamic and extrathalamic targets. *Journal of Neuroscience*, **40**(30), 5785–5796.

Reichova, I. (2004). Somatosensory corticothalamic projections: Distinguishing Drivers from modulators. *Journal of Neurophysiology*, **92**(4), 2185–2197.

Rockland, K. S. (2019). Corticothalamic axon morphologies and network architecture. *European Journal of Neuroscience*, **49**(8), 969–977.

Rojas-Piloni, G., Guest, J. M., Egger, R., Johnson, A. S., Sakmann, B., & Oberlaender, M. (2017). Relationships between structure, in vivo function and long-range axonal target of cortical pyramidal tract neurons. *Nature Communications*, **8**(1), 870.

Rouiller, E. M., & Welker, E. (2000). A comparative analysis of the morphology of corticothalamic projections in mammals. *Brain Research Bulletin*, **53**(6), 727–741.

Sampathkumar, V., Miller-Hansen, A., Sherman, S. M., & Kasthuri, N. (2021). Integration of signals from different cortical areas in higher order thalamic neurons. *Proceedings of the National Academy of Sciences of the United States of America*, **118**(30), e2104137118. https://doi.org/10.1073/pnas.2104137118

Schmitt, L. I., Ian Schmitt, L., Wimmer, R. D., Nakajima, M., Happ, M., Mofakham, S., & Halassa, M. M. (2017). Thalamic amplification of cortical connectivity sustains attentional control. *Nature*, **545**(7653), 219–223. https://doi.org/10.1038/nature22073

Seol, M., & Kuner, T. (2015). Ionotropic glutamate receptor GluA4 and T-type calcium channel Cav 3.1 subunits control key aspects of synaptic transmission at the mouse L5B-POm giant synapse. *European Journal of Neuroscience*, **42**(12), 3033–3044.

Shepherd, G. M. G. (2013). Corticostriatal connectivity and its role in disease. *Nature Reviews Neuroscience*, **14**(4), 278–291.

Shepherd, G. M. G., & Yamawaki, N. (2021). Untangling the cortico-thalamo-cortical loop: Cellular pieces of a knotty circuit puzzle. *Nature Reviews Neuroscience*, **22**(7), 389–406. https://doi.org/10.1038/s41583-021-00459-3

Sherman, S. M. (2001a). Thalamic relay functions. *Progress in Brain Research*, **134**, 51–69.

Sherman, S. M. (2001b). Tonic and burst firing: Dual modes of thalamocortical relay. *Trends in Neurosciences*, **24**(2), 122–126.

Sherman, S. M. (2007). The thalamus is more than just a relay. *Current Opinion in Neurobiology*, **17**(4), 417–422.

Sherman, S. M. (2016). Thalamus plays a central role in ongoing cortical functioning. *Nature Neuroscience*, **19**(4), 533–541.

Sherman, S. M., & Guillery, R. W. (1998). On the actions that one nerve cell can have on another: distinguishing "drivers" from "modulators." *Proceedings of the National Academy of Sciences of the United States of America*, **95**(12), 7121–7126.

Sherman, S. M., & Guillery, R. W. (2006). *Exploring the Thalamus and Its Role in Cortical Function* (2nd ed.). MIT Press.

Smith, Y., Wichmann, T., & DeLong, M. R. (2014). Corticostriatal and mesocortical dopamine systems: do species differences matter? [Review of Corticostriatal and mesocortical dopamine systems: Do species differences matter?]. *Nature Reviews. Neuroscience*, **15**(1), 63.

Spacek, M. A., Born, G., Crombie, D., Bauer, Y., & Liu, X. (2021). Robust effects of corticothalamic feedback during naturalistic visual stimulation. BioRxiv. https://www.biorxiv.org/content/10.1101/776237v5.abstract

Stroh, A., Adelsberger, H., Groh, A., Rühlmann, C., Fischer, S., Schierloh, A., Deisseroth, K., & Konnerth, A. (2013). Making waves: Initiation and propagation of corticothalamic Ca^{2+} waves in vivo. *Neuron*, **77**(6), 1136–1150.

Sumser, A., Mease, R. A., Sakmann, B., & Groh, A. (2017). Organization and somatotopy of corticothalamic projections from L5B in mouse barrel cortex. *Proceedings of the National Academy of Sciences*, **114**(33), 8853–8858. https://doi.org/10.1073/pnas.1704302114

Suzuki, M., & Larkum, M. E. (2020). General anesthesia decouples cortical pyramidal neurons. *Cell*, **180**(4), 666–676.e13. https://doi.org/10.1016/j.cell.2020.01.024

Swadlow, H. A., & Gusev, A. G. (2001). The impact of "bursting" thalamic impulses at a neocortical synapse. *Nature Neuroscience*, **4**(4), 402–408.

Takahashi, N., Oertner, T. G., Hegemann, P., & Larkum, M. E. (2016). Active cortical dendrites modulate perception. *Science*, **354**(6319), 1587–1590. https://doi.org/10.1126/science.aah6066

Temereanca, S., & Simons, D. J. (2004). Functional topography of corticothalamic feedback enhances thalamic spatial response tuning in the somatosensory whisker/barrel system. *Neuron*, **41**(4), 639–651.

Theyel, B. B., Llano, D. A., & Sherman, S. M. (2010). The corticothalamocortical circuit drives higher-order cortex in the mouse. *Nature Neuroscience*, **13**(1), 84–88.

Thomson, A. M. (2010). Neocortical layer 6, a review. *Frontiers in Neuroanatomy*, **4**, 13.

Trageser, J. C. (2004). Reducing the uncertainty: Gating of peripheral inputs by zona incerta. *Journal of Neuroscience*, **24**(40), 8911–8915. https://doi.org/10.1523/jneurosci.3218-04.2004

Tscherter, A., David, F., Ivanova, T., Deleuze, C., Renger, J. J., Uebele, V. N., Shin, H.-S., Bal, T., Leresche, N., & Lambert, R. C. (2011). Minimal alterations in T-type calcium channel gating markedly modify physiological firing dynamics. *Journal of Physiology*, **589**(Pt 7), 1707–1724.

Urbain, N., & Deschênes, M. (2007). Motor cortex gates vibrissal responses in a thalamocortical projection pathway. *Neuron*, **56**(4), 714–725. https://doi.org/10.1016/j.neuron.2007.10.023

Urbain, N., Salin, P. A., Libourel, P.-A., Comte, J.-C., Gentet, L. J., & Petersen, C. C. H. (2015). Whisking-related changes in neuronal firing and membrane potential dynamics in the somatosensory thalamus of awake mice. *Cell Reports*, **13**(4), 647–656. https://doi.org/10.1016/j.celrep.2015.09.029

Veinante, P., Lavallée, P., & Deschênes, M. (2000). Corticothalamic projections from layer 5 of the vibrissal barrel cortex in the rat. *Journal of Comparative Neurology*, **424**(2), 197–204.

Wark, B., Lundstrom, B. N., & Fairhall, A. (2007). Sensory adaptation. *Current Opinion in Neurobiology*, **17**(4), 423–429.

Williams, L. E., & Holtmaat, A. (2019). Higher-order thalamocortical inputs gate synaptic long-term potentiation via disinhibition. *Neuron*, **101**(1), 91–102.e4.

Wolff, M., Morceau, S., Folkard, R., Martin-Cortecero, J., & Groh, A. (2020). A thalamic bridge from sensory perception to cognition. *Neuroscience and Biobehavioral Reviews*, **120**, 222–235.

Zhang, W., & Bruno, R. M. (2019). High-order thalamic inputs to primary somatosensory cortex are stronger and longer lasting than cortical inputs. *eLife*, **8**. https://doi.org/10.7554/elife.44158

Zhang, Z. W., & Deschênes, M. (1997). Intracortical axonal projections of lamina VI cells of the primary somatosensory cortex in the rat: A single-cell labeling study. *Journal of Neuroscience*, **17**(16), 6365–6379.

Zolnik, T. A., Ledderose, J., Toumazou, M., Trimbuch, T., Oram, T., Rosenmund, C., Eickholt, B. J., Sachdev, R. N. S., & Larkum, M. E. (2020). Layer 6b is driven by intracortical long-range projection neurons. *Cell Reports*, **30**(10), 3492–3505.e5.

Chapter 13

Thalamocortical Circuits for Auditory Processing, Plasticity, and Perception

Daniel B. Polley and Anne E. Takesian

1. Introduction

The medial geniculate body (MGB) of the thalamus is an obligatory station for sound processing and the primary source of subcortical auditory-related input to the neocortex, striatum, amygdala, and posterior regions of the basal forebrain. The MGB consists of three major subdivisions: (i) a primary first-order nucleus, the ventral subdivision (MGBv); (ii) a higher-order nucleus, the dorsal subdivision (MGBd); and (iii) an integrative, multi-sensory nucleus – the medial subdivision (MGBm) – that can be functionally grouped with neighboring multi-sensory nuclei outside of the MGB, including the suprageniculate (Sg) and posterior intralaminar nuclei (PIN) (Figure 1A). The anatomy of the MGB – namely, its cytoarchitecture, chemoarchitecture, and inter-regional connectivity – has been characterized in detail, particularly in non-human primates and cats. Several excellent and detailed reviews on these aspects of MGB organization already exist, and we will therefore only briefly touch upon these findings as a means to establish the foundation for a more integrative description of auditory thalamocortical pathways (Bartlett, 2013; Hackett, 2011; C. C. Lee, 2015; Winer et al., 2005; Winer & Lee, 2007).

More recent work has taken advantage of approaches to trace, monitor, and manipulate genetically identified cell types in the MGB and auditory cortex (ACtx), often in awake animals that are engaged in listening tasks. Because the contributions of cell-type-specific thalamocortical circuits to sound processing and auditory cognition are less often featured in auditory thalamocortical reviews, we have made it a central focus of this chapter. One important caveat is that although we include relevant characterizations made in many species, functional characterizations based on genetic; neurochemical; and fine-scale anatomical, biophysical, or morphological identifiers of cell types have largely been made in rodents (often mice and rats but also gerbils). Everything – from the molecular identifiers of particular thalamocortical subclasses to innate behaviors and learning strategies – can vary between species. As just one example that illustrates the broader point, GABAergic interneurons are interspersed throughout the MGB in many non-rodent species, whereas GABAergic interneurons are virtually non-existent in the MGB of mice and rats, leaving the thalamic reticular nucleus (TRN) as the main source of intra-thalamic inhibition of mouse MGB neurons. This difference, along with many other comparative differences in the transcriptional and neurochemical organization of the MGB, could have important implications for thalamic circuits for sound processing and plasticity between species.

Therefore, although the broader themes and principles of auditory thalamocortical circuit organization and function discussed here will be of general interest to neuroscientists working in many model systems or related brain areas, the composition of particular thalamocortical circuit elements should not be taken for granted between species.

A second major aim of this chapter is to identify important unsolved questions and intriguing future directions for research on auditory thalamic contributions to sound processing and auditory cognition. The function of the MGB is woefully understudied, both in relation to other sensory regions of the dorsal thalamus and also relative to any other stage of the central auditory system. Although research on the auditory thalamus has grown by leaps and bounds in recent years, the literature should be understood as less of a cohesive canon – as it might in the somatosensory, motor, or visual thalamus – and more as a series of streetlights that reveal the dark gaps in our knowledge base and illuminate a way forward toward a more complete understanding of this brain structure.

1.1 Feedforward Input to the MGB

The bulk of feedforward auditory-related input to the MGB arises from the excitatory and inhibitory projection neurons in the central nucleus of the inferior colliculus (IC) that terminate in the MGBv (Figure 1B). Work in several species has described that excitatory tectothalamic projections to the MGB arise from (i) disk-shaped neurons with dendrites restricted to the isofrequency lamina of the IC tonotopic map and focal MGBv axon termination fields and (ii) stellate neurons with dendritic fields spanning isofrequency lamina and more diffuse MGBv axon terminations (Ito & Oliver, 2012). In gerbils, the majority of disk-shaped tectothalamic afferents express cholecystokinin (Kreeger et al., 2021). A genetic identifier for the broader class of stellate tectothalamic afferents has yet to be determined, although one subclass in mice can be identified by the expression of vasoactive intestinal peptide (VIP) (Goyer et al., 2019). MGBv neurons also receive feedforward inhibition via large GABAergic projection neurons found throughout the central nucleus of the IC (Malmierca et al., 2002; Peruzzi et al., 1997).

Whereas the first-order nucleus of the MGB receives the heaviest bottom-up input from the central nucleus of the IC, work in non-human primates, cats, and rodents has found that higher-order and multisensory/integrative subdivisions of the MGB receive their strongest feedforward input from the dorsal and lateral cortex of the IC. The cortex of the IC features

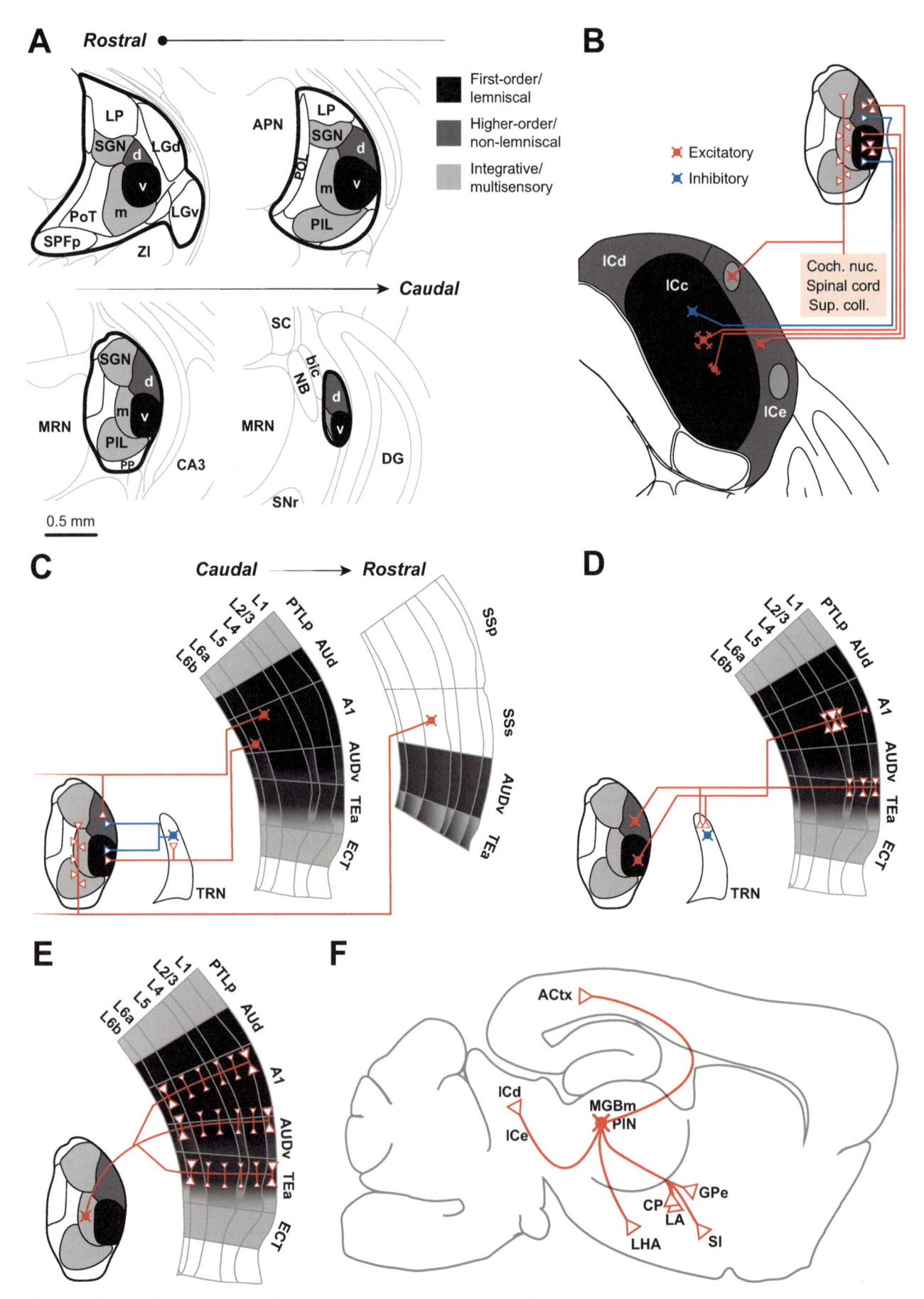

Figure 1 Organization and connectivity of auditory processing centers in the thalamus.

A. Schematic of four evenly spaced coronal sections of the mouse brain depicting anatomical landmarks within the rostral to caudal extent of the MGB. Thick line demarcates the boundary of the thalamus.

circumscribed modules of multisensory processing with inputs from the somatosensory cortex and multisensory nuclei of the auditory brainstem. Neurons located within these auditory–somatosensory modules of the IC, along with inputs from the intermediate and deep layers of the superior colliculus, provide a strong source of multisensory feedforward excitation to the MGBm and MGBd (Lesicko et al., 2016, 2020). Reports in rats and guinea pigs identify a final source of feedforward excitatory input that bypasses the normal flow of bottom-up activity through the lateral lemniscus and IC and instead arises directly from the cochlear nucleus, the first station of central sound processing. This subclass of direct excitatory brainstem input specifically targets the MGBm, presumably providing a short-latency input to the auditory thalamus with a functional contribution to integrative brain function and behavior that has yet to be determined (Anderson et al., 2006; Malmierca et al., 2002).

1.2 Corticothalamic Feedback to the MGB

The bulk of feedback input to the MGB arises from excitatory neurons located in layers 5 and 6 of the ACtx (Figure 1C). In mice, virtually all layer (L) 6 corticothalamic (CT) neurons in ACtx are *Ntsr1*- and *FoxP2*-positive, with one vertically oriented axonal branch remaining in the cortical column and a second branch that deposits collaterals in TRN en route to the MGBv (Clayton et al., 2021; Guo et al., 2017). L5 CT neurons express genetic markers consistent with pyramidal tract-like (PT-like) projection neurons found throughout L5 of the neocortex (X. Chen et al., 2019). L5 PT-like corticofugal neurons feature large, tufted apical dendrites and large-caliber axons that bypass the TRN and deposit collaterals in the MGBd en route to additional downstream targets in the amygdala, striatum, and IC (X. Chen et al., 2019; Williamson & Polley, 2019). Integrative, multisensory regions of the auditory thalamus, including the MGBm and PIN, are also densely innervated by L5 CT projections originating in the somatosensory cortex, which converge with bottom-up somatosensory inputs from the superior colliculus and multisensory modules within the lateral cortex of the IC to further enrich the convergence of multi-modal inputs to medial regions of the auditory thalamus (Lohse et al., 2021).

1.3 MGBv Efferent Projections

At a coarse spatial scale, MGBv axonal projections are focused on L4 of the ACtx with an additional thin band of axon terminals in L1 (Hackett, 2015) (Figure 1D). MGBv projections are limited to the first-order "core" auditory fields that include the primary auditory cortex (A1) and several additional cortical fields that feature well-defined, short-latency pure-tone receptive fields that are arranged into tonotopic maps when studied at a more macroscopic scale. The nomenclature for core fields with strong MGBv input varies between species but would include A1; the anterior auditory field (AAF) in mice, ferrets, and gerbils; A1, AAF, and the ventral auditory field (VAF) in rats; A1, AAF, VAF, and the posterior auditory field in cats; A1, the rostral, and rostrotemporal areas in macaque monkeys; and Heschl's gyrus in humans (for review, see Hackett, 2011).

At a finer scale, thalamocortical projections appear as dense bands of vesicular glutamate-2 (VGluT2) expression in L4 and L1 against a background of VGluT1-expressing cortical neurons. In the ACtx, virtually all excitatory neurons are pyramidal neurons; unlike the somatosensory or visual cortex in most species, there are vanishingly few stellate or granule cells, and as such, distinctions such as "supragranular" or "infragranular" do not apply (Barbour & Callaway, 2008; Smith & Populin, 2001). Unlike the visual cortex, where the proportions of pyramidal versus stellate neurons may depend on the species (e.g., there are few stellate neurons in mouse and rat visual cortex compared with cats and primates; Lund et al., 1979; Marie & Peters, 1985; Peters & Kara, 1985; Scala et al., 2019), the predominance of pyramidal neurons in the ACtx appears to apply broadly across species, including mice (R. J. Richardson et al., 2009), rats (Barbour & Callaway, 2008), cats (Smith & Populin, 2001), and humans (Meyer et al., 1989). Whereas intracortical connections are distributed throughout the dendritic field of pyramidal neurons, thalamic afferents make peri-somatic contacts within 0.1 mm of ACtx pyramidal neuron cell bodies. This subcellular arrangement of thalamocortical afferents provides comparatively strong postsynaptic voltage-gated calcium influx and cortical action potential probability, despite the fact that the MGBv accounts for less than 15% of A1 inputs (C. C. Lee & Winer, 2011; R. J. Richardson et al., 2009). MGBv afferents also synapse onto local inhibitory neurons, providing a potent source of indirect feedforward inhibition that is delayed relative to direct thalamocortical excitation by 1–2 ms (A. Y. Y. Tan et al., 2004; Wehr & Zador, 2003). Virtually all L1 cell bodies are GABAergic, and L1 MGBv afferents may activate these inhibitory neurons (Takesian

---

Caption for Figure 1 (cont.)

B. Schematic of several major classes of excitatory and inhibitory bottom-up inputs to the MGB.

C. Schematic of several major classes of excitatory and inhibitory descending corticothalamic and intra-thalamic inputs to the MGB.

D. Schematic of thalamocortical projections from the MGBv and MGBd.

E and F. Schematic of the thalamocortical (E) and brain-wide projections (F) from the MGBm and PIN.

Abbreviations: *A1*, primary auditory cortex; *ACtx*, auditory cortex; *APN*, anterior pretectal nucleus; *AUd*, dorsal auditory area; *AUDv*, ventral auditory area; *Bic*, brachium of the inferior colliculus; *CA3*, field CA3; *Coch. Nuc.*, cochlear nuclei; *CP*, caudoputamen; *d*, medial geniculate complex, dorsal part; *DG*, dentate gyrus; *ECT*, ectorhinal area; *GPe*, globus pallidus, external segment; *ICc*, inferior colliculus, central nucleus; *ICd*, inferior colliculus, dorsal nucleus; *ICe*, inferior colliculus, external nucleus; *LA*, lateral amygdalar nucleus; *LGd*, dorsal part of the lateral geniculate complex; *LGv*, ventral part of the lateral geniculate complex; *LHA*, lateral hypothalamic area; *LP*, lateral posterior nucleus of the thalamus; *MRN*, midbrain reticular nucleus; *NB*, nucleus of the brachium of the inferior colliculus; *PIL*, posterior intralaminar thalamic nucleus; *POL*, posterior limiting nucleus of the thalamus; *PoT*, posterior triangular thalamic nucleus; *PP*, peripeduncular nucleus; *PTLp*, Posterior parietal association areas; *SC*, superior colliculus; *SGN*, suprageniculate nucleus; *SI*, substantia innominata; *SNr*, substantia nigra, reticular part; *SPFp*, subparafascicular nucleus, parvicellular part; *SSp*, primary somatosensory area; *SSs*, supplemental somatosensory area; *Sup. Coll.*, superior colliculus; *TEa*, temporal association areas; *TRN*, reticular nucleus of the thalamus; *v*, medial geniculate complex, ventral part; *ZI*, zona incerta.

et al., 2018). Whereas the populations of inhibitory interneurons in the middle layers are predominantly parvalbumin (PV)-positive fast-spiking and somatostatin-positive (SST) subtypes, L1 inhibitory neurons are predominantly subtypes expressing neuron-derived neurotrophic factor (NDNF) and VIP.

1.4 Efferent Projections from Non-Primary Subdivisions of the Auditory Thalamus

Whereas the lemniscal MGBv projections target core regions of the auditory cortex, non-lemniscal MGBd efferents predominantly target higher-order "belt" fields of the ACtx (Andersen et al., 1980; J. E. Rose & Woolsey, 1949a, 1949b). Again, the nomenclature varies between species but would include the temporal association area (TEA) in rodents; posterior pseudosylvian and suprasylvian fields in ferrets; A2 and TEA in cats; the rostromedial, caudomedial, mediolateral, and anterolateral fields in macaque monkeys, and the regions of the superior temporal gyrus in humans (Hackett, 2011). The laminar distribution of MGBd axons within belt fields of the ACtx varies to a degree between non-human primates, cats, and rodents but is generally more biased toward upper layers when compared with MGBv innervation of core fields (C. L. Huang & Winer, 2000; Jones & Burton, 1976; Smith et al., 2012). The MGBm targets the auditory cortex as well, with sparse large-diameter thalamocortical axons entering layers 1 and 6 and additional diffuse projections observed in all layers (C. L. Huang & Winer, 2000) (Figure 1E). The primary distinguishing feature of MGBm and neighboring multi-sensory nuclei is their significant projection to forebrain targets outside of the lemniscal auditory system, such as the striatum, amygdala, and the basal forebrain (Chavez & Zaborszky, 2017; LeDoux et al., 1991; C. C. Lee, 2015) (Figure 1F).

Less is known about the circuit, cellular, and sub-cellular organization outside of the MGBv. In rodents, MGBd and MGBm neurons express a complement of calcium-binding proteins – calbindin and calretinin – that are virtually absent in the MGBv (Lu et al., 2009). Thalamocortical axons of calretinin-positive neurons are concentrated in L1 of higher-order ACtx belt fields, where they synapse onto NDNF GABAergic interneurons. NDNF cells regulate plasticity within the local cortical column via their postsynaptic contacts onto local pyramidal neurons and PV cell types, but they also regulate thalamocortical transmission via presynaptic $GABA_B$ receptors on higher-order MGB axons (Abs et al., 2018; Belén Pardi et al., 2020; Cohen-Kashi Malina et al., 2021).

Thus, although many details remain to be filled in through experiments that provide genetic access to key thalamocortical cell types, anatomical work across many animal species reveals a rough outline of parallel auditory thalamocortical circuitries: (i) a projection from the MGBv to L4 of ACtx core fields that recruits strong thalamocortical excitation with strong delayed inhibition via local inhibitory neurons and (ii) projections from other auditory thalamic nuclei that either target upper-layer microcircuits within higher-order fields of the ACtx (MGBd) or project diffusely across all layers and cortical fields (MGBm) that collectively serve a modulatory role by regulating columnar excitability and plasticity. In this regard, the flow of information from higher-order fields of the auditory cortex is neither strictly parallel nor hierarchical. As demonstrated clearly in non-human primates and cats, core fields of the auditory cortex project directly to higher-order fields as per a hierarchical system (de La Mothe et al., 2006; Kaas & Hackett, 2000), but higher-order fields also receive direct innervation from the MGBd, constituting a parallel stream of thalamic input (de la Mothe et al., 2012; C. C. Lee & Winer, 2011). The maturation and plasticity of these thalamocortical circuits during postnatal development, as well as their functional contribution to the coding of acoustic features, sound perception, and auditory learning in mature animals, are discussed in the following sections.

2. Integrative Sensory and Extra-Sensory Processing in Auditory Thalamocortical Circuits

2.1 Neural Coding of Sound Features across the Midbrain–Thalamus–Cortex Auditory Hierarchy

In all sensory systems, representational features of increasing complexity emerge at successive stages of processing. In the mammalian auditory system, the de novo computation of most auditory features from the surrounding soundscape occurs very early in the system, either in the inner ear itself or in the first- or second-order auditory brainstem nuclei. Although the receptive field organization and neural coding of sound features in the spectral, spatial, and intensity domain are clearly modified between sound-processing centers in the midbrain, thalamus, and cortex, to a first approximation, these are differences of degree, not kind, and generally do not reflect the de novo emergence of new representational features.

The neural coding of temporal sound features is another matter entirely, and in this regard, the auditory thalamus sits at the boundary between the high-fidelity isomorphic temporal coding of acoustic features found in the brainstem and midbrain and the more sparse, plastic, and sluggish rate-based coding found throughout the forebrain (Joris et al., 2004; X. Wang et al., 2008). For the sense of hearing, many fundamental elements of vocal communication and environmental sound awareness are encoded in the time domain. Beginning with the purely temporal patterns of vibrations on the tympanic membrane (i.e., the eardrum), neural encoding of sound features – more than any other modality – remains rooted in how neurons represent fluctuations in the stimulus waveform over time, rather than across the spatial extent of the peripheral receptor epithelia. Neurons in the spiral ganglion and auditory brainstem are the high-speed, high-fidelity temporal processors par excellence in the nervous system, where single units synchronize action-potential timing to acoustic modulations in excess of 1 kHz and compute sub-millisecond discrepancies in the timing of sound waves that reach each ear. The remarkable high-speed processing in the auditory brainstem is enabled by cellular morphologies, intrinsic electrical properties, and synaptic architectures that are unique to the first stages of auditory processing and are indispensable for encoding the rapid acoustic building blocks of sound perception (Yin et al., 2019).

At the level of the auditory midbrain, single-unit action potentials in the IC synchronize to modulations in the sound-pressure envelope at rates as high as several hundred hertz (Batra et al., 1989). Although IC neuron spike rates are often tuned to particular rates of amplitude modulation (Müller-Preuss et al., 1994), the coding strategy they employ is comparable to that of the brainstem and primary afferent neurons, in the sense that spikes are synchronized to a particular phase of the stimulus waveform, permitting individual units to encode a wide rate of stimulus-modulation rates via spike timing (Figure 2A) (Joris et al., 2004). Beginning at the level of the MGB and continuing in the cortex, the high-fidelity isomorphic copies of the stimulus-amplitude envelope are transformed into abstract, spike-rate-based representations. Rather than synchronizing action-potential timing to temporal sound features, significant numbers of auditory forebrain units encode temporal sound features with a rate code by producing a non-synchronized burst of action potentials to a range of preferred temporal modulation rates (Figure 2B). In the MGB, approximately 40% of single units exhibit non-synchronized rate-based encoding of stimulus temporal features even though all feedforward input from the IC is organized as synchronized temporal coding (Bartlett & Wang, 2007) (Figure 2C). Within the MGB, the higher-order dorsal subdivision features a significantly higher fraction of non-synchronized responses compared to the MGBv, where units predominantly exhibit synchronized neural coding of temporal sound features (Figure 2D).

The mechanisms underlying this temporal-to-rate conversion in neural coding are not yet fully resolved. Computational models emphasize that synchronized spiking responses in MGB neurons can be reproduced with large, rapidly depressing inputs, whereas non-synchronized rate-based coding can be produced by depressing α-amino-3-hydroxy-5-methyl-4-isoxazolepropionic acid (AMPA)-receptor conductances with facilitating gamma-aminobutyric acid (GABA)-modulated N-methyl-D-aspartate (NMDA)-receptor conductances (Cai & Caspary, 2015; Rabang & Bartlett, 2011). At the level of A1, where it is possible to make intracellular or whole-cell recordings from awake animals, studies have provided direct evidence for a conversion of synchronized feedforward synaptic input to non-synchronized spiking outputs (L. Gao et al., 2016; X. Gao & Wehr, 2015). Non-synchronized rate-based units can be distinguished from synchronized units based on the time constant and saturation rates of excitatory and inhibitory conductances, where weaker and approximately balanced excitatory and inhibitory inputs can produce the complete menagerie of low-pass, high-pass, and mixed-rate-based unsynchronized tuning profiles (L. Gao et al., 2016).

Across the IC–MGB–ACtx hierarchy, as sound-evoked spiking becomes increasingly less precisely synchronized to amplitude fluctuations in the sound waveform, there is a clear loss in stimulus-coding accuracy. However, slow

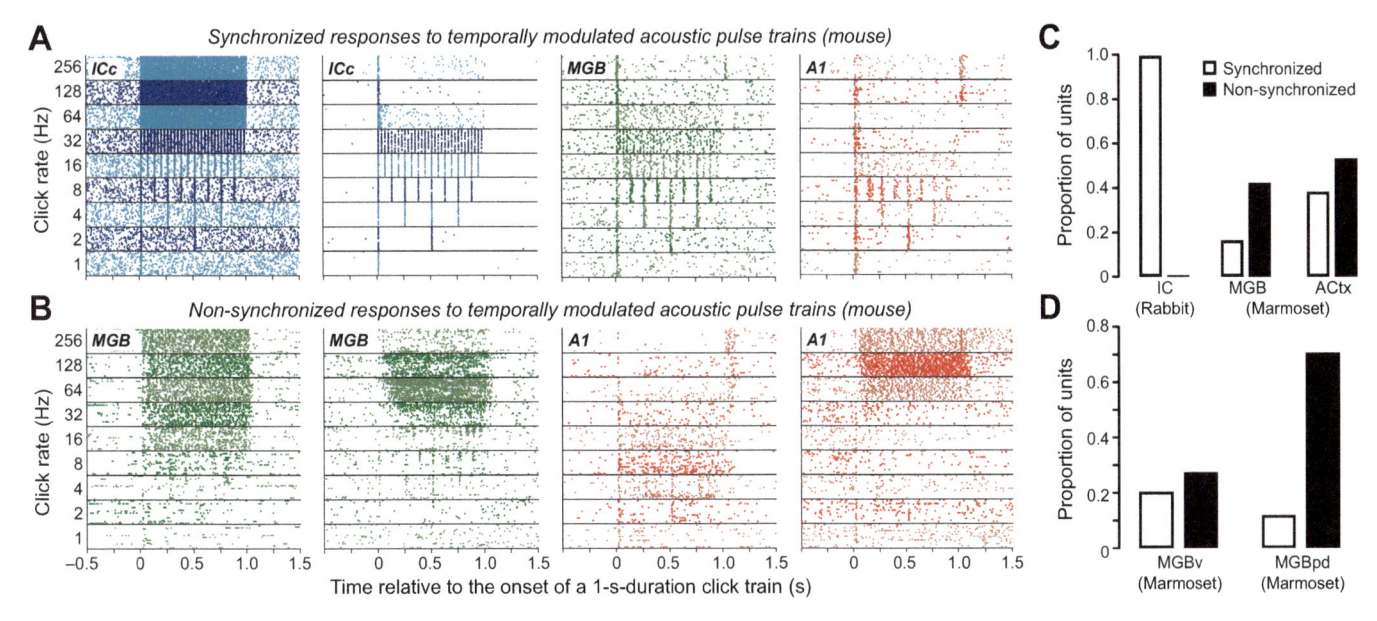

Figure 2 Neural coding of acoustic temporal modulation is reformatted from timing to rate codes across the IC–MGB–ACtx hierarchy.

A. Spike rasters for four representative single units recorded from the central nucleus of the inferior colliculus (ICc; *blue*), medial geniculate body (MGB; *green*), and primary auditory cortex (A1; *red*) of awake, head-fixed mice. Alternating colors are presented for ease of visualization. Stimuli are 1-s duration rectified sine-wave–modulated click trains presented at rates ranging from 1 to 256 Hz. Across each unit, the synchronization limit and bandpass firing rate tuning for modulation rate vary, but all show spike synchronization to the timing of individual clicks.

B. As per panel A, except these four units all demonstrate non-synchronized rate-based responses to the same stimuli.

C. In prior studies, the proportion of non-synchronized unit responses increases across the IC–MGB–A1 hierarchy.

D. Within the MGB, the proportion of non-synchronized responses is highest in the higher-order nucleus of the MGB. Units categorized as mixed (a combination of synchronized and non-synchronized responses across pulse rates) are not included in these summary plots; hence, the proportions may not add to 1.0. Example units in panels A and B are unpublished. IC recordings were described by Batra et al. (1989). MGB recordings were reported by Bartlett and Wang (2007) (panel C) and Bartlett and Wang (2011) (panel D). ACtx recordings were reported by Lu et al. (2001).

processing can reflect something more than just a failure for fast processing. For example, perceiving higher-order structure in music (e.g., rhythms), vocal communication (e.g., sentences), and auditory scenes (e.g., repeating patterns) requires neural processes that are attuned to inherently slow timescales. Although the extended neural timescales in the MGB and ACtx may interfere with precise synchronization to rapid stimulus features, slower and integrative temporal processing could afford an advantage over midbrain and brainstem stations for encoding slowly evolving features. New findings support this notion by showing that temporal coding of brief local intervals (0.001–0.1 s) separating consecutive noise bursts was robust in the IC for intervals as short as just a few milliseconds (Figure 3A–C). Although the temporal resolution of cortical neurons was poorer than that of IC neurons by over an order of magnitude, neural ensembles in A1 (and to a lesser extent in the MGB) exhibited dampened sound-evoked spiking when noise bursts were arranged in slowly repeating (~1-s-period) rhythms (Figure 3D and E). Decoding analyses confirmed that changes in spiking patterns across ensembles of cortical neurons were sufficient to classify the stimulus context. Conversely, IC units showed excellent encoding of local temporal intervals but conveyed no information about whether the noise bursts occurred in a random or rhythmic stimulus context (Asokan et al., 2021).

Across a wide range of auditory protocols to study the neural encoding of stimulus context, neural sensitivity in the MGB to temporally distributed contextual cues is consistently greater than what is observed in the IC but far less than what is observed from recordings in the auditory cortex (Anderson et al., 2009; Cai et al., 2016; Harpaz et al., 2021; Lohse et al., 2021; Parras et al., 2017) (Figure 3F). This consistent observation raises unanswered questions about the neural network, circuit, and synaptic mechanisms that adjust the neural

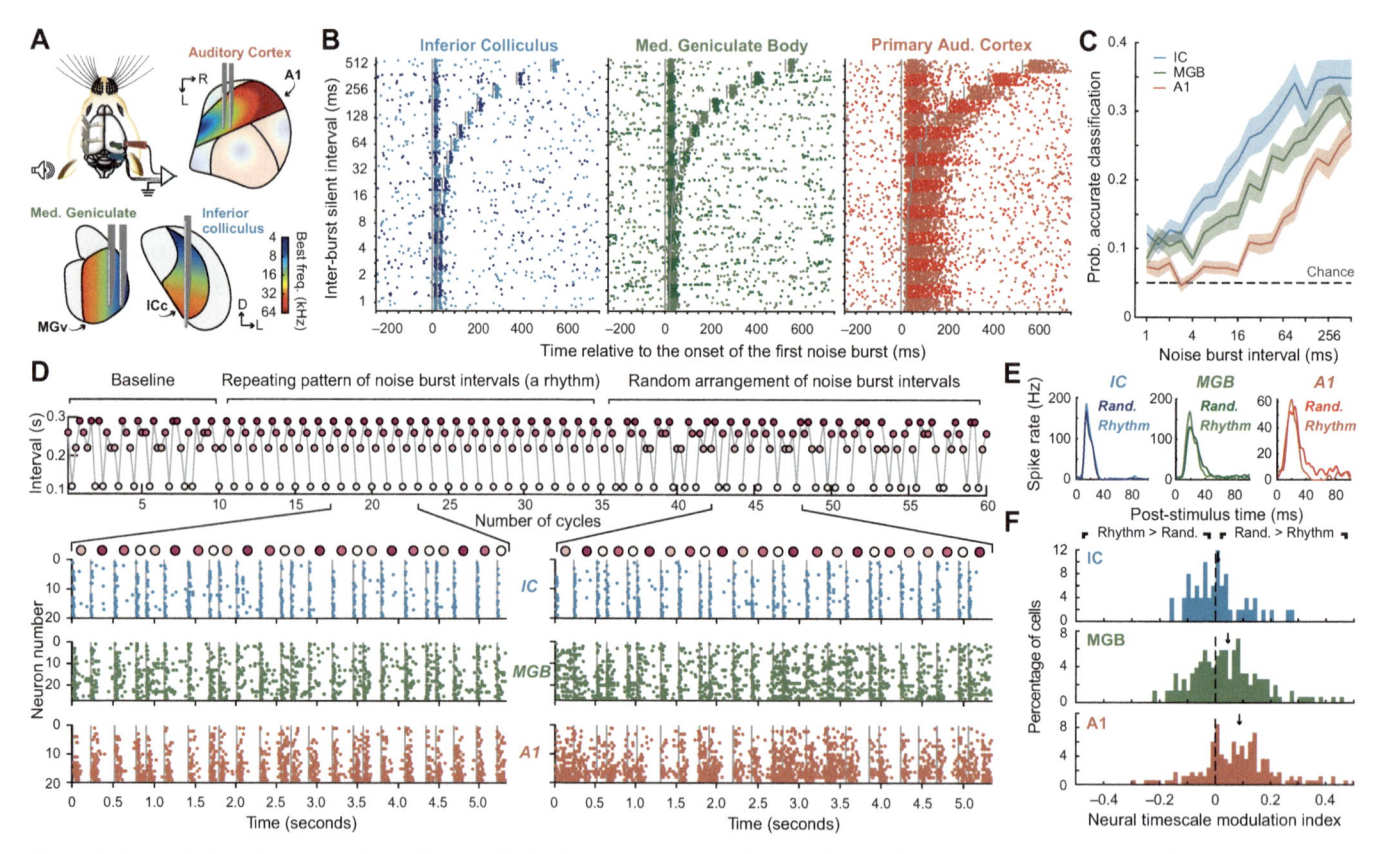

Figure 3 Inverted hierarchies across the auditory midbrain, thalamus, and cortex for encoding local temporal intervals versus global temporal patterns.

A. Schematic of simultaneous multi-regional extracellular recordings from the IC, MGB, and A1 of awake, passively listening, head-fixed mice. One- or two-shanked 64-channel probe positioning relative to a schematic of the best frequency tonotopic gradients in each structure. D, L, and R = dorsal, lateral, and rostral, respectively.

B. Spike rasters for three representative single units for paired noise bursts. Alternating colors are presented for ease of visualization. Vertical gray lines = timing of each 20-ms noise burst in the pair.

C. Mean ± standard error of the mean (SEM) probability of veridical classification of the inter-burst interval for all IC, MGB, and A1 units. Temporal interval decoding accuracy is significantly poorer across higher stages of the IC–MGB–A1 hierarchy.

D. Top: Schematic of rhythmic and random noise burst sequences. A single cycle is composed of four intervals which are joined by the gray line. The four intervals are presented in a stereotyped order to form a rhythm or in a random order during the baseline and random periods. Bottom: Six cycles from the rhythmic and random epochs are presented with the single-unit spike rasters from 68 simultaneously recorded units in the IC, MGB, and A1. Vertical gray bars denote the timing of individual noise bursts.

E. Representative post-stimulus firing rate histograms from IC, MGB, and A1 units for 100 noise bursts presented during either the random or rhythmic contexts.

F. Histogram of neural timescale asymmetry index ([random − rhythm]/[random + rhythm]), where values <0 indicate more dampened responses during random intervals and values >0 indicate more dampened responses during rhythmic intervals. Arrows denote sample means. Neural timescales are significantly reduced during rhythmic epochs in A1, slightly reduced in the MGB, but not affected in the IC. Neural timescales were quantified by fitting the autocorrelation function for each unit with an exponential function and computing the decay constant. Data are from Asokan et al. (2021).

representation of sounds according to their statistical predictability. On the one hand, the emergent sensitivity to slow contextual features could arise purely within the ACtx. Local GABA circuits are a clear candidate, particularly somatostatin or neuron-derived neurotrophic factor (NDNF) neurons, which target the distal dendrites of A1 pyramidal neurons to sharpen spike timing and dampen intracortical excitation for predictable or behaviorally inconsequential sound features (Abs et al., 2018; Fan et al., 2020; Kato et al., 2015; Natan et al., 2015). Alternatively, a presynaptic thalamocortical mechanism could also be at play, wherein the same cortical GABA circuits act either through GABA$_B$ receptors to dynamically regulate thalamocortical synaptic depression (Belén Pardi et al., 2020) or via corticothalamic feedback, which could dampen feedforward thalamocortical synaptic inputs via inhibition from the TRN (Ibrahim et al., 2021; Reinhold et al., 2015).

2.2 Functional Contributions of Auditory Corticothalamic Circuits to Sound Processing

The dense network of descending corticothalamic (CT) feedback projections into the MGB has been the subject of anatomical studies for over a century (Andersen et al., 1980; Diamond et al., 1969; Llano & Sherman, 2008; Ramón y Cajal, 1906; Winer et al., 2001). However, the functional contribution of CT projections to sound processing and perception have only come to light recently, with the advent of contemporary methods for neural circuit perturbations in awake and behaving animals. The majority of glutamatergic L6 neurons in the ACtx are projection neurons that provide collaterals onto GABAergic neurons in the TRN en route to the MGBv (Clayton et al., 2021; Guo et al., 2017). In addition, substantial numbers of large "PT-like" L5 pyramidal neurons provide collaterals in the MGBd en route to other subcortical targets in the midbrain and forebrain. Medial portions of the auditory thalamus (i.e., the MGBm, PIN, and SG) receive comparatively sparse CT innervation from the ACtx but prominent input from the L5 PT-like corticofugal pyramidal neurons in the somatosensory cortex. Direct stimulation of somatosensory L5 corticofugal inputs enhances sound-evoked MGBm spike rates, but the adaptive contribution or natural recruitment of cross-modal descending input to the MGB during active listening behaviors remains to be determined (Lohse et al., 2021).

Targeted recordings and manipulations of L5 ACtx neurons that innervate the MGB suggest that they function as canonical broadcast neurons that integrate and transmit cortical sound representations to distributed subcortical targets. Optogenetically targeted L5 corticofugal neurons exhibit broad sound-frequency tuning with sluggish response latencies and non-linear spectrotemporal receptive fields (Williamson & Polley, 2019). Cross-correlating L5 corticofugal spike trains with other cell types demonstrates that their activity lags – rather than leads – neighboring regular and fast-spiking units within the local column, supporting the notion that they function as a columnar output to multiple sub-cortical auditory stations, including the MGB. Selective activation, inactivation, and lesion experiments have identified a critical behavioral role for L5 corticofugal neurons in the experience-dependent plasticity of sound localization following the occlusion of one ear (Bajo et al., 2010) and in the gating of innate flight responses triggered by loud sounds (Xiong et al., 2015), although these studies have not identified any particular role for the CT synapse or an L5 CT→MGB local circuit in these behaviors.

L6 CT neurons differ in nearly every respect from L5 corticofugal neurons, effectively functioning as a parallel feedback system designed to dynamically regulate auditory thalamocortical gain and selectivity. L6 CT neurons receive monosynaptic inputs from the MGBv and strongly express FoxP2, a protein marker found in brain regions involved in motor control and sensorimotor integration (Clayton et al., 2021). Optogenetically targeted recordings of L6 CT A1 neurons reveal short-latency responses and sparse auditory receptive fields that are likely shaped by intra-laminar GABAergic neurons (X. Y. Ji et al., 2016; Williamson & Polley, 2019; Y. Zhou et al., 2010). L6 CT axons are bifurcated, with one branch remaining within the local cortical column to directly activate a combination of excitatory neurons and fast-spiking PV neurons (Figure 4A) and a thalamic branch that drives inhibitory neurons in the TRN and excitatory neurons in the MGBv (Bortone et al., 2014; Guo et al., 2017; J. Kim et al., 2014). Because L6 CTs drive mixed populations of excitatory and inhibitory neurons, they can exert either net excitatory or net suppressive effects on downstream circuits (Crandall et al., 2015; Guo et al., 2017; J. Kim et al., 2014) (Figure 4B). Optogenetic activation of ACtx L6 CTs can either suppress or enhance sound-evoked activity in A1, the MGBv, and the TRN, depending on the relative timing of L6 CT spiking and sound delivery (Guo et al., 2017). Interestingly, the strongest effects of L6 CT activation on neural responses occur *after* optogenetically induced spiking ends, not during activation, and the specific form of modulation (i.e., suppression or enhancement) switches based on the temporal interval between the offset of L6 CT spiking and the arrival of auditory stimulation (Figure 4C). Activating L6 CT neurons at longer intervals prior to sound onset facilitates A1 and MGB sound-evoked responses, broadens frequency tuning, and – at a behavioral level – improves sound-detection thresholds but reduces frequency discrimination thresholds. Conversely, activating CT neurons at shorter intervals before sound onset suppresses sound-evoked spiking, sharpens frequency tuning, and improves frequency discrimination while elevating detection thresholds (Guo et al., 2017) (Figure 4C–F).

2.3 Internal States and Other Forms of Extra-Sensory Modulation of Auditory Thalamocortical Circuits

Recent work has shown that L6 CT units in A1 are activated hundreds of milliseconds prior to the onset of movements expected to produce sounds and reward but not to movements that are unrelated to a reinforced behavioral (Clayton et al., 2021) (Figure 5). In this regard, self-initiated movement may

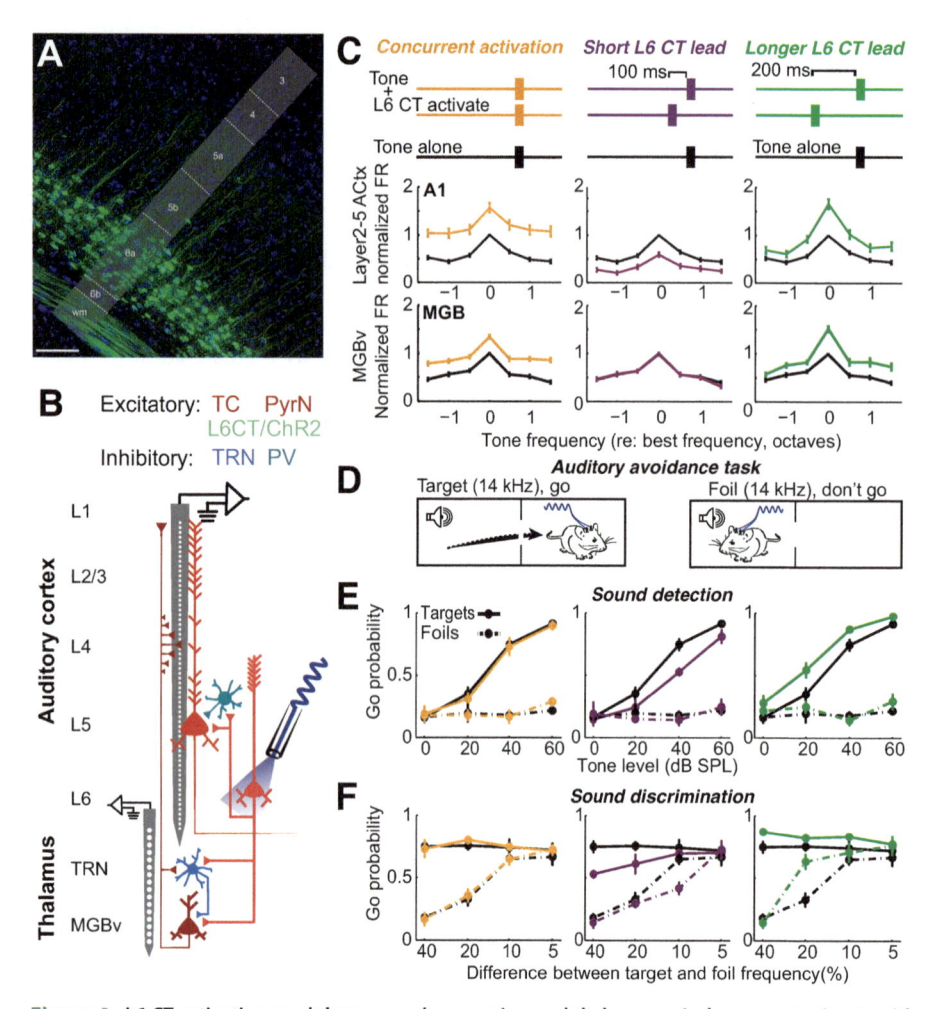

Figure 4 L6 CT activation modulates sound perception and thalamocortical sensory tuning to either enhance detection at the expense of discrimination or vice versa, depending on timing.

A. A1 corticothalamic cells labeled in NTSR1-Cre mice crossed with a GFP reporter have somata in L6a and sparse vertically oriented neuropil labeling up to L5a. Scale bar, 0.1 mm.

B. Schematic for multi-regional single-unit recordings in A1, the TRN, and the MGBv during optogenetic activation of L6 CTs in Ntsr1-Cre mice that express channelrhodopsin-2 (ChR2). Note that the thalamic branch of L6 CT axons is connected to inhibitory neurons in the TRN and excitatory thalamocortical projection neurons (TCs), and the cortical branch is connected with PV-expressing inhibitory interneurons as well as excitatory pyramidal neurons (PyrNs).

C. Tones were presented without L6 CT activation (50% of trials; *black*) or with L6 CT activation in awake, passively listening, head-fixed mice. The delay between the onset of tone bursts and laser pulses varied from 0 to 800 ms, with three conditions shown here (0, 100, and 200 ms). Mean (1 SEM) tone-evoked firing rates were normalized to the best frequency in the tone-alone condition (*black*). Compared to tone-alone responses, firing rates were significantly elevated with concurrent L6 CT activation in A1 (*top left*) and the MGB (*bottom left*), as well as with a 200-ms lead time (*right*). With a short lead time, tuning was significantly suppressed in A1 but not the MGB.

D. Mice were trained in an auditory avoidance task that required them to cross sides of a shuttle box following the presentation of 14-kHz tone bursts (target) to avoid foot shock but not tones of other frequencies (foils). Mice expressed ChR2 in L6 CT neurons in the left and right auditory cortex and were implanted with bilateral optic fiber assemblies.

E. Probability of a "Go" (i.e., crossing) response for target tones, foil tones, and the three combined tone and laser test conditions as a function of sound level. Compared to tone-alone trials, target detection is impaired in the short-delay configuration but enhanced in the long-delay configuration.

F. Probability of a "Go" response as a function of frequency separation between the target tone and the foil tone at a fixed sound level (40 dB SPL). Discrimination is enhanced for difficult conditions (10%) in the short-delay condition but is reduced in easy conditions (20%) in the long-delay condition. Data in panels C–F are from Guo et al. (2017).

play the role of the artificial optogenetic activation in the experiments described previously by providing a natural trigger that activates L6 CT neurons hundreds of milliseconds prior to anticipated sounds. Motor corollary discharge also modulates cortical sound processing via direct inputs from motor cortical regions to local GABA circuits within the ACtx. Motor preparatory inputs recruit local GABA circuits to suppress self-generated sounds that fall within a narrow range of predicted sound frequencies (Eliades & Wang, 2008; Rummell et al., 2016; Schneider et al., 2018). Sounds produced by self-initiated movements are also suppressed subcortically, particularly when the acoustic consequences of movement are nearly immediate and highly stereotyped (e.g., chewing) (Singla et al., 2017). Flexibility appears to be the key distinguishing feature between cortical and subcortical circuits for self-generated sound cancellation. In the ACtx, suppressive filters for reafferent sounds can be acquired through learning and applied to arbitrary associations between movement and delayed auditory feedback (Schneider & Mooney, 2018). It is unclear how the motor-related activation of L6 CT units or the thalamus in general (either

Spontaneous and sound-evoked MGB firing rates are also modulated by global brain states related to arousal, movement, and task engagement, although the magnitude of these effects is generally smaller than what is observed in the ACtx (Otazu et al., 2009; Rummell et al., 2016; Schneider et al., 2014) and depends on the degree of pupil-indexed arousal (McGinley et al., 2015) or movement velocity (Williamson et al., 2015). In fact, modulation of spontaneous and sound-evoked firing rates by arousal, movement, and task engagement is observed throughout the central auditory pathway, including the midbrain, brainstem, and even the auditory periphery (Carmel & Starr, 1963; R. Chen et al., 2019; Ryan et al., 1984; Shaheen et al., 2021; Singla et al., 2017; Y. Yang et al., 2020). Based on the limited evidence available, the coarse and relatively subtle modulation of MGB firing rates by extra-sensory internal state variables appears roughly equivalent in degree and specificity to that of other subcortical auditory stations but collectively differs from that of ACtx, where firing-rate properties can be modulated at precise moments in time (Buran et al., 2014; Carcea et al., 2017; Jaramillo & Zador, 2011) or focused on auditory feature submodalities (J. B. Fritz et al., 2005; Polley et al., 2006; Saderi et al., 2021) to reflect task demands. In terms of encoding extra-sensory task elements, MGB and ACtx neurons encode limited information about non-sensory variables related to decision planning, reward expectation, and reward value (Brosch et al., 2005; Stoilova et al., 2020; Xin et al., 2019). The information that is encoded about extra-sensory task features is strongly dependent on descending frontal cortex inputs (Liu et al., 2021), is more ephemeral than what is observed in downstream association cortex areas (Runyan et al., 2017), and may be no stronger overall in the ACtx than the MGB (Jaramillo et al., 2014).

In sum, auditory thalamocortical circuits occupy an intermediate station on the road from sound to meaning. At the level of the auditory thalamus, the high-fidelity isomorphic encoding of the acoustic stimulus waveform is reformatted to a rate-based abstraction of the source signal that can reflect integrative sound properties distributed over longer timescales. The rate-based representations reflect more than just the sensory properties of the stimulus and also reflect extra-sensory features such as sensorimotor integration, multisensory attributes, global internal states, and very specific modulations related to selective attention (Downer et al., 2017; Schwartz & David, 2018) and temporal anticipation (Jaramillo & Zador, 2011). Although auditory thalamocortical circuits reflect the contribution of wider brain states, their activity is still best conceptualized as representing behaviorally relevant acoustic features that will shape perceptually guided decision making, not decision planning, action, or reinforcement expectation.

Having introduced the reader to the organization of auditory thalamocortical circuits and provided a summary of their role in sensory coding, perception, and action, we now turn our attention to the organization and plasticity of local circuits in the MGB and ACtx across early postnatal development and adulthood.

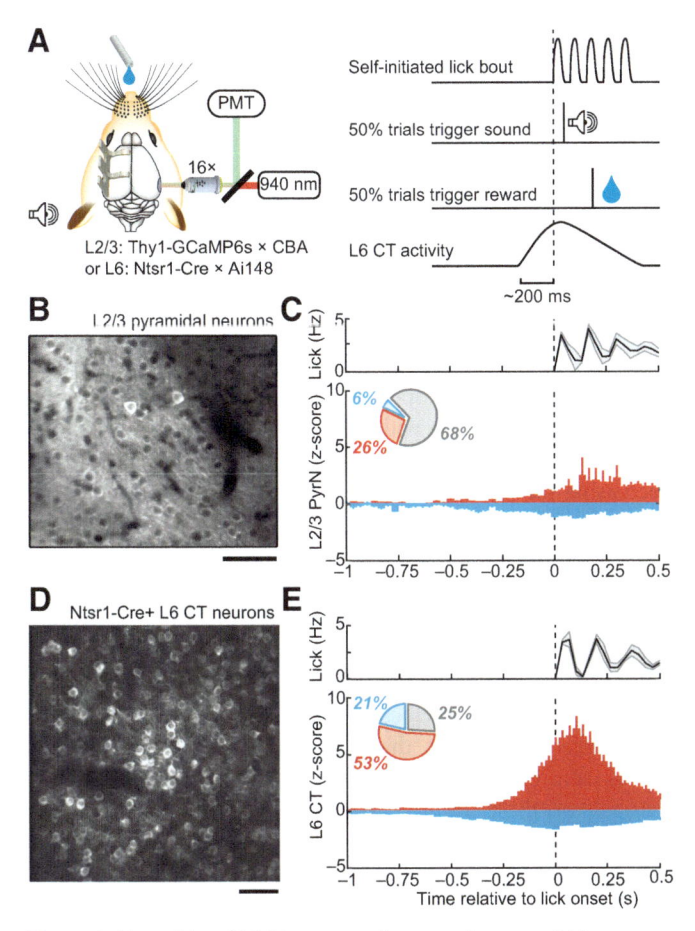

Figure 5 Ensembles of L6 CT neurons – but not other pyramidal neurons – are activated hundreds of milliseconds prior to movements that can trigger sound and reward.

A. Left: Schematic for two-photon imaging of motor-related activation in layer 2/3 pyramidal neurons (L2/3 PyrNs) and L6 CT neurons. Right: Schematic of lickspout sampling task in which the onset of a lick bout is probabilistically linked to sound presentation and reward.

B. GCaMP6s fluorescence in layer 2/3 PyrNs in a Thy1-GCaMP transgenic mouse. Scale bar, 50 μm.

C. Pie charts present percentage of neurons significantly enhanced (red) or suppressed (blue) during the peri-lick period (n = 624 L2/3 PyrNs). Peri-event time histograms (PSTHs) present mean ± SEM normalized calcium activity rates from lick-only trials. Top panel presents the mean ± SEM lick rate for the corresponding recordings sessions.

D. GCaMP6f fluorescence in layer L6 CT neurons in an NTSR1-Cre x Ai148 mouse obtained 690 μm below the cortical surface. Scale bar, 50 μm.

E. As per panel C, but from 739 Ntsr1-Cre+ L6 CT neurons. Data are from Clayton et al. (2021).

the MGB or TRN) fits into this scheme. ACtx GABA neurons and L6 neurons both receive monosynaptic inputs from the secondary motor cortex, yet their dominant source of motor-related input onto L6 CTs appears to come from the globus pallidus, not motor regions of the cortex (Clayton et al., 2021; Nelson et al., 2013). Further, it remains to be seen whether the bi-directional modulation of frequency tuning in A1, the MGB, and the TRN following artificial optogenetic activation of L6 CTs (Figure 4) is upheld with the natural patterns of L6 CT activation by motor corollary inputs, and these forms of dynamic sensory tuning can be leveraged to adaptively amplify or suppress anticipated sounds according to task demands.

3. Development of the Thalamocortical Pathway

In popular altricial animal models, such as rats, mice, and ferrets, mature thalamocortical response properties emerge during early postnatal development in an activity- and experience-dependent manner. In neonatal rodents, central auditory circuits develop in response to intense bursts of activity in the auditory periphery driven by the Ca^{2+} action potentials of the inner hair cells (Wang & Bergles, 2015). This coordinated activity resembles the propagating retinal waves that occur before eye opening and is necessary for establishing normal retinotopic maps within the superior colliculus and lateral geniculate nuclei (reviewed in Firth et al., 2005). Remarkably, the coarse topography of the thalamocortical circuits is also established in the absence of sound-driven activity (Barkat et al., 2011).

The onset of hearing spurs on the rapid sound-driven development of the molecular, electrophysiological, and anatomical properties of neurons throughout the auditory pathway. In rodents, hearing onset occurs around postnatal day (P) 11, when the external auditory meatus (ear canal) typically opens and the middle ear is cleared of fluid (Alford & Ruben, 1963; Ehret, 1976), leading to an abrupt drop in peripheral hearing thresholds that stabilize at adult-like levels several days later. Hearing onset is accompanied by a global upregulation of genes related to neurotransmission and synaptic plasticity within both the MGB and ACtx (Hackett et al., 2015). At the network level, frequency tuning and tonotopic map organization parallel the rapid maturation of peripheral sound transduction and are mature several days after hearing onset (Barkat et al., 2011; Bonham et al., 2004; de Villers-Sidani et al., 2007; Ehret & Romand, 1992; Polley et al., 2013; Romand & Ehret, 1990; Sanes et al., 1989). Higher-order sound feature representations are refined on a more protracted developmental time course. For example, selectivity for ipsilateral sound sources matures several days after pure-tone frequency tuning (Polley et al., 2013), followed by the maturation of spectral bandwidth selectivity and responses to frequency modulation (Insanally et al., 2009). Neural synchronization to temporal modulation is the slowest to mature; it continues to develop throughout adolescence, potentially reflecting the perceptual utility of encoding conspecific vocalizations (Razak & Fuzessery, 2010, 2015; Rosen et al., 2010; Sanes & Woolley, 2011; Sarro & Sanes, 2010).

Although thalamocortical maps and single-neuron selectivity for basic sound features are fairly mature by the time peripheral transduction thresholds are adult-like, they can still be powerfully shaped by abnormal hearing experiences. In the sections that follow, we describe marked changes in local-circuit and synaptic properties that occur in the period surrounding the onset of hearing. We also summarize a large body of work describing how alterations in early auditory experience change the developmental trajectories of thalamocortical circuits and guide the emergence of functionally specialized neural circuits for sound processing.

3.1 Maturation of MGB Circuits

Postnatal development and plasticity of MGB sensory, synaptic, and intrinsic properties are remarkably understudied, compared to both the other central auditory regions and other regions of the sensory thalamus. The evidence that exists has identified pronounced changes in the electrophysiological properties of MGB neurons around the onset of hearing, including a large reduction in membrane input resistances, a hyperpolarization of resting membrane potentials, and a quickening of the membrane time constants (Tennigkeit et al., 1998a, 1998b; Venkataraman & Bartlett, 2014). Changes in intrinsic properties parallel the dramatic maturation of gene expression within the MGB. Interestingly, a high percentage of genes (~85%) in the MGB, unlike the ACtx, show decreasing rather than increasing gene-expression trajectories (Hackett et al., 2015). Following hearing onset, the excitatory and inhibitory inputs innervating the MGB also undergo developmental alterations. For example, protein expression of the vesicular transporter for glutamate 1 (VGluT1) is dramatically upregulated after hearing onset, which may partially reflect the proliferation of VGluT1-expressing CT terminals throughout the MGB (Hackett et al., 2016; Torii et al., 2013). Brain-slice experiments that isolate feedforward GABAergic inputs from the IC to the MGB revealed rapid developmental changes in these inputs around hearing onset, including a faster kinetics of inhibitory postsynaptic potentials (IPSPs) and reduced synaptic depression (Venkataraman & Bartlett, 2013). These developmental changes increase the efficacy of IC inputs to curtail the excitation of MGB neurons, which may contribute to the experience-dependent plasticity of MGBv frequency tuning bandwidth that also occurs in the first few days following the onset of hearing (Barkat et al., 2011).

3.2 MGB Innervation of the Transient Cortical Subplate

As the developing thalamic axons grow toward the cortex, the first neurons they target are the subplate neurons (SPNs) located within the white matter below the cortical plate. SPNs are among the earliest generated cortical neurons (Luskin & Shatz, 1985; Valverde et al., 1989) and the first to respond to sensory stimuli (Wess et al., 2017). In the developing ferret cortex, SPNs exhibit broad tuning, suggesting that these neurons form an early-, coarse tonotopic map (Wess et al., 2017). Similarly, experiments in mouse thalamocortical slices have revealed that SPNs receive direct monosynaptic input from the MGB in the first few days after birth that strengthens over the first two postnatal weeks (Zhao et al., 2009). These neurons display extensive dendritic ramifications (del Río et al., 2000; Zljak et al., 1992) that integrate inputs from the thalamus (Viswanathan et al., 2017; Zhao et al., 2009), cortex (Viswanathan et al., 2012, 2017) and neuromodulatory regions (Calarco & Robertson, 1995; Mechawar & Descarries, 2001). In turn, SPNs send cascading axons into the cortex that synapse onto both excitatory pyramidal neurons and GABAergic inhibitory interneurons (Deng et al., 2017; Zhao et al., 2009). Although SPNs are a diverse population consisting of both glutamatergic and GABAergic neurons, retrograde labeling has shown that the majority of the SPNs projecting to L4 are glutamatergic (Finney et al., 1998). In slices of mouse ACtx, selective stimulation of SPNs produces large feedforward excitatory postsynaptic potentials (EPSCs) in L4 neurons (Zhao et al., 2009). Thus, the subplate forms a transient microcircuit linking the neonatal thalamus and cortex, where thalamic axons appear to "wait" before extending into the cortical plate.

Various studies highlight the important function of SPN microcircuits in orchestrating the development of thalamic projections (for reviews, see Kanold, 2009; Kanold & Luhmann, 2010). SPNs have been proposed to play an essential role in thalamocortical pathfinding across sensory cortices, providing a scaffold for thalamic axons to find their targets in the more superficial cortical layers (Ghosh et al., 1990; Grant et al., 2012; López-Bendito & Molnár, 2003). Indeed, early ablation of SPNs by excitotoxic kainic acid injections prevents thalamic axons from growing into L4 above the ablated subplate regions (Ghosh et al., 1990). Even ablations performed after the thalamic axons have reached L4 affect the thalamocortical circuitry, reducing the developmental strengthening of thalamocortical synapses onto L4 neurons (Kanold et al., 2003). Thus, SPNs are thought to couple the developing thalamus and cortex, enhancing correlated activity between these two regions to induce thalamocortical plasticity during early developmental periods (Kanold & Luhmann, 2010).

Although most studies have focused on subplate innervation of cortical L4, SPNs project to all layers of the cortex and affect the development of both intracortical and thalamocortical connections. SPNs may play a key role in the maturation of cortical GABAergic inhibition (Kanold & Shatz, 2006). SPNs also project to the most superficial cortical layer, L1, targeting both the apical dendrites and inhibitory neurons within this layer (Deng et al., 2017; Meng et al., 2020; Viswanathan et al., 2017). Interestingly, GABAergic SPNs directly inhibit another transient neuronal network in the developing cortex, the inhibitory L1 Cajal Retzius cells (Myakhar et al., 2011). However, the function of the inhibitory interactions between these two pioneer networks during early development is still unknown.

SPNs are thought to be transient populations that disappear following early development. Indeed, the vast majority undergo programmed cell death after the thalamocortical circuitry is established. However, a subset of these neurons (15–39%) will survive into adulthood and become integrated into deep layer 6 (Clancy et al., 2001; Clancy & Cauller, 1999; Hoerder-Suabedissen & Molnár, 2013; Marx et al., 2017; Price et al., 1997; Reep, 2000; Torres-Reverón & Friedlander, 2007; Vandevelde et al., 1996). These adult SPNs project to thalamorecipient layers 1, 5, and 5a, as well as back to the thalamus (Clancy & Cauller, 1999; Viswanathan et al., 2017). Newly discovered molecular markers are identifying SPNs (Heuer et al., 2003; Viswanathan et al., 2017), and future studies may reveal the function of SPNs in the adult cortex.

3.3 Silent Synapses in Auditory Thalamocortical Development

In the cortex, glutamate is the major excitatory transmitter and binds to two major types of glutamate-sensing postsynaptic receptors, AMPA receptors (AMPARs) and NMDA receptors (NMDARs). As a result of the Mg^{2+} block of NMDARs at resting membrane potentials, both glutamate binding and concurrent depolarization are required to activate NMDARs and conduct current (Nowak et al., 1984). "Silent synapses," a unique subset of immature synapses, express NMDARs but not AMPARs (Isaac, 2003; Isaac et al., 1995, 1997; Liao et al., 1995; Rumpel et al., 1998). NMDAR-only silent synapses can be evaluated in slices using voltage-clamp whole-cell recordings, holding the neurons at either hyperpolarized (~−60-mV) or depolarized (~+30-mV) voltages (Isaac et al., 1995). If AMPARs are present at the synapse, EPSCs are observed at both holding voltages. However, when only NMDA receptors are present at the synapse, EPSCs are only observed at +30 mV when the Mg^{2+} block of NMDA receptors is relieved. Experiments using this recording protocol in mouse auditory cortical slices have uncovered the presence of silent synapses at cortical inputs onto SPNs during the first two postnatal weeks (Meng et al., 2014).

Developmental strengthening of thalamocortical synapses onto L4 neurons may also occur by the insertion of AMPA receptors at silent synapses (Isaac et al., 1997). In the developing mouse ACtx, more than 50% of thalamocortical synapses onto L4 pyramidal neurons are "silent" during an early critical period for tonotopic map plasticity (P12–15) (H. Sun et al., 2018). This fraction of silent synapses shows a significant decline (to ~3%) as the mice age beyond this critical period (P16–21). In addition to excitatory neurons, GABAergic cortical neurons also exhibit silent synapses (Deng et al., 2017). Indeed, the gradual conversion of silent to active synapses across postnatal development is a ubiquitous feature of many brain networks (Hanse et al., 2013). The trafficking of AMPARs into silent synapses is a form of synaptic plasticity, long-term potentiation (LTP), that requires calcium-dependent post-translational modifications of AMPAR subunits (for review, see Huganir & Nicoll, 2013). The depolarization necessary to activate NMDARs at silent synapses to promote AMPAR insertion may depend on sensory inputs, depolarizing GABAergic inputs (for reviews, see Ben-Ari, 2002; Ben-Ari et al., 1997; Wang & Kriegstein, 2009), or neuromodulatory inputs (Levy & Aoki, 2002; Maggi et al., 2003).

3.4 Maturation of MGB Innervation of Cortical Excitatory and Inhibitory Neurons

Thalamocortical circuits undergo a surge of sound-driven development shortly after the onset of hearing, as peripheral transduction thresholds mature and SPNs are gradually eliminated. An in vitro technique was pioneered to track developmental and experience-dependent changes of functional topography between receptive field maps in the MGBv and ACtx (Barkat et al., 2011; Hackett et al., 2011). Stimulating

MGBv along the tonotopic axis produces a linear shift of maximal cortical responses, measured using voltage-sensitive dye imaging, within L4 along the ACtx tonotopic axis in developing mice (Barkat et al., 2011). These experiments demonstrate that functional thalamocortical topography is organized in neonatal mice, even before the onset of hearing. This is consistent with evidence that the expression and laminar patterns of VGluT2, a protein responsible for packaging glutamate into vesicles within thalamocortical synapses, is well established before hearing onset (Hackett et al., 2016).

At the cellular level, thalamocortical synapses onto both excitatory pyramidal neurons and GABAergic inhibitory interneurons within the ACtx undergo robust developmental changes (Kotak et al., 2005; Takesian et al., 2013). Although most studies focus on the thalamic innervation of L4 excitatory neurons within the ACtx, the GABAergic inhibitory interneurons are also a major thalamic target (X. Y. Ji et al., 2016; H. J. Rose & Metherate, 2005; Takesian et al., 2013). In fact, a key functional distinction between diverse inhibitory interneuron subtypes is the manner in which they are recruited by the thalamocortical pathway (Beierlein et al., 2003; Cruikshank et al., 2010; Gibson et al., 1999; Tan et al., 2008). PV-positive fast-spiking subtypes receive strong thalamic inputs that rapidly depress during repetitive stimuli, whereas SST-positive low-threshold spiking interneurons receive a relatively weak thalamic drive that facilitates. These distinct properties of thalamocortical synapses onto cortical interneurons emerge during postnatal development in response to hearing experience (Takesian et al., 2013). It is increasingly clear that across the sensory cortex, different subtypes of inhibitory interneurons exhibit distinct developmental profiles (Lazarus & Josh Huang, 2011; Takesian et al., 2013).

3.5 Maturation of Cortical Excitatory/Inhibitory Circuit Balance within the Auditory Cortex

The sound-evoked responses and receptive field properties of cortical neurons reflect the integration of excitatory thalamocortical inputs and a mixture of excitatory and inhibitory intracortical inputs. A prominent feature of neurons across sensory cortical regions is the approximate balance of sensory-evoked excitatory and inhibitory postsynaptic currents (Dorrn et al., 2010; Isaacson & Scanziani, 2011; Y. J. Sun et al., 2010; A. Y. Y. Tan & Wehr, 2009; Wehr & Zador, 2003; Xue et al., 2014). Sensory inputs elicit a fast excitatory current in neurons that is generally followed by a lagging feedforward inhibitory current proportional to the excitation. A relatively constant excitation/inhibition (E/I) ratio is thought to restrict activity, preventing runaway excitation, epileptiform activity, and excitotoxicity. Moreover, balanced inhibition expands the dynamic range of single neurons and cortical networks, permitting the recruitment of a large number of active afferents without saturating firing rates (Carcea & Froemke, 2013). Finally, slight adjustments in this E/I ratio can promote heightened synaptic and representational plasticity during normal development or in adult animals, either following peripheral deprivation or during sensory learning (reviewed in Persic et al., 2020; Takesian & Hensch, 2013).

A constant E/I ratio across a range of sensory stimuli implies that excitation and inhibition are co-tuned for sensory features. Indeed, various studies have demonstrated that excitatory and inhibitory receptive fields are aligned in the adult ACtx. However, the manner by which excitatory and inhibitory circuits are refined during early postnatal development to achieve a constant E/I ratio and co-tuning is a long-standing debate. Two pioneering studies (Dorrn et al., 2010; Y. J. Sun et al., 2010) utilized challenging whole-cell recordings in the ACtx to provide insights into the postnatal maturation of excitatory and inhibitory synaptic inputs. Both studies revealed changes in the balance of excitation and inhibition over development; however, the two studies observed contradictory developmental changes in excitatory and inhibitory tuning. Dorrn and colleagues showed that excitatory tuning remains stable while inhibitory tuning sharpens across the first postnatal month. Conversely, Sun and colleagues found that excitatory tuning sharpens across development, whereas inhibitory tuning remains stable. Some methodological differences between the studies, including the range of sound stimuli presented and the cortical layers where the recordings were performed, may underlie the conflicting results (for review, see King, 2010). A recent follow-up study combined in vivo whole-cell recordings with pharmacological silencing of the cortex to isolate the separate contributions of thalamocortical input and recurrent intracortical activity to the developmental refinement of excitatory input (Y. J. Sun et al., 2019). The results emphasize that the selective strengthening of intracortical excitatory connections plays a dominant, important role in the sharpening of excitatory input tuning to L4 neurons. However, the precise contributions of thalamocortical, intracortical excitatory, and inhibitory inputs to the refinement of receptive field properties across postnatal development have yet to be resolved.

3.6 Maturation of Corticothalamic Connectivity into the MGB

Because SPNs provide one of earliest connections between the thalamus and cortex, they are thought to function as a trailblazer for the thalamocortical pathway (McConnell et al., 1994). Thalamic-projecting SPNs may bypass primary thalamic nuclei, specifically targeting higher-order thalamic regions (Hoerder-Suabedissen et al., 2018; Viswanathan et al., 2017). Just as the thalamocortical neurons "wait" in the subplate before extending into the cortex, the first CT neurons may also "wait" in regions outside of the thalamus (reviewed in Grant et al., 2012). Neonatal auditory CT projections are initially confined to the deep dorsal zone (DDZ) of the MGB before innervating surrounding regions of the MGB at the time of hearing onset (Torii et al., 2013). This developmental pattern of CT targeting may depend on molecular cues. For example, in mice over-expressing a receptor for the axon guidance molecule ephrin-A, EphA7, corticothalamic axons remain concentrated in the DDZ (Torii et al., 2013).

Differential expression of other axon-guidance factors in neonatal mice, including semaphorins, ephrins, and netrins, has also been proposed to steer the cortical axons into the MGB versus the primary visual thalamus, the LGN (Horng et al., 2009).

4. Experience- and Activity-Dependent Development of Auditory Thalamocortical Circuits

4.1 Plasticity of Sound Representations Following Manipulations of Early Auditory Experience

Studies in developing animals have revealed a remarkable degree of plasticity within thalamocortical circuits in response to the early sound environment. During restricted developmental epochs, occurring in the rodent life from the onset of hearing to before sexual maturity, changes in the ambient sound environment can profoundly modify auditory circuits. Robust plasticity by passive sound exposure is often found to be unique to these developmental windows, referred to as *critical* or *sensitive* periods (for reviews, see Hensch, 2004; Kuhl, 2010; Takesian & Hensch, 2013). Enduring alterations in the MGB or cortical representation of specific sound features following periods of abnormal developmental experience may have long-lasting effects on perceptual abilities (for review, see Sanes & Woolley, 2011).

Although thalamocortical connections are initially established embryonically (Gurung & Fritzsch, 2004), with further refinements in connectional topography occurring before the onset of hearing (Barkat et al., 2011), the tonotopic organization of preferred frequency tuning can be specifically and persistently modified by rearing altricial animals in modified acoustic environments. Sound-induced morphing of the cortical synaptic properties, receptive field tuning, and map organization has become a premier model of auditory plasticity, providing a valuable platform to study modes and mechanisms of age-dependent plasticity (for reviews, see Pienkowski & Eggermont, 2011; Schreiner & Polley, 2014). In rodents, exposure to repetitive pure tones of a single frequency leads to an expanded representation of that frequency within the cortical tonotopic map (Han et al., 2007; H. Kim & Bao, 2009; Zhang et al., 2001). This form of robust plasticity is limited to just a brief three-day critical period beginning at the onset of hearing when sound-evoked thresholds abruptly drop (Barkat et al., 2011; de Villers-Sidani et al., 2007). Interestingly, robust changes in tonotopic maps to brief periods of passive tone rearing do not occur in the upstream auditory thalamus, highlighting either thalamocortical or intracortical synapses as key sites of plasticity (Barkat et al., 2011).

Similar to the effects of dark rearing on the development of central visual circuits, rearing young animals in featureless noise can disrupt the normal development of subcortical sound localization circuits (Seidl & Grothe, 2005), detune frequency selectivity in the ACtx (Zhang et al., 2002), and forestall the normal maturation of other sound features (Chang & Merzenich, 2003). For example, exposing animals to continuous noise disrupts the normal timing of ACtx critical-period windows and prevents the normal maturation of GABAergic protein markers in map regions corresponding to the frequency range of the noise band (Chang & Merzenich, 2003; de Villers-Sidani et al., 2007; X. Zhou et al., 2011). In humans, early childhood experience with degraded auditory inputs is a commonly occurring condition that can lead to long-lasting deficits in auditory perceptual skills and difficulties in the acquisition of speech and language (for review, see Moore, 2007; Whitton & Polley, 2011). Although these deficits are particularly severe following extended periods of auditory deprivation, even a temporary elevation of hearing thresholds can lead to auditory-processing impairments (Hogan et al., 1996; Sharma et al., 2002; Wilmington et al., 1994). Developmental bilateral conductive hearing loss in gerbils impairs the detection of slow-sinusoidal-amplitude modulations (SAMs) across populations of auditory cortical neurons, resulting in deficits in behavioral perception (Rosen et al., 2012). Similarly, selectivity for frequency-modulation (FM) sweep direction is vulnerable to early hearing loss. Neurons with low characteristic frequencies (CFs) generally respond to up sweeps, whereas neurons with high CFs respond more robustly to down sweeps (Zhang et al., 2003). Bats deprived of normal developmental experience with echolocation calls exhibit a dramatic reduction in the FM direction selectivity of cortical neurons (Razak et al., 2008). Conversely, animals exposed to downward FM sweeps during a specific developmental window showed an increase in the neuronal selectivity for downward sweeps (Insanally et al., 2009). Studies using two-tone stimulus and tone sequence paradigms also provide evidence that temporal responses are shaped by sensory inputs during early postnatal periods (Chang et al., 2005; Nakahara et al., 2004).

Although the binaural coding properties of central auditory neurons are mostly adult-like at the onset of hearing, the integration of sound inputs from the two ears is needed to preserve these properties during distinct developmental windows (Knudsen et al., 1984; D. R. Moore et al., 1999; Parsons et al., 1999; Polley et al., 2013; Popescu & Polley, 2010). "Amblyaudia" is commonly associated with transient hearing loss related to childhood middle ear infections and seems to arise from an imbalance in the quality and timing of auditory afferent activity transmitted from each ear. Like the more commonly studied amblyopia, a reversible unilateral deprivation of sound inputs to one ear during early postnatal development engages an interaural competitive plasticity that culminates in the neural over-representation of the non-deprived ear in A1, with comparatively weak effects in the IC (Popescu & Polley, 2010). Even a very brief deprivation of inputs from one ear shortly after hearing onset disrupts the alignment of interaural frequency receptive fields. The same manipulation applied after the tonotopic map critical period remodeled neural selectivity for interaural level differences, such that A1 neurons preferred inputs to the normally subordinate ipsilateral ear (Polley et al., 2013). Interestingly, even subtle changes in the arrival of sounds between the two ears can influence the development of central sound-localization encoding. One elegant study implanted an acoustic filtering device in one ear of juvenile barn owls that altered the timing and level of sounds. Experience with this device resulted in adaptive shifts in the tuning of thalamic neurons to interaural time differences (ITDs), another important sound-localization cue. ITD tuning was not altered in the IC, suggesting that this plasticity may first emerge in the thalamus along the auditory pathway (Miller & Knudsen, 2003).

4.2 Plasticity of Sound Representations in Adult Thalamocortical Circuits

Although robust modifications of central auditory circuits by changes in the ambient sound environment may be restricted to developmental "critical periods," perhaps one of the most influential discoveries in auditory neuroscience is the remarkable preservation of plasticity in adult thalamocortical circuits. Work performed in many species has demonstrated that this malleability can support associative and enduring synaptic changes for inputs with acquired behavioral significance but also underlies widespread neural hyperactivity that overshoots homeostatic set points to cause disordered perceptual states. Understanding both the "yin" and the "yang" of the large-scale plasticity in adult auditory thalamocortical circuits – as well as the underlying mechanisms that shape adaptive versus catastrophic manifestations of these changes – is key to understanding the importance of these circuits in normal and disordered sound perception and is the topic that we turn our attention to in the next two sections.

Recent studies highlight the consequences of degraded sensory inputs from the auditory periphery for mature thalamocortical circuits. Both the loss of auditory sensory signals from the auditory periphery and changes in the acoustic environment that mask patterned sensory inputs can result in reorganization in the coarse tonotopic maps within the adult MGB and auditory cortex. One approach used by several studies is to assess the impact of a mechanical lesion that is restricted to a specific region of the cochlea, eliminating signals from the cochlea over the affected frequency range. When the MGB is examined months after the lesion, the region deprived by the cochlear lesion is not silent but instead responsive to spared frequencies that flank damaged cochlear regions (Kamke et al., 2003). This "expanded representation" of the lesion-edge epithelium results in a distorted tonotopic map within the MGB. A similar expanded representation of lesion-edge regions and a distorted tonotopic map is observed in A1 (Eggermont & Komiya, 2000; Pienkowski & Eggermont, 2011; Robertson & Irvine, 1989). The reorganization of tonotopic maps within A1 has been described across a number of species in response to cochlear damage produced by distinct methods, including ototoxic lesions and acute exposure to pure tones (Calford et al., 1993; Eggermont & Komiya, 2000; Noreña et al., 2003; Schreiner & Polley, 2014). However, such plasticity to restricted lesions either does not occur or occurs to a lesser degree in the IC, implicating the MGB as the primary locus for this form of plasticity.

Even non-traumatic sound experiences during adulthood may spur central auditory plasticity. For example, prolonged passive exposure to tone pip ensembles or noise at non-traumatic intensities can reduce the activity of neurons within the auditory cortex (Pienkowski et al., 2011). Similarly, continuous exposure to moderate-intensity broadband white noise is associated with plasticity of receptive field bandwidths, tonotopic maps, and synchronization of spontaneous activity (Thomas et al., 2019; Zheng, 2012; Zhou & Merzenich, 2012). Interestingly, the disruption of patterned sound inputs by this white-noise stimulus is thought to briefly reopen a "critical period" that enables robust plasticity to the ambient sound environment.

Remarkably, central circuits may adjust to diminished input from the auditory periphery by drastically amplifying the residual sensory signals. For example, profound cochlear denervation that eliminates >95% of synapses between auditory nerve fibers and cochlear sensory cells triggers a progressive, compensatory plasticity that enables robust sound-evoked activity in the higher auditory pathway, including the IC (Chambers, Resnik, et al., 2016), MGB (Chambers, Salazar, et al., 2016), and primary ACtx (Chambers, Resnik, et al., 2016). Although these animals would be deemed profoundly deaf based on traditional measures of brainstem evoked potentials and acoustic reflexes, neurons in the IC, MGB, and A1 amplify the small fraction of residual inputs from the ear to restore relatively normal behavioral tone-detection thresholds (Chambers, Resnik, et al., 2016). In fact, sound-evoked activity in these regions, particularly the ACtx and, to a lesser extent, the IC and MGB, rebounds, even surpassing control levels. This increase in "central gain" occurs by the progressive development of network hyperexcitability following hearing loss, associated with underlying changes in thalamic and cortical GABAergic inhibitory function (Resnik & Polley, 2017; Sametsky et al., 2015).

Learning-induced changes in adult thalamocortical circuits are thought to require the release of neuromodulators recruited by arousal or attention (for reviews, see Pienkowski & Eggermont, 2011; Schreiner & Polley, 2014). For example, pairing tones with aversive shocks produces rapid shifts in the tuning of neurons within the MGB and ACtx cortex toward the paired frequency and an expanded representation of that frequency within tonotopic maps (Abs et al., 2018; Bakin & Weinberger, 1990; J. M. Edeline et al., 1993; J.-M. Edeline & Weinberger, 1991a, 1991b, 1992). A recent study using a miniature microscope to monitor the calcium activity of MGB neurons during fear conditioning revealed highly diverse plasticity patterns that may be in coordination with downstream networks, such as the amygdala (Taylor et al., 2021). Behavioral training on an auditory task can also reinstate a plasticity in frequency tuning in both the MGB and auditory cortex (Bieszczad & Weinberger, 2010; J. Fritz et al., 2003; Polley et al., 2006; Recanzone et al., 1993; Reed et al., 2011). Intriguingly, the representation of specific sound features in the ACtx may be shaped by specific task training. For example, training animals to attend to either frequency or intensity cues results in selective increases in the representation of either the target frequencies or the target intensities within the ACtx, respectively (Polley et al., 2006). Thus, the receptive field properties of neurons within the adult central auditory system may be continuously shaped by active listening during reinforcement-based learning.

5. Circuit, Cellular, and Molecular Mechanisms for Thalamocortical Plasticity

The remarkable plasticity of thalamocortical sound representations in the first weeks of hearing reflects a precisely orchestrated process across multiple cell types that collectively open, close, and regulate the lasting influence of auditory experience on forebrain circuits for sound perception. Identifying how these mechanisms work both independently and synergistically could suggest new therapeutic avenues for auditory perceptual disorders that feature prominently in neurodevelopmental disorders, hearing loss, and normal aging. Although thalamocortical sound representations can be shaped by auditory experience throughout the lifespan, the mechanisms that support statistical learning in development are not the same as the processes underlying auditory learning in adulthood, and both collectively differ from the mechanisms that regulate neural gain after the loss of peripheral input. Identifying the circuit, cellular, and molecular regulators underlying each form of plasticity informs our understanding of how auditory forebrain circuits regulate sound representations to match the physical and psychological demands of sound processing, as well as the catastrophic neurological failures that result from their improper regulation.

Intriguingly, the timing of critical-period windows for heightened brain plasticity is not strictly controlled by developmental age but is itself plastic and can be shifted by sensory experience (for reviews, see de Villers-Sidani & Merzenich, 2011; Takesian & Hensch, 2013; Voss et al., 2017). For example, exposure to pulsed tones or pulsed white noise accelerates critical-period closure in the ACtx (Zhang et al., 2002; X. Zhou & Merzenich, 2012), whereas noisy environments delay critical-period closure (Chang & Merzenich, 2003). Diverse mechanisms underlie the timing of windows for heightened brain plasticity, encompassing "triggers" that spur the onset of critical periods and "brakes" that actively dampen plasticity as thalamocortical sound representations more reliably match auditory environmental inputs. The vast majority of our knowledge about auditory thalamocortical critical-period regulation has been inspired by the far larger and richer literature on the plasticity of central visual pathways following visual deprivation, which has been the subject of many comprehensive reviews (Hensch, 2005; Hooks & Chen, 2007; Levelt & Hübener, 2012).

5.1 Disinhibitory Mechanisms for Thalamocortical Plasticity

GABAergic circuits feature prominently in the regulation of many distinct forms of thalamocortical developmental plasticity. The experience-dependent maturation of cortical GABAergic inhibitory neurons is thought to act as a "trigger" for enhanced periods of plasticity. In the auditory system, the abrupt onset of peripheral hearing stimulates the maturation of inhibition (Kandler, 2004). It has been proposed that this inhibition acts to preferentially suppress spontaneous activity, switching the primary driving factor for circuit maturation from internally generated patterns to sensory-evoked (Toyoizumi et al., 2013). Factors that promote the maturation of inhibitory interneurons, including brain-derived neurotrophic factor (BDNF) (Z. J. Huang et al., 1999; Itami et al., 2007), contribute to sound-induced plasticity during the critical period for tonotopic map plasticity (Anomal et al., 2013) These studies parallel those in the visual cortex showing that stimulating the maturation of inhibitory circuits with BDNF (Hanover et al., 1999) or pharmacologically enhancing inhibition (Fagiolini et al., 2004; Fagiolini & Hensch, 2000; Hensch et al., 1998) can initiate critical-period onset. Moreover, reducing inhibitory transmission in the adult reopens a state of robust synaptic plasticity (Morishita & Hensch, 2008). For example, inactivating PV-expressing GABAergic interneurons using a chemogenetic approach in the ACtx enables CP-like tonotopic reorganization (Cisneros-Franco & de Villers-Sidani, 2019). Even natural forms of adult auditory learning are associated with a profound reduction of spontaneous inhibitory synaptic currents onto pyramidal neurons that is restored to baseline levels once performance on the auditory task has plateaued (Sarro et al., 2015).

Although reduced intracortical inhibition promotes sensory plasticity following enriched hearing experience and auditory learning, many of the molecular "brakes" that restrict plasticity into adulthood also target GABAergic interneurons. For example, perineuronal nets (PNNs) are lattice-like structures of extracellular matrix molecules that gradually form around cortical PV interneurons (Härtig et al., 1992) during the maturation of sound-response properties (Friauf, 2000). PNNs are thought to augment the metabolic microenvironment surrounding these interneurons (Balmer, 2016), enable these neurons to maintain high firing frequencies (Dityatev et al., 2007; Lensjø et al., 2017), and regulate synaptic inputs impinging onto these interneurons (Carceller et al., 2020; Favuzzi et al., 2017).

Referring to "inhibition" or "E:I ratio" in the previous examples as a monolithic mechanism ignores the more nuanced control of local circuit plasticity by specific subtypes of GABAergic interneurons, each endowed with distinct connectivity patterns, morphological and electrophysiological properties, and molecular identities. For example, GABAergic microcircuits in the superficial ACtx regulate plasticity by disinhibition. Located directly underneath the pial surface, cortical L1 is sparsely populated by a diverse group of GABAergic interneurons often identified by the expression of NDNF or VIP that are distinct from the two other commonly studied interneuron classes expressing PV or SST (S. H. Lee et al., 2010). These interneurons are key targets of the diverse axons populating L1, including thalamic and neuromodulatory projections (S. H. Lee et al., 2010; Letzkus et al.,

2011; Takesian et al., 2018). Although NDNF and VIP interneurons release the inhibitory neurotransmitter GABA, subsets of these interneurons have a "disinhibitory" function—because they target other inhibitory interneurons, their activity leads to a net withdrawal of inhibition from glutamatergic neurons (Fu et al., 2014; Letzkus et al., 2011; Pfeffer et al., 2013; Takesian et al., 2018).

L1 interneurons in primary and secondary auditory cortical regions are positioned at the nexus of thalamocortical inputs from the MGBv, MGBd, and MGBm and long-range neuromodulatory inputs and specifically target local PV and SST GABAergic subtypes, endowing them with a privileged capacity to regulate sensory plasticity and sound processing. Indeed, cholinergic activation of this disinhibitory circuit underlies tonotopic map reorganization, likely by inhibiting PV neurons (Cohen-Kashi Malina et al., 2021; Kuchibhotla et al., 2017; Letzkus et al., 2011; Takesian et al., 2018). Moreover, boosting the cholinergic activation of these interneurons by genetic deletion of an nAChR modulator, Lynx1, prolongs this critical period beyond early life (Takesian et al., 2018). Thus, recent studies highlight this diverse group of disinhibitory neurons in the superficial cortex as a promising target to regulate both developmental and adult plasticity.

5.2 Plasticity of GABAergic Inhibitory Circuits

GABAergic interneurons are both a regulator of – and regulated by – auditory experience. A complete loss of acoustic input during early life is associated with reduced expression of GABAergic markers and reduced synaptic inhibitory currents (reviewed by Sanes & Bao, 2009; Takesian et al., 2009). Even a brief period of moderate hearing loss during development can result in enduring alterations in inhibitory synapses (Mowery et al., 2015, 2019; Takesian et al., 2012) that may underlie perceptual deficits in later life (Caras & Sanes, 2015; Whitton & Polley, 2011). Indeed, the importance of early sensory experience for the normal maturation of cortical inhibition has been shown across primary sensory cortices (Chattopadhyaya et al., 2004; Gianfranceschi et al., 2003; Jiao et al., 2006; Morales et al., 2002; Sadaka et al., 2003; Takesian et al., 2013). The failure to develop normal inhibition following early hearing loss may underlie the increases in the spontaneous and sensory-evoked excitability of auditory cortical neurons (Noreña et al., 2003; Qiu et al., 2000; Raggio & Schreiner, 1999; Seki & Eggermont, 2003).

A comprehensive understanding of the deficits in cortical inhibition that accompany hearing loss requires an understanding of the complex changes within specific interneuron circuits. For example, developmental sensorineural hearing loss produces opposing effects within two distinct inhibitory circuits mediated by fast-spiking (FS) neurons (putative PV interneurons) and low-threshold spiking (LTS) neurons (putative SST interneurons). Whereas the FS circuit shows both a *reduction* of fast thalamocortical drive onto FS interneurons and a *reduction* of inhibitory drive from FS interneurons to pyramidal neurons, the LTS interneuron circuit exhibits an opposite *increase* in thalamocortical drive and *increase* in inhibitory drive onto pyramidal neurons (Takesian et al., 2010, 2013). Indeed, there is converging evidence from across sensory cortices that decreased cortical inhibitory gain following developmental deprivation occurs specifically at synapses formed by FS interneurons (Katagiri et al., 2007; Maffei et al., 2004).

Reductions in cortical PV interneuron-mediated inhibition also occur following adult-onset hearing loss. Within hours after either moderate or profound loss of auditory nerve fibers, a dip in PV interneuron-mediated inhibition is observed in the adult mouse primary auditory cortex (Resnik & Polley, 2017). The rapid reduction in inhibitory function persists for weeks and forecasts the eventual recovery of sound-evoked cortical responses weeks later. Conversely, SST interneurons in the ACtx exhibit elevated spontaneous and tone-evoked firing rates after adult peripheral hearing loss and may, therefore, serve to thwart increases in cortical excitability (Novák et al., 2016). A comprehensive understanding of how the distinct populations of cortical inhibitory circuits dynamically adjust to a loss of signals from the sensory periphery will further illuminate the sequelae leading to hyperexcitability and its associated auditory disorders following both developmental and adult hearing loss.

5.3 Age-Dependent Plasticity of Thalamocortical Synapses

In addition to inhibitory mechanisms, the excitatory thalamocortical synapses have been identified as loci of age-dependent plasticity. The unsilencing of NMDAR-only synapses is a mechanism for developmental plasticity in sensory cortices (X. Huang, 2019) that occurs in the days following hearing onset in the ACtx during the critical period for tonotopic map plasticity (H. Sun et al., 2018). As these silent synapses disappear, long-term plasticity at developing thalamocortical synapses is abruptly lost with age (Blundon & Zakharenko, 2013). For example, trains of stimuli applied to the thalamic afferents in acute thalamocortical slices lead to both (LTP) and long-term depression in mouse pups aged <P15 but not in juvenile or adult mice (Blundon et al., 2011; Chun et al., 2013). This sharp loss of neonatal plasticity is associated with an upregulation of adenosine levels within MGB neurons (Blundon et al., 2017), which may limit sustained glutamate release at thalamocortical synapses (Patton et al., 2019). Indeed, genetic and pharmacological disruptions of adenosine signaling can rejuvenate tonotopic map plasticity in the adult auditory cortex (Blundon et al., 2017). Interestingly, the normal expression of LTP at both developing excitatory and inhibitory synapses within the ACtx may be impaired by the loss of normal hearing experience (Kotak et al., 2007; Xu et al., 2010). Thus, gating mechanisms for bidirectional long-term synaptic plasticity along the developing thalamocortical pathway may be a crucial mechanism underlying the experience-dependent plasticity of sensory representations.

5.4 Neuromodulatory Mechanisms

The central auditory system is innervated by an extensive network of long-range inputs from neuromodulatory nuclei in the brainstem, midbrain, and basal forebrain. Neuromodulators powerfully filter and modify acoustic signal processing in the MGB and ACtx, acutely influencing sound perception and sound-driven behaviors. Moreover, the convergence of these neuromodulators with sensory signals can induce long-lasting changes in sound responses within forebrain regions that may underlie auditory learning. Accumulating studies are identifying the synaptic, cellular, and circuit mechanisms underlying acute and long-term modifications within the auditory thalamocortical system induced by neuromodulators.

The cholinergic neuromodulatory system has long been a target to promote plasticity in the adult auditory system. Seminal experiments have demonstrated robust shifts in the preferred frequency of adult ACtx neurons by pairing a tone with stimulation of the basal forebrain, a source of cholinergic input to the ACtx (Bakin & Weinberger, 1996; Froemke et al., 2007, 2013; Guo et al., 2019; Kilgard & Merzenich, 1998). This pairing induces a rapid drop of synaptic inhibition that is thought to gate synaptic plasticity processes (Froemke et al., 2007). Pairing a tone with vagus nerve stimulation (VNS), which may lead to the release of multiple neurotransmitters, including acetylcholine, was also found to induce persistent changes in auditory cortical maps and reverse deficits in auditory cortical properties following noise-induced trauma (Engineer et al., 2011).

Acetylcholine is known to target multiple sites within thalamocortical circuits, but the precise mechanisms by which acetylcholine induces auditory plasticity are not fully understood. Basal forebrain cholinergic neurons can indirectly modulate MGB thalamocortical processing via dense projections to the TRN, whereas brainstem nuclei release acetylcholine onto postsynaptic cholinergic receptors on MGB neurons and excitatory presynaptic corticothalamic and inhibitory tectothalamic axon terminals (reviewed by B. D. Richardson et al., 2021). In the ACtx, cholinergic inputs to cortical L1 interneurons may gate cortical plasticity by disinhibiting PV-expressing interneurons during developmental periods (Takesian et al., 2018) and adulthood (Belén Pardi et al., 2020; Cohen-Kashi Malina et al., 2021; Letzkus et al., 2011). Acetylcholine may also promote adult auditory plasticity by targeting thalamocortical synapses. The activation of muscarinic (metabotropic) acetylcholine receptors may restore critical period–like tonotopic map plasticity in the ACtx by inhibiting adenosine signaling, a molecular brake that blocks glutamate release (Blundon et al., 2011; Chun et al., 2013).

The noradrenergic and serotonergic neuromodulatory systems have also been implicated in auditory plasticity (W. Ji & Suga, 2007; Martins & Froemke, 2015). For example, tonotopic reorganization by pure tones is abolished in mice that lack noradrenaline from birth (Shepard et al., 2015). Moreover, pairing tones with electrical stimulation of the locus coeruleus (Martins and Froemke, 2015), a region that releases noradrenaline, causes shifts in the frequency tuning of A1 neurons. These findings highlight the distributed neuromodulatory systems as key therapeutic targets to enhance experience-dependent plasticity in the mature sensory systems (Morishita et al., 2010; Takesian et al., 2018). Experiments that leverage novel neurochemical sensors may illuminate how and when these distinct neuromodulators are released to elicit different forms of synaptic and network plasticity, as well as the interplay between these neuromodulators.

Experience- or age-dependent changes in neuromodulatory transmission may alter the capacity for subsequent network plasticity. Indeed, as critical-period plasticity wanes during the transition into adulthood, the function of nicotinic cholinergic receptors is actively dampened by the developmental upregulation of Lynx1, a membrane-anchored protein that reduces nAChR function (Miwa et al., 1999). Genetic deletion of Lynx1 upregulates the nicotinic activation of cortical interneurons and prolongs the critical period for tonotopic map plasticity into adulthood. Cholinergic basal forebrain neurons are themselves plastic, exhibiting rapid, selective, and lasting response enhancements to sounds associated with aversive reinforcement (Guo et al., 2019; Robert et al., 2021). Thus, even neuromodulatory gating factors like acetylcholine and noradrenaline that act through local circuit regulatory hubs in L1 to create a permissive state for cortical plasticity are transiently released by – and preferentially tuned to – behaviorally meaningful sounds. In later life, the age-related decline in basal cholinergic cell numbers and cholinergic receptors in the MGB and ACtx may interfere with normal plasticity processes, resulting in auditory learning and memory deficits (Ghimire et al., 2020; Sottile, Hackett, et al., 2017; Sottile, Ling, et al., 2017).

5.5 Experience-Dependent Myelination within the Thalamocortical System

The exquisitely precise and rapid saltatory propagation of signals that characterizes the adult auditory thalamocortical system emerges during postnatal life with the maturation of myelin, the lipid-rich sheath around axons formed by oligodendrocytes. The maturation of myelin in the central auditory system of both humans and rodents is protracted, beginning with the onset of hearing and continuing until the age of sexual maturity (Hackett, 2015; Long et al., 2018). A growing appreciation for the experience-driven dynamics of myelin has emerged as recent studies have demonstrated an interplay between neural activity and myelination throughout life (for reviews, see Chorghay et al., 2018; Fields, 2015). For example, transient auditory deprivation by ear-plugging around hearing onset results in thinner myelin sheaths around mouse brainstem axons (Sinclair et al., 2017).

Less is known about the role of experience in the development of myelination in the thalamocortical system. Axons projecting from the thalamus to the white matter are heavily ensheathed by myelin, resulting in fast conduction times that make a wide swath of cortical regions simultaneously accessible to the thalamus, irrespective of the variability in traveling distances (Salami et al., 2003). In addition to speeding up conduction velocities, oligodendrocytes in the central auditory system may provide axonal metabolic support (Fünfschilling et al., 2012; Saab et al., 2016). For example, the temporal acuity of auditory cortical neuron responses is impaired both in mice with a partial myelin loss and in mice with a mutation of a monocarboxylate transporter that is required for metabolic glial support (Moore et al., 2020).

Myelination on thalamic axons becomes substantially thinner upon entering the cortex, where myelin is generally relatively sparse overall compared with other brain regions (Salami et al., 2003; Tomassy et al., 2014). In the ACtx, the expression of myelin-associated genes and intracortical myelin basic protein (MBP) increases dramatically in the week following hearing onset. However, mouse pups exposed to tones from P12 to P15 showed reduced expression of myelin-associated genes, including MBP (Kalish et al., 2020). Similarly, young adult rats chronically exposed to white noise also showed a reduction in the density of MBP (Kamal et al., 2013).

Interactions between a protein found in myelin called *NoGo* and the NoGo receptor (NgR) expressed on cortical neurons may mediate activity-dependent changes in myelination and underlie cortical plasticity (reviewed by Petratos et al., 2020). NoGo was first identified as an inhibitor of axonal growth (M. S. Chen et al., 2000) but is now known to be involved in multiple processes during cortical development. NoGo is upregulated in the mouse auditory cortex by oligodendrocytes during postnatal development (Kalish et al., 2020). Genetic deletion of NgR prolongs the critical periods for tonotopic map plasticity (Kalish et al., 2020) and for establishing acoustic behavioral preferences (E. J. Yang et al., 2012). Studies across sensory cortices now implicate the binding of myelin-associated proteins – including NoGo and myelin-associated glycoprotein (MAG) – to NgR as "brakes" that limit developmental plasticity across diverse cortical regions (Akbik et al., 2013; Kalish et al., 2020; McGee et al., 2005; E. J. Yang et al., 2012).

6. Future Research Directions on the Auditory Thalamus

Looking forward, the clearest need for research on the auditory thalamus lies in performing more research on the thalamus itself and not just on the cell types that project to the MGB or receive inputs from the MGB. The MGB and surrounding multisensory nuclei are among the most overlooked and understudied stations of sound processing in the central auditory pathway, especially from the perspective of modern neuroscience approaches that can leverage genetic methods to monitor and manipulate specific cell types during well-defined behavioral conditions. Beyond the general need for more work on this brain area, it will also be important to approach the MGB as a constellation of nuclei that each have different patterns of connectivity and functional specializations rather than as a monolithic entity. This is well understood in sensory thalamic research in other systems, where visual and somatosensory researchers take care to avoid intermingling recordings or stimulation of the first- and higher-order thalamic nuclei. Among the relatively small number of MGB experiments, research often conflates recordings and manipulations of the MGBv, MGBd, and MGBm. Recent experiments that satisfy each of the criteria just noted are occasionally being published, particularly as they relate to MGB plasticity associated with auditory fear learning (Belén Pardi et al., 2020; Taylor et al., 2021), a research sub-discipline that has historically been thoughtful and careful in targeting specific MGB subdivisions (J. M. Edeline et al., 1993; J.-M. Edeline & Weinberger, 1991a, 1991b, 1992). Auditory neuroscience research would benefit from the application of these approaches to a broader spectrum of research questions. In the following sections, we identify a significant unanswered question related to MGB sound processing and auditory perception for each major subdivision of the auditory thalamus.

6.1 MGBv Neurons Provide a Unique Locus for Bottom-Up and Top-Down Convergence – Do They Generate Prediction-Error Signals?

Descending projections from auditory corticofugal neurons are found in every subcortical station for sound processing. In the midbrain and brainstem, corticofugal feedback projections are weakest overall in the regions with the strongest centrifugal feedforward processing. In this regard, the ascending lemniscal and descending systems in the auditory midbrain and brainstem are more akin to two parallel lanes of traffic, each moving in opposite directions, that can influence each other via local circuits but generally do not collide on the same set of neurons (Feliciano & Potashner, 1995; Winer, 2006). The MGBv is a clear exception in the ascending lemniscal pathway, where individual neurons receive feedforward synaptic inputs from the central nucleus of the IC as well as descending synaptic input, either via direct excitatory inputs from L6 CT neurons or via indirect inhibitory feedback from the TRN.

The cell types and circuits that perform essential computations for predictive coding are a topic of central interest throughout neuroscience. In the context of sensory processing, top-down predictions are continuously compared with feedforward sensory information, where the discrepancies produce prediction-error signals that are then used to update top-down predictive models. Intracolumnar cortical microcircuits are generally regarded as the biological embodiment of predictive coding, but that does not rule out the possibility that fundamental computations for active sensing are not performed elsewhere as well (Bastos et al., 2012). Although MGBv neurons are normally assigned the role of simply relaying the feedforward representation of the sensory environment, their unique anatomical connectivity positions them directly at the confluence of feedforward information from the midbrain and cortical feedback signals, suggesting that they could be a site of prediction-error computation that could be passed forward to prediction circuits in the neocortex.

Exceedingly few studies have recorded from the MGBv while animals are engaged in active listening tasks. Although "predictive coding" has been studied in MGB neurons, these experiments have only been performed in passively listening (typically anesthetized) animals and therefore may describe something different than the predictive coding underlying the active sensing behaviors described previously (Carbajal & Malmierca, 2018; Parras et al., 2017). Indeed, paradigms like stimulus-specific adaptation and other variations that study neural sensitivity to local sensory context in passively listening animals can be informative about where and how sounds are abstracted from sensory to perceptual features but probably have less to contribute to the question of how internalized, forward models of the sensory world interface with (and are updated from) bottom-up sensory evidence (Asokan et al., 2021; Harpaz et al., 2021). Active listening behaviors that juxtapose predictive models against sensory evidence are straightforward to implement in rodents, and the feedforward and feedback inputs to MGBv neurons are well established and accessible via optogenetic activation and silencing approaches (Clayton et al., 2021; Jaramillo et al., 2014; Jaramillo & Zador, 2011). Furthermore, the primary feedback input to the MGBv from L6 CTs is activated hundreds of milliseconds prior to anticipated sounds, suggesting that their output could be encoding predicted sound features that would be conveyed to the MGBv through a combination of direct excitatory input and trans-thalamic inhibition (Clayton et al., 2021). As the thalamus is increasingly afforded a more expansive role in cognitive processes (Halassa & Sherman, 2019; Schmitt et al., 2017), it may prove fruitful to revisit the contribution of the MGBv to prediction-error computations.

6.2 What Are Higher-Order Auditory Features, and What Do the MGBd and "High-Order" Auditory Cortical Fields Have to Do with Them?

The MGBd is commonly described as the higher-order subdivision of the auditory thalamus. Because there are no obvious inherent differences between MGBv and MGBd neurons (Bartlett & Smith, 1999), this label is primarily derived from neuroanatomical tracer studies that identify the MGBd as the primary source of thalamic input to the higher-order fields of the ACtx (Andersen et al., 1980; C. L. Huang & Winer, 2000; J. E. Rose & Woolsey, 1949) and neurophysiological recordings in anesthetized animals that report unreliable or strongly adapting responses to tone bursts with no discernable tonotopic organization (Aitkin & Webster, 1972; Bordi & LeDoux, 1994; Calford, 1983; Parras et al., 2017). Direct neurophysiological evidence for higher-order sound feature representations in the MGBd is scant, mostly on account of the very small number of recordings made from MGBd neurons in unanesthetized animals. As discussed previously, the clearest evidence for higher-order sound features arising de novo in auditory thalamocortical circuits comes from paradigms that characterize non-isomorphic, abstract representations of temporal sound features. To this point, the few studies that have made single-unit recordings from the MGBd in alert animals have confirmed a substantially greater proportion of non-synchronized rate-based selectivity for temporal modulation (approximately 70% of units) than other MGB regions (approximately 30% of units) (Bartlett & Wang, 2011) (Figure 3D) and stronger responses for infrequently occurring, deviant tone frequencies presented in the context of repeating tones at a standard frequency (Lakatos et al., 2020).

In humans, higher-order fields of the ACtx also show longer time constants for temporal integration and emergent selectivity for speech and music (Lerner et al., 2011; Norman-Haignere et al., 2015; Overath et al., 2015). Importantly, electrical stimulation or even surgical ablation of the human A1 does not impair speech perception, whereas electrical stimulation of secondary cortical areas in the superior temporal gyrus profoundly disrupts speech perception (Hamilton et al., 2021). These findings clearly support the existence of parallel projections in humans from first- and higher-order thalamic regions to core and higher-order cortical fields, respectively. A clear implication from these studies is that the MGBd and other non-primary auditory thalamic nuclei may perform specialized processing that supports the perception of speech and music, yet functional characterizations of the human MGB – to say nothing of subregions of the MGB – have not been performed in this context.

Among the few studies that have made recordings from higher-order fields of the ACtx in unanesthetized animals, the key distinction that can be drawn to core fields is less about acoustic signal processing and more about focused decision making (Tsunada et al., 2016) or the modulation and plasticity of sound feature representations with acquired emotional salience via innate learning (Tasaka et al., 2020) or behavioral conditioning (Atiani et al., 2014; Belén Pardi et al., 2020; Cambiaghi et al., 2016; Elgueda et al., 2019; Pereira et al., 2020). To this point, MGBd neurons also express strong associative plasticity for sound features with acquired behavioral relevance, which likely contributes to the expression of conditioned changes in downstream higher-order ACtx circuits (Belén Pardi et al., 2020; J.-M. Edeline & Weinberger, 1991a; Pereira et al., 2020).

Thus, there are two emerging suggestions for the type of features that might be selectively represented in higher-order thalamocortical circuits: (i) specific and lasting plasticity of sound features with learned behavioral significance and (ii) the increasing timescales for the integration and abstraction of auditory temporal features. However, these are two disconnected literatures that offer no obvious road for the synthesis of the essential computations performed by MGBd neurons. Simply put, there are too few studies that have recorded from the MGBd or higher-order fields of the ACtx in alert, task-engaged subjects. Future studies that – for example – perform calcium imaging in MGBv versus MGBd thalamocortical axons or from cell bodies in core and higher-order regions of the ACtx could resolve key sensory- and task-related features that distinguish MGB regions and could identify the extent to which cortical selectivity is inherited from the MGB versus actively constructed via local circuit dynamics.

6.3 The MGBm and ACtx Provide Parallel Paths for Auditory-Related Activity Flowing to and from the Basal Ganglia and Amygdala – to What End?

Classic neuroanatomical tracer studies have revealed two intriguing triads of inter-regional connectivity between the ACtx, the MGBm complex (MGBm, PIN, and SG), and either the basolateral amygdala or the striatum. These triads are organized such that the MGBm projects to the ACtx as well as the striatum and amygdala, and the striatum and amygdala are each innervated by the ACtx and the MGBm. The broader motif of parallel connectivity also extends to the inputs to the MGBm, where the feedforward inputs arise both from the IC as well as from the first-order nucleus for central sound processing, the cochlear nucleus. The same applies to cross-modal input, where the MGBm receives top-down input from the somatosensory cortex in addition to bottom-up cross-modal inputs from the multisensory modules within the lateral cortex of the IC, from the superior colliculus, and even direct nociceptive and somatosensory inputs from the spinal cord (Bordi & LeDoux, 1994; LeDoux et al., 1987; Lohse et al., 2021). Finally, the parallel connectivity works in the reverse direction as well, where amygdalar neurons project to the higher-order auditory and association cortical areas but can also modulate MGB sound representations via their input to the TRN (Aizenberg et al., 2019).

All of these parallel pathways into and out of the MGBm complex raise a series of questions, both in terms of the functional contributions to behavior but also related to fine-grained connectivity analysis. For the latter, the anatomy has only been characterized at the regional level, thus making it unclear whether, for example, individual MGBm neurons receive inputs from both the cochlear nucleus and IC or whether those inputs are segregated onto different cells. Future work could pick up on classic neuroanatomy (Doron and LeDoux, 1999) to investigate whether individual MGBm neurons diffusely project to the ACtx, amygdala, and basal ganglia or instead target only one or a subset of these structures. Related to this point, although there is some evidence from gross electrical stimulation studies in acute brain-slice preparations (Cho et al., 2012), it remains to be seen whether the cortical and thalamic input to the striatum and basolateral amygdala generally impinge upon the same neurons or instead connect to different types of postsynaptic neurons that interact through local circuits. Answers to each of these questions would be essential to understanding the connectivity logic for each of these triads and parallel paths of connectivity and could be tackled with a combination of contemporary neuroanatomical approaches for barcoded in situ sequencing and optogenetically assisted cell-type-specific connectivity studies in acute brain slices (X. Chen et al., 2019; Cho et al., 2013).

In terms of functional contributions to behavior, the major outstanding questions are to understand the different types of information that the MGBm and ACtx each transmit to downstream circuits in the basal ganglia and amygdala and how the temporal arrangement of these inputs produces adaptive behavior and learning-related plasticity. For example, strong sound-evoked responses with well-defined auditory receptive field properties have been described in the lateral amygdala, the posterior tail of the dorsal striatum, and the posterior tail of the cholinergic basal forebrain (Guo et al., 2019; Quirk et al., 1995). Does the MGBm complex play the role of an early warning system by supplying the shortest-latency inputs to these regions that are then filled out in greater sensory detail by a delayed wave of cortical inputs? These questions (and others of this ilk) could be addressed in future experiments that make use of multi-regional recording methods and projection-specific silencing approaches during active listening and auditory learning tasks.

References

Abs, E., Poorthuis, R. B., Apelblat, D., Muhammad, K., Pardi, M. B., Enke, L., Kushinsky, D., Pu, D. L., Eizinger, M. F., Conzelmann, K. K., Spiegel, I., & Letzkus, J. J. (2018). Learning-related plasticity in dendrite-targeting layer 1 interneurons. *Neuron*, **100**(3), 684–699.e6. https://doi.org/10.1016/j.neuron.2018.09.001

Aitkin, L. M., & Webster, W. R. (1972). Medial geniculate body of the cat: organization and responses to tonal stimuli of neurons in ventral division. *Journal of Neurophysiology*, **35**(3), 365–380. https://doi.org/10.1152/JN.1972.35.3.365

Aizenberg, M., Rolón-Martínez, S., Pham, T., Rao, W., Haas, J. S., & Geffen, M. N. (2019). Projection from the amygdala to the thalamic reticular nucleus amplifies cortical sound responses. *Cell Reports*, **28**(3), 605–615.e4. https://doi.org/10.1016/j.celrep.2019.06.050

Akbik, F. v., Bhagat, S. M., Patel, P. R., Cafferty, W. B. J., & Strittmatter, S. M. (2013). Anatomical plasticity of adult brain is titrated by NoGo receptor 1. *Neuron*, **77**(5), 859–866. https://doi.org/10.1016/J.NEURON.2012.12.027

Alford, B. R., & Ruben, R. J. (1963). Physiological, behavioral and anatomical correlates of the development of hearing in the mouse. *Annals of Otology, Rhinology & Laryngology*, **72**(1), 237–247. https://doi.org/10.1177/000348946307200119

Andersen, R. A., Knight, P. L., & Merzenich, M. M. (1980). The thalamocortical and corticothalamic connections of AI, AII, and the anterior auditory field (AFF) in the cat: evidence of two largely segregated systems of connections. *Journal of Comparative Neurology*, **194**(3), 663–701.

Anderson, L. A., Christianson, G. B., & Linden, J. F. (2009). Stimulus-specific adaptation occurs in the auditory thalamus. *Journal of Neuroscience*, **29**(22), 7359–7363. https://doi.org/10.1523/JNEUROSCI.0793-09.2009

Anderson, L. A., Malmierca, M. S., Wallace, M. N., & Palmer, A. R. (2006). Evidence for a direct, short latency projection from the dorsal cochlear nucleus to the auditory thalamus in the guinea pig. *European Journal of Neuroscience*, **24**(2), 491–498. https://doi.org/10.1111/j.1460-9568.2006.04930.x

Anomal, R., de Villers-Sidani, E., Merzenich, M. M., & Panizzutti, R. (2013). Manipulation of BDNF signaling modifies the experience-dependent plasticity induced by pure tone exposure during the critical period in the primary auditory cortex. *PLoS ONE*, **8**(5). https://doi.org/10.1371/JOURNAL.PONE.0064208

Asokan, M. M., Williamson, R. S., Hancock, K. E., & Polley, D. B. (2021). Inverted central auditory hierarchies for encoding local intervals and global temporal patterns. *Current Biology*, **31**(8), 1762–1770.e4. https://doi.org/10.1016/J.CUB.2021.01.076

Atiani, S., David, S. V., Elgueda, D., Locastro, M., Radtke-Schuller, S., Shamma, S. A., & Fritz, J. B. (2014). Emergent selectivity for task-relevant stimuli in higher-order auditory cortex. *Neuron*, **82** (2), 486–499. https://doi.org/10.1016/J.NEURON.2014.02.029

Bajo, V. M., Nodal, F. R., Moore, D. R., & King, A. J. (2010). The descending corticocollicular pathway mediates learning-induced auditory plasticity. *Nature Neuroscience*, **13**(2), 253–260. https://doi.org/10.1038/NN.2466

Bakin, J. S., & Weinberger, N. M. (1990). Classical conditioning induces CS-specific receptive field plasticity in the auditory cortex of the guinea pig. *Brain Research*, **536** (1–2), 271–286.

Bakin, J. S., & Weinberger, N. M. (1996). Induction of a physiological memory in the cerebral cortex by stimulation of the nucleus basalis. *Proceedings of the National Academy of Sciences of the United States of America*, **93** (20), 11219–11224. https://doi.org/10.1073/PNAS.93.20.11219

Balmer, T. S. (2016). Perineuronal nets enhance the excitability of fast-spiking neurons. *ENeuro*, **3**(4), 745–751. https://doi.org/10.1523/ENEURO.0112-16.2016

Barbour, D. L., & Callaway, E. M. (2008). Excitatory local connections of superficial neurons in rat auditory cortex. *Journal of Neuroscience*, **28**(44), 11174–11185. https://doi.org/10.1523/JNEUROSCI.2093-08.2008

Barkat, T. R., Polley, D. B., & Hensch, T. K. (2011). A critical period for auditory thalamocortical connectivity. *Nature Neuroscience*, **14**(9), 1189–1194. https://doi.org/10.1038/nn.2882

Bartlett, E. L. (2013). The organization and physiology of the auditory thalamus and its role in processing acoustic features important for speech perception. *Brain and Language*, **126**(1), 29–48. https://doi.org/10.1016/j.bandl.2013.03.003

Bartlett, E. L., & Smith, P. H. (1999). Anatomic, intrinsic, and synaptic properties of dorsal and ventral division neurons in rat medial geniculate body. *Journal of Neurophysiology*, **81**(5), 1999–2016. https://doi.org/10.1152/JN.1999.81.5.1999

Bartlett, E. L., & Wang, X. (2007). Neural representations of temporally modulated signals in the auditory thalamus of awake primates. *Journal of Neurophysiology*, **97**(2), 1005–1017. https://doi.org/10.1152/JN.00593.2006

Bartlett, E. L., & Wang, X. (2011). Correlation of neural response properties with auditory thalamus subdivisions in the awake marmoset. *Journal of Neurophysiology*, **105**(6), 2647–2667. https://doi.org/10.1152/JN.00238.2010

Bastos, A. M., Usrey, W. M., Adams, R. A., Mangun, G. R., Fries, P., & Friston, K. J. (2012). Canonical microcircuits for predictive coding. *Neuron*, **76**(4), 695–711. https://doi.org/10.1016/J.NEURON.2012.10.038

Batra, R., Kuwada, S., & Stanford, T. R. (1989). Temporal coding of envelopes and their interaural delays in the inferior colliculus of the unanesthetized rabbit. *Journal of Neurophysiology*, **61**(2), 257–268. https://doi.org/10.1152/JN.1989.61.2.257

Beierlein, M., Gibson, J. R., & Connors, B. W. (2003). Two dynamically distinct inhibitory networks in layer 4 of the neocortex. *Journal of Neurophysiology*, **90**(5), 2987–3000. https://doi.org/10.1152/JN.00283.2003

Belén Pardi, M., Vogenstahl, J., Dalmay, T., Spanò, T., Pu, D. L., Naumann, L. B., Kretschmer, F., Sprekeler, H., & Letzkus, J. J. (2020). A thalamocortical top-down circuit for associative memory. *Science*, **370**(6518), 844–848. https://doi.org/10.1126/SCIENCE.ABC2399

Ben-Ari, Y. (2002). Excitatory actions of GABA during development: the nature of the nurture. *Nature Reviews Neuroscience*, **3** (9), 728–739. https://doi.org/10.1038/NRN920

Ben-Ari, Y., Khazipov, R., Leinekugel, X., Caillard, O., & Gaiarsa, J. (1997). GABAA, NMDA and AMPA receptors: a developmentally regulated "ménage à trois." *Trends in Neurosciences*, **20**(11), 523–529. https://doi.org/10.1016/S0166-2236(97)01147-8

Bieszczad, K. M., & Weinberger, N. M. (2010). Representational gain in cortical area underlies increase of memory strength. *Proceedings of the National Academy of Sciences of the United States of America*, **107** (8), 3793–3798. https://doi.org/10.1073/PNAS.1000159107

Blundon, J. A., Bayazitov, I. T., & Zakharenko, S. S. (2011). Presynaptic gating of postsynaptically expressed plasticity at mature thalamocortical synapses. *Journal of Neuroscience*, **31**(44), 16012–16025. https://doi.org/10.1523/jneurosci.3281-11.2011

Blundon, J. A., Roy, N. C., Teubner, B. J. W., Yu, J., Eom, T. Y., Sample, K. J., Pani, A., Smeyne, R. J., Han, S. B., Kerekes, R. A., Rose, D. C., Hackett, T. A., Vuppala, P. K., Freeman 3rd, B. B., & Zakharenko, S. S. (2017). Restoring auditory cortex plasticity in adult mice by restricting thalamic adenosine signaling. *Science*, **356**(6345), 1352–1356. https://doi.org/10.1126/science.aaf4612

Blundon, J. A., & Zakharenko, S. S. (2013). Presynaptic gating of postsynaptic synaptic plasticity: a plasticity filter in the adult auditory cortex. *Neuroscientist*, **19**(5), 465–478. https://doi.org/10.1177/1073858413482983

Bonham, B. H., Cheung, S. W., Godey, B., & Schreiner, C. E. (2004). Spatial organization of frequency response areas and rate/level functions in the developing AI. *Journal of Neurophysiology*, **91**(2), 841–854. https://doi.org/10.1152/JN.00017.2003

Bordi, F., & LeDoux, J. E. (1994). Response properties of single units in areas of rat auditory thalamus that project to the amygdala—I. Acoustic discharge patterns and frequency receptive fields. *Experimental Brain Research*, **98**(2), 261–274. https://doi.org/10.1007/BF00228414

Bortone, D. S., Olsen, S. R., & Scanziani, M. (2014). Translaminar inhibitory cells recruited by layer 6 corticothalamic neurons suppress visual cortex. *Neuron*, **82**(2), 474–485. https://doi.org/10.1016/J.NEURON.2014.02.021

Brosch, M., Selezneva, E., & Scheich, H. (2005). Nonauditory events of a behavioral procedure activate auditory cortex of highly trained monkeys. *Journal of Neuroscience*, **25** (29), 6797–6806. https://doi.org/10.1523/JNEUROSCI.1571-05.2005

Buran, B. N., von Trapp, G., & Sanes, D. H. (2014). Behaviorally gated reduction of spontaneous discharge can improve detection thresholds in auditory cortex. *Journal of Neuroscience*, **34**(11), 4076–4081. https://doi.org/10.1523/JNEUROSCI.4825-13.2014

Cai, R., & Caspary, D. M. (2015). GABAergic inhibition shapes SAM responses in rat auditory thalamus. *Neuroscience*, **299**, 146–155. https://doi.org/10.1016/J.NEUROSCIENCE.2015.04.062

Cai, R., Richardson, B. D., & Caspary, D. M. (2016). Responses to predictable versus random temporally complex stimuli from single units in auditory thalamus: Impact of aging and anesthesia. *Journal of Neuroscience*, **36**(41), 10696–10706. https://doi.org/10.1523/JNEUROSCI.1454-16.2016

Calarco, C. A., & Robertson, R. T. (1995). Development of basal forebrain projections to visual cortex: DiI studies in rat. *Journal of Comparative Neurology*, **354**(4), 608–626. https://doi.org/10.1002/CNE.903540409

Calford, M. B. (1983). The parcellation of the medial geniculate body of the cat defined by the auditory response properties of single units. *Journal of Neuroscience*, **3**(11), 2350–2364.

Calford, M. B., Rajan, R., & Irvine, D. R. F. (1993). Rapid changes in the frequency tuning of neurons in cat auditory cortex resulting from pure-tone-induced temporary threshold shift. *Neuroscience*, **55**

(4), 953–964. https://doi.org/10.1016/0306-4522(93)90310-C

Cambiaghi, M., Grosso, A., Likhtik, E., Mazziotti, R., Concina, G., Renna, A., Sacco, T., Gordon, J. A., & Sacchetti, B. (2016). Higher-order sensory cortex drives basolateral amygdala activity during the recall of remote, but not recently learned fearful memories. *Journal of Neuroscience*, **36**(5), 1647–1659. https://doi.org/10.1523/JNEUROSCI.2351-15.2016

Caras, M. L., & Sanes, D. H. (2015). Sustained perceptual deficits from transient sensory deprivation. *Journal of Neuroscience*, **35**(30), 10831–10842. https://doi.org/10.1523/JNEUROSCI.0837-15.2015

Carbajal, G. v., & Malmierca, M. S. (2018). The neuronal basis of predictive coding along the auditory pathway: from the subcortical roots to cortical deviance detection. *Trends in Hearing*, **22**. https://doi.org/10.1177/2331216518784822

Carcea, I., & Froemke, R. C. (2013). Cortical plasticity, excitatory-inhibitory balance, and sensory perception. *Progress in Brain Research*, **207**, 65–90. https://doi.org/10.1016/B978-0-444-63327-9.00003-5

Carcea, I., Insanally, M. N., & Froemke, R. C. (2017). Dynamics of auditory cortical activity during behavioural engagement and auditory perception. *Nature Communications*, **8**. https://doi.org/10.1038/NCOMMS14412

Carceller, H., Guirado, R., Ripolles-Campos, E., Teruel-Marti, V., & Nacher, J. (2020). Perineuronal nets regulate the inhibitory perisomatic input onto parvalbumin interneurons and c activity in the prefrontal cortex. *Journal of Neuroscience*, **40**(26), 5008–5018. https://doi.org/10.1523/JNEUROSCI.0291-20.2020

Carmel, P. W., & Starr, A. (1963). Acoustic and nonacoustic factors modifying middle-ear muscle activity in waking cats. *Journal of Neurophysiology*, **26**, 598–616. https://doi.org/10.1152/JN.1963.26.4.598

Chambers, A. R., Resnik, J., Yuan, Y., Whitton, J. P., Edge, A. S., Liberman, M. C., & Polley, D. B. (2016). Central gain restores auditory processing following near-complete cochlear denervation. *Neuron*, **89**(4), 867–879. https://doi.org/10.1016/j.neuron.2015.12.041

Chambers, A. R., Salazar, J. J., & Polley, D. B. (2016). Persistent thalamic sound processing despite profound cochlear denervation. *Frontiers in Neural Circuits*, **10**, 72. https://doi.org/10.3389/fncir.2016.00072

Chang, E. F., Bao, S., Imaizumi, K., Schreiner, C. E., & Merzenich, M. M. (2005). Development of spectral and temporal response selectivity in the auditory cortex. *Proceedings of the National Academy of Sciences of the United States of America*, **102**(45), 16460–16465. https://doi.org/10.1073/PNAS.0508239102

Chang, E. F., & Merzenich, M. M. (2003). Environmental noise retards auditory cortical development. *Science*, **300**(5618), 498–502. https://doi.org/10.1126/SCIENCE.1082163

Chattopadhyaya, B., di Cristo, G., Higashiyama, H., Knott, G. W., Kuhlman, S. J., Welker, E., & Huang, Z. J. (2004). Experience and activity-dependent maturation of perisomatic GABAergic innervation in primary visual cortex during a postnatal critical period. *Journal of Neuroscience*, **24**(43), 9598–9611. https://doi.org/10.1523/JNEUROSCI.1851-04.2004

Chavez, C., & Zaborszky, L. (2017). Basal forebrain cholinergic-auditory cortical network: Primary versus nonprimary auditory cortical areas. *Cerebral Cortex*, **27**(3), 2335–2347. https://doi.org/10.1093/CERCOR/BHW091

Chen, M. S., Huber, A. B., van der Haar, M. E. D., Frank, M., Schnell, L., Spillmann, A. A., Christ, F., & Schwab, M. E. (2000). NoGo-A is a myelin-associated neurite outgrowth inhibitor and an antigen for monoclonal antibody IN-1. *Nature*, **403**(6768), 434–439. https://doi.org/10.1038/35000219

Chen, R., Puzerey, P. A., Roeser, A. C., Riccelli, T. E., Podury, A., Maher, K., Farhang, A. R., & Goldberg, J. H. (2019). Songbird ventral pallidum sends diverse performance error signals to dopaminergic midbrain. *Neuron*, **103**(2), 266–276.e4. https://doi.org/10.1016/J.NEURON.2019.04.038

Chen, X., Sun, Y. C., Zhan, H., Kebschull, J. M., Fischer, S., Matho, K., Huang, Z. J., Gillis, J., & Zador, A. M. (2019). High-throughput mapping of long-range neuronal projection using in situ sequencing. *Cell*, **179**(3), 772–786.e19. https://doi.org/10.1016/J.CELL.2019.09.023

Cho, J. H., Bayazitov, I. T., Meloni, E. G., Myers, K. M., Carlezon, W. A., Zakharenko, S. S., & Bolshakov, V. Y. (2012). Coactivation of thalamic and cortical pathways induces input timing-dependent plasticity in amygdala. *Nature Neuroscience*, **15**(1), 113–122. https://doi.org/10.1038/NN.2993

Cho, J. H., Deisseroth, K., & Bolshakov, V. Y. (2013). Synaptic encoding of fear extinction in mPFC-amygdala circuits. *Neuron*, **80**(6), 1491–1507. https://doi.org/10.1016/J.NEURON.2013.09.025

Chorghay, Z., Káradóttir, R. T., & Ruthazer, E. S. (2018). White matter plasticity keeps the brain in tune: axons conduct while glia wrap. *Frontiers in Cellular Neuroscience*, **12**. https://doi.org/10.3389/FNCEL.2018.00428

Chun, S., Bayazitov, I. T., Blundon, J. A., & Zakharenko, S. S. (2013). Thalamocortical long-term potentiation becomes gated after the early critical period in the auditory cortex. *Journal of Neuroscience*, **33**(17), 7345–7357. https://doi.org/10.1523/jneurosci.4500-12.2013

Cisneros-Franco, J. M., & de Villers-Sidani, É. (2019). Reactivation of critical period plasticity in adult auditory cortex through chemogenetic silencing of parvalbumin-positive interneurons. *Proceedings of the National Academy of Sciences of the United States of America*, **116**(52), 26329–26331. https://doi.org/10.1073/PNAS.1913227117

Clancy, B., & Cauller, L. J. (1999). Widespread projections from subgriseal neurons (layer VII) to layer I in adult rat cortex. *Journal of Comparative Neurology*, **407**(2), 275–286.

Clancy, B., Silva-Filho, M., & Friedlander, M. J. (2001). Structure and projections of white matter neurons in the postnatal rat visual cortex. *Journal of Comparative Neurology*, **434**(2), 233–252. https://doi.org/10.1002/CNE.1174

Clayton, K. K., Williamson, R. S., Hancock, K. E., Tasaka, G. I., Mizrahi, A., Hackett, T. A., & Polley, D. B. (2021). Auditory corticothalamic neurons are recruited by motor preparatory inputs. *Current Biology*, **31**(2), 310–321.e5. https://doi.org/10.1016/j.cub.2020.10.027

Cohen-Kashi Malina, K., Tsivourakis, E., Kushinsky, D., Apelblat, D., Shtiglitz, S., Zohar, E., Sokoletsky, M., Tasaka, G., Mizrahi, A., Lampl, I., & Spiegel, I. (2021). NDNF interneurons in layer 1 gain-modulate whole cortical columns according to an animal's behavioral state. *Neuron*, **109**(13), 2150–2164.e5. https://doi.org/10.1016/J.NEURON.2021.05.001

Crandall, S. R., Cruikshank, S. J., & Connors, B. W. (2015). A corticothalamic switch: controlling the thalamus with dynamic synapses. *Neuron*, **86**(3), 768–782. https://doi.org/10.1016/J.NEURON.2015.03.040

Cruikshank, S. J., Urabe, H., Nurmikko, A. v., & Connors, B. W. (2010). Pathway-specific feedforward circuits between thalamus and neocortex revealed by selective optical stimulation of axons. *Neuron*, **65**(2), 230–245. https://doi.org/10.1016/J.NEURON.2009.12.025

de La Mothe, L. A., Blumell, S., Kajikawa, Y., & Hackett, T. A. (2006). Thalamic connections of the auditory cortex in marmoset monkeys: core and medial belt regions. *Journal of Comparative Neurology*, **496**(1), 72–96. https://doi.org/10.1002/CNE.20924

de la Mothe, L. A., Blumell, S., Kajikawa, Y., & Hackett, T. A. (2012). Thalamic connections of auditory cortex in marmoset monkeys: lateral belt and parabelt regions. *Anatomical Record*, **295**(5), 822–836. https://doi.org/10.1002/AR.22454

de Villers-Sidani, E., Chang, E. F., Bao, S., & Merzenich, M. M. (2007). Critical period window for spectral tuning defined in the primary auditory cortex (A1) in the rat. *Journal of Neuroscience*, **27**(1), 180–189. https://doi.org/10.1523/jneurosci.3227-06.2007

de Villers-Sidani, E., & Merzenich, M. M. (2011). Lifelong plasticity in the rat auditory cortex. Basic mechanisms and role of sensory experience. *Progress in Brain Research*, **191**, 119–131. https://doi.org/10.1016/B978-0-444-53752-2.00009-6

del Río, J. A., Martínez, A., Auladell, C., & Soriano, E. (2000). Developmental history of the subplate and developing white matter in the murine neocortex. Neuronal organization and relationship with the main afferent systems at embryonic and perinatal stages. *Cerebral Cortex*, **10**(8), 784–801.

Deng, R., Kao, J. P. Y., & Kanold, P. O. (2017). Distinct translaminar glutamatergic circuits to GABAergic interneurons in the neonatal auditory cortex. *Cell Reports*, **19**(6), 1141–1150. https://doi.org/10.1016/J.CELREP.2017.04.044

Diamond, I. T., Jones, E. G., & Powell, T. P. S. (1969). The projection of the auditory cortex upon the diencephalon and brain stem in the cat. *Brain Research*, **15**(2), 305–340. https://doi.org/10.1016/0006-8993(69)90160-7

Dityatev, A., Brückner, G., Dityateva, G., Grosche, J., Kleene, R., & Schachner, M. (2007). Activity-dependent formation and functions of chondroitin sulfate-rich extracellular matrix of perineuronal nets. *Developmental Neurobiology*, **67**(5), 570–588. https://doi.org/10.1002/DNEU.20361

Doron, N. N., & LeDoux, J. E. (1999). Organization of projections to the lateral amygdala from auditory and visual areas of the thalamus in the rat. *Journal of Comparative Neurology*, **412**(3), 383–409.

Dorrn, A. L., Yuan, K., Barker, A. J., Schreiner, C. E., & Froemke, R. C. (2010). Developmental sensory experience balances cortical excitation and inhibition. *Nature*, **465**(7300), 932–936. https://doi.org/10.1038/NATURE09119

Downer, J. D., Niwa, M., & Sutter, M. L. (2017). Hierarchical differences in population coding within auditory cortex. *Journal of Neurophysiology*, **118**(2), 717–731. https://doi.org/10.1152/JN.00899.2016

Edeline, J. M., Pham, P., & Weinberger, N. M. (1993). Rapid development of learning-induced receptive field plasticity in the auditory cortex. *Behavioral Neuroscience*, **107**(4), 539–551.

Edeline, J.-M., & Weinberger, N. M. (1991a). Subcortical adaptive filtering in the auditory system: Associative receptive field plasticity in the dorsal medial geniculate body. *Behavioral Neuroscience*, **105**(1), 154–175. https://doi.org/10.1037//0735-7044.105.1.154

Edeline, J.-M., & Weinberger, N. M. (1991b). Thalamic short-term plasticity in the auditory system: Associative retuning of receptive fields in the ventral medial geniculate body. *Behavioral Neuroscience*, **105**(5), 618–639. https://doi.org/10.1037//0735-7044.105.5.618

Edeline, J.-M., & Weinberger, N. M. (1992). Associative retuning in the thalamic source of input to the amygdala and auditory cortex: receptive field plasticity in the medial division of the medial geniculate body. *Behavioral Neuroscience*, **106**(1), 81–105. https://doi.org/10.1037//0735-7044.106.1.81

Eggermont, J. J., & Komiya, H. (2000). Moderate noise trauma in juvenile cats results in profound cortical topographic map changes in adulthood. *Hearing Research*, **142**(1–2), 89–101. https://doi.org/10.1016/S0378-5955(00)00024-1

Ehret, G. (1976). Development of absolute auditory thresholds in the house mouse (*Mus musculus*). *Journal of the American Audiology Society*, **1**(5), 179–184. https://pubmed.ncbi.nlm.nih.gov/956003/

Ehret, G., & Romand, R. (1992). Development of tone response thresholds, latencies and tuning in the mouse inferior colliculus. *Brain Research Developmental Brain Research*, **67**(2), 317–326. https://doi.org/10.1016/0165-3806(92)90233-M

Elgueda, D., Duque, D., Radtke-Schuller, S., Yin, P., David, S. V., Shamma, S. A., & Fritz, J. B. (2019). State-dependent encoding of sound and behavioral meaning in a tertiary region of the ferret auditory cortex. *Nature Neuroscience*, **22**(3), 447–459. https://doi.org/10.1038/S41593-018-0317-8

Eliades, S. J., & Wang, X. (2008). Neural substrates of vocalization feedback monitoring in primate auditory cortex. *Nature*, **453**(7198), 1102–1106. https://doi.org/10.1038/NATURE06910

Engineer, N. D., Riley, J. R., Seale, J. D., Vrana, W. A., Shetake, J. A., Sudanagunta, S. P., Borland, M. S., & Kilgard, M. P. (2011). Reversing pathological neural activity using targeted plasticity. *Nature*, **470**(7332), 101–104. https://doi.org/10.1038/nature09656

Fagiolini, M., Fritschy, J. M., Löw, K., Möhler, H., Rudolph, U., & Hensch, T. K. (2004). Specific GABA$_A$ circuits for visual cortical plasticity. *Science*, **303**(5664), 1681–1683. https://doi.org/10.1126/SCIENCE.1091032

Fagiolini, M., & Hensch, T. K. (2000). Inhibitory threshold for critical-period activation in primary visual cortex. *Nature*, **404**(6774), 183–186. https://doi.org/10.1038/35004582

Fan, L. Z., Kheifets, S., Böhm, U. L., Wu, H., Piatkevich, K. D., Xie, M. E., Parot, V., Ha, Y., Evans, K. E., Boyden, E. S., Takesian, A. E., & Cohen, A. E. (2020). All-optical electrophysiology reveals the role of lateral inhibition in sensory processing in cortical layer 1. *Cell*, **180**(3), 521–535.e18. https://doi.org/10.1016/J.CELL.2020.01.001

Favuzzi, E., Marques-Smith, A., Deogracias, R., Winterflood, C. M., Sánchez-Aguilera, A., Mantoan, L., Maeso, P., Fernandes, C., Ewers, H., & Rico, B. (2017). Activity-dependent gating of parvalbumin interneuron function by the perineuronal net protein brevican. *Neuron*, **95**(3), 639–655.e10. https://doi.org/10.1016/J.NEURON.2017.06.028

Feliciano, M., & Potashner, S. J. (1995). Evidence for a glutamatergic pathway from the guinea pig auditory cortex to the inferior colliculus. *Journal of Neurochemistry*, **65**(3), 1348–1357. https://doi.org/10.1046/J.1471-4159.1995.65031348.X

Fields, R. D. (2015). A new mechanism of nervous system plasticity: activity-dependent myelination. *Nature Reviews Neuroscience*, **16**(12), 756–767. https://doi.org/10.1038/NRN4023

Finney, E. M., Stone, J. R., & Shatz, C. J. (1998). Major glutamatergic projection from subplate into visual cortex during development. *Journal of Comparative Neurology*, **398**(1), 105–118.

Firth, S. I., Wang, C. T., & Feller, M. B. (2005). Retinal waves: mechanisms and function in visual system development. *Cell Calcium*, **37**(5 Spec. Iss.), 425–432. https://doi.org/10.1016/J.CECA.2005.01.010

Friauf, E. (2000). Development of chondroitin sulfate proteoglycans in the central auditory system of rats correlates with acquisition of mature properties. *Audiology and Neuro-Otology*, **5**(5), 251–262. https://doi.org/10.1159/000013889

Fritz, J. B., Elhilali, M., & Shamma, S. A. (2005). Differential dynamic plasticity of A1 receptive fields during multiple spectral tasks. *Journal of Neuroscience*, 25(33), 7623–7635.

Fritz, J., Shamma, S., Elhilali, M., & Klein, D. (2003). Rapid task-related plasticity of spectrotemporal receptive fields in primary auditory cortex. *Nature Neuroscience*, 6(11), 1216–1223. https://doi.org/10.1038/NN1141

Froemke, R. C., Carcea, I., Barker, A. J., Yuan, K., Seybold, B. A., Martins, A. R., Zaika, N., Bernstein, H., Wachs, M., Levis, P. A., Polley, D. B., Merzenich, M. M., & Schreiner, C. E. (2013). Long-term modification of cortical synapses improves sensory perception. *Nature Neuroscience*, 16(1), 79–88. https://doi.org/10.1038/nn.3274

Froemke, R. C., Merzenich, M. M., & Schreiner, C. E. (2007). A synaptic memory trace for cortical receptive field plasticity. *Nature*, 450(7168), 425–429. https://doi.org/10.1038/nature06289

Fu, Y., Tucciarone, J. M., Espinosa, J. S., Sheng, N., Darcy, D. P., Nicoll, R. A., Huang, Z. J., & Stryker, M. P. (2014). A cortical circuit for gain control by behavioral state. *Cell*, 156(6), 1139–1152. https://doi.org/10.1016/j.cell.2014.01.050

Fünfschilling, U., Supplie, L. M., Mahad, D., Boretius, S., Saab, A. S., Edgar, J., Brinkmann, B. G., Kassmann, C. M., Tzvetanova, I. D., Möbius, W., Diaz, F., Meijer, D., Suter, U., Hamprecht, B., Sereda, M. W., Moraes, C. T., Frahm, J., Goebbels, S., & Nave, K. A. (2012). Glycolytic oligodendrocytes maintain myelin and long-term axonal integrity. *Nature*, 485(7399), 517–521. https://doi.org/10.1038/NATURE11007

Gao, L., Kostlan, K., Wang, Y., & Wang, X. (2016). Distinct subthreshold mechanisms underlying rate-coding principles in primate auditory cortex. *Neuron*, 91(4), 905–919. https://doi.org/10.1016/J.NEURON.2016.07.004

Gao, X., & Wehr, M. (2015). A coding transformation for temporally structured sounds within auditory cortical neurons. *Neuron*, 86(1), 292–303. https://doi.org/10.1016/J.NEURON.2015.03.004

Ghimire, M., Cai, R., Ling, L., Hackett, T. A., & Caspary, D. M. (2020). Nicotinic receptor subunit distribution in auditory cortex: impact of aging on receptor number and function. *Journal of Neuroscience*, 40(30), 5724–5739. https://doi.org/10.1523/JNEUROSCI.0093-20.2020

Ghosh, A., Antonini, A., McConnell, S. K., & Shatz, C. J. (1990). Requirement for subplate neurons in the formation of thalamocortical connections. *Nature*, 347(6289), 179–181. https://doi.org/10.1038/347179A0

Gianfranceschi, L., Siciliano, R., Walls, J., Morales, B., Kirkwood, A., Huang, Z. J., Tonegawa, S., & Maffei, L. (2003). Visual cortex is rescued from the effects of dark rearing by overexpression of BDNF. *Proceedings of the National Academy of Sciences of the United States of America*, 100(21), 12486–12491. https://doi.org/10.1073/PNAS.1934836100

Gibson, J. R., Beierlein, M., & Connors, B. W. (1999). Two networks of electrically coupled inhibitory neurons in neocortex. *Nature*, 402(6757), 75–79. https://doi.org/10.1038/47035

Goyer, D., Silveira, M. A., George, A. P., Beebe, N. L., Edelbrock, R. M., Malinski, P. T., Schofield, B. R., & Roberts, M. T. (2019). A novel class of inferior colliculus principal neurons labeled in vasoactive intestinal peptide-cre mice. *eLife*, 8. https://doi.org/10.7554/ELIFE.43770

Grant, E., Hoerder-Suabedissen, A., & Molnár, Z. (2012). Development of the corticothalamic projections. *Frontiers in Neuroscience*, 6, 1–14. https://doi.org/10.3389/FNINS.2012.00053

Guo, W., Clause, A. R., Barth-Maron, A., & Polley, D. B. (2017). A corticothalamic circuit for dynamic switching between feature detection and discrimination. *Neuron*, 95(1), 180–194.e5. https://doi.org/10.1016/j.neuron.2017.05.019

Guo, W., Robert, B., & Polley, D. B. (2019). The cholinergic basal forebrain links auditory stimuli with delayed reinforcement to support learning. *Neuron*, 103(6), 1164–1177.e6. https://doi.org/10.1016/j.neuron.2019.06.024

Gurung, B., & Fritzsch, B. (2004). Time course of embryonic midbrain and thalamic auditory connection development in mice as revealed by carbocyanine dye tracing. *Journal of Comparative Neurology*, 479, 309–327. https://doi.org/10.1002/cne.20328

Hackett, T. A. (2011). Information flow in the auditory cortical network. *Hearing Research*, 271(1–2), 133–146. https://doi.org/10.1016/j.heares.2010.01.011

Hackett, T. A. (2015). Anatomic organization of the auditory cortex. *Handbook of Clinical Neurology*, 129, 27–53. https://doi.org/10.1016/B978-0-444-62630-1.00002-0

Hackett, T. A., Barkat, T. R., O'Brien, B. M., Hensch, T. K., & Polley, D. B. (2011). Linking topography to tonotopy in the mouse auditory thalamocortical circuit. *Journal of Neuroscience*, 31(8), 2983–2995. https://doi.org/10.1523/jneurosci.5333-10.2011

Hackett, T. A., Clause, A. R., Takahata, T., Hackett, N. J., & Polley, D. B. (2016). Differential maturation of vesicular glutamate and GABA transporter expression in the mouse auditory forebrain during the first weeks of hearing. *Brain Structure & Function*, 221(5), 2619–2673. https://doi.org/10.1007/S00429-015-1062-3

Hackett, T. A., Guo, Y., Clause, A., Hackett, N. J., Garbett, K., Zhang, P., Polley, D. B., & Mirnics, K. (2015). Transcriptional maturation of the mouse auditory forebrain. *BMC Genomics*, 16(1), 606. https://doi.org/10.1186/s12864-015-1709-8

Halassa, M. M., & Sherman, S. M. (2019). Thalamocortical circuit motifs: a general framework. *Neuron*, 103(5), 762–770. https://doi.org/10.1016/J.NEURON.2019.06.005

Hamilton, L. S., Oganian, Y., Hall, J., & Chang, E. F. (2021). Parallel and distributed encoding of speech across human auditory cortex. *Cell*, 184(18), 4626–4639.e13. https://doi.org/10.1016/J.CELL.2021.07.019

Han, Y. K., Köver, H., Insanally, M. N., Semerdjian, J. H., & Bao, S. (2007). Early experience impairs perceptual discrimination. *Nature Neuroscience*, 10(9), 1191–1197. https://doi.org/10.1038/NN1941

Hanover, J. L., Huang, Z. J., Tonegawa, S., & Stryker, M. P. (1999). Brain-derived neurotrophic factor overexpression induces precocious critical period in mouse visual cortex. *Journal of Neuroscience*, 19(22). https://doi.org/10.1523/JNEUROSCI.19-22-J0003.1999

Hanse, E., Seth, H., & Riebe, I. (2013). AMPA-silent synapses in brain development and pathology. *Nature Reviews Neuroscience*, 14(12), 839–850. https://doi.org/10.1038/NRN3642

Harpaz, M., Jankowski, M. M., Khouri, L., & Nelken, I. (2021). Emergence of abstract sound representations in the ascending auditory system. *Progress in Neurobiology*, 202. https://doi.org/10.1016/J.PNEUROBIO.2021.102049

Härtig, W., Brauer, K., & Brückner, G. (1992). *Wisteria floribunda* agglutinin-labelled nets surround parvalbumin-containing neurons. *NeuroReport*, 3(10), 869–872. https://doi.org/10.1097/00001756-199210000-00012

Hensch, T. K. (2004). Critical period regulation. *Annual Review of Neuroscience*, 27, 549–579. https://doi.org/10.1146/ANNUREV.NEURO.27.070203.144327

Hensch, T. K. (2005). Critical period plasticity in local cortical circuits. *Nature Reviews Neuroscience*, 6(11), 877–888. https://doi.org/10.1038/NRN1787

Hensch, T. K., Fagiolini, M., Mataga, N., Stryker, M. P., Baekkeskov, S., & Kash, S. F.

(1998). Local GABA circuit control of experience-dependent plasticity in developing visual cortex. *Science*, **282**(5393), 1504–1508. https://doi.org/10.1126/SCIENCE.282.5393.1504

Heuer, H., Christ, S., Friedrichsen, S., Brauer, D., Winckler, M., Bauer, K., & Raivich, G. (2003). Connective tissue growth factor: a novel marker of layer VII neurons in the rat cerebral cortex. *Neuroscience*, **119**(1), 43–52.

Hoerder-Suabedissen, A., Hayashi, S., Upton, L., Nolan, Z., Casas-Torremocha, D., Grant, E., Viswanathan, S., Kanold, P. O., Clascá, F., Kim, Y., & Molnár, Z. (2018). Subset of cortical layer 6b neurons selectively innervates higher order thalamic nuclei in mice. *Cerebral Cortex*, **28**(5), 1882–1897. https://doi.org/10.1093/CERCOR/BHY036

Hoerder-Suabedissen, A., & Molnár, Z. (2013). Molecular diversity of early-born subplate neurons. *Cerebral Cortex*, **23**(6), 1473–1483. https://doi.org/10.1093/CERCOR/BHS137

Hogan, S. C., Meyer, S. E., & Moore, D. R. (1996). Binaural unmasking returns to normal in teenagers who had otitis media in infancy. *Audiology and Neuro-Otology*, **1**(2), 104–111. https://doi.org/10.1159/000259189

Hooks, B. M., & Chen, C. (2007). Critical periods in the visual system: changing views for a model of experience-dependent plasticity. *Neuron*, **56**(2), 312–326. https://doi.org/10.1016/J.NEURON.2007.10.003

Horng, S., Kreiman, G., Ellsworth, C., Page, D., Blank, M., Millen, K., & Sur, M. (2009). Differential gene expression in the developing lateral geniculate nucleus and medial geniculate nucleus reveals novel roles for Zic4 and Foxp2 in visual and auditory pathway development. *Journal of Neuroscience*, **29**(43), 13672–13683. https://doi.org/10.1523/JNEUROSCI.2127-09.2009

Huang, C. L., & Winer, J. A. (2000). Auditory thalamocortical projections in the cat: laminar and areal patterns of input. *Journal of Comparative Neurology*, **427**(2), 302–331.

Huang, X. (2019). Silent synapse: a new player in visual cortex critical period plasticity. *Pharmacological Research*, **141**, 586–590. https://doi.org/10.1016/J.PHRS.2019.01.031

Huang, Z. J., Kirkwood, A., Pizzorusso, T., Porciatti, V., Morales, B., Bear, M. F., Maffei, L., & Tonegawa, S. (1999). BDNF regulates the maturation of inhibition and the critical period of plasticity in mouse visual cortex. *Cell*, **98**(6), 739–755. https://doi.org/10.1016/S0092-8674(00)81509-3

Huganir, R. L., & Nicoll, R. A. (2013). Perspective AMPARs and synaptic plasticity: the last 25 years. *Neuron*, **80**(3), 704–717. https://doi.org/10.1016/j.neuron.2013.10.025

Ibrahim, B. A., Murphy, C. A., Yudintsev, G., Shinagawa, Y., Banks, M. I., & Llano, D. A. (2021). Corticothalamic gating of population auditory thalamocortical transmission in mouse. *eLife*, **10**. https://doi.org/10.7554/eLife.56645

Insanally, M. N., Kover, H., Kim, H., & Bao, S. (2009). Feature-dependent sensitive periods in the development of complex sound representation. *Journal of Neuroscience*, **29**(17), 5456–5462. https://doi.org/10.1523/jneurosci.5311-08.2009

Isaac, J. T. R. (2003). Mini-review postsynaptic silent synapses: evidence and mechanisms. *Neuropharmacology*, **45**, 450–460. https://doi.org/10.1016/S0028-3908(03)00229-6

Isaac, J. T. R., Crair, M. C., Nicoll, R. A., & Malenka, R. C. (1997). Silent synapses during development of thalamocortical inputs. *Neuron*, **18**(2), 269–280. https://doi.org/10.1016/S0896-6273(00)80267-6

Isaac, J. T. R., Nicoll, R. A., & Malenka, R. C. (1995). Evidence for silent synapses: Implications for the expression of LTP. *Neuron*, **15**(2), 427–434. https://doi.org/10.1016/0896-6273(95)90046-2

Isaacson, J. S., & Scanziani, M. (2011). How inhibition shapes cortical activity. *Neuron*, **72**(2), 231–243. https://doi.org/10.1016/J.NEURON.2011.09.027

Itami, C., Kimura, F., & Nakamura, S. (2007). Brain-derived neurotrophic factor regulates the maturation of layer 4 fast-spiking cells after the second postnatal week in the developing barrel cortex. *Journal of Neuroscience*, **27**(9), 2241–2252. https://doi.org/10.1523/JNEUROSCI.3345-06.2007

Ito, T., & Oliver, D. L. (2012). The basic circuit of the IC: tectothalamic neurons with different patterns of synaptic organization send different messages to the thalamus. *Frontiers in Neural Circuits*, **6**, 1–9. https://doi.org/10.3389/fncir.2012.00048

Jaramillo, S., Borges, K., & Zador, A. M. (2014). Auditory thalamus and auditory cortex are equally modulated by context during flexible categorization of sounds. *Journal of Neuroscience*, **34**(15), 5291–5301. https://doi.org/10.1523/JNEUROSCI.4888-13.2014

Jaramillo, S., & Zador, A. M. (2011). The auditory cortex mediates the perceptual effects of acoustic temporal expectation. *Nature Neuroscience*, **14**(2), 246–253. https://doi.org/10.1038/NN.2688

Ji, W., & Suga, N. (2007). Serotonergic modulation of plasticity of the auditory cortex elicited by fear conditioning. *Journal of Neuroscience*, **27**(18), 4910–4918. https://doi.org/10.1523/JNEUROSCI.5528-06.2007

Ji, X. Y., Zingg, B., Mesik, L., Xiao, Z., Zhang, L. I., & Tao, H. W. (2016). Thalamocortical innervation pattern in mouse auditory and visual cortex: laminar and cell-type specificity. *Cerebral Cortex*, **26**(6), 2612–2625. https://doi.org/10.1093/cercor/bhv099

Jiao, Y., Zhang, C., Yanagawa, Y., & Sun, Q. Q. (2006). Major effects of sensory experiences on the neocortical inhibitory circuits. *Journal of Neuroscience*, **26**(34), 8691–8701. https://doi.org/10.1523/JNEUROSCI.2478-06.2006

Jones, E. G., & Burton, H. (1976). Areal differences in the laminar distribution of thalamic afferents in cortical fields of the insular, parietal and temporal regions of primates. *Journal of Comparative Neurology*, **168**(2), 197–247. https://doi.org/10.1002/CNE.901680203

Joris, P. X., Schreiner, C. E., & Rees, A. (2004). Neural processing of amplitude-modulated sounds. *Physiological Reviews*, **84**(2), 541–577. https://doi.org/10.1152/PHYSREV.00029.2003

Kaas, J. H., & Hackett, T. A. (2000). Subdivisions of auditory cortex and processing streams in primates. *Proceedings of the National Academy of Sciences of the United States of America*, **97**(22), 11793–11799. https://doi.org/10.1073/PNAS.97.22.11793

Kalish, B. T., Barkat, T. R., Diel, E. E., Zhang, E. J., Greenberg, M. E., & Hensch, T. K. (2020). Single-nucleus RNA sequencing of mouse auditory cortex reveals critical period triggers and brakes. *Proceedings of the National Academy of Sciences of the United States of America*, **117**(21). https://doi.org/10.1073/PNAS.1920433117

Kamal, B., Holman, C., & de Villers-Sidani, E. (2013). Shaping the aging brain: Role of auditory input patterns in the emergence of auditory cortical impairments. *Frontiers in Systems Neuroscience*, **7**. https://doi.org/10.3389/FNSYS.2013.00052

Kamke, M. R., Brown, M., & Irvine, D. R. F. (2003). Plasticity in the tonotopic organization of the medial geniculate body in adult cats following restricted unilateral cochlear lesions. *Journal of Comparative Neurology*, **459**(4), 355–367. https://doi.org/10.1002/CNE.10586

Kandler, K. (2004). Activity-dependent organization of inhibitory circuits: lessons from the auditory system. *Current Opinion in Neurobiology*, **14**(1), 96–104. https://doi.org/10.1016/J.CONB.2004.01.017

Kanold, P. O. (2009). Subplate neurons: crucial regulators of cortical development and plasticity. *Frontiers in Neuroanatomy*, 3. https://doi.org/10.3389/NEURO.05.016.2009

Kanold, P. O., Kara, P., Reid, R. C., & Shatz, C. J. (2003). Role of subplate neurons in functional maturation of visual cortical columns. *Science*, 301(5632), 521–525. https://doi.org/10.1126/SCIENCE.1084152

Kanold, P. O., & Luhmann, H. J. (2010). The subplate and early cortical circuits. *Annual Review of Neuroscience*, 33, 23–48. https://doi.org/10.1146/ANNUREV-NEURO-060909-153244

Kanold, P. O., & Shatz, C. J. (2006). Subplate neurons regulate maturation of cortical inhibition and outcome of ocular dominance plasticity. *Neuron*, 51(5), 627–638. https://doi.org/10.1016/J.NEURON.2006.07.008

Katagiri, H., Fagiolini, M., & Hensch, T. K. (2007). Optimization of somatic inhibition at critical period onset in mouse visual cortex. *Neuron*, 53(6), 805–812. https://doi.org/10.1016/J.NEURON.2007.02.026

Kato, H. K., Gillet, S. N., & Isaacson, J. S. (2015). Flexible sensory representations in auditory cortex driven by behavioral relevance. *Neuron*, 88(5), 1027–1039. https://doi.org/10.1016/J.NEURON.2015.10.024

Kilgard, M. P., & Merzenich, M. M. (1998). Cortical map reorganization enabled by nucleus basalis activity. *Science*, 279(5357), 1714–1718.

Kim, H., & Bao, S. (2009). Selective increase in representations of sounds repeated at an ethological rate. *Journal of Neuroscience*, 29(16), 5163–5169. https://doi.org/10.1523/JNEUROSCI.0365-09.2009

Kim, J., Matney, C. J., Blankenship, A., Hestrin, S., & Brown, S. P. (2014). Layer 6 corticothalamic neurons activate a cortical output layer, layer 5a. *Journal of Neuroscience*, 34(29), 9656–9664. https://doi.org/10.1523/JNEUROSCI.1325-14.2014

King, A. J. (2010). Auditory neuroscience: balancing excitation and inhibition during development. *Current Biology*, 20(18), R808. https://doi.org/10.1016/J.CUB.2010.07.034

Knudsen, E. I., Esterly, S. D., & Knudsen, P. F. (1984). Monaural occlusion alters sound localization during a sensitive period in the barn owl. *Journal of Neuroscience*, 4(4), 1001–1011. https://doi.org/10.1523/JNEUROSCI.04-04-01001.1984

Kotak, V. C., Breithaupt, A. D., & Sanes, D. H. (2007). Developmental hearing loss eliminates long-term potentiation in the auditory cortex. *Proceedings of the National Academy of Sciences of the United States of America*, 104(9), 3550–3555. https://doi.org/10.1073/PNAS.0607177104

Kotak, V. C., Fujisawa, S., Lee, F. A., Karthikeyan, O., Aoki, C., & Sanes, D. H. (2005). Hearing loss raises excitability in the auditory cortex. *Journal of Neuroscience*, 25(15), 3908–3918. https://doi.org/10.1523/JNEUROSCI.5169-04.2005

Kreeger, L. J., Connelly, C. J., Mehta, P., Zemelman, B. v., & Golding, N. L. (2021). Excitatory cholecystokinin neurons of the midbrain integrate diverse temporal responses and drive auditory thalamic subdomains. *Proceedings of the National Academy of Sciences of the United States of America*, 118(10). https://doi.org/10.1073/pnas.2007724118

Kuchibhotla, K. v, Gill, J. v, Lindsay, G. W., Papadoyannis, E. S., Field, R. E., Sten, T. A., Miller, K. D., & Froemke, R. C. (2017). Parallel processing by cortical inhibition enables context-dependent behavior. *Nature Neuroscience*, 20(1), 62–71. https://doi.org/10.1038/nn.4436

Kuhl, P. K. (2010). Brain mechanisms in early language acquisition. *Neuron*, 67(5), 713–727. https://doi.org/10.1016/J.NEURON.2010.08.038

Lakatos, P., O'Connell, M. N., Barczak, A., McGinnis, T., Neymotin, S., Schroeder, C. E., Smiley, J. F., & Javitt, D. C. (2020). The thalamocortical circuit of auditory mismatch negativity. *Biological Psychiatry*, 87(8), 770–780. https://doi.org/10.1016/J.BIOPSYCH.2019.10.029

Lazarus, M. S., & Josh Huang, Z. (2011). Distinct maturation profiles of perisomatic and dendritic targeting GABAergic interneurons in the mouse primary visual cortex during the critical period of ocular dominance plasticity. *Journal of Neurophysiology*, 106(2), 775–787. https://doi.org/10.1152/JN.00729.2010

LeDoux, J. E., Farb, C. R., & Romanski, L. M. (1991). Overlapping projections to the amygdala and striatum from auditory processing areas of the thalamus and cortex. *Neuroscience Letters*, 134(1), 139–144. https://doi.org/10.1016/0304-3940(91)90526-Y

LeDoux, J. E., Ruggiero, D. A., Forest, R., Stornetta, R., & Reis, D. J. (1987). Topographic organization of convergent projections to the thalamus from the inferior colliculus and spinal cord in the rat. *Journal of Comparative Neurology*, 264(1), 123–146. https://doi.org/10.1002/CNE.902640110

Lee, C. C. (2015). Exploring functions for the non-lemniscal auditory thalamus. *Front Neural Circuits*, 9, 69. https://doi.org/10.3389/fncir.2015.00069

Lee, C. C., & Winer, J. A. (2011). Convergence of thalamic and cortical pathways in cat auditory cortex. *Hearing Research*, 274(1–2), 85–94. https://doi.org/10.1016/j.heares.2010.05.008

Lee, S. H., Hjerling-Leffler, J., Zagha, E., Fishell, G., & Rudy, B. (2010). The largest group of superficial neocortical GABAergic interneurons expresses ionotropic serotonin receptors. *Journal of Neuroscience*, 30(50), 16796–16808. https://doi.org/10.1523/JNEUROSCI.1869-10.2010

Lensjø, K. K., Lepperød, M. E., Dick, G., Hafting, T., & Fyhn, M. (2017). Removal of perineuronal nets unlocks juvenile plasticity through network mechanisms of decreased inhibition and increased gamma activity. *Journal of Neuroscience*, 37(5), 1269–1283. https://doi.org/10.1523/JNEUROSCI.2504-16.2016

Lerner, Y., Honey, C. J., Silbert, L. J., & Hasson, U. (2011). Topographic mapping of a hierarchy of temporal receptive windows using a narrated story. *Journal of Neuroscience*, 31(8), 2906–2915. https://doi.org/10.1523/JNEUROSCI.3684-10.2011

Lesicko, A. M. H., Hristova, T. S., Maigler, K. C., & Llano, D. A. (2016). Connectional modularity of top-down and bottom-up multimodal inputs to the lateral cortex of the mouse inferior colliculus. *Journal of Neuroscience*, 36(43), 11037–11050. https://doi.org/10.1523/JNEUROSCI.4134-15.2016

Lesicko, A. M. H., Sons, S. K., & Llano, D. A. (2020). Circuit mechanisms underlying the segregation and integration of parallel processing streams in the inferior colliculus. *Journal of Neuroscience*, 40(33), 6328–6344. https://doi.org/10.1523/JNEUROSCI.064620.2020

Letzkus, J. J., Wolff, S. B., Meyer, E. M., Tovote, P., Courtin, J., Herry, C., & Luthi, A. (2011). A disinhibitory microcircuit for associative fear learning in the auditory cortex. *Nature*, 480(7377), 331–335. https://doi.org/10.1038/nature10674

Levelt, C. N., & Hübener, M. (2012). Critical-period plasticity in the visual cortex. *Annual Review of Neuroscience*, 35, 309–330. https://doi.org/10.1146/ANNUREV-NEURO-061010-113813

Levy, R. B., & Aoki, C. (2002). α7 nicotinic acetylcholine receptors occur at postsynaptic densities of AMPA receptor-positive and -negative excitatory synapses in rat sensory cortex. *Journal of Neuroscience*, 22(12), 5001–5015. https://doi.org/10.1523/JNEUROSCI.22-12-05001.2002

Liao, D., Hessler, N. A., & Malinow, R. (1995). Activation of postsynaptically silent synapses during pairing-induced LTP in

CA1 region of hippocampal slice. *Nature*, *375*(6530), 400–404. https://doi.org/10.1038/375400A0

Liu, Y., Xin, Y., & Xu, N. long. (2021). A cortical circuit mechanism for structural knowledge-based flexible sensorimotor decision-making. *Neuron*, *109*(12), 2009–2024.e6. https://doi.org/10.1016/J.NEURON.2021.04.014

Llano, D. A., & Sherman, S. M. (2008). Evidence for nonreciprocal organization of the mouse auditory thalamocortical-corticothalamic projection systems. *Journal of Comparative Neurology*, *507*(2), 1209–1227. https://doi.org/10.1002/cne.21602

Lohse, M., Dahmen, J. C., Bajo, V. M., & King, A. J. (2021). Subcortical circuits mediate communication between primary sensory cortical areas in mice. *Nature Communications*, *12*(1), 1–14. https://doi.org/10.1038/s41467-021-24200-x

Long, P., Wan, G., Roberts, M. T., & Corfas, G. (2018). Myelin development, plasticity, and pathology in the auditory system. *Developmental Neurobiology*, *78*(2), 80–92. https://doi.org/10.1002/DNEU.22538

López-Bendito, G., & Molnár, Z. (2003). Thalamocortical development: how are we going to get there? *Nature Reviews Neuroscience*, *4*(4), 276–289. https://doi.org/10.1038/NRN1075

Lu T, Liang L, Wang X. (2001). Temporal and rate representations of time-varying signals in the auditory cortex of awake primates. *Nature Neuroscience*, *4*, 1131–1138.

Lu, E., Llano, D. A., & Sherman, S. M. (2009). Different distributions of calbindin and calretinin immunostaining across the medial and dorsal divisions of the mouse medial geniculate body. *Hearing Research*, *257*(1–2), 16–23. https://doi.org/10.1016/J.HEARES.2009.07.009

Lund, J. S., Henry, G. H., Macqueen, C. L., & Harvey, A. R. (1979). Anatomical organization of the primary visual cortex (area 17) of the cat. A comparison with area 17 of the macaque monkey. *Journal of Comparative Neurology*, *184*(4), 599–618. https://doi.org/10.1002/CNE.901840402

Luskin, M. B., & Shatz, C. J. (1985). Studies of the earliest generated cells of the cat's visual cortex: cogeneration of subplate and marginal zones. *Journal of Neuroscience*, *5*(4), 1062–1075.

Maffei, A., Nelson, S. B., & Turrigiano, G. G. (2004). Selective reconfiguration of layer 4 visual cortical circuitry by visual deprivation. *Nature Neuroscience*, *7*(12), 1353–1359. https://doi.org/10.1038/NN1351

Maggi, L., le Magueresse, C., Changeux, J. P., & Cherubini, E. (2003). Nicotine activates immature "silent" connections in the developing hippocampus. *Proceedings of the National Academy of Sciences of the United States of America*, *100*(4), 2059–2064. https://doi.org/10.1073/PNAS.0437947100

Malmierca, M. S., Merchán, M. A., Henkel, C. K., & Oliver, D. L. (2002). Direct projections from cochlear nuclear complex to auditory thalamus in the rat. *Journal of Neuroscience*, *22*(24), 10891–10897. https://doi.org/10.1523/jneurosci.22-24-10891.2002

Marie, R. L. S., & Peters, A. (1985). The morphology and synaptic connections of spiny stellate neurons in monkey visual cortex (area 17): a golgi-electron microscopic study. *Journal of Comparative Neurology*, *233*(2), 213–235. https://doi.org/10.1002/CNE.902330205

Martins, A. R., & Froemke, R. C. (2015). Coordinated forms of noradrenergic plasticity in the locus coeruleus and primary auditory cortex. *Nature Neuroscience*, *18*(10), 1483–1492. https://doi.org/10.1038/nn.4090

Marx, M., Qi, G., Hanganu-Opatz, I. L., Kilb, W., Luhmann, H. J., & Feldmeyer, D. (2017). Neocortical layer 6B as a remnant of the subplate—a morphological comparison. *Cerebral Cortex*, *27*(2), 1011–1026. https://doi.org/10.1093/CERCOR/BHV279

McConnell, S. K., Ghosh, A., and Shatz, C. J. (1994). Subplate pioneers and the formation of descending connections from cerebral cortex. *Journal of Neuroscience*, *14*(4), 1892–1907.

McGee, A. W., Yang, Y., Fischer, Q. S., Daw, N. W., & Strittmatter, S. H. (2005). Neuroscience: Experience-driven plasticity of visual cortex limited by myelin and NoGo receptor. *Science*, *309*(5744), 2222–2226. https://doi.org/10.1126/SCIENCE.1114362

McGinley, M. J., David, S. v., & McCormick, D. A. (2015). Cortical membrane potential signature of optimal states for sensory signal detection. *Neuron*, *87*(1), 179–192. https://doi.org/10.1016/J.NEURON.2015.05.038

Mechawar, N., & Descarries, L. (2001). The cholinergic innervation develops early and rapidly in the rat cerebral cortex: a quantitative immunocytochemical study. *Neuroscience*, *108*(4), 555–567. https://doi.org/10.1016/S0306-4522(01)00389-X

Meng, X., Kao, J. P. Y., & Kanold, P. O. (2014). Differential signaling to subplate neurons by spatially specific silent synapses in developing auditory cortex. *Journal of Neuroscience*, *34*(26), 8855–8864. https://doi.org/10.1523/JNEUROSCI.0233-14.2014

Meng, X., Xu, Y., Kao, J. P. Y., & Kanold, P. O. (2020). Transient coupling between subplate and subgranular layers to L1 neurons before and during the critical period. *BioRxiv*, *2020*.05.05.077784. https://doi.org/10.1101/2020.05.05.077784

Meyer, G., González-Hernández, T. H., & Ferres-Torres, R. (1989). The spiny stellate neurons in layer IV of the human auditory cortex. A Golgi study. *Neuroscience*, *33*(3), 489–498. https://doi.org/10.1016/0306-4522(89)90401-6

Miller, G. L., & Knudsen, E. I. (2003). Adaptive plasticity in the auditory thalamus of juvenile barn owls. *Journal of Neuroscience*, *23*(3), 1059. https://doi.org/10.1523/JNEUROSCI.23-03-01059.2003

Miwa, J. M., Ibañez-Tallon, I., Crabtree, G. W., Sánchez, R., Šali, A., Role, L. W., & Heintz, N. (1999). lynx1, an endogenous toxin-like modulator of nicotinic acetylcholine receptors in the mammalian CNS. *Neuron*, *23*(1), 105–114. https://doi.org/10.1016/S0896-6273(00)80757-6

Moore, D. R. (2007). Auditory processing disorders: acquisition and treatment. *Journal of Communication Disorders*, *40*(4), 295–304. https://doi.org/10.1016/J.JCOMDIS.2007.03.005

Moore, D. R., Hine, J. E., Jiang, Z. D., Matsuda, H., Parsons, C. H., & King, A. J. (1999). Conductive hearing loss produces a reversible binaural hearing impairment. *Journal of Neuroscience*, *19*(19), 8704–8711. https://doi.org/10.1523/JNEUROSCI.19-19-08704.1999

Moore, S., Meschkat, M., Ruhwedel, T., Trevisiol, A., Tzvetanova, I. D., Battefeld, A., Kusch, K., Kole, M. H. P., Strenzke, N., Möbius, W., de Hoz, L., & Nave, K. A. (2020). A role of oligodendrocytes in information processing. *Nature Communications*, *11*(1). https://doi.org/10.1038/S41467-020-19152-7

Morales, B., Choi, S. Y., & Kirkwood, A. (2002). Dark rearing alters the development of GABAergic transmission in visual cortex. *Journal of Neuroscience*, *22*(18), 8084–8090. https://doi.org/10.1523/JNEUROSCI.22-18-08084.2002

Morishita, H., & Hensch, T. K. (2008). Critical period revisited: impact on vision. *Current Opinion in Neurobiology*, *18*(1), 101–107. https://doi.org/10.1016/J.CONB.2008.05.009

Morishita, H., Miwa, J. M., Heintz, N., & Hensch, T. K. (2010). Lynx1, a cholinergic brake, limits plasticity in adult visual cortex. *Science*, *330*(6008), 1238–1240. https://doi.org/10.1126/SCIENCE.1195320

Mowery, T. M., Caras, M. L., Hassan, S. I., Wang, D. J., Dimidschstein, J., Fishell, G., & Sanes, D. H. (2019). Preserving inhibition during developmental hearing loss rescues auditory learning and perception. *Journal of Neuroscience*, 39(42), 8347–8361. https://doi.org/10.1523/jneurosci.0749-19.2019

Mowery, T. M., Kotak, V. C., & Sanes, D. H. (2015). Transient hearing loss within a critical period causes persistent changes to cellular properties in adult auditory cortex. *Cerebral Cortex*, 25(8), 2083–2094. https://doi.org/10.1093/CERCOR/BHU013

Müller-Preuss, P., Flachskamm, C., & Bieser, A. (1994). Neural encoding of amplitude modulation within the auditory midbrain of squirrel monkeys. *Hearing Research*, 80(2), 197–208. https://doi.org/10.1016/0378-5955(94)90111-2

Myakhar, O., Unichenko, P., & Kirischuk, S. (2011). GABAergic projections from the subplate to Cajal-Retzius cells in the neocortex. *NeuroReport*, 22(11), 525–529. https://doi.org/10.1097/WNR.0B013E32834888A4

Nakahara, H., Zhang, L. I., & Merzenich, M. M. (2004). Specialization of primary auditory cortex processing by sound exposure in the "critical period." *Proceedings of the National Academy of Sciences of the United States of America*, 101(18), 7170–7174. https://doi.org/10.1073/PNAS.0401196101

Natan, R. G., Briguglio, J. J., Mwilambwe-Tshilobo, L., Jones, S. I., Aizenberg, M., Goldberg, E. M., & Geffen, M. N. (2015). Complementary control of sensory adaptation by two types of cortical interneurons. *eLife*, 4. https://doi.org/10.7554/eLife.09868

Nelson, A., Schneider, D. M., Takatoh, J., Sakurai, K., Wang, F., & Mooney, R. (2013). A circuit for motor cortical modulation of auditory cortical activity. *Journal of Neuroscience*, 33(36), 14342–14353. https://doi.org/10.1523/JNEUROSCI.2275-13.2013

Noreña, A. J., Tomita, M., & Eggermont, J. J. (2003). Neural changes in cat auditory cortex after a transient pure-tone trauma. *Journal of Neurophysiology*, 90(4), 2387–2401. https://doi.org/10.1152/JN.00139.2003

Norman-Haignere, S., Kanwisher, N. G., & McDermott, J. H. (2015). Distinct cortical pathways for music and speech revealed by hypothesis-free voxel decomposition. *Neuron*, 88(6), 1281–1296. https://doi.org/10.1016/J.NEURON.2015.11.035

Novák, O., Zelenka, O., Hromádka, T., & Syka, J. (2016). Immediate manifestation of acoustic trauma in the auditory cortex is layer specific and cell type dependent. *Journal of Neurophysiology*, 115(4), 1860–1874. https://doi.org/10.1152/JN.00810.2015

Nowak, L., Bregestovski, P., Ascher, P., Herbet, A., & Prochiantz, A. (1984). Magnesium gates glutamate-activated channels in mouse central neurones. *Nature*, 307(5950), 462–465. https://doi.org/10.1038/307462A0

Otazu, G. H., Tai, L. H., Yang, Y., & Zador, A. M. (2009). Engaging in an auditory task suppresses responses in auditory cortex. *Nature Neuroscience*, 12(5), 646–654. https://doi.org/10.1038/NN.2306

Overath, T., McDermott, J. H., Zarate, J. M., & Poeppel, D. (2015). The cortical analysis of speech-specific temporal structure revealed by responses to sound quilts. *Nature Neuroscience*, 18(6), 903–911. https://doi.org/10.1038/NN.4021

Parras, G. G., Nieto-Diego, J., Carbajal, G. v., Valdés-Baizabal, C., Escera, C., & Malmierca, M. S. (2017). Neurons along the auditory pathway exhibit a hierarchical organization of prediction error. *Nature Communications*, 8(1). https://doi.org/10.1038/S41467-017-02038-6

Parsons, C. H., Lanyon, R. G., Schnupp, J. W. H., & King, A. J. (1999). Effects of altering spectral cues in infancy on horizontal and vertical sound localization by adult ferrets. *Journal of Neurophysiology*, 82(5), 2294–2309. https://doi.org/10.1152/JN.1999.82.5.2294

Patton, M. H., Blundon, J. A., & Zakharenko, S. S. (2019). Rejuvenation of plasticity in the brain: opening the critical period. *Current Opinion in Neurobiology*, 54, 83–89. https://doi.org/10.1016/J.CONB.2018.09.003

Pereira, A. G., Farias, M., & Moita, M. A. (2020). Thalamic, cortical, and amygdala involvement in the processing of a natural sound cue of danger. *PLoS Biology*, 18(5). https://doi.org/10.1371/JOURNAL.PBIO.3000674

Persic, D., Thomas, M. E., Pelekanos, V., Ryugo, D. K., Takesian, A. E., Krumbholz, K., & Pyott, S. J. (2020). Regulation of auditory plasticity during critical periods and following hearing loss. *Hearing Research*, 397, 107976. https://doi.org/10.1016/j.heares.2020.107976

Peruzzi, D., Bartlett, E., Smith, P. H., & Oliver, D. L. (1997). A monosynaptic GABAergic input from the inferior colliculus to the medial geniculate body in rat. *Journal of Neuroscience*, 17(10), 3766–3777. https://doi.org/10.1523/JNEUROSCI.17-10-03766.1997

Peters, A., & Kara, D. A. (1985). The neuronal composition of area 17 of rat visual cortex. I. The pyramidal cells. *Journal of Comparative Neurology*, 234(2), 218–241. https://doi.org/10.1002/CNE.902340208

Petratos, S., Theotokis, P., Kim, M. J., Azari, M. F., & Lee, J. Y. (2020). That's a wrap! Molecular drivers governing neuronal NoGo receptor-dependent myelin plasticity and integrity. *Frontiers in Cellular Neuroscience*, 14. https://doi.org/10.3389/FNCEL.2020.00227

Pfeffer, C. K., Xue, M., He, M., Huang, Z. J., & Scanziani, M. (2013). Inhibition of inhibition in visual cortex: the logic of connections between molecularly distinct interneurons. *Nature Neuroscience*, 16(8), 1068–1076. https://doi.org/10.1038/nn.3446

Pienkowski, M., & Eggermont, J. J. (2011). Cortical tonotopic map plasticity and behavior. *Neuroscience and Biobehavioral Reviews*, 35(10), 2117–2128. https://doi.org/10.1016/J.NEUBIOREV.2011.02.002

Pienkowski, M., Munguia, R., & Eggermont, J. J. (2011). Passive exposure of adult cats to bandlimited tone pip ensembles or noise leads to long-term response suppression in auditory cortex. *Hearing Research*, 277(1–2), 117–126. https://doi.org/10.1016/J.HEARES.2011.02.002

Polley, D. B., Steinberg, E. E., & Merzenich, M. M. (2006). Perceptual learning directs auditory cortical map reorganization through top-down influences. *Journal of Neuroscience*, 26(18), 4970–4982. https://doi.org/10.1523/jneurosci.3771-05.2006

Polley, D. B., Thompson, J. H., & Guo, W. (2013). Brief hearing loss disrupts binaural integration during two early critical periods of auditory cortex development. *Nature Communications*, 4, 2547. https://doi.org/10.1038/ncomms3547

Popescu, M. v, & Polley, D. B. (2010). Monaural deprivation disrupts development of binaural selectivity in auditory midbrain and cortex. *Neuron*, 65(5), 718–731. https://doi.org/10.1016/j.neuron.2010.02.019

Price, D. J., Aslam, S., Tasker, L., & Gillies, K. (1997). Fates of the earliest generated cells in the developing murine neocortex. *Journal of Comparative Neurology*, 377, 414–422.

Qiu, C. X., Salvi, R., Ding, D., & Burkard, R. (2000). Inner hair cell loss leads to enhanced response amplitudes in auditory cortex of unanesthetized chinchillas: evidence for increased system gain. *Hearing Research*, 139(1–2), 153–171. https://doi.org/10.1016/S0378-5955(99)00171-9

Quirk, G. J., Repa, J. C., & LeDoux, J. E. (1995). Fear conditioning enhances short-latency auditory responses of lateral amygdala neurons: parallel recordings in the freely behaving rat. *Neuron*, **15**(5), 1029–1039. https://doi.org/10.1016/0896-6273(95)90092-6

Rabang, C. F., & Bartlett, E. L. (2011). A computational model of cellular mechanisms of temporal coding in the medial geniculate body (MGB). *PLoS ONE*, **6**(12). https://doi.org/10.1371/JOURNAL.PONE.0029375

Raggio, M. W., & Schreiner, C. E. (1999). Neuronal responses in cat primary auditory cortex to electrical cochlear stimulation. III. Activation patterns in short- and long-term deafness. *Journal of Neurophysiology*, **82**(6), 3506–3526. https://doi.org/10.1152/JN.1999.82.6.3506

Ramón y Cajal, S. (1906). *Nobel lecture*. https://www.nobelprize.org/prizes/medicine/1906/cajal/lecture/

Razak, K. A., & Fuzessery, Z. M. (2010). Development of parallel auditory thalamocortical pathways for two different behaviors. *Frontiers in Neuroanatomy*, **4**. https://doi.org/10.3389/fnana.2010.00134

Razak, K. A., & Fuzessery, Z. M. (2015). Development of echolocation calls and neural selectivity for echolocation calls in the pallid bat. *Developmental Neurobiology*, **75**(10), 1125–1139. https://doi.org/10.1002/DNEU.22226

Razak, K. A., Richardson, M. D., & Fuzessery, Z. M. (2008). Experience is required for the maintenance and refinement of FM sweep selectivity in the developing auditory cortex. *Proceedings of the National Academy of Sciences of the United States of America*, **105**(11), 4465–4470. https://doi.org/10.1073/PNAS.0709504105

Recanzone, G. H., Schreiner, C. E., & Merzenich, M. M. (1993). Plasticity in the frequency representation of primary auditory cortex following discrimination training in adult owl monkeys. *Journal of Neuroscience*, **13**(1), 87–103. https://doi.org/10.1523/JNEUROSCI.13-01-00087.1993

Reed, A., Riley, J., Carraway, R., Carrasco, A., Perez, C., Jakkamsetti, V., & Kilgard, M. P. (2011). Cortical map plasticity improves learning but is not necessary for improved performance. *Neuron*, **70**(1), 121–131. https://doi.org/10.1016/J.NEURON.2011.02.038

Reep, R. L. (2000). Cortical layer VII and persistent subplate cells in mammalian brains. *Brain, Behavior and Evolution*, **56**(4), 212–234. https://doi.org/10.1159/000047206

Reinhold, K., Lien, A. D., & Scanziani, M. (2015). Distinct recurrent versus afferent dynamics in cortical visual processing. *Nature Neuroscience*, **18**(12), 1789–1797. https://doi.org/10.1038/NN.4153

Resnik, J., & Polley, D. B. (2017). Fast-spiking GABA circuit dynamics in the auditory cortex predict recovery of sensory processing following peripheral nerve damage. *eLife*, **6**. https://doi.org/10.7554/eLife.21452

Richardson, B. D., Sottile, S. Y., & Caspary, D. M. (2021). Mechanisms of GABAergic and cholinergic neurotransmission in auditory thalamus: impact of aging. *Hearing Research*, **102**, 108003. https://doi.org/10.1016/j.heares.2020.108003

Richardson, R. J., Blundon, J. A., Bayazitov, I. T., & Zakharenko, S. S. (2009). Connectivity patterns revealed by mapping of active inputs on dendrites of thalamorecipient neurons in the auditory cortex. *Journal of Neuroscience*, **29**(20), 6406–6417. https://doi.org/10.1523/JNEUROSCI.0258-09.2009

Robert, B., Kimchi, E. Y., Watanabe, Y., Chakoma, T., Jing, M., Li, Y., & Polley, D. B. (2021). A functional topography within the cholinergic basal forebrain for processing sensory cues associated with reward and punishment. *BioRxiv*, 2021.04.16.439895. https://doi.org/10.1101/2021.04.16.439895

Robertson, D., & Irvine, D. R. F. (1989). Plasticity of frequency organization in auditory cortex of guinea pigs with partial unilateral deafness. *Journal of Comparative Neurology*, **282**(3), 456–471. https://doi.org/10.1002/CNE.902820311

Romand, R., & Ehret, G. (1990). development of tonotopy in the inferior colliculus. I. Electrophysiological mapping in house mice. *Developmental Brain Research*, **54**(2), 221–234.

Rose, H. J., & Metherate, R. (2005). Auditory thalamocortical transmission is reliable and temporally precise. *Journal of Neurophysiology*, **94**(3), 2019–2030. https://doi.org/10.1152/JN.00860.2004

Rose, J. E., & Woolsey, C. N. (1949a). Organization of the mammalian thalamus and its relationships to the cerebral cortex. *Electroencephalography and Clinical Neurophysiology*, **1**(1–4), 391–404. https://doi.org/10.1016/0013-4694(49)90212-6

Rose, J. E., & Woolsey, C. N. (1949b). The relations of thalamic connections, cellular structure and evocable electrical activity in the auditory region of the cat. *Journal of Comparative Neurology*, **91**(3), 441–466.

Rosen, M. J., Sarro, E. C., Kelly, J. B., & Sanes, D. H. (2012). Diminished behavioral and neural sensitivity to sound modulation is associated with moderate developmental hearing loss. *PLoS ONE*, **7**(7). https://doi.org/10.1371/JOURNAL.PONE.0041514

Rosen, M. J., Semple, M. N., & Sanes, D. H. (2010). Exploiting development to evaluate auditory encoding of amplitude modulation. *Journal of Neuroscience*, **30**(46), 15509–15520. https://doi.org/10.1523/JNEUROSCI.3340-10.2010

Rummell, B. P., Klee, J. L., & Sigurdsson, T. (2016). Attenuation of responses to self-generated sounds in auditory cortical neurons. *Journal of Neuroscience*, **36**(47), 12010–12026. https://doi.org/10.1523/JNEUROSCI.1564-16.2016

Rumpel, S., Hatt, H., & Gottmann, K. (1998). Silent synapses in the developing rat visual cortex: Evidence for postsynaptic expression of synaptic plasticity. *Journal of Neuroscience*, **18**(21), 8863–8874. https://doi.org/10.1523/JNEUROSCI.18-21-08863.1998

Runyan, C. A., Piasini, E., Panzeri, S., & Harvey, C. D. (2017). Distinct timescales of population coding across cortex. *Nature*, **548**(7665), 92–96. https://doi.org/10.1038/NATURE23020

Ryan, A. F., Miller, J. M., Pfingst, B. E., & Martin, G. K. (1984). Effects of reaction time performance on single-unit activity in the central auditory pathway of the rhesus macaque. *Journal of Neuroscience*, **4**(1), 298–308. https://doi.org/10.1523/JNEUROSCI.04-01-00298.1984

Saab, A. S., Tzvetavona, I. D., Trevisiol, A., Baltan, S., Dibaj, P., Kusch, K., Möbius, W., Goetze, B., Jahn, H. M., Huang, W., Steffens, H., Schomburg, E. D., Pérez-Samartín, A., Pérez-Cerdá, F., Bakhtiari, D., Matute, C., Löwel, S., Griesinger, C., Hirrlinger, J., … Nave, K. A. (2016). Oligodendroglial NMDA receptors regulate glucose import and axonal energy metabolism. *Neuron*, **91**(1), 119–132. https://doi.org/10.1016/J.NEURON.2016.05.016

Sadaka, Y., Weinfeld, E., Lev, D. L., & White, E. L. (2003). Changes in mouse barrel synapses consequent to sensory deprivation from birth. *Journal of Comparative Neurology*, **457**(1), 75–86. https://doi.org/10.1002/CNE.10518

Saderi, D., Schwartz, Z. P., Heller, C. R., Pennington, J. R., & David, S. v. (2021). Dissociation of task engagement and arousal effects in auditory cortex and midbrain. *eLife*, **10**, 1–25. https://doi.org/10.7554/ELIFE.60153

Salami, M., Itami, C., Tsumoto, T., & Kimura, F. (2003). Change of conduction velocity by regional myelination yields constant latency irrespective of distance between thalamus and cortex. *Proceedings of the National Academy of Sciences of the United States of America*, **100**(10),

6174–6179. https://doi.org/10.1073/PNAS.0937380100

Sametsky, E. A., Turner, J. G., Larsen, D., Ling, L., & Caspary, D. M. (2015). Enhanced GABAA-Mediated tonic inhibition in auditory thalamus of rats with behavioral evidence of tinnitus. *Journal of Neuroscience*, **35**(25), 9369–9380. https://doi.org/10.1523/JNEUROSCI.5054-14.2015

Sanes, D. H., & Bao, S. (2009). Tuning up the developing auditory CNS. *Current Opinion in Neurobiology*, **19**(2), 188–199. https://doi.org/10.1016/J.CONB.2009.05.014

Sanes, D. H., Merickel, M., & Rubel, E. W. (1989). Evidence for an alteration of the tonotopic map in the gerbil cochlea during development. *Journal of Comparative Neurology*, **279**(3), 436–444. https://doi.org/10.1002/CNE.902790308

Sanes, D. H., & Woolley, S. M. N. (2011). A behavioral framework to guide research on central auditory development and plasticity. *Neuron*, **72**(6), 912–929. https://doi.org/10.1016/J.NEURON.2011.12.005

Sarro, E. C., & Sanes, D. H. (2010). Prolonged maturation of auditory perception and learning in gerbils. *Developmental Neurobiology*, **70**(9), 636–648. https://doi.org/10.1002/DNEU.20801

Sarro, E. C., von Trapp, G., Mowery, T. M., Kotak, V. C., & Sanes, D. H. (2015). Cortical synaptic inhibition declines during auditory learning. *Journal of Neuroscience*, **35**(16), 6318–6325. https://doi.org/10.1523/JNEUROSCI.4051-14.2015

Scala, F., Kobak, D., Shan, S., Bernaerts, Y., Laturnus, S., Cadwell, C. R., Hartmanis, L., Froudarakis, E., Castro, J. R., Tan, Z. H., Papadopoulos, S., Patel, S. S., Sandberg, R., Berens, P., Jiang, X., & Tolias, A. S. (2019). Layer 4 of mouse neocortex differs in cell types and circuit organization between sensory areas. *Nature Communications*, **10**(1). https://doi.org/10.1038/S41467-019-12058-Z

Schmitt, L. I., Wimmer, R. D., Nakajima, M., Happ, M., Mofakham, S., & Halassa, M. M. (2017). Thalamic amplification of cortical connectivity sustains attentional control. *Nature*, **545**(7653), 219–223. https://doi.org/10.1038/NATURE22073

Schneider, D. M., & Mooney, R. (2018). How movement modulates hearing. *Annual Review of Neuroscience*, **41**, 553–572. https://doi.org/10.1146/ANNUREV-NEURO-072116-031215

Schneider, D. M., Nelson, A., & Mooney, R. (2014). A synaptic and circuit basis for corollary discharge in the auditory cortex. *Nature*, **513**(7517), 189–194. https://doi.org/10.1038/nature13724

Schneider, D. M., Sundararajan, J., & Mooney, R. (2018). A cortical filter that learns to suppress the acoustic consequences of movement. *Nature*, **561**(7723), 391–395. https://doi.org/10.1038/S41586-018-0520-5

Schreiner, C. E., & Polley, D. B. (2014). Auditory map plasticity: diversity in causes and consequences. *Current Opinion in Neurobiology*, **24**(1), 143–156. https://doi.org/10.1016/j.conb.2013.11.009

Schwartz, Z. P., & David, S. v. (2018). Focal suppression of distractor sounds by selective attention in auditory cortex. *Cerebral Cortex*, **28**(1), 323–339. https://doi.org/10.1093/CERCOR/BHX288

Seidl, A. H., & Grothe, B. (2005). Development of sound localization mechanisms in the Mongolian gerbil is shaped by early acoustic experience. *Journal of Neurophysiology*, **94**(2), 1028–1036. https://doi.org/10.1152/JN.01143.2004

Seki, S., & Eggermont, J. J. (2003). Changes in spontaneous firing rate and neural synchrony in cat primary auditory cortex after localized tone-induced hearing loss. *Hearing Research*, **180**(1–2), 28–38. https://doi.org/10.1016/S0378-5955(03)00074-1

Shaheen, L. A., Slee, S. J., & David, S. V. (2021). Task engagement improves neural discriminability in the auditory midbrain of the marmoset monkey. *Journal of Neuroscience*, **41**(2), 284–297. https://doi.org/10.1523/JNEUROSCI.1112-20.2020

Sharma, A., Dorman, M. F., & Spahr, A. J. (2002). A sensitive period for the development of the central auditory system in children with cochlear implants: implications for age of implantation. *Ear and Hearing*, **23**(6), 532–539. https://doi.org/10.1097/00003446-200212000-00004

Shepard, K. N., Liles, L. C., Weinshenker, D., & Liu, R. C. (2015). Norepinephrine is necessary for experience-dependent plasticity in the developing mouse auditory cortex. *Journal of Neuroscience*, **35**(6), 2432–2437. https://doi.org/10.1523/JNEUROSCI.0532-14.2015

Sinclair, J. L., Fischl, M. J., Alexandrova, O., Heß, M., Grothe, B., Leibold, C., & Kopp-Scheinpflug, C. (2017). Sound-evoked activity influences myelination of brainstem axons in the trapezoid body. *Journal of Neuroscience*, **37**(34), 8239–8255. https://doi.org/10.1523/JNEUROSCI.3728-16.2017

Singla, S., Dempsey, C., Warren, R., Enikolopov, A. G., & Sawtell, N. B. (2017). A cerebellum-like circuit in the auditory system cancels responses to self-generated sounds. *Nature Neuroscience*, **20**(7), 943–950. https://doi.org/10.1038/NN.4567

Smith, P. H., & Populin, L. C. (2001). Fundamental differences between the thalamocortical recipient layers of the cat auditory and visual cortices. *Journal of Comparative Neurology*, **436**(4), 508–519. https://doi.org/10.1002/CNE.1084

Smith, P. H., Uhlrich, D. J., Manning, K. A., & Banks, M. I. (2012). Thalamocortical projections to rat auditory cortex from the ventral and dorsal divisions of the medial geniculate nucleus. *Journal of Comparative Neurology*, **520**(1), 34–51. https://doi.org/10.1002/cne.22682

Sottile, S. Y., Hackett, T. A., Cai, R., Ling, L., Llano, D. A., & Caspary, D. M. (2017). Presynaptic neuronal nicotinic receptors differentially shape select inputs to auditory thalamus and are negatively impacted by aging. *Journal of Neuroscience*, **37**(47), 11377–11389. https://doi.org/10.1523/JNEUROSCI.1795-17.2017

Sottile, S. Y., Ling, L., Cox, B. C., & Caspary, D. M. (2017). Impact of ageing on postsynaptic neuronal nicotinic neurotransmission in auditory thalamus. *Journal of Physiology*, **595**(15), 5375–5385. https://doi.org/10.1113/JP274467

Stoilova, V. v., Knauer, B., Berg, S., Rieber, E., Jäkel, F., & Stüttgen, M. C. (2020). Auditory cortex reflects goal-directed movement but is not necessary for behavioral adaptation in sound-cued reward tracking. *Journal of Neurophysiology*, **124**(4), 1056–1071. https://doi.org/10.1152/JN.00736.2019

Sun, H., Takesian, A. E., Wang, T. T., Lippman-Bell, J. J., Hensch, T. K., & Jensen, F. E. (2018). Early seizures prematurely unsilence auditory synapses to disrupt thalamocortical critical period plasticity. *Cell Reports*, **23**(9), 2533–2540. https://doi.org/10.1016/j.celrep.2018.04.108

Sun, Y. J., Liu, B. H., Tao, H. W., & Zhang, L. I. (2019). Selective strengthening of intracortical excitatory input leads to receptive field refinement during auditory cortical development. *Journal of Neuroscience*, **39**(7), 1195–1205. https://doi.org/10.1523/JNEUROSCI.2492-18.2018

Sun, Y. J., Wu, G. K., Liu, B. H., Li, P., Zhou, M., Xiao, Z., Tao, H. W., & Zhang, L. I. (2010). Fine-tuning of pre-balanced excitation and inhibition during auditory cortical development. *Nature*, **465**(7300), 927–931.

Takesian, A. E., Bogart, L. J., Lichtman, J. W., & Hensch, T. K. (2018). Inhibitory circuit gating of auditory critical-period plasticity. *Nature Neuroscience*, **21**(2), 218–227. https://doi.org/10.1038/s41593-017-0064-2

Takesian, A. E., & Hensch, T. K. (2013). Balancing plasticity/stability across brain development. *Progress in Brain Research*, **207**, 3–34. https://doi.org/10.1016/B978-0-444-63327-9.00001-1

Takesian, A. E., Kotak, V. C., & Sanes, D. H. (2009). Developmental hearing loss disrupts synaptic inhibition: Implications for auditory processing. *Future Neurology*, **4**(3), 331–349. https://doi.org/10.2217/FNL.09.5

Takesian, A. E., Kotak, V. C., & Sanes, D. H. (2010). Presynaptic GABA(B) receptors regulate experience dependent development of inhibitory short-term plasticity. *Journal of Neuroscience*, **30**(7), 2716–2727. https://doi.org/10.1523/jneurosci.3903-09.2010

Takesian, A. E., Kotak, V. C., & Sanes, D. H. (2012). Age-dependent effect of hearing loss on cortical inhibitory synapse function. *Journal of Neurophysiology*, **107**(3), 937–947. https://doi.org/10.1152/jn.00515.2011

Takesian, A. E., Kotak, V. C., Sharma, N., & Sanes, D. H. (2013). Hearing loss differentially affects thalamic drive to two cortical interneuron subtypes. *Journal of Neurophysiology*, **110**(4), 999–1008. https://doi.org/10.1152/jn.00182.2013

Tan, A. Y. Y., & Wehr, M. (2009). Balanced tone-evoked synaptic excitation and inhibition in mouse auditory cortex. *Neuroscience*, **163**(4), 1302–1315. https://doi.org/10.1016/J.NEUROSCIENCE.2009.07.032

Tan, A. Y. Y., Zhang, L. I., Merzenich, M. M., & Schreiner, C. E. (2004). Tone-evoked excitatory and inhibitory synaptic conductances of primary auditory cortex neurons. *Journal of Neurophysiology*, **92**(1), 630–643. https://doi.org/10.1152/JN.01020.2003

Tan, Z., Hu, H., Huang, Z. J., & Agmon, A. (2008). Robust but delayed thalamocortical activation of dendritic-targeting inhibitory interneurons. *Proceedings of the National Academy of Sciences of the United States of America*, **105**(6). www.pnas.orgcgidoi10.1073pnas.0710628105

Tasaka, G. ichi, Feigin, L., Maor, I., Groysman, M., DeNardo, L. A., Schiavo, J. K., Froemke, R. C., Luo, L., & Mizrahi, A. (2020). The temporal association cortex plays a key role in auditory-driven maternal plasticity. *Neuron*, **107**(3), 566–579.e7. https://doi.org/10.1016/J.NEURON.2020.05.004

Taylor, J. A., Hasegawa, M., Benoit, C. M., Freire, J. A., Theodore, M., Ganea, D. A., Innocenti, S. M., Lu, T., & Gründemann, J. (2021). Single cell plasticity and population coding stability in auditory thalamus upon associative learning. *Nature Communications*, **12**(1). https://doi.org/10.1038/S41467-021-22421-8

Tennigkeit, F., Schwarz, D. W. F., & Puil, E. (1998a). Modulation of bursts and high-threshold calcium spikes in neurons of rat auditory thalamus. *Neuroscience*, **83**(4), 1063–1073. https://doi.org/10.1016/S0306-4522(97)00458-2

Tennigkeit, F., Schwarz, D. W. F., & Puil, E. (1998b). Postnatal development of signal generation in auditory thalamic neurons. *Developmental Brain Research*, **109**(2), 255–263. https://doi.org/10.1016/S0165-3806(98)00056-X

Thomas, M. E., Friedman, N. H. M., Cisneros-Franco, J. M., Ouellet, L., & de Villers-Sidani, É. (2019). The prolonged masking of temporal acoustic inputs with noise drives plasticity in the adult rat auditory cortex. *Cerebral Cortex*, **29**(3), 1032–1046. https://doi.org/10.1093/CERCOR/BHY009

Tomassy, G. S., Berger, D. R., Chen, H. H., Kasthuri, N., Hayworth, K. J., Vercelli, A., Seung, H. S., Lichtman, J. W., & Arlotta, P. (2014). Distinct profiles of myelin distribution along single axons of pyramidal neurons in the neocortex. *Science*, **344**(6181), 319–324. https://doi.org/10.1126/SCIENCE.1249766

Torii, M., Hackett, T. A., Rakic, P., Levitt, P., & Polley, D. B. (2013). EphA signaling impacts development of topographic connectivity in auditory corticofugal systems. *Cerebral Cortex*, **23**(4), 775–785. https://doi.org/10.1093/cercor/bhs066

Torres-Reveron, J., & Friedlander, M. (2007). Properties of persistent postnatal cortical subplate neurons. *Journal of Neuroscience*, **27**(37), 9962–9974. https://doi.org/10.1523/JNEUROSCI.1536-07.2007

Toyoizumi, T., Miyamoto, H., Yazaki-Sugiyama, Y., Atapour, N., Hensch, T. K., & Miller, K. D. (2013). A Theory of the transition to critical period plasticity: inhibition selectively suppresses spontaneous activity. *Neuron*, **80**(1), 51–63. https://doi.org/10.1016/J.NEURON.2013.07.022

Tsunada, J., Liu, A. S. K., Gold, J. I., & Cohen, Y. E. (2016). Causal contribution of primate auditory cortex to auditory perceptual decision-making. *Nature Neuroscience*, **19**(1), 135–142. https://doi.org/10.1038/nn.4195

Valverde, F., Facal-valverde, M. V., Santacana, M., & Heredia, M. (1989). Development and differentiation of early generated cells of sublayer VIb in the somatosensory cortex of the rat: A correlated Golgi and autoradiographic study. *Journal of Comparative Neurology*, **290**(1), 118–140.

Vandevelde, I. L., Duckworth, E., & Reep, R. L. (1996). Layer VII and the gray matter trajectories of corticocortical axons in rats. *Anatomy and Embryology*, **194**(6), 581–593. https://doi.org/10.1007/BF00187471

Venkataraman, Y., & Bartlett, E. L. (2013). Postnatal development of synaptic properties of the GABAergic projection from the inferior colliculus to the auditory thalamus. *Journal of Neurophysiology*, **109**(12), 2866–2882.

Venkataraman, Y., & Bartlett, E. L. (2014). Postnatal development of auditory central evoked responses and thalamic cellular properties. *Developmental Neurobiology*, **74**(5), 541–555. https://doi.org/10.1002/DNEU.22148

Viswanathan, S., Bandyopadhyay, S., Kao, J. P. Y., & Kanold, P. O. (2012). Changing microcircuits in the subplate of the developing cortex. *Journal of Neuroscience*, **32**(5), 1589–1601. https://doi.org/10.1523/JNEUROSCI.4748-11.2012

Viswanathan, S., Sheikh, A., Looger, L. L., & Kanold, P. O. (2017). Molecularly defined subplate neurons project both to thalamocortical recipient layers and thalamus. *Cerebral Cortex*, **27**(10), 4759–4768. https://doi.org/10.1093/CERCOR/BHW271

Voss, P., Thomas, M. E., Cisneros-Franco, J. M., & de Villers-Sidani, É. (2017). Dynamic brains and the changing rules of neuroplasticity: implications for learning and recovery. *Frontiers in Psychology*, **8**. https://doi.org/10.3389/FPSYG.2017.01657

Wang, D. D., & Kriegstein, A. R. (2009). Defining the role of GABA in cortical development. *Journal of Physiology*, **587**(9), 1873–1879. https://doi.org/10.1113/JPHYSIOL.2008.167635

Wang, H. C., & Bergles, D. E. (2015). Spontaneous activity in the developing auditory system. *Cell and Tissue Research*, **361**(1), 65–75. https://doi.org/10.1007/S00441-014-2007-5

Wang, X., Lu, T., Bendor, D., & Bartlett, E. (2008). Neural coding of temporal information in auditory thalamus and cortex. *Neuroscience*, **157**(2), 484–493. https://doi.org/10.1016/J.NEUROSCIENCE.2008.07.050

Wehr, M., & Zador, A. M. (2003). Balanced inhibition underlies tuning and sharpens spike timing in auditory cortex. *Nature*, **426**(6965), 442–446. https://doi.org/10.1038/NATURE02116

Wess, J. M., Isaiah, A., Watkins, P. v., & Kanold, P. O. (2017). Subplate neurons are the first cortical neurons to respond to sensory stimuli. *Proceedings of the National Academy of Sciences of the United States of America*, **114**(47), 12602–12607. https://doi.org/10.1073/PNAS.1710793114

Whitton, J. P., & Polley, D. B. (2011). Evaluating the perceptual and pathophysiological consequences of auditory deprivation in early postnatal life: a comparison of basic and clinical studies. *Journal of the Association for Research in Otolaryngology*, **12**(5), 535–547. https://doi.org/10.1007/s10162-011-0271-6

Williamson, R. S., Hancock, K. E., Shinn-Cunningham, B. G., & Polley, D. B. (2015). Locomotion and task demands differentially modulate thalamic audiovisual processing during active search. *Current Biology*, **25**(14), 1885–1891. https://doi.org/10.1016/j.cub.2015.05.045

Williamson, R. S., & Polley, D. B. (2019). Parallel pathways for sound processing and functional connectivity among layer 5 and 6 auditory corticofugal neurons. *eLife*, **8**. https://doi.org/10.7554/eLife.42974

Wilmington, D., Gray, L., & Jahrsdoerfer, R. (1994). Binaural processing after corrected congenital unilateral conductive hearing loss. *Hearing Research*, **74**(1–2), 99–114. https://doi.org/10.1016/0378-5955(94)90179-1

Winer, J. A. (2006). Decoding the auditory corticofugal systems. *Hearing Research*, **212**(1–2), 1–8. https://doi.org/10.1016/J.HEARES.2005.06.014

Winer, J. A., Diehl, J. J., & Larue, D. T. (2001). Projections of auditory cortex to the medial geniculate body of the cat. *Journal of Comparative Neurology*, **430**, 27–55.

Winer, J. A., & Lee, C. C. (2007). The distributed auditory cortex. *Hearing Research*, **229**(1–2), 3–13. https://doi.org/10.1016/j.heares.2007.01.017

Winer, J. A., Miller, L. M., Lee, C. C., & Schreiner, C. E. (2005). Auditory thalamocortical transformation: structure and function. *Trends in Neuroscience*, **28**(5), 255–263. https://doi.org/10.1016/j.tins.2005.03.009

Xin, Y., Zhong, L., Zhang, Y., Zhou, T., Pan, J., & Xu, N. long. (2019). Sensory-to-Category transformation via dynamic reorganization of ensemble structures in mouse auditory cortex. *Neuron*, **103**(5), 909–921.e6. https://doi.org/10.1016/J.NEURON.2019.06.004

Xiong, X. R., Liang, F., Zingg, B., Ji, X. Y., Ibrahim, L. A., Tao, H. W., & Zhang, L. I. (2015). Auditory cortex controls sound-driven innate defense behaviour through corticofugal projections to inferior colliculus. *Nature Communications*, **6**. https://doi.org/10.1038/NCOMMS8224

Xu, H., Kotak, V. C., & Sanes, D. H. (2010). Normal hearing is required for the emergence of long-lasting inhibitory potentiation in cortex. *Journal of Neuroscience*, **30**(1), 331–341. https://doi.org/10.1523/JNEUROSCI.4554-09.2010

Xue, M., Atallah, B. v., & Scanziani, M. (2014). Equalizing excitation-inhibition ratios across visual cortical neurons. *Nature*, **511**(7511), 596–600. https://doi.org/10.1038/NATURE13321

Yang, E. J., Lin, E. W., & Hensch, T. K. (2012). Critical period for acoustic preference in mice. *Proceedings of the National Academy of Sciences of the United States of America*, **109**(2), 17213–17220. https://doi.org/10.1073/PNAS.1200705109

Yang, Y., Lee, J., & Kim, G. (2020). Integration of locomotion and auditory signals in the mouse inferior colliculus. *eLife*, **9**. https://doi.org/10.7554/ELIFE.52228

Yin, T. C. T., Smith, P. H., & Joris, P. X. (2019). Neural mechanisms of binaural processing in the auditory brainstem. *Comprehensive Physiology*, **9**(4), 1503–1575. https://doi.org/10.1002/CPHY.C180036

Zhang, L. I., Bao, S., & Merzenich, M. M. (2001). Persistent and specific influences of early acoustic environments on primary auditory cortex. *Nature Neuroscience*, **4**(11), 1123–1130. https://doi.org/10.1038/nn745

Zhang, L. I., Bao, S., & Merzenich, M. M. (2002). Disruption of primary auditory cortex by synchronous auditory inputs during a critical period. *Proceedings of the National Academy of Sciences of the United States of America*, **99**(4), 2309–2314. https://doi.org/10.1073/PNAS.261707398

Zhang, L. I., Tan, A. Y. Y., Schreiner, C. E., & Merzenich, M. M. (2003). Topography and synaptic shaping of direction selectivity in primary auditory cortex. *Nature*, **424**(6945), 201–205. https://doi.org/10.1038/NATURE01796

Zhao, C., Kao, J. P. Y., & Kanold, P. O. (2009). Functional excitatory microcircuits in neonatal cortex connect thalamus and layer 4. *Journal of Neuroscience*, **29**(49), 15479–15488. https://doi.org/10.1523/JNEUROSCI.4471-09.2009

Zheng, W. (2012). Auditory map reorganization and pitch discrimination in adult rats chronically exposed to low-level ambient noise. *Frontiers in Systems Neuroscience*, 1–14. https://doi.org/10.3389/FNSYS.2012.00065

Zhou, X., & Merzenich, M. M. (2012). Environmental noise exposure degrades normal listening processes. *Nature Communications*, **3**, 843. https://doi.org/10.1038/ncomms1849

Zhou, X., Panizzutti, R., de Villers-Sidani, É., Madeira, C., & Merzenich, M. M. (2011). Natural restoration of critical period plasticity in the juvenile and adult primary auditory cortex. *Journal of Neuroscience*, **31**(15), 5625–5634. https://doi.org/10.1523/JNEUROSCI.6470-10.2011

Zhou, Y., Liu, B. hua, Wu, G. K., Kim, Y. J., Xiao, Z., Tao, H. W., & Zhang, L. I. (2010). Preceding inhibition silences layer 6 neurons in auditory cortex. *Neuron*, **65**(5), 706–717. https://doi.org/10.1016/J.NEURON.2010.02.021

Zljak, L., Uylings, H. B. M., Kostovic, I., & van Eden, C. G. (1992). Prenatal development of neurons in the human prefrontal cortex. II. A quantitative Golgi study. *Journal of Comparative Neurology*, **316**(4), 485–496. https://doi.org/10.1002/CNE.903160408

Section 6: **Motor Control**

Chapter 14

Motor Thalamic Interactions with the Brainstem and Basal Ganglia

Jesse H. Goldberg

Introduction

The motor thalamus routes diverse inputs from the brainstem, cerebellum, cortex, and basal ganglia to the cortex and striatum, which in turn, implement further signal transformations prior to the issuance of decisions or motor commands (Figure 1) (Bosch-Bouju et al., 2013; Guillery and Sherman, 2002). All of these pathways are parts of poly-regional, reciprocal loops that interact during natural behavior (Chabrol et al., 2019; Gao et al., 2018). The sheer complexity of the vertebrate motor system, and the central place of the thalamus within it, presents a challenge for neuroscientists seeking principles of thalamic function. Here, I highlight the roles of input-defined thalamic circuits in motor sequence production and learning. The roles of the motor thalamus in Parkinson's disease are addressed in other reviews (McGregor and Nelson, 2019; Rubin et al., 2012), and cerebellar-related thalamic functions are addressed elsewhere in this volume (Chapter 15). Reviews focused on detailed intra-thalamic anatomy and sub-regions can be found elsewhere (Bosch-Bouju et al., 2013; Ilinsky and Kultas-Ilinsky, 2002).

Brainstem-Recipient Motor Thalamus

Decerebrate rodents exhibit a surprisingly intact behavioral repertoire, including vocalization, breathing, orienting, righting, and locomotor patterns that give the appearance of goal-directed movements (Dirlam, 1969; Grill and Norgren, 1978; Woods, 1964). The fact that organized motor sequences can arise from the brainstem alone poses a problem for forebrain motor circuits, which require moment-to-moment information about both current body posture and ongoing movements to issue appropriate motor commands (Andersen et al., 1985; Kakei et al., 2003). If a brainstem circuit drives a behavioral response, the forebrain needs to know about it in order to accurately plan and execute subsequent actions. The following sections present four examples of how the motor thalamus plays a critical role in relaying efference copies of brainstem-dependent motor commands to the basal ganglia and cortex in the service of motor sequence generation and learning.

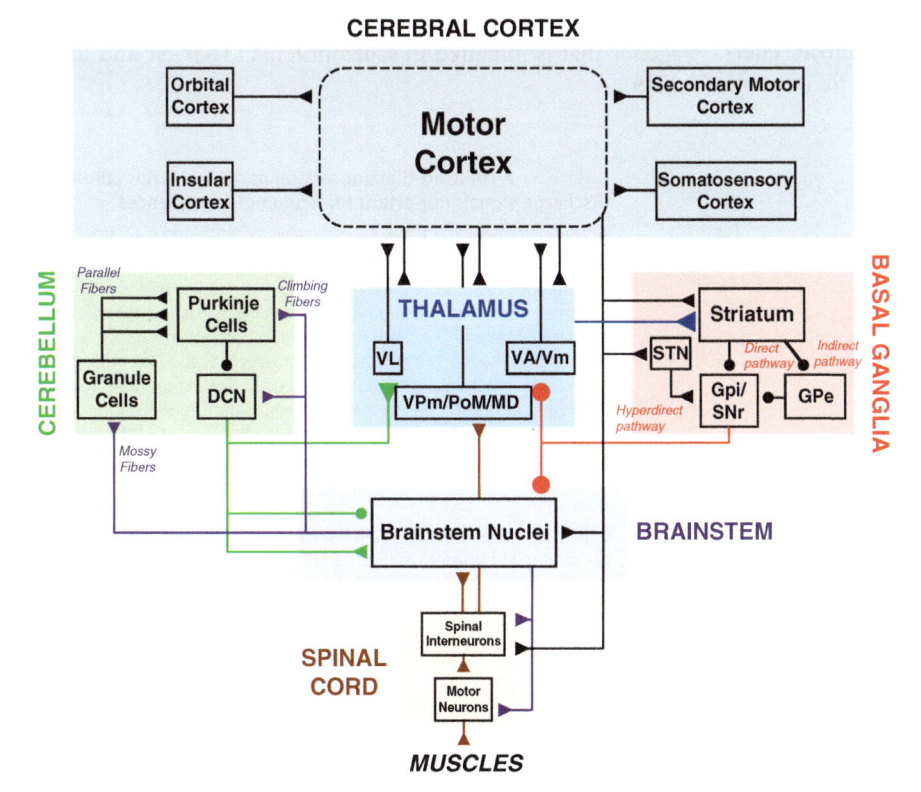

Figure 1 The place of the thalamus in the mammalian motor system.

This simplified schematic of the mammalian motor system reveals some challenges for understanding motor thalamic function. Motor thalamic outputs are further processed in target striatal and cortical areas before they are transformed into motor commands.

A Colliculo-Thalamocortical Pathway for Efference Copy of Occulomotor Commands

Occulomotor control provides a clear-cut example of the action-selection problem. At any given instant, an animal with conjugate gaze must pick one, and only one, target location to orient to. Under natural conditions, primates generate roughly two to five saccades per second (Schall, 1995). Although many of these saccades may be driven by forebrain structures, for example, during reward-maximizing decision tasks (Gold and Shadlen, 2007), other saccades, for example, "reflexive" ones to a sudden appearance of a salient object, may be driven, "bottom-up" pathways independent of the forebrain (Schall, 1995; Theeuwes, 2010).

The superior colliculus (SC) is a key site of convergence of "bottom-up" sensory inputs and "top-down" forebrain motor commands and, together with underlying isthmic circuits, contains an architecture uniquely suited for solving an action-selection problem critical for saccade control (Krauzlis et al., 2004; Mysore and Knudsen, 2012). Specifically, the colliculus and underlying inhibitory isthmic circuits implement a lateral inhibition process that is robust across a wide range of stimulus intensities, enabling animals to orient to only one direction at a given movement in time (Koyama and Pujala, 2018; Mysore and Knudsen, 2011). Thus, the colliculus may have the final say on which saccade to make in a given instant. If the colliculus commands a saccade and displaces the eyes to the left at an object, then this fundamentally changes the state of the oculomotor plant in a way that cortical structures such as frontal eye fields (FEFs) need to know about in order to issue a command for any subsequent saccade.

Classic experiments by Sommer and Wurtz clarified how a colliculo-thalamocortical pathway in macaques carries efference copies of motor commands that are necessary for accurate saccadic sequences (Sommer and Wurtz, 2008). The SC forms a topographic map that projects directly to downstream motor areas of the occulomotor plant. Copies of these signals project to the mediodorsal (MD) thalamus, which in turn projects to the FEF, a cortical region important for descending control of gaze. Antidromically identified FEF-projecting MD neurons exhibited direction-specific efference copy signals that, in essence, could "tell" the FEF what saccade the SC had just commanded, resulting in FEF neurons that can shift their receptive field toward the future center of gaze (Shin and Sommer, 2012; Sommer and Wurtz, 2004a). To test if these efference copy signals in the SC–MD–FEF pathway were important for sequential saccades, Sommer and Wurtz transiently inactivated the MD thalamus in a variety of saccade tasks (Sommer and Wurtz, 2004b). MD inactivation did not impair saccadic accuracy or speed in simple single-target tasks. Yet if a monkey was given two targets to reach in a sequence, the second command would require information about the state of the eye at the end of the first command (Figure 2). In this task, inactivation of the MD dramatically impaired the accuracy of the second but not the first command. This body of work in primates inspired studies of a human patient with a remarkably similar thalamic lesion (Ostendorf et al., 2010), as well as studies in individuals with schizophrenia, who are hypothesized to have impaired corollary discharge signals important for the sense of agency (Thakkar and Rolfs, 2019). In both patient populations, double-step performance was impaired.

These data provide an example of the transthalamic efference copy signals necessary for coordination of a simple occulomotor sequence. The MD enables the FEFs to predict the upcoming "state" of the occulomotor plan. More generally, the ability to predict an upcoming "state" of the body on the basis of self-generated movements may be related to a sense of agency that is impaired in schizophrenia (Thakkar and Rolfs, 2019).

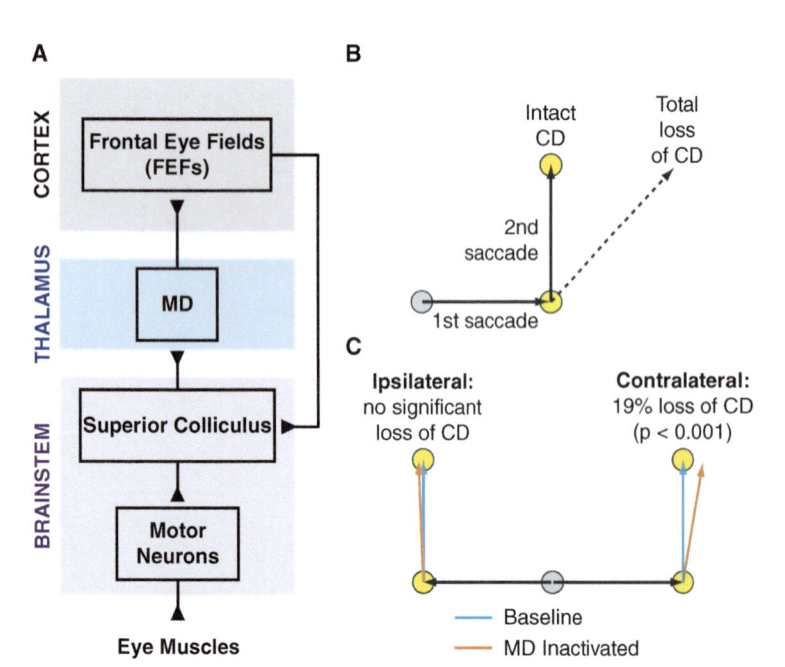

Figure 2 A colliculo-thalamocortical pathway carries corollary discharge signals important for oculomotor sequences.

A. A transthalamic pathway carries corollary discharge (CD) signals from the SC, to the MD, to the FEFs.

B. Schematic of a double-step task in which a monkey had to make two saccades from a starting position to two targets flashed sequentially before a GO signal. Successful saccades to both targets (*black lines*) require that the memory of the second target location be adjusted to account for where the eye lands at the end of the first saccade. Because the task is performed in the dark, this adjustment requires internal information about the consequences of the first saccade. Without such adjustment, an erroneous saccade would be made (*dashed line*) based on the location of the second target relative to the position of the eye prior to the first saccade.

C. Inactivation of the MD caused errors in the second saccade consistent with the loss of internal corollary discharge signals. Adapted from Sommer and Wurtz (2008).

Brainstem-Thalamostriatal Pathways for Learned and Innate Motor Sequences

Conceptually similar circuits that carry efference copies of brainstem motor commands may, in other settings, provide the foundation for reliable multi-step sequence execution. For example, in a behavior with a fixed sequence of component actions, efference copy signals of action *a1* can function as a premotor command for second action *a2*. Consider rodent grooming – a highly complex yet stereotyped, species-specific action sequence that includes up to 25 specific forelimb and body movements (Figure 3A). Rats produce a behavioral chain consisting of (1) a bout of ~5–10 bilaterally alternating forepaw strokes over the mystacial vibrissae at ~6 Hz (2) a set of 1–4 slower, unilateral strokes of intermediate amplitude; (3) a larger set of ~3–8 large-amplitude strokes; and (4) a sequence of body licks. This chain can be produced with incredible stereotypy (Figure 3B) (Aldridge et al., 1993; Berridge and Aldridge, 2000).

In a classic body of work, Aldridge and colleagues performed a series of lesion and electrophysiology studies to identify neural circuits for grooming production (Aldridge et al., 1993, 2004). Remarkably, animals with massive lesions to the cortex, cerebellum, or trigeminal sensory feedback produced intact grooming sequences, implicating subcortical central pattern-generating (CPG) circuits. Importantly, lesions to the anterior lateral striatum abolished the grooming syntax, but individual components such as flank licks and vibrissae strokes remained largely intact. Based on these results, Aldridge and colleagues proposed that brainstem circuits are sufficient to produce individual grooming components but rely on a thalamo striato nigral brainstem loop to pattern them into a reliable sequence. Complementing the lesion data, striatal and nigral neurons exhibited temporally precise activity locked to specific transitions within a grooming sequence (Aldridge and Berridge, 1998; Meyer-Luehmann et al., 2002). In essence, individual grooming components appear to be driven by fixed-action pattern-generating circuits distributed throughout the brainstem (Berridge, 1989). Efference copies of these pattern-generating commands are sent to the striatum via the thalamus. Striatal activation associated with the offset of a specific grooming action, for example, *a1*, is able to promote the onset of the next action *a2* through a process of striato-nigral disinhibition. This model

Figure 3 Brainstem thalamostriatal pathways for executing forelimb sequences

A. Schematic of brain pathways important for rodent grooming and sequential lever pressing. The thalamo-cortico-striatal pathway is important for learning (blue) but not execution of sequences produced by pattern-generating circuits in the brainstem.

B. Rodents produce a species-specific and highly stereotyped sequence of rhythmic actions during grooming that requires intact brainstem-thalamo-striatal-nigral loop but not cortex.

C. Top: In a learned double-tap task, rats are gradually trained to produce unnaturally long inter-tap intervals to earn a reward. Bottom: Early in training, paw trajectories exhibit substantial trial-by-trial variability as the animals execute the two taps. In experts, animals produce individually unique and highly stereotyped trajectories that are unaffected by cortical lesion.

D. Inter-tap interval is plotted against trial number in naive (*left*) and expert (*center*) rats. Viral methods were used to delete the thalamostriatal projection, resulting in complete reversion to the "naive" inter-tap interval of ~0.3 s. Execution of both grooming and learned forepaw tap sequences relies on similar brainstem-thalamic loops with the basal ganglia. Adapted from Berridge et al. (2005) and Wolff et al. (2019).

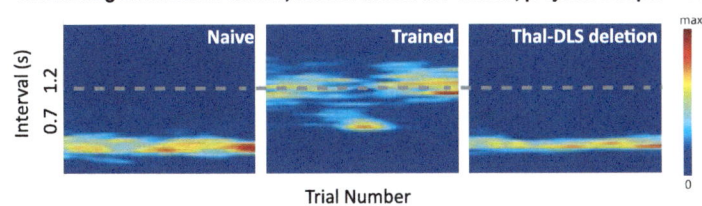

predicts that (1) thalamic lesions will resemble striatal lesions, preserving grooming components but abolishing the syntax, and (2) the activity of thalamic neurons projecting to the anterior striatum will be precisely time-locked to transitions in the grooming sequence – two straightforward experiments that have yet to be carried out. This model also relies on the "gating: view of basal ganglia output (Figure 4).

A conceptually similar brainstem thalamostriatal loop is also sufficient for the production of some types of learned motor sequences. In a series of studies, Olveczky and colleagues (2005) dissected circuit components necessary for rats to learn and execute precise forelimb sequences in a sequential lever-pressing task (Figure 3C) (Kawai et al., 2015). Rats exhibit an innate tendency to press levers at a rate of ~3 Hz (possibly due to repurposing of digging, burrowing, and/or locomotor CPGs), but Olveczky and colleagues (2005) gradually shaped them, over thousands of trials, to press a lever twice with an unnaturally long inter-press interval of 0.7 seconds to earn a reward (Kawai et al., 2015). During learning, rats acquired individually unique "superstitious" movement patterns that spanned the inter-press interval (IPI) (Figure 3C). By tracking precise paw kinematics in between presses, they discovered that animals tile the interval with a remarkably stereotyped sequence of forepaw and whole-body movements resembling a "dance." Lesions to the motor cortex in untrained animals blocked their ability to learn the long IPI and the corresponding paw sequence, but cortex lesions in trained experts had no measurable impact on either task performance or the kinematics of the "dance." In a series of follow-up experiments combining electrophysiology and pathway-specific inactivations, they discovered that a brainstem thalamostriatal loop, possibly similar to the one that implements grooming, controls the production of the full motor sequence. Lesions to the dorsolateral striatum or its thalamic inputs in trained experts resulted in a complete reversion to the naive state: animals that had acquired individually unique solutions to the task with a 0.7-second interval reverted to a species-typical 0.3-second inter-press interval (Figure 3D) (Wolff et al., 2019). Dense recordings from the dorsolateral striatum (DLS) showed that striatal neurons encoded precise time steps of the learned sequence that, importantly, tiled the entire inter-press interval. These neural sequences persisted in cortex-lesioned animals (Dhawale et al., 2019). Taken together, these data show that corticostriatal inputs can "train" thalamostriatal inputs to independently drive learned sequences.

Although the precise mechanisms of cortex-dependent acquisition and consolidation of these sequences are not yet clear, they may involve dopamine-modulated thalamostriatal plasticity. Specifically, in a heterosynaptic learning rule, if cortico- and thalamostriatal inputs to a striatal neuron are coincident, and if a dopamine burst signifying reward subsequently occurs, they strengthen the thalamostriatal input (Izhikevich, 2007; Surmeier et al., 2009; Wolff et al., 2019). For example, imagine a medium spiny neuron (MSN) with three inputs from the motor cortex, motor thalamus, and dopamine neurons. Thalamostriatal inputs could contain efference copies of specific movements driven by a CPG in the brainstem that drives an innate ~3-Hz forelimb tap rhythm. During learning, corticostriatal inputs could drive behavioral variations, such as a command to override the brainstem CPG and add an additional sub-movement that delays the second tap. If this delayed tap results in an unexpected reward, then the dopamine input to the MSN would follow coincident activation of the cortical input to the MSN that drove the fluctuation and the thalamic input that carried an efference copy of the precise time step within the CPG at which the fluctuation occurred. By increasing the weight specifically of the thalamostriatal input, the thalamus would acquire the ability to drive the MSN, which in turn drives the successful variation through downstream inputs back to the brainstem. This learning rule would, in essence, implement node perturbation (Fiete and Seung, 2006), a mechanism of biologically plausible yet effective credit assignment during reinforcement learning (Kornfeld et al., 2020; Lillicrap et al., 2020). In node perturbation, connections mediating exploratory behavioral variations are not themselves plastic, but instead they gate the plasticity of other inputs that can take over to drive a successful variation.

A Brainstem-Thalamocortical Loop in Songbirds for Learned Motor Sequences

Songbirds provide one of the best-understood model systems for the generation of learned motor sequences and yet another example of a brainstem-thalamic pathway that drives a learned sequence. Adult zebra finches produce a highly stereotyped and learned sequence of specific syllables, for example, *a-b-c-d-* and so forth. Song motifs are ~1-second-duration sequences of three to eight syllables. Songbirds have a dedicated neural circuit, the song system, entirely dedicated to singing and not to other behaviors such as grooming, eating, or flight (Feenders et al., 2008). The song system includes two distinct pathways: a brainstem-thalamocortical loop necessary for normal song production and a separate basal ganglia–thalamocortical loop necessary for learning (Figure 4A) (Aronov et al., 2008; Bottjer et al., 1984; Doupe et al., 2005; Goldberg and Fee, 2011; Jarvis et al., 2005; Scharff and Nottebohm, 1991).

The brainstem-thalamocortical "motor" pathway necessary for adult song production consists of a motor cortex–like nucleus RA (robust nucleus of the arcopallium) and its input from the premotor cortical nucleus HVC (proper name). HVC neurons that project to the RA discharge in an ultra-sparse sequence that tiles the entire song, forming a chain that specifies each time step of the song sequence (Katlowitz et al., 2018; Lynch et al., 2016) (much like the DLS representations tile the grooming or inter-tap-interval sequences) (Aldridge and Berridge, 1998; Dhawale et al., 2019). The RA, in turn, projects to both brainstem respiratory nuclei and motor neurons. In the feedforward model of song production, RA and downstream structures function like follower circuits – a stereotyped chain in the HVC drives the correspondingly stereotyped ensemble firing in the RA, which in turn drives the premotor signals in the brainstem that coordinate respiratory and syringeal muscles during singing (Fee et al., 2004).

An important nuance of adult song production is that although both left and right HVCs exhibit chains that tile the song, the two hemispheres mostly alternate in the actual control of song production; that is, they "take turns" driving vocal output during singing (Long and Fee, 2008; Schmidt et al., 2004; Vu et al., 1998; Wang et al., 2008). Thus, the song is probably best conceptualized not as a single ~1-second song-duration neural sequence entirely within one HVC but rather as a sequence of order ~0.2-second-duration HVC sequences that themselves must be concatenated with other (contralateral) HVC sequences to form the full song (Wang et al., 2008). For simplicity, one can imagine each syllable arising from a single HVC, and a syllable sequence requires the offset of syllable n to be linked to the onset of syllable $n + 1$ – much like the grooming sequence requires the offset of a bilateral ear stroke to be linked to the onset of a body lick.

Linking HVC sequences together is complicated by the fact that birds lack a corpus callosum, and thus the only way for two HVCs to coordinate is through a distributed brainstem-thalamocortical loop (Figure 4B)(Schmidt et al., 2004). A motor thalamic nucleus called the *Uva* (nucleus Uvaeformis) projects to the HVC and is the key bottleneck of the loop that enables interhemispheric synchronization. Bilaterally symmetric Uvas receive efference copy inputs from both left and right brainstem nuclei that, through their descending collaterals, drive respiratory and motor neurons during singing (Figure 4B) (McLean et al., 2013). Yet in addition to sending descending signals to downstream motor neurons, the dorsomedial nucleus of the inter-collicular complex (DM; possibly analogous to the mammalian lateral periaqueductal gray [Wild, 1997]) also sends ascending inputs to the Uva. Although no one has recorded DM signals in singing birds, thalamus-projecting DM neurons are poised to carry the same types of efference copy signals discussed in the previous sections, that is, signals that carry information about precisely what action (vocal syllable) is currently being commanded. If this is the case, then the Uva would be able to "know" which HVC chain is finishing and, accordingly, which one to initiate next via its direct projections to the HVC. Because the brainstem projections to the Uva are bilateral, each Uva is positioned to relay motor commands from the contralateral HVC to the ipsilateral HVC, including at chain transitions (Schmidt et al., 2004).

Several findings support this model. First, bilateral Uva or HVC lesions completely abolish all song structure – reverting vocal output to a highly random babbling stage normally observed in juveniles singing HVC-independent song (see more in later discussion) (Figure 4C) (Aronov et al., 2008; Danish et al., 2017). Second, unilateral Uva lesions abolish coordination of the two HVCs and result in a degraded song that nevertheless retains some temporal structure (Ashmore et al., 2008; Schmidt, 2003). Third, during singing, Uva neurons encode specific time steps of the song, and in multi-unit recordings, activity is concentrated at transitions between syllables – exactly when the end of one HVC chain (for example, on the left) needs to be coupled to the beginning of the next one (for example, on the right) (Figure 4D–F) (Andalman et al., 2010; Danish et al., 2017).

In summary, in sequential saccades, grooming, interval-timing tasks, and birdsong, the thalamus relays copies of brainstem-generated motor commands to forebrain structures that can then produce the next step in the sequence. Although these data are specific to motor sequence generation, the core idea fits with an emerging and more general view that the thalamus implements forward inference that enables forebrain targets to update their estimates of the current state (Rikhye et al., 2018).

Signal Transmission in the Brainstem-Thalamic Pathway

In all of the examples provided previously, the brainstem efference copy inputs to the thalamus were presumed to be carried by excitatory inputs. Yet surprisingly little is known about the influence of these inputs on thalamic discharge. The precise brainstem pathways mediating grooming or lever pressing are not well understood and likely involve inputs from a combination of midbrain, reticular, and medullary regions (Berridge, 1989). Genetic tools in mice are making these brainstem regions more experimentally tractable, providing opportunities for clarification of possible themes in brainstem-thalamic connectivity (Ruder and Arber, 2019). One feature of brainstem–motor thalamic pathways observed across diverse behaviors is that they stitch together distinct components of a motor sequence so seamlessly that there are no visibly clear-cut interruptions in behavioral output. Careful examination of birdsong, the grooming sequence, or the rats moving their paws in between lever presses yields no clear "moment" where one output is ending and the next is beginning. To achieve these seamless transitions, the brainstem-thalamic synapses should be highly reliable and perhaps not corrupted by the types of stochastic release seen in cortical structures that may implement specific aspects of learning, such as dropout (Srivastava et al., 2014). Although classic retrograde tracer studies show widespread and diffuse brainstem inputs to the thalamus (Krout et al., 2002), remarkably little is known of the synaptic physiology of these inputs. Delineating how distinct brainstem circuits for diverse motor outputs interact with the thalamus is an important area for future study.

Basal Ganglia–Recipient Motor Thalamus (BG-Thal)

The basal ganglia (BG) are broadly implicated in diverse aspects of motor control and learning (Hikosaka, 2007a). Many models of BG function focus on roles in producing or selecting ongoing behavioral output (Redgrave et al., 1999), as exemplified in the roles of the striatum in both grooming and lever sequencing (Aldridge et al., 1993; Jin and Costa, 2010). Yet other models emphasize the role of the BG in controlling action vigor, that is, how quickly to move toward an object based on its predicted reward (Dudman and Krakauer, 2016). This view is supported by the finding that manipulations of BG activity strongly affect the vigor of ongoing behavior, most

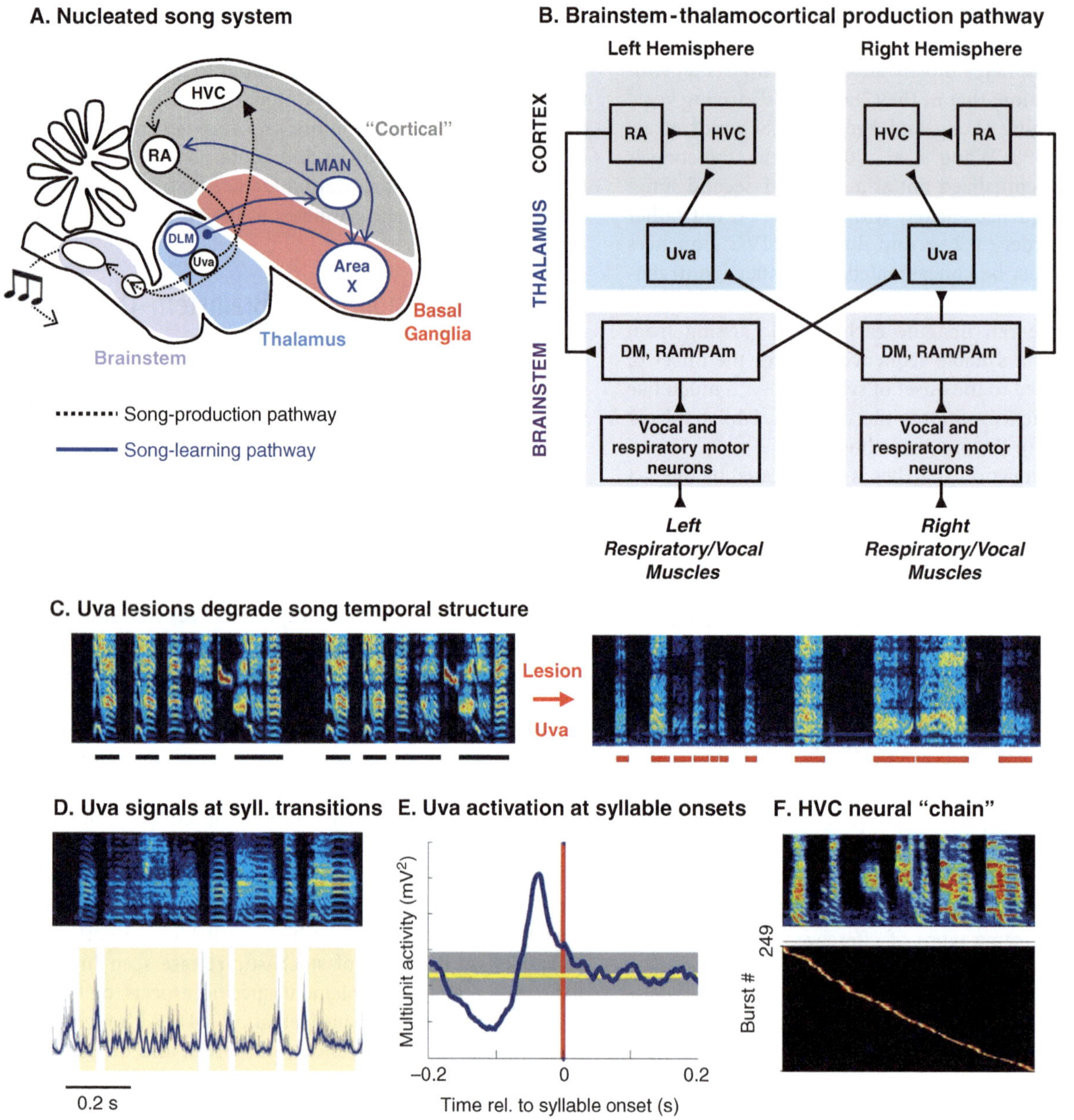

Motor Control

A. Nucleated song system

B. Brainstem-thalamocortical production pathway

C. Uva lesions degrade song temporal structure

D. Uva signals at syll. transitions **E. Uva activation at syllable onsets** **F. HVC neural "chain"**

Figure 4 Brainstem thalamocortical pathway for birdsong production.

A. Schematic of the songbird "song system." A brainstem-thalamocortical loop is necessary for song production (*black dotted lines*). A separate basal ganglia–thalamocortical loop is necessary for song learning but not production (*blue lines*).

B. Expanded view of the motor production pathway, highlighting the place of thalamic nucleus Uva in mediating inter-hemispheric synchronization during singing.

C. Spectrograms from an adult zebra finch song before and after bilateral Uva lesion. Note the stereotyped acoustic structure characteristic of adult zebra finch song in which an identical sequence of four syllables is repeated twice. Following Uva lesion, all song temporal structure degrades, and birds sing highly unstructured songs akin to vocal babbling. The HVCs also cause similar degradation of song.

D. Top: Spectrogram of zebra finch song. Bottom: Time-aligned multiunit activity from the Uva.

E. On average, Uva activity exhibits precise activations immediately before syllable onsets, exactly when "chains" in the target HVC need to be initiated.

F. The timing of 249 bursts recorded in the HVC in a single bird plotted beneath that bird's single song. Note that HVC neurons exhibit a "chain" of activity that tiles the entire song. Figure adapted from Schmidt et al. (2004). Lynch et al. (2016), and Danish et al. (2017).

famously in Parkinson's disease. Yet *Drosophila* exhibit increases in locomotion velocity upon the presentation of a food-predicting olfactory cue (Sayin et al., 2019), showing that the phenomenon of reward-cue-modulated vigor can be implemented without the BG. Other studies focus on the role of the BG in learning from reinforcement (Joel et al., 2002). This idea that the BG implement important aspects of reinforcement learning (RL) may be the most powerful and all-encompassing idea that explains diverse experimental outcomes across a wide range of species and behaviors. The precise roles of the BG in implementing RL in rodents (Costa, 2011), primates (Bar-Gad et al., 2003), humans (Maia and Frank, 2011), and songbirds (Chen and Goldberg, 2020) are reviewed extensively elsewhere. Here, I present a simplified framework necessary to contextualize findings from BG-related thalamic areas.

Basal Ganglia–Dependent Reinforcement Learning

In 1911, Edward Thorndike captured the essence of RL in his "law of effect": responses that produce a satisfying effect in a particular situation become more likely to occur again in that situation, and responses that produce a discomforting effect become less likely to occur again in that situation (Thorndike, 1911). In classic experiments, Schultz (2007) discovered how dopamine (DA) promotes RL by recording the activity of DA neurons in thirsty primates. DA neurons were phasically activated in response to unexpected rewards (surprisingly good outcomes) and suppressed when a predicted reward was omitted (disappointingly bad outcomes). Thus, DA neurons can encode "reward prediction error" (RPE): the difference between the actual and the predicted reward outcome (Schultz, 2007).

In actor-critic BG models, these DA error signals modulate plasticity in two BG compartments: a dorsal striatal "actor" with topographically organized outputs to the motor system and a ventral striatal "critic" with outputs back to DA neurons (Alexander et al., 1986; Lee et al., 2020) (Figure 5). Both striatal domains receive inputs from the cortex and thalamus, which, together, can encode the "state" that an animal is in (e.g., a cue, a place, or even the action just taken in, for example, a tap sequence) (Matsumoto et al., 2001). A key learning rule expressed by striatal MSNs is DA-dependent plasticity of these glutamatergic inputs from the thalamus or cortex (Hong and Hikosaka, 2011; Shen et al., 2008). In this learning rule, the synaptic weight of cortico- or thalamo-striatal inputs is changed by pairing with a phasic DA signal, such that state representations are weighed according to their reward value. DA-modulated plasticity in the critic computes how much reward to expect in a given situation, that is, the predicted state value. Predicted-state-value signals are exemplified by ventral striato-pallidal responses to conditioned stimuli in conditioning tasks (Ahrens et al., 2016; Humphries and Prescott, 2010; Ito and Doya, 2009; Richard et al., 2018; Tindell et al., 2004; Yin et al., 2008), and they can provide the ventral tegmental area (VTA) with prediction information necessary to compute RPE (Suri and Schultz, 1998; Tian et al., 2016). Meanwhile, DA-modulated plasticity in the actor results in value-weighted "state action" mappings that link each state representation to its reward-maximizing action, that is, the policy (Daw et al., 2006; Joel et al., 2002; Takahashi et al., 2008). Neurons throughout the dorsal striatum can encode the predicted value of actions in a wide range of species and behavioral paradigms (Hikosaka et al., 2006; Samejima and Doya, 2007).

Basal Ganglia–Brainstem versus Basal Ganglia–Thalamic Pathways

It remains unknown exactly how BG signals are transformed by downstream circuits to produce behavior. For example, it remains unclear exactly how striatal action-value or premotor signals propagate through BG–brainstem and/or thalamocortical pathways to eventually reach motor neurons to control specific muscle activity. BG output neurons in the globus pallidus internal segment (GPi) and the substantia nigra pars reticulata (SNr) have projections directly to brainstem motor centers and to the thalamus, which in turn projects to the cortex and/or back to the striatum (Figure 6). Due to the complexity of BG-thalamic transmission and the complex functions of the frontal cortical areas to which the BG-thal projects, the direct BG–brainstem pathways invoked in the previous sections are better understood and provide a reasonable starting point for evaluating BG-thalamic function.

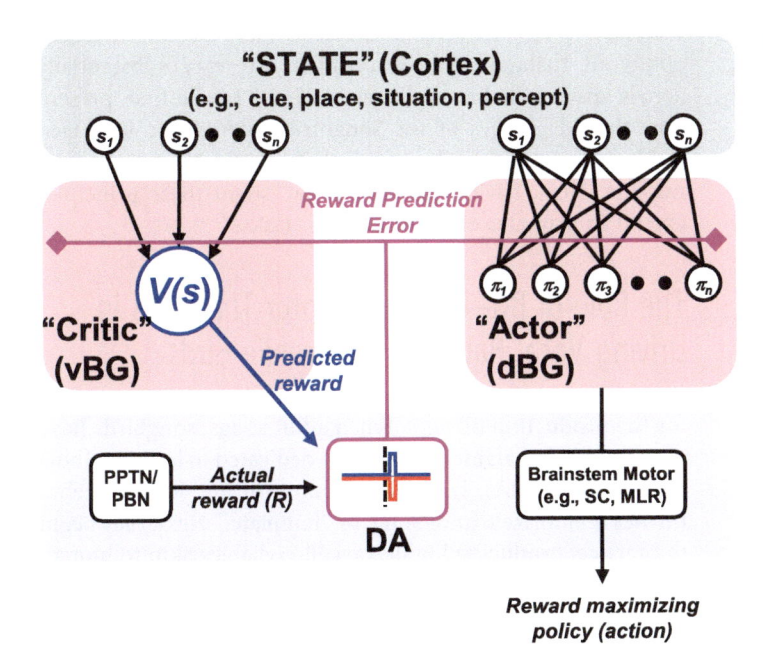

Figure 5 Actor-Critic Model of BG-dependent reinforcement learning.

The environment provides current state information, S, and current reward, r. The "actor" learns the quality of state/action pairs (Q(s,a)) that get converted into the reward-maximizing action given the state (i.e., the policy, p(a|S)). DA-weighted state representations in the critic compute the predicted state value, V(s). DA neurons signal RPE by taking the difference between actual, R, and predicted, V(s), reward.

The "canonical" model of BG signal transmission emerged largely from a series of classic studies by Hikosaka and colleagues, who examined how activity in the striato-nigro-collicular pathway controls rewarded eye movements (Hikosaka, 2007b; Hikosaka et al., 2006). First, BG output neurons in the SNr are GABAergic, target collicular cell bodies, and exhibit high baseline activity that is presumed to suppress collicular activation and the generation of unwanted saccades. MSNs in the caudate nucleus, a portion of the primate striatum involved in oculomotor control, are specifically activated by visual cues associated with rewarded target locations. Bursts of activity in SNr-projecting direct-pathway MSNs can drive pauses in the high tonic activity of SNr neurons, which in turn can disinhibit SC neurons to bias a saccade to a rewarded target (Figure 6). Meanwhile, MSNs in the indirect pathway increase SNr activity by suppressing globus pallidus externa (GPe) firing, with the result of suppression of visual targets. Based largely on anatomical evidence that D1 MSNs target BG output neurons in the globus pallidus interna (GPi) and SNr, whereas D2 MSNs of the indirect pathway target the globus pallidus (GP), which in turn suppresses BG outputs, it was proposed that the direct pathway promotes movement, whereas the indirect pathway suppresses movement (Figure 4B and C) (DeLong, 1990; Mink, 1996).

To put this classic view to the test, Kreitzer and colleagues leveraged transgenic mice expressing Cre in either D1 or D2 MSNs in a part of the striatum that projects, through the SNr, to a midbrain locomotor region (MLR) capable of initiating locomotion (Kravitz et al., 2010). Activation of D1-expressing MSNs in the dorsomedial striatum promoted locomotion by inducing pauses in SNr firing, which in turn disinhibited glutamatergic neurons in the midbrain locomotor region (Roseberry et al., 2016). Activation of D2 MSNs had the opposite effect, causing suppression of the GP, activation of the SNr, and suppression of the MLR. These experiments supported the decades-old "classic" view of the functions of the direct and indirect pathways.

Although the basic idea that the direct and indirect pathways promote or suppress action is likely oversimplified because both pathways are commonly co-activated during behavior (Cui et al., 2013), the core idea is useful because it appears to hold true for direct BG–brainstem circuits in control of simple actions such as orienting, locomotion and licking (Hikosaka et al., 2006; Lee et al., 2020; Rossi et al., 2016). Overall, these studies support a "gating" mechanism by which BG outputs control brainstem-generated behavior: When SNr neurons are highly active, downstream activity and its corresponding action is suppressed. When SNr neurons pause, downstream neurons are disinhibited, resulting in the selection of a given action.

BG-Thal Transmission

The functions of BG-thalamic pathways are more poorly understood. A first obstacle is that in mammals, the BG-thal projects to large territories of the frontal cortical areas where they target upper layers (Hooks et al., 2013; Oh et al., 2014). Second, most BG inputs to the thalamus are collaterals of massively arborizing axons targeting brainstem structures (Bentivoglio et al., 1979; McElvain et al., 2021), implicating the thalamus as a "monitor" and not always a driver of motor output (Guillery and Sherman, 2002). Finally, whereas lesions to BG structures have a devastating effect on brainstem-driven sequences (e.g., the grooming and interval-timing tasks outlined previously), lesions to the BG–recipient thalamus in cortex-dependent behaviors fail to result in specific, clear-cut losses of function. First, human patients with therapeutic lesions or deep-brain stimulation to BG outputs or the BG-thal exhibit surprisingly intact behavioral repertoires, personalities, and speech (Marsden and Obeso, 1994). Non-human primates with BG-thal lesions can push or rotate a manipulandum in response to cues but exhibit impaired learning of new stimulus–response contingencies (Canavan et al., 1989). BG-thal inactivation causes impairments in the kinematics of limb control during simple reach tasks, but the ability to reach is preserved (van Donkelaar et al., 2000). In cats, motor thalamic lesions also preserve the ability to reach and also impair re-learning (Fabre-Thorpe and Levesque, 1991). Notably, paired thalamic and red nucleus lesions are more devastating (Lorincz and Fabre-Thorpe, 1997). Generally, these results show that distributed motor circuits (e.g., Figure 1) can compensate for specific BG-thal lesions in the preservation of action execution. Yet importantly and consistent with the RL framework for BG function, motor thalamic lesions appear to disrupt learning more than action execution. Notably, acute inactivation does not allow for circuits to recover and results in more severe impairments of ongoing reaching in mice (Sauerbrei et al., 2020; Wolff and Ölveczky, 2018).

Several recent studies suggest that the simple "gating" view of BG output does not generalize to BG-thalamic transmission (Goldberg et al., 2013; Schwab et al., 2020). Instead, BG control of thalamic discharge is highly dependent on the specific architecture of the BG-thalamic projection (i.e., how many pallidal axons innervate a given thalamic neuron, which can vary substantially across distinct species and possibly across distinct BG–recipient thalamic regions) and also on the excitability of thalamic neurons, which can vary substantially across distinct behavioral states. Here, I will first present how the advantages of the songbird system were leveraged to identify new principles of BG-thalamic function and transmission. Next, I will explore to what extent these principles extend to primates engaged in reach tasks.

The Role of BG–Recipient Motor Thalamus in Driving Vocal Babbling in Juvenile Birds

In addition to the brainstem-thalamocortical loop necessary for the production of stereotyped adult songs, songbirds have a separate BG-thalamocortical loop dedicated to learning (blue lines in Figure 4A). In the first month of life, juvenile zebra finches memorize a tutor song, or "template." Next, they begin to practice, producing highly variable syllables akin to human babbling (Doupe and Kuhl, 1999). Over several weeks, variability decreases as the bird learns to produce a highly stereotyped sequence of syllables resembling the tutor song

(Tchernichovski et al., 2001). The essence of babbling is its exploratory variability: like a beginner piano player banging randomly on the keys, a juvenile bird produces a variety of syllables of different durations and sounds. Remarkably, inactivation of a frontal cortical nucleus called the LMAN (lateral magnocellular nucleus of the anterior nidopallium, the output of the BG-thal loop) eliminates this variability – as if our beginner piano player became instantly stuck, striking the same rudimentary sequence over and over (Bottjer et al., 1984; Goldberg and Fee, 2011; Kao and Brainard, 2006; Olveczky et al., 2005; Scharff and Nottebohm, 1991).

To investigate the neural origins of vocal variability, several studies quantitatively analyzed the immediate effect of BG and thalamic lesions on juvenile songs (Chen et al., 2014; Goldberg and Fee, 2011). Lesions to the thalamus, but not the BG, abolished vocal variability in juvenile birds (Figure 3). This result was surprising because classic models predicted that the thalamus was principally a relay from the BG to the cortex, and yet here, aspects of thalamic motor function did not require BG inputs. In addition, this study was inconsistent with models where behavioral variability was generated within BG circuitry itself (Leblois et al., 2010; Sheth et al., 2011) (But see Kojima et al. [2018]). How, then, did the thalamus contribute to vocal variability if its inputs from the BG were not required?

Songbirds also provided a tractable system to study how neural signals propagate through the BG-thal. The BG have several cell classes but only one output: GABAergic pallidal neurons that project to the thalamus (Person et al., 2008). In the classical model, thalamic activity is suppressed by the tonic inhibition of the pallidal inputs, and pauses in pallidal firing enable thalamic activation (Figure 6B). In the songbird, the pallidal axon terminal forms a large calyx that can be recorded extracellularly in the thalamus (Person and Perkel, 2005), providing a unique opportunity to study BG-thalamic transmission (inset, Figure 7A). In a series of experiments, Fee and colleagues recorded simultaneously from connected pairs of pallidal terminals and thalamic neurons during singing and discovered that connected pallidal and thalamic neurons fired in concert at high rates (>200 Hz), that thalamic spiking was not restricted to pallidal pauses, and that thalamic spikes were time-locked to pallidal spikes with sub-millisecond precision (Figure 6) (Goldberg et al., 2012; Goldberg and Fee, 2012).

Together, these findings suggested a novel "entrainment" mode of BG-thalamic transmission (Figure 7). Cortical inputs to the thalamus provide a strong excitatory drive during singing, and somatic inhibition from the BG controls the precise timing of thalamic discharge. Although the exact functions of precise spike timing remain unknown, Parkinsonism is associated with abnormal synchrony in BG-cortical loops, leading to the hypothesis that BG function involves the coordinated activity of populations of neurons (Rosin et al., 2007).

Finally, an important caveat is that the mode of BG-thalamic transmission depended on the level of excitability of the thalamic neuron. In anesthetized songbirds, when the thalamus was strongly hyperpolarized, thalamic neurons discharged at <5 Hz (as compared to ~100 Hz during wakefulness), and under these conditions, the thalamic spikes were driven by post-inhibitory rebound mechanisms following pallidal pauses (Person et al., 2008). Biophysical modeling showed that thalamic neurons operated in rebound mode when their excitation was very low, in gating mode at intermediate levels of excitation, and in entrainment mode when the corticothalamic drive was high (Figure 7D). (See also Goldberg et al. [2013] for details.)

BG–Recipient Thalamus in "Reach" Tasks in Rodents and Primates

Although the "gating" model of BG output was initially presumed to generalize to BG-thalamic transmission in mammals (Chevalier and Deniau, 1982), more recent studies suggest that some discoveries from the songbird generalize to the mammal.

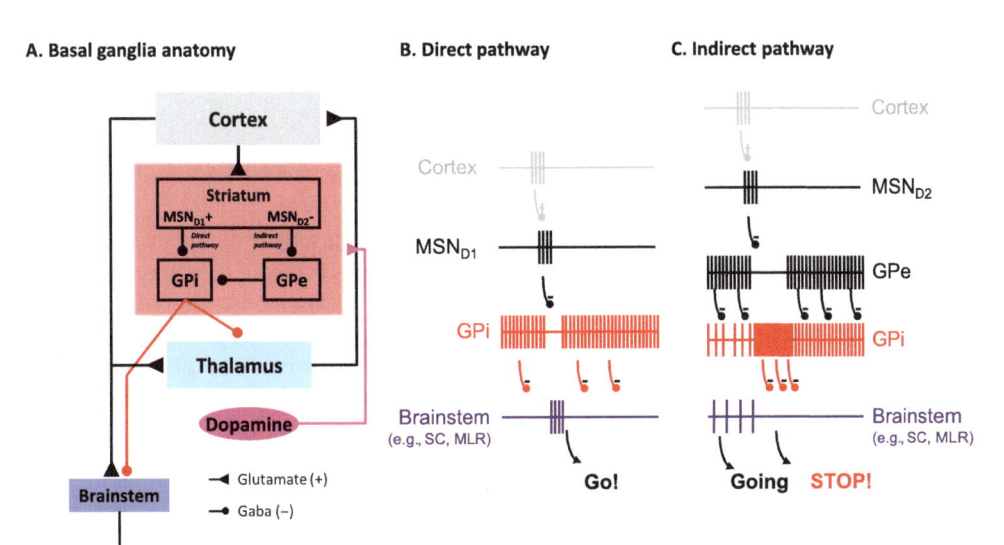

Figure 6 Functional anatomy of direct and indirect pathways through the basal ganglia: the gating model.

A. Schematic of the BG brain pathways, including outputs to both the brainstem and the thalamus.

B and C. In the classic "gating" model of BG output, pauses in GPi or SNr output disinhibit downstream brainstem structures such as the SC or MLR. Release from tonic inhibition functions as a "go" signal that contributes to saccade or locomotion initiation. Activation of BG output increases inhibition and suppresses a saccade or stops ongoing locomotion.

Motor Control

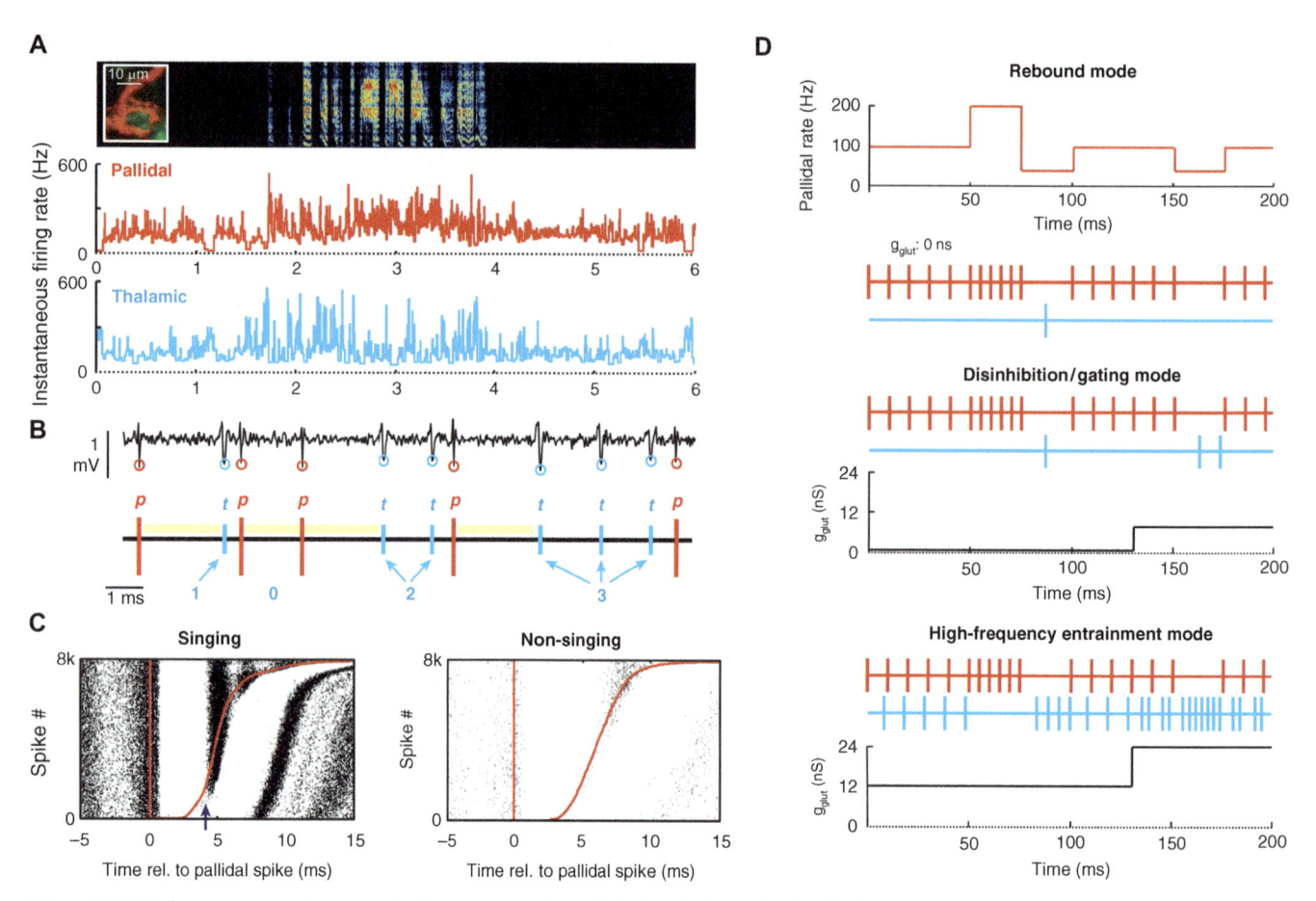

Figure 7 High-frequency entrainment of thalamic neurons by pallidal inputs in the singing bird.

A. Instantaneous firing rates of a thalamic neuron (*blue*) and its simultaneously recorded pallidal terminal (*red*) plotted during a bout of song. Note that both the thalamic neuron and its pallidal input fire in concert at more than 100 Hz. Inset in spectrogram: Confocal image of a single pallidal calyceal axon terminal (*red*) wrapped around a single postsynaptic thalamic neuron (*green*).

B. Example of extracellular waveform containing signals from a thalamic neuron (t; *blue circles*) and its presynaptic pallidal axon terminal (p; *red circles*). Bottom: Schematic of the pallidal and thalamic spike trains. Yellow bars represent periods of complete thalamic spike suppression following each pallidal spike. The number of thalamic spikes that occurred in each pallidal ISI is annotated in blue and was a simple function of the pallidal ISI duration.

C. Raster plots of thalamic spikes (*black ticks*) aligned to the timing of pallidal spikes (*red line*). Red line at right shows the time of the next pallidal spike. The plot is sorted by the duration of the pallidal ISI. Note that each pallidal spike is followed by a brief period of absolute thalamic spike suppression and that the duration of this suppression was reduced during singing (*left*), when cortico-thalamic excitation is high, compared to during non-singing (*right*), when cortico-thalamic excitation is low (*not shown*).

D. In mathematical simulations of pallidothalamic transmission, thalamic spikes could be initiated by post-inhibitory rebound following pallidal pauses when corticothalamic drive was very low. Thalamic spikes were gated by pallidal inputs at intermediate levels of cortical excitation, and at high levels of thalamic activation, thalamic spikes became entrained to pallial inputs. Red trace indicates pallidal spike train. Blue trace indicates postsynaptic thalamic spike train. Note that these simulations modeled the songbird system, where a single thalamic neuron is innervated by a single presynaptic pallidal calyceal terminal. Figure adapted from Goldberg and Fee (2012) and Goldberg et al. (2012).

First, in studies where pallidal and thalamic neurons were recorded separately but in similar tasks, researchers repeatedly observed that both pallidal neurons and their thalamic targets were usually co-activated at movement initiation – just as they were at syllable onsets in singing birds (Anderson and Turner, 1991; Bosch-Bouju et al., 2014; Kunimatsu and Tanaka, 2010; Sauerbrei et al., 2020; Schlag-Rey and Schlag, 1984; Strick, 1976). Such paradoxical co-activation cannot be explained by the gating model and instead is consistent with common sources of excitation (e.g., from the cortex). In seminal experiments, Marjorie Anderson and colleagues recorded thalamic neurons while inactivating inputs from the GPi. As in songbirds, movement-locked activations persisted, consistent with a drive from the motor cortex (Inase et al., 1996). Thus, as in songbirds, the mammalian motor thalamus appears to receive correlated excitation (from the cortex) and inhibition (from the GPi).

A critical difference between songbirds and mammals is the architecture of the BG-thalamic projection. Whereas songbirds have a 1:1 calyceal synapse (e.g., Figure 7A, inset), in mammals, ~10 pallidal axons converge onto a single thalamic neuron (Kultas-Ilinsky et al., 1983; Person et al., 2008; Person and Perkel, 2005). In a recent tour de force, Turner and colleagues recorded simultaneously from putatively connected pallidal and thalamic neurons in macaques performing a reach task (Schwab et al., 2020). Consistent with past studies in primates and songbirds, most pallidal and thalamic neurons exhibited phasic co-activations at movement onset (Figure 8A). Yet unlike songbirds, thalamic spikes were not strongly entrained to single pallidal spikes – most likely because of the

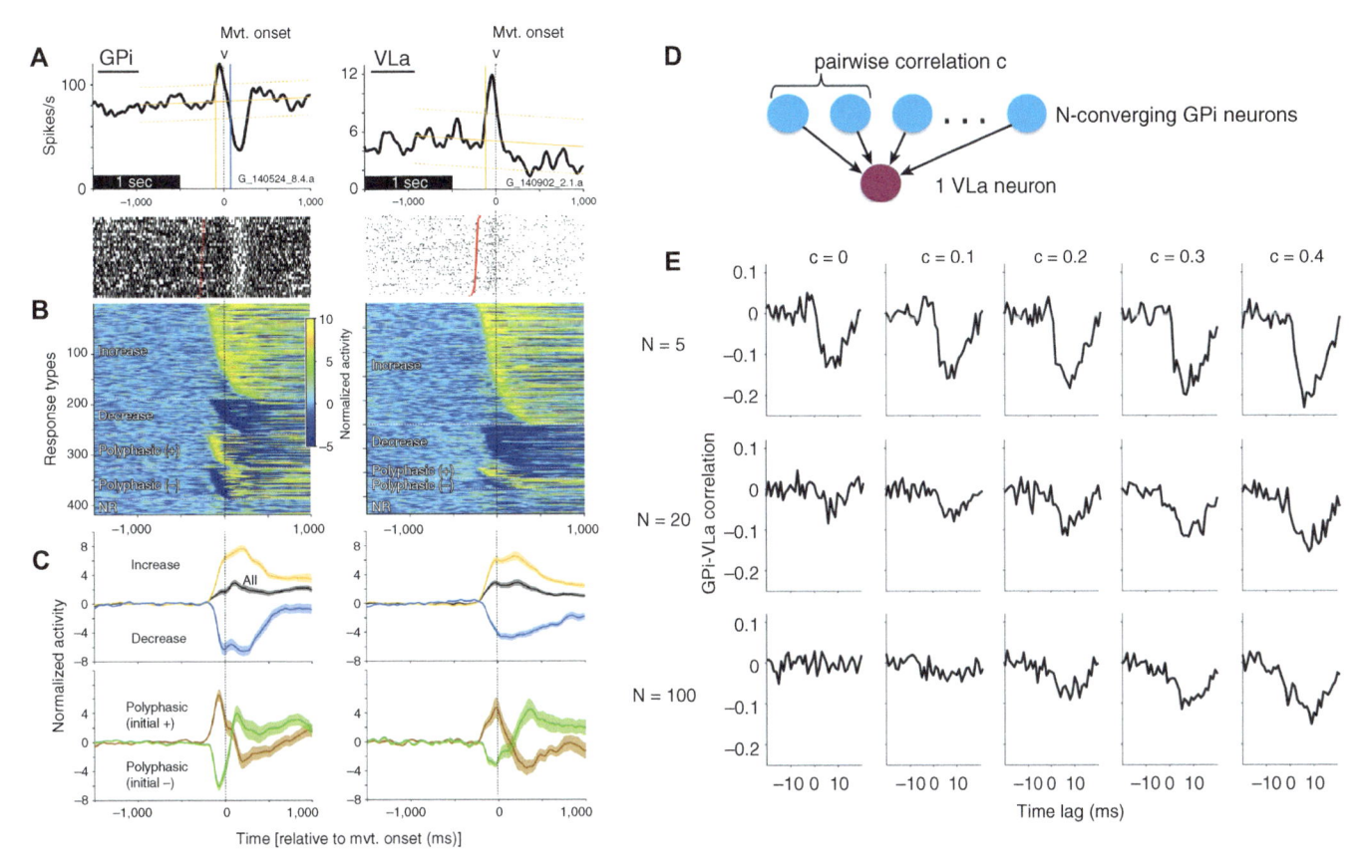

Figure 8 Basal ganglia–thalamic transmission in behaving primates.

Turner and colleagues recorded simultaneously from the GPi and target regions in the ventrolateral anterior (VLa) thalamus in macaques engaged in a cued reach task.

A. Top: Single neuronal examples of a GPi neuron (*left*) and a VLa neuron (*right*), aligned to reach onset. Note that both units exhibited phasic activations at movement onset.

B. Normalized activities of the population of GPi and VLa neurons, sorted according to response form (activation, suppression, polyphasic) and latency. Note that most neurons exhibited activations at onset.

C. Population-averaged spike density functions for all neurons, color coded by response form.

D. Architecture of a computational model of BG-thalamic transmission in which a single thalamic neuron (*purple*) is innervated by N converging Gpi neurons (*blue*). Note that songbirds represent an extreme case where $N = 1$ (see Figure 6).

E. Population average GPi–VLa cross-correlations across varying values of N (number of GPi neurons converging onto a single thalamic neuron) and c (the correlation strength of those N GPi inputs). The strong GPi-induced suppression of thalamic discharge necessary for entrainment occurred when N was low and c was high. Figure adapted from Schwab et al. (2020).

asynchronous inhibition provided by the ~10 distinct pallidal inputs. In a detailed biophysical model, Turner and colleagues examined precisely how the entrainment of single thalamic neurons depended on the number of pallidal inputs each receives as well as how correlated these pallidal inputs are with each other (Figure 8B). Entrainment occurred only when the number of inputs was low (~<5) or when pallidal inputs were highly synchronized (Vaadia et al., 1995; Rosin et al., 2007). In summary, cortical inputs drive BG-thalamic activity in songbirds and primates, and pallidothalamic inhibition appears to play a modulatory role that, under some conditions, can precisely control thalamic spike timing.

A challenge going forward is to determine why thalamic spike timing matters to the thalamo-recipient cortical neurons and how this feature of BG-thalamic transmission may help implement reinforcement learning. Several features of the BG-thalamocortical system make it well situated to both generate variability and bias it toward better performance and/or reward outcomes – two processes important for RL. First, GPi neurons are strongly uncorrelated with one another (Vaadia et al., 1995). Second, the BG-thal lacks recurrent connectivity, making it likely that neighboring thalamocortical neurons entrained by GPi inputs are also uncorrelated with one another. Yet many thalamic neurons converge onto single cortical neurons, which appear to act as coincident detectors (thalamocortical synapses undergo short-term depression and are subject to strong feedforward inhibition – two features that, together, make thalamo-recipient cortical neurons highly sensitive to thalamic synchrony (Bruno and Sakmann, 2006; Izhikevich and Edelman, 2008). Because the activity of populations of BG-thal neurons is uncorrelated, synchrony would occur at random moments – perfect for generating the motor variability necessary to try new things. Yet the GPi can control moments of transient synchrony in thalamic neurons (as has been observed in the motor cortex; Vaadia et al., 1995), and this could constitute the key action-value signal coming out of the BG. Thalamic inputs also control and/or undergo spike-timing-dependent plasticity in the frontal cortical area important for learning (Brzosko et al., 2019; Pasupathy and Miller, 2005). Consistent with the idea that a lack of correlation among GPi neurons is central to BG function, synchronization of GPi neurons occurs in Parkinsonism and completely corrupts system output and degrades motor behavior and learning (Rosin et al., 2007).

References

Ahrens, A.M., Meyer, P.J., Ferguson, L.M., Robinson, T.E., and Aldridge, J.W. (2016). Neural activity in the ventral pallidum encodes variation in the incentive value of a reward cue. J Neurosci 36, 7957–7970.

Aldridge, J.W., and Berridge, K.C. (1998). Coding of serial order by neostriatal neurons: a "natural action" approach to movement sequence. J Neurosci 18, 2777–2787.

Aldridge, J.W., Berridge, K.C., Herman, M., and Zimmer, L. (1993). Neuronal coding of serial order: syntax of grooming in the neostriatum. Psychol Sci 4, 391–395.

Aldridge, J.W., Berridge, K.C., and Rosen, A.R. (2004). Basal ganglia neural mechanisms of natural movement sequences. Can J Physiol Pharmacol 82, 732–739.

Alexander, G.E., DeLong, M.R., and Strick, P.L. (1986). Parallel organization of functionally segregated circuits linking basal ganglia and cortex. Annu Rev Neurosci 9, 357–381.

Andalman, A.S., Foerster, J.N., and Fee, M.S. (2010). Does HVC control the timing of respiratory events during singing? Presentation at Society for Neuroscience Conference, Abstract 4113.

Andersen, R.A., Essick, G.K., and Siegel, R.M. (1985). Encoding of spatial location by posterior parietal neurons. Science 230, 456–458.

Anderson, M.E., and Turner, R.S. (1991). Activity of neurons in cerebellar-receiving and pallidal-receiving areas of the thalamus of the behaving monkey. J Neurophysiol 66, 879–893.

Aronov, D., Andalman, A.S., and Fee, M.S. (2008). A specialized forebrain circuit for vocal babbling in the juvenile songbird. Science 320, 630–634.

Ashmore, R.C., Renk, J.A., and Schmidt, M.F. (2008). Bottom-up activation of the vocal motor forebrain by the respiratory brainstem. J Neurosci 28, 2613–2623.

Bar-Gad, I., Morris, G., and Bergman, H. (2003). Information processing, dimensionality reduction and reinforcement learning in the basal ganglia. Prog Neurobiol 71, 439–473.

Bentivoglio, M., van der Kooy, D., and Kuypers, H.G. (1979). The organization of the efferent projections of the substantia nigra in the rat. A retrograde fluorescent double labeling study. Brain Res 174, 1–17.

Berridge, K.C. (1989). Progressive degradation of serial grooming chains by descending decerebration. Behav Brain Res 33, 241–253.

Berridge, K.C., and Aldridge, J.W. (2000). Super-stereotypy I: enhancement of a complex movement sequence by systemic dopamine D1 agonists. Synapse 37, 194–204.

Berridge, K.C., Aldridge, J.W., Houchard, K.R., and Zhuang, X. (2005). Sequential super-stereotypy of an instinctive fixed action pattern in hyper-dopaminergic mutant mice: a model of obsessive compulsive disorder and Tourette's. BMC Biol 3, 4.

Bosch-Bouju, C., Hyland, B.I., and Parr-Brownlie, L.C. (2013). Motor thalamus integration of cortical, cerebellar and basal ganglia information: implications for normal and parkinsonian conditions. Front Comput Neurosci 7, 163.

Bosch-Bouju, C., Smither, R.A., Hyland, B.I., and Parr-Brownlie, L.C. (2014). Reduced reach-related modulation of motor thalamus neural activity in a rat model of Parkinson's disease. J Neurosci 34, 15836–15850.

Bottjer, S.W., Miesner, E.A., and Arnold, A.P. (1984). Forebrain lesions disrupt development but not maintenance of song in passerine birds. Science 224, 901–903.

Bruno, R.M., and Sakmann, B. (2006). Cortex is driven by weak but synchronously active thalamocortical synapses. Science 312, 1622–1627.

Brzosko, Z., Mierau, S.B., and Paulsen, O. (2019). Neuromodulation of spike-timing-dependent plasticity: past, present, and future. Neuron 103, 563–581.

Canavan, A.G., Nixon, P.D., and Passingham, R.E. (1989). Motor learning in monkeys (*Macaca fascicularis*) with lesions in motor thalamus. Exp Brain Res 77, 113–126.

Chabrol, F.P., Blot, A., and Mrsic-Flogel, T.D. (2019). Cerebellar contribution to preparatory activity in motor neocortex. Neuron 103, 506–519.e504.

Chen, J.R., Stepanek, L., and Doupe, A.J. (2014). Differential contributions of basal ganglia and thalamus to song initiation, tempo, and structure. J Neurophysiol 111, 248–257.

Chen, R., and Goldberg, J.H. (2020). Actor-critic reinforcement learning in the songbird. Curr Opin Neurobiol 65, 1–9.

Chevalier, G., and Deniau, J.M. (1982). Inhibitory nigral influence on cerebellar evoked responses in the rat ventromedial thalamic nucleus. Exp Brain Res 48, 369–376.

Costa, R.M. (2011). A selectionist account of de novo action learning. Curr Opin Neurobiol 21, 579–586.

Cui, G., Jun, S.B., Jin, X., Pham, M.D., Vogel, S.S., Lovinger, D.M., and Costa, R.M. (2013). Concurrent activation of striatal direct and indirect pathways during action initiation. Nature 494, 238–242.

Danish, H.H., Aronov, D., and Fee, M.S. (2017). Rhythmic syllable-related activity in a songbird motor thalamic nucleus necessary for learned vocalizations. PLoS One 12, e0169568.

Daw, N.D., Niv, Y., and Dayan, P. (2006). Actions, policies, values and the basal ganglia. In E. Bezard (Ed.), Recent Breakthroughs in Basal Ganglia Research (New York: Nova Science), 1214–1221.

DeLong, M.R. (1990). Primate models of movement disorders of basal ganglia origin. Trends Neurosci 13, 281–285.

Dhawale, A.K., Wolff, S.B., Ko, R., and Ölveczky, B.P. (2019). The basal ganglia can control learned motor sequences independently of motor cortex. BioRxiv, 827261.

Dirlam, D.K. (1969). The effects of septal, thalamic, and tegmental lesions on general activity in the hooded rat. Can J Psychol 23, 303.

Doupe, A.J., and Kuhl, P.K. (1999). Birdsong and human speech: common themes and mechanisms. Annu Rev Neurosci 22, 567–631.

Doupe, A.J., Perkel, D.J., Reiner, A., and Stern, E.A. (2005). Birdbrains could teach basal ganglia research a new song. Trends Neurosci 28, 353–363.

Dudman, J.T., and Krakauer, J.W. (2016). The basal ganglia: from motor commands to the control of vigor. Curr Opin Neurobiol 37, 158–166.

Fabre-Thorpe, M., and Levesque, F. (1991). Visuomotor relearning after brain damage crucially depends on the integrity of the ventrolateral thalamic nucleus. Behav Neurosci 105, 176.

Fee, M.S., Kozhevnikov, A.A., and Hahnloser, R.H. (2004). Neural mechanisms of vocal sequence generation in the songbird. Ann NY Acad Sci **1016**, 153–170.

Feenders, G., Liedvogel, M., Rivas, M., Zapka, M., Horita, H., Hara, E., Wada, K., Mouritsen, H., and Jarvis, E.D. (2008). Molecular mapping of movement-associated areas in the avian brain: a motor theory for vocal learning origin. PLoS One **3**, e1768.

Fiete, I.R., and Seung, H.S. (2006). Gradient learning in spiking neural networks by dynamic perturbation of conductances. Phys Rev Lett **97**, 048104.

Gao, Z., Davis, C., Thomas, A.M., Economo, M.N., Abrego, A.M., Svoboda, K., De Zeeuw, C.I., and Li, N. (2018). A cortico-cerebellar loop for motor planning. Nature **563**, 113–116.

Gold, J.I., and Shadlen, M.N. (2007). The neural basis of decision making. Annu Rev Neurosci **30**, 535–574.

Goldberg, J.H., Farries, M.A., and Fee, M.S. (2012). Integration of cortical and pallidal inputs in the basal ganglia-recipient thalamus of singing birds. J Neurophysiol **108**, 1403–1429.

Goldberg, J.H., Farries, M.A., and Fee, M.S. (2013). Basal ganglia output to the thalamus: still a paradox. Trends Neurosci **36**, 695–705.

Goldberg, J.H., and Fee, M.S. (2011). Vocal babbling in songbirds requires the basal ganglia-recipient motor thalamus but not the basal ganglia. J Neurophysiol **105**, 2729–2739.

Goldberg, J.H., and Fee, M.S. (2012). A cortical motor nucleus drives the basal ganglia-recipient thalamus in singing birds. Nat Neurosci **15**, 620–627.

Grill, H.J., and Norgren, R. (1978). Neurological tests and behavioral deficits in chronic thalamic and chronic decerebrate rats. Brain Res **143**, 299–312.

Guillery, R.W., and Sherman, S.M. (2002). The thalamus as a monitor of motor outputs. Philos Trans R Soc Lond B Biol Sci **357**, 1809–1821.

Hikosaka, O. (2007a). Basal ganglia mechanisms of reward-oriented eye movement. Ann NY Acad Sci **1104**, 229–249.

Hikosaka, O. (2007b). GABAergic output of the basal ganglia. Prog Brain Res **160**, 209–226.

Hikosaka, O., Nakamura, K., and Nakahara, H. (2006). Basal ganglia orient eyes to reward. J Neurophysiol **95**, 567–584.

Hong, S., and Hikosaka, O. (2011). Dopamine-mediated learning and switching in cortico-striatal circuit explain behavioral changes in reinforcement learning. Front Behav Neurosci **5**, 15.

Hooks, B.M., Mao, T., Gutnisky, D.A., Yamawaki, N., Svoboda, K., and Shepherd, G.M. (2013). Organization of cortical and thalamic input to pyramidal neurons in mouse motor cortex. J Neurosci **33**, 748–760.

Humphries, M.D., and Prescott, T.J. (2010). The ventral basal ganglia, a selection mechanism at the crossroads of space, strategy, and reward. Prog Neurobiol **90**, 385–417.

Ilinsky, I.A., and Kultas-Ilinsky, K. (2002). Motor thalamic circuits in primates with emphasis on the area targeted in treatment of movement disorders. Mov Disord **17** Suppl 3, S9–14.

Inase, M., Buford, J.A., and Anderson, M.E. (1996). Changes in the control of arm position, movement, and thalamic discharge during local inactivation in the globus pallidus of the monkey. J Neurophysiol **75**, 1087–1104.

Ito, M., and Doya, K. (2009). Validation of decision-making models and analysis of decision variables in the rat basal ganglia. J Neurosci **29**, 9861–9874.

Izhikevich, E.M. (2007). Solving the distal reward problem through linkage of STDP and dopamine signaling. Cereb Cortex **17**, 2443–2452.

Izhikevich, E.M., and Edelman, G.M. (2008). Large-scale model of mammalian thalamocortical systems. Proc Natl Acad Sci USA **105**, 3593–3598.

Jarvis, E.D., Gunturkun, O., Bruce, L., Csillag, A., Karten, H., Kuenzel, W., Medina, L., Paxinos, G., Perkel, D.J., Shimizu, T., et al. (2005). Avian brains and a new understanding of vertebrate brain evolution. Nat Rev Neurosci **6**, 151–159.

Jin, X., and Costa, R.M. (2010). Start/stop signals emerge in nigrostriatal circuits during sequence learning. Nature **466**, 457–462.

Joel, D., Niv, Y., and Ruppin, E. (2002). Actor-critic models of the basal ganglia: new anatomical and computational perspectives. Neural Netw **15**, 535–547.

Kakei, S., Hoffman, D.S., and Strick, P.L. (2003). Sensorimotor transformations in cortical motor areas. Neurosci Res **46**, 1–10.

Kao, M.H., and Brainard, M.S. (2006). Lesions of an avian basal ganglia circuit prevent context-dependent changes to song variability. J Neurophysiol **96**, 1441–1455.

Katlowitz, K.A., Picardo, M.A., and Long, M.A. (2018). Stable sequential activity underlying the maintenance of a precisely executed skilled behavior. Neuron **98**, 1133–1140 e1133.

Kawai, R., Markman, T., Poddar, R., Ko, R., Fantana, A.L., Dhawale, A.K., Kampff, A.R., and Olveczky, B.P. (2015). Motor cortex is required for learning but not for executing a motor skill. Neuron **86**, 800–812.

Kojima, S., Kao, M.H., Doupe, A.J., and Brainard, M.S. (2018). The avian basal ganglia are a source of rapid behavioral variation that enables vocal motor exploration. J Neurosci **38**, 9635–9647.

J Kornfeld, M Januszewski, P Schubert, V Jain, W Denk, MS Fee. An anatomical substrate of credit assignment in reinforcement learning. bioRxiv 2020.02.18.954354; doi: https://doi.org/10.1101/2020.02.18.954354

Koyama, M., and Pujala, A. (2018). Mutual inhibition of lateral inhibition: a network motif for an elementary computation in the brain. Curr Opin Neurobiol **49**, 69–74.

Krauzlis, R.J., Liston, D., and Carello, C.D. (2004). Target selection and the superior colliculus: goals, choices and hypotheses. Vision Res **44**, 1445–1451.

Kravitz, A.V., Freeze, B.S., Parker, P.R., Kay, K., Thwin, M.T., Deisseroth, K., and Kreitzer, A.C. (2010). Regulation of parkinsonian motor behaviours by optogenetic control of basal ganglia circuitry. Nature **466**, 622–626.

Krout, K.E., Belzer, R.E., and Loewy, A.D. (2002). Brainstem projections to midline and intralaminar thalamic nuclei of the rat. J Comp Neurol **448**, 53–101.

Kultas-Ilinsky, K., Ilinsky, I., Warton, S., and Smith, K.R. (1983). Fine structure of nigral and pallidal afferents in the thalamus: an EM autoradiography study in the cat. J Comp Neurol **216**, 390–405.

Kunimatsu, J., and Tanaka, M. (2010). Roles of the primate motor thalamus in the generation of antisaccades. J Neurosci **30**, 5108–5117.

Leblois, A., Wendel, B.J., and Perkel, D.J. (2010). Striatal dopamine modulates basal ganglia output and regulates social context-dependent behavioral variability through D1 receptors. J Neurosci **30**, 5730–5743.

Lee, J., Wang, W., and Sabatini, B.L. (2020). Anatomically segregated basal ganglia pathways allow parallel behavioral modulation. Nat Neurosci **23**, 1388–1398.

Lillicrap, T.P., Santoro, A., Marris, L., Akerman, C.J., and Hinton, G. (2020). Backpropagation and the brain. Nat Rev Neurosci, 1–12.

Long, M.A., and Fee, M.S. (2008). Using temperature to analyse temporal dynamics in the songbird motor pathway. Nature **456**, 189–194.

Lorincz, E., and Fabre-Thorpe, M. (1997). Effect of pairing red nucleus and motor thalamic lesions on reaching toward moving targets in cats. Behav Neurosci **111**, 892–907.

Lynch, G.F., Okubo, T.S., Hanuschkin, A., Hahnloser, R.H., and Fee, M.S. (2016). Rhythmic continuous-time coding in the songbird analog of vocal motor cortex. Neuron **90**, 877–892.

Maia, T.V., and Frank, M.J. (2011). From reinforcement learning models to psychiatric and neurological disorders. Nat Neurosci **14**, 154–162.

Marsden, C.D., and Obeso, J.A. (1994). The functions of the basal ganglia and the paradox of stereotaxic surgery in Parkinson's disease. Brain **117** (Pt 4), 877–897.

Matsumoto, N., Minamimoto, T., Graybiel, A.M., and Kimura, M. (2001). Neurons in the thalamic CM-Pf complex supply striatal neurons with information about behaviorally significant sensory events. J Neurophysiol **85**, 960–976.

McElvain, L.E., Chen, Y., Moore, J.D., Brigidi, G.S., Bloodgood, B.L., Lim, B.K., Costa, R.M., and Kleinfeld, D. (2021). Specific populations of basal ganglia output neurons target distinct brain stem areas while collateralizing throughout the diencephalon. Neuron **109**, 1721–1738.e4.

McGregor, M.M., and Nelson, A.B. (2019). Circuit mechanisms of Parkinson's disease. Neuron **101**, 1042–1056.

McLean, J., Bricault, S., and Schmidt, M.F. (2013). Characterization of respiratory neurons in the rostral ventrolateral medulla, an area critical for vocal production in songbirds. J Neurophysiol **109**, 948–957.

Meyer-Luehmann, M., Thompson, J.F., Berridge, K.C., and Aldridge, J.W. (2002). Substantia nigra pars reticulata neurons code initiation of a serial pattern: implications for natural action sequences and sequential disorders. Eur J Neurosci **16**, 1599–1608.

Mink, J.W. (1996). The basal ganglia: focused selection and inhibition of competing motor programs. Prog Neurobiol **50**, 381–425.

Mysore, S.P., and Knudsen, E.I. (2011). The role of a midbrain network in competitive stimulus selection. Curr Opin Neurobiol **21**, 653–660.

Mysore, S.P., and Knudsen, E.I. (2012). Reciprocal inhibition of inhibition: a circuit motif for flexible categorization in stimulus selection. Neuron **73**, 193–205.

Oh, S.W., Harris, J.A., Ng, L., Winslow, B., Cain, N., Mihalas, S., Wang, Q., Lau, C., Kuan, L., and Henry, A.M. (2014). A mesoscale connectome of the mouse brain. Nature **508**, 207–214.

Olveczky, B.P., Andalman, A.S., and Fee, M.S. (2005). Vocal experimentation in the juvenile songbird requires a basal ganglia circuit. PLoS Biol **3**, e153.

Ostendorf, F., Liebermann, D., and Ploner, C.J. (2010). Human thalamus contributes to perceptual stability across eye movements. Proc Natl Acad Sci USA **107**, 1229–1234.

Pasupathy, A., and Miller, E.K. (2005). Different time courses of learning-related activity in the prefrontal cortex and striatum. Nature **433**, 873–876.

Person, A.L., Gale, S.D., Farries, M.A., and Perkel, D.J. (2008). Organization of the songbird basal ganglia, including area X. J Comp Neurol **508**, 840–866.

Person, A.L., and Perkel, D.J. (2005). Unitary IPSPs drive precise thalamic spiking in a circuit required for learning. Neuron **46**, 129–140.

Redgrave, P., Prescott, T.J., and Gurney, K. (1999).The basal ganglia: a vertebrate solution to the selection problem? Neuroscience **89**, 1009–1023.

Richard, J.M., Stout, N., Acs, D., and Janak, P.H. (2018). Ventral pallidal encoding of reward-seeking behavior depends on the underlying associative structure. eLife **7**, e33107.

Rikhye, R.V., Wimmer, R.D., and Halassa, M.M. (2018). Toward an integrative theory of thalamic function. Annu Rev Neurosci **41**, 163–183.

Roseberry, T.K., Lee, A.M., Lalive, A.L., Wilbrecht, L., Bonci, A., and Kreitzer, A.C. (2016). Cell-type-specific control of brainstem locomotor circuits by basal ganglia. Cell **164**, 526–537.

Rosin, B., Nevet, A., Elias, S., Rivlin-Etzion, M., Israel, Z., and Bergman, H. (2007). Physiology and pathophysiology of the basal ganglia-thalamo-cortical networks. Parkinsonism Relat Disord **13** Suppl 3, S437–439.

Rossi, M.A., Li, H.E., Lu, D., Kim, I.H., Bartholomew, R.A., Gaidis, E., Barter, J.W., Kim, N., Cai, M.T., Soderling, S.H., and Yin, H.H. (2016). A GABAergic nigrotectal pathway for coordination of drinking behavior. Nat Neurosci **19**, 742–748.

Rubin, J.E., McIntyre, C.C., Turner, R.S., and Wichmann, T. (2012). Basal ganglia activity patterns in parkinsonism and computational modeling of their downstream effects. Eur J Neurosci **36**, 2213–2228.

Ruder, L., and Arber, S. (2019). Brainstem circuits controlling action diversification. Annu Rev Neurosci **42**, 485–504.

Samejima, K., and Doya, K. (2007). Multiple representations of belief states and action values in corticobasal ganglia loops. Ann NY Acad Sci **1104**, 213–228.

Sauerbrei, B.A., Guo, J.Z., Cohen, J.D., Mischiati, M., Guo, W., Kabra, M., Verma, N., Mensh, B., Branson, K., and Hantman, A.W. (2020). Cortical pattern generation during dexterous movement is input-driven. Nature **577**, 386–391.

Sayin, S., De Backer, J.-F., Siju, K., Wosniack, M.E., Lewis, L.P., Frisch, L.-M., Gansen, B., Schlegel, P., Edmondson-Stait, A., and Sharifi, N. (2019). A neural circuit arbitrates between persistence and withdrawal in hungry *Drosophila*. Neuron **104**, 544–558.e546.

Schall, J.D. (1995). Neural basis of saccade target selection. Rev Neurosci **6**, 63–63.

Scharff, C., and Nottebohm, F. (1991). A comparative study of the behavioral deficits following lesions of various parts of the zebra finch song system: implications for vocal learning. J Neurosci **11**, 2896–2913.

Schlag-Rey, M., and Schlag, J. (1984). Visuomotor functions of central thalamus in monkey. I. Unit activity related to spontaneous eye movements. J Neurophysiol **51**, 1149–1174.

Schmidt, M.F. (2003). Pattern of interhemispheric synchronization in HVc during singing correlates with key transitions in the song pattern. J Neurophysiol **90**, 3931–3949.

Schmidt, M.F., Ashmore, R.C., and Vu, E.T. (2004). Bilateral control and interhemispheric coordination in the avian song motor system. Ann NY Acad Sci **1016**, 171–186.

Schultz, W. (2007). Behavioral dopamine signals. Trends Neurosci **30**, 203–210.

Schwab, B.C., Kase, D., Zimnik, A., Rosenbaum, R., Codianni, M.G., Rubin, J.E., and Turner, R.S. (2020). Neural activity during a simple reaching task in macaques is counter to gating and rebound in basal ganglia–thalamic communication. PLoS Biol **18**, e3000829.

Shen, W., Flajolet, M., Greengard, P., and Surmeier, D.J. (2008). Dichotomous dopaminergic control of striatal synaptic plasticity. Science **321**, 848–851.

Sheth, S.A., Abuelem, T., Gale, J.T., and Eskandar, E.N. (2011). Basal ganglia neurons dynamically facilitate exploration during associative learning. J Neurosci **31**, 4878–4885.

Shin, S., and Sommer, M.A. (2012). Division of labor in frontal eye field neurons during presaccadic remapping of visual receptive fields. J Neurophysiol **108**, 2144–2159.

Sommer, M.A., and Wurtz, R.H. (2004a). What the brain stem tells the frontal cortex. I. Oculomotor signals sent from superior colliculus to frontal eye field via mediodorsal thalamus. J Neurophysiol **91**, 1381–1402.

Sommer, M.A., and Wurtz, R.H. (2004b). What the brain stem tells the frontal cortex.II. Role of the SC-MD-FEF pathway in corollary discharge. J Neurophysiol **91**, 1403–1423.

Sommer, M.A., and Wurtz, R.H. (2008). Brain circuits for the internal monitoring of movements. Annu Rev Neurosci **31**, 317–338.

Srivastava, N., Hinton, G., Krizhevsky, A., Sutskever, I., and Salakhutdinov, R. (2014). Dropout: a simple way to prevent neural networks from overfitting. J Mach Learn Res **15**, 1929–1958.

Strick, P.L. (1976). Activity of ventrolateral thalamic neurons during arm movement. J Neurophysiol **39**, 1032–1044.

Suri, R.E., and Schultz, W. (1998). Learning of sequential movements by neural network model with dopamine-like reinforcement signal. Exp Brain Res **121**, 350–354.

Surmeier, D.J., Plotkin, J., and Shen, W. (2009). Dopamine and synaptic plasticity in dorsal striatal circuits controlling action selection. Curr Opin Neurobiol **19**, 621–628.

Takahashi, Y., Schoenbaum, G., and Niv, Y. (2008). Silencing the critics: understanding the effects of cocaine sensitization on dorsolateral and ventral striatum in the context of an actor/critic model. Front Neurosci **2**, 86–99.

Tchernichovski, O., Mitra, P.P., Lints, T., and Nottebohm, F. (2001). Dynamics of the vocal imitation process: how a zebra finch learns its song. Science **291**, 2564–2569.

Thakkar, K.N., and Rolfs, M. (2019). Disrupted corollary discharge in schizophrenia: Evidence from the oculomotor system. Biol Psychiatry: Cogn Neurosci Neuroimaging **4**, 773–781.

Theeuwes, J. (2010). Top–down and bottom–up control of visual selection. Acta Psychol **135**, 77–99.

Thorndike, E.L. (1911). Animal Intelligence (Darien, CT: Hafner).

Tian, J., Huang, R., Cohen, J.Y., Osakada, F., Kobak, D., Machens, C.K., Callaway, E.M., Uchida, N., and Watabe-Uchida, M. (2016). Distributed and mixed information in monosynaptic inputs to dopamine neurons. Neuron **91**, 1374–1389.

Tindell, A.J., Berridge, K.C., and Aldridge, J.W. (2004). Ventral pallidal representation of pavlovian cues and reward: population and rate codes. J Neurosci **24**, 1058–1069.

Vaadia, E., Haalman, I., Abeles, M., Bergman, H., Prut, Y., Slovin, H., and Aertsen, A. (1995). Dynamics of neuronal interactions in monkey cortex in relation to behavioural events. Nature **373**, 515–518.

van Donkelaar, P., Stein, J.F., Passingham, R.E., and Miall, R.C. (2000). Temporary inactivation in the primate motor thalamus during visually triggered and internally generated limb movements. J Neurophysiol **83**, 2780–2790.

Vu, E.T., Schmidt, M.F., and Mazurek, M.E. (1998). Interhemispheric coordination of premotor neural activity during singing in adult zebra finches. J Neurosci **18**, 9088–9098.

Wang, C.Z., Herbst, J.A., Keller, G.B., and Hahnloser, R.H. (2008). Rapid interhemispheric switching during vocal production in a songbird. PLoS Biol **6**, e250.

Wild, J.M. (1997). Neural pathways for the control of birdsong production. J Neurobiol **33**, 653–670.

Wolff, S., and Ölveczky, B. (2018). The promise and perils of causal circuit manipulations. Curre Opin Neurobiol **49**, 84–94.

Wolff, S.B., Ko, R., and Ölveczky, B.P. (2019). Distinct roles for motor cortical and thalamic inputs to striatum during motor learning and execution. bioRxiv, 825810.

Woods, J.W. (1964). Behavior of chronic decerebrate rats. J Neurophysiol **27**, 635–644.

Yin, H.H., Ostlund, S.B., and Balleine, B.W. (2008). Reward-guided learning beyond dopamine in the nucleus accumbens: the integrative functions of cortico-basal ganglia networks. Eur J Neurosci **28**, 1437–1448.

Chapter 15

Cerebellar Regulation of the Thalamus

Freek E. Hoebeek and Henk-Jan Boele

Introduction

In the final section of the 2nd edition of his landmark textbook *The Thalamus*, Ed Jones states that investigations into the efferents and afferents of the thalamus should not only focus on the classic "first-order" motor nucleus of the thalamus. Instead, other parts of the mammalian thalamus should also be studied carefully because these parts are probably vital for proper motor control and thus the survival of an organism. While reviewing the literature that has been published since then, it appeared to the authors of the current chapter that the field has indeed made significant steps in unraveling how the thalamus integrates inputs from the cerebellum to drive neurons in the motor, premotor, and other associative cortices. Following Jones, we will not only focus on the cerebellar input to the first-order motor nuclei, that is, the ventroanterior (VA) and ventrolateral nuclei (VL), but also discuss the cerebellum's input to "higher-order" thalamic nuclei, such as the ventromedian (VM) and centrolateral (CL) nuclei. Perhaps one of the most urgent gaps in our knowledge that needs to be filled concerns the development of the cerebellothalamic tract, for which the critical periods of plasticity still remain unexplored. In this chapter, we will first discuss the most recent updates and remaining questions on the developing cerebellothalamic tract.

To understand the impact of the cerebellum on thalamocortical networks, investigations of pathology are often at least as important as the basic anatomy and physiology of the unaffected brain. Already in the late 19th century, cerebellar lesions were linked to atypical behavior and disturbed thalamocortical activity patterns. In the current chapter, we will review the literature on aberrant cerebellar activity leading to abnormal thalamocortical functioning. In addition, we will focus on the potential therapeutic value of cerebellar stimulation for several neurological conditions. Thus, since in 2007, Ed Jones called upon the scientific community to investigate the motor thalamus from a broader perspective than just the first-order VA/VL nuclei, we would like to point in two directions for the next period of time: (1) a deepening of the field's knowledge about the impact of cerebellar input on nuclei outside of the VA/VL will contribute significantly to understanding the functioning of the motor system, and (2) a focus on the developmental stages of the cerebellothalamic tract could provide a better understanding of the cerebellar role in neurological disorders in the motor, cognitive, and social domains. Cell-type-specific stimulation and inhibition of axonal populations *in vivo* and *ex vivo* with great spatiotemporal precision, automated video analysis of motor execution, and a myriad of chemo- and optogenetic tools will allow the fields of neuroscience, neurology, neurosurgery, psychiatry, and psychology to take coordinated steps toward a deeper understanding of cerebello-cerebral interaction, eventually leading to better diagnosis and treatment options for patients suffering from neurological and developmental disorders.

Nomenclature

From the earliest functional lesion studies in the 18th and 19th centuries, it became clear that the cerebellum and thalamus were indispensable for proper motor functioning. The research of anatomists like Rolando (1773–1831) and Magendie (1783–1855), which utilized the experimental strategies of Flourens (1794–1867), paved the way for the investigators of the late 19th and early 20th centuries to examine how the cerebellar and thalamic structures corroborate and contribute to corticospinal tract activity that drives coordinated and well-timed muscle contractions (Ito, 2002; Serra et al., 2019).

The cerebellothalamic tract is formed by axons from the four bilateral cerebellar nuclei, which are positioned within the central white matter of the cerebellum, the lateral (dentatus in phylogenetically younger species), anterior interposed (emboliformus) and posterior interposed (globosus), and medial (fastigial) nuclei (Figure 1). These cerebellar nuclei are part of functional and anatomical modules that encompass the cerebellar cortex and inferior olive. Within cerebellar nuclei, several types of neurons are found, of which the glutamatergic neurons with a relatively large soma form the cerebellothalamic projections. Apart from the thalamic projections discussed later in detail, cerebellar nuclei neurons also project to various mesencephalic structures, such as the anterior pretectal nucleus and superior colliculus (Teune et al., 2000), which in turn also innervate thalamic nuclei (Schäfer and Hoebeek, 2018).

In the current chapter, we mostly focus on the rodent brain. (For a complete review of the primate motor thalamus nomenclature, see, for instance, Sakai [2013], in which the motor thalamus encompasses the VA, VL, and VM thalamus.) In the rodent brain, the VA and VL are combined into the ventral anterior-lateral complex and typically referred to as the *VAL* or *VA/VL* because the cytological border between the pallidal-receiving VA and cerebellar-receiving VL is virtually absent, in contrast to the primate brain (Gallay et al., 2008; Bosch-Bouju et al., 2013) (Figure 2). In the rodent VM nucleus, the pallidal and cerebellar projections overlap extensively: synapses of the substantia nigra pars reticulata appear in the same rostrocaudal and medial-lateral planes of the VM, which allows the

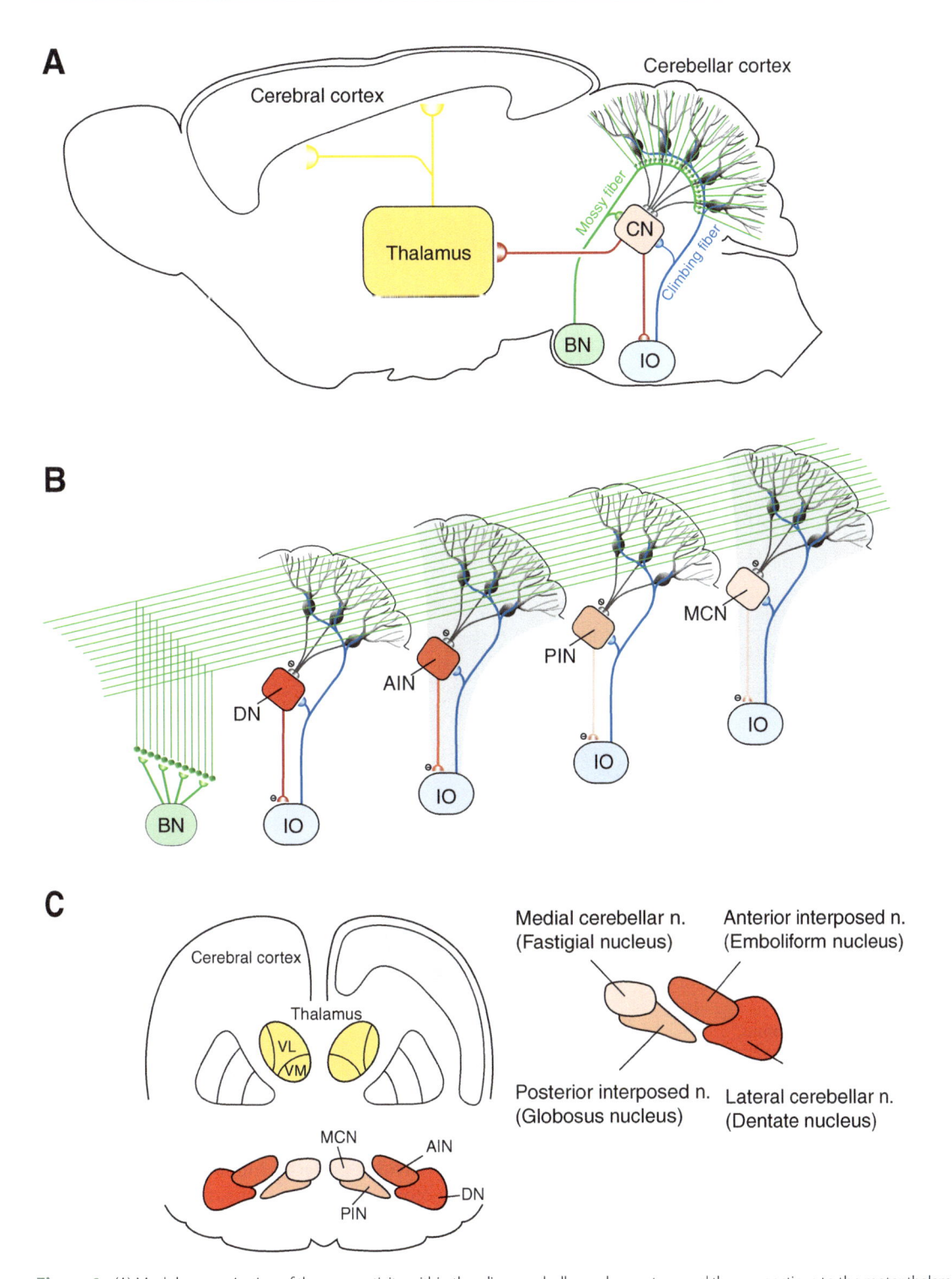

Figure 1 (A) Modular organization of the connectivity within the olivo-cerebello-nuclear system and the connections to the motor thalamus. (B) The basilar pontine nuclei (BPN) and inferior olive nucleus (IO) provide mossy fiber (*green*) and climbing fiber afferents (*blue*) to the cerebellar cortex that form excitatory synapses with granule cells (*green*) and Purkinje cells (*black*), respectively. Whereas the inferior olive axons from specific subnuclei respect anatomical borders and synapse solely within functionally distinct regions of the cerebellar cortex, the granule cell axons traverse various modules. Purkinje cell axons converge and inhibit cerebellar nuclei (CN) neurons in well-defined regions, which in turn innervate the original inferior olive neurons, closing the olivo-cerebello-nuclear loop. Each of the cerebellar nuclei – lateral (L)CN, anterior interposed (AIN), posterior interposed (PIN), and medial (M)CN – receives input from a dedicated set of Purkinje cells and innervates a dedicated set of inferior olive neurons, the latter of which not only innervates the Purkinje cells but also provides axon collaterals to the cerebellar nuclei neurons in the same module. (C) The cerebellothalamic tract is formed by axons from all four cerebellar nuclei that cross the midline and innervate various thalamic nuclei, including the classical motor thalamus nuclei VL and VM.

former inhibitory input to modulate the thalamic responses to cerebellar inputs (Buee et al., 1986). Later in the chapter, we will address this cerebellar and pallidal convergence (for further discussion of basal ganglia–thalamic interactions, see Chapter 14 in this volume). In addition, we will address other thalamic subnuclei taking part in motor function and receiving cerebellar input. Two of these are the intralaminar CL and centromedian (CM) nuclei.

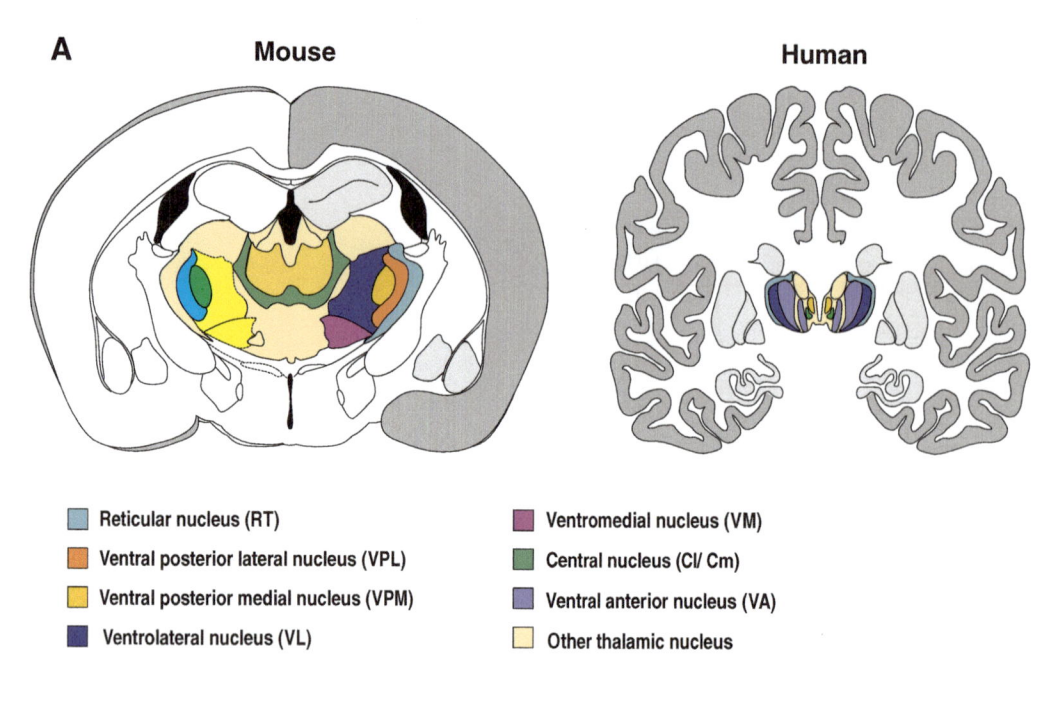

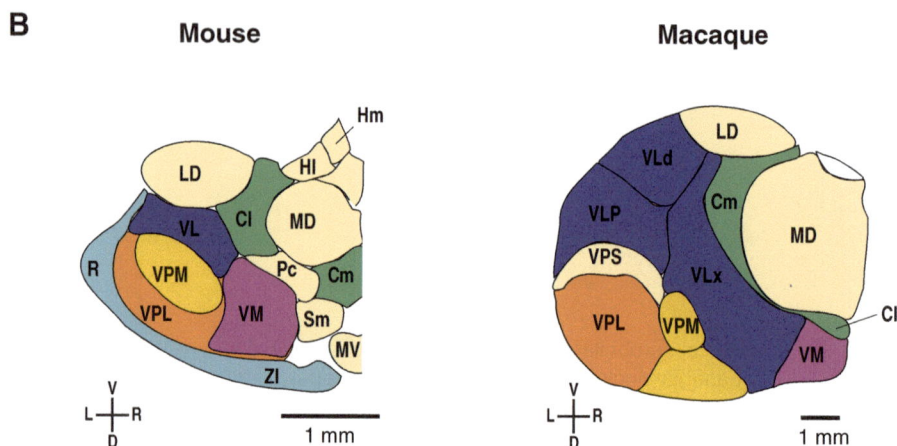

Figure 2 Comparative anatomy of the motor thalamus.

A. Schematic representation of the macroscopy of the mouse and human thalamus at the anteroposterior level that includes the motor thalamus nuclei, highlighting the difference in the relative size of the thalamus compared to cerebral cortical volume.

B. Unilateral section of mouse and macaque thalamus at the level of the motorthalamus, revealing that the motor thalamus is relatively larger in the latter LD: laterodorsal; MD: Mediodorsal; Pc: Paracentral; Sm: Submedial; MV: Medioventral; VPS: Ventroposterior superior.

Somatotopy

The first-order motor thalamus (i.e., the VL nucleus) has been somatotopically characterized in several species (mouse: Tlamsa and Brumberg, 2010; rat: Angaut and Cicirata, 1990; monkey: Vitek et al., 1994; Hoover and Strick, 1999) (Figure 2). The connectivity of the VL with the motor cortex has also been studied in great detail. Several anatomical studies show that functionally distinct patches of neurons in the VL nucleus can be identified following retrograde tracer injections into the motor cortex (e.g., Cicirata et al., 1986; Tlamsa and Brumberg, 2010), and thereby VL neurons can be linked to the cortico-spinal tract somatotopy. However, the axonal branching pattern of single VL and especially VM neurons is remarkably complex and appears to span throughout several cortical regions and layers (Figure 3) (Kuramoto et al., 2015). This divergent branching pattern of motor thalamus neurons encompasses motor, prefrontal, sensory, and associative regions, which underlines the connection between cerebellar nuclei and many cortical regions (Pisano et al., 2021).

The somatotopy of the cerebellar nuclei is somewhat more complex, in that several nuclei project onto the same patches of VL neurons and even onto the same neuron. This concept aligns with the general statement from Brooks and Thach (1981) about the organization of the cerebellar output: "one body part might be influenced by several areas in the cerebellum, each part exerting its own kind of control" (quoted in Angaut and Cicirata, 1990, p. 325). In this chapter, we will discuss the electrophysiological data that confirm the convergence of cerebellar axons onto single cells, which is a remarkable concept in the diverging cerebellothalamic tract.

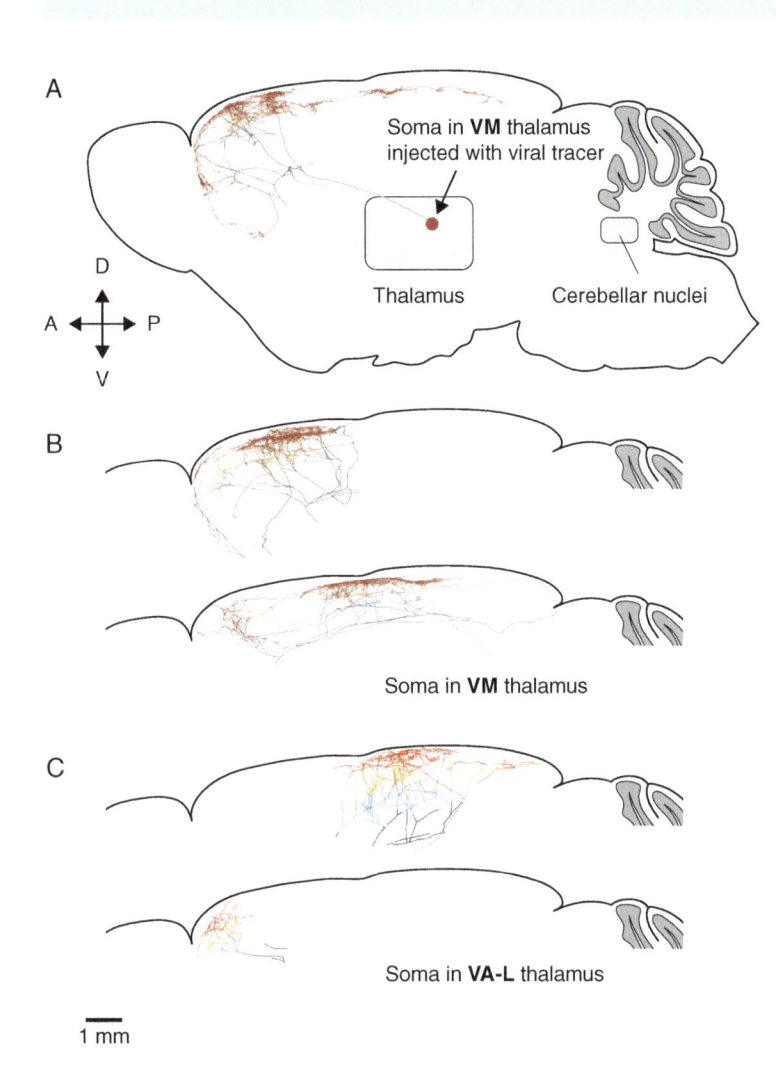

Figure 3 Axonal branching differs in rat brain between neurons from motor thalamus nuclei.

A and B. The axon fibers of three single VM neurons (neurons 14, 5, and 6 in original publication) infected with a Sindbis virus expressing a fluorescent protein were reconstructed using serial sectioning light microscopy. These axon fibers were widely distributed in the motor-associated areas (primary and associative motor cortex) but also invaded the orbitofrontal, sensory, and primary visual cortex, especially in L1.

C. As in panel B for the axon fibers of a single VL neuron (neuron 1 in original publication). The colors of axon fibers indicate fine varicose axon fibers in different cortical layers. Panels A and B are adapted from Kuramoto et al. (2015), and panel C is adapted from Kuramoto et al. (2009), with permission.

Morphological and Genetic Profile of the Motor Thalamus

The neurons in the VA, VL, and VM motor thalamus are much like those in other first-order thalamic nuclei: a radially organized ("bushy") dendritic tree, a round soma, and a single axon (Sawyer et al., 1989; Kuramoto et al., 2009; Tlamsa and Brumberg, 2010; Gornati et al., 2018). In addition, the distribution of the VA, VL, and VM afferents is standardized: subcortical inputs, for instance, from cerebellar nuclei, synapse predominantly on proximal dendrites and modulatory inputs, for instance, from layer 6 (L6) cortico-thalamic neurons, synapse on the more distal parts of the dendrites. Neurons in the CL and CM have a different morphological profile with more asymmetric dendritic profiles and occasional grape-like appendages. The dendritic trees tend to follow the borders of the nuclei (Deschênes et al., 1996; Parent and Parent, 2005; Gornati et al., 2018), which putatively limits the number of *en passant* synaptic contacts by axons that populate the neighboring nuclei. Also, the dendritic morphology affects the electrophysiological characteristics: in comparison to VM and VL neurons, CL neurons have a higher membrane resistance and increased excitability in mice (Gornati et al., 2018).

The repetitive architecture of the thalamus is also represented in its genetic composition. Recent evidence revealed that the transcriptome of thalamic neurons appears to be repeated throughout functionally distinct parts of the thalamus, such as the motor and cognitive thalamus (Phillips et al., 2019). The transcriptional differences between these thalamic neuronal identities correlate with morphological characteristics and expression of ion channels and neurotransmitter receptor subunits. For instance, calbindin D-28 K, which is an intracellular calcium buffer molecule, is differentially expressed in the adult motor thalamus. Neurons that receive pallidal inputs (VA neurons from globus pallidus interna and VM neurons from substantia nigra pars reticulata) express calbindin D-28 K in higher levels than other neurons (Bodor et al., 2008). Importantly, during developmental stages, several genes are expressed transiently per the thalamic nucleus, which may well influence the functioning of the nuclei (Blackshaw et al., 2010; Yuge et al., 2011). Apart from functional differentiation, the genetic architecture of thalamic nuclei has recently been linked to neurological disorders, such as Parkinson's disease, bipolar disorder, and schizophrenia (Elvsåshagen et al., 2021).

Development of the Cerebellothalamic Tract

With a birthdate between E10.5 and E12.5 (E = embryonic age), among the first cerebellar neurons produced from the metencephalic rhombic lip and ventricular zone in the mouse are the glutamatergic and GABAergic cerebellar nuclei neurons, respectively (Green and Wingate, 2014). As a reference, the cerebellar cortex develops and matures at a slower pace than the cerebellar nuclei, in that migration and morphology of cortical neurons last until the third postnatal week (Elsen et al., 2013), whereas the cerebellar nuclei neurons do so during the first and second postnatal week in rodents (Pierce, 1975; Goffinet, 1983; Gardette et al., 1985; Altman and Bayer, 1997; Garin and Escher, 2001; Machold and Fishell, 2005; Wang et al., 2005; Fink et al., 2006; Leto et al., 2016). The growth of cerebellar nuclei axons during pre- and postnatal periods has been studied using the anterograde neuronal tracers wheat germ agglutinin-conjugated horseradish peroxidase (WGA-HRP) and carbocyanine dyes (e.g., DiI) and retrograde fast-blue (FB) tracing. Such qualitative tracing studies indicated that in E17.5 rats, cerebellar nuclei axons are found in the thalamic complex (Asanuma et al., 1988; Altman and Bayer, 1997). Using in utero electroporation, Hara and colleagues showed that after reaching the mesencephalic red nucleus in E15.5 mice, cerebellar nuclei axons reach the thalamus at E17.5 (Hara et al., 2016). Recently, this finding was further quantified by Dumas et al. (2019) using transgenic mouse embryos in which cerebellar nuclei axons were labeled with a fluorescent protein (*Ntsr1-Cre/Ai14* mice). Fluorescently labeled cerebellar nuclei axons were absent in the thalamus at E15.5 and E16.5 but appeared to be waiting outside of the thalamus. From E17.5 on, cerebellar nuclei axon innervation steadily increased and revealed the sequential innervation of the VL, VM, and other thalamic nuclei. Immunofluorescent labeling of the vesicular glutamate transporter type II (vGluT2) indicated that at E18.5, cerebellar nuclei axons form glutamatergic synapses (Dumas et al., 2019) (Figure 4). Within this same period, thalamocortical innervation also commences. Thalamocortical fibers grow to reach and "handshake" the subplate neurons (a transient cellular layer underneath the developing cortical plate) at E13 (Hoerder-Suabedissen and Molnár, 2015). After accumulation in the subplate, thalamocortical fibers start innervating the cortical plate (the "anlage" of the mature cerebral cortex) at E17 to form synapses and finally reach layer 4 around postnatal day 8 (Hoerder-Suabedissen and Molnár, 2015). The overlap in timelines of the developing cerebellothalamic and thalamocortical projections (Auladell et al., 2000; Dumas et al., 2019; Lopez-Bendito and Molnar, 2003) (Figure 4C) indicates that cerebellar pathology during development could affect thalamocortical development (see also the section on pathology later in the chapter).

Generalization beyond Rodents

In addition to studies in mice and rats, the development of the cerebellothalamic tract has also been studied qualitatively in the Virginia opossum (*Didephis virginiana*). Because the Virginia opossum is born extremely premature at 13 days after conception, a major part of brain development is an extrauterine process. The period P0–P15 in the Virginia opossum corresponds to that of E11–P0 in the mouse. In the Virginia opossum, cerebellar nuclei neurons are first seen at E11–E13 (Larsell, 1935). Interestingly, the thalamic innervation of cerebellar nuclei axons starts relatively late at P17–20 (Martin et al., 1987), which is around 18 days after cell formation (for comparison, in the mouse brain, this occurs around 8 days after cell formation). Thalamocortical innervation has been studied in the South American opossum (*Monodelphis domestica*) (Molnár et al., 1998), which has a slightly longer gestational period than the Virginia opossum (15 days instead of 13 days). In the South American opossum, thalamocortical fibers reach the subplate at P8, subplate innervation starts at P10, and cortical layer formation starts around P15. This sequence of events suggests that also in the opossum family, cerebellar nuclei axons arrive in the thalamus at the stage that also marks the ontogeny of thalamocortical innervation, suggesting that the putative role of cerebellar output in orchestrating thalamocortical maturation is not unique to rodents but also applies to other mammalian species.

Development of Cerebellothalamic Tract in Humans

In humans, cerebellar nuclei emerge between gestational weeks 6 and 8, and the full contours of the four nuclei (*dentatus*, *globosus*, *emboliformus*, and *fastigii*) are clearly demarcated around gestational week 16. Similar to rodents, human development of cerebellar nuclei neurons precedes Purkinje cell development (Mihajlovic and Zecevic, 1986; Yamaguchi et al., 1989). After gestational week 16, there is no further proliferation of cerebellar nuclei neurons; all nuclei have reached their mature number of neurons per nucleus: an estimated ~750,000 neurons for the dentate nucleus, ~100,000 for the globosus and emboliformus nuclei combined, and ~30,000 for the fastigial nucleus (Yamaguchi et al., 1989).

Until gestational week 20, the dentate nucleus has a smooth surface; the first folding appears around gestational week 24, and the typical convoluted dentate nucleus characteristic for adult stages appears at gestational week 35 (Yamaguchi et al., 1989). Golgi staining revealed that in the dentate, dendritic branching and spine formation start around week 20 and continue at least until week 34 (Mihajlovic and Zecevic, 1986; Hayaran et al., 1992; Elsen et al., 2013). As pointed out by Hayaran et al. (1992), the human cerebellar nuclei have a protracted developmental period extending over 7–8 months of intrauterine life, thereby rendering it vulnerable to environmental hazards and stimuli, a statement that has also been postulated about cerebellar development in general (Volpe, 2009).

It is unknown at what exact developmental stage cerebellar nuclei axons start innervating the thalamus in humans. Takahashi et al. (2014) studied postmortem fixed cerebellar tissue, including the cerebellar peduncles, of fetuses between gestational weeks 17 and 38 using high-angular diffusion imaging (HARDI) tractography. Their MRI-based analysis revealed that the cerebellothalamic tract is developing in both pre- and postnatal months (Takahashi et al., 2014). Using *in vivo* HARDI tractography in preterm-born infants, Pieterman et al. (2017) quantified the cerebellothalamic tract development using functional anisotropy values, revealing a steady growth

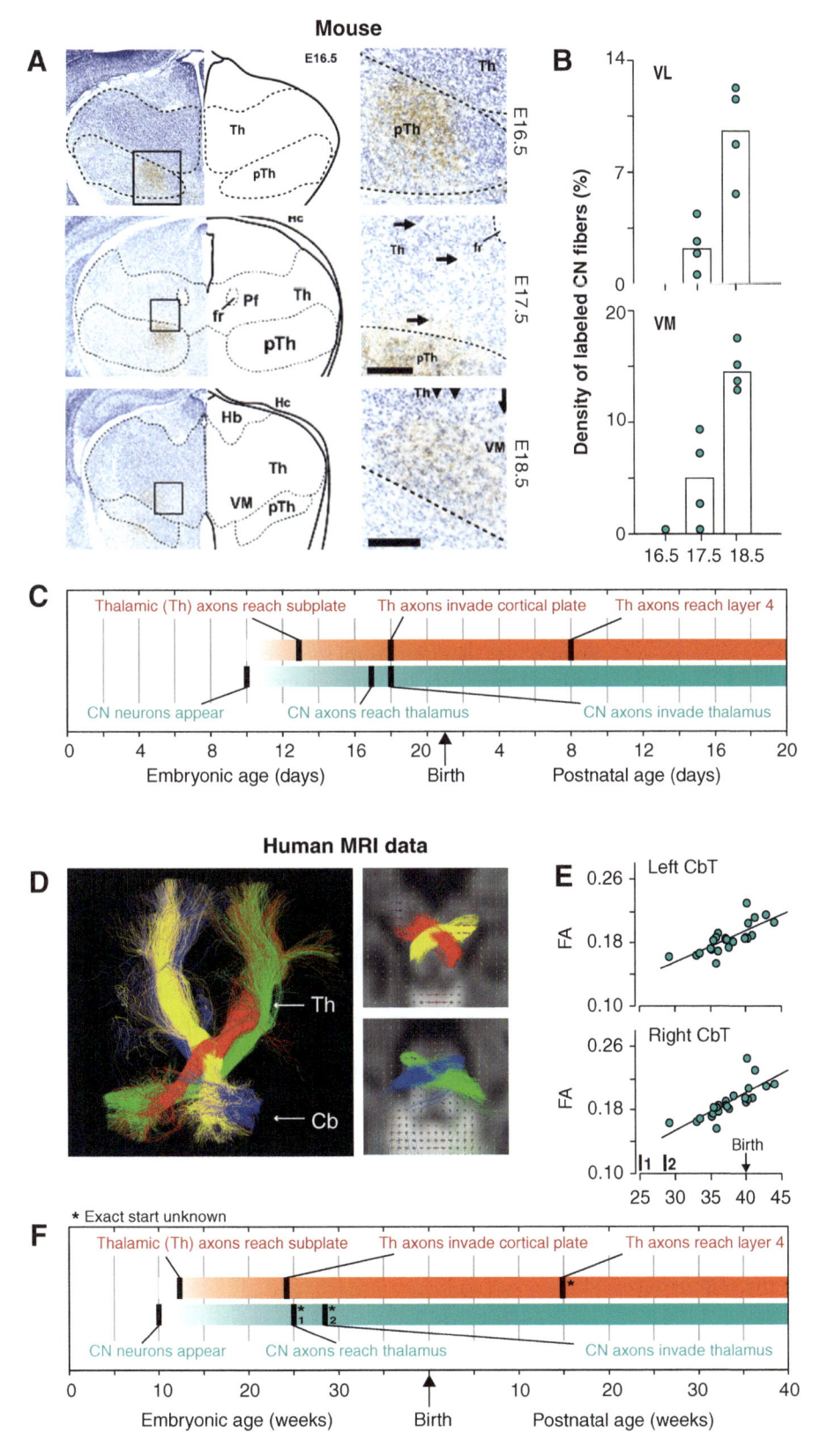

Figure 4 Immunohistochemical labeling of cerebellar nuclei axons during late embryonic stages indicate a waiting period.

A. Coronal section of an E16.5 mouse brain showing presence of DAB-stained cerebellar nuclei axons in the prethalamus (pTh) and absence of RFP+ fibers in the thalamus (Th) of $Ntsr1^{Cre}/Ai14$ transgenic mice. Sections are counterstained with thionin. At E17.5 and E18.5, CN axons invade the thalamus (indicated by arrows). fr: Fasciculus retroflexus; Pf: Parafasciculus; VM: Ventromedial; Hb: Habenula; HC: Hippocampus.

B. The density of labeled cerebellar nuclei axons in the thalamus increases with age, (in embryonic days) as quantified by the percentage of pixels that are DAB-labeled. VL: Ventrolateral.

C. Timeline of the developing cerebellothalamic (green bar) and thalamocortical tracts (red bar) during the prenatal and postnatal periods in the mouse. Several milestones of tract development have been indicated. CN: cerebellar nuclei.

D. Magnetic resonance imaging (MRI)–diffusion tractography imaging reconstruction of cerebello-thalamo-cortical (red-yellow) and cortico-ponto-cerebellar (blue-green) tracts in an infant born at 33 weeks of gestational age and images at 40 weeks of gestational age. Insets on the right indicate the decussation of the cerebellothalamic tract (superior cerebellar peduncle; red-yellow) at the level of the midbrain and of the pontocerebellar tract (middle cerebral peduncle; blue-green) at the level of the pons.

E. The fractional anisotropy FA, which is a quantitative measure for the fiber density, of the left (upper panel) and right (lower panel) cerebellothalamic (CbT) steadily increases during the last trimester of pregnancy, as measured in preterm-born children with in vivo MRI.

F. As in panel C for humans. The * symbol indicates that the exact timing of the milestone remains unknown and is estimated by the authors based on the literature discussed in the main text. Panels A and B are adapted from Dumas et al. (2019), and panels D and E are adapted from Pieterman et al. (2017), with permission.

between weeks 29 and 44 of postmenstrual age (Pieterman et al., 2017) (Figure 4C). Thus, although the exact start of the cerebellar innervation of thalamic neurons in humans remains to be elucidated, these imaging studies indicate that the cerebellothalamic tract ontogeny probably occurs in the second trimester of pregnancy.

Similar to rodents and opossum, the ontogeny of the cerebellothalamic tract appears to overlap with that of the thalamocortical tract in humans. Converging lines of evidence, obtained from postmortem tissue and functional brain imaging, show that thalamocortical fibers reach and "handshake" the subplate neurons at gestational week 11–13. The "waiting period" lasts until gestational week 23–25, after which the thalamocortical fibers start innervating the cortical plate to form synapses (Marin-Padilla, 1970; Kostović and Goldman-Rakic, 1983; Kostović and Rakic, 1984; Kostović and Judas, 2002; Aeby et al., 2009; Alcauter et al., 2014; Kostović et al., 2014; Hoerder-Suabedissen and Molnár, 2015; Krsnik et al., 2017). In humans, the exact moment of thalamocortical fiber ingrowth seems region dependent (Krsnik et al., 2017), which might also be true for the developing cerebellothalamic tract.

Conclusions on the Development and Maturation of the Cerebellothalamic Tract

Two general concepts about the developing connection between cerebellum and thalamocortical networks can be drawn. First, maturation of the cerebellothalamic tract occurs before maturation of the cerebellar cortex. Second, maturation of the cerebellothalamic tract coincides with maturation of the thalamocortical tracts. To clarify the impact of cerebellar innervation on thalamic activity and thalamocortical tract development, basic neurodevelopmental concepts like heterosynaptic (cerebello-thalamic and cortico-thalamic) interactions, synaptic pruning, and cerebellar nuclei axon myelination require investigation. This applies not only to the neuronal networks encoding the motor system but also to the cognitive and social systems. Because the cerebellar output (i.e., cerebellar nuclei action-potential firing patterns) harbors information relevant to each of these systems, one of the major challenges will be to decipher how the cerebellum contributes to the timing of critical periods and the sequential maturation of each of these systems (Hensch, 2004; Reh et al., 2020).

Anatomy of the Cerebellothalamic Tract in the Adult

Anatomical studies on cerebellothalamic connectivity in the adult human brain focused primarily on the laterally positioned dentate nucleus and the *brachium conjunctivum* (the superior cerebellar peduncle), that is, the white-matter bundle that encompasses the cerebellothalamic tract (Hassler, 1950; Voogd and van Baarsen, 2014). With the improving resolution of magnetic resonance scanners and the rapid development of scanning sequences and analytical tools, it has become possible to (1) investigate the cerebellothalamic tract in the human brain in more detail; (2) investigate the structure and connectivity of the three smaller cerebellar nuclei (*emboliforme*, *globosus*, and *fastigii*) (Dimitrova et al., 2006; Diedrichsen et al., 2011); and (3) study in vivo the contribution of the individual cerebellar nuclei to various well-characterized behavioral tasks, such as delayed eyeblink conditioning (Ernst et al., 2017). In the coming years, both the spatial and temporal resolution of such imaging studies will increase, allowing in-depth investigations of the importance of the connections between individual cerebellar nuclei and individual thalamic nuclei.

Despite these improvements in human research on the cerebellothalamic tract in the adult stage, the bulk of knowledge on the cerebellothalamic tract still stems from experiments in rodents and larger mammalian species. For an exhaustive review of cerebellar nuclei–thalamic projections in larger species (monkeys, cats), we refer to Sakai (2013).

Monosynaptic Tracers

Detailed descriptions of axonal projections from cerebellar nuclei neurons to various thalamic nuclei in the rat were published in the 1980s–1990s (Angaut et al., 1985; Angaut and Cicirata, 1990; Sawyer et al., 1994; Aumann and Horne, 1996; Teune et al., 2000) (Figure 5). Neurochemical tracers like biotinylated dextran amines (BDA) and WGA-HRP showed that cerebellar axons branch within the thalamic complex, both within and outside of the VL and VM. Single-axon tracing of interposed neurons revealed that collaterals of VL-bound axons also branch into CL and CM nuclei (Aumann and Horne, 1996). Electron micrographs revealed that the synaptic architecture characteristic of so-called "driver" synapses (terminals with a relatively large volume, mostly on proximal dendrites that have several active zones with asymmetric dimensions and are filled with numerous ellipsoid vesicles and several mitochondria) also applies to cerebellothalamic synapses (Aumann et al., 1994; Sawyer et al., 1994). These findings were recently confirmed in mice (Gornati et al., 2018) with the use of electron and confocal microscopy (Figure 6). Of note is that the cerebellar axons from the interposed and lateral cerebellar nuclei form morphologically similar terminals on single VL neurons (Shinoda et al., 1985; Aumann et al., 1994). Still, these cerebellar nuclei most likely convey "information" of different kinds because interposed and dentate nuclei receive input from functionally distinct regions of the cerebellar cortex (Ruigrok, 2011) (Figure 1). Moreover, even within the lateral, interposed, and medial cerebellar nuclei, there are separate functional domains that have been shown to selectively innervate downstream targets in the midbrain and thalamus (Dum and Strick, 2003; Houck and Person, 2015; Fujita et al., 2020), highlighting the relevance of an earlier statement by (Evarts and Thach, 1969): "VL is, in no sense, a mere relay nucleus, but rather, the neurons of VL appear to constitute a final common path upon which many components of motor and sensory systems converge" (p. 479).

Transsynaptic Tracers

The route from the cerebellum to the motor cortex is multisynaptic and organized in parallel for the separate body parts. Using retrograde transsynaptic tracing with herpes simplex virus (HSV) type 1 injections into functionally defined parts of the monkey motor cortex revealed that VL neurons that project to the primary motor cortex areas that control face, arm, or leg musculature receive input from different sets of cerebellar nuclei neurons (Dum and Strick, 2003). Similar

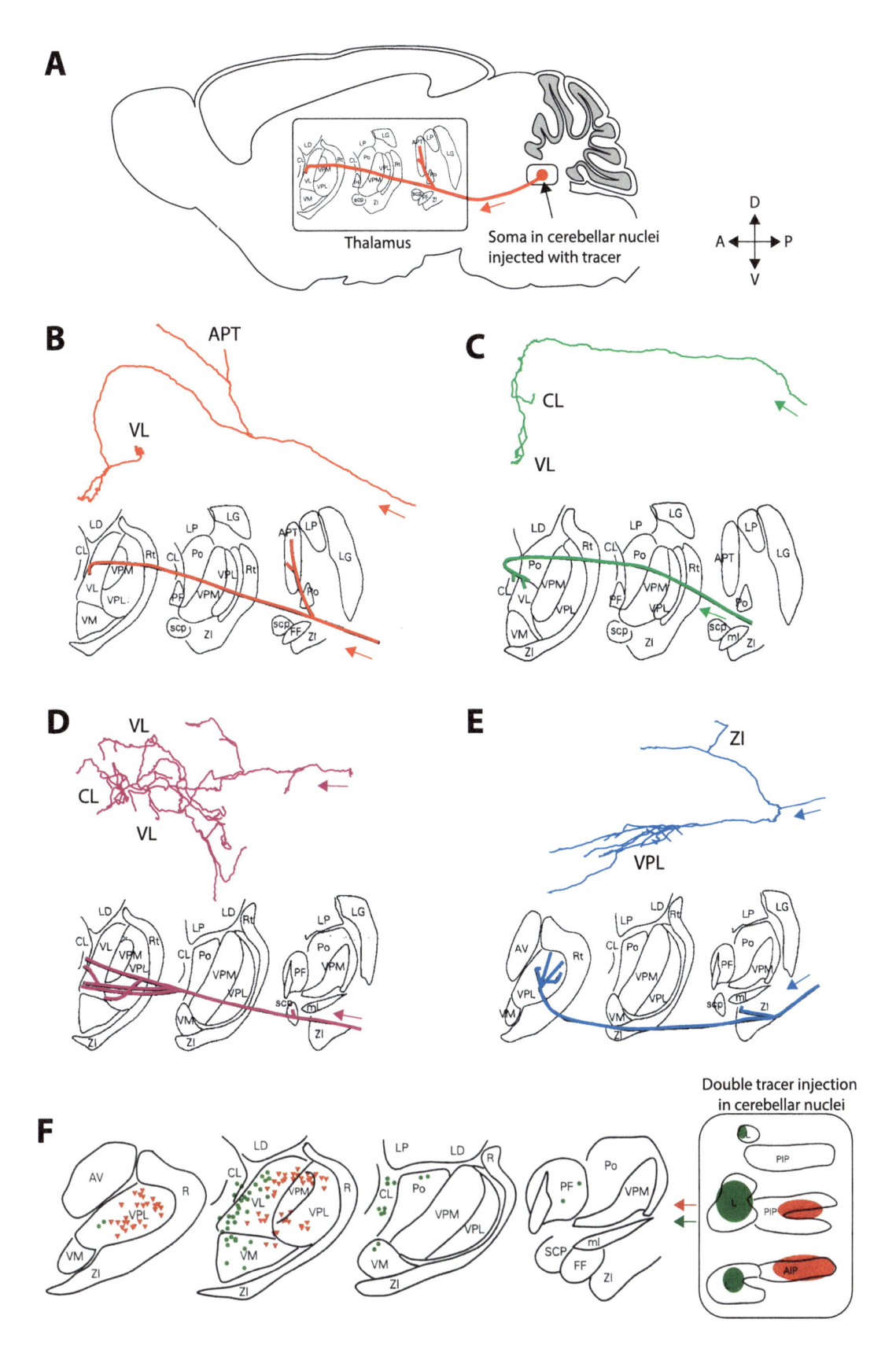

Figure 5 Variable branching pattern of cerebellar nuclei axons in various thalamic nuclei of the rat.

A. Schematic drawing of a reconstructed axon originating from the anterior interposed nucleus in the rat brain that was injected with dextran-biotin.

B–E. Top: Single-axon reconstructions indicating the branching and termination patterns that are located (*bottom*) within various thalamic nuclei.

results were found when using rabies virus in monkey and rat brains (Kelly and Strick, 2003; Aoki et al., 2019) and anterograde HSV subtypes (Badura et al., 2018; Pisano et al., 2021) to map neuronal networks important for motor and nonmotor modalities, such as executive functioning and cognitive flexibility.

These transsynaptic, anterograde tracing experiments could also be utilized to investigate cerebellar efferents that innervate neurons outside of the diencephalon that, in turn, project to the motor thalamus or motor cortex. These putative feedforward hubs could, in principle, form a source of feedforward inhibition, such as the anterior pretectal nucleus (as reviewed by Schäfer and Hoebeek, 2018), and contribute to the mixture of responses seen in thalamic firing patterns upon cerebellar stimulation (see next paragraphs). Future experiments using recombinant adeno-associated virus (rAAV) and pseudotyped deletion-mutant rabies viruses could also provide conclusive evidence. So far, this approach has been used to investigate the connection from the cerebellar nuclei to the limbic cortex and hippocampal regions, which runs via the VL and laterodorsal thalamus (for a rabies-based retrograde study on this connection, see Bohne et al., 2019; Watson et al., 2019).

Physiology

Cerebellar Output

An important part of the cerebellar output is formed by the action-potential firing patterns of cerebellar nuclei projection neurons. The various types of cerebellar nuclei neurons are characterized by a particular set of ion channels, neurotransmitter receptors, and morphological aspects (Uusisaari and De Schutter, 2011; Canto et al., 2016; Yarden-Rabinowitz and Yarom, 2017). Thalamus-projecting cerebellar nuclei neurons are glutamatergic, and thus cerebellar nuclei action-potential firing excites thalamic neurons. The spiking pattern of cerebellar nuclei neurons has been studied in various mammalian species, with a particular focus on the frequency and regularity of action-potential firing. The spiking patterns of cerebellar nuclei neurons are the product of their own intrinsic pacemaker activity, as well as inhibitory (Purkinje cells, cerebellar nuclei interneurons) and excitatory (mossy and climbing fiber collaterals) inputs. *In silico* and *ex vivo* studies revealed that apart from regularity and frequency of individual input, also, their synchronicity can modulate cerebellar nuclei firing patterns (Gauck and Jaeger, 2000; Rowland and Jaeger, 2008; De Zeeuw et al., 2011; Person and Raman, 2011; Najac and Raman, 2015; Wu and Raman, 2017).

Investigating cerebellar nuclei spiking patterns *in vivo* revealed that the vigilance state is a major determinant of both the regularity and frequency of cerebellar nuclei firing: changing from rest to locomotion (e.g., scratch movements in cats [Antziferova et al., 1980], walking in cats [Armstrong and Edgley, 1984] and mice [Sarnaik and Raman, 2018]), as well as cycling between sleep stages (Del Rio-Bermudez et al., 2016; Canto et al., 2017), results in drastic changes in cerebellar spiking patterns (Heck, 2015) (Figure 7). These data provide an overarching view that the firing pattern of large-bodied cerebellar nuclei neurons, which include the thalamus-projecting glutamatergic neurons, is characterized by a relatively high frequency, generally ranging between 30 and 100 Hz, with highly variable levels of regularity. It is unclear whether the average activity of cerebellar nuclei neurons differs between lateral, interposed, and medial cerebellar nuclei. Answering this question is of major importance for understanding the impact of cerebellar nuclei spiking patterns on thalamic neurons.

Cerebello-Thalamic Synapse Physiology

Cerebellothalamic synapses are excitatory synapses in which the postsynaptic response is mediated by ionotropic glutamate (alpha-amino-3-hydroxy-5-methyl-4-isoxazole propionic acid [AMPA] and *N*-methyl-D-aspartate [NMDA]) receptors. Electrical stimulation of putative cerebellar nuclei axons in ex vivo tissue of the VL thalamus from adult rats resulted in sharp-electrode recordings in depolarizing responses that often triggered action-potential firing (Aumann et al., 2000). Optical stimulation of channelrhodopsin2 (ChR2)-expressing cerebellar nuclei axons in ex vivo tissue of the thalamus from adult mice resulted in similar responses, in that whole-cell patch-clamp recordings revealed inward currents upon a single stimulus (Gornati et al., 2018) that readily elicited action-potential firing (Schäfer et al., 2021). Also, it was recently shown that upon modulation of the thalamic membrane potential (via optical stimulation of layer 6 cerebrothalamic axons), the response to optical cerebellar nuclei stimulation was modulated (Schäfer et al., 2021) (Figure 8). This dichotomous response pattern finds its origin in the activation of low-threshold T-type voltage-gated calcium channels, which are active at hyperpolarized membrane potentials but inactive at depolarized membrane potentials. Upon activation of T-type channels, thalamic neurons are prone to fire a burst of action potentials (Llinás and Jahnsen, 1982; Jahnsen and Llinás, 1984). Regardless of the membrane potential at the start of stimulation, repetitive stimulation resulted in a decreasing amplitude of the post-synaptic response (paired-pulse depression) and a decrease in spiking probability (Gornati et al., 2018; Schäfer et al., 2021), which is in accordance with previously published *in vivo* studies (Uno et al., 1970; Sawyer et al., 1994). This basic concept of driver-like synapses (large-amplitude inward currents that decrease with repetitive stimulation) fits cerebellothalamic synapses in the VL,

Caption for Figure 5 (cont.)

F. Left: Location of thalamic terminals in a double-anterograde labeling experiment in which (*right*) an injection of dextran-fluorescein (DF) was confined to the lateral nucleus and an injection of fluoro-Ruby (FR) was confined to the adjacent anterior and posterior interposed nucleus (AIP and PIP, respectively). Right: Green and red show the extent of each injection site. Green circles show the location of terminals from the lateral nucleus, and red triangles show the location of terminals from the posterior interposed nuclei. The anatomical atlas images and nomenclature adhere to the stereotaxic atlas of Paxinos and Watson (1986). Thalamic nuclei: *APT*, anterior pretectal; *AV*, anteroventral; *CL*, centrolateral; *FF*, fields of Forel; *LD*, laterodorsal; *LG*, lateral geniculate; *LP*, lateral posterior; *Nu.*, nucleus; *ml*, medial lemniscus; *PF*, parafascicular; *Po*, posterior group; *Rt*, reticular; *scp*, superior cerebellar peduncle; *VL*, ventrolateral; *VM*, ventromedial; *VPL*, ventral posterolateral; *VPM*, ventral posteromedial; *ZI*, zona incerta. Panels A–E are adapted from Aumann and Horne (1996), and panel F is adapted from Aumann et al. (1994), with permission.

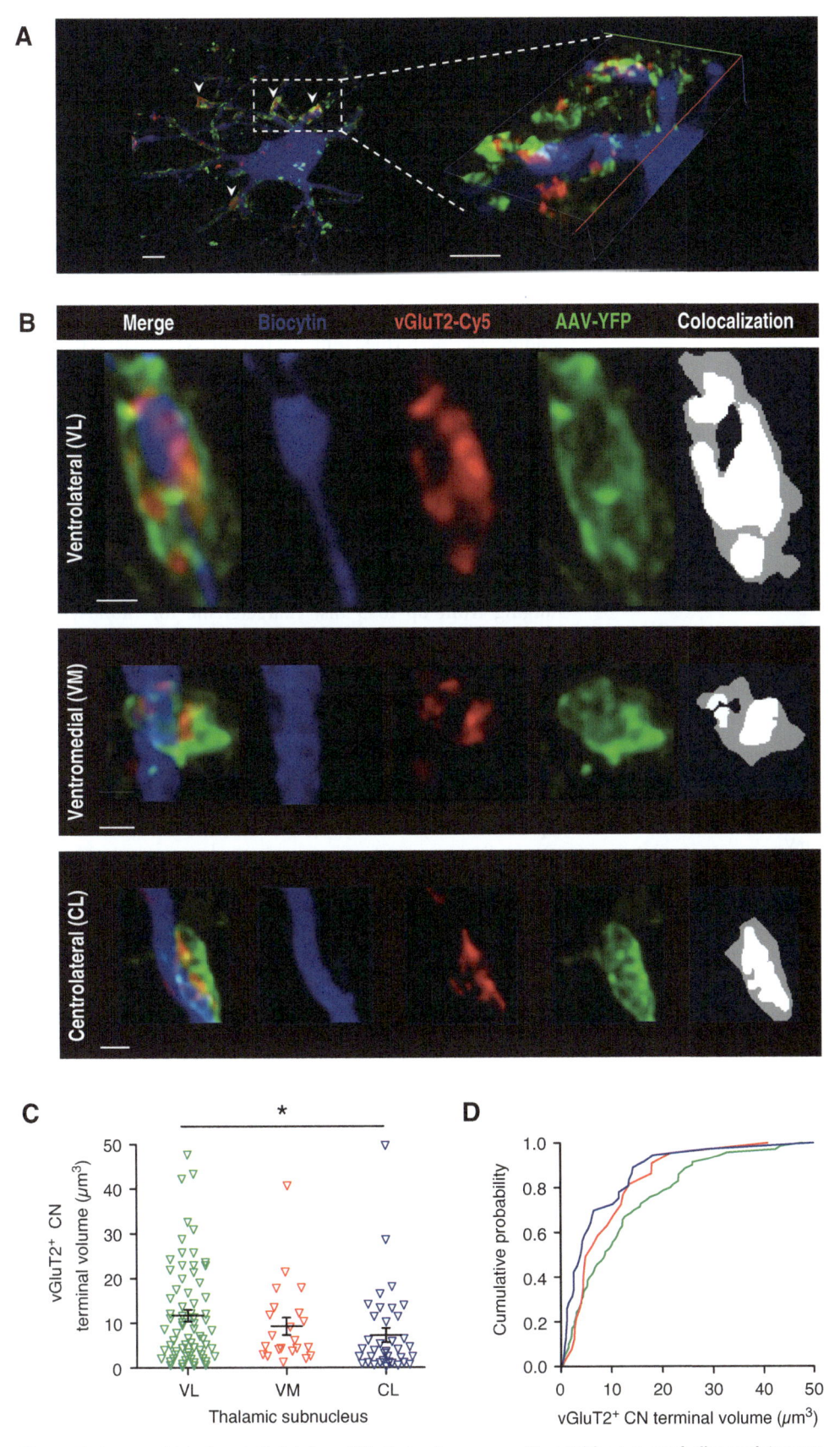

Figure 6 Immunohistochemical staining of VL thalamic neuron with neighboring cerebellar nuclei axons.

A. Two-dimensional (2D) (*left*) and three-dimensional (3D) (*right*) representation of the putative synapses between channelrhodopsin-EYFP–expressing cerebellar nuclei axons (*green*) and VL thalamic neurons. Synapses with asterisks stain positive for the vesicular glutamate transporter type 2 (*red*), which is a marker for cerebellar nuclei–thalamic synapses, and are located within 1 μm of the biocytin-stained dendrite.

B. Examples of cerebello-thalamic synapses in VL, VM, and CL nuclei.

C. Quantification of the volume of cerebellar nuclei axon terminals that stain positive for vGluT2 in VL, VM, and CL.

D. Cumulative probability of data represented in panel C. Figure is adapted from Gornati et al. (2018), with permission.

VM, and CL (Gornati et al., 2018). Surprisingly, single-pulse cerebellar nuclei stimulation did result in a highly variable postsynaptic response amplitude in VL, VM, and CL nuclei. On average, the amplitudes in VL and VM neurons were larger than those in CL neurons, which appeared in line with morphological differences in the cerebellar nuclei axon terminals reconstructed in these nuclei (Gornati et al., 2018) (Figure 6).

Thalamic Responses to Cerebellar Stimulation – Ventrolateral Responses

In the first half of the 20th century, a comprehensive range of studies was performed on the role of cerebellar activity in thalamocortical motor systems. Various investigators, such as Sherrington, Moruzzi, Snider, Dow, and Miller, stimulated specific areas of the cerebellar cortex, monitored the impact on the motor system, and recognized that the movements evoked by motor cortical stimulation could be manipulated by cerebellar stimulation (Snider and Magoun, 1949; Moruzzi et al., 1950). In several mammalian species (mouse, rat, cat, macaque), direct electrical stimulation of individual cerebellar nuclei results in thalamic responses with a variable delay, ranging from up to 5 ms, characteristic for monosynaptic connections, to up to more than 10 ms, indicating polysynaptic connections (Sakata et al., 1966; Bava et al., 1967, 1980, 1986; Condé and Angaut, 1970; Uno et al., 1970; Filion et al., 1971; Sasaki et al., 1972b, 1972a; Rispal-Padel et al., 1973; Rispal-Padel and Latreille, 1974; Shinoda et al., 1982, 1985; Jörntell and Ekerot, 1999; Proville et al., 2014).

The action-potential firing patterns of VL neurons are reported to vary between vigilance states. When the animal is at rest (i.e., not performing a particular motor task), these neurons have an average firing rate of 5–20 Hz (rat: Nakamura et al., 2014; Gaidica et al., 2018); monkey: Anderson and Turner, 1991; mouse: Eelkman Rooda et al., 2021). Electrical stimulation of cerebellar nuclei neurons, or their axons, elicits several types of responses. For instance, Bava et al. (1967) described both excitatory and inhibitory effects on VL spiking patterns in vivo after fastigial nucleus stimulation in the cat brain. Likewise, electrical brachium conjunctivum (i.e., superior cerebellar peduncle containing the cerebellothalamic tract) stimulation evoked a bimodal response in the membrane potential of VL neurons (excitatory postsynaptic potential [EPSP] followed by inhibitory postsynaptic potential [IPSP]) (Purpura et al., 1965). Also, in the mouse brain, stimulation of cerebellar nuclei neurons evokes various types of responses in the VL, the VM, and other thalamic nuclei (Eelkman Rooda et al., 2021). A possible source for these multiple response types is the innervation of thalamus-projecting inhibitory neurons in the midbrain by glutamatergic cerebellar nuclei neurons. Whether this feedforward inhibition is regulated via extrathalamic (anterior pretectal nucleus, zona incerta) or intrathalamic neurons (i.e., reticular thalamus) is unknown (Schäfer and Hoebeek, 2018).

Because the fastigial, anterior interposed, posterior interposed, and lateral nuclei all have different projection patterns

Figure 7 Extracellular recordings of cerebellar nuclei neurons in alert mice during rest and voluntary motor activity.

A. Top: Schematic of the setup, including a head-fixed mouse running on the cylindrical treadmill, with paw movement recorded with an infrared camera. The patch pipette contained an electrode wire and an optical fiber. Bottom: Side view of the ipsilateral hindlimb (*left*). A cursor (*green cross*) tracked the X and Y positions of the tip of the paw within a marked ROI (*green box*). The paw record (*right*) was captured at ~240 frames/s.

B. Sample traces of loose cell-attached recordings from a cerebellar nuclei cell in awake, head-fixed mice on a nonmotorized treadmill during periods of rest (*top*) or run (*bottom*). Paw, ipsilateral hind paw position in the x-domain; *IFR*, instantaneous firing rate; *IFR hist*, histogram of the IFR in 20-ms bins, overlaid for rest and run. Figure is adapted from Sarnaik and Raman (2018), with permission.

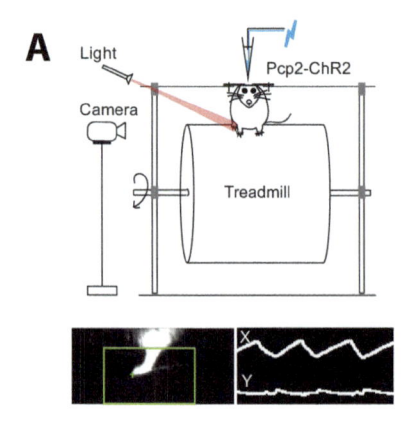

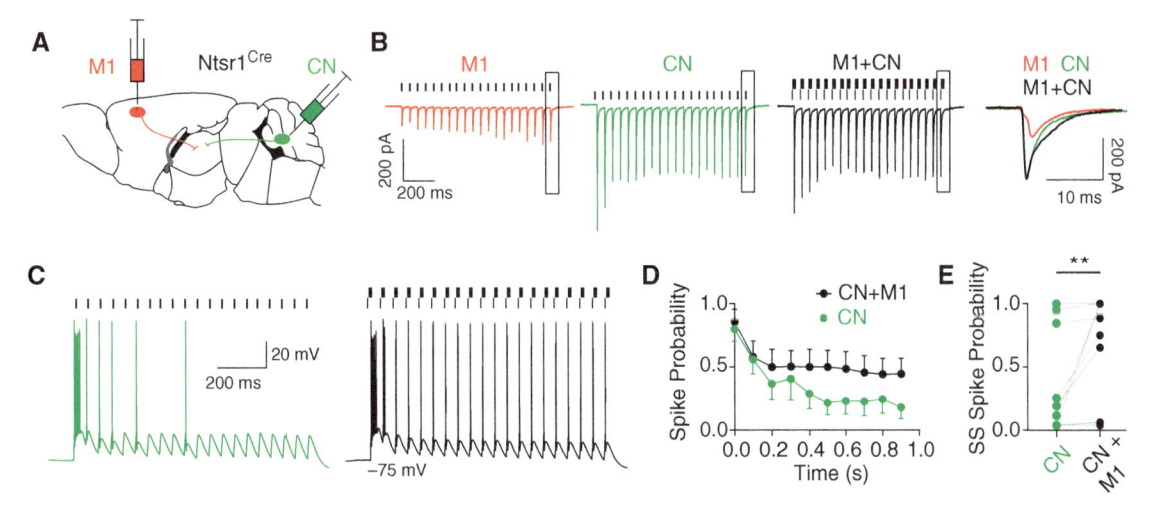

Figure 8 Schematic representation of the dual-optogenetic stimulation approach by expressing ChrimsonR-TdTomato (Chrimson) in M1–L6 and ChannelRhodopsin2-EYFP (ChR2) in the CN in *Ntsr1-Cre* transgenic mice.

A. Schematic representation of experimental setup for panels B–E. In Ntsr1-Cre mice, AAV particles encoding Cre-dependent Chrimson expression are injected into M1, and AAV particles encoding Chr2 expression are injected into the CN.

B. In VL cells that are recorded in whole-cell voltage-clamp mode and are innervated by both Chrimson -expressing M1–L6 axons (M1; *red*) and ChR2- expressing cerebellar nuclei axons (CN; *green*), 15-ms-long light pulses at 585 nm evoked excitatory postsynaptic currents (EPSCs) with increasing amplitude and 1-ms-long light pulses at 460 nm evoked EPSCs with decreasing amplitude. The inset illustrates the accumulation of both currents in the charge of the compound responses.

C. Example traces of current-clamp recordings illustrating that costimulation of motor cortical afferents using 15-ms-long light pulses at 585 nm can shift the cerebellar nuclei evoked responses to 1-ms-long light pulses at 460 nm of VL cells from nonspiking to spiking.

D and E. The spike probability is quantified in the average spike probability per stimulus (D), as well as in the average steady-state (ss) spike probability per cell and stimulus condition (E). Error bars in D represent the standard error of the mean. Figure is adapted from Schäfer et al. (2021), with permission.

to medullary, mesencephalic, and diencephalic structures (e.g., in the rat: Teune et al., 2000), the feedforward inhibition (or excitation) may be specific for each cerebellar nuclei-thalamic connection. Indeed, single thalamic neurons that receive monosynaptic input from various cerebellar nuclei show various response types to stimulation in the various cerebellar nuclei (Shinoda et al., 1982; Bava et al., 1986; Rispal-Padel et al., 1987). In addition to several cerebellar nuclei inputs that may evoke various types of responses in thalamic neurons, motor thalamus neurons could also receive converging cerebellar and pallidal input. Even though these two subcortical afferents do not synapse onto single neurons in the VA or VL in the cat, monkey, and rat (Hendry et al., 1979; Tracey et al., 1980; Yamamoto et al., 1983, 1984), they converge within the motor cortex. Via the corticothalamic feedback from L5 collaterals and/or L6 axons, input from the basal ganglia could, in principle, still mediate the thalamic responses to cerebellar nuclei stimulation (Bosch-Bouju et al., 2013).

Thalamic Responses to Cerebellar Stimulation – Ventromedial Responses

Much like the VL neurons, VM neurons are also known to show initial excitatory responses to cerebellar nuclei stimulation that increase the VM firing rate and are typically followed by a period of quiescence (e.g., MacLeod and James, 1984). Whereas in the VA/VL of rats and mice there is hardly any overlap between pallidal and cerebellar projections, in the VM, that is different for rodents. In rats, and quite possibly also in dogs and mice, but not cats and primates, it has been shown that inhibitory neurons in the substantia nigra pars reticulata synapse onto VM neurons that also receive cerebellar nuclei excitatory inputs (Chevalier and Deniau, 1982; Ueki, 1983; Yamamoto et al., 1984; Gao et al., 2018; Hintzen et al., 2018). The cerebellar axons that innervate the VM in rats were characterized as thin axon collaterals that form *en passant* terminals (Deniau et al., 1992). In the mouse brain, the axons from all cerebellar nuclei were found to be no different from those in the VL when compared by terminal volume or synaptic components (Figure 6) (Gao et al., 2018; Gornati et al., 2018). How the VM spiking patterns may be co-modulated (differentially) by these different cerebellar nuclei inputs, pallidal inputs, and possibly other afferents remains to be elucidated.

Thalamic Responses to Cerebellar Stimulation – Centrolateral and Centromedian Nuclei

Neurons in the CL thalamus, which project to various cortical regions and layers (Wang and Shyu, 2004) and to the striatum (Castle et al., 2005; Doig et al., 2010), receive cerebellar input. Chemically lesioning the lateral cerebellar nuclei neurons that project to CL neurons in mice results in diminished control of motor skills, including motor coordination and forelimb reaching, but not spatial recognition and its flexibility – two other behaviors related to the CL thalamus (Sakayori et al., 2019). Optical stimulation of lateral cerebellar nuclei axons in the CL resulted in short-latency responses in the striatum whereby a portion of striatal neurons showed an increased firing rate and others showed a decreased response (Chen et al., 2014). This variability of the responses may be due to the converging input that the CL receives from the primary and secondary motor cortices, as well as from the substantia nigra pars reticulate. In addition, CL neurons also receive input from the mesencephalic reticular formation, thus also relating the CL spiking pattern to cortical oscillatory activity and behavioral arousal states (Glenn and Steriade, 1982; Steriade et al., 1991, 1993), which in theory could also manipulate the CL responses to cerebellar nuclei stimulation.

The more medially located CM nucleus, which in rodents is considered to be part of a complex with the parafascicular nucleus (CM-PF), is part of thalamo-striatal and thalamocortical networks that modulate arousal, consciousness levels, and nociception (Ilyas et al., 2019). Matsumoto et al. (2001) revealed that CM neurons encode information about the onset of sensory stimuli of various modalities. Notably, CM neurons were activated by auditory or visual stimuli that attracted the attention of the animals (Matsumoto et al., 2001; Minamimoto and Kimura, 2002). With an average baseline firing rate of approximately 5 Hz, there is ample dynamic range available in the firing frequency of CM neurons to rapidly increase (Matsumoto et al., 2001). To our knowledge, no studies have been published on the neural spiking patterns of CM thalamic neurons after cerebellar nuclei stimulation.

Synopsis and Future Perspective on Cerebellar Impact on Thalamic Activity

Cerebellar output is essential for the proper planning and timing of motor behavior. Already prior to the onset of movement, the average firing rate of both cerebellar nuclei and VL neurons increases. Two recent investigations revealed that these cerebellar and thalamic peaks in spiking are related to the accurate planning and execution of the movement. When action-potential firing is blocked in the medial cerebellar nuclei during the waiting time after a sensory cue has been given, mice have reduced performance on a delayed licking task (Gao et al., 2018). When the spiking of VL neurons is blocked, mice fail to start a goal-directed movement (Dacre et al., 2021). These findings indicate that both cerebellar and thalamic spiking patterns encode the preparatory activity that is required to correctly plan, time, and perform movements, aligning with the overall motor behavior impairments evoked by cerebellar and motor thalamic lesions (see next sections of this chapter).

To exert this function, it is imperative to transfer information to the motor thalamus and cortex with millisecond precision. Thus, the spiking pattern of cerebellar nuclei neurons is controlled by their synaptic inputs, of which the inhibitory Purkinje cells are thought to play a predominant role. The converging Purkinje cell input (in mice: ratio of ~30 Purkinje cells to 1 cerebellar nuclei neuron in the lateral nucleus; Person and Raman, 2011) can evoke a pause in cerebellar nuclei spiking patterns when Purkinje cell synchronicity is increased, for instance, by climbing fiber activity (Bell and Kawasaki, 1972; Llinás and Sasaki, 1989; Lang et al., 2006; Ozden et al., 2012). When such a pause occurs, this potentially has a profound effect on cerebellothalamic synaptic transmission, in that the paired-pulse depression evoked by the high-frequency cerebellar nuclei spiking pattern is likely to decrease. Thus, following a pause in cerebellar nuclei spiking, thalamic neurons are likely to show an increased probability of action-potential firing, which, in the case of an increased inhibitory tonus onto motor thalamic neurons, could elicit bursts of action potentials (Sawyer et al., 1994; Schäfer et al., 2021). Such thalamic spiking activity might have a profound impact on thalamocortical network activity and "drive movement" or "initiate movement" via the cortico-spinal tract (Marlinski et al., 2011; Gaidica et al., 2018; Beloozerova and Marlinski, 2020; Dacre et al., 2021).

Motor learning has been shown to be mediated by cerebellar neurons. Purkinje cells and cerebellar nuclei neurons have both been shown to undergo synaptic plasticity upon repetitive stimulation of their afferents (De Zeeuw et al., 2011). Such changes have been translated into altered cerebellar nuclei activity during and after the induction of motor tasks like Pavlovian eye-blink conditioning (Ten Brinke et al., 2017; Wang et al., 2018). After the acquisition of conditioned responses, cerebellar nuclei spiking patterns indeed revealed an increased occurrence of pauses in action-potential firing, which in principle could evoke a reduction of paired-pulse depression at cerebellothalamic synapses. Recordings in the motor thalamus during the acquisition of motor learning have not been performed yet but might show that the synchronicity between cerebellar nuclei and thalamic spiking patterns is increased during and after learning occurs.

Novel insights into the correlation between motor thalamus activity and premotor and motor cortex activity reveal another means by which the cerebellar output can affect thalamocortical motor networks. Nashef et al. (2021) showed that the synchronicity level between VL thalamus spiking patterns and those in the primary motor and premotor regions could be opposite and even change upon a switch between preparation for and performing a movement. We speculate that a synchronous burst in cerebellar nuclei firing could switch the preparatory activity (mediated by medial cerebellar nuclei neurons that project to the VM) to spiking patterns that encode motor performance. Such a dichotomous function was also mentioned by Dominique Purpura, who in 1966 wrote in his book *The Thalamus* (p. 169) that "generalized synchronization and desynchronization of thalamocortical activity play an important role in regulating transmission in the cerebellothalamocortical pathway through VL." Thus, the cerebellar output may have various faces in the thalamocortical network: a clock that informs thalamocortical networks about time-sensitive information and a modulator that contributes to the interpretation of ongoing processes and helps to prepare planned actions ahead.

Pathology

The cerebellum plays an important role in various neurological disorders that affect motor, cognitive, and social functioning. For instance, irregularity of cerebellar spiking patterns leads to ataxia and/or tremor (Hoebeek et al., 2005; Walter et al., 2006;

Brown et al., 2020), cerebellar-specific knockout mutations of P/Q-type voltage-gated calcium channels resulted in generalized absence seizures (Mark et al., 2011; Maejima et al., 2013), and cerebellar-specific knockout mutations of tuberous sclerosis type 1 (TSC1) induced autism-like impairments in social behavior and increased repetitive behavior (Tsai et al., 2012). Without the intention of providing an all-encompassing review of clinical symptoms related to impaired cerebellothalamic functioning, the remainder of this chapter aims to incorporate data from the previous sections to interpret the dysfunction of the cerebellothalamic network and, ultimately, guide future studies into the potential therapeutic value of manipulating cerebellothalamic network activity.

Movement Disorders with Tremors

Tremors are defined as rhythmic oscillatory movements of a body part. These uncontrollable movements characterize various disorders, such as dystonia, ataxia, essential tremor (ET), and Parkinson's disease (PD). The cerebellothalamocortical tract has a central role in tremor frequency and amplitude (Passamonti et al., 2011; Muthuraman et al., 2018). In patients with ET, the local field potentials recorded in the ventral intermediate thalamus (Vim) (also known as the *posterior part of the ventrolateral [VLp] nucleus*) are coherent with sensorimotor cortical electroencephalogram (EEG) and muscle contractions at 4–6 Hz (Pedrosa et al., 2014) and at 8–27 Hz (Marsden et al., 2000). Cerebellar high-density EEG recordings pinpointed the interposed cerebellar nuclei (globosus and emboliformus) as part of the cerebellothalamocortical tract involved in the oscillatory activity (Muthuraman et al., 2018). The prime thalamic target of interposed cerebellar nuclei axons is the VLp thalamus. Indeed, electrical stimulation of the VLp nucleus in patients with ET and PD has been shown effective in dampening tremors, with efficacies of up to 48% and 63% at 10 years after the start of stimulation (Cury et al., 2017). These data indicate that electrical stimulation of the cerebellothalamic tract at the level of the thalamus can modulate tremors in patients with ET and PD.

Direct stimulation of the cerebellum with transcranial magnetic stimulation (TMS) and transcranial direct current stimulation (tDCS) has been, until now, less efficient in dampening tremors (França et al., 2018) than the direct stimulation of the cerebellothalamic tract. This could be explained by (1) the small diameter of the cerebellar cortical foliation, which currently limits the spatial accuracy of positioning the TMS and tDCS stimulation, and (2) the orientation in parasagittal stripes of Purkinje cells (Figure 1). Therefore, it is unlikely that cerebellar cortical stimulation with TMS and tDCS, which evoke neuronal modulation in spheroid volumes, will be sufficient to effectively control the interposed cerebellar nuclei activity and thereby dampen tremor-related oscillatory activity in the cerebellothalamic tract.

The most effective type of stimulation will allow effective control over the spiking pattern of cerebellar nuclei neurons. Using experimental procedures like optogenetics, this can be performed reliably and with millisecond precision using either direct cerebellar nuclei activation or Purkinje cell stimulation (Miterko et al., 2019). To investigate the cerebellar contribution to the harmaline-induced tremor (Ahmed and Taylor, 1959; Llinás and Volkind, 1973), the lab of Sillitoe recently used optogenetic stimulation and showed that the rhythmic firing of Purkinje cells (and thus cerebellar nuclei neurons) is both necessary and sufficient to induce tremor (Brown et al., 2020). Further studies are needed to elucidate the role of the cerebellothalamic tract in such tremors.

Autism Spectrum Disorder

Findings from several groups are pointing toward the cerebellum as a key player in autism-spectrum disorder (ASD) pathogenesis. MRI studies in patients with ASD found the cerebellum to be one of the most frequently disrupted brain regions, and studies on postmortem brain tissue from patients with ASD have revealed substantial olivo-cerebellar degeneration (Palmen et al., 2004; Courchesne et al., 2005). ASD is associated with reductions in gray-matter volume in right Crus 1, left lobule VIII, and medial IX, as well as reduced functional connectivity between right Crus 1 and left-hemisphere language regions (Stoodley, 2012, 2014; Stoodley et al., 2012; Stoodley and Limperopoulos, 2016; Kelly et al., 2020), suggesting that the altered cerebellar morphology affects the cerebellothalamocortical circuit.

Direct causal evidence for a cerebellar role in ASD pathogenesis is sparse. It is known that a cerebellar insult during adulthood results in symptoms in both the motor and cognitive domains but does not lead to ASD, although adult lesions in the posterior cerebellum can lead to a cerebellar cognitive-affective syndrome. Cerebellar damage around birth, instead, shows a positive correlation with ASD (Hashimoto et al., 1995; Beversdorf et al., 2005; Limperopoulos et al., 2007, 2014; Stoodley and Limperopoulos, 2016; Hortensius et al., 2018; Kelly et al., 2020). Limperopoulos et al. (2007) reported that early-life cerebellar damage, often a cerebellar hemorrhage – a common complication of preterm birth – is associated with a 40-fold increase in ASD risk. A mechanistic explanation for this finding has been formulated by the "developmental diaschisis" hypothesis, which basically states that the cerebellum may act as a developmental guide of forebrain circuit maturation (Wang et al., 2014; Badura et al., 2018). Two lines of evidence support this hypothesis. First, interconnected cerebral and cerebellar structures show correlative impairments. The dorsolateral prefrontal cortex and Crus 1 in the cerebellar cortex both show gray-matter damage in patients with ASD, as well as impaired functional connectivity in functional magnetic resonance imaging (fMRI) studies (Limperopoulos et al., 2014; Stoodley et al., 2017). In addition, inactivation of (right) Crus 1, which has strong projections to prefrontal regions, is sufficient to cause ASD symptoms in mice (Stoodley et al., 2017; Kelly et al., 2020). Second, ASD in both human and mouse models (*Tsc1, MECP2, 15q11-13, dFraX*) has been repeatedly associated with reduced spine pruning in the cerebral cortex, leading to higher spine densities during adulthood (Galvez and Greenough, 2005; Hutsler and Zhang, 2010; Tang et al., 2014; Wang et al., 2017). Among a long list of genetic and environmental causes, these pruning deficits can also be a result of cerebellar dysfunction. Future experiments aimed at quantifying the thalamic and cortical dendritic spine densities in mice with ASD-like phenotypes and cerebellum-specific deficiencies should provide results that can test this hypothesis.

Epilepsy

During generalized seizures, neural activity in the cerebellum, thalamus, and cortex shows repetitive, synchronous action-potential firing and pausing, which can be recorded as generalized spike-and-wave discharges (GSWDs) in the electroencephalogram or electrocorticogram. Whereas the bulk of neuroscience research in the pathophysiology of epilepsy focused on the thalamus and cortex, the cerebellum was associated with epileptic seizures as early as 1691. The German medical doctor Johann Paul Wurffbain (1655–1711) described a case of a 2-year-old child with "symptoms being identical with that of the type of convulsion traditionally styled opisthotony," who appeared to have a cerebellar tumor (Fulton, 1929, p. 577). Almost two centuries later, the English neurologist John Hughlings Jackson (1835–1911) described another case of "cerebellar epilepsy" in a 5-year-old child who suffered from "tetanus-like" seizures and appeared to have a tubercular abscess in the cerebellar vermis (Jackson, 1871, 1906).

After these initial reports, several other studies showed that cerebellar tumors can indeed cause epileptic seizures and that surgical dissection of these tumors often abolished seizures (for review: McCrory et al., 1999; Streng and Krook-Magnuson, 2020). It is still unknown whether it is the pathophysiological cerebellar activity itself that causes the epileptic seizures or whether the epilepsy is a result of increased intracranial pressure or brainstem compression caused by the cerebellar tumor. Other lines of evidence supporting cerebellar involvement in epilepsy come from morphological and electrophysiological studies. Epilepsy is often associated with cerebellar atrophy, and this atrophy shows a positive correlation with the number and intensity of seizures (Crooks et al., 2000). Indeed, dampening the cerebellar output increased the occurrence of GSWDs in epileptic *tottering* mice (Kros et al., 2015). These results align with the induction of GSWDs by cerebellar-specific deletion of the *Cacna1a* gene (Mark et al., 2011; Maejima et al., 2013).

Electrophysiological recordings show that the GSWDs are not "restricted" to the cerebral cortex and thalamus but that there is also strong oscillatory activity in the cerebellum during seizures. Based on these observations, the cerebellum was appreciated as a candidate site for the intervention and treatment of epilepsy, and several attempts were undertaken to modulate cerebellar cortical activity in order to stop GSWDs. Although some animal studies that used surface electrodes for electrical stimulation had very promising results, generally speaking, the effects were too inconsistent to consider it as a therapeutic tool (Graber and Fisher, 2012). It appeared that the anti-epileptic effects of cerebellar stimulation depended on the precise location and stimulation conditions, as well as the type and severity of seizures involved. Instead, electrical stimulation of the dentate nucleus was consistently reported to be highly effective in dampening the occurrence of various types of seizures in patients with epilepsy (Šramka and Chkhenkeli, 1990; Chkhenkeli et al., 2004).

Various recent animal studies revisited the efficacy of cerebellar stimulation to stop GSWDs. In epileptic *tottering* and *C3 H/HeOuJ* mice, single-pulse stimulation of the interposed nucleus appeared to reliably stop GSWDs (Kros et al., 2015). Likewise, also in a mouse model of spontaneous temporal lobe epilepsy, optogenetic stimulation of the midline cerebellum reduced the occurrence of seizures (Krook-Magnuson et al., 2014). It remains to be investigated which cerebellar nucleus is the best target for direct electrical stimulation as a treatment for epilepsy. Given that neuronavigation during brain surgery will become more accurate, the anti-epileptic potency and the reliability of cerebellothalamic tract stimulation may increase.

Closing Remarks

Investigating the cellular aspects important for the integration of the cerebellar output with thalamocortical networks requires tools to selectively modulate the activity of cerebellar nuclei neurons. Over the past years, several approaches have been applied that allow the quantification of the cerebellar impact on thalamic spiking patterns and investigate its role in various types of (motor) behavior. One particularly exciting research line is to compare how the impact of aberrant cerebellar output affects thalamocortical functions in the motor, cognitive, and social domains, as is seen in patients with ET and PD (Puertas-Martín et al., 2016). Many of these studies will also benefit from a more detailed view of the maturation of the cerebellothalamic tract, a research topic that, although being very popular as a topic to discuss in light of developmental disorders like ASD, is only marginally studied at the moment. We foresee that the study of synaptic and nonsynaptic forms of plasticity of the developing cerebellothalamic tracts will be of particular interest. The pioneering work by Aumann et al. (2000) has already indicated how long-term potentiation can be induced at cerebellothalamic synapses in the motor thalamus. Future experiments need to unravel which developmental periods are particularly sensitive for the maturing cerebellothalamic tract.

References

Aeby A, Liu Y, De Tiège X, Denolin V, David P, Balériaux D, Kavec M, Metens T, Van Bogaert P (2009) Maturation of thalamic radiations between 34 and 41 weeks' gestation: a combined voxel-based study and probabilistic tractography with diffusion tensor imaging. AJNR Am J Neuroradiol **30**:1780–1786.

Ahmed A, Taylor NRW (1959) The analysis of drug-induced tremor in mice. Brit J Pharmacol Chemother **14**:350–354. Available at: https://bpspubs.onlinelibrary.wiley.com/doi/abs/10.1111/j.1476-5381.1959.tb00255.x [Accessed March 8, 2021].

Alcauter S, Lin W, Smith JK, Short SJ, Goldman BD, Reznick JS, Gilmore JH, Gao W (2014) Development of thalamocortical connectivity during infancy and its cognitive correlations. J Neurosci

34:9067–9075. Available at: https://www.ncbi.nlm.nih.gov/pmc/articles/PMC4078084/ [Accessed March 6, 2021].

Altman J, Bayer SA (1997) Development of the Cerebellar System: In Relation to Its Evolution, Structure, and Functions. Boca Raton, FL: CRC Press. Available at: https://books.google.com/books?id=WN1qAAAAMAAJ.

Anderson ME, Turner RS (1991) Activity of neurons in cerebellar-receiving and pallidal-receiving areas of the thalamus of the behaving monkey. J Neuorphysiol 66: 879–893.

Angaut P, Cicirata F (1990) Dentate control pathways of cortical motor activity. Anatomical and physiological studies in rat: comparative considerations. Arch Ital Biol 128:315–330.

Angaut P, Cicirata F, Serapide F (1985) Topographic organization of the cerebellothalamic projections in the rat. An autoradiographic study. Neuroscience 15:389–401.

Antziferova LI, Arshavsky YuI, Orlovsky GN, Pavlova GA (1980) Activity of neurons of cerebellar nuclei during fictitious scratch reflex in the cat. I. Fastigial nucleus. Brain Res 200:239–248. Available at: https://www.sciencedirect.com/science/article/pii/0006899380909166 [Accessed March 4, 2021].

Aoki S, Smith JB, Li H, Yan X, Igarashi M, Coulon P, Wickens JR, Ruigrok TJ, Jin X (2019) An open cortico-basal ganglia loop allows limbic control over motor output via the nigrothalamic pathway. eLife 8:e49995.

Armstrong DM, Edgley SA (1984) Discharges of nucleus interpositus neurones during locomotion in the cat. J Physiol 351:411–432.

Asanuma C, Ohkawa R, Stanfield BB, Cowan WM (1988) Observations on the development of certain ascending inputs to the thalamus in rats. I. Postnatal development. Brain Res 469:159–170.

Auladell C, Pérez-Sust P, Supèr H, Soriano E (2000) The early development of thalamocortical and corticothalamic projections in the mouse. Anat Embryol (Berl) 201:169–179.

Aumann TD, Horne MK (1996) Ramification and termination of single axons in the cerebellothalamic pathway of the rat. J Comp Neurol 376:420–430.

Aumann TD, Rawson JA, Finkelstein DI, Horne MK (1994) Projections from the lateral and interposed cerebellar nuclei to the thalamus of the rat: a light and electron microscopic study using single and double anterograde labelling. J Comp Neurol 349:165–181.

Aumann TD, Redman SJ, Horne MK (2000) Long-term potentiation across rat cerebello-thalamic synapses in vitro. Neurosci Lett 287:151–155.

Badura, A. et al. Normal cognitive and social development require posterior cerebellar activity. eLife 7, doi:10.7554/eLife.36401 (2018), PMC6195348.

Bava A, Cicirata F, Giuffrida R, Licciardello S, Panto MR (1986) Electrophysiologic properties and nature of ventrolateral thalamic nucleus neurons reactive to converging inputs of paleo- and neocerebellar origin. Exp Neur 91:1–12.

Bava A, Cicirata F, Licciardello S, Pantò MR (1980) [Organization of corticothalamic projections, arising from the sensorimotor cerebral areas, on neurons belonging to the diencephalic relay-nucleus of cerebello-cerebral pathway (n. ventralis lateralis, VL): an electrophysiological study]. Boll Soc Ital Biol Sper 56:1708–1714.

Bava A, Fadiga E, Manzoni T (1967) Lemniscal afferents and extracallosal mechanisms for interhemispheric transmission of somato-sensory evoked potentials. Electroencephalogr Clin Neurophysiol: Suppl 26:182–187.

Bell CC, Kawasaki T (1972) Relations among climbing fiber responses of nearby Purkinje cells. J Neurophysiol 35:155–169. Available at: https://journals.physiology.org/doi/abs/10.1152/jn.1972.35.2.155 [Accessed March 4, 2021].

Beloozerova IN, Marlinski V (2020) Contribution of the ventrolateral thalamus to the locomotion-related activity of motor cortex. J Neurophysiol 124:1480–1504.

Beversdorf DQ, Manning SE, Hillier A, Anderson SL, Nordgren RE, Walters SE, Nagaraja HN, Cooley WC, Gaelic SE, Bauman ML (2005) Timing of prenatal stressors and autism. J Autism Dev Disord 35:471–478.

Blackshaw S, Scholpp S, Placzek M, Ingraham H, Simerly R, Shimogori T (2010) Molecular pathways controlling development of thalamus and hypothalamus: from neural specification to circuit formation. J Neurosci 30:14925–14930. Available at: https://www.jneurosci.org/content/30/45/14925 [Accessed September 21, 2021].

Bodor AL, Giber K, Rovó Z, Ulbert I, Acsády L (2008) Structural correlates of efficient GABAergic transmission in the basal ganglia-thalamus pathway. J Neurosci 28:3090–3102.

Bohne P, Schwarz MK, Herlitze S, Mark MD (2019) A new projection from the deep cerebellar nuclei to the hippocampus via the ventrolateral and laterodorsal thalamus in mice. Front Neural Circuits 13:51.

Bosch-Bouju C, Hyland BI, Parr-Brownlie LC (2013) Motor thalamus integration of cortical, cerebellar and basal ganglia information: implications for normal and parkinsonian conditions. Front Comput Neurosci 7. Available at: https://www.frontiersin.org/articles/10.3389/fncom.2013.00163/full [Accessed March 4, 2021].

Brooks VB, Thach WT (1981). Cerebellar control of posture and movement. In: Handbook of Physiology, sec. I, vol. 2, part 2 (Brooks VB, eds), pp 877–946. Rockville, MD: American Physiological Society.

Brown AM, White JJ, van der Heijden ME, Zhou J, Lin T, Sillitoe RV (2020) Purkinje cell misfiring generates high-amplitude action tremors that are corrected by cerebellar deep brain stimulation. eLife 9: e51928.

Buee J, Deniau JM, Chevalier G (1986) Nigral modulation of cerebello-thalamo-cortical transmission in the ventral medial thalamic nucleus. Exp Brain Res 65:241–244.

Canto CB, Onuki Y, Bruinsma B, Werf YD, van der, Zeeuw CID (2017) The sleeping cerebellum. Trends Neurosci 40:309–323. Available at: https://www.cell.com/trends/neurosciences/abstract/S0166-2236(17)30030-9 [Accessed March 4, 2021].

Canto CB, Witter L, De Zeeuw CI (2016) Whole-cell properties of cerebellar nuclei neurons in vivo. PloS One 11:e0165887.

Castle M, Aymerich MS, Sanchez-Escobar C, Gonzalo N, Obeso JA, Lanciego JL (2005) Thalamic innervation of the direct and indirect basal ganglia pathways in the rat: ipsi- and contralateral projections. J Comp Neurol 483:143–153. Available at: https://onlinelibrary.wiley.com/doi/abs/10.1002/cne.20421 [Accessed March 3, 2021].

Chen CH, Fremont R, Arteaga-Bracho EE, Khodakhah K (2014) Short latency cerebellar modulation of the basal ganglia. Nat Neurosci 17:1767–1775.

Chevalier G, Deniau JM (1982) Inhibitory nigral influence on cerebellar evoked responses in the rat ventromedial thalamic nucleus. Exp Brain Res 48:369–376.

Chkhenkeli SA, Sramka M, Lortkipanidze GS, Rakviashvili TN, Bregvadze ES, Magalashvili GE, Gagoshidze TS, Chkhenkeli IS (2004) Electrophysiological effects and clinical results of direct brain stimulation for intractable epilepsy. Clin Neurol Neurosurg 106:318–329.

Cicirata F, Angaut P, Cioni M, Serapide MF, Papale A (1986) Functional organization of thalamic projections to the motor cortex. An anatomical and electrophysiological study in the rat. Neuroscience **19**:81–99.

Condé H, Angaut P (1970) An electrophysiological study of the cerebellar projections to the nucleus ventralis lateralis thalami in the cat. 2. Nucleus lateralis. Brain Res **20**:107–119.

Courchesne E, Redday E, Morgan JT, Kennedy DP (2005) Autism at the beginning: microstructural and growth abnormalities underlying the cognitive and behavioral phenotype of autism. Dev Psychopathol **17**:577–597.

Crooks R, Mitchell T, Thom M (2000) Patterns of cerebellar atrophy in patients with chronic epilepsy: a quantitative neuropathological study. Epilepsy Res **41**:63–73.

Cury RG, Fraix V, Castrioto A, Fernández MAP, Krack P, Chabardes S, Seigneuret E, Alho EJL, Benabid A-L, Moro E (2017) Thalamic deep brain stimulation for tremor in Parkinson disease, essential tremor, and dystonia. Neurology **89**:1416–1423. Available at: https://n.neurology.org/content/89/13/1416 [Accessed March 5, 2021].

Dacre J, Colligan M, Clarke T, Ammer JJ, Schiemann J, Chamosa-Pino V, Claudi F, Harston JA, Eleftheriou C, Pakan JMP, Huang C-C, Hantman AW, Rochefort NL, Duguid I (2021) A cerebellar-thalamocortical pathway drives behavioral context-dependent movement initiation. Neuron **109**:2326–2338.e8. Available at: https://linkinghub.elsevier.com/retrieve/pii/S0896627321003561 [Accessed September 22, 2021].

De Zeeuw CI, Hoebeek FE, Bosman LW, Schonewille M, Witter L, Koekkoek SK (2011) Spatiotemporal firing patterns in the cerebellum. Nat Rev Neurosci **12**:327–344.

Del Rio-Bermudez C, Plumeau AM, Sattler NJ, Sokoloff G, Blumberg MS (2016) Spontaneous activity and functional connectivity in the developing cerebellorubral system. J Neurophysiol **116**:1316–1327.

Deniau JM, Kita H, Kitai ST (1992) Patterns of termination of cerebellar and basal ganglia efferents in the rat thalamus. Strictly segregated and partly overlapping projections. Neurosci Lett **144**:202–206.

Deschênes M, Bourassa J, Parent A (1996) Striatal and cortical projections of single neurons from the central lateral thalamic nucleus in the rat. Neuroscience **72**:679–687.

Diedrichsen J, Maderwald S, Küper M, Thürling M, Rabe K, Gizewski ER, Ladd ME, Timmann D (2011) Imaging the deep cerebellar nuclei: a probabilistic atlas and normalization procedure. NeuroImage **54**:1786–1794. Available at: http://www.sciencedirect.com/science/article/pii/S1053811910013273 [Accessed October 30, 2020].

Dimitrova A, Zeljko D, Schwarze F, Maschke M, Gerwig M, Frings M, Beck A, Aurich V, Forsting M, Timmann D (2006) Probabilistic 3D MRI atlas of the human cerebellar dentate/interposed nuclei. NeuroImage **30**:12–25.

Doig NM, Moss J, Bolam JP (2010) Cortical and thalamic innervation of direct and indirect pathway medium-sized spiny neurons in mouse striatum. J Neurosci **30**:14610–14618. Available at: https://www.jneurosci.org/content/30/44/14610 [Accessed March 3, 2021].

Dum RP, Strick PL (2003) An unfolded map of the cerebellar dentate nucleus and its projections to the cerebral cortex. J Neurophysiol **89**:634–639. Available at: https://journals.physiology.org/doi/full/10.1152/jn.00626.2002 [Accessed October 31, 2020].

Dumas DB, Gornati SV, Adolfs Y, Shimogori T, Pasterkamp RJ, Hoebeek FE (2019) Anatomical development of the cerebellothalamic tract in embryonic mice. bioRxiv: 731968. Available at: https://www.biorxiv.org/content/10.1101/731968v1 [Accessed October 5, 2020].

Eelkman Rooda OHJ, Kros L, Faneyte SJ, Holland PJ, Gornati SV, Poelman HJ, Jansen NA, Tolner EA, van den Maagdenberg AMJM, De Zeeuw CI, Hoebeek FE (2021) Single-pulse stimulation of cerebellar nuclei stops epileptic thalamic activity. Brain Stimul **14**:861–872. Available at: https://linkinghub.elsevier.com/retrieve/pii/S1935861X21001005 [Accessed July 14, 2021].

Elsen GE, Juric-Sekhar G, Daza RAM, Hevner RF (2013) Development of cerebellar nuclei. In: Handbook of the Cerebellum and Cerebellar Disorders (Manto M, Schmahmann JD, Rossi F, Gruol DL, Koibuchi N, eds), pp 179–205. Dordrecht: Springer Netherlands. Available at: https://doi.org/10.1007/978-94-007-1333-8_10 [Accessed October 29, 2020].

Elvsåshagen T, Shadrin A, Frei O, van der Meer D, Bahrami S, Kumar VJ, Smeland O, Westlye LT, Andreassen OA, Kaufmann T (2021) The genetic architecture of the human thalamus and its overlap with ten common brain disorders. Nat Commun **12**:2909. Available at: https://www.nature.com/articles/s41467-021-23175-z [Accessed September 21, 2021].

Ernst TM, Thürling M, Müller S, Kahl F, Maderwald S, Schlamann M, Boele H-J, Koekkoek SKE, Diedrichsen J, De Zeeuw CI, Ladd ME, Timmann D (2017) Modulation of 7 T fMRI signal in the cerebellar cortex and nuclei during acquisition, extinction, and reacquisition of conditioned eyeblink responses. Hum Brain Mapp **38**:3957–3974.

Evarts EV, Thach WT (1969) Motor mechanisms of the CNS: cerebrocerebellar interrelations. Annu Rev Physiol **31**:451–498.

Filion M, Lamarre Y, Cordeau JP (1971) Neuronal discharges of the ventrolateral nucleus of the thalamus during sleep and wakefulness in the cat. II. Evoked activity. Exp Brain Res **12**:499–508.

Fink AJ, Englund C, Daza RAM, Pham D, Lau C, Nivison M, Kowalczyk T, Hevner RF (2006) Development of the deep cerebellar nuclei: transcription factors and cell migration from the rhombic lip. J Neurosci **26**:3066–3076. Available at: https://www.ncbi.nlm.nih.gov/pmc/articles/PMC6673970/ [Accessed October 30, 2020].

França C, Ciampide Andrade D, Jacobsen Teixeira M, Galhardoni R, Silva V, Reis Barbosa E, Gisbert Cury R. (2018) Effects of cerebellar neuromodulation in movement disorders: a systematic review. Brain Stimul **11**: 249–260.

Fujita, H., Kodama, T. & du Lac, S. Modular output circuits of the fastigial nucleus for diverse motor and nonmotor functions of the cerebellar vermis. *eLife* **9**, doi:10.7554/eLife.58613 (2020), PMC7438114.

Fulton J (1929) Case of cerebellar tumor with seizures of head retraction described by Wurffbain in 1691. J Nerv Ment Dis **70**:577–583.

Gaidica M, Hurst A, Cyr C, Leventhal DK (2018) Distinct populations of motor thalamic neurons encode action initiation, action selection, and movement vigor. J Neurosci **38**:6563–6573.

Gallay MN, Jeanmonod D, Liu J, Morel A (2008) Human pallidothalamic and cerebellothalamic tracts: anatomical basis for functional stereotactic neurosurgery. Brain Struct Funct **212**:443–463.

Galvez R, Greenough WT (2005) Sequence of abnormal dendritic spine development in primary somatosensory cortex of a mouse model of the fragile X mental retardation syndrome. Am J Med Genet **135A**:155–160. Available at: https://onlinelibrary.wiley.com/doi/abs/10.1002/ajmg.a.30709 [Accessed July 31, 2019].

Gao Z, Davis C, Thomas AM, Economo MN, Abrego AM, Svoboda K, De Zeeuw CI, Li N (2018) A cortico-cerebellar loop for motor planning. Nature **563**:113–116.

Gardette R, Debono M, Dupont JL, Crepel F (1985) Electrophysiological studies on the postnatal development of intracerebellar nuclei neurons in rat cerebellar slices maintained in vitro. II. Membrane conductances. Brain Res **352**:97–106.

Garin N, Escher G (2001) The development of inhibitory synaptic specializations in the mouse deep cerebellar nuclei. Neuroscience **105**:431–441.

Gauck V, Jaeger D (2000) The control of rate and timing of spikes in the deep cerebellar nuclei by inhibition. J Neurosci **20**:3006–3016.

Glenn LL, Steriade M (1982) Discharge rate and excitability of cortically projecting intralaminar thalamic neurons during waking and sleep states. J Neurosci **2**:1387–1404. Available at: https://www.jneurosci.org/content/2/10/1387 [Accessed March 4, 2021].

Goffinet AM (1983) The embryonic development of the cerebellum in normal and reeler mutant mice. Anat Embryol **168**:73–86. Available at: https://doi.org/10.1007/BF00305400 [Accessed October 30, 2020].

Gornati SV, Schäfer CB, Eelkman Rooda OHJ, Nigg AL, De Zeeuw CI, Hoebeek FE (2018) Differentiating cerebellar impact on thalamic nuclei. Cell Rep **23**:2690–2704.

Graber KD, Fisher RS (2012) Deep brain stimulation for epilepsy: animal models. In: Jasper's Basic Mechanisms of the Epilepsies, 4th ed. (Noebels JL, Avoli M, Rogawski MA, Olsen RW, Delgado-Escueta AV, eds). Bethesda, MD: National Center for Biotechnology Information. Available at: http://www.ncbi.nlm.nih.gov/books/NBK98160/ [Accessed March 1, 2021].

Green MJ, Wingate RJ (2014) Developmental origins of diversity in cerebellar output nuclei. Neural Dev **9**:1. Available at: https://doi.org/10.1186/1749-8104-9-1 [Accessed October 27, 2020].

Hara S, Kaneyama T, Inamata Y, Onodera R, Shirasaki R (2016) Interstitial branch formation within the red nucleus by deep cerebellar nuclei-derived commissural axons during target recognition. J Comp Neurol **524**:999–1014.

Hashimoto T, Tayama M, Murakawa K, Yoshimoto T, Miyazaki M, Harada M, Kuroda Y (1995) Development of the brainstem and cerebellum in autistic patients. J Autism Dev Disord **25**:1–18.

Hassler E (1950) [Penicillin therapy of scarlet fever]. Kinderarztl Prax **18**:132–136.

Hayaran A, Wadhwa S, Bijlani V (1992) Cytoarchitectural development of the human dentate nucleus: a Golgi study. Dev Neurosci **14**:181–194.

Heck DH (2015) The Neural Codes of the Cerebellum, 1st ed. Academic Press.

Hendry SHC, Jones EG, Graham J (1979) Thalamic relay nuclei for cerebellar and certain related fiber systems in the cat. J Compe Neurol **185**:679–713. Available at: https://onlinelibrary.wiley.com/doi/abs/10.1002/cne.901850406 [Accessed March 3, 2021].

Hensch TK (2004) Critical period regulation. Annu Rev Neurosci **27**:549–579.

Hintzen A, Pelzer EA, Tittgemeyer M (2018) Thalamic interactions of cerebellum and basal ganglia. Brain Struct Funct **223**:569–587.

Hoebeek FE, Stahl JS, van Alphen AM, Schonewille M, Luo C, Rutteman M, van den Maagdenberg AM, Molenaar PC, Goossens HH, Frens MA, De Zeeuw CI (2005) Increased noise level of Purkinje cell activities minimizes impact of their modulation during sensorimotor control. Neuron **45**:953–965.

Hoerder-Suabedissen A, Molnár Z (2015) Development, evolution and pathology of neocortical subplate neurons. Nat Rev Neurosci **16**:133–146.

Hoover JE, Strick PL (1999) The organization of cerebellar and basal ganglia outputs to primary motor cortex as revealed by retrograde transneuronal transport of herpes simplex virus type 1. J Neurosci **19**:1446–1463. Available at: http://www.jneurosci.org/lookup/doi/10.1523/JNEUROSCI.19-04-01446.1999 [Accessed October 28, 2020].

Hortensius LM, Dijkshoorn ABC, Ecury-Goossen GM, Steggerda SJ, Hoebeek FE, Benders MJNL, Dudink J (2018) Neurodevelopmental consequences of preterm isolated cerebellar hemorrhage: a systematic review. Pediatrics **142**: e20180609.

Houck BD, Person AL (2015) Cerebellar premotor output neurons collateralize to innervate the cerebellar cortex. J Comp Neurol **523**:2254–2271.

Hutsler JJ, Zhang H (2010) Increased dendritic spine densities on cortical projection neurons in autism spectrum disorders. Brain Res **1309**:83–94. Available at: http://linkinghub.elsevier.com/retrieve/pii/S0006899309023117 [Accessed December 7, 2018].

Ilyas A, Pizarro D, Romeo AK, Riley KO, Pati S (2019) The centromedian nucleus: anatomy, physiology, and clinical implications. J Clin Neurosci **63**:1–7. Available at: https://www.jocn-journal.com/article/S0967-5868(19)30016-5/abstract [Accessed February 15, 2021].

Ito M (2002) Historical review of the significance of the cerebellum and the role of Purkinje cells in motor learning. Ann NY Acad Sci **978**:273–288.

Jackson J. (1871) Case of tumor of the middle lobe of the cerebellum: rigidity in cerebellar attitude—occasional tetanus-like seizures. Brit Med J **ii**:528.

Jackson J. (1906) Case of tumour of the middle lobe of the cerebellum. Brain, Volume 29, Issue 4, March 1907, Pages 425–440, https://doi.org/10.1093/brain/29.4.425.

Jahnsen H, Llinás R (1984) Voltage-dependent burst-to-tonic switching of thalamic cell activity: an in vitro study. Arch Ital Biol **122**:73–82.

Jörntell H, Ekerot CF (1999) Topographical organization of projections to cat motor cortex from nucleus interpositus anterior and forelimb skin. J Physiol **514** (Pt 2):551–566.

Kelly E, et al. (2020) Regulation of autism-relevant behaviors by cerebellar-prefrontal cortical circuits. Nat Neurosci **23**:1102–1110.

Kelly RM, Strick PL (2003) Cerebellar loops with motor cortex and prefrontal cortex of a nonhuman primate. J Neurosci **23**:8432–8444.

Kostović I, Goldman-Rakic PS (1983) Transient cholinesterase staining in the mediodorsal nucleus of the thalamus and its connections in the developing human and monkey brain. J Comp Neurol **219**:431–447.

Kostović I, Judas M (2002) Correlation between the sequential ingrowth of afferents and transient patterns of cortical lamination in preterm infants. Anat Rec **267**:1–6.

Kostović I, Kostović-Srzentić M, Benjak V, Jovanov-Milošević N, Radoš M (2014) Developmental dynamics of radial vulnerability in the cerebral compartments in preterm infants and neonates. Front Neurol **5**: 139. Available at: https://www.ncbi.nlm.nih.gov/pmc/articles/PMC4114264/ [Accessed March 6, 2021].

Kostović I, Rakic P (1984) Development of prestriate visual projections in the monkey and human fetal cerebrum revealed by transient cholinesterase staining. J Neurosci **4**:25–42. Available at: https://www.jneurosci.org/content/4/1/25 [Accessed March 6, 2021].

Krook-Magnuson E, Szabo GG, Armstrong C, Oijala M, Soltesz I (2014) Cerebellar directed optogenetic intervention inhibits spontaneous hippocampal seizures in a mouse model of temporal lobe epilepsy. eNeuro **1**. Available at: https://www.eneuro.org/content/1/1/ENEURO.0005-14.2014 [Accessed February 26, 2021].

Kros L, Eelkman Rooda OHJ, De Zeeuw CI, Hoebeek FE (2015) Controlling cerebellar output to treat refractory epilepsy. Trends Neurosci 38:787–799. Available at: http://www.sciencedirect.com/science/article/pii/S016622361500226X [Accessed January 28, 2021].

Krsnik Ž, Majić V, Vasung L, Huang H, Kostović I (2017) Growth of thalamocortical fibers to the somatosensory cortex in the human fetal brain. Front Neurosci 11. Available at: https://www.ncbi.nlm.nih.gov/pmc/articles/PMC5406414/ [Accessed March 6, 2021].

Kuramoto E, Furuta T, Nakamura KC, Unzai T, Hioki H, Kaneko T (2009) Two types of thalamocortical projections from the motor thalamic nuclei of the rat: a single neuron-tracing study using viral vectors. Cereb Cortex 19:2065–2077.

Kuramoto E, Ohno S, Furuta T, Unzai T, Tanaka YR, Hioki H, Kaneko T (2015) Ventral medial nucleus neurons send thalamocortical afferents more widely and more preferentially to layer 1 than neurons of the ventral anterior-ventral lateral nuclear complex in the rat. Cereb Cortex 25:221–235.

Lang EJ, Sugihara I, Llinas R (2006) Olivocerebellar modulation of motor cortex ability to generate vibrissal movements in rat. J Physiol 571:101–120.

Larsell O (1935) The development and morphology of the cerebellum in the opossum. Part I. Early development. J Comp Neurol 63:65–94.

Leto K, et al. (2016) Consensus paper: cerebellar development. Cerebellum 15:789–828. Available at: https://www.ncbi.nlm.nih.gov/pmc/articles/PMC4846577/ [Accessed October 30, 2020].

Limperopoulos C, Bassan H, Gauvreau K, Robertson RL, Sullivan NR, Benson CB, Avery L, Stewart J, Soul JS, Ringer SA, Volpe JJ, duPlessis AJ (2007) Does cerebellar injury in premature infants contribute to the high prevalence of long-term cognitive, learning, and behavioral disability in survivors? Pediatrics 120:584–593.

Limperopoulos C, Chilingaryan G, Sullivan N, Guizard N, Robertson RL, du Plessis AJ (2014) Injury to the premature cerebellum: outcome is related to remote cortical development. Cereb Cortex 24:728–736.

Llinás R, Jahnsen H (1982) Electrophysiology of mammalian thalamic neurones in vitro. Nature 297:406–408.

Llinás R, Sasaki K (1989) The functional organization of the olivo-cerebellar system as examined by multiple Purkinje cell recordings. Eur J Neurosci 1:587–602.

Llinás R, Volkind RA (1973) The olivo-cerebellar system: functional properties as revealed by harmaline-induced tremor. Exp Brain Res 18:69–87. Available at: https://doi.org/10.1007/BF00236557 [Accessed March 8, 2021].

Lopez-Bendito G, Molnar Z (2003) Thalamocortical development: how are we going to get there? Nat Rev Neurosci 4:276–289.

Machold R, Fishell G (2005) Math1 is expressed in temporally discrete pools of cerebellar rhombic-lip neural progenitors. Neuron 48:17–24.

MacLeod NK, James TA (1984) Regulation of cerebello-cortical transmission in the rat ventromedial thalamic nucleus. Exp Brain Res 55:535–552.

Maejima T, Wollenweber P, Teusner LUC, Noebels JL, Herlitze S, Mark MD (2013) Postnatal loss of P/Q-type channels confined to rhombic-lip-derived neurons alters synaptic transmission at the parallel fiber to Purkinje cell synapse and replicates genomic Cacna1a mutation phenotype of ataxia and seizures in mice. J Neurosci 33:5162–5174.

Marin-Padilla M (1970) Prenatal and early postnatal ontogenesis of the human motor cortex: a golgi study. II. The basket-pyramidal system. Brain Res 23:185–191.

Mark MD, Maejima T, Kuckelsberg D, Yoo JW, Hyde RA, Shah V, Gutierrez D, Moreno RL, Kruse W, Noebels JL, Herlitze S (2011a) Delayed postnatal loss of P/Q-type calcium channels recapitulates the absence epilepsy, dyskinesia, and ataxia phenotypes of genomic Cacna1a mutations. J Neurosci 31:4311–4326.

Marlinski V, Nilaweera WU, Zelenin PV, Sirota MG, Beloozerova IN (2011) Signals from the ventrolateral thalamus to the motor cortex during locomotion. J Neurophysiol 107:455–472. Available at: https://journals.physiology.org/doi/full/10.1152/jn.01113.2010 [Accessed March 4, 2021].

Marsden JF, Werhahn KJ, Ashby P, Rothwell J, Noachtar S, Brown P (2000) Organization of cortical activities related to movement in humans. J Neurosci 20:2307–2314.

Martin GF, Cabana T, Hazlett JC, Ho R, Waltzer R (1987) Development of brainstem and cerebellar projections to the diencephalon with notes on thalamocortical projections: studies in the North American opossum. J Comp Neurol 260:186–200.

Matsumoto N, Minamimoto T, Graybiel AM, Kimura M (2001) Neurons in the thalamic CM-Pf complex supply striatal neurons with information about behaviorally significant sensory events. J Neurophysiol 85:960–976. Available at: https://journals.physiology.org/doi/full/10.1152/jn.2001.85.2.960 [Accessed February 15, 2021].

McCrory PR, Bladin PF, Berkovic SF (1999) The cerebellar seizures of Hughlings Jackson. Neurology 52:1888–1888. Available at: https://n.neurology.org/content/52/9/1888 [Accessed February 27, 2021].

Mihajlovic P, Zecevic N (1986) Development of the human dentate nucleus. Hum Neurobiol 5:189–197.

Minamimoto T, Kimura M (2002) Participation of the thalamic CM-Pf complex in attentional orienting. J Neurophysiol 87:3090–3101. Available at: https://journals.physiology.org/doi/full/10.1152/jn.2002.87.6.3090 [Accessed February 15, 2021].

Miterko LN et al. (2019) Consensus paper: experimental neurostimulation of the cerebellum. Cerebellum 18:1064–1097. Available at: https://doi.org/10.1007/s12311-019-01041-5 [Accessed March 8, 2021].

Molnár Z, Knott GW, Blakemore C, Saunders NR (1998) Development of thalamocortical projections in the South American gray short-tailed opossum (*Monodelphis domestica*). J Comp Neurol 398:491–514.

Moruzzi G, Montanari L, Rossi CA, Rabbi A, Jacoli G (1950) [Active ultrafilterable fraction of corticotropic hormone with low nitrogen content]. Bollettino della Societa italiana di biologia sperimentale 26:1567–1569.

Muthuraman M, Koirala N, Ciolac D, Pintea B, Glaser M, Groppa S, Tamás G, Groppa S (2018) Deep brain stimulation and L-DOPA therapy: concepts of action and clinical applications in Parkinson's disease. Front Neurol 9:711.

Najac M, Raman IM (2015) Integration of Purkinje cell inhibition by cerebellar nucleo-olivary neurons. J Neurosci 35:544–549.

Nakamura KC, Sharott A, Magill PJ (2014) Temporal coupling with cortex distinguishes spontaneous neuronal activities in identified basal ganglia-recipient and cerebellar-recipient zones of the motor thalamus. Cereb Cortex 24:81–97.

Nashef A, Mitelman R, Harel R, Joshua M, Prut Y (2021) Area-specific thalamocortical synchronization underlies the transition from motor planning to execution. Proc Natl Acad Sci USA 118. Available at: https://www.pnas.org/content/118/6/e2012658118 [Accessed March 4, 2021].

Ozden, I., Dombeck, D. A., Hoogland, T. M., Tank, D. W. & Wang, S. S. Widespread state-dependent shifts in cerebellar activity in locomoting mice. PLoS One 7, e42650, doi:10.1371/journal.pone.0042650 (2012), PMC3411825.

Palmen SJMC, van Engeland H, Hof PR, Schmitz C (2004) Neuropathological findings in autism. Brain 127:2572–2583.

Parent M, Parent A (2005) Single-axon tracing and three-dimensional reconstruction of centre median-parafascicular thalamic neurons in primates. J Comp Neurol 481:127–144.

Passamonti L, Novellino F, Cerasa A, Chiriaco C, Rocca F, Matina MS, Fera F, Quattrone A (2011) Altered cortical-cerebellar circuits during verbal working memory in essential tremor. Brain: J Neurol 134:2274–2286.

Paxinos G, Watson, C (1986) The Rat Brain in Stereotaxic Coordinates. New York: Academic Press.

Pedrosa DJ, Auth M, Pauls KAM, Runge M, Maarouf M, Fink GR, Timmermann L (2014) Verbal fluency in essential tremor patients: the effects of deep brain stimulation. Brain Stimul 7:359–364. Available at: https://www.brainstimjrnl.com/article/S1935-861X(14)00110-7/abstract [Accessed March 5, 2021].

Person AL, Raman IM (2011) Purkinje neuron synchrony elicits time-locked spiking in the cerebellar nuclei. Nature 481:502–505.

Phillips JW, Schulmann A, Hara E, Winnubst J, Liu C, Valakh V, Wang L, Shields BC, Korff W, Chandrashekar J, Lemire AL, Mensh B, Dudman JT, Nelson SB, Hantman AW (2019) A repeated molecular architecture across thalamic pathways. Nat Neurosci 22:1925–1935.

Pierce ET (1975) Histogenesis of the deep cerebellar nuclei in the mouse: an autoradiographic study. Brain Res 95:503–518. Available at: http://www.sciencedirect.com/science/article/pii/0006899375901249 [Accessed October 30, 2020].

Pieterman K, Batalle D, Dudink J, Tournier J-D, Hughes EJ, Barnett M, Benders MJ, Edwards AD, Hoebeek FE, Counsell SJ (2017) Cerebello-cerebral connectivity in the developing brain. Brain Struct Funct 222:1625–1634.

Pisano TJ, Dhanerawala ZM, Kislin M, Bakshinskaya D, Engel EA, Hansen EJ, Hoag AT, Lee J, Oude NL de, Venkataraju KU, Verpeut JL, Hoebeek FE, Richardson BD, Boele H-J, Wang SS-H (2021) Homologous organization of cerebellar pathways to sensory, motor, and associative forebrain. Cell Rep 36. Available at: https://www.cell.com/cell-reports/abstract/S2211-1247(21)01170-0 [Accessed September 21, 2021].

Proville RD, Spolidoro M, Guyon N, Dugué GP, Selimi F, Isope P, Popa D, Léna C (2014) Cerebellum involvement in cortical sensorimotor circuits for the control of voluntary movements. Nat Neurosci 17:1233–1239.

Puertas-Martín V, Villarejo-Galende A, Fernández-Guinea S, Romero JP, Louis ED, Benito-León J (2016) A comparison study of cognitive and neuropsychiatric features of essential tremor and Parkinson's disease. Tremor Other Hyperkinet Mov 6:431. Available at: http://tremorjournal.org/article/10.5334/tohm.288/ [Accessed November 1, 2020].

Purpura DP, Scarff T, McMurtry JG. (1965) Intracellular study of internuclear inhibition in ventrolateral thalamic neurons. J Neurophysiol 28: 487–496.

Reh RK, Dias BG, Nelson CA, Kaufer D, Werker JF, Kolb B, Levine JD, Hensch TK (2020) Critical period regulation across multiple timescales. Proc Natl Acad Sci USA 117:23242–23251.

Rispal-Padel L, Harnois C, Troiani D (1987) Converging cerebellofugal inputs to the thalamus. I. Mapping of monosynaptic field potentials in the ventrolateral nucleus of the thalamus. Exp Brain Res 68:47–58.

Rispal-Padel L, Latreille J (1974) The organization of projections from the cerebellar nuclei to the contralateral motor cortex in the cat. Exp Brain Res 19:36–60.

Rispal-Padel L, Massion J, Grangetto A (1973) Relations between the ventrolateral thalamic nucleus and motor cortex and their possible role in the central organization of motor control. Brain Res 60:1–20.

Rowland NC, Jaeger D (2008) Responses to tactile stimulation in deep cerebellar nucleus neurons result from recurrent activation in multiple pathways. J Neurophysiol 99:704–717.

Ruigrok TJH (2011) Ins and outs of cerebellar modules. Cerebellum 10:464–474.

Sakai ST (2013) Cerebellar thalamic and thalamocortical projections. In: Handbook of the Cerebellum and Cerebellar Disorders (Manto M, Schmahmann JD, Rossi F, Gruol DL, Koibuchi N, eds), pp 529–547. Dordrecht: Springer Netherlands. Available at: https://doi.org/10.1007/978-94-007-1333-8_24 [Accessed September 20, 2021].

Sakata H, Ishijima T, Toyoda Y (1966) Single unit studies on ventrolateral nucleus of the thalamus in cat: its relation to the cerebellum, motor cortex and basal ganglia. Jpn J Physiol 16:42–60.

Sakayori N, Kato S, Sugawara M, Setogawa S, Fukushima H, Ishikawa R, Kida S, Kobayashi K (2019) Motor skills mediated through cerebellothalamic tracts projecting to the central lateral nucleus. Mol Brain 12:13. Available at: https://molecularbrain.biomedcentral.com/articles/10.1186/s13041-019-0431-x [Accessed October 5, 2020].

Sarnaik R, Raman IM (2018) Control of voluntary and optogenetically perturbed locomotion by spike rate and timing of neurons of the mouse cerebellar nuclei. eLife 7:e29546.

Sasaki K, Kawaguchi S, Matsuda Y, Mizuno N (1972a) Electrophysiological studies on cerebello-cerebral projections in the cat. Exp Brain Res 16:75–88.

Sasaki K, Matsuda Y, Kawaguchi S, Mizuno N (1972b) On the cerebello-thalamo-cerebral pathway for the parietal cortex. Exp Brain Res 16:89–103.

Sawyer SF, Young SJ, Groves PM (1989) Quantitative Golgi study of anatomically identified subdivisions of motor thalamus in the rat. J Comp Neurol 286:1–27.

Sawyer SF, Young SJ, Groves PM, Tepper JM (1994) Cerebellar-responsive neurons in the thalamic ventroanterior-ventrolateral complex of rats: in vivo electrophysiology. Neuroscience 63:711–724.

Schäfer CB, Gao Z, Zeeuw CID, Hoebeek FE (2021) Temporal dynamics of the cerebello-cortical convergence in ventro-lateral motor thalamus. J Physiol 599:2055–2073. Available at: https://physoc.onlinelibrary.wiley.com/doi/abs/10.1113/JP280455 [Accessed March 4, 2021].

Schäfer CB, Hoebeek FE (2018) Convergence of primary sensory cortex and cerebellar nuclei pathways in the whisker system. Neuroscience 368:229–239.

Serra C, Guida L, Staartjes VE, Krayenbühl N, Türe U (2019) Historical controversies about the thalamus: from etymology to function. Neurosurg Focus 47: E13.

Shinoda Y, Kano M, Futami T (1985) Synaptic organization of the cerebello-thalamo-cerebral pathway in the cat. I. Projection of individual cerebellar nuclei to single pyramidal tract neurons in areas 4 and 6. Neurosci Res 2:133–156.

Shinoda Y, Yamazaki M, Futami T (1982) Convergent inputs from the dentate and the interpositus nuclei to pyramidal tract neurons in the motor cortex. Neurosci Lett 34:111–115.

Snider RS, Magoun HW (1949) Facilitation produced by cerebellar stimulation. J Neurophysiol 12:335–345.

Šramka M, Chkhenkeli SA (1990) Clinical experience in intraoperational determination of brain inhibitory structures and application of implanted neurostimulators in epilepsy. Stereotact Funct Neurosurg **54**:56–59. Available at: https://www.karger.com/Article/FullText/100190 [Accessed March 1, 2021].

Steriade M, Dossi RC, Nunez A (1991) Network modulation of a slow intrinsic oscillation of cat thalamocortical neurons implicated in sleep delta waves: cortically induced synchronization and brainstem cholinergic suppression. J Neurosci **11**:3200–3217. Available at: https://www.jneurosci.org/content/11/10/3200 [Accessed March 4, 2021].

Steriade M, McCormick DA, Sejnowski TJ (1993) Thalamocortical oscillations in the sleeping and aroused brain. Science **262**:679–685. Available at: https://science.sciencemag.org/content/262/5134/679 [Accessed March 4, 2021].

Stoodley CJ (2012) The cerebellum and cognition: evidence from functional imaging studies. Cerebellum **11**:352–365.

Stoodley CJ (2014) Distinct regions of the cerebellum show gray matter decreases in autism, ADHD, and developmental dyslexia. Front Syst Neurosci **8**:92.

Stoodley CJ, D'Mello AM, Ellegood J, Jakkamsetti V, Liu P, Nebel MB, Gibson JM, Kelly E, Meng F, Cano CA, Pascual JM, Mostofsky SH, Lerch JP, Tsai PT (2017) Altered cerebellar connectivity in autism and cerebellar-mediated rescue of autism-related behaviors in mice. Nat Neurosci **20**:1744–1751.

Stoodley CJ, Limperopoulos C (2016) Structure-function relationships in the developing cerebellum: Evidence from early-life cerebellar injury and neurodevelopmental disorders. Semin Fetal Neonatal Med **21**:356–364.

Stoodley CJ, Valera EM, Schmahmann JD (2012) Functional topography of the cerebellum for motor and cognitive tasks: an fMRI study. NeuroImage **59**:1560–1570.

Streng ML, Krook-Magnuson E (2020) The cerebellum and epilepsy. Epilepsy Behav: 106909. Available at: https://www.sciencedirect.com/science/article/pii/S1525505019311667 [Accessed February 26, 2021].

Takahashi E, Hayashi E, Schmahmann JD, Grant PE (2014) Development of cerebellar connectivity in human fetal brains revealed by high angular resolution diffusion tractography. NeuroImage **96**:326–333.

Tang G, Gudsnuk K, Kuo S-H, Cotrina ML, Rosoklija G, Sosunov A, Sonders MS, Kanter E, Castagna C, Yamamoto A, Yue Z, Arancio O, Peterson BS, Champagne F, Dwork AJ, Goldman J, Sulzer D (2014) Loss of mTOR-dependent macroautophagy causes autistic-like synaptic pruning deficits. Neuron **83**:1131–1143. Available at: https://linkinghub.elsevier.com/retrieve/pii/S0896627314006515 [Accessed June 27, 2019].

Ten Brinke MM, Heiney SA, Wang X, Proietti-Onori M, Boele H-J, Bakermans J, Medina JF, Gao Z, De Zeeuw CI (2017) Dynamic modulation of activity in cerebellar nuclei neurons during pavlovian eyeblink conditioning in mice. eLife **6**: e28132.

Teune TM, van der Burg J, van der Moer J, Voogd J, Ruigrok TJ (2000) Topography of cerebellar nuclear projections to the brain stem in the rat. Prog Brain Res **124**:141–172.

Tlamsa AP, Brumberg JC (2010) Organization and morphology of thalamocortical neurons of mouse ventral lateral thalamus. Somatosens Mot Res **27**:34–43.

Tracey DJ, Asanuma C, Jones EG, Porter R (1980) Thalamic relay to motor cortex: afferent pathways from brain stem, cerebellum, and spinal cord in monkeys. J Neurophysiol **44**:532–554. Available at: https://journals.physiology.org/doi/abs/10.1152/jn.1980.44.3.532 [Accessed March 3, 2021].

Tsai PT, Hull C, Chu Y, Greene-Colozzi E, Sadowski AR, Leech JM, Steinberg J, Crawley JN, Regehr WG, Sahin M (2012) Autistic-like behaviour and cerebellar dysfunction in Purkinje cell Tsc1 mutant mice. Nature **488**:647–651.

Ueki A (1983) The mode of nigro-thalamic transmission investigated with intracellular recording in the cat. Exp Brain Res **49**:116–124.

Uno M, Yoshida M, Hirota I (1970) The mode of cerebello-thalamic relay transmission investigated with intracellular recording from cells of the ventrolateral nucleus of cat's thalamus. Exp Brain Res **10**:121–139.

Uusisaari M, De Schutter E (2011) The mysterious microcircuitry of the cerebellar nuclei. J Physiol **589**:3441–3457.

Vitek JL, Ashe J, DeLong MR, Alexander GE (1994) Physiologic properties and somatotopic organization of the primate motor thalamus. J Neurophysiol **71**:1498–1513. Available at: https://journals.physiology.org/doi/abs/10.1152/jn.1994.71.4.1498 [Accessed October 28, 2020].

Volpe JJ (2009) Cerebellum of the premature infant: rapidly developing, vulnerable, clinically important. J Child Neurol **24**:1085–1104.

Voogd J, van Baarsen K (2014) The horseshoe-shaped commissure of Wernekinck or the decussation of the brachium conjunctivum methodological changes in the 1840s. Cerebellum **13**:113–120.

Walter JT, Alvina K, Womack MD, Chevez C, Khodakhah K (2006) Decreases in the precision of Purkinje cell pacemaking cause cerebellar dysfunction and ataxia. Nat Neurosci **9**:389–397.

Wang C-C, Shyu B-C (2004) Differential projections from the mediodorsal and centrolateral thalamic nuclei to the frontal cortex in rats. Brain Res **995**:226–235. Available at: https://www.sciencedirect.com/science/article/pii/S000689930303840X [Accessed March 3, 2021].

Wang D, Smith-Bell CA, Burhans LB, O'Dell DE, Bell RW, Schreurs BG (2018) Changes in membrane properties of rat deep cerebellar nuclear projection neurons during acquisition of eyeblink conditioning. Proc Natl Acad Sci USA **115**:E9419–E9428. Available at: http://www.pnas.org/lookup/doi/10.1073/pnas.1808539115 [Accessed September 22, 2021].

Wang M, Li H, Takumi T, Qiu Z, Xu X, Yu X, Bian W-J (2017) Distinct defects in spine formation or pruning in two gene duplication mouse models of autism. Neurosci Bull **33**:143–152. Available at: http://link.springer.com/10.1007/s12264-017-0111-8 [Accessed June 27, 2019].

Wang SS-H, Kloth AD, Badura A (2014) The cerebellum, sensitive periods, and autism. Neuron **83**:518–532. Available at: https://www.ncbi.nlm.nih.gov/pmc/articles/PMC4135479/ [Accessed October 31, 2020].

Wang VY, Rose MF, Zoghbi HY (2005) Math1 expression redefines the rhombic lip derivatives and reveals novel lineages within the brainstem and cerebellum. Neuron **48**:31–43.

Watson TC, Obiang P, Torres-Herraez A, Watilliaux A, Coulon P, Rochefort C, Rondi-Reig L (2019) Anatomical and physiological foundations of cerebello-hippocampal interaction. eLife **8**.

Wu Y, Raman IM (2017) Facilitation of mossy fibre-driven spiking in the cerebellar nuclei by the synchrony of inhibition. J Physiol **595**:5245–5264.

Yamaguchi K, Goto N, Yamamoto TY (1989) Development of human cerebellar nuclei. Morphometric study. Acta Anat (Basel) **136**:61–68.

Yamamoto T, Hassler R, Huber C, Wagner A, Sasaki K (1983) Electrophysiologic studies on the pallido- and cerebellothalamic projections in squirrel monkeys (*Saimiri sciureus*). Exp Brain Res 51:77–87.

Yamamoto T, Noda T, Miyata M, Nishimura Y (1984) Electrophysiological and morphological studies on thalamic neurons receiving entopedunculo- and cerebello-thalamic projections in the cat. Brain Res 301:231–242.

Yarden-Rabinowitz Y, Yarom Y (2017) In vivo analysis of synaptic activity in cerebellar nuclei neurons unravels the efficacy of excitatory inputs. J Physiol 595:5945–5963. Available at: https://physoc.onlinelibrary.wiley.com/doi/abs/10.1113/JP274115 [Accessed March 7, 2021].

Yuge K, Kataoka A, Yoshida AC, Itoh D, Aggarwal M, Mori S, Blackshaw S, Shimogori T (2011) Region-specific gene expression in early postnatal mouse thalamus. J Comp Neurol 519:544–561.

Section 7: Cognition

Chapter 16: The Thalamus in Cognitive Control

Kai Hwang and Mark D'Esposito

Introduction

Cognitive control, also commonly termed *executive function* or *executive control*, refers to our ability to regulate thoughts and actions for adaptive, goal-directed behaviors (Norman & Shallice, 1986; Stuss & Alexander, 2007). Cognitive control comprises multiple cognitive functions, including working memory, attentional control, inhibition, and cognitive flexibility (Miyake et al., 2000; Posner et al., 2004; Verbruggen et al., 2014). Broadly defined, cognitive control is necessary to maintain behaviorally relevant information in mind and to use this information to regulate perceptual and motor functions to conduct purposeful behavior (J. D. Cohen, 2017; Fellows, 2017). In our daily lives, we constantly face situations where cognitive control is needed—for example, searching for grocery items from a memorized shopping list, switching between the brake or gas pedal while driving a car, or avoiding distractions when attending a lecture. Cognitive control abilities are predictive of school-age children's academic outcomes (Clark et al., 2010; Diamond & Lee, 2011), and cognitive control deficits are found in many psychiatric and neurological disorders, such as schizophrenia (Lesh et al., 2011), depression (Rock et al., 2014), attention deficit–hyperactivity disorder (Willcutt et al., 2005), and stroke and traumatic brain injury (Stuss & Alexander, 2000). These deficits are disabling and among the hardest to treat (D'Esposito & Chen, 2013), further highlighting the clinical and scientific significance of elucidating the neural substrates and mechanisms of cognitive control.

This chapter reviews the role of the human thalamus in cognitive control. We will pose and discuss the following questions: Is the human thalamus involved in cognitive control? Are specific thalamic nuclei involved in cognitive control? Are there specific cognitive control functions that the thalamus performs, and if so, how are these functions accomplished? To address these questions, it is necessary to first clearly define cognitive control, given that it is not a unitary function but, rather, a collection of component processes that support goal-directed behavior (Halassa & Kastner, 2017; Verbruggen et al., 2014). We will focus on one central aspect of cognitive control: the ability to prioritize information that is compatible with behavioral goals. This definition includes the ability to maintain goal-relevant information in mind, an ability referred to as *working memory*. We will also consider processes that utilize working memory content to bias and regulate perceptual and motor functions, also known as *top-down biasing*. We will review anatomical, human functional neuroimaging, and human neuropsychology findings that have investigated the role of the thalamus in working memory and top-down biasing. To understand how the human thalamus mechanistically supports cognitive control, we will extract operational principles of thalamocortical circuits from anatomical and neurophysiological studies. Finally, we present an overarching conceptual framework to describe how thalamocortical circuits implement different components of information processing necessary for cognitive control. In conclusion, we will refute the traditional view that the thalamus passively relays signals to the cortex for purposeful processing. Instead, emerging and convergent evidence suggests an alternative but more convincing view that the thalamus actively modulates cortical activity and cortical network interactions to shape and coordinate the information processes underlying cognitive control.

Anatomical, Human Neuroimaging, and Neuropsychology Studies of Thalamic Function

In this section, we will first review anatomical studies of thalamocortical connectivity, which will serve as a foundation for a review of human neuroimaging and neuropsychology studies that have investigated the role of the thalamus in cognitive control.

Anatomical Connectivity between Thalamic Nuclei and Frontoparietal Cortices

The thalamus can be divided into two types of nuclei: first order and higher-order thalamic nuclei (S. M. Sherman & Guillery, 2006). First-order thalamic nuclei, such as the lateral geniculate nucleus, receive inputs from ascending sensory pathways or other subcortical brain regions. In contrast, higher-order thalamic nuclei receive inputs primarily from the cortex. The frontal and parietal cortices, in particular, are critical for cognitive control functions (Duncan, 2010; Gazzaley & Nobre, 2012). Anatomical tracing studies performed on nonhuman primates have identified several higher-order thalamic nuclei that have dense interconnectivity with frontal and parietal cortices. The mediodorsal nucleus projects to and receives projections from the medial prefrontal, lateral prefrontal, and inferior and superior parietal cortices (Giguere & Goldman-Rakic, 1988; Goldman-Rakic & Porrino, 1985; Schmahmann & Pandya, 1990; Selemon & Goldman-Rakic, 1988; Xiao et al., 2009; Zikopoulos & Barbas, 2006). The anterior nucleus is reciprocally connected to the medial prefrontal cortex and receives projections from the lateral prefrontal cortex (Xiao et al., 2009). The pulvinar receives projections from the lateral prefrontal cortex and the intraparietal sulcus (Selemon & Goldman-Rakic, 1988) and projects to both lateral prefrontal and parietal association areas (Asanuma et al., 1985; Romanski et al., 1997; Trojanowski & Jacobson, 1976). The ventrolateral nucleus projects to the premotor region in the frontal cortex (Schell & Strick, 1984) and receives projections from the lateral prefrontal and the intraparietal sulcus (Selemon & Goldman-Rakic, 1988). The intralaminar nucleus is described as the "nonspecific" nucleus because it projects to multiple cortical regions throughout the cerebral cortex (Jones & Leavitt, 1974). These thalamic nuclei have "many-to-one" and "one-to-many" connectivity motifs with the frontal and parietal cortices. That is, one thalamic nucleus may receive projections from multiple segregated cortical regions and broadly project to multiple distal cortical regions, in which different thalamic nuclei may be connected with the same cortical region (Selemon & Goldman-Rakic, 1988; S. M. Sherman & Guillery, 2002). Furthermore, because the basal ganglia and cerebellum do not directly relay their output back to the cortex, their influence on cortical function is mediated through both first-order and higher-order thalamic nuclei (G. E. Alexander et al., 1986). In this way, these subcortical regions can also influence frontoparietal regions involved in cognitive control. Thus, the thalamus is well positioned to integrate information from multiple modalities across subcortical and cortical structures, a property likely to be important for cognitive control. This anatomical connectivity profile of the thalamus, basal ganglia, and cerebellum highlights that the frontoparietal cortices do not function in isolation in support of cognitive control but, rather, are directly influenced by the thalamus and its inputs.

Human Neuroimaging Studies of Thalamic Involvement in Cognitive Control

The vast majority of human functional neuroimaging studies of cognitive control have focused on determining the functional specialization of the frontal and parietal regions (e.g., Aron et al., 2007; Badre & D'Esposito, 2007; Cole & Schneider, 2007; Koenigs et al., 2009; Nee & D'Esposito, 2016), whereas the thalamus has been largely ignored (but see de Bourbon-Teles et al., 2014; Fischer & Whitney, 2012; Kastner et al., 2004). Large-scale meta-analyses that synthesize results from decades of neuroimaging research provide a method for evaluating the association between thalamic activity and cognitive control (Eickhoff et al., 2012; Yarkoni et al., 2011). This method aggregates the results from a large number of studies rather than considering the findings from a single study, which minimizes biases (e.g., such as only reporting cortical findings), increases statistical power, and reduces false-positive rates (Poldrack et al., 2017). To this end, automated procedures have been developed to quantify, in the corpus of tens of thousands of functional magnetic resonance imaging (fMRI) studies, the strength of correlation between terms that are reported in publications to describe cognitive constructs, such as those related to cognitive control (e.g., *working memory*), and the likelihood of observing brain activity associated with the queried terms (Yarkoni et al., 2011).

We have performed two large-scale meta-analyses using the Neurosynth database (Yarkoni et al., 2011), which are presented in Figure 1. Each of these analyses included a large number of fMRI studies (1091 and 598, respectively) and sought to identify brain regions most frequently associated with the reported terms *working memory* and *cognitive control*. We found that activity in the thalamus, the frontoparietal association areas, and the basal ganglia was associated with the terms *working memory* and *cognitive control* (Figure 1A). Because the thalamus comprises more than 20 nuclei, each with unique anatomical and cortical projection profiles (S. M. Sherman & Guillery, 2013), we also performed a more detailed anatomical analysis to determine which thalamic nuclei are associated with these two cognitive terms (Figure 1B). Specifically, we calculated the strength of association between thalamic activity (quantified as z-score) and cognitive terms, separately for each thalamic nuclei as defined by the Morel atlas (Krauth et al., 2010; Morel et al., 1997), which is a histologically based atlas derived from postmortem human brains. We found that activity in the mediodorsal, anterior, ventral lateral, intralaminar, and pulvinar nuclei was significantly associated with the terms *working memory* and *cognitive control*. As described earlier, these thalamic nuclei are known to have strong anatomical connectivity with frontal and parietal cortical regions.

The meta-analyses described previously aggregated the findings from fMRI studies that included the terms *working memory* and *cognitive control*. However, behavioral tasks aimed at investigating cognitive control and working memory likely engage multiple component processes. For example, the Stroop task that is commonly used to assess cognitive control likely involves processes for maintaining a behavioral goal ("name the color of the word"), selecting the appropriate stimuli attribute ("attend to the color of the word"), and inhibiting the inappropriate response ("naming the word itself"). These latent cognitive processes (hereafter referred to as *cognitive components*) are hypothetical mental processes that are usually not directly observable. It is hypothesized that a behavioral task likely engages multiple cognitive components, and a single component may be necessary for the execution of many different types of behavioral tasks (Poldrack, 2011). Another meta-analytical approach that can determine the relationship between the human thalamus and cognitive control is to identify latent components of cognitive processes (hereafter referred to as *cognitive components*) engaged by behavioral tasks that assess cognitive control (e.g., *n*-back, Stroop, flanker, go/no-go) and the anatomical regions associated with component processes that are engaged during the performance of such tasks.

One cannot derive latent components of all possible cognitive processes from a single experiment, but it is possible to estimate their organization (also known as *cognitive ontology*)

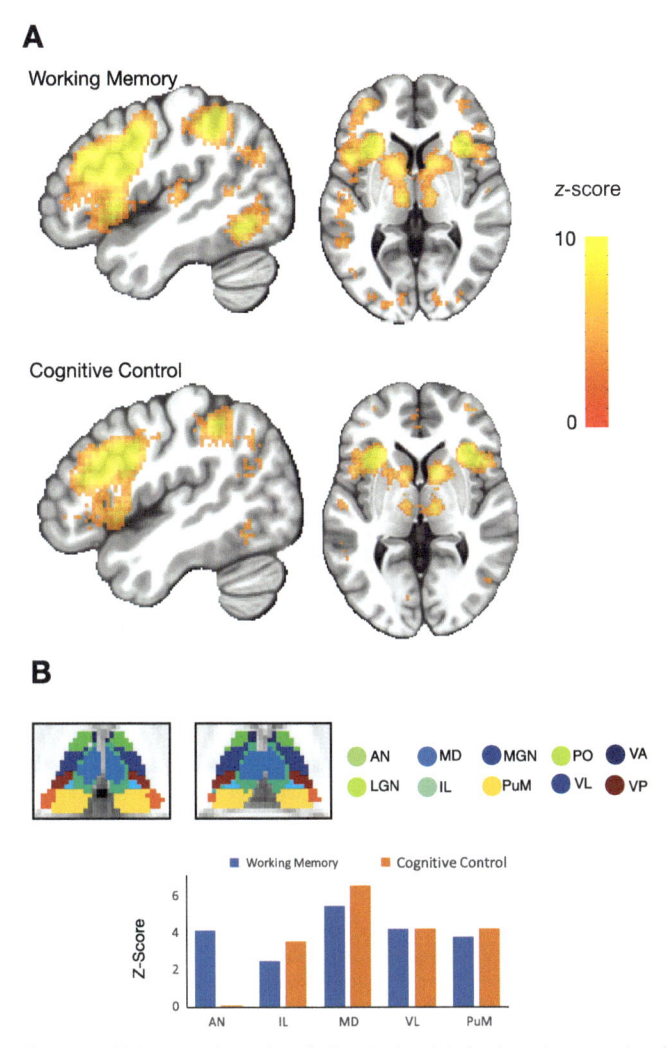

Figure 1 (A) Meta-analyses identified cortical and thalamic regions associated with the terms *working memory* and *cognitive control*. Maps thresholded at false discovery rate $q < 0.01$. z-scores indicate the strength of correlation between brain activity and queried terms. (B) Thalamic nuclei that showed significant associations with the terms *working memory* and *cognitive control*. *AN*, anterior nucleus; *MD*, mediodorsal nucleus; *IL*, intralaminar; *MGN*, medial geniculate nucleus; *PO*, posterior nucleus; *PuM*, medial pulvinar; *VL*, ventrolateral; *VA*, ventral anterior; *VP*, ventroposterior.

with a large-scale meta-analytical approach. Yeo and colleagues (2015) attempted to develop a cognitive ontology by performing a meta-analysis of more than 8,000 fMRI studies in the BrainMap database that employed more than 77 different behavioral tasks (Laird et al., 2005). They utilized a hierarchical Bayesian model to formally estimate the probability of a cognitive component being engaged by a particular behavior task and the probability that each cognitive component engaged a specific brain region (Bertolero et al., 2015; Yeo et al., 2015). With this approach, they identified five different cognitive components that supported eight different behavioral tasks commonly used to measure cognitive control (Figure 2). These five different cognitive components had a high probability of engaging the lateral frontal, medial frontal, insula, and posterior parietal cortices. Critically, four out of five of these cognitive components also had a high probability of engaging thalamic activity (Figure 2). Similar to the meta-analysis performed using the Neurosynth database, the anterior, mediodorsal, intralaminar, ventrolateral, and pulvinar nuclei were associated with these cognitive components. It is important to note that the specific processes underlying each of these cognitive components cannot be determined by this approach, which would require studies that experimentally manipulate these components and observe the effect on behavior and brain activity. In summary, the results from these studies suggest that the human thalamus has a strong and reliable association with behavioral tasks that assess cognitive control and working memory functions. These behavioral tasks likely engage multiple component processes that recruit multiple thalamic nuclei, specifically the anterior, mediodorsal, intralaminar, ventrolateral, and pulvinar nuclei.

Human Neuropsychologic Studies of Thalamic Involvement in Cognitive Control

The meta-analyses described previously included a large number of fMRI studies and convincingly demonstrated that there is a reliable and robust relationship between thalamic activity and cognitive control. These results, although compelling in establishing brain–behavior associations, are nevertheless correlational evidence. Increased brain activity in response to a particular behavior is not evidence that this brain region is *necessary* for the studied behavior (Sutterer & Tranel, 2017). Hypothetically, a brain region may exhibit activity that correlates with processes that directly contribute to a behavior but without a causal, mechanistic relationship. To determine if thalamic activity is necessary for cognitive control requires experimental or naturalistic causal experiments. To this end, experimental neuropsychology studies that quantify behavioral changes after focal brain injuries can directly test a brain region's necessary contribution to cognition. Transcranial magnetic stimulation (TMS) in healthy volunteers is another method for determining causal relationships. However, TMS to the thalamus is not feasible because the thalamus is deep beneath the cerebral cortex. Numerous neuropsychological studies have shown that frontal and parietal lobe lesions impair cognitive control, demonstrating the necessity of these regions (e.g., Badre et al., 2009; Gläscher et al., 2012; Mackey et al., 2016; Tsuchida & Fellows, 2013). Focal thalamic lesions, as compared to lesions in the cortex, are less common, which has led to fewer neuropsychological studies of thalamic function.

The thalamus receives its blood supply from the posterior cerebral artery (Schmahmann, 2003), and occlusion of this artery can lead to a stroke that is restricted to the thalamus, without damage to nearby structures. Studying patients with focal thalamic infarcts makes it possible to probe the thalamus's unique contribution to behavior. For example, the sensory thalamus's role in relaying peripheral sensory information to the cortex is affirmed by human lesion studies, where disruptions in sensory-related processes following focal thalamic stroke have been reported (Krause et al., 2012; Nasreddine & Saver, 1997). In addition to sensory-related symptoms, widely ranging cognitive impairments have been reported following

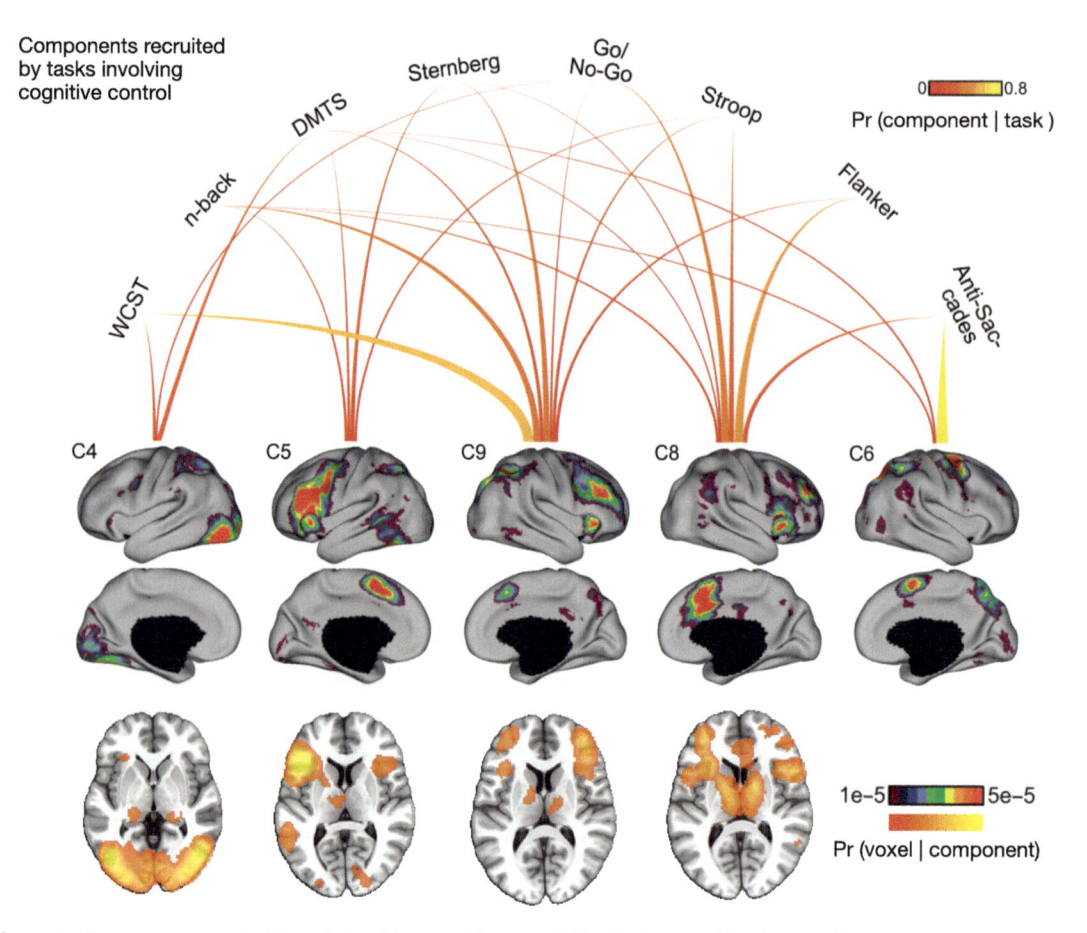

Figure 2 Components recruited by tasks involving cognitive control. The thickness and brightness of lines depict the probability of a task engaging a specific component. The colormap depicts the probability of a component recruiting a cortical or subcortical voxel. Figures adapted from Yeo et al. (2015), with permission from Oxford University Press.

thalamic lesions, such as aphasia (Crosson et al., 1986; Graff-Radford et al., 1984; Kuljic-Obradovic, 2003), amnesia (Carlesimo et al., 2011; Graff-Radford et al., 1990; von Cramon et al., 1985), and visual neglect (Rafal & Posner, 1987; Watson & Heilman, 1979). Finally, focal thalamic lesions can also cause impairments in arousal (Van der Werf et al., 2002). This wide range of deficits observed following thalamic infarction, ranging from sensory to higher cognition and arousal, highlights the thalamus's global and extensive connectivity relationship with other brain structures (Schmahmann, 2003). Each thalamic nucleus has a partially distinct pattern of connectivity to a system of cortical and subcortical regions (S. M. Sherman & Guillery, 2013); therefore, each thalamic subregion likely contributes to a specific (or multiple) cognitive function(s), and the specific location of a thalamic lesion likely determines the specific domain of behavioral deficits.

Given that the pulvinar, mediodorsal, anterior, and ventrolateral nuclei have strong anatomical projections with the frontal and parietal cortices implicated in cognitive control, lesions to these nuclei should impair cognitive control functions. Lesions in the anterior nucleus are most commonly associated with amnesia causing deficits in episodic memory (Child & Benarroch, 2013). Pulvinar lesions in human patients and chemical inactivation in nonhuman primates cause impairments in visual attention in the contralateral visual field (Arend et al., 2008; Danziger et al., 1999; Rafal & Posner, 1987; Wilke et al., 2010; Zhou et al., 2016), which are more pronounced when the attended target is surrounded by visual distractors (Chalupa et al., 1976; Snow et al., 2009). In human patients, mediodorsal nucleus lesions cause impairments on the Wisconsin Card Sorting Test (Liebermann et al., 2013; Van der Werf et al., 2003), a standardized, clinical neuropsychological test designed to assess the ability to use feedback to flexibly switch between task rules (Anderson et al., 1991; Dehaene & Changeux, 1991; Gläscher et al., 2019). However, in two other studies, only 40% and 20%, respectively, of patients with mediodorsal nucleus lesions were impaired (Hwang et al., 2020; Liebermann et al., 2013). Mediodorsal nucleus lesions also impair performance on the Trail Making Test (TMT; Hwang et al., 2020), another standardized clinical neuropsychological test of cognitive control (Bowie & Harvey, 2006). In this study, 9 out of 11 patients with mediodorsal nucleus lesions exhibited scores that were worse than 95% of the normative population matched in age and years of education (z-score > 2; Figure 3). Furthermore, patients with mediodorsal nucleus lesions also perform significantly worse than patients with nonthalamic lesions similar in size (Hwang et al., 2020), which strengthens the evidence of the specificity of the effect of thalamic lesions.

Patients with focal thalamic lesions

Trail Making Test Scores

Figure 3 Patients with lesions that involved the mediodorsal thalamus showed impaired task performance on the TMT. Top left panel shows four patients with focal thalamic lesions that damaged different parts of the thalamus. Top right panel depicts the lesion extent of 15 thalamic patients included in the analysis. Bottom panel shows the TMT test scores. Patients with lesions that overlapped with the mediodorsal thalamus showed significantly worse performance on the Part B test after controlling for scores from psychomotor functions (Part B – Part A; $p < .05$). Figure adapted from Hwang et al. (2020).

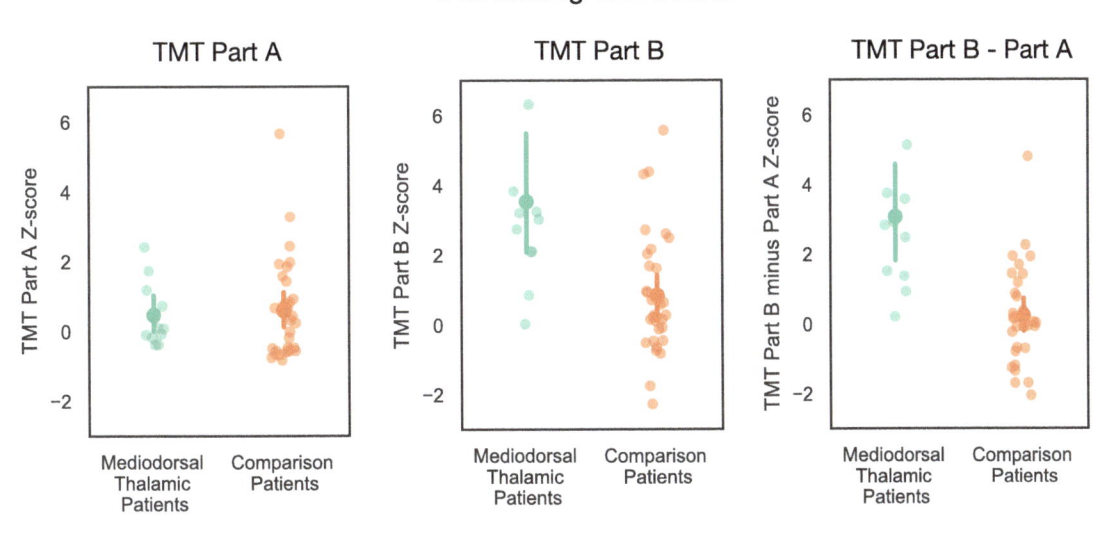

Patients with mediodorsal nucleus lesions, compared to healthy controls, are also impaired on working memory tasks (Kubat-Silman et al., 2002). A study that performed deep-brain stimulation found that stimulating the mediodorsal nucleus in human participants, but not the anterior nucleus, impaired working memory (Peräkylä et al., 2017). Lesions of the monkey mediodorsal nucleus had similar negative effects on working memory, impairing performances on a spatial working memory task (Isseroff et al., 1982) and a delayed match-to-sample task (Buschman & Miller, 2007; J. R. Cohen & D'Esposito, 2016; Cole et al., 2013; Gazzaley et al., 2004; Hwang et al., 2014; Saalmann et al., 2012). Working memory-related impairments have also been reported in human patients with lesions in the ventrolateral nucleus. Specifically, a study of three patients with ventrolateral thalamic lesions found impairments in the use of memorized working memory content to guide visual search (de Bourbon-Teles et al., 2014).

The findings from patients with focal thalamic lesions demonstrate that the mediodorsal, ventrolateral, and pulvinar nuclei are necessary for cognitive control. Critically, these findings extend the correlative findings between the thalamus and cognitive control reported in neuroimaging studies. However, the neuropsychological studies performed thus far have been limited to cognitive tasks that are complex (e.g., Wisconsin Card Sorting Test and TMT) that engage many different hypothetical component processes (e.g., selective attention, task-set maintenance, working memory prospection, and cognitive flexibility) involved in cognitive control including (Crowe, 1998; Kortte et al., 2002; Miyake et al., 2000; Poldrack, 2006). To fully uncover the underlying neural mechanisms of this cascade of cognitive processes engaged by these tasks will require appropriate experimental designs and techniques. Formal models can be used to parametrize hypothetical component processes engaged during cognitive control, including maintaining the fidelity of working memory representation (Luck & Vogel, 1997; Ma et al., 2014), monitoring error and outcome (W. H. Alexander & Brown, 2011), and selecting competing actions (Ratcliff & McKoon, 2008). The neural substrate of these models can be mapped using tailored behavioral tasks and model-based neuroimaging analyses (e.g., Jiang et al., 2015; Yu et al., 2020). Such studies should further combine the inferential power of human lesion approaches to test how and if thalamic lesions modulate model parameters and to more precisely determine thalamic contributions to different component processes of cognitive control.

Thalamocortical Mechanisms of Cognitive Control

The human brain is known to express rich, dynamic activity. At the local level, neural responses such as neuronal spiking and voltage fluctuations in local field potentials exhibit task-dependent amplitude and tuning-property changes, which can be experimentally manipulated and measured (Curtis & D'Esposito, 2003; Luo & Maunsell, 2019; Roux et al., 2012; Serences et al., 2009). Local neural responses are in turn transmitted across brain networks via axonal projections and white-matter connections (Bullmore & Sporns, 2009), where inter-regional communication is dynamically adjusted depending on task demands (Buschman & Miller, 2007; J. R. Cohen & D'Esposito, 2016; Cole et al., 2013; Gazzaley et al., 2004; Hwang et al., 2014; Saalmann et al., 2012). These rich patterns of spatiotemporal brain activity facilitate the execution of a range of complex behaviors, including cognitive control. In this section, we will first discuss how the dynamic activity among both local and distributed brain regions is related to cognitive control functions. Next, we will describe how thalamocortical circuitry may be involved in shaping local responses and brain network activity.

The Role of the Thalamus in Working Memory

As discussed, cognitive control comprises many component processes. One such process, working memory, allows the individual to retain, manipulate, and utilize behaviorally relevant information, especially when this information is no longer available in the sensorium (Baddeley, 2007). Studies that utilize a wide range of techniques and approaches have consistently found that the frontal and parietal cortices are involved in working memory (D'Esposito et al., 1999; Ester et al., 2015; Fuster & Alexander, 1971; Lundqvist et al., 2016). Working memory is commonly studied using delayed-response tasks, where subjects are first presented with one or multiple stimuli and asked to memorize the stimuli after the stimuli are withdrawn from their senses, and then, after a delay, they must make a contingent response based on the memorized content. Neural activity that occurs between the sensory input and the contingent response, also known as the *delay period* (Sreenivasan & D'Esposito, 2019), is thought to reflect the active maintenance of working memory content that can be used to guide the contingent response (Nobre & Stokes, 2020).

Persistent, elevated delay activity is observed in the form of increased neuronal spike rates, increased oscillatory power in local field potentials, and elevated blood-oxygen-level–dependent (BOLD) signals measured by functional magnetic resonance imaging (fMRI). Elevated, persistent delay activity during working memory delayed-response tasks is found in rodents, nonhuman primates, and humans (Curtis & D'Esposito, 2003; Fuster & Alexander, 1971; Guo et al., 2017) and is distributed across multiple brain regions, including the prefrontal cortex (D'Esposito et al., 2000; E. K. Miller et al., 1996), the posterior parietal cortex (Chafee & Goldman-Rakic, 1998; Curtis et al., 2004), the occipitotemporal cortices (Ranganath et al., 2004), and the mediodorsal thalamus (Funahashi, 2013; Fuster & Alexander, 1971). In some regions, delay activity can be selective for the memorized stimuli identity (Ester et al., 2015; E. K. Miller et al., 1996), which is interpreted as activity related to processes that sustain the memory representation. Delay activity is also selective for stimuli attributes that are most relevant for making the contingent response or coding for the planned motor response itself (Armstrong et al., 2009; Funahashi, 2013; Funahashi et al., 1993; Fuster & Alexander, 1971; Watanabe & Funahashi, 2004b). Thus, delay activity is more than a passive representation of memory content but can also reflect prospective processes that bridge perceptual input and planned motor actions (Nobre & Stokes, 2020).

How is elevated, persistent delay activity generated? Computational models offer a few possible mechanisms. One such proposal is that persistent delay activity is a result of local circuit interactions where reciprocal, excitatory synaptic connections between a group of closely interconnected pyramidal neurons can create recurrent, reverberate interactions to sustain persistent neuronal firing (Camperi & Wang, 1998). An alternative proposal is that persistent activity is sustained by long-range inputs from external sources, such as reciprocal cortico-cortical excitatory interactions or recurrent thalamo-cortical loops (Wang, 2001). This mechanism is consistent with the finding of persistent delay activity in the mediodorsal thalamus in both humans and nonhuman primates (Callicott et al., 1999; Manoach et al., 2003; Watanabe & Funahashi, 2004a; Watanabe et al., 2009). In fact, the first seminal empirical study of delay activity during a working memory task by Fuster and Alexander (1971) found delay activity in the mediodorsal thalamus. This finding, coupled with the known thalamocortical projection anatomy (Jones, 1998), suggests that persistent delay activity observed in cortical regions during working memory may be driven by thalamic inputs.

To directly test this hypothesis, several studies using optogenetics techniques in mice found that inhibition of activity in the ventrolateral or mediodorsal nucleus caused diminished delay activity in the prefrontal (Bolkan et al., 2017) and premotor cortices (Guo et al., 2017). Another study induced activity in the mediodorsal thalamus during the performance of a delayed-response task and found enhanced information coding in the prefrontal cortex (Schmitt et al., 2017). These results provide strong evidence that the thalamus can modulate working memory-related delay activity in cortical regions, playing an active role in sustaining the representation of working memory content. Notably, in contrast to cortical neurons, these studies did not find sharp tuning properties in thalamic neurons, suggesting that the precise information content in working memory is not likely directly encoded in the thalamus. Thus, the fidelity of the working memory content is likely supported by the cortex, whereas the thalamus may be involved in control-related operations, such as selecting or sustaining information representation.

To support goal-directed behavior, working memory must be able to adaptively select behaviorally relevant information and update the content when necessary. In addition to modulating the temporary maintenance of task-relevant information, as indexed by delay activity, the thalamus may also be involved in inputting and updating task-relevant information into working memory. Computational models operationalize the process of encoding information into and updating content into working memory as an "input gate" (Chatham & Badre, 2015). When the gate is open, new information can enter the system. Mechanistically, this process is hypothesized to be dependent on a striatal-thalamic circuit (Figure 4A; Frank et al., 2001; Hazy et al., 2006). Specifically, it is proposed that the striatum disinhibits the thalamocortical projection system to facilitate new information to be activated in cortical circuits through thalamocortical projections (Figure 4B). In contrast, inhibition of the thalamus by the basal ganglia would prevent information from entering cortical circuits (Figure 4C). This model is built on a specific feature of the thalamocortical projection system in which a class of thalamocortical projection neurons, known as the "core" thalamic neurons (Jones, 1998), projects in a topographically ordered fashion to specific cortical areas (Figure 4A). Given that different cortical regions may be sensitive to different features, categories, or modalities of working memory content (Christophel et al., 2017), having a specific thalamocortical projection pathway that is selective for a restrictive class of information may be particularly advantageous because different core cells may be selectively activated to allow precise control over working memory content. This model, however, depends on a critical assumption that input/updating to the cortex by the thalamus is modulated by a graded level of inhibitory output to the thalamus from the basal ganglia as a result of the summed interactions of the direct and indirect pathways within the basal ganglia (Frank et al., 2001). In this way, the level of the basal ganglia's inhibitory output will inhibit or disinhibit thalamocortical projections to open or close the input gate to working memory. In addition to the outputs from the basal ganglia, the thalamus also directly receives corticothalamic projections from the cortex (Theyel et al., 2010) as well as inhibitory outputs from the reticular thalamic nucleus (Wimmer et al., 2015), both of which could also influence the gating of working memory content.

This model of thalamic function, in contrast to the thalamus being a passive relay station, is consistent with the empirical studies we reviewed previously demonstrating that the thalamus is actively involved in modulating cortical activity during working memory function (Bolkan et al., 2018; Guo

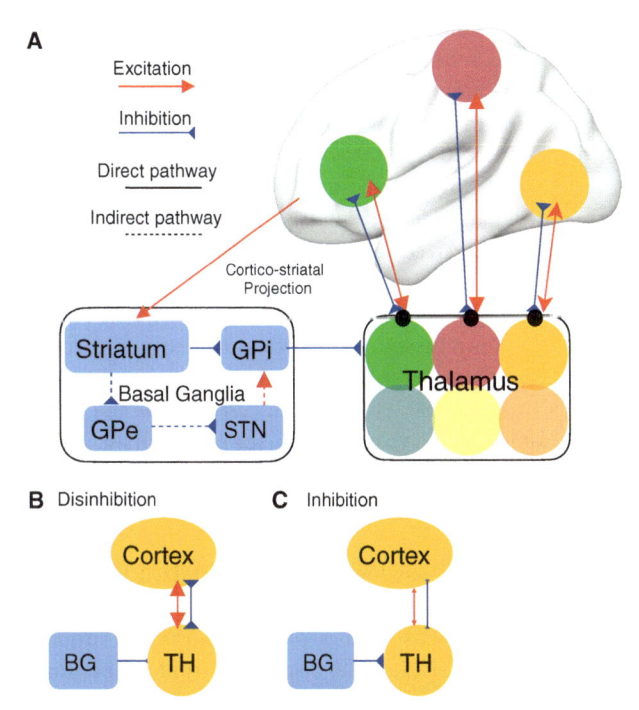

Figure 4 (A) Model of basal ganglia–thalamocortical control for working memory. Colored cells in the thalamus depict different thalamocortical projection cells, which target different cortical regions that represent different information content. (B) The striatum disinhibits the thalamocortical projection system to facilitate new information to be activated in cortical circuits through thalamocortical projections. (C) In contrast, inhibition of the thalamus from the basal ganglia would prevent information from entering cortical circuits. The thalamus is also capable of exerting both excitatory and inhibitory influence over cortical regions (thalamocortical activation vs. inhibition). The thalamus may also receive direct excitatory and inhibitory (via the thalamic reticular nucleus) outputs from the cortex. The inputting, updating, and maintenance of working memory content may be directly controlled by engaging excitatory and inhibitory thalamocortical interactions.

et al., 2017; Schmitt et al., 2017). Further refuting the passive role of the thalamus in cortical function, Rikhye and colleagues (2018) trained mice to perform a hierarchical task-switching task in which a task rule was more or less relevant depending on the behavioral context the rat was placed in during the experiment. Using optogenetics, disruption of mediodorsal thalamic activity enhanced information coding for the irrelevant task rule (Rikhye et al., 2018), suggesting that the thalamus can exert an inhibitory influence over cortical activity to inhibit task-irrelevant information. This further demonstrates that the thalamus can exert both excitatory and inhibitory control over cortical activity, indicating a broader task-adaptive, flexible modulatory role in cognitive function. In summary, the findings reviewed previously suggest that the thalamus may implement cognitive control operations that include inputting, updating, and maintaining task-relevant information by selectively activating or deactivating cortical processes through targeted thalamocortical circuits (Figure 4).

Thalamic Control of Local Evoked Responses

At the local level, top-down biasing signals emanating from cortical regions are known to modulate how strongly neurons in connected regions respond to inputs, defined as *evoked responses* (Badre et al., 2005; O'Craven et al., 1999). For example, attending to sensory stimuli amplifies evoked-response amplitudes associated with the attended stimuli (Feredoes et al., 2011; Gregoriou et al., 2014; Lee & D'Esposito, 2012; B. T. Miller et al., 2011; Morishima et al., 2009; Ruff et al., 2006; Zanto et al., 2011) and sharpens the tuning of evoked responses to the attended stimulus attribute (Serences et al., 2009), both hypothesized to be modulated by biasing signals (Desimone, 1998). Biasing signals can also inhibit processes that are not compatible with behavioral goals, for example, dampening the amplitude of activity associated with prepotent but inappropriate motor actions (Cai et al., 2011; Everling & Munoz, 2000; Hwang et al., 2014). The net effect of modulation of local evoked responses is to enhance task-relevant processes and inhibit task-irrelevant or distracting processes counterproductive to behavioral goals (Gazzaley et al., 2005).

The frontal cortex has long been hypothesized to be one source of biasing signals (D'Esposito, 2007; E. K. Miller & Cohen, 2001), and many studies provide empirical support for this hypothesis. For example, disrupting frontal lobe function, either through transcranial magnetic stimulation (TMS) in healthy adults or by lesions in animals or humans, causally affects the brain activity recorded in downstream connected regions (e.g., Feredoes et al., 2011; Gregoriou et al., 2014; Lee & D'Esposito, 2012; B. T. Miller et al., 2011; Morishima et al., 2009; Ruff et al., 2006; Zanto et al., 2011). Because TMS to the thalamus is not feasible and focal thalamic lesions in humans are uncommon, there have not been any human studies that have tested the role of the thalamus as a source of a top-down biasing signal. However, animal studies have investigated the modulatory effects of the thalamus.

In one study, white-matter pathways were severed in macaque monkeys to eliminate the transmission of biasing signals emanating from the frontal cortex to V4 during the performance of a spatial attention task. It was found that attentional modulation of evoked responses recorded in V4 was reduced but not completely eliminated (Gregoriou et al., 2014). This finding suggests that in addition to the frontal cortex, there may be another source of biasing signals that can modulate local evoked responses in V4, such as the thalamus. In two other studies, pharmacological or ontogenetic inhibition of pulvinar or reticular nucleus activity during the performance of a visual selective-attention task significantly reduced attentional modulation of evoked responses recorded in the visual cortex (Wimmer et al., 2015; Zhou et al., 2016). Specifically, the attentional enhancement in evoked-response amplitude for the attended target was greatly reduced, suggesting that thalamocortical interactions are necessary for attentional amplification of task-relevant evoked responses in the visual cortex. Together, these findings are consistent with the notion that in both rodents and nonhuman primates, the thalamus can exert excitatory influences over local cortical activity involved in goal-directed behavior. It remains to be tested whether the human thalamus exerts the same excitatory influence over cortical evoked activity for cognitive control.

Thalamic Control of Network Activity

The human brain can be conceptualized as a complex network consisting of interconnected circuits, brain regions, and neural systems (Bullmore & Sporns, 2009). Evaluating the architecture of brain networks offers another window into understanding cognitive control mechanisms. Methodological advances in whole-brain functional neuroimaging, coupled with mathematical tools to study networks (i.e., graph theory), now provide a means of formal analysis that can identify and characterize brain networks in humans (van den Heuvel & Sporns, 2013). With this approach, it is possible to quantify the degree and connectivity patterns of every region in the human brain, which allows one to ask the question: What type of brain network architecture supports cognitive control?

The architecture of brain networks can be effectively studied by graph theory-based methods, where brain networks are represented as graphs, brain regions are modeled as nodes, and relationships among regions are modeled as edges (Figure 5A). Edges can be defined anatomically, for example, white-matter structural connectivity, or functionally, by calculating the correlation of activity between brain regions. One popular technique for defining the functional relationship among brain regions is to measure correlations of spontaneous fluctuations in BOLD signals, also known as *resting-state functional connectivity*. Resting-state functional connectivity infers patterns of information communication, assuming that brain regions that share similar functions will exhibit strong functional connectivity among them (Buckner et al., 2013; Cole et al., 2016). After defining a network graph using resting-state functional connectivity, several different community-detection algorithms can be applied to identify the modular structure of brain networks (Sporns & Betzel, 2016). Brain regions within the same module have many connections with other brain regions in the same module and fewer connections with brain regions outside the module. Studies that utilized this approach have revealed the modular organization of functional brain networks in humans. For example, sensory and motor cortices form visual, auditory, and somatomotor networks that are localized and confined to unimodal cortices (Yeo et al., 2011). In contrast, frontoparietal association cortices form several distributed networks, including the dorsal-attention, ventral-attention, operculo-cingular, and frontal-parietal networks (Power et al., 2011; Yeo et al., 2011; Figure 5B).

In addition to revealing the modular structure of functional brain networks, graph theoretic approaches can also be used to study the network properties of individual nodes (brain regions) in a network. For example, nodes with many connections to other nodes in their own module are defined as *provincial hubs*, presumably to promote within-network interactions for executing specialized functions of the module (Figure 5A, left panel). In contrast, a brain region with many between-network connections has a strong "connector hub" property, presumably to mediate interactions between functional networks (Figure 5A, left panel). Provincial and connector hub properties can be quantified by two measures, the within-module z-score and participation coefficient, respectively (Guimerà & Nunes Amaral, 2005). Studies have

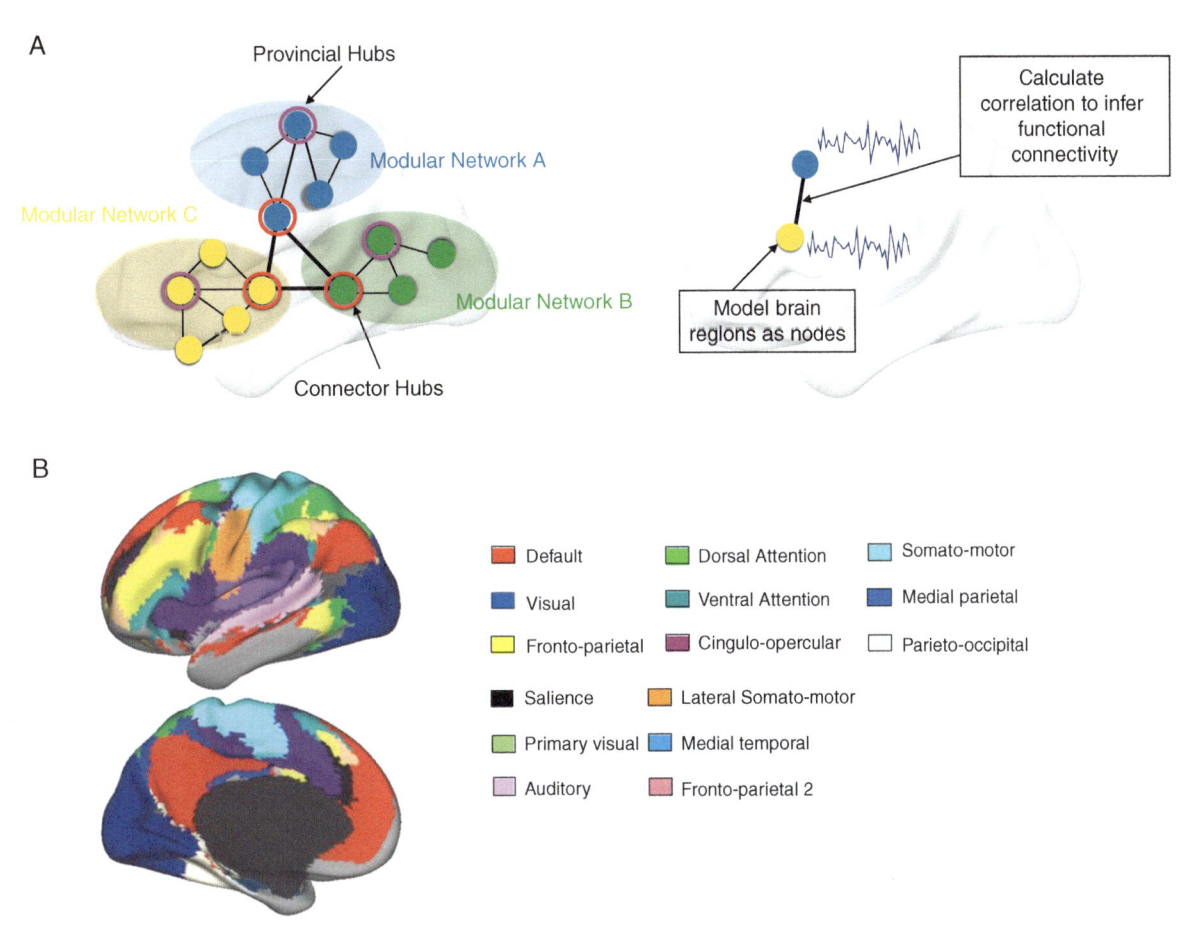

Figure 5 (A) Constructing and analyzing brain networks as graphs. In the left panel, brain networks can be represented as graphs, where brain regions are modeled as nodes, and functional connectivity among regions is modeled as edges. Nodes that share strong connectivity can be grouped as modular networks. Nodes with many connections to other nodes in their own module are defined as *provincial hubs*. Nodes with many between-network connections are *connector hubs*. In the right panel, functional connectivity is usually defined as correlation between BOLD signals. (B) Functional networks that have been identified in the human cerebral cortex. Figure 5B adapted from Wig et al. (2017).

found that functional networks that are primarily located in the frontal and parietal cortices have a high proportion of "connector hubs," more so than other networks (Bertolero et al., 2015; Power et al., 2013). Connector hubs may be involved in cognitive control functions through their diverging, distributed connections that interlink different functional networks, a network position that is ideal for exerting top-down control over behavior, facilitating biasing signals to flow through the internetwork connectivity to lower-level sensory and motor networks (Gordon et al., 2018; Power et al., 2013; Shine et al., 2016).

Does the thalamus exhibit connector hub properties for cognitive control? If so, this would support the notion that it is a source of top-down bias signal that can influence not only local evoked responses in connected regions but also network-level activity. In one set of analyses to address this question, rather than parcellating the thalamus based on histology, cytoarchitecture, and anatomical projection properties, the thalamus was parcellated based on its affiliation with different brain networks (Behrens et al., 2003; Morel et al., 1997), in a manner similar to what has been performed with the cerebral cortex (Zhang et al., 2008). In this way, it was determined which cortical network shares the strongest functional relationship with a particular thalamic subdivision. The anterior, medial, and posterior subdivisions of the thalamus are most strongly associated with control-related cortical networks that include the cingulo-opercular, frontoparietal, and dorsal attention networks (Greene et al., 2020; Hwang et al., 2017). Furthermore, these thalamic subdivisions, which overlap with the anterior, mediodorsal, intralaminar, ventrolateral, ventroposterior, and pulvinar nuclei, also exhibit strong connector hub properties (Figure 6A; Greene et al., 2020; Hwang et al., 2017). Surprisingly, both first-order and higher-order thalamic nuclei exhibit connector hub properties, which are even stronger than those of cortical regions (Figure 6B; Hwang et al., 2017). This finding suggests that the thalamus has a diverse and extensive functional relationship with distributed cortical networks. Similar to cortical regions such as the prefrontal cortex, thalamic nuclei are in a privileged position for providing bias signals that could broadly influence cortical networks. Because of its strong internetwork functional connectivity with both frontoparietal and unimodal networks, thalamic connector

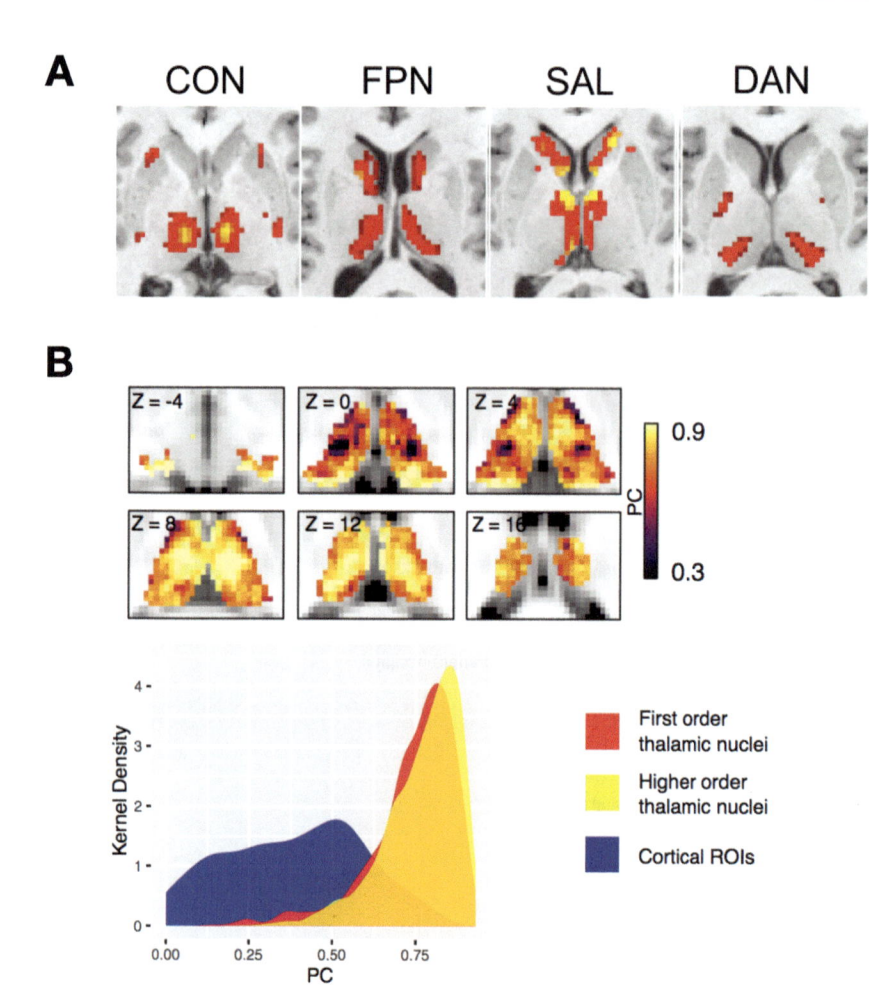

Figure 6 Functional parcellation of the thalamus and its connector hub properties. (A) Thalamic regions that associated cortical functional networks putatively involved in cognitive control–related functions. *CON*, cingulo-opercular network; *FPN*, frontoparietal network; *SAL*, saliency network; *DAN*, dorsal attention network. (B) The thalamus exhibits connector hub properties that are stronger than those of cortical regions. The color bar depicts the participation coefficient (PC), which ranges from 0 to 1. The PC is a measure of connector hubness. The medial, mediodorsal, and posterior portion of the thalamus exhibit particularly strong connector hub properties. Figure 6A adapted from Greene et al. (2019), with permission from Elsevier. Figure 6B adapted from Hwang et al. (2017).

hubs may also be involved in mediating the effects of top-down biasing signals emanating from frontoparietal networks to sensory and motor cortices. These proposed roles for the thalamus are consistent with findings that thalamic lesions impair cognitive control functions in a similar fashion to cortical lesions (de Bourbon-Teles et al., 2014; Snow et al., 2009).

Interregional communication within or between networks is proposed to be facilitated via the temporal coherence of local neural oscillations, in which modulating the consistency in the phase relationship between local neural oscillations provides a flexible mechanism to up- or down regulate information transfer between brain regions (Bastos et al., 2015; Fries, 2015). This phenomenon, increased coherence in neural oscillations between two putatively communicating brain regions, is referred to as *neural synchrony* (Varela et al., 2001; Womelsdorf et al., 2007). Information communication between cortical regions is commonly assumed to be carried out by direct cortico-cortical projections. However, higher-order thalamic nuclei, such as the mediodorsal and pulvinar nuclei, form the majority of its input–output relationship with the cerebral cortex and have been proposed to mediate the exchange of information between cortical regions through cortico-thalamo-cortical pathways (Guillery & Sherman, 2002). Moreover, inactivation of the thalamus diminishes the effectiveness of cortico-cortical communication (Theyel et al., 2010), suggesting that the thalamus is directly or indirectly involved in facilitating information transfer between cortical regions. What evidence exists that the thalamus can influence patterns of cortical neural synchrony?

Different frequencies of neural oscillations (i.e., alpha-, beta-, and gamma-band oscillations) have been demonstrated to be controlled by different sets of cortical GABAergic inhibitory interneurons (Cardin et al., 2009; M. A. Sherman et al., 2016; Sohal et al., 2009). GABAergic interneurons may therefore be a target for thalamocortical projections to control cortical neural synchrony and facilitate interregional communication. Indeed, GABAergic interneurons are known to be innervated by thalamocortical projections (Ährlund-Richter et al., 2019; Cruikshank et al., 2007). This mechanism may underlie findings in studies of the role of the thalamus in cognitive control. For example, while monkeys performed a visual attention task, the level of alpha-band neural synchrony between V4 and the TEO was modulated by the level of attention directed to the specific spatial receptive field (Usrey & Kastner, 2020). Similar findings have been observed in a human study using fMRI (Hwang et al., 2019). In another study, the pulvinar projection zone that is anatomically connected to both V4 and the TEO also exhibited increased alpha neural synchrony with these two regions, and applying regions that likely belong to different cortical networks (Giguere & Goldman-Rakic, 1988). Therefore, it is possible that a single higher-order thalamic nucleus could regulate cortico-cortical neural synchrony between multiple cortical regions that it projects to (Figure 7A). Alternatively, multiple different thalamic nuclei may simultaneously modulate distributed cortical neural oscillations to facilitate cortico-cortical neural synchrony. For example, if the lateral prefrontal cortex needs to effectively communicate biasing signals to the early visual cortex through increases in neural synchrony, both the mediodorsal nucleus and the pulvinar may modulate lateral frontal and occipital neural oscillations, respectively (Figure 7B).

To summarize, as reviewed in a previous section, the thalamus is in a privileged position within the overall network architecture of the human brain that allows it to influence interregional interactions for cognitive control. In this way, thalamic nuclei can provide top-down bias signals to influence both the local evoked activity of connected regions and internetwork interactions. These operations may be implemented via modulating neural synchrony between brain regions.

Conclusions

First, we comprehensively characterized the human thalamus's relationship with cognitive control to determine where and which thalamic nuclei may be involved in cognitive control and whether these nuclei provide necessary contributions. Results from meta-analyses of a large corpus of human functional neuroimaging studies indicate that there is a significant and reliable relationship between cognitive control and several thalamic nuclei, including the mediodorsal nucleus, the ventrolateral nucleus, and the pulvinar. These nuclei are known to have extensive interconnectivity with the frontal and parietal cortical regions, which have long been implicated as neural substrates for cognitive control. Human neuropsychology studies further demonstrate the necessity of the human thalamus for cognitive control, as lesions to several thalamic nuclei impair this cognitive ability.

Next, we presented several operation principles derived from anatomical and electrophysiology studies to form an empirical framework that describes the possible role of the human thalamus in cognitive control. This framework postulates that the human thalamus selects, maintains, and prioritizes information processing most relevant to one's behavior goals. We propose that there are several thalamocortical operations that support processes involved in cognitive control. First, specific thalamic nuclei modulate the amplitude of local cortical evoked responses to excite or inhibit cortical activity via targeted innervation to cortical pyramidal and inhibitory neurons. Through this operation, the thalamus may flexibly enhance cortical activity most relevant to behavior goals while inhibiting task-irrelevant activity. Second, leveraging its diverging connectivity with multiple cortical networks, the thalamus modulates network interactions. The thalamus modulates interregional communication within a network or between networks via influencing the coherence of local neural oscillations. In this way, the thalamus may be able to adaptively route

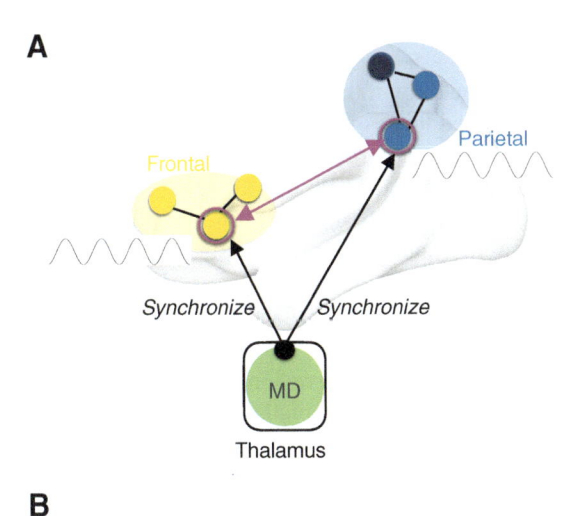

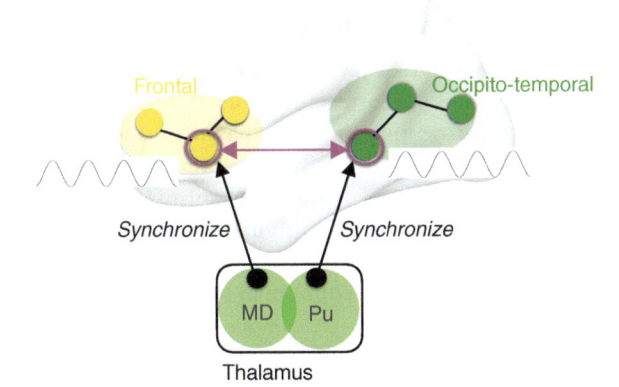

Figure 7 Two hypothetical models of how the thalamus regulates internetwork coordination in the human brain. (A) A single higher-order thalamic nucleus—in this example, the mediodorsal thalamus (MD)—regulates cortico-cortical neural synchrony between the frontal and parietal regions that it projects to. (B) Multiple different thalamic nuclei may simultaneously modulate distributed cortical neural oscillations to facilitate cortico-cortical coordination. For example, both the mediodorsal nucleus and the pulvinar (Pu) may modulate lateral frontal and occipitotemporal neural oscillations, respectively.

Granger causality analysis (Kamiński et al., 2001) revealed that the pulvinar modulates alpha-band activity in both V4 and the TEO (Saalmann et al., 2012). These findings were further corroborated by a study demonstrating that pharmacological inactivation of the macaque pulvinar reduces the attention-driven neural synchrony between V4 and the inferior temporal cortex (Zhou et al., 2016). These studies demonstrate that the pulvinar can modulate neural synchrony between brain regions within the occipitotemporal visual system for selective attention.

The question remains whether this type of modulation extends to information communication between large-scale networks. That is, in addition to influencing communication between brain regions within the visual system, can the thalamus influence communication between brain regions that belong to different yet distinct modular networks? To date, there is no direct evidence for it. However, there are known convergent projection zones in both the mediodorsal and the pulvinar that are anatomically connected with distal cortical information communication between task-related cortical regions to prioritize the information-processing channels most relevant to behavioral goals or by mediating the effects of top-down biasing signals originating from connector hubs.

There are many open questions in regard to the human thalamus's contribution to cognitive control, several already mentioned throughout this chapter. Here, we briefly highlight a few open questions:

- Cognitive control depends on both excitatory and inhibitory processes. Although the basal ganglia have been shown to inhibit thalamocortical projections, recently, the thalamus has also been found to exhibit inhibitory influences over cortical processes (Figure 4). Are there distinct functions between basal ganglia and thalamic inhibitory outputs? Do they have distinct contributions to cognitive control, and how are they utilized, respectively?
- Connector hubs are critical for coordinating network interactions in the human brain. Multiple thalamic nuclei exhibit strong connector hub properties, which also densely project to frontal and parietal connector hubs. Are there distinct functions between cortical and thalamic connector hubs for cognitive control?
- We reviewed a diverse range of thalamocortical mechanisms. The complexity of thalamocortical mechanisms is very much parallel to the complex ontogeny of cognitive control functions. More work is needed to determine if and how each thalamocortical mechanism is engaged for distinct cognitive control functions.
- Acknowledging the human thalamus's critical importance, there is an increased focus on investigating how thalamic dysfunction may cause neurological and psychiatric disorders (Clinton & Meador-Woodruff, 2004; Cronenwett & Csernansky, 2010; Krol et al., 2018). The specific thalamocortical mechanism that is disrupted in different disorders remains an open question.
- Our focus in this chapter was on thalamic nuclei (i.e., mediodorsal and pulvinar nuclei) that project and receive inputs from frontal and parietal regions presumed to be necessary for cognitive control functions. Presumably, the mechanisms by which these thalamic nuclei interact with the cortex extend to other thalamic nuclei, but this also remains an open question. For example, are first-order thalamic nuclei capable of executing the same type of operation identified in higher-order nuclei for cognitive control?

To conclude, given that several dozen thalamic nuclei project to every region of the cortex, these nuclei are positioned to influence specific cognitive processes based on their unique connectivity profiles. The diversity of the thalamus anatomy and its associated thalamocortical mechanisms is therefore crucial for a myriad of brain information processes. Undoubtedly, the thalamus plays a central role in all types of adaptive, flexible, and intelligent human behavior.

References

Ährlund-Richter, S., Xuan, Y., van Lunteren, J. A., Kim, H., Ortiz, C., Pollak Dorocic, I., Meletis, K., & Carlén, M. (2019). A whole-brain atlas of monosynaptic input targeting four different cell types in the medial prefrontal cortex of the mouse. *Nature Neuroscience*, **22**(4), 657–668.

Alexander, G. E., DeLong, M. R., & Strick, P. L. (1986). Parallel organization of functionally segregated circuits linking basal ganglia and cortex. *Annual Review of Neuroscience*, **9**, 357–381.

Alexander, W. H., & Brown, J. W. (2011). Medial prefrontal cortex as an action-outcome predictor. *Nature Neuroscience*, **14**(10), 1338–1344.

Anderson, S. W., Damasio, H., Jones, R. D., & Tranel, D. (1991). Wisconsin Card Sorting Test performance as a measure of frontal lobe damage. *Journal of Clinical and Experimental Neuropsychology*, **13**(6), 909–922.

Arend, I., Rafal, R., & Ward, R. (2008). Spatial and temporal deficits are regionally dissociable in patients with pulvinar lesions. *Brain: A Journal of Neurology*, **131**(Pt 8), 2140–2152.

Armstrong, K. M., Chang, M. H., & Moore, T. (2009). Selection and maintenance of spatial information by frontal eye field neurons. *Journal of Neuroscience*, **29**(50), 15621–15629.

Aron, A. R., Behrens, T. E., Smith, S., Frank, M. J., & Poldrack, R. A. (2007). Triangulating a cognitive control network using diffusion-weighted magnetic resonance imaging (MRI) and functional MRI. *Journal of Neuroscience*, **27**(14), 3743–3752.

Asanuma, C., Andersen, R. A., & Cowan, W. M. (1985). The thalamic relations of the caudal inferior parietal lobule and the lateral prefrontal cortex in monkeys: divergent cortical projections from cell clusters in the medial pulvinar nucleus. *Journal of Comparative Neurology*, **241**(3), 357–381.

Baddeley, A. (2007). *Working Memory, Thought, and Action*. Oxford University Press.

Badre, D., & D'Esposito, M. (2007). Functional magnetic resonance imaging evidence for a hierarchical organization of the prefrontal cortex. *Journal of Cognitive Neuroscience*, **19**(12), 2082–2099.

Badre, D., Hoffman, J., Cooney, J. W., & D'Esposito, M. (2009). Hierarchical cognitive control deficits following damage to the human frontal lobe. *Nature Neuroscience*, **12**(4), 515–522.

Badre, D., Poldrack, R. A., Paré-Blagoev, E. J., Insler, R. Z., & Wagner, A. D. (2005). Dissociable controlled retrieval and generalized selection mechanisms in ventrolateral prefrontal cortex. *Neuron*, **47**(6), 907–918.

Bastos, A. M., Vezoli, J., & Fries, P. (2015). Communication through coherence with inter-areal delays. *Current Opinion in Neurobiology*, **31**, 173–180.

Behrens, T. E. J., Johansen-Berg, H., Woolrich, M. W., Smith, S. M., Wheeler-Kingshott, C. A. M., Boulby, P. A., Barker, G. J., Sillery, E. L., Sheehan, K., Ciccarelli, O., Thompson, A. J., Brady, J. M., & Matthews, P. M. (2003). Non-invasive mapping of connections between human thalamus and cortex using diffusion imaging. *Nature Neuroscience*, **6**(7), 750–757.

Bertolero, M. A., Yeo, B. T. T., & D'Esposito, M. (2015). The modular and integrative functional architecture of the human brain. *Proceedings of the National Academy of Sciences of the United States of America*, **112**(49), E6798–807.

Bolkan, S. S., Stujenske, J. M., Parnaudeau, S., Spellman, T. J., Rauffenbart, C., Abbas, A. I., Harris, A. Z., Gordon, J. A., & Kellendonk, C. (2017). Thalamic projections sustain prefrontal activity during working memory maintenance. *Nature Neuroscience*, **20**(7), 987–996.

Bolkan, S. S., Stujenske, J. M., Parnaudeau, S., Spellman, T. J., Rauffenbart, C., Abbas, A. I., Harris, A. Z., Gordon, J. A., & Kellendonk, C. (2018). Publisher correction: thalamic projections sustain prefrontal activity during working memory maintenance. *Nature Neuroscience*, **21**(8), 1138.

Bowie, C. R., & Harvey, P. D. (2006). Administration and interpretation of the Trail Making Test. *Nature Protocols*, **1**(5), 2277–2281.

Buckner, R. L., Krienen, F. M., & Yeo, B. T. T. (2013). Opportunities and limitations of intrinsic functional connectivity MRI. *Nature Neuroscience*, **16**(7), 832–837.

Bullmore, E., & Sporns, O. (2009). Complex brain networks: graph theoretical analysis of structural and functional systems. *Nature Reviews. Neuroscience*, **10**(3), 186–198.

Buschman, T. J., & Miller, E. K. (2007). Top-down versus bottom-up control of attention in the prefrontal and posterior parietal cortices. *Science*, **315**(5820), 1860–1862.

Cai, W., Oldenkamp, C. L., & Aron, A. R. (2011). A proactive mechanism for selective suppression of response tendencies. *Journal of Neuroscience*, **31**(16), 5965–5969.

Callicott, J. H., Mattay, V. S., Bertolino, A., Finn, K., Coppola, R., Frank, J. A., Goldberg, T. E., & Weinberger, D. R. (1999). Physiological characteristics of capacity constraints in working memory as revealed by functional MRI. *Cerebral Cortex*, **9**(1), 20–26.

Camperi, M., & Wang, X. J. (1998). A model of visuospatial working memory in prefrontal cortex: recurrent network and cellular bistability. *Journal of Computational Neuroscience*, **5**(4), 383–405.

Cardin, J. A., Carlén, M., Meletis, K., Knoblich, U., Zhang, F., Deisseroth, K., Tsai, L.-H., & Moore, C. I. (2009). Driving fast-spiking cells induces gamma rhythm and controls sensory responses. *Nature*, **459**(7247), 663–667.

Carlesimo, G. A., Lombardi, M. G., & Caltagirone, C. (2011). Vascular thalamic amnesia: a reappraisal. *Neuropsychologia*, **49**(5), 777–789.

Chafee, M. V., & Goldman-Rakic, P. S. (1998). Matching patterns of activity in primate prefrontal area 8a and parietal area 7ip neurons during a spatial working memory task. *Journal of Neurophysiology*, **79**(6), 2919–2940.

Chalupa, L. M., Coyle, R. S., & Lindsley, D. B. (1976). Effect of pulvinar lesions on visual pattern discrimination in monkeys. *Journal of Neurophysiology*, **39**(2), 354–369.

Chatham, C. H., & Badre, D. (2015). Multiple gates on working memory. *Current Opinion in Behavioral Sciences*, **1**, 23–31.

Child, N. D., & Benarroch, E. E. (2013). Anterior nucleus of the thalamus: functional organization and clinical implications. *Neurology*, **81**(21), 1869–1876.

Christophel, T. B., Klink, P. C., Spitzer, B., Roelfsema, P. R., & Haynes, J.-D. (2017). The distributed nature of working memory. *Trends in Cognitive Sciences*, **21**(2), 111–124.

Clark, C. A. C., Pritchard, V. E., & Woodward, L. J. (2010). Preschool executive functioning abilities predict early mathematics achievement. *Developmental Psychology*, **46**(5), 1176–1191.

Clinton, S. M., & Meador-Woodruff, J. H. (2004). Thalamic dysfunction in schizophrenia: neurochemical, neuropathological, and in vivo imaging abnormalities. *Schizophrenia Research*, **69**(2–3), 237–253.

Cohen, J. D. (2017). Cognitive control: core constructs and current considerations. In T. Egner (Ed.), *The Wiley Handbook of Cognitive Control* (Vol. 50, pp. 1–28). John Wiley & Sons, Ltd.

Cohen, J. R., & D'Esposito, M. (2016). The segregation and integration of distinct brain networks and their relationship to cognition. *Journal of Neuroscience*, **36**(48), 12083–12094.

Cole, M. W., Ito, T., Bassett, D. S., & Schultz, D. H. (2016). Activity flow over resting-state networks shapes cognitive task activations. *Nature Neuroscience*, **19**(12), 1718–1726.

Cole, M. W., Reynolds, J. R., Power, J. D., Repovs, G., Anticevic, A., & Braver, T. S. (2013). Multi-task connectivity reveals flexible hubs for adaptive task control. *Nature Neuroscience*, **16**(9), 1348–1355.

Cole, M. W., & Schneider, W. (2007). The cognitive control network: Integrated cortical regions with dissociable functions. *NeuroImage*, **37**(1), 343–360.

Cronenwett, W. J., & Csernansky, J. (2010). Thalamic pathology in schizophrenia. *Current Topics in Behavioral Neurosciences*, **4**, 509–528.

Crosson, B., Parker, J. C., Kim, A. K., Warren, R. L., Kepes, J. J., & Tully, R. (1986). A case of thalamic aphasia with postmortem verification. *Brain and Language*, **29**(2), 301–314.

Crowe, S. F. (1998). The differential contribution of mental tracking, cognitive flexibility, visual search, and motor speed to performance on parts A and B of the Trail Making Test. *Journal of Clinical Psychology*, **54**(5), 585–591.

Cruikshank, S. J., Lewis, T. J., & Connors, B. W. (2007). Synaptic basis for intense thalamocortical activation of feedforward inhibitory cells in neocortex. *Nature Neuroscience*, **10**(4), 462–468.

Curtis, C. E., & D'Esposito, M. (2003). Persistent activity in the prefrontal cortex during working memory. *Trends in Cognitive Sciences*, **7**(9), 415–423.

Curtis, C. E., Rao, V. Y., & D'Esposito, M. (2004). Maintenance of spatial and motor codes during oculomotor delayed response tasks. *Journal of Neuroscience*, **24**(16), 3944–3952.

Danziger, S., Ward, R., Owen, V., & Rafal, R. (1999). The effects of unilateral pulvinar damage in humans on reflexive orienting and filtering of irrelevant information. *Behavioural Neurology*, **13**(3, 4), 95–104.

de Bourbon-Teles, J., Bentley, P., Koshino, S., Shah, K., Dutta, A., Malhotra, P., Egner, T., Husain, M., & Soto, D. (2014). Thalamic control of human attention driven by memory and learning. *Current Biology: CB*, **24**(9), 993–999.

Dehaene, S., & Changeux, J. P. (1991). The Wisconsin Card Sorting Test: theoretical analysis and modeling in a neuronal network. *Cerebral Cortex*, **1**(1), 62–79.

Desimone, R. (1998). Visual attention mediated by biased competition in extrastriate visual cortex. *Philosophical Transactions of the Royal Society of London. Series B, Biological Sciences*, **353**(1373), 1245–1255.

D'Esposito, M. (2007). From cognitive to neural models of working memory. *Philosophical Transactions of the Royal Society of London. Series B, Biological Sciences*, **362**(1481), 761–772.

D'Esposito, M., & Chen, A. J. W. (2013). Remediating frontal lobe dysfunction: from bench to bedside. In D. T. Stuss & R. T. Knight (Eds.), *Oxford Handbook of Frontal Lobe Function* (pp. 726–741). Oxford University Press.

D'Esposito, M., Postle, B. R., Ballard, D., & Lease, J. (1999). Maintenance versus manipulation of information held in working memory: an event-related fMRI study. *Brain and Cognition*, **41**(1), 66–86.

D'Esposito, M., Postle, B. R., & Rypma, B. (2000). Prefrontal cortical contributions to working memory: evidence from event-related fMRI studies. *Experimental Brain Research. Experimentelle Hirnforschung. Experimentation Cerebrale*, **133**(1), 3–11.

Diamond, A., & Lee, K. (2011). Interventions shown to aid executive function development in children 4 to 12 years old. *Science*, **333**(6045), 959–964.

Duncan, J. (2010). The multiple-demand (MD) system of the primate brain: mental programs for intelligent behaviour. *Trends in Cognitive Sciences*, **14**(4), 172–179.

Eickhoff, S. B., Bzdok, D., Laird, A. R., Kurth, F., & Fox, P. T. (2012). Activation likelihood estimation meta-analysis revisited. *NeuroImage*, **59**(3), 2349–2361.

Ester, E. F., Sprague, T. C., & Serences, J. T. (2015). Parietal and frontal cortex encode stimulus-specific mnemonic representations during visual working memory. *Neuron*, **87**(4), 893–905.

Everling, S., & Munoz, D. P. (2000). Neuronal correlates for preparatory set associated with pro-saccades and anti-saccades in the primate frontal eye field. *Journal of Neuroscience*, **20**(1), 387–400.

Fellows, L. K. (2017). Cognitive control in the injured brain. In T. Egner (Ed.), *The Wiley Handbook of Cognitive Control* (Vol. 67, pp. 513–538). John Wiley & Sons, Ltd.

Feredoes, E., Heinen, K., Weiskopf, N., Ruff, C., & Driver, J. (2011). Causal evidence for frontal involvement in memory target maintenance by posterior brain areas during distracter interference of visual working memory. *Proceedings of the National Academy of Sciences of the United States of America*, **108**(42), 17510–17515.

Fischer, J., & Whitney, D. (2012). Attention gates visual coding in the human pulvinar. *Nature Communications*, **3**, 1051.

Frank, M. J., Loughry, B., & O'Reilly, R. C. (2001). Interactions between frontal cortex and basal ganglia in working memory: a computational model. *Cognitive, Affective & Behavioral Neuroscience*, **1**(2), 137–160.

Fries, P. (2015). Rhythms for cognition: communication through coherence. *Neuron*, **88**(1): 220–235.

Funahashi, S. (2013). Thalamic mediodorsal nucleus and its participation in spatial working memory processes: comparison with the prefrontal cortex. *Frontiers in Systems Neuroscience*, **7**, 36.

Funahashi, S., Chafee, M. V., & Goldman-Rakic, P. S. (1993). Prefrontal neuronal activity in rhesus monkeys performing a delayed anti-saccade task. *Nature*, **365**(6448), 753–756.

Fuster, J. M., & Alexander, G. E. (1971). Neuron activity related to short-term memory. *Science*, **173**(3997), 652–654.

Gazzaley, A., Cooney, J. W., McEvoy, K., Knight, R. T., & D'Esposito, M. (2005). Top-down enhancement and suppression of the magnitude and speed of neural activity. *Journal of Cognitive Neuroscience*, **17**(3), 507–517.

Gazzaley, A., & Nobre, A. C. (2012). Top-down modulation: bridging selective attention and working memory. *Trends in Cognitive Sciences*, **16**(2), 129–135.

Gazzaley, A., Rissman, J., & D'Esposito, M. (2004). Functional connectivity during working memory maintenance. *Cognitive, Affective & Behavioral Neuroscience*, **4**(4), 580–599.

Giguere, M., & Goldman-Rakic, P. S. (1988). Mediodorsal nucleus: areal, laminar, and tangential distribution of afferents and efferents in the frontal lobe of rhesus monkeys. *Journal of Comparative Neurology*, **277**(2), 195–213.

Gläscher, J., Adolphs, R., Damasio, H., Bechara, A., Rudrauf, D., Calamia, M., Paul, L. K., & Tranel, D. (2012). Lesion mapping of cognitive control and value-based decision making in the prefrontal cortex. *Proceedings of the National Academy of Sciences of the United States of America*, **109**(36), 14681–14686.

Gläscher, J., Adolphs, R., & Tranel, D. (2019). Model-based lesion mapping of cognitive control using the Wisconsin Card Sorting Test. *Nature Communications*, **10**(1), 20.

Goldman-Rakic, P. S., & Porrino, L. J. (1985). The primate mediodorsal (MD) nucleus and its projection to the frontal lobe. *Journal of Comparative Neurology*, **242**(4), 535–560.

Gordon, E. M., Lynch, C. J., Gratton, C., Laumann, T. O., Gilmore, A. W., Greene, D. J., Ortega, M., Nguyen, A. L., Schlaggar, B. L., Petersen, S. E., Dosenbach, N. U. F., & Nelson, S. M. (2018). Three distinct sets of connector hubs integrate human brain function. *Cell Reports*, **24**(7), 1687–1695.e4.

Graff-Radford, N. R., Eslinger, P. J., Damasio, A. R., & Yamada, T. (1984). Nonhemorrhagic infarction of the thalamus: behavioral, anatomic, and physiologic correlates. *Neurology*, **34**(1), 14–23.

Graff-Radford, N. R., Tranel, D., Van Hoesen, G. W., & Brandt, J. P. (1990). Diencephalic amnesia. *Brain: A Journal of Neurology*, **113** (Pt 1), 1–25.

Greene, D. J., Marek, S., Gordon, E. M., Siegel, J. S., Gratton, C., Laumann, T. O., Gilmore, A. W., Berg, J. J., Nguyen, A. L., Dierker, D., Van, A. N., Ortega, M., Newbold, D. J., Hampton, J. M., Nielsen, A. N., McDermott, K. B., Roland, J. L., Norris, S. A., Nelson, S. M., . . . Dosenbach, N. U. F. (2020). Integrative and network-specific connectivity of the basal ganglia and thalamus defined in individuals. *Neuron*, **105**(4), 742–758.e6.

Gregoriou, G. G., Rossi, A. F., Ungerleider, L. G., & Desimone, R. (2014). Lesions of prefrontal cortex reduce attentional modulation of neuronal responses and synchrony in V4. *Nature Neuroscience*, **17**(7), 1003–1011.

Guillery, R. W., & Sherman, S. M. (2002). Thalamic relay functions and their role in corticocortical communication: generalizations from the visual system. *Neuron*, **33**(2), 163–175.

Guimerà, R., & Nunes Amaral, L. A. (2005). Functional cartography of complex metabolic networks. *Nature*, **433**(7028), 895–900.

Guo, Z. V., Inagaki, H. K., Daie, K., Druckmann, S., Gerfen, C. R., & Svoboda, K. (2017). Maintenance of persistent activity in a frontal thalamocortical loop. *Nature*, **545**(7653), 181–186.

Halassa, M. M., & Kastner, S. (2017). Thalamic functions in distributed cognitive control. *Nature Neuroscience*, **20**(12), 1669–1679.

Hazy, T. E., Frank, M. J., & O'Reilly, R. C. (2006). Banishing the homunculus: making working memory work. *Neuroscience*, **139**(1), 105–118.

Hwang, K., Bertolero, M. A., Liu, W. B., & D'esposito, M. (2017). The human thalamus is an integrative hub for functional brain networks. *Journal of Neuroscience*, **37**(23), 5594–5607.

Hwang, K., Bruss, J., Tranel, D., & Boes, A. D. (2020). Network localization of executive function deficits in patients with focal thalamic lesions. *Journal of Cognitive Neuroscience*, **32**(12), 2303–2319.

Hwang, K., Ghuman, A. S., Manoach, D. S., Jones, S. R., & Luna, B. (2014). Cortical neurodynamics of inhibitory control. *Journal of Neuroscience*, **34**(29), 9551–9561.

Hwang, K., Shine, J. M., & D'Esposito, M. (2019). Frontoparietal activity interacts with task-evoked changes in functional connectivity. *Cerebral Cortex*, **29**(2), 802–813.

Isseroff, A., Rosvold, H. E., Galkin, T. W., & Goldman-Rakic, P. S. (1982). Spatial memory impairments following damage to the mediodorsal nucleus of the thalamus in rhesus monkeys. *Brain Research*, **232**(1), 97–113.

Jiang, J., Beck, J., Heller, K., & Egner, T. (2015). An insula-frontostriatal network mediates flexible cognitive control by adaptively predicting changing control demands. *Nature Communications*, **6**, 8165.

Jones, E. G. (1998). Viewpoint: the core and matrix of thalamic organization. *Neuroscience*, 85(2), 331–345.

Jones, E. G., & Leavitt, R. Y. (1974). Retrograde axonal transport and the demonstration of non-specific projections to the cerebral cortex and striatum from thalamic intralaminar nuclei in the rat, cat and monkey. *Journal of Comparative Neurology*, 154(4), 349–377.

Kamiński, M., Ding, M., Truccolo, W. A., & Bressler, S. L. (2001). Evaluating causal relations in neural systems: Granger causality, directed transfer function and statistical assessment of significance. *Biological Cybernetics*, 85(2), 145–157.

Kastner, S., O'Connor, D. H., Fukui, M. M., Fehd, H. M., Herwig, U., & Pinsk, M. A. (2004). Functional imaging of the human lateral geniculate nucleus and pulvinar. *Journal of Neurophysiology*, 91(1), 438–448.

Koenigs, M., Barbey, A. K., Postle, B. R., & Grafman, J. (2009). Superior parietal cortex is critical for the manipulation of information in working memory. *Journal of Neuroscience*, 29(47), 14980–14986.

Kortte, K. B., Horner, M. D., & Windham, W. K. (2002). The Trail Making Test, Part B: cognitive flexibility or ability to maintain set? *Applied Neuropsychology*, 9(2), 106–109.

Krause, T., Brunecker, P., Pittl, S., Taskin, B., Laubisch, D., Winter, B., Lentza, M. E., Malzahn, U., Villringer, K., Villringer, A., & Jungehulsing, G. J. (2012). Thalamic sensory strokes with and without pain: differences in lesion patterns in the ventral posterior thalamus. *Journal of Neurology, Neurosurgery, and Psychiatry*, 83(8), 776–784.

Krauth, A., Blanc, R., Poveda, A., Jeanmonod, D., Morel, A., & Székely, G. (2010). A mean three-dimensional atlas of the human thalamus: generation from multiple histological data. *NeuroImage*, 49(3), 2053–2062.

Krol, A., Wimmer, R. D., Halassa, M. M., & Feng, G. (2018). Thalamic reticular dysfunction as a circuit endophenotype in neurodevelopmental disorders. *Neuron*, 98(2), 282–295.

Kubat-Silman, A. K., Dagenbach, D., & Absher, J. R. (2002). Patterns of impaired verbal, spatial, and object working memory after thalamic lesions. *Brain and Cognition*, 50(2), 178–193.

Kuljic-Obradovic, D. C. (2003). Subcortical aphasia: three different language disorder syndromes? *European Journal of Neurology*, 10(4), 445–448.

Laird, A. R., Lancaster, J. J., & Fox, P. T. (2005). BrainMap. *Neuroinformatics*, 3(1), 65–77.

Lee, T. G., & D'Esposito, M. (2012). The dynamic nature of top-down signals originating from prefrontal cortex: a combined fMRI-TMS study. *Journal of Neuroscience*, 32(44), 15458–15466.

Lesh, T. A., Niendam, T. A., Minzenberg, M. J., & Carter, C. S. (2011). Cognitive control deficits in schizophrenia: mechanisms and meaning. *Neuropsychopharmacology*, 36(1), 316–338.

Liebermann, D., Ploner, C. J., Kraft, A., Kopp, U. A., & Ostendorf, F. (2013). A dysexecutive syndrome of the medial thalamus. *Cortex*, 49(1), 40–49.

Luck, S. J., & Vogel, E. K. (1997). The capacity of visual working memory for features and conjunctions. *Nature*, 390(6657), 279–281.

Lundqvist, M., Rose, J., Herman, P., Brincat, S. L., Buschman, T. J., & Miller, E. K. (2016). Gamma and beta bursts underlie working memory. *Neuron*, 90(1), 152–164.

Luo, T. Z., & Maunsell, J. H. R. (2019). Attention can be subdivided into neurobiological components corresponding to distinct behavioral effects. *Proceedings of the National Academy of Sciences of the United States of America*, 116(52), 26187–26194. https://doi.org/10.1073/pnas.1902286116

Ma, W. J., Husain, M., & Bays, P. M. (2014). Changing concepts of working memory. *Nature Neuroscience*, 17(3), 347–356.

Mackey, W. E., Devinsky, O., Doyle, W. K., Golfinos, J. G., & Curtis, C. E. (2016). Human parietal cortex lesions impact the precision of spatial working memory. *Journal of Neurophysiology*, 116(3), 1049–1054.

Manoach, D. S., Greve, D. N., Lindgren, K. A., & Dale, A. M. (2003). Identifying regional activity associated with temporally separated components of working memory using event-related functional MRI. *NeuroImage*, 20(3), 1670–1684.

Miller, B. T., Vytlacil, J., Fegen, D., Pradhan, S., & D'Esposito, M. (2011). The prefrontal cortex modulates category selectivity in human extrastriate cortex. *Journal of Cognitive Neuroscience*, 23(1), 1–10.

Miller, E. K., & Cohen, J. D. (2001). An integrative theory of prefrontal cortex function. *Annual Review of Neuroscience*, 24, 167–202.

Miller, E. K., Erickson, C. A., & Desimone, R. (1996). Neural mechanisms of visual working memory in prefrontal cortex of the macaque. *Journal of Neuroscience*, 16(16), 5154–5167.

Miyake, A., Friedman, N. P., Emerson, M. J., & Witzki, A. H. (2000). The unity and diversity of executive functions and their contributions to complex "frontal lobe" tasks: a latent variable analysis. *Cognitive Psychology*, 41(1), 49–100.

Morel, A., Magnin, M., & Jeanmonod, D. (1997). Multiarchitectonic and stereotactic atlas of the human thalamus. *Journal of Comparative Neurology*, 387(4), 588–630.

Morishima, Y., Akaishi, R., Yamada, Y., Okuda, J., Toma, K., & Sakai, K. (2009). Task-specific signal transmission from prefrontal cortex in visual selective attention. *Nature Neuroscience*, 12(1), 85–91.

Nasreddine, Z. S., & Saver, J. L. (1997). Pain after thalamic stroke: right diencephalic predominance and clinical features in 180 patients. *Neurology*, 48(5), 1196–1199.

Nee, D. E., & D'Esposito, M. (2016). The hierarchical organization of the lateral prefrontal cortex. *eLife*, 5. https://doi.org/10.7554/eLife.12112

Nobre, A., & Stokes, M. S. (2020). Memory and attention: the back and forth. In M. S. Gazzaniga (Ed.), *The Cognitive Neurosciences* (6th ed., pp. 291–300). MIT Press.

Norman, D. A., & Shallice, T. (1986). Attention to action. In R. J. Davidson, G. E. Schwartz, & D. Shapiro (Eds.), *Consciousness and Self-Regulation: Advances in Research and Theory Volume 4* (pp. 1–18). Springer US.

O'Craven, K. M., Downing, P. E., & Kanwisher, N. (1999). fMRI evidence for objects as the units of attentional selection. *Nature*, 401(6753), 584–587.

Peräkylä, J., Sun, L., Lehtimäki, K., Peltola, J., Öhman, J., Möttönen, T., Ogawa, K. H., & Hartikainen, K. M. (2017). Causal evidence from humans for the role of mediodorsal nucleus of the thalamus in working memory. *Journal of Cognitive Neuroscience*, 29(12), 2090–2102.

Poldrack, R. A. (2006). Can cognitive processes be inferred from neuroimaging data? *Trends in Cognitive Sciences*, 10(2), 59–63.

Poldrack, R. A. (2011). Inferring mental states from neuroimaging data: from reverse inference to large-scale decoding. *Neuron*, 72(5), 692–697.

Poldrack, R. A., Baker, C. I., Durnez, J., Gorgolewski, K. J., Matthews, P. M., Munafò, M. R., Nichols, T. E., Poline, J.-B., Vul, E., & Yarkoni, T. (2017). Scanning the horizon: towards transparent and reproducible neuroimaging research. *Nature Reviews. Neuroscience*, **18**(2), 115.

Posner, M. I., Snyder, C. R., & Solso, R. (2004). Attention and cognitive control. In D. Balota & E. Marsh (Eds.), *Cognitive Psychology: Key Readings* (pp. 55–85). Psychology Press.

Power, J. D., Cohen, A. L., Nelson, S. M., Wig, G. S., Barnes, K. A., Church, J. A., Vogel, A. C., Laumann, T. O., Miezin, F. M., Schlaggar, B. L., & Petersen, S. E. (2011). Functional network organization of the human brain. *Neuron*, **72**(4), 665–678.

Power, J. D., Schlaggar, B. L., Lessov-Schlaggar, C. N., & Petersen, S. E. (2013). Evidence for hubs in human functional brain networks. *Neuron*, **79**(4), 798–813.

Rafal, R. D., & Posner, M. I. (1987). Deficits in human visual spatial attention following thalamic lesions. *Proceedings of the National Academy of Sciences of the United States of America*, **84**(20), 7349–7353.

Ranganath, C., DeGutis, J., & D'Esposito, M. (2004). Category-specific modulation of inferior temporal activity during working memory encoding and maintenance. *Brain Research. Cognitive Brain Research*, **20**(1), 37–45.

Ratcliff, R., & McKoon, G. (2008). The diffusion decision model: theory and data for two-choice decision tasks. *Neural Computation*, **20**(4), 873–922.

Rikhye, R. V., Gilra, A., & Halassa, M. M. (2018). Thalamic regulation of switching between cortical representations enables cognitive flexibility. *Nature Neuroscience*, **21**(12), 1753–1763.

Rock, P. L., Roiser, J. P., Riedel, W. J., & Blackwell, A. D. (2014). Cognitive impairment in depression: a systematic review and meta-analysis. *Psychological Medicine*, **44**(10), 2029–2040.

Romanski, L. M., Giguere, M., Bates, J. F., & Goldman-Rakic, P. S. (1997). Topographic organization of medial pulvinar connections with the prefrontal cortex in the rhesus monkey. *Journal of Comparative Neurology*, **379**(3), 313–332.

Roux, F., Wibral, M., Mohr, H. M., Singer, W., & Uhlhaas, P. J. (2012). Gamma-band activity in human prefrontal cortex codes for the number of relevant items maintained in working memory. *Journal of Neuroscience*, **32**(36), 12411–12420.

Ruff, C. C., Blankenburg, F., Bjoertomt, O., Bestmann, S., Freeman, E., Haynes, J.-D., Rees, G., Josephs, O., Deichmann, R., & Driver, J. (2006). Concurrent TMS-fMRI and psychophysics reveal frontal influences on human retinotopic visual cortex. *Current Biology: CB*, **16**(15), 1479–1488.

Saalmann, Y. B., Pinsk, M. A., Wang, L., Li, X., & Kastner, S. (2012). The pulvinar regulates information transmission between cortical areas based on attention demands. *Science*, **337**(6095), 753–756.

Schell, G. R., & Strick, P. L. (1984). The origin of thalamic inputs to the arcuate premotor and supplementary motor areas. *Journal of Neuroscience*, **4**(2), 539–560.

Schmahmann, J. D. (2003). Vascular syndromes of the thalamus. *Stroke*, **34**(9), 2264–2278.

Schmahmann, J. D., & Pandya, D. N. (1990). Anatomical investigation of projections from thalamus to posterior parietal cortex in the rhesus monkey: a WGA-HRP and fluorescent tracer study. *Journal of Comparative Neurology*, **295**(2), 299–326.

Schmitt, L. I., Wimmer, R. D., Nakajima, M., Happ, M., Mofakham, S., & Halassa, M. M. (2017). Thalamic amplification of cortical connectivity sustains attentional control. *Nature*, **545**(7653), 219–223.

Selemon, L. D., & Goldman-Rakic, P. S. (1988). Common cortical and subcortical targets of the dorsolateral prefrontal and posterior parietal cortices in the rhesus monkey: evidence for a distributed neural network subserving spatially guided behavior. *Journal of Neuroscience*, **8**(11), 4049–4068.

Serences, J. T., Saproo, S., Scolari, M., Ho, T., & Muftuler, L. T. (2009). Estimating the influence of attention on population codes in human visual cortex using voxel-based tuning functions. *NeuroImage*, **44**(1), 223–231.

Sherman, M. A., Lee, S., Law, R., Haegens, S., Thorn, C. A., Hämäläinen, M. S., Moore, C. I., & Jones, S. R. (2016). Neural mechanisms of transient neocortical beta rhythms: Converging evidence from humans, computational modeling, monkeys, and mice. *Proceedings of the National Academy of Sciences of the United States of America*, **113**(33), E4885–94.

Sherman, S. M., & Guillery, R. W. (2002). The role of the thalamus in the flow of information to the cortex. *Philosophical Transactions of the Royal Society of London. Series B, Biological Sciences*, **357**(1428), 1695–1708.

Sherman, S. M., & Guillery, R. W. (2006). *Exploring the Thalamus and Its Role in Cortical Function* (2nd ed.). MIT Press.

Sherman, S. M., & Guillery, R. W. (2013). *Functional Connections of Cortical Areas: A New View from the Thalamus*. MIT Press.

Shine, J. M., Bissett, P. G., Bell, P. T., Koyejo, O., Balsters, J. H., Gorgolewski, K. J., Moodie, C. A., & Poldrack, R. A. (2016). The dynamics of functional brain networks: integrated network states during cognitive task performance. *Neuron*, **92**(2), 544–554.

Snow, J. C., Allen, H. A., Rafal, R. D., & Humphreys, G. W. (2009). Impaired attentional selection following lesions to human pulvinar: evidence for homology between human and monkey. *Proceedings of the National Academy of Sciences of the United States of America*, **106**(10), 4054–4059.

Sohal, V. S., Zhang, F., Yizhar, O., & Deisseroth, K. (2009). Parvalbumin neurons and gamma rhythms enhance cortical circuit performance. *Nature*, **459**(7247), 698–702.

Sporns, O., & Betzel, R. F. (2016). Modular brain networks. *Annual Review of Psychology*, **67**, 613–640.

Sreenivasan, K. K., & D'Esposito, M. (2019). The what, where and how of delay activity. *Nature Reviews. Neuroscience*, **20**(8), 466–481.

Stuss, D. T., & Alexander, M. P. (2000). Executive functions and the frontal lobes: a conceptual view. *Psychological Research*, **63**(3–4), 289–298.

Stuss, D. T., & Alexander, M. P. (2007). Is there a dysexecutive syndrome? *Philosophical Transactions of the Royal Society of London. Series B, Biological Sciences*, **362**(1481), 901–915.

Sutterer, M. J., & Tranel, D. (2017). Neuropsychology and cognitive neuroscience in the fMRI era: A recapitulation of localizationist and connectionist views. *Neuropsychology*, **31**(8), 972–980.

Theyel, B. B., Llano, D. A., & Sherman, S. M. (2010). The corticothalamocortical circuit drives higher-order cortex in the mouse. *Nature Neuroscience*, **13**(1), 84–88.

Trojanowski, J. Q., & Jacobson, S. (1976). Areal and laminar distribution of some pulvinar cortical efferents in rhesus monkey. *Journal of Comparative Neurology*, **169**(3), 371–392.

Tsuchida, A., & Fellows, L. K. (2013). Are core component processes of executive function dissociable within the frontal lobes? Evidence from humans with focal prefrontal damage. *Cortex*, **49**(7), 1790–1800.

Usrey, W. M., & Kastner, S. (2020). Functions of the visual thalamus in selective attention. In M. S. Gazzaniga, G. R. Mangun, & D. Poeppel (Eds.), *The Cognitive Neurosciences* (6th ed., pp. 367–378). MIT Press.

van den Heuvel, M. P., & Sporns, O. (2013). Network hubs in the human brain. *Trends in Cognitive Sciences*, **17**(12), 683–696.

Van der Werf, Y. D., Scheltens, P., Lindeboom, J., Witter, M. P., Uylings, H. B. M., & Jolles, J. (2003). Deficits of memory, executive functioning and attention following infarction in the thalamus; a study of 22 cases with localised lesions. *Neuropsychologia*, **41**(10), 1330–1344.

Van der Werf, Y. D., Witter, M. P., & Groenewegen, H. J. (2002). The intralaminar and midline nuclei of the thalamus. Anatomical and functional evidence for participation in processes of arousal and awareness. *Brain Research. Brain Research Reviews*, **39**(2–3), 107–140.

Varela, F., Lachaux, J. P., Rodriguez, E., & Martinerie, J. (2001). The brainweb: phase synchronization and large-scale integration. *Nature Reviews. Neuroscience*, **2**(4), 229–239.

Verbruggen, F., McLaren, I. P. L., & Chambers, C. D. (2014). Banishing the control homunculi in studies of action control and behavior change. *Perspectives on Psychological Science*, **9**(5), 497–524.

von Cramon, D. Y., Hebel, N., & Schuri, U. (1985). A contribution to the anatomical basis of thalamic amnesia. *Brain: A Journal of Neurology*, **108** (Pt 4), 993–1008.

Wang, X. J. (2001). Synaptic reverberation underlying mnemonic persistent activity. *Trends in Neurosciences*, **24**(8), 455–463.

Watanabe, Y., & Funahashi, S. (2004a). Neuronal activity throughout the primate mediodorsal nucleus of the thalamus during oculomotor delayed-responses. I. Cue-, delay-, and response-period activity. *Journal of Neurophysiology*, **92**(3), 1738–1755.

Watanabe, Y., & Funahashi, S. (2004b). Neuronal activity throughout the primate mediodorsal nucleus of the thalamus during oculomotor delayed-responses. II. Activity encoding visual versus motor signal. *Journal of Neurophysiology*, **92**(3), 1756–1769.

Watanabe, Y., Takeda, K., & Funahashi, S. (2009). Population vector analysis of primate mediodorsal thalamic activity during oculomotor delayed-response performance. *Cerebral Cortex*, **19**(6), 1313–1321.

Watson, R. T., & Heilman, K. M. (1979). Thalamic neglect. *Neurology*, **29**(5), 690–694.

Wilke, M., Turchi, J., Smith, K., Mishkin, M., & Leopold, D. A. (2010). Pulvinar inactivation disrupts selection of movement plans. *Journal of Neuroscience*, **30**(25), 8650–8659.

Willcutt, E. G., Doyle, A. E., Nigg, J. T., Faraone, S. V., & Pennington, B. F. (2005). Validity of the executive function theory of attention-deficit/hyperactivity disorder: a meta-analytic review. *Biological Psychiatry*, **57**(11), 1336–1346.

Wimmer, R. D., Schmitt, L. I., Davidson, T. J., Nakajima, M., Deisseroth, K., & Halassa, M. M. (2015). Thalamic control of sensory selection in divided attention. *Nature*, **526**(7575), 705–709.

Womelsdorf, T., Schoffelen, J.-M., Oostenveld, R., Singer, W., Desimone, R., Engel, A. K., & Fries, P. (2007). Modulation of neuronal interactions through neuronal synchronization. *Science*, **316**(5831), 1609–1612.

Xiao, D., Zikopoulos, B., & Barbas, H. (2009). Laminar and modular organization of prefrontal projections to multiple thalamic nuclei. *Neuroscience*, **161**(4), 1067–1081.

Yarkoni, T., Poldrack, R. A., Nichols, T. E., Van Essen, D. C., & Wager, T. D. (2011). Large-scale automated synthesis of human functional neuroimaging data. *Nature Methods*, **8**(8), 665–670.

Yeo, B. T. T., Krienen, F. M., Eickhoff, S. B., Yaakub, S. N., Fox, P. T., Buckner, R. L., Asplund, C. L., & Chee, M. W. L. (2015). Functional specialization and flexibility in human association cortex. *Cerebral Cortex*, **25**(10), 3654–3672.

Yeo, B. T. T., Krienen, F. M., Sepulcre, J., Sabuncu, M. R., Lashkari, D., Hollinshead, M., Roffman, J. L., Smoller, J. W., Zöllei, L., Polimeni, J. R., Fischl, B., Liu, H., & Buckner, R. L. (2011). The organization of the human cerebral cortex estimated by intrinsic functional connectivity. *Journal of Neurophysiology*, **106**(3), 1125–1165.

Yu, Q., Panichello, M. F., Cai, Y., Postle, B. R., & Buschman, T. J. (2020). Delay-period activity in frontal, parietal, and occipital cortex tracks noise and biases in visual working memory. *PLoS Biology*, **18**(9), e3000854.

Zanto, T. P., Rubens, M. T., Thangavel, A., & Gazzaley, A. (2011). Causal role of the prefrontal cortex in top-down modulation of visual processing and working memory. *Nature Neuroscience*, **14**(5), 656–661.

Zhang, D., Snyder, A. Z., Fox, M. D., Sansbury, M. W., Shimony, J. S., & Raichle, M. E. (2008). Intrinsic functional relations between human cerebral cortex and thalamus. *Journal of Neurophysiology*, **100**(4), 1740–1748.

Zhou, H., Schafer, R. J., & Desimone, R. (2016). Pulvinar-cortex interactions in vision and attention. *Neuron*, **89**(1), 209–220.

Zikopoulos, B., & Barbas, H. (2006). Prefrontal projections to the thalamic reticular nucleus form a unique circuit for attentional mechanisms. *Journal of Neuroscience*, **26**(28), 7348–7361.

Chapter 17: The Thalamus in Attention

Sabine Kastner and Michael J. Arcaro

Introduction

The term *attention* refers to the selective prioritization of information that is most relevant to current behavioral goals. Such information and its associated neural representations can be related to external sources from the sensory environment or internally generated ones, such as thoughts. Typically, at any given moment in time, multiple items compete for neural representation, and prioritization of one representation over the others is necessary because of the brain's limited processing capacity. Attention mechanisms aid this prioritization or selection process in order to overcome competition for neural resources. Selective attention is fundamental to most cognition because it interfaces and guides cognitive processes such as memory, decision making, and action control (Lückmann et al., 2014; Ganguli et al., 2008; Smith & Ratcliff, 2009; Gottlieb & Balan, 2010). The study of the neural basis of selective attention also serves as a general model for cognitive function, whose fundamental mechanistic principles may apply more broadly to other cognitive domains.

In this chapter, we focus on the attention function of the primate thalamus and on its dominant sensory domain: vision. Much of primate behavior is guided by information selected from complex visual environments. The resulting behavioral repertoire and its underlying neural basis are fundamentally different from that of other mammals such as rodents. These differences in behavioral repertoires are also reflected in the functional organization of thalamocortical pathways (for detailed accounts of such organization in rodents, see Harris et al., 2019; Bennett et al., 2019), as we will elaborate later in the chapter. In particular, comparative studies in monkeys and humans using cognitive tasks that result in similar or identical behavioral patterns are ideally suited to guide models of human thalamic function, where the thalamus has been largely uncharted territory (Saalmann et al., 2012; Martin et al., 2019; Helfrich et al., 2018; Fiebelkorn et al., 2018, 2019). With few exceptions, our discussion of the functional role of the thalamus in selective attention will focus on results from non-human primates and humans.

There are multiple ways in which information from a visual scene can be selectively routed. It is possible to direct attention to a spatial location (space-based attention), to a particular feature (e.g., red items in the visual field; feature-based attention), or to a set of features that comprise an object (object-based attention). Each of these selection processes is associated with a distinct set of underlying neural mechanisms. Our chapter mainly focuses on the most well-studied mechanisms, which are those for space-based selections. Directing attention to a spatial location increases the speed and accuracy with which a subject can detect a target at that location (Posner et al., 1980), increases discrimination sensitivity (Lu & Dosher, 1998), improves acuity (Yeshurun & Carrasco, 1998), increases contrast sensitivity (Cameron et al., 2002), and reduces the interference caused by distractors (Shiu & Pashler, 1995). Although these behavioral benefits have been primarily demonstrated in classical cognitive psychology studies in humans, several of them have also been documented in the behaviors of monkeys, most compellingly by conducting direct comparative studies in the two primate species (Saalmann et al., 2012; Martin et al., 2019; Fiebelkorn et al., 2018, 2019; Helfrich et al., 2018).

Classic attention theories (Posner et al., 1980; Treisman & Gelade, 1980) assume that the spatial selection process utilizes a "spotlight" that, once allocated in space, samples information continuously over time. Recent work, however, has instead shown that attentional deployment is highly dynamic, characterized by alternating periods of relatively enhanced or diminished visual processing at the presently attended location (Fiebelkorn & Kastner, 2019). Even though these alternations in the sensitivity of visual processing are not noted subjectively, they can be readily observed in behavioral data and occur about four to six times per second (i.e., at a frequency in the theta range; VanRullen et al., 2007; Landau & Fries, 2012; Fiebelkorn et al., 2013; Song et al., 2014). Importantly, these theta-dependent rhythmic alternations of visual processing, associated with better or worse behavioral performance during visual-target detection, have been observed in both humans (Fiebelkorn et al., 2013; Helfrich et al., 2018) and non-human primates (Fiebelkorn et al., 2018), thus constituting a fundamental property of attention function that has been evolutionarily preserved for more than 20 million years.

In a typical visual attention experiment, a stimulus presented to the periphery of the visual field serves as a cue to direct attention to a specific location. Attention is then to be sustained at that location until a target is presented and the subject responds with a manual response or an eye movement. Such a simple task engages a vast network of areas distributed across all major lobes and includes the thalamus and other subcortical structures (Corbetta & Shulman, 2002; Kastner & Ungerleider, 2000; Buschman & Kastner, 2015; Fiebelkorn & Kastner, 2020; Caspari et al., 2015). This distributed large-scale network was initially defined mainly using neuroimaging methods and emphasized the cortical network parts as a result of methodological limitations. Specifically, areas along the intraparietal sulcus in the posterior parietal cortex and the frontal eye fields (FEFs) were identified as part of an attention-control network that generates modulatory signals to influence sensory processing in the visual cortex (e.g., Kastner et al., 1999; Szczepanski et al., 2010; Szczepanski & Kastner, 2013). The allocation of attention leads to an enhancement of the neural representation (e.g., of the spatial location in the previous example) that can occur in several different ways: (1) by enhancing response rates (on both baseline and visually evoked responses; Luck et al., 1997); (2) by decreasing noise correlations, trial-to-trial co-fluctuations in response strength shared by pairs of neurons (Cohen & Maunsell, 2009; Mitchell et al., 2009); and (3) by increasing synchronous firing in local neural populations (Fries et al., 2001). This initial focus on cortical processing during attention resulted in a corticocentric view of attention function and cognition more broadly. More recently, it has become clear that the thalamus is an integral part of the attentional large-scale network (Parvizi, 2009).

In primates, the visual thalamus consists of two main nuclei, the lateral geniculate nucleus (LGN) and the pulvinar. These structures are characterized by differences in their efferent and afferent connectivity patterns (Jones, 2007; Sherman & Guillery, 2013; Saalmann & Kastner, 2011). The LGN is considered a first-order nucleus because it relays visual signals from the retina primarily to V1 (or the primary visual cortex; Figure 1A, green arrows). In addition to retinal afferents, it receives projections from multiple other sources, including the brainstem, the thalamic reticular nucleus (TRN), and feedback from V1 (Figure 1A, red arrows). Thus, the LGN is the first stage in the visual pathway at which modulatory influences from other sources can affect information processing. The pulvinar is the largest nucleus in the primate thalamus and is considered a second-order, or higher-order, nucleus because it forms input–output loops almost exclusively with the cortex (Figure 2A). Both of these structures are also interconnected with the TRN, which forms a thin shell of neurons surrounding the thalamus. The TRN receives thalamocortical and corticothalamic projections but sends its output exclusively to the thalamus, constituting an important source of inhibitory control over thalamocortical transmission (Figures 1A and 2A; Hirsch et al., 2015; Halassa & Acsády, 2016). From an anatomical perspective, the visual thalamus is therefore ideally positioned to regulate information transmission to the cortex and between cortical areas, as originally proposed in theoretical accounts decades ago (Sherman & Koch, 1986; Crick, 1984). In the following, we will review the empirical evidence in support of the functional roles that the visual thalamus plays in selective attention.

The LGN: A "Gatekeeper"

The LGN is the prototypical thalamic nucleus for studying relay function. Given that the typical center/surround receptive field properties known from retinal ganglion cells are preserved in LGN cells (Wiesel & Hubel, 1966), it was long thought to be a "passive relay" that transmitted retinal signals faithfully to the visual cortex. Particularly, early studies demonstrated that selective attention appeared to affect neural responses in the cortex but had little or no influence in the LGN (Bender & Youakim, 2001; Lehky & Maunsell, 1996; Mehta et al., 2000). These studies shaped notions that cognitive operations recruited primarily cortical networks. This view is now overcome, and we will present evidence for a function of the LGN in controlling neural gain at the earliest possible processing stage, thereby exerting a powerful mechanism to filter unwanted information. Before we describe the specific studies in support of this evidence, we will briefly introduce the functional organization of the LGN as a basis for our discussion.

Functional Organization

In primates, the LGN is organized into six primary layers, four parvocellular and two magnocellular layers, each of which contains a retinotopic map of the contralateral visual field and a magnified foveal representation (Figure 1A; Malpeli & Baker, 1996). In addition, there are six thin layers, located ventral to each parvo- or magnocellular layer, that contain koniocellular cells. These different cell types form not only anatomically segregated but also functionally distinct parallel pathways and can selectively process specific aspects of the visual scene (Figure 1A; see Casagrande & Xu, 2004; Jones, 2007; Usrey & Alitto, 2015). Parvocellular cells receive input from midget ganglion cells and project to layer 4Cß in V1. They have small receptive fields, exhibit sustained responses, have low contrast sensitivity, and largely process form and color information. Magnocellular cells receive input from parasol retinal ganglion cells and project to layer 4Cα in V1. Their response properties are characterized by transient discharge patterns and high contrast sensitivity, and they largely process motion and depth information. Koniocellular cells receive input from a variety of ganglion cells and project into the superficial layers of V1 as well as to extrastriate areas (Hendry & Reid, 2000; Xu et al., 2001; Callaway, 2005). The response properties of koniocellular cells are not well understood. Some cells carry signals from short-wavelength–sensitive cone receptors (Martin et al., 1997; Roy et al., 2009). Unlike parvo- and magnocellular cells that resemble the functional response properties of their retinal ganglion cells' input, koniocellular cells can have complex response properties, including binocular responses or motion and orientation selectivity (Cheong et al., 2013; Zeater et al., 2015).

Postmortem and functional neuroimaging studies have revealed a highly similar anatomical and functional organization of the human LGN, including detailed retinotopic maps (Figure 1B; Hickey & Guillery, 1979; Schneider et al., 2004; DeSimone et al., 2015; Qian et al., 2020). Although it has not been possible to identify koniocellular layers, parvo- and magnocellular parts can be readily distinguished based on functional criteria, particularly the differences in contrast sensitivity and chromatic responses between magno- and parvocellular neurons (Derrington & Lennie, 1984; Sclar et al., 1990; Schneider & Kastner, 2009; Denison et al., 2014; Zhang et al., 2015). At higher-field (7T) magnetic field strength, even layer-specific responses with respect to parvo-, magno-, and eye-specific response properties may be resolvable (Qian et al., 2020), providing opportunities to determine their functions in

Cognition

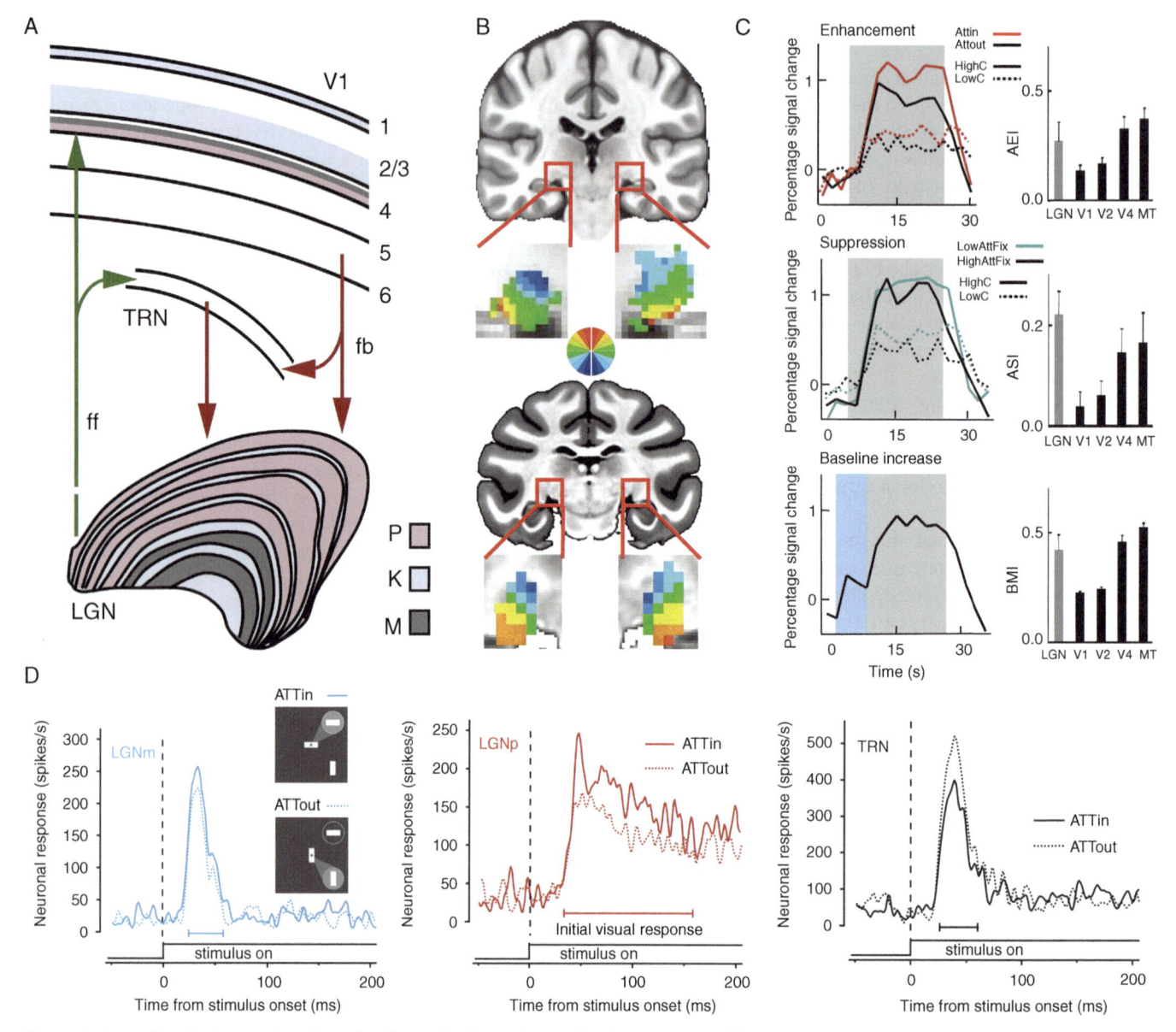

Figure 1 Lateral geniculate nucleus: Functional organization and attentional response modulation.

A. Feedforward (ff) projections from parvo-, konio-, and magnocellular (P, K, M) neurons in the LGN target specific layers in V1 (color-coded). Layer 6 feedback (fb) from V1, respectively, targets P, K, and M layers of the LGN.

B. Functional magnetic resonance imaging (fMRI)-defined retinotopic maps of contralateral visual space in human (*top*) and macaque (*bottom*) LGN (Arcaro et al. 2015; Arcaro & Livingstone 2017). Color-code wheel illustrates the preferred region of the contralateral visual field.

C. Time-series and attentional response modulation of fMRI signals in the human LGN (adapted with permission from O'Connor et al. 2002). Top: Attentional enhancement. During directed attention to the stimuli (*red curves*), responses to both a high-contrast stimulus (100%; *solid curves*) and a low-contrast stimulus (5%; *dashed curves*) were enhanced relative to an unattended condition (*black curves*). Middle: Attentional suppression. During an attentionally demanding fixation task (*black curves*), responses evoked by both a high-contrast stimulus (100%; *solid curves*) and a low-contrast stimulus (10%; *dashed curves*) were attenuated relative to an easier attention task at fixation (*green curves*). Bottom: Baseline increases. Baseline activity was elevated during directed attention to the periphery of the visual hemifield in expectation of the stimulus onset (*blue*). Gray shades indicate periods of checkerboard presentation. Attentional effects were quantified and normalized by defining several indices: attentional enhancement index (AEI), attentional suppression index (ASI), and baseline modulation index (BMI). Attentional effects in the LGN were larger than in V1. Vertical bars indicate the standard error of the mean (SEM) across subjects.

D. Responses to shifts of attention in an example magnocellular LGN neuron (*top*), parvocellular LGN neuron (*middle*), and TRN neuron (*bottom*) (adapted from McAlonan et al. 2008). Solid and dashed traces are spike-density plots of the neuron's ATTin and ATTout responses, respectively (illustrated by the "spotlight" of attention in the inset cartoon directed to the circle representing the receptive field). Responses are aligned to stimulus onset (*dashed vertical line*).

perceptual tasks such as binocular rivalry that are difficult to study in animal models (e.g., Wunderlich et al., 2005; Haynes et al., 2005).

Most of the projections that the LGN receives come from sources other than the retina, which comprises only about a third of the overall input. About another third consists of feedback projections from V1 and the TRN (Figure 1A) that are particularly important in the context of spatial attention because they provide spatially selective input to the same representations that inform the cortex (Sherman & Guillery, less spatial specificity. They play an important role in adjusting LGN activity to varying levels of alertness and during the sleep–wake cycle (Livingstone & Hubel, 1981; Steriade, 2004; Bereshpolova et al., 2011; McCormick et al., 2015). Whether they provide neuromodulation during selective attention is an open question. Given its multiple modulatory inputs, the LGN is well positioned to modify visual information transmission at the earliest processing stage in the primate visual system, and we will discuss next the possible functions of this modulation.

Gain Control and Distracter Filtering

The first compelling demonstration that the LGN plays a role in cognitive control came from human neuroimaging studies (O'Connor et al., 2002). In a series of three experiments (Figure 1C), it was found that spatially directed attention to a location in the right or left visual field enhanced LGN responses in spatially selective and predictable ways. Importantly, these attention effects were not only found on visually evoked responses but also on baseline activity, that is, during the time period when subjects directed attention to the visual field location in anticipation of the visual stimulus. The latter finding is quite remarkable, suggesting that pure feedback input to the LGN can drive neural activity without simultaneous input from the retina. Both of the enhancement effects—on visually evoked responses and on baseline activity—were larger than in V1 and on the order of typical effects found in the extrastriate cortex (Figure 1C; O'Connor et al., 2002). The modulatory effects on visually evoked responses in the magnocellular LGN tended to be greater than those in the parvocellular LGN (Schneider et al., 2009), supporting the idea of stream-specific feedback from the cortex. This idea has been further corroborated by a study showing orientation-selective modulation of functional magnetic resonance imaging (fMRI) signals in the LGN (Ling et al., 2015). Importantly, not only modulation of target-related activity was found but also attenuation of distracter-related activity. That is, when the attentional resources allocated at a target stimulus were gradually increased, the responses evoked by unattended distracter stimuli were gradually attenuated (Figure 1C; O'Connor et al., 2002). Thus, it appears that at the level of the LGN, spatial attention is not only able to modulate the sensory gain of neural responses evoked by attended stimuli but can also filter out unwanted information at the same time.

These findings were corroborated by single-cell recording studies in the monkey LGN that also provided insight into the temporal dynamics of the effects as well as the role of the TRN (Figure 1D; McAlonan et al., 2008). Consistent with the human studies, the spike rate of magnocellular neurons increased slightly more than in parvocellular neurons (11% vs. 9%). Interestingly, magnocellular neurons were affected earlier by spatial attention than parvocellular neurons, in line with the idea of pathway-specific cognitive modulation. There were two time windows of attentional response modulation: one within the first 100 ms and a second one occurring later and starting around 200 ms. It is possible that the modulatory effects varying over time reflect feedback from different sources, and we

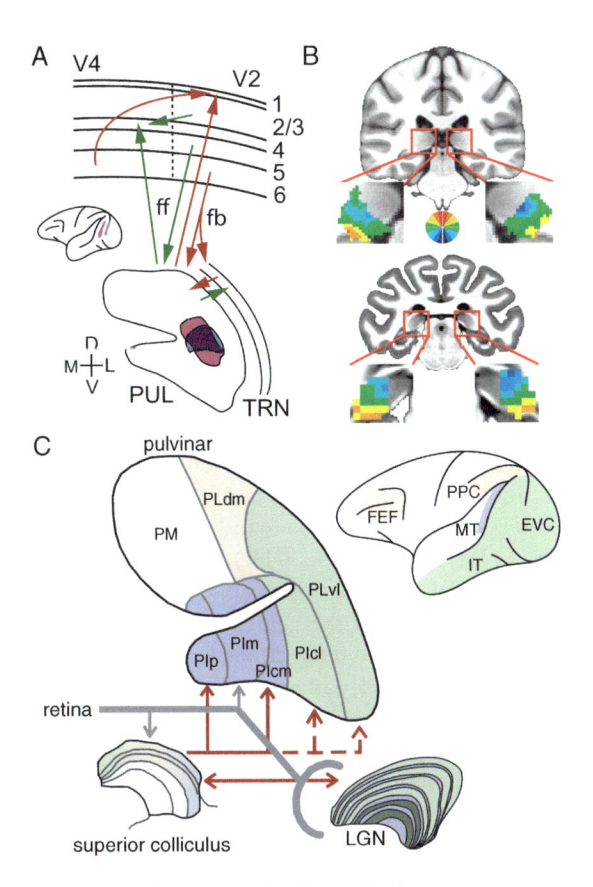

Figure 2 Pulvinar: Functional organization.

A. Direct cortico-cortical connections (*top*) and indirect cortico-pulvino-cortical loops exemplified by V2–pulvino–V4 circuitry. Tracer injections into V2 (*blue*) and V4 (*pink*; inset) showed overlapping (*purple*) projection zones in the pulvinar (*bottom*). Adapted with permission from Figure 8 in Adams et al. (2000).

B. fMRI-defined retinotopic maps of contralateral visual space in human (*top*) and macaque (*bottom*) ventral lateral pulvinar (Arcaro et al. 2015; Arcaro & Livingstone 2017). Color-code wheel illustrates the preferred region of the contralateral visual field.

C. Subdivisions of the macaque pulvinar and regional cortical connectivity. Frontoparietal (*beige*), medio-temporal (*violet*), and inferotemporal and occipital (*green*) cortical regions preferentially connect with different divisions of the pulvinar (with matching colors). The Plcl and PLvl pulvinar subdivisions shown in green are retinotopically organized (Figure 2B, bottom). Gray arrows indicate the direct projections from the eye to the subcortex. Red arrows indicate interconnectivity between the superior colliculus, LGN, and pulvinar. Abbreviations: *Plcl*, pulvinar inferior centro-lateral; *Plcm*, pulvinar inferior centro-medial; *Plm*, pulvinar inferior medial; *Pip*, pulvinar inferior posterior; *PLvl*, pulvinar lateral ventrolateral; *PLdm*, pulvinar lateral dorso-medial; *PM*, pulvinar medial.

2013). Importantly, corticothalamic feedback arises from different classes of neurons that each selectively target parvo-, magno- and koniocellular layers (Briggs & Usrey, 2009), suggesting that the parallel geniculo-cortical feedforward pathways could be modulated selectively by cortical feedback. Spatially selective input also arises from the TRN that exerts inhibitory control over LGN neurons and represents visual information in retinotopic maps (McAlonan et al., 2006). A third major modulatory influence arises from a number of extraretinal sources, including noradrenergic input from the reticular formation, cholinergic input from the parabrachial nucleus, and serotonergic input from the dorsal raphe nucleus. These projections are more diffusely organized than the V1 and TRN projections and will modulate LGN responses with will argue that the early modulation may be mediated by the TRN bypassing the cortex, whereas the later modulation may be attributable to feedback from the cortex. In contrast to LGN neurons and in line with their role in inhibitory control, TRN neurons showed a decrease in firing rates during the allocation of spatial attention, and the modulation started before that of the magnocellular LGN neurons, suggesting that the TRN may influence LGN responses during the early period (Figure 1D, right; McAlonan et al., 2008). Direct evidence for this idea comes from studies in rodents trained to selectively attend to either visual or auditory stimuli (Wimmer et al., 2015). Similar to the primate studies, attending to visual stimuli led to increases in LGN responses and decreases in TRN responses relative to when the visual stimuli were ignored. Importantly, causal manipulations showed that the TRN modulated the gain of LGN neurons via feedforward inhibition. This TRN–LGN circuit was controlled by the prefrontal cortex exerting direct influences on the TRN and bypassing the sensory cortex. Thus, the TRN may play an important role in controlling sensory gain at the level of the LGN to prioritize target-related representations. An independent second line of evidence for such a role of the TRN comes from rodent studies deleting the gene *PTCHD1* from the thalamus. *PTCHD1* is a gene that has been associated with attention deficit–hyperactivity disorder (ADHD) in humans and is enriched in the mouse TRN. Its expression is critical for thalamic inhibitory control (Wells et al., 2016). Mice in which this gene is deleted show impairments in filtering distracter information and are more susceptible to sensory noise (Wells et al., 2016). The rodent studies demonstrate circuit-level mechanisms for the control of sensory gain at the level of the LGN as well as for the filtering of unwanted information through PFC–TRN feedforward inhibition. Even though it is unclear whether the corresponding neural mechanisms exist in the primate PFC–TRN pathway (Zikopoulos & Barbas, 2006, 2012), these studies provide important hypotheses for future circuit-level studies in the primate thalamus.

Geniculo-Cortical Interactions

Thus far, we have discussed how sensory gain can be controlled even at early stages of visual processing in the LGN by rate changes of neural responses. Importantly, spatial attention also modulates the interactions between LGN and cortical neurons. Studies in which LGN neurons were electrically stimulated while their V1 target neurons were simultaneously recorded in monkeys trained in a spatial attention task revealed that attention increased the percentage of electrically evoked spikes in the cortex (Briggs et al., 2013). Thus, in addition to spike rate, spatial attention increased the likelihood of, or efficacy in, evoking postsynaptic responses in cortical target neurons by stimulating upstream neurons in the LGN that comprise the input signal. Such optimization of efficacy in signal transmission may be mediated by mechanisms that are related to spike timing. For example, precisely correlated firing within a group of LGN neurons that converge on a cortical neuron can increase the efficacy of the thalamic input to the cortex (Alonso et al., 1996). Similarly, paired spike interactions that occur in very short time windows within a geniculate neuron can increase the efficacy to drive cortical targets (Usrey et al., 1998).

Synchronizing the activity of two groups of neurons in different regions, such as in LGN and V1 input layers, may increase information exchange (Womelsdorf et al., 2007). Spikes are more likely to be relayed if the activity from presynaptic neurons arrives during periods of reduced inhibition of postsynaptic neurons. This spike-timing relationship can be achieved by synchronizing the oscillatory activity of pre- and postsynaptic neurons with an appropriate phase lag. Thus, synchrony between thalamic and cortical neurons may be yet another mechanism to increase the efficacy of thalamic input to the cortex. In support of this idea, oscillatory phase synchrony between LGN and V1 has been found for neural activity in the alpha (8–14 Hz) and beta (15–30 Hz) frequency bands of the local field potential (LFP; Bastos et al., 2014). Beta-band interactions were mediated by the geniculo-cortical feedforward pathway, and alpha-band interactions were mediated by the cortico-geniculate feedback pathway. Thus, given the existence of oscillatory activity that is phase synchronized in the LGN and V1, it is an important open question in primates whether spatial attention can modulate the oscillatory interactions, thereby strengthening the information transfer between them. In support of such a possibility, in cats, attentive viewing enhances the synchrony of beta-band oscillations of LFPs in the LGN and V1 (Bekisz & Wrobel, 1993; Wróbel et al., 1994).

In summary, our concept of the LGN as a "passive" relay has been thoroughly revised during the last two decades, and it has become clear that the thalamus plays active roles at this early stage of visual information processing. Thus far, there is evidence for TRN-controlled neural gain modulation that may not only enhance behaviorally relevant information processing but also attenuate distracter information, thereby filtering unwanted information. Geniculo-cortical interactions may be modulated in several possible ways during attention to increase the efficacy of thalamic signal transmission to the cortex. Thus, there is mounting empirical evidence for Crick's longstanding and, when first published, visionary theoretical ideas for the TRN–LGN circuit in controlling the "spotlight of attention" (Crick, 1984), consistent with the idea of an early "gatekeeper."

The Pulvinar: A "Timekeeper"

The pulvinar is the largest nucleus in the primate thalamus, and its vast expansion during evolution scales with that of the primate neocortex (Chalfin et al., 2007; Baldwin et al., 2017; Smaers et al., 2017), suggesting an important functional role in the increasing cognitive abilities of primates. It is considered a higher-order thalamic nucleus because it forms input–output loops almost exclusively with the cortex through at least two well-established pulvino-cortical pathways, a feedback and a feedforward one, that we will describe in greater detail in the next section. Even though our focus is on the functional role of the pulvinar and its interaction with the cortex in cognition, and specifically selective attention, it is necessary to provide first a brief overview of the anatomical and functional pulvinar organization, which has been shaped by specific primate behaviors. This will form the basis for our discussion of theoretical considerations regarding pulvinar function, impairments of behavior as a consequence of pulvinar lesions, and interpretations of electrophysiological recordings from pulvinar and interconnected cortex.

Functional Organization

The pulvinar is primarily interconnected with the extended visual cortical system (Adams et al., 2000; Gutierrez et al., 1995; Stepniewska & Kaas, 1997; Kaas & Lyon, 2007). Based on this connectivity, three main visual subdivisions have been traditionally distinguished: inferior (PI), lateral (PL), and mediodorsal (PM) pulvinar (Figure 2A and C). The PI can be further subdivided into two main sectors. One sector (PIcl) is defined by its retinotopic organization containing one visual field map that receives projections from early visual areas (Figure 2C, green color code). A second PI sector, located inferomedially, consists of three distinct nuclei (PIcm, PIm, and Pip) that connect with motion-selective areas, such as the middle temporal (MT), medial superior temporal (MST), and fundus of the superior temporal (FST; Figure 2C, violet color code), and also contains a coarse map of the contralateral visual space (Ungerleider et al., 1984). This second PI sector is the only region that receives input from the sensory periphery—either directly from the retina (Warner et al., 2012) or via the superior colliculus (Lyon et al., 2010). The PLvl connects with ventral and dorsal extrastriate areas and contains a second retinotopic map in its ventral half (Figure 2C, green color code). Accordingly, neurons in retinotopically organized parts of the PI and PL have a high proportion of visually responsive neurons with circumscribed receptive fields that roughly correspond in size to their interconnected cortical sites (Bender, 1982; Petersen et al., 1985). Similarly, the response properties of these neurons resemble those of their cortical inputs, such as orientation, movement direction, and color selectivity, including color opponency, albeit with weaker tuning than in the cortex (Bender, 1982; Felsten, 1983; Petersen et al., 1985). The mediodorsal pulvinar (PM and PLdm) connects with higher-order frontal and parietal areas and many other non-visual cortical sites (Figure 2C, beige color code; Kaas & Lyon, 2007). For example, in the marmoset, a New World monkey, more than 60 cortical projection sites have been identified (Homman-Ludiye et al., 2019). In the context of this chapter's topic, the mediodorsal pulvinar is a particularly critical part of the pulvinar. This subdivision appears to be primate-specific, reflecting the vast expansion of parietal association and frontal cortex in primates relative to other species (Romanski et al., 1997; Darian-Smith & Edwards, 1999; Homman-Ludiye et al., 2019). Among other areas, the mediodorsal pulvinar is interconnected with parietal and frontal cortical sites that constitute an attention control network (Yeterian & Pandya 1985; Schahmann & Pandya 1990; Baleydier & Maugeiere 1985). Therefore, it is of critical importance to understand the functional interactions of the mediodorsal pulvinar with the cortex in the context of attention behaviors. Similar to their cortical counterparts, mediodorsal pulvinar neurons can respond both to visual stimuli and during eye movements, and their response rates depend on cognitive state (Bender & Youakim, 2001; Petersen et al., 1985; Dominguez-Vargas et al., 2017; Fiebelkorn et al., 2019).

In humans, with the use of magnetic resonance imaging (MRI), a highly homologous functional organization of the pulvinar has been established (Figure 2B; Arcaro et al., 2015; DeSimone et al., 2015). Subdivisions of the human pulvinar analogous to the parcellation in monkeys, described earlier, have been identified based on the spatial clustering of activity patterns (Barron et al., 2015; Guedj & Vuilleumier, 2020). The inferior pulvinar contains two retinotopic maps in its lateral half (Arcaro et al., 2015; DeSimone et al., 2015) that are similar in location and organization to the PIcl and PLvl in macaques. Also similar to the macaque PIcl and PLvl, this region contains small receptive fields (DeSimone et al., 2015) covering the contralateral visual space (Cotton & Smith, 2007; Arcaro et al., 2015; DeSimone et al., 2015) and is responsive to a broad range of visual inputs, including color, motion direction, and image contrast (Cotton & Smith, 2007; Schneider, 2011; Gouws et al., 2014; Arcaro et al., 2018). Further, this region of the pulvinar is functionally coupled with early visual cortical areas that have similar response properties (Arcaro et al., 2015, 2018). Medial to these maps, there is a small region of the inferior pulvinar that contains a coarse representation of the contralateral visual space and is functionally coupled with motion-sensitive cortical areas (Arcaro et al., 2015). This region may be analogous to the motion-sensitive medial second sector of the macaque PI. The mediodorsal pulvinar lacks strong contralateral tuning and, similar to cortical connectivity in macaques, is functionally coupled with the frontoparietal attention control network as well as the lateral parietal cortex and the cingulate cortex (Arcaro et al., 2018). Taken together, the organization of the pulvinar appears to be well preserved between monkeys and humans.

It is noteworthy that the input–output loops that the pulvinar and cortex form reflect and are possibly shaped by species-specific behavioral repertoires. A good example to appreciate this important issue is the pulvino-cortical connectivity of the tectorecipient zone, the aforementioned second PI sector. Projections from the superior colliculus to the pulvinar or its homologue exist in all studied mammals (Figure 2C; Baldwin et al., 2017). In primates, this retino-collicular-pulvinar pathway that projects to the dorsal extrastriate motion pathway appears to be particularly important during early development in shaping motion selectivity in cortical neurons before inputs from the primary visual cortex and the geniculo-striate pathway arrive in these dorsal extrastriate areas (Bridge et al., 2016). After cortical lesions of the early visual cortex that lead to blindness, this pathway can carry responses about motion stimuli that afford residual vision in adults. Remarkably, if such lesions occur early in development, this pathway can drive visual plasticity with much better outcomes than in adulthood (Bourne & Morrone, 2017). In rodents, there is also a tectorecipient zone in the posterior part of the lateral posterior nucleus (LP), which is assumed to be homologous to the primate pulvinar. However, in contrast to primates, this zone projects to the ventral (not dorsal) visual cortical pathway and carries information about object motion (Bennett et al., 2019). This example illustrates how the use of motion information in the behavioral repertoire shapes the connectivity of thalamocortical pathways. In humans, the medial pulvinar is expected to have even richer connectivity than that observed in non-human primates, given the formation of unique cortical networks that reflect human-specific knowledge and behaviors, such as the parietal tool network (Kastner et al., 2017).

Thus far, we have described the gross connectivity of pulvinar subdivisions with the cortex. Intriguingly, the input–output loops between the pulvinar and cortex follow certain connectivity principles that lay the foundation for the functions of these circuits. Specifically, there are two well-established cortico-pulvinar pathways that parallel the canonical input–output relationships constituting the visual-processing hierarchy (Marion et al., 2013; Markov et al., 2014): (1) a transthalamic feedforward pathway (the green pathway in Figure 2A) that originates from layer 5 of a "lower" area (e.g., area V2 in Figure 2A), loops through a dedicated projection zone in the pulvinar, and feeds into layer 4 of a "higher" area (e.g., area V4 in Figure 2A), and (2) a feedback pathway (the red pathway in Figure 2A) that originates from layer 6 of a cortical area and projects to its pulvinar projection zone, also passing through the TRN (Figure 2A). An important characteristic of the transthalamic pathway, known as the *replication principle*, is that it indirectly connects two cortical areas that share a direct cortico-cortical projection (Adams et al., 2000; Shipp, 2003). In this respect, the pulvinar can be thought of as a mosaic of projection zones that mirrors the cortico-cortical connectivity. The replication principle may be a fundamental feature of corticothalamic organization that extends to all higher-order thalamic nuclei (Phillips et al., 2019). It is important to note that the input–output loops of the "canonical transthalamic pathways," as described previously, certainly present a simplification of the rich thalamocortical connectivity that exists (see Rovó et al., 2012). For example, pulvino-cortical projections can have spatially segregated targets in the cortex (Rockland, 1998; Rockland et al., 1999), and cortico-pulvinar projections exhibit convergence from multiple sources, particularly in the PM (Homman-Ludiye et al., 2019). However, this framework presents a starting point to explore the functions of the transthalamic pathways, which we will discuss in the next sections.

Effects of Pulvinar Lesions

Compelling evidence for a functional role of the pulvinar in selective attention has been provided by lesion studies in humans and monkeys. Functional or structural lesions of the pulvinar can lead to (1) spatial coding deficits that range in severity from slowing of responses in the affected visual space to thalamic neglect, a deficit in directing attention to the contralesional space (Wilke et al., 2010; Danziger et al., 2002; Rafal & Posner, 1987); (2) errors in binding featural information (Ward et al., 2002; Arend et al., 2008); and (3) an inability to filter distracting stimuli that compete with a target stimulus for neural representation (Danziger et al., 2004; Snow et al., 2009). In monkeys, lesions of the pulvinar, particularly the PM, have also been shown to affect visually guided behavior, such as reaching and grasping movements in the contralateral visual space (Wilke et al., 2010), similar to the optic ataxia observed after lesions of the superior parietal cortex in humans (e.g., Battaglia-Mayer & Caminiti, 2002). These deficits speak to the important role of the posterior parietal cortex and the interconnected pulvinar sites in integrating information across sensory modalities; however, we will focus our discussion on the deficits more closely related to visual attention function.

Visuospatial hemineglect is a profound attention deficit that is characterized by the inability to direct attention to the contralesional space. For patients with neglect, the visual scene contralateral to their lesion has simply vanished from existence, and they do not have conscious access to it. As typical consequences, these patients will eat from only half of their plate, apply makeup to only half of their face, and draw only half of an object when asked to copy it. There are various cortical lesion sites that can result in this syndrome, the most typical being the inferior temporoparietal cortex of the right hemisphere. Such a lesion typically causes a functional distant lesion of the right dorsal attention network in the posterior parietal cortex (PPC); that is, these areas are structurally, but not functionally, intact as a result of the lesion (Corbetta et al., 2005). Neglect can also occur as a consequence of thalamic lesions that involve the pulvinar (Karnath et al., 2002; Petersen et al., 1987). However, in humans, thalamic neglect is rare and typically does not persist. A milder deficit that may be a residual form of thalamic neglect has been observed as a slowing of responses to the contralesional space (Danziger et al., 2002; Rafal & Posner, 1987). Lesions in humans often encompass multiple parts of the pulvinar and other thalamic nuclei, and it therefore can be difficult to link a lesion site with a specific deficit. Inactivation studies in monkeys that target specific pulvinar subdivisions have shown that particularly lesions of the PM lead to deficits in directing attention to the contralateral space, similar to the typical deficits observed after parietal lesions (Wilke et al., 2010). Inactivation of the retinotopic map of the PIcl may lead to a visual field defect (scotoma; Zhou et al., 2016) or a neglect-like syndrome because lesions of the interconnected ventral extrastriate cortical areas will not result in visual field deficits.

Information in the visual system is initially filtered along multiple feature dimensions, such as orientation, movement direction, color, and others (Hubel & Wiesel, 1962; Livingstone & Hubel, 1988). Particularly, the filtered featural information has to be linked to the dimension of space as a fundamental building block for coding visual information. Patients with pulvinar lesions have difficulties in coding spatial information in the contralesional visual field, including difficulties in localizing stimuli and in binding visual features based on spatial information (Ward et al., 2002). For example, a patient may have difficulties binding a color to a shape when multiple objects are presented simultaneously: a green circle and red triangle may be mistaken to be a green triangle and red circle. Binding the featural information, as in this example, requires the precise coding of the spatial information associated with each feature. Errors in feature binding have been classically observed after PPC lesions (Friedman-Hill et al., 1995) but have also been demonstrated after pulvinar lesions (Arend et al., 2008; Ward et al., 2002), further underlining the close functional relationship between the PPC and, presumably, the mediodorsal pulvinar.

The process of selecting the information that is most relevant to behavior entails not only the preferential processing of target information but also the filtering of the majority of the visual information present in a typical visual scene, the unwanted distracter information. Accordingly, attention deficits are often associated with impairments in distracter filtering. Deficits in distracter filtering have been observed after pulvinar lesions (Danziger et al., 2004; Snow et al., 2009), and they are similar to those described after PPC lesions in humans (Friedman-Hill et al., 2003) or lesions in the extrastriate cortex, including area V4 in humans (Gallant et al., 2000) and monkeys (DeWeerd et al., 1999). Typically, when a target stimulus is presented alone, the patient will not have difficulties in discriminating it. However, once the target stimulus is shown together with competing salient distracter stimuli, the discrimination deficits of the target stimulus will become apparent.

Taken together, the spatial-coding deficits, feature-binding errors, and deficits in distracter filtering observed after pulvinar lesions often resemble the impairments classically observed after specific cortical lesions and thus underline the role of the pulvinar as an integral part of a large-scale attention network. Next, we will discuss studies from human neuroimaging and monkey electrophysiology on neural mechanisms in the pulvinar and particularly pulvino-cortical interactions related to attention behaviors.

Regulation of Intra- and Inter-Areal Interactions

As noted previously, the allocation of attention at a spatial location leads to an enhancement of the attended neural representation that can occur in several different ways. Attention-related increases in firing rates on both baseline and visually evoked responses (Bender & Youakim, 2001; Petersen et al., 1985; Saalmann et al., 2012; Zhou et al., 2016; Fiebelkorn et al., 2019), decreased noise correlations (Saalmann et al., 2012; Fiebelkorn et al., 2019), and increases in synchronous firing of local populations (Saalmann et al., 2012; Zhou et al., 2016; Fiebelkorn et al., 2019) have been found in all major pulvinar subdivisions, similar to the typical attention effects observed in the cortex. Indeed, the response modulation observed in the pulvinar appears to resemble that of the interconnected cortical areas (Figure 3A). This could be interpreted as evidence for a function of the transthalamic feedforward pathway in routing information through the thalamus, thereby indirectly relaying information from one cortical area to another, as proposed in the driver/modulator framework (Sherman & Guillery, 1998; Theyel et al., 2010; see review by Bickford, 2016). Specifically, in this account, driving input to the pulvinar originates from pyramidal cells in layer V and is routed through the thalamus to other cortical areas, implying that the receptive field properties and/or response properties will be largely preserved in this signal transformation. However, such a relay function is not compatible with a number of observations. For example, the effect sizes of response modulation in the cortex and pulvinar can differ substantially (Saalmann et al., 2012; Zhou et al., 2016; Fiebelkorn et al., 2019). Also, pulvinar neurons typically show less feature selectivity and larger receptive fields than their cortical inputs (Chalupa & Abramson, 1989; Purushothaman et al., 2012). These differences between pulvinar neurons and their cortical inputs suggest convergent inputs from additional sources, consistent with theoretical frameworks suggesting that the loops that the pulvinar forms with cortex are not closed, or "not so strong" (Crick & Koch, 1998). For example, in the "no-close-loops" framework, convergent inputs in the thalamus may lead to novel computations and output signals that are not present in the cortex. As for one prediction, eye position and eye-movement–related signals may transform from retinotopic cortical input signals to head- or body-centered reference frames in the pulvinar (Grieve & Cudeiro, 2000). Evidence in support of unique pulvinar output signals has been found in a study reporting neural signals related to decision certainty in a categorization task that were present only in the pulvinar and not in the cortex (Komura et al., 2013). It will be an important area of future inquiry to understand how the information that is carried through the transthalamic feedforward pathway is different from that of the corresponding cortico-cortical pathway.

Human neuroimaging studies have demonstrated that most, if not all, of the pulvinar is engaged during attention-related processes. Attention-related effects have been shown to vary across pulvinar subregions. Similar to attentional modulation effects observed in monkey physiology, ventral and dorsal regions that are functionally associated with the early visual and frontoparietal cortex, respectively, both show increased activity during the allocation of attention to the contralateral visual space (Smith et al., 2009; Schneider, 2011; Arcaro et al., 2018). Although the ventral pulvinar has a stronger visual drive, attention-related modulation is proportionally greater in the dorsal pulvinar (Smith et al., 2009; Arcaro et al., 2018). The dorsal, but not ventral, pulvinar shows increased activity during bilateral attention (Kastner et al., 2004). In line with lesion studies in human patients, both the dorsal and inferior parts of the pulvinar are engaged during the filtering of task-irrelevant visual information (Strumpf et al., 2012), potentially by gating spatial and featural information to represent only the attended target (Fischer & Whitney, 2012). In addition to selective enhancement of the attended stimulus, the medial pulvinar may be involved in the suppression of irrelevant information (Gouws et al., 2014). Together, these studies provide insight into the regionally specific effects of attention in the pulvinar that may be mediated by distinct cortical connectivity.

Although the signals that the pulvinar receives from the cortex and their transformation within the pulvinar are still quite unclear, recent studies have begun to shed light on the reverse influence of the pulvinar on the cortex. By recording simultaneously from two cortical areas in the monkey ventral extrastriate cortex (i.e., areas V4 and TEO) that share both direct cortico-cortical connectivity and a common pulvinar projection zone, Saalmann et al. (2012) probed functions of the transthalamic feedforward pathway and found evidence for a thalamic role in coordinating attention-related functional interactions across

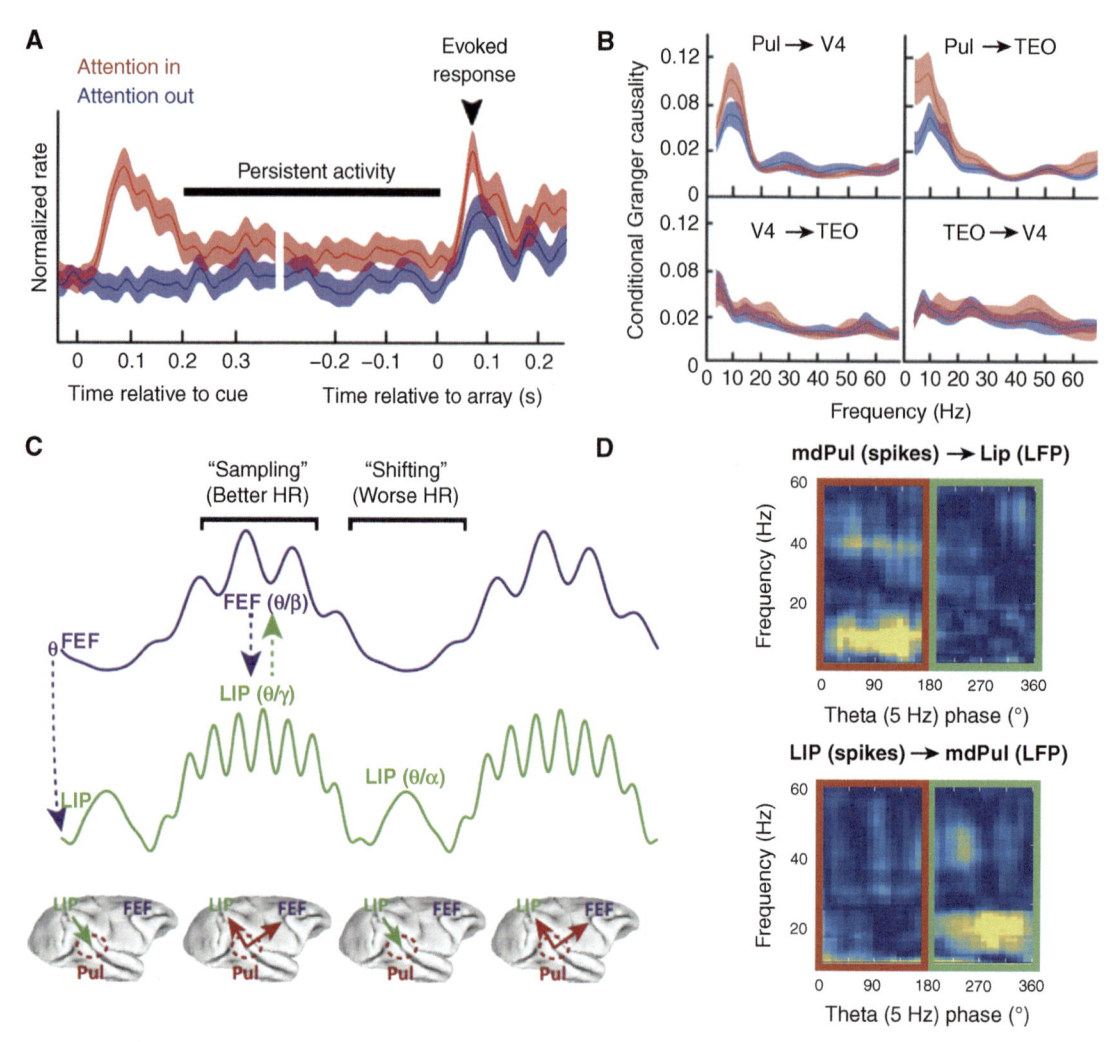

Figure 3 Pulvinar: Attentional response modulation and thalamocortical interactions.

A. Attentional modulation of pulvinar responses when spatial attention is allocated at the receptive field that is recorded from ("Attention in") versus elsewhere in the visual field ("Attention out"). Elevated activity during the cue target interval ("persistent activity") and attention-related response enhancement of visually evoked activity are apparent, similar to typical attention effects obtained in the visual cortex. (Adapted with permission from Saalmann et al., 2012.)

B. Conditional Granger causality analysis suggests that the pulvinar increases coherence in alpha frequencies in V4 and the TEO (a transitional area between the temporal and occipital visual areas) during the delay period. In contrast, V4 and the TEO do not seem to exert functional influences on each other or the pulvinar (*not shown*). (Adapted with permission from Saalmann et al., 2012.)

C. Spatial attention is characterized by alternating attentional states that promote either sampling at the attended location or a higher likelihood of shifting attentional resources to another location. These theta-rhythmic, alternating attentional states are associated with different oscillatory frequencies (e.g., beta and gamma oscillations) and different patterns of functional connectivity, with the pulvinar coordinating cortical activity specifically during periods of sensory sampling. (Adapted from Fiebelkorn & Kastner, 2019.)

D. Red box denotes sampling phase, and green box denotes shifting phase. (Adapted from Fiebelkorn et al., 2019.) Abbreviations: *Pul*, pulvinar; *V4*, visual area 4; *FEF*, frontal eye field; *LIP*, lateral intraparietal area; *mdPul*, mediodorsal pulvinar.

cortical areas. In addition to attentional modulation of spike rates (Figure 3A), attention enhanced coordinated spiking activity within the pulvinar and between the pulvinar and interconnected cortical areas. Such temporal coordination can be measured as a correlation of spiking activity relative to local population activity obtained from the field potential (i.e., spike-field coherence), either within or across areas. Saalmann et al. (2012) measured these functional interactions during the task period following the cue and before target presentation (i.e., the delay period), when the wider cortical attention network is set up for target selection. During the delay period, neurons in all three areas showed enhanced coordinated spiking in the alpha and low-beta ranges (<20 Hz). Strikingly, the pulvinar appeared to have the strongest influence on coordinated activity in V4 and the TEO in a frequency band that matched that of the local attentional modulation (Figure 3B). In contrast, both cortical areas had little influence on these interactions, suggesting that the pulvinar controlled the temporal coordination of functional interactions between cortical areas. These data are therefore consistent with the pulvinar, particularly the transthalamic feedforward pathway, having a primary role as a "timekeeper," coordinating and optimizing functional interactions across cortical networks to enhance the efficiency of signal processing between nodes. Fiebelkorn et al. (2019) have since provided evidence that this role of the pulvinar in coordinating cortical interactions is not limited to sensory cortical regions but also extends to functional interactions between higher-order frontoparietal regions (Figure 3C). Zhou et al. (2016) found evidence that the interactions between the pulvinar and cortex reverse during visual processing. For example, the latencies of pulvinar neurons lagged behind those of cortical neurons, and the cortex exerted a strong influence on the pulvinar in establishing functional interactions. However, this study may have primarily targeted the corticopulvino feedback pathway, and these results may therefore reflect fundamental differences between the functions of the transthalamic feedforward and feedback pathways.

Studies using causal manipulations have further corroborated these ideas, showing that functional connectivity between cortical areas is weakened as a consequence of pulvinar inactivation. These studies suggest that cortico-cortical information transmission is greatly compromised without the pulvinar's influences. During pulvinar inactivation, neural activity—spiking as well as gamma activity—was largely reduced in the visual cortex (Purushothaman et al., 2013; Zhou et al., 2016; Eradath et al., 2021), indicating a profound loss of responsiveness to visual stimuli. Pulvinar inputs to the cortex may therefore be instrumental in controlling the excitability of neurons in superficial and/or granular layers, allowing them to respond normally to incoming visual information from downstream areas. Such control of excitability could occur via excitatory inputs on pyramidal neurons or inhibitory control of interneurons, as suggested by increases in baseline firing during pulvinar inactivation (Zhou et al., 2016). Sensory gain control of cortical neurons by the pulvinar appears to follow a response gain model, in which neural responses are scaled multiplicatively or additively (de Souza et al., 2019). Thus, another major functional role of the transthalamic pathways appears to be that of an "enabler" of cortical function (Lakatos et al., 2016). It is important to note that the two functions that have been identified thus far, that of an enabler of cortical functioning and that of a temporal coordinator, may be mutually dependent. Once cortical functions are enabled by pulvinar inputs, a cascade of mechanisms could be set up that leads to synchronous oscillatory activity across cortical areas. In the next section, we will discuss the highly dynamic nature of these pulvino-cortical interactions and their associated functions.

Dynamics of Pulvino-Cortical Interactions

In considering the "fourth dimension"—time—recent studies have shown that cognition, and particularly attention function, is not static over time, but instead, cognition unfolds over time in a highly dynamic fashion (VanRullen, 2016). Specifically, when attention is allocated in space and sustained at a location, behavioral studies have shown that there are alternating periods of relatively enhanced or diminished visual processing at the attended location that occur at a frequency of about 4–6 Hz (VanRullen et al., 2007; Landau and Fries, 2012; Fiebelkorn et al., 2013; Song et al., 2014). These attention rhythms are present in humans as well as in non-human primates (Fiebelkorn et al., 2018).

What is the function of these theta-dependent attentional rhythms? It has been proposed that attention-related, theta-rhythmic fluctuations in behavioral performance reflect the temporal coordination of potentially conflicting sensory and motor functions that occur in the frontoparietal attention network and also include cortico-pulvino-cortical loops (Fiebelkorn & Kastner, 2019). The attention network directs both attention-related boosts in sensory processing, or "sampling," and the orienting of attention to new targets, or "shifting," for example, by executing saccadic eye movements (Fiebelkorn & Kastner, 2020; Corbetta et al., 1998; Moore & Fallah, 2001). This functionality is reflected in the response properties of neurons in the frontal cortex and the parietal cortex, which range from purely sensory (i.e., visually driven) to purely motor (i.e., saccade related; Thompson et al., 2005; Gregoriou et al., 2012). Sampling and shifting cannot occur at the same time and require temporal coordination of the associated neural populations and the wider circuits that they are embedded in. Theta-dependent attentional rhythms appear to coordinate two alternating states: a "sampling" state that emphasizes the preferential processing of visual information from the attended location and a "shifting" state when there is an increased likelihood of attentional shifting through either covert attentional shifts (i.e., in the absence of eye movements) or through overt attentional shifts (i.e., with eye movements). These latter "shifting periods," which are associated with relatively diminished visual processing, reflect windows of opportunity when it is easier to disengage from the presently attended location and shift to another location. Rhythmic sampling during attentional deployment thus provides critical flexibility not only to prioritize visual processing at an attended location but also to provide opportunities to reallocate attentional resources, if needed, without locking them into one particular state for extended periods of time (Fiebelkorn & Kastner, 2019).

Both pulvino-cortical and cortico-cortical dynamics play pivotal roles in controlling these alternating attentional states. Sampling periods—associated with relatively better visual-target detection at the attended location—are characterized by greater synchronization of gamma (>35 Hz) and beta (~15–30 Hz) activity within and between the frontal cortex and the parietal cortex (Figure 3C; Fiebelkorn et al., 2019). Importantly, the spiking activity of visual neurons is exclusively correlated with gamma activity, which has often been observed during enhanced visual processing (Fries et al., 2001), whereas the spiking activity of visuomotor neurons is exclusively correlated with beta activity, which has been linked to the suppression of motor actions (Pogosyan et al., 2009; Zhang et al., 2008). Similar to the temporal coordination that the PI provides for extrastriate visual cortex, as discussed in the last section, the mediodorsal pulvinar, or PM, coordinates these cortico-cortical interactions across the attention network (Fiebelkorn et al., 2019). However, it does so exclusively during sampling periods (Figure 3D) and not during shifting periods, further underlining the role of the transthalamic pathway in sensory gating. In contrast, shifting periods—associated with relatively worse visual-target detection at the attended location—are not only associated with a release of suppression in the motor system (Fiebelkorn et al., 2018) but also with greater synchronization of alpha-band activity (~9–14 Hz), specifically within the parietal cortex and between the parietal cortex and the mediodorsal pulvinar (Figure 3D; Fiebelkorn et al., 2019).

Parieto-occipital alpha-band activity is frequently associated with the suppression of sensory processing in human studies (Foxe & Snyder, 2011; Jensen & Mazaheri, 2010) as well as the suppression of cortical neuronal firing (Haegens et al., 2011). We propose that parietal-driven synchronization in the pulvinar temporarily shuts down the transthalamic pathway and its sensory gating function, thereby providing a neural substrate for the frequently observed visual suppression following alpha synchronization in the parietal cortex. As schematically summarized in Figure 3C, the neural evidence of rhythmic sampling during attentional deployment suggests a highly dynamic process across the attention network that results in alternating periods associated with either (1) enhanced visual processing and the suppression of attentional shifts (i.e., sampling periods) or (2) suppression of visual processing and a release from the suppression of attentional shifts (i.e., shifting periods; Fiebelkorn & Kastner, 2019). This pattern of results is consistent with a previous proposal based on human lesion studies, which suggested that the pulvinar was associated with the engagement of attentional resources at a behaviorally relevant location, whereas the parietal cortex was associated with a disengagement of attentional resources (Posner & Petersen, 1990).

In summary, we have reviewed the evidence that the indirect transthalamic pathways that link the cortex and pulvinar are associated with at least two major functions. First, these pathways serve to coordinate cortical networks recruited during cognition in time to enhance the efficiency of information transmission across the cortical network. Second, the pathway gates, or even enables, sensory information processing by controlling the local excitability of cortical neurons. Importantly, such temporal coordination and the enabling of cortical activity only occur during network states that emphasize sensory processing and not during states that emphasize motor processing and are implemented through a pulvino-parietal control network.

Computational Models of Pulvinar Function

Computational models play an increasingly important role in capturing the complexity of the local and long-distance circuits that characterize cognitive networks and the behaviors that they produce. Most distributed circuit models have emphasized cortical large-scale networks with modules in the frontal cortex and parietal cortex that successfully capture behavioral and neural features of cognitive tasks (e.g., Lee et al., 2013; Murray et al., 2017). Thalamic contributions to such networks have only been considered in recent modeling studies that have begun to include thalamic modules and examine their interactions with the cortex. Both of the main functional roles in attention that have been discussed in this chapter have been emphasized in recent studies.

Jaramillo and colleagues (2019) showed in their model, which builds on a model with two reciprocally connected cortical modules, that adding a pulvinar module provided critical flexibility during various cognitive behaviors, including attention. The pulvinar module was interconnected with the cortical modules through the "canonical" thalamocortical feedforward and feedback pathways, described previously. The overall connectivity in this large-scale circuit resulted from two sources: the direct cortico-cortical projection and the indirect transthalamic projections. Modulation of a single variable—pulvinar excitability, influenced by behavioral state—had a remarkable influence on cortical computation. As mentioned previously, persistent neuronal spiking is a classic signature of sustained-attention tasks (see Figure 3A). According to Jaramillo and colleagues (2019), when pulvinar excitability was low, the pulvinar was not actively engaged and did not contribute to overall connectivity in the network. As a consequence, persistent activity across the network could not be established. That is, even though cortical area 1 generated task-related activity, it could not propagate to area 2 because of low overall connectivity across the network. Similarly, cortical area 2 was not able to generate recurrent feedback signals that would reinforce the representation of task-related activity in area 1, again contributing to a lack of persistent activity. When pulvinar excitability was sufficiently large, however, signals were able to propagate between cortical areas 1 and 2, setting up the recurrent network state that is necessary for sustaining activity over time (i.e., for persistent activity). However, the precise local circuit mechanisms through which pulvinar excitability changes based on behavioral state remain largely unaddressed in this model.

The model by Quax et al. (2017) provided a mechanistic account of the pulvinar's role in synchronizing cortical large-scale networks to optimize information transmission across the network according to attentional demands. In their model, cortical circuits consisted of excitatory and inhibitory neuronal populations that were reciprocally connected within each area. Such local circuits have been shown to spontaneously produce gamma oscillations through a pyramidal–interneuron (excitatory/inhibitory) gamma mechanism (PING; Whittington et al., 2000). Further, the local circuits of a downstream cortical area 1 and an upstream cortical area 2 were connected via feedforward and feedback connections, respectively. Modulatory input from the pulvinar at alpha frequencies to inhibitory neurons of area 1 and with an appropriate phase lag to those of area 2 had a strong effect on coherent activity in the gamma band between the cortical areas. The modulation of gamma coherence by the relative alpha phase also led to a higher probability of spiking activity propagating from area 1 to area 2 and to an increase of information transfer between the two areas. The directionality of these interactions was also controlled by the alpha phase. Even though this model relies on a vast simplification of both cortical and thalamic local circuits, it presents an important starting point for the development of a biologically plausible large-scale network that will model empirical key results using interactions of detailed local circuits that dynamically change over time according to the behavioral demands of a task.

Conclusions

The last two decades have witnessed a renaissance of interest in the thalamus and its interaction with the cortex. Cortico-centric views have begun to shift toward concepts that emphasize the critical importance of thalamocortical interactions in normal cognitive functioning and in mental disease (Parvizi, 2009; Halassa & Kastner, 2017; Fiebelkorn & Kastner, 2020; Saalmann & Kastner, 2011). Particularly, studies in awake monkeys trained on sophisticated cognitive tasks have revealed important roles for the thalamus in cognition. As for attention function, the LGN is the earliest stage in the visual processing pathway at which neural responses are modulated. These modulations are important for controlling neural gain, thereby enhancing neural representations of attended stimuli and filtering out unwanted information from non-attended stimuli. Because of its rich and widespread connectivity with the cortex, the pulvinar coordinates cortical large-scale networks in time by synchronizing neural population activity between nodes, and pulvinar signals are critically needed to enable normal cortical functioning within a given area. The study of cognitive functions of the thalamus is still in its infancy, and much remains to be learned. However, it has become clear that a full understanding of primate—including human—cognition will not be possible without profound knowledge about the role of the thalamus.

Acknowledgments

We thank Bichan Wu for assistance with manuscript preparation. We gratefully acknowledge funding support from the National Institutes of Health (RO1MH64043, RO1EY017699, 21560–685 Silvio O. Conte Center), the James S. McDonnell Foundation, and the Overdeck Family Foundation. It should be noted that the pulvinar part of this chapter is an extended version of the review by Kastner et al. (2020).

References

Adams, M. M., Hof, P. R., Gattass, R., Webster, M. J. & Ungerleider, L. G. Visual cortical projections and chemoarchitecture of macaque monkey pulvinar. *Journal of Comparative Neurology* **419**, 377–393 (2000).

Alonso, J.-M., Usrey, W. M. & Reid, R. C. Precisely correlated firing in cells of the lateral geniculate nucleus. *Nature* **383**, 815–819 (1996).

Arcaro, M. J. & Livingstone, M. S. Retinotopic organization of scene areas in macaque inferior temporal cortex. *Journal of Neuroscience* **37**, 7373 (2017).

Arcaro, M. J., Pinsk, M. A., Chen, J. & Kastner, S. Organizing principles of pulvino-cortical functional coupling in humans. *Nature Communications* **9**, 5382 (2018).

Arcaro, M. J., Pinsk, M. A. & Kastner, S. The anatomical and functional organization of the human visual pulvinar. *Journal of Neuroscience* **35**, 9848 (2015).

Arend, I., Rafal, R. & Ward, R. Spatial and temporal deficits are regionally dissociable in patients with pulvinar lesions. *Brain* **131**, 2140–2152 (2008).

Baldwin, M. K. L., Balaram, P. & Kaas, J. H. The evolution and functions of nuclei of the visual pulvinar in primates. *Journal of Comparative Neurology* **525**, 3207–3226 (2017).

Baleydier, C. & Mauguiere, F. Anatomical evidence for medial pulvinar connections with the posterior cingulate cortex, the retrosplenial area, and the posterior parahippocampal gyrus in monkeys. *Journal of Comparative Neurology* **232**, 219–228 (1985).

Barron, D. S., Eickhoff, S. B., Clos, M. & Fox, P. T. Human pulvinar functional organization and connectivity. *Human Brain Mapping* **36**, 2417–2431 (2015).

Bastos, A. M., Briggs, F., Alitto, H. J., Mangun, G. R. & Usrey, W. M. Simultaneous recordings from the primary visual cortex and lateral geniculate nucleus reveal rhythmic interactions and a cortical source for gamma-band oscillations. *Journal of Neuroscience* **34**, 7639 (2014).

Battaglia-Mayer, A. & Caminiti, R. Optic ataxia as a result of the breakdown of the global tuning fields of parietal neurones. *Brain* **125**, 225–237 (2002).

Bekisz, M. & Wróbel, A. 20 Hz rhythm of activity in visual system of perceiving cat. *Acta Neurobiologiae Experimentalis* **53**, 175–182 (1993).

Bender, D. B. Receptive-field properties of neurons in the macaque inferior pulvinar. *Journal of Neurophysiology* **48**, 1–17 (1982).

Bender, D. B. & Youakim, M. Effect of attentive fixation in macaque thalamus and cortex. *Journal of Neurophysiology* **85**, 219–234 (2001).

Bennett, C. et al. Higher-order thalamic circuits channel parallel streams of visual information in mice. *Neuron* **102**, 477–492.e5 (2019).

Bereshpolova, Y. et al. Getting drowsy? Alert/nonalert transitions and visual thalamocortical network dynamics. *Journal of Neuroscience* **31**, 17480 (2011).

Bickford, M. Thalamic circuit diversity: modulation of the driver/modulator framework. *Frontiers in Neural Circuits* **9**, 86 (2016).

Bourne, J. A. & Morrone, M. C. Plasticity of visual pathways and function in the developing brain: is the pulvinar a crucial player? *Frontiers in Systems Neuroscience* **11**, 3 (2017).

Bridge, H., Leopold, D. A. & Bourne, J. A. Adaptive pulvinar circuitry supports visual cognition. *Trends in Cognitive Sciences* **20**, 146–157 (2016).

Briggs, F., Mangun, G. R. & Usrey, W. M. Attention enhances synaptic efficacy and the signal-to-noise ratio in neural circuits. *Nature* **499**, 476–480 (2013).

Briggs, F. & Usrey, W. M. Parallel processing in the corticogeniculate pathway of the macaque monkey. *Neuron* **62**, 135–146 (2009).

Buschman, T. J. & Kastner, S. From behavior to neural dynamics: an integrated theory of attention. *Neuron* **88**, 127–144 (2015).

Callaway, E. M. Structure and function of parallel pathways in the primate early visual system. *Journal of Physiology* **566**, 13–19 (2005).

Cameron, E. L., Tai, J. C. & Carrasco, M. Covert attention affects the psychometric function of contrast sensitivity. *Vision Research* **42**, 949–967 (2002).

Casagrande, V. A. & Xu, X. Parallel visual pathways: a comparative perspective. In *The Visual Neurosciences* (eds. Chalupa, L. M. & Werner, J. S.), 494–506 (MIT Press, 2004).

Caspari, N., Janssens, T., Mantini, D., Vandenberghe, R. & Vanduffel, W. Covert shifts of spatial attention in the macaque monkey. *Journal of Neuroscience* **35**, 7695 (2015).

Chalfin, B. P., Cheung, D. T., Muniz, J. A. P. C., de Lima Silveira, L. C. & Finlay, B. L. Scaling of neuron number and volume of the pulvinar complex in new world primates: Comparisons with humans, other primates, and mammals. *Journal of Comparative Neurology* **504**, 265–274 (2007).

Chalupa, L. & Abramson, B. Visual receptive fields in the striate-recipient zone of the lateral posterior-pulvinar complex. *Journal of Neuroscience* **9**, 347 (1989).

Cheong, S. K., Tailby, C., Solomon, S. G. & Martin, P. R. Cortical-like receptive fields in the lateral geniculate nucleus of marmoset monkeys. *Journal of Neuroscience* **33**, 6864 (2013).

Cohen, M. R. & Maunsell, J. H. R. Attention improves performance primarily by reducing interneuronal correlations. *Nature Neuroscience* **12**, 1594–1600 (2009).

Corbetta, M. et al. A common network of functional areas for attention and eye movements. *Neuron* **21**, 761–773 (1998).

Corbetta, M., Kincade, M. J., Lewis, C., Snyder, A. Z. & Sapir, A. Neural basis and recovery of spatial attention deficits in spatial neglect. *Nature Neuroscience* **8**, 1603–1610 (2005).

Corbetta, M. & Shulman, G. L. Control of goal-directed and stimulus-driven attention in the brain. *Nature Reviews Neuroscience* **3**, 201–215 (2002).

Cotton, P. L. & Smith, A. T. Contralateral visual hemifield representations in the human pulvinar nucleus. *Journal of Neurophysiology* **98**, 1600–1609 (2007).

Crick, F. Function of the thalamic reticular complex: the searchlight hypothesis. *Proceedings of the National Academy of Sciences of the United States of America* **81**, 4586 (1984).

Crick, F. & Koch, C. Constraints on cortical and thalamic projections: the no-strong-loops hypothesis. *Nature* **391**, 245–250 (1998).

Danziger, S., Ward, R., Owen, V. & Rafal, R. The effects of unilateral pulvinar damage in humans on reflexive orienting and filtering of irrelevant information. *Behavioural Neurology* **13**, 917570 (2002).

Danziger, S., Ward, R., Owen, V. & Rafal, R. Contributions of the human pulvinar to linking vision and action. *Cognitive, Affective, & Behavioral Neuroscience* **4**, 89–99 (2004).

Darian-Smith, C., Tan, A. & Edwards, S. Comparing thalamocortical and corticothalamic microstructure and spatial reciprocity in the macaque ventral posterolateral nucleus (VPLc) and medial pulvinar. *Journal of Comparative Neurology* **410**, 211–234 (1999).

de Souza, B. O. F., Cortes, N. & Casanova, C. Pulvinar modulates contrast responses in the visual cortex as a function of cortical hierarchy. *Cerebral Cortex* **30**, 1068–1086 (2019).

Denison, R. N., Vu, A. T., Yacoub, E., Feinberg, D. A. & Silver, M. A. Functional mapping of the magnocellular and parvocellular subdivisions of human LGN. *NeuroImage* **102**, 358–369 (2014).

Derrington, A. M. & Lennie, P. Spatial and temporal contrast sensitivities of neurones in lateral geniculate nucleus of macaque. *Journal of Physiology* **357**, 219–240 (1984).

DeSimone, K., Viviano, J. D. & Schneider, K. A. Population receptive field estimation reveals new retinotopic maps in human subcortex. *Journal of Neuroscience* **35**, 9836 (2015).

DeWeerd, P., Peralta, M. R., Desimone, R. & Ungerleider, L. G. Loss of attentional stimulus selection after extrastriate cortical lesions in macaques. *Nature Neuroscience* **2**, 753–758 (1999).

Dominguez-Vargas, A.-U., Schneider, L., Wilke, M. & Kagan, I. Electrical microstimulation of the pulvinar biases saccade choices and reaction times in a time-dependent manner. *Journal of Neuroscience* **37**, 2234 (2017).

Eradath, M. K., Pinsk, M. A. & Kastner, S. Causal role of pulvinar in resting state cortico-cortical interactions. *Journal of Comparative Neurology* **529**, 3772–3784 (2020).

Felsten, G. Different approaches to physiological psychology. *Psyccritiques* **28**, 38–40 (1983).

Fiebelkorn, I. C. & Kastner, S. A rhythmic theory of attention. *Trends in Cognitive Sciences* **23**, 87–101 (2019).

Fiebelkorn, I. C. & Kastner, S. Functional specialization in the attention network. *Annual Review of Psychology* **71**, 221–249 (2020).

Fiebelkorn, I. C., Pinsk, M. A. & Kastner, S. A dynamic interplay within the frontoparietal network underlies rhythmic spatial attention. *Neuron* **99**, 842–853.e8 (2018).

Fiebelkorn, I. C., Pinsk, M. A. & Kastner, S. The mediodorsal pulvinar coordinates the macaque fronto-parietal network during rhythmic spatial attention. *Nature Communications* **10**, 215 (2019).

Fiebelkorn, I. C., Saalmann, Y. B. & Kastner, S. Rhythmic sampling within and between objects despite sustained attention at a cued location. *Current Biology* **23**, 2553–2558 (2013).

Fischer, J. & Whitney, D. Attention gates visual coding in the human pulvinar. *Nature Communications* **3**, 1051 (2012).

Foxe, J. & Snyder, A. The role of alpha-band brain oscillations as a sensory suppression mechanism during selective attention. *Frontiers in Psychology* **2**, 154 (2011).

Friedman-Hill, S. R., Robertson, L. C., Desimone, R. & Ungerleider, L. G. Posterior parietal cortex and the filtering of distractors. *Proceedings of the National Academy of Sciences of the United States of America* **100**, 4263 (2003).

Friedman-Hill, S. R., Robertson, L. C., & Treisman, A. Parietal contributions to visual feature binding: evidence from a patient with bilateral lesions. *Science* **269**, 853 (1995).

Fries, P., Reynolds, J. H., Rorie, A. E. & Desimone, R. Modulation of oscillatory neuronal synchronization by selective visual attention. *Science* **291**, 1560 (2001).ss

Gallant, J. L., Shoup, R. E. & Mazer, J. A. A human extrastriate area functionally homologous to macaque V4. *Neuron* **27**, 227–235 (2000).

Ganguli, S. et al. One-dimensional dynamics of attention and decision making in LIP. *Neuron* **58**, 15–25 (2008).

Gottlieb, J. & Balan, P. Attention as a decision in information space. *Trends in Cognitive Sciences* **14**, 240–248 (2010).

Gouws, A. D. et al. On the role of suppression in spatial attention: evidence from negative BOLD in human subcortical and cortical structures. *Journal of Neuroscience* **34**, 10347–10360 (2014).

Gregoriou, G. G., Gotts, S. J. & Desimone, R. Cell-type-specific synchronization of neural activity in FEF with V4 during attention. *Neuron* **73**, 581–594 (2012).

Grieve, K. L., Acuña, C. & Cudeiro, J. The primate pulvinar nuclei: vision and action. *Trends in Neurosciences* **23**, 35–39 (2000).

Guedj, C. & Vuilleumier, P. Functional connectivity fingerprints of the human pulvinar: Decoding its role in cognition. *NeuroImage* **221**, 117162 (2020).

Gutierrez, C., Yaun, A. & Cusick, C. G. Neurochemical subdivisions of the inferior pulvinar in macaque monkeys. *Journal of Comparative Neurology* **363**, 545–562 (1995).

Haegens, S., Nácher, V., Luna, R., Romo, R. & Jensen, O. α-Oscillations in the monkey sensorimotor network influence discrimination performance by rhythmical inhibition of neuronal spiking. *Proceedings of the National Academy of Sciences of the United States of America* **108**, 19377 (2011).

Halassa, M. M. & Acsády, L. Thalamic inhibition: diverse sources, diverse scales. *Trends in Neurosciences* **39**, 680–693 (2016).

Halassa, M. M. & Kastner, S. Thalamic functions in distributed cognitive control. *Nature Neuroscience* **20**, 1669–1679 (2017).

Harris, J. A. et al. Hierarchical organization of cortical and thalamic connectivity. *Nature* **575**, 195–202 (2019). 1.

Haynes, J.-D., Deichmann, R. & Rees, G. Eye-specific effects of binocular rivalry in the human lateral geniculate nucleus. *Nature* **438**, 496–499 (2005).

Helfrich, R. F. et al. Neural mechanisms of sustained attention are rhythmic. *Neuron* **99**, 854–865.e5 (2018).

Hendry, S. H. C. & Reid, R. C. The koniocellular pathway in primate vision. *Annual Review of Neuroscience* **23**, 127–153 (2000).

Hickey, T. L. & Guillery, R. W. Variability of laminar patterns in the human lateral geniculate nucleus. *Journal of Comparative Neurology* **183**, 221–246 (1979).

Hirsch, J. A., Wang, X., Sommer, F. T. & Martinez, L. M. How inhibitory circuits in the thalamus serve vision. *Annual Review of Neuroscience* **38**, 309–329 (2015).

Homman-Ludiye, J., Mundinano, I. C., Kwan, W. C. & Bourne, J. A. Extensive connectivity between the medial pulvinar and the cortex revealed in the marmoset monkey. *Cerebral Cortex* **30**, 1797–1812 (2019).

Hubel, D. H. & Wiesel, T. N. Receptive fields, binocular interaction and functional architecture in the cat's visual cortex. *Journal of Physiology* **160**, 106–154 (1962).

Jaramillo, J., Mejias, J. F. & Wang, X.-J. Engagement of pulvino-cortical feedforward and feedback pathways in cognitive computations. *Neuron* **101**, 321–336.e9 (2019).

Jensen, O. & Mazaheri, A. Shaping functional architecture by oscillatory alpha activity: gating by inhibition. *Frontiers in Human Neuroscience* **4**, 186 (2010).

Jones, E. G. *The thalamus* (Springer Science & Business Media, 2007).

Kaas, J. H. & Lyon, D. C. Pulvinar contributions to the dorsal and ventral streams of visual processing in primates. *Brain Research Reviews* **55**, 285–296 (2007).

Karnath, H., Himmelbach, M. & Rorden, C. The subcortical anatomy of human spatial neglect: putamen, caudate nucleus and pulvinar. *Brain* **125**, 350–360 (2002).

Kastner, S. et al. Functional imaging of the human lateral geniculate nucleus and pulvinar. *Journal of Neurophysiology* **91**, 438–448 (2004).

Kastner, S., Chen, Q., Jeong, S. K. & Mruczek, R. E. B. A brief comparative review of primate posterior parietal cortex: a novel hypothesis on the human toolmaker. *Neuropsychologia* **105**, 123–134 (2017).

Kastner, S., Fiebelkorn, I. C., & Eradath, M. K. Dynamic pulvino-cortical interactions in the primate attention network. *Current Opinion in Neurobiology* **65**, 10–19 (2020).Kastner, S., Pinsk, M. A.,

De Weerd, P., Desimone, R. & Ungerleider, L. G. Increased activity in human visual cortex during directed attention in the absence of visual stimulation. *Neuron* **22**, 751–761 (1999).

Kastner, S., & Ungerleider, L. G. Mechanisms of visual attention in the human cortex. *Annual Review of Neuroscience* **23**, 315–341 (2000).

Komura, Y., Nikkuni, A., Hirashima, N., Uetake, T. & Miyamoto, A. Responses of pulvinar neurons reflect a subject's confidence in visual categorization. *Nature Neuroscience* **16**, 749–755 (2013).

Lakatos, P., O'Connell, M. N. & Barczak, A. Pondering the pulvinar. *Neuron* **89**, 5–7 (2016).

Landau, A. N. & Fries, P. Attention samples stimuli rhythmically. *Current Biology* **22**, 1000–1004 (2012).

Lee, S., Kruglikov, I., Huang, Z. J., Fishell, G. & Rudy, B. A disinhibitory circuit mediates motor integration in the somatosensory cortex. *Nature Neuroscience* **16**, 1662–1670 (2013).

Lehky, S. R. & Maunsell, J. H. R. No binocular rivalry in the LGN of alert macaque monkeys. *Vision Research* **36**, 1225–1234 (1996).

Ling, S., Pratte, M. S. & Tong, F. Attention alters orientation processing in the human lateral geniculate nucleus. *Nature Neuroscience* **18**, 496–498 (2015).

Livingstone, M. & Hubel, D. Segregation of form, color, movement, and depth: anatomy, physiology, and perception. *Science* **240**, 740 (1988).

Livingstone, M. S. & Hubel, D. H. Effects of sleep and arousal on the processing of visual information in the cat. *Nature* **291**, 554–561 (1981).

Lu, Z.-L. & Dosher, B. A. External noise distinguishes attention mechanisms. *Vision Research* **38**, 1183–1198 (1998).

Luck, S. J., Chelazzi, L., Hillyard, S. A. & Desimone, R. Neural mechanisms of spatial selective attention in areas V1, V2, and V4 of macaque visual cortex. *Journal of Neurophysiology* **77**, 24–42 (1997).

Lückmann, H. C., Jacobs, H. I. L. & Sack, A. T. The cross-functional role of frontoparietal regions in cognition: internal attention as the overarching mechanism. *Progress in Neurobiology* **116**, 66–86 (2014).

Lyon, D. C., Nassi, J. J. & Callaway, E. M. A disynaptic relay from superior colliculus to dorsal stream visual cortex in macaque monkey. *Neuron* **65**, 270–279 (2010).

Malpeli, J. G., Lee, D. & Baker, F. H. Laminar and retinotopic organization of the macaque lateral geniculate nucleus: magnocellular and parvocellular magnification functions. *Journal of Comparative Neurology* **375**, 363–377 (1996).

Marion, R., Li, K., Purushothaman, G., Jiang, Y. & Casagrande, V. A. Morphological and neurochemical comparisons between pulvinar and V1 projections to V2. *Journal of Comparative Neurology* **521**, 813–832 (2013).

Markov, N. T. et al. Anatomy of hierarchy: feedforward and feedback pathways in macaque visual cortex. *Journal of Comparative Neurology* **522**, 225–259 (2014).

Martin, A. B. et al. Temporal dynamics and response modulation across the human visual system in a spatial attention task: an ECoG study. *Journal of Neuroscience* **39**, 333–352 (2019).

Martin, P. R., White, A. J. R., Goodchild, A. K., Wilder, H. D. & Sefton, A. E. Evidence that blue-on cells are part of the third geniculocortical pathway in primates. *European Journal of Neuroscience* **9**, 1536–1541 (1997).

McAlonan, K., Cavanaugh, J. & Wurtz, R. H. Attentional modulation of thalamic reticular neurons. *Journal of Neuroscience* **26**, 4444 (2006).

McAlonan, K., Cavanaugh, J. & Wurtz, R. H. Guarding the gateway to cortex with attention in visual thalamus. *Nature* **456**, 391–394 (2008).

McCormick, D. A., McGinley, M. J. & Salkoff, D. B. Brain state dependent activity in the cortex and thalamus. *Current Opinion in Neurobiology* **31**, 133–140 (2015).

Mehta, A. D., Ulbert, I. & Schroeder, C. E. Intermodal selective attention in monkeys. I: distribution and timing of effects across visual areas. *Cerebral Cortex* **10**, 343–358 (2000).

Mitchell, J. F., Sundberg, K. A. & Reynolds, J. H. Spatial attention decorrelates intrinsic activity fluctuations in macaque area V4. *Neuron* **63**, 879–888 (2009).

Murray, J. D., Jaramillo, J. & Wang, X.-J. Working memory and decision-making in a frontoparietal circuit model. *Journal of Neuroscience* **37**, 12167 (2017).

Moore, T., & Fallah, M. Control of eye movements and spatial attention. *Proceedings of the national Academy of Sciences of the United States of America* **98**, 1273–1276 (2001).

O'Connor, D. H., Fukui, M. M., Pinsk, M. A. & Kastner, S. Attention modulates responses in the human lateral geniculate nucleus. *Nature Neuroscience* **5**, 1203–1209 (2002).

Parvizi, J. Corticocentric myopia: old bias in new cognitive sciences. *Trends in Cognitive Sciences* **13**, 354–359 (2009).

Petersen, S. E., Robinson, D. L. & Keys, W. Pulvinar nuclei of the behaving rhesus monkey: visual responses and their modulation. *Journal of Neurophysiology* **54**, 867–886 (1985).

Petersen, S. E., Robinson, D. L. & Morris, J. D. Contributions of the pulvinar to visual spatial attention. *Neuropsychologia* **25**, 97–105 (1987).

Phillips, J. M. *et al.* Topographic organization of connections between prefrontal cortex and mediodorsal thalamus: evidence for a general principle of indirect thalamic pathways between directly connected cortical areas. *NeuroImage* **189**, 832–846 (2019).

Pogosyan, A., Gaynor, L. D., Eusebio, A. & Brown, P. Boosting cortical activity at beta-band frequencies slows movement in humans. *Current Biology* **19**, 1637–1641 (2009).

Posner, M. I. & Petersen, S. E. The attention system of the human brain. *Annual Review of Neuroscience* **13**, 25–42 (1990).

Posner, M. I., Snyder, C. R. & Davidson, B. J. Attention and the detection of signals. *Journal of Experimental Psychology: General* **109**, 160–174 (1980).

Purushothaman, G., Marion, R., Li, K. & Casagrande, V. A. Gating and control of primary visual cortex by pulvinar. *Nature Neuroscience* **15**, 905–912 (2012).

Qian, Y. *et al.* Robust functional mapping of layer-selective responses in human lateral geniculate nucleus with high-resolution 7T fMRI. *Proceedings of the Royal Society B: Biological Sciences* **287**, 20200245 (2020).

Quax, S., Jensen, O. & Tiesinga, P. Top-down control of cortical gamma-band communication via pulvinar induced phase shifts in the alpha rhythm. *PLOS Computational Biology* **13**, e1005519 (2017).

Rafal, R. D. & Posner, M. I. Deficits in human visual spatial attention following thalamic lesions. *Proceedings of the National Academy of Sciences of the United States of America* **84**, 7349 (1987).

Rockland, K. S. Convergence and branching patterns of round, type 2 corticopulvinar axons. *Journal of Comparative Neurology* **390**, 515–536 (1998).

Rockland, K. S., Andresen, J., Cowie, R. J. & Robinson, D. L. Single axon analysis of pulvinocortical connections to several visual areas in the macaque. *Journal of Comparative Neurology* **406**, 221–250 (1999).

Romanski, L. M., Giguere, M., Bates, J. F. & Goldman-Rakic, P. S. Topographic organization of medial pulvinar connections with the prefrontal cortex in the rhesus monkey. *Journal of Comparative Neurology* **379**, 313–332 (1997).

Rovó, Z., Ulbert, I. & Acsády, L. Drivers of the primate thalamus. *Journal of Neuroscience* **32**, 17894 (2012).

Roy, S. *et al.* Segregation of short-wavelength-sensitive (S) cone signals in the macaque dorsal lateral geniculate nucleus. *European Journal of Neuroscience* **30**, 1517–1526 (2009).

Saalmann, Y. B. & Kastner, S. Cognitive and perceptual functions of the visual thalamus. *Neuron* **71**, 209–223 (2011).

Saalmann, Y. B., Pinsk, M. A., Wang, L., Li, X. & Kastner, S. The pulvinar regulates information transmission between cortical areas based on attention demands. *Science* **337**, 753 (2012).

Schmahmann, J. D. & Pandya, D. N. Anatomical investigation of projections from thalamus to posterior parietal cortex in the rhesus monkey: a WGA-HRP and fluorescent tracer study. *Journal of Comparative Neurology* **295**, 299–326 (1990).

Schneider, K. A. Subcortical mechanisms of feature-based attention. *Journal of Neuroscience* **31**, 8643 (2011).

Schneider, K. A. & Kastner, S. Effects of sustained spatial attention in the human lateral geniculate nucleus and superior colliculus. *Journal of Neuroscience* **29**, 1784 (2009).

Schneider, K. A., Richter, M. C. & Kastner, S. Retinotopic organization and functional subdivisions of the human lateral geniculate nucleus: a high-resolution functional magnetic resonance imaging study. *Journal of Neuroscience* **24**, 8975 (2004).

Sclar, G., Maunsell, J. H. R. & Lennie, P. Coding of image contrast in central visual pathways of the macaque monkey. *Vision Research* **30**, 1–10 (1990).

Sherman, S. M. & Guillery, R. W. On the actions that one nerve cell can have on another: Distinguishing "drivers" from "modulators." *Proceedings of the National Academy of Sciences of the United States of America* **95**, 7121 (1998).

Sherman, S. M. & Guillery, R. W. *Functional connections of cortical areas: a new view from the thalamus* (MIT Press, 2013).

Sherman, S. M. & Koch, C. The control of retinogeniculate transmission in the mammalian lateral geniculate nucleus. *Experimental Brain Research* **63**, 1–20 (1986).

Shipp, S. The functional logic of cortico-pulvinar connections. *Philosophical Transactions of the Royal Society of London. Series B: Biological Sciences* **358**, 1605–1624 (2003).

Shiu, L.-P. & Pashler, H. Spatial attention and vernier acuity. *Vision Research* **35**, 337–343 (1995).

Smaers, J. B., Gómez-Robles, A., Parks, A. N. & Sherwood, C. C. Exceptional evolutionary expansion of prefrontal cortex in great apes and humans. *Current Biology* **27**, 714–720 (2017).

Smith, A. T., Cotton, P. L., Bruno, A. & Moutsiana, C. Dissociating vision and visual attention in the human pulvinar. *Journal of Neurophysiology* **101**, 917–925 (2009).

Smith, P. L. & Ratcliff, R. An integrated theory of attention and decision making in visual signal detection. *Psychological Review* **116**, 283–317 (2009).

Snow, J. C., Allen, H. A., Rafal, R. D. & Humphreys, G. W. Impaired attentional selection following lesions to human pulvinar: evidence for homology between human and monkey. *Proceedings of the National Academy of Sciences of the United States of America* **106**, 4054 (2009).

Song, K., Meng, M., Chen, L., Zhou, K. & Luo, H. Behavioral oscillations in attention: rhythmic α pulses mediated through θ band. *Journal of Neuroscience* **34**, 4837 (2014).

Stepniewska, I. & Kaas, J. H. Architectonic subdivisions of the inferior pulvinar in New World and Old World monkeys. *Visual Neuroscience* **14**, 1043–1060 (1997).

Steriade, M. Acetylcholine systems and rhythmic activities during the waking–sleep cycle. *Progress in Brain Research* **145**, 179–196 (2004).

Strumpf, H. *et al.* The role of the pulvinar in distractor processing and visual search. *Human Brain Mapping* **34**, 1115–1132 (2013).

Szczepanski, S. M. & Kastner, S. Shifting attentional priorities: control of spatial attention through hemispheric competition. *Journal of Neuroscience* **33**, 5411 (2013).

Szczepanski, S. M., Konen, C. S. & Kastner, S. Mechanisms of spatial attention control in frontal and parietal cortex. *Journal of Neuroscience* **30**, 148 (2010).

Theyel, B. B., Llano, D. A. & Sherman, S. M. The corticothalamocortical circuit drives higher-order cortex in the mouse. *Nature Neuroscience* **13**, 84–88 (2010).

Thompson, K. G., Biscoe, K. L. & Sato, T. R. Neuronal basis of covert spatial attention in the frontal eye field. *Journal of Neuroscience* **25**, 9479 (2005).

Treisman, A. M. & Gelade, G. A feature-integration theory of attention. *Cognitive Psychology* **12**, 97–136 (1980).

Ungerleider, L. G., Desimone, R., Galkin, T. W. & Mishkin, M. Subcortical projections of area MT in the macaque. *Journal of Comparative Neurology* **223**, 368–386 (1984).

Usrey, W. M. & Alitto, H. J. Visual functions of the thalamus. *Annual Review of Vision Science* **1**, 351–371 (2015).

Usrey, W. M., Reppas, J. B. & Reid, R. C. Paired-spike interactions and synaptic efficacy of retinal inputs to the thalamus. *Nature* **395**, 384–387 (1998).

VanRullen, R. Perceptual cycles. *Trends in Cognitive Sciences* **20**, 723–735 (2016).

VanRullen, R., Carlson, T. & Cavanagh, P. The blinking spotlight of attention. *Proceedings of the National Academy of Sciences of the United States of America* **104**, 19204 (2007).

Ward, R., Danziger, S., Owen, V. & Rafal, R. Deficits in spatial coding and feature binding following damage to spatiotopic maps in the human pulvinar. *Nature Neuroscience* **5**, 99–100 (2002).

Warner, C. E., Kwan, W. C. & Bourne, J. A. The early maturation of visual cortical area MT is dependent on input from the retinorecipient medial portion of the inferior pulvinar. *Journal of Neuroscience* **32**, 17073 (2012).

Wells, M. F., Wimmer, R. D., Schmitt, L. I., Feng, G. & Halassa, M. M. Thalamic reticular impairment underlies attention deficit in Ptchd1Y/− mice. *Nature* **532**, 58–63 (2016).

Whittington, M. A., Traub, R. D., Kopell, N., Ermentrout, B. & Buhl, E. H. Inhibition-based rhythms: experimental and mathematical observations on network dynamics. *International Journal of Psychophysiology* **38**, 315–336 (2000).

Wiesel, T. N. & Hubel, D. H. Spatial and chromatic interactions in the lateral geniculate body of the rhesus monkey. *Journal of Neurophysiology* **29**, 1115–1156 (1966).

Wilke, M., Turchi, J., Smith, K., Mishkin, M. & Leopold, D. A. Pulvinar inactivation disrupts selection of movement plans. *Journal of Neuroscience* **30**, 8650 (2010).

Wimmer, R. D. et al. Thalamic control of sensory selection in divided attention. *Nature* **526**, 705–709 (2015).

Womelsdorf, T. et al. Modulation of neuronal interactions through neuronal synchronization. *Science* **316**, 1609 (2007).

Wróbel, A., Bekisz, M. & Waleszczyk, W. 20 Hz bursts of activity in the cortico-thalamic pathway during attentive perception. In *Oscillatory Event-Related Brain Dynamics* (eds. Pantev, C., Elbert, T. & Lütkenhöner, B.), 311–324 (Springer US, 1994).

Wunderlich, K., Schneider, K. A. & Kastner, S. Neural correlates of binocular rivalry in the human lateral geniculate nucleus. *Nature Neuroscience* **8**, 1595–1602 (2005).

Xu, X. et al. A comparison of koniocellular, magnocellular and parvocellular receptive field properties in the lateral geniculate nucleus of the owl monkey (*Aotus trivirgatus*). *Journal of Physiology* **531**, 203–218 (2001).

Yeshurun, Y. & Carrasco, M. Attention improves or impairs visual performance by enhancing spatial resolution. *Nature* **396**, 72–75 (1998).

Yeterian, E. H. & Pandya, D. N. Corticothalamic connections of the posterior parietal cortex in the rhesus monkey. *Journal of Comparative Neurology* **237**, 408–426 (1985).

Zeater, N., Cheong, S. K., Solomon, S. G., Dreher, B. & Martin, P. R. Binocular visual responses in the primate lateral geniculate nucleus. *Current Biology* **25**, 3190–3195 (2015).

Zhang, P., Zhou, H., Wen, W. & He, S. Layer-specific response properties of the human lateral geniculate nucleus and superior colliculus. *NeuroImage* **111**, 159–166 (2015).

Zhang, Y., Chen, Y., Bressler, S. L. & Ding, M. Response preparation and inhibition: the role of the cortical sensorimotor beta rhythm. *Neuroscience* **156**, 238–246 (2008).

Zhou, H., Schafer, R. J. & Desimone, R. Pulvinar-cortex interactions in vision and attention. *Neuron* **89**, 209–220 (2016).

Zikopoulos, B. & Barbas, H. Prefrontal projections to the thalamic reticular nucleus form a unique circuit for attentional mechanisms. *Journal of Neuroscience* **26**, 7348 (2006).

Zikopoulos, B. & Barbas, H. Pathways for emotions and attention converge on the thalamic reticular nucleus in primates. *Journal of Neuroscience* **32**, 5338 (2012).

Chapter 18: The Thalamus in Navigation

Adrien Peyrache

1. Introduction and Definition

The anterior thalamus (AT) is an essential node of the Papez circuit, a large brain's network (sometimes referred to as the *limbic* system) organized in loops (Papez, 1937). One of the main functions of this circuit is to enable spatial navigation. In vertebrates and arthropods, decades of research have revealed a complex network of brain structures supporting navigation (Hulse and Jayaraman, 2020; McNaughton et al., 2006; O'Keefe and Nadel, 1978; Pisokas et al., 2020). In mammals, these networks connect widely distributed areas, from the vestibular organs to the medial and temporal cortex, including the hippocampus. The hippocampus lies at the center stage of spatial processing in the brain, especially because most of its neurons fire in association with specific locations of the animal in its environment, the so-called *place cells* (O'Keefe and Dostrovsky, 1971; O'Keefe and Nadel, 1978), and its integrity is crucial for a broad set of spatial cognitive skills. The AT provides vestibular-related signals to the hippocampal formation and the medial cortex and connects these cortical areas to each other.

The AT shares some fundamental properties with other parts of the dorsal thalamus. For instance, it is divided into cytoarchitectonically defined nuclei and is composed of excitatory neurons that target only cortical structures (the thalamocortical neurons). The AT classically includes three distinct subregions: the anterodorsal (AD), anteromedial (AM), and anteroventral (AV) nuclei. These nuclei are reciprocally connected with the medial cortex, the subiculum, and other parahippocampal areas but not the hippocampus per se. The nucleus reuniens (RE) is the only thalamic nucleus that directly projects to the hippocampus proper. What is more, a growing body of evidence suggests that the RE plays an instrumental role in modulating hippocampal activity, and for this reason, it will also be discussed in this chapter. Like AT nuclei, the RE is also reciprocally connected with the medial cortex and the parahippocampal areas. The AT and the RE can thus be referred to as the *limbic* thalamus.

The pathways linking the main inputs of the limbic thalamus, the mammillary bodies (MBs), with its cortical targets are segregated, that is, anatomically nonoverlapping. One striking question regarding thalamic function in general, and particularly the limbic thalamus, is whether it constitutes a mere relay of input signals to target structures or whether local computations are also performed. The AT and RE are targeted by additional subcortical areas that break the symmetries of the mamillary-thalamic-cortical tracts. This suggests that inputs signals are differently processed in each pathway and thus that the thalamus performs specific operations on mammillary inputs before conveying these signals.

More modern definitions of the limbic system entail dynamical properties of neurons, in particular their modulation by theta oscillations (5–10 Hz), which dominate neuronal population dynamics during an animal's movement (Buzsáki, 2002; Buzsáki and Moser, 2013; Vanderwolf, 1969). In addition to the anatomical characteristics of the limbic thalamus, I will present in this chapter how studying the dynamical properties of AT/RE neurons provides a detailed picture of the potential contribution of different nuclei to navigation.

Navigation relies on the integration of various sensory streams, a process that is both flexible (the absence of any one input can be compensated by others) and robust (Angelaki and Cullen, 2008; Berthoz and Viaud-Delmon, 1999). This is particularly the case for the head-direction (HD) signal, which orients the animal in its environment (Peyrache et al., 2019; Taube et al. 1990a, 1990b; Taube, 2007, 1995) and is broadcast to the posterior medial cortex and parahippocampal structures (i.e., the "cortical navigation system") by the AT.

HD cells constitute a vast majority of the neurons of the AD and its cortical target, the postsubiculum (PoSub; also referred to as the *dorsal presubiculum*) (Peyrache et al., 2019; Sharp et al., 2001; Taube et al. 1990a; Taube, 2007, 1995). HD and place cells are two examples of functional cell types with spatial correlates found in the brain's navigation network (Bicanski and Burgess, 2020; McNaughton et al., 2006). Other such cell types include grid cells in the medial entorhinal cortex that fire at the vertices of triangles tessellating the environment (Hafting et al., 2005) as well as boundary vector and border cells that signal the boundary of the environment (Lever et al., 2009; Savelli et al., 2008; Solstad et al., 2008). I will present some of the known behavioral and spatial correlates in the thalamus and will subsequently discuss the potential role of the thalamus in navigation, based on the results of interventional and computational studies.

2. The AT and RE Are Key Nodes in Superimposed Anatomical Loops

AT nuclei and the RE are well-defined cytoarchitecturally (Jones, 2007); for example, the neurons in these different nuclei show clear morphological differences as well as different gene-expression patterns (Phillips et al., 2019). One way to identify the role of individual (or groups of) neurons in the brain is to determine their input/output connectivity. Here, I will present how the AT/RE nuclei are key nodes in anatomical loops defining the "extended" hippocampal system (Aggleton and Brown, 1999).

2.1 The AT Is a Node in Superimposed Loops of the Limbic System

2.1.1 The AT in the Papez Circuit

In a seminal paper, James Papez first proposed that the limbic system was constituted of an anatomical loop (Papez, 1937) that connects the mammillary bodies, the anterior thalamus, the medial cortex, and the subiculum, which, in turn, sends feedback projection to the mammillary bodies. Part of the Papez circuit was first described in the 18th century when Felix Vicq d'Azyr, pioneering new brain-dissection techniques, identified the mammillothalamic tract, a bundle of fibers originating from the MBs and forming the main subcortical inputs to the AT. The AT projects to a wide cortical network, including the medial cortex, the subicular complex, and other parahippocampal regions (van Groen and Wyss, 1995). In turn, the subicular complex projects back to the MBs (Allen and Hopkins, 1989; Meibach and Siegel, 1977; Rosene and Hoesen, 1977; Swanson and Cowan, 1977; Wright et al., 2010), closing the loop of the Papez circuit. Although Papez's idea that this loop supports the expression of emotions was progressively abandoned, the Papez circuit remains a key structural definition of the limbic system. It is now well established that the Papez circuit is essential for navigation and memory, as evidenced by the dramatic impairment in spatial cognition following lesions at every stage of this pathway (Aggleton and Brown, 1999; Rosenstock et al., 1977; Sziklas and Petrides, 1998; Vann and Aggleton, 2004).

The Papez circuit is anatomically organized into segregated pathways. The MBs are divided into two cytoarchitecturally distinct areas, which form separated circuits: the lateral mammillary nucleus (LMN) projects most strongly to the AD, whereas the medial mammillary nuclei (MMN) target the AM and AV (Cruce, 1975; Powell and Cowan, 1954; Seki and Zyo, 1984; Shibata, 1992; Watanabe and Kawana, 1980). The MMN can be subdivided into different areas projecting to different subregions of the AT, in particular the *pars lateralis* (lMMN) and *pars medialis* (mMMN) that connect to the AV and AM, respectively. Each nucleus of the MBs receives inputs from different brainstem nuclei. The LMN receives inputs from the dorsal tegmental nucleus of Gudden, whereas the MMN receive inputs from the ventral part (Allen and Hopkins, 1989). The mammillothalamic tract can thus be considered as a collection of independent, nondivergent fibers, connecting distinct locations of the MBs and the AT, an anatomical arrangement that also reflects differences in MB-projecting zones in the brainstem. Of note, whereas MMN connections to AM and AV nuclei are mostly ipsilateral, the LMN projects bilaterally to the AD nuclei (Blair et al., 1999; Cruce, 1975; Kuypers et al., 1980; Shibata, 1992). Finally, the organization of the mammillothalamic tract is largely preserved across mammalian species, as shown in anatomical studies in cats and nonhuman primates (Veazey et al., 1982).

All AT nuclei project to the parahippocampal areas, in particular the subicular complex (van Groen and Wyss, 1995). AT projections to the subicular complex remain segregated, with the AD, AV, and AM projecting mainly to the PoSub, the proximal subiculum (near CA1), and the distal subiculum, respectively.

The subicular → MB feedback projections are also anatomically organized, respecting the segregation of AT inputs to the subicular complex (Christiansen et al., 2016; Wright et al., 2010). The individual loops within the Papez circuit are thus believed to be segregated and to serve distinct functions, especially in navigation (Aggleton and Nelson, 2015). An example of this is the LMN → AD → PoSub → LMN circuit, which is well established anatomically (Yoder and Taube, 2011) and is central in processing the HD signal and conveying it to the cortical navigation system (Peyrache et al., 2019; Taube, 2007). Importantly, the dorsal tegmental nucleus of Gudden (which projects to the LMN) indirectly receives signals originating in the semicircular canals of the vestibular system, and its neurons code for angular head velocity. The MBs project back to the ventral/dorsal tegmental nuclei. The reciprocal connection of the LMN with the dorsal part is crucial for transforming the vestibular signals into a code for HD. The role of the other Papez circuit remains unclear and will not be discussed in this chapter. It is important to note that these loops may extend beyond the AT–subicular–MB components because the cingulate and prefrontal cortices also project to the MBs (Allen and Hopkins, 1989), possibly entailing loops with the AM nucleus that are independent of the subicular complex.

2.1.2 Thalamocortical Loops of the Limbic System

In addition to directly contacting the subicular complex, each AT nucleus projects to different sets of medial cortical targets. However, unlike the segregated organization of subcortical limbic pathways, AT projections to the medial cortex overlap (Wright et al., 2013) (Figure 1A).

Specifically, AT nuclei can be further segregated based on their mutual connections with medial cortical areas, especially the pre- and infralimbic cortex, the cingulate cortex, and the retrosplenial cortex (RSP). The RSP is, with the subicular complex, the other main output of the AT that is a part of the navigation system. It can be divided into the granular (RSPg) and agranular (RSPag) subareas that differ in one crucial aspect: their connections with the AT. The AD and AV nuclei project to the RSPg cortex, whereas the AM nucleus projects to the RSPag (Shibata 1993b; Sripanidkulchai and Wyss, 1986; van Groen and Wyss, 1995).

The output connectivity of the AM is widespread, and within the AM, neurons projecting to different cortical areas are anatomically arranged (Shibata and Kato, 1993). The anterior part of the AM projects to frontal regions, including the cingulate cortex and the pre- and infralimbic cortices, whereas the posterior part shares more similarities with the AV/AD system, projecting to the RSP and presubiculum (Musil and Olson, 1988; Shibata and Kato, 1993; van Groen et al., 1999).

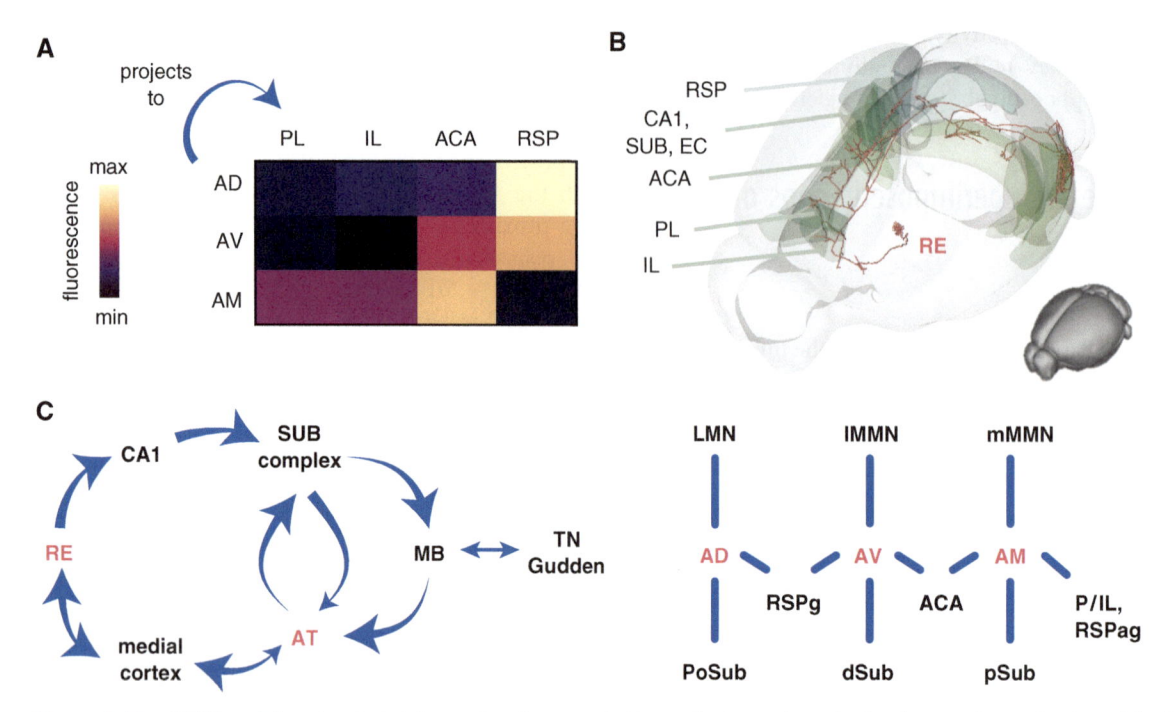

Figure 1 The AT/RE nuclei are located at the center of segregated loops that constitute the fundamental organization of the limbic system.
A. Average normalized fluorescence using anterograde viral tracing (*dark to light, minimum to maximum fluorescence, respectively*). Data from the Allen Institute Connectivity Atlas (see "Materials and Methods" section).
B. Reconstructed axonal projection from an RE neuron. Data from the MouseLight dataset (see "Materials and Methods" section).
C. AT/RE nuclei within anatomical loops of the limbic system. Left: Organization of superimposed loops in the system. Right: Three segregated loops between the MBs, the AT, and the subicular complex. Abbreviations (not cited in text): *ACA*, cingulate cortex; *I/PL*, infra-/prelimbic cortex; *SUB*, subiculum; *EC*, entorhinal cortex; *d/pSub*, distal/proximal subiculum; *TN Gudden*, tegmental nucleus of Gudden.

The parasubiculum and the presubiculum are also targeted by AT neurons to various extents (Shibata, 1993a; van Groen and Wyss, 1995). Finally, the entorhinal (both medial and lateral) cortex receives inputs from these nuclei, but these inputs are much sparser than those to the subicular complex.

As with any other thalamic nuclei, AT nuclei receive cortical feedback, usually from the same areas to which they project. PoSub neurons project back to the AD with direct but sparse excitatory feedback (Petrof and Sherman, 2009; Peyrache et al., 2015). The strength of cortical feedback to the AV and AM is more unclear. Interestingly, feedback projections to the thalamus and the MBs are supported by anatomically segregated neurons (Christiansen et al., 2016; Wright et al., 2010; Yoder and Taube, 2011); for example, different layers of the PoSub project back to the AD and the LMN (Yoder and Taube, 2011).

Although most of the anatomical studies of the AT have been performed in rodents, especially in rats, there do not appear to be any major differences between rodents and other mammals. For example, the same pattern of thalamocortical projections has been reported in cats (Kaitz and Robertson, 1981; Niimi, 1978; Robertson and Kaitz, 1981) as well as in nonhuman primates (Amaral and Cowan, 1980). These circuits seem largely homologous across mammals, but the homology of the prefrontal areas between primates and other mammalian species, in particular from the point of view of thalamocortical networks, is still a matter of debate (Carlén, 2017; Preuss, 1995; Uylings et al., 2003).

2.1.3 Diffuse Projection to and from the RE

The RE receives inputs from virtually all medial cortices, with which it is usually mutually connected (Herkenham, 1978; McKenna and Vertes, 2004) (Figure 1B). Furthermore, it is the only thalamic nucleus to project directly to the hippocampus, specifically to the CA1 subarea (Herkenham, 1978; Varela et al., 2014; Vertes et al., 2007), and it directly modulates the activity of place cells in relation to ongoing behavior (Ito et al., 2015) (this point is discussed in more detail in later sections). In turn, CA1 projects to the subicular complex. It should be noted that CA1 projects directly to the prelimbic cortex (Jay et al., 1989), which is itself a major input to the RE, thus forming another loop within this circuit.

The RE receives inputs from the MBs (McKenna and Vertes, 2004), but whether these projections are topographically organized is unknown. Finally, similar to the segregation of the subicular output neurons to the AT and the MBs, different layers project back to the RE and the MBs (Mathiasen et al., 2019).

2.1.4 Superimposed Loops in the Limbic System

In summary, the AT and RE occupy a central position in the organization of the limbic system (Figure 1C). The AT/RE nuclei are part of anatomical loops at three distinct levels: thalamocortical, Papez circuit, and the AT → medial cortex → RE → CA1 pathway. These loops are anatomically and functionally segregated except for the convergent inputs from the AT to the medial cortex, especially the RSP.

The thalamus is often seen as a simple relay, and the anatomical considerations presented earlier raise the question of whether the role of AT nuclei in navigation is limited to relaying their distinct inputs from the MBs to downstream cortical targets. As outlined in the following sections, further considerations regarding non-MB subcortical inputs suggest the opposite view.

2.2 Inhibitory Control of the AT

The dorsal thalamus is surrounded by a thin layer of inhibitory neurons forming the thalamic reticular nucleus (TRN) (Jones, 2007). These neurons receive excitatory collaterals from thalamocortical neurons, en route to the cortex. In turn, TRN neurons project back onto neurons in the dorsal thalamus. In rodents, AT neurons receive inhibitory inputs from the TRN (Gonzalo-Ruiz and Lieberman, 1995; Lozsádi, 1995; Oda et al., 1996; Vantomme et al., 2020; Wang et al., 1999), but as elsewhere in the thalamus, these mutual connections are not homogeneous. In the AT, the AD and AV nuclei seem to be the main targets of this inhibitory control, with some indications that the AD nucleus receives the most dense inhibitory input (Duszkiewicz and Peyrache, unpublished observations).

The role of the TRN in thalamic processing remains poorly understood but is certainly essential in modulating the gain of thalamic signals (Wimmer et al., 2015). One key property of the TRN is that its neurons are also contacted by corticothalamic fibers projecting toward the dorsal thalamus. Projection from the RSP and the PoSub leads to a strong and disynaptic inhibition of AT activity, especially in the AD, potentially playing a role in the computation of the HD signal (Peyrache et al., 2019; Vantomme et al., 2020).

In rodents, no local GABAergic neurons have been identified in the AT/RE (Wang et al., 1999), so inhibition in these nuclei is thought to be exclusively exogenous, originating from the TRN and other nonthalamic areas (Halassa and Acsády, 2016). Other mammalian species, in particular felines and primates, seem to possess a higher density of GABAergic neurons in thalamic nuclei outside the TRN (Arcelli et al., 1997). The role of these different inhibitory sources and the resulting differences in the computation of AT/RE signals across species remain largely unexplored.

2.3 Cholinergic Modulation of the AT/RE

Acetylcholine is one of the most widely studied neuromodulators of forebrain activity. It plays a fundamental role in forebrain operations, ranging from neuronal dynamics and the organization of sleep–wake cycles to learning and memory (Hasselmo, 2006; Jones, 1993; Steriade et al., 1993). Cholinergic inputs to the AT arise from brainstem nuclei, specifically the laterodorsal tegmentum (LDT) and represent the main source of neuromodulation within the AT. Cholinergic inputs innervate the AV and AM but not the AD (Cornwall et al., 1990; Levey et al., 1987; Satoh and Fibiger, 1986; Shibata, 1992; Sikes and Vogt, 1987; Wright et al., 2013) (Figure 2). The RE is believed to receive cholinergic inputs (Levey et al., 1987) but perhaps not from the LDT (Figure 2). In

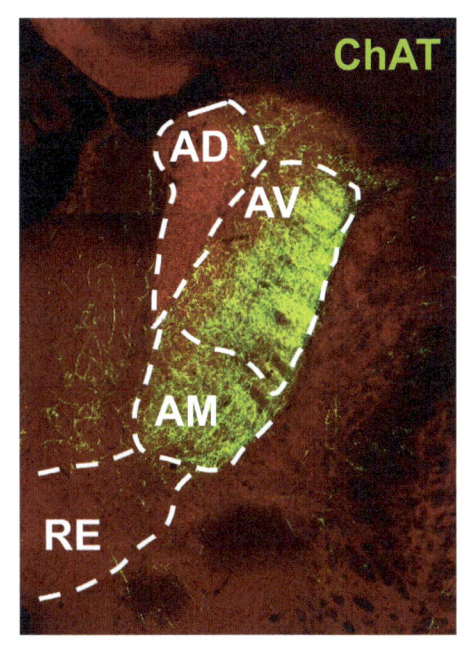

Figure 2 Cholinergic projection from the LDT to AT/RE. Green color indicates axonal fluorescence of choline acetyltransferase (ChAT)-positive neurons from the LDT (see "Materials and Methods" section).

humans, the AT is also the main projection site of cholinergic inputs (but not necessarily from the brainstem) (Heckers et al., 1992).

The effect of acetylcholine can be excitatory or inhibitory, depending on the activated channels, but overall, it has a depolarizing effect on targeted neurons, in particular in the thalamus (Andersen and Curtis, 1964; Curro Dossi et al., 1991). Stimulation of the LDT has a fast (<20 ms) depolarizing effect on AT neurons (Pare et al., 1990). However, this could result from direct glutamatergic inputs from the LDT (Boucetta et al., 2014). This brainstem system has thus been referred to as the *ascending activating system* since the early days of integrated physiological studies (Moruzzi and Magoun, 1949). LDT cholinergic neurons show dramatic changes in firing rates depending on the brain states (Boucetta et al., 2014; Cissé et al., 2018): they are maximally active during waking and rapid eye movement (REM) sleep and virtually silent during non-REM (NREM) sleep.

Unlike the segregated organization of the Papez circuit (Figure 1), LDT neurons project to both AV and AM nuclei (Wright et al., 2013), suggesting that this projection plays a common role for all the targeted circuits. As such, cholinergic inputs to the AV and AM nuclei shift activity in these nuclei depending on behavioral states (Steriade et al., 1993), possibly gating MB inputs to the AT (Pare et al., 1990) but not to the AD. This modulating projection may have fundamental importance for mechanisms underlying the consolidation of hippocampal-dependent memories during sleep and thus play a role in memory-guided navigation.

During wakefulness, LDT inputs may convey a signal related to speed, like the neighboring pedunculopontine tegmental nucleus, which also contains cholinergic neurons and shares anatomical and physiological properties with the LDT

(Boucetta et al., 2014; Cissé et al., 2018). The pedunculopontine tegmental nucleus plays an essential role in modulating the navigation system with the animal's velocity (Carvalho et al., 2020), a crucial signal for self-localization. Hence, this projection could potentially generate speed-modulated signals in the AV and AM.

2.4 Anatomy: Conclusions

The AT and RE constitute crucial nodes of superimposed loops within the limbic system (Aggleton and Brown, 1999). These loops are organized in highly segregated circuits that interconnect mainly in the cortical areas targeted by the AT/RE. Furthermore, several anatomical features of this circuit support the idea that the AT is not just a relay of its main inputs from the mammillary bodies. First, the AT is reciprocally connected with the TRN, and this local thalamic circuit is bound to perform specific functions on the incoming MB and corticothalamic signals. Second, the AT is also innervated by cholinergic fibers from the LDT, and these projections break the strict organization of the Papez circuits: LDT inputs to the AD are virtually absent, and the same LDT neurons can target both the AV and the AM. This modulatory signal must play a key role in neuronal dynamics and in gating MB inputs in a brain-state–dependent manner. The AT receives many other inputs, including other neuromodulatory signals from the brainstem, but for the most part, its inputs are weaker than LDT projections.

On top of the cortical Papez circuit, the RE is part of a larger loop that integrates signals from the medial cortex, including the prefrontal cortex. Unlike any other thalamic nucleus, it targets the CA1 area of the hippocampus that, in turn, projects to the subicular complex to feed back into the Papez circuit. The exact nature of the interactions between the AT/RE and other subcortical areas, in particular the TRN and LDT, remains largely a matter of speculation and will be discussed in the following sections.

3. Spatial Correlates and Oscillatory Properties of Neuronal Activity

One central hypothesis is that the segregated loops of the Papez circuit relay independent signals and thus play different roles in navigation. However, anatomy alone cannot address the question of the nature of the signals conveyed in each loop and their role in navigation. Although nucleus-specific lesion studies are challenging to achieve because of the small size and closeness of some nuclei, sensory and behavioral correlates of neuronal activity provide important insights into the role of specific brain regions and the nature of the local computations performed by the circuits.

Soon after the discovery of place cells in the hippocampus (O'Keefe and Dostrovsky, 1971), it was postulated that these spatial correlates must result from the integration of lower-level components, including signals related to external sensory inputs and self-movement (O'Keefe, 1976; O'Keefe and Nadel, 1978). One key property of place cells is that they are preserved in darkness, suggesting that the system can be updated in the absence of visual information and that vestibular inputs must thus play a central role in their generation. The AT receives direct inputs from the tegmento-mamillary system, which is itself targeted by brainstem vestibular nuclei. Hence, the AT is believed to be part of the circuit conveying information related to how the animal moves relative to its environment. In the AT, the HD signal is by far the most studied and understood behavioral correlate (Peyrache et al., 2019, 2015; Sharp et al., 2001; Taube, 1995, 2007). The HD signal is broadcast to the cortical navigation system by the LMN–AD–PoSub loop. There are no HD-modulated cells in the MMN, and the anatomical segregation of the Papez loops thus suggests that, although in vivo characterization remains scarce, the AV should convey other types of signals. In contrast, the AM and RE seem to relay signals between cortical regions, possibly playing a role in the integration of information from distributed areas.

3.1 Tuning to Head Direction in the AD Nucleus

Like other thalamic sensory nuclei that convey peripheral signals to the cortex, the AD is indirectly linked to a primary sensory organ—the semicircular canals of the vestibular system. The semicircular canals provide a signal related to angular head velocity, directly resulting from inertial forces during head rotation, which is, in essence, related to displacement in the absolute reference frame. Angular head acceleration is transformed along the subcortical circuit that converges to the LMN–AD–PoSub loop into angular velocity and subsequently to a direction signal by a computation analogous to temporal integration. This signal is encoded by HD neurons that each fire for a specific direction of the head in the horizontal plane. Importantly, although this signal certainly results from the integration of multiple inputs, the integrity of the semicircular canals is crucial for the emergence of the HD signal (Muir et al., 2009). Unlike other sensory inputs that are all relative to the position of the body in the environment (i.e., "egocentric"), the HD system acts as a biological compass for the brain, providing it with a primitive "allocentric" signal.

HD neurons are ubiquitous in the AD–PoSub loop (Figure 3A) (Peyrache et al., 2019, 2015; Ranck, 1985; Taube, 1990a, 1995, 2007). HD neurons are also found in the RSPg, the other cortical target of the AD (Chen et al., 1994; Jacob et al., 2017). The AD is a key node in the HD system and is certainly the only location within the HD circuit where cells are almost uniquely modulated by HD. Indeed, input neurons in the MBs are also modulated by angular head velocity (Blair et al., 1998; Stackman and Taube, 1998), and subsets of HD cells within the PoSub and RSP are modulated by other factors, such as the egocentric (i.e., body-centered) position of environment boundaries (Alexander et al., 2020; Gofman et al., 2019; Peyrache et al., 2017) and the direction of visual landmarks (Jacob et al., 2017).

In addition to the AD inputs, the PoSub and RSP receive inputs from the visual cortex, among other afferent connections. These structures are essential in aligning the HD signal to the external world, especially to distal visual landmarks (Goodridge and Taube, 1997). However, lesions of the AD

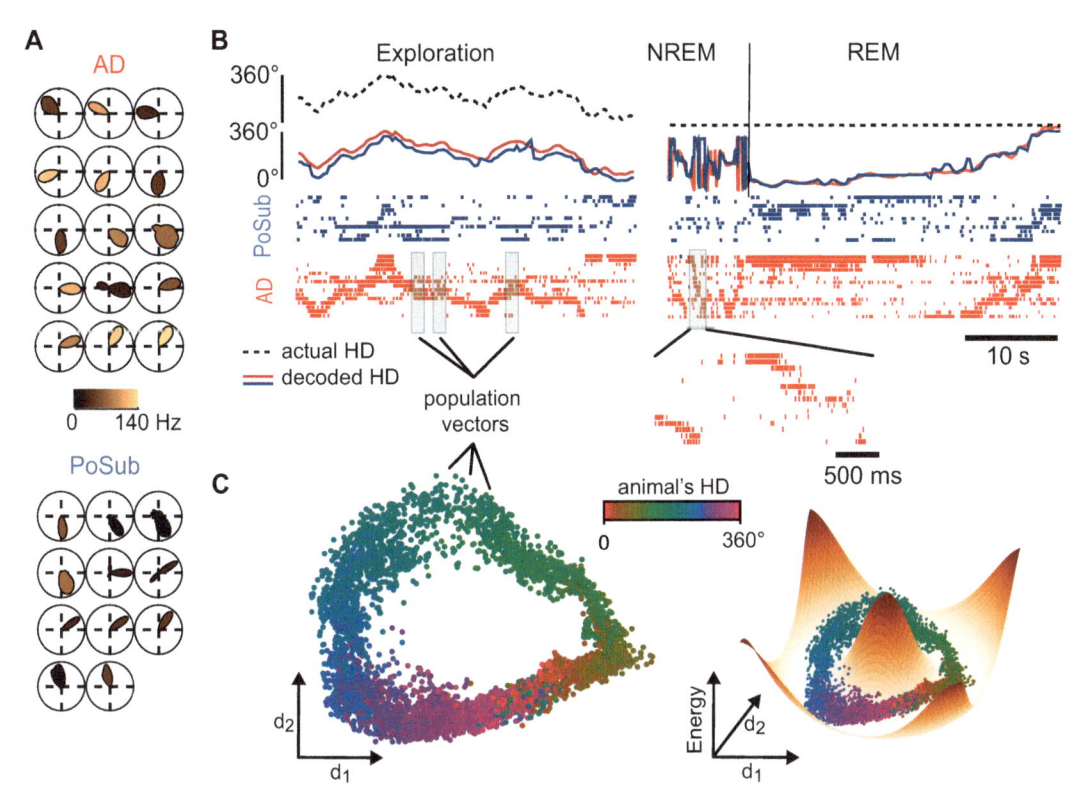

Figure 3 The organization of HD cell population activity in the AD is rigid and is governed by attractor dynamics.

A. Tuning curve (in polar coordinates) of HD cells simultaneously recorded in the AD–PoSub network.

B. The organization of HD cell population activity in the AD–PoSub network is preserved across brain states. Top: Actual (*dotted line*) and decoded (*colored lines*) HD. Bottom: Raster plot of HD cells in the AD–PoSub network (same cells as in panel A).

C. Left: Isomap projection of AD HD cell population vectors during wakefulness. Color indicates animal's HD for each population vector. This projection reveals the ring topology of the AD HD cell population activity. Right: Schema illustrating how HD cell activity may be constrained in a ring-shaped well of energy, resulting in the coding of an angular feature by the neuronal population (in this case, mapped to animal's HD during wakefulness but not during sleep). Panels A and B adapted from Peyrache et al. (2015). Panel C adapted with permission from Chaudhuri et al. (2019) and Viejo and Peyrache (2020).

nucleus disrupt HD tuning in the PoSub, suggesting that the AD is necessary for the emergence of an HD code (Goodridge and Taube, 1997).

Although the exact proportion of HD cells within the AD is still a matter of debate, this number depends on arbitrary criteria (on the firing rates and the degree of modulation by HD, among others) and is limited by the quality of extracellular spike detection, yet multichannel recordings in the AD suggest that a vast majority of cells in the AD are modulated by HD (Peyrache et al., 2015; Viejo and Peyrache, 2020). In the AD nucleus, the tuning width is highly homogeneous (approximatively 60 degrees at half-peak width), but peak firing rates can vary across almost two orders of magnitude and are typically in the 1–100 Hz range (Peyrache et al., 2015; Taube, 2007). The true lower bound of the distribution is unknown and is limited, again, by extracellular spike detection.

HD cells are commonly referred to as the brain's compass, but does this organization depend on the context? The question arises naturally because hippocampal place cells have long been known to remap across different environments (Leutgeb et al., 2004; Muller and Kubie, 1987). In sharp contrast with hippocampal place cells, HD cells are believed to maintain their mutual consistency in all situations. Rotation of visual landmarks, especially distal landmarks, shifts the preferred directions of all HD cells in the same direction (Knierim et al., 1995; Taube et al., 1990b; Taube, 1995; Yoganarasimha et al., 2006; Zugaro et al., 2001). Multichannel electrophysiological studies in the AD revealed that the organization of HD neuronal populations in this nucleus is "rigid." Specifically, the pairwise correlation of HD cells is maintained in all brain states (Figure 3B) (Peyrache et al., 2015), which was further demonstrated by the fact that training a decoder during any period of wakefulness is sufficient to reliably decode an HD signal at all times, even during sleep (Figure 3B) (Brandon et al., 2012; Peyrache et al., 2015).

From a computational perspective, the HD system is a canonical example of an "attractor" network, that is, a system in which internal circuits and dynamics constrain neuronal population activity into a small number of possible states. For the HD system, these states are continuously distributed along a functional ring, corresponding to low energy levels in the system (Figure 3C). These states can be identified in multi-neuronal data by projecting population vectors (the number of spikes emitted by each neuron in a given time window) onto a low-dimensional map using machine learning techniques (Chaudhuri et al., 2019; Viejo and Peyrache, 2020). Interestingly, attractor dynamics in the AD exist before neurons show a reliable code for HD, when rat pups have not yet opened their eyes (Basset et al., 2018). This is revealed by rigid pairwise coordination in the AD, although individual neurons show no apparent tuning to HD.

In the absence of visual inputs, the attractor dynamics of the HD circuit ensure that the signal is maintained and updated by other (mostly vestibular) inputs. However, this process is prone to error accumulation over time because of the inherent noise in estimating angular head velocity, leading to a gradual shift of HD cells' preferred direction in environments that provide no additional cues (e.g., the geometry of the environment) (Bassett et al., 2018; Knierim et al., 1995; Valerio and Taube, 2012). Other factors influence the HD signal, such as motor efferent copy and optical flow (Taube, 2007), but the underlying circuits and processes remain unclear.

Finally, the firing of AD neurons in relation to HD is anticipatory; HD cells in the AD tend to fire ~50 ms before the animal's HD, a phenomenon that can be particularly observed during fast rotation of the head (Blair and Sharp, 1995). The degree of anticipatory firing is the highest in the MBs (~100 ms) (Blair et al., 1998; Stackman and Taube, 1998) and nearly nonexistent in the PoSub. Its origin remains unclear, but it likely depends on intrinsic properties of neurons in the HD circuit (van der Meer et al., 2007) and reflects circuit properties enabling the temporal integration of angular head velocity into the HD signal (Redish et al., 1996). The fact that AD HD cells show anticipatory firing intervals that are intermediate between the MBs and the PoSub suggests that AD may play a role in correcting for this temporal misalignment.

3.2 Computation in a Convergent–Divergent Circuit

One central aspect of the circuits linking the AT/RE with other limbic structures is the relative size of the different areas under consideration, along with the organization of the system in convergent–divergent loops. Each AT nucleus in rodents contains several thousand neurons and projects to cortical structures that contain hundreds of thousands of neurons. For example, Taube and Basset (2003) estimated the number of neurons in the LMN, AD nucleus, and PoSub to be 4260, 19,300, and 227,000, respectively. The most natural transformation of a divergent system such as this one is to increase the sparseness of the representation (in the case of HD cells, by decreasing the width of tuning curves), that is, to increase the resolution of the signal. Such sharpening of the tuning curves is exactly what is observed in the LMN–AD–PoSub pathway (Stackmann and Taube, 1998) (Figure 5). Sparsification can be achieved by diverse mechanisms, such as subtractive inhibition or nonlinear integration of inputs, and both mechanisms may play a role in the sharpening of AD tuning curves. In the AD, this is potentially achieved by inhibitory drive from the TRN and would explain why the AD is the main recipient of TRN inputs in the AT. However, the difference between AD and PoSub HD tuning curves is mild and certainly does not explain a 10-fold increase in the number of neurons. Thus, additional levels of organization of the HD signal within the PoSub are possible.

In contrast to the effect of divergent properties of the circuit, convergent inputs from the cortex to smaller populations of neurons, in the thalamus or the MBs, can result in low-dimensional representation of the inputs. Hence, the feedback of the PoSub to the AD and its input, the LMN, may not just be about resetting the HD signal but could be thought of as reprojecting complex spatial signals in the parahippocampal areas onto the low-dimensional HD system, ensuring coherent representation of HD in all the nodes of the navigation system. Although the exact behavioral correlates of AT/RE nuclei (except the AD) remain elusive, it is possible to think of the signals conveyed by these nuclei as low-dimensional codes of spatial navigation features distributed over large ensembles of parahippocampal areas. It would then not be surprising to detect signals coding for speed, distance to boundary, and other low-dimensional representations of space.

3.3 Oscillatory Modulation in the AT/RE

In rodents, and certainly many other mammals, electrical activity in the hippocampal formation is dominated by theta oscillations (6–9 Hz) as soon as the animal starts moving (Buzsáki, 2002; Vanderwolf, 1969). The spiking activity of most neurons in the hippocampus and associated structures is modulated in phase by this oscillation. Theta emerges from oscillatory firing in the medial septum (Buzsáki, 2002) and the intrinsic oscillatory properties of neurons in the entorhino-hippocampal network (Alonso and Llinás, 1989; Buzsáki, 2002; Stark et al., 2013). Theta oscillations play a key role in organizing neuronal population activity during exploration (Dragoi and Buzsáki, 2006; O'Keefe and Recce, 1993) and are thus crucial for spatial navigation and memory processes (Buzsáki and Moser, 2013). Most brain structures that are functionally related to the entorhino-hippocampal network show modulation of neuronal discharge by hippocampal theta oscillations, suggesting a role in cross-area communication (Siapas et al., 2005; Sirota et al., 2008). The strength of this oscillatory coupling is modulated by learning, decision making, and other cognitive processes requiring interaction between the hippocampus and its associated structures (Benchenane et al., 2010; DeCoteau et al., 2007; Jones and Wilson, 2005; Seidenbecher, 2003). Modulation by theta oscillations defines, to some extent, the extended limbic system (Buzsáki, 2002; Vertes et al., 2001).

The AT contains neurons modulated by theta, as shown in anesthetized (Vertes et al., 2001) and freely moving animals (Tsanov, Chah, et al., 2011; Viejo and Peyrache, 2020). Theta-modulation strength (i.e., the rhythmicity of the cell's spike train) is continuously distributed and does not reveal distinct cell classes (Figure 4). Anatomical reconstruction of electrode tracks suggests that theta-modulated cells are found everywhere in the AT except in the AD, which contains virtually no theta-modulated cells (Viejo and Peyrache, 2020).

The overlap between the anatomical location of theta-modulated cells and cholinergic inputs from the LDT in the AT is remarkable. The cholinergic system, especially within the septohippocampal network, plays a central role in the generation of theta oscillations (Buzsáki, 2002). The LDT, the main cholinergic (and potentially GABAergic and glutamatergic)

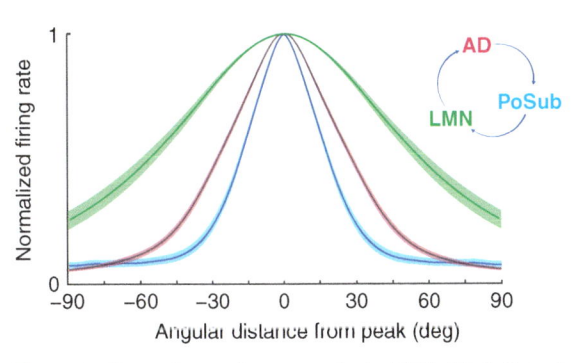

Figure 4 Narrowing tuning curves in the LMN–AD–PoSub circuit. Average HD tuning curves, centered at their preferred direction and normalized by their peak firing rate. Data courtesy from Adrian Duszkiewicz and Guillaume Viejo (see "Materials and Methods" section).

input to the AT is also modulated by theta (Cissé et al., 2018) but is not the only source of theta modulation in the AT. The MMN, but not the LMN, receive inputs from the medial septum (Swanson and Cowan, 1979), and their main input from the brainstem, the ventral tegmental nucleus of Gudden, is also modulated by theta (Bassant and Poindessous-Jazat, 2001; Kocsis et al., 2001).

Although the firing of theta-modulated neurons in a given theta cycle does not usually depend on the previous theta cycle, certain neurons systematically fire during every two cycles and are referred to as *theta-skipping neurons* (Brandon et al., 2013). Theta-skipping HD neurons are found in the RE (Jankowski et al., 2014). As described earlier, the RE directly projects to the hippocampus and other structures of the parahippocampal formation. Interestingly, theta-skipping HD neurons can also be observed in the medial entorhinal cortex (Brandon et al., 2013). In CA1, assemblies of place cells (that is, groups of functionally related neurons) do not always fire at each theta cycle (Harris et al., 2003). While animals run toward a decision point to turn either left or right at the fork of a T-shaped maze, assemblies of CA1 neurons prospectively code for future locations, alternating every other theta cycle between the two possible choices (Kay et al., 2020). Although still unproven, this theta-skipping phenomenon at the population level could originate from direct RE inputs to CA1.

The origin of theta-skipping oscillatory properties is unknown. However, it is interesting to speculate that theta-skipping firing corresponds to the first subharmonic of theta, that is, at around 4 cycles per second. A 4-Hz oscillation has been described in the medial prefrontal cortex (Fujisawa and Buzsáki, 2011), whose signals are relayed to the hippocampal formation by the RE. Anesthetized preparations suggest that the RE is also modulated by this 4-Hz oscillation (Roy et al., 2017). Although the origin of this 4-Hz oscillation is still a matter of debate (Bagur and Benchenane, 2018), the interaction of this endogenous 4-Hz oscillation with theta could potentially lead to the emergence of these theta-skipping neurons in the RE.

It is important to note that although they show theta rhythmicity, AT/RE neurons do not contribute to theta generation in the parahippocampal networks. Inactivation of the AT spares theta oscillations in the entorhinal cortex (Winter et al., 2015), and lesions of the RE do not change CA1 theta power (Ito et al., 2015).

During NREM sleep, theta oscillations are absent, and instead, the hippocampus shows irregular activity characterized by intermittent sharp wave-ripples (SWRs)—fast (150 Hz) and short-lasting (50- to 200 ms) oscillations (Buzsáki, 2015). The response profiles of AT neurons to SWRs and theta are related, indicating that their mutual relationship with the hippocampal formation is, to some extent, brain-state independent (Viejo and Peyrache, 2020). Furthermore, nearby neurons within the AT could show very different modulation by hippocampal rhythms, suggesting that beyond the cytoarchitectural definition of AT nuclei, nearby neurons may be parts of independent circuits. The only exception is the AD, where neurons all share similar dynamics and oscillatory properties (Viejo and Peyrache, 2020).

3.4 HD Tuning in Rate and Time outside the LMN–AD –PoSub loop

Anatomical considerations suggest that loops of the Papez circuit should convey different messages, yet HD cells have also been observed in the AV of rats (Tsanov, Chah, et al., 2011; Yoganarasimha et al., 2006), where approximatively two-thirds of the recorded cells in the medial part of the AV are finely tuned to the HD (Tsanov, Chah, et al., 2011). This is in contrast to recordings in mice, where HD cells are almost exclusively concentrated within the AD nucleus of the AT (Viejo and Peyrache, 2020).

Interestingly, some AV HD cells are comodulated by theta (Tsanov, Chah, et al., 2011), unlike AD HD cells (Tsanov, Chah, et al., 2011; Viejo and Peyrache, 2020). The origin of this HD-by-theta signal modulation is also uncertain and could potentially result from cortical feedback. Indeed, such HD-by-theta cells are commonly found in parahippocampal structures (Brandon et al., 2013; Cacucci et al., 2004; Kornienko et al., 2018).

In contrast to AV HD-by-theta modulated cells, pure AV theta cells are only mildly (if at all) modulated by HD. This echoes hippocampal fast-spiking inhibitory neurons (sometimes referred to as *theta cells*), which are only mildly modulated by the animal's spatial position (Ego-Stengel and Wilson, 2007; Maurer et al., 2006). However, Welday et al. (2011) have unraveled an unexpected modulation of AT theta cells: while not showing any typical HD tuning in their firing rate response, many theta cells in the AT show a modulation of intrinsic theta rhythmic discharge with respect to HD. Specifically, the time separating two consecutive volleys of spikes is, on average, the period of theta (~120 ms) but varies with HD, revealing a tuning of oscillatory properties of these neurons (Welday et al., 2011). It is unlikely that all theta cells show such oscillatory directional tuning, but it demonstrates that the operation of the navigation system relies on the interaction of neuronal codes of many different kinds—even when conveying the same behavioral feature, such as the HD signal.

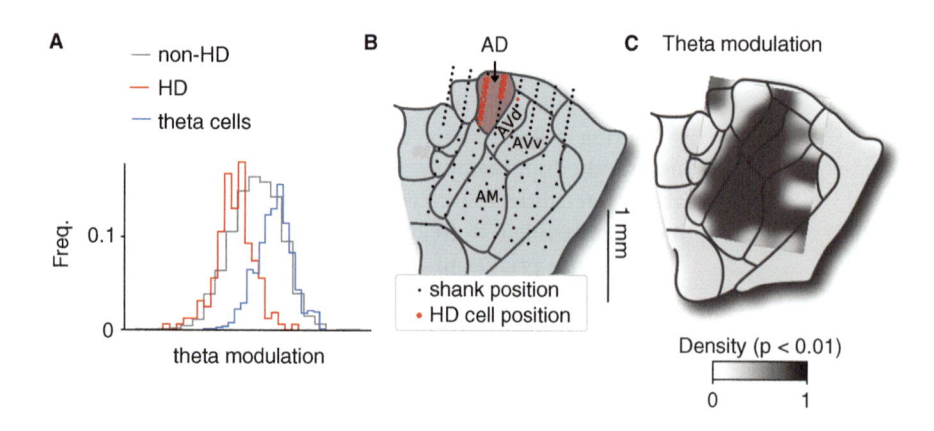

Figure 5 Modulation by HD and theta in the AT.

A. Distribution of theta modulation for HD (*red*) neurons, non-HD (*gray*) neurons, and significantly theta-modulated neurons (*blue*).

B. Coronal section of the AT showing the anatomical location of electrodes across the course of multiple recording sessions in an example mouse. Red dots indicate the locations where HD cells were detected. AVd and AVg indicate the dorsal and ventral AV nucleus, respectively.

C. Distribution of theta-modulated neurons in the same example mouse as in panel B. Note the virtual absence of theta-modulated neurons in the AD. Adapted from Viejo and Peyrache (2020).

3.5 Flow of Information in the Limbic Thalamocortical Network

Thalamic nuclei can either relay peripheral information to the cortex or relay information between cortical regions, depending on the origin of their main driver inputs. The thalamus is thus classically divided into first-order nuclei that relay subcortical and sensory signals and higher-order nuclei, which are driven by corticothalamic inputs from layer 5 neurons and enable indirect interaction across cortical areas (Sherman and Guillery, 2002). Is the limbic thalamus a relay of subcortical inputs or a hub connecting various cortical areas together?

Although gene expression in the AD is unique and does not resemble that of other thalamic nuclei (Phillips et al., 2019), the AD has the anatomical properties of a first-order nucleus because it is more influenced by its subcortical inputs, from the MBs, than by cortical feedback projections (Petrof and Sherman, 2009). In agreement with these findings, PoSub activity is well predicted from past AD ensemble activity, with a delay of ~20–50 ms (Viejo et al., 2018). This is the case not only during wakefulness but also during all stages of sleep. Hence, the rate-coded HD signal of the AD is a "primary" signal influencing the cortical navigation system (Peyrache et al., 2019). The bottom-up influence of the AD is also illustrated by its ability to synchronize widespread limbic areas (Gent et al., 2018) and the homogeneous increase in activity of its member neurons before hippocampal SWRs (Viejo and Peyrache, 2020), suggesting that AD discharge precedes neuronal activity in the entire hippocampal formation. One could speculate that the unique gene-expression profile of the AD (different from other first-order nuclei) is related to the nature of the HD signal, but further research is required to understand it.

The first- or higher-order nature of the AV, AM, and RE nuclei has not been well characterized and is still a matter of debate (Perry and Mitchell, 2019). At first sight, there is no reason to think that they differ from the AD nucleus because they also receive strong inputs from the MBs. Yet, gene-expression profiles suggest that the AV and AM nuclei share characteristics of first- and higher-order nuclei, respectively (Phillips et al., 2019). This would suggest that the AV nucleus primarily relays MB signals to the cortical navigation system and that its activity is not too strongly dependent on cortical feedback. In contrast, the AM nucleus may convey high-level spatial information inherited from subicular (or other cortical) feedback. In line with this view, there exists some evidence that AM neurons encode an animal's location, some with sharp place fields (Jankowski et al., 2015). Whether this high-level spatial representation in the AM emerges locally or is inherited from cortical feedback remains unknown, yet the AM may constitute an important relay of information from the hippocampal formation to the medial prefrontal cortex.

Like the AD nucleus, the RE nucleus is an outlier in gene-expression profiles. However, the RE nucleus has all the anatomical properties of a higher-order nucleus, driven by cortical projection. For example, accumulating evidence suggests that the RE is strongly modulated by prefrontal signals (Ito et al., 2015; Roy et al., 2017). The RE also exerts a strong influence on hippocampal activity (Bertram and Zhang, 1999; Weel et al., 1997), yet how strongly the hippocampal formation (through the subiculum) affects neuronal activity in the RE remains unknown. Whether RE neurons are modulated by place is a matter of debate (Ito et al., 2015; Jankowski et al., 2015, 2014), suggesting that subicular feedback may not be, at any rate, their strong driving signal.

3.6 Electrophysiological Properties: Conclusion

AT/RE neurons convey different signals. Although the exact behavioral correlates remain unclear for many neurons, spiking activity seems to be distributed over a continuum of a rate code for HD (especially in the AD) to strong theta-modulated activity in other nuclei. Theta rhythmicity may itself convey information relative to HD and could play a role in the oscillatory basis of spatial information processing in parahippocampal structures.

4. Role in Spatial Cognition

The evidence presented so far in this chapter indirectly suggests a role of the AT/RE nuclei in spatial navigation, which has been clarified by lesion, electrophysiological, and computational studies.

4.1 Role of the AT/RE in Spatial Cognition: Interventional Studies

In humans, clinical cases of strokes and alcohol abuse point to a role of the AT and RE in explicit memory (Carlesimo et al., 2011; Harding et al., 2000), suggesting that they are necessary for normal functioning of the hippocampal-dependent memory processes. In rodents, hippocampal lesions are best characterized by their effect on spatial navigation deficits. As expected, lesions of the AT lead to severe deficits in a wide range of navigation tasks, similar to the effect of hippocampal lesions (Aggleton and Brown, 1999; Clark and Harvey, 2016). However, in most cases, the deficits cannot be attributed to one specific AT nucleus but are instead most severe when the entire AT is lesioned (Aggleton et al., 1996, 1991; Byatt and Dalrymple-Alford, 1996; Sutherland and Rodriguez, 1989; van Groen et al., 2002). This is the case, for example, in the Morris Water Maze, in which animals learn to find a hidden platform below the water surface, for which only extended lesions of the AT produce severe learning deficits in contrast to AD or AV lesions alone (van Groen et al., 2002). The ability to remember previously visited locations defined in a map-based (allocentric) reference frame, but not an egocentric one (e.g., "this place on my left"), is impaired in animals with extensive AT lesions, particularly after a delay (Aggleton et al., 1996). Interestingly, lesions of the AT usually lead to more severe cognitive deficits than lesions of the MBs (Aggleton et al., 1991; Perry et al., 2018). Transient inactivation of the RE also disrupts spatial working memory (Maisson et al., 2018).

Thalamic lesions or transient inactivation certainly deprive cortical targets of a major excitatory input, leading to potential confounds in the interpretation of such manipulation. The specific role of the AT in spatial cognition is confirmed by the demonstration that immediate early gene expression (cFos, a proxy indicator for increases in neuronal activity and/or plasticity) is expressed at high levels in the AT after animals explore a radial arm maze (Vann et al., 2000). Furthermore, the integrity of the reciprocal interaction between the AT and the subicular complex is required for allocentric orientation because the selective disruption of both thalamocortical and corticothalamic pathways impairs behavioral performance in a forced alternation task in which the animal has to rely on distal visual cues (Nelson et al., 2020).

Lesion studies suggest a critical role of the AT/RE in allocentric navigation, especially during spatial working memory tasks, when animals need to remember previously visited places. Both theta and acetylcholine are associated with memory processes (Buzsáki and Moser, 2013; Hasselmo, 2006). Specifically, the depolarizing effect of acetylcholine could enable the maintenance of neuronal activity and thus stabilize the neuronal representation at behavioral timescales, on the order of seconds, during which neuronal ensembles of the limbic system oscillate at theta. Infusion of scopolamine (a muscarinic antagonist) in the AT strongly impairs spatial working memory (Mitchell et al., 2002). This points to a synergetic interaction between the main inputs to the AT (from the MBs) and cholinergic modulation, possibly resulting in the maintenance of specific activity states in thalamocortical loops and enabling spatial working memory. These interactions would take place in the AV, AM, and perhaps RE nuclei, where neurons show high modulation by theta oscillations.

4.2 Transformation of AT Signals into Spatial Representation

The HD signal is certainly the major type of information conveyed by AT neurons, using various codes (rate or oscillatory). How is the HD signal translated into spatial tuning in medial cortical structures and the hippocampus? Mammals, as well as many arthropods, have the ability to locate themselves in the absence of external inputs (e.g., complete darkness), a behavior referred to as *path integration* (Etienne and Jeffery, 2004; Gallistel, 1989; McNaughton et al., 2006; Mittelstaedt and Mittelstaedt, 1980). The animals can then rely on internal signals, such as vestibular and proprioceptive information, which translate into codes for HD and speed. Like sailors in the open sea, who can navigate with a compass and estimate how far they have traveled, the brain is capable of integrating, in time, HD and speed to compute an estimate of the animal's current location (Gallistel, 1989). The identification of the system supporting path integration remains elusive, yet there is a general agreement that the extended hippocampal formation is necessary for this ability (McNaughton et al., 2006, 1996). The discovery of grid cells (Hafting et al., 2005) sparked new interest in the field because they seemed like an ideal candidate to support a neuronal code for path integration (Burak and Fiete, 2009; Fuhs and Touretzky, 2006; McNaughton et al., 2006).

It is important to note that the HD signal itself results from the temporal integration of angular head-velocity signals and is thus prone to error accumulation in the absence of visual landmarks that normally anchor the signal to the external world. In darkness, the HD signal drifts and leads to behavioral disorientation of the same magnitude as the accumulated error (Valerio and Taube, 2012), thus showing that in these situations, animals have no other strategy but to rely on their internal orientation and spatial maps to find their way.

4.2.1 Grid Cells and Path Integration

Computing path integration is a mere temporal integration process and can thus be implemented in many ways. What are the current theories of the brain mechanisms that would enable it, and what could be the role of the thalamus in such processes? Samsonovich and McNaughton (1997) and Touretzky and Redish (1996) proposed two of the first connectionist models accounting for path integration in the hippocampal formation, which were based on attractor maps and a series of intermediate layers progressively transforming the HD and speed signals into place cell-like units. Later models accounted for the generation of grid cells in the medial entorhinal cortex (Banino et al., 2018; Burak and Fiete, 2009; Fuhs and Touretzky, 2006; McNaughton et al., 2006). In these computational studies, the HD signal is usually treated as a simple population code indicating the animal's current orientation, in line with the rate-coding HD cells of the AD nucleus.

Another class of models suggests that grid cells result from the interference between theta-rhythmic oscillators (Burgess et al., 2007). The interference model suggests that small differences in oscillating frequency in the inputs of grid cells would result in a slowly varying envelope of theta-rhythmic membrane potential, leading to repetitive activation of the neurons in space and thus grid fields. In support of this view, suppressing theta oscillations by inactivating the medial septum leads to degradation of grid firing (Brandon et al., 2011; Koenig et al., 2011). Importantly, during theta disruption, grid cells become strongly tuned to HD, confirming that the HD signal is certainly a key ingredient in grid firing—an assertion also supported by AT inactivation experiments (Winter et al., 2015). One prediction of these models is that grid cells receive an HD-by-velocity theta-modulated signal, as found in the entorhinal cortex (Sargolini et al., 2006) and the PoSub (Cacucci et al., 2004; Sharp, 1996). The AV nucleus also conveys such signals (see Section 3.3) and could thus directly influence the emergence of grid cells.

4.2.2 Place Cells and the Spatial Cognitive Map

A growing body of evidence supports the view that the HD cells of the AT influence spatial navigation processes in the hippocampo-entorhinal formation. By simultaneously recording AD HD cells and CA1 place cells in freely moving rats, Knierim et al. (1995) showed how the drift of the HD signal in disoriented animals is associated with rotation of hippocampal place fields in the same direction (Figure 6A). In addition, lesions of the HD system alter the stability of place cells (Calton et al., 2003) and disrupt the firing of grid cells (Winter et al., 2015). The lack of an HD signal also impairs the ability of the animals to differentiate between similar but differently oriented environments (Harland et al., 2017). The influence of HD cells in the hippocampal formation is not limited to waking behavior and is further evidenced by the interaction between AT HD cells and hippocampal activity during NREM sleep. AD neurons fire immediately before hippocampal SWRs (Viejo and Peyrache, 2020). Not only does firing increase at the time of SWRs, but the spontaneous drift of the HD signal during NREM sleep stops immediately before SWRs, as if the HD system indicated a "virtual" direction to the hippocampal formation (Figure 6B).

4.2.3 HD, Egocentric Modulation, and Boundary Signaling

Hippocampal place cells are driven by multiple factors, including path integration. One leading model is that they also encode the distance of the animal from the environment boundaries (Barry et al., 2006; Bicanski and Burgess, 2020; O'Keefe and Burgess, 1996). Neurons firing in the proximity of one or several of the environment boundaries have been reported in the subiculum (Lever et al., 2009) and the entorhinal cortex (Savelli et al., 2008; Solstad et al., 2008). Interestingly, neurons signaling environment boundaries have also been reported in the RE (Jankowski et al., 2015), possibly as a consequence of feedback from the subiculum and/or a combination of the multiple inputs converging in the RE.

What is the role of the HD signal in the emergence of a signal for boundaries? The firing of HD cells is usually not uniform in the environment, not because it is intrinsically modulated by space but because the animal's behavior is itself nonhomogeneous. Specifically, animals, including humans (Walz et al., 2016), tend to walk and run along boundaries of the environment (e.g., Wiltschko et al., 2015), a behavior referred to as *thigmotaxis*. As a result, an HD cell with a preferred direction parallel to a boundary will tend to fire almost half of the time the animal is located along that boundary, resulting, on average, in higher firing rates than elsewhere in the environment. Controlling for this potential confound, it can be shown that HD cells in the AD are not modulated by space but only by HD (Peyrache et al., 2017). Of note, similar arguments and analyses were originally made to demonstrate that hippocampal place cells were not directionally tuned (Muller et al., 1994). Unlike the AD, the PoSub contains neurons that are actually modulated by position, usually in conjunction with the HD (Cacucci et al., 2004; Peyrache et al., 2017). The preferred firing fields of these neurons were usually along the walls and could be explained by a simple transformation of the HD signal (Peyrache et al., 2017). The combination of HD modulation with a signal indicating the position of a wall in egocentric space (e.g., "there is a wall on my right") result in subsets of neurons firing for specific borders in an HD-dependent manner. Furthermore, a combination of egocentric-modulated HD cells with opposite orientations can potentially lead to an actual signal for a border (Gofman et al., 2019; Peyrache et al., 2017). More generally, the combination of egocentric and HD signals seems to be key in the emergence of spatial information in the subicular complex and the retrosplenial cortex (Alexander et al., 2020; Gofman et al., 2019; LaChance et al., 2019; Peyrache et al., 2017).

4.2.4 Head or Movement Direction?

One major issue with the role of HD signal, and thus the AT/RE, in spatial navigation is that all models and theories regarding how path integration is supported assume that the HD signal, irrespective of its origin and associated code, indicates the direction of movement. However, this is far from being the case; animals tend to rotate their heads even during running. Raudies et al. (2015) reported that in the medial entorhinal cortex, the activity of individual neurons is more correlated with HD than with movement direction. The authors further showed that grid-cell regularity is strongly affected when updated by HD instead of actual movement direction. Whether a separate system conveys movement direction or whether the grid-cell network can correct for this discrepancy remains to be answered.

4.3 Executive Modulation of CA1 by the RE

Whereas the AT is believed to be crucial for spatial representation, the RE may modulate spatial representation in the hippocampo-entorhinal network with respect to ongoing behavior and executive functions, resulting in multiplexed signals. Indeed, the firing of hippocampal place cells depends not only on the location of the animal in its environment but also on the ongoing behavioral context. For example, the locations of place fields in an environment are remapped when the animal alternates between two different behavioral tasks (Markus et al., 1995). Another illustration of such context dependence is how place cells are prospectively modulated on a T-maze, where place cells firing on the central arm alter their

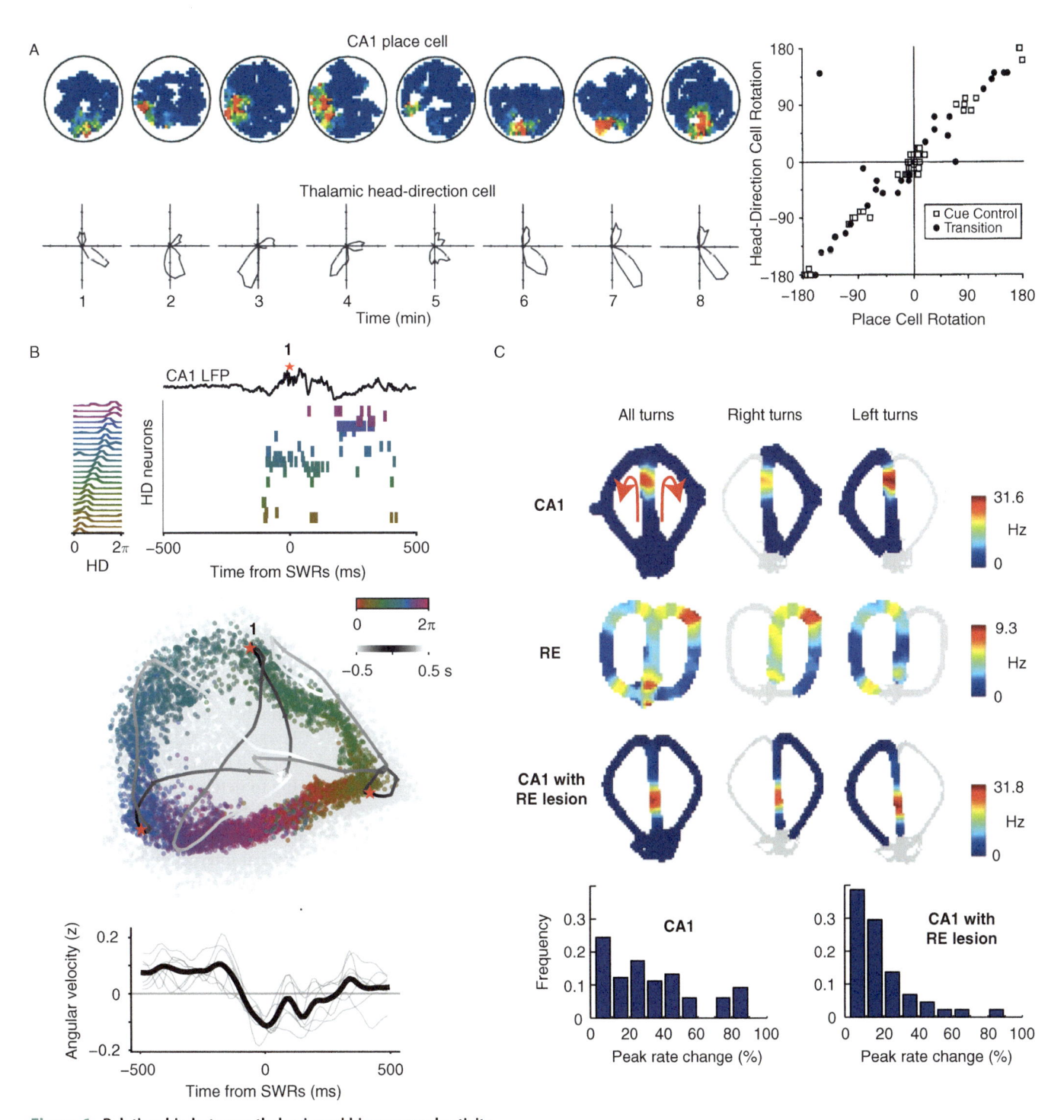

Figure 6 Relationship between thalamic and hippocampal activity.

A. Coherent representation of orientation in HD and place cells. Left: An example HD cell (*bottom*) from the AT was simultaneously recorded with a hippocampal place cell (*top*) in a disoriented animal. The internal representations of HD and place rotated coherently over the course of several minutes. Right: Rotation offset in various behavioral tests in simultaneously recorded HD and place cells. Adapted with permission from Knierim et al. (1995).

B. HD cells of the AD point to precise locations at the time of SWRs. Top: Example raster plot of HD cell population activity sorted by their preferred HD during exploration (*top left*, angular tuning curves) during NREM sleep. The CA1 LFP is shown above; red asterisk indicates an SWR. Middle: Isomap projection of HD cell population activity during exploration (color indicates animal's HD during exploration) and NREM sleep (gray points). The three lines indicate isomap trajectories around three example SWRs. Bottom: average angular speed in isomap projection space around SWRs (n = 7 sessions). Adapted from Viejo and Peyrache (2020).

C. Prospective modulation of CA1 place cells by RE signals. Top, first row: Example place fields of a CA1 place cell on a continuous eight-arm maze during all laps (*left column*) and restricted to left and right turns (*middle and right columns*, respectively). Middle row: Same as first row for an example RE neuron. Third row: Example CA1 neuron in an RE-lesioned animal. Bottom left: Change in CA1 peak firing rate in control animals. Bottom right: Same as bottom left but in RE-lesioned animals. Adapted with permission from Ito et al. (2015).

firing rate depending on the future choice (either right or left arm) (Wood et al., 2000).

These results beg the question of the origin of such phenomena. Ample evidence points to the role of the medial prefrontal cortex in behavioral flexibility and rule-shifting capability, including in rodents (Benchenane et al., 2010; Birrell and Brown, 2000; Dalley et al., 2004; Euston et al., 2012; Peyrache et al., 2009). Anatomically, the RE is ideally situated to relay frontal signals to the hippocampus (see Section 2.1.3). Ito et al. (2015) trained animals on an alternation task on a T-maze and observed that prospective coding of hippocampal place cells is abolished when the RE is lesioned or transiently silenced with optogenetics (Figure 6C). Modulation of RE neurons is limited to navigation planning because they do not exhibit changes in firing rates when the environmental context is modified, a manipulation that usually leads to the remapping of CA1 neurons. However, the manipulation of the RE in the Ito et al. (2015) study did not impair behavioral performance, perhaps as a result of the animals having already learned the task at the time of the manipulation. The question of the exact role of the RE in navigation, and not only in modulating hippocampal activity, thus remains open. One possibility is that RE inputs gate inputs from the entorhinal cortex by nonlinear interaction in the distal dendrites of CA1 pyramidal cells (Dolleman-van der Weel et al., 2017).

The hippocampus has also been shown to disengage from immediate sensory experience and to "project" the internal representation of the animal's position toward possible future paths (Johnson and Redish, 2007). This transient disengagement from the animal's current location is observed in particular when the animal deliberates between different options and shows behavioral signs of indecision, a behavior referred to as *vicarious trial and error* (see (Redish, 2016) for review). Furthermore, at a choice point, hippocampal neuronal assemblies alternate between representations of left or right choices during every other theta cycle (Kay et al., 2020). The RE contains prospective neurons (Ito et al., 2015) and theta-skipping HD cells (Jankowski et al., 2014), suggesting that it may play a role in theta-alternating assemblies in CA1. More generally, the RE would enable the multiplexing of spatial and executive signals in CA1, possibly supported by the oscillatory properties of the system.

5. Thalamus, Sleep, and Memory

The limbic system is not only necessary for spatial navigation but is also instrumental for the formation of long-term declarative memories (i.e., memories of facts and events) (Frankland and Bontempi, 2005; Nadel and Moscovitch, 1997; Scoville and Milner, 1957; Squire, 1992). Accumulating evidence suggests that the integrity of the AT and RE is necessary for memory formation, for example, clinical cases of strokes and alcohol abuse (Carlesimo et al., 2011; Harding et al., 2000) and lesion studies in rodents (Aggleton and Brown, 1999). The consolidation of declarative memories depends on a cascade of molecular, neuronal, and circuit-level reorganization (Dudai, 2004), and sleep is believed to be crucial for this process (Diekelmann and Born, 2010). What can be the role of the AT/RE nuclei in the consolidation of memories during sleep?

Neuronal activity in the thalamus shifts dramatically with brain states, from regular spiking during wakefulness to burst-firing regimes during NREM sleep (Steriade et al., 1993). At the population level, thalamocortical networks show intermittent spindle oscillations, one of the hallmarks of NREM sleep. Spindles result from the coordination of burst firing across a population of thalamic neurons, resulting in network oscillations at 10–15 Hz that rhythmically modulate their cortical targets (Fernandez and Lüthi, 2019; Steriade et al., 1993). Although the role of spindles remains elusive, it has been hypothesized that they are related to learning and memory (for review, see Peyrache and Seibt, 2020).

At the population level, recently formed neuronal assemblies in the hippocampus (in the form of sequentially activated neurons representing the trajectory of the animal) are spontaneously replayed during NREM sleep (Lee and Wilson, 2002; Skaggs and McNaughton, 1996; Wilson and McNaughton, 1994). Replay occurs during SWRs, and these physiological events are necessary for memory consolidation during sleep (Ego-Stengel and Wilson, 2010; Girardeau et al., 2009). Hence, the replay phenomenon bridges the gap between the two main roles of the limbic system: spatial navigation and memory. The thalamus, as during wakefulness while the animal navigates, may thus be essential in providing the hippocampal formation with low-level signals and coordinating activity across the limbic system.

Spindles, detected in the medial cortex, are coordinated with hippocampal SWRs (Peyrache et al., 2011; Siapas and Wilson, 1998; Sirota et al., 2003). The precise origin of these "limbic" spindles is challenging to determine, but it is reasonable to expect them to be generated in the AT/RE. Spindles are supposed to arise from two key ingredients: burst firing of thalamic neurons and their mutual interaction with the TRN. The AT/RE system seems to violate this rule: although the AD is the main recipient of TRN inputs, its neurons do not show any bursts during NREM (Viejo and Peyrache, 2020). In contrast, many neurons in the AM and AV are bursty but certainly receive much less inhibition from the TRN. It is computationally not impossible that the AD generates spindles without bursting, but this will require further investigation.

The other oscillatory hallmark of NREM is the slow oscillation (0.1–4 Hz), corresponding to the aperiodic fluctuation of thalamic and cortical neuron membrane potential between depolarized (UP) states and hyperpolarized (DOWN) states. The AD is a key player in the coordination of medial cortical and parahippocampal activity in the slow-frequency range (0.1–4 Hz) (Gent et al., 2018; see also Chapter 19 in this volume). As discussed earlier, the activity in the AD during NREM is highly structured as the HD signal remains coherent and randomly drifts along the two possible directions on the ring (Peyrache et al., 2015). This drift stops immediately before hippocampal SWRs and AD neurons indicate a precise direction during the entire SWR (Viejo and Peyrache, 2020) (Figure 5B). Other AT neurons may play a similar role, providing specific inputs that will set the stage for hippocampal replay. The nature of such signals remains to be understood. Many AT neurons (outside the AD) discharge more strongly after SWRs (Viejo and Peyrache, 2020), and this is typically what is expected from a higher-order pathway: conveying messages between cortical regions, enabling the broadcasting of replayed information across large cortical networks.

The RE is a key relay between regions of the medial cortex and parahippocampal structures. The hippocampus projects directly to the medial prefrontal cortex (Jay et al., 1989), as evidenced by the strong modulation of mPFC neurons by hippocampal rhythms (Peyrache et al., 2011; Siapas et al., 2005; Sirota et al., 2003; Wierzynski et al., 2009). Neuronal populations in the mPFC replay previous wake-experience–associated activity traces during NREM (Euston et al., 2007; Peyrache et al., 2009), especially after learning, at the time of SWRs (Peyrache et al., 2009). In turn, the relay of medial prefrontal signals to the hippocampus by the RE may be particularly important for memory processes (Mei et al., 2018; Xu and Südhof, 2013). Hippocampal replay is strengthened during spindles, and during SWRs, RE neurons show high levels of burstiness (Varela and Wilson, 2020). RE inputs can thus play a role in the dynamic control of replay in the hippocampo-cortical network, possibly modulating the gain and routing of replayed information.

In conclusion, the information conveyed by the AT/RE nuclei during NREM sleep may be essentially the same as that conveyed during spatial navigation and certainly plays a role in the establishment of long-term memories by influencing hippocampal states during replay and enabling communication between the hippocampus and the cortex. Neuronal dynamics in the thalamus during NREM sleep are modified at the both neuronal level (e.g., bursts) and at the level of the population (e.g., spindles). These dynamical properties may be instrumental in the mechanisms supporting memory consolidation (Peyrache and Seibt, 2020).

Conclusion

I have presented in this chapter evidence for the role of the AT and RE nucleus in navigation. The AT occupies a central position in the superimposed and interacting loops that constitute the limbic system, or the extended hippocampal system. These loops enable the maintenance of specific activity states and information streams during exploration. They are updated by brainstem inputs that convey information related to the movement of the animal (i.e., HD and linear speed). These signals are segregated in the AT and its inputs from the MBs but are combined in the cortex, where projections of different AT/RE subareas overlap.

Because of space constraints, this chapter omitted several important facts, notably the role of the laterodorsal nucleus of the thalamus, which is believed to be involved in HD signal processing (Mizumori and Williams, 1993), among other functions in spatial navigation (Clark and Harvey, 2016; Perry and Mitchell, 2019). However, its connectivity, its neuronal activity, and the effect of its lesions in navigation are much less studied than the AT/RE nuclei. The role of some intralaminar nuclei, specifically the interanteromedial nucleus, is also unclear but is certainly related to the role of the AM. Last, the plasticity of the circuits discussed in this chapter, at both the input and output levels, is still unclear, although preliminary evidence suggests that some of these inputs, specifically the feedback from the parahippocampal formation, are plastic (Tsanov, Wright, et al., 2011).

Many questions remain open. Future studies will shed new light on the circuits discussed in this chapter. Future directions include the cell-by-cell characterization of these circuits (how much the activity of an individual AT neuron contributes to its own inputs), how neuronal connectivity relates to gene-expression profiles (do AT neurons connect to cortical neurons expressing similar genes?), the exact role of the TRN and cholinergic inputs in AT/RE operations, the nature of MMN inputs, and more generally, how mammillary inputs are processed by the AT and what other kinds of information are conveyed by the activity of AT neurons.

Materials and Methods

The connectivity matrix in Figure 1A was obtained from publicly available data at the Allen Institute. The analyses were performed using the Allen SDK package in Python 3. The database was queried for sources in AD, the AV, and AM (across all available mouse lines), and fluorescence data were retrieved in the target structures (prelimbic [PL], infralimbic [ILA], cingulate cortex [ACA], retrosplenial cortex [RSP]). For each experiment, fluorescence was normalized to its maximum and then averaged. List of experiments: 155735826 and 182280916 for the AD; 614435699, 605092364, 146046430, 292478008, 114427219, 182805965, 267609756, 292321278, 175818392, 286553311, 479267539, and 100142569 for the AV; 158840459, 506947040, 592698832, 606278526, 156393801, 592698087, 573035760, 167571459, 514333422, 266174045, 601900484, and 146658170.

The reconstruction of an RE neuron axon in Figure 1B was obtained from the MouseLight database. The reconstruction was displayed using BrainRender software (Claudi et al., 2020).

The data presented in Figure 4 were collected by Adrian Duszkiewicz and Guillaume Viejo in the Peyrache Lab, following the same methods as in Peyrache et al. (2015).

Acknowledgments

I would like to thank Barbara Jones, Adrian Duszkiewicz, Karim Benchenane, and the Peyrache Lab for discussion and comments on an earlier version of this chapter and Lynda Mainville for proofreading. This work was supported by a Canadian Research Chair in Systems Neuroscience (245716); a Canadian Institutes of Health Research (CIHR) Project Grant (155957); a Natural Sciences and Engineering Research Council of Canada (NSERC) Discovery Grant (RGPIN-2018-04600); and the Canada-Israel Health Research Initiative, jointly funded by the CIHR, the Israel Science Foundation, the International Development Research Centre of Canada, and the Azrieli Foundation (108877-001).

References

Aggleton, J.P., Brown, M.W., 1999. Episodic memory, amnesia, and the hippocampal–anterior thalamic axis. Behav. Brain Sci. **22**, 425–444.

Aggleton, J.P., Hunt, P.R., Nagle, S., Neave, N., 1996. The effects of selective lesions within the anterior thalamic nuclei on spatial memory in the rat. Behav. Brain Res. **81**, 189–198. https://doi.org/10.1016/S0166-4328(96)89080-2

Aggleton, J.P., Keith, A.B., Sahgal, A., 1991. Both fornix and anterior thalamic, but not mammillary, lesions disrupt delayed non-matching-to-position memory in rats. Behav. Brain Res. **44**, 151–161. https://doi.org/10.1016/S0166-4328(05)80020-8

Aggleton, J.P., Nelson, A.J.D., 2015. Why do lesions in the rodent anterior thalamic nuclei cause such severe spatial deficits? Neurosci. Biobehav. Rev. **54**, 131–144. https://doi.org/10.1016/j.neubiorev.2014.08.013

Alexander, A.S., Carstensen, L.C., Hinman, J. R., Raudies, F., Chapman, G.W., Hasselmo, M. E., 2020. Egocentric boundary vector tuning of the retrosplenial cortex. Sci. Adv. **6**, eaaz2322. https://doi.org/10.1126/sciadv.aaz2322

Allen, G.V., Hopkins, D.A., 1989. Mamillary body in the rat: Topography and synaptology of projections from the subicular complex, prefrontal cortex, and midbrain tegmentum. J. Comp. Neurol. **286**, 311–336. https://doi.org/10.1002/cne.902860303

Alonso, A., Llinás, R.R., 1989. Subthreshold Na$^+$-dependent theta-like rhythmicity in stellate cells of entorhinal cortex layer II. Nature **342**, 175–177. https://doi.org/10.1038/342175a0

Amaral, D.G., Cowan, W.M., 1980. Subcortical afferents to the hippocampal formation in the monkey. J. Comp. Neurol. **189**, 573–591. https://doi.org/10.1002/cne.901890402

Andersen, P., Curtis, D.R., 1964. The excitation of thalamic neurones by acetylcholine. Acta Physiol. Scand. **61**, 85–99. https://doi.org/10.1111/j.1748-1716.1964.tb02945.x

Angelaki, D.E., Cullen, K.E., 2008. Vestibular system: the many facets of a multimodal sense. Annu. Rev. Neurosci. **31**, 125–150. https://doi.org/10.1146/annurev.neuro.31.060407.125555

Arcelli, P., Frassoni, C., Regondi, M.C., Biasi, S.D., Spreafico, R., 1997. GABAergic neurons in mammalian thalamus: a marker of thalamic complexity? Brain Res. Bull. **42**, 27–37. https://doi.org/10.1016/S0361-9230(96)00107-4

Bagur, S., Benchenane, K., 2018. Taming the oscillatory zoo in the hippocampus and neocortex: a review of the commentary of Lockmann and Tort on Roy et al. Brain Struct. Funct. **223**, 5–9. https://doi.org/10.1007/s00429-017-1569-x

Banino, A., Barry, C., Uria, B., Blundell, C., Lillicrap, T., Mirowski, P., Pritzel, A., Chadwick, M.J., Degris, T., Modayil, J., Wayne, G., Soyer, H., Viola, F., Zhang, B., Goroshin, R., Rabinowitz, N., Pascanu, R., Beattie, C., Petersen, S., Sadik, A., Gaffney, S., King, H., Kavukcuoglu, K., Hassabis, D., Hadsell, R., Kumaran, D., 2018. Vector-based navigation using grid-like representations in artificial agents. Nature **557**, 429–433. https://doi.org/10.1038/s41586-018-0102-6

Barry, C., Lever, C., Hayman, R., Hartley, T., Burton, S., O'Keefe, J., Jeffery, K., Burgess, N., 2006. The boundary vector cell model of place cell firing and spatial memory. Rev. Neurosci. **17**, 71–97. https://doi.org/10.1515/revneuro.2006.17.1-2.71

Bassant, M.-H., Poindessous-Jazat, F., 2001. Ventral tegmental nucleus of Gudden: a pontine hippocampal theta generator? Hippocampus **11**, 809–813. https://doi.org/10.1002/hipo.1096

Bassett, J.P., Wills, T.J., Cacucci, F., 2018. Self-organized attractor dynamics in the developing head direction circuit. Curr. Biol. **28**, 609–615.e3. https://doi.org/10.1016/j.cub.2018.01.010

Benchenane, K., Peyrache, A., Khamassi, M., Tierney, P.L., Gioanni, Y., Battaglia, F.P., Wiener, S.I., 2010. Coherent theta oscillations and reorganization of spike timing in the hippocampal-prefrontal network upon learning. Neuron **66**, 921–936. https://doi.org/10.1016/j.neuron.2010.05.013

Berthoz, A., Viaud-Delmon, I., 1999. Multisensory integration in spatial orientation. Curr. Opin. Neurobiol. **9**, 708–712. https://doi.org/10.1016/S0959-4388(99)00041-0

Bertram, E.H., Zhang, D.X., 1999. Thalamic excitation of hippocampal CA1 neurons: a comparison with the effects of CA3 stimulation. Neuroscience **92**, 15–26. https://doi.org/10.1016/S0306-4522(98)00712-X

Bicanski, A., Burgess, N., 2020. Neuronal vector coding in spatial cognition. Nat. Rev. Neurosci. **21**, 453–470. https://doi.org/10.1038/s41583-020-0336-9

Birrell, J.M., Brown, V.J., 2000. Medial frontal cortex mediates perceptual attentional set shifting in the rat. J. Neurosci. **20**, 4320.

Blair, H.T., Cho, J., Sharp, P.E., 1998. Role of the lateral mammillary nucleus in the rat head direction circuit: a combined single unit recording and lesion study. Neuron **21**, 1387–1397.

Blair, H.T., Cho, J., Sharp, P.E., 1999. The anterior thalamic head-direction signal is abolished by bilateral but not unilateral lesions of the lateral mammillary nucleus. J. Neurosci. **19**, 6673–6683.

Blair, H.T., Sharp, P.E., 1995. Anticipatory head direction signals in anterior thalamus: evidence for a thalamocortical circuit that integrates angular head motion to compute head direction. J. Neurosci. **15**, 6260.

Boucetta, S., Cissé, Y., Mainville, L., Morales, M., Jones, B.E., 2014. Discharge profiles across the sleep–waking cycle of identified cholinergic, GABAergic, and glutamatergic neurons in the pontomesencephalic tegmentum of the rat. J. Neurosci. **34**, 4708–4727. https://doi.org/10.1523/JNEUROSCI.2617-13.2014

Brandon, M.P., Bogaard, A.R., Andrews, C. M., Hasselmo, M.E., 2012. Head direction cells in the postsubiculum do not show replay of prior waking sequences during sleep. Hippocampus **22**, 604–618. https://doi.org/10.1002/hipo.20924

Brandon, M.P., Bogaard, A.R., Libby, C.P., Connerney, M.A., Gupta, K., Hasselmo, M. E., 2011. Reduction of theta rhythm dissociates grid cell spatial periodicity from directional tuning. Science **332**, 595–599. https://doi.org/10.1126/science.1201652

Brandon, M.P., Bogaard, A.R., Schultheiss, N.W., Hasselmo, M.E., 2013. Segregation of cortical head direction cell assemblies on alternating theta cycles. Nat. Neurosci. **16**, 739–748. https://doi.org/10.1038/nn.3383

Burak, Y., Fiete, I.R., 2009. Accurate path integration in continuous attractor network models of grid cells. PLOS Comput. Biol. **5**, e1000291. https://doi.org/10.1371/journal.pcbi.1000291

Burgess, N., Barry, C., O'Keefe, J., 2007. An oscillatory interference model of grid cell firing. Hippocampus **17**, 801–812. https://doi.org/10.1002/hipo.20327

Buzsáki, G., 2002. Theta oscillations in the hippocampus. Neuron **33**, 325–340.

Buzsáki, G., 2015. Hippocampal sharp wave-ripple: A cognitive biomarker for episodic memory and planning. Hippocampus **25**, 1073–1188. https://doi.org/10.1002/hipo.22488

Buzsáki, G., Moser, E.I., 2013. Memory, navigation and theta rhythm in the hippocampal-entorhinal system. Nat. Neurosci. **16**, 130–138. https://doi.org/10.1038/nn.3304

Byatt, G., Dalrymple-Alford, J.C., 1996. Both anteromedial and anteroventral thalamic lesions impair radial-maze learning in rats. Behav. Neurosci. **110**, 1335–1348. https://doi.org/10.1037//0735-7044.110.6.1335

Cacucci, F., Lever, C., Wills, T.J., Burgess, N., O'Keefe, J., 2004. Theta-modulated place-by-direction cells in the hippocampal formation in the rat. J. Neurosci. **24**, 8265–8277. https://doi.org/10.1523/JNEUROSCI.2635-04.2004

Calton, J.L., Stackman, R.W., Goodridge, J.P., Archey, W.B., Dudchenko, P.A., Taube, J.S., 2003. Hippocampal place cell instability after lesions of the head direction cell network. J. Neurosci. **23**, 9719–9731.

Carlén, M., 2017. What constitutes the prefrontal cortex? Science **358**, 478–482. https://doi.org/10.1126/science.aan8868

Carlesimo, G.A., Lombardi, M.G., Caltagirone, C., 2011. Vascular thalamic amnesia: A reappraisal. Neuropsychologia **49**, 777–789. https://doi.org/10.1016/j.neuropsychologia.2011.01.026

Carvalho, M.M., Tanke, N., Kropff, E., Witter, M.P., Moser, M.-B., Moser, E.I., 2020. A brainstem locomotor circuit drives the activity of speed cells in the medial entorhinal cortex. Cell Rep. **32**, 108123. https://doi.org/10.1016/j.celrep.2020.108123

Chaudhuri, R., Gercek, B., Pandey, B., Peyrache, A., Fiete, I., 2019. The intrinsic attractor manifold and population dynamics of a canonical cognitive circuit across waking and sleep. Nat. Neurosci. **22**, 1512–1520.

Chen, L.L., Lin, L.H., Green, E.J., Barnes, C.A., McNaughton, B.L., 1994. Head-direction cells in the rat posterior cortex. I. Anatomical distribution and behavioral modulation. Exp. Brain Res. **101**, 8–23.

Christiansen, K., Dillingham, C.M., Wright, N.F., Saunders, R.C., Vann, S.D., Aggleton, J.P., 2016. Complementary subicular pathways to the anterior thalamic nuclei and mammillary bodies in the rat and macaque monkey brain. Eur. J. Neurosci. **43**, 1044–1061. https://doi.org/10.1111/ejn.13208

Cissé, Y., Toossi, H., Ishibashi, M., Mainville, L., Leonard, C.S., Adamantidis, A., Jones, B.E., 2018. Discharge and role of acetylcholine pontomesencephalic neurons in cortical activity and sleep-wake states examined by optogenetics and juxtacellular recording in mice. eNeuro **5**. https://doi.org/10.1523/ENEURO.0270-18.2018

Clark, B.J., Harvey, R.E., 2016. Do the anterior and lateral thalamic nuclei make distinct contributions to spatial representation and memory? Neurobiol. Learn. Mem. **133**, 69–78. https://doi.org/10.1016/j.nlm.2016.06.002

Claudi, F., Tyson, A.L., Branco, T., 2020. Brainrender. A Python-based software for visualisation of neuroanatomical and morphological data. bioRxiv 2020.02.23.961748. https://doi.org/10.1101/2020.02.23.961748

Cornwall, J., Cooper, J.D., Phillipson, O.T., 1990. Projections to the rostral reticular thalamic nucleus in the rat. Exp. Brain Res. **80**. https://doi.org/10.1007/BF00228857

Cruce, J.A.F., 1975. An autoradiographic study of the projections of the mammillothalamic tract in the rat. Brain Res. **85**, 211–219. https://doi.org/10.1016/0006-8993(75)90072-4

Curro Dossi, R., Pare, D., Steriade, M., 1991. Short-lasting nicotinic and long-lasting muscarinic depolarizing responses of thalamocortical neurons to stimulation of mesopontine cholinergic nuclei. J. Neurophysiol. **65**, 393–406. https://doi.org/10.1152/jn.1991.65.3.393

Dalley, J.W., Cardinal, R.N., Robbins, T.W., 2004. Prefrontal executive and cognitive functions in rodents: neural and neurochemical substrates. Neurosci. Biobehav. Rev. **28**, 771–784. https://doi.org/10.1016/j.neubiorev.2004.09.006

DeCoteau, W.E., Thorn, C., Gibson, D.J., Courtemanche, R., Mitra, P., Kubota, Y., Graybiel, A.M., 2007. Learning-related coordination of striatal and hippocampal theta rhythms during acquisition of a procedural maze task. Proc. Natl. Acad. Sci. **104**, 5644.

Diekelmann, S., Born, J., 2010. The memory function of sleep. Nat. Rev. Neurosci. **11**, 114–126. https://doi.org/10.1038/nrn2762

Dolleman-van der Weel, M.J., Lopes da Silva, F.H., Witter, M.P., 2017. Interaction of nucleus reuniens and entorhinal cortex projections in hippocampal field CA1 of the rat. Brain Struct. Funct. **222**, 2421–2438. https://doi.org/10.1007/s00429-016-1350-6

Dragoi, G., Buzsáki, G., 2006. Temporal encoding of place sequences by hippocampal cell assemblies. Neuron **50**, 145–157.

Dudai, Y., 2004. The neurobiology of consolidations, or, how stable is the engram? Annu. Rev. Psychol. **55**, 51–86. https://doi.org/10.1146/annurev.psych.55.090902.142050

Ego-Stengel, V., Wilson, M.A., 2007. Spatial selectivity and theta phase precession in CA1 interneurons. Hippocampus **17**, 161–174. https://doi.org/10.1002/hipo.20253

Ego-Stengel, V., Wilson, M.A., 2010. Disruption of ripple-associated hippocampal activity during rest impairs spatial learning in the rat. Hippocampus **20**, 1–10. https://doi.org/10.1002/hipo.20707

Etienne, A.S., Jeffery, K.J., 2004. Path integration in mammals. Hippocampus **14**, 180–192. https://doi.org/10.1002/hipo.10173

Euston, D.R., Gruber, A.J., McNaughton, B.L., 2012. The role of medial prefrontal cortex in memory and decision making. Neuron **76**, 1057–1070. https://doi.org/10.1016/j.neuron.2012.12.002

Euston, D.R., Tatsuno, M., McNaughton, B.L., 2007. Fast-forward playback of recent memory sequences in prefrontal cortex during sleep. Science **318**, 1147–1150. https://doi.org/10.1126/science.1148979

Fernandez, L.M.J., Lüthi, A., 2019. Sleep spindles: mechanisms and functions. Physiol. Rev. **100**, 805–868. https://doi.org/10.1152/physrev.00042.2018

Frankland, P.W., Bontempi, B., 2005. The organization of recent and remote memories. Nat. Rev. Neurosci. **6**, 119–130. https://doi.org/10.1038/nrn1607

Fuhs, M.C., Touretzky, D.S., 2006. A spin glass model of path integration in rat medial entorhinal cortex. J. Neurosci. **26**, 4266–4276. https://doi.org/10.1523/JNEUROSCI.4353-05.2006

Fujisawa, S., Buzsáki, G., 2011. A 4 Hz oscillation adaptively synchronizes prefrontal, VTA, and hippocampal activities. Neuron **72**, 153–165. https://doi.org/10.1016/j.neuron.2011.08.018

Gallistel, C.R., 1989. Animal cognition: the representation of space, time and number. Annu. Rev. Psychol. **40**, 155–189. https://doi.org/10.1146/annurev.ps.40.020189.001103

Gent, T.C., Bandarabadi, M., Herrera, C.G., Adamantidis, A.R., 2018. Thalamic dual control of sleep and wakefulness. Nat. Neurosci. **21**, 974. https://doi.org/10.1038/s41593-018-0164-7

Girardeau, G., Benchenane, K., Wiener, S.I., Buzsáki, G., Zugaro, M.B., 2009. Selective suppression of hippocampal ripples impairs spatial memory. Nat. Neurosci. **12**, 1222–1223. https://doi.org/10.1038/nn.2384

Gofman, X., Tocker, G., Weiss, S., Boccara, C.N., Lu, L., Moser, M.-B., Moser, E.I., Morris, G., Derdikman, D., 2019. Dissociation between postrhinal cortex and downstream parahippocampal regions in the representation of egocentric boundaries. Curr. Biol. **29**, 2751–2757.e4. https://doi.org/10.1016/j.cub.2019.07.007

Gonzalo-Ruiz, A., Lieberman, A.R., 1995. Topographic organization of projections from the thalamic reticular nucleus to the anterior thalamic nuclei in the rat. Brain Res. Bull. **37**, 17–35. https://doi.org/10.1016/0361-9230(94)00252-5

Goodridge, J.P., Taube, J.S., 1997. Interaction between the postsubiculum and anterior thalamus in the generation of head direction cell activity. J. Neurosci. **17**, 9315–9330.

Hafting, T., Fyhn, M., Molden, S., Moser, M.-B., Moser, E.I., 2005. Microstructure of a spatial map in the entorhinal cortex. Nature **436**, 801–806. https://doi.org/10.1038/nature03721

Halassa, M.M., Acsády, L., 2016. Thalamic inhibition: diverse sources, diverse scales. Trends Neurosci. **39**, 680–693. https://doi.org/10.1016/j.tins.2016.08.001

Harding, A., Halliday, G., Caine, D., Kril, J., 2000. Degeneration of anterior thalamic nuclei differentiates alcoholics with amnesia. Brain **123**, 141–154. https://doi.org/10.1093/brain/123.1.141

Harland, B., Grieves, R.M., Bett, D., Stentiford, R., Wood, E.R., Dudchenko, P.A., 2017. Lesions of the head direction cell system increase hippocampal place field repetition. Curr. Biol. **27**, 2706–2712. https://doi.org/10.1016/j.cub.2017.07.071

Harris, K.D., Csicsvari, J., Hirase, H., Dragoi, G., Buzsaki, G., 2003. Organization of cell assemblies in the hippocampus. Nature **424**, 552–556. https://doi.org/10.1038/nature01834

Hasselmo, M.E., 2006. The role of acetylcholine in learning and memory. Curr. Opin. Neurobiol. **16**, 710–715. https://doi.org/10.1016/j.conb.2006.09.002

Heckers, S., Geula, C., Mesulam, M.-M., 1992. Cholinergic innervation of the human thalamus: dual origin and differential nuclear distribution. J. Comp. Neurol. **325**, 68–82. https://doi.org/10.1002/cne.903250107

Herkenham, M., 1978. The connections of the nucleus reuniens thalami: evidence for a direct thalamo-hippocampal pathway in the rat. J. Comp. Neurol. **177**, 589–609. https://doi.org/10.1002/cne.901770405

Hulse, B.K., Jayaraman, V., 2020. Mechanisms underlying the neural computation of head direction. Annu. Rev. Neurosci. **43**, 31–54. https://doi.org/10.1146/annurev-neuro-072116-031516

Ito, H.T., Zhang, S.-J., Witter, M.P., Moser, E.I., Moser, M.-B., 2015. A prefrontal–thalamo–hippocampal circuit for goal-directed spatial navigation. Nature **522**, 50–55. https://doi.org/10.1038/nature14396

Jacob, P.-Y., Casali, G., Spieser, L., Page, H., Overington, D., Jeffery, K., 2017. An independent, landmark-dominated head-direction signal in dysgranular retrosplenial cortex. Nat. Neurosci. **20**, 173–175. https://doi.org/10.1038/nn.4465

Jankowski, M.M., Islam, M.N., Wright, N.F., Vann, S.D., Erichsen, J.T., Aggleton, J.P., O'Mara, S.M., 2014. Nucleus reuniens of the thalamus contains head direction cells. eLife **3**, e03075. https://doi.org/10.7554/eLife.03075

Jankowski, M.M., Passecker, J., Islam, M.N., Vann, S., Erichsen, J.T., Aggleton, J.P., O'Mara, S.M., 2015. Evidence for spatially-responsive neurons in the rostral thalamus. Front. Behav. Neurosci. **9**. https://doi.org/10.3389/fnbeh.2015.00256

Jay, T.M., Glowinski, J., Thierry, A.-M., 1989. Selectivity of the hippocampal projection to the prelimbic area of the prefrontal cortex in the rat. Brain Res. **505**, 337–340. https://doi.org/10.1016/0006-8993(89)91464-9

Johnson, A., Redish, A.D., 2007. Neural ensembles in CA3 transiently encode paths forward of the animal at a decision point. J. Neurosci. **27**, 12176.

Jones, B.E., 1993. The organization of central cholinergic systems and their functional importance in sleep-waking states. Prog. Brain Res. **98**, 61–71. https://doi.org/10.1016/s0079-6123(08)62381-x

Jones, E.G., 2007. The Thalamus. Cambridge University Press.

Jones, M.W., Wilson, M.A., 2005. Theta rhythms coordinate hippocampal-prefrontal interactions in a spatial memory task. PLOS Biol. **3**, e402. https://doi.org/10.1371/journal.pbio.0030402

Kaitz, S.S., Robertson, R.T., 1981. Thalamic connections with limbic cortex. II. Corticothalamic projections. J. Comp. Neurol. **195**, 527–545. https://doi.org/10.1002/cne.901950309

Kay, K., Chung, J.E., Sosa, M., Schor, J.S., Karlsson, M.P., Larkin, M.C., Liu, D.F., Frank, L.M., 2020. Constant sub-second cycling between representations of possible futures in the hippocampus. Cell **180**, 552–567.e25. https://doi.org/10.1016/j.cell.2020.01.014

Knierim, J.J., Kudrimoti, H.S., McNaughton, B.L., 1995. Place cells, head direction cells, and the learning of landmark stability. J. Neurosci. **15**, 1648–1659.

Kocsis, B., Prisco, G.V.D., Vertes, R.P., 2001. Theta synchronization in the limbic system: the role of Gudden's tegmental nuclei. Eur. J. Neurosci. **13**, 381–388. https://doi.org/10.1111/j.1460-9568.2001.tb01708.x

Koenig, J., Linder, A.N., Leutgeb, J.K., Leutgeb, S., 2011. The spatial periodicity of grid cells is not sustained during reduced theta oscillations. Science **332**, 592–595. https://doi.org/10.1126/science.1201685

Kornienko, O., Latuske, P., Bassler, M., Kohler, L., Allen, K., 2018. Non-rhythmic head-direction cells in the parahippocampal region are not constrained by attractor network dynamics. eLife **7**, e35949. https://doi.org/10.7554/eLife.35949

Kuypers, H.G., Bentivoglio, M., Catsman-Berrevoets, C.E., Bharos, A.T., 1980. Double retrograde neuronal labeling through divergent axon collaterals, using two fluorescent tracers with the same excitation wavelength which label different features of the cell. Exp. Brain Res. **40**, 383–392. https://doi.org/10.1007/BF00236147

LaChance, P.A., Todd, T.P., Taube, J.S., 2019. A sense of space in postrhinal cortex. Science **365**, eaax4192. https://doi.org/10.1126/science.aax4192

Lee, A.K., Wilson, M.A., 2002. Memory of sequential experience in the hippocampus during slow wave sleep. Neuron **36**, 1183–1194.

Leutgeb, S., Leutgeb, J.K., Treves, A., Moser, M.-B., Moser, E.I., 2004. Distinct ensemble codes in hippocampal areas CA3 and CA1. Science **305**, 1295–1298. https://doi.org/10.1126/science.1100265

Lever, C., Burton, S., Jeewajee, A., O'Keefe, J., Burgess, N., 2009. Boundary vector cells in the subiculum of the hippocampal formation. J. Neurosci. **29**, 9771–9777. https://doi.org/10.1523/JNEUROSCI.1319-09.2009

Levey, A.I., Hallanger, A.E., Wainer, B.H., 1987. Choline acetyltransferase immunoreactivity in the rat thalamus. J. Comp. Neurol. **257**, 317–332. https://doi.org/10.1002/cne.902570302

Lozsádi, D.A., 1995. Organization of connections between the thalamic reticular and the anterior thalamic nuclei in the rat. J. Comp. Neurol. **358**, 233–246. https://doi.org/10.1002/cne.903580206

Maisson, D.J.-N., Gemzik, Z.M., Griffin, A.L., 2018. Optogenetic suppression of the nucleus reuniens selectively impairs encoding during spatial working memory. Neurobiol. Learn. Mem. **155**, 78–85. https://doi.org/10.1016/j.nlm.2018.06.010

Markus, E.J., Qin, Y.L., Leonard, B., Skaggs, W.E., McNaughton, B.L., Barnes, C.A., 1995. Interactions between location and task affect the spatial and directional firing of hippocampal neurons. J. Neurosci. **15**, 7079–7094. https://doi.org/10.1523/JNEUROSCI.15-11-07079.1995

Mathiasen, M.L., Amin, E., Nelson, A.J.D., Dillingham, C.M., O'Mara, S.M., Aggleton, J.P., 2019. Separate cortical and hippocampal cell populations target the rat nucleus reuniens and mammillary bodies. Eur. J. Neurosci. **49**, 1649–1672. https://doi.org/10.1111/ejn.14341

Maurer, A.P., Cowen, S.L., Burke, S.N., Barnes, C.A., McNaughton, B.L., 2006. Phase precession in hippocampal interneurons showing strong functional coupling to individual pyramidal cells. J. Neurosci. **26**, 13485–13492. https://doi.org/10.1523/JNEUROSCI.2882-06.2006

McKenna, J.T., Vertes, R.P., 2004. Afferent projections to nucleus reuniens of the thalamus. J. Comp. Neurol. **480**, 115–142. https://doi.org/10.1002/cne.20342

McNaughton, B.L., Barnes, C.A., Gerrard, J.L., Gothard, K., Jung, M.W., Knierim, J.J., Kudrimoti, H., Qin, Y., Skaggs, W.E., Suster, M., Weaver, K.L., 1996. Deciphering the hippocampal polyglot: the hippocampus as a path integration system. J. Exp. Biol. **199**, 173.

McNaughton, B.L., Battaglia, F.P., Jensen, O., Moser, E.I., Moser, M.-B., 2006. Path integration and the neural basis of the "cognitive map." Nat. Rev. Neurosci. **7**, 663–678. https://doi.org/10.1038/nrn1932

Mei, H., Logothetis, N.K., Eschenko, O., 2018. The activity of thalamic nucleus reuniens is critical for memory retrieval, but not essential for the early phase of "off-line" consolidation. Learn. Mem. **25**, 129–137. https://doi.org/10.1101/lm.047134.117

Meibach, R.C., Siegel, A., 1977. Efferent connections of the hippocampal formation in the rat. Brain Res. **124**, 197–224. https://doi.org/10.1016/0006-8993(77)90880-0

Mitchell, A.S., Dalrymple-Alford, J.C., Christie, M.A., 2002. Spatial working memory and the brainstem cholinergic innervation to the anterior thalamus. J. Neurosci. **22**, 1922–1928. https://doi.org/10.1523/JNEUROSCI.22-05-01922.2002

Mittelstaedt, M.L., Mittelstaedt, H., 1980. Homing by path integration in a mammal. Naturwissenschaften **67**, 566–567. https://doi.org/10.1007/bf00450672

Mizumori, S.J., Williams, J.D., 1993. Directionally selective mnemonic properties of neurons in the lateral dorsal nucleus of the thalamus of rats. J. Neurosci. **13**, 4015–4028.

Moruzzi, G., Magoun, H.W., 1949. Brain stem reticular formation and activation of the EEG. Electroencephalogr. Clin. Neurophysiol. **1**, 455–473. https://doi.org/10.1016/0013-4694(49)90219-9

Muir, G.M., Brown, J.E., Carey, J.P., Hirvonen, T.P., Santina, C.C.D., Minor, L.B., Taube, J.S., 2009. Disruption of the head direction cell signal after occlusion of the semicircular canals in the freely moving chinchilla. J. Neurosci. **29**, 14521–14533. https://doi.org/10.1523/JNEUROSCI.3450-09.2009

Muller, R.U., Bostock, E., Taube, J.S., Kubie, J.L., 1994. On the directional firing properties of hippocampal place cells. J. Neurosci. **14**, 7235–7251.

Muller, R.U., Kubie, J.L., 1987. The effects of changes in the environment on the spatial firing of hippocampal complex-spike cells. J. Neurosci. **7**, 1951–1968.

Musil, S.Y., Olson, C.R., 1988. Organization of cortical and subcortical projections to anterior cingulate cortex in the cat. J. Comp. Neurol. **272**, 203–218. https://doi.org/10.1002/cne.902720205

Nadel, L., Moscovitch, M., 1997. Memory consolidation, retrograde amnesia and the hippocampal complex. Curr. Opin. Neurobiol. **7**, 217–227. https://doi.org/10.1016/s0959-4388(97)80010-4

Nelson, A.J.D., Kinnavane, L., Amin, E., O'Mara, S.M., Aggleton, J.P., 2020. Deconstructing the direct reciprocal hippocampal-anterior thalamic pathways for spatial learning. J. Neurosci. **40**, 6978–6990. https://doi.org/10.1523/JNEUROSCI.0874-20.2020

Niimi, M., 1978. Cortical projections of the anterior thalamic nuclei in the cat. Exp. Brain Res. **31**, 403–416. https://doi.org/10.1007/BF00237298

Oda, S., Kuroda, M., Chen, S.Y., Shinkai, M., Kishi, K., 1996. Ultrastructure and distribution of axon terminals from the reticular thalamic nucleus to the anteroventral thalamic nucleus of the rat. J. Hirnforsch. **37**, 459–466.

O'Keefe, J., 1976. Place units in the hippocampus of the freely moving rat. Exp. Neurol. **51**, 78–109. https://doi.org/10.1016/0014-4886(76)90055-8

O'Keefe, J., Burgess, N., 1996. Geometric determinants of the place fields of hippocampal neurons. Nature **381**, 425–428. https://doi.org/10.1038/381425a0

O'Keefe, J., Dostrovsky, J., 1971. The hippocampus as a spatial map. Preliminary evidence from unit activity in the freely-moving rat. Brain Res. **34**, 171–175.

O'Keefe, J., Nadel, L., 1978. The Hippocampus as a Cognitive Map. Clarendon Press Oxford.

O'Keefe, J., Recce, M.L., 1993. Phase relationship between hippocampal place units and the EEG theta rhythm. Hippocampus **3**, 317–330. https://doi.org/10.1002/hipo.450030307

Papez, J.W., 1937. A proposed mechanism of emotion. Arch. Neurol. Psychiatry **38**, 725–743. https://doi.org/10.1001/archneurpsyc.1937.02260220069003

Pare, D., Steriade, M., Deschênes, M., Bouhassira, D., 1990. Prolonged enhancement of anterior thalamic synaptic responsiveness by stimulation of a brain-stem cholinergic group. J. Neurosci. **10**, 20–33. https://doi.org/10.1523/JNEUROSCI.10-01-00020.1990

Perry, B.A.L., Mercer, S.A., Barnett, S.C., Lee, J., Dalrymple-Alford, J.C., 2018. Anterior thalamic nuclei lesions have a greater impact than mammillothalamic tract lesions on the extended hippocampal system. Hippocampus **28**, 121–135. https://doi.org/10.1002/hipo.22815

Perry, B.A.L., Mitchell, A.S., 2019. Considering the evidence for anterior and laterodorsal thalamic nuclei as higher order relays to cortex. Front. Mol. Neurosci. **12**. https://doi.org/10.3389/fnmol.2019.00167

Petrof, I., Sherman, S.M., 2009. Synaptic properties of the mammillary and cortical afferents to the anterodorsal thalamic nucleus in the mouse. J. Neurosci. **29**, 7815–7819. https://doi.org/10.1523/JNEUROSCI.1564-09.2009

Peyrache, A., Battaglia, F.P., Destexhe, A., 2011. Inhibition recruitment in prefrontal cortex during sleep spindles and gating of hippocampal inputs. Proc. Natl. Acad. Sci. **108**, 17207–17212. https://doi.org/10.1073/pnas.1103612108

Peyrache, A., Duszkiewicz, A.J., Viejo, G., Angeles-Duran, S., 2019. Thalamocortical processing of the head-direction sense. Prog. Neurobiol. **183**, 101693. https://doi.org/10.1016/j.pneurobio.2019.101693

Peyrache, A., Khamassi, M., Benchenane, K., Wiener, S.I., Battaglia, F.P., 2009. Replay of rule-learning related neural patterns in the prefrontal cortex during sleep. Nat. Neurosci. **12**, 919–926. https://doi.org/10.1038/nn.2337

Peyrache, A., Lacroix, M.M., Petersen, P.C., Buzsáki, G., 2015. Internally organized mechanisms of the head direction sense. Nat. Neurosci. **18**, 569–575. https://doi.org/10.1038/nn.3968

Peyrache, A., Schieferstein, N., Buzsáki, G., 2017. Transformation of the head-direction signal into a spatial code. Nat. Commun. **8**, 1752. https://doi.org/10.1038/s41467-017-01908-3

Peyrache, A., Seibt, J., 2020. A mechanism for learning with sleep spindles. Philos.

Trans. R. Soc. B Biol. Sci. 375, 20190230. https://doi.org/10.1098/rstb.2019.0230

Phillips, J.W., Schulmann, A., Hara, E., Winnubst, J., Liu, C., Valakh, V., Wang, L., Shields, B.C., Korff, W., Chandrashekar, J., Lemire, A.L., Mensh, B., Dudman, J.T., Nelson, S.B., Hantman, A.W., 2019. A repeated molecular architecture across thalamic pathways. Nat. Neurosci. 22, 1925–1935. https://doi.org/10.1038/s41593-019-0483-3

Pisokas, I., Heinze, S., Webb, B., 2020. The head direction circuit of two insect species. eLife 9, e53985. https://doi.org/10.7554/eLife.53985

Powell, T.P.S., Cowan, W.M., 1954. The origin of the mamillo-thalamic tract in the rat. J. Anat. 88, 489–497.

Preuss, T.M., 1995. Do rats have prefrontal cortex? The Rose-Woolsey-Akert Program reconsidered. J. Cogn. Neurosci. 7, 1–24. https://doi.org/10.1162/jocn.1995.7.1.1

Ranck, J.B., 1985. Head direction cells in the deep cell layer of dorsal presubiculum in freely moving rats. In: Buzsáki, G., Vanderwolf, C. H. (Eds.), Electrical Activity of Archicortex. Akademiai Kiado, pp. 217–220.

Raudies, F., Brandon, M.P., Chapman, G.W., Hasselmo, M.E., 2015. Head direction is coded more strongly than movement direction in a population of entorhinal neurons. Brain Res. 1621, 355–367. https://doi.org/10.1016/j.brainres.2014.10.053

Redish, A.D., 2016. Vicarious trial and error. Nat. Rev. Neurosci. 17, 147–159. https://doi.org/10.1038/nrn.2015.30

Redish, A.D., Elga, A.N., Touretzky, D.S., 1996. A coupled attractor model of the rodent head direction system. Netw. Comput. Neural Syst. 7, 671–685. https://doi.org/10.1088/0954-898X_7_4_004

Robertson, R.T., Kaitz, S.S., 1981. Thalamic connections with limbic cortex. I. Thalamocortical projections. J. Comp. Neurol. 195, 501–525. https://doi.org/10.1002/cne.901950308

Rosene, D.L., Hoesen, G.V., 1977. Hippocampal efferents reach widespread areas of cerebral cortex and amygdala in the rhesus monkey. Science 198, 315–317. https://doi.org/10.1126/science.410102

Rosenstock, J., Field, T.D., Greene, E., 1977. The role of mammillary bodies in spatial memory. Exp. Neurol. 55, 340–352. https://doi.org/10.1016/0014-4886(77)90005-X

Roy, A., Svensson, F.P., Mazeh, A., Kocsis, B., 2017. Prefrontal-hippocampal coupling by theta rhythm and by 2–5 Hz oscillation in the delta band: the role of the nucleus reuniens of the thalamus. Brain Struct. Funct. 222, 2819–2830. https://doi.org/10.1007/s00429-017-1374-6

Samsonovich, A., McNaughton, B.L., 1997. Path integration and cognitive mapping in a continuous attractor neural network model. J. Neurosci. 17, 5900.

Sargolini, F., Fyhn, M., Hafting, T., McNaughton, B.L., Witter, M.P., Moser, M.-B., Moser, E.I., 2006. Conjunctive representation of position, direction, and velocity in entorhinal cortex. Science 312, 758–762. https://doi.org/10.1126/science.1125572

Satoh, K., Fibiger, H.C., 1986. Cholinergic neurons of the laterodorsal tegmental nucleus: Efferent and afferent connections. J. Comp. Neurol. 253, 277–302. https://doi.org/10.1002/cne.902530302

Savelli, F., Yoganarasimha, D., Knierim, J.J., 2008. Influence of boundary removal on the spatial representations of the medial entorhinal cortex. Hippocampus 18, 1270–1282. https://doi.org/10.1002/hipo.20511

Scoville, W.B., Milner, B., 1957. Loss of recent memory after bilateral hippocampal lesions. J. Neurol. Neurosurg. Psychiatry 20, 11–21.

Seidenbecher, T., 2003. Amygdalar and hippocampal theta rhythm synchronization during fear memory retrieval. Science 301, 846–850. https://doi.org/10.1126/science.1085818

Seki, M., Zyo, K., 1984. Anterior thalamic afferents from the mammillary body and the limbic cortex in the rat. J. Comp. Neurol. 229, 242–256. https://doi.org/10.1002/cne.902290209

Sharp, P.E., 1996. Multiple spatial/behavioral correlates for cells in the rat postsubiculum: multiple regression analysis and comparison to other hippocampal areas. Cereb. Cortex 6, 238–259.

Sharp, P.E., Blair, H.T., Cho, J., 2001. The anatomical and computational basis of the rat head-direction cell signal. Trends Neurosci. 24, 289–294.

Sherman, S.M., Guillery, R.W., 2002. The role of the thalamus in the flow of information to the cortex. Philos. Trans. R. Soc. B Biol. Sci. 357, 1695–1708. https://doi.org/10.1098/rstb.2002.1161

Shibata, H., 1992. Topographic organization of subcortical projections to the anterior thalamic nuclei in the rat. J. Comp. Neurol. 323, 117–127. https://doi.org/10.1002/cne.903230110

Shibata, H., 1993a. Direct projections from the anterior thalamic nuclei to the retrohippocampal region in the rat. J. Comp. Neurol. 337, 431–445. https://doi.org/10.1002/cne.903370307

Shibata, H., 1993b. Efferent projections from the anterior thalamic nuclei to the cingulate cortex in the rat. J. Comp. Neurol. 330, 533–542. https://doi.org/10.1002/cne.903300409

Shibata, H., Kato, A., 1993. Topographic relationship between anteromedial thalamic nucleus neurons and their cortical terminal fields in the rat. Neurosci. Res. 17, 63–69. https://doi.org/10.1016/0168-0102(93)90030-t

Siapas, A.G., Lubenov, E.V., Wilson, M.A., 2005. Prefrontal phase locking to hippocampal theta oscillations. Neuron 46, 141–151. https://doi.org/10.1016/j.neuron.2005.02.028

Siapas, A.G., Wilson, M.A., 1998. Coordinated interactions between hippocampal ripples and cortical spindles during slow-wave sleep. Neuron 21, 1123–1128.

Sikes, R.W., Vogt, B.A., 1987. Afferent connections of anterior thalamus in rats: sources and association with muscarinic acetylcholine receptors. J. Comp. Neurol. 256, 538–551. https://doi.org/10.1002/cne.902560406

Sirota, A., Csicsvari, J., Buhl, D., Buzsáki, G., 2003. Communication between neocortex and hippocampus during sleep in rodents. Proc. Natl. Acad. Sci. U.S.A. 100, 2065.

Sirota, A., Montgomery, S., Fujisawa, S., Isomura, Y., Zugaro, M., Buzsaki, G., 2008. Entrainment of neocortical neurons and gamma oscillations by the hippocampal theta rhythm. Neuron 60, 683–697. https://doi.org/10.1016/j.neuron.2008.09.014

Skaggs, W.E., McNaughton, B.L., 1996. Replay of neuronal firing sequences in rat hippocampus during sleep following spatial experience. Science 271, 1870–1873.

Solstad, T., Boccara, C.N., Kropff, E., Moser, M.-B., Moser, E.I., 2008. Representation of geometric borders in the entorhinal cortex. Science 322, 1865–1868. https://doi.org/10.1126/science.1166466

Squire, L.R., 1992. Memory and the hippocampus: a synthesis from findings with rats, monkeys, and humans. Psychol. Rev. 99, 195–231. https://doi.org/10.1037/0033-295x.99.2.195

Sripanidkulchai, K., Wyss, J.M., 1986. Thalamic projections to retrosplenial cortex in the rat. J. Comp. Neurol. 254, 143–165. https://doi.org/10.1002/cne.902540202

Stackman, R.W., Taube, J.S., 1998. Firing properties of rat lateral mammillary single units: head direction, head pitch, and angular head velocity. J. Neurosci. 18, 9020–9037.

Stark, E., Eichler, R., Roux, L., Fujisawa, S., Rotstein, H.G., Buzsáki, G., 2013. Inhibition-induced theta resonance in cortical circuits. Neuron 80, 1263–1276. https://doi.org/10.1016/j.neuron.2013.09.033

Steriade, M., McCormick, D.A., Sejnowski, T.J., 1993. Thalamocortical oscillations in the sleeping and aroused brain. Science 262, 679–685.

Sutherland, R.J., Rodriguez, A.J., 1989. The role of the fornix/fimbria and some related subcortical structures in place learning and memory. Behav. Brain Res. 32, 265–277. https://doi.org/10.1016/S0166-4328(89)80059-2

Swanson, L.W., Cowan, W.M., 1977. An autoradiographic study of the organization of the efferent connections of the hippocampal formation in the rat. J. Comp. Neurol. 172, 49–84. https://doi.org/10.1002/cne.901720104

Swanson, L.W., Cowan, W.M., 1979. The connections of the septal region in the rat. J. Comp. Neurol. 186, 621–655. https://doi.org/10.1002/cne.901860408

Sziklas, V., Petrides, M., 1998. Memory and the region of the mammillary bodies. Prog. Neurobiol. 54, 55–70. https://doi.org/10.1016/S0301-0082(97)00064-6

Taube, J.S., 1995. Head direction cells recorded in the anterior thalamic nuclei of freely moving rats. J. Neurosci. 15, 70–86.

Taube, J.S., 2007. The head direction signal: origins and sensory-motor integration. Annu. Rev. Neurosci. 30, 181–207. https://doi.org/10.1146/annurev.neuro.29.051605.112854

Taube, J.S., Bassett, J.P., 2003. Persistent neural activity in head direction cells. Cereb. Cortex 13, 1162–1172. https://doi.org/10.1093/cercor/bhg102

Taube, J.S., Muller, R.U., Ranck, J.B., 1990a. Head-direction cells recorded from the postsubiculum in freely moving rats. I. Description and quantitative analysis. J. Neurosci. 10, 420–435.

Taube, J.S., Muller, R.U., Ranck, J.B., Jr, 1990b. Head-direction cells recorded from the postsubiculum in freely moving rats. II. Effects of environmental manipulations. J. Neurosci. 10, 436–447.

Touretzky, D.S., Redish, A.D., 1996. Theory of rodent navigation based on interacting representations of space. Hippocampus 6, 247–270. https://doi.org/10.1002/(SICI)1098-1063(1996)6:3<247::aid-hipo4>3.0.CO;2-K

Tsanov, M., Chah, E., Vann, S.D., Reilly, R.B., Erichsen, J.T., Aggleton, J.P., O'Mara, S.M., 2011. Theta-modulated head direction cells in the rat anterior thalamus. J. Neurosci. 31, 9489–9502. https://doi.org/10.1523/JNEUROSCI.0353-11.2011

Tsanov, M., Wright, N., Vann, S.D., Erichsen, J.T., Aggleton, J.P., O'Mara, S.M., 2011. Hippocampal inputs mediate theta-related plasticity in anterior thalamus. Neuroscience 187, 52–62. https://doi.org/16/j.neuroscience.2011.03.055

Uylings, H., Groenewegen, H.J., Kolb, B., 2003. Do rats have a prefrontal cortex? Behav. Brain Res. 146, 3–17.

Valerio, S., Taube, J.S., 2012. Path integration: how the head direction signal maintains and corrects spatial orientation. Nat. Neurosci. 15, 1445–1453. https://doi.org/10.1038/nn.3215

van der Meer, M.A.A., Knierim, J.J., Yoganarasimha, D., Wood, E.R., van Rossum, M.C.W., 2007. Anticipation in the rodent head direction system can be explained by an interaction of head movements and vestibular firing properties. J. Neurophysiol. 98, 1883–1897. https://doi.org/10.1152/jn.00233.2007

van Groen, T., Kadish, I., Wyss, J.M., 1999. Efferent connections of the anteromedial nucleus of the thalamus of the rat. Brain Res. Rev. 30, 1–26. https://doi.org/10.1016/s0165-0173(99)00006-5

van Groen, T., Kadish, I., Wyss, J.M., 2002. Role of the anterodorsal and anteroventral nuclei of the thalamus in spatial memory in the rat. Behav. Brain Res. 132, 19–28. https://doi.org/10.1016/S0166-4328(01)00390-4

van Groen, T., Wyss, J.M., 1995. Projections from the anterodorsal and anteroventral nucleus of the thalamus to the limbic cortex in the rat. J. Comp. Neurol. 358, 584–604. https://doi.org/10.1002/cne.903580411

Vanderwolf, C.H., 1969. Hippocampal electrical activity and voluntary movement in the rat. Electroencephalogr. Clin. Neurophysiol. 26, 407–418. https://doi.org/10.1016/0013-4694(69)90092-3

Vann, S.D., Aggleton, J.P., 2004. The mammillary bodies: two memory systems in one? Nat. Rev. Neurosci. 5, 35–44. https://doi.org/10.1038/nrn1299

Vann, S.D., Brown, M.W., Aggleton, J.P., 2000. Fos expression in the rostral thalamic nuclei and associated cortical regions in response to different spatial memory tests. Neuroscience 101, 983–991. https://doi.org/10.1016/s0306-4522(00)00288-8

Vantomme, G., Rovó, Z., Cardis, R., Béard, E., Katsioudi, G., Guadagno, A., Perrenoud, V., Fernandez, L.M.J., Lüthi, A., 2020. A thalamic reticular circuit for head direction cell tuning and spatial navigation. Cell Rep. 31, 107747. https://doi.org/10.1016/j.celrep.2020.107747

Varela, C., Kumar, S., Yang, J.Y., Wilson, M.A., 2014. Anatomical substrates for direct interactions between hippocampus, medial prefrontal cortex, and the thalamic nucleus reuniens. Brain Struct. Funct. 219, 911–929. https://doi.org/10.1007/s00429-013-0543-5

Varela, C., Wilson, M.A., 2020. mPFC spindle cycles organize sparse thalamic activation and recently active CA1 cells during non-REM sleep. eLife 9, e48881. https://doi.org/10.7554/eLife.48881

Veazey, R.B., Amaral, D.G., Cowan, W.M., 1982. The morphology and connections of the posterior hypothalamus in the cynomolgus monkey (*Macaca fascicularis*). II. Efferent connections. J. Comp. Neurol. 207, 135–156. https://doi.org/10.1002/cne.902070204

Vertes, R.P., Albo, Z., Viana Di Prisco, G., 2001. Theta-rhythmically firing neurons in the anterior thalamus: implications for mnemonic functions of Papez's circuit. Neuroscience 104, 619–625. https://doi.org/10.1016/S0306-4522(01)00131-2

Vertes, R.P., Hoover, W.B., Szigeti-Buck, K., Leranth, C., 2007. Nucleus reuniens of the midline thalamus: Link between the medial prefrontal cortex and the hippocampus. Brain Res. Bull. 71, 601–609.

Viejo, G., Cortier, T., Peyrache, A., 2018. Brain-state invariant thalamo-cortical coordination revealed by non-linear encoders. PLOS Comput. Biol. 14, e1006041. https://doi.org/10.1371/journal.pcbi.1006041

Viejo, G., Peyrache, A., 2020. Precise coupling of the thalamic head-direction system to hippocampal ripples. Nat. Commun. 11, 2524. https://doi.org/10.1038/s41467-020-15842-4

Walz, N., Mühlberger, A., Pauli, P., 2016. A human open field test reveals thigmotaxis related to agoraphobic fear. Biol. Psychiatry 80, 390–397. https://doi.org/10.1016/j.biopsych.2015.12.016

Wang, B., Gonzalo-Ruiz, A., Sanz, J.M., Campbell, G., Lieberman, A.R., 1999. Immunoelectron microscopic study of gamma-aminobutyric acid inputs to identified thalamocortical projection neurons in the anterior thalamus of the rat. Exp. Brain Res. 126, 369–382. https://doi.org/10.1007/s002210050744

Watanabe, K., Kawana, E., 1980. A horseradish peroxidase study on the mammillothalamic tract in the rat. Cells Tissues Organs 108, 394–401. https://doi.org/10.1159/000145322

Weel, M.J.D.-V. der, Silva, F.H.L. da, Witter, M.P., 1997. Nucleus reuniens thalami modulates activity in hippocampal field CA1 through excitatory and inhibitory mechanisms. J. Neurosci. **17**, 5640–5650. https://doi.org/10.1523/JNEUROSCI.17-14-05640.1997

Welday, A.C., Shlifer, I.G., Bloom, M.L., Zhang, K., Blair, H.T., 2011. Cosine directional tuning of theta cell burst frequencies: evidence for spatial coding by oscillatory interference. J. Neurosci. **31**, 16157–16176. https://doi.org/10.1523/JNEUROSCI.0712-11.2011

Wierzynski, C.M., Lubenov, E.V., Gu, M., Siapas, A.G., 2009. State-dependent Spike-timing relationships between hippocampal and prefrontal circuits during sleep. Neuron **61**, 587–596. https://doi.org/10.1016/j.neuron.2009.01.011

Wilson, M.A., McNaughton, B.L., 1994. Reactivation of hippocampal ensemble memories during sleep. Science **265**, 676.

Wiltschko, A.B., Johnson, M.J., Iurilli, G., Peterson, R.E., Katon, J.M., Pashkovski, S.L., Abraira, V.E., Adams, R.P., Datta, S.R., 2015. Mapping sub-second structure in mouse behavior. Neuron **88**, 1121–1135. https://doi.org/10.1016/j.neuron.2015.11.031

Wimmer, R.D., Schmitt, L.I., Davidson, T.J., Nakajima, M., Deisseroth, K., Halassa, M.M., 2015. Thalamic control of sensory selection in divided attention. Nature **526**, 705–709. https://doi.org/10.1038/nature15398

Winter, S.S., Clark, B.J., Taube, J.S., 2015. Disruption of the head direction cell network impairs the parahippocampal grid cell signal. Science **347**, 870–874. https://doi.org/10.1126/science.1259591

Wood, E.R., Dudchenko, P.A., Robitsek, R.J., Eichenbaum, H., 2000. Hippocampal neurons encode information about different types of memory episodes occurring in the same location. Neuron **27**, 623–633. https://doi.org/10.1016/S0896-6273(00)00071-4

Wright, N.F., Erichsen, J.T., Vann, S.D., O'Mara, S.M., Aggleton, J.P., 2010. Parallel but separate inputs from limbic cortices to the mammillary bodies and anterior thalamic nuclei in the rat. J. Comp. Neurol. **518**, 2334–2354. https://doi.org/10.1002/cne.22336

Wright, N.F., Vann, S.D., Erichsen, J.T., O'Mara, S.M., Aggleton, J.P., 2013. Segregation of parallel inputs to the anteromedial and anteroventral thalamic nuclei of the rat. J. Comp. Neurol. **521**, 2966–2986. https://doi.org/10.1002/cne.23325

Xu, W., Südhof, T.C., 2013. A neural circuit for memory specificity and generalization. Science **339**, 1290–1295. https://doi.org/10.1126/science.1229534

Yoder, R.M., Taube, J.S., 2011. Projections to the anterodorsal thalamus and lateral mammillary nuclei arise from different cell populations within the postsubiculum: Implications for the control of head direction cells. Hippocampus **21**, 1062–1073. https://doi.org/10.1002/hipo.20820

Yoganarasimha, D., Yu, X., Knierim, J.J., 2006. Head direction cell representations maintain internal coherence during conflicting proximal and distal cue rotations: comparison with hippocampal place cells. J. Neurosci. **26**, 622–631. https://doi.org/10.1523/JNEUROSCI.3885-05.2006

Zugaro, M.B., Berthoz, A., Wiener, S.I., 2001. Background, but not foreground, spatial cues are taken as references for head direction responses by rat anterodorsal thalamus neurons. J. Neurosci. **21**, RC154.

Section 8: Arousal

Chapter 19

The Thalamus and Sleep

Mattia Aime and Antoine R. Adamantidis

1. Introduction

Sleep is an evolutionary conserved behaviour, and sleep or sleep-like states have been described in all animal species studied so far. In mammals, behavioural features of sleep include stereotypic body posture, consolidated quiescence at a particular time of day, increased arousal threshold reflecting a sensory disconnection from the environment, and a compensatory increase after its deprivation (called *sleep homeostasis*) (Campbell & Tobler, 1984; Yamazaki et al., 2020). In some mammals, sleep is associated with an altered level of consciousness (Pace-Schott & Hobson, 2002). Most of these behavioural features have been observed in non-mammalian species, including birds, flies, fishes (Kirszenblat & van Swinderen, 2015), worms during lethargus states (Nichols et al., 2017; Raizen et al., 2008), octopuses, jellyfishes (Nath et al., 2017), and sponges, suggesting an essential role for sleep at multiple scales (i.e., brain, body, cells, molecules). Besides these behavioural features, the recording of electroencephalogram (EEG) and electromyogram (EMG) elements allows the definition of multiple sleep states in animals with a well-developed cerebral cortex (e.g., mammals and birds), although recent development of non-invasive imaging techniques (Churgin et al., 2019; Leung et al., 2019) have provided a comprehensive way to look at the neural substrates of sleep or sleep-like states in organisms with a simple nervous system, including lower vertebrates (review in Anafi et al., 2019).

From an evolutionary perspective, the manifestations of sleep at the cellular and circuit levels widely varies across species according to the size and complexity of the nervous system (review in Kirszenblat & van Swinderen, 2015). This phylogeny conservation suggests that sleep covers ancient functions or at least has provided a window of opportunity for a restorative state essential for brain development, brain clearance, diverse homeostatic processes, and synaptic plasticity. In fact, sleep deprivation during juvenile stages results in long-lasting cognitive and behavioural impairments in *Drosophila* flies (Kayser et al., 2014; Seugnet et al., 2011).

This chapter focuses on the implication of the thalamus in the generation of sleep oscillations during non–rapid eye movement (NREM) sleep, its contribution to the brain-wide mechanisms controlling the architecture of the sleep–wake cycle, and its regulation by the brainstem neuromodulatory systems during sleep.

2. Sleep Oscillations and the Thalamus

Since the first EEG recordings in a human by the German physiologist Hans Berger (1924) and the discovery of rapid eye movement (REM) sleep by Professor Nathaniel Kleitman and Eugene Aserinsky (1953), scalp EEG has remained the gold standard in experimental and clinical contexts to identify electrophysiological features of sleep states. In mammals, sleep is divided into episodes of NREM sleep, which accounts for most of the sleeping time, and REM (or paradoxical) sleep (Figure 1), which is classically associated with dreaming, although dreaming has also been reported during NREM in humans (Siclari et al., 2017, 2018). Each of these sleep states is associated with distinct EEG fingerprints that reflect the oscillatory activities of underlying thalamo-cortical (TC) and, to a lesser extent, hippocampal neuronal circuits described in this section.

2.1 NREM Sleep Oscillations

At sleep onset, the excitatory influence of wake-promoting systems on thalamic and cortical neuronal populations progressively decreases (Adamantidis et al., 2019; Saper et al., 2010; Weber & Dan, 2016). The TC circuits generate region-specific, highly synchronized, low-frequency oscillations that characterize the cortical EEG during NREM sleep (Figure 2). As observed in humans, the transition from quiet wakefulness to eyes closed and NREM sleep onset occurs gradually and is characterized by progressive slowing in the frequencies of brain oscillations observed with scalp EEG recordings. Cortical gamma (25 to 80 Hz) and beta (15- to 25 Hz) waves are progressively replaced by alpha oscillations (8–11 Hz), followed shortly thereafter by theta waves (4.0–7.5 Hz) in the N1 stage. Stage 2 of NREM sleep (N2) is characterized by a progressive increase in the average wave amplitude and the onset of two distinctive TC waveforms (Steriade, 2006) that include transient sleep spindles (11–14 Hz) and K-complex defined by large negative deflection (downward) followed by a positive deflection (upward). The N3 stage is represented by prominent large-amplitude, slow oscillations (<1 Hz), and delta waves (1.0–4.5 Hz). In rodents, NREM sleep is generally considered as a single homogeneous stage defined by distinct slow-wave oscillations (0.5–4.5 Hz), in which spindles occur irregularly (spindle rate: 3 events/minute) (Figure 2A).

At the cellular scale, scalp EEG oscillations during NREM sleep reflect the stereotypical deflections of membrane potentials from TC neurons and the influence of the thalamic reticular nucleus (TRN), a capsule-shaped nucleus in the ventral thalamus that encompasses GABAergic neurons that exert a strong inhibitory action on TC cells (Figure 2B). This variation in the membrane potential of TC neurons oscillates

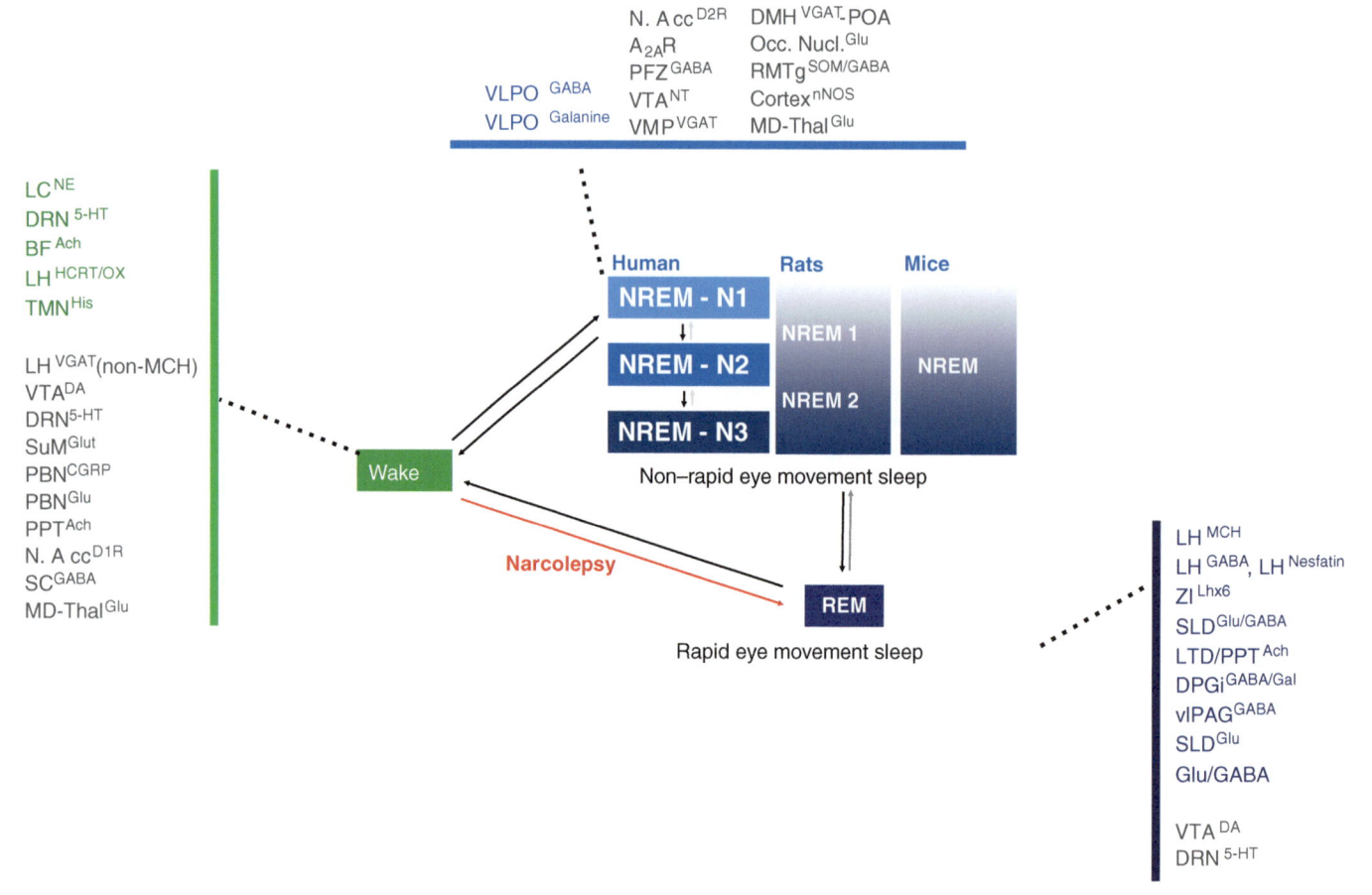

Figure 1 Cortical and sub-cortical sleep–wake circuits.

Schematic representation of sleep–wake cycle in mammals. Spontaneous (*black*) and pathological (*red*; narcolepsy) state transitions are indicated by arrows. Neuronal substrates associated with specific state of vigilance are listed for wakefulness (*green*), NREM sleep (*light blue*), and REM sleep (*dark blue*). Neuronal populations identified recently (2020) using optogenetics are indicated in grey. See main text for functional descriptions of the nuclei.

between hyperpolarized (DOWN) and depolarized (UP) states that generate the <1-Hz slow oscillations recorded on both scalp or intracranial EEG electrodes across all primary and secondary sensory TC networks and associative and motor cortices (Destexhe et al., 2007; Mahon et al., 2006; Steriade et al. 1993a, 2001) (Figure 2C). During the UP state, TC relay and cortico-thalamic (CT) neurons exhibit intense synaptic activity (both excitatory and inhibitory) and fire bursts of action potentials, whereas during the DOWN state, their membrane hyperpolarization induces a period of relative quiescence. Mechanistic studies on the UP–DOWN transitions suggested that the onset of the UP state originates in layer 5 neocortical neurons (Lőrincz et al., 2015), possibly from a subset of pacemaker pyramidal neurons or medio-dorsal thalamic neurons (Baker et al., 2014; Gent, Bassetti, et al., 2018), whereas its termination involves astrocytes and inhibitory neurons.

Slow waves. At the time of writing (2021), it is still debated whether slow oscillations (<1 Hz) are of cortical (Lőrincz et al., 2015; Poulet & Petersen, 2008; Steriade et al., 1993a; Timofeev et al., 2000) or thalamic (Baker et al., 2014; David et al., 2013; Gent, Bassetti, et al., 2018; Honjoh et al., 2018; Magnin et al., 2004) origin. On one side, slow oscillations in the cortex were shown to be maintained after TC lesions, pharmacological blockade, or isolated cortical preparations, but they disappeared in the thalamus after cortical deafferentation, leading to the conclusion that this rhythm is generated in the cortex and further imposed on thalamic regions. However, important changes in the slow oscillation features—such as the duration of UP/DOWN states, synchrony, and the firing rate during the UP states—may occur after thalamic lesion or blockade, as shown by the lower rhythmicity of cortical UP and DOWN transitions after thalamic input deprivation in cats (Crunelli & Hughes, 2010) that eventually question the similarity of the nature and the underlying mechanism of the remaining graphoelements identified as a slow wave. On the other hand, emerging experimental evidence supports a contribution of thalamic structures, in particular the midline and dorsal thalamic nuclei, to the generation of cortical slow waves, as suggested by their burst firing at the onset of local cortical UP states in anaesthetized (Baker et al., 2014) and spontaneously sleeping rodents (Gent, et al., 2018) (Figure 3). Furthermore, optogenetically induced burst firing of midline thalamic neurons controls the onset of cortical UP states, whereas their tonic firing induces awakening from NREM sleep (Figure 3). Collectively, these

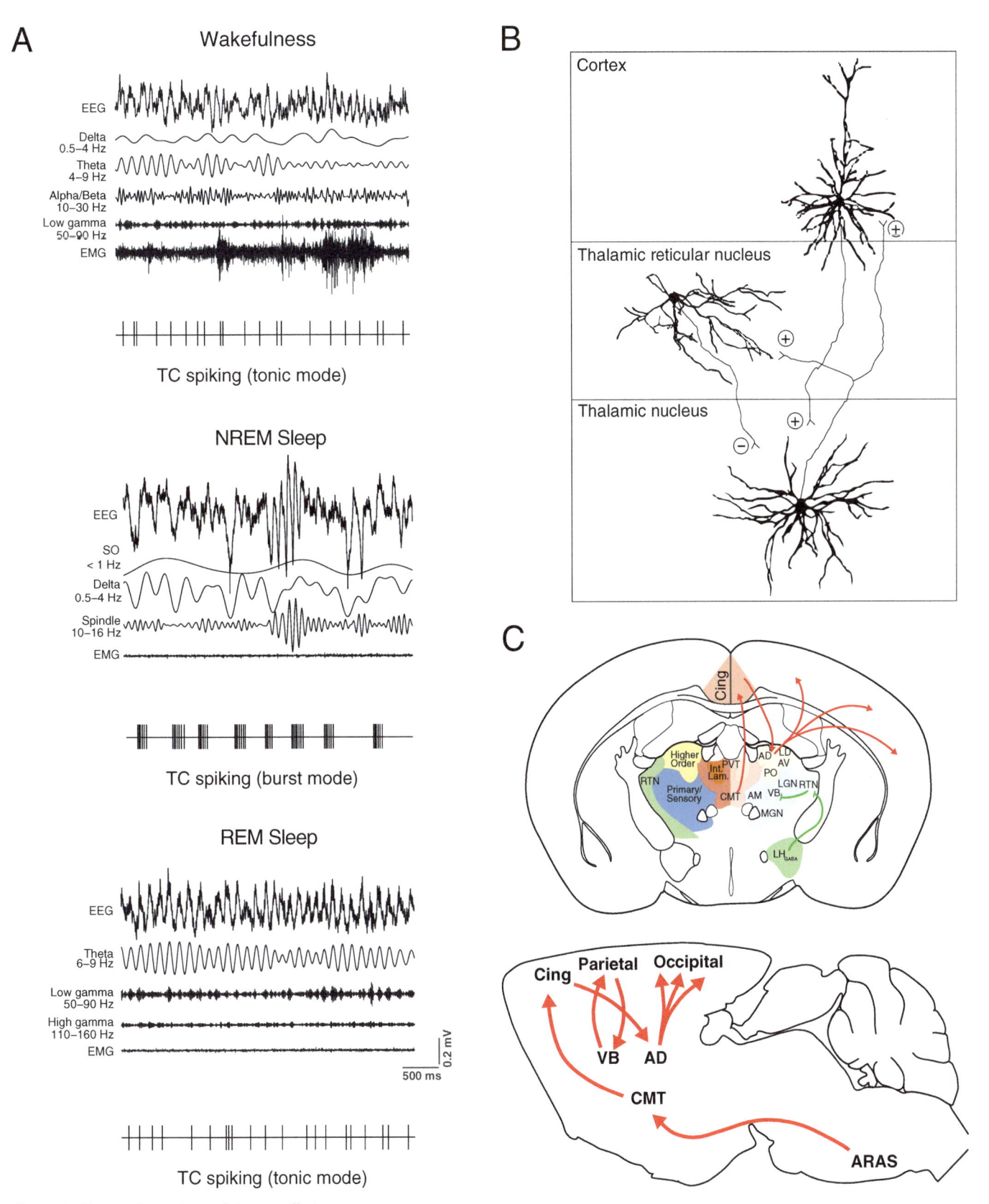

Figure 2 Neuronal correlates of sleep oscillations.

A. Typical EEG grapho-elements associated with vigilance states in freely moving mice are composed of state-dependent oscillations generated by a series of cardinal cellular networks. During wakefulness, multiple cortical and subcortical networks show high-frequency and/or low-amplitude activity, including theta and gamma oscillations, which signal interactions with the environment, whereas high-EMG activity signals body movements. At the onset of NREM sleep, EMG activity is low, and EEG activity is dominated by high-amplitude, low-frequency slow waves (<4.5 Hz) that include slow oscillations (<1 Hz) and delta waves (0.5–4.5 Hz). Spindles (10–16 Hz) are transient events generated by the interplay between neocortical and thalamic circuitries. During REM sleep, EEG activity predominantly comprises theta oscillations (6–9 Hz) and gamma oscillations (30–150 Hz) generated by the hippocampus and cortical networks, respectively. EMG tone is further reduced, reflecting postural muscle atonia (sleep paralysis). During wakefulness and REM sleep, TC neurons display tonic firing, regardless of whether the NREM activity of TC cells is characterized by burst firing.

findings suggested that each hub of the TC network contributes to the generation of a region-specific slow wave. Importantly, recent studies suggested that slow waves can originate from cortical or thalamic sources and can overlap both temporally and spatially in humans (Siclari et al., 2014).

Delta waves. Delta waves are most common during deeper stages of NREM sleep in humans and are intermixed with slow oscillations. Delta waves have two proposed mechanisms, including either the thalamus or layer 5 cortical neurons (Adamantidis et al., 2019; Hubbard et al., 2020). In the thalamus, membrane hyperpolarization of TC neurons activates a hyperpolarization-activated current (I_h) that results in a gradual depolarization. This in turn activates the I_T-current (resulting from the opening of T-type calcium channels) and, subsequently, low-threshold calcium spikes. Cortical layer 5 neurons also exhibit an intrinsic delta oscillation, as revealed in the de-afferentiated cortex (Steriade et al., 1993b), which is dependent on an acetylcholine-sensitive potassium conductance (Lőrincz et al., 2015). Which of these two generators, or unidentified others, is essential for delta oscillations during sleep remains unclear, and recent investigations using optogenetic silencing of midline and dorsal thalamic neurons have demonstrated a reduction of oscillation amplitude in delta frequencies in cortical regions (Gent, Bassetti, et al., 2018), suggesting a driving role for the thalamus.

Spindles. Sleep spindles are waxing-and-waning electrophysiological events (11–15 Hz) typical of NREM sleep observed in humans, cats, and rodents, which generally propagate across the TC circuits (Lüthi, 2014). Spindles are single events that are frequently, but not exclusively, associated with the UP state of a slow wave. In humans, spindles predominate in the central and parietal neocortical areas, although fast and slow spindles are distributed across the frontal and occipital areas (Mölle et al., 2011), respectively, suggesting two functionally distinct spindle generators involving the thalamus, although this awaits further investigations.

During spindle oscillations, TC cells transiently exhibit strong burst firing, which generates typical spindling activity within the TC and CT neuronal circuits, as observed in rodent studies. Volleys of TRN inputs in the spindle range frequency provide a strong inhibition to TC cells from the sensory thalamus, which results in a large hyperpolarization that triggers the I_h depolarizing current, immediately followed by a calcium (T-type) current (I_T) that produces a burst of action potentials in TC neurons (Bal et al., 1995). These bursts of spikes directly excite layer 4 pyramidal neurons in the corresponding cortical area where excitatory postsynaptic potentials generate spindle oscillations detectable by scalp EEG electrodes. The pacemaker activity of reticular thalamus nucleus (RTN) cells and functional inputs to RTN cells from the cortex are sufficient to generate spindle-like activity (Durkin et al., 2017), whereas cortical inputs to the RTN are responsible for spindle termination. Similarly, dual recordings in humans suggested that convergent cortical DOWN states led to thalamic DOWN states and thalamic cell hyperpolarization, hence triggering spindles that are transmitted to the cortex at the transition from the DOWN state to the UP state (Mak-Mccully et al., 2017). Thus, reciprocal interactions between the thalamus and the cortex shape the duration and amplitude of spindles (Bonjean et al., 2011; Lüthi, 2014).

K-complex. A K-complex consists of a short, negative, high-voltage peak, usually greater than 100 μV, followed by a regular 14-Hz rhythm (i.e., spindle-like followed by alpha burst) typically observed during stage 2 of NREM sleep in humans but less apparent in rodents (Loomis et al., 1938). K-complexes are generally associated with the onset of a DOWN state in NREM. They originate from the occurrence of cortical outward dendritic currents from the supragranular layers of the cerebral cortex, resulting in a general decrease in the EEG power and a reduction of neuronal network activity. The K-complex events are then transferred in the thalamic territories, where they may synchronize sleep oscillations such as spindle and delta waves.

2.2 REM Sleep Oscillations

During REM sleep, the cortical EEG shows a marked change that resembles wakefulness in rodents and includes low-voltage, high-frequency activity, including theta oscillations (6–9 Hz in rodents and 4–6 Hz in humans) and gamma oscillations (30–90 Hz) and, to a lesser extent, pontine waves. In rodents, theta-locked firing of neurons from the medial septum (gamma-aminobutyric acid [GABA], glutamate, acetylcholine), posterior hypothalamus, brainstem, and internal hippocampus all contribute, to a different extent, to the generation of theta rhythm during wakefulness and REM sleep. Theta-synchronized gamma oscillations result from the synchronization of local neuronal assemblies composed of inhibitory interneurons and post-synaptic $GABA_A$ receptor-mediated inhibition, typically via coupling of local interneurons alone (the I–I model) or with pyramidal cells (E–I model) or both. REM-sleep pontine waves, traditionally referred to as *PGO waves* (or *P-waves*), are large phasic waves detectable as (pontine) local field potentials (LFPs)

Caption for Figure 2 (cont.)

B. TC neurons are reciprocally connected through long-range excitatory projections. In parallel, thalamic projections send collaterals to the TRN. The TRN represents a collection of GABAergic neurons that exert a strong inhibitory action on TC cells.

C. Frontal cortical (Cing = cingulate cortex) slow waves are initiated in the midline central medial thalamic (CMT) nucleus, and propagation to the posterior cortex occurs via a higher-order thalamus relay. The primary somatosensory thalamus and cortex have reciprocal connectivity, separate from the higher-order thalamus, arranged as a classical TC loop. The TRN projects to both the primary sensory thalamus and the higher-order thalamus but not the midline thalamus. These projections may synchronize large thalamic regions. Hypothalamic and brainstem sleep–wake nuclei project to the TRN, midline thalamus, and frontal cortex. Modified from Adamantidis et al. (2019).

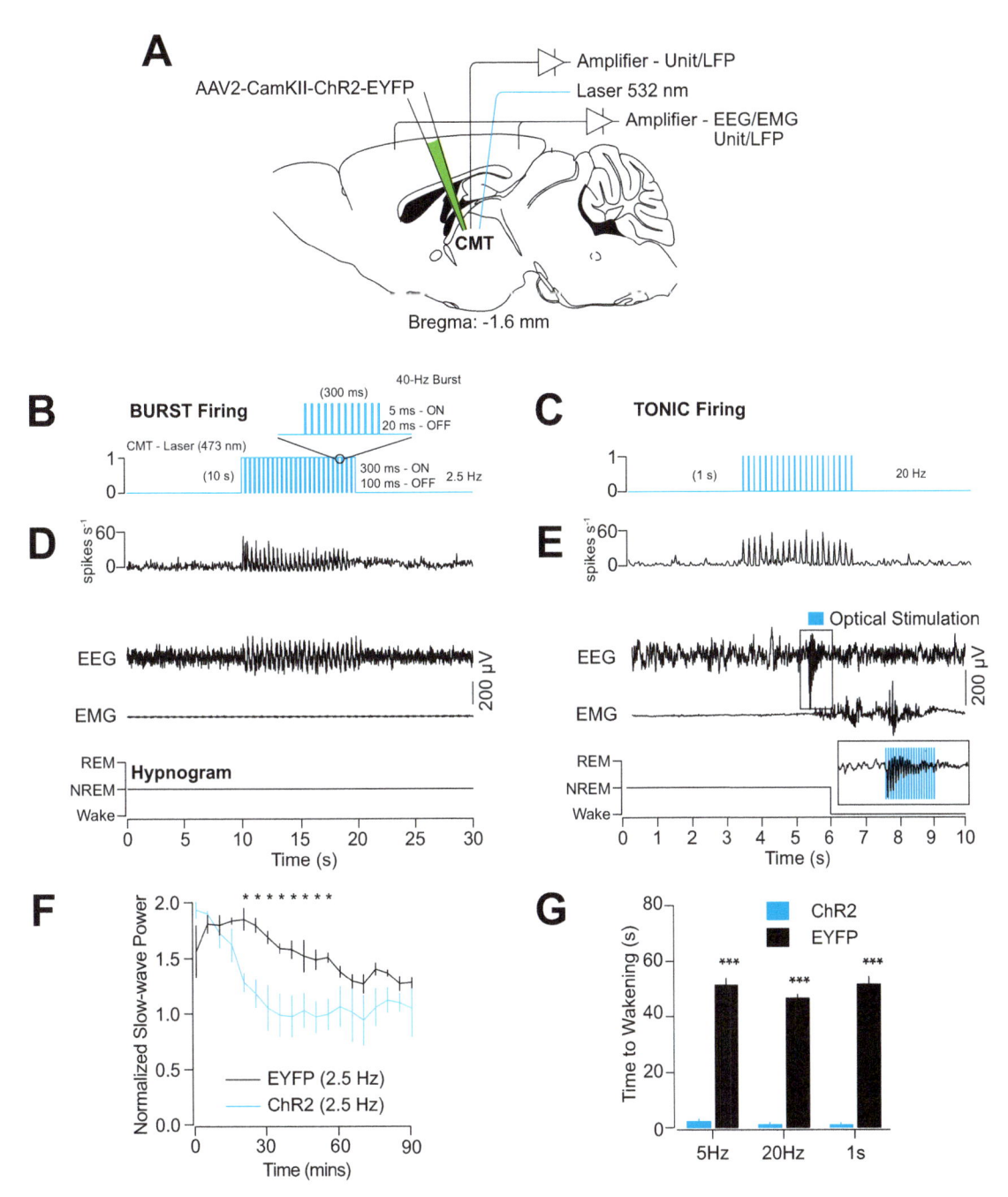

Figure 3 Neuronal firing pattern of CMT neurons drives cortical tone and behavioural state.

A. Schematic of optic fibre and tetrode implantations in the brain. An optic fiber was placed above the CMT. Additionally, tetrodes were implanted within the CMT as well as the cingulate (CING), barrel (BARR), and visual (VIS) cortices.

B and C. Laser stimulation patterns for induction of burst (panel B) or tonic (panel C) firing patterns in ChR2-expressing CMT neurons during NREM sleep.

D and E. Top row: Example firing rates of CMT neurons during optogenetically induced burst (panel D) or tonic (panel E) firing. Bottom: Example EEG/EMG and behavioural state during optogenetically induced burst (panel D) or tonic (panel E) firing of CMT neurons during NREM. Notice that tonic activation induced rapid awakening, whereas awakening did not result from induction of burst firing.

F. Average delta power ± standard error of the mean (SEM) during sleep recovery in CING during optogenetic burst stimulation of CMT neurons (b: $P < 0.035$; $t = 4.59$; degrees of freedom (df) = 7; one-way analysis of variance [ANOVA]; $n = 6$ animals).

G. Averaged latencies to awakening ± SEM following tonic optogenetic CMT neuron activation ($n = 6$ animals per group). Data based on a minimum of 10 stimulations per frequency per animal. (5 Hz: $P = 0.00008$; $t = 26.75$; df = 10; 20 Hz: $P = 0.00006$; $t = 41.68$; df = 10; 1 s: $P = 0.00006$; $t = 27.23$; df = 10; two-sided t-test). Figure adapted from Gent, Bassetti, et al. (2018) with permission.

during eye movements in rats, cats, and humans (Adamantidis et al., 2019).

Unlike NREM sleep, experimental investigation of a possible contribution of thalamic neurons to brain activity during REM sleep remains scarce. Interestingly, neurons from the midline thalamus, as well as the sensory thalamo-cortical circuits, showed the highest discharge rates during REM sleep, as compared to NREM sleep and even wakefulness (Gent,

Bandarabadi, et al., 2018; Sriji et al., 2020; Vyazovskiy et al., 2009). Thalamic-projecting mesopontine cholinergic neurons have been involved in the maintenance of tonic firing in the TC network similar to what has been observed during wakefulness (Steriade et al., 1990); however, whether this strong activation is due to high cholinergic, or low noradrenergic, tone during REM sleep remains unclear. Indirect measurements of thalamic activation in humans (Maquet et al., 1996, 2000) and increased brain perfusion in mice (Bergel et al., 2018; Tsai et al., 2021) collectively suggested a role for the thalamus in modulating cortical activity during REM sleep, yet this remains to be experimentally investigated.

3. The Thalamus and Sleep–Wake Architecture

Decades of clinical and experimental studies using lesions, pharmacology, genetics, and opto-/pharmaco-genetics support a circuit model proposing that the periodic cycling through sleep–wake states relies on a balance between sleep-promoting circuits, such as the anterior hypothalamus, and wake-promoting circuits located in the posterior hypothalamus, the basal forebrain, and the brainstem (Luppi et al., 2017; Saper et al., 2010; Weber & Dan, 2016).

However, amassing evidence supports a role for local TC oscillations that stem from both high-density scalp EEG recordings in humans that were incremental to the description of locally regulated sleep slow waves during NREM sleep and the ability of the simple circuit to generate sleep-like oscillations (Huber et al., 2004; Krueger et al., 2019; Vyazovskiy et al., 2011). The corresponding intracranial recordings of multiple cell types in rodents further emphasized the broad diversity of region-specific cellular activities across sleep–wake states. These discoveries support the hypothesis that (global) sleep may emerge from local region-specific mechanisms (Krueger & Tononi, 2012).

In the following sections, we will review the experimental evidence supporting an implication of the diverse thalamic nuclei in the region-specific modulation of TC oscillations during sleep, on the one hand, and on the other, its central position as an anatomical and functional hub that integrate inputs from major sub-cortical sleep–wake circuits identified in the brain.

3.1 Brain Mechanisms of Sleep–Wake States

A common feature of sleep–wake circuits is their widespread projections to the basal forebrain, brainstem, thalamus, neocortex, and hippocampus, where their activities ultimately contribute to the high-frequency gamma waves during wakefulness, the low-frequency slow waves during NREM sleep, and the theta/gamma rhythmic activity typical of REM sleep. In fact, recent studies collectively emphasized a much more complex mechanism than previously thought that implicates multiple circuits and heterogeneous subpopulations of neurons distributed across all brain areas (Figure 1).

The periodic cycling through sleep and wake relies on a balance between sleep- and arousal-promoting neurons, located in the posterior hypothalamus, the basal forebrain, and the brainstem (Eban-Rothschild et al., 2016; Fort et al., 2009; Saper et al., 2010; Weber & Dan, 2016). Activity in the brainstem correlates with wakefulness and states of enhanced arousal, such as alertness or stress, but it decreases during NREM sleep to become silent during REM sleep (except the LDT/PPT cholinergic neurons and REM-active neurons from the sub-latero-dorsal nuclei; Figure 1). These arousal systems classically include distinct neuronal populations that produce and release a complex set of neurotransmitters and neuropeptides/modulators, including norepinephrine, dopamine, histamine, acetylcholine, serotonin, and hypocretins/orexins. Recent opto- and pharmacogenetic studies identified a series of additional neuronal populations that further extend the number of wake circuits to neurons producing classical neurotransmitters (GABA, glutamate) across the brain (Weber & Dan, 2016), including dopaminergic neurons from the ventral tegmental area (VTA) (Dahan et al., 2007) and the dorsal raphe (Kocsis et al., 2006); neurons located in the supra-mammillary nuclei (Pedersen et al., 2017), the lateral parabrachial nucleus (Qiu et al., 2016), or the pedunculopontine tegmental (PPT) nucleus producing GABA, glutamate, or acetylcholine (Kroeger et al., 2017); dopamine D1 receptor (D1-R)-expressing neurons that co-release GABA in the nucleus accumbens (Luo et al., 2018); GABAergic neurons from the superior colliculus (Ze Zhang et al., 2019); and glutamate neurons in the medio-dorsal thalamic nucleus (Gent, Bassetti, et al., 2018). Thus, neural circuits supporting the onset and maintenance of wakefulness show a high redundancy, yet it is thought that these represent specific pathways regulating arousal-related states, including attention, anxiety, or stress, but also NREM-to-wake or REM-to-wake transitions.

At the onset of NREM sleep, the modulatory influence of wake-promoting systems on subcortical and cortical neuronal populations progressively decreases concomitant to the increased activity of sleep-promoting systems (Figure 1). Original lesion studies and retrograde/anterograde tract-tracing techniques indicated that ventrolateral preoptic nucleus (VLPO) and medial preoptic nucleus (MnPn) neurons of the anterior hypothalamus are essential for NREM sleep (Weber & Dan, 2016). These cells encompass multiple sub-populations of inhibitory neurons that fire in a reciprocal pattern to the wake-active neurons on which they exert a strong inhibitory tone during NREM as compared to waking (Chung et al., 2017; Morairty et al., 2013; Takahashi et al., 2020; Zhe Zhang et al., 2015, 2019). Accordingly, their opto-/chemo-genetic activation induced NREM sleep, possibly through the inhibition of wake-active neurons such as histamine neurons. Their concomitant activation also induced a drop in body temperature (Morairty et al., 2013; Zhe Zhang et al., 2015), which is associated with natural sleep.

Recent causal evidence identified a role for extra-hypothalamic neuron populations. Some of those are located in the neocortex (Oishi et al., 2017), but others include neurons from the nucleus accumbens (A2AR) (Anaclet et al., 2018), GABAergic neurons from the parafacial zone (Zhong et al., 2019), neurotensinergic from the midbrain (Takata et al., 2018), and GABAergic of the ventral medial midbrain/pons (K. Liu et al., 2017), as well as some excitatory neurons from the perioculomotor nuclei (Takahashi et al., 2020), zona incerta (Chen et al., 2018), preoptic area (POA)-projecting galanin-expressing GABAergic neurons in the dorso-medial hypothalamus (DMH) (Xu et al., 2015), somatostatin-positive (SOM+) GABAergic neurons (Yang et al., 2018), neurons from the midbrain rostromedial tegmental (RMTg) nuclei, striatal A2AR neurons/globus pallidus externa (GPe) parvalbumin (PV) neuron circuits involved in adenosine-induced sleep (Yuan et al., 2017), and glutamate neurons in the medio-dorsal thalamic nucleus (Gent, Bandarabadi, et al., 2018). Each of these neuronal populations was found to facilitate, or prolong, NREM sleep with variable latencies when selectively activated.

Transitions to REM sleep complete the sleep–wake cycle. REM sleep (or paradoxical sleep; Jouvet et al., 1959) is characterized by rapid eye movements, muscle atonia, and a prominent theta rhythm in the hippocampus and cortex (Saper et al., 2010; Weber & Dan, 2016). Pioneer studies initially located the REM sleep "generator(s)" within the pons (Jouvet et al., 1959), where reciprocal inhibition between neurons in the oralis pontine and sublaterodorsal nuclei (REM active neurons) and ventro-lateral periacqueductal gray/lateropontine tegmentum (REM inactive neurons) is hypothesized to gate REM sleep. More recently, neurons producing the neurotransmitters GABA and glutamate have been integrated into the brainstem circuitry critical for the onset of REM sleep (Hayashi et al., 2015; Luppi et al., 2017). Importantly, the activity of neurons outside the brainstem also correlates with the REM sleep state, including neurons located in the anterior and lateral parts of the hypothalamus (Hassani et al., 2009, 2010; Herrera et al., 2016; Verret et al., 2003). Recent work identified the neurons expressing the peptide melanin-concentrating hormone (MCH) as a REM sleep circuit in the lateral hypothalamus (Hassani et al., 2009, 2010; Herrera et al., 2016; Verret et al., 2003).

Collectively, these studies supported a paradigm shift in the field of experimental sleep research from a hypothalamic-centric to a multi-centric origin of sleep (Luppi et al., 2017), and NREM sleep in particular, that implicates distinct local neuronal populations that are necessary, or sufficient, for the brain control of sleep–wake states. Interestingly, evidence for a role of the thalamus, in particular the medio-dorsal thalamus, in the control of sleep–wake states (Gent, Bassetti, et al., 2018) suggested a functional link between sleep–wake circuits and the oscillating TC circuits in the sleeping brain (described in Section 3.2).

3.2 Thalamic Contribution to Sleep Architecture

The thalamus is a federation of anatomically and functionally diverse nuclei, each of which is composed of molecularly defined clusters with their own cellular properties and activity dynamics (Mai & Majtanik, 2019; Rikhye et al., 2018), consistent with a region-specific organization of sleep (Fernandez et al., 2018). Indeed, neighbouring TC areas display different (local) sleep waves that result from a heterogeneous anatomical distribution of thalamic oscillators (Contreras et al., 1992; Piantoni et al., 2017; Siclari & Tononi, 2017).

Classical work on thalamic inputs to the cortex during sleep focused on primary sensory thalamic nuclei and their reciprocal connections with primary sensory cortical areas (Sanchez-Vives et al., 2008; Steriade et al., 1993a, 1993b) and highlighted a central role for both the thalamus and the cortex in the mechanisms of slow waves. Recent studies integrated the non-sensory medio-dorsal thalamus and higher-order thalamic nuclei into the model as a control mechanism for the generation of slow waves and their brain-wide propagation throughout the cortex (Gent, Bassetti, et al., 2018; Massimini et al., 2007; Sherman, 2016). This revisited view is supported by the anatomical distribution of higher-order thalamus efferents and their afferents from sleep–wake circuits located in the hypothalamus and brainstem (McKenna & Vertes, 2004; Vertes et al., 2015).

The implication of thalamic nuclei in sleep stems from decades of experimental and clinical investigations using lesion studies, pharmacology studies, genetic models, and both in vitro and in vivo electrophysiology. This section summarizes the contribution of these investigations to the understanding of the anatomy, connectivity, plasticity, and function of thalamic neurons in sleep; thalamic modulation of other functions is reviewed elsewhere (Halassa & Kastner, 2017).

Lesion studies. Human patients with stroke lesions restricted to the paramedian thalamus (often centred on the centromedian and intralaminar nuclei) are often associated with profound sleep disturbances of arousal and NREM sleep occurrence (Bassetti et al., 1996; Hermann et al., 2008). Furthermore, human subjects with thalamic lesions showed highly variable modifications of sleep due to the extent of the lesion, its location, and the delay of sleep recording. Human stroke studies represent a first effort to establish a link between normal sleep architecture and the necessity of an intact thalamus (Sarasso et al., 2020; Wu et al., 2016).

Similar results were observed in experimental studies. In vivo lesion studies in cats suggested that sleep slow oscillations have a cortical origin because slow oscillations persisted in a de-afferented cortical "slab" preparation (Timofeev et al., 2000) but were abolished in the majority of thalamocortical and RTN neurons following decortication or transection of their cortical afferents (Steriade et al., 1993b; Timofeev & Steriade, 1996). Consistent with these findings, acute (Anaclet et al., 2015) or chronic (Fuller et al., 2011) midline and intralaminar thalamic lesions in rats resulted in mild or no changes of slow-wave features or fast cortical activity, with no significant changes in the amount of NREM and REM sleep or in the circadian pattern of sleep. However, cortical de-afferentation from thalamic inputs results in the inhibition of local UP-state initiation and a profound depression of sleep slow oscillations in the mouse brain (Lemieux et al., 2014). Such effect was found to be transient—slow waves reappeared 36 h after thalamic lesions, possibly as a result of the restricted size of the lesions or the compensatory nature of the travelling slow wave in the cortex (Gent, Bassetti, et al., 2018; Massimini et al., 2004). Furthermore, these discrepancies may result from the absence of a systematic and quantitative comparison of the properties of slow oscillations in the cortex before, during, and after lesioning. In fact, cortical oscillations appear less regular and rhythmic in the absence of thalamic inputs in these lesion studies (Crunelli & Hughes, 2010; Steriade et al., 1993b; Timofeev & Steriade, 1996). Altogether, these studies suggested that slow waves may persist after lesioning of TC circuits, but their mechanisms and features, and thus their functions, may differ from those of spontaneously occurring slow waves.

Pharmacology studies. Pharmacological approaches provide the possibility to artificially activate selective receptors expressed in thalamic nuclei as compared to the non-selective inactivation obtained by lesions. Although it was once thought that the generation of rhythmic activities in the EEG was due to the interaction of very large networks of neurons and therefore could only be investigated *in vivo*, it has been shown that slow waves with characteristics identical to those observed *in vivo* can be reliably recorded in vitro under certain conditions (Sanchez-Vives & McCormick, 2000) in TC and TRN neurons. Thereby, several in vitro studies on TC neurons upon pharmacological intervention allowed the investigation of thalamic influence on sleep-like oscillations. For instance, continuous pharmacological activation of mGluR1a evokes slow oscillations that can last for many hours (Blethyn et al., 2006; L. Zhu et al., 2006). At the cellular level, these are characterized by large (15- to 20-mV) and constant membrane fluctuation of TC and RTN neurons, similar to the UP and DOWN states observed in vivo. RTN neuron UP states were associated with sleep spindles, whereas delta waves occurred during the DOWN state of both TC and RTN cells. These slow oscillations, recorded from single thalamic cells, are not blocked by tetrodotoxin (action-potential blocker), indicating that this activity is intrinsically generated (Hughes et al., 2002; L. Zhu et al., 2006). Consistent with this finding, slow waves were recorded in thalamic slices as large LFPs, suggesting that thalamic cells are able to synchronize in the absence of cortical afferents (Hughes et al., 2004).

In vivo pharmacological disinhibition of the midline thalamus promoted arousal from general anaesthesia (Alkire et al., 2007, 2009; Lioudyno et al., 2013), whereas inhibition through local GABA$_A$ receptor agonist muscimol infusion prolonged membrane potential hyperpolarization that prevented fluctuations of cortical slow membrane potential (Poulet et al., 2012). Accordingly, thalamic inactivation by local application of a T-type calcium channel blocker strongly reduced the amplitude and frequency of cortical slow oscillation (David et al., 2013). Similarly, increased delta waves and stabilized NREM sleep were observed after thalamic micro-infusion of the GABAergic sleep-promoting drug THIP (4,5,6,7-tetrahydroisoxazolo[5,4-c]pyridin-3-ol) in rats (Mesbah-Oskui et al., 2014).

Taken together, these studies provided evidence for a direct implication of thalamic nuclei, in particular midline thalamic neurons, in the modulation of slow waves or spindles and, ultimately, the duration or number of NREM sleep episodes.

Genetic studies. Genetically engineered animal models allowed the manipulation of single genes, leading to precise changes in the excitability of thalamic neurons, TC oscillations, and sleep. The genetic deletion of $Ca_v3.1$-, $Ca_v3.3$-, and Ca^{2+}-dependent small-conductance (SK)-type K^+ channels in inhibitory thalamic reticular neurons or excitatory thalamic relay neurons led to a reduction in the rhythmic high-frequency burst firing of TC neurons and decreased amplitude of low-frequency oscillations during NREM sleep (Astori et al., 2011; Cueni et al., 2008; Lee et al., 2004). Furthermore, sleep patterns from both global and midline thalamic conditional deletion of the $Ca_v3.1$ gene exhibited a decreased amount of NREM sleep (~20%), in particular during the light period (Anderson et al., 2005). This phenotype was associated with sleep fragmentation, NREM sleep reduction, and prolonged duration of arousal episodes (Anderson et al., 2005). These studies supported a role for midline thalamic nuclei in sleep maintenance through stabilization of TC oscillatory activity. Of note, global knockouts (KOs) result in a milder decrease in NREM sleep than the thalamic-selective KOs, indicating a possible compensation of sleep stability (of unknown origin) consistent with the implication of some of the cortical circuits in NREM sleep onset and maintenance (Krone et al., 2021; Morairty et al., 2013).

Interestingly, $Ca_v3.3$ KO mice showed a strong suppression of sleep spindle rhythmogenesis (Pellegrini et al., 2016) and a selective reduction in the power density of the sigma frequency band (10–12 Hz) at transitions from NREM to REM sleep, whereas other sleep oscillations (between 0.75 and 20 Hz) remained unchanged (Astori et al., 2011). Consistent with these findings, global genetic deletion of Ca^{2+}-dependent SK-type K^+ channels impaired the rhythmic bursting oscillatory activity of TRN neurons, which led to a significant decrease of EEG power density in delta and spindle frequency bands and general NREM sleep fragmentation (Cueni et al., 2008). In contrast, constitutive deletion of the phospholipase C (PLC) β4, a protein highly expressed in TC cells and involved in neuronal excitability, led to a dramatic increase in burst firing of TC neurons concomitant to an increase of NREM duration and a decrease of spindle occurrence (Hong et al., 2020). Although the latter finding is striking in regard to the implication of spindles in NREM sleep stability (Dang-vu et al., 2010; Schabus et al., 2012), the increase of total NREM duration was associated with an impairment of memory consolidation, further emphasizing the importance of an intact TC for cognitive functions and a decoupling between sleep quantity and cognitive improvement (Economo et al., 2018; Wells et al., 2016).

Optogenetic studies. Optogenetic techniques enable the manipulation of the activity of genetically targeted excitable cells with unprecedented spatio-temporal resolution as compared to pharmacological and genetic approaches. The high temporal precision of optogenetically induced spiking reliably reproduces the naturalistic tonic, or burst, firing patterns of thalamic neurons relevant to the functional dissection of thalamic neural circuit control of sleep, sleep oscillations, or other behaviours.

Ramping intensity of optogenetic stimulation over a 5-s time period of somatosensory thalamus excitatory neurons is sufficient to drive a cortical state, similar to those observed during awake, in behaving mice (Poulet et al., 2012), whereas 5- to 100-ms short optogenetic stimulation of ventrobasal complex (VB) TC neurons in anesthetized mice entrained cortical EEG slow waves, where each light pulse elicited high-frequency bursts of action potentials, invariably followed by a 100- to 250-ms period of electrical quiescence before firing resumed (David et al., 2013). Similarly, tonic activation of midline thalamic neurons induces NREM–wake transitions, whereas burst activation mimics UP states in the cortex of naturally sleeping mice and ultimately stabilizes NREM sleep (Gent, Bassetti, et al., 2018; Figure 3). Interestingly, optogenetically induced burst spiking of medio-dorsal thalamic neurons generates a slow-wave–like waveform in the anterior cingulate cortex that propagates through the cortex, similar to cortical slow waves during sleep in rodents (Gent, Bassetti, et al., 2018) and similar to what has been observed in humans (Massimini et al., 2007). These findings suggest that the tonic, or burst, firing pattern of midline thalamic neurons modulates brain-wide cortical activity and neocortical spindle occurrence and provides dual control of sleep–wake states (Figure 3).

Brief optical activation of the TRN neurons induced burst firing in TC neurons and neocortical sleep spindle occurrence *in vivo* (Halassa et al., 2011), and it eventually increased the total duration of NREM sleep upon chronic stimulation (Kim et al., 2012) and the probability of transitions from NREM to REM sleep (Bandarabadi et al., 2020), providing evidence that oscillatory circuits directly contribute to the switching of sleep–wake states.

The thalamus and sleep-state control. The contribution of the thalamus to the brain oscillatory landscape during NREM sleep is consistent with a "local" origin of sleep. In line with this view, distinct region-specific NREM sleep oscillations result from the pattern of local TC circuits' activity (Vantomme et al., 2019). Indeed, local modulation of slow-wave amplitude is conditioned by prior TC circuit activity during wakefulness (Huber et al., 2004); slow (~12 Hz) and fast (~14 Hz) spindles predominate in the frontal and centro-parietal neocortex, respectively (Schabus et al., 2007; Warby et al., 2014); and delta 1 (<1.5 Hz), unlike delta 2 (>1.5 Hz), does not show the expected homeostatic regulation (Hubbard et al., 2020). These results supported the hypothesis that locally generated sleep oscillations eventually lead to the onset of a particular sleep state, yet a definitive conclusion awaits further investigations (D. Liu et al., 2020).

In contrast, growing evidence implicate the thalamus in the brain mechanism underlying sleep architecture. Indeed, previous correlative studies showed that the number and occurrence of spindles are essential in stabilizing NREM sleep, in particular during sensory perturbation, such as acoustic stimulations (Kim et al., 2012; Lecci et al., 2017), and supported the brain plasticity associated with sleep-dependent memory consolidation (Helfrich et al., 2019; Latchoumane et al., 2017; Muehlroth et al., 2019; Seibt et al., 2017). Furthermore, spindle occurrence is maximal during NREM sleep preceding REM sleep transitions (Kim et al., 2012; Watts et al., 2012), and causal optogenetic stimulation implicated spindles, and the RTN in particular, in the onset of REM sleep (Bandarabadi et al., 2019; Stucynski et al., 2021). These data confirmed previous assumptions that REM sleep depends on the distribution of sleep spindles in time and space (Glin et al., 1991; Watson et al., 2016).

These studies are important because they started to provide missing links between the "sleep circuit" and the "local sleep" views on the origins of sleep. In other words, they showed that the modulation of TC circuits and single oscillatory events in particular have a direct influence on sleep architecture. In turn, classical circuits promoting sleep–wake states also modulate these oscillatory circuits. This is the case for a subset of GABAergic neurons in the lateral hypothalamus (LH) projecting directly onto RTN cells, where they exert a strong inhibitory control that triggers a rapid transition from NREM sleep to the wake state (Herrera et al., 2016).

4. Neuromodulation of Thalamic Neurons across Sleep–Wake States

Brain-state intrinsic oscillations depend on the interplay between CT, TC, and TRN neurons, yet their fine-tuning also relies on the direct influence of the ascending reticular activating system (ARAS). The ARAS is composed of glutamatergic, cholinergic, serotoninergic, noradrenergic, dopaminergic, and histaminergic neurons (Figure 4) that send axonal projections to the cerebral cortex and the thalamus as well as other subcortical nuclei. ARAS activation is responsible for promoting wakefulness from sleep or light anaesthesia and hyperarousal states associated with stress (Moruzzi & Magoun, 1949). The ARAS is composed of a ventral pathway that directly controls cortical activity through widespread projections from the locus coeruleus (LC) and the dorsal raphe (DR), crossing the ventral periacqueductal grey matter (vPAG), the tuberomammillary nucleus (TMN), the lateral hypothalamus (LH), and the basal forebrain (BF; Figure 4). The ARAS dorsal pathway originates from the midbrain, pontine, and medullary reticular formation and is composed of glutamatergic and cholinergic neurons from the pons and the pedunculopontine and laterotegmental nuclei (PPT/LDT), respectively, and densely project to the thalamus and innervate the midline and intralaminar thalamocortical nuclei (Figure 4).

The activity of the ARAS is strongly modulated across the sleep–wake cycle. Cholinergic, noradrenergic, and serotonergic neurons are strongly activated during wakefulness, and their firing rate progressively decreases during NREM sleep, to become completely silent during REM sleep, with the exception of cholinergic neurons that are strongly active during REM sleep (Figure 4; Jones, 2005; Pace-Schott & Hobson, 2002; Varela, 2014). This section summarizes the evidence for the neuromodulation of thalamic neurons and the implications for sleep architecture and sleep oscillations.

Cholinergic system. Acetylcholine (Ach) is widely implicated in cognitive processes, including arousal, attention, learning, control of cortical rhythms, and processing of sensory information (for a review, see Colangelo et al., 2019; Picciotto et al., 2012). Ach is released from two major cholinergic projections of the central nervous system: the magnocellular basal forebrain cholinergic system and the brainstem LDT/PPT cholinergic system (Newman et al., 2012). The magnocellular basal forebrain (BF) cholinergic system encompasses the medial septal nucleus (MS), the vertical and horizontal limbs of the diagonal band of Broca (DB), and the nucleus basalis magnocellularis (nBM). The magnocellular BF cholinergic system sends extensive diffuse projections to the neocortex as well as the basolateral amygdala, the olfactory bulb, the hippocampus, the entorhinal cortices, the reticular nucleus, and the anterior nuclei of the thalamus (Kolmac & Mitrofanis, 1999; Parent et al., 1988).

The brainstem cholinergic system includes the pedunculopontine tegmental nucleus (PPT) and laterodorsal pontine tegmentum (LDT) and projects predominantly to the anterior, parafascicular, medio-dorsal, and intralaminar thalamic nuclei, where it modulates the activity of thalamic neurons. Cholinergic fiber activation depolarizes most of the thalamic cells (Curró Dossi et al., 1991; Francesconi et al., 1988; Sillito et al., 1983), although some TC relay cells and thalamic interneurons are hyperpolarized by cholinergic agonists (J. Zhu & Heggelund, 2001; McCormick & Pape, 1988; McCormick & Prince, 1986; Varela & Sherman, 2007). Cholinergic-evoked depolarization is mediated by ionotropic (nicotinic) and metabotropic muscarinic (M1, M3) receptors (C. Varela & Sherman, 2007), whereas the M2 muscarinic receptor is responsible for the hyperpolarization of GABAergic neurons (J. Zhu & Heggelund, 2001; McCormick & Prince, 1986). Consistent with this, Ach triggers the depolarization of RTN cells that produce prolonged asynchronous activation (decorrelated activity between neurons) in the thalamic networks (Pita-Almenar et al., 2014). Furthermore, cholinergic neurons from the basal forebrain were found to mediate biphasic excitatory–inhibitory postsynaptic responses onto thalamic RTN cells as a result of the activation of fast-acting nicotinic cholinergic receptors (nAChRs) and slow M2 muscarinic receptors (mAChRs), respectively (Sun et al., 2013). In mouse brain slices, cholinergic agonists depolarize TC relay neurons via a muscarinic-receptor–mediated blockade of leak potassium conductance (Broicher et al., 2008) that promotes tonic firing over bursting activity, reminiscent of what is observed during NREM sleep (Weyand et al., 2000). Ach affects neurotransmitter release and synaptic strength in intracortical and thalamocortical synapses (Favero et al., 2012), essential to bottom-up (subcortical-to-cortical) and top-down (cortical-to-subcortical) attentional regulation during awake behaviours (Varela, 2013).

Similar to BF cholinergic neurons, the firing of brainstem LDT/PPT cholinergic neurons is phase-advanced to a cortical "asynchronous" state (El Mansari et al., 1989; Kayama et al., 1992). *In vivo* electrical stimulation of brainstem areas containing cholinergic neurons enhanced 20–40 Hz oscillations (beta-/gamma-frequency band) in TC circuits and cortical EEGs, similar to what was observed during periods of heightened vigilance (Steriade et al., 1991). It has been hypothesized that UP/DOWN states during NREM sleep may be mainly caused by increased activity of leak K^+ channels brought about by decreased brainstem cholinergic activity (McCormick et al., 2015; McCormick & Prince, 1986). Importantly, activation of cholinergic cells from the LDT/PPT correlates with the onset of REM sleep, besides wakefulness (Boucetta et al., 2014). Notably, neurons from the midline and sensory thalamus (CMT and AD) show the highest discharge rates during REM sleep, and this may be due to the strong cholinergic tone in the medio-dorsal thalamus during this sleep state (Gent, Bassetti, et al., 2018; Steriade et al., 1990), although this remains to be confirmed.

In summary, the release of Ach from the ventral BF and dorsal LDT/PPT pathway correlates with high-frequency oscillations in the cortex, similar to those observed during wakefulness or REM sleep. Both this REM sleep-specific mechanism and the hypothesis that Ach absence is permissive to TC slow oscillations during NREM sleep await confirmation. Novel imaging tools, including cholinergic G-protein–coupled receptor (GPCR)-based neurotransmitter fluorescent sensors (Jing et al., 2020), will further address fundamental biological questions on neuromodulation during sleep in the future.

Noradrenergic system. The locus coeruleus (LC) is the primary source of norepinephrine (NE) in the brain (Aston-Jones & Cohen, 2005). Activation of NE neurons and the release of NE signal arousal and increased attention during multiple behaviours, including flight-or-fight responses, the increased arousal associated with stress conditions, and the maintenance of muscle tone during wakefulness, whereas they are silent during REM sleep. During NREM sleep, LC^{NE} neurons are phase-locked to cortical UP states, suggesting that they contribute to the rising phase of the EEG slow wave by providing a neuromodulatory input that increases cortical excitability (Eschenko et al., 2012).

LC^{NE} neurons send projections throughout the brain, including the dorsal thalamus (Jones & Yang, 1985) that is involved in slow-oscillation generation and sleep–wake control (Gent, Bassetti, et al., 2018). The release of NE in thalamic neurons induces an increase in membrane conductance, resulting from an enhancement of hyperpolarization-activated cation currents (I_h) (Pape & McCormick, 1989). Enhancement of I_h current by β-adrenoceptors decreases responses to hyperpolarizing stimuli, resulting in a subsequent dampening of bursting activity and a facilitation of tonic firing. In addition, activation of α-adrenoceptors by NE release also reduces the resting potassium conductance, producing pronounced slow depolarization (McCormick & Pape, 1990). These changes ultimately promote tonic firing of thalamic cells that is similar to the activity observed during increased cortical activity and responsiveness in awake, behaving animals (McBride & Sutin, 1976; McCormick et al., 1991). Besides these well-characterized excitatory potentials, evidence from in vivo multi-channel recording in awake rats reported inhibitory responses during sensory stimulations because 20–40% of cells showed a suppression of their response, likely resulting from LC modulation of inhibitory neurons (Moxon et al., 2007) (Devilbiss & Waterhouse, 2011). In particular, phasic electrical stimulation of the LC^{NE} neurons, concomitant to salient polymodal sensory stimulation, had a facilitating effect in some neurons that otherwise would not have responded in the absence of LC stimulation (Devilbiss & Waterhouse, 2011). Similarly, LC stimulation enhanced neuronal synchronization in the sensory thalamus, with potential implications for temporal action-potential summation at the cortical level (Devilbiss & Waterhouse, 2011), and reduced burst firing, possibly through a synergistic activation of α-adrenergic receptors and modulation of T-type calcium channels in the thalamus (Rodenkirch et al., 2019). Additional modulation of synaptic plasticity in thalamic circuits has been linked to NE release and the activation of NE receptors (see earlier discussion). β-Adrenoceptors have also been shown to participate in mechanisms of long-term potentiation (Hopkins & Johnston, 1984; Stanton & Sarvey, 1985). Furthermore, noradrenaline changes the synaptic strength of intracortical and thalamocortical synapses *in vitro* (Favero et al., 2012). In this study, noradrenaline facilitated thalamocortical, relative to intracortical, transmission to the input layers of the cortex, a result that has implications for the routing of external versus internal information during sleep (Varela, 2013). Thus, in addition to promoting wakefulness, NE possibly contributes to the brain plasticity required for memory formation during wakefulness and NREM sleep (Totah et al., 2019).

Serotoninergic system. Dorsal and median raphe neurons are modulatory cells located in the brainstem producing serotonin (5-HT) and co-releasing GABA or glutamate neurotransmitters (De-miguel et al., 2015). It is now well established that the serotonergic system has an important role in maintaining arousal, suppressing REM sleep (Portas et al., 2000), and responding to stress, all of which are implicated in some aspects of stress-related disorders and associated sleep perturbances (Portas et al., 2000). Although the precise mechanisms of 5-HT control of the sleep–wake transition remain unclear, it has been shown that dorsal raphe neurons project to several regions, including the cerebral cortex, basal forebrain, amygdala, hypothalamus, LC, pontine reticular formation, and thalamus, where it can act on sleep- or wake-promoting cells (Abrams et al., 2004; Clark et al., 2006; Gazea et al., 2021). In the thalamus, 5-HT release onto midline and intralaminar thalamic neurons resulted in very heterogeneous modifications of membrane potential, depending on the post-synaptic thalamic cell types and the receptors involved. In brain slices, 5-HT induced a direct depolarization of lateral geniculate neurons and first-order thalamic relay neurons via a 5-HT7 receptor-mediated modulation of hyperpolarization-activated cation conductance (Chapin & Andrade, 2001). The majority of higher-order thalamic neurons are depolarized in response to 5-HT release (McCormick & Pape, 1990; Pape & McCormick, 1989); however, 15% of higher-order thalamic relay cells showed a hyperpolarization upon 5-HT bath application (Varela & Sherman, 2009). When compared in the same preparation, the depolarization is much stronger in higher-order thalamic regions as compared to first-order regions (Varela & Sherman, 2009), consistent with the higher density of serotonergic innervation and a possible local control of sleep oscillations. Further investigation of this strong heterogeneity of response to 5-HT neuromodulation is warranted to better understand the underlying synaptic mechanisms involved and the relevance to neuromodulation during sleep and sleep-dependent functions.

In summary, a common mechanism of action of ACh, noradrenaline (NA), and 5-HT neuromodulators involves a depolarizing shift of the membrane potential of TC relay neurons, leading to a cessation of rhythmic bursts and the occurrence of tonic spiking activity, which ultimately enhances information transfer from the thalamus to the cortex and hence sensory-motor processing as well as attention (Figure 4). In addition to this canonical "burst-tonic" switch, a significant portion of thalamic neurons showed different, sometimes opposite responses, possibly relevant to the "local" nature of sleep oscillations and sleep function, that emphasize the need for a better understanding of the subpopulations amongst defined anatomical nuclei of the thalamus (Phillips et al., 2019).

5. The Thalamus and Brain Plasticity during Sleep

The thalamus plays a crucial role in generating and modulating a large spectrum of oscillations across sleep–wake states, ranging from states of low vigilance to progressively large-amplitude low-frequency waves and deeper stages of NREM sleep. Far from being an epiphenomenon of intrinsic membrane properties or synaptic operations within cortical and thalamic networks, sleep oscillations are thought to lead to the synaptic plasticity essential for sleep-dependent consolidation, or weakening, of previously acquired information (Puentes-Mestril & Aton, 2017; Tononi & Cirelli, 2014).

Unlike the cerebral cortex, where synaptic plasticity mainly occurs through Hebbian plasticity, thalamic circuits appear to follow alternative plasticity rules. Hebb's neurophysiological postulate for plasticity proposes that the strength of synapses is enhanced if the use of those synapses is associated with the nearly simultaneous occurrence of postsynaptic spiking (Hebb, 1949). Hence, Hebbian plasticity requires a temporal association between pre- and postsynaptic compartments. Compelling evidence identified back-propagating action potentials (bAPs) as potential electrophysiological mechanisms responsible for postsynaptic activation of Hebbian synapses in several brain areas, including the cortex and hippocampus (Larkum, 2013). However, the weak bAPs

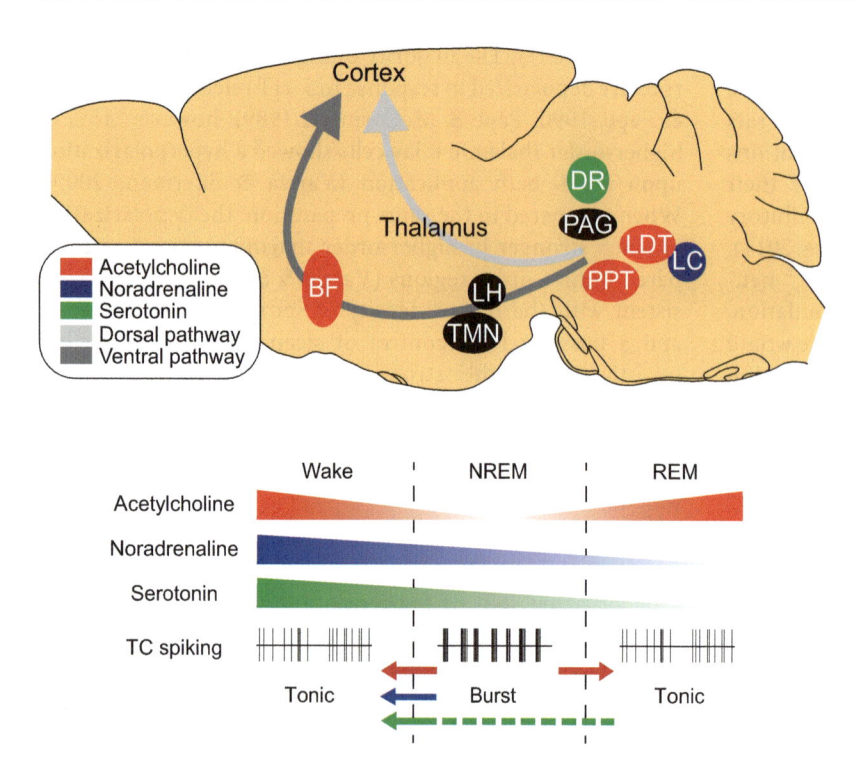

Figure 4 Neuromodulation of thalamic activity across sleep–wake states.

Top: Schematic representation of the ARAS, encompassing dorsal (*light-grey arrow*) and ventral (*dark-grey arrow*) pathways. Dorsal pathway: Projections from the pedunculopontine and laterodorsal tegmental nuclei (PPT/LDT) innervate the midline and intralaminar thalamocortical neurons. Ventral pathway: Projections from the locus coeruleus (LC) and the dorsal raphe (DR) project to the cortex, crossing the periacqueductal grey (PAG), the lateral hypothalamus (LH), the tuberomammillary nucleus (TMN), and the basal forebrain (BF). Cholinergic structures are represented in red, noradrenergic structures in blue, and serotoninergic structures in green. Bottom: Neuromodulatory activity during sleep–wake cycles. Ach levels are high during wakefulness and REM sleep, whereas NA and 5-HT levels are high during wakefulness, lower during NREM sleep, and lowest during REM sleep. A common mechanism of action of ACh, NA, and 5-HT neuromodulators involves a depolarizing shift of the membrane potential of TC relay neurons, leading to a cessation of rhythmic bursts and the occurrence of tonic spiking activity, which ultimately enhances information transfer from the thalamus to the cortex.

observed in thalamic neurons may not efficiently depolarize the dendritic arbour (Crandall et al., 2010; Errington et al., 2010) and are unlikely to represent a major mechanism for synaptic plasticity in thalamic circuits. Instead, TC and RTN neurons bear the common electrophysiological feature of rhythmic action-potential bursts driven by voltage-dependent Ca^{2+} spikes across low-vigilance-state oscillations (Crunelli et al., 2018). During slow-wave activity, spindles, and delta oscillations, both TC and TRN neurons elicit very high intra-burst frequencies (100–500 Hz), during which Ca^{2+} spikes rely upon the opening of low-voltage-gated T-type Ca^{2+} channels (T-VGCCs), commonly defined as low-threshold spikes (LTSs) (Deschfines et al., 1984; Llinás & Steriade, 2006). T-VGCCs are inactivated when membrane potentials are depolarized (above −60 to −65 mV), and neurons respond to excitatory postsynaptic potentials (EPSPs) with a volley of tonic activity. When T-VGCCs are de-inactivated—for example, after membrane hyperpolarization due to decreased excitability or increased inhibition—thalamic neurons respond to large EPSPs with a LTS, generally co-occuring with a burst of several spikes. During alpha waves of quiet wakefulness or theta waves of light NREM sleep, such burst activity displays remarkably lower frequency (50–70 Hz) and is generated by high-threshold Ca^{2+} spikes that rely upon the opening of T-VGCCs and high-voltage-gated L-type Ca^{2+} channels (L-VGCCs). This global and considerable depolarization provided by the low-threshold Ca^{2+} spikes represents a major candidate for thalamic plasticity during sleep stages (Astori & Lüthi, 2013; Sieber et al., 2013). Whether this mechanism is occurring during states of high attention remains unclear.

It is reasonable to hypothesize that the aforementioned plastic mechanisms can be functionally operational at two different circuit levels. *Firstly*, they may strongly contribute to local intra-thalamic synaptic homeostasis. One hypothesis, known as the *synaptic homeostasis hypothesis* (SHY; Tononi & Cirelli, 2014) proposes that during sleep, homeostatic control of synaptic strengths increase the signal-to-noise ratio, and eventually results in a downscaling of the strength of particular synapses while preserving increased strength at synapses that had been strongly activated by novel information acquired during wakefulness (Tononi & Cirelli, 2014). In agreement with this view, and similar to cortical regions, continuous peripheral inputs to thalamic nuclei during wakefulness induce synaptic modifications that require subsequent rescaling during periods of sleep. The previously described forms of thalamic plasticity associated with oscillatory activity during NREM sleep may subserve this purpose.

Second, this form of plasticity associated with oscillatory activity is also operating as a bottom-up control of cortical circuits. Experimental data suggested that changes in response to sensory inputs occur immediately at the thalamic level but not the cortical level, and subsequent NREM oscillations are necessary to induce cortical response plasticity (Durkin et al., 2017). Consistent with these findings, coherent oscillations of TC circuits during NREM sleep predicted the extent of memory consolidation (Aton et al., 2014). Other studies proposed that the transmission of information in TC networks during active states occurs in a linear fashion and that waking is dominated by steady-states dynamics, relatively low in amplitude but highly reliable, that did not undergo strong plastic changes (Timofeev & Chauvette,

2017). Conversely, synchronous DOWN states during sleep may abolish wake-related steady-state synaptic plasticity and increase overall synaptic responsiveness. Indeed, prethalamic stimulation-evoked cortical responses during the wake state are enhanced after a NREM sleep episode, compared to the previous wake episode (Chauvette et al., 2012). This enhancement is shown to be calcium-dependent (LTS described previously) and required the co-activation of both α-amino-3-hydroxy-5-methyl-4-isoxazolepropionic acid (AMPA) and N-methyl-D-aspartate (NMDA) receptors, suggesting that long-term potentiation occurs during sleep, requiring coordinated oscillatory activity between the thalamus and the cortex.

In conclusion, experimental evidence strongly suggests that TC oscillations during sleep support the modification of synaptic strength—both upscaling and downscaling—at excitatory and inhibitory synapses within thalamic and cortical neuronal ensembles, presumably in a region- or circuit-specific manner.

6. Thalamus in Disorders of Sleep

Given the brain-wide origin of sleep, it is therefore not surprising that disorders of sleep and consciousness include multiple symptoms, such as state instability, excessive daytime sleepiness, insomnia, cataplexy, night terrors, sleepwalking, and other parasomnias, most of which may implicate multiple neuronal populations.

An essential feature of TC neurons is their ability to switch between an intrinsic burst state (e.g., oscillatory activity) and a tonic state. In the latter state, TC neurons transfer information received from spike trains encoding peripheral stimuli to the cortex. In contrast, when TC neurons switch to a bursting/oscillatory mode, both thalamic and cortical neurons show a high level of synchronization that may induce a disconnection of the brain from the external world (i.e., environmental stimuli). Fine-tuning of TC-circuit activity is key for proper brain physiology, information processing, and sleep–wake states. It is therefore not surprising that subtle alterations of the molecular properties of TC neurons lead to dysregulated dynamics and pathological states, including arousal disturbances, hypersomnolence, cognitive impairments, and disorders of consciousness. In humans, sleep–wake disorders are frequent after thalamic brain damage (Lugaresi et al., 1986). Similar to rodents, human subjects with dorso-medial thalamic damage display decreased spindles, NREM (N3) sleep, and REM sleep. An interesting example is the syndrome of fatal familial insomnia (FFI) (Lugaresi et al., 1986) associated with neuronal loss in the anterior and dorsomedial nuclei of the thalamus and a clinical hypo-vigilance and attention deficit, inability to generate EEG sleep patterns, sympathetic hyperactivity, and attenuation of vegetative and hormonal circadian oscillations. Similar to patients with FFI, approximately 60–70% of stroke cases exhibit sleep disturbances (Bassetti, 2005). Paramedian thalamic stroke (PTS) causes hypersomnia with excessive daytime sleepiness and/or prolonged sleep. Recent findings attribute the pathological sleep signs of PTS to the lack of ascending noradrenergic and dopaminergic inputs to the thalamus, thus resulting in decreased arousal episodes (Bassetti et al., 1996). Interestingly, subjects with FFI and bilateral PTS display a bilateral decrease of sleep spindle density (Guilleminault et al., 1993; Lugaresi et al., 1986), although unilateral thalamic lesions also produced a bilateral, rather than an ipsilateral, decrease of spindles (Santamaria et al., 2000). A possible explanation is that the thalamic lesions could induce a non-specific dysfunction of the brainstem and result in an inefficient modulation of the RTN, thus producing a bilateral reduction of sleep spindles. Clinical evidence highlighted the thalamus as a prominent gate for consciousness (Alkire et al., 2008; Brown et al., 2018), where effective communication between cortical areas requires functional thalamic relays (Tononi et al., 2016). Accordingly, thalamic lesions are thought to lead to a functional disconnection, despite obvious cortical activity, as evidenced by neuroimaging studies (White & Alkire, 2003).

The thalamus is also implicated in the physiopathology of neuropsychiatric disorders, including schizophrenia (SZ). Subjects with SZ show typical sleep disturbances, with difficulty initiating and maintaining sleep states (Benson, 2015) and altered circadian rhythms (Manoach et al., 2016). Their scalp EEGs revealed a reduction of sleep spindle density that is considered as a biomarker, and potential target, for future therapies (Ferrarelli & Tononi, 2017). Reduced spindle activity is considered as an endophenotype that contributes to reduced sleep-dependent memory consolidation despite normal learning (Manoach et al., 2010; Wamsley et al., 2012). Others SZ deficits include impairments in sensory gating, attention, and cortical gamma oscillations during wakefulness, all of which may result from abnormal activity of the RTN, amongst other possible pathways.

Taken together, these studies demonstrated the importance of the thalamus in the control and maintenance of physiological sleep states and sleep-related functions; thalamic deficits or lesions of various extents can lead to severe pathological consequences. In this context, a better understanding of the anatomical and functional parcellation of the thalamus and its connectivity with cortical and subcortical circuits will undoubtedly open new paths of investigation to better understand its functional implication in sleep and higher-brain functions and lead to the discovery of novel therapeutic strategies.

Concluding Remarks

The thalamus plays a key role in controlling brain oscillations, attention, and consciousness. Nonetheless, the thalamus has not traditionally been considered to be an important node in the brain mechanism controlling sleep–wake states. This chapter provided an overview of compelling data supporting the idea that the thalamus represents a hub that integrates sleep–wake inputs from both subcortical and cortical origin into stable sleep–wake states through topographically distinct subcortical inputs and temporally precise circuit dynamics.

The oscillatory rhythms generated by TC networks and sub-cortical modulation are a driving force essential for the onset and maintenance of sleep and, presumably, sleep-dependent functions. Absent or reduced physiological thalamic activity during sleep results in inadequate protection of NREM sleep and impaired sleep maintenance, as evidenced in sleep-related disorders. Far from being an end in itself, this chapter discussed the implications of TC oscillations in memory consolidation and synaptic homeostasis during NREM-sleep TC rhythms in regard to their possible support in information transfer, and long-term storage, between cortical networks.

Acknowledgements

We thank all members of the Adamantidis Lab for helpful discussions. Antoine R. Adamantidis was supported by the Human Frontier Science Program (RGY0076/2012), the Inselspital University Hospital of Bern, the Swiss National Science Foundation (31003A_156156), the European Research Council (725850), Sinergia (CRSII3_160803), the University of Bern, and the Bern University Hospital.

References

Abrams, J. K., Johnson, P. L., Hollis, J. H., & Lowry, C. A. (2004). Anatomic and functional topography of the dorsal raphe nucleus. *Annals of the New York Academy of Sciences*, 1018, 46–57. https://doi.org/10.1196/annals.1296.005

Adamantidis, A. R., Gutierrez Herrera, C., & Gent, T. C. (2019). Oscillating circuitries in the sleeping brain. *Nature Reviews Neuroscience*, 20(12), 746–762. https://doi.org/10.1038/s41583-019-0223-4

Alkire, M., Hudetz, A., & Tononi, G. (2008). Consciousness and anesthesia. *Science*, 322(November), 139–152. https://doi.org/10.1016/B978-0-12-800948-2.00009-1

Alkire, M. T., Asher, C. D., Franciscus, A. M., & Hahn, E. L. (2009). Thalamic microinfusion of antibody to a voltage-gated potassium channel restores consciousness during anesthesia. *Anesthesiology*, 110(4), 766–773. https://doi.org/10.1097/ALN.0b013e31819c461c

Alkire, M. T., McReynolds, J. R., Hahn, E. L., & Trivedi, A. N. (2007). Thalamic microinjection of nicotine reverses sevoflurane-induced loss of righting reflex in the rat. *Anesthesiology*, 107(2), 264–272. https://doi.org/10.1097/01.anes.0000270741.33766.24

Anaclet, C., Griffith, K., & Fuller, P. M. (2018). Activation of the GABAergic parafacial zone maintains sleep and counteracts the wake-promoting action of the psychostimulants armodafinil and caffeine. *Neuropsychopharmacology*, 43(2), 415–425. https://doi.org/10.1038/npp.2017.152

Anaclet, C., Pedersen, N. P., Ferrari, L. L., Venner, A., Bass, C. E., Arrigoni, E., & Fuller, P. M. (2015). Basal forebrain control of wakefulness and cortical rhythms. *Nature Communications*, 6, 1–14. https://doi.org/10.1038/ncomms9744

Anafi, R. C., Kayser, M. S., & Raizen, D. M. (2019). Exploring phylogeny to find the function of sleep. *Nature Reviews Neuroscience*, 20(2), 109–116. https://doi.org/10.1038/s41583-018-0098-9

Anderson, M. P., Mochizuki, T., Xie, J., Fischler, W., Manger, J. P., Talley, E. M., Scammell, T. E., & Tonegawa, S. (2005). Thalamic Cav3.1 T-type Ca^{2+} channel plays a crucial role in stabilizing sleep. *Proceedings of the National Academy of Sciences of the United States of America*, 102(5), 1743–1748.

Aston-Jones, G., & Cohen, J. D. (2005). An integrative theory of locus coeruleus-norepinephrine function: adaptive gain and optimal performance. *Annual Review of Neuroscience*, 28(1), 403–450. https://doi.org/10.1146/annurev.neuro.28.061604.135709

Astori, S., & Lüthi, A. (2013). Synaptic plasticity at intrathalamic connections via CaV3.3 T-type Ca^{2+} channels and GluN2B-containing NMDA receptors. *Journal of Neuroscience*, 33(2), 624–630. https://doi.org/10.1523/JNEUROSCI.3185-12.2013

Astori, S., Wimmer, R. D., Prosser, H. M., Corti, C., Corsi, M., & Liaudet, N. (2011). The CaV3.3 calcium channel is the major sleep spindle pacemaker in thalamus. *Proceedings of the National Academy of Sciences of the United States of America*, 108(33), 13823–13828. https://doi.org/10.1073/pnas.1105115108

Aton, S. J., Suresh, A., Broussard, C., & Frank, M. G. (2014). Sleep promotes cortical response potentiation following visual experience. *Sleep*, 37(7), 1163–1170. https://doi.org/10.5665/sleep.3830

Baker, A. P., Brookes, M. J., Rezek, I. A., Smith, S. M., Behrens, T., Smith, P. J. P., & Woolrich, M. (2014). Fast transient networks in spontaneous human brain activity. *eLife*, 2014(3), 1–18. https://doi.org/10.7554/eLife.01867

Bal, T., von Krosigk, M., & McCormick, D. A. (1995). Role of the ferret perigeniculate nucleus in the generation of synchronized oscillations in vitro. *Journal of Physiology*, 483(3), 665–685. https://doi.org/10.1113/jphysiol.1995.sp020613

Bandarabadi, M., Boyce, R., Herrera, C. G., Bassetti, C. L., Williams, S., Schindler, K., & Adamantidis, A. (2019). Dynamic modulation of theta-gamma coupling during rapid eye movement sleep. *Sleep*, 42(12), 1–11. https://doi.org/10.1093/sleep/zsz182

Bandarabadi, M., Herrera, C. G., Gent, T. C., Bassetti, C., Schindler, K., & Adamantidis, A. R. (2020). A role for spindles in the onset of rapid eye movement sleep. *Nature Communications*, 11(5247). https://doi.org/10.1038/s41467-020-19076-2

Bassetti, C. L. (2005). Sleep and stroke. *Seminars in Neurology*, 25. https://doi.org/10.1016/B978-0-12-804074-4.00006-6

Bassetti, C., Mathis, J., Gugger, M., Lovblad, K., & Hess, C. W. (1996). Hypersomnia following paramedian thalamic stroke: a report of 12 patients. *Annals of Neurology*, 39, 471–480.

Benson, K. L. (2015). Sleep in schizophrenia: pathology and treatment. *Sleep Medicine Clinics*, 10(1), 49–55. https://doi.org/10.1016/j.jsmc.2014.11.001

Bergel, A., Deffieux, T., Demené, C., Tanter, M., & Cohen, I. (2018). Local hippocampal fast gamma rhythms precede brain-wide hyperemic patterns during spontaneous rodent REM sleep. *Nature Communications*, 9(1). https://doi.org/10.1038/s41467-018-07752-3

Blethyn, K. L., Hughes, S. W., Tóth, T. I., Cope, D. W., & Crunelli, V. (2006). Neuronal basis of the slow (< Hz) oscillation in neurons of the nucleus reticularis thalami in vitro. *Journal of Neuroscience*, 26(9), 2474–2486. https://doi.org/10.1523/JNEUROSCI.3607-05.2006

Bonjean, M., Baker, T., Lemieux, M., Timofeev, I., Sejnowski, T., & Bazhenov, M. (2011). Corticothalamic feedback controls sleep spindle duration in vivo. *Journal of Neuroscience*, 31(25), 9124–9134. https://doi.org/10.1523/JNEUROSCI.0077-11.2011

Boucetta, S., Cisse, Y., Mainville, L., Morales, M., & Jones, B. E. (2014). Discharge profiles across the sleep–waking cycle of identified cholinergic, GABAergic, and glutamatergic neurons in the pontomesencephalic tegmentum of the rat. *Journal of Neuroscience*, 34(13), 4708–4727. https://doi.org/10.1523/JNEUROSCI.2617-13.2014

Broicher, T., Wettschureck, N., Munsch, T., Coulon, P., Meuth, S. G., Kanyshkova, T., Seidenbecher, T., Offermanns, S., Pape, H. C., & Budde, T. (2008). Muscarinic ACh receptor-mediated control of thalamic activity via G q/G11-family G-proteins. *Pflugers Archive European Journal of Physiology*, **456**(6), 1049–1060. https://doi.org/10.1007/s00424-008-0473-x

Brown, E. N., Lydic, R., & Schiff, N. D. (2018). General anesthesia, sleep, and coma. *New England Journal of Medicine*, **363**(27), 2638–2650. https://doi.org/10.1001/jama.306.20.2283

Campbell, S. S., & Tobler, I. (1984). Animal sleep: a review of sleep duration across phylogeny. *Neuroscience and Biobehavioral Reviews*, **8**(3), 269–300. https://doi.org/10.1016/0149-7634(84)90054-X

Chapin, E. M., & Andrade, R. (2001). A 5-HT7 receptor-mediated depolarization in the anterodorsal thalamus. II. Involvement of the hyperpolarization-activated current Ih. *Journal of Pharmacology and Experimental Therapeutics*, **297**(1), 403–409.

Chauvette, S., Seigneur, J., & Timofeev, I. (2012). Sleep Oscillations in the thalamocortical system induce long-term neuronal plasticity. *Neuron*, **75**(6), 1105–1113. https://doi.org/10.1016/j.neuron.2012.08.034

Chen, K. S., Xu, M., Zhang, Z., Chang, W. C., Gaj, T., Schaffer, D. V., & Dan, Y. (2018). A hypothalamic switch for REM and non-REM sleep. *Neuron*, **97**(5), 1168–1176.e4. https://doi.org/10.1016/j.neuron.2018.02.005

Chung, S., Weber, F., Zhong, P., Tan, C. L., Nguyen, T. N., Beier, K. T., Hörmann, N., Chang, W. C., Zhang, Z., Do, J. P., Yao, S., Krashes, M. J., Tasic, B., Cetin, A., Zeng, H., Knight, Z. A., Luo, L., & Dan, Y. (2017). Identification of preoptic sleep neurons using retrograde labelling and gene profiling. *Nature*, **545**(7655), 477–481. https://doi.org/10.1038/nature22350

Churgin, M. A., Szuperak, M., Davis, K. C., Raizen, D. M., Fang-Yen, C., & Kayser, M. S. (2019). Quantitative imaging of sleep behavior in *Caenorhabditis elegans* and larval *Drosophila melanogaster*. *Nature Protocols*, **14**(5), 1555–1588. https://doi.org/10.1038/s41596-019-0146-6

Clark, M., McDevitt, R., & Neumaier, J. (2006). Quantitative mapping of tryptophan hydroxylase-2, 5-HT1A, 5-HT1B, and serotonin transporter expression across the anteroposterior axis of the rat dorsal and median raphe nuclei. *Journal of Comparative Neurology*, **498**(5), 611–623. https://doi.org/10.1002/cne

Colangelo, C., Shichkova, P., Keller, D., & Markram, H. (2019). Cellular, synaptic and network effects of acetylcholine in the neocortex. *Frontiers in Neural Circuits*, **13**, 24. https://doi.org/10.3389/fncir.2019.00024

Contreras, D., Dossi, R. C., & Steriade, M. (1992). Bursting and tonic discharges in two classes of reticular thalamic neurons. *Journal of Neurophysiology*, **68**(3), 973–977. https://doi.org/10.1152/jn.1992.68.3.973

Crandall, S. R., Govindaiah, G., & Cox, C. L. (2010). Low-threshold Ca^{2+} current amplifies distal dendritic signaling in thalamic reticular neurons. *Journal of Neuroscience*, **30**(46), 15419–15429. https://doi.org/10.1523/JNEUROSCI.3636-10.2010

Crunelli, V., & Hughes, S. W. (2010). The slow (1 Hz) rhythm of non-REM sleep: a dialogue between three cardinal oscillators. *Nature Neuroscience*, **13**(1), 9–17. https://doi.org/10.1038/nn.2445

Crunelli, V., Larincz, M. L., Connelly, W. M., David, F., Hughes, S. W., Lambert, R. C., Leresche, N., & Errington, A. C. (2018). Dual function of thalamic low-vigilance state oscillations: rhythm-regulation and plasticity. *Nature Reviews Neuroscience*, **19**(2), 107–118. https://doi.org/10.1038/nrn.2017.151

Cueni, L., Canepari, M., Lujan, R., Emmenegger, Y., Watanabe, M., Bond, C. T., Franken, P., Adelman, J. P., & Luthi, A. (2008). T-type Ca^{2+} channels, SK2 channels and SERCAs gate sleep-related oscillations in thalamic dendrites. *Nature Neuroscience*, **11**(6), 683–692. https://doi.org/10.1038/nn.2124

Currò Dossi, R., Pare, D., & Steriade, M. (1991). Short-lasting nicotinic and long-lasting muscarinic depolarizing responses of thalamocortical neurons to stimulation of mesopontine cholinergic nuclei. *Journal of Neurophysiology*, **65**(3), 393–406. https://doi.org/10.1152/jn.1991.65.3.393

Dahan, L., Astier, B., Vautrelle, N., Urbain, N., Kocsis, B., & Chouvet, G. (2007). Prominent burst firing of dopaminergic neurons in the ventral tegmental area during paradoxical sleep. *Neuropsychopharmacology*, **32**, 1232–1241. https://doi.org/10.1038/sj.npp.1301251

Dang-vu, T. T., Buxton, O. M., & Solet, J. M. (2010). Spontaneous brain rhythms predict sleep stability in the face of noise. *Current Biology*, **20**(15), 626–627. https://doi.org/10.1016/j.cub.2010.06.032

David, F., Schmiedt, J. T., Taylor, H. L., Orban, G., Di Giovanni, G., Uebele, V. N., Renger, J. J., Lambert, R. C., Leresche, N., & Crunelli, V. (2013). Essential thalamic contribution to slow waves of natural sleep. *Journal of Neuroscience*, **33**(50), 19599–19610. https://doi.org/10.1523/JNEUROSCI.3169-13.2013

De-miguel, F. F., Leon-pinzon, C., Noguez, P., & Mendez, B. (2015). Serotonin release from the neuronal cell body and its long-lasting effects on the nervous system. *Philosophical Transactions of the Royal Society B*, **370**(1672).

Deschfines, M., Paradis, M., Roy, J. P., & Steriade, M. (1984). Electrophysiology of neurons of lateral thalamic nuclei in cat: resting properties and burst discharges. *Journal of Neurophysiology*, **51**(6), 1196–1219.

Destexhe, A., Hughes, S. W., Rudolph, M., & Crunelli, V. (2007). Are corticothalamic "up" states fragments of wakefulness? *Trends in Neurosciences*, **30**(7), 334–342. https://doi.org/10.1016/j.tins.2007.04.006

Devilbiss, D. M., & Waterhouse, B. D. (2011). Phasic and tonic patterns of locus coeruleus output differentially modulate sensory network function in the awake rat. *Journal of Neurophysiology*, **105**(1), 69–87. https://doi.org/10.1152/jn.00445.2010

Durkin, J., Suresh, A. K., Colbath, J., Broussard, C., Wu, J., Zochowski, M., & Aton, S. J. (2017). Cortically coordinated NREM thalamocortical oscillations play an essential, instructive role in visual system plasticity. *Proceedings of the National Academy of Sciences of the United States of America*, **114**(39), 10485–10490. https://doi.org/10.1073/pnas.1710613114

Eban-Rothschild, A., Rothschild, G., Giardino, W. J., Jones, J. R., & De Lecea, L. (2016). VTA dopaminergic neurons regulate ethologically relevant sleep-wake behaviors. *Nature Neuroscience*, **19**(10), 1356–1366. https://doi.org/10.1038/nn.4377

Economo, M. N., Viswanathan, S., Tasic, B., Bas, E., Winnubst, J., Menon, V., Graybuck, L. T., Nguyen, T. N., Smith, K. A., Yao, Z., Wang, L., Gerfen, C. R., Chandrashekar, J., Zeng, H., Looger, L. L., & Svoboda, K. (2018). Distinct descending motor cortex pathways and their roles in movement. *Nature*, **563**(7729), 79–84. https://doi.org/10.1038/s41586-018-0642-9

El Mansari, M., Sakai, K., & Jouvet, M. (1989). Unitary characteristics of presumptive cholinergic tegmental neurons during the sleep-waking cycle in freely moving cats. *Experimental Brain Research*, **76**(3), 519–529. https://doi.org/10.1007/BF00248908

Errington, A. C., Renger, J. J., Uebele, V. N., & Crunelli, V. (2010). State-dependent firing determines intrinsic dendritic Ca^{2+} signaling in thalamocortical neurons. *Journal of Neuroscience*, **30**(44), 14843–14853. https://doi.org/10.1523/JNEUROSCI.2968-10.2010

Eschenko, O., Magri, C., Panzeri, S., & Sara, S. J. (2012). Noradrenergic neurons of the locus coeruleus are phase locked to cortical up-down states during sleep. *Cerebral Cortex*, **22**, 426–435. https://doi.org/10.1093/cercor/bhr121

Favero, M., Varghese, G., & Castro-Alamancos, M. A. (2012). The state of somatosensory cortex during neuromodulation. *Journal of Neurophysiology*, **108**(4), 1010–1024. https://doi.org/10.1152/jn.00256.2012

Fernandez, L. M. J., Vantomme, G., Osorio-Forero, A., Cardis, R., Béard, E., & Lüthi, A. (2018). Thalamic reticular control of local sleep in mouse sensory cortex. *eLife*, **7**, 1–25. https://doi.org/10.7554/eLife.39111

Ferrarelli, F., & Tononi, G. (2017). Reduced sleep spindle activity point to a TRN-MD thalamus-PFC circuit dysfunction in schizophrenia. *Schizophrenia Research*, **180**, 36–43. https://doi.org/10.1016/j.schres.2016.05.023

Fort, P., Bassetti, C. L., & Luppi, P. H. (2009). Alternating vigilance states: new insights regarding neuronal networks and mechanisms. *European Journal of Neuroscience*, **29**(9), 1741–1753. https://doi.org/10.1111/j.1460-9568.2009.06722.x

Francesconi, W., Muller, C. M., & Singer, W. (1988). Cholinergic mechanisms in the reticular control of transmission in the cat lateral geniculate nucleus. *Journal of Neurophysiology*, **59**(6), 1690–1718. https://doi.org/10.1152/jn.1988.59.6.1690

Fuller, P., Sherman, D., Pedersen, N. P., Saper, C. B., & Lu, J. (2011). Reassessment of the structural basis of the ascending arousal system. *Journal of Comparative Neurology*, **519**(5), 933–956. https://doi.org/10.1002/cne.22559

Gazea, M., Furdan, S., Sere, P., Oesch, L., Molnár, B., Giovanni, G. Di, Fenno, L. E., Ramakrishnan, C., Mattis, J., Deisseroth, K., Dymecki, S. M., Adamantidis, A. R., & Lőrincz, M. L. (2021). Reciprocal lateral hypothalamic and raphe GABAergic projections promote wakefulness. *Journal of Neuroscience*, **41**(22), 4840–4849. https://doi.org/10.1523/JNEUROSCI.2850-20.2021

Gent, T. C., Bandarabadi, M., Herrera, C. G., & Adamantidis, A. R. (2018). Thalamic dual control of sleep and wakefulness. *Nature Neuroscience*, **21**(7), 974–984. https://doi.org/10.1038/s41593-018-0164-7

Gent, T. C., Bassetti, C. L. A., & Adamantidis, A. R. (2018). Sleep-wake control and the thalamus. *Current Opinion in Neurobiology*, **52**, 188–197. https://doi.org/10.1016/j.conb.2018.08.002

Glin, L., Arnaud, C., Berracochea, D., Galey, D., Jaffard, R., & Gottesmann, C. (1991). The intermediate stage of sleep in mice. *Physiology and Behavior*, **50**(5), 951–953. https://doi.org/10.1016/0031-9384(91)90420-S

Guilleminault, C., Quera-salva, M. A., & Goldberg, M. P. (1993). Pseudo-hypersomnia and pre-sleep behaviour with bilateral paramedian thalamic lesions. *Brain*, **116**(6), 1549–1563. https://doi.org/10.1093/brain/116.6.1549

Halassa, M. M., & Kastner, S. (2017). Thalamic functions in distributed cognitive control. *Nature Neuroscience*, **20**(12), 1669–1679. https://doi.org/10.1038/s41593-017-0020-1

Halassa, M. M., Siegle, J. H., Ritt, J. T., Ting, J. T., Feng, G., & Moore, C. I. (2011). Selective optical drive of thalamic reticular nucleus generates thalamic bursts and cortical spindles. *Nature Neuroscience*, **14**(9), 1118–1120. https://doi.org/10.1038/nn.2880

Hassani, O. K., Henny, P., Lee, M. G., & Jones, B. E. (2010). GABAergic neurons intermingled with orexin and MCH neurons in the lateral hypothalamus discharge maximally during sleep. *European Journal of Neuroscience*, **32**(3), 448–457. https://doi.org/10.1111/j.1460-9568.2010.07295.x

Hassani, O. K., Lee, M. G., & Jones, B. E. (2009). Melanin-concentrating hormone neurons discharge in a reciprocal manner to orexin neurons across the sleep-wake cycle. *Proceedings of the National Academy of Sciences of the United States of America*, **106**(7), 2418–2422. https://doi.org/10.1073/pnas.0811400106

Hayashi, Y., Kashiwagi, M., Yasuda, K., Ando, R., Kanuka, M., Sakai, K., & Itohara, S. (2015). Cells of a common developmental origin regulate REM/non-REM sleep and wakefulness in mice. *Science*, **350**(6263), 957–962.

Hebb, D. O. (1949). *The organization of behavior: a neuropsychological theory.* New York: Wiley.

Helfrich, R. F., Lendner, J. D., Mander, B. A., Guillen, H., Paff, M., Mnatsakanyan, L., Vadera, S., Walker, M. P., Lin, J. J., & Knight, R. T. (2019). Bidirectional prefrontal-hippocampal dynamics organize information transfer during sleep in humans. *Nature Communications*, **10**(1), 1–16. https://doi.org/10.1038/s41467-019-11444-x

Hermann, D. M., Siccoli, M., Brugger, P., Wachter, K., Mathis, J., Achermann, P., & Bassetti, C. L. (2008). Evolution of neurological, neuropsychological and sleep-wake disturbances after paramedian thalamic stroke. *Stroke*, **39**(1), 62–68. https://doi.org/10.1161/STROKEAHA.107.494955

Herrera, C. G., Cadaviaco, M. C., Jego, S., Ponomarenko, A., Korotkova, T., & Adamantidis, A. (2016). Hypothalamic feedforward inhibition of thalamocortical network controls arousal and consciousness. *Nature Neuroscience*, **19**(2), 290–298. https://doi.org/10.1038/nn.4209

Hong, J., Ha, G. E., Kwak, H., Lee, Y., Jeong, H., Suh, P. G., & Cheong, E. (2020). Destabilization of light NREM sleep by thalamic PLCβ4 deletion impairs sleep-dependent memory consolidation. *Scientific Reports*, **10**(1), 1–14. https://doi.org/10.1038/s41598-020-64377-7

Honjoh, S., Sasai, S., Schiereck, S. S., Nagai, H., Tononi, G., & Cirelli, C. (2018). Regulation of cortical activity and arousal by the matrix cells of the ventromedial thalamic nucleus. *Nature Communications*, **9**(1). https://doi.org/10.1038/s41467-018-04497-x

Hopkins, W., & Johnston, D. (1984). Frequency-dependent noradrenergic modulation of long-term potentiation in the hippocampus abstract. *Science*, **226**(4672), 350–352.

Hubbard, J., Gent, T. C., Hoekstra, M. M. B., Emmenegger, Y., Mongrain, V., Landolt, H. P., Adamantidis, A. R., & Franken, P. (2020). Rapid fast-delta decay following prolonged wakefulness marks a phase of wake-inertia in NREM sleep. *Nature Communications*, **11**(1), 1–16. https://doi.org/10.1038/s41467-020-16915-0

Huber, R., Ghilardi, M. F., Massimini, M., & Tononi, G. (2004). Local sleep and learning. *Nature*, **430**(6995), 78–81. https://doi.org/10.1038/nature02663

Hughes, S. W., Cope, D. W., Blethyn, K. L., & Crunelli, V. (2002). Cellular mechanisms of the slow (< Hz) oscillation in thalamocortical neurons in vitro. *Neuron*, **33**(6), 947–958. https://doi.org/10.1016/S0896-6273(02)00623-2

Hughes, S. W., Lo, M., Cope, D. W., Blethyn, K. L., Ke, K. A., & Parri, H. R. (2004). Synchronized oscillations at α and θ frequencies in the lateral geniculate nucleus. *Neuron*, **42**, 253–268.

Jing, M., Li, Y., Zeng, J., Huang, P., Skirzewski, M., Kljakic, O., Peng, W., Qian, T., Tan, K., Zou, J., Trinh, S., Wu, R., Zhang, S., Pan, S., Hires, S. A., Xu, M., Li, H., Saksida, L. M., Prado, V. F., ... Li, Y. (2020). An optimized acetylcholine sensor for monitoring in vivo cholinergic activity. *Nature Methods*, **17**(11), 1139–1146. https://doi.org/10.1038/s41592-020-0953-2

Jones, B. E. (2005). From waking to sleeping: neuronal and chemical substrates. *Trends in Pharmacological Sciences*, **26**(11), 578–586. https://doi.org/10.1016/j.tips.2005.09.009

Jones, B. E., & Yang, T. -Z. (1985). The efferent projections from the reticular formation and the locus coeruleus studied by anterograde and retrograde axonal transport in the rat. *Journal of Comparative Neurology*, **242**(1), 56–92. https://doi.org/10.1002/cne.902420105

Jouvet, M., Michel, F., & Courjon, J. (1959). Sur un stade d'activité éléctrique cérébrale rapide au cours du sommeil physiologique. *Comptes Rendus des Seances de la Societe de Biologie et de Ses Filiales*, **153**, 1024–1028.

Kayama, Y., Ohta, M., & Jodo, E. (1992). Firing of "possibly" cholinergic neurons in the rat laterodorsal tegmental nucleus during sleep and wakefulness. *Brain Research*, **569**(2), 210–220. https://doi.org/10.1016/0006-8993(92)90632-J

Kayser, M. S., Yue, Z., & Sehgal, A. (2014). A critical period of sleep for development of courtship circuitry and behavior in *Drosophila*. *Science*, **344**(6181), 269–274. https://doi.org/10.1126/science.1250553

Kim, A., Latchoumane, C., Lee, S., Kim, G. B., Cheong, E., Augustine, G. J., & Shin, H. S. (2012). Optogenetically induced sleep spindle rhythms alter sleep architectures in mice. *Proceedings of the National Academy of Sciences of the United States of America*, **109**(50), 20673–20678. https://doi.org/10.1073/pnas.1217897109

Kirszenblat, L., & van Swinderen, B. (2015). The yin and yang of sleep and attention. *Trends in Neurosciences*, **38**(12), 776–786. https://doi.org/10.1016/j.tins.2015.10.001

Kocsis, B., Varga, V., Dahan, L., & Sik, A. (2006). Serotonergic neuron diversity: identification of raphe neurons with discharge time-locked to the hippocampal theta rhythm. *Proceedings of the National Academy of Sciences of the United States of America*, **103**(4), 1059–1064. https://doi.org/10.1073/pnas.0508360103

Kolmac, C., & Mitrofanis, J. (1999). Organization of the basal forebrain projection to the thalamus in rats. *Neuroscience Letters*, **272**(3), 151–154. https://doi.org/10.1016/S0304-3940(99)00614-X

Kroeger, D., Ferrari, L. L., Petit, G., Mahoney, C. E., Fuller, P. M., Arrigoni, E., & Scammell, T. E. (2017). Cholinergic, glutamatergic, and GABAergic neurons of the pedunculopontine tegmental nucleus have distinct effects on sleep/wake behavior in mice. *Journal of Neuroscience*, **37**(5), 1352–1366. https://doi.org/10.1523/JNEUROSCI.1405-16.2016

Krone, L. B., Yamagata, T., Blanco-duque, C., Guillaumin, M. C. C., Kahn, M. C., Vinne, V. Van Der, Mckillop, L. E., Tam, S. K. E., Peirson, S. N., Akerman, C. J., Hoerder-suabedissen, A., Molnár, Z., & Vyazovskiy, V. V. (2021). A role for the cortex in sleep–wake regulation. *Nature Neuroscience*, **24**(September). https://doi.org/10.1038/s41593-021-00894-6

Krueger, J. M., Nguyen, J. T., Dykstra-Aiello, C. J., & Taishi, P. (2019). Local sleep. *Sleep Medicine Reviews*, **43**, 14–21. https://doi.org/10.1016/j.smrv.2018.10.001

Krueger, J. M., & Tononi, G. (2012). Local use-dependent sleep; synthesis of the new paradigm. *Current Topics in Medicinal Chemistry*, **11**(19), 2490–2492. https://doi.org/10.2174/156802611797470330

Larkum, M. (2013). A cellular mechanism for cortical associations: an organizing principle for the cerebral cortex. *Trends in Neurosciences*, **36**(3), 141–151. https://doi.org/10.1016/j.tins.2012.11.006

Latchoumane, C. F. V., Ngo, H. V. V., Born, J., & Shin, H. S. (2017). Thalamic spindles promote memory formation during sleep through triple phase-locking of cortical, thalamic, and hippocampal rhythms. *Neuron*, **95**(2), 424–435.e6. https://doi.org/10.1016/j.neuron.2017.06.025

Lecci, S., Fernandez, L. M. J., Weber, F. D., Cardis, R., Chatton, J.-Y., Born, J., & Luthi, A. (2017). Coordinated infraslow neural and cardiac oscillations mark fragility and offline periods in mammalian sleep. *Science Advances*, **3**. https://doi.org/10.3389/fphys.2017.00847

Lee, J., Kim, D., & Shin, H. (2004). Lack of delta waves and sleep disturbances during non-rapid eye movement sleep in mice lacking α1 G-subunit of T-type calcium channels. *Proceedings of the National Academy of Sciences of the United States of America*, **101**(52), 18195–18199.

Lemieux, M., Chen, J. Y., Lonjers, P., Bazhenov, M., & Timofeev, I. (2014). The impact of cortical deafferentation on the neocortical slow oscillation. *Journal of Neuroscience*, **34**(16), 5689–5703. https://doi.org/10.1523/JNEUROSCI.1156-13.2014

Leung, L. C., Wang, G. X., Madelaine, R., Skariah, G., Kawakami, K., Deisseroth, K., Urban, A. E., & Mourrain, P. (2019). Neural signatures of sleep in zebrafish. *Nature*, **571**(7764), 198–204. https://doi.org/10.1038/s41586-019-1336-7

Lioudyno, M. I., Birch, A. M., Tanaka, B. S., Sokolov, Y., Goldin, A. L., Chandy, K. G., Hall, J. E., & Alkire, M. T. (2013). Shaker-related potassium channels in the central medial nucleus of the thalamus are important molecular targets for arousal suppression by volatile general anesthetics. *Journal of Neuroscience*, **33**(41), 16310–16322. https://doi.org/10.1523/JNEUROSCI.0344-13.2013

Liu, D., Li, W., Ma, C., Zheng, W., Yao, Y., Tso, C. F., Zhong, P., Chen, X., Song, J. H., Choi, W., Paik, S. B., Han, H., & Dan, Y. (2020). A common hub for sleep and motor control in the substantia nigra. *Science*, **367**(6476), 440–445. https://doi.org/10.1126/science.aaz0956

Liu, K., Kim, J., Kim, D. W., Zhang, Y. S., Bao, H., Denaxa, M., Lim, S. A., Kim, E., Liu, C., Wickersham, I. R., Pachinis, V., Hattar, S., Song, J., Brown, S. P., & Blackshaw, S. (2017). Lhx6-positive GABA-releasing neurons of the zona incerta promote sleep. *Nature*, **548**(7669), 582–587. https://doi.org/10.1038/nature23663

Llinás, R. R., & Steriade, M. (2006). Bursting of thalamic neurons and states of vigilance. *Journal of Neurophysiology*, **95**(6), 3297–3308. https://doi.org/10.1152/jn.00166.2006

Loomis, L. A., Newton, E. H., & Hobart, A. G. (1938). Distribution of disturbance-patterns in the human electroencephalogram, with special reference to sleep. *Journal of Neurophysiology*, **1**, 413–430.

Lőrincz, M. L., Gunner, D., Bao, Y., Connelly, W. M., Isaac, J. T. R., Hughes, S. W., & Crunelli, V. (2015). A distinct class of slow (~0.2–2 Hz) intrinsically bursting layer 5 pyramidal neurons determines UP/DOWN state dynamics in the neocortex. *Journal of Neuroscience*, **35**(14), 5442–5458. https://doi.org/10.1523/JNEUROSCI.3603-14.2015

Lugaresi, E., Medori, R., Montagna, P., Baruzzi, A., Cortelli, P., Lugaresi, A., Tinuper, P., Zucconi, M., & Gambetti, P. (1986). Fatal familial insomnia and dysautonomia with selective degeneration of thalamic nuclei. *New England Journal of Medicine*, **315**(16), 997–1003. https://doi.org/10.1056/NEJM198610163151605

Luo, Y. J., Li, Y. D., Wang, L., Yang, S. R., Yuan, X. S., Wang, J., Cherasse, Y., Lazarus, M., Chen, J. F., Qu, W. M., & Huang, Z. L. (2018). Nucleus accumbens controls wakefulness by a subpopulation of neurons expressing dopamine D1 receptors. *Nature Communications*, **9**(1). https://doi.org/10.1038/s41467-018-03889-3

Luppi, P. H., Peyron, C., & Fort, P. (2017). Not a single but multiple populations of GABAergic neurons control sleep. *Sleep Medicine Reviews*, **32**, 85–94. https://doi.org/10.1016/j.smrv.2016.03.002

Lüthi, A. (2014). Sleep spindles: where they come from, what they do. *Neuroscientist*, **20**

(3), 243–256. https://doi.org/10.1177/1073858413500854

Magnin, M., Bastuji, H., Garcia-Larrea, L., & Mauguière, F. (2004). Human thalamic medial pulvinar nucleus is not activated during paradoxical sleep. *Cerebral Cortex*, 14(8), 858–862. https://doi.org/10.1093/cercor/bhh044

Mahon, S., Vautrelle, N., Pezard, L., Slaght, S. J., Deniau, J. M., Chouvet, G., & Charpier, S. (2006). Distinct patterns of striatal medium spiny neuron activity during the natural sleep-wake cycle. *Journal of Neuroscience*, 26(48), 12587–12595. https://doi.org/10.1523/JNEUROSCI.3987-06.2006

Mai, J. K., & Majtanik, M. (2019). Toward a common terminology for the thalamus. *Frontiers in Neuroanatomy*, 12(January), 1–23. https://doi.org/10.3389/fnana.2018.00114

Mak-Mccully, R. A., Rolland, M., Sargsyan, A., Gonzalez, C., Magnin, M., Chauvel, P., Rey, M., Bastuji, H., & Halgren, E. (2017). Coordination of cortical and thalamic activity during non-REM sleep in humans. *Nature Communications*, 8 (May). https://doi.org/10.1038/ncomms15499

Manoach, D. S., Pan, J. Q., Purcell, S. M., & Stickgold, R. (2016). Reduced sleep spindles in schizophrenia: a treatable endophenotype that links risk genes to impaired cognition? *Biological Psychiatry*, 80(8), 599–608. https://doi.org/10.1016/j.biopsych.2015.10.003

Manoach, D. S., Thakkar, K. N., Stroynowski, E., Ely, A., McKinley, S. K., Wamsley, E., Djonlagic, I., Vangel, M. G., Goff, D. C., & Stickgold, R. (2010). Reduced overnight consolidation of procedural learning in chronic medicated schizophrenia is related to specific sleep stages. *Journal of Psychiatric Research*, 44(2), 112–120. https://doi.org/10.1016/j.jpsychires.2009.06.011

Maquet, P., Laureys, S., Peigneux, P., Fuchs, S., Petiau, C., Phillips, C., Aerts, J., Del Fiore, G., Degueldre, C., Meulemans, T., Luxen, A., Franck, G., Van Der Linden, M., Smith, C., & Cleeremans, A. (2000). Experience-dependent changes in changes in cerebral activation during human REM sleep. *Nature Neuroscience*, 3(8), 831–836. https://doi.org/10.1038/77744

Maquet, P., Peters, J., Aerts, J., Delfiore, G., Degueldre, C., Luxen, A., & Franck, G. (1996). Functional neuroanatomy of human rapid-eye-movement sleep and dreaming. *Nature*, 383, 163–166.

Massimini, M., Ferrarelli, F., Esser, S. K., Riedner, B. A., Huber, R., Murphy, M., Peterson, M. J., & Tononi, G. (2007). Triggering sleep slow waves by transcranial magnetic stimulation. *Proceedings of the National Academy of Sciences of the United States of America*, 104(20), 8496–8501.

Massimini, M., Huber, R., Ferrarelli, F., Hill, S., & Tononi, G. (2004). The sleep slow oscillation as a traveling wave. *Journal of Neuroscience*, 24(31), 6862–6870. https://doi.org/10.1523/JNEUROSCI.1318-04.2004

McBride, R. L., & Sutin, J. (1976). Projections of the locus coeruleus and adjacent pontine tegmentum in the cat. *Journal of Comparative Neurology*, 165(3), 265–284. https://doi.org/10.1002/cne.901650302

McCormick, D. A., McGinley, M. J., & Salkoff, D. B. (2015). Brain state dependent activity in the cortex and thalamus. *Current Opinion in Neurobiology*, 31, 133–140. https://doi.org/10.1016/j.conb.2014.10.003

McCormick, D. A., & Pape, H. C. (1988). Acetylcholine inhibits identified interneurons in the cat lateral geniculate nucleus. *Nature*, 334(6179), 246–248. https://doi.org/10.1038/334246a0

McCormick, D. A., & Pape, H. C. (1990). Noradrenergic and serotoninergic modulation of a hyperpolarization-activated cation current in thalamic relay neurons. *Journal of Physiology*, 431, 319–342.

McCormick, D. A., Pape, H. C., & Williamson, A. (1991). Actions of norepinephrine in the cerebral cortex and thalamus: implications for function of the central noradrenergic system. *Progress in Brain Research*, 88(C), 293–305. https://doi.org/10.1016/S0079-6123(08)63817-0

McCormick, D. A., & Prince, D. A. (1986). Acetylcholine induces burst firing in thalamic reticular neurones by activating a potassium conductance. *Nature*, 319, 402–405.

McKenna, J. T., & Vertes, R. P. (2004). Afferent projections to nucleus reuniens of the thalamus. *Journal of Comparative Neurology*, 480(2), 115–142. https://doi.org/10.1002/cne.20342

Mesbah-Oskui, L., Horner, R. L., Orser, B. A., & Horner, R. L. (2014). Thalamic δ-subunit containing GABA$_A$ receptors promote electrocortical signatures of deep non-REM sleep but do not mediate the effects of etomidate at the thalamus in vivo. *Journal of Neuroscience*, 34(37), 12253–12266. https://doi.org/10.1523/JNEUROSCI.0618-14.2014

Mölle, M., Bergmann, T. O., Marshall, L., & Born, J. (2011). Fast and slow spindles during the sleep slow oscillation: disparate coalescence and engagement in memory processing. *Sleep*, 34(10), 1411–1421. https://doi.org/10.5665/SLEEP.1290

Morairty, S. R., Dittrich, L., Pasumarthi, R. K., Valladao, D., Heiss, J. E., Gerashchenko, D., & Kilduff, T. S. (2013). A role for cortical nNOS/NK1 neurons in coupling homeostatic sleep drive to EEG slow wave activity. *Proceedings of the National Academy of Sciences of the United States of America*, 110(50), 20272–20277. https://doi.org/10.1073/pnas.1314762110

Moruzzi, G., & Magoun, H. W. (1949). Brain stem reticular formation and activation of the EEG. *Electroencephalography and Clinical Neurophysiology*, 1(1–4), 455–473.

Moxon, K. A., Devilbiss, D. M., Chapin, J. K., & Waterhouse, B. D. (2007). Influence of norepinephrine on somatosensory neuronal responses in the rat thalamus: a combined modeling and in vivo multi-channel, multi-neuron recording study. *Brain Research*, 1147(1), 105–123. https://doi.org/10.1016/j.brainres.2007.02.006

Muehlroth, B. E., Sander, M. C., Fandakova, Y., Grandy, T. H., Rasch, B., Shing, Y. L., & Werkle-Bergner, M. (2019). Precise slow oscillation–spindle coupling promotes memory consolidation in younger and older adults. *Scientific Reports*, 9(1), 1–15. https://doi.org/10.1038/s41598-018-36557-z

Nath, R. D., Bedbrook, C. N., Abrams, M. J., Basinger, T., Bois, J. S., Prober, D. A., Sternberg, P. W., Gradinaru, V., & Goentoro, L. (2017). The jellyfish *Cassiopea* exhibits a sleep-like state. *Current Biology*, 27(19), 2984–2990.e3. https://doi.org/10.1016/j.cub.2017.08.014

Newman, E. L., Gupta, K., Climer, J. R., Monaghan, C. K., & Hasselmo, M. E. (2012). Cholinergic modulation of cognitive processing: insights drawn from computational models. *Frontiers in Behavioral Neuroscience*. https://doi.org/10.3389/fnbeh.2012.00024

Nichols, A. L. A., Eichler, T., Latham, R., & Zimmer, M. (2017). A global brain state underlies *C. elegans* sleep behavior. *Science*, 356(6344), 1247–1256. https://doi.org/10.1126/science.aam6851

Oishi, Y., Xu, Q., Wang, L., Zhang, B. J., Takahashi, K., Takata, Y., Luo, Y. J., Cherasse, Y., Schiffmann, S. N., De Kerchove D'Exaerde, A., Urade, Y., Qu, W. M., Huang, Z. L., & Lazarus, M. (2017). Slow-wave sleep is controlled by a subset of nucleus accumbens core neurons in mice. *Nature Communications*, 8(1), 1–12. https://doi.org/10.1038/s41467-017-00781-4

Pace-Schott, E. F., & Hobson, J. A. (2002). The neurobiology of sleep: genetics, cellular physiology and subcortical networks. *Nature Reviews Neuroscience*, 3(8), 591–605. https://doi.org/10.1038/nrn895

Pape, H. C., & McCormick, D. A. (1989). Noradrenaline and serotonin selectively modulate thalamic burst firing by enhancing a hyperpolarization-activated cation current. *Nature*, 340, 715–718. https://doi.org/10.1038/246170a0

Parent, A., Paré, D., Smith, Y., & Steriade, M. (1988). Basal forebrain cholinergic and noncholinergic projections to the thalamus and brainstem in cats and monkeys. *Journal of Comparative Neurology*, 277(2), 281–301. https://doi.org/10.1002/cne.902770209

Pedersen, N. P., Ferrari, L., Venner, A., Wang, J. L., Abbott, S. B. G., Vujovic, N., Arrigoni, E., Saper, C. B., & Fuller, P. M. (2017). Supramammillary glutamate neurons are a key node of the arousal system. *Nature Communications*, 8(1). https://doi.org/10.1038/s41467-017-01004-6

Pellegrini, C., Lecci, S., Lüthi, A., & Astori, S. (2016). Suppression of sleep spindle rhythmogenesis in mice with deletion of CaV3.2 and CaV3.3 T-type Ca^{2+} channels. *Sleep*, 39(4), 875–885.

Phillips, J. W., Schulmann, A., Hara, E., Winnubst, J., Liu, C., Valakh, V., Wang, L., Shields, B. C., Korff, W., Chandrashekar, J., Lemire, A. L., Mensh, B., Dudman, J. T., Nelson, S. B., & Hantman, A. W. (2019). A repeated molecular architecture across thalamic pathways. *Nature Neuroscience*, 22(11), 1925–1935. https://doi.org/10.1038/s41593-019-0483-3

Piantoni, G., Halgren, E., & Cash, S. S. (2017). Spatiotemporal characteristics of sleep spindles depend on cortical location. *NeuroImage*, 146(June), 236–245. https://doi.org/10.1016/j.neuroimage.2016.11.010

Picciotto, M. R., Higley, M. J., & Mineur, Y. S. (2012). Acetylcholine as a neuromodulator: cholinergic signaling shapes nervous system function and behavior. *Neuron*, 76(1), 116–129. https://doi.org/10.1016/j.neuron.2012.08.036

Pita-Almenar, J. D., Yu, D., Lu, H. C., & Beierlein, M. (2014). Mechanisms underlying desynchronization of cholinergic-evoked thalamic network activity. *Journal of Neuroscience*, 34(43), 14463–14474. https://doi.org/10.1523/JNEUROSCI.2321-14.2014

Portas, C. M., Bjorvatn, B., & Ursin, R. (2000). Serotonin and the sleep/wake cycle: special emphasis on microdialysis studies. *Progress in Neurobiology*, 60, 13–35.

Poulet, J. F. A., Fernandez, L. M. J., Crochet, S., & Petersen, C. C. H. (2012). Thalamic control of cortical states. *Nature Neuroscience*, 15(3), 370–372. https://doi.org/10.1038/nn.3035

Poulet, J. F. A., & Petersen, C. C. H. (2008). Internal brain state regulates membrane potential synchrony in barrel cortex of behaving mice. *Nature*, 454(7206), 881–885. https://doi.org/10.1038/nature07150

Puentes-Mestril, C., & Aton, S. J. (2017). Linking network activity to synaptic plasticity during sleep: Hypotheses and recent data. *Frontiers in Neural Circuits*, 11(September), 1–18. https://doi.org/10.3389/fncir.2017.00061

Qiu, M. H., Chen, M. C., Fuller, P. M., & Lu, J. (2016). Stimulation of the Pontine parabrachial nucleus promotes wakefulness via extra-thalamic forebrain circuit nodes. *Current Biology*, 26(17), 2301–2312. https://doi.org/10.1016/j.cub.2016.07.054

Raizen, D. M., Zimmerman, J. E., Maycock, M. H., Ta, U. D., You, Y. J., Sundaram, M. V., & Pack, A. I. (2008). Lethargus is a *Caenorhabditis elegans* sleep-like state. *Nature*, 451(7178), 569–572. https://doi.org/10.1038/nature06535

Rikhye, R. V., Wimmer, R. D., & Halassa, M. M. (2018). Toward an integrative theory of thalamic function. *Annual Review of Neuroscience*, 41(March), 163–183. https://doi.org/10.1146/annurev-neuro-080317-062144

Rodenkirch, C., Liu, Y., Schriver, B. J., & Wang, Q. (2019). Locus coeruleus activation enhances thalamic feature selectivity via norepinephrine regulation of intrathalamic circuit dynamics. *Nature Neuroscience*, 22(1), 120–133. https://doi.org/10.1038/s41593-018-0283-1

Sanchez-Vives, M. V., Descalzo, V. F., Reig, R., Figueroa, N. A., Compte, A., & Gallego, R. (2008). Rhythmic spontaneous activity in the piriform cortex. *Cerebral Cortex*, 18(5), 1179–1192. https://doi.org/10.1093/cercor/bhm152

Sanchez-Vives, M. V., & McCormick, D. A. (2000). Cellular and network mechanisms of rhythmic recurrent activity in neocortex. *Nature Neuroscience*, 3(10), 1027–1034. https://doi.org/10.1038/79848

Santamaria, J., Pujol, M., Orteu, N., Solanas, A., Cardenal, C., Santacruz, P., Chimeno, E., & Moon, P. (2000). Unilateral thalamic stroke does not decrease ipsilateral sleep spindles. *Sleep*, 23(3), 333–339. https://doi.org/10.1093/sleep/23.3.1

Saper, C. B., Fuller, P. M., Pedersen, N. P., Lu, J., & Scammell, T. E. (2010). Sleep state switching. *Neuron*, 68(6), 1023–1042. https://doi.org/doi:10.1016/j.neuron.2010.11.032

Sarasso, S., D'Ambrosio, S., Fecchio, M., Casarotto, S., Viganò, A., Landi, C., Mattavelli, G., Gosseries, O., Quarenghi, M., Laureys, S., Devalle, G., Rosanova, M., & Massimini, M. (2020). Local sleep-like cortical reactivity in the awake brain after focal injury. *Brain*, 143(12), 3672–3684. https://doi.org/10.1093/brain/awaa338

Schabus, M., Dang-Vu, T. T., Albouy, G., Balteau, E., Boly, M., Carrier, J., Darsaud, A., Degueldre, C., Desseilles, M., Gais, S., Phillips, C., Rauchs, G., Schnakers, C., Sterpenich, V., Vandewalle, G., Luxen, A., & Maquet, P. (2007). Hemodynamic cerebral correlates of sleep spindles during human non-rapid eye movement sleep. *Proceedings of the National Academy of Sciences of the United States of America*, 104(32), 13164–13169. https://doi.org/10.1073/pnas.0703084104

Schabus, M., Dang-vu, T. T., Philip, D., Heib, J., Boly, M., Vandewalle, G., Schmidt, C., Albouy, G., Darsaud, A., & Gais, S. (2012). The fate of incoming stimuli during NREM sleep is determined by spindles and the phase of the slow oscillation. *Frontiers in Neurology*, 3(April), 1–11. https://doi.org/10.3389/fneur.2012.00040

Seibt, J., Richard, C. J., Sigl-Glöckner, J., Takahashi, N., Kaplan, D. I., Doron, G., De Limoges, D., Bocklisch, C., & Larkum, M. E. (2017). Cortical dendritic activity correlates with spindle-rich oscillations during sleep in rodents. *Nature Communications*, 8(1). https://doi.org/10.1038/s41467-017-00735-w

Seugnet, L., Suzuki, Y., Donlea, J. M., Gottschalk, L., & Shaw, P. J. (2011). Sleep deprivation during early-adult development results in long-lasting learning deficits in adult Drosophila. *Sleep*, 34(2), 137–146. https://doi.org/10.1093/sleep/34.2.137

Sherman, S. M. (2016). Thalamus plays a central role in ongoing cortical functioning. *Nature Neuroscience*, 19(4), 533–541. https://doi.org/10.1038/nn.4269

Siclari, F., Baird, B., Perogamvros, L., Bernardi, G., LaRocque, J. J., Riedner, B., Boly, M., Postle, B. R., & Tononi, G. (2017). The neural correlates of dreaming. *Nature Neuroscience*, 20(6), 872–878. https://doi.org/10.1038/nn.4545

Siclari, F., Bernardi, G., Cataldi, J., & Tononi, G. (2018). Dreaming in NREM sleep: a high-density EEG study of slow waves and spindles. *Journal of Neuroscience*, 38(43), 9175–9185. https://doi.org/10.1523/JNEUROSCI.0855-18.2018

Siclari, F., Bernardi, F., Riedner, B. A., LaRocque, J. J., Benca, R. M., & Tononi, G. (2014). Two distinct synchronization processes in the transition to sleep. *Sleep*, 37.

Siclari, F., & Tononi, G. (2017). Local aspects of sleep and wakefulness. *Current Opinion in Neurobiology*, 44, 222–227. https://doi.org/10.1016/j.conb.2017.05.008

Sieber, A. R., Min, R., & Nevian, T. (2013). Non-Hebbian long-term potentiation of inhibitory synapses in the thalamus. *Journal of Neuroscience*, **33**(40), 15675–15685. https://doi.org/10.1523/JNEUROSCI.0247-13.2013

Sillito, A. M., Kemp, J. A., & Berardi, N. (1983). The cholinergic influence on the function of the cat dorsal lateral geniculate nucleus (dLGN). *Brain Research*, **280**(2), 299–307. https://doi.org/10.1016/0006-8993(83)90059-8

Sriji, S., Akhtar, N., & Mallick, H. N. (2020). Mediodorsal thalamus lesion increases paradoxical sleep in rats. *Sleep Science*, 1–6. https://doi.org/10.5935/1984-0063.20190155

Stanton, P. K., & Sarvey, J. M. (1985). Depletion of norepinephrine, but not serotonin, reduces long-term potentiation in the dentate gyrus of rat hippocampal slices. *Journal of Neuroscience*, **5**(8), 2169–2176. https://doi.org/10.1523/jneurosci.05-08-02169.1985

Steriade, M. (2006). Grouping of brain rhythms in corticothalamic systems. *Neuroscience*, **137**(4), 1087–1106. https://doi.org/10.1016/j.neuroscience.2005.10.029

Steriade, M., Curro Dossi, R., Pare, D., & Oakson, G. (1991). Fast oscillations (20–40 Hz) in thalamocortical systems and their potentiation by mesopontine cholinergic nuclei in the cat. *Proceedings of the National Academy of Sciences of the United States of America*, **88**(10), 4396–4400. https://doi.org/10.1073/pnas.88.10.4396

Steriade, M., Datta, S., Paré, D., Oakson, G., & Curró Dossi, R. (1990). Neuronal activities in brain-stem cholinergic nuclei related to tonic activation processes in thalamocortical systems. *Journal of Neuroscience*, **10**(8), 2541–2559. https://doi.org/10.1523/jneurosci.10-08-02541.1990

Steriade, M., Nunez, A., & Amzica, F. (1993a). A novel slow (< 1 Hz) oscillation of neocortical neurons in vivo: depolarizing and hyperpolarizing components. *Journal of Neuroscience*, **13**(8), 3252–3265. https://doi.org/10.1523/jneurosci.13-08-03252.1993

Steriade, M., Nunez, A., & Amzica, F. (1993b). Intracellular analysis of relations between the slow (< Hz) neocortical oscillation and other sleep rhythms of the electroencephalogram. *Journal of Neuroscience*, **13**(8), 3266–3283. https://doi.org/10.1016/S0040-4039(97)01107-6

Steriade, M., Timofeev, I., & Grenier, F. (2001). Natural waking and sleep states: a view from inside neocortical neurons. *Journal of Neurophysiology*, **85**(5), 1969–1985. https://doi.org/10.1152/jn.2001.85.5.1969

Stucynski, J. A., Schott, A. L., Baik, J., Chung, S., & Weber, F. (2021). Regulation of REM sleep by inhibitory neurons in the dorsomedial medulla. *Current Biology*, **32**, 1–14. https://doi.org/10.1016/j.cub.2021.10.030

Sun, Y. G., Pita-Almenar, J. D., Wu, C. S., Renger, J. J., Uebele, V. N., Lu, H. C., & Beierlein, M. (2013). Biphasic cholinergic synaptic transmission controls action potential activity in thalamic reticular nucleus neurons. *Journal of Neuroscience*, **33**(5), 2048–2059. https://doi.org/10.1523/JNEUROSCI.3177-12.2013

Takahashi, T. M., Sunagawa, G. A., Soya, S., Abe, M., Sakurai, K., Ishikawa, K., Yanagisawa, M., Hama, H., Hasegawa, E., Miyawaki, A., Sakimura, K., Takahashi, M., & Sakurai, T. (2020). A discrete neuronal circuit induces a hibernation-like state in rodents. *Nature*, **583**(7814), 109–114. https://doi.org/10.1038/s41586-020-2163-6

Takata, Y., Oishi, Y., Zhou, X. Z., Hasegawa, E., Takahashi, K., Cherasse, Y., Sakurai, T., & Lazarus, M. (2018). Sleep and wakefulness are controlled by ventral medial midbrain/pons GABAergic neurons in mice. *Journal of Neuroscience*, **38**(47), 10080–10092. https://doi.org/10.1523/JNEUROSCI.0598-18.2018

Timofeev, I., & Chauvette, S. (2017). Sleep slow oscillation and plasticity. *Current Opinion in Neurobiology*, **44**, 116–126. https://doi.org/10.1016/j.conb.2017.03.019

Timofeev, I., Grenier, F., Bazhenov, M., Sejnowski, T. J., & Steriade, M. (2000). Origin of slow cortical oscillations in deafferented cortical slabs. *Cerebral Cortex*, **10**(12), 1185–1199. https://doi.org/10.1093/cercor/10.12.1185

Timofeev, I., & Steriade, M. (1996). Low-frequency rhythms in the thalamus of intact-cortex and decorticated cats. *Journal of Neurophysiology*, **76**(6), 4152–4168. https://doi.org/10.1152/jn.1996.76.6.4152

Tononi, G., Boly, M., Massimini, M., & Koch, C. (2016). Integrated information theory: From consciousness to its physical substrate. *Nature Reviews Neuroscience*, **17**(7), 450–461. https://doi.org/10.1038/nrn.2016.44

Tononi, G., & Cirelli, C. (2014). Sleep and the price of plasticity: from synaptic and cellular homeostasis to memory consolidation and integration. *Neuron*, **81**(1), 12–34. https://doi.org/10.1016/j.neuron.2013.12.025

Totah, N. K. B., Logothetis, N. K., & Eschenko, O. (2019). Noradrenergic ensemble-based modulation of cognition over multiple timescales. *Brain Research*, **1709**(December), 50–66. https://doi.org/10.1016/j.brainres.2018.12.031

Tsai, C. J., Nagata, T., Liu, C. Y., Suganuma, T., Kanda, T., Miyazaki, T., Liu, K., Saitoh, T., Nagase, H., Lazarus, M., Vogt, K. E., Yanagisawa, M., & Hayashi, Y. (2021). Cerebral capillary blood flow upsurge during REM sleep is mediated by A2a receptors. *Cell Reports*, **36**(7), 109558. https://doi.org/10.1016/j.celrep.2021.109558

Vantomme, G., Osorio-Forero, A., Lüthi, A., & Fernandez, L. M. J. (2019). Regulation of local sleep by the thalamic reticular nucleus. *Frontiers in Neuroscience*, **13**(June), 1–8. https://doi.org/10.3389/fnins.2019.00576

Varela, C. (2013). The gating of neocortical information by modulators. *Journal of Neurophysiology*, **109**(5), 1229–1232. https://doi.org/10.1152/jn.00701.2012

Varela, C. (2014). Thalamic neuromodulation and its implications for executive networks. *Neural Circuits*, **8**(June), 1–22. https://doi.org/10.3389/fncir.2014.00069

Varela, C., & Sherman, S. M. (2007). Differences in response to muscarinic activation between first and higher order thalamic relays. *Journal of Neurophysiology*, **98**(6), 3538–3547. https://doi.org/10.1152/jn.00578.2007

Varela, C., & Sherman, S. M. (2009). Differences in response to serotonergic activation between first and higher order thalamic nuclei. *Cerebral Cortex*, **19**(8), 1776–1786. https://doi.org/10.1093/cercor/bhn208

Verret, L., Goutagny, R., Fort, P., Cagnon, L., Salvert, D., Léger, L., Boissard, R., Salin, P., Peyron, C., & Luppi, P. H. (2003). A role of melanin-concentrating hormone producing neurons in the central regulation of paradoxical sleep. *BMC Neuroscience*, **4**, 1–10. https://doi.org/10.1186/1471-2202-4-19

Vertes, R. P., Linley, S. B., & Hoover, W. B. (2015). Limbic circuitry of the midline thalamus. *Neuroscience and Biobehavioral Reviews*, **54**, 89–107. https://doi.org/10.1016/j.neubiorev.2015.01.014

Vyazovskiy, V. V., Olcese, U., Hanlon, E. C., Nir, Y., Cirelli, C., & Tononi, G. (2011). Local sleep in awake rats. *Nature*, **472**(7344), 443–447. https://doi.org/10.1038/nature10009

Vyazovskiy, V. V., Olcese, U., Lazimy, Y. M., Faraguna, U., Esser, S. K., Williams, J. C., Cirelli, C., & Tononi, G. (2009). Cortical firing and sleep homeostasis. *Neuron*, **63**(6), 865–878. https://doi.org/10.1016/j.neuron.2009.08.024

Wamsley, E. J., Tucker, M. A., Shinn, A. K., Ono, K. E., McKinley, S. K., Ely, A. V., Goff, D. C., Stickgold, R., & Manoach, D. S. (2012). Reduced sleep spindles and spindle coherence in schizophrenia: mechanisms of impaired memory consolidation? *Biological Psychiatry*, **71**(2), 154–161. https://doi.org/10.1016/j.biopsych.2011.08.008

Warby, S. C., Wendt, S. L., Welinder, P., Munk, E. G. S., Carrillo, O., Sorensen, H. B. D., Jennum, P., Peppard, P. E., Perona, P., & Mignot, E. (2014). Sleep-spindle detection: crowdsourcing and evaluating performance of experts, non-experts and automated methods. *Nature Methods*, **11**(4), 385–392. https://doi.org/10.1038/nmeth.2855

Watson, B. O., Levenstein, D., Greene, J. P., Gelinas, J. N., & Buzsáki, G. (2016). Network homeostasis and state dynamics of neocortical sleep. *Neuron*, **90**(4), 839–852. https://doi.org/10.1016/j.neuron.2016.03.036

Watts, A., Gritton, H. J., Sweigart, J., & Poe, G. R. (2012). Antidepressant suppression of non-REM sleep spindles and REM sleep impairs hippocampus-dependent learning while augmenting striatum-dependent learning. *Journal of Neuroscience*, **32**(39), 13411–13420. https://doi.org/10.1523/JNEUROSCI.0170-12.2012

Weber, F., & Dan, Y. (2016). Circuit-based interrogation of sleep control. *Nature*, **538**(7623), 51–59. https://doi.org/10.1038/nature19773

Wells, M. F., Wimmer, R. D., Schmitt, L. I., Feng, G., & Halassa, M. M. (2016). Thalamic reticular impairment underlies attention deficit in Ptchd1 Y'mice. *Nature*, **532**(7597), 58–63. https://doi.org/10.1038/nature17427

Weyand, T. G., Boudreaux, M., Guido, W., Theodore, G., Boudreaux, M., & Guido, W. (2000). Burst and tonic response modes in thalamic neurons during sleep and wakefulness. *Journal of Physiology*, **85**(3), 1107–1118.

White, N. S., & Alkire, M. T. (2003). Impaired thalamocortical connectivity in humans during general-anesthetic- induced unconsciousness. *NeuroImage*, **19**(2), 402–411. https://doi.org/10.1016/S1053-8119(03)00103-4

Wu, W., Cui, L., Fu, Y., Tian, Q., Liu, L., Zhang, X., Du, N., Chen, Y., Qiu, Z., Song, Y., Shi, F. D., & Xue, R. (2016). Sleep and cognitive abnormalities in acute minor thalamic infarction. *Neuroscience Bulletin*, **32**(4), 341–348. https://doi.org/10.1007/s12264-016-0036-7

Xu, M., Chung, S., Zhang, S., Zhong, P., Ma, C., Chang, W. C., Weissbourd, B., Sakai, N., Luo, L., Nishino, S., & Dan, Y. (2015). Basal forebrain circuit for sleep-wake control. *Nature Neuroscience*, **18**(11), 1641–1647. https://doi.org/10.1038/nn.4143

Yamazaki, R., Toda, H., Libourel, P. A., Hayashi, Y., Vogt, K. E., & Sakurai, T. (2020). Evolutionary origin of distinct NREM and REM sleep. *Frontiers in Psychology*, **11**(December), 1–8. https://doi.org/10.3389/fpsyg.2020.567618

Yang, S. R., Hu, Z. Z., Luo, Y. J., Zhao, Y. N., Sun, H. X., Yin, D., Wang, C. Y., Yan, Y. D., Wang, D. R., Yuan, X. S., Ye, C. B., Guo, W., Qu, W. M., Cherasse, Y., Lazarus, M., Ding, Y. Q., & Huang, Z. L. (2018). The rostromedial tegmental nucleus is essential for non-rapid eye movement sleep. *PLoS Biology*, **16**(4), 1–29. https://doi.org/10.1371/journal.pbio.2002909

Yuan, X.-S., Wang, L., Dong, H., Qu, W.-M., Yang, S.-R., Cherasse, Y., Lazarus, M., Schiffmann, S. N., d'Exaerde, A. de K., Li, R.-X., & Huang, Z.-L. (2017). Striatal adenosine A2A receptor neurons control active-period sleep via parvalbumin neurons in external globus pallidus. *eLife*, **6**, 1–24. https://doi.org/10.7554/elife.29055

Zhang, Ze, Liu, W. Y., Diao, Y. P., Xu, W., Zhong, Y. H., Zhang, J. Y., Lazarus, M., Liu, Y. Y., Qu, W. M., & Huang, Z. L. (2019). Superior colliculus GABAergic neurons are essential for acute dark induction of wakefulness in mice. *Current Biology*, **29**(4), 637–644.e3. https://doi.org/10.1016/j.cub.2018.12.031

Zhang, Zhe, Ferretti, V., Güntan, I., Moro, A., Steinberg, E. A., Ye, Z., Zecharia, A. Y., Yu, X., Vyssotski, A. L., Brickley, S. G., Yustos, R., Pillidge, Z. E., Harding, E. C., Wisden, W., & Franks, N. P. (2015). Neuronal ensembles sufficient for recovery sleep and the sedative actions of α 2 adrenergic agonists. *Nature Neuroscience*, **18**(4), 553–561. https://doi.org/10.1038/nn.3957

Zhang, Zhe, Zhong, P., Hu, F., Barger, Z., Ren, Y., Ding, X., Li, S., Weber, F., Chung, S., Palmiter, R. D., & Dan, Y. (2019). An excitatory circuit in the perioculomotor midbrain for non-REM sleep control. *Cell*, **177**(5), 1293–1307.e16. https://doi.org/10.1016/j.cell.2019.03.041

Zhong, P., Zhang, Z., Barger, Z., Ma, C., Liu, D., Ding, X., & Dan, Y. (2019). Control of non-REM sleep by midbrain neurotensinergic neurons. *Neuron*, **104**(4), 795–809.e6. https://doi.org/10.1016/j.neuron.2019.08.026

Zhu, J., & Heggelund, P. (2001). Muscarinic regulation of dendritic and axonal outputs of rat thalamic interneurons: a new cellular mechanism for uncoupling distal dendrites. *Journal of Neuroscience*, **21**(4), 1148–1159. https://doi.org/10.1523/jneurosci.21-04-01148.2001

Zhu, L., Blethyn, K. L., Cope, D. W., Tsomaia, V., Crunelli, V., & Hughes, S. W. (2006). Nucleus- and species-specific properties of the slow (< 1 Hz) sleep oscillation in thalamocortical neurons. *Neuroscience*, **141**, 621–636. https://doi.org/10.1016/j.neuroscience.2006.04.069

Chapter 20

Central Thalamic Contributions to Arousal Regulation

Nicholas D. Schiff

Historical Antecedents

The modern introduction of a role for the central thalamus in forebrain arousal mechanisms originates in the studies of Moruzzi and Magoun (1949). Their work advanced the concept of a defined pathway extending from the medullary reticular formation into central regions of the thalamus and envisioned diffuse thalamic projections emanating to innervate the cerebral cortex. In a series of experiments carried out in anesthetized cats, it was demonstrated that electrical stimulation of several points along this pathway produced low-amplitude, high-frequency activity in the electroencephalogram (EEG), shifting the EEG background from high-amplitude, very low-frequency oscillations induced by the anesthetic. Placement of the stimulating electrode within the central regions of the thalamus (notably not identified by nuclear boundaries or histological verification in the study) produced similar but less broad EEG activation. Although comparable EEG activation was shown with rostral pontine reticular stimulation or stimulation within the dorsal lateral hypothalamic regions, only a limited cortical modulation could be elicited by direct brainstem stimulation after the creation of bi-thalamic lesions that combined the severing of the massa intermedia connecting the thalami across the cerebral hemispheres. Alternatively, with only unilateral central thalamic ablation, a full EEG "desynchronization" effect could be obtained. This particular subset of the experiments showed that withdrawal of the direct central thalamic projection to the cortex produced powerful and immediate effects on EEG activation.

During the 1950s and 1960s, Moruzzi and Magoun's experimental results led to extensive basic neuroscience research that dominated contemporary textbook discussions of forebrain organization (Thompson 1967). In early behavioral experiments in awake non-human primates, Fuster (1958) applied direct electrical stimulation of the midbrain reticular formation (MRF) and demonstrated improved performance accuracy of a tachistoscopic visual recognition task accompanied by reduced reaction times. Increased detection of near-threshold stimuli with stimulation persisted across increasingly difficult parametric modulations of the task, providing the first evidence that activation of this ascending pathway from the MRF to the central thalamus and forebrain could affect wakeful cognition. The present chapter traces the evolution of these critical observations into basic neuroscience, examining the role of the central thalamus in arousal regulation and translational clinical deep-brain stimulation (DBS) within the central thalamus to support impaired arousal regulation in human subjects.

The Concept of a "Central Thalamus" Linked to Forebrain Arousal Regulation

The underspecificity of thalamic targeting that characterized the original Moruzzi and Magoun report contributed to the notion of an ill-defined "central thalamus," which emerged as a physiological construct typically without strict anatomical boundaries. Identification of the precise central thalamic targets of ascending projections from the MRF per se, as inferred from these studies, first occurred in the 1980s in two papers by Steriade and Glenn. These studies demonstrated that an anatomical pathway from the glutamatergic MRF neurons to neurons within the central thalamus primarily targeted the central lateral (CL) nucleus (Steriade and Glenn 1982, Glenn and Steriade 1982). The targeted CL neurons, in turn, were demonstrated to have broad cortical and striatal projections; see Figure 1. Using detailed electroanatomical stimulation techniques in the cat, Steriade and Glenn (1982) recorded extracellularly from histologically identified neurons in the largest cell populations in the lateral wing of CL and within the paracentralis nucleus (Pc) of the cat thalamus; both the CL and Pc neuronal populations could be antidromically activated by electrically stimulating association regions of the cerebral cortex and the caudate nucleus of the striatum or synaptically driven by stimulation of the MRF. Critically, the MRF stimulations in these studies occurred after the lesioning of all rostral pontine projections to the thalamus, thus eliminating the often-raised concern for confounding activation of fibers of passage (see also the section on controversies later in the chapter).

Simultaneous extracellular recordings from cell bodies in the MRF, CL, and Pc during spontaneous sleep–wake cycles further showed a strong correlation of tonic excitation of MRF neurons and excitability of CL/Pc neurons projecting to the cortex during wakefulness (Glenn and Steriade 1982). Among these neurons, those within the lateral wing of the cat CL demonstrate unique characteristic firing patterns: intracellular recordings reveal spike bursts at 800–1000 Hz in the 20–40 Hz frequency range during wakefulness and rapid eye movement (REM) sleep (Steriade et al. 1993). CL neurons with comparable firing patterns during wakefulness have now been identified in the macaque monkey (Redinbaugh et al. 2020). Glenn and Steriade (1982) also found that the increased firing rates observed during transitions to wakefulness in MRF and CL neurons lagged earlier increases in brainstem cholinergic neuron firing rates that appeared to drive these changes in firing rate via depolarizing effects of nicotinic and muscarinic receptors (Curró Dossi et al. 1991). Comparable activity shifts in several other brainstem, basal forebrain, and hypothalamic populations have been characterized, all of which have strong projections to the CL (Saper et al. 2005, Smiley et al. 1999, Sutcliff and De Lecea 2002). Importantly, the CL receives the densest innervation of noradrenergic afferents from the locus ceruleus, an observation consistent in both humans (Oke et al. 1997) and monkeys (Vogt et al. 2008). Similarly, the CL, along with the core region of the medial dorsalis nucleus, receives the densest innervation from the brainstem cholinergic penduculopontine and lateral dorsal tegmental nuclei as well as sparse cholinergic innervation from the basal forebrain (Heckers et al. 1992, Huerta-Ocampo et al. 2019). Recent studies have also pointed to dopaminergic innervation of the CL, which likely emanates from the ventral tegmental area (Rieck et al. 2004, Fridman et al. 2014, 2019). Consistent with the first observations of Moruzzi and Magoun (1949) noted earlier, optogenetic studies have identified a deeper ascending projection from the medullary nucleus, the anterior nucleus gigantocellularis (aNGC), to the CL (Gao et al. 2019), providing additional glutamatergic innervation of the CL, along with the MRF, hypothalamus, pontine reticular formation, parabrachial nucleus (PB), and pontis oralis nucleus (Krout et al. 2020, Giber et al. 2015, Bayer et al. 2002, Newman and Ginsberg 1994). These heavy and broad innervations of the CL by brainstem arousal nuclei support the selectivity of the CL as a critical node in forebrain arousal regulation. Other activating inputs to the CL arise from the zona incerta and are less well characterized in their properties (Liu et al. 2015, Barthó et al. 2002).

Experimental studies have delineated important functional distinctions within the "central thalamus" for the CL and the paralaminar regions of several abutting thalamic nuclei (Schlag-Rey and Schlag 1984, 1986, Schlag and Schlag-Rey 1984, Wyder et al. 2003, 2004, Schiff et al. 2013) as compared with the more posterior components of the intralaminar nuclei, the centromedian-parafascicularis (Cm-Pf) nuclei (Matsumoto et al. 2001, Minamimoto and Kimura 2002, Minamimoto et al. 2009). Several anatomical and physiological specializations of these nuclei in the central thalamus have become increasingly well understood, and sharp distinctions between the CL and Cm-Pf have been identified in anatomical projection patterns, synaptic contacts at their striatal targets, and intrinsic expression of calcium-binding proteins. Jones first introduced an anatomical distinction for the CL and several other components of the primate intralaminar nuclei based on the expression of calcium-binding proteins (Jones 1998a, 1998b). In his studies, thalamic neurons rich in the parvalbumin protein were noted to project to granular layers of the cerebral cortex (the layer IV input regions), whereas other thalamic nuclei dominantly expressing the calbindin protein demonstrated primarily wide superficial layer (layer I–III) projections (Jones 1998a, 1998b, 2007, 2009). These patterns in calcium-binding proteins showed a very marked distinction between the CL and Cm; the Cm showed only parvalbumin staining, whereas the CL demonstrated pure calbindin staining. The Cm has only sparse cortical projections (Sadikot et al. 1992). Using the same methods Jones argued to relabel the lateral aspects of primate median dorsalis (MD) as part of the CL (Jones 1998a, 1998b, 2007), Münkle and colleagues (1999, 2000) canvassed human thalamus calcium-protein-binding patterns, confirming these distinctions for the CL and Cm and identifying that a third protein, calretinin, uniquely appeared along with calbindin in the CL and in related rostral intralaminar thalamic nuclei (including the Pc) of the human thalamus.

Additional anatomical distinctions between CL/Pc and Cm-Pf neuronal populations identified in comprehensive evaluations of the corticothalamic (Scannell et al. 1999) and cerebral connectivity of these and other intralaminar thalamic nuclei supported their unique geometric properties (Groenewegen and Berendse 1994, Van der Werf et al. 2002). Scannell et al. (1999) developed a full multidimensional scaling model of the entire cat thalamocortical system and found that the anterior intralaminar nuclei (CL, Pc, and central medial) cluster together within the center of four other segregated thalamocortical loop systems (frontal, limbic, temporal, and parietal). The CL/Pc's central positioning in the model reflects an effective shortest-path connectivity of these nuclei via their very wide point-to-point connections with cortical regions within each of the other clusters. Notably, this analysis indicated that these nuclei are closer to the frontal/limbic regions of the cortex, which are more strongly connected with the striatum (see Figure 2C for comparison with optogenetic functional magnetic resonance imaging [fMRI] activation studies; Liu et al. 2015). Groenewegen and Berendse (1994) earlier proposed that the CL and other thalamic intralaminar projections represented the anatomical substrate supporting interactions across relatively segregated cortico–striatopallidal–thalamocortical loop pathways via the control of the prefrontal cortex. In an exhaustive review of thalamic intralaminar connections across the rat forebrain, Van der Werf et al. (2002) organized evidence in support of this conjecture, showing the specific correspondence of different intralaminar nuclei with cortico–striatopallidal–thalamocortical loop systems described in nonhuman primates, including a visceral, motor, limbic, and cognitive loop (Alexander et al. 1986). Taken together, these exhaustive examinations of CL connectivity in the rat and cat show that they admit a unique geometric position within the corticothalamic system that provides insight into the experimental and clinical findings reviewed here.

In comparing the results of single-unit neuron electrophysiological recordings in the CL and Cm-Pf in alert non-human primates, a clear distinction further emerges that is consistent with the varying patterns of anatomical specializations of these thalamic projections. Consistent with the anatomical grouping by profiles of calcium-binding-protein expression, a large segment of the neuronal populations in the CL nucleus and surrounding paralaminar regions of the MD, ventral anterior (VA), and ventral lateral (VL) nuclei all demonstrate persistent activity in their firing rates during attentive behaviors, including ramping of firing rates and maintenance of discharge rates over temporal delays during sustained attention and working memory tasks (Schlag-Rey and Schlag 1984, 1986, Schlag and Schlag-Rey 1984, Wyder et al. 2003, 2004, Schiff et al. 2013).

In addition, CL and adjacent neuronal populations have multi-sensory receptive fields that show responses to both sensory inputs and motor decisions across ipsi- and contraversive body space (Schlag-Rey and Schlag 1984, 1989, Schlag and Schlag-Rey 1984, Wyder et al. 2003, 2004, Schiff et al. 2013). Similar broad input–output relationships are shared by the neurons of many prefrontal and frontal targets receiving projections from these nuclei but not their basal ganglia targets, which tend to show mostly contraversive responses (Hikosaka et al. 1989). Thus CL, Pc, and adjacent paralaminar neurons demonstrate evidence for a general role in supporting executive functions (sustained attention, working memory, rule maintenance, etc.) in non-human primate single-unit response profiles. In contrast, Cm-Pf neurons appear to provide stronger contributions to the sensorimotor-integration components of attended behaviors and the evaluative processes associated with reward and detection of salient or task-related sensory events (Matsumoto et al. 2001, Minamimoto et al. 2002, 2009). Cm–Pf neurons signal behaviorally relevant sensory events, the onset of sensory cues, and attentional orienting responses (Matsumoto et al. 2001, Minamimoto et al. 2002, 2009).

Experimental studies in rodents further support the role of CL and paralaminar regions of abutting nuclei in arousal regulation of executive functions, including decision making and working memory, as well as demonstrating other broad effects on both operantly conditioned and spontaneous behaviors. The classes of experimental evidence fall roughly into two categories: influences of the CL on behavioral components imposing working memory requirements and a variety of behavioral effects reflecting influences on memory encoding and other task-related components.

In a series of detailed lesioning, pharmacological activation/inactivation, and electrical stimulation experiments in awake rats, Mair and colleagues provided evidence that the rat rostral intralaminar nuclei (CL/Pc and related nuclei) contribute to the performance of working memory in the form of delayed conditional discrimination tasks (reviewed in Mair et al. 2011, 2021). Local lesioning of the rostral intralaminar nuclei produced impaired working memory, whereas more posterior lesions within the rat intralaminar nuclei primarily impaired visually guided responding in which sensory cues remained visible and were monitored by the animals during task performance (Mair et al. 2011). Although the Cm component of the Cm-Pf complex is not present in the rat thalamus (Jones 2007), these findings show a strong functional homology with the distinctions seen in non-human primates reviewed earlier in the chapter. Using the gamma-amino butyric acid (GABA) agonists muscimol or baclofen to inactivate CL and adjacent intralaminar regions produced similar lesion effects on working memory performance (Mair and Hembrook 2008), whereas the use of a partial inverse benzodiazepine agonist (FG-7142) demonstrated a dose-dependent behavioral facilitation (improved response speed) with an inverted "U" type of response profile, with higher doses producing worsening of both performance accuracy and speed (Burk et al. 1999). Electrical stimulation of the CL with brief periods of microstimulation at 120 Hz demonstrated facilitation of memory retrieval and decision making independent of the duration of widely varying delay periods of a delayed match-to-sample task in rats over 1 to 23 s, indicating that electrical stimulation within the CL could support sustained activity associated with successful native task performance (Mair and Hembrook 2008). These observations complemented earlier results in experiments using large thalamic lesions including the CL/Pc that demonstrated impaired performance of tasks requiring delay periods; of note, the lesions in these experiments impaired performance across all tested retention intervals, including no delay (Burk and Mair 1998).

The wide point-to-point connections of the CL and related intralaminar and paralaminar regions of the central thalamus, along with their laminar-specific innervations of supragranular and infragranular cortical regions, led to earlier proposals that these projections supported cortical sustained activity across long-range cortico-cortical connections associated with different types of "delay-period" activity involving remembered spatial location, task rules, and so forth (Purpura and Schiff 1997, Schiff and Purpura 2002). Sustained activity during cognitive tasks was envisioned to be initiated by attentional shifts or oculomotor signals emanating from frontal cortical regions and supported by the projections across the frontal and parietal cortex by the CL and related intralaminar nuclei (Purpura and Schiff 1997). Recent detailed physiological studies in mice have verified such a crucial and more general role for thalamic neurons in amplifying and supporting delay-period activity (Acsády 2017, Guo et al. 2017, Schmitt et al. 2017, Bolkan et al. 2017). Guo et al. demonstrated that directionally selective delay-period activity co-exists within frontal cortical and thalamic neuronal populations coding movement direction. Inactivation of either anterior lateral motor cortical populations or ventral medial/VA-VL nuclei via optogenetic methods produced contralesional neglect. Schmidt et al. (2017) demonstrated an opposite effect similar to the earlier theoretical proposal of active thalamic support of delay-period activity (Purpura and Schiff 1997); enhancing activity within the mouse mediodorsal nucleus provided broader behavioral facilitation without interfering with categorical information computed within the prefrontal cortex. Finally, Bolkan et al. (2017) used similar methods to demonstrate the support of prefrontal cortical activity by MD thalamic neurons. Early theoretical work considered the possible role of the CL's laminar-specific projections in supporting cortical columnar integration and in cross-areal feedforward and feedback integration across the cortex underlying delay-period activity (Mair 1994, Purpura and Schiff 1997). Mair (1994) proposed a key role for the CL's anatomical specializations in supporting memory-hold functions and in underlying amnesias associated with central thalamic lesions. Purpura and Schiff (1997) extended the model of Llinás et al. (1994, 1998) to consider the specific contribution of the CL and related intralaminar nuclei to the modulation of cortico-cortical feedforward and feedback interactions supporting delay-period activity underlying sustained attention and integration of oculomotor activity with working memory systems; see further discussion later in the chapter. However, a crucially important distinction between the effects of MD lesions and CL/Pc lesions is that although the MD conveys salient task-related information, MD lesions have limited effects on delayed conditional discrimination, whereas CL/Pc lesions disrupt performance accuracy and response speed across all delay intervals and with no delay (Mair et al. 2021).

In other rat studies, Shirvalkar et al. demonstrated that 100-Hz electrical stimulation of the CL during the retrieval phase of an object-recognition memory task facilitated performance; stimulation of the CL using the same methods correlated with up-regulation of cortical gene expression of both the *c-fos* and *zif-268* immediate early genes in the anterior cingulate and motor cortex (Figures 2A and 2B), hippocampal CA1, basal ganglia, and other regions and showed accumulating carryover effects of increasing improvements of behavioral performance over three days (Shirvalkar et al. 2006). Tsai et al. (2016) demonstrated similar improvements in rats performing a standard spatial memory task (Morris Water Maze) and correlated CL stimulation at 100 Hz for 30 min with both increased *c-fos* activation in the hippocampus and cortex and a 50% increase in dendritic spines in layer III neurons and the apical dendrites of layer V neurons. In addition to a role in memory function, transient signals within the CL are linked with a variety of orienting and monitoring responses. Alerting responses related to the elementary startle response and orienting behavior have been characterized in the cat CL as the "central lateral elicited wave," which resists habituation and persists long after peripheral acoustic startle responses or orienting behaviors have terminated (Sanford et al. 1992); these CL elicited waves are observed as spontaneous events and might be linked with eye movements (Schiff and Purpura 2002), spontaneous attentional shifts, or other internally organized alerting responses (Sanford et al. 1992; see Schiff 2008 for further review)

In addition to their cortical projections, the CL and Cm-Pf have strong striatal projections with differential patterns of innervations in terms of specific cellular elements and cell types. As shown in Figure 1, single-fiber studies note that CL afferents make *en passant* synapses in the thalamic reticular nucleus, broadly innervate the rostral striatum, and continue on to their targets in frontal and prefrontal cortices, where they selectively avoid granular (input) layer projects (Deschênes et al. 1996). Conversely, Cm fibers project strongly into localized regions of the striatum, where they form bushy local arborizations (Smith et al. 2009, Jones 2007). Although both CL and Pf afferents project to the main neuronal populations of the striatum, the medium spiny neurons (MSNs; Ellender et al. 2013), Cm neurons project to the local cholinergic interneurons (Smith et al. 2009). Additional distinctions between neurons in the CL, Pf, and Cm nuclei have been identified by whole-cell patch-clamp studies of striatal MSNs optogenetically activated by either CL or Pf afferents. CL afferents act through alpha-amino-3-hydroxy-5-methyl-4-isoxazole propionic acid (AMPA) receptors and are more effective in driving MSN action potentials; Pf afferents act via *N*-methyl-D-aspartate (NMDA) receptors and generate long-term depression through mechanisms of synaptic plasticity (Ellender et al. 2013); see Figure 1. These specializations likely underlie the impact of selective removal of CL thalamostriatal neurons on flexible set shifting and learning of stimulus–response relationships (Kato et al. 2018). Suppression of CL thalamostriatal inputs also alters striatal dopamine signaling (Cover et al. 2019).

Collectively, these anatomical specializations of CL neurons support their key role in strongly driving frontal cortical and striatal neuronal populations to adjust arousal levels during wakefulness. Consistent with this view, the combined use of optogenetic and fMRI techniques demonstrates the unique capacity for CL stimulation to broadly activate the entire frontostriatal system, as shown in Figure 2B. Comparing the effects of 62 separate local optogenetic activation sites within the rat central thalamus and responses obtained from whole-brain fMRI imaging, Liu et al. (2015) identified sites within the CL as selectively generating the strongest and most reliable activation of frontostriatal neuronal populations.

Modulation of Conscious State and Arousal Regulation during Wakeful Behaviors in Intact Experimental Animals and Disease Models Using CL Electrical Stimulation

Several experimental studies have examined the behavioral effects of continuous stimulation of the CL and modulation of arousal regulation. Three research teams have specifically examined the use of continuous electrical stimulation of the CL to induce wakefulness under general anesthesia (Redinbaugh et al. 2020, Donoghue et al. 2019, Tasserie et al. 2019). Redinbaugh et al. (2020) used electrical stimulation of the CL to induce arousal in anesthetized macaques under both propofol and isoflurane anesthesia. A customized quantitative behavioral arousal index captured eye opening and other behavioral changes consistent with arousal from the plane of general anesthesia. The behavioral changes, however, included few features consistent with human metrics identifying consciousness that separate non-reflexive movements from those observed in comatose patients and in vegetative state from the initial transition into minimally conscious state (MCS; Schiff 2020). The behavioral arousal state rarely reached the top of the scale used and suggested a very limited recovery varying between that consistent with vegetative state or the initial transition into MCS marked by the appearance of non-reflexive movements (Redinbaugh et al. 2020, Schiff 2020, Calderon and Schiff, 2021).

Baker et al. (2016) first applied scale models of human electrical stimulation (DBS) methods in the awake, behaving non-human primate CL during the performance of cognitive tasks. In their studies, co-activation of the CL nucleus and its adjacent fiber tract, the medial dorsal tegmental tract (DTTm; see Edlow et al. 2012), selectively induced the strongest and most reliable behavioral facilitation when applying a novel method of "field-shaping" DBS within the central thalamus (fsCT-DBS). The DTTm largely relays CL projections to the frontal cortex and striatum. Donoghue et al. (2017) employed these fsCT-DBS methods to test awakening from propofol anesthesia in experiments similar to those of Redinbaugh et al. (2020), which had employed microelectrode contacts with very short electrotonic length compared to the human scale model electrodes used in this study. In the Donoghue et al. (2019) experiments, fsCT-DBS produced eye opening, organized movements, and importantly, reliable behavioral responses to air puffs during an otherwise-stable general anesthesia maintained by propofol infusion. The emergence of a behavioral response contingent upon a sensory stimulus in these experiments verified a level of function at least at the equivalent of the upper range of MCS.

Critically, the experiments of Redinbaugh et al. (2020) provide detailed insight into the interactions of neocortical neurons within the cortical column (Redinbaugh et al. 2020, Schiff 2020). In their studies, laminar probes placed in both the frontal cortex and the parietal cortex allowed for the direct evaluation of the effects of CL stimulation on cortical feedforward and feedback connections (see Figure 1 inset and feedforward/feedback connectivity diagram). Synchronization of cortical intercolumnar activity was observed with effective CL stimulation, as well as modulation of feedforward connections from the parietal to the frontal cortex and feedback connections from the frontal to the parietal cortex. The laminar-specific changes in synchronization of activity across frontal-parietal cortico-cortical connections seen in these experiments (Redinbaugh et al. 2020) likely depend on the integrative role of the layer V pyramidal cells (Schiff 2020). Suzuki and Larkum (2020) used optogenetic experiments to demonstrate that multiple types of anesthesia disrupt the active maintenance of coupling along the apical dendritic axis by metabotropic activity in proximal dendritic and somatic compartments of layer V neurons (Figure 1). This dendritosomatic coupling within the layer V pyramidal cell was also abolished by optogenetic inactivation of thalamic higher-order inputs to supra- and infragranular regions; in these experiments, afferents from the thalamic nucleus POm were inactivated, which, like the CL (Llinás et al. 2002), have selective supra- and infragranular laminar projections into the cortical column. Interestingly, the complete loss of dendritosomatic coupling in these experiments could be reproduced by blockade of metabotropic glutamate receptor activity and partially reproduced by blockade of metabotropic acetylcholinergic receptors (Figure 1), specifying a role for cholinergic modulation at both the cortical (dendritosomatic coupling) and central thalamic (membrane depolarization) sites for control of arousal states.

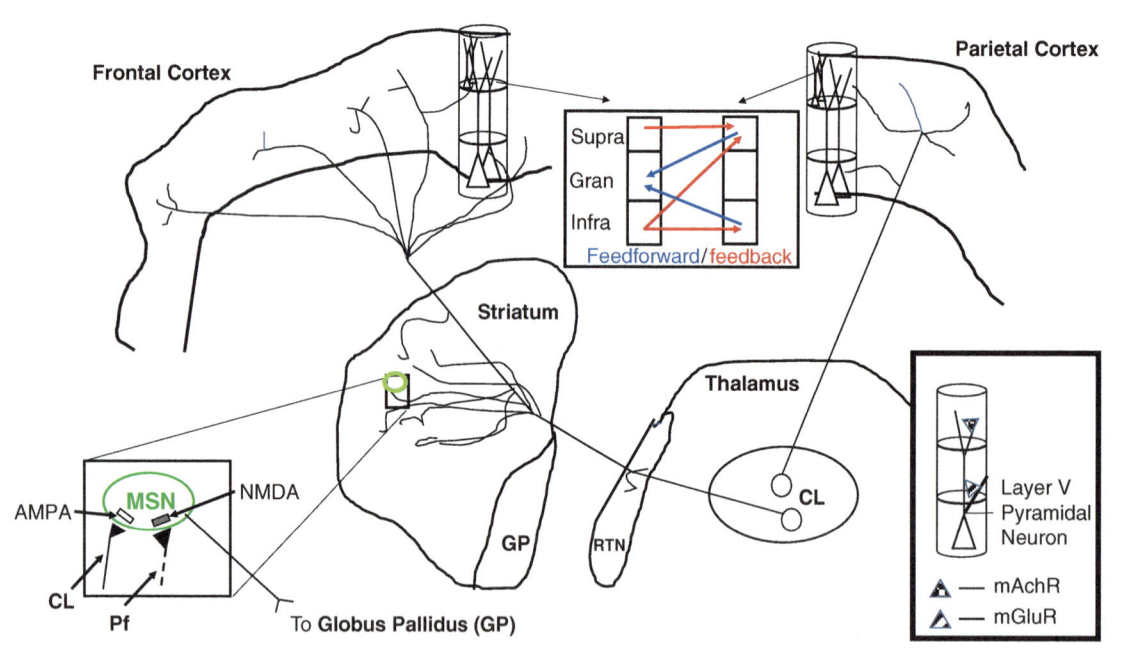

Figure 1 Specializations of neurons within the central lateral thalamic nucleus supporting its unique role in arousal regulation. Schematic diagram of projections of central lateral thalamic neurons to anterior forebrain mesocircuit and posterior medial complex (Schiff 2010, Laureys and Schiff 2012). CL neurons, uniquely among other central thalamic populations, demonstrate a broad pattern of innervation of the frontal cortex and rostral striatum, forming *en passant* synapses in the reticular nucleus of the thalamus (RTN) before broadly arborizing across the frontal cortex and striatum (frontostriatal projection modeled after single-fiber tracing in Deschênes et al. 1996). This anatomical foundation supports the marked functional activation of the frontal cortex and striatum and the behavioral effects achieved with direct stimulation of the CL using optogenetic and electrical stimulation techniques (see Figures 2 and 3). The CL co-activates frontal-parietal cortico-cortical connections and modulates their feed-forward and feedback connectivity via layer-specific effects within cortical columns (Redinbaugh et al. 2020, Larkum et al. 1999, Llinás et al. 1998, Purpura and Schiff 1997). The CL specifically targets supragranular and infragranular cortical layers, avoiding projections into the input layers (Llinás et al. 2002); these anatomical specializations support a proposed selective role in the modulation of long-range corticocortical functional connectivity (Purpura and Schiff 1997) via impact on the canonical cortical microcircuit (Fellman and Van Essen 1991). Layer V pyramidal neurons likely play a key role in the impact of CL stimulation (Schiff 2020); integrative activity within layer V neurons depends on activation of metabotropic acetylcholine (mACh) and glutamate (mGlu) receptors (Suzuki and Larkum 2020, and see text). CL projections to the striatum strongly activate this structure via projections to MSNs (Liu et al. 2015; Figure 2B) and act via AMPA receptors, whereas Cm-Pf afferents act via NMDA receptors (Ellender et al. 2013). Corticocortical feedforward and feedback connections shown modeled after Felleman and Van Essen (1991).

In Baker et al.'s (2016) studies of awake, behaving monkeys, optimal CL/DTTm stimulation sharpened local field potential (LFP) activity within the beta and gamma range of the power spectrum of frontal cortical regions in association with improved performance accuracy and shortened reaction times (consistent with early findings of Fuster [1958] with mesencephalic reticular formation [MRF] stimulation). As noted earlier, CL neurons fire on a 20 to 40 Hz duty cycle in wakefulness (Steriade et al. 1993), and LFPs in both CL and cortical regions demonstrate peaks in power spectrum in these frequency ranges during wakefulness (Steriade et al. 1996). Thus, the observed shifts in LFP power correlating facilitation of performance of sustained attention tasks with fsCT-DBS are consistent with a further depolarization of the cortical neurons as the foundation of the modulation of arousal regulation. Baker et al. (2016) found these changes to reliably associate with improved sustained attention in two animals (increasing above the level seen in native good performance, cf. Schiff et al. 2013) and also to generalize to both working memory and pattern-categorization tasks in one animal trained across three behavioral paradigms. Importantly in these studies of fsCT-DBS effects in the intact brain, optimal CL stimulation frequencies ranged from 150 to 225 Hz. These observations are consistent with the results from studies with awake, intact rodents discussed earlier that used 100- to 120-Hz CL stimulation (Shirvalkar et al. 2006, Mair and Hembrook 2008, Tsai et al. 2016) and point to the likely importance of the integrative effects within the layer V pyramidal neurons (Schiff 2020). As noted earlier, Suzuki and Larkum (2020) linked dendritosomatic coupling within layer V pyramidal cells to maintenance of the conscious state. In layer V and layer II/III pyramidal cells, frequencies above 130 Hz pass a threshold necessary to engage various forms of dendritic electrogenesis, such as back-propagating action potentials and dendritic action potentials (Larkum et al. 1999, 2007). The increased beta and gamma power generated within frontal cortical regions by fsCT-DBS may reflect these changes. This is also consistent with the theoretical proposal that cortico-cortical information flow could be modulated by the CL in the gamma frequency range in the form of persistent activity supporting cross-areal synchronization around shifts of attention or eye movements (Purpura and Schiff 1997) and capitalizing on proposed columnar integrative processes (Llinás et al. 1994, Larkum et al. 1999).

Finally, a small number of studies utilized CL electrical stimulation in rodent disease models. Blumenfeld and colleagues tested CL stimulation to modulate unconsciousness during epileptic seizures and in the post-ictal phase of epileptic unconsciousness in rats (Kundishora et al. 2017, Xu et al. 2020). In rodents, CL stimulation during interictal periods and ictal periods produced behavioral recoveries. Kundishora et al. (2017) combined bilateral CL and pontis oralis stimulation during focal limbic seizures and demonstrated normalization of the EEG and improved behavioral arousal in the rats; Xu et al. (2020) stimulated the CL in post-ictal rats and demonstrated desynchronization of frontal cortical slow waves and partial recovery of behavior in a shock-avoidance task. Tabansky et al. (2014) tested CL stimulation in models of traumatic brain injury and found increased generalized arousal and spontaneous motor activity linked to the stimulation. Tsai and colleagues (2020) stimulated the CL in beta-amyloid infused rats, a model of Alzheimer's disease, and tested spatial memory with the Morris Water Maze task. CL stimulation improved performance, increased dendritic spines, and was associated with increases in measured post-synaptic density proteins. Lin et al. (2019) stimulated the CL in a rat model of autism, finding increased functional connectivity within corticostriatal networks measured with fMRI and induced changes in social behaviors; social avoidance in the rats decreased while increased social interactions emerged.

Role of the Human Central Thalamus in Arousal Regulation within the Wakeful State

Human imaging studies verify that the CL/Pc and Cm-Pf both show selective activation during short-term attention tasks over the course of hundreds of milliseconds to seconds (Kinomura et al. 1996, Naito et al. 2000, Nagai et al. 2004) and during tasks placing sustained demands of high vigilance over extended time periods of hours (Paus et al. 1997). Kinomura et al. (1996) first showed activation of both the rostral (CL, Pc) and caudal intralaminar nuclei (centromedian–parafascicularis complex, Cm-Pf) linked to the delay period of a forewarned reaction-time task ("phasic alerting") using functional positron emission tomography. In addition to activation of these thalamic regions, the MRF showed a selective activation, providing an in vivo human correlation of the pathway identified in the original Morruzi and Magoun (1949) and Steriade and Glenn (1982) studies. Direct recordings in the monkey central thalamus (centered around the CL) during the performance of similar tasks demonstrate that 25% of these neurons participate in a delay-period elevation of firing rates (Schiff et al. 2013). Paus and colleagues (1997) studied healthy volunteers undergoing an hour-long vigil detecting infrequent targets and correlated vigilance decrements arising over time with selectively decreased blood flow in the central thalamus (placed by stereotaxic coordinates in the central lateral and medial dorsalis nuclei). Using a regression model, they demonstrated a covariance of this reduced thalamic blood flow with parallel decreases in the anterior cingulate cortex (ACC) and posterior pontomesencephalon (consistent with cholinergic nuclei and the reticular formation). The anterior cingulate cortex has strong reciprocal connections with the CL and itself provides a wide layer I projection across the prefrontal cortex (Barbas and Pandya, 1989). Thus, the ACC, which acts as the cortical site for effort-regulation determinations (Narayanan et al. 2013), may drive the CL and other central thalamic regions to recruit broader cortical activation in response to effort demands. In addition to the ACC, the CL has strong reciprocal projections with the supplementary motor area (SMA) of the medial frontal cortex (Morel et al. 2005); these regions drive cortical activity during the delay components of forewarned reaction-time tasks in human studies and grade activation with the rapidity of response (Naito et al. 2000, Nagai et al. 2004).

A small literature also verifies the role of the human Cm-Pf in the attentive processing of sensory events. Using LFPs within the human Cm-Pf of patients with neuropathic pain, Beck et al. (2020) found evidence for local event-related potential linked to attended targets arising in the Cm-Pf.

Clinical Pathological Correlation of Human Central Thalamic Lesions and Altered Arousal Regulation

Clinical-pathological correlations show that unilateral or bilateral lesions of nuclei within the central thalami can produce alterations of consciousness (for further review, see Schiff and Plum 2000, Schiff 2008). Several forms of global alteration of consciousness have been associated with central thalamic lesions, with the most marked impairment of arousal regulation correlated with bilateral paramedian thalamic lesions producing the initial onset of coma (Castaigne et al. 1981, von Domberg et al. 1996, Krolak-Salmon et al. 2000). Identification of the association of pure bilateral paramedian thalamic injuries with no encroachment on the midbrain or hypothalamus with initial coma has, however, been debated (see also the section on controversies later in the chapter). Histological evaluations of autopsy data and high-quality magnetic resonance imaging studies reveal that such cases often have minimal, unilateral midbrain involvement (Castaigne et al. 1981, von Domberg et al. 1996, Krolak-Salmon et al. 2000). Nonetheless, an acute coma arising with concomitant high-quality neuroimaging studies revealing dominant evidence of relatively isolated bi-thalamic infarction is common (Schiff 2018). Most such lesions arise as a result of ischemic infarcts of Percheron's artery, which may provide a bilateral vascular supply to the central regions of both thalami and a unilateral vascular supply to the tegmental midbrain from only one vessel arising from the basilar artery (Castaigne et al. 1981).

Although few reports disaggregate injuries to the rostral CL/Pc nucleus and the posterior Cm-Pf nuclei, neuropsychological distinctions identified in many studies parallel the observations made in experimental animals reviewed earlier in the chapter. Globally impaired consciousness arises with large bilateral lesions involving both rostral and posterior nuclei (von Domberg et al. 1996, Krolak-Salmon et al. 2000); recovery from coma following these bilateral lesions is typically associated with a marked slowing of mentation (Katz et al. 1987) and instability of cognitive function across domains of working memory, sustained attention, and executive function (Stuss et al. 1988). When lesions are unilateral, functional distinctions between the involvement of the CL/Pc and Cm-Pf are more evident. Even very discrete, unilateral lesions of the CL may produce enduring impairment in executive function and fluctuations in cognitive function. Van der Werf et al. (1999) reported on a patient with a small right-CL lesion that was associated with chronic right-frontal hypoperfusion and broad attentional deficits, memory deficits, and impaired executive function for 17 years. Discrete lesions of the Cm-Pf can produce alterations in controlled task performance under attentive conditions (Mennemeier et al. 1997), consistent with the neuronal response profiles in alert monkeys associated with attentive orientation to sensory stimuli and neuroimaging studies in healthy controls discussed earlier. Additionally, a thalamic neglect syndrome mirroring the classical parietal cortex neglect syndrome is described, with a right-sided predominance involving central regions of the thalamus, likely combining CL/Pc and Cm-Pf nuclei (Watson et al. 1981). These clinical distinctions are consistent with the marked anatomical differences of the wide CL/Pc frontostriatal projections and the dominantly focal Cm-Pf inputs to the striatum discussed earlier (see Figure 1).

As noted previously, the CL and Pc are unique in forming the closest point-to-point connections across the corticothalamic system (Scannell et al. 1999). These unique geometrical aspects of the CL/Pc underlie their important role in the model of recovery of consciousness following coma known as the *mesocircuit hypothesis* (Schiff 2010). This model proposes that the neurons across the anterior forebrain (prefrontal and frontal cortex, striatum) are particularly vulnerable to downregulation due to the impact of widespread cerebral deafferentation (which occurs following all types of severe multi-focal brain injuries associated with coma; Posner et al. 2019), producing a combined effect of loss of input to the central thalamus hyperpolarizing these neurons and a consequent downstream loss of their role in arousal regulation. Autopsy studies comparing human traumatic brain injury outcomes with patterns of neuronal loss within the thalamus support this inference that the geometric properties of CL/Pc projections confer a selective effect on the central thalamus via its integration of neuronal loss across wide cortical territories; in these studies, the loss of the CL/Pc appears first in patients with higher-level outcomes, with further loss observed involving more posterior components of the Cm-Pf as outcomes approach vegetative state (Maxwell et al. 2006). A secondary contribution of anterior forebrain down-regulation is anticipated from an active inhibition arising as a circuit-level consequence of reduced synaptic background activity within the striatum (Schiff 2010). A sharp decrease of central thalamic firing rates is expected as a result of the broad loss of corticothalamic inputs to these neurons from either widespread disconnection (as in diffuse axonal injury) or neuronal dysfunction (as in hypoxic-ischemic injury), thus providing an insufficient level of background synaptic input to maintain neuronal membrane depolarization. For the Cm-Pf nuclei, a direct inhibition arising from disinhibition of globus pallidus interna neurons can also be expected. The globus pallidus interna is under tonic inhibition from the striatum in the awake, healthy brain, but following severe brain injuries, insufficient corticostriatal and thalamostriatal input to the MSNs of the striatum may drop below the high frequency of required incoming synaptic excitatory inputs required to keep the MSNs at their firing threshold (Grillner et al. 2005). Studies of recovery of consciousness after severe brain injuries support this common "mesocircuit" mechanism of restoration of activity across the anterior forebrain mesocircuit (Schiff 2010, Edlow et al. 2020). At the extreme end of cerebral deafferentation, restoration of subtle behavioral elements of consciousness is associated with increased activation of the central thalamus and medial regions of the posterior parietal cortex (Laureys and Schiff 2012); evidence for recovery of higher integrative function linked to central thalamic activation after severe brain injuries has also been developed; see further discussion that follows.

Resolving Some "Controversies" across Experimental and Clinical Observations of Central Thalamic Contributions to Arousal Regulation

Several controversial points have arisen in the literature that can now be highlighted and placed in their proper context. Collectively, these controversies have centered around observations that have been framed to bring the role of the central thalamus in arousal regulation into question.

In a study often cited as a counterpoint to the importance of central thalamic mechanisms supporting arousal regulation, Fuller et al. (2011) described bilateral lesions of the basal forebrain done in awake rats that produced a behavioral abnormality described as a "coma-like" state and correlated with a slow (predominantly less than 1 Hz) diffuse EEG rhythm. In their study, three different lesion types were compared: (1) wide nonselective basal forebrain (BF) lesions, (2) combined brainstem lesions of the parabrachial-precoeruleus (PC/PB) complex disrupting projections to the basal forebrain, and (3) whole thalamic chemical lesions. The investigators concluded from these observations that the thalamus as a whole plays no role in ascending arousal. However, several crucial points undermine this conclusion. Most importantly, the potential of stimulation within the central thalamus as a method to reverse the "coma-like" state was not considered. In an earlier series of experiments in cats, Steriade and colleagues demonstrated that activation of the thalamocortical pathway can desynchronize the <1-Hz EEG rhythm induced by similar large nonselective basal forebrain lesions (Steriade, Dossi, and Nuñez 1991). Critically, in these studies, stimulation of the mesopontine cholinergic system reversed the <1-Hz EEG rhythm in the setting of large combined ibotenic acid lesions of the BF and diagonal band nuclei (and callosal disconnection). This effect was suppressed by scopolamine. In related experiments, recruitment of fast 20 to 40 Hz rhythms of the EEG through mesopontine stimulation persisted despite similar BF lesioning with concomitant callosal transection and also showed scopolamine dependence (Steriade, Dossi, and Nuñez 1991, Steriade, Dossi, Paré, et al. 1991). Based on these collective findings, Steriade (2001) had concluded that neither loss of the BF nor loss of the thalamic pathway was sufficient to prevent arousal activation and further suggested that a glutamatergic projection from the brainstem areas that overlapped the pedunculopontine nucleus and PB in the cat may be responsible for activation of both subcortical projection systems. Both of these nuclei send strong projections to the CL. Additionally, anatomical projections of the BF into the rat thalamus are concentrated within the CL and other intralaminar nuclei (Kolmac and Mitrofanis 1999). These observations raise the strong possibility that the "coma-like" behavior and bilateral EEG slow rhythms seen in the Fuller et al. (2011) rats might be similarly reversible with CL stimulation, a possibility that was not directly tested.

Rodents as a species do have a relative invariance to the removal of the entire cerebral cortex to the preservation of organized behaviors as well as total thalamic lesions (Thompson 1993, Vanderwolf and Stewart 1988). In addition, rodents have many differences in the evolution of the thalamus, including the relative lack of the calcium-binding-protein distinctions noted earlier (Rubio-Garrido et al. 2007) and the lack of a developed Cm nucleus (Jones 2007). Importantly, during the experimentally derived "coma-like" state in the study by Fuller et al. (2011), the rats preserved the righting response, which is used as a standard demonstration of emergence from coma in the rodent (Gao and Calderon, 2020, Calderon and Schiff, 2021). Thus, the observations by Fuller et al. do demonstrate the vulnerability of distributed networks linking neurons across the cortex, thalamus, basal forebrain, and basal ganglia to certain combinations of destructive lesions that might nonetheless be recoverable through the various redundant arousal pathways left intact. The findings direct future studies aimed at understanding the pluripotentiality of the systems activating forebrain arousal, including the hypothalamus (Pfaff 2005) and basolateral amygdala (Feindel and Gloor, 1954).

As also noted previously, another perennial controversy that has arisen is whether or not pure bilateral central thalamic lesions alone can produce coma in humans. Hindman and colleagues (2018) presented the results of a retrospective study of 33 patients with magnetic resonance images obtained after acute infarction in the Percheron artery distribution of the central thalamus (Castaigne et al. 1981, Schiff 2018). Based on the interpretation of chart reviews, the level of arousal measured within 12 hours of symptom onset was correlated with anatomical lesion data transferred into a common standard atlas. This study found that lesions restricted to the thalamus were not associated with coma or deep stupor within the first 12 hours of injury. These findings are consistent with the largest previously reported study of Percheron artery distribution infarcts from an autopsy case series in which the patients with relatively isolated bilateral thalamic infarcts and initial coma nonetheless all showed some evidence of very limited extrathalamic extension (Castaigne et al. 1981). Although "pure" bilateral paramedian thalamic lesions may be insufficient to produce initial coma, their impact on forebrain arousal is profound. Even small unilateral lesions within the CL can result in enduring cognitive impairment for decades and persistent underactivation of the frontal cortex (Van der Werf et al. 1999). Moreover, studies of the natural history of bilateral paramedian thalamic injuries, with minor extrathalamic components and associated with only brief-period coma, demonstrate persistent disorders of consciousness that rarely may give way to full recovery over years (von Domberg et al. 1996, Krolak-Salmon et al. 2000) or remain with enduring and severe cognitive impairments (Castaigne et al. 1981). Although the evidence noted previously supports that such bi-thalamic stroke lesions associated with coma show some minor extension past the thalamus into the brainstem, the involvement of the observed brainstem components alone, which are often only unilateral, would, in isolation of any thalamic lesions, be clearly insufficient to produce coma (or perhaps not even be clinically evident at all). Thus, the conclusion that coma associated with bilateral paramedian thalamic strokes requires extrathalamic lesion burden is both consistent with the earlier inference that coma and impaired arousal with focal lesions within the paramedian thalamus and brainstem grades with the rostrocaudal extent of the lesions (Plum and Posner 1966) and does not alter the importance of the acute coma that arises in nearly isolated bilateral strokes of the central thalamus (Schiff 2018).

Finally, despite the often-enduring and broad impact of such bilateral central thalamic lesions in humans, it is often unrecognized that full cognitive recoveries are still possible (von Domberg et al. 1996, Krolak-Salmon et al. 2000). How might consciousness recover after bilateral lesions to the central thalamus sufficiently damaging to produce coma and enduring cognitive impairment? The observations of slow reconstitution of global forebrain dynamics in such recoveries further underscore the pluripotentiality of arousal systems, many of which project directly to the cerebral cortex, entirely bypassing the thalamus (Pfaff 2005). Differences in the natural history of lesions restricted to the brainstem that produce coma from those concentrated on the central thalami provide some mechanistic insight: for patients who survive isolated brainstem lesions associated with coma, a deep coma may persist for several days, but the following recovery *is typically very rapid and complete* (Parvisi and Damasio 2003). However, when wide bilateral central thalamic lesions (with small, often only unilateral, mesencephalic extension) produce coma, the coma is typically brief, rarely lasting more than 24–48 hours. *The patients, however, evolve much slower recoveries, typically demonstrating disorders of consciousness for weeks or months,* although complete recovery to baseline cognition can occur within one to two years in some instances (Castaigne et al. 1981, von Domberg et al. 1996, Krolak-Salmon et al. 2000). The slow recoveries seen after the central thalamic injuries demonstrate the functional distinction of these neurons in supporting activation of frontal executive resources within wakefulness via their powerful excitatory inputs to frontostriatal regions. That acute coma can arise with such lesions dominantly involving the central thalamus emphasizes the impact of immediate withdrawal of their glutamatergic afferents. Although the brainstem nuclei provide an essential foundation for the overall state of wakefulness, the necessary and sufficient combination of these systems appears to allow great flexibility in the faster restoration of general forebrain arousal (Parvisi and Damasio 2003). Restoration of cognition after bilateral central thalamic lesions, when it occurs, must then involve distinct mechanisms of reconstitution of crucial dynamical elements supporting the broad patterns of sensorimotor integration and frontoparietal integration typically linked to these neurons. One possibility suggested earlier by the theoretical model of Jones (2009) is that the remaining calbindin-positive thalamic neurons ("matrix" neurons) might support workarounds through their patterns of innervation within the cerebral cortex (Jones 2009, Cruikshank et al. 2012). Paralaminar regions surrounding the CL/Pc and Pf may contain sufficient neuronal populations with similar properties to overtake the loss of large injuries within the intralaminar nuclei per se. A crucially important point, however, is that such recoveries demonstrate that up to a point, the functional contributions of these critical central thalamic regions can be reconfigured in the human brain. Although such patients typically show fluctuations in cognitive capacity and vulnerabilities to stressors (Stuss et al. 1988), it is nonetheless remarkable. Thus, understanding the process of recovery after such injuries remains important future work.

Deep-Brain Stimulation of the Central Thalamus to Improve Arousal Regulation in Human Subjects

Efforts to improve arousal regulation in the injured brain through direct application of DBS within the human central thalamus (CT-DBS) were initiated about 20 years after the studies of Moruzzi and Magoun (see Shah and Schiff 2010 for review). A case study by Sturm and colleagues (1979) notably reported targeting of the left rostral intralaminar regions, presumably including the CL, in a patient described as being in some kind of unconsciousness that was neither a manifest coma nor a typical "apallic syndrome" (an early term similar to *vegetative state*) (p. 236). Unilateral electrical stimulation at 50 Hz of the left rostral intralaminar region and thalamic reticular nucleus produced localizing reactions to painful stimuli consistent with the behavioral level of MCS (see Giacino et al. 2002). Stimulation also intermittently produced brief recovery of simple command following in the form of tongue protrusion and lifting of the arms or legs. These observed effects faded over a few weeks of stimulation. Other single case studies described stimulation in different central thalamic regions and allied structures without evidence of restoration of command following, although reliably generating physiological arousal responses (reviewed in Shah and Schiff 2010). In the late 1980s through the early 1990s, 49 patients in vegetative state were studied in a multi-center trial across France (Cohadon and Richer 1993), Japan (Tsubokawa et al. 1990, Yamamoto and Katayama 2005), and the United States (Hosobuchi and Yingling 1993). In these studies, most patients had DBS electrodes placed in the Cm-Pf. Stimulation produced evidence of increases in behavioral arousal and associated physiological responses, including eye opening and autonomic arousal responses (increases in heart rate, blood pressure), similar to the monkeys activated under anesthesia in the studies of Redinbaugh et al. (2020) discussed earlier. No studies, however, obtained serial behavioral assessments or tested for statistical evidence of contingent changes linked to DBS ON or OFF conditions. Because these patients were also studied within the known timeframes for spontaneous recovery for both vegetative state and MCS, it was not possible to link changes over time to a causal instrumental effect of DBS (see review in Shah and Schiff 2010).

The first study to employ a statistical design capable of disambiguating the effects of elapsed time and DBS stimulation effects was carried out in a 38-year-old man who had remained in MCS for six years following a severe traumatic brain injury. Schiff and colleagues reported the results of CL DBS in this subject, with measurement across six 30-day blocked ON and OFF periods using an interleaved cross-over design (Schiff et al. 2007). The patient demonstrated significant improvements in behaviorally relevant attentive responsiveness, executive motor control of one upper extremity, and restoration of oral feeding capacity during the cross-over period. Of note, during a five-month period of titration of stimulation parameters before the blinded testing protocol, other improvements had included the full restoration of spoken language and consistent communication (Figure 3A). These observations demonstrated the proof of concept that DBS in CL could significantly activate the human brain, even following years of behavioral function at the MCS level. Figure 3A shows the impact of the initial titration period of testing of CL DBS on spoken language in this subject. A combination of DBS-linked improvements in spoken language and the initiation of increasing improvement in baseline function is seen, indicating the presence of a carry-over effect. Notably, this subject had not demonstrated consistent fluent speech in the six-year period prior to the initiation of CL DBS. In a second patient in MCS from the same clinical trial, CL DBS demonstrated a long-term impact on sleep architecture despite initiation of DBS 20 years after injury (Figure 3B; see also following discussion). Subsequent studies have demonstrated that CT-DBS in other patients in MCS (mostly targeting the Cm-Pf, with some examples of CL targeting) can facilitate measurable behavioral improvements, although no study to date has demonstrated a similar level of functional restoration reliably shifting the level of consciousness from MCS to a conversant confusional state (Chudy et al. 2018, Lemaire et al. 2017 Magrassi et al. 2016).

CL/DTTm DBS has now been initiated in patients with moderate to severe traumatic brain injuries (msTBI) following a rationale to activate chronically down-regulated frontostriatal systems, aiming to ameliorate cognitive dysfunction and decrease fatigability (Schiff et al. 2019, Schiff 2016). Enduring cognitive impairment in the form of impaired executive function, primarily reduced vigilance, and impaired executive attention is the dominant form of disability following msTBI (Dikmen et al. 2003, Corrigan et al., 2014). These cognitive deficits span a wide range of impairments in attention, executive function, working memory, and information-processing speed, processes that are primarily supported by the frontostriatal systems and their connections to the central thalamus (Duncan and Owen 2000, Schiff 2016). Cognitive deficits after msTBI also show a dose–response relationship (Dikmen et al. 2003), suggesting that the graded severity of functional deficits is linked to the degree of deafferentation and available resource allocation of frontal-striatal networks. The first msTBI subject to complete the CL/DTTm DBS study had remained with long-standing executive dysfunction and marked fatigue, requiring daily naps, for over 18 years after severe traumatic brain injury (Schiff et al. 2019). CL/DTTm stimulation induced consistent improvement in fatigue and mental focus as well as the incidental recovery of distal motor control of the left lower extremity. The primary outcome measure, Trail-Making Test B, capturing information-processing speed and the secondary outcome measure quantifying fatigue resistance both exceeded their pre-selected criteria for establishing response to treatment in this subject; in addition, three additional subjects with msTBI showed similar improvements in this study (Schiff et al. 2021). These findings provide the first proof of concept that CL/DTTm DBS can improve cognitive functions and fatigue resistance very late in the course of coma recovery (Schiff et al. 2019, 2021).

An Integrative Model of CT-DBS Effects on Arousal-Regulation Mechanisms

Following the previous review, we are invited to briefly consider how CL DBS exerts positive arousal-regulation effects in the injured human brain despite the CL's varying cortical and subcortical inputs, different types of intrinsic information processing within the CL, and the rich patterns of connectivity of the CL and closely related regions of the central thalamus. Several principles can be proposed to formulate an integrative model: (1) the arousal regulation effects exerted by CL-DBS techniques dominantly arise from activation of monosynaptic CL/DTTm connections to the frontostriatal components of the anterior forebrain mesocircuit and frontoparietal network; (2) the level of overall deafferentation of the corticothalamic system in an individual human subject plays a critical role in determining the type of clinically meaningful effects to be anticipated; (3) in patients with disorders of consciousness, restoration of neuronal firings rates and overall population activity reflected within patterns evident in the resting EEG likely play a primary role in behavioral facilitation and are linked to marked shifts in corticothalamic dynamics (Williams et al. 2013, Schiff et al. 2014, Drover and Schiff 2018); and (4) in patients with higher levels of functional recovery, the impact of CL DBS-induced arousal-regulation effects likely depend more upon influences on the integrative properties of neocortical and striatal neurons, as the following discussion notes. Perhaps the most general principle, however, is that the clinically observable impacts of CL DBS are primarily a consequence of the unique geometry of the CL connections to the frontal cortex and striatum and wider point-to-point connections across the cerebral cortex. This anatomical foundation, combined with the patterns of microcircuit innervation within the cortical column and across the striatum, supports the strong physiological impact of activating these neurons through electrical stimulation to produce high firing rates, with fidelity maintained by an external pacemaker (directly akin to the cardiac pacemaking of the sinoatrial node). We briefly organize the evidence supporting these suggested principles and discuss the important contribution of large-scale plasticity in the injured brain's evolving response to CL DBS over time.

In the intact central nervous system, the measured arousal regulation effects of CL DBS reviewed previously can be framed exclusively in terms of the concept of "hormesis," a term applied to the inverted "U" curve observed for the impact of drugs, electrical stimulation, or sensory stimulation effects on arousal regulation (Mair et al. 2011). Hormesis implies a relatively narrow therapeutic window in which an optimal level of stimulation is achieved with the application of stimulation; stimulation outside of this range results in underactivation or overactivation. The level of overall deafferentation of the corticothalamic system, however, plays a critical role in determining the type of clinically meaningful effects to be anticipated. In patients with very deafferented cortical neurons, marked state changes may arise in response to restoration of the excitatory drive across frontal cortical neurons, leading to changes in global brain dynamics; such state changes may be anticipated to produce large changes in baseline thalamic background firing rates, from relative quiescence of central thalamic activity (Giacino et al. 2012) to the restoration of burst or tonic modes of firing, associating with overall changes in the shape of the EEG power spectrum (Williams et al. 2013, Schiff et al. 2014, Drover and Schiff 2018). Similarly, restoration of excitatory input can result in a wide range of shifts in the patterns of neocortical firing rates. In patients in MCS with severe deafferentation and globally depressed cerebral metabolic rates, EEG phenomena consistent with the emergence of a sustained firing pattern of ~7.4 Hz (Williams et al. 2013) suggests an independence from synaptic activity with spikes arising from intrinsic membrane properties of layer V neurons in the presence of brief inputs (cf. Silva et al. 1991). EEG patterns consistent with abnormal features generated by thalamic bursting during wakefulness (Llinás et al. 1999, 2005) are associated with increases in overall cerebral metabolic rates (Drover and Schiff 2018). Finally, recovery of consistent interactive conscious behaviors spanning the range of confusional state to persistent cognitive slowing in otherwise-independent levels of recovery is associated with relative restoration of the normal resting EEG signal (Shah, Mohamadpour, et al. 2017, Shah, Goldin, et al. 2017). However, recovery of normal EEG resting activity does not indicate the restoration of the full range of firing motifs of neocortical and striatal neurons. In particular, neocortical neurons demonstrate many different firing patterns (Steriade 2001), and the integrative properties of neocortical neurons are highly sensitive to levels of overall synaptic background activity (Bernander et al. 1991). Thus, CL DBS can be expected to exert specific effects that are dependent on the functional integrity of the corticothalamic system.

In patients with disorders of consciousness, several predictions of the mesocircuit hypothesis have been tested across the range of outcomes following coma, from vegetative state to nearly full recovery in patients at the level of independent function with persistent impairment in executive function; these studies demonstrate a graded relationship of increasing normalization of activity patterns within the anterior forebrain mesocircuit and frontoparietal network (Laureys and Schiff 2012, Giacino et al. 2014, Fridman et al. 2014). Comparing patients with disorders of consciousness arising across a wide range of etiologies with and without evidence of command following and healthy controls, a normalization of the ratio of metabolic activity within the central thalamus and globus pallidus grades the level of recovery; in addition, graded improvements positively correlate with increasing central thalamic and precuneus metabolism in the dominant hemisphere, linking frontoparietal network activity to the restoration of anterior forebrain mesocircuit function (Fridman et al. 2014). This positive correlation is consistent with patterns of innervation of the posterior medial complex by afferents from the central thalamus, dominantly the CL (Buckwalter et al. 2008, Schiff 2012, Laureys and Schiff 2012). Recovery to the level of the confusional state (CS) is accompanied by relative normalization of these metabolic ratios, but quantitative studies of the resting EEG show persistent abnormality of resting posterior parietal-occipital activity using spectral power analyses comparing power within the alpha (8 to 12 Hz) and delta (1 to 4 Hz) frequency ranges (Shah, Mohamadour, et al. 2017). This persistent down-regulation of the posterior parietal-occipital regions likely reflects the high metabolic demands of these regions and failure to restore sufficient afferent input to these regions. Further recovery past the level of CS is associated with full restoration of the normal resting spectral power distribution in the EEG, but effective modulation of midline frontal EEG power during controlled attentional processing is impaired in patients with persistently impaired executive function after coma (Shah, Goldin, et al. 2017). These observations are also consistent with the mesocircuit hypothesis, suggesting that despite restoration of corticothalamic activity to near-normal resting levels, an enduring vulnerability of recruitment of the anterior forebrain mesocircuit is present, exposed by demands of increased cognitive effort (Shah, Goldin, et al. 2017). The preliminary findings in the msTBI subject with CL/DTTm DBS–induced improvements discussed previously (Schiff et al. 2019) indicate improvements on these controlled attention tasks linked to DBS (Shah et al. unpublished observations).

At the neuronal level, clinically effective CT-DBS can be expected to exert its primary effects on layer II/III and layer V pyramidal neurons and the striatal output neurons, the MSNs. As reviewed earlier, CL afferents innervate layer V and layers II/III, as well as layer I, where apical dendrites of layer V pyramidal neurons are contacted. The work of Suzuki and Larkum (2020) identifies the importance of co-activation of the dendritic and somatic compartment of the layer V pyramidal neurons in maintaining consciousness. Silencing of thalamic afferents with properties similar to those of the CL produced identical effects to different general anesthetics blocking dendritosomatic coupling and layer V outputs. In the anesthetized monkey experiments of Redinbaugh et al. (2020), CL microstimulation at 50 Hz showed restoration of parietal lobe deep-layer firing rates and limited behavioral recovery to the level of vegetative state or low-level MCS (Schiff 2020); the effective CL stimulation, however, did not restore frontal lobe firing rates or normal resting background activity at the population level in either cortical location. In the Baker et al.'s (2016) experiments in awake monkeys, higher-frequency stimulation of the CL/DTTm at 150–225 Hz produced behavioral facilitation. The impact of high-frequency synaptic barrage on the integrative properties of layer V pyramidal neurons (Bernander et al. 1991,

Larkum et al. 1999) and layer II/III pyramidal neurons (Larkum et al. 2007) likely underlies the greater impact of higher-frequency stimulation in the awake or more recovered corticothalamic system (Schiff 2020). Importantly, higher-frequency activation within the dendritic arbor of layer V pyramidal neurons by CL afferents may activate mechanisms of dendritic electrogenesis (Larkum et al. 1999, 2007), initiate the release of growth factors associated with local plasticity (Kuczewski et al. 2008), and drive changes in immediate early gene expression and dendrite spine formation (Shirvalkar et al. 2006, Tsai et al. 2016)).

Several observations demonstrate that behavioral facilitation initiated in structurally injured human brains by CL DBS induces carry-over effects beyond the actual period of electrical stimulation, as 12-hour duty cycles have been utilized with DBS off overnight (Figure 3; Schiff et al. 2007, Adams et al. 2016, Gottshall et al. 2019), including large-scale plasticity in the form of full reorganization of sleep–wake architecture (Adams et al. 2016, Gottshall et al. 2019; Figure 3B). These observations suggest that CL DBS induces plasticity mechanisms that are likely dependent on changes arising over the sleep–wake cycle. As shown in Figure 2B, CL stimulation during wakefulness upregulated the immediate early gene *zif-268* and correlated with improved object-recognition memory performance and carry-over effects measured over three days (Shirvalkar et al. 2006). The laminar-specific pattern of *zif268* in the motor cortex, demonstrating significant up-regulation in supra- and infragranular cortical layers and down-regulation within the granular layer, matches the expression pattern of this immediate early gene during REM periods after earlier induction of long-term potentiation (LTP)–dependent memory processes (Ribeiro et al. 2002). These observations support a role for wakeful activation of supra- and infragranular *zif268* expression by CL stimulation on REM sleep pressure, linking the observations of the very late reemergence of REM in the MCS patient initiating CL DBS 20 years after injury shown in Figure 3B (Adams et al. 2016, Gottshall et al. 2019). In late recoveries of behavior in disorders of consciousness, quantitative neuroimaging studies have demonstrated similar evidence of widespread plasticity suggestive of axonal remyelination or sprouting (Thengone et al. 2016, Voss et al. 2006). Thus, a wide range of possible mechanisms for inducing both short-term and long-term plasticity may be associated with CL DBS. That such mechanisms can be initiated and effectively engaged 6, 18, and 20 years following severe traumatic brain injury by CL stimulation has now been demonstrated in three human subjects (Schiff et al. 2007, Adams et al. 2016, Gottshall et al. 2019, Schiff et al. 2019). Future studies

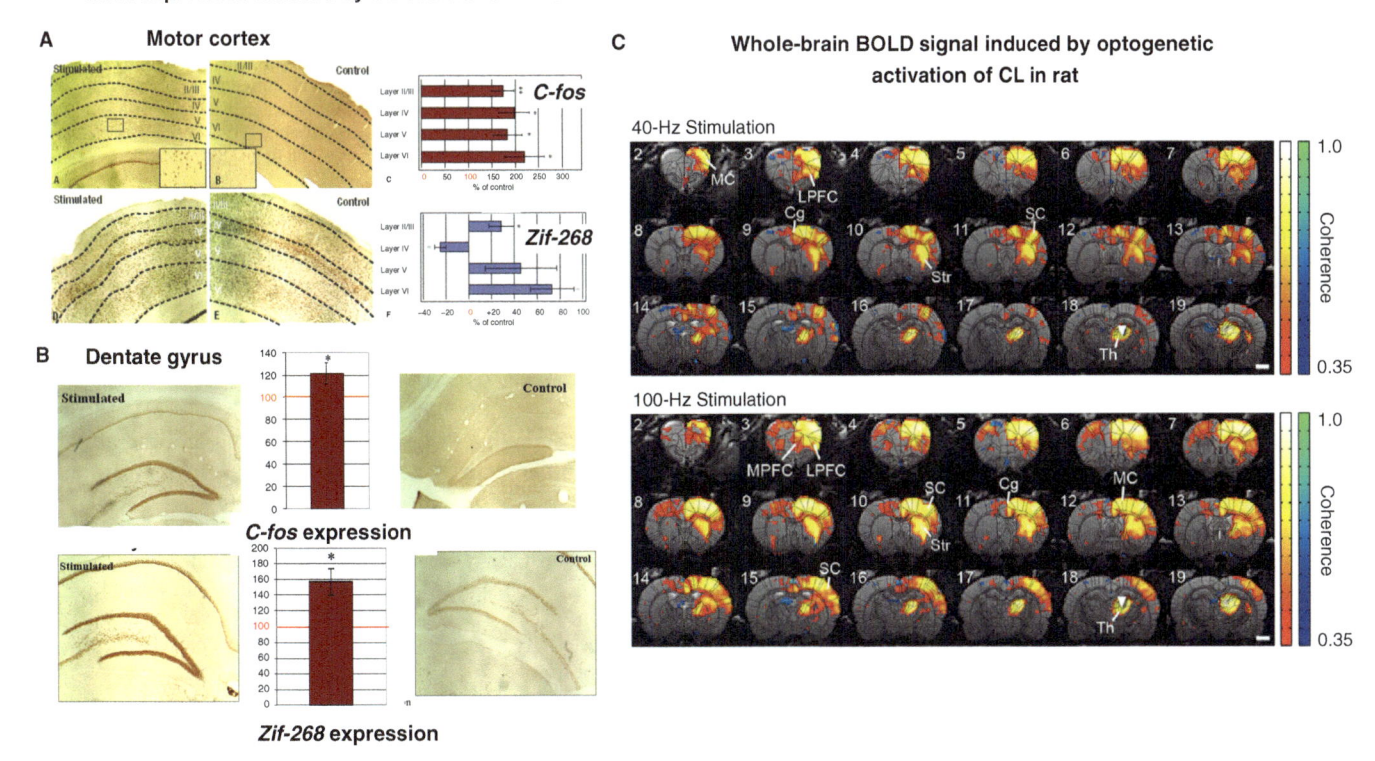

Figure 2 A, B. **Activation of immediate early gene expression by CL stimulation in the rodent.** Figure shows activation of the immediate early genes *c-fos* and *zif-268* following 30 minutes of CL electrical stimulation at 100 Hz (from Shirvalkar et al. 2006). In panel A, both *c-fos and zif-268* show increased cortical expression in several areas, including the motor cortex, and subcortical regions, including the dentate gyrus, as shown. A significant difference of *c-fos* expression appeared across all layers (II–VI), but a distinct laminar-specific pattern of selective expression of *zif-268* showed suppression within the granular layer (layer IV) but activation of layers II/III and V in the motor cortex. *, $P < 0.05$. **, $P < 0.01$. Figure elements from Shirvalkar et al. (2006).

C. **Spatial characterization of evoked fMRI signals from CL optogenetic activation**. Optogenetic activation of the CL produces broad frontostriatal activation, as demonstrated by increased blood oxygen level–dependent (BOLD) signal responses. Average coherence maps of brain-wide activity during stimulation of excitatory central thalamus relay neurons driven via optogenetic methods at 40 and 100 Hz. Warm colors indicate positive BOLD responses, whereas cool colors indicate negative BOLD responses. The amount of active volume (positive signal with coherence > 0.35) in the ipsilateral thalamus is significantly greater during 40 Hz compared with 100-Hz stimulation. Figure from Liu et al. (2015) under Creative Commons License.

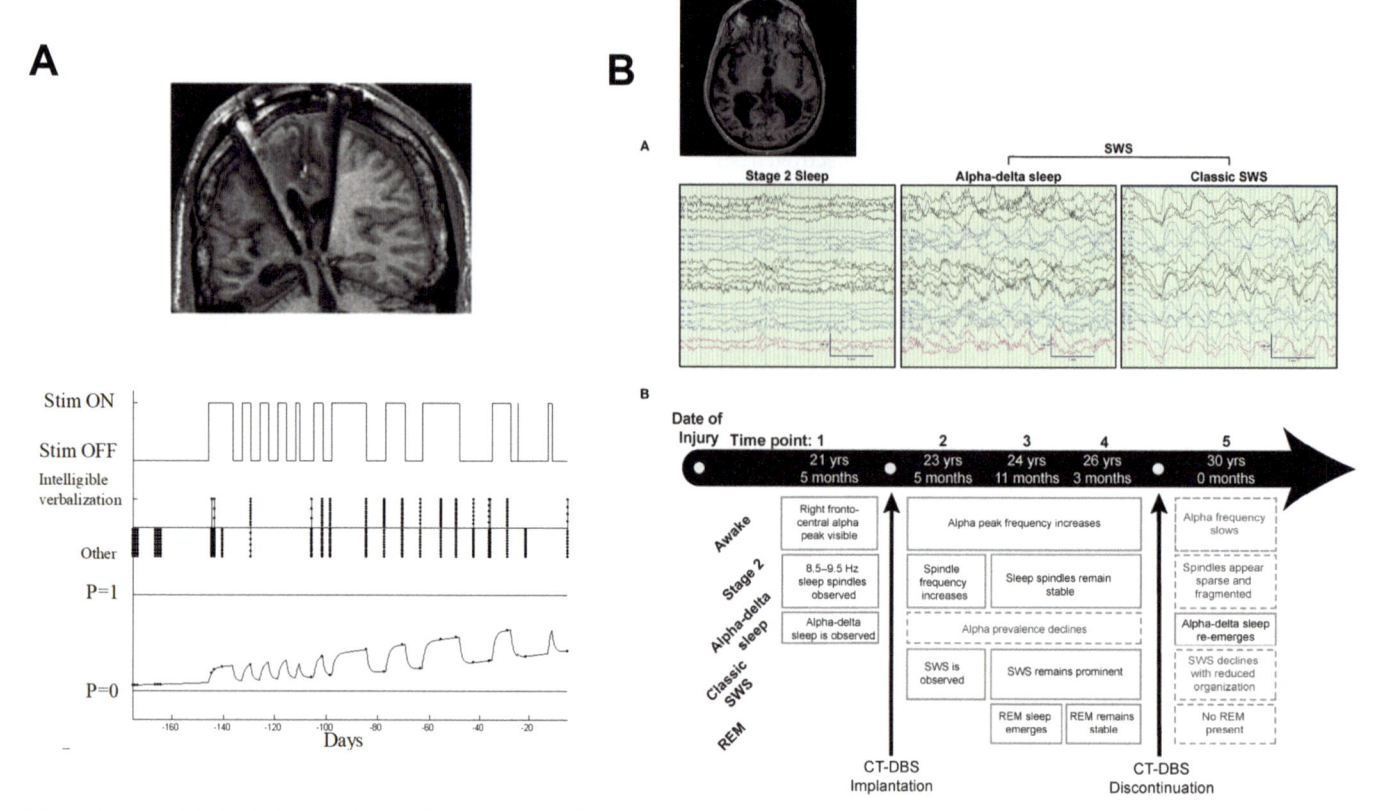

Figure 3 Central thalamic deep brain stimulation in minimally conscious state.

A. Top figure element shows placement of DBS electrodes in the central thalamus (targeting the central lateral nucleus) of patient remaining in MCS for six years (Schiff et al. 2007). Lower figure element shows logistic regression modeling of recovery of intelligible verbalization with initiation of stimulation. "Stim ON" and "Stim OFF" mark the stimulation history over time; behavioral time-series data are binarized, and raw data are displayed as dots on stems. Smooth curve plots the outcome variable (with 1= intelligible response, and 0 = all other categories) and the best-fitting probability model. Although a clear upward trend is visible, the log likelihood is significantly improved ($p < 0.001$) with a stimulation-dependent term (see Schiff et al. 2007 for details). Figure elements from Schiff et al. (2007; from *Nature*; author retains copyright for free reproduction with citation).

B. Top figure element shows structural brain image from patient remaining in MCS for 20 years prior to placement of DBS electrodes in the central thalamus (targeting the central lateral nucleus (Adams et al. 2016, Gottshall et al. 2019). Middle figure elements show representative segments of patient subject EEG tracings during non-REM sleep, demonstrating the presence of stage 2 (*left*) and classical slow-wave sleep (SWS) (*right*) epochs. A mixed-frequency signature consistent with alpha-delta sleep is also seen (*middle*). The patient subject was studied at five time points over the course of 8.5 years, consisting of one time point before, three during, and one after CT-DBS treatment. Lower panels show changes in the restoration of sleep architecture and quantitative changes in sleep features over the period of central thalamic stimulation and loss of features with cessation of stimulation. Figure from Gottshall et al. (2019). (Frontiers Open Source image)

should examine how effects induced by stimulation of the CL/DTTm during the day integrate into the 24-hour cycle for brain repair and may interact with basic learning and memory systems and other forms of cellular repair and network restoration.

References

Acsády L. The thalamic paradox. *Nat Neurosci.* **20**, 901–902 (2017)

Adams ZA, Forgacs PB, Conte MC, Nauvel TN, Drover JD, Schiff ND. Late and progressive alterations of sleep dynamics following central thalamic deep brain stimulation (CT-DBS) in chronic minimally conscious state. *Clin Neurophysiol.* **127**, 3086–3092 (2016)

Alexander GE, DeLong MR, Strick PL. Parallel organization of functionally segregated circuits linking basal ganglia and cortex. *Ann Rev Neurosci.* **9**, 357–381 (1986)

Baker JL, Ryou JW, Wei XF, Butson CR, Schiff ND, Purpura KP. Robust modulation of arousal regulation, performance, and frontostriatal activity through central thalamic deep brain stimulation in healthy nonhuman primates. *J Neurophysiol.* **116**, 2383–2404 (2016)

Barbas H, Pandya DN. Architecture and intrinsic connections of the prefrontal cortex in the rhesus monkey. *J Comp Neurol.* **286**, 353–375 (1989)

Barthó P, Freund TF, Acsády L. Selective GABAergic innervation of thalamic nuclei from zona incerta. *Eur J Neurosci.* **16**, 999–1014 (2002)

Bayer L, Eggermann E, Saint-Mleux B, Machard D, Jones BE, Mühlethaler M, Serafin M. Selective action of orexin (hypocretin) on nonspecific thalamocortical projection neurons. *J Neurosci.* **22**, 7835–7839 (2002)

Beck AK, Sandmann P, Dürschmid S, Schwabe K, Saryyeva A, Krauss JK. Neuronal activation in the human centromedian-parafascicular complex predicts cortical responses to behaviorally significant auditory events. *Neuroimage.* **211**, 116583 (2020)

Bernander O, Douglas RJ, Martin KA, Koch C. Synaptic background activity influences spatiotemporal integration in single pyramidal cells. *Proc Natl Acad Sci USA.* **88**, 11569–11573 (1991)

Bolkan SS, Stujenske JM, Parnaudeau S, Spellman TJ, Rauffenbart C, Abbas AI, Harris AZ, Gordon JA, Kellendonk C. Thalamic projections sustain prefrontal activity during working memory maintenance. *Nat Neurosci.* **20**, 987–996 (2017)

Buckwalter JA, Parvizi J, Morecraft RJ, van Hoesen GW. Thalamic projections to the posteromedial cortex in the macaque. *J Comp Neurol.* **507**, 1709–1733 (2008)

Burk JA, Glode BM, Drugan RC and Mair RG. Effects of chlordiazepoxide and FG 7142 on a rat model of diencephalic amnesia as measured by delayed matching to sample performance. *Psychopharmacology.* **142**, 413–420 (1999)

Burk JA, Mair RG. Thalamic amnesia reconsidered: excitotoxic lesions of the intralaminar nuclei, but not the mediodorsal nucleus, disrupt place delayed matching-to-sample performance in rats (*Rattus norvegicus*). *Behav Neurosci.* **112**, 54–67 (1998)

Calderon DP, Schiff ND. Objective and graded calibration of recovery of consciousness in experimental models. *Curr Opin Neurol.* **34**, 142–149 (2021)

Castaigne P, Lhermitte F, Buge A, Escourolle R, Hauw JJ, Lyon-Caen O. Paramedian thalamic and midbrain infarct: clinical and neuropathological study. *Ann Neurol.* **10**, 127–148. (1981)

Chudy D, Deletis V, Almahariq F, Marčinković P, Škrlin J, Paradžik V. Deep brain stimulation for the early treatment of the minimally conscious state and vegetative state: experience in 14 patients. *J Neurosurg.* **128**, 1189–1198 (2018)

Cohadon F, Richer E. Deep cerebral stimulation in patients with post-traumatic vegetative state: 25 cases. *Neurochirurgie.* **39**, 281–292 (1993)

Corrigan JD, Cuthbert JP, Harrison-Felix C, Whiteneck GG, Bell JM, Miller AC, Coronado VG, Pretz CR. US population estimates of health and social outcomes 5 years after rehabilitation for traumatic brain injury. *J Head Trauma Rehabil.* **29**, E1–9. (2014)

Cover KK, Gyawali U, Kerkhoff WG, Patton MH, Mu C, White MG, Marquardt AE, Roberts BM, Cheer JF, Mathur BN. Activation of the rostral intralaminar thalamus drives reinforcement through striatal dopamine release. *Cell Rep.* **26**, 1389–1398.e3 (2019)

Cruikshank SJ, Ahmed OJ, Stevens TR, Patrick SL, Gonzalez AN, Elmaleh M, Connors BW. Thalamic control of layer 1 circuits in prefrontal cortex. *J Neurosci.* **32**, 17813–17823 (2012)

Curró Dossi R, Paré D, Steriade M. Short-lasting nicotinic and long-lasting muscarinic depolarizing responses of thalamocortical neurons to stimulation of mesopontine cholinergic nuclei. *J Neurophysiol.* **3**, 393–406. (1991)

Deschênes M, Bourassa J, Parent A. Striatal and cortical projections of single neurons from the central lateral thalamic nucleus in the rat. *Neuroscience.* **72**, 679–687 (1996)

Dikmen SS, Machamer JE, Powell JM, Temkin NR. Outcome 3 to 5 years after moderate to severe traumatic brain injury. *Arch Phys Med Rehabil.* **84**, 1449–1457 (2003)

Donoghue JA, Bastos AM, Yanar J, Kornblith S, Mahnke M, Brown EN, Miller EK. Neural signatures of loss of consciousness and its recovery by thalamic stimulation. *BioArxiv.* http://dx.doi.org/10.1101/806687 (2019)

Donoghue JA, Kornblith S, Mahke M, Lundqvist M, Roy JE, Brown EN, Miller EK. Thalamic deep brain stimulation restores awake-like behavior and cortical dynamics in the anesthetized macaque. In Society for Neuroscience Abstracts [Abstract 751.04] (2017)

Drover JD, Schiff ND. A method for decomposing multivariate time series into a causal hierarchy within specific frequency bands. *J Comput Neurosci.* **45**, 59–82 (2018)

Duncan J, Owen AM. Common regions of the human frontal lobe recruited by diverse cognitive demands. *Trends Neurosci.* **23**, 475–483 (2000)

Edlow BL, Claassen J, Schiff ND, Greer DM. Recovery from disorders of consciousness: mechanisms, prognosis, and emerging therapies. *Nat Rev Neurol.* **17**, 135–156. (2021)

Edlow BL, Takahashi E, Wu O, Benner T, Dai G, Bu L, Grant PE, Greer DM, Greenberg SM, Kinney HC, Folkerth RD. Neuroanatomic connectivity of the human ascending arousal system critical to consciousness and its disorders. *J Neuropathol Exp Neurol.* **71**, 531–546 (2012)

Ellender TJ, Harwood J, Kosillo P, Capogna M, Bolam JP. Heterogeneous properties of central lateral and parafascicular thalamic synapses in the striatum. *J Physiol.* **591**, 257–272 (2013)

Feindel W, Gloor P. Comparison of electrographic effects of stimulation of the amygdala and brain stem reticular formation in cats. *Electroencephalogr Clin Neurophysiol.* **3**, 389–402. (1954)

Felleman DJ, Van Essen DC. Distributed hierarchical processing in the primate cerebral cortex. *Cereb Cortex.* **1**, 1–47. (1991)

Fridman EA, Beattie BJ, Broft A, Laureys S, Schiff ND. Regional cerebral metabolic patterns demonstrate the role of anterior forebrain mesocircuit dysfunction in the severely injured brain. *Proc Natl Acad Sci USA.* **111**, 6473–6478 (2014)

Fridman EA, Osbourne JR, Mozley PD, Victor JD, Schiff ND. Presynaptic dopamine deficit in minimally conscious state patients following traumatic brain injury. *Brain.* **142**,1887–1893 (2019)

Fuller PM, Sherman D, Pedersen NP, Saper CB, Lu J. Reassessment of the structural basis of the ascending arousal system. *J Comp Neurol.* **519**, 933–956 (2011)

Fuster JM. Effects of stimulation of brain stem on tachistoscopic perception. *Science.* **127**, 150 (1958)

Gao S, Calderon DP. Robust alternative to the righting reflex to assess arousal in rodents. *Sci Rep.* **10**, 20280 (2020)

Gao S, Proekt A, Renier N, Calderon DP, Pfaff DW. Activating an anterior nucleus gigantocellularis subpopulation triggers emergence from pharmacologically-induced coma in rodents. *Nat Comm.* **10**, 2897 (2019)

Giacino JT, Ashwal S, Childs N, Cranford R, Jennett B, Katz DI, Kelly JP, Rosenberg JH, Whyte J, Zafonte RD, Zasler ND. The minimally conscious state: definition and diagnostic criteria. *Neurology.* **58**, 349–353 (2002)

Giacino JT, Fins JJ, Laureys S, Schiff ND. Disorders of consciousness after acquired brain injury: the state of the science. *Nat Rev Neurol.* **10**, 99–114. (2014)

Giacino J, Fins JJ, Machado A, Schiff ND. Central thalamic deep brain stimulation to promote recovery from chronic posttraumatic minimally conscious state: challenges and opportunities. *Neuromodulation.* **15**, 339–349 (2012)

Giber K, Diana MA, Plattner V, Dugué GP, Bokor H, Rousseau CV, Maglóczky Z, Havas L, Hangya B, Wildner H, Zeilhofer HU, Dieudonné S, Acsády L. A subcortical inhibitory signal for behavioral arrest in the thalamus. *Nat Neurosci.* **18**, 562–568 (2015)

Glenn LL, Steriade M. Discharge rate and excitability of cortically projecting intralaminar thalamic neurons during waking and sleep states. *J Neurosci.* **2**, 1287–1404 (1982)

Gottshall JL, Adams ZM, Forgacs PB, Schiff ND. Daytime central thalamic deep brain stimulation modulates sleep dynamics in the severely injured brain: mechanistic insights and a novel framework for alpha-delta sleep generation. *Front Neurol.* **10**, 20 (2019)

Grillner S, Hellgren J, Ménard A, Saitoh K, Wikström MA. Mechanisms for selection of basic motor programs–roles for the striatum and pallidum. *Trends Neurosci.* **28**, 364–370. (2005)

Gronewegen H, Berendse H. The specificity of the "nonspecific" midline and intralaminar thalamic nuclei. *Trends Neurosci.* **17**, 52–66. (1994)

Guo ZV, Inagaki HK, Daie K, Druckmann S, Gerfen CR, Svoboda K. Maintenance of persistent activity in a frontal thalamocortical loop. *Nature.* **545**, 181–186. 2017

Heckers S, Geula C, Mesulam MM. Cholinergic innervation of the human thalamus: dual origin and differential nuclear distribution. *J Comp Neurol.* **325**, 68–82 (1992)

Hikosaka O, Sakamoto M, Usui S. Functional properties of monkey caudate neurons. III. Activities related to expectation of target and reward. *J Neurophysiol.* **61**, 814–832 (1989)

Hindman J, Bowren MD, Bruss J, Wright B, Geerling JC, Boes AD. Thalamic strokes that severely impair arousal extend into the brainstem. *Ann Neurol.* **84**, 926–930 (2018)

Hosobuchi Y, Yingling C. The treatment of prolonged coma with neurostimulation. In: Devinsky O, Beric A, Dogali M, eds., Electrical and Magnetic stimulation of the Brain and Spinal Cord. New York: Raven Press, pp. 247–252 (1993)

Huerta-Ocampo I, Hacioglu-Bay H, Dautan D, Mena-Segovia J. Distribution of midbrain cholinergic axons in the thalamus. *eNeuro.* **7**, ENEURO.0454-19.2019 (2020)

Jones EG. A new view of the specific and non-specific thalamocortical connections. *Adv Neurol.* **77**, 49–71(1998a)

Jones EG. Viewpoint: the core and matrix of thalamic organization. *Neuroscience.* **85**, 331–345 (1998b)

Jones EG. The *Thalamus*, 2nd ed. Cambridge: Cambridge University Press (2007)

Jones EG. Synchrony in the interconnected circuitry of the thalamus and cerebral cortex. *Ann NY Acad Sci.* **1157**, 10–23 (2009)

Kato S, Fukabori R, Nishizawa K, Okada K, Yoshioka N, Sugawara M, Maejima Y, Shimomura K, Okamoto M, Eifuku S, Kobayashi K. Action selection and flexible switching controlled by the intralaminar thalamic neurons. *Cell Rep.* **22**, 2370–2382 (2018)

Katz DI, Alexander MP, Mandell AM. Dementia following strokes in the mesencephalon and diencephalon. *Arch Neurol.* **44**, 1127–1133 (1987)

Kinomura S, Larsson J, Gulyás B, Roland PE. Activation by attention of the human reticular formation and thalamic intralaminar nuclei. *Science.* **271**, 512–515 (1996)

Kolmac C, Mitrofanis J. Organization of the basal forebrain projection to the thalamus in rats. *Neurosci Lett.* **272**, 151–154 (1999)

Krolak-Salmon P, Croisile B, Houzard C, Setiey A, Girard-Madoux P, Vighetto A. Total recovery after bilateral paramedian thalamic infarct. *Eur Neurol.* **44**, 216–218 (2000)

Krout KE, Loewy AD, Westby GW, Redgrave P. Superiorcolliculus projections to midline and intralaminar thalamic nuclei of the rat. *J Comp Neurol.* **431**, 198–216 (2001)

Kuczewski N, Porcher C, Ferrand N, Fiorentino H, Pellegrino C, Kolarow R, Lessmann V, Medina I, Gaiarsa J-L. (2008) Backpropagating action potentials trigger dendritic release of BDNF during spontaneous network activity. *J Neurosci.* **28**, 7013–7023 (2008)

Kundishora AJ, Gummadavelli A, Ma C, Liu M, McCafferty C, Schiff ND, Willie JT, Gross RE, Gerrard J, Blumenfeld H. Restoring conscious arousal during focal limbic seizures with deep brain stimulation. *Cereb Cortex.* **27**, 1964–1975 (2017)

Larkum ME, Waters J, Sakmann B, Helmchen F. Dendritic spikes in apical dendrites of neocortical layer 2/3 pyramidal neurons. *J Neurosci.* **27**, 8999–9008 (2007)

Larkum, ME, ZhuJJ, Sakmann B. A new cellular mechanism for coupling inputs arriving at different cortical layers. *Nature.* **398**, 338–341 (1999)

Laureys S, Schiff ND. Coma and consciousness: paradigms (re)framed by neuroimaging. *NeuroImage.* **61**, 478–491 (2012)

Lemaire JJ, Sontheimer A, Pereira B, Coste J, Rosenberg S, Sarret C, Coll G, Gabrillargues J, Jean B, Gillart T, Coste A, Roche B, Kelly A, Pontier B, Feschet F. Deep brain stimulation in five patients with severe disorders of consciousness. *Ann Clin Transl Neurol.* **5**, 1372–1384 (2017)

Lin TC, Lo YC, Lin HC, Li SJ, Lin SH, Wu HF, Chu MC, Lee CW, Lin IC, Chang CW, Liu YC, Chen TC, Lin YJ, Ian Shih YY, Chen YY. MR imaging central thalamic deep brain stimulation restored autistic-like social deficits in the rat. *Brain Stimul.* **12**, 1410–1420 (2019)

Liu J, Lee HJ, Weitz AJ, Fang Z, Lin P, Choy MK, Fisher R, Pinskiy V, Tolpygo A, Mitra P, Schiff ND, Lee JH. Frequency-selective control of cortical and subcortical networks by central thalamus. *eLife.* **4**, e09215 (2015)

Llinás R, Ribary U, Contreras D, Pedroarena C. The neuronal basis for consciousness. *Philos Trans RSoc Lond B.* **353**, 1841–1849 (1998)

Llinás RR, Ribary U, Jeanmonod D, Kronberg E, Mitra PP. Thalamocortical dysrhythmia: A neurological and neuropsychiatric syndrome characterized by magnetoencephalography. *Proc Natl Acad Sci USA.* **96**, 15222–15227 (1999)

Llinás R, Ribary U, Joliot M, Wang XJ. Content and context in temporal thalamocortical binding. In: Buzsaki G, Llinás R, Singer W, Berthoz A, Christen Y, eds., Temporal Coding in the Brain. Heidelberg: Springer, pp. 252–272 (1994)

Llinás R, Urbano FJ, Leznik E, Ramírez RR, van Marle HJF rhythmic and dysrhythmic thalamocortical dynamics: GABA systems and the edge effect. *Trends Neurosci.* **28**, 325–333 (2005)

Llinás RR, Leznik E, UrbanoFJ. Temporal binding via cortical coincidence detection of specific and nonspecific thalamocortical inputs: a voltage-dependent dye-imaging study in mouse brain slices. *Proc Natl Acad Sci USA.* **99**, 449–454 (2002)

Magrassi L, Maggioni G, Pistarini C, Di Perri C, Bastianello S, Zippo AG, Iotti GA, Biella GE, Imberti R. Results of a prospective study (CATS) on the effects of thalamic stimulation in minimally conscious and vegetative state patients. *J Neurosurg.* **125**, 972–981 (2016)

Mair R. On the role of thalamic pathology in diencephalic amnesia. *Rev Neurosci.* **5**, 105–140 (1994)

Mair RG, Francoeur MJ, Gibson BM. Central thalamic-medial prefrontal control of adaptive responding in the rat: many players in the chamber. *Front Behav Neurosci.* **15**, 642204 (2021)

Mair RG, Hembrook JR. Memory enhancement with event-related stimulation of the rostral intralaminar thalamic nuclei. *J Neurosci.* **28**, 14293–14300. (2008)

Mair RG, Onos KD, Hembrook JR. Cognitive activation by central thalamic stimulation: the Yerkes-Dodson law revisited. *Dose Response.* **9**, 313–331 (2011)

Matsumoto N, Minamimoto T, Graybiel AM, Kimura M. Neurons in the thalamic CM-Pf complex supply striatal neurons with information about behaviorally significant sensory events. *J Neurophysiol.* **85**, 960–976 (2001)

Maxwell WL, MacKinnon MA, Smith DH, McIntosh TK, Graham DI. Thalamic nuclei after human blunt head injury. *J Neuropathol Exp Neurol.* **65**, 478–488 (2006)

Mennemeier M, Crosson B, Williamson DJ, Nadeau SE, Fennell E, Valenstein E, Heilman KM. Tapping, talking and the thalamus: possible influence of the intralaminar nuclei on basal ganglia function. *Neuropsychologia.* **35**, 183–193 (1997)

Minamimoto T, Kimura M. Participation of the thalamic CM-Pf complex in attentional orienting. *J Neurophysiol.* **87**, 3090–3101 (2002)

Minamimoto T, La Camera G, Richmond BJ. Measuring and modeling the interaction among reward size, delay to reward, and satiation level on motivation in monkeys. *J Neurophysiol.* **101**, 437–447 (2009)

Morel A, Liu J, Wannier T, Jeanmonod D, Rouiller EM. Divergence and convergence of thalamocortical projections to premotor and supplementary motor cortex: a multiple tracing study in the macaque monkey. *Eur J Neurosci.* **21**, 1007–1029 (2005)

Moruzzi G, Magoun HW. Brainstem reticular formation and activation of the EEG. *Electroencephalogr Clin Neurophysiol.* **1**, 455–473 (1949)

Münkle MC, Waldvogel HJ, Faull RL. Calcium-binding protein immunoreactivity delineates the intralaminar nuclei of the thalamus in the human brain. *Neuroscience.* **90**, 485–491 (1999)

Münkle MC, Waldvogel HJ, Faull RL. The distribution of calbindin, calretinin and parvalbumin immunoreactivity in the human thalamus. *J Chem Neuroanat.* **19**, 155–173 (2000)

Nagai Y, Critchley HD, Featherstone E, Fenwick PB, Trimble MR, Dolan RJ. Brain activity relating to the contingent negative variation: an fMRI investigation. *Neuroimage.* **21**, 1232–1241 (2004)

Naito E, Kinomura S, Geyer S, Kawashima R, Roland PE, Zilles K. Fast reaction to different sensory modalities activates common fields in the motor areas, but the anterior cingulate cortex is involved in the speed of reaction. *J Neurophysiol.* **83**, 1701–1709 (2000)

Narayanan NS, Cavanagh JF, Frank MJ, Laubach M. Common medial frontal mechanisms of adaptive control in humans and rodents. *Nat Neurosci.* **16**, 1888–1895 (2013)

Newman DB, Ginsberg CY. Brainstem reticular nuclei that project to the thalamus in rats: a retrograde tracer study. *Brain Behav Evol.* **44**, 1–39 (1994)

Oke AF, Carver LA, Gouvion CM, Adams RN. Three-dimensional mapping of norepinephrine and serotonin in human thalamus. *Brain Res.* **763**, 69–78 (1997)

Parvizi J, Damasio AR. Neuroanatomical correlates of brainstem coma. *Brain.* **126**, 1524–1536 (2003)

Paus T, Zatorre R, Hofle N, Caramanos Z, Gotman J, Petrides M, Evans, A. Time-related changes in Neural systems underlying attention and arousal during the performance of an auditory vigilance task. *J Cog Neurosci.* **9**, 392–408 (1997)

Pfaff D. Brain *Arousal* and *Information Processing*. Cambridge, MA: Harvard University Press (2005)

Plum F, Posner J. Diagnosis of Stupor and Coma. Philadelphia: F.A. Davis. (1966)

Posner J, Saper C, Schiff ND, Claassen J. Plum and Posner's Diagnosis and Treatment of Stupor and Coma, 5th ed. Oxford: Oxford University Press (2019)

Purpura K, Schiff ND. The thalamic intralaminar nuclei: a role in visual awareness. *Neuroscientist.* **3**, 8–15 (1997)

Redinbaugh MJ, Phillips JM, Kambi NA, Mohanta S, Andryk S, Dooley GL, Afrasiabi M, Raz A, Saalmann YB. Thalamus modulates consciousness via layer-specific control of cortex. *Neuron.* **106**, 66–75.e12 (2020)

Ribeiro S, Mello CV, Velho T, Gardner TJ, Jarvis ED, Pavlides C. *J Neurosci.* **22**, 10914–10923. (2002)

Rieck RW, Ansari MS, Whetsell WO Jr, Deutch AY, Kessler RM. Distribution of dopamine D2-like receptors in the human thalamus: autoradiographic and PET studies. *Neuropsychopharmacology.* **29**, 362–372 (2004)

Rubio-Garrido P, Pérez-de-Manzo F, Clascá F. Calcium-binding proteins as markers of layer-I projecting vs. deep layer-projecting thalamocortical neurons: a double-labeling analysis in the rat. *Neuroscience.* **149**, 242–250 (2007)

Sadikot AF, Parent A, Smith Y, Bolam JP. Efferent connections of the centromedian and parafascicular thalamic nuclei in the squirrel monkey: a light and electron microscopic study of the thalamostriatal projection in relation to striatal heterogeneity. *J Comp Neurol.* **320**, 228–242 (1992)

Sanford LD, Morrison AR, Ball WA, Ross RJ, Mann GL. Varying expressions of alerting mechanisms in wakefulness and across sleep states. *Electroencephalogr Clin Neurophysiol.* **82**, 458–468 (1992)

Saper CB, Scammell TE, Lu J. Hypothalamic regulation of sleep and circadian rhythms. *Nature.* **437**, 1257–1263 (2005)

Scannell JW, Burns GA, Hilgetag CC, O'Neil MA, Young MP. The connectional organization of the cortico-thalamic system of the cat. *Cereb Cortex.* **9**, 277–299 (1999)

Schiff ND. Central thalamic contributions to arousal regulation and neurological disorders of consciousness. *Ann NY Acad Sci.* **1129**, 105–118 (2008)

Schiff ND. Recovery of consciousness after brain injury: a mesocircuit hypothesis. *Trends Neurosci.* **33**, 1–9 (2010)

Schiff ND. Posterior medial corticothalamic connectivity and consciousness. *Ann Neurol.* **72**, 305–306. (2012)

Schiff ND. Central thalamic deep brain stimulation to support anterior forebrain mesocircuit function in the severely injured brain. *J Neural Transm* (Vienna). **123**, 797–806. (2016)

Schiff ND. Resolving the role of the paramedian thalamus in forebrain arousal mechanisms. *Ann Neurol.* **84**, 812–813 (2018)

Schiff ND. Central lateral thalamic nucleus stimulation awakens cortex via modulation of cross-regional, laminar-specific activity during general anesthesia. *Neuron.* **106**, 1–3 (2020)

Schiff ND, Giacino JT, Butson CR, Baker JL, Bergin M, Bronte-Stewart HM, Choi EY, DeGeorge L, Gerber LM, Janson AP, Shah SA, Su J, Kolakowsky-Hayner SA, Fins JJ, Machado AG, Rutt BK, Henderson JM. Central thalamic brain stimulation modulates executive function and fatigue in a patient with severe to moderate traumatic brain injury. In Fifth Annual Brain Initiative Investigators Meeting Abstract book [Abstract S-124] (2019)

Schiff ND, Giacino JT, Butson CR, Baker JL, Bergin M, Bronte-Stewart HM, Choi EY, DeGeorge L, Gerber LM, Janson AP, Shah SA, Su J, Kolakowsky-Hayner SA, Fins JJ, Machado AG, Rutt BK, Henderson JM. Central thalamic brain stimulation improves executive function and mental fatigue in severe to moderate traumatic brain injury. In Seventh Annual Brain Initiative Investigators Meeting [3051] (2021)

Schiff ND, Giacino JT, Kalmar K, Victor JD, Baker K, Gerber M, Fritz B, Eisenberg B, Biondi T, O'Connor J, Kobylarz EJ, Farris S, Machado A, McCagg C, Plum F, Fins JJ, Rezai AR. Behavioral improvements with thalamic stimulation after severe traumatic brain injury. *Nature.* **448**, 600–603 (2007)

Schiff ND, Nauvel T, Victor JD. Large-scale brain dynamics in disorders of consciousness. *Curr Opin Neurobiol.* **25**, 7–14 (2014)

Schiff ND, Plum F. The role of arousal and "gating" systems in the neurology of impaired consciousness. *J Clin Neurophysiol.* **17**, 438–452 (2000)

Schiff ND, Purpura KP. Towards a neurophysiological basis for cognitive neuromodulation. *Thalamus Relate Syst.* **2**, 55–69 (2002)

Schiff ND, Shah SA, Hudson AE, Nauvel T, Kalik SF, Purpura KP. Gating of attentional effort through the central thalamus. *J Neurophysiol.* **109**, 1152–1163 (2013)

Schlag J, Schlag-Rey M. Visuomotor functions of central thalamus in monkey. II. Unit activity related to visual events, targeting, and fixation. *J Neurophysiol.* **51**, 1175–1195. (1984)

Schlag J, Schlag-Rey MR. Role of the central thalamus in gaze control. *Prog Brain Res.* **64**, 191–201 (1986)

Schlag-Rey M, Schlag J. Visuomotor functions of central thalamus in monkey. I. Unit activity related to spontaneous eye movements. *J Neurophysiol.* **51**, 1149–1174. 1984

Schmitt LI, Wimmer RD, Nakajima M, Happ M, Mofakham S, Halassa MM. Thalamic amplification of cortical connectivity sustains attentional control. *Nature.* **545**, 219–223 (2017)

Shah S, Mohamadpour M, Askin G, Nakase-Richardson R, Stokic DS, Sherer M, Yablon SA, Schiff ND. Focal electroencephalographic changes index post-traumatic confusion and outcome. *J Neurotrauma.* **34**, 2691–2699 (2017)

Shah SA, Goldin Y, Conte MM, Goldfine AM, Mohamadpour M, Fidali BC, Cicerone K, Schiff ND. Executive attention deficits after traumatic brain injury reflect impaired recruitment of resources. *Neuroimage Clin.* **14**, 233–241 (2017)

Shah SA, Schiff ND. Central thalamic deep brain stimulation for cognitive neuromodulation: a review of proposed mechanisms and investigational studies. *Eur J Neurosci.* **32**, 1135–1144 (2010)

Shirvalkar P, Seth M, Schiff ND, Herrera DG. Cognitive enhancement with central thalamic electrical stimulation. *Proc Nat Acad Sci USA.* **103**, 17007–17012 (2006)

Silva LR, Amitai Y, Connors BW. Intrinsic oscillations of neocortex generated by layer 5 pyramidal neurons. *Science.* **251**, 432–435 (1991)

Smiley JF, Subramanian M, Mesulam MM. Monaminergic-cholinergi interactions in the primate basal forebrain. *Neuroscience.* **93**, 817–829. (1999)

Smith Y, Raju D, Nanda B, Pare JF, Galvan A, Wichmann T. The thalamostriatal systems: anatomical and functional organization in normal and parkinsonian states. *Brain Res Bull.* **78**, 60–68 (2009)

Steriade M. Neocortical neurons are flexible entities. *Trends Neurosci.* **5**, 121–134. (2001)

Steriade M, Contreras D, Amzica F, Timofeev I. Synchronization of fast (30–40 Hz) spontaneous oscillations in intrathalamic and thalamocortical networks. *J Neurosci.* **16**, 2788–2808 (1996)

Steriade M, Curro R, Contreras D. Electrophysiological properties of intralaminar thalamocortical cells discharging rhythmic (40 Hz) spikebursts at 1000 Hz during waking and rapid eye movement sleep. *Neuroscience.* **56**, 1–9 (1993)

Steriade M, Dossi RC, Nuñez A. Network modulation of a slow intrinsic oscillation of cat thalamocortical neurons implicated in sleep delta waves: cortically induced synchronization and brainstem cholinergic suppression. *J Neurosci.* **10**, 3200–3217 (1991)

Steriade M, Dossi RC, Paré D, Oakson G. Fast oscillations (20–40 Hz) in thalamocortical systems and their potentiation by mesopontine cholinergic nuclei in the cat. *Proc Natl Acad Sci USA.* **88**, 4396–4400 (1991)

Steriade M, Glenn LL. Neocortical and caudate projections of intralaminar thalamic neurons and their synaptic excitation from midbrain reticular core. *J Neurophysiol.* **48**, 352–371 (1982)

Sturm V, Kuhner A, Schmitt HP, Assmus H, Stock G. Chronic electrical stimulation of the thalamic unspecific activating system in a patient with coma due to midbrain and upper brain stem infarction. *Acta Neurochirurgica.* **47**, 235–244 (1979)

Stuss DT, Guberman A, Nelson R, Larochelle S. The neuropsychology of paramedian thalamic infarction. *Brain Cogn.* **8**, 348–378 (1988)

Sutcliff JG, De Lecea L. The hypocretins: setting the arousal threshold. *Nat Rev Neurosci.* **3**, 339–349 (2002)

Suzuki M, Larkum ME. General Anesthesia Decouples Cortical Pyramidal Neurons. *Cell.* **180**, 666–676.e13 (2020)

Tabansky I, Quinkert AW, Rahman N, Muller SZ, Lofgren J, Rudling J, Pfaff DW. Temporally-patterned deep brain stimulation in a mouse model of multiple traumatic brain injury. *Behav Brain Res.* **273**, 123–132 (2014)

Tasserie J, Uhrig L, Sitt JD, Dupont M, Deheane S, Jayarra M. Thalamic stimulation modulates consciousness in anesthetized macaques by restoring spontaneous and evoked fMRI activity in a cortical global neuronal workspace. In Society for Neuroscience Abstracts [Abstract 420.02 SFN] (2019)

Thengone DJ, Voss HU, Fridman EA, Schiff ND. Local changes in network structure contribute to late communication recovery after severe brain injury. *Sci Transl Med.* **8**, 368re5 (2016)

Thompson R. Centrencephalic theory, generalized learning system and subcortical dementia. *Ann NY Acad Sci.* **702**, 197–223. (1993)

Thompson RF. Foundations of Physiological Psychology. New York: Joanna Cotler Books (1967)

Tsai ST, Chen LJ, Wang YJ, Chen SY, Tseng GF. Rostral intralaminar thalamic deep brain stimulation triggered cortical and hippocampal structural plasticity and enhanced spatial memory. *Stereotact Funct Neurosurg.* **94**, 108–117 (2016)

Tsai ST, Chen SY, Lin SZ, Tseng GF. Rostral intralaminar thalamic deep brain stimulation ameliorates memory deficits and dendritic regression in beta-amyloid-infused rats. *Brain Struct Funct.* **225**, 751–761 (2020)

Tsubokawa T, Yamamoto T, Katayama Y, Hirayama T, Maejima S, Moriya T. Deep-brain stimulation in a persistent vegetative state: follow-up results and criteria for selection of candidates. *Brain Inj.* **4**, 315–327 (1990)

Van Der Werf YD, Weerts JG, Jolles J, Witter MP, Lindeboom J, Scheltens P. Neuropsychological correlates of a right unilateral lacunar thalamic infarction. *J Neurol Neurosurg Psychiatry.* **66**, 36–42 (1999)

Van der Werf YD, Witter MP, Groenewegen HJ. The intralaminar and midline nuclei of the thalamus. Anatomical and functional evidence for participation in processes of arousal and awareness. *Brain Res Brain Res Rev.* **39**, 107–140 (2002)

Vanderwolf CH, Stewart DJ. Thalamic control of neocortical activation: a critical re-evaluation. *Brain Res Bull.* **20**, 529–538 (1988)

Vogt BA, Hof PR, Friedman DP, Sikes RW, Vogt LJ. Norepinephrinergic afferents and cytology of the macaque monkey midline, mediodorsal, and intralaminar thalamic nuclei. *Brain Struct Funct.* **212**, 465–479 (2008)

von Domburg PH, ten Donkelaar HJ, Notermans SL. Akinetic mutism with bithalamic infarction. Neurophysiological correlates. *J Neurol Sci.* **139**, 58–65 (1996)

Voss HU, Uluç AM, Dyke JP, Watts R, Kobylarz EJ, McCandliss BD, Heier LA, Beattie BJ, Hamacher KA, Vallabhajosula S, Goldsmith SJ, Ballon D, Giacino JT, Schiff ND. Possible axonal regrowth in late recovery from minimally conscious state. *J Clin Invest.* **116**, 2005–2011 (2006)

Watson RT, Valenstein E, Heilman KM. Thalamic neglect. Possible role of the medial thalamus and nucleus reticularis in behavior. *Arch Neurol.* **38**, 501–506 (1981)

Williams ST, Conte MM, Goldfine AM, Noirhomme Q, Gosseries O, Thonnard M, Beattie B, Hersh J, Katz DI, Victor JD, Laureys S, Schiff ND. Common resting brain dynamics indicate a possible mechanism underlying zolpidem response in severe brain injury. *eLife.* **2**, e01157 (2013)

Wyder MT, Massoglia DP, Stanford TR. Quantitative assessment of the timing and tuning of visual-related, saccade-related, and delay period activity in primate central thalamus. *J Neurophysiol.* **90**, 2029–2052 (2003)

Wyder MT, Massoglia DP, Stanford TR. Contextual modulation of central thalamic delay-period activity: representation of visual and saccadic goals. *J Neurophysiol.* **91**, 2628–2648 (2004)

Xu J, Galardi MM, Pok B, Patel KK, Zhao CW, Andrews JP, Singla S, McCafferty CP, Feng L, Musonza ET, Kundishora AJ, Gummadavelli A, Gerrard JL, Laubach M, Schiff ND, Blumenfeld H. Thalamic stimulation improves postictal cortical arousal and behavior. *J Neurosci.* **40**, 1370–1320 (2020)

Yamamoto T, Katayama Y. Deep brain stimulation therapy for the vegetative state. *Neuropsychol Rehabil.* **15**, 406–413 (2005)

Section 9: Computation

Chapter 21: A Dynamical Systems Perspective on Thalamic Circuit Function

Qinglong L. Gu and John D. Murray

Introduction

The thalamus has long been regarded to function principally as a relay station of the brain, through which most sensory information propagates to reach different areas of the cerebral cortex. Yet it is clear that thalamic circuits do much more than relay signals. In this chapter, we will view thalamic function from the perspective of dynamical systems and biophysically grounded computational modeling. An emphasis will be placed on how biophysical mechanisms shape neurophysiological dynamics, which in turn support functional computations.

Connectivity structures within the thalamus and pathways interconnecting the thalamus and cortex have been extensively studied (Jones, 2012; Sherman, 2012; Usrey and Sherman, 2018). In particular, thalamocortical (TC) neurons receive inputs from ascending sensory pathways such as the visual, auditory, and somatosensory systems (Jones, 2012). In addition, the thalamus receives inputs from the cortex, which can differ in their laminar origin and biophysical properties (Rovó et al., 2012; Sherman, 2001, 2016). In addition, TC neurons send their glutamatergic axons to the thalamic reticular nucleus (TRN). The TRN, which forms a thin capsule around the thalamus, contains GABAergic reticular (RE) neurons, which provide inhibition of TC neurons (Jones, 2012). Monosynaptic connections between neurons of the same type (TC or RE) are not believed to exist abundantly within the mature mammalian brain (Lee et al., 2010; Hou et al., 2016). The two types of neurons are coupled to each other through sparse synaptic connections (Jones, 2012). In addition, experimental studies have shown that corticothalamic (CT) neurons can project to different subtypes of interneurons in the cortex (Porter et al., 2001; Tottene et al., 2019; Gabernet et al., 2005), which characterizes the importance of thalamic output in regulating cortical dynamics.

Moreover, research has demonstrated the pivotal role of the thalamus in cognitive flexibility and attention control. Optogenetic experiments have shown that thalamic input is necessary for sustaining cortical activity (Reinhold et al., 2015), is able to modulate fear extinction (Lee et al., 2019) and flight behavior (Dong et al., 2019), and can support behavioral tasks by enhancing functional cortical connectivity (Schmitt et al., 2017). In turn, it has been found that thalamic activity can be shaped by an extensive network of CT projections. The top-down CT projections can switch the spike mode of these neurons between burst and tonic firing (Ahissar and Oram, 2013) by modulating the level of hyperpolarization in TC cells and can sharpen receptive fields in thalamic sensory nuclei (Soto-Sánchez et al., 2017; Vantomme et al., 2020). In addition, the top-down modulation can leverage the TRN to control selective attention (Wimmer et al., 2015; Ahrens et al., 2015; Knudsen, 2018; Nakajima et al., 2019). Moreover, the interaction between TC and RE neurons is believed to be necessary for the generation and propagation of different types of oscillatory activities (McCormick and Bal, 1997; Timofeev et al., 2012), which are found to be associated with many functions and diseases. Importantly, the thalamus has been thought of as a key site of vulnerability associated with neurodevelopmental disorders and as a target for therapeutics (Scheibel, 1997; Huguenard and McCormick, 2007; Fagerberg et al., 2014; Ahrens et al., 2015; Wells et al., 2016; Krol et al., 2018; Ritter-Makinson et al., 2019).

Therefore, in order to link different functions of the thalamic circuit with the cellular and synaptic properties and the connectivity structure, various mathematical models of neural systems, in close interplay with experimentation, should be investigated. Biophysically based neural circuit models can simulate the activity and computations of neural populations, incorporating key properties of neurons, synapses, and circuit connectivity. Mapping the output activity of the circuit model to the activity of real neuron recordings or the corresponding behavioral data provides opportunities to mechanistically understand how the thalamus works in various conditions.

Different from the cortical microcircuitry, which has been modeled in fine detail, the TC circuitry has received much less attention. The rising importance of the TC loop in generating different types of oscillatory activities, in diseases associated with TC/RE dysfunctions, and in various cognitive processes motivates the detailed investigations of the thalamic microcircuitry. Several computational models simulating either thalamic (Destexhe, Babloyantz, et al., 1993; 1994a; Golomb et al., 1996; Destexhe, McCormick, et al., 1996; Sohal and Huguenard, 1998; Pham and Haas, 2018) or thalamocortical networks (Destexhe et al., 1998; Bazhenov et al., 2002; Traub et al., 2005) have reproduced oscillatory waveforms intrinsic to the thalamus with high fidelity, including sleep spindles, epileptiform activity, and gamma oscillations, and have engendered important dynamical clarifications or experimentally verifiable predictions in relation to these phenomena. In addition, computational models are used for investigating the effect of locus ceruleus (LC) activation on the thalamus (Rodenkirch et al., 2019), the amplification effect of input from the basolateral amygdala to RE neurons on the auditory thalamus (Aizenberg et al., 2019), and the epileptiform activity associated with channel pathologies (Ritter-Makinson et al., 2019).

Information Processing in Tonic and Burst Spiking Modes

TC and RE neurons from different thalamic nuclei and species exhibit similarities in electrophysiological properties (Figure 1). A characteristic property of TC and RE neurons is their capacity to operate in two distinct modes of spiking activity: tonic and bursting modes (Jahnsen and Llinás, 1984; Sherman, 2001; Cueni et al., 2008; Halassa and Acsády, 2016). TC neurons generate bursts of action potential through an interaction between the low-threshold Ca^{2+} current known as I_T and the hyperpolarization-activated current known as I_h (Pape, 1996; Tarasenko et al., 1997). RE neurons generate bursts of action potential through an interaction between the slow low-threshold Ca^{2+} current known as I_{Ts} and the Ca^{2+}-activated K^+ current known as I_{KCa} (Huguenard and Prince, 1992; Cueni et al., 2008). In modeling studies (Destexhe, Babloyantz, et al., 1993; Golomb et al., 1996), the slow inactivation variable of I_T is de-inactivated during hyperpolarization (Figure 1A and B), which can result in the burst spike activity. Tonic depolarization of TC or RE neurons can result in a suppression of the burst firing through inactivation of the low-threshold Ca^{2+} current and a switch to, or near, the tonic mode of action-potential generation (Figure 1). Neurons' propensities to exhibit tonic or burst spiking modes depend on brain state (Steriade, McCormick, et al., 1993; Halassa et al., 2014) and vary across the anatomical locations (Ramcharan et al., 2005; Li et al., 2020; Martinez-Garcia et al., 2020). In addition, different subtypes of RE neurons can display different electrophysiological properties (Clemente-Perez et al., 2017; Martinez-Garcia et al., 2020).

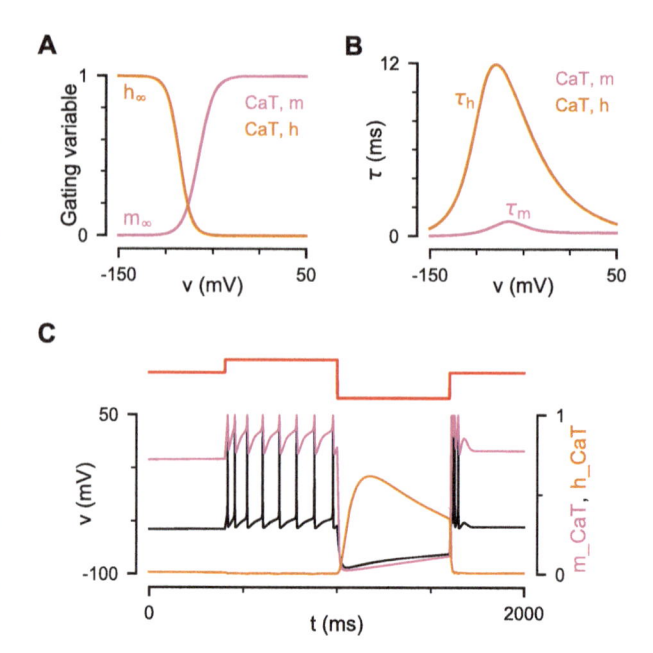

Figure 1 Dual modes of spiking in TC neurons. A single-compartment model of a thalamocortical neuron with a minimal set of conductances, including T-type calcium (CaT), can exhibit two distinct modes of spiking activity.

A. CaT gating variables at steady state as a function of membrane potential. Defined in a Hodgkin–Huxley formalism, the pink curve indicates the activation variable m, and the orange curve indicates the inactivation variable h.

B. Time constants of the gating variables as a function of membrane potential. The inactivation variable is much slower than the activation variable.

C. Example model neuron membrane potential trace in response to depolarizing and hyperpolarizing current input, exhibiting tonic and burst spiking activity, respectively. Tonic and burst spiking activity depend on the dynamics of the activation variable m_{CaT} (*pink*) and inactivation variable h_{CaT} (*orange*) of the low-threshold Ca^{2+} current. The neuron model was adapted from Destexhe, Babloyantz, et al. (1993).

Tonic and Burst Spike Coding

It has been proposed that these two firing modes of the TC neurons could be a mechanism for dynamically controlling information processing (Sherman, 2001). Modulatory inputs, which alter the baseline membrane potential in TC neurons at different levels, enable distinct tonic and burst firing modes by selective engagement of low-threshold calcium channels. These modulations, arising from local membrane and synaptic properties (Masson et al., 2002; Wolfart et al., 2005), stimulus history (Whitmire et al., 2016), and neuromodulatory inputs from the cortex (Wimmer et al., 2015; Nakajima et al., 2019), can potentially help the thalamus to gate information flow to the cortex. In the visual pathway, both burst and tonic spikes can carry stimulus information (Reinagel et al., 1999; Wang et al., 2007). The burst response, which can be reliably elicited across trials in response to sensory stimulation, was found to be able to code the feature selectivity by a prolonged inhibitory stimulus before the depolarizing input that occurs immediately prior to the spike onset (Lesica, 2004; Wang et al., 2007). Some studies have shown that the tonic spike mode is more ideal for the transmission of detailed information (Whitmire et al., 2016; Rodenkirch et al., 2019). However, at the thalamocortical synapse, burst spiking can enhance the reliability of information transmission by driving cortical spiking more effectively (Swadlow and Gusev, 2001) and evoke larger cortical depolarizations (Bruno, 2006) than tonic spiking. It has been shown that bursts could indeed facilitate the transmission of information to the cortex by amplifying the sensory signals (Alitto et al., 2019; Aizenberg et al., 2019). In addition, it is believed that bursts can carry additional information and thereby expand the coding space (Zeldenrust et al., 2018). Mease et al. (2017) found that bursts may convey more information than the presence or absence of a burst event through inter-burst spike timing and the number of spikes per burst event.

In addition, rather than providing more widespread and longer-lasting inhibition of thalamic targets through burst spiking, the tonic and burst spiking modes of RE neurons may have other functional roles. Clemente-Perez et al. (2017) found that parvalbumin (PV) subtype RE cells, which contain more T-type calcium channels than somatostatin (SOM) RE cells and show more burstiness, are a more potent pacemaker of oscillations within different bands. Martinez-Garcia et al. (2020) found that different types of RE neurons in the central versus edge regions of the TRN (in either the somatosensory or the visual thalamic sector) respond differently. Under depolarization, the responses of central RE cells became far less phasic and were more persistent, whereas the effect on edge cells was small, indicating that the two groups of RE neurons may contribute to different states, such as central RE cells for the sleep state and edge RE cells for behavioral states.

Short-Term Synaptic Plasticity

The specific short-term plasticity of the thalamocortical synapse implements, in effect, a gating mechanism that dynamically filters signals (Castro-Alamancos, 1997). Short-term facilitation enables synapses to filter out single spikes and favor bursts of action potentials (Matveev and Wang, 2000; Jackman and Regehr, 2017). As discussed by Sherman (2012), the glutamatergic synapse participating in thalamocortical pathways can be identified as "driver" (Class 1, short-term depression [STD]) and "modulator" (Class 2, short-term facilitation [STF]). The driver synapse with STD is proposed to carry the main information to be relayed (Figure 2A and A1). In addition, in layer 4 of the cortex, where axons of TC neurons preferentially terminate, the thalamic inputs mainly exhibit the STD driver property (Granseth et al., 2002; Viaene et al., 2011; Sherman, 2012; Diaz-Quesada et al., 2014). However, layers 2 and 3 of the cortex have been found to receive predominantly STF modulator input from the thalamus (Viaene et al., 2011; Sherman, 2012). In this perspective, tonic and burst thalamic spiking activities are allowed to process information in a parallel manner. Furthermore, taking into account the pathway from the external world to the thalamus, then to the cerebral cortex, bottom-up synaptic projections into the thalamus may be largely STD (Granseth et al., 2002), and top-down synaptic projections may be largely STF (Sherman, 2012; Crandall et al., 2015) (Figure 2A2 and A3).

Both STD and STF can be computationally modeled as presynaptic processes that modify the probability of transmitter release (Tsodyks et al., 1998; Fuhrmann et al., 2002; Abbott, 2008; Hennig, 2013) (Figure 2B). STD is based on the concept of a limited pool of synaptic resources available for transmission (e.g., the overall amount of neurotransmitters at the presynaptic terminals). Then, depletion during ongoing activity can lead to a suppression of the postsynaptic response. The model of STF is an extension of the model for the depressing synapse, with the release probability increasing at each presynaptic spike and decaying to the baseline level in the absence of spikes (Figure 2B–D). Based on experimentally constrained modeling, STP has been found to affect neural information transmission because it modifies synaptic efficacy based on the history of presynaptic activity (Abbott, 1997; Fuhrmann et al., 2002; Abbott and Regehr, 2004; Rosenbaum et al., 2012). For instance, it has been shown that STD provides a dynamic gain-control mechanism in a frequency-dependent manner by assigning high gain to slowly firing afferents and low gain to rapidly firing afferents, which could dramatically increase the sensitivity of a neuron to subtle changes in the firing patterns of its afferents (Abbott, 1997; Abbott and Regehr, 2004). Models and intracellular data also suggest that an STD-dominated synapse favors processing information at low firing rates (low-pass filter) because high-frequency spikes rapidly deactivate the synapse Fuhrmann et al. (2002); Fortune and Rose (2001); Rosenbaum et al. (2012). However, an STF-dominated synapse tends to be optimized to code information at higher presynaptic firing rates (as a high-pass filter) Dittman et al. (2000); Fortune and Rose (2001); Fuhrmann et al. (2002). In addition, STD was found to

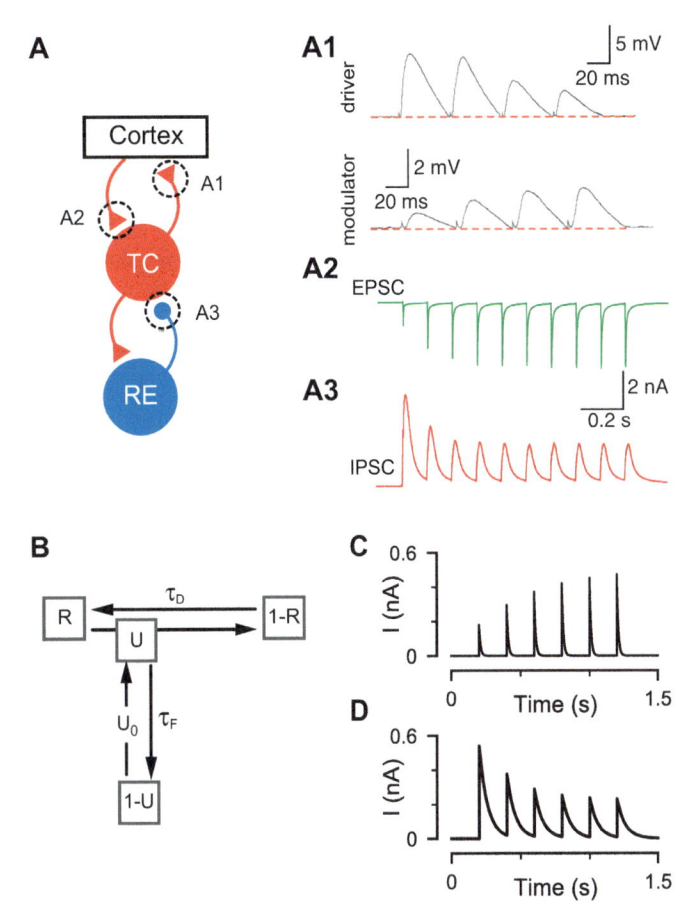

Figure 2 Short-term plasticity in thalamocortical circuits.

A. Short-term plasticity of synapses in TC and CT pathways. **(A1)** Example "driver" and "modulator" type TC synapses. Driver synapses exhibit short-term depression, whereas modulator synapses exhibit short-term facilitation. **(A2)** Short-term facilitation in CT synapse. **(A3)** Short-term depression in RE→TC synapse.

B. The phenomenological model for short-term plasticity. The STD effect can be computationally modeled by a normalized variable R ($0 \leq R \leq 1$), denoting the fraction of resources that remain available after neurotransmitter depletion. The STF effect can be modeled by a utilization parameter U, representing the fraction of available resources ready for use (release probability). τ_D and τ_F are the time constants of STD and STD, respectively.

C. The postsynaptic current generated by an STF-dominated synapse.

D. The postsynaptic current generated by an STD-dominated synapse.

Panels A and A1–A3 are adapted from Sherman (2012) and Crandall et al. (2015). Panels B–D are adapted from Tsodyks and Wu (2013), with the presynaptic neuron firing at 10 Hz.

contribute to removing autocorrelation in temporal inputs (Goldman et al., 2002; Rosenbaum et al., 2013). On the other hand, STF, whose effect is enlarged by temporally proximal spikes, improves both the detection and the discrimination sensitivity of postsynaptic neurons (Mejías and Torres, 2007; Bourjaily and Miller, 2012).

Thalamic Circuit Model for Oscillations

The slow oscillation has generally been considered a predominantly cortical phenomenon because of its survival following extensive thalamic lesions (Steriade, Nunez, et al., 1993) and the absence of slow oscillations in the thalamus of decorticated cats (Timofeev and Steriade, 1996). However, in slow oscillation, thalamocortical projections are believed to play a role in initiating up states and, consequently, determining the oscillation period (Contreras and Steriade, 1995; Wester and Contreras, 2013; Timofeev et al., 2020). In addition, it has been shown that in a thalamic circuit, there are some types of thalamic oscillations (e.g., thalamic delta [2–3 Hz] and spindle [7–14 Hz]) that depend on the interaction of a few intrinsic currents or a few neurons of different types. Biophysically based circuit models have been developed to probe the generation of these oscillations in thalamocortical systems. Note that the active voltage-dependent conductances of TC and RE cells strongly shape their firing activity (McCormick and Huguenard, 1992; Destexhe, Babloyantz, et al., 1993, Destexhe, McCormick, et al., 1993). To be specific, when starting at a relatively depolarized baseline potential (>60 mV), I_T inactivates, and the cell fires in a tonic mode characterized by regular firing of single spikes. In contrast, if the cell is held at a hyperpolarized potential for 50–100 ms, then I_T de-inactivates, and the cell can generate a low-threshold Ca^{2+} spike and a burst of action potentials while receiving a depolarized current (Cueni et al., 2008). This provides a complex cellular-level regulatory mechanism for specific cellular states in thalamic neurons, which gives rise to the generation of oscillations at different frequencies.

Thalamic Delta Oscillation

Thalamic delta (1–4 Hz) oscillation can be generated intrinsically in thalamic relay neurons, arising as an interaction of I_T and I_h (McCormick and Pape, 1990) (Figure 3A and B). This cycle begins with hyperpolarization of the TC cells, which de-inactivates I_T and activates I_h. The I_h depolarizes the cell, which then activates I_T. Depolarization by I_T causes a burst of Na–K action potentials. During the high-voltage burst, IT inactivates and I_h deactivates, causing the cell to then become hyperpolarized, and the burst can begin again. Similarly, RE neurons can robustly generate delta oscillations through single-cell mechanisms, in this case through the interplay of I_T and the Ca^{2+}-dependent K^+ current I_{KCa}. I_T generates a burst, and the accumulating calcium then activates I_{KCa}. I_{KCa} then hyperpolarizes the cell, and the cycle can begin again.

The interplay of I_T and I_h during delta oscillations was later studied with computational models (Destexhe, Babloyantz, et al., 1993; Lytton et al., 1996). In the computational model, single-compartment, Hodgkin–Huxley (HH) types of TC neurons with specific ion channels were studied. It has been shown that various types of slow oscillatory behavior (0.5–4 Hz) were observed for moderate values of the conductance associated with I_h. The regular slow oscillation was similar to the slow oscillatory behavior recorded in TC cells in vitro.

Thalamic Spindle Oscillation

Spindle waves (7–14 Hz) are typically observed during the early stages of sleep or during the active phases of slow-wave sleep oscillations and depend on both intrinsic mechanisms of and interaction between thalamic RE and TC cells (Contreras et al., 1996; Timofeev et al., 2012, 2020). The dominant model for spindles describes a reciprocally connected RE–TC microcircuit Destexhe, McCormick, et al. (1993) (Figure 3C). In these models, RE neurons are interconnected via $GABA_A$ synapses and project to TC neurons with $GABA_A$ and $GABA_B$ synapses. TC neurons, in turn, project back onto RE cells with glutamatergic alpha-amino-3-hydroxy-5-methyl-4-isoxazole propionic acid (AMPA) synapses. In the cycle of the spindle

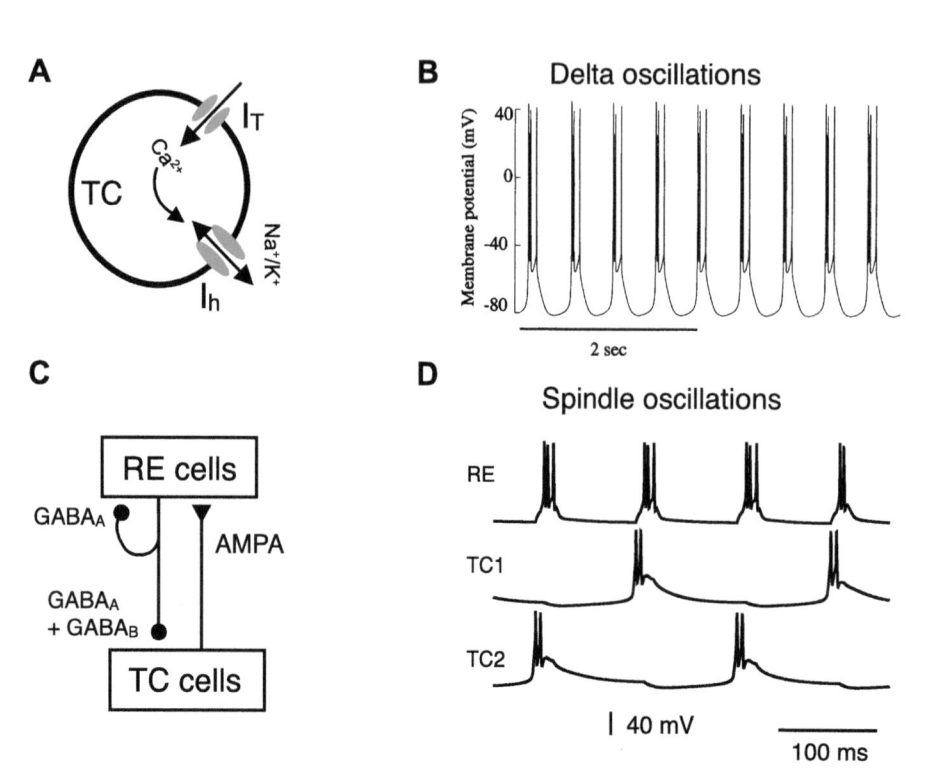

Figure 3 Cellular-level models of oscillations in thalamic-reticular systems.

A. Among other currents, TC cells possess T-type calcium current (I_T) and a hyperpolarization-activated cation current (I_h).

B. The interplay between I_T and I_h can generate delta (1- to 4-Hz) oscillations in isolated TC model cells.

C. Schematic of interconnected networks of TC cells and RE cells in the TRN.

D. Synaptic interactions between TC and RE cells can generate spindle (8- to 15-Hz) oscillations in a circuit model. Panels A and C are adapted from Murray and Anticevic (2017). Panels B and D are adapted from Destexhe, Babloyantz, et al. (1993) and Destexhe, Bal, et al. (1996).

oscillation, TC neurons excite hyperpolarized RE neurons, triggering an I_T-mediated burst. RE neurons then strongly inhibit both TC neurons and RE neurons. This inhibition-related hyperpolarization activates I_T in both, causing a rebound burst in TC neurons, beginning the cycle again. This leads to an offset spiking pattern between the populations. RE neurons typically burst in every cycle, whereas TC neurons tend to skip cycles (Figure 3D). The waxing-and-waning envelope of the bout of spindles can be achieved through the dependence of I_h on intracellular Ca^{2+} that accumulates during the spindles. However, in the model consisting of only one TC neuron and one RE neuron (Destexhe, McCormick, et al. 1993), both TC and RE cells fired during every cycle of oscillations, which is not consistent with experimental data where TC neurons are only intermittently bursting, with subthreshold wax and wane (Kim et al., 1995). The phenomenon was captured by a simple but sufficient model that consisted of two reciprocally coupled RE neurons and two TC cells (Destexhe, Bal, et al., 1996). In this model, more than one cycle of the oscillation was needed to integrate sufficient inhibition to de-inactivate I_T channels when the inhibition was moderate.

Experimental and modeling studies show that spindles can be generated in an isolated RE nucleus (Steriade et al., 1987; Destexhe et al., 1994a, 1994b). Also in the modeling study of Lytton et al. (1996), other than suggesting the ionic cellular process in TC cells as the mechanism of producing oscillations in the delta range, it was shown that although TC cells have no intrinsic mechanisms for generating faster oscillations in the range of spindling, they can be easily entrained to these frequencies. In addition, modeling studies have indeed shown the importance of feedback from the cortex to the TRN in mediating the coherence of spindles across the thalamus (Destexhe et al., 1998). These results may support the view of synaptic inputs from the cortex neurons and RE cells involved in determining the phase and frequency of oscillations in TC cells (Timofeev et al., 2020).

Gap Junction Electrical Coupling

Most of the modeling studies described previously for the spindle oscillations were based on RE–RE connections mediated by $GABA_A$ chemical synapses (Destexhe, McCormick et al., 1993; Destexhe et al. 1994a; Destexhe, Bal, et al., 1996). However, the prevailing evidence suggests that intra-TRN synaptic inhibition is not prevalent in adult mice (Hou et al., 2016), and the GABAergic synapses are reported at less than 1% of nearby TRN pairs (Landisman et al., 2002). Experimental results show that the source of intra-TRN connectivity, especially between closely spaced RE neurons, is the electrical coupling via gap junctions (Landisman et al., 2002; Fuentealba et al., 2004; Long, 2004; Lee et al., 2014). Gap junctions could enable coordinated firing between adjacent RE neurons (Landisman et al., 2002) and dynamically alter the scale of RE actions (Landisman, 2005). Experimental observations have also shown that the probability of the coupling (connectivity) and the coupling coefficient (strength) decreases with the distance between RE cells (Long, 2004; Coulon and Landisman, 2017). Note that for most experimental results, the inferred electrical couplings were less than 50% of observed RE neuron pairs, whereas Long (2004) reported 71% at extremely close (intrasomatic) distances of ≤5 μm. The mean electrical coupling coefficients between RE neurons vary substantially (e.g., 0.032 in Landisman et al. [2002]; ∼0.02 in Fuentealba et al. [2004]; 0.11 in Long [2004]). These findings raise the question of how weak, closely spaced gap junctions affect thalamic activity. It has been shown that gap junctions between TRN neurons can promote thalamocortical neuronal rhythms, including components of spindle waves (Fuentealba et al., 2004; Long, 2004), and can increase the temporal discrimination of multiple near-coincident sensory stimuli by the cortex (Pham and Haas, 2018).

Thalamic Circuit Model for Top-Down Modulation

Selective Attention in the Thalamus

Selective attention, which is central to neurocognitive function, improves information processing of selected sensory signals and helps to filter out distractors in a goal-directed manner (Knudsen, 2018). A growing experimental literature shows that selective attention engages the thalamus (Saalmann and Kastner, 2011; Halassa and Kastner, 2017; Knudsen, 2018). Selection signals computed in high-order brain areas project to the thalamus in a top-down manner, modulating the processing and representation of the selected bottom-up stimulus. Note that TC neurons can receive both driver and modulator input from the cortex, in addition to inputs from subcortical structures, including the basal ganglia (Nakajima et al., 2019). CT inputs were found to modulate the transfer efficiency of TC neurons during selective attention at different levels (Béhuret et al., 2015). In addition, an influential theoretical proposal by Crick (1984) hypothesized that selective attention could be implemented with the TRN acting as a "spotlight," suggesting that "if the thalamus is the gateway to the cortex, the reticular complex might be described as the guardian of the gateway" (p. 4587).

Convergent experimental findings across rodents, monkeys, and humans characterize the sensory thalamus as a locus of attentional filtering and corroborate the proposal of top-down control in the thalamus via the TRN (O'Connor et al., 2002; Zikopoulos and Barbas, 2006; McAlonan et al., 2008; Ahrens et al., 2015; Wimmer et al., 2015; Nakajima et al., 2019). For instance, Wimmer et al. (2015) recorded neuronal spiking activity from the visual TRN and lateral geniculate nucleus (LGN) in mice trained on a cross-modal attention task, in which a cue informed the subject of the sensory modality (vision vs. audition) on which to base its behavioral response. Visual TRN and LGN exhibited opposite modulations by attentional selection: when vision was the attended modality, the visual TRN decreased firing activity, and the LGN exhibited increased activity and higher gain of the stimulus response. Moreover, a subsequent experimental study found that a pathway directly operated in this attentional control of the thalamus, that from the prefrontal cortex through the basal ganglia's inhibitory projections onto the TRN (Nakajima et al., 2019).

A growing literature exhibits anatomical and physiological identification of synaptic inputs to the TRN, which has continuously corroborated the novel point of view for the TRN's active role in gating sensory information flow to and from the cortex. For instance, glutamatergic inputs from the cingulate cortex selectively activate the limbic TRN, which in turn inhibits the intermediodorsal thalamic nucleus and then produces flight behavior (Dong et al., 2019). It has been shown that synapses from the amygdalar pathway onto RE neurons have large and efficient terminals (Zikopoulos and Barbas, 2012), and optogenetic activation of amygdala–TRN projections could indeed amplify tone-evoked responses in the auditory thalamus and cortex (Aizenberg et al., 2019). In an experiment on fear extinction, there is evidence that RE neurons likely receive input from the infralimbic cortex (Lee et al., 2019). In addition, excitatory synaptic projections from the presubiculum and multisensory-associative retrosplenial cortex to the anterodorsal TRN have been found to be able to sharpen mouse thalamic head-direction cell tuning and guide navigation by feedforward inhibition (Vantomme et al., 2020). In general, the top-down modulation pathway "X→RE→TC" (X can be various brain areas) has been implicated in a wide range of studies, suggesting that RE neurons provide a potent site for top-down control.

Thalamic Circuit Model for Top-Down Modulation

In order to investigate how the thalamic microcircuitry supports top-down modulation to subserve functions such as attention, a biophysically detailed model of thalamic reticular circuits is needed that operates in the dynamical regime consistent with observations from awake, behaving animals (Gu et al., 2021). This is different from many previous computational models that investigated thalamic oscillations and traveling waves in the sleep state or in slice preparations (Wang et al., 1995; Destexhe, McCormick, et al., 1996; Destexhe et al., 1998; Bazhenov et al., 2002; Krishnan et al., 2016). In the awake state, spontaneous activity in the thalamus can be characterized by irregular, quasi-asynchronous spiking with intermittent bursting and a lack of strong intrinsic oscillation (Bastos et al., 2014; Saleem et al., 2017). The characterization of "quasi-asynchronous" is supported by the weak cross-correlation coefficient between the spiking activity of different neurons (Bruno, 2006; Temereanca et al., 2008), and "irregular" is consistent with the autocorrelation of the single-neuron spiking activity (Ramcharan et al., 2005; Hirai et al., 2017). To achieve this dynamical regime in a circuit model, TC–RE reciprocal connectivity should not be too strong; otherwise, highly synchronous oscillations would be generated. However, if TC–RE connectivity is too weak or feedback inhibition is too strong, the circuit would not exhibit spindle-like evoked activity in response to a transient RE drive as was observed in the experiments (Halassa et al., 2011).

As shown in Figure 4A and E, top-down excitation of TC neurons and top-down inhibition of RE neurons dissociably affect the baseline activity of RE neurons in the thalamic circuit (Gu et al., 2021). That is, even though both pathways can increase the baseline firing rate of TC neurons, top-down excitation of TC neurons weakly increases the baseline firing rate, whereas top-down inhibition of RE neurons strongly reduces the baseline firing rate of RE neurons. Top-down attentional inputs can regulate thalamic response gain (Figure 4B), that is, change the slope of the response–stimulus function with different levels of top-down modulation (Figure 4A). One can find that increasing the strength of the top-down drive suppresses RE firing rates and elevates TC firing rates via disinhibition, which captures experimental observations when attention is directed toward the associated sensory modality (Wimmer et al., 2015; Nakajima et al., 2019) (Figure 4B). In addition, top-down inputs via excitation of TC cells can also increase the thalamic response gain and downstream detection sensitivity, however, with much less efficacy (Figure 4C and D).

The result that reducing RE neurons' input suppresses RE neurons' firing activity while increasing TC neurons' firing activity reflects that the thalamic circuit operates in a dynamical regime called a *non–inhibition-stabilized network* (non-ISN) (Ozeki et al., 2009) (Figure 4E). The non-ISN properties result from the lack of recurrent excitation within the TC population, which is distinct from models of neocortical circuits in which strong recurrent excitation is stabilized by feedback inhibition (Litwin-Kumar et al., 2016; Sanzeni et al., 2020). How could thalamic output be affected by the two top-down pathways? In the thalamic circuit, it can be seen that the response gain of the thalamocortical projection is an emergent property that is shaped by the interplay between the neuronal sensitivities and the feedback inhibition loop created by TC–RE interconnections (Gu et al., 2021) (Figure 4A). The neuronal sensitivities can be derived from the neuronal transfer function describing the output firing rate as a function of the input current (commonly called an *f-I curve*), whose shape follows an expansive nonlinearity (Abbott, 2008). Top-down input to RE neurons, compared to TC neurons, shifts the circuit to a state of higher response gain. The mechanistic basis of this difference is due to the fact that with top-down inhibition of RE neurons, RE neuronal sensitivity decreases, which in turn boosts the response gain. Moreover, the stronger increase in the response gain leads to a stronger increase in the detection ability in the case of top-down modulation via RE neurons (Figure 4F). Therefore, theoretical analyses give insight into how the interplay of neuronal and circuit properties gives rise to the differential potency of RE neurons as a site for top-down control of thalamic gain.

Thalamic Coding Properties

Attentional modulation of the thalamus can cause thalamic neurons to fire more vigorously in the attended modality compared to the unattended modality (Wimmer et al., 2015; Nakajima et al., 2019; O'Connor et al., 2002; McAlonan et al., 2008), and it has been hypothesized that the response-gain mechanisms might underlie behavioral advantages of attention by amplifying the representation of the relevant information (Wimmer et al., 2015). These findings raise computational questions about how bottom-up and top-down signals, and their interaction, are represented in the high-dimensional space of neuronal activity with a thalamic population

(Figure 5A). The geometric relationships in how signals are represented in population activity affect how a downstream circuit can decode information. Experimental studies of attention control within the thalamus establish multiplexing of bottom-up and top-down signals in neuronal population activity, yet these signals must interact within the thalamus to produce gain modulation of stimulus responses.

Experimental and modeling findings suggest that heterogeneity of thalamic response patterns plays an essential role in the attentional enhancement of stimulus information. In the high-dimensional space of neuronal activities, a trained downstream decoder for detecting a stimulus can be viewed geometrically as a hyperplane, defined by a decoder axis, which can best classify the activity dots (Figure 5B). Gu et al. (2021) found that in a biophysically detailed thalamic circuit model, strengthening top-down modulation of RE cells reduced both false alarms (i.e., responding "yes" when the stimulus was absent) and misses (i.e., responding "no" when the stimulus was present) in a stimulus-detection paradigm (Figure 5C).

From the perspective of regression analysis of recordings from the auditory thalamus (MGBv) (Figure 5D), the firing activity of MGBv neurons can be regarded as comprising at least three signals: (i) bottom-up (*BU*), reflecting the stimulus; (ii) top-down (*TD*), reflecting the influence of the attention state; and (iii) the interaction of bottom-up and top-down (*BU* × *TD*), reflecting top-down gain modulation of the stimulus response (Figure 5E). Because of the relationships between these coding axes, when a linear decoder is trained on thalamic spiking activity to classify in a detection paradigm, attention toward the relevant modality improves decoding performance by reducing both misses and false alarms (Figure 5F). Specifically, the top-down weight vector has a weak negative cosine similarity with the decoder axis. In the absence of a bottom-up stimulus, stronger top-down modulation thereby yields stronger negative decoder scores, which reduces false alarms, whereas the bottom-up weight vector and the bottom-up–top-down interaction weight vector have a strong cosine similarity with the decoder axis, which thereby increases decoder scores during stimulus presentation and reduces misses. The geometric properties of population coding reveal how top-down modulation can increase the separability of TC activity patterns for stimulus-on versus stimulus-off conditions to improve behavioral performance.

A difference between thalamic and cortical microcircuitry is the lack of recurrent synaptic connectivity among excitatory neurons in the thalamus (Jones, 2012). Thus, there exists a question regarding how the architectural feature of the thalamic lack of recurrent excitation affects its engagement in attentional control. Simulations in silico that vary the excitatory recurrent strength show that strong local recurrent excitation can impair downstream decoding of multiplexed bottom-up and top-down signals (Figure 5G and H). In addition, the increased *BU–TD* similarity observed in the model is consistent with the experimental recordings of MGBv and A1 neurons (Figure 5I). The results of the "how" question may suggest why thalamic circuits, lacking such recurrent excitation, are an effective locus for attentional modulation.

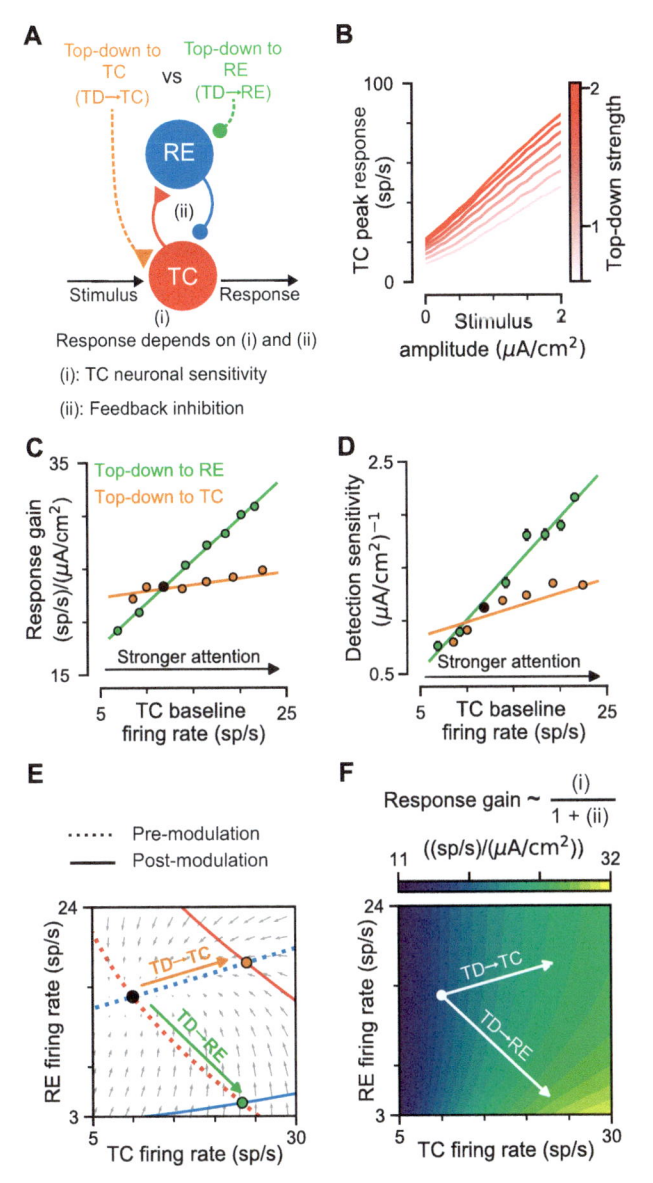

Figure 4 Thalamic circuit model for top-down modulation.

A. Schematic of the thalamic reticular circuit. Top-down (TD) inhibition and excitation (*brown*) modulate the circuit through RE (TD→RE) and TC (TD→TC) populations, respectively.

B. Circuit response function, that is, TC firing rate as a function of stimulus strength, under different levels of top-down modulation strength.

C. Slope of the circuit response function, that is, the response gain, as a function of top-down modulation strength, for inhibition to RE (*green*) or excitation to TC (*orange*). Response gain is derived from the TC response as a function of stimulus amplitude (as shown by the examples in panel B). To facilitate comparison of RE versus TC modulations, the strength of top-down modulation is parameterized in terms of its net effect on TC baseline firing rate.

D. Slope of detection accuracy function, that is, the detection sensitivity, as a function of top-down modulation strength for inhibition to RE (*green*) or excitation to TC (*orange*). Detection sensitivity is derived from a support vector machine (SVM) decoder trained for stimulus detection from TC responses, quantifying accuracy as a function of stimulus amplitude.

E and F. Analytical results from mean-field firing-rate circuit model, within which TC (*red*) and RE (*blue*) activity are modeled as two dynamical variables. Panel E is a phase-plane analysis showing nullclines of TC (*red*) and RE (*blue*) firing rates, with solid lines representing nullclines under top-down modulation. Intersections of the nullclines are the steady-state fixed points of the circuit (black for control; orange and green for states under top-down modulation via TC and RE, respectively). The small gray arrows represent the vector field for activity flow in the control state. Panel F shows the circuit response gain as a function of TC and RE firing rates. Adapted from Gu et al. (2021).

Computation

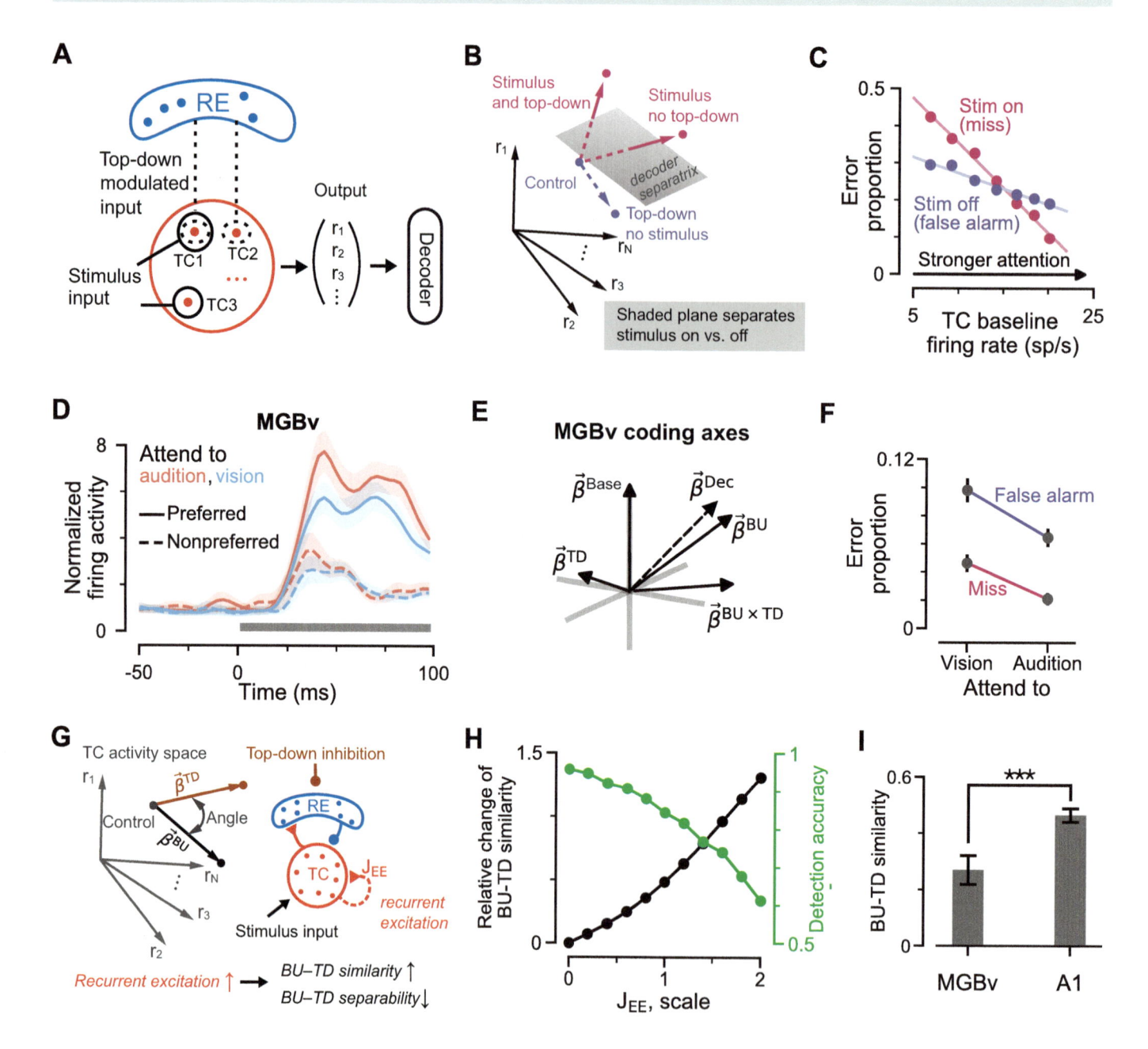

Figure 5 Thalamic coding properties.

A. Schematic of readout via population decoders. Heterogeneity of circuit properties leads TC neurons to differ in their net inputs from bottom-up stimuli and top-down (mediated by RE) pathways. TC output can be decoded via high-dimensional patterns of population activity.

B. Schematic of population-activity decoding in the detection paradigm. The decoder corresponds to a hyperplane separatrix that maps activity patterns on each side of the hyperplane to "stimulus-on" versus "stimulus-off" reports.

C. Detection errors as a function of top-down strength. The top-down modulation via RE neurons improves detection performance by reducing error rates for both misses and false alarms. Misses (pink) versus false alarms (purple) are error types when the stimulus was on versus off, respectively. TC baseline activity serves as a proxy for top-down modulation via RE neurons.

D. Normalized firing activity averaged across all MGBv neurons ($N = 2$ mice, $n = 52$ neurons). Top-down attention increases the activity in both the preferred stimuli (solid) and the nonpreferred ones (dashed). Zero time indicates stimulus onset. The horizontal bar indicates the duration of auditory tones. The shaded area represents the standard error of the mean (SEM).

E. Geometric relationships among coding axes in the MGBv activity space. The three-dimensional subspace here is spanned by ($\beta^{BU}, \beta^{TD}, \beta^{Base}$).

F. Error proportion as a function of attended modality for the support vector machine (SVM) decoder. Both the mean misses and false-alarm errors were reduced when the attention was directed to the corresponding sensory modality.

G. Schematic of the TC neuron activity space. Recurrent excitation (J_{EE}) affects the similarity as well as the separability of BU and TD inputs induced by TC activities.

H. Relative change of BU–TD similarity and detection accuracy as a function of recurrent coupling strength J_{EE}. In a thalamo-reticular network of rate neurons, increasing recurrent excitation can increase the similarity and reduce the detection accuracy of thalamic output. $J_{EE} > 1$ indicates that the system is an ISN, whereas $J_{EE} < 1$ is a non-ISN.

I. BU–TD similarity of MGBv and A1 recordings ($N = 2$ mice; $n = 52$ MGBv neurons; $n = 25$ A1 neurons). The standard deviation was computed by the delete-one jackknife procedure. BU–TD similarity was higher in A1 neurons (t-test, $p < 0.001$). Adapted from Gu et al. (2021).

Open-Loop versus Closed-Loop Connectivity Motifs

The detailed synaptic organization of the bidirectional pathways connecting thalamic nuclei and the TRN remains poorly understood. One important question concerns whether TC–RE connectivity forms a "closed-loop" or "open-loop" motif (Figure 6A and B). A closed loop here is characterized as an arrangement in which the RE neuron inhibits the same TC neuron that excites it, whereas an open loop indicates that the RE neuron instead innervates TC cells other than those from which it receives excitatory input (Pinault, 2004; Halassa and Acsády, 2016).

It was previously assumed that there were reciprocal closed loops of feedback inhibition delivered to TC neurons (Jones, 1975; Hale et al., 1982; Sherman and Guillery, 1996). The structure of the closed-loop motif is suggested by the spatially restricted scale of the RE axon arbors (Pinault and Deschênes, 1998b; Lam and Sherman, 2015) and spatially restricted spindle oscillation in vivo under anesthesia (Barthó et al., 2014) and has been confirmed by in vitro (Lo and Sherman, 1994; Gentet and Ulrich, 2003) and in vivo (Shosaku, 1986; Shosaku et al., 1989) physiological data, albeit with small numbers of examined TC–RE pairs. Reciprocal TC–RE connectivity was found to be not able to fully apply at the cellular level when examining both the anterogradely and the retrogradely labeled neuronal elements (Pinault and Deschênes, 1998a). Those data then indicated an open-loop configuration, which represents the anatomical substrate of mechanisms of lateral inhibition. The open-loop disynaptic motif was also supported by the physiological data of cross-modal projections and interactions (Kimura et al., 2007; Kimura, 2014).

Computational modeling studies (Destexhe, Babloyantz, et al., 1993; Destexhe et al., 1994a; Sohal and Huguenard, 1998; Pham and Haas, 2018) utilized the HH neurons with a closed-loop structure and succeeded in reproducing experimental observations such as the spindle oscillation. However, the combination of open-loop and closed-loop circuits with certain fractions of TC–RE pairs is a more realistic scenario in a thalamic network. In order to reproduce the propagating waves observed in slices of the visual thalamus of ferrets (Kim et al., 1995), two independent modeling studies constructed computational models of networks of interconnected TC and RE cells in a one-dimensional architecture (Golomb et al., 1996; Destexhe, Bal, et al., 1996). These thalamic networks used HH-type models of TC and RE neurons and assumed that there was topographic connectivity between TC and RE layers according to the anatomic data (Fitzgibbon et al., 1995; Gonzalo-Ruiz and Lieberman, 1995). The one-dimensional structured connectivity (i.e., the connectivity profile was chosen in a distance-dependent manner with the exponential or stepped profile) exhibited some level of the open-loop property and applied lateral inhibition (Figure 6E). Wave propagation then can be accommodated along the lattice of interconnected TC and RE neurons by way of laterally inhibitory RE–TC synapses (Figure 6F).

Destexhe et al. (1998) further combined a previous model of thalamic slices with a model of deep cortical layers with

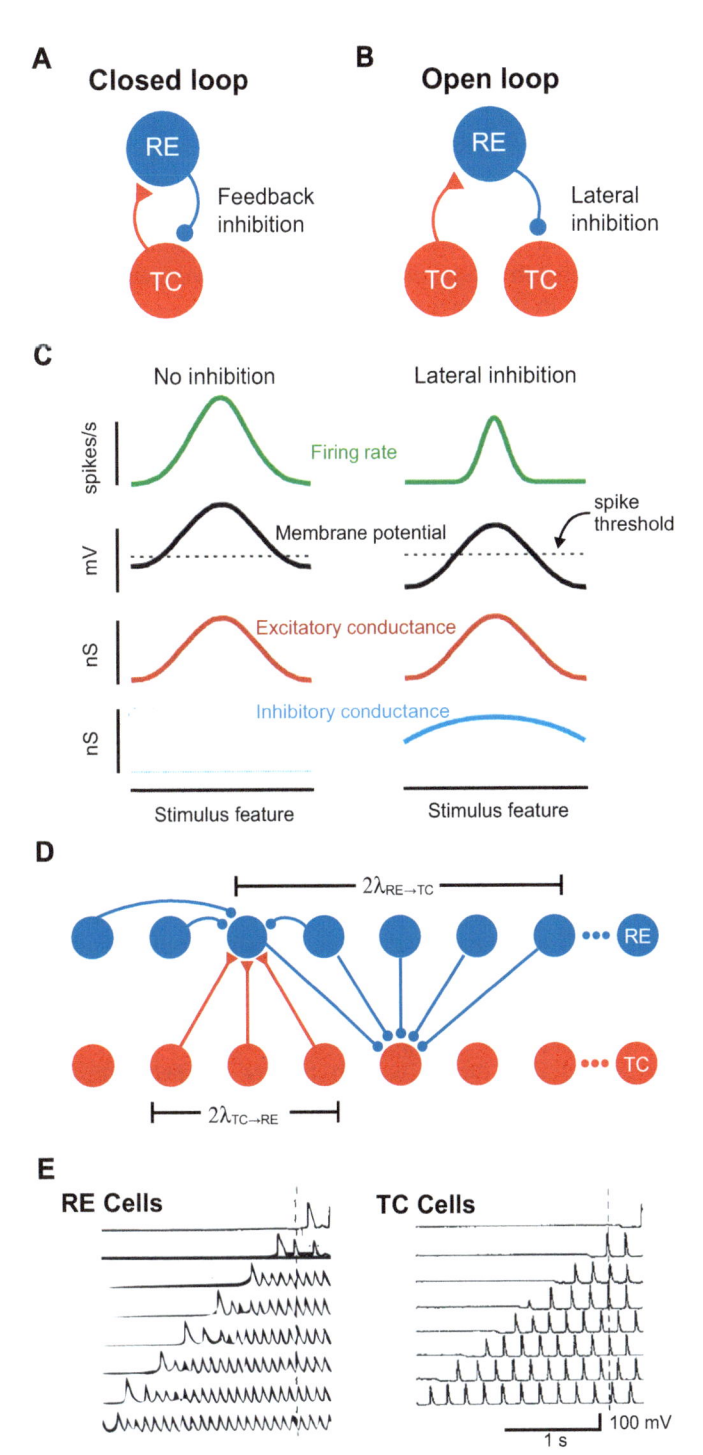

Figure 6 Lateral inhibition. Schematic of the "closed-loop" (panel A) and "open-loop" (panel B) connectivity configurations between TC and RE neurons.

C. Schematic showing how inhibition can sharpen stimulus-selective spiking outputs via the "iceberg effect." Action-potential firing occurs only when the membrane potential exceeds a fixed spike threshold. Responses are shown in the presence (*left*) and absence (*right*) of a weakly tuned inhibitory conductance (*blue*).

D. One-dimensional connectivity architecture between TC and RE neurons. Lateral inhibition (*open loop*) can be found in such a structure.

E. The traveling wave exhibited by the membrane-potential time courses of eight RE neurons and eight TC neurons equally spaced along the one-dimensional system.

Panel C is adapted from Isaacson and Scanziani (2011). Panels D and E are adapted from Golomb et al. (1996).

pyramidal cells and interneurons to investigate propagating waves in the thalamocortical system. This model could reproduce experimental observations of propagating activity, under the assumption that the cortex intervened in the thalamus mainly through excitation of GABAergic RE neurons, therefore recruiting TC cells essentially through lateral inhibition and rebound (Destexhe et al., 1998). In general, modeling studies rely on lateral inhibitory RE–TC synapses playing a vital role in the generation of waves in the thalamus, which potentially provides the importance of the open-loop configuration. Recently, Brown et al. (2020) have further shown that networks with strong open-loop connectivity can better support the propagation wave. However, in order to easily control the fraction of open or closed loop, a strong restriction was applied on network architecture that every TC neuron projected to only one RE neuron, whereas single RE neurons could project to either one TC neuron (whether in a feedback or lateral way) or two TC neurons (one in a feedback way and one in a lateral way) (Brown et al., 2020). In addition, it has been shown that in the open-loop circuit of three nodes (TC, RE, CT neurons), RE activation could paradoxically enhance TC output and then cortical responses to sensory stimuli (Willis et al., 2015). It seems that there is still a lack of a biophysically detailed thalamic circuit model that would provide a deeper understanding of how the open-loop configuration affects the thalamic activity.

In general, lateral inhibition makes it possible for neurons to inhibit their neighbors in a network and, consequently, makes neurons more sensitive to a spatially varying stimulus than to a spatially uniform stimulus (Isaacson and Scanziani, 2011). It has been shown that synaptic excitation to a preferred stimulus shapes the tuning of a cell's spike output in the visual cortex and that tuning is then further sharpened by the untuned (robust in response to nonpreferred stimuli) or broadly tuned lateral inhibition (Priebe and Ferster, 2008; Liu et al., 2011; Katzner et al., 2011), the so-called "iceberg effect" (Carandini and Ferster, 2000) (Figure 6C). Similarly, TRN neurons were found to exhibit selectivity to bottom-up stimulus features (Hirsch et al., 2015; Soto-Sánchez et al., 2017) and to be able to shape the selectivity of thalamic responses (Cotillon-Williams et al., 2008; Vantomme et al., 2020). TRN-mediated lateral inhibition in the thalamus, which can arise from open-loop configuration, could potentially operate at multiple scales, such as tuned lateral inhibition or normalization within a thalamic nucleus or cross-modal competition between nuclei.

Conclusions

In this chapter, we have reviewed experimental and computational modeling studies from the perspective of dynamical systems modeling, with the goal of linking the biophysical properties of the thalamic microcircuit to its physiological dynamics and functional roles. In topics covering tonic and burst spike coding, oscillations, top-down modulation of thalamic activity, and comparison between feedback inhibition and lateral inhibition, computational modeling plays a useful role in linking across levels of analysis to better understand how lower-level mechanisms shape higher-level function. Here we turn to some critical areas for future modeling and experiments to address.

Heterogeneity across Thalamus Subregions

Both RE and TC neurons exhibit a high degree of heterogeneity across regions of the thalamic circuit. For instance, RE neurons contain distinct inhibitory cell types with different neuronal and synaptic properties (Ahrens et al., 2015; Clemente-Perez et al., 2017; Martinez-Garcia et al., 2020; Vantomme et al., 2020), which may relate to different states and contribute to different functions. Studies have found that both in vitro and in vivo, TC cells in higher-order thalamic nuclei exhibit a higher propensity for burstiness than those in sensory relay nuclei (Wei et al., 2011; Ramcharan et al., 2005). In addition, TC neurons exhibit heterogeneity in neuronal properties and receive heterogeneous inputs of either inhibition or excitation (Landisman and Connors, 2007; Lee et al., 2007; Urbain et al., 2015; Galvan et al., 2016). In general, such heterogeneity will lead to a heterogeneous distribution of neuronal responses across regions and will be likely to influence the population code (Marsat and Maler, 2010; Panzeri et al., 2015). These intrinsic differences in thalamic physiology may also render cells in specific thalamic subdivisions differentially sensitive to an underlying perturbation (Murray and Anticevic, 2017). Therefore, it is worthwhile to incorporate the regional heterogeneity of thalamic properties into large-scale network models of the thalamus and its interactions with the cortex (Roberts and Robinson, 2012; Jaramillo et al., 2019).

Microcircuit Complexity

Most of the computational modeling studies described earlier (Destexhe, McCormick, et al., 1993; Destexhe, Babloyantz, et al., 1993; Dextexhe et al., 1994a; Golomb et al., 1996; Bazhenov et al., 2002; Ritter-Makinson et al., 2019; Gu et al., 2021) utilized single-compartment HH neurons, which neglect the intrinsic cable properties of real neurons. However, neurons possess diverse, elaborate morphologies that allow the propagation of electrical signals through fine, intricate neuronal structures. In the thalamic circuit, early studies have investigated the dendritic distribution of the low-threshold calcium current and hyperpolarization-activated cation current in TC neurons (Destexhe et al., 1998; Traub et al., 2005) and in RE neurons (Destexhe, Contreras, et al., 1996; Traub et al., 2005) with multicompartment dendritic models. In addition, recent experimental observations have found different functional roles of different subtypes of RE neurons (Ahrens et al., 2015; Clemente-Perez et al., 2017; Vantomme et al., 2020; Martinez-Garcia et al., 2020). Therefore, it is worth investigating how the different subtypes of RE cells regulate thalamic activity via control of dendritic integration using the multicompartment models.

Large-Scale Brain Networks

Recent advances in the mapping of human brain cortical organization have revealed macroscale gradients in microcircuit and functional properties (Burt et al., 2018; Huntenburg et al., 2018; Wang, 2020; Tian et al., 2020). In addition, experimental evidence indicates a close association between the functional gradients and the thalamo-cortical structural connectome (Phillips et al., 2019; Yang et al., 2020). These results suggest the incorporation of biophysically grounded models of the thalamus into large-scale brain models of cognitive functions such as attentional control and decision making (Murray et al., 2017; Jaramillo et al., 2019). That is, the thalamic circuit model can be embedded in networks with long-range interactions involving thalamic, cortical, and other brain areas to gain further insight into the distributed computational mechanisms of attentional function (Saalmann and Kastner, 2011; Sherman, 2016; Halassa and Kastner, 2017; Nakajima and Halassa, 2017; Rikhye et al., 2018; Schmitt et al., 2017; Halassa and Sherman, 2019).

References

Abbott L.F. (1997). Synaptic depression and cortical gain control. Science **275**, 221–224.

Abbott L.F. (2008). Theoretical neuroscience rising. Neuron **60**, 489–495.

Abbott L.F., and Regehr W.G. (2004). Synaptic computation. Nature **431**, 796–803.

Ahissar E., and Oram T. (2013). Thalamic relay or cortico-thalamic processing? Old question, new answers. Cerebral Cortex **25**, 845–848.

Ahrens S., Jaramillo S., Yu K., Ghosh S., Hwang G.R., Paik R., Lai C., He M., Huang Z.J., and Li B. (2015). ErbB4 regulation of a thalamic reticular nucleus circuit for sensory selection. *Nature Neuroscience* **18**, 104–11.

Aizenberg M., Rolón-Martínez S., Pham T., Rao W., Haas J.S., and Geffen M.N. (2019). Projection from the amygdala to the thalamic reticular nucleus amplifies cortical sound responses. Cell Reports **28**, 605–615.e4.

Alitto H., Rathbun D.L., Vandeleest J.J., Alexander P.C., and Usrey W.M. (2019). The augmentation of retinogeniculate communication during thalamic burst mode. Journal of Neuroscience **39**, 5697–5710.

Barthó P., Slézia A., Mátyás F., Faradzs-Zade L., Ulbert I., Harris K.D., and Acsády L. (2014). Ongoing network state controls the length of sleep spindles via inhibitory activity. Neuron **82**, 1367–1379.

Bastos A.M., Briggs F., Alitto H.J., Mangun G.R., and Usrey W.M. (2014). Simultaneous recordings from the primary visual cortex and lateral geniculate nucleus reveal rhythmic interactions and a cortical source for gamma-band oscillations. Journal of Neuroscience **34**, 7639–7644.

Bazhenov M., Timofeev I., Steriade M., and Sejnowski T.J. (2002). Model of thalamocortical slow-wave sleep oscillations and transitions to activated states. Journal of Neuroscience **22**, 8691–8704.

Béhuret S., Deleuze C., and Bal T. (2015). Corticothalamic synaptic noise as a mechanism for selective attention in thalamic neurons. Frontiers in Neural Circuits 9.

Bourjaily M.A., and Miller P. (2012). Dynamic afferent synapses to decision-making networks improve performance in tasks requiring stimulus associations and discriminations. Journal of Neurophysiology **108**, 513–527.

Brown J.W., Taheri A., Kenyon R.V., Berger-Wolf T.Y., and Llano D.A. (2020). Signal propagation via open-loop intrathalamic architectures: A computational model. eNeuro **7**, ENEURO.0441-19.2020.

Bruno R.M. (2006). Cortex is driven by weak but synchronously active thalamocortical synapses. Science **312**, 1622–1627.

Burt J.B., Demirtaș M., Eckner W.J., Navejar N.M., Ji J.L., Martin W.J., Bernacchia A., Anticevic A., and Murray J.D. (2018). Hierarchy of transcriptomic specialization across human cortex captured by structural neuroimaging topography. *Nature Neuroscience* **21**, 1251–1259.

Carandini M., and Ferster D. (2000). Membrane potential and firing rate in cat primary visual cortex. Journal of Neuroscience **20**, 470–484.

Castro-Alamancos M.A. (1997). Short-term plasticity in thalamocortical pathways: Cellular mechanisms and functional roles. Reviews in the Neurosciences 8.

Clemente-Perez A., Makinson S.R., Higashikubo B., Brovarney S., Cho F.S., Urry A., Holden S.S., Wimer M., Dávid C., Fenno L.E., Acsády L., Deisseroth K., and Paz J.T. (2017). Distinct thalamic reticular cell types differentially modulate normal and pathological cortical rhythms. Cell Reports **19**, 2130–2142.

Contreras D., Destexhe A., Sejnowski T.J., and Steriade M. (1996). Control of spatiotemporal coherence of a thalamic oscillation by corticothalamic feedback. Science **274**, 771–774.

Contreras D., and Steriade M. (1995). Cellular basis of EEG slow rhythms: a study of dynamic corticothalamic relationships. Journal of Neuroscience **15**, 604–622.

Cotillon-Williams N., Huetz C., Hennevin E., and Edeline J.M. (2008). Tonotopic control of auditory thalamus frequency tuning by reticular thalamic neurons. *Journal of Neurophysiology* **99**, 1137–1151.

Coulon P., and Landisman C.E. (2017). The potential role of gap junctional plasticity in the regulation of state. Neuron **93**, 1275–1295.

Crandall S.R., Cruikshank S.J., and Connors B.W. (2015). A corticothalamic switch: controlling the thalamus with dynamic synapses. Neuron **86**, 768–782.

Crick F. (1984). Function of the thalamic reticular complex: the searchlight hypothesis. *Proceedings of the National Academy of Sciences of the United States of America* **81**, 4586–4590.

Cueni L., Canepari M., Luján R., Emmenegger Y., Watanabe M., Bond C.T., Franken P., Adelman J.P., and Lüthi A. (2008). T-type Ca^{2+} channels, SK2 channels and SERCAs gate sleep-related oscillations in thalamic dendrites. *Nature Neuroscience* **11**, 683–692.

Destexhe A., Babloyantz A., and Sejnowski T.J. (1993). Ionic mechanisms for intrinsic slow oscillations in thalamic relay neurons. *Biophysical Journal* **65**, 1538–52.

Destexhe A., Bal T., McCormick D.A., and Sejnowski T.J. (1996). Ionic mechanisms underlying synchronized oscillations and propagating waves in a model of ferret thalamic slices. Journal of Neurophysiology **76**, 2049–70.

Destexhe A., Contreras D., Sejnowski T.J., and Steriade M. (1994a). A model of spindle rhythmicity in the isolated thalamic reticular nucleus. *Journal of Neurophysiology* **72**, 803–18.

Destexhe A., Contreras D., Sejnowski T.J., and Steriade M. (1994b). Modeling the control of reticular thalamic oscillations by neuromodulators. NeuroReport **5**, 2217–2220.

Destexhe A., Contreras D., and Steriade M. (1998). Mechanisms underlying the synchronizing action of corticothalamic feedback through inhibition of thalamic relay cells. *Journal of Neurophysiology* **79**, 999–1016.

Destexhe A., Contreras D., Steriade M., Sejnowski T.J., and Huguenard J.R. (1996). In vivo, in vitro, and computational analysis of dendritic calcium currents in thalamic reticular neurons. *Journal of Neuroscience* **16**, 169–185.

Destexhe A., McCormick D.A., and Sejnowski T.J. (1993). A model for 8-10 Hz spindling in interconnected thalamic relay and reticularis neurons. *Biophysical Journal* **65**, 2473–2477.

Diaz-Quesada M., Martini F.J., Ferrati G., Bureau I., and Maravall M. (2014). Diverse thalamocortical short-term plasticity elicited by ongoing stimulation. Journal of Neuroscience **34**, 515–526.

Dittman J.S., Kreitzer A.C., and Regehr W.G. (2000). Interplay between facilitation, depression, and residual calcium at three presynaptic terminals. Journal of Neuroscience **20**, 1374–1385.

Dong P., Wang H., Shen X.F., Jiang P., Zhu X.T., Li Y., Gao J.H., Lin S., Huang Y., He X.B., Xu F.Q., Duan S., Lian H., Wang H., Chen J., and Li X.M. (2019). A novel cortico-intrathalamic circuit for flight behavior. Nature Neuroscience **22**, 941–949.

Fagerberg L., Hallström B.M., Oksvold P., Kampf C., Djureinovic D., Odeberg J., Habuka M., Tahmasebpoor S., Danielsson A., Edlund K., Asplund A., Sjöstedt E., Lundberg E., Szigyarto C.A.K., Skogs M., Takanen J.O., Berling H., Tegel H., Mulder J., Nilsson P., Schwenk J.M., Lindskog C., Danielsson F., Mardinoglu A., Sivertsson A., von Feilitzen K., Forsberg M., Zwahlen M., Olsson I., Navani S., Huss M., Nielsen J., Ponten F., and Uhlén M. (2014). Analysis of the human tissue-specific expression by genome-wide integration of transcriptomics and antibody-based proteomics. *Molecular & Cellular Proteomics* **13**, 397–406.

Fitzgibbon T., Tevah L.V., and Sefton A.J. (1995). Connections between the reticular nucleus of the thalamus and pulvinar-lateralis posterior complex: A WGA-HRP study. Journal of Comparative Neurology **363**, 489–504.

Fortune E.S., and Rose G.J. (2001). Short-term synaptic plasticity as a temporal filter. Trends in Neurosciences **24**, 381–385.

Fuentealba P., Crochet S., Timofeev I., Bazhenov M., Sejnowski T.J., and Steriade M. (2004). Experimental evidence and modeling studies support a synchronizing role for electrical coupling in the cat thalamic reticular neurons in vivo. European Journal of Neuroscience **20**, 111–119.

Fuhrmann G., Segev I., Markram H., and Tsodyks M. (2002). Coding of temporal information by activity-dependent synapses. Journal of Neurophysiology **87**, 140–148.

Gabernet L., Jadhav S.P., Feldman D.E., Carandini M., and Scanziani M. (2005). Somatosensory integration controlled by dynamic thalamocortical feed-forward inhibition. Neuron **48**, 315–327.

Galvan A., Hu X., Smith Y., and Wichmann T. (2016). Effects of optogenetic activation of corticothalamic terminals in the motor thalamus of awake monkeys. Journal of Neuroscience **36**, 3519–3530.

Gentet L.J., and Ulrich D. (2003). Strong, reliable and precise synaptic connections between thalamic relay cells and neurones of the nucleus reticularis in juvenile rats. Journal of Physiology **546**, 801–811.

Goldman M.S., Maldonado P., and Abbott L.F. (2002). Redundancy reduction and sustained firing with stochastic depressing synapses. Journal of Neuroscience **22**, 584–591.

Golomb D., Wang X.J., and Rinzel J. (1996). Propagation of spindle waves in a thalamic slice model. *Journal of Neurophysiology* **75**, 750–769.

Gonzalo-Ruiz A., and Lieberman A. (1995). Topographic organization of projections from the thalamic reticular nucleus to the anterior thalamic nuclei in the rat. Brain Research Bulletin **37**, 17–35.

Granseth B., Ahlstrand E., and Lindström S. (2002). Paired pulse facilitation of corticogeniculate EPSCs in the dorsal lateral geniculate nucleus of the rat investigated in vitro. Journal of Physiology **544**, 477–486.

Gu Q.L., Lam N.H., Halassa M.M., and Murray J.D. (2021). Computational circuit mechanisms underlying thalamic control of attention. bioRxiv 10.1101/2020.09.16.300749.

Halassa M.M., and Acsády L. (2016). Thalamic inhibition: diverse sources, diverse scales. Trends *in Neurosciences* **39**, 680–693.

Halassa M.M., Chen Z., Wimmer R.D., Brunetti P.M., Zhao S., Zikopoulos B., Wang F., Brown E.N., and Wilson M.A. (2014). State-dependent architecture of thalamic reticular subnetworks. Cell **158**, 808–821.

Halassa M.M., and Kastner S. (2017). Thalamic functions in distributed cognitive control. *Nature Neuroscience* **20**, 1669–1679.

Halassa M.M., and Sherman S.M. (2019). Thalamocortical circuit motifs: a general framework. Neuron **103**, 762–770.

Halassa M.M., Siegle J.H., Ritt J.T., Ting J.T., Feng G., and Moore C.I. (2011). Selective optical drive of thalamic reticular nucleus generates thalamic bursts and cortical spindles. *Nature Neuroscience* **14**, 1118–1120.

Hale P., Sefton A., Baur L., and Cottee L. (1982). Interrelations of the rat's thalamic reticular and dorsal lateral geniculate nuclei. Experimental Brain Research 45–45.

Hennig M.H. (2013). Theoretical models of synaptic short term plasticity. Frontiers in Computational Neuroscience 7.

Hirai D., Nakamura K.C., ichi Shibata K., Tanaka T., Hioki H., Kaneko T., and Furuta T. (2017). Shaping somatosensory responses in awake rats: cortical modulation of thalamic neurons. Brain Structure and Function **223**, 851–872.

Hirsch J.A., Wang X., Sommer F.T., and Martinez L.M. (2015). How inhibitory circuits in the thalamus serve vision. *Annual Review of Neuroscience* **38**, 309–329.

Hou G., Smith A.G., and Zhang Z.W. (2016). Lack of intrinsic GABAergic connections in the thalamic reticular nucleus of the mouse. *Journal of Neuroscience* **36**, 7246–52.

Huguenard J., and Prince D. (1992). A novel t-type current underlies prolonged Ca^{2+}-dependent burst firing in GABAergic neurons of rat thalamic reticular nucleus. Journal of Neuroscience **12**, 3804–3817.

Huguenard J.R., and McCormick D.A. (2007). Thalamic synchrony and dynamic regulation of global forebrain oscillations. Trends in Neurosciences **30**, 350–356.

Huntenburg J.M., Bazin P.L., and Margulies D.S. (2018). Large-scale gradients in human cortical organization. Trends *in Cognitive Sciences* **22**, 21–31.

Isaacson J.S., and Scanziani M. (2011). How inhibition shapes cortical activity. Neuron **72**, 231–243.

Jackman S.L., and Regehr W.G. (2017). The mechanisms and functions of synaptic facilitation. Neuron **94**, 447–464.

Jahnsen H., and Llinás R. (1984). Electrophysiological properties of guinea-pig thalamic neurones: an in vitro study. Journal of Physiology **349**, 205–226.

Jaramillo J., Mejias J.F., and Wang X.J. (2019). Engagement of pulvino-cortical feedforward and feedback pathways in cognitive computations. Neuron **101**, 321–336.e9.

Jones E.G. (1975). Some aspects of the organization of the thalamic reticular complex. Journal of Comparative Neurology **162**, 285–308.

Jones E.G. (2012). The thalamus (Springer Science & Business Media).

Katzner S., Busse L., and Carandini M. (2011). $GABA_A$ inhibition controls response gain in visual cortex. Journal of Neuroscience **31**, 5931–5941.

Kim U., Bal T., and McCormick D.A. (1995). Spindle waves are propagating synchronized oscillations in the ferret LGNd in vitro. Journal of Neurophysiology **74**, 1301–1323.

Kimura A. (2014). Diverse subthreshold cross-modal sensory interactions in the thalamic reticular nucleus: implications for new pathways of cross-modal attentional gating function. European Journal of Neuroscience **39**, 1405–1418.

Kimura A., Imbe H., Donishi T., and Tamai Y. (2007). Axonal projections of single auditory neurons in the thalamic reticular nucleus: implications for tonotopy-related gating function and cross-modal modulation. European Journal of Neuroscience **26**, 3524–3535.

Knudsen E.I. (2018). Neural circuits that mediate selective attention: a comparative perspective. Trends in Neurosciences **41**, 789–805.

Krishnan G.P., Chauvette S., Shamie I., Soltani S., Timofeev I., Cash S.S., Halgren E., and Bazhenov M. (2016). Cellular and neurochemical basis of sleep stages in the thalamocortical network. eLife **5**.

Krol A., Wimmer R.D., Halassa M.M., and Feng G. (2018). Thalamic reticular dysfunction as a circuit endophenotype in neurodevelopmental disorders. Neuron **98**, 282–295.

Lam Y.W., and Sherman S.M. (2015). Functional topographic organization of the motor reticulothalamic pathway. Journal of Neurophysiology **113**, 3090–3097.

Landisman C.E. (2005). Long-term modulation of electrical synapses in the mammalian thalamus. Science **310**, 1809–1813.

Landisman C.E., and Connors B.W. (2007). VPM and PoM nuclei of the rat somatosensory thalamus: intrinsic neuronal properties and corticothalamic feedback. Cerebral Cortex **17**, 2853–2865.

Landisman C.E., Long M.A., Beierlein M., Deans M.R., Paul D.L., and Connors B.W. (2002). Electrical synapses in the thalamic reticular nucleus. Journal of Neuroscience **22**, 1002–1009.

Lee J.H., Latchoumane C.F.V., Park J., Kim J., Jeong J., Lee K.H., and Shin H.S. (2019). The rostroventral part of the thalamic reticular nucleus modulates fear extinction. Nature Communications **10**.

Lee S.C., Cruikshank S.J., and Connors B.W. (2010). Electrical and chemical synapses between relay neurons in developing thalamus. Journal of Physiology **588**, 2403–2415.

Lee S.C., Patrick S.L., Richardson K.A., and Connors B.W. (2014). Two functionally distinct networks of gap junction-coupled inhibitory neurons in the thalamic reticular nucleus. Journal of Neuroscience **34**, 13170–13182.

Lee S.H., Govindaiah G., and Cox C.L. (2007). Heterogeneity of firing properties among rat thalamic reticular nucleus neurons. Journal of Physiology **582**, 195–208.

Lesica N.A. (2004). Encoding of natural scene movies by tonic and burst spikes in the lateral geniculate nucleus. Journal of Neuroscience **24**, 10731–10740.

Li Y., Lopez-Huerta V.G., Adiconis X., Levandowski K., Choi S., Simmons S.K., Arias-Garcia M.A., Guo B., Yao A.Y., Blosser T.R., Wimmer R.D., Aida T., Atamian A., Naik T., Sun X., Bi D., Malhotra D., Hession C.C., Shema R., Gomes M., Li T., Hwang E., Krol A., Kowalczyk M., Peça J., Pan G., Halassa M.M., Levin J.Z., Fu Z., and Feng G. (2020). Distinct subnetworks of the thalamic reticular nucleus. Nature **583**, 819–824.

Litwin-Kumar A., Rosenbaum R., and Doiron B. (2016). Inhibitory stabilization and visual coding in cortical circuits with multiple interneuron subtypes. Journal of Neurophysiology **115**, 1399–1409.

Liu B.H., Li Y.T., Ma W.P., Pan C.J., Zhang L.I., and Tao H.W. (2011). Broad inhibition sharpens orientation selectivity by expanding input dynamic range in mouse simple cells. Neuron **71**, 542–554.

Lo F.S., and Sherman S.M. (1994). Feedback inhibition in the cat's lateral geniculate nucleus. Experimental Brain Research **100**.

Long M.A. (2004). Small clusters of electrically coupled neurons generate synchronous rhythms in the thalamic reticular nucleus. Journal of Neuroscience **24**, 341–349.

Lytton W., Destexhe A., and Sejnowski T. (1996). Control of slow oscillations in the thalamocortical neuron: a computer model. Neuroscience **70**, 673–684.

Marsat G., and Maler L. (2010). Neural heterogeneity and efficient population codes for communication signals. Journal of Neurophysiology **104**, 2543–2555.

Martinez-Garcia R.I., Voelcker B., Zaltsman J.B., Patrick S.L., Stevens T.R., Connors B.W., and Cruikshank S.J. (2020). Two dynamically distinct circuits drive inhibition in the sensory thalamus. Nature **583**, 813–818.

Masson G.L., Masson S.R.L., Debay D., and Bal T. (2002). Feedback inhibition controls spike transfer in hybrid thalamic circuits. Nature **417**, 854–858.

Matveev V., and Wang X.J. (2000). Differential short-term synaptic plasticity and transmission of complex spike trains: to depress or to facilitate? Cerebral Cortex **10**, 1143–1153.

McAlonan K., Cavanaugh J., and Wurtz R.H. (2008). Guarding the gateway to cortex with attention in visual thalamus. Nature **456**, 391–394.

McCormick D.A., and Bal T. (1997). Sleep and arousal: thalamocortical mechanisms. Annual Review of Neuroscience **20**, 185–215.

McCormick D.A., and Huguenard J.R. (1992). A model of the electrophysiological properties of thalamocortical relay neurons. Journal of Neurophysiology **68**, 1384–1400.

McCormick D.A., and Pape H.C. (1990). Properties of a hyperpolarization-activated cation current and its role in rhythmic oscillation in thalamic relay neurones. Journal of Physiology **431**, 291–318.

Mease R.A., Kuner T., Fairhall A.L., and Groh A. (2017). Multiplexed spike coding and adaptation in the thalamus. Cell Reports **19**, 1130–1140.

Mejías J.F., and Torres J.J. (2007). The role of synaptic facilitation in spike coincidence detection. Journal of Computational Neuroscience **24**, 222–234.

Murray J.D., and Anticevic A. (2017). Toward understanding thalamocortical dysfunction in schizophrenia through computational models of neural circuit dynamics. Schizophrenia Research **180**, 70–77.

Murray J.D., Jaramillo J., and Wang X.J. (2017). Working memory and decision-making in a frontoparietal circuit model. Journal of Neuroscience **37**, 12167–12186.

Nakajima M., and Halassa M.M. (2017). Thalamic control of functional cortical connectivity. Current Opinion in Neurobiology **44**, 127–131.

Nakajima M., Schmitt L.I., and Halassa M.M. (2019). Prefrontal cortex regulates sensory filtering through a basal ganglia-to-thalamus pathway. Neuron **103**, 445–458.e10.

O'Connor D.H., Fukui M.M., Pinsk M.A., and Kastner S. (2002). Attention modulates responses in the human lateral geniculate nucleus. *Nature Neuroscience* 5, 1203–1209.

Ozeki H., Finn I.M., Schaffer E.S., Miller K.D., and Ferster D. (2009). Inhibitory stabilization of the cortical network underlies visual surround suppression. Neuron 62, 578–592.

Panzeri S., Macke J.H., Gross J., and Kayser C. (2015). Neural population coding: combining insights from microscopic and mass signals. Trends in Cognitive Sciences 19, 162–172.

Pape H.C. (1996). Queer current and pacemaker: the hyperpolarization-activated cation current in neurons. Annual Review of Physiology 58, 299–327.

Pham T., and Haas J.S. (2018). Electrical synapses between inhibitory neurons shape the responses of principal neurons to transient inputs in the thalamus: a modeling study. Scientific Reports 8.

Phillips J.W., Schulmann A., Hara E., Winnubst J., Liu C., Valakh V., Wang L., Shields B.C., Korff W., Chandrashekar J., Lemire A.L., Mensh B., Dudman J.T., Nelson S.B., and Hantman A.W. (2019). A repeated molecular architecture across thalamic pathways. *Nature Neuroscience* 22, 1925–1935.

Pinault D. (2004). The thalamic reticular nucleus: structure, function and concept. Brain *Research Reviews* 46, 1–31.

Pinault D., and Deschênes M. (1998a). Anatomical evidence for a mechanism of lateral inhibition in the rat thalamus. European Journal of Neuroscience 10, 3462–3469.

Pinault D., and Deschênes M. (1998b). Projection and innervation patterns of individual thalamic reticular axons in the thalamus of the adult rat: a three-dimensional, graphic, and morphometric analysis. *Journal of Comparative Neurology* 391, 180–203.

Porter J.T., Johnson C.K., and Agmon A. (2001). Diverse types of interneurons generate thalamus-evoked feedforward inhibition in the mouse barrel cortex. Journal of Neuroscience 21, 2699–2710.

Priebe N.J., and Ferster D. (2008). Inhibition, spike threshold, and stimulus selectivity in primary visual cortex. Neuron 57, 482–497.

Ramcharan E.J., Gnadt J.W., and Sherman S.M. (2005). Higher-order thalamic relays burst more than first-order relays. *Proceedings of the National Academy of Sciences of the United States of America* 102, 12236–12241.

Reinagel P., Godwin D., Sherman S.M., and Koch C. (1999). Encoding of visual information by LGN bursts. Journal of Neurophysiology 81, 2558–2569.

Reinhold K., Lien A.D., and Scanziani M. (2015). Distinct recurrent versus afferent dynamics in cortical visual processing. Nature Neuroscience 18, 1789–1797.

Rikhye R.V., Wimmer R.D., and Halassa M.M. (2018). Toward an integrative theory of thalamic function. *Annual Review of Neuroscience* 41, 163–183.

Ritter-Makinson S., Clemente-Perez A., Higashikubo B., Cho F.S., Holden S.S., Bennett E., Chkhaidze A., Rooda O.H.E., Cornet M.C., Hoebeek F.E., Yamakawa K., Cilio M.R., Delord B., and Paz J.T. (2019). Augmented reticular thalamic bursting and seizures in Scn1a-Dravet syndrome. Cell Reports 26, 54–64.e6.

Roberts J.A., and Robinson P.A. (2012). Corticothalamic dynamics: structure of parameter space, spectra, instabilities, and reduced model. *Physical Review* E: *Statistical, Nonlinear, and* Soft Matter *Physics* 85, 011910.

Rodenkirch C., Liu Y., Schriver B.J., and Wang Q. (2019). Locus coeruleus activation enhances thalamic feature selectivity via norepinephrine regulation of intrathalamic circuit dynamics. *Nature Neuroscience* 22, 120–133.

Rosenbaum R., Rubin J., and Doiron B. (2012). Short term synaptic depression imposes a frequency dependent filter on synaptic information transfer. PLoS Computational Biology 8, e1002557.

Rosenbaum R., Rubin J.E., and Doiron B. (2013). Short-term synaptic depression and stochastic vesicle dynamics reduce and shape neuronal correlations. Journal of Neurophysiology 109, 475–484.

Rovó Z., Ulbert I., and Acsády L. (2012). Drivers of the primate thalamus. Journal of Neuroscience 32, 17894–17908.

Saalmann Y.B., and Kastner S. (2011). Cognitive and perceptual functions of the visual thalamus. Neuron 71, 209–223.

Saleem A.B., Lien A.D., Krumin M., Haider B., Rosón M.R., Ayaz A., Reinhold K., Busse L., Carandini M., and Harris K.D. (2017). Subcortical source and modulation of the narrowband gamma oscillation in mouse visual cortex. Neuron 93, 315–322.

Sanzeni A., Akitake B., Goldbach H.C., Leedy C.E., Brunel N., and Histed M.H. (2020). Inhibition stabilization is a widespread property of cortical networks. eLife 9.

Scheibel A.B. (1997). The thalamus and neuropsychiatric illness. Journal of Neuropsychiatry and Clinical Neurosciences 9, 342–353.

Schmitt L.I., Wimmer R.D., Nakajima M., Happ M., Mofakham S., and Halassa M.M. (2017). Thalamic amplification of cortical connectivity sustains attentional control. Nature 545, 219–223.

Sherman S. (2001). Tonic and burst firing: dual modes of thalamocortical relay. Trends in Neurosciences 24, 122–126.

Sherman S.M. (2012). Thalamocortical interactions. Current Opinion in Neurobiology 22, 575–579.

Sherman S.M. (2016). Thalamus plays a central role in ongoing cortical functioning. Nature *Neuroscience* 19, 533–541.

Sherman S.M., and Guillery R.W. (1996). Functional organization of thalamocortical relays. Journal of Neurophysiology 76, 1367–1395.

Shosaku A. (1986). Cross-correlation analysis of a recurrent inhibitory circuit in the rat thalamus. Journal of Neurophysiology 55, 1030–1043.

Shosaku A., Kayama Y., Sumitomo I., Sugitani M., and Iwama K. (1989). Analysis of recurrent inhibitory circuit in rat thalamus: neurophysiology of the thalamic reticular nucleus. Progress in Neurobiology 32, 77–102.

Sohal V.S., and Huguenard J.R. (1998). Long-range connections synchronize rather than spread intrathalamic oscillations: computational modeling and in vitro electrophysiology. Journal of Neurophysiology 80, 1736–1751.

Soto-Sánchez C., Wang X., Vaingankar V., Sommer F.T., and Hirsch J.A. (2017). Spatial scale of receptive fields in the visual sector of the cat thalamic reticular nucleus. *Nature Communications* 8, 800.

Steriade M., Domich L., Oakson G., and Deschênes M. (1987). The deafferented reticular thalamic nucleus generates spindle rhythmicity. Journal of Neurophysiology 57, 260–273.

Steriade M., McCormick D., and Sejnowski T. (1993). Thalamocortical oscillations in the sleeping and aroused brain. Science 262, 679–685.

Steriade M., Nunez A., and Amzica F. (1993). Intracellular analysis of relations between the slow (<1 Hz) neocortical oscillation and other sleep rhythms of the electroencephalogram. Journal of Neuroscience 13, 3266–3283.

Swadlow H.A., and Gusev A.G. (2001). The impact of "bursting" thalamic impulses at a neocortical synapse. Nature Neuroscience 4, 402–408.

Tarasenko A.N., Kostyuk P.G., Eremin A.V., and Isaev D.S. (1997). Two types of low-voltage-activated Ca^{2+} channels in neurones of rat laterodorsal thalamic nucleus. Journal of Physiology **499**, 77–86.

Temereanca S., Brown E.N., and Simons D.J. (2008). Rapid changes in thalamic firing synchrony during repetitive whisker stimulation. Journal of Neuroscience **28**, 11153–11164.

Tian Y., Margulies D.S., Breakspear M., and Zalesky A. (2020). Topographic organization of the human subcortex unveiled with functional connectivity gradients. *Nature Neuroscience* **23**, 1421–1432.

Timofeev I., Bazhenov M., Seigneur J., and Sejnowski T. (2012). Neuronal synchronization and thalamocortical rhythms in sleep, wake and epilepsy. In Noebels J.L., Avoli M., Rogawski M.A., Olsen R.W., and Delgado-Escueta A.V., eds., Jasper's *basic mechanisms* of the *epilepsies* [Internet], 4th ed. (National Center for Biotechnology Information).

Timofeev I., Bonjean M.E., and Bazhenov M. (2020).Cellular *mechanisms* of *thalamocortical oscillations* in the *sleeping brain* (Springer).

Timofeev I., and Steriade M. (1996). Low-frequency rhythms in the thalamus of intact-cortex and decorticated cats. Journal of Neurophysiology **76**, 4152–4168.

Tottene A., Favero M., and Pietrobon D. (2019). Enhanced thalamocortical synaptic transmission and dysregulation of the excitatory–inhibitory balance at the thalamocortical feedforward inhibitory microcircuit in a genetic mouse model of migraine. Journal of Neuroscience **39**, 9841–9851.

Traub R.D., Contreras D., Cunningham M.O., Murray H., LeBeau F.E.N., Roopun A., Bibbig A., Wilent W.B., Higley M.J., and Whittington M.A. (2005). Single-column thalamocortical network model exhibiting gamma oscillations, sleep spindles, and epileptogenic bursts. Journal of Neurophysiology **93**, 2194–2232.

Tsodyks M., Pawelzik K., and Markram H. (1998). Neural networks with dynamic synapses. Neural Computation **10**, 821–835.

Tsodyks M., and Wu S. (2013). Short-term synaptic plasticity. Scholarpedia **8**, 3153. Revision #182521.

Urbain N., Salin P.A., Libourel P.A., Comte J.C., Gentet L.J., and Petersen C.C. (2015). Whisking-related changes in neuronal firing and membrane potential dynamics in the somatosensory thalamus of awake mice. Cell Reports **13**, 647–656.

Usrey W.M., and Sherman S.M. (2018). Corticofugal circuits: communication lines from the cortex to the rest of the brain. Journal of Comparative Neurology **527**, 640–650.

Vantomme G., Rovó Z., Cardis R., Béard E., Katsioudi G., Guadagno A., Perrenoud V., Fernandez L.M.J., and Lüthi A. (2020). A thalamic reticular circuit for head direction cell tuning and spatial navigation. Cell *Reports* **31**, 107747.

Viaene A.N., Petrof I., and Sherman S.M. (2011). Synaptic properties of thalamic input to layers 2/3 and 4 of primary somatosensory and auditory cortices. Journal of Neurophysiology **105**, 279–292.

Wang X., Wei Y., Vaingankar V., Wang Q., Koepsell K., Sommer F.T., and Hirsch J.A. (2007). Feedforward excitation and inhibition evoke dual modes of firing in the cat's visual thalamus during naturalistic viewing. Neuron **55**, 465–478.

Wang X.J. (2020).Macroscopic gradients of synaptic excitation and inhibition in the neocortex. *Nature Reviews Neuroscience* **21**, 169–178.

Wang X.J., Golomb D., and Rinzel J. (1995). Emergent spindle oscillations and intermittent burst firing in a thalamic model: specific neuronal mechanisms. *Proceedings of the National Academy of Sciences of the United States of America* **92**, 5577–5581.

Wei H., Bonjean M., Petry H.M., Sejnowski T.J., and Bickford M.E. (2011). Thalamic burst firing propensity: a comparison of the dorsal lateral geniculate and pulvinar nuclei in the tree shrew. *Journal of Neuroscience* **31**, 17287–17299.

Wells M.F., Wimmer R.D., Schmitt L.I., Feng G., and Halassa M.M. (2016). Thalamic reticular impairment underlies attention deficit in Ptchd1$^{Y/-}$ mice. Nature **532**, 58–63.

Wester J.C., and Contreras D. (2013). Differential modulation of spontaneous and evoked thalamocortical network activity by acetylcholine level in vitro. Journal of Neuroscience **33**, 17951–17966.

Whitmire C.J., Waiblinger C., Schwarz C., and Stanley G.B. (2016). Information coding through adaptive gating of synchronized thalamic bursting. Cell Reports **14**, 795–807.

Willis A.M., Slater B.J., Gribkova E.D., and Llano D.A. (2015). Open-loop organization of thalamic reticular nucleus and dorsal thalamus: a computational model. Journal of Neurophysiology **114**, 2353–2367.

Wimmer R.D., Schmitt L.I., Davidson T.J., Nakajima M., Deisseroth K., and Halassa M.M. (2015). Thalamic control of sensory selection in divided attention. Nature **526**, 705–709.

Wolfart J., Debay D., Masson G.L., Destexhe A., and Bal T. (2005). Synaptic background activity controls spike transfer from thalamus to cortex. Nature Neuroscience **8**, 1760–1767.

Yang S., Meng Y., Li J., Li B., Fan Y.S., Chen H., and Liao W. (2020). The thalamic functional gradient and its relationship to structural basis and cognitive relevance. NeuroImage **218**, 116960.

Zeldenrust F., Wadman W.J., and Englitz B. (2018). Neural coding with bursts—current state and future perspectives. Frontiers in Computational Neuroscience 12.

Zikopoulos B., and Barbas H. (2006). Prefrontal projections to the thalamic reticular nucleus form a unique circuit for attentional mechanisms. Journal of Neuroscience **26**, 7348–7361.

Zikopoulos B., and Barbas H. (2012). Pathways for emotions and attention converge on the thalamic reticular nucleus in primates. Journal of Neuroscience **32**, 5338–5350.

Chapter 22: Computational Contributions of the Thalamus to Learning and Memory

Randall C. O'Reilly and Thomas E. Hazy

From an anatomical perspective, the thalamus should be in a position to make essential contributions to the overall function of the mammalian neocortex, given its extensive interconnectivity with every cortical area and role as an intermediary between extensive subcortical systems. However, despite many promising leads and well-developed theories, the critical role of the thalamus arguably remains significantly underrepresented in the broader literature; all too often, it is still relegated to its well-worn *relay* role. In this chapter, we provide a more thalamus-centric perspective, informed by a gradual appreciation for the many critical roles of the thalamus. This appreciation has emerged from the intersection between neural and computational necessity in the course of attempting to create large-scale systems-neuroscience–based computational models of the brain to understand the neural basis of a variety of cognitive functions.

The scope of functions we consider is as follows:

- **Attention.** One of the most widely discussed and supported functions of the thalamus is its role in modulating attention across the cortex at multiple different scales (Bender & Youakim, 2001; Fiebelkorn & Kastner, 2019; Halassa & Kastner, 2017; LaBerge & Buchsbaum, 1990; Robinson & Petersen, 1992; Saalmann & Kastner, 2011; Snow, Allen, Rafal, & Humphreys, 2009; Zhou, Schafer, & Desimone, 2016). The influential *attentional searchlight* idea of Crick (1984) included a critical role for the thalamic reticular nucleus (TRN) in driving the focus of this attentional signal. However, the bursting-based mechanisms leveraged in that paper have been shown to operate mainly in the anesthetized and sleeping brain (and in vitro preparations) and are specifically associated with reductions in arousal (Halassa et al., 2011; Lewis et al., 2015). Nevertheless, one of the simplest possibilities was perhaps too quickly rejected by Crick (1984): the TRN can provide *pooled inhibition* across multiple different spatial scales, without the need for more complex bursting dynamics. Pooled inhibition aggregates the excitatory signals across a given pool of neurons and feeds that "averaged" excitation uniformly back to those same neurons, such that only the most strongly excited neurons can remain strongly active in the face of the inhibition.

  The TRN constitutes a shell of inhibitory neurons surrounding and projecting topographically to the underlying thalamic nuclei, putting it in a unique position to support pooled inhibition across widely separated areas in the neocortex, where direct corticocortical pooling over such long distances would not be feasible. Distances in the thalamus are much smaller than in the neocortex because it is a compact structure without significant internal connectivity compared to the complex networks present in the cortex. This form of inhibition can replicate the influential, abstract *normalization* model of Reynolds and Heeger (2009) and also fits with many elements of the *folded-feedback* model of Grossberg (1999). Functionally and computationally, the broad-scale inhibition between pathways in the brain can enable dynamic switching between different ways of processing information, potentially playing a critical role in cognitive flexibility.

- **Learning.** The central, integrative role of the higher-order thalamic areas, such as the *pulvinar* and *mediodorsal* (MD) nuclei, was highlighted in the early *blackboard* model of Mumford (1991) and was further supported by extensive analysis of this thalamocortical connectivity (Sherman & Guillery, 2006; Shipp, 2003; Usrey & Sherman, 2018). Likewise, more recent work has highlighted the contributions of these thalamic areas to integrating and coordinating processing across distributed brain areas (Fiebelkorn & Kastner, 2019; Fiebelkorn, Pinsk, & Kastner, 2018; Halassa & Kastner, 2017; Saalmann, Pinsk, Wang, Li, & Kastner, 2012). Building on these ideas and data, we hypothesized that the distinctive pattern of thalamocortical connectivity in these circuits, consisting of separate *driver* versus *modulatory* pathways (Sherman & Guillery, 2006; Usrey & Sherman, 2018), may also play a critical role in learning (O'Reilly, Russin, Zolfaghar, & Rohrlich, 2021; O'Reilly, Wyatte, & Rohrlich, 2014, 2017). Specifically, the numerous top-down corticothalamic (CT) projections can generate a *prediction* of what will happen next over the pulvinar and other higher-order thalamic areas, whereas the strong bottom-up driver pathways provide a *ground-truth* signal representing what actually did happen. This pulvinar-based predictive-learning mechanism provides a biologically plausible solution to the much-discussed, unresolved challenge of understanding what drives something like error-backpropagation learning in the neocortex (Lillicrap, Santoro, Marris, Akerman, & Hinton, 2020; Whittington & Bogacz, 2019). Predictive learning provides an essentially unbounded, continuous supply of prediction error signals, which can drive the neocortex to develop sophisticated internal models of the environment. Thus, the thalamus may play a central role in one of the most important functions in the brain.

- **Executive function.** Building on the earlier foundation of its well-established role in motor control (Mink, 1996), there is an emerging consensus that the basal ganglia circuitry, which centrally involves the thalamus, plays a critical role in *gating* activity in the frontal cortex in the service of higher-level cognitive functions (Brown & Marsden, 1990; Chatham, Frank, & Badre, 2014; Dahlin, Neely, Larsson, Backman, & Nyberg, 2008; Frank, 2005; Frank, Loughry, & O'Reilly, 2001; Graybiel, 1995; Houk, 2005; Middleton & Strick, 2000; O'Reilly & Frank, 2006; Pasupathy & Miller, 2005; Rac-Lubashevsky & Frank, 2020; Voytek & Knight, 2010). In the classical basal ganglia (BG) circuit, the thalamus serves as the interface between the BG output and the frontal cortex, where tonic inhibition from the globus pallidus internal segment (GPi) or substantia nigra pars reticulata (SNr) blocks strong recurrent activation through the corticothalamic loops. When the direct (Go) pathway in the BG fires, it disinhibits this thalamocortical loop. By analogy with motor-action initiation (Mink, 1996), these same kinds of mechanisms could also serve to initiate the updating of working memory in the prefrontal cortex (PFC). This function is known as *gating* in existing models of dopamine modulation of the PFC (Braver & Cohen, 2000) and in a widely used computational model, the long short-term memory (LSTM) model (Hochreiter & Schmidhuber, 1997). Gating is similar in many ways to attentional modulation, suggesting a commonality across these functions, but it takes on a more significant functional role in the context of the specialized dopamine-based learning mechanisms present in the BG. Whereas our original models of this gating dynamic used highly simplified representations of the thalamus (O'Reilly, 2006; O'Reilly & Frank, 2006), we are now exploring the diversity of thalamic interconnections with the frontal cortex and discovering some important new functional roles as a result.

These three functions are synergistic: prediction operates on the focus of attention (not everything can be predicted), and prediction helps guide attention toward anticipated outcomes and spatial locations (Richter & de Lange, 2019). Both are driven by the same top-down corticothalamic projections. Further, executive function depends critically on manipulating the levers of attention in posterior cortical areas (including via direct control projections into the TRN via frontal area 46), and predictive learning likely plays a critical role in shaping executive-function abilities. Taken together, these mechanisms can also be seen as driving some of the most important aspects of our subjective, conscious experience. For example, the fact that we perceive a stable and coherent external world, despite receiving constantly changing sensory signals, depends on predictive learning. To see this, you can gently nudge the bottom of one of your eyeballs with your finger—the world moves around with this manipulation, but it is otherwise rock-steady despite constant saccadic eye movements. We have learned to predict the effects of our planned eye movements (Cavanagh, Hunt, Afraz, & Rolfs, 2010; Duhamel, Colby, & Goldberg, 1992; Wurtz, 2008), but we have no such learning experience for the manually induced motion. This principle extends well beyond eye movements and likely underlies the various perceptual *constancies*, such as size constancy, color constancy, and so forth: the brain learns about what is solid and reliably predictable (the external world), not the idiosyncratic and fleeting raw sensory input.

In light of the long history and large amount of empirical data documenting the dependence of conscious alertness and arousal on thalamic input to the cerebral cortex, we can usefully relate each of these three functions to the nature of *conscious awareness*. Specifically, many theoretical frameworks for understanding the nature of consciousness center around the notion of a mental workspace or blackboard, producing an integrated information-processing system (Baars, 1988; Dehaene & Naccache, 2001; Edelman & Tononi, 2001; Tononi, 2004). Based on extensive neural and behavioral data, Lamme (2006) attributed a critical role for recurrent processing in supporting conscious awareness, and the extensive recurrent nature of corticothalamic connectivity suggests that it should also play a critical role, especially in focusing attention across areas in a coordinated way (Fiebelkorn & Kastner, 2019; Halassa & Kastner, 2017; Saalmann & Kastner, 2011). Ward (2011) offers a more elaborated theory of consciousness associated with thalamic function, along with a review of relevant literature. At a more basic level, the modulation of overall cortical arousal by nonspecific, intralaminar nuclei has long been recognized (Schiff, 2008), and the recurrent connections involving the deep cortical layers have now been shown to be critical in sustaining arousal states (Redinbaugh et al., 2020).

If these computational contributions of the thalamus are correct, then it is hard to imagine a more consequential noncortical substrate for understanding overall cortical function. The thalamus is the modulatory and training master of the neocortex. Although the neocortex is where all the learning and knowledge is actually encoded, without the thalamus, it would be an undisciplined, untutored wild beast! Indeed, that colorfully characterizes the behavior of our computational models in the absence of the various thalamic mechanisms described previously. In the remaining sections, we review each of the aforementioned computational contributions of the thalamus.

Attentional Focusing through TRN Pooled Inhibition

The importance of thalamic attentional mechanisms can be illustrated by the limitations of computational models of the visual system that lack such mechanisms. For example, we developed models that captured the overall hierarchy of superficial-layer cortical processing up through invariant object categorization neurons in the inferotemporal (IT) cortex (Kobatake & Tanaka, 1994) but that lacked thalamic attentional mechanisms (O'Reilly, Wyatte, Herd, Mingus, & Jilk, 2013). These models showed that bidirectional excitation between cortical areas could drive appropriate bottom-up and top-down *constraint-satisfaction* processing, which is important for resolving the many ambiguities in visual inputs (Wyatte, Curran, & O'Reilly, 2012). However, because these models only simulated superficial-layer (i.e., cortical lamina

2–3) pathways, they suffered significantly when faced with complex, real-world visual scenes containing multiple different objects. All of the different features across the different objects merged and collided with each other, creating a big messy jumble.

Interestingly, this jumbled perception is exactly what people who have damage to various attentional pathways in the brain report as their subjective experience, including those with damage to the pulvinar nucleus of the thalamus (Karnath, Himmelbach, & Rorden, 2002; Petersen, Robinson, & Morris, 1987). If they are faced with single discrete objects or letters, they can process those just fine, but once multiple different objects or a normal page of text is presented, they cannot handle the sensory overload (known as *simultanagnosia*—the inability to process multiple simultaneously present stimuli; Farah, 1990). Thus, it is clear that the brain needs some kind of attentional mechanism to focus processing on a small subset of the external world at a time (Buschman & Kastner, 2015; Desimone & Duncan, 1995; Reynolds & Desimone, 2003; Reynolds & Heeger, 2009; Treisman, 1993). These attentional mechanisms are known to involve thalamocortical circuits (Halassa & Kastner, 2017), in addition to larger-scale brain pathways in the frontal and parietal lobes (Bisley & Goldberg, 2010; He et al., 2007). At a computational level, introducing these thalamically based attentional circuits into our models has likewise enabled the processing of complex visual scenes.

Interestingly, most machine-learning approaches to vision have managed to get by without including attentional mechanisms (LeCun, Bengio, & Hinton, 2015), but these models have great difficulty recognizing some *adversarial* images that people consider obvious, and extensive analysis shows that these models are using texture and other aggregate patterns to recognize object categories and are not really processing individuated objects per se (Sinz, Pitkow, Reimer, Bethge, & Tolias, 2019). When spatial attention mechanisms are introduced into these models, these adversarial recognition problems are greatly reduced (Luo, Boix, Roig, Poggio, & Zhao, 2015), consistent with the idea that the mammalian visual system depends critically on attention for supporting robust object recognition.

To understand the neural basis of such attentional mechanisms, we begin with the influential *biased-competition* model (Desimone & Duncan, 1995), which posits that attended neurons receive some kind of additional excitation or bias (which can come from any number of sources, including bottom-up salience or top-down control signals), which then enables them to outcompete other neurons, which become less active as a consequence. The frontal and parietal attentional networks, involving the systems subserving overt eye movements, including the frontal eye fields (FEFs) and the lateral inferior parietal area (LIP), play a particularly strong role in driving spatially based attentional biases (Buschman & Kastner, 2015; He et al., 2007). This biased-competition model has been widely supported (Reynolds & Desimone, 2003) and has been captured mathematically in the *normalization* model of attention shown in Figure 1, which shows how a competitive process of normalization driven by the *pooling* of activity over retinotopically organized spatial regions can account for a range of attentional phenomena (Reynolds & Heeger, 2009).

It is in this critical role of inhibitory pooling that the thalamus can potentially play a unique role in the larger network of brain circuits involved in attention. This is because with the strong and topographically organized inhibitory projection of the TRN to all of the excitatory thalamic nuclei, the thalamus is in a unique position to exert a net inhibitory pooling effect across a wider range of downstream cortical areas than would be possible through direct corticocortical connections within the cortex itself. Thus, whereas direct corticocortical pathways can support pooling and normalization within localized cortical areas, the thalamus may be particularly important for mediating competition between different brain areas. This idea is consistent with the data from Saalmann et al. (2012) showing a central role for the pulvinar in coordinating activity across brain areas and, in particular, a cross-modal attention role for the TRN (Wimmer et al., 2015), which we revisit after first introducing a more detailed anatomical picture for how the thalamus fits in with the overall biased-competition and normalization dynamic.

Although the Reynolds and Heeger (2009) model is abstract and not directly tied to specific neural mechanisms, we found that it provided a useful framework for understanding the different contributions of the cortical lamina and the thalamus in a manner that is consistent overall with the *folded-feedback* model of Grossberg (1999) (Figure 1b). This model is anchored by the finding that layer 6 corticothalamic (6CT) neurons exert a multiplicative or gain-field effect on neural activations in the superficial network (Bortone, Olsen, & Scanziani, 2014; Dougherty, Cox, Ninomiya, Leopold, & Maier, 2017; Olsen, Bortone, Adesnik, & Scanziani, 2012; van Kerkoerle et al., 2014), which corresponds to the net modulatory effect of the *suppressive-drive* signal from the normalization model. Thus, where activations are strong in the suppressive-drive layer, the corresponding superficial layer activations will remain strong, but where they are weaker, the superficial layer activations will be reduced, as if multiplied by a gain factor of less than 1.

To walk through the model shown in Figure 1 in detail: Bottom-up sensory inputs project to layer 4, which may provide a more faithful representation of their bottom-up strength differences (which are equal in the example shown). Initially, these equal-strength bottom-up signals activate the superficial layers equally, but the top-down attentional signal (e.g., from the LIP in this case) causes the attended stimulus to become more strongly activated, especially as it converges on the layer 5 neurons (with some top-down modulation of superficial layers likely as well). The broad lateral connectivity among these deep layers 5 and 6 corticocortical (CC) neurons serves to integrate across discrete sensory features to create a more broadly tuned spatial activity pattern reflecting both bottom-up and top-down signals. This is then reflected in the 6CT (corticothalamic) projections to the thalamic relay cells (TRCs) and the TRN. The TRN connectivity causes significant pooling across many of these descending projections, such that the TRN projects back a broadly pooled inhibitory signal to the TRCs.

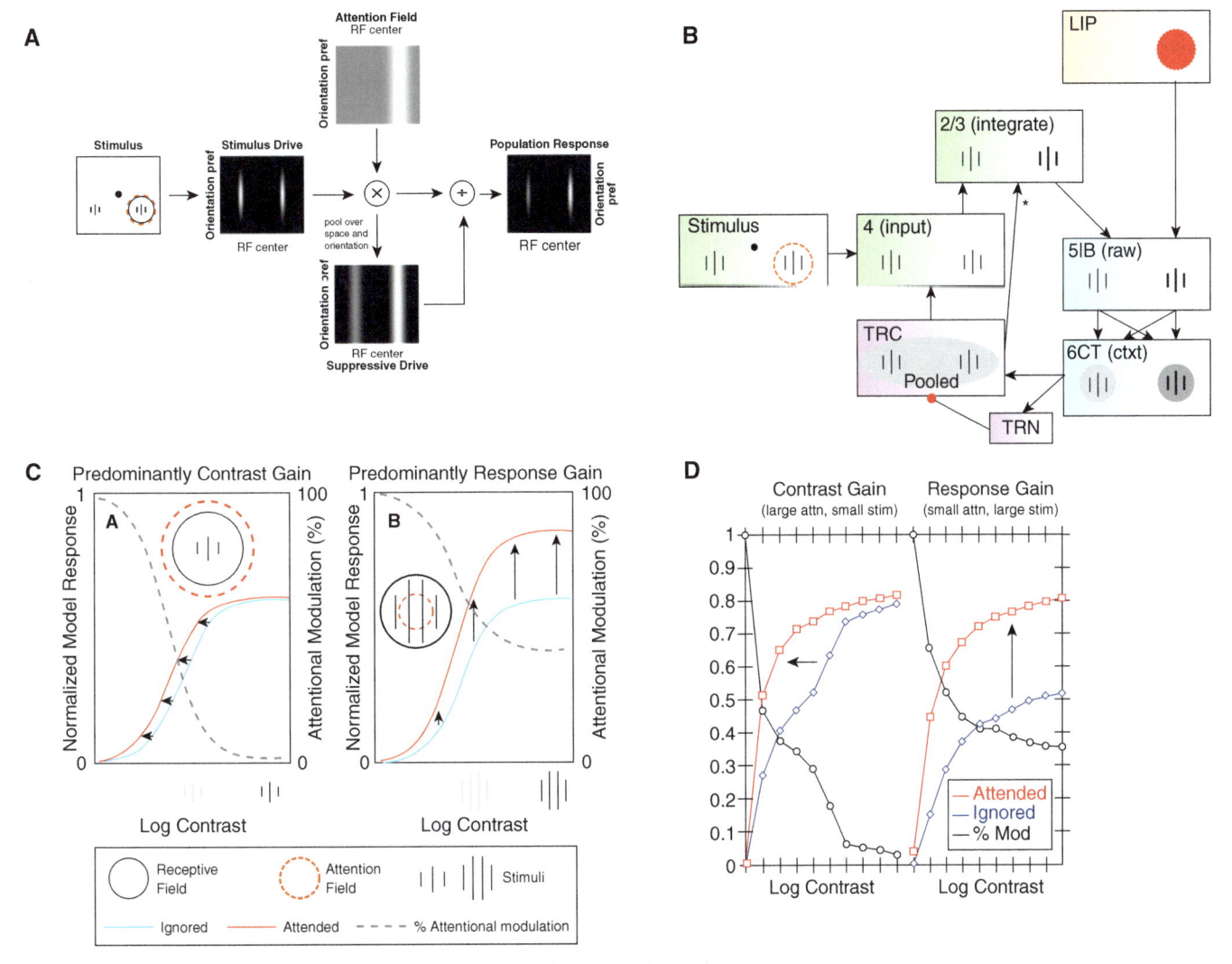

Figure 1 A. The Reynolds and Heeger (2009) mathematical model of pooling and normalization processes in attention.
B. How attentional modulation is computed across the deep layers in our biological model, in response to a top-down attentional focus (as encoded in the LIP of the parietal cortex). Layer 4 receives bottom-up sensory input (initially equally weighted), which then drives superficial layers (2/3), which initially do not reflect the attentional modulation (*not shown*). The deep 5IB neurons integrate deep-to-deep top-down attentional inputs from the LIP plus the local stimulus features from layers 2/3, to produce the "raw" deep output, prior to the contextual normalization process. The 6CC neurons integrate across the 5IB activations (context integration or pooling), within the limits of corticocortical connectivity, resulting in a 6CT signal that drives the thalamic relay cells (TRCs) and TRN, with the TRN pooling across a wider area, resulting in a more fully normalized activity over the TRC, decreasing the unattended location activity. The TRC projections have a net multiplicative effect on other cortical lamina.
C. Key data accounted for by Reynolds and Heeger (2009) model: two qualitatively different types of attentional modulation resulting from differences in the size of the attentional spotlight relative to the stimulus size, which directly reflect pooling and normalization processes.
D. Results from our thalamically equipped model driven by a large LIP attentional top-down spotlight relative to a small bottom-up stimulus (*left*) versus a small LIP spotlight relative to a larger stimulus, reproducing the same qualitative effects (from O'Reilly et al., 2017).

Critically, the top-down attentional bias effectively increases the strength of this overall pooled inhibitory signal, which in turn more strongly inhibits the *unattended* TRCs that are not also receiving the direct excitatory benefits from this top-down signal. Thus, the net effect of this circuit is that TRCs in the attended region remain robustly active, but those in the unattended region are relatively inhibited, and these differential activity levels then feed back up into the cortex, where the attended region thus has stronger thalamic drive. The TRCs then provide the equivalent of the multiplicative attentional filter in the Reynolds and Heeger (2009) model. In addition, there are direct intracortical, interlaminar circuits (Bortone et al., 2014; Frandolig et al., 2019) driven by 6CT collaterals that provide focused, local, center-surround excitation and inhibition throughout the cortical column, which serve to further augment the multiplicative-like effect of the TRC feedback into the cortex.

Figure 1D shows that our model of these laminar circuits through the deep layers and thalamus captures the same key data as the Reynolds and Heeger (2009) model, where the relative balance of the enhancing versus suppressive effects of attentional modulation can shift depending on the relative sizes of the attentional spotlight and the stimulus input (and as a function of stimulus contrast), producing the shift from *contrast-gain* to *response-gain* effects of attention. Thus, although there is much more work to be done here to explore the full range of attentional dynamics, this provides a solid foundation building on the well-established Reynolds and Heeger (2009) model. Furthermore, our model is related to the *folded-feedback* model of Grossberg (1999) (for a more elaborated version, see Raizada & Grossberg, 2003), which also posits this same kind of attentional modulation dynamic between layer 6 and the superficial layers. Interestingly, top-down attentional signals, like those coming from the LIP down to lower-level visual pathways, are preferentially communicated via a network of deep-to-deep projections (Markov et al., 2014; van Kerkoerle et al., 2014; von Stein, Chiang, & König, 2000).

A critical question for the effects of attention in the abstract normalization model (Reynolds & Heeger, 2009) is the spatial scope over which these normalization effects can occur. Anatomically, it is likely that local inhibitory interneurons within the neocortex could support some local amount of pooled inhibitory competition, but to cover the full visual field in an area the size of V1 in a primate, the TRN contribution to pooled inhibition is likely to be critical. Thus, more selective tests of thalamic contributions to attention could focus on measuring across a wide range of spatial scales, with the prediction that the broader scales are differentially affected.

Predictive Learning in the Pulvinar

The central question of how learning is able to shape the networks of neurons in the neocortex to support our incredibly powerful and adaptive human cognitive abilities remains one of the most important unresolved scientific challenges. This question has been addressed from many different angles at many different levels of analysis, and the recent advances in deep neural network (DNN) machine-learning algorithms (LeCun et al., 2015) based on error backpropagation (Rumelhart, Hinton, & Williams, 1986) have reignited interest in how this form of learning might operate in the neocortex (Lillicrap et al., 2020; Whittington & Bogacz, 2019). Our models are based on an early proposal for how bidirectional connectivity between cortical areas could communicate error signals in a way that mathematically approximates error backpropagation (O'Reilly, 1996; O'Reilly & Munakata, 2000). The main principles of this form of error-driven learning are as follows:

- Error signals take the form of *changes over time* in the firing patterns of neurons, in particular, parts of the network that first encode an expectation or guess and then experience the correct answer relative to that prior expectation. This is known as a *temporal-difference* form of error signal, as contrasted with the alternative possibility of an explicitly coded error signal where the firing of individual neurons directly reflects the error. In simple artificial networks (and current-day DNNs), there are "output layers" that represent things such as the category label for an object presented to the visual "input layer" of the network. The network's expectation is the output-layer activity in response to the visual input, which is then followed by the correct answer being presented, producing the temporal-difference sequence of activations. Current DNNs use huge data sets of hand-labeled images to provide such correct answers to drive output-layer targets.

- The ubiquitous bidirectional connectivity in the neocortex allows individual neurons everywhere to be influenced by these changes over time in the firing of output-layer neurons, and the math shows that, with certain assumptions, such as symmetrical connectivity (which can be significantly relaxed in practice), the local changes in activity state in an individual neuron accurately reflect the error-backpropagation derivative that is needed to drive learning to minimize the error on the output layer of the network.

This framework for neocortical error-driven learning avoids some of the most glaring forms of biological implausibility associated with the error-backpropagation algorithm (Crick, 1989), and a large number of models developed over several years demonstrate that a wide range of cognitive functions can be accounted for within this general framework (O'Reilly, Hazy, & Herd, 2016; O'Reilly & Munakata, 2000; O'Reilly, Munakata, Frank, Hazy, & Contributors, 2012). However, there remains a critical unresolved question: What are the primary ecologically plausible sources of the error signals needed to drive error-backpropagation learning? Unlike the artificial models, developing humans and other animals are not provided with massive labeled data sets to drive their learning. Somehow, we must learn in a more "self-organizing," naturalistic fashion.

One widely discussed solution to this problem is that we learn by predicting what will happen next, which goes back to Helmholtz in his proposal of *recognition by synthesis* (von Helmholtz, 1867) and has been widely embraced in a range of different frameworks (Clark, 2013; Dayan, Hinton, Neal, & Zemel, 1995; J. Elman et al., 1996; J. L. Elman, 1990; Friston, 2005; Kawato, Hayakawa, & Inui, 1993; Mumford, 1992; Rao & Ballard, 1999). In this *predictive-learning* framework, the raw sensory input itself can generate the error signal as a "ground truth" relative to a prior prediction, avoiding the need for any form of human labeling and providing an essentially unlimited and automatic source of error signals to drive learning. This abstract computational idea turns out to be synergistic with the circuitry of higher-order thalamic areas (primarily the pulvinar and MD), providing another important example where the thalamus comes to the rescue in our computational understanding of overall cortical functioning (O'Reilly et al., 2021).

Specifically, Figure 2 shows the critical elements of this thalamocortical circuitry as emphasized by Sherman and Guillery (2006), which features two separate sources of input into the higher-order thalamic relay cells: the strong, focal, bottom-up *driver* inputs and the much more numerous but weaker "modulatory" top-down inputs. These two inputs provide a natural organization for predictive learning, where the top-down inputs are responsible for generating the prediction or expectation, and the bottom-up drivers impose the "ground-truth" outcome that actually occurred relative to this prediction.

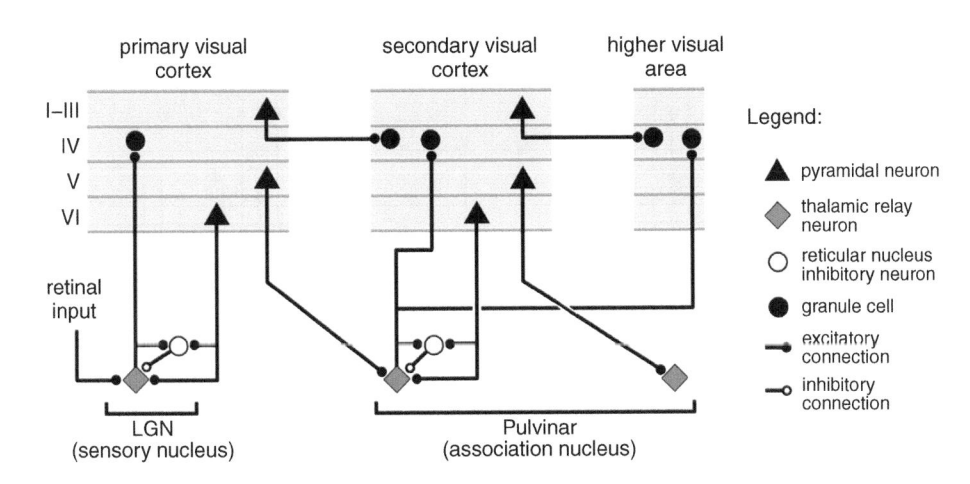

Figure 2 Summary figure from Sherman and Guillery (2006) showing the strong feedforward *driver* projection emanating from layer 5IB cells in the lower layers (e.g., V1) and the much more numerous feedback "modulatory" projections from layer 6CT (corticothalamic) cells. We interpret these same connections as providing a prediction (6CT) versus outcome (5IB) activity pattern over the pulvinar.

The sources of these driver inputs are the layer 5 intrinsic bursting (5IB) neurons, which fire discrete bursts with intrinsic dynamics having a period of roughly 100 ms between bursts (Connors, Gutnick, & Prince, 1982; Franceschetti et al., 1995; Larkum, Zhu, & Sakmann, 1999; Saalmann et al., 2012; Silva, Amitai, & Connors, 1991). These are thought to drive the widely studied *alpha* frequency of 10 Hz that originates in cortical deep layers and has important effects on a wide range of perceptual and attentional tasks (Buffalo, Fries, Landman, Buschman, & Desimone, 2011; Clayton, Yeung, & Kadosh, 2018; Jensen, Bonnefond, & VanRullen, 2012; K. Mathewson, Gratton, Fabiani, Beck, & Ro, 2009; VanRullen & Koch, 2003). Critically, unlike many other such bursting phenomena, this 5IB bursting occurs in awake animals (Luczak, Bartho, & Harris, 2009, 2013; Sakata & Harris, 2009, 2012), consistent with the presence of alpha in awake, behaving states.

From a computational perspective, the burst firing of these driver inputs provides the necessary timing for a temporal-difference form of error signal, as in our earlier models. Specifically, when these 5IB neurons are not active in between their burst phases, the top-down inputs to the TRC neurons can generate a prediction, which is then followed immediately in time by the bottom-up driver outcome signal. The extensive projections from the thalamus back into the cortex (Shipp, 2003) can convey this temporal-difference error signal to the neocortical neurons, driving local synaptic changes that will end up minimizing the prediction error (O'Reilly et al., 2021).

Figure 3 illustrates the temporal evolution of activity states according to this predictive-learning theory over a single 125-ms time window of a 100-ms alpha cycle (the actual timing is likely to be more dynamic). The activity state in pulvinar TRC neurons, representing a prediction, as driven by the top-down 6CT projections, should develop during the first ~75 ms, when the 5IB neurons are paused between bursting. Then the final ~25 ms largely reflects the strong 5IB bottom-up ground-truth driver inputs when they burst. Thus, the prediction error signal is reflected in the temporal difference of these activation states as they develop over time. In other words, our hypothesis is that the pulvinar is directly representing either the top-down prediction or the bottom-up outcome at any given time, and the temporal difference between these states implicitly encodes a prediction error. While the deep 6CT layer is involved in generating a top-down prediction over the pulvinar, the superficial layer neurons continuously represent the current state, simultaneously incorporating bottom-up and top-down constraints via their own connections with other areas. To ensure that the prediction is not directly influenced by this current-state representation (i.e., "peeking at the right answer"), it is important that the 6CT neurons encode temporally delayed information, consistent with available data (Harris & Shepherd, 2015; Sakata & Harris, 2009; Thomson, 2010).

In addition to the extensive primary sources of anatomical and electrophysiological evidence cited earlier, there is a wide range of other neural data consistent with this theory of higher-order thalamic contributions to predictive learning, as reviewed by O'Reilly et al. (2021). For example, there is an extensive literature on alpha-frequency entrainment emerging from deep neocortical layers and the pulvinar and how these organize cortical processing over time in a manner consistent with this model (Fiebelkorn et al., 2018; Klimesch, 2011; Makeig et al., 2002; K. E. Mathewson et al., 2012; Saalmann et al., 2012; Spaak, de Lange, & Jensen, 2014). Furthermore, this framework makes a number of testable predictions, outlined by O'Reilly et al. (2021), that could be conducted using available techniques to more directly test this theory. Two such tests are now underway, so hopefully we will have further relevant data soon.

We have shown how this predictive error-driven learning mechanism, based directly on the biology of the corticothalamic loops, can drive the learning of abstract object-category representations in higher layers of a simulated visual cortex, based solely on short movies of three-dimensional (3D) objects moving and rotating through space (O'Reilly et al., 2021). This model did not have any input telling it how to categorize or label the objects—the learning was purely "self-organizing" based on the raw visual inputs from the movies. Thus, this model provides an initial proof of concept that predictive error-driven learning can drive the formation of more abstract "conceptual" representations, avoiding the implausible use of hand-labeled training data. Furthermore, comparison models

Computation

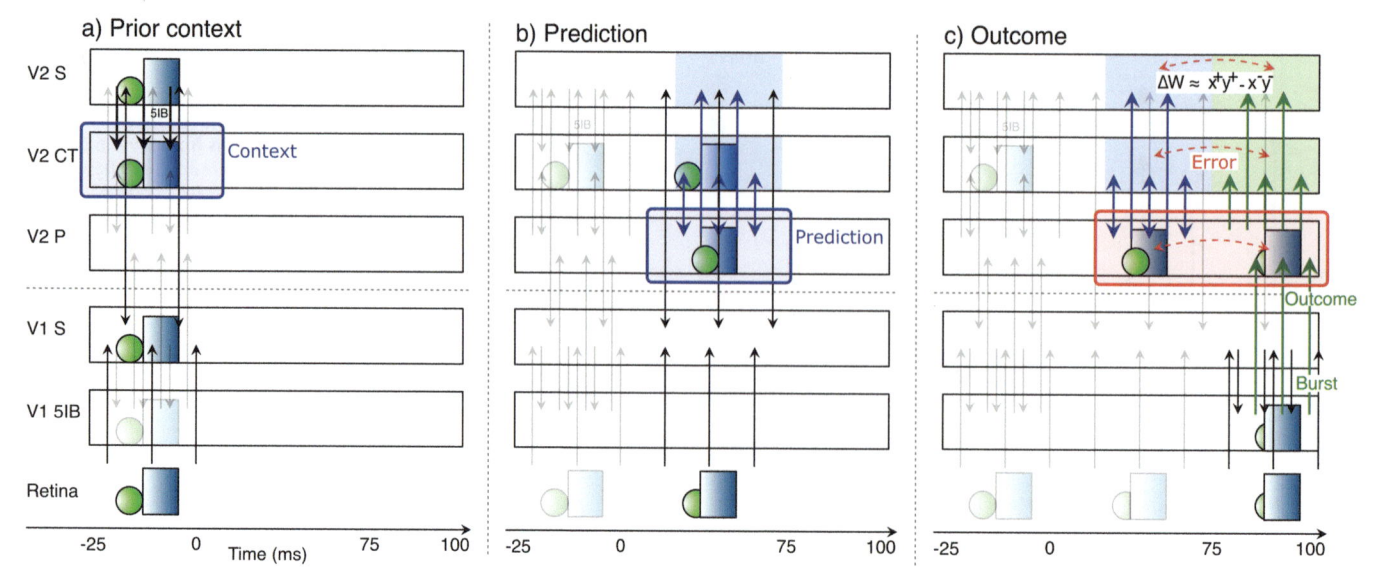

Figure 3 Corticothalamic information flow under our predictive learning hypothesis, shown as a sequence of movie frames (Retina), illustrating the three key steps taking place within a single 125-ms time window, broken out separately across the three panels: (A) prior context is updated in the V2 CT layer, (B) which is then used to generate a prediction over the pulvinar (V2 P), (C) against which the outcome, driven by bottom-up 5IB bursting, represents the prediction error *as a temporal difference between the prediction and outcome states over the pulvinar*. Changes in synaptic weights (learning) in all superficial (S) and CT layers are driven by the *local temporal difference* experienced by each neuron, using a form of the contrastive Hebbian learning (CHL) term as shown, where the + superscripts indicate outcome activations and '/' superscripts indicate prediction. CHL approximates the gradient of the backpropagated prediction error experienced by each neuron (O'Reilly, 1996), reflecting both direct pulvinar error signals and indirect corticocortical error signals as well. In specific: (A) CT context updating occurs via 5IB bursting (*not shown*) in the higher layer (V2) during the prior alpha (100-ms) cycle; this context is maintained in the CT layer and used to generate predictions. (B) The prediction over the pulvinar is generated via numerous top-down CT projections. This prediction state also projects up to the S and CT layers and from S to all other S layers via extensive bidirectional connectivity, so their activation state reflects this prediction as well. (C) The subsequent outcome drives pulvinar activity bottom-up via V1 5IB bursting and is likewise projected to the S and CT layers, ensuring that the relevant temporal-difference error signal is available locally in the cortex. The difference in activation values across these two time points, in the S and CT layers throughout the network, drives learning to reduce prediction errors. Note that the single most important property of the 5IB bursting is that these driver cells are *not* active during the prediction phase—the bursting itself may also be useful in the driving property, but that is a secondary consideration to the critical feature of having a time when the prediction alone can be projected onto the pulvinar.

based on current machine-learning algorithms did not develop these abstract, conceptual representations, indicating the importance of some of the other biologically motivated properties of this model. These properties include the bidirectional connections needed to drive the biological form of error-driven learning in the first place, which also has the effect of enabling higher-level representations to influence lower levels in the network through top-down connectivity. Furthermore, extensive inhibitory connectivity is required to balance and control the bidirectional excitatory connections, and the resulting competitive dynamics can also shape representations in useful ways to promote categorical learning (Kohonen, 1989; Rumelhart & Zipser, 1985).

This thalamocortically mediated temporal-difference mechanism for predictive error-driven learning contrasts with widely discussed explicit error-coding ideas for predictive learning (Bastos et al., 2012; Friston, 2005, 2010; Kawato et al., 1993; Lotter, Kreiman, & Cox, 2016; Ouden, Kok, & Lange, 2012; Rao & Ballard, 1999), where a dedicated population of neurons (typically suggested to be superficial-lamina cortical neurons) explicitly codes for the error signal in their direct firing rates, via an inhibitory-mediated subtraction-like process between the bottom-up outcome signal and a top-down prediction. Despite many attempts to identify such explicit error-coding neurons in the cortex, no substantial body of unambiguous evidence has been discovered (Kok & de Lange, 2015; Kok, Jehee, & de Lange, 2012; Lee & Mumford, 2003;

Summerfield & Egner, 2009; Walsh, McGovern, Clark, & O'Connell, 2020). Thus, the thalamic mechanism may provide a more biologically supported framework.

Thalamic Gating of Frontal Function

To more completely understand learning in the brain, it is essential to understand the significant role that goals, motivation, and reward play in shaping the learning process (O'Reilly, 2020). The thalamus plays a central role in this domain as well, through its interactions with the frontal cortex. In our initial computational models of these frontal/thalamic circuits (Frank et al., 2001), we considered how the BG disinhibition of the thalamus could lead to the *gating* of prefrontal cortex active maintenance of task and goal representations, in the same way that it was thought to affect the selection of overt actions in the motor frontal cortex (Mink, 1996) (Figure 4). Anatomically, the same kinds of excitatory thalamocortical loops are present in the frontal cortex as discussed previously for the posterior cortex, but unlike in the posterior cortex, much of the frontally projecting thalamus is under tonic inhibitory control by the output nuclei of the BG (the GPi and SNr). According to the classic understanding of the BG circuitry (Nambu, 2008), when the direct BG pathway fires, it disinhibits the thalamocortical loop, which then enables a new surge of cortical activation that could drive the updating of task and goal states.

Furthermore, the neuromodulatory effects of phasic dopamine on the BG direct and indirect pathways (Gerfen & Surmeier,

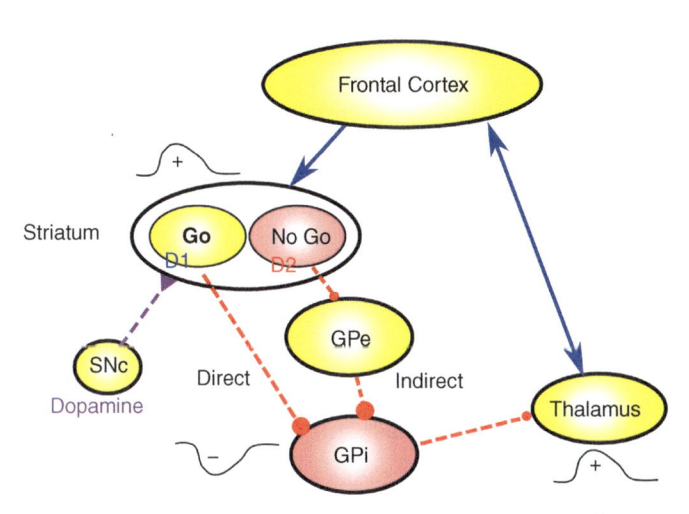

Figure 4 Classical BG circuit producing a disinhibitory, *gating*-like effect on frontal activity to influence when new task/goal states are updated in the frontal cortex, in the same way that the BG is widely thought to support action initiation in motor cortical areas. The thalamus provides the critical interface upon which this disinhibitory control can operate, leveraging the bidirectional excitatory thalamocortical loops.

2011; Shen, Flajolet, Greengard, & Surmeier, 2008) are ideally situated to sculpt adaptive learning to reinforce such updates associated with good outcomes and punish those associated with less good ones, providing a computationally effective overall account of frontal executive function (Frank, 2005; Hazy, Frank, & O'Reilly, 2006, 2007; O'Reilly & Frank, 2006). These models have shown that many complex working memory tasks can be learned from trial-and-error experience, including the 1–2-AX and phonological loop (O'Reilly & Frank, 2006), intradimensional (ID)/extradimensional (ED) dynamic categorization (O'Reilly, Noelle, Braver, & Cohen, 2002), the Wisconsin Card Sorting Task (WCST; (Rougier & O'Reilly, 2002), N-back (Chatham et al., 2011), task switching, the Stroop task (Herd et al., 2014), hierarchical rule learning (Badre & Frank, 2012), and the reference-back-2 task (Rac-Lubashevsky & Frank, 2020).

Consistent with the theme of a progressive appreciation of the importance of the thalamus over time, our computational models have only recently begun to incorporate a more complete understanding of the anatomical and physiological data on thalamic interconnectivity with the frontal cortex and the potentially significant functional implications thereof. For example, these data indicate that the BG gating dynamic shown in Figure 4 only applies to a subset of frontal thalamocortical circuits, predominantly those involving the ventral anterior (VA) and medial thalamic (VM) areas. There are significant other circuits, particularly involving the MD thalamus, that appear to have only sparse or patchy disinhibitory BG inputs and are similar in many ways to the pulvinar circuitry discussed earlier in the context of predictive learning (Giguere & Goldman-Rakic, 1988; Rovó, Ulbert, & Acsády, 2012).

Thus, consistent with computational models of the pulvinar, the MD might function as a predictive-learning and attentional control system for the frontal cortex (Rikhye, Gilra, & Halassa, 2018) while the ventral thalamic circuits support the gating dynamics captured in prior models. Furthermore, the differential patterns of termination in these pathways suggest that the MD may drive updating of the N-methyl-D-aspartate (NMDA)-dependent working memory circuits in frontal layer 3 in response to new sensory inputs (Arnsten, Wang, & Paspalas, 2012; Kritzer & Goldman-Rakic, 1995; Lisman, Fellous, & Wang, 1999; Sanders, Berends, Major, Goldman, & Lisman, 2013), whereas the gating pathway from the BG to the VA and VM may be more responsible for the activation of layer 5 output neurons. Thus, at a computational level, we can think of the MD-based pathways as supporting an attentionally modulated *input/maintenance* gating function, whereas the BG may be more focused on gating the cortical *output* pathways (Chatham et al., 2014).

In the following section, we review a range of data relevant to these multiple frontothalamic circuits, which provide a more fine-grained and high-dimensional picture relative to a simple MD-versus-ventral dichotomy: some areas and patches of the MD are more similar to those in the ventral nuclei and vice versa. Furthermore, modern updates to the classical distinction between *core* versus *matrix* thalamic pathways (Jones, 1998a, 1998b, 2007) provide relevant ways of understanding the functional differences between the input/maintenance versus output gating types. Despite these additional sources of complexity, it does appear that across these areas, the BG disinhibitory control over the frontal cortex is conveyed predominantly through a distinct type of corticothalamic pathway, having broad patterns of connectivity terminating preferentially in cortical layer 1, consistent with the matrix type of thalamic neurons. This would then imply that the BG output-gating control over the cortex is at a very coarse-grained level, such that it can influence the *timing* of action initiation, but it is unlikely to be useful for providing more fine-grained control over the detailed encoding of information in the frontal cortex.

Thus, contrary to our original hypothesis that the BG could provide more fine-grained control over working memory updating, it now seems that the attentionally gated corticothalamic pathways predominantly in the MD are critical for that function. This is consistent with the frontal areas preferentially targeted by the MD projections as well, which include the primate-specific dorsolateral PFC cognitive control and working memory areas. We are currently developing new computational models to incorporate these new anatomically motivated ways of understanding frontal/thalamocortical function.

Details of Frontothalamic Pathways

The distinction between core- and matrix-type projections is one of the early foundational ideas about thalamic organization (Jones, 1998a, 1998b, 2007). Core-type projections have more focal connectivity and target the central cortical lamina, including layers 3 and 4 most strongly. In contrast, matrix-type projections send broad, diffuse connections spanning roughly entire cortical areas and preferentially target lamina 1, where the apical tufts of pyramidal cells from lamina 2, 3, and 5b reside, the thick tufts of subcortically projecting layer 5b being particularly prominent (Harris & Shepherd, 2015; Larkum, Petro, Sachdev, & Muckli, 2018; Ramaswamy & Markram, 2015).

More recent anatomical data, including gene-expression analyses, support a more complex, high-dimensional set of thalamic cell and projection types (Clascá, Rubio-Garrido, & Jabaudon, 2012; Phillips et al., 2019), which include elements of the original core-versus-matrix distinction. At the broadest level, three different categories of thalamic cells can be identified: primary sensory/motor core type (e.g., lateral geniculate nucleus [LGN] for vision and ventral lateral nucleus [VL] primary motor cortex), higher-order types (including the pulvinar, MD, VA, and VM), and the highly diffuse matrix type associated with the intralaminar and midline nuclei (Phillips et al., 2019). Within each such category, there is significant variability.

Within the higher-order types of most relevance for our computational models, the pulvinar and MD predominantly have cells labeled as a *focal* matrix type, which target layer 3 and also layer 1 and receive cortical driver inputs, whereas the VA and VM predominantly have broader *multiareal* matrix-type cells that receive BG disinhibitory inputs and project most strongly to layer 1 and also to layer 3 (Clascá et al., 2012). In the context of the classical dichotomy of core versus matrix type, the focal matrix-type cells are more core-like in their focal connectivity and strong termination in layer 3, whereas the multiareal matrix-type cells are more clearly matrix-like in their broad connectivity and strong termination in layer 1. We adopt the terminology of *focal type* versus *broad type* in what follows. In the MD, the focal nature of the thalamic projections has been characterized as being organized at around the 1-mm scale (Giguere & Goldman-Rakic, 1988), which would provide relatively fine-grained influence of these thalamic cells on corresponding frontal activity states.

Figure 5 shows a schematic diagram integrating a number of different findings across the literature regarding how the distinction of focal versus broad aligns with the different frontal thalamocortical and BG circuits in both rodents and primates. Critically, two major ventral thalamic areas (VM, VA) predominantly send broad-type projections (Kuramoto et al., 2009, 2015) and also receive dense BG projections (Ilinsky, Jouandet, & Goldman-Rakic, 1985; Kuramoto et al., 2009, 2015; Tanibuchi, Kitano, & Jinnai, 2009a). In contrast, the MD receives more patchy BG projections, and it also has patchy distributions of broad-type cells (Münkle, Waldvogel, & Faull, 2000; Phillips et al., 2019), which are sufficiently aligned so as to be consistent with the overall idea that the BG disinhibitory control over the thalamus is primarily conveyed through broad-type thalamocortical pathways.

A complementary distribution of cell types is present with respect to the focal-type neurons, with the MD having a much higher concentration of these, with more patchy distributions of focal-type cells in the VM and VA (Kuramoto et al., 2009). Interestingly, as shown in Figure 5, the MD focal-type connectivity predominates in the areas of the prefrontal cortex (PFC) that are present in primates but not rodents. These areas include the same areas that have specialized layer 3 NMDA-based working memory circuits not found in rodents (Arnsten et al., 2012; Kritzer & Goldman-Rakic, 1995; Lisman et al., 1999; Sanders et al., 2013), which is consistent with the focal-type projections terminating strongly in layer 3. The more focal, clumpy, topographically organized nature of these projections (Giguere & Goldman-Rakic, 1988) would enable them to have more fine-grained control over updating and maintenance of working memory information in these PFC areas, which was the original computational motivation for working memory gating in our models (O'Reilly & Frank, 2006), based on the earlier and widely used LSTM machine-learning algorithm (Gers, Schmidhuber, & Cummins, 2000; Hochreiter & Schmidhuber, 1997). These ideas are also consistent with direct evidence linking the MD and active maintenance in the frontal cortex (Rikhye et al., 2018; Tanibuchi, Kitano, & Jinnai, 2009b; Watanabe & Funahashi, 2012; Watanabe, Takeda, & Funahashi, 2009; Wyder, Massoglia, & Stanford, 2004).

Although the widespread effects of broad-type output gating initially may not sound very useful, it actually could have important benefits. Specifically, any given frontal area can only activate a single motor output at any given point in time (e.g., you can saccade and move your limbs at the same time, but you cannot execute two different saccades at the same time). Thus, perhaps broad-type output gating enforces this singular constraint, where only one output per broader area can be gated at a time. In this case, it would make sense for there to be a *sequential* consideration of different possible output actions, and the broad-type gating fires whenever one such action is determined to be over threshold via the pathway competition of Go versus No Go within the BG (Herd, Krueger, Nair, Mollick, & O'Reilly, 2019; O'Reilly, Nair, Russin, & Herd, 2020). Furthermore, the broad impact of the gating signal may also serve to reset the circuit to facilitate moving on to the next step in a sequence of actions: neural recordings of delayed-action tasks inevitably show a rapid reset of maintenance activation coincident with motor actions.

The broad-versus-focal distinction applies to the output projections from the thalamus, but the driver inputs to these neurons are equally important in determining their functional contributions, as we saw in the case of predictive learning discussed earlier. A recent technique for mapping the sources and types of driver inputs across the primate thalamus (Rovó et al., 2012) showed that the MD predominantly has cortical-type driver inputs similar to those found in the pulvinar, which is consistent with the idea that it provides similar attentional and predictive-learning functions to the frontal cortex. In contrast, the VM and VA have *no* strong drivers and instead receive GABAergic inhibitory inputs from the BG output nuclei (Kuramoto et al., 2009, 2015). The VL, which interconnects with primary and secondary motor areas, receives subcortical drivers primarily from the deep cerebellar nuclei. This VL pathway would enable the cerebellum to train the motor cortex to produce better motor commands, which is consistent with a substantial literature showing that the dysmetria associated with cerebellar damage is significant; it is relatively less impactful after motor development has stabilized but remains crucial for adapting to novel trajectories (Chen, Hua, Smith, Lenz, & Shadmehr, 2006; Manto, 2009).

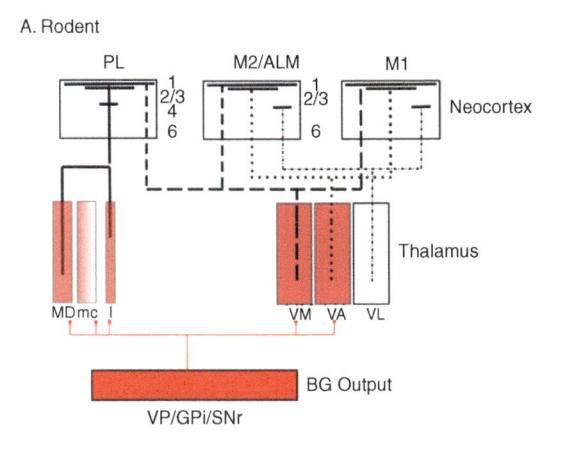

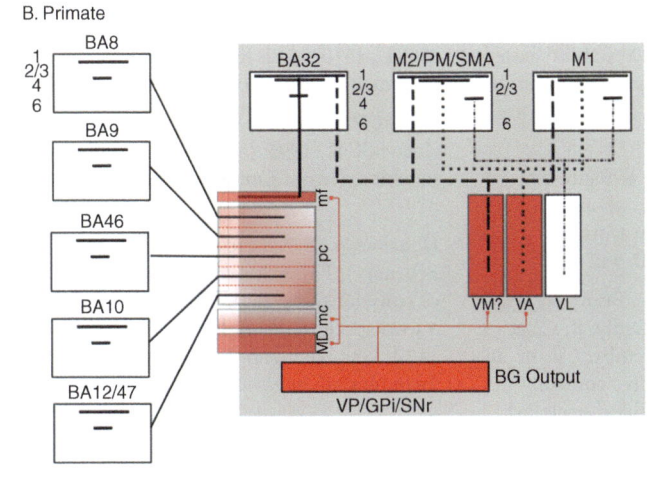

Figure 5 Focal versus broad thalamocortical connectivity and BG modulation in rodent versus primate prefrontal cortex.

A. The rodent prelimbic cortex (PL) is interconnected with both the MD and ventral motor thalamus (VM and VA). The MD projects more focally to the middle cortical laminae, most prominently from its lateral segment (l), whereas the VM and VA project more broadly and more to layer 1. The VA and VM also project broadly to secondary (M2/ALM) and primary (M1) motor cortices. In contrast, the VL projects focally to the middle cortical laminae of motor cortices and uniquely receives cerebellar inputs (not shown), with only minimal BG input, whereas the VA and VM receive the densest BG input. BG projections to the MD are of intermediate density and exhibit a patchy connectivity pattern. The central part of MD (panel C) projects to the orbital frontal cortex (not shown).

B. Primate PFC connectivity essentially replicates the rodent pattern as a subset (gray box), although some homologous areas typically have different labels; for example, primate BA32 is homologous to the PL in rodents, and the PM and SMA are secondary motor areas. Primates have several additional PFC areas (left side of diagram), all of them interconnected with segments of an essentially new part of a greatly enlarged MD nucleus, the parvocellular middle segment (MDpc). BG output nuclei = VP/GPi/SNr (ventral pallidum/globus pallidus, internal segment/ substantia nigra, pars reticulata); BA = Brodmann areas; VM? = ventromedial thalamic nucleus, not prominent in primates and sometimes considered part of the midline nuclei; MDmc/pc/mf = magnocellular/ parvocellular/multiforme segments of the MD.

Finally, it is important to note that even if we adopt this clear distinction between BG-mediated output gating and cortically/attentionally mediated maintenance gating, there remains considerable ambiguity about the potential time course of these respective gating signals. For example, it is possible that BG-gated disinhibition of the 5b neurons could drive a *preparatory* form of pre-output activity in advance of actually executing an action. For example, there is evidence in the mouse for a BG-mediated preparatory form of gating through the VM thalamic nucleus (K. Guo, Yamawaki, Svoboda, & Shepherd, 2018; Z. V. Guo et al., 2017). Likewise, there is extensive evidence in people of a *proactive* engagement of frontal control and action representations, which may well be associated with BG preparatory gating of output-pathway neurons (Braver, Paxton, Locke, & Barch, 2009). Furthermore, the purely maintenance form of gating may largely be restricted to primates (Elston, 2003; Wang et al., 2013), where it may provide a more "offline" form of active maintenance of information that may be useful for subsequent actions but falls short of actually driving output-level action preparation. In short, there are numerous important functional questions about the nature of gating that remain to be explored, in conjunction with critical experimental tests that can directly inform these models.

Conclusions

In summary, across all of these potential contributions of the thalamus, there is a core *modulatory* role, where thalamic activity modulates corresponding neocortical activity, whether that is characterized as being an attentional or gating modulation. Furthermore, the thalamus may play a *training* role, conveying prediction error signals that shape neural representations in the cortex to develop a systematic predictive model of the world. Across the thalamus, the source of these training signals arises from the distinctive *driver* inputs on thalamic neurons—the map of such drivers across the thalamus (Rovó et al., 2012) thus provides a window into the nature of training signals for different cortical areas.

Despite its truly "core" (and matrix) connectivity, one could argue that the thalamus itself doesn't really *do* anything—it just happens to be in the right place to connect other circuits in an effective way. However, it is not clear that any part of the brain can avoid this argument: neurons mainly just pass the buck around to other neurons, making their own modest contributions along the way. What thalamic neurons may lack in such processing contributions, they more than make up for by their unique connectivity that results in such critical functional dynamics, including the attention, predictive-learning, and executive-function mechanisms discussed here.

References

Arnsten, A. F. T., Wang, M. J., & Paspalas, C. D. (2012, October). Neuromodulation of thought: Flexibilities and vulnerabilities in prefrontal cortical network synapses. *Neuron*, **76**(1), 223–239. doi: 10.1016/j.neuron.2012.08.038

Baars, B. J. (1988). *A Cognitive Theory of Consciousness*. New York: Cambridge University Press.

Badre, D., & Frank, M. J. (2012, March). Mechanisms of hierarchical reinforcement learning in corticostriatal circuits 2: Evidence from fMRI. *Cerebral Cortex*, **22**(3), 527–536. Retrieved from http://www.ncbi.nlm.nih.gov/pubmed/21693491

Bastos, A. M., Usrey, W. M., Adams, R. A., Mangun, G. R., Fries, P., & Friston, K. J. (2012, November). Canonical microcircuits for predictive coding. *Neuron*, **76**(4), 695–711. Retrieved from http://www.ncbi.nlm.nih.gov/pubmed/23177956

Bender, D. B., & Youakim, M. (2001, January). Effect of attentive fixation in macaque thalamus and cortex. *Journal of Neurophysiology*, **85**, 219–234. Retrieved from http://www.ncbi.nlm.nih.gov/pubmed/11152722

Bisley, J. W., & Goldberg, M. E. (2010). Attention, intention, and priority in the parietal lobe. *Annual Review of Neuroscience*, **33**, 1–21. Retrieved from http://www.ncbi.nlm.nih.gov/pubmed/20192813

Bortone, D. S., Olsen, S. R., & Scanziani, M. (2014, April). Translaminar inhibitory cells recruited by layer 6 corticothalamic neurons suppress visual cortex. *Neuron*, **82**(2), 474–485. Retrieved from http://www.ncbi.nlm.nih.gov/pubmed/24656931

Braver, T. S., & Cohen, J. D. (2000, December). On the control of control: The role of dopamine in regulating prefrontal function and working memory. In S. Monsell & J. Driver (Eds.), *Control of Cognitive Processes: Attention and Performance XVIII* (pp. 713–737). Cambridge, MA: MIT Press.

Braver, T. S., Paxton, J. L., Locke, H. S., & Barch, D. M. (2009, May). Flexible neural mechanisms of cognitive control within human prefrontal cortex. *Proceedings of the National Academy of Sciences of the United States of America*, **106**(18), 7351–7356.

Brown, R. G., & Marsden, C. D. (1990, February). Cognitive function in Parkinson's disease: From description to theory. *Trends in Neurosciences*, **13**, 21–29. Retrieved from http://www.ncbi.nlm.nih.gov/pubmed/1688671

Buffalo, E. A., Fries, P., Landman, R., Buschman, T. J., & Desimone, R. (2011, July). Laminar differences in gamma and alpha coherence in the ventral stream. *Proceedings of the National Academy of Sciences of the United States of America*, **108**(27), 11262–11267. Retrieved from http://www.ncbi.nlm.nih.gov/pubmed/21690410

Buschman, T. J., & Kastner, S. (2015, October). From behavior to neural dynamics: An integrated theory of attention. *Neuron*, **88**(1), 127–144. doi: 10.1016/j.neuron.2015.09.017

Cavanagh, P., Hunt, A. R., Afraz, A., & Rolfs, M. (2010, April). Visual stability based on remapping of attention pointers. *Trends in Cognitive Sciences*, **14**(4), 147–153. doi: 10.1016/j.tics.2010.01.007

Chatham, C. H., Frank, M., & Badre, D. (2014, January). Corticostriatal output gating during selection from working memory. *Neuron*, **81**(4), 930–942.

Chatham, C. H., Herd, S. A., Brant, A. M., Hazy, T. E., Miyake, A., O'Reilly, R. C., & Friedman, N. P. (2011, November). From an executive network to executive control: A computational model of the n-back task. *Journal of Cognitive Neuroscience*, **23**, 3598–3619. Retrieved from http://www.ncbi.nlm.nih.gov/pubmed/21563882

Chen, H., Hua, S. E., Smith, M. A., Lenz, F. A., & Shadmehr, R. (2006, October). Effects of human cerebellar thalamus disruption on adaptive control of reaching. *Cerebral Cortex*, **16**(10), 1462–1473. doi: 10.1093/cercor/bhj087

Clark, A. (2013, June). Whatever next? Predictive brains, situated agents, and the future of cognitive science. *Behavioral and Brain Sciences*, **36**(3), 181–204. Retrieved from http://www.ncbi.nlm.nih.gov/pubmed/23663408

Clascá, F., Rubio-Garrido, P., & Jabaudon, D. (2012). Unveiling the diversity of thalamocortical neuron subtypes. *European Journal of Neuroscience*, **35**(10), 1524–1532. doi: 10.1111/j.1460-9568.2012.08033.x

Clayton, M. S., Yeung, N., & Kadosh, R. C. (2018). The many characters of visual alpha oscillations. *European Journal of Neuroscience*, **48**(7), 2498–2508. doi: 10.1111/ejn.13747

Connors, B. W., Gutnick, M. J., & Prince, D. A. (1982, December). Electrophysiological properties of neocortical neurons in vitro. *Journal of Neurophysiology*, **48**(6), 1302–1320. Retrieved from http://www.ncbi.nlm.nih.gov/pubmed/6296328

Crick, F. (1984, July). Function of the thalamic reticular complex: The searchlight hypothesis. *Proceedings of the National Academy of Sciences of the United States of America*, **81**, 4586–4590. Retrieved from http://www.ncbi.nlm.nih.gov/pubmed/6589612

Crick, F. (1989, February). The recent excitement about neural networks. *Nature*, **337**, 129–132. Retrieved from http://www.ncbi.nlm.nih.gov/pubmed/2911347

Dahlin, E., Neely, A. S., Larsson, A., Backman, L., & Nyberg, L. (2008, June). Transfer of learning after updating training mediated by the striatum. *Science*, **320**(5882), 1510–1512. Retrieved from http://www.ncbi.nlm.nih.gov/pubmed/18556560

Dayan, P., Hinton, G. E., Neal, R. N., & Zemel, R. S. (1995, January). The Helmholtz machine. *Neural Computation*, **7**(5), 889–904.

Dehaene, S., & Naccache, L. (2001, February). Towards a cognitive neuroscience of consciousness: Basic evidence and a workspace framework. *Cognition*, **79**(1–2), 1–37. Retrieved from http://www.ncbi.nlm.nih.gov/pubmed/11164022

Desimone, R., & Duncan, J. (1995). Neural mechanisms of selective visual attention. *Annual Review of Neuroscience*, **18**(1), 193–222. doi: 10.1146/annurev.ne.18.030195.001205

Dougherty, K., Cox, M. A., Ninomiya, T., Leopold, D. A., & Maier, A. (2017, February). Ongoing alpha activity in v1 regulates visually driven spiking responses. *Cerebral Cortex*, **27**(2), 1113–1124. doi: 10.1093/cercor/bhv304

Duhamel, J. R., Colby, C. L., & Goldberg, M. E. (1992, April). The updating of the representation of visual space in parietal cortex by intended eye movements. *Science*, **255**(5040), 90–92. Retrieved from http://www.ncbi.nlm.nih.gov/pubmed/1553535

Edelman, G. M., & Tononi, G. (2001). *A Universe of Consciousness: How Matter Becomes Imagination*. New York, NY: Basic Books.

Elman, J., Bates, E., Karmiloff-Smith, A., Johnson, M., Parisi, D., & Plunkett, K. (1996). *Rethinking Innateness: A Connectionist Perspective on Development*. Cambridge, MA: MIT Press.

Elman, J. L. (1990, January). Finding structure in time. *Cognitive Science*, **14**(2), 179–211.

Elston, G. N. (2003). Cortex, cognition and the cell: New insights into the pyramidal neuron and prefrontal function. *Cerebral Cortex*, **13**(11), 1124–1138. Retrieved from http://www.ncbi.nlm.nih.gov/pubmed/14576205

Farah, M. J. (1990). *Visual Agnosia*. Cambridge, MA: MIT Press.

Fiebelkorn, I. C., & Kastner, S. (2019, February). A rhythmic theory of attention. *Trends in Cognitive Sciences*, **23**(2), 87–101. doi: 10.1016/j.tics.2018.11.009

Fiebelkorn, I. C., Pinsk, M. A., & Kastner, S. (2018, August). A dynamic interplay within the frontoparietal network underlies rhythmic spatial attention. *Neuron*, **99**(4), 842–853.e8. doi: 10.1016/j.neuron.2018.07.038

Franceschetti, S., Guatteo, E., Panzica, F., Sancini, G., Wanke, E., & Avanzini, G. (1995, October). Ionic mechanisms underlying burst firing in pyramidal neurons: Intracellular study in rat sensorimotor cortex. *Brain Research*, **696**(1–2), 127–139. Retrieved from http://www.ncbi.nlm.nih.gov/pubmed/8574660

Frandolig, J. E., Matney, C. J., Lee, K., Kim, J., Chevée, M., Kim, S.-J., . . . Brown, S. P. (2019, September). The synaptic organization of layer 6 circuits reveals inhibition as a major output of a neocortical sublamina. *Cell Reports*, **28**(12), 3131–3143.e5. doi: 10.1016/j.celrep.2019.08.048

Frank, M. J. (2005, January). When and when not to use your subthalamic nucleus: Lessons from a computational model of the basal ganglia. In A. K. Seth, T. J. Prescott, & J. J. Bryson (Eds.), *Modelling Natural Action Selection: Proceedings of an International Workshop* (pp. 53–60). Sussex: AISB.

Frank, M. J., Loughry, B., & O'Reilly, R. C. (2001, January). Interactions between the frontal cortex and basal ganglia in working memory: A computational model. *Cognitive, Affective, and Behavioral Neuroscience*, **1**, 137–160. Retrieved from https://www.ncbi.nlm.nih.gov/pubmed/12467110

Friston, K. (2005, April). A theory of cortical responses. *Philosophical Transactions of the Royal Society B*, **360**(1456), 815–836. Retrieved from http://www.ncbi.nlm.nih.gov/pubmed/15937014

Friston, K. (2010, February). The free-energy principle: A unified brain theory? *Nature Reviews Neuroscience*, **11**(2), 127–138. Retrieved from http://www.ncbi.nlm.nih.gov/pubmed/20068583

Gerfen, C. R., & Surmeier, D. J. (2011). Modulation of striatal projection systems by dopamine. *Annual Review of Neuroscience*, **34**, 441–466. Retrieved from http://www.ncbi.nlm.nih.gov/pubmed/21469956

Gers, F. A., Schmidhuber, J., & Cummins, F. (2000, November). Learning to forget: Continual prediction with LSTM. *Neural Computation*, **12**, 2451–2471. Retrieved from http://www.ncbi.nlm.nih.gov/pubmed/11032042

Giguere, M., & Goldman-Rakic, P. S. (1988). Mediodorsal nucleus: Areal, laminar, and tangential distribution of afferents and efferents in the frontal lobe of rhesus monkeys. *Journal of Comparative Neurology*, **277**(2), 195–213. doi: 10.1002/cne.902770204

Graybiel, A. M. (1995). Building action repertoires: Memory and learning functions of the basal ganglia. *Current Opinion in Neurobiology*, **5**(6), 733–741. Retrieved from http://www.ncbi.nlm.nih.gov/pubmed/8805417

Grossberg, S. (1999). How does the cerebral cortex work? Learning, attention, and grouping by the laminar circuits of visual cortex. *Spatial Vision*, **12**. Retrieved from http://www.ncbi.nlm.nih.gov/pubmed/10221426

Guo, K., Yamawaki, N., Svoboda, K., & Shepherd, G. M. G. (2018, October). Anterolateral motor cortex connects with a medial subdivision of ventromedial thalamus through cell type-specific circuits, forming an excitatory thalamo-cortico-thalamic loop via layer 1 apical tuft dendrites of layer 5b pyramidal tract type neurons. *Journal of Neuroscience*, **38**(41), 8787–8797. doi: 10.1523/JNEUROSCI.1333-18.2018

Guo, Z. V., Inagaki, H. K., Daie, K., Druckmann, S., Gerfen, C. R., & Svoboda, K. (2017, May). Maintenance of persistent activity in a frontal thalamocortical loop. *Nature*, **545**(7653), 181–186. doi: 10.1038/nature22324

Halassa, M. M., & Kastner, S. (2017, December). Thalamic functions in distributed cognitive control. *Nature Neuroscience*, **20**(12), 1669. doi: 10.1038/s41593-017-0020-1

Halassa, M. M., Siegle, J. H., Ritt, J. T., Ting, J. T., Feng, G., & Moore, C. I. (2011, September). Selective optical drive of thalamic reticular nucleus generates thalamic bursts and cortical spindles. *Nature Neuroscience*, **14**(9), 1118–1120. doi: 10.1038/nn.2880

Harris, K. D., & Shepherd, G. M. G. (2015, February). The neocortical circuit: Themes and variations. *Nature Neuroscience*, **18**(2), 170–181. doi: 10.1038/nn.3917

Hazy, T. E., Frank, M. J., & O'Reilly, R. C. (2006, April). Banishing the homunculus: Making working memory work. *Neuroscience*, **139**, 105–118. Retrieved from http://www.ncbi.nlm.nih.gov/pubmed/16343792

Hazy, T. E., Frank, M. J., & O'Reilly, R. C. (2007, August). Towards an executive without a homunculus: Computational models of the prefrontal cortex/basal ganglia system. *Philosophical Transactions of the Royal Society of London. Series B, Biological Sciences*, **362**(1485), 1601–1613. Retrieved from http://www.ncbi.nlm.nih.gov/pubmed/17428778

He, B. J., Snyder, A. Z., Vincent, J. L., Epstein, A., Shulman, G. L., & Corbetta, M. (2007, March). Breakdown of functional connectivity in frontoparietal networks underlies behavioral deficits in spatial neglect. *Neuron*, **53**(6), 905–918. doi: 10.1016/j.neuron.2007.02.013

Herd, S. A., Krueger, K., Nair, A., Mollick, J., & O'Reilly, R. (2019). Neural mechanisms of human decision-making. *Cognitive Affective and Behavioral Neuroscience*. Retrieved from https://arxiv.org/abs/1912.07660

Herd, S. A., O'Reilly, R. C., Hazy, T. E., Chatham, C. H., Brant, A. M., & Friedman, N. P. (2014, April). A neural network model of individual differences in task switching abilities. *Neuropsychologia*, **62**, 375–389. Retrieved from http://www.ncbi.nlm.nih.gov/pubmed/24791709

Hochreiter, S., & Schmidhuber, J. (1997, January). Long short-term memory. *Neural Computation*, **9**, 1735–1780.

Houk, J. C. (2005, June). Agents of the mind. *Biological Cybernetics*, **92**(6), 427–437. Retrieved from http://dx.doi.org/10.1007/s00422-005-0569-8

Ilinsky, I. A., Jouandet, M. L., & Goldman-Rakic, P. S. (1985). Organization of the nigrothalamocortical system in the rhesus monkey. *Journal of Comparative Neurology*, **236**(3), 315–330. doi: 10.1002/cne.902360304

Jensen, O., Bonnefond, M., & VanRullen, R. (2012, April). An oscillatory mechanism for prioritizing salient unattended stimuli. *Trends in Cognitive Sciences*, **16**(4), 200–206. Retrieved from http://www.ncbi.nlm.nih.gov/pubmed/22436764

Jones, E. G. (1998a). A new view of specific and nonspecific thalamocortical connections. *Advances in Neurology*, **77**, 49–71. Retrieved from http://www.ncbi.nlm.nih.gov/pubmed/9709817

Jones, E. G. (1998b, April). Viewpoint: The core and matrix of thalamic organization. *Neuroscience*, **85**(2), 331–345. doi: 10.1016/S0306-4522(97)00581-2

Jones, E. G. (2007). *The Thalamus* (2nd ed., Vol. 2). Cambridge: Cambridge University Press.

Karnath, H. O., Himmelbach, M., & Rorden, C. (2002, February). The subcortical anatomy of human spatial neglect: Putamen, caudate nucleus and pulvinar. *Brain: A Journal of Neurology*, **125**, 350–360. Retrieved from http://www.ncbi.nlm.nih.gov/pubmed/11844735

Kawato, M., Hayakawa, H., & Inui, T. (1993, January). A forward-inverse optics model of reciprocal connections between visual cortical areas. *Network: Computation in Neural Systems*, **4**(4), 415–422. doi: 10.1088/0954-898X 4 4 001

Klimesch, W. (2011, August). Evoked alpha and early access to the knowledge system: The P1 inhibition timing hypothesis. *Brain Research*, **1408**, 52–71. doi: 10.1016/j.brainres.2011.06.003

Kobatake, E., & Tanaka, K. (1994, January). Neuronal selectivities to complex object features in the ventral visual pathway. *Journal of Neurophysiology*, **71**(3), 856–867.

Kohonen, T. (1989). *Self-organization and associative memory*. New York: Springer-Verlag.

Kok, P., & de Lange, F. P. (2015). Predictive coding in sensory cortex. In B. U. Forstmann & E-J. Wagenmakers (Eds.), *An Introduction to Model-Based Cognitive Neuroscience* (pp. 221–244). New York: Springer. doi: 10.1007/978-1-4939-2236-9 11

Kok, P., Jehee, J. F. M., & de Lange, F. P. (2012, July). Less is more: Expectation sharpens representations in the primary visual cortex. *Neuron*, **75**(2), 265–270. doi: 10.1016/j.neuron.2012.04.034

Kritzer, M. F., & Goldman-Rakic, P. S. (1995, August). Intrinsic circuit organization of the major layers and sublayers of the dorsolateral prefrontal cortex in the rhesus monkey. *Journal of Comparative Neurology*, **359**(1), 131–143. Retrieved from http://www.ncbi.nlm.nih.gov/pubmed/8557842

Kuramoto, E., Furuta, T., Nakamura, K. C., Unzai, T., Hioki, H., & Kaneko, T. (2009, September). Two types of thalamocortical projections from the motor thalamic nuclei of the rat: A single neuron-tracing study using viral vectors. *Cerebral cortex*, **19**(9), 2065–2077. Retrieved from http://www.ncbi.nlm.nih.gov/pubmed/19174446

Kuramoto, E., Ohno, S., Furuta, T., Unzai, T., Tanaka, Y. R., Hioki, H., & Kaneko, T. (2015, January). Ventral medial nucleus neurons send thalamocortical afferents more widely and more preferentially to layer 1 than neurons of the ventral anterior–ventral lateral nuclear complex in the rat. *Cerebral Cortex*, **25**(1), 221–235. doi: 10.1093/cercor/bht216

LaBerge, D., & Buchsbaum, M. S. (1990, March). Positron emission tomographic measurements of pulvinar activity during an attention task. *Journal of Neuroscience*, **10**, 613–619. Retrieved from http://www.ncbi.nlm.nih.gov/pubmed/2303863

Lamme, V. A. F. (2006, January). Towards a true neural stance on consciousness. *Trends in Cognitive Sciences*, **10**(11), 494–501. doi: 10.1016/j.tics.2006.09.001

Larkum, M. E., Petro, L. S., Sachdev, R. N. S., & Muckli, L. (2018). A perspective on cortical layering and layer-spanning neuronal elements. *Frontiers in Neuroanatomy*, **12**. doi: 10.3389/fnana.2018.00056

Larkum, M. E., Zhu, J. J., & Sakmann, B. (1999, March). A new cellular mechanism for coupling inputs arriving at different cortical layers. *Nature*, **398**(6725), 338–341. doi: 10.1038/18686

LeCun, Y., Bengio, Y., & Hinton, G. (2015, May). Deep learning. *Nature*, **521**(7553), 436–444. doi: 10.1038/nature14539

Lee, T. S., & Mumford, D. (2003, July). Hierarchical Bayesian inference in the visual cortex. *Journal of the Optical Society of America*, **20**(7), 1434–1448. Retrieved from http://www.ncbi.nlm.nih.gov/pubmed/12868647/

Lewis, L. D., Voigts, J., Flores, F. J., Schmitt, L. I., Wilson, M. A., Halassa, M. M., & Brown, E. N. (2015, October). Thalamic reticular nucleus induces fast and local modulation of arousal state. *eLife*, **4**, e08760. doi: 10.7554/eLife.08760

Lillicrap, T. P., Santoro, A., Marris, L., Akerman, C. J., & Hinton, G. (2020, June). Backpropagation and the brain. *Nature Reviews Neuroscience*, **21**(6), 335–346. doi: 10.1038/s41583-020-0277-3

Lisman, J. E., Fellous, J. M., & Wang, X. J. (1999, April). A role for NMDA-receptor channels in working memory. *Nature Neuroscience*, **1**, 273–275. Retrieved from http://www.ncbi.nlm.nih.gov/pubmed/10195158

Lotter, W., Kreiman, G., & Cox, D. (2016, May). Deep predictive coding networks for video prediction and unsupervised learning. *arXiv:1605.08104 [cs, q-bio]*. Retrieved from http://arxiv.org/abs/1605.08104

Luczak, A., Bartho, P., & Harris, K. D. (2009, May). Spontaneous events outline the realm of possible sensory responses in neocortical populations. *Neuron*, **62**(3), 413–425. Retrieved from http://www.ncbi.nlm.nih.gov/pubmed/19447096

Luczak, A., Bartho, P., & Harris, K. D. (2013, January). Gating of sensory input by spontaneous cortical activity. *Journal of Neuroscience*, **33**(4), 1684–1695. Retrieved from http://www.ncbi.nlm.nih.gov/pubmed/23345241

Luo, Y., Boix, X., Roig, G., Poggio, T., & Zhao, Q. (2015, November). Foveation-based mechanisms alleviate adversarial examples. *arXiv:1511.06292 [cs]*. Retrieved from http://arxiv.org/abs/1511.06292

Makeig, S., Westerfield, M., Jung, T. P., Enghoff, S., Townsend, J., Courchesne, E., & Sejnowski, T. J. (2002, January). Dynamic brain sources of visual evoked responses. *Science*, **295**, 690–693.

Manto, M. (2009, April). Mechanisms of human cerebellar dysmetria: Experimental evidence and current conceptual bases. *Journal of NeuroEngineering and Rehabilitation*, **6**(1), 10. doi: 10.1186/1743-0003-6-10

Markov, N. T., Vezoli, J., Chameau, P., Falchier, A., Quilodran, R., Huissoud, C., ... Kennedy, H. (2014, January). Anatomy of hierarchy: Feedforward and feedback pathways in macaque visual cortex: Cortical counterstreams. *Journal of Comparative Neurology*, **522**(1), 225–259. doi: 10.1002/cne.23458

Mathewson, K., Gratton, G., Fabiani, M., Beck, D., & Ro, T. (2009). To see or not to see: Prestimulus alpha phase predicts visual awareness. *Journal of Neuroscience*, **29**(9), 2725–2732.

Mathewson, K. E., Prudhomme, C., Fabiani, M., Beck, D. M., Lleras, A., & Gratton, G. (2012, August). Making waves in the stream of consciousness: Entraining oscillations in EEG alpha and fluctuations in visual awareness with rhythmic visual stimulation. *Journal of Cognitive Neuroscience*, **24**(12), 2321–2333. doi: 10.1162/jocn a 00288

Middleton, F. A., & Strick, P. L. (2000, May). Basal ganglia and cerebellar loops: Motor and cognitive circuits. *Brain Research*, **31**(2–3), 236–250. Retrieved from http://www.ncbi.nlm.nih.gov/pubmed/10719151

Mink, J. W. (1996, March). The basal ganglia: Focused selection and inhibition of competing motor programs. *Progress in Neurobiology*, **50**(4), 381–425. Retrieved from http://www.ncbi.nlm.nih.gov/pubmed/9004351

Mumford, D. (1991, June). On the computational architecture of the neocortex. *Biological Cybernetics*, **65**(2), 135–145. doi: 10.1007/BF00202389

Mumford, D. (1992). On the computational architecture of the neocortex. II. The role of cortico-cortical loops. *Biological Cybernetics*, **66**(3), 241–251. Retrieved from http://www.ncbi.nlm.nih.gov/pubmed/1540675

Münkle, M. C., Waldvogel, H. J., & Faull, R. L. M. (2000, July). The distribution of calbindin, calretinin and parvalbumin immunoreactivity in the human thalamus. *Journal of Chemical Neuroanatomy*, **19**(3), 155–173. doi: 10.1016/S0891-0618(00)00060-0

Nambu, A. (2008, December). Seven problems on the basal ganglia. *Current Opinion in Neurobiology*, **18**(6), 595–604. Retrieved from http://www.ncbi.nlm.nih.gov/pubmed/19081243

Olsen, S., Bortone, D., Adesnik, H., & Scanziani, M. (2012, February). Gain control by layer six in cortical circuits of vision. *Nature*, **483**(7387), 47–52.

O'Reilly, R. C. (1996, January). Biologically plausible error-driven learning using local activation differences: The generalized recirculation algorithm. *Neural Computation*, **8**(5), 895–938. doi: 10.1162/neco.1996.8.5.895

O'Reilly, R. C. (2006, October). Biologically based computational models of high-level cognition. *Science*, **314**(5796), 91–94. Retrieved from http://www.ncbi.nlm.nih.gov/pubmed/17023651

O'Reilly, R. C. (2020, April). Unraveling the mysteries of motivation. *Trends in Cognitive Sciences*, **24**(6), 425–434. doi: 10.1016/j.tics.2020.03.001

O'Reilly, R. C., & Frank, M. J. (2006). Making working memory work: A computational model of learning in the prefrontal cortex and basal ganglia. *Neural Computation*, **18**(2), 283–328. Retrieved from http://www.ncbi.nlm.nih.gov/pubmed/16378516

O'Reilly, R. C., Hazy, T. E., & Herd, S. A. (2016). The Leabra cognitive architecture: How to play 20 principles with nature and win! In S. Chipman (Ed.), *Oxford Handbook of Cognitive Science*. Oxford: Oxford University Press. Retrieved from http://www.oxfordhandbooks.com/view/10.1093/oxfordhb/9780199842193.001.0001/oxfordhb-9780199842193-e-8

O'Reilly, R. C., & Munakata, Y. (2000). *Computational Explorations in Cognitive Neuroscience: Understanding the Mind by Simulating the Brain*. Cambridge, MA: MIT Press.

O'Reilly, R. C., Munakata, Y., Frank, M. J., Hazy, T. E., & Contributors. (2012). *Computational Cognitive Neuroscience*. Wiki Book, 1st Ed. Retrieved from http://ccnbook.colorado.edu

O'Reilly, R. C., Nair, A., Russin, J. L., & Herd, S. A. (2020, March). How Sequential interactive processing within frontostriatal loops supports a continuum of habitual to controlled processing. *Frontiers in Psychology*, **11**, 380. doi: 10.3389/fpsyg.2020.00380

O'Reilly, R. C., Noelle, D. C., Braver, T. S., & Cohen, J. D. (2002, February). Prefrontal cortex and dynamic categorization tasks: Representational organization and neuromodulatory control. *Cerebral Cortex*, **12**, 246–257. Retrieved from http://www.ncbi.nlm.nih.gov/pubmed/11839599

O'Reilly, R. C., Russin, J. L., Zolfaghar, M., & Rohrlich, J. (2021). Deep predictive learning in neocortex and pulvinar. *Journal of Cognitive Neuroscience*, **33**(6), 1158–1196.

O'Reilly, R. C., Wyatte, D., Herd, S. A., Mingus, B., & Jilk, D. J. (2013). Recurrent processing during object recognition. *Frontiers in Psychology*, **4**(124). Retrieved from http://www.ncbi.nlm.nih.gov/pubmed/23554596

O'Reilly, R. C., Wyatte, D., & Rohrlich, J. (2014, July). Learning through time in the thalamocortical loops. *arXiv:1407.3432 [q-bio]*. Retrieved from http://arxiv.org/abs/1407.3432

O'Reilly, R. C., Wyatte, D. R., & Rohrlich, J. (2017, September). Deep predictive learning: A comprehensive model of three visual streams. *arXiv:1709.04654 [q-bio]*. Retrieved from http://arxiv.org/abs/1709.04654

Ouden, H. E. M., Kok, P., & Lange, F. P. (2012). How prediction errors shape perception, attention, and motivation. *Frontiers in Psychology*, **3**(548). Retrieved from http://www.ncbi.nlm.nih.gov/pubmed/23248610

Pasupathy, A., & Miller, E. K. (2005, January). Different time courses for learning-related activity in the prefrontal cortex and striatum. *Nature*, **433**, 873–876. Retrieved from http://www.nature.com/nature/journal/v433/n7028/full/nature03287.html

Petersen, S. E., Robinson, D. L., & Morris, J. D. (1987, January). Contributions of the pulvinar to visual spatial attention. *Neuropsychologia*, **25**(1), 97–105. doi: 10.1016/0028-3932(87)90046-7

Phillips, J. W., Schulmann, A., Hara, E., Winnubst, J., Liu, C., Valakh, V., ... Hantman, A. W. (2019, November). A repeated molecular architecture across thalamic pathways. *Nature Neuroscience*, **22**(11), 1925–1935. doi: 10.1038/s41593-019-0483-3

Rac-Lubashevsky, R., & Frank, M. J. (2020, December). Analogous computations in working memory input, output and motor gating: Electrophysiological and computational modeling evidence. *bioRxiv*, 2020.12.21.423791. doi: 10.1101/2020.12.21.423791

Raizada, R. D. S., & Grossberg, S. (2003, January). Towards a theory of the laminar architecture of cerebral cortex: Computational clues from the visual system. *Cerebral Cortex*, **13**(1), 100–113. Retrieved from http://www.ncbi.nlm.nih.gov/pubmed/12466221

Ramaswamy, S., & Markram, H. (2015). Anatomy and physiology of the thick-tufted layer 5 pyramidal neuron. *Frontiers in Cellular Neuroscience*, **9**. doi: 10.3389/fncel.2015.00233

Rao, R. P., & Ballard, D. H. (1999, January). Predictive coding in the visual cortex: A functional interpretation of some extra-classical receptive-field effects. *Nature Neuroscience*, **2**(1), 79–87. doi: 10.1038/4580

Redinbaugh, M. J., Phillips, J. M., Kambi, N. A., Mohanta, S., Andryk, S., Dooley, G. L., ... Saalmann, Y. B. (2020, April). Thalamus modulates consciousness via layer-specific control of cortex. *Neuron*, **106**(1), 66–75.e12. doi: 10.1016/j.neuron.2020.01.005

Reynolds, J. H., & Desimone, R. (2003, March). Interacting roles of attention and visual salience in V4. *Neuron*, **37**, 853–863. Retrieved from http://www.ncbi.nlm.nih.gov/pubmed/12628175

Reynolds, J. H., & Heeger, D. J. (2009, January). The normalization model of attention. *Neuron*, **61**(2), 168–185. Retrieved from http://www.ncbi.nlm.nih.gov/pubmed/19186161/

Richter, D., & de Lange, F. P. (2019, August). Statistical learning attenuates visual activity only for attended stimuli. *eLife*, **8**, e47869. doi: 10.7554/eLife.47869

Rikhye, R. V., Gilra, A., & Halassa, M. M. (2018, December). Thalamic regulation of switching between cortical representations enables cognitive flexibility. *Nature Neuroscience*, **21**(12), 1753–1763. doi: 10.1038/s41593-018-0269-z

Ringach DL. Sparse thalamo cortical convergence. Current Biology. 2021 May 24;31(10):2199–202.

Robinson, D. L., & Petersen, S. E. (1992, June). The pulvinar and visual salience. *Trends in Neurosciences*, **15**, 127–132. Retrieved from http://www.ncbi.nlm.nih.gov/pubmed/1374970

Rougier, N. P., & O'Reilly, R. C. (2002, January). Learning representations in a gated prefrontal cortex model of dynamic task switching. *Cognitive Science*, **26**, 503–520. Retrieved from http://onlinelibrary.wiley.com/doi/abs/10.1207/s15516709cog26044

Rovó, Z., Ulbert, I., & Acsády, L. (2012, December). Drivers of the primate thalamus. *Journal of Neuroscience*, **32**(49), 17894–17908. doi: 10.1523/JNEUROSCI.2815-12.2012

Rumelhart, D. E., Hinton, G. E., & Williams, R. J. (1986, January). Learning representations by back-propagating errors. *Nature*, **323**(9), 533–536.

Rumelhart, D. E., & Zipser, D. (1985, January). Feature discovery by competitive learning. *Cognitive Science*, **9**(1), 75–112. doi: 10.1207/s15516709cog0901_5

Saalmann, Y. B., & Kastner, S. (2011, July). Cognitive and perceptual functions of the visual thalamus. *Neuron*, **71**(2), 209–223. Retrieved from http://www.ncbi.nlm.nih.gov/pubmed/21791281

Saalmann, Y. B., Pinsk, M. A., Wang, L., Li, X., & Kastner, S. (2012, August). The pulvinar regulates information transmission between cortical areas based on attention demands. *Science*, **337**(6095), 753–756. doi: 10.1126/science.1223082

Sakata, S., & Harris, K. D. (2009, November). Laminar structure of spontaneous and sensory-evoked population activity in auditory cortex. *Neuron*, **64**(3), 404–418. Retrieved from http://www.ncbi.nlm.nih.gov/pubmed/19914188

Sakata, S., & Harris, K. D. (2012). Laminar-dependent effects of cortical state on auditory cortical spontaneous activity. *Frontiers in Neural Circuits*, **6**. Retrieved from http://www.ncbi.nlm.nih.gov/pubmed/23267317

Sanders, H., Berends, M., Major, G., Goldman, M. S., & Lisman, J. E. (2013, January). NMDA and $GABA_B$ (KIR) conductances: The "perfect couple" for bistability. *Journal of Neuroscience*, **33**(2), 424–429. doi: 10.1523/JNEUROSCI.1854-12.2013

Schiff, N. D. (2008). Central thalamic contributions to arousal regulation and neurological disorders of consciousness. *Annals of the New York Academy of Sciences*, **1129**(1), 105–118. doi: 10.1196/annals.1417.029

Shen, W., Flajolet, M., Greengard, P., & Surmeier, D. J. (2008, August). Dichotomous dopaminergic control of striatal synaptic plasticity. *Science*, **321**(5890), 848–851. Retrieved from http://www.ncbi.nlm.nih.gov/pubmed/18687967

Sherman, S. M., & Guillery, R. W. (2006). *Exploring the Thalamus and Its Role in Cortical Function*. Cambridge, MA: MIT Press. Retrieved from http://www.scholarpedia.org/article/Thalamus

Shipp, S. (2003, October). The functional logic of cortico-pulvinar connections. *Philosophical Transactions of the Royal Society of London B*, **358**(1438), 1605–1624. Retrieved from http://www.ncbi.nlm.nih.gov/pubmed/14561322

Silva, L. R., Amitai, Y., & Connors, B. W. (1991, January). Intrinsic oscillations of neocortex generated by layer 5 pyramidal neurons. *Science*, **251**(4992), 432–435. Retrieved from http://www.ncbi.nlm.nih.gov/pubmed/1824881

Sinz, F. H., Pitkow, X., Reimer, J., Bethge, M., & Tolias, A. S. (2019, September). Engineering a less artificial intelligence. *Neuron*, **103**(6), 967–979. doi: 10.1016/j.neuron.2019.08.034

Snow, J. C., Allen, H. A., Rafal, R. D., & Humphreys, G. W. (2009, March). Impaired attentional selection following lesions to human pulvinar: Evidence for homology between human and monkey. *Proceedings of the National Academy of Sciences*, **106**(10), 4054–4059. doi: 10.1073/pnas.0810086106

Spaak, E., de Lange, F. P., & Jensen, O. (2014, March). Local entrainment of alpha oscillations by visual stimuli causes cyclic modulation of perception. *Journal of Neuroscience*, **34**(10), 3536–3544. doi: 10.1523/JNEUROSCI.4385-13.2014

Summerfield, C., & Egner, T. (2009, September). Expectation (and attention) in visual cognition. *Trends in Cognitive Sciences*, **13**(9), 403–409. doi: 10.1016/j.tics.2009.06.003

Tanibuchi, I., Kitano, H., & Jinnai, K. (2009a, November). Substantia nigra output to prefrontal cortex via thalamus in monkeys. I. Electrophysiological identification of thalamic relay neurons. *Journal of Neurophysiology*, **102**(5), 2933–2945. Retrieved from http://www.ncbi.nlm.nih.gov/pubmed/19692504

Tanibuchi, I., Kitano, H., & Jinnai, K. (2009b, November). Substantia nigra output to prefrontal cortex via thalamus in monkeys. II. Activity of thalamic relay neurons in delayed conditional go/no-go discrimination task. *Journal of Neurophysiology*, **102**(5116), 2946–2954. Retrieved from http://www.ncbi.nlm.nih.gov/pubmed/19692503

Thomson, A. M. (2010). Neocortical layer 6, a review. *Frontiers in Neuroanatomy*, **4**(13). Retrieved from http://www.ncbi.nlm.nih.gov/pubmed/20556241

Tononi, G. (2004, November). An information integration theory of consciousness. *BMC Neuroscience*, **5**, 42. doi: 10.1186/1471-2202-5-42

Treisman, A. (1993, January). The perception of features and objects. In A. Baddeley & L. Weiskrantz (Eds.), *Attention: Selection, Awareness, and Control: A Tribute to Donald Broadbent* (pp. 5–35). Oxford: Oxford University Press.

Tsumoto T, Creutzfeldt OD, Legendy CR (1978) Functional organization of the cortifugal system from visual cortex to lateral geniculate nucleus in the cat. Exp Brain Res 32:345–364.

Usrey, W. M., & Sherman, S. M. (2018). Corticofugal circuits: Communication lines from the cortex to the rest of the brain. *Journal of Comparative Neurology*, **527**(3), 640–650. doi: 10.1002/cne.24423

van Kerkoerle, T., Self, M. W., Dagnino, B., Gariel-Mathis, M.-A., Poort, J., van der Togt, C., & Roelfsema, P. R. (2014, October). Alpha and gamma oscillations characterize feedback and feedforward processing in monkey visual cortex. *Proceedings of the National Academy of Sciences of the United States of America*, **111**(40), 14332–14341. Retrieved from http://www.ncbi.nlm.nih.gov/pubmed/25205811

VanRullen, R., & Koch, C. (2003, May). Is perception discrete or continuous? *Trends in Cognitive Sciences*, **7**(5), 207–213. Retrieved from http://www.ncbi.nlm.nih.gov/pubmed/12757822

von Helmholtz, H. (1867). *Treatise on Physiological Optics, Vol III*. Courier Corporation.

von Stein, A., Chiang, C., & König, P. (2000, December). Top-down processing mediated by interareal synchronization. *Proceedings of the National Academy of Sciences of the United States of America*, **97**(26), 14748–14753. doi: 10.1073/pnas.97.26.14748

Voytek, B., & Knight, R. T. (2010, October). Prefrontal cortex and basal ganglia contributions to visual working memory. *Proceedings of the National Academy of Sciences of the United States of America*, **107**(42), 18167–18172. Retrieved from http://www.ncbi.nlm.nih.gov/pubmed/20921401

Walsh, K. S., McGovern, D. P., Clark, A., & O'Connell, R. G. (2020, March). Evaluating the neurophysiological evidence for predictive processing as a model of perception. *Annals of the New York Academy of Sciences*, **1464**(1), 242–268. doi: 10.1111/nyas.14321

Wang, M., Yang, Y., Wang, C.-J., Gamo, N. J., Jin, L. E., Mazer, J. A., ... Arnsten, A. F. T. (2013, February). NMDA receptors subserve persistent neuronal firing during working memory in dorsolateral prefrontal cortex. *Neuron*, **77**(4), 736–749. doi: 10.1016/j.neuron.2012.12.032

Ward, L. M. (2011, June). The thalamic dynamic core theory of conscious experience. *Consciousness and Cognition*, **20**(2), 464–486. doi: 10.1016/j.concog.2011.01.007

Watanabe, Y., & Funahashi, S. (2012, January). Thalamic mediodorsal nucleus and working memory. *Neuroscience & Biobehavioral Reviews*, **36**(1), 134–142. doi: 10.1016/j.neubiorev.2011.05.003

Watanabe, Y., Takeda, K., & Funahashi, S. (2009, June). Population vector analysis of primate mediodorsal thalamic activity during oculomotor delayed-response performance. *Cerebral Cortex*, **19**, 1313–1321. Retrieved from http://cercor.oxfordjournals.org/cgi/content/abstract/19/6/1313

Whittington, J. C. R., & Bogacz, R. (2019, March). Theories of error back-propagation in the brain. *Trends in Cognitive Sciences*, **23**(3), 235–250. doi: 10.1016/j.tics.2018.12.005

Wig, G. S. (2017). Segregated systems of human brain networks. *Trends in Cognitive Sciences*, **21**(12), 981–996.

Wimmer, R. D., Schmitt, L. I., Davidson, T. J., Nakajima, M., Deisseroth, K., & Halassa, M. M. (2015, October). Thalamic control of sensory selection in divided attention. *Nature*, **526**(7575), 705–709. doi: 10.1038/nature15398

Wurtz, R. H. (2008, September). Neuronal mechanisms of visual stability. *Vision Research*, **48**(20), 2070–2089. doi: 10.1016/j.visres.2008.03.021

Wyatte, D., Curran, T., & O'Reilly, R. C. (2012). The limits of feedforward vision: Recurrent processing promotes robust object recognition when objects are degraded. *Journal of Cognitive Neuroscience*, **24**(11), 2248–2261. Retrieved from http://www.ncbi.nlm.nih.gov/pubmed/22905822

Wyder, M. T., Massoglia, D. P., & Stanford, T. R. (2004, June). Contextual modulation of central thalamic delay-period activity: Representation of visual and saccadic goals. *Journal of Neurophysiology*, **91**(6), 2628–2648. Retrieved from http://www.ncbi.nlm.nih.gov/pubmed/14762161

Zhou, H., Schafer, R. J., & Desimone, R. (2016). Pulvinar-cortex interactions in vision and attention. *Neuron*, **89**, 209–220.

Index

abstract normalization model of attention, 420
action-selection problem occulomotor control, 270
activity-dependent control of thalamic interneuron development, 175–177
adaptive learning, 422–423
age-dependent plasticity of thalamocortical synapses, 252
amblyaudia, 249
amblyopia, 194
amphibians
  evolution of the dorsal thalamus, 110–111
  organization of the thalamus, 134
amphioxus, 125
Anderson, Marjorie, 278
anterior thalamus (AT)
  cholinergic modulation, 343–344
  consolidating memories during sleep, 352–353
  electrophysical properties of neurons, 348
  inhibitory control of, 343
  interventional studies, 348–349
  node in superimposed loops of the limbic system, 341–343
  oscillatory modulation, 346–347
  role in navigation, 340
  role in spatial cognition, 348–352
  role in the limbic system, 344
  role in the Papez circuit, 341
  structure and function, 340
  transformation of AT signals into spatial representation, 349–350
  tuning to head direction in the anterodorsal nucleus, 344–345
arousal regulation
  central thalamic lesions and altered regulation in humans, 388–389

concept of a central thalamus linked to, 382–385
controversies over the contribution of the central thalamus, 389–390
deep-brain stimulation of the central thalamus in human subjects, 390–391
integrative model of CT-DBS effects, 391–394
modulation using CL electrical stimulation, 385–387
role of the central thalamus in the wakeful state in humans, 387–388
role of the neurons of the central lateral (CL) nucleus, 382–385
Aserinsky, Eugene, 361
ataxia, 297
attention
  connections of the lateral geniculate nucleus, 325
  connections of the pulvinar, 325
  connections of the thalamic reticular nucleus, 325
  definition of, 324
  distributed large-scale network of neural responses, 324–325
  evolutionary explanation, 85
  future research on the role of the thalamus, 334–335
  gatekeeper role of the lateral geniculate nucleus, 325–328
  involvement of subcortical circuits, 85
  object-based attention, 324
  prioritization of information, 324
  role of cortical layer 5 projections, 84–85
  role of the thalamic reticular nucleus in selective attention, 416
  role of the thalamus, 416
  role of the thalamus in primates, 324

selective attention in the thalamus, 405–406
space-based attention, 324
structure of the primate visual thalamus, 325–327
theories of, 324
timekeeper role of the pulvinar, 328–334
visual attention mechanisms, 324
attention deficit–hyperactivity disorder, 307
attentional focusing
  abstract normalization model, 420
  biased competition model, 418
  difficulty in simultanagnosia, 418
  folded-feedback model, 418–420
  machine learning models, 418
  through thalamic reticular nucleus pooled inhibition, 417–420
auditory pathway development
  development of the thalamocortical auditory pathway, 246–249
  maturation of corticothalamic connectivity into the MGB, 248–249
  maturation of excitatory/inhibitory balance within the auditory cortex, 248
  maturation of MGB circuits, 246
  maturation of MGB innervation of cortical neurons, 247–248
  MGB innervation of the transient cortical subplate, 246–247
  onset of hearing across species, 246
  silent synapses, 247
auditory processing
  extra-sensory modulation of auditory thalamocortical circuits, 243–245
  functional contributions of auditory corticothalamic circuits, 243–244

influence of internal states, 243–245
neural coding of sound features across the midbrain–thalamus–cortex hierarchy, 240–243
auditory thalamocortical circuit development
  amblyaudia, 249
  critical periods in development, 249–250
  experience- and activity-dependent development, 249–251
  plasticity of sound representations following manipulation of early auditory experience, 249–250
  plasticity of sound representations in adult thalamocortical circuits, 250–251
auditory thalamocortical circuits
  age-dependent plasticity of thalamocortical synapses, 252
  cholinergic neuromodulatory system, 253
  disinhibitory plasticity mechanisms, 251–252
  experience-dependent myelination within the thalamocortical system, 253–254
  neuromodulatory mechanisms, 252–253
  noradrenergic neuromodulatory system, 253
  plasticity mechanisms, 251–254
  plasticity of GABAergic inhibitory circuits, 252
  serotonergic neuromodulatory system, 253
  timing of critical periods for heightened plasticity, 251
auditory thalamus
  corticothalamic feedback to the MGB, 239

Index

efferent connections from non-primary divisions, 240
feedforward input to the MGB, 237–239
future research directions, 254–256
organization and connectivity, 237
role of the medial geniculate body (MGB) of the thalamus, 237
ventral MGB efferent connections, 239–240
autism spectrum disorder (ASD)
cerebellar pathology and, 297–298
autoradiography, 7
axon arborization patterns
insights from single-cell labeling studies, 11–12
axonal branching
driver afferents to the thalamus, 82
potential to carry efference copies, 82
sharing a single message with multiple targets, 81–82
axonal transport tracing, 7–9

basal ganglia, 27
organization in the lamprey, 131–132
signal transmission pathways, 275–276
basal ganglia–brainstem pathways, 275–276
basal ganglia–dependent reinforcement learning, 275
basal ganglia–recipient motor thalamus, 273–280
role in reach tasks in rodents and primates, 277–280
basal ganglia–recipient thalamus
role in vocal babbling in juvenile birds, 276–277
basal ganglia–thalamic pathways, 275–276
basal ganglia–thalamic transmission, 276
Berger, Hans, 361
biased competition model of attention, 418
biocytin, 11
biological homology, 94, 101–102
bipolar disorder, 287
birds
complex cognitive abilities, 115–116
learned motor sequences in songbirds, 272–273
somatosensory pathways, 127
thalamostriatal pathways, 131
visual pathways, 131
vocal babbling in juvenile birds, 276–277

blind mole rats, 33
blindsight, 193
bony fishes
organization of the thalamus in teleosts, 133
preglomerular relay nuclei in teleosts, 133
brain network activity
thalamic control of, 314–317
brain plasticity
role of the thalamus during sleep, 371–373
brainstem
diffuse inputs to the thalamus, 9
brainstem-dependent motor commands
relay of efference copies by the motor thalamus, 270
brainstem-recipient motor thalamus, 269–273
brainstem-thalamic pathway signal transmission, 273
brainstem-thalamocortical loop
learned motor sequences in songbirds, 272–273
brainstem-thalamostriatal pathways
learned and innate motor sequences, 271–272
Broca, Paul, 3
Bruce, Laura, 91
Burdach, Karl Friedrich, 1
burst firing in thalamic relay cells, 75–77

Calb1 gene, 166
calbindin, 166, 240, 383
calbindin28K, 9
calcium-binding proteins, 383
expression by thalamic cells, 9
calcium channels
thalamic relay neurons, 13
transient T-type Ca^{2+} channels, 13
calretinin, 9, 240, 383
canonical inputs, 36
cartilaginous fishes
evolution of the dorsal thalamus, 112
organization of the thalamus, 132
cat
lateral geniculate nucleus circuitry, 71–73
cell lineage studies
thalamic nuclei, 3
central thalamus
arousal modulation using CL electrical stimulation, 385–387
concept of, 382
concept of a link to forebrain arousal regulation, 382–385

controversies over its contribution to arousal regulation, 389–390
deep-brain stimulation (CT-DBS) to improve arousal regulation in human subjects, 390–391
functional distinctions within, 382–385
historical studies, 382
integrative model of CT-DBS effects on arousal regulation mechanisms, 391–394
lesions correlate with altered arousal regulation in humans, 388–389
role in arousal regulation in the wakeful state in humans, 387–388
role of the neurons of the central lateral (CL) nucleus, 382–385
cerebellar loop, 27
cerebellar nuclei
somatotopy, 286
cerebellar output, 292–294
cerebellar pathology
autism spectrum disorder (ASD), 297–298
epilepsy, 298
essential tremor, 297
movement disorders with tremors, 297
neurological disorders, 296–298
Parkinson's disease, 297
cerebellar stimulation of the thalamus
centrolateral nucleus responses, 295–296
centromedial nucleus responses, 296
ventrolateral responses, 294–295
ventromedial responses, 295
cerebellothalamic synapse physiology, 292–295
cerebellothalamic tract, 284–286
anatomy in the adult, 290–292
monosynaptic tracer studies, 290–293
transsynaptic tracer studies, 290–292
cerebellothalamic tract development, 287–290
critical periods, 290
generalization beyond rodents, 288
humans, 288–290
maturation, 290
rodents, 287–289
cerebellum
future research on thalamocortical circuits, 298
influence on thalamocortical networks, 284, 296

cholinergic inputs to geniculate relay cells, 71
cholinergic modulation
anterior thalamus/nucleus reuniens, 343–344
cholinergic neuromodulatory system
auditory thalamocortical circuits, 253
cladistic analysis, 93–94
claustroamygdalar hypothesis of thalamus evolution, 91
cognition
abilities of some fishes, 116
circuit motifs that may support cognition, 116–117
complex cognitive abilities of birds, 115–116
insights from the evolution of the thalamus, 113–117
cognitive control
anatomical connectivity between thalamic nuclei and frontoparietal cortices, 307–308
association with working memory (meta-analysis of behavioral task studies), 308–310
association with working memory (meta-analysis of fMRI studies), 308
cognitive ontology, 308–309
components of, 307
definition of, 307
disorders of, 307
empirical framework on the role of the thalamus, 317–318
focal thalamic lesion studies, 309–312
human neuroimaging studies of thalamic involvement, 308–310
human neuropsychological studies of thalamic involvement, 309–312
influence of the thalamus and its inputs, 307–308
latent cognitive processes (cognitive components), 308–310
modulation by top-down biasing signals, 313–314
open questions on the role of the thalamus, 318
thalamic control of brain network activity, 314–317
thalamic control of local evoked responses, 313–314
thalamocortical mechanisms of cortical control, 312–317
thalamocortical operations that support it, 317–318
See also executive function.
cognitive ontology, 308–309

433

Index

coincidence detector, 15
colliculo-thalamocortical pathway, 270
collothalamus, 91
computation in a convergent–divergent circuit navigation, 346
computational modeling
  abstract normalization model of attention, 420
  adaptive learning, 422–423
  approach to modeling thalamic functions, 401
  attentional focusing through thalamic reticular nucleus pooled inhibition, 417–420
  biased competition model of attention, 418
  computational contributions of the thalamus, 416–417
  critical functions of the thalamus, 416–417
  deep neural network (DNN) machine learning algorithms, 420
  feedback inhibition and lateral inhibition, 409–410
  folded-feedback model of attention, 418–420
  frontothalamic pathways, 423–425
  future research on thalamic circuits, 410–411
  gating of executive function, 416–417
  gating of frontal function by the thalamus, 422–425
  Hodgkin–Huxley models, 409
  information processing in neuron tonic and burst spiking modes, 402–403
  LSTM (long short-term memory) machine learning algorithm, 424
  machine learning models of attentional focusing, 418
  open-loop versus closed-loop connectivity motifs, 409–410
  perspective on thalamic circuit function, 410
  predictive error-driven learning in the pulvinar, 420–422
  predictive learning, 416, 417
  pulvinar function, 334
  recognition by synthesis proposal, 420
  role of error backpropagation in predictive learning, 420–422
  role of the thalamus in attention, 416
  role of the thalamus in consciousness, 417
  role of the thalamus in learning, 416
  thalamic circuit model for oscillations, 403–405
  thalamic circuit model for top-down modulation, 405–407
computational problem of vertebrate forebrains, 27–30
connection-tracing studies, 4–12
conscious experience
  role of predictive learning, 417
consciousness
  circuit motifs that may support consciousness, 116–117
  insights from the evolution of the thalamus, 113–117
  role of the thalamus, 417
context-dependent sensory processing
  role of the cortical layer 5–posterior medial thalamus pathway, 231–232
core versus matrix projections in the thalamus, 423–425
corollary discharges. *See* efference copies
corridor cells, 143, 145–146
cortex
  axonal branching of driver afferents to the thalamus, 82
  bursting in layer 5 corticofugal cells, 84
  computational problem of vertebrate forebrains, 27–30
  features of layer 5 (pyramidal) corticothalamic inputs, 226–229
  features of layer 5 projections, 82–85
  features of layer 6 corticothalamic pathways, 224–226
  glutamatergic drivers and modulators in, 78
  layer 5 corticothalamic axons and efference copies, 82
  layer 5 projections to the midbrain, 84
  layer 6 corticothalamic neurons, 206
  logic of cortically related efference copies, 82–84
  pathways of layer 5 outputs, 84
  role of layer 5 projections in attention, 84–85
  role of the thalamus in cortical slow oscillations, 403–404
  theories of cortical function, 232
cortical control
  role of the thalamus in working memory, 312–313
thalamic modulation of neural synchrony, 316–317
cortical inputs to the thalamus, 31–32
  dynamic stability during evolution, 32–33
  layer 5b inputs, 32
  layer 6a inputs, 31–32
  layer 6b inputs, 32
corticocortical communication
  higher-order (HO) thalamic relay neurons and, 79–80
corticogeniculate feedback pathway, 206
corticogeniculate effects on visual processing, 209–210
  effect on the receptive field of LGN neurons, 209–210
  future research, 210
  gating of information flows, 210
  general properties of corticogeniculate feedback, 207–208
  influence on synchronization of activity in the thalamus, 210
  influence on the temporal transmission of visual information, 210
  modulatory role, 209–210
  parallel pathways for corticogeniculate feedback, 208–209
  parallel pathways from retina to cortex, 206–207
  response to synchronous inputs from the thalamus, 210
  retinogeniculocortical pathway, 206–207
cortico-subcortico-cortical loops, 27
corticothalamic feedback
  visual system, 206
corticothalamic pathways, 27
  functions in the somatosensory system, 229–232
  future research, 232
  inhibitory control in the somatosensory system, 224
  layer 5 (pyramidal) corticothalamic inputs, 226–229
    connections, 226
    cytoarchitecture, 226
    engagement of extrathalamic inhibitory networks via, 228
    functions in the somatosensory system, 229
    functions of the L5–posterior medial thalamus pathway, 231–232
long-term plasticity of the L5–posterior medial thalamus pathway, 229
    relationship with posterior medial thalamus sectors, 227
    role in context-dependent sensory processing, 231–232
    role in learning, 231
    role in memory, 231
    role in theories of cortical function, 232
    short-term plasticity of the L5–posterior medial thalamus pathway, 228–229
    subcortical target specificity, 226–227
    synaptic properties of the L5–posterior medial thalamus pathway, 227–228
  layer 6 corticothalamic pathways, 224–226
    connections, 224–225
    control of thalamic firing mode, 229–230
    control of thalamic gain, 230–231
    control of thalamic sensory adaptation, 230
    cytoarchitecture, 224–225
    engagement of inhibitory networks via, 225
    functions in the somatosensory system, 229–231
    long-term plasticity of, 226
    modulation of thalamic receptive fields, 229
    short-term plasticity of, 225–226
    synaptic properties, 225
corticothalamic projections
  layer 5 projection system, 7
  layer 6 projection system, 7
corticothalamocortical loops
  open and closed loops, 223–224
cross-hierarchical plasticity of corticothalamic projections, 155
cross-modal thalamocortical plasticity, 153
Cyclostomata (jawless fishes), 32, 36, 94, 102, 125
  evolution of, 125
  evolution of the dorsal thalamus, 112

de Luzzi, Mondino, 1
deep-brain stimulation of the central thalamus (CT-DBS)
  integrative model of effects on arousal regulation mechanisms, 391–394

434

to improve arousal regulation in human subjects, 390–391
deep neural network (DNN) machine learning algorithms, 420
Déjerine-Roussy syndrome, 4
Depp, Johnny, 191
depression, 15, 307
development
  pronuclei of the dorsal thalamus, 102–103
development of connections between thalamus and cortex
  areal differences in thalamocortical topographic organization, 149–151
  autonomous establishment of earliest thalamocortical connectivity, 148–149
  early outgrowths from the thalamus towards the cortex, 143–144
  first interactions of the thalamocortical axons with the cortical subplate, 147–148
  guidance cues for early projections, 143–144
  guidance mechanisms for crossing the diencephalon-telencephalon boundary, 144–145
  handshake of thalamocortical and corticothalamic projections through the pallial-subpallial boundary, 146–147
  rearrangement of thalamocortical ingrowth, 149–151
  role of corridor cells in delineating the path of thalamocortical axons in the subpallium, 145–146
  role of gene-expression gradients, 145
  thalamic axon innervation of the subplate and cortical plate, 149–151
development of connections from cortex to thalamus
  development of the complex corticothalamic innervation pattern, 151
  early outgrowth of corticothalamic projections, 152
  early transient circuits, 152
  plasticity of thalamocortical connectivity, 153–155
  role of spontaneous activity patterns, 152–153
  waiting period for corticothalamic projections, 152
development of thalamocortical auditory circuits
  amblyaudia, 249
  critical periods in development, 249–250
  experience- and activity-dependent development, 249–251
  plasticity of sound representations following manipulation of early auditory experience, 249–250
  plasticity of sound representations in adult thalamocortical circuits, 250–251
development of thalamocortical connectivity, 139
  co-evolution of the thalamus and cortex, 139
  complexities of adult thalamocortical relations, 139–140
  cross-hierarchical plasticity of corticothalamic projections, 155
  cross-modal plasticity, 153
  development of thalamocortical and corticothalamic projections, 141
  mouse model of thalamocortical interactions, 141
  role of sensory experience, 153–154
  routes taken by thalamocortical fibers in the adult, 139–141
  transient developmental circuits, 141
development of the thalamocortical auditory pathway, 246–249
  maturation of corticothalamic connectivity into the MGB, 248–249
  maturation of excitatory/inhibitory balance within the auditory cortex, 248
  maturation of MGB circuits, 246
  maturation of MGB innervation of cortical neurons, 247–248
  MGB innervation of the transient cortical subplate, 246–247
  onset of hearing across species, 246
  silent synapses, 247
development of the thalamus
  lineage-related functional organization, 143
  molecular patterning of the early thalamus, 142–143
  neural progenitor cells, 142–143
  nuclei specification, 143
  prosomeric model, 142
  role of signaling molecules, 142–143
  thalamic neurogenesis, 143
  See also ontogeny of thalamic GABAergic neurons.
diapsids, 95, 102, 109
discrete homology, 94, 101
dopamine
  role in reinforcement learning, 275
dorsal thalamus
  functional integration with the reticular nucleus, 15
dorsolateral geniculate nucleus, 187
  input to the visual cortex, 187
dual elaboration hypothesis. See evolution of the dorsal thalamus
dynamical systems perspective
  approach to modeling thalamic functions, 401
  feedback inhibition and lateral inhibition, 409–410
  future research on thalamic circuits, 410–411
  Hodgkin–Huxley models, 409
  information processing in neuron tonic and burst spiking modes, 402–403
  open-loop versus closed-loop connectivity motifs, 409–410
  role of computational modeling, 410
  short-term synaptic plasticity in thalamocortical circuits, 403
  thalamic circuit model for oscillations, 403–405
  thalamic circuit model for top-down modulation, 405–407
  thalamic coding properties, 406–407
  tonic and burst spike coding, 402
dystonia, 297

efference copies
  axonal branching of driver afferents to the thalamus, 82
  description, 81
  logic of cortically related efference copies, 82–84
  potential role of axonal branching, 82
  purpose of, 81
  relay of brainstem-dependent motor commands, 270
  role in self-generated movement, 81
  role of driver afferents to the thalamus, 81–84
electrical recording
  excitatory postsynaptic potentials (EPSPs), 15
  fast oscillations, 15
  first-order (FO) and higher-order (HO) thalamocortical circuits, 17–19
  inhibitory postsynaptic potentials (IPSPs), 15
  primary (short-latency) responses, 14
  recruiting responses, 14
  sensory relay function studies, 11–13
  spindles, 14, 15
  studies of intrathalamic and thalamus-driven large-scale oscillations, 13–15
  thalamic pacemaker mechanism, 15–16
electrical recording techniques
  development of, 11–19
electron microscopy
  introduction of, 5–6
embryological development. See development
epifluorescence, 7
epigenetics, 94
epilepsy
  cerebellar pathology and, 298
error backpropagation
  role in predictive learning, 420–422
essential tremor
  cerebellar pathology and, 297
evolution
  dynamic stability of cortical afferents, 32–33
  selective process of attention, 85
  stability of thalamic terminal complexity, 36
evolution of the dorsal thalamus
  alternative to the developmental pallial evolution hypothesis, 101–102
  amphibians, 110–111
  background, 91–93
  biological homology, 101–102
  cladistic analysis, 93–94
  claustroamygdalar hypothesis, 91
  collothalamus, 91
  comparative structure of the thalamus across vertebrates, 91–92
  comparing dorsal thalamic evolution across amniotes, 102–104
  criteria for homology, 94
  developmental relationships, 92

evolution dorsal thalamus (cont.)
  developmental studies of pallial segments, 98–99
  discrete homology, 101
  dorsal thalamus in tetrapods, 95
  dual elaboration hypothesis
    collothalamic and lemnothalamic elaboration in sauropsids, 104–107
    collothalamus, 102–104
    comparison with anatomical and functional divisions, 108–109
    developmental studies and, 107–108
    different patterns of elaboration, 102–104
    lemnothalamic and collothalamic elaboration in mammals, 103–104
    lemnothalamus, 102–104
    relationship to tetrapartite pallial evolution, 109–110
    revised collothalamic homologues in amniotes, 110
  elaboration of pallial segment derivatives in sauropsids, 99–101
  embryological development of pronuclei, 102–103
  epigenetic influences, 94
  evolution of the major vertebrate groups, 94–95
  field homology, 94
  fishes, 111–112
  fossil studies, 93
  generative homology (syngeny), 102
  hodology, 94, 102
  homologous derivatives of embryological structures, 101
  homology studies, 93–94
  hypotheses of homology, 98–99
  Karten hypothesis of pallial evolution, 91
  Karten hypothesis of pallial evolution in sauropsids, 96–98
  lemnothalamus, 91
  overview, 91
  pallial evolution and, 95, 96–102
  pallium configuration across vertebrates, 92–93
  parcellation hypothesis (Ebbesson), 109
  perspectives on dorsal thalamic components, 95
  question of homology, 91–92
  relationship between dorsal thalamic evolution and pallial evolution, 96–102

  role of the neocortex, 92–93
  specialization from a hypothesized common ancestor, 93–94
  Strong Karten Hypothesis (homology of cell types), 101
  study methodology, 93–94
  thalamus in tetrapods, 94–95
  two evolutionary divisions of the dorsal thalamus, 91
  value of specifying the homology, 101
evolution of the thalamus
  amphioxus, 125
  circuit motifs that may support cognition and consciousness, 116–117
  co-evolution of the thalamus and cortex, 139
  cognitive abilities of some fishes, 116
  comparing thalamic pathways, 134
  complex cognitive abilities of birds, 115–116
  conclusions from the lamprey thalamus, 134
  developmental pallial evolution hypothesis, 101
  earliest developments, 125
  insights into perception, cognition, and consciousness, 113–117
  lamprey, 125
  phylogenetic tree of vertebrates, 135
  tunicates, 125
evolution of the ventral thalamus across vertebrates, 112–113
evolutionary perspective
  sleep, 361
excitatory postsynaptic potentials (EPSPs), 15
executive control. See cognitive control; executive function
executive function
  frontothalamic pathways, 423–425
  gating activity, 416–417
  gating of frontal function by the thalamus, 422–425
  See also cognitive control.
experience-dependent myelination within the thalamocortical system, 253–254
external medullary lamina, 1
extra-geniculate pathway of the visual system, 187

fatal familial insomnia (FFI), 373
feedback inhibition in thalamic circuits, 409–410

feedforward versus feedback transthalamic pathways, 80–81
Ferrier, David, 3–4
Feynman, Richard, 200
first-order (FO) thalamic nuclei, 139
  comparison with higher-order (HO) nuclei, 81
  cortical projections to, 221–222
first-order (FO) thalamic relay neurons, 17–19, 79–81
  driver input source and relay cell function, 79–80
fishes
  cognitive abilities, 116
  evolution of the dorsal thalamus, 111–112
  organization of the thalamus in the different groups, 132–133
  See also Cyclostomata (jawless fishes).
folded-feedback model of attention, 418–420
Forel, Auguste, 1
frontal function
  gating by the thalamus, 422–425
frontothalamic pathways, 423–425

GABA (gamma-aminobutyric acid) neurotransmitter, 163
GABAergic inputs to geniculate relay cells, 71
GABAergic inputs to the thalamus, 31
GABAergic neurogenesis, 171–175
GABAergic neurons
  identification of, 9
  See also ontogeny of thalamic GABAergic neurons.
Galenus, Claudius, 1
gap junction electrical coupling, 405
gar (ray-finned fish)
  organization of the thalamus, 132–133
gating of executive function, 416–417
gating of frontal function
  role of the thalamus, 422–425
gating role of the thalamic reticular nucleus, 405–406
generative homology (syngeny), 102
geniculo-striate pathway of the visual system, 187
Gerlach, Joseph von, 1
glutamatergic drivers and modulators, 77–79
  drivers and modulators in the cortex, 78

functional division between retinal and non-retinal inputs, 77
  in the thalamus, 77–78
  purpose of, 78–79
  topographic modulation, 78–79
glutamatergic inputs to geniculate relay cells, 71
glutamatergic neurons
  identification of, 9
Golgi, Camillo, 163
  early Golgi stain studies, 4–5
grid cells
  role in path integration, 349–350
guidepost cells, 143, 145
Guillery, Ray, 17–19, 224

habenula
  identification of, 1
head direction
  tuning, 347
  tuning in the anterodorsal nucleus, 344–345
head-direction signal
  head direction and movement direction, 350
  role in navigation, 340
  spatial cognition, 349–350
higher-order (HO) thalamic nuclei, 139
  comparison with first-order (FO) nuclei, 81
  cortical projections to, 221–222
higher-order (HO) thalamic relay neurons, 17–19, 79–81
  corticocortical communication, 79–80
  driver input source and relay cell function, 79–80
hippocampus
  place cells, 340
  role in navigation, 340
histochemistry, 7
history of thalamus research
  axonal transport tracing, 7–9
  conceptual framework of Guillery and Sherman, 17–19
  connection-tracing studies, 4–12
  cytoarchitectonic approach, 2–3
  delineation of input pathways, 2–3
  delineation of output pathways, 3
  development of a common nomenclature, 2
  development of tissue staining and fixing techniques, 1–2, 4
  diffuse brainstem inputs to the thalamus, 9

Index

early Golgi stain studies, 4–5
early lesion-degeneration studies, 4–9
electrical recording techniques, 11–19
first-order (FO) and higher-order (HO) thalamocortical circuits, 17–19
functional association of nuclei delineations, 2–3
identification of GABAergic neurons, 9
identification of glutamatergic neurons, 9
identification of interneurons, 4
identification of myelinated fiber tracts associated with the thalamus, 1
identification of thalamic projection neurons, 4
identification of the thalamus and its constituent nuclei, 1–3
immunolabeling studies, 9
introduction of electron microscopy, 5–6
lesion studies, 3–4
macroscopic descriptions of the inner structures, 1
Marchi staining method for myelin sheaths, 4–5
matrix-core hypothesis (Jones), 7, 14
microelectrode studies, 11–13
neurochemical characterization of thalamic circuits, 9–10
neuronal circuits and functional frameworks, 3–19
origin of the term *thalamus*, 1
role of the reticular nucleus, 15
single-cell labeling studies, 11–12
stages of, 1
studies of intrathalamic and thalamus-driven large-scale oscillations, 13–15
thalamic pacemaker mechanism, 15–16
thalamic sensory relay function studies, 11–13
thalamotomy procedures, 2
theories of thalamic function, 11–19
work of Auguste Forel, 1
work of Claudius Galenus, 1
work of David Ferrier, 3–4
work of Franz Nissl, 2
work of Julius Bernard Luys, 1, 3
work of Karl Friedrich Burdach, 1
work of Rafael Lorente de Nó, 4
work of Santiago Ramón y Cajal, 4–6

work of Theodor Meynert, 1
Hodgkin–Huxley models, 409
hodology, 91, 94, 102
homeobox genes, 94
homology
  biological homology, 94, 101–102
  criteria for, 94
  discrete homology, 94, 101
  field homology, 94
  generative homology (syngeny), 102
  homologous derivatives of embryological structures, 101
  hypotheses of the evolution of the dorsal thalamus, 98–99
  iterative homology, 94
  revised hypothesis for collothalamic nuclei in amniotes, 110
  role in evolution of the dorsal thalamus, 91–92
  thalamic evolution studies, 93–94

IMAX 3D technology, 194
immunolabeling studies, 9
immunolabeling with specific antibodies, 7
inhibitory postsynaptic potentials (IPSPs), 15
innate motor sequences
  brainstem-thalamostriatal pathways, 271–272
inputs to the thalamus
  axon terminals with single and multiple synapses, 33
  canonical inputs, 36
  challenge to sort, weigh, and integrate incoming information, 27–30
  computational problem of vertebrate forebrains, 27–30
  cortical inputs, 27, 31–32
  delineation of input pathways, 2–3
  diffuse brainstem inputs, 9
  dynamic stability of cortical afferents during evolution, 32–33
  GABAergic inputs, 31
  heterogeneity of input integration, 29–30, 36–40
  heterogeneity of input space, 28, 30–33
  heterogeneity of terminal types, 28–29, 33–36
  hubs of integration, 39–40
  integration in the intralaminar nuclei, 39–40
  integration in the midline nuclear group, 39–40
  integration of multisynaptic cortical and

  multisynaptic subcortical glutamatergic inputs, 38
  integration of multisynaptic GABAergic and multisynaptic glutamatergic inputs, 39
  integration of multisynaptic inhibitory and unisynaptic excitatory inputs, 39
  integration of multisynaptic, subcortical, glutamatergic terminals with distinct origin, 37
  integrative role of the thalamus, 27
  large, multisynaptic, cortical, glutamatergic inputs, 37–38
  large, multisynaptic, subcortical glutamatergic inputs, 37
  local computation by neurons, 36
  mosaic-like (non-canonical) organization in the thalamus, 40
  relay function of the thalamus, 27
  role of the thalamus, 27
  stability of terminal complexity during evolution, 36
  subcortical inputs, 27, 30–31
  thalamic reticular nucleus, 31
  types of, 27
  types of input integration, 36–40
  uni- and multisynaptic excitatory terminals, 34–35
  uni- and multisynaptic inhibitory terminals, 33–34
  variability of terminals, 35–36
  variable size and complexity of axon terminals, 33
integrative role of the thalamus, 27
intergeniculate leaflet (IGL), 163, 164–165
interneurons
  axons, 15
  identification of, 4
  variation across mammalian phyla, 15
interneurons in the thalamus, 163–164
  activity-dependent control of interneuron development, 175–177
  distribution in mammals, 165–166
  extra-thalamic origin, 168–170
  molecular diversity, 166–168
  neurogenesis in the midbrain, 173–175

  neurogenesis in the rostral forebrain, 171–173
ionotropic receptors, 71–73
iterative homology, 94

Jackson, John Hughlings, 298
Jones, Edward, 91–92, 284
  matrix-core hypothesis, 7, 14

Karten, Harvey
  hypothesis of pallial evolution, 91
  hypothesis of pallial evolution in sauropsids, 96–98
  Strong Karten hypothesis (homology of cell types), 101
Kleitman, Nathaniel, 361
Koniocellular pathway, 193

lamina medullaris interna, 1
lamprey thalamus
  basal ganglia and, 131–132
  comparison with other classes of vertebrates, 125
  evolution of the cyclostomes, 125
  evolution of the dorsal thalamus, 112
  evolutionary implications, 134
  interactions between the optic tectum (superior colliculus) and thalamus, 130
  organization of the forebrain, 125
  organization of the thalamus, 125–126
  pallial/cortical projections to the thalamus, 132–133
  projections to the cortex/pallium, 125–127
  retinotopic representation in the thalamus and pallium/cortex, 128–130
  somatosensory pathways, 125–127
  visual pathways, 128–130
lampreys, 32, 36, 94, 102
Larkum, Matthew, 84
lateral geniculate body, 1
  identification of, 1
lateral geniculate nucleus
  circuitry in the cat, 71–73
  functional organization, 325–327
  gain control and distracter filtering, 327–328
  geniculo-cortical interactions, 328
  role in visual attention, 325–327
  visual pathway connections, 325
lateral inhibition in thalamic circuits, 409–410
Le Gros Clark, Wilfred, 2

Index

learned motor sequences
  brainstem-thalamocortical loop in songbirds, 272–273
  brainstem-thalamostriatal pathways, 271–272
learning
  adaptive learning, 422–423
  basal ganglia–dependent reinforcement learning, 275
  predictive error-driven learning in the pulvinar, 420–422
  predictive learning, 416, 417
  role of the cortical layer 5-posterior medial thalamus loop, 231
  role of the pulvinar, 416
  role of the thalamus, 416
lemnothalamus, 91
lesion-degeneration studies, 4–9
lesion studies, 3–4
limbic system
  anterior thalamus (AT) as a node in superimposed loops, 341–343
  consolidating memories during sleep, 352–353
  flow of information in the limbic thalamocortical network, 348
  neuronal properties, 340
  role in navigation, 340
  role of the anterior thalamus (AT), 344
  role of the nucleus reuniens, 342–343, 344
  superimposed loops, 342–343
  thalamocortical loops, 341–342
  See also Papez circuit.
limbic thalamus, 340
Llinás, Rodolfo, 13
lobe-finned fishes
  evolution of the dorsal thalamus, 111
local evoked responses
  thalamic control of, 313–314
Lorente de Nó, Rafael, 4, 14
LSTM (long short-term memory) machine-learning algorithm, 424
Luys, Julius Bernard, 1, 3

machine learning
  deep neural network (DNN) machine learning algorithms, 420
  LSTM (long short-term memory) algorithm, 424
  models of attention, 418
mammals
  distribution of GABAergic thalamic interneurons, 165–166
  somatosensory pathways, 126–127

visual pathways, 131
Marchi staining method for myelin sheaths, 4–5
matrix-core hypothesis (Jones), 7, 14
McGurk effect, 187
medial geniculate body (MGB) of the thalamus
  corticothalamic feedback to, 239
  efferent connections from non-primary divisions of the auditory thalamus, 240
  extra-sensory modulation of auditory thalamocortical circuits, 243–245
  feedforward input to, 237–239
  future research directions, 254–256
  identification of, 1
  maturation of corticothalamic connectivity into the MGB, 248–249
  maturation of MGB circuits, 246
  maturation of MGB innervation of cortical neurons, 247–248
  MGB innervation of the transient cortical subplate, 246–247
  neural coding of sound features across the midbrain–thalamus–cortex hierarchy, 240–243
  organization and connectivity, 237
  role in auditory processing, 237
  sound processing functions of auditory corticothalamic circuits, 243–244
  subdivisions, 237
  ventral MGB efferent connections, 239–240
memory
  consolidating memories during sleep, 352–353
  role of the cortical layer 5-posterior medial thalamus loop, 231
Meynert, Theodor, 1
microelectrode studies, 11–13
midbrain
  pathways of cortical layer 5 projections to, 84
monotropic receptors, 71–73
mosaic-like (non-canonical) organization in the thalamus, 40
motor learning
  role of the cerebellum, 296
motor sequences
  brainstem-thalamocortical loop in songbirds, 272–273

brainstem-thalamostriatal pathways, 271–272
motor thalamus
  action-selection problem, 270
  basal ganglia–dependent reinforcement learning, 275
  basal ganglia signal transmission pathways, 275–276
  basal ganglia–thalamic transmission, 276
  brainstem-recipient motor thalamus, 269–273
  cerebellothalamic tract, 284–286
  influence of the cerebellum, 284
  interactions with the basal ganglia, 273–280
  morphology and genetic profile, 287
  relay of efference copies of brainstem-dependent motor commands, 270
  role in reach tasks in rodents and primates, 277–280
  role in the mammalian motor system, 269
  role in vocal babbling in juvenile birds, 276–277
  signal transmission in the brainstem-thalamic pathway, 273
  somatotopy in the ventrolateral nucleus, 286–287
Mountcastle, Vernon, 11
mouse
  model of thalamocortical interactions, 141
movement
  role of efference copies in self-generated movement, 81
movement disorders with tremors
  cerebellar pathology and, 297
myelin sheaths
  Marchi staining method, 4–5
myelinated fiber tracts associated with the thalamus
  identification of, 1
myelination
  experience-dependent myelination within the thalamocortical system, 253–254

navigation
  AT as a node in superimposed loops of the limbic system, 341–343
  cholinergic modulation of the anterior thalamus/nucleus reuniens, 343–344
  computation in a convergent–divergent circuit, 346

diffuse projections to and from the nucleus reuniens, 342
electrophysical properties of neurons, 348
flow of information in the limbic thalamocortical network, 348
functional cell types with spatial correlates, 340
head-direction signal, 340
head-direction tuning, 347
inhibitory control of the anterior thalamus (AT), 343
limbic thalamus, 340
neuronal properties in the limbic system, 340
nucleus reuniens structure and function, 340
open questions, 353
oscillatory modulation in the anterior thalamus/nucleus reuniens, 346–347
plasticity of some circuits, 353
role in the Papez circuit, 341
role of some intralaminar nuclei, 353
role of the anterior thalamus (AT), 340, 344
role of the anterior thalamus and nucleus reuniens in spatial cognition, 348–352
role of the hippocampus, 340
role of the laterodorsal nucleus of the thalamus, 353
role of the limbic system, 340
role of the nucleus reuniens, 344
role of the Papez circuit, 340, 344
spatial correlates and oscillator properties of neuronal activity, 344–348
superimposed loops in the limbic system, 342–343
thalamocortical loops of the limbic system, 341–342
tuning to head direction in the anterodorsal nucleus, 344–345
Neary, Tim, 91
neocortex
  evolution of, 92–93
neural synchrony
  thalamic modulation of, 316–317
neurochemical characterization of thalamic circuits, 9–10
neurogenic pain, 15
neurological disorders, 287
  cerebellar pathology and, 296–298
  cognitive control deficits, 307
neuromodulatory mechanisms
  auditory thalamocortical circuits, 252–253

438

Index

neuropsychiatric disorders
  sleep disorders associated with, 373
neurotransmitters
  inputs to geniculate relay cells, 71
Nissl, Franz, 2, 4
nitric oxide synthase (Nos), 166
nomenclature
  development of a common nomenclature for thalamus structures, 2
noradrenergic neuromodulatory system
  auditory thalamocortical circuits, 253
nuclei delineations
  cell lineage studies, 3
  functional association, 2–3
nucleus reuniens
  cholinergic modulation, 343–344
  consolidating memories during sleep, 352–353
  diffuse projections to and from, 342
  electrophysiological properties of neurons, 348
  executive modulation of CA 1, 350–352
  interventional studies, 348–349
  oscillatory modulation, 346–347
  role in spatial cognition, 348–352
  role in the limbic system, 342–343, 344
  structure and function, 340

occulomotor control
  action-selection problem, 270
ontogeny of thalamic GABAergic neurons
  activity-dependent control of interneuron development, 175–177
  classes of GABAergic neurons, 163
  developmental complexity of GABAergic neurons, 168–171
  distribution of interneurons in mammals, 165–166
  evolutionary implications, 177
  extra-thalamic origin of interneurons, 168–170
  GABA (gamma-aminobutyric acid) neurotransmitter, 163
  interneuron neurogenesis, 171–175
  interneurons, 163–164
  intrinsic control of GABAergic neurogenesis, 171
  molecular diversity of interneurons, 166–168

  multiple sources of thalamic GABAergic neurons, 168–171
  projection neurons, 163, 164–165
  prosomeric model, 163
  thalamic origin of projection neurons, 170–171
  transcriptional regulation in the midbrain, 173–175
  transcriptional regulation in the rostral forebrain, 171–173
  transcriptional regulation of projection neurons, 175
oscillations
  role of the thalamus in cortical slow oscillations, 403–404
  thalamic circuit model for, 403–405
  thalamic delta oscillation, 404
  thalamic spindle oscillation, 404–405
outputs from the thalamus
  delineation of output pathways, 3
  See also thalamic projection neurons (TPNs).
Owen, Richard, 94

pacemaker mechanism in the thalamus, 15–16
pain
  thalamic pain syndrome (Déjerine-Roussy syndrome), 4
pallial evolution, 96–102
  relationship to dual elaboration hypothesis of dorsal thalamus evolution, 109–110
pallium
  configuration across vertebrates, 92–93
Papez, James, 341
Papez circuit, 27
  role in navigation, 340, 344
  role of the anterior thalamus (AT), 341
  spatial correlates and oscillator properties of neuronal activity, 344–348
  See also limbic system.
parcellation hypothesis (Ebbesson), 109
Parkinson's disease, 15, 39, 269, 287
  cerebellar pathology and, 297
Parkinsonism, 280
parvalbumin, 9, 166, 383
path integration, 349–350
Pavlovian conditioning, 39
perception
  insights from the evolution of the thalamus, 113–117
perihabenula nucleus (pHB), 164–165

plasticity of thalamocortical connectivity, 153–155
  cross-hierarchical plasticity of corticothalamic projections, 155
  cross-modal plasticity, 153
  sensory-induced plasticity, 153–154
platypus, 32
predictive learning, 416
  recognition by synthesis proposal, 420
  role in conscious experience, 417
predictive learning in the pulvinar
  error-driven learning, 420–422
preglomerular relay nuclei in teleost fishes, 133
primates
  reach tasks and the basal ganglia–recipient motor thalamus, 277–280
prioritization of information. See attention
pronuclei
  embryological development of the dorsal thalamus, 102–103
prosomeric model, 163
psychiatric disorders
  cognitive control deficits, 307
Puelles, Luis, 91, 102
pulvinar, 192
  computational models of pulvinar function, 334
  dynamics of pulvino-cortical interactions, 333–334
  effects of pulvinar lesions, 330–331
  functional organization, 329–330
  identification of, 1
  input to the visual cortex, 187
  non-human primates, 2
  predictive error-driven learning, 420–422
  regulation of intra- and inter-areal interactions, 331–333
  role in learning, 416
  timekeeper role in visual attention, 328–334
  visual input to, 187
  visual pathway connections, 325
Purpura, Dominique, 296
Pvalb gene, 166

Ramón y Cajal, Santiago, 4–6, 82, 163
rat vibrissa system, 30
  anatomy of the vibrissae, 214
  ascending streams of vibrissa information, 214–217
  extralemniscal pathway, 216

  functional representation in barrelettes, barreloids, and barrels, 218
  information-processing pathways, 214–215
  inhibitory control of thalamic relay cells, 217
  lemniscal pathway, 214–216
  microvibrissae, 217–218
  open questions and missing data, 218
  organization of corticothalamic pathways, 217
  paralemniscal pathway, 216–217
  prototypical sensorimotor system, 214–215
  touch and self-motion signaling, 214–215
ray-finned fishes
  evolution of the dorsal thalamus, 111–112
  organization of the thalamus, 132–133
receptors
  monotropic and ionotropic receptor types, 71–73
  postsynaptic receptors on relay cells (cat), 71–73
recognition by synthesis
  proposal for predictive learning, 420
reinforcement learning
  basal ganglia–dependent, 275
  role of dopamine, 275
relay function of the thalamus, 27
reptiles
  somatosensory pathways, 127
  thalamostriatal pathways, 131
  visual pathways, 131
reticular nucleus. See thalamic reticular nucleus
retinogeniculocortical pathway, 206–207
Riolan, Jean, 1
rodents
  cerebellothalamic tract development, 287–289
  reach tasks and the basal ganglia–recipient motor thalamus, 277–280
  thalamostriatal pathways, 131
  See also rat vibrissa system.
Rose, Jerzy, 11
  embryological development of the dorsal thalamus, 102–103

Santorini, Giovanni Domenico, 1
schizophrenia, 270, 287, 307
  sleep disorders associated with, 373
selective attention
  role of the thalamic reticular nucleus, 416
  role of the thalamus, 405–406

439

Index

self-generated movement
  role of efference copies, 81
sensorimotor pathways (rat vibrissa)
  anatomy of the vibrissae, 214
  ascending streams of vibrissa information, 214–217
  extralemniscal pathway, 216
  functional representation in barrelettes, barreloids, and barrels, 218
  information-processing pathways, 214–215
  inhibitory control of thalamic relay cells, 217
  lemniscal pathway, 214–216
  microvibrissae, 217–218
  open questions and missing data, 218
  organization of corticothalamic pathways, 217
  paralemniscal pathway, 216–217
  prototypical sensorimotor system, 214–215
  touch and self-motion signaling, 214–215
sensory experience
  role of development of thalamocortical connectivity, 153–154
sensory-induced thalamocortical plasticity, 153–154
sensory inputs
  combination to extract meaning, 187–188
serotonergic neuromodulatory system
  auditory thalamocortical circuits, 253
Sherman, Murray, 17–19
silent synapses
  role in auditory pathway development, 247
simultanagnosia, 418
single-cell labeling studies, 11–12
sleep
  consolidating memories during, 352–353
  delta waves, 364
  EEG recording, 361
  evolutionary perspective, 361
  features of, 361
  K-complexes, 364
  NREM sleep, 361–362
  NREM sleep oscillations, 361–364
  REM sleep, 361–362
  REM sleep oscillations, 364–365
  sleep oscillations and the thalamus, 361–365
  sleep states in different organisms, 361
  slow waves, 362–364
  spindles, 364
sleep disorders
  associated with neuropsychiatric disorders, 373
  associated with schizophrenia, 373
  fatal familial insomnia (FFI), 373
  parasomnias, 373
  related to stroke, 373
  role of the thalamus, 373
sleep–wake architecture, 366–369
  brain mechanisms of sleep–wake states, 366–367
  evidence for the role of the thalamus, 367–369
  genetic studies, 368
  lesion studies, 367–368
  optogenetic studies, 368–369
  pharmacology studies, 368
  sleep states control and the thalamus, 369
sleep–wake cycles
  cholinergic modulation of the anterior thalamus/ nucleus reuniens, 343–344
sleep–wake states
  ascending reticular activating system (ARAS), 369
  brain plasticity during sleep, 371–373
  cholinergic neuromodulation, 370
  neuromodulation of thalamic neurons across, 369–372
  noradrenergic neuromodulation, 370–371
  role of the thalamus in brain plasticity, 371–373
  serotonergic neuromodulation, 371
Smith, Hobart, 94
somatosensory system
  activity-dependent control of thalamic interneuron development, 175–177
  cortical layer 5 and layer 6 projections, 221–222
  corticothalamic feedback pathways, 221–222
  corticothalamic layer 5 (pyramidal tract) pathway, 221–222
  corticothalamic layer 6 pathway, 221–222
  first-order (FO) thalamic nuclei, 221–222
  functional impact of corticothalamic feedback, 221
  functions of the corticothalamic circuits, 229–232
  future research, 232
  higher-order (HO) thalamic nuclei, 221–222
  inhibitory control via corticothalamic pathways, 224
  integration of external and internal information, 221
  layer 5 (pyramidal) corticothalamic inputs, 226–229
    connections, 226
    cytoarchitecture, 226
    engagement of extrathalamic inhibitory networks via, 228
    functions in the somatosensory system, 229
    functions of the L5–posterior medial thalamus pathway, 231–232
    long-term plasticity of the L5–posterior medial thalamus pathway, 229
    relationship with posterior medial thalamus sectors, 227
    role in context-dependent sensory processing, 231–232
    role in learning, 231
    role in memory, 231
    role in theories of cortical function, 232
    short-term plasticity of the L5–posterior medial thalamus pathway, 228–229
    subcortical target specificity, 226–227
    synaptic properties of the L5–posterior medial thalamus pathway, 227–228
  layer 6 corticothalamic pathways, 224–226
    connections, 224–225
    control of thalamic firing mode, 229–230
    control of thalamic gain, 230–231
    control of thalamic sensory adaptation, 230
    cytoarchitecture, 224–225
    engagement of inhibitory networks via, 225
    functions in the somatosensory system, 229–231
    long-term plasticity of, 226
    modulation of thalamic receptive fields, 229
    short-term plasticity of, 225–226
    synaptic properties, 225
  open and closed corticothalamocortical loops, 223–224
  sense of touch, 221
spatial cognition
  boundary signaling, 350
  egocentric modulation, 350
  executive modulation of CA1 by the nucleus reuniens, 350–352
  grid cells, 349–350
  head direction, 349–350
  head direction and movement direction, 350
  interventional studies, 348–349
  path integration, 349–350
  place cells and the cognitive map, 350–351
  relationship between thalamic and hippocampal activity, 350–351
  role of the anterior thalamus and nucleus reuniens, 348–352
  transformation of AT signals into spatial representation, 349–350
spiking modes in thalamocortical neurons
  tonic and burst spiking, 402–403
spindles, 14, 15
  thalamic spindle oscillation, 404–405
stereopsis
  visual depth perception and, 194–196
stroke, 307
  sleep disorders related to, 373
Stroop task, 308
subcortical inputs to the thalamus, 30–31
superior colliculus, 270
synapses
  short-term plasticity in thalamocortical circuits, 403
synapsids, 95, 102, 109
syngeny (generative homology), 102

thalamic cell properties
  action potential, 75
  burst and tonic firing in relay cells, 75–77
  K^+ channels, 74
  low-threshold Ca^{2+} spike, 75
  Na^+ channels, 75
  relay cell ionic membrane conductances, 73–75
  T-type Ca^{2+} channels, 75
thalamic circuit function
  computational modeling approach, 401
  feedback inhibition and lateral inhibition, 409–410
  future research, 410–411
  Hodgkin–Huxley models, 409
  information processing in neuron tonic and burst

spiking modes, 402–403
open-loop versus closed-loop connectivity motifs, 409–410
role of computational modeling, 410
short-term synaptic plasticity, 403
tonic and burst spike coding, 402
thalamic circuit model for oscillations, 403–405
gap junction electrical coupling, 405
role of the thalamus in cortical slow oscillations, 403–404
thalamic delta oscillation, 404
thalamic spindle oscillation, 404–405
thalamic circuit model for top-down modulation, 405–407
features of the model, 406
gating role of the thalamic reticular nucleus, 405–406
selective attention in the thalamus, 405–406
thalamic coding properties, 406–407
thalamic circuitry, 71
alternative view of thalamocortical processing, 85–87
axonal branching of driver afferents to the thalamus, 82
differences between first-order (FO) and higher-order (HO) thalamic nuclei, 81
driver afferents to the thalamus and efference copies, 81–84
driver input source and relay cell function, 79–80
features of cortical layer 5 projections, 82–85
feedforward versus feedback transthalamic pathways, 80–81
first-order (FO) and higher-order (HO) relay neurons, 79–81
functional division between retinal and non-retinal inputs, 77
glutamatergic drivers and modulators, 77–79
glutamatergic drivers and modulators in the cortex, 78
glutamatergic drivers and modulators in the thalamus, 77–78
inputs to geniculate relay cells (cat), 71
insights from axonal transport tracing studies, 7–9

logic of cortically related efference copies, 82–84
neurochemical characterization, 9–10
neurotransmitter inputs to geniculate relay cells, 71
outstanding questions, 87
overview (lateral geniculate nucleus of the cat), 71–73
postsynaptic receptors on relay cells (cat), 71–73
purpose of glutamatergic drivers and modulators, 78–79
topographic modulation, 78–79
thalamic function framework of Guillery and Sherman, 17–19
thalamic pacemaker mechanism, 15–16
thalamic pain syndrome, 4
thalamic projection neurons (TPNs)
anterior thalamostriatal axon wiring, 55
approach to single-cell level categorization, 45
axon architecture diversity, 47–48
axon-wiring motifs, 51–56
catalog of top-level TPN classes, 61
defining TPN cell types, 51–56
dendrite-arborization pattern, 45
developmental origins, 45
different axon-wiring patterns, 45
electronic properties, 45
gene-expression differences, 45
gene-expression diversity, 58–60
general layout of TPN axons, 48–51
genomic profile groups, 45
identification of, 4
insights from axonal transport tracing studies, 7
membrane conductances, 45
membrane properties, 56–58
midline thalamostriatal axon wiring, 55
multifocal thalamocortical axon wiring, 52–53
neurochemical diversity, 58–60
outputs from the thalamus, 45
posterior thalamostriatal axon wiring, 55
somatodendritic morphology, 46–47
subpial thalamocortical axon wiring, 54
unifocal thalamocortical axon wiring, 51–52
thalamic relay neurons

calcium channels, 13
thalamic reticular nucleus
attentional focusing through TRN pooled inhibition, 417–420
functional integration with the dorsal thalamus, 15
gating role, 405–406
inputs to the thalamus, 31
pacemaker role, 15
role in selective attention, 416
visual pathway connections, 325
thalamic sensory relay function studies, 11–13
thalamocortical circuit, 31
thalamocortical circuit maturation
activity-dependent development, 175–177
thalamocortical loops of the limbic system, 341–342
thalamocortical neurons
information processing in tonic and burst spiking modes, 402–403
thalamocortical processing
alternative view, 85–87
thalamotomy procedures, 2
thalamus
computational contributions, 416–417
core versus matrix projections, 423–425
gating of frontal function, 422–425
role in selective attention, 416
Thorndike, Edward, 275
tinnitus, 15
tissue staining and fixing techniques
history of development, 1–2, 4
tonic firing in thalamic relay cells, 75–77
top-down modulation of thalamic activity
dynamical systems perspective, 405–407
TPNs. See thalamic projection neurons
transthalamic pathways
feedforward versus feedback, 80–81
traumatic brain injury, 307
tremors
movement disorders and cerebellar pathology, 297
tunicates, 125
turtles
thalamic terminal structures, 36
visual pathways, 131

vertebrates
circuit motifs that may support cognition and consciousness, 116–117

evolution of the major vertebrate groups, 94–95
phylogenetic tree, 135
thalamus in tetrapods, 94–95
visual pathways, 131
vibrissal sensory system in rodents. See rat vibrissa system
Vicq d'Azyr, Felix, 341
visual attention
gatekeeper role of the lateral geniculate nucleus, 325–328
mechanisms, 324
timekeeper role of the pulvinar, 328–334
visual cortex
input from the dorsolateral geniculate nucleus, 187
input from the pulvinar, 187
input via the thalamus, 187
ocular dominance columns, 189
parallel pathways of sensory inputs, 187–193
visual pathways
arrangement of parallel pathways, 187–188
binocular vision and visual acuity, 194–196
birds, 131
blindsight and, 193
combination of sensory signals to extract meaning, 187–188
combining ON and OFF pathways, 196
combining pathways for spatial resolution and visual acuity, 193–194
combining pathways from the two eyes, 194–196
combining pathways in the primary visual cortex, 193–197
combining pathways in visual space, 193–194
combining transient and sustained pathways, 196–197
corticogeniculate effects on visual processing, 209–210
corticogeniculate feedback pathway, 206
direction selectivity of cortical neurons, 196–197
eye independence and, 189–191
features of geniculocortical pathways, 199
future research on the corticogeniculate feedback pathway, 210
general properties of corticogeniculate feedback, 207–208
Koniocellular pathway, 193

visual pathways (cont.)
  lamprey, 128–130
  layer 6 corticothalamic neurons, 206
  linear and non-linear spatial summation, 192
  magnocellular layer of the dorsal lateral geniculate nucleus, 192
  mammals, 131
  orientation tuning of cortical neurons, 193
  outstanding questions, 199–200
  parallel ON and OFF pathways, 191–192
  parallel pathways, 187–193
  parallel pathways for corticogeniculate feedback, 208–209
  parallel pathways from retina to cortex, 206–207
  parallel pathways in ocular space, 189–191
  parallel pathways in visual space, 188–189
  parallel signaling of light and dark, 191–192
  parallel tecto-geniculate pathways, 192–193
  parallel transient and sustained pathways, 192
  parvocellular layer of the dorsal lateral geniculate nucleus, 192
  reptiles, 131
  retinogeniculocortical pathway, 206–207
  size and structure of cortical receptive fields, 193–194
  vertebrates, 131
  visual cortical targets of converging pathways, 197–199
  visual depth perception and stereopsis, 194–196
visual system
  activity-dependent control of thalamic interneuron development, 175–177
  extra-geniculate pathway, 187
  geniculo-striate pathway, 187
visual thalamus
  structure of, 325–327
von Gudden, Bernhard, 4
Von Monakow, Constantin, 4

Wheatstone, Charles, 194
Willis, Thomas, 1
Woolsey, Clinton, 11
working memory
  association with cognitive control, 308–310
  role of the thalamus, 312–313
Wurffbain, Johann Paul, 298